Managerial Accounting

Eighteenth Edition

Ray H. Garrison, D.B.A., CPA

Professor Emeritus
Brigham Young University

Eric W. Noreen, Ph.D., CMA

Professor Emeritus
University of Washington

Peter C. Brewer, Ph.D.

Wake Forest University

With Contributions By
Norma R. Montague

Wake Forest University

lighthouse image: Martin73/Shutterstock; big data image: INGARA/Shutterstock

Mc
Graw
Hill

MANAGERIAL ACCOUNTING, EIGHTEENTH EDITION

Published by McGraw Hill LLC, 1325 Avenue of the Americas, New York, NY 10019. Copyright ©2024 by McGraw Hill LLC. All rights reserved. Printed in the United States of America. Previous editions ©2021, 2018, and 2015. No part of this publication may be reproduced or distributed in any form or by any means, or stored in a database or retrieval system, without the prior written consent of McGraw Hill LLC, including, but not limited to, in any network or other electronic storage or transmission, or broadcast for distance learning.

Some ancillaries, including electronic and print components, may not be available to customers outside the United States.

This book is printed on acid-free paper.

1 2 3 4 5 6 7 8 9 LWI 28 27 26 25 24 23

ISBN 978-1-266-63450-5 (bound edition)
MHID 1-266-63450-9 (bound edition)
ISBN 978-1-265-61592-5 (loose-leaf edition)
MHID 1-265-61592-6 (loose-leaf edition)

Portfolio Manager: *Noelle Bathurst*
Product Developer: *Erin Quinones and Rachel Hinton*
Marketing Manager: *Kaitlin Murray*
Content Project Managers: *Pat Frederickson and Angela Norris*
Manufacturing Project Manager: *Sandy Ludovissy*
Design: *Matt Diamond*
Content Licensing Specialist: *Beth Cray*
Cover Images: *lighthouse image: Martin73/Shutterstock; big data image: INGARA/Shutterstock*
Compositor: *Straive*

All credits appearing on page or at the end of the book are considered to be an extension of the copyright page.

Library of Congress Cataloging-in-Publication Data

Cataloging-in-Publication Data has been requested from the Library of Congress.

The Internet addresses listed in the text were accurate at the time of publication. The inclusion of a website does not indicate an endorsement by the authors or McGraw Hill LLC, and McGraw Hill LLC does not guarantee the accuracy of the information presented at these sites.

mheducation.com/highered

About the Authors

Ray H. Garrison

Ray H. Garrison is emeritus professor of accounting at Brigham Young University, Provo, Utah. He received his BS and MS degrees from Brigham Young University and his DBA degree from Indiana University.

As a certified public accountant, Professor Garrison has been involved in management consulting work with both national and regional accounting firms. He has published articles in *The Accounting Review, Management Accounting,* and other professional journals. Innovation in the classroom has earned Professor Garrison the Karl G. Maeser Distinguished Teaching Award from Brigham Young University.

Eric W. Noreen

Eric W. Noreen has taught at INSEAD in France and the Hong Kong Institute of Science and Technology and is emeritus professor of accounting at the University of Washington. Currently, he is the Accounting Circle Professor of Accounting, Fox School of Business, Temple University.

He received his BA degree from the University of Washington and MBA and PhD degrees from Stanford University. A Certified Management Accountant, he was awarded a Certificate of Distinguished Performance by the Institute of Certified Management Accountants.

Professor Noreen has served as associate editor of *The Accounting Review* and the *Journal of Accounting and Economics.* He has numerous articles in academic journals including the *Journal of Accounting Research; The Accounting Review;* the *Journal of Accounting and Economics; Accounting Horizons; Accounting, Organizations and Society; Contemporary Accounting Research;* the *Journal of Management Accounting Research;* and the *Review of Accounting Studies.*

Professor Noreen has won a number of awards from students for his teaching.

Peter C. Brewer teaches in the Department of Accountancy at Wake Forest University. Prior to joining the faculty at Wake Forest, he was an accounting professor at Miami University for 19 years. He holds a BS degree in accounting from Penn State University, an MS degree in accounting from the University of Virginia, and a PhD from the University of Tennessee. He has published more than 40 articles in a variety of journals including *Management Accounting Research;* the *Journal of Information Systems; Cost Management; Strategic Finance;* the *Journal of Accountancy; Issues in Accounting Education;* and the *Journal of Business Logistics.*

Professor Brewer has served on the editorial boards of the *Journal of Accounting Education* and *Issues in Accounting Education.* His article "Putting Strategy into the Balanced Scorecard" won the 2003 International Federation of Accountants' Articles of Merit competition, and his articles "Using Six Sigma to Improve the Finance Function" and "Lean Accounting: What's It All About?" were awarded the Institute of Management Accountants' Lybrand Gold and Silver Medals in 2005 and 2006. He has received Miami University's Richard T. Farmer School of Business Teaching Excellence Award.

Professor Brewer and his wife own a Howdy Homemade Ice Cream shop in Asheville, North Carolina (www.howdyavl.com). Howdy Homemade's highest priority is recruiting, training, retaining, and promoting its employees—the majority of whom have intellectual and developmental disabilities. The company's employees "pay it forward" by serving all members of their community and *inspiring all of us to realize the potential in each of us.*

Dedication

To our families and to our many colleagues who use this book.

Let **Garrison** be Your Guide

For centuries, the lighthouse has provided guidance and safe passage for sailors. Similarly, Garrison/Noreen/Brewer has successfully guided millions of students through managerial accounting, lighting the way and helping them sail smoothly through the course.

Decades ago, lighthouses were still being operated manually. In these days of digital transformation, lighthouses are run using automatic lamp changers and other modern devices. In much the same way, Garrison/Noreen/Brewer has evolved over the years. Today, this edition of the Garrison book affirms its tradition of guiding students—accounting majors and other business majors alike—safely through the course while also embracing innovation through the incorporation of **Data Analytics Exercises.** These exercises teach students how to use the power of Excel to derive managerial insights and then communicate those findings in visually compelling ways. They also provide students with the opportunity to interpret and create data visualizations within Tableau and Power BI two of the most popular data visualization software packages used in business today. These innovative features build on a tradition of inventive, powerful tools created to augment student learning and increase student motivation.

Connect

The eighteenth edition of Garrison's learning system in Connect features the following: **SmartBook 2.0's** adaptive learning and reading experience, **Concept Overview Videos, Guided Examples, Audio Hints, Data Analytics Content, Integrated Excel, Applying Excel,** and more. Quality assessment continues to be a focus of Connect, with over 9,300 questions available for assignment, including more than 1,600 new test bank questions.

I have used the Garrison textbook for many years and can say that the textbook is by far one of my favorite textbooks in terms of content, exercises and problems, and online resources. As instructors we are being asked more and more to provide students with critical thinking exercises. Some of the Garrison problems are quite comprehensive and require great problem solving skills. . .

Stacy Kline, Drexel University

It is one of the best texts for Managerial Accounting available. It covers desired materials and allows choices about how to cover the data. I really like this text.

Pamela Baker, Texas Women's University

This is a total learning system that provides the student with a vast variety of ways to learn the material and concepts. It's almost entertaining.

Rhonda K Thomas, Butler Community College

Just as the lighthouse continues to provide reliable guidance to seafarers, the Garrison/Noreen/Brewer book continues its tradition of leading the way and helping students sail successfully through managerial accounting by always focusing on three important qualities: **relevance, accuracy,** and **clarity.**

RELEVANCE.

Every effort is made to help students relate the concepts in this book to the decisions made by working managers. The Garrison author team also ensures that *Managerial Accounting* stays current with the latest pedagogy and digital tools. The eighteenth edition expands the incorporation of **Data Analytics Exercises** that allow students to analyze, interpret, and visualize accounting data using Excel, Tableau, and Power BI with auto-graded questions assignable within Connect. These exercises enable students to develop both analytical and communication skills within an accounting context that are highly valued in the marketplace.

ACCURACY.

The Garrison book continues to set the standard for accurate and reliable material in its eighteenth edition. With each revision, the authors evaluate the book and its supplements in their entirety, working diligently to ensure that the end-of-chapter material, solutions manual, and test bank are consistent, current, and accurate.

CLARITY.

Generations of students have praised Garrison for the friendliness and readability of its writing, but that's just the beginning. In the eighteenth edition, the authors have rewritten various chapters with input and guidance from instructors around the country to ensure that teaching and learning from Garrison remains as easy as it can be.

The authors' steady focus on these three core elements has led to tremendous results. *Managerial Accounting* has consistently led the market, being used by over two million students and earning a reputation for reliability that other texts aspire to match.

> The text makes the subject matter practical and interesting. It also does not get bogged down in complicated explanations, but rather provides simple and easy to follow explanations. The supporting textbook problems are also well-written and work well for assigning homework.
>
> *Kari Olsen, Utah State University*

> I feel this is the strongest textbook on the market for managerial accounting. It provides the needed depth for accounting majors yet is accessible for the non-accounting major. The book blends theory and practice successfully in a well-integrated and useful way.
>
> *Joseph Gerard, University of Wisconsin–Whitewater*

> LOVE IT! best managerial book out there. I cannot imagine using anything else at this point based on my reviews.
>
> *Jerrilyn Eisenhauer, Tulsa Community College*

> It is very difficult to create a textbook that will satisfy the needs of students and faculty. This book is very well done, and each instructor can utilize the materials they deem the most important. Classroom time is limited; the more resources available to students to utilize on their own, the better the opportunity for full understanding of the materials.
>
> *Jacklyn Collins, University of Miami*

Managerial Accounting includes pedagogical elements that engage and instruct students without cluttering the pages or interrupting student learning. Garrison's key pedagogical tools enhance and support students' understanding of the concepts rather than compete with the narrative for their attention.

This text allows the text to be utilized as an introductory course with availability to expand the course with a higher level pedagogy.

David Laurel, South Texas College

New* Continuing Case: Howdy Homemade Ice Cream

The eighteenth edition includes a new Continuing Case in Connect that follows managerial accounting decisions at a real company. Howdy Homemade Ice Cream is a real company, and the Asheville, NC franchise that forms the foundation for this case study is owned and operated by author Pete Brewer. The serial case study that spans most of the textbook's chapters enables students to see that managerial accounting provides an **integrated** set of tools that support organizational planning, control, and decision making.

The business serves a product line that is familiar to all students—ice cream! This familiar context is more engaging for students than a generic manufacturing setting. The company's primary mission is to employ adults with intellectual and developmental disabilities, thereby exposing students to the important topic of environmental, social, & governance (ESG) responsibilities.

Courtesy of Howdy Catering LLC/Howdy Homemade Ice Cream

Chapter Opener Features

Each chapter opens with an **Entrepreneur Spotlight** that serves four purposes. First, it acknowledges small business entrepreneurs as the life-blood of our economy. Second, it features an inclusive group of entrepreneurs to ensure all of our students can see themselves within these vignettes. Third, it connects each entrepreneur's company to the subject matter covered within the corresponding chapter. Fourth, it describes how each entrepreneur's company fulfills its environmental, social, and governance (ESG) responsibilities. **Learning Objectives** alert students to what they should expect as they progress through the chapter.

> **The vignettes do a good job of highlighting to students the practical application of concepts. In other words, it helps them see why the concepts matter.**
>
> *Andrew Felo, Nova Southeastern University*

> **I believe the real-world examples at the start of the chapter get the students to see the real-world application and "buy-in" to the learning process because it makes the information more "real" and relevant.**
>
> *Elizabeth Cannata, Johnson and Wales University*

Chapter 4

lighthouse image: Martin73/Shutterstock;
big data image: INGARA/Shutterstock

LEARNING OBJECTIVES

After studying Chapter 4, you should be able to:

LO4–1 Record the flow of materials, labor, and overhead through a process costing system.

LO4–2 Compute the equivalent units of production using the weighted-average method.

LO4–3 Compute the cost per equivalent unit using the weighted-average method.

LO4–4 Assign costs to units using the weighted-average method.

LO4–5 Prepare a cost reconciliation report using the weighted-average method.

LO4–6 *(Appendix 4A) Compute the equivalent units of production using the FIFO method.*

LO4–7 *(Appendix 4A) Compute the cost per equivalent unit using the FIFO method.*

LO4–8 *(Appendix 4A) Assign costs to units using the FIFO method.*

LO4–9 *(Appendix 4A) Prepare a cost reconciliation report using the FIFO method.*

LO4–10 *(Appendix 4B) Allocate service department costs to operating departments using the direct method.*

LO4–11 *(Appendix 4B) Allocate service department costs to operating departments using the step-down method.*

Data Analytics Exercise available in Connect to complement this chapter

Process Costing

Rob Kim/Getty Images for NYCWFF

ENTREPRENEUR SPOTLIGHT

Formed by sisters Robin McBride and Andrea McBride-John, the McBride Sisters Collection is the largest Black- and women-owned vineyard to produce and distribute its own wines in the United States. The sisters, who share a father, grew up worlds apart—Robin in Monterey, CA, and Andrea in Marlborough, New Zealand. Being unaware of each other's existence until they reached adulthood, the two women quickly bonded around a shared passion for wine. Today, their most sought-after wines, which combine "old world elegance with new world finesse," can be found in Target, Kroger, and Total Wines stores nationwide.

Applying Managerial Accounting

The McBride sisters could use process costing to calculate unit product costs. For example, the company might define its departments as Harvesting, Crushing and Pressing, Fermenting, Clarifying, and finally Aging and Bottling. In the Fermenting Department, the company could calculate the equivalent units of production and the cost per equivalent unit. This cost information could then be used to calculate the cost of ending work in process inventory within the Fermenting Department and the cost of the units completed and transferred to the Clarifying Department.

In Business Boxes

These helpful boxed features offer a glimpse into how real companies use the managerial accounting concepts discussed within the chapter. Each chapter contains multiple current examples.

"Managerial Accounting in Action" and "In Business" boxes are also really nice additional features in the ext. These insights into how the concepts in the chapter relate to real business help he information come alive to students.

ny Bentley, Tallahassee Community College

**MANAGERIAL ACCOUNTING IN ACTION
THE ISSUE**

ACOUSTIC concepts inc

Prem started Acoustic Concepts, Inc., to market a new speaker he designed for automobile sound systems. The speaker, called the Sonic Blaster, uses an advanced microprocessor and proprietary software to boost amplification to awesome levels. Prem contracted with a Taiwanese electronics manufacturer to produce the speaker. With seed money provided by his family, Prem placed an order with the manufacturer and ran advertisements in auto magazines.

The Sonic Blaster's immediate success enabled Prem to move the company's headquarters out of his apartment and into a nearby industrial park. He also hired a receptionist, an accountant, a sales manager, and a small sales staff to sell the speakers to retail stores. The accountant, Bob Luchinni, had worked for several small companies where he acted as a business advisor and bookkeeper. The following discussion occurred soon after Bob was hired:

Prem: Bob, I have a lot of questions about the company's finances that I hope you can answer.

Bob: We're in great shape. The loan from your family will be paid off within a few months.

---

[1] One additional assumption often used in manufacturing companies is that inventories do not change. The number of units produced equals the number of units sold.

---

anagerial Accounting in Action Vignettes

e vignettes depict cross-functional teams working together in real-life settings, :ing with the products and services that students recognize from their own . Students are shown step by step how accounting concepts are implemented ganizations and how these concepts are applied to solve everyday business lems. First, "The Issue" is introduced through a dialogue; the student then s through the implementation process; finally, "The Wrap-up" summarizes the icture.

I think the "In Business" boxes are very helpful—they are short, concise, and on point. I think it is helpful they appear throughout the chapter.

Elizabeth Cannata, Johnson and Wales University

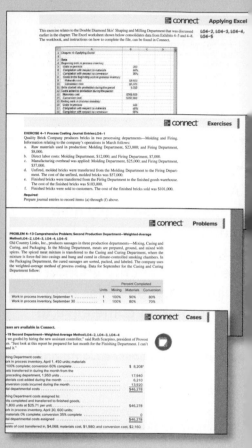

End-of-Chapter Material

Managerial Accounting has earned a reputation for the best end-of-chapter practice material of any text on the market. Our problem and case material continues to conform to AACSB recommendations and makes a great starting point for class discussions and group projects. When Ray Garrison first wrote *Managerial Accounting,* he started with the end-of-chapter material, then wrote the narrative in support of it. This unique approach to textbook authoring not only ensured consistency between the end-of-chapter material and text content but also underscored Garrison's fundamental belief in the importance of applying theory through practice. It is not enough for students to read; they must also understand. To this day, the guiding principle of that first edition remains, and Garrison's superior end-of-chapter material continues to provide accurate, current, and relevant practice for students.

Utilizing the Icons

This icon indicates **Data Analytic Exercises** in Connect tied to chapter learning objectives.

To reflect our service-based economy, the text is replete with examples from service-based businesses. A helpful icon distinguishes service-related examples in the text.

Ethics assignments and examples serve as a reminder that good conduct is vital in business. Icons call out content that relates to ethical behavior for students.

The writing icon denotes problems that require students to use critical thinking as well as writing skills to explain their decisions.

Garrison   Noreen   Brewer

...hor-Written Supplements

...e other managerial accounting texts, the book's authors write the major
...lements such as the test bank and solution files, ensuring a perfect fit between
...nd supplements.

...Foundational 15

...chapter contains one **Foundational 15** exercise that includes 15 "building-
..." questions related to one concise set of data. These exercises can be used
...-class discussion or as homework assignments. They are found before the
...ises and are available in **Connect**.

Data Analytics Exercises

Data Analytics Exercises teach students how to use software tools to derive manag insights and communicate them to stakeholders. These exercises, which appear in Con are linked to a diverse range of learning objectives that span numerous chapters. So these exercises require students to use various Microsoft Excel–based tools, such as Seek, Pivot Tables, and Solver, to analyze data sets to derive solutions. Other exer also teach students how to use a variety of **Data Visualization** techniques, such as charts, graphs, and maps, to communicate their findings in succinct and compelling ways. Students will also be given the opportunity to acquire the value-added skill of interpreting Tableau data visualizations and creating visualizations in both Tableau and Microsoft Power BI.

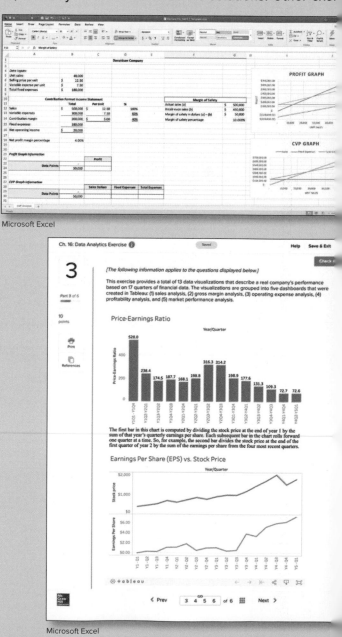

Microsoft Excel

Microsoft Excel

...gration Exercises

...ave a total of 20 **Integration Exercises in the eighteenth edition.** These ...cises, which are located in the back of the book, integrate learning objectives ...ss more than one chapter. They help increase the students' level of interest ...e course by forging connections across chapters. Rather than seeing each ...ter as an isolated set of learning objectives, students begin to see how ...1 fits together" to provide greater managerial insight and more effective ...ning, controlling, and decision making. The **Integration Exercises** are also ...-made for flipping the classroom because they offer challenging questions ...require students to work in teams to derive solutions that synthesize what ...are learning throughout the semester.

> **The Integration Exercises provide a significant opportunity to keep specific concepts on the forefront of a student's comprehension. This exposure is essential for critical thinking ability.**
>
> *Rhonda Thomas, Butler Community College*
>
> **This (Integration Exercises) is an exciting addition; it is missing from most texts and definitely not included in the one we are using now. These are the types of problems that I write for myself so that students are given the opportunity to review and continue working with concepts throughout the text.**
>
> *Kim Lyons, University of Wisconsin—LaCrosse*

...V* Author-Created Learning Objective Videos

...or Pete Brewer created narrated PowerPoint videos for each chapter. There is one video for every learning objective ...chapter overview videos. Each video is three to eight minutes in duration and includes a brief explanation of the learning ...tive's key concepts accompanied by a numerical example.

Concept Overview Videos

Concept Overview Videos, available within Connect, teach the core concepts of the content in an animated, narrated, and interactive multimedia format, bringing the key learning objectives of the course to life. Checkpoint questions allow instructors to assign points to knowledge checks and grade for accuracy, not just completion. **Concept Overview Videos** are particularly helpful for online courses and for those audio and visual learners who struggle reading the textbook page by page.

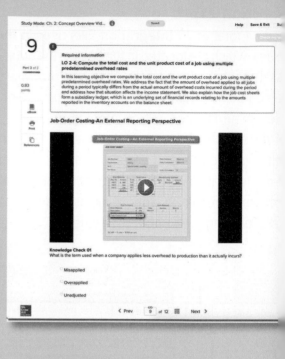

NEW* Integrated Excel Assignments

Integrated Excel assignments pair the power of Microsoft Excel with the pow Connect. A seamless integration of Excel within Connect, Integrated Excel ques allow students to work in live, auto-graded Excel spreadsheets—no additional logins, no need to upload or download files. Instructors can choose to grade by formula or solution value, and students receive instant cell-level feedback via integrated Check My Work functionality.

lighthouse image: Martin73/Shutterstock; big data image: INGARA/Shutterstock

Microsoft Excel

ded Examples/Hint
eos

ed Example/Hint Videos
ide an animated walk-through
narration of select exercises
ar to those assigned. These
presentations, which can
urned on or off by instructors,
de reinforcement when
ents need it most.

nect-Only Test Bank

nline-only test bank is available in Connect, containing more than **1,600 multiple-**
e test bank questions. These new, author-created **Connect-only Test Bank**
ions were written in such a way to prevent students from finding answers on
nal sites. The questions are presented in a combination of static and algorithmic
quantitative and qualitative algo) modes and cover all learning objectives in all of
hapters. The questions are qualitative and quantitative in nature and span the entire
ree-of-difficulty" continuum, including easy, medium, and hard.

Builder in Connect

able within Connect, Test Builder is a cloud-based tool that enables instructors
rmat tests that can be printed or administered within a LMS. Test Builder offers a
ern, streamlined interface for easy content configuration that matches course needs,
ut requiring a download.

Builder allows you to:

cess all test bank content from a particular title.

sily pinpoint the most relevant content through robust filtering options.

nipulate the order of questions or scramble questions and/or answers.

questions to a specific location within a test.

ermine your preferred treatment of algorithmic questions.

oose the layout and spacing.

d instructions and configure default settings.

Builder provides a secure interface for better protection of content and allows for just-
e updates to flow directly into assessments.

lighthouse image: Martin73/Shutterstock; big data image: INGARA/Shutterstock

Tegrity: Lectures 24/7

Tegrity in Connect is a tool that makes class time available 24/7 by automatically turing every lecture. With a simple one-click start-and-stop process, you captur computer screens and corresponding audio in a format that is easy to search, fi by frame. Students can replay any part of any class with easy-to-use, browser-b viewing on a PC, Mac, iPod, or other mobile device.

Educators know that the more students can see, hear, and experience class resou the better they learn. In fact, studies prove it. Tegrity's unique search feature I students efficiently find what they need, when they need it, across an entire sem of class recordings. Help turn your students' study time into learning mom immediately supported by your lecture. With Tegrity, you also increase intent liste and class participation by easing students' concerns about note-taking. Using Tegr Connect will make it more likely you will see students' faces, not the tops of their he

Assurance of Learning Ready

Many educational institutions today are focused on the notion of assurance of learnin important element of some accreditation standards. *Managerial Accounting,* 18e, is des specifically to support your assurance of learning initiatives with a simple, yet powerful, sol

Each question for *Managerial Accounting,* 18e, maps to a specific chapter learning outc objective listed in the text. The reporting features of **Connect** can aggregate studer make the collection and presentation of assurance of learning data simple and easy.

AACSB Statement

McGraw Hill Education is a proud corporate member of AACSB International. Recogr the importance and value of AACSB accreditation, we have sought to recognize the cur guidelines detailed in AACSB standards for business accreditation by connecting sel questions in *Managerial Accounting,* 18e, to the general knowledge and skill guide found in the AACSB standards. The statements contained in *Managerial Accounting,* are provided only as a guide for the users of this text. The AACSB leaves content cov and assessment clearly within the realm and control of individual schools, the mission school, and the faculty. The AACSB does also charge schools with the obligation of assessment against their own content and learning goals. While *Managerial Accou* 18e, and its teaching package make no claim of any specific AACSB qualificati evaluation, we have, within *Managerial Accounting,* 18e, tagged questions according six general knowledge and skills areas. The labels or tags within *Managerial Accou* 18e, are as indicated. There are, of course, many more within the test bank, the tex the teaching package which that be used as a "standard" for your course. Howeve labeled questions are suggested for your consideration.

New in the Eighteenth Edition

Faculty feedback helps us continue to improve *Managerial Accounting.* In response to reviewer suggestions, the authors have made the following changes to the text:

- New **Entrepreneur Spotlights** have been added to the beginning of each chapter to highlight diverse businesspeople, their managerial decisions, and the ways they give back to their communities.
- New **Communicating with Data Visualizations** features in every chapter illustrate how analytics and data visualization can be used to answer managerial accounting questions.
- New **Howdy Homemade Ice Cream Continuing Case** in Connect brings managerial accounting to the real world with engaging case materials, videos, exercises, and more. The Continuing Case focuses on the start-up of a real franchise business, Howdy Homemade Ice Cream, in Asheville, NC.
- Additional *Data Analytics Exercises* and auto-graded **Tableau Dashboard Activities** have been added for each chapter in Connect for this edition.
- New **author-created videos** cover each learning objective in the chapter along with overview videos for each chapter.

- **In-Business boxes** are updated throughout to provide relevant and current real-world examples for use in classroom discussion and to support student understanding of key concepts as they read through a chapter.

Chapter-Specific Changes

Prologue

Revised Exhibit P–1 and its corresponding text to better describe the differences between financial accounting and managerial accounting. Revised the definition of strategy to better reflect its true meaning. Added coverage of organizational environmental, social, and governance (ESG) responsibilities as well as three new In Business boxes.

Chapter 1

Added four new In Business boxes.

Chapter 2

Added a new learning objective related to calculating ending inventories for the balance sheet and cost of goods sold for the income statement. Also, revised the Foundational 15, Exercise 2–17, and Problem 2–22. Added two new In Business boxes.

Chapter 3

Added three new In Business boxes.

Chapter 4

Added three new In Business boxes.

Chapter 5

Reorganized the sequence of learning objectives to improve the students' ability to understand the material. Introduced Microsoft Excel as a tool for creating CVP and profit graphs. Added four new In Business boxes.

Chapter 6

Heavily edited the chapter to cover the same learning objectives in fewer pages. Added three new In Business boxes.

Chapter 7

Heavily edited the chapter to cover the same learning objectives in fewer pages. Added three new In Business boxes.

Chapter 8

Heavily edited the chapter to cover the same lear objectives in fewer pages. Added two new In Busi boxes.

Chapter 9

Added three new In Business boxes.

Chapter 10

Added two new In Business boxes.

Chapter 11

Added two new In Business boxes.

Chapter 12

Added coverage of organizational environmental, s and governance (ESG) reporting as well as four ne Business boxes.

Chapter 13

Changed the language accompanying lea objective 6–3 from the manufacturing-centric " or buy decisions" to the broader business langua "sourcing decisions." Created three new end-of-ch exercises (6–11, 6–18, and 6–20) to illustrate (1 decision to add a product line, (2) sourcing decisic a nonmanufacturing context, and (3) the relevan replacement costs in decision making. Also, added new In Business boxes.

Chapter 14

Added four new In Business boxes.

Chapter 15

Added three new learning objectives correspondi the three sections of the statement of cash flows. added seven new end-of-chapter exercises.

Chapter 16

Added two new In Business boxes.

Instructors
Student Success Starts with You

Tools to enhance your unique voice

Want to build your own course? No problem. Prefer to use an OLC-aligned, prebuilt course? Easy. Want to make changes throughout the semester? Sure. And you'll save time with Connect's auto-grading, too.

65%
Less Time Grading

Laptop: Getty Images; Woman/dog: George Doyle/Getty Images

A unique path for each student

In Connect, instructors can assign an adaptive reading experience with SmartBook® 2.0. Rooted in advanced learning science principles, SmartBook 2.0 delivers each student a personalized experience, focusing students on their learning gaps, ensuring that the time they spend studying is time well-spent. **mheducation.com/highered/connect/smartbook**

Affordable solutions, added value

Make technology work for you with LMS integration for single sign-on access, mobile access to the digital textbook, and reports to quickly show you how each of your students is doing. And with our Inclusive Access program, you can provide all these tools at the lowest available market price to your students. Ask your McGraw Hill representative for more information.

Solutions for your challenges

A product isn't a solution. Real solutions are affordable, reliable, and come with training and ongoing support when you need it and how you want it. Visit **supportateverystep.com** for videos and resources both you and your students can use throughout the term.

Students
Get Learning that Fits You

Effective tools for efficient studying

Connect is designed to help you be more productive with simple, flexible, intuitive tools that maximize your study time and meet your individual learning needs. Get learning that works for you with Connect.

Study anytime, anywhere

Download the free ReadAnywhere® app and access your online eBook, SmartBook® 2.0, or Adaptive Learning Assignments when it's convenient, even if you're offline. And since the app automatically syncs with your Connect account, all of your work is available every time you open it. Find out more at **mheducation.com/readanywhere**

"I really liked this app—it made it easy to study when you don't have your text-book in front of you."

- Jordan Cunningham, Eastern Washington University

iPhone: Getty Images

Everything you need in one place

Your Connect course has everything you need—whether reading your digital eBook or completing assignments for class, Connect makes it easy to get your work done.

Learning for everyone

McGraw Hill works directly with Accessibility Services Departments and faculty to meet the learning needs of all students. Please contact your Accessibility Services Office and ask them to email accessibility@mheducation.com, or visit **mheducation.com/about/accessibility** for more information.

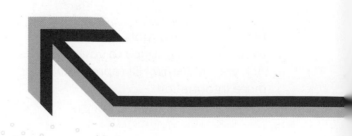

Acknowledgments

Suggestions from professors, students, and the professional accounting community continue to drive the excellence and refinement of each edition of this book. Each of those who have offered comments and suggestions has our immense gratitude and thanks.

The efforts of many people are needed to continually refine a text and maintain its excellence. Among these people are the reviewers and consultants who point out areas of concern, cite areas of strength, and make recommendations for change. In this regard, the following academics have provided feedback that was enormously helpful in preparing the eighteenth edition of *Managerial Accounting:*

Dawn Addington, *Central New Mexico Community College*

Nasrollah Ahadiat, *California State PolytecnicUniversity*

Markus Ahrens, *St. Louis Community College–Meramec*

Akinloye Akindayomi, *University Of Massachusetts–Dartmouth*

David Albrecht, *Bowling Green State University*

Natalie Allen, *Texas A & M University*

Vern Allen, *Central Florida Community College*

Shamir Ally, *DeSales University*

Deepthi Amaradasa, *North Central Texas College*

Felix Amenkhienan, *Radford University*

Jane Austin, *Oklahoma City University*

John Babich, *Kankakee Community College*

Pamela Baker, *Texas Women's University*

Ibolya Balog, *Cedar Crest College*

Bonnie Banks, *Alabama A&M University*

Scottie Barty, *Northern Kentucky University*

Eric Bashaw, *University of Nevada–Las Vegas*

Lamrot Bekele, *Dallas County Community College*

Phyllis Belak, *West Chester University*

Sharon Bell, *University of North Carolina–Pembroke*

Pamela Benner, *Stark State Park*

Stephen Benner, *Eastern Illinois University*

Amy Bentley, Tallahassee Community College

Scott Berube, *University of New Hampshire*

Kelly Blacker, *Mercy College*

Phillip Blanchard, *The University of Arizona*

Charles Blumer, *Saint Charles Community College*

Rachel Brassine, *East Carolina University*

Alison Jill Brock, *Imperial Valley College*

Ann Brooks, *University of New Mexico*

Rada Brooks, *University of California–Berkeley*

Myra Bruegger, *Southeastern Community College*

Georgia Buckles, *Manchester Community College*

Esther Bunn, *Stephen S. Austin State University*

Raymond E. Burgess, *University of Kentucky*

Laurie Burney, *Mississippi State University*

Marci Butterfield, *University of Utah–Salt Lake City*

Charles Caliendo, *University of Minnesota*

Donald Campbell, *Brigham Young University–Idaho*

Don Campodonico, *Notre Dame de Namur University*

Elizabeth Cannata, *Johnson and Wales University*

Dana Carpenter, *Madison Area Technical College*

Wanda Causseaux, *Valdosta State University*

David Centers, *Grand Valley State University*

Sandra Cereola, *James Madison University*

Gayle Chaky, *Dutchess Community College*

Pamela Champeau, *University of Wisconsin Whitewater*

Kathryn Chang, *Sonoma State University*

Linda Chase, *Baldwin Wallace University*

Valerie Chau, *Palomar College*

Clement Chen, *University of Michigan–Flint*

Carolyn Christesen, *Westchester Community College*

Star Ciccio, *Johnson and Wales University*

Richard S. Claire, *Canada College*

Dina Clark, *Bloomsburg University of Pennsylvania*

Robert Clarke, *Brigham Young University–Idaho*

Curtis Clements, *Abilene Christian University*

Darlene Coarts, *University of Northern Iowa*

Jacklyn Collins, *University of Miami*

Ron Collins, *Miami University–Ohio*

Carol Coman, *California Lutheran University*

Jackie Conrecode, *Florida Gulf Coast University*

Debora Constable, *Georgia Perimeter College*

Rita Cook, *University of Delaware*

Wendy Coons, *University of Maine*

Susan Corder, *Johnson County Community College*

Michael Cornick, *Winthrop University*

Deb Cosgrove, *University of Nebraska–Lincoln*

Kathy Crusto-Way, *Tarrant County College*

Robin D'Agati, *Palm Beach State College–Lake Worth*

Masako Darrough, *Baruch College*

Patricia Davis, *Keystone College*

Kathleen Davisson, *University of Denver*

Nina Doherty, *Arkansas Tech University*

Patricia Doherty, *Boston University*
Carleton Donchess, *Bridgewater State University*
Kenneth James Doolittle, *Penn Foster*
Peter Dorff, *Kent State University*
David Doyon, *Southern New Hampshire University*
Emily Drogt, *Grand Valley State University*
Rita Dufour, *Northeast Wisconsin Technical College*
Joseph Bernard Dulin, *University of Oklahoma*
Dean Edmiston, *Emporia State University*
Barb Eide, *University of Wisconsin–Lacrosse*
Jerrilyn Eisenhauer, *Tulsa Community College*
Rafik Elias, *California State University–Los Angeles*
Dr. Gene Elrod, *University of Texas at Arlington*
Raymond Elson, *Valdosta State University*
Richard F. Emery, *Linfield College*
Ruth Epps, *Virginia Commonwealth University*
John Eubanks, *Independence Community College*
Christopher M. Fairchild, *Southeastern University*
Amanda Farmer, *University of Georgia*
Jack Fatica, *Terra Community College*
Christos Fatouros, *Curry College*
Andrew Felo, *Nova Southeastern University*
Susan Ferguson, *James Madison University*
Janice Fergusson, *University of South Carolina*
Jerry Ferry, *University of North Alabama*
Calvin Fink, *Bethune Cookman University*
Virginia Fullwood, *Texas A&M University–Commerce*
Robert Gannon, *Alvernia University*
Joseph Gerard, *University of Wisconsin Whitewater*
Frank Gersich, *Monmouth College*
Hubert Gill, *North Florida*
Paul Gilles, *University of North Carolina–Charlotte*
Jeff Gillespie, *University of Delaware*
Earl Godfrey, *Gardner-Webb University*
Nina Goza, *Arkansas Tech University*
Marina Grau, *Huston Community College–Northwest College*
Alfred C. Greenfield Jr., *High Point University*
Olen Greer, *Missouri State University*
Connie Groer, *Frostburg State University*
Steve Groves, *Ivy Tech Community College of Indiana–Kokomo*
Thomas Guarino, *Plymouth State University*
Bob Gutschick, *College of Southern Nevada*
Alexandra Hampshire, *Texas State University*
Ty Handy, *Vermont Technical College*
David Harr, *George Mason University*
Michael Haselkorn, *Bentley University*
Susan Hass, *Simmons College*
John Haverty, *St. Joseph's University*

Hassan Hefzi, *Cal Poly Pomona University*
Candice Heino, *Anoka Ramsey Community College*
Sueann Hely, *West Kentucky Community & Technical College*
David Henderson, *College of Charleston*
Donna Hetzel, *Western Michigan University–Kalamazoo*
Kristina Hoang, *Tulane University*
Cynthia Hollenbach, *University of Denver*
Peg Horan, *Wagner College*
Rong Huang, *Baruch College*
Steven Huddart, *Penn State*
George Hunt, *Stephen F. Austin State University*
Gilberto Marquez Illescas, *University of Rhode Island*
Marianne James, *California State University, Los Angeles*
Mary Jepperson, *College of Saint Benedict & Saint John's University*
Gene Johnson, *Clark College*
Becky Jones, *Baylor University*
Jeffrey Jones, *College of Southern Nevada*
Kevin Jones, *Drexel University*
Kevin Keith Jones, *University of California–Santa Cruz*
Bill Joyce, *Minnesota State University–Mankato*
Celina Jozsi, *University of South Florida*
Robert L. Kachur, *Richard Stockton College of New Jersey*
Gokham Karahan, *University of Anchorage Alaska*
Loisanne Kattelman, *Weber State University*
Sue Kattelus, *Michigan State University–East Lansing*
Nancy Kelly, *Middlesex Community College*
Anna Kenner, *Brevard Community College*
Sara Kern, *Gonzaga University*
Lara Kessler, *Grand Valley State University*
Mozaffar Khan, *University of Minnesota*
Frank Klaus, *Cleveland State University*
Shirly Kleiner, *Johnson County Community College*
Stacy Kline, *Drexel University*
Christine Kloezeman, *Glendale Community College*
Bill Knowles, *University of New Hampshire*
Barbara Kren, *Marquette University*
Jerry Kreuze, *Western Michigan University*
Ranjani Krishnan, *Georgetown University*
David Krug, *Johnson County Community College*
Wikil Kwak, *Nebraska Omaha*
C. Andrew Lafond, *LaSalle University*
Dr. Ben Lansford, *Rice University*
David Laurel, *South Texas College*
Brian R. Lazarus, *Baltimore City Community College*
Yvette Lazdowski, *Plymouth State University*
Ron Lazer, *University of Houston–Houston*

Raymond Levesque, *Bentley College*
Jing Lin, *Saint Joseph's University*
Serena Loftus, *Tulane University*
Dennis Lopez, *University of Texas–San Antonio*
Gina Lord, *Santa Rosa Junior College*
Don Lucy, *Indian River State College*
Cathy Lumbattis, *Southern Illinois University*
Joseph F. Lupino, *St. Mary's College of California*
Patrick M. Lynch, *Loyola University of New Orleans*
Kim Lyons, *University of Wisconsin–LaCrosse*
Suneel Maheshwari, *Marshall University*
Linda Malgeri, *Kennesaw State University*
Michael Manahan, *California State University–Dominquez Hills*
Carol Mannino, *Milwaukee School of Engineering*
Steven Markoff, *Montclair State University*
Linda Marquis, *Northern Kentucky University*
Melissa Martin, *Arizona State University*
Michele Martinez, *Hillsborough Community College*
Josephine Mathias, *Mercer Community College*
Florence McGovern, *Bergen Community College*
Annie McGowan, *Texas A&M University*
Dawn McKinley, *William Rainey Harper College*
Michael McLain, *Hampton University*
Gloria McVay, *Winona State University*
Heidi Meier, *Cleveland State University*
Francis Melaragni, *MCPHS University*
Shawn Miller, *Lone Star College*
Edna Mitchell, *Polk State College*
Kim Mollberg, *Minnesota State University–Moorhead*
Shirley Montagne, *Lyndon State College*
Andrew Morgret, *Christian Brothers University*
Jennifer Moriarty, *Hudson Valley Community College*
Kenneth Morlino, *Wilmington University*
Michael Morris, *University of Notre Dame*
Mark Motluck, *Anderson University*
Heminigild Mpundu, *University of Northern Iowa*
Matt Muller, *Adirondack Community College*
Pam Neely, *SUNY Brockport*
Michael Newman, *University of Houston–Houston*
Hossein Noorian, *Wentworth Institue of Technology*
Christopher O'Byrne, *Cuyamaca College*
Kari Olsen, *Utah State University*
Janet O'Tousa, *University of Notre Dame*
Mehmet Ozbilgin, *Bernard M. Baruch College*
Angela Pannell, *Mississippi State University*
Janet Papiernik, *Indiana University–Purdue University Fort Wayne*
Abbie Gail Parham, *Georgia Southern*
Glenn Pate, *Palm Beach State College*

Mary Pearson, *Southern Utah University*
Judy Peterson, *Monmouth College*
Yvonne Phang, *Bernard M. Baruch College*
Debbie Pike, *Saint Louis University*
Jo Ann Pinto, *Montclair State University*
Janice Pitera, *Broome Community College*
Matthew Probst, *Ivy Tech Community College*
Laura Prosser, *Black Hills State University*
Herbert Purick, *Palm Beach State College–Lake Worth*
Rama Ramamurthy, *Georgetown University*
Robert Jay Rankin, *Texas A&M University, Commerce*
Paulette Ratliff-Miller, *Grand Valley State University*
Vasant Raval, *Creighton University*
Margaret Reed, *University of Cincinnati*
Vernon Richardson, *University of Arkansas–Fayetteville*
Marc B. Robinson, *Richard Stockton College of New Jersey*
Ramon Rodriguez, *Murray State University*
Alan Rogers, *Franklin University*
David Rogers, *Mesa State College*
Lawrence A. Roman, *Cuyahoga Community College*
Luther Ross Sr., *Central Piedmont Community College*
Pamela Rouse, *Butler University*
T. Brian Routh, *University of Southern Indiana*
Martin Rudnick, *William Paterson University*
Amal Said, *University of Toledo*
Yehia Salama, *University of Illinois–Chicago*
Mary Scarborough, *Tyler Junior College*
Rex Schildhouse, *Miramar College*
Nancy Schrumpf, *Parkland College*
Jeremy Schwartz, *Youngstown State University*
Pamela Schwer, *St. Xavier University*
Vineeta Sharma, *Florida International University–Miami*
Lewis Shaw, *Suffolk University*
Jeffrey Shields, *University of Southern Maine*
Kathe Shinham, *Northern Arizona University at Flagstaff*
Franklin Shuman, *Utah State University–Logan*
Danny Siciliano, *University of Nevada at Las Vegas*
Kenneth Sinclair, *LeHigh University*
Lakshmy Sivaratnam, *Kansas City Kansas Community College*
Talitha Smith, *Auburn University–Auburn*
Paul Spindler, *Grand Valley State University*
Diane Stark, *Phoenix College*
Dennis Stovall, *Grand Valley State University*
Gracelyn Stuart-Tuggle, *Palm Beach State College–Boca Campus*

Suzy Summers, *Furman University*
Kenton Swift, *University of Montana*
Scott Szilagyi, *Fordham University–Rose Hill*
Karen Tabak, *Maryville University*
Linda Tarrago, *Hillsborough Community College*
Rita Taylor, *University of Cincinnati*
Lisa Tekmetarovic, *Truman College*
Teresa Thamer, *Brenau University*
Rhonda Thomas, *Butler Community College*
Amanda Thompson-Abbott, *Marshall University*
Jerry Thorne, *North Carolina A&T State University*
Don Trippeer, *State University of New York at Oneonta*
Robin Turner, *Rowan-Cabarrus Community College*
Tracy Campbell Tuttle, *San Diego Mesa Community College*
Eric Typpo, *University of the Pacific*
Suneel Udpa, *University of California–Berkeley*
Michael Van Breda, *Southern Methodist University*
Jayaraman Vijayakumar, *Virginia Commonwealth University*
Ron Vogel, *College of Eastern Utah*

David Vyncke, *Scott Community College*
Terri Walsh, *Seminole State College of Florida*
Doris Warmflash, *Westchester Community College*
Lorry Wasserman, *University of Portland*
Richard Watson, *University of California–Santa Barbara*
Victoria Wattigny, *Midwestern State University*
Betsy Wenz, *Indiana University–Kokomo*
Robert Weprin, *Lourdes College*
Gwendolen White, *Ball State University*
Elizabeth Widdison, *University of Washington–Seattle*
Val Williams, *Duquesne University*
Janet Woods, *Macon State College*
John Woodward, *Polk State College*
Jia Wu, *University of Massachusetts–Dartmouth*
Emily Xu, *University of New Hampshire*
Claire Yan, *University or Arkansas–Fayetteville*
James Yang, *Montclair State University*
Jeff Yu, *Southern Methodist University*
Bert Zarb, *Embry-Riddle Aeronautical University*
Thomas Zeller, *Loyola University–Chicago*

We are grateful for the outstanding support from McGraw Hill. In particular, we would like to thank Tim Vertovec, Portfolio VP; Becky Olson, Senior Director; Noelle Bathurst, Senior Portfolio Manager; Erin Quinones and Rachel Hinton, Product Developers; Kaitlin Murray, Marketing Manager; Kevin Moran, Director of Digital Development; Xin Lin, Lead Product Manager; Pat Frederickson and Angela Norris, Lead Content Project Managers; Matt Diamond, Senior Designer; and Beth Cray, Content Licensing Specialist.

Special thanks also to the team of contributors who spend countless hours helping us build and test our digital assets and ancillary materials. This team includes the best and brightest in the business. Julie Hampton and Dan Kelly (Lead Digital Contributors) deserve special mention for their tireless efforts in building, testing, and supporting others in producing the Connect assessment content. We also thank the following contributors: Beth Kobylarz and Emily Bello (subject matter experts and digital consultants), for their detailed Connect accuracy reviews; Ann Brooks and Julie Hampton for their work on the test bank; Jeannie Folk (Emeritus at College of DuPage), for her work on the Concept Overview Videos; and Helen Roybark (Radford University) and Ann Brooks (Wake Forest University), for their detailed review of the text. Thank you to Emily Bello for her work on the updated PowerPoints and Lectures notes. Jacob Shortt (Virginia Tech) was invaluable in the creation and implementation of the new Data Analytics material.

We are grateful to the Institute of Certified Management Accountants for permission to use questions and/or unofficial answers from past Certificate in Management Accounting (CMA) examinations.

Ray Garrison • Eric Noreen • Peter Brewer

Brief Contents

Contents

Job-Order Costing: Cost Flows and External Reporting 106

Job-Order Costing—The Flow of Costs 107

The Purchase and Issue of Materials 109

Issue of Direct and Indirect Materials 109

Process Costing 152

Comparison of Job-Order and Process Costing 153

Similarities between Job-Order and Process Costing 153

Differences between Job-Order and Process Costing 153

Chapter 5

**Cost-Volume-Profit
Relationships 195**

Chapter 6

Variable Costing and Segment Reporting: Tools for Management 253

Chapter 7

Activity-Based Costing: A Tool to Aid Decision Making 305

Chapter 8

Master Budgeting 353

Chapter 9

Flexible Budgets and Performance Analysis 404

Chapter 10

Standard Costs and Variances 438

Chapter 11

Responsibility Accounting Systems 494

Decentralization in Organizations 495

Advantages and Disadvantages of Decentralization 495

Chapter 14

Capital Budgeting Decisions   630

Chapter 15

Statement of Cash Flows   682

Chapter 16

Financial Statement Analysis 725

Managerial Accounting: An Overview

AzmanJaka/E+/Getty Images

ENTREPRENEUR SPOTLIGHT

Maria Contreras-Sweet "sees entrepreneurship as a force that can change lives and lift whole communities around the world." In 2006, she started ProAmérica Bank—the first commercial bank started in California by a person of Latino origin in more than 35 years. The bank focuses on serving small and medium-sized businesses in Latino neighborhoods, based on her belief "that the lack of access to capital means a lack of opportunity."

Applying Managerial Accounting

ProAmérica Bank maintains internal controls (as summarized in Exhibit P–8) to minimize various risks, such as incurring financial reporting errors. For example, the bank uses physical safeguards to limit access to its cash and other tangible assets. It also requires proper authorizations for transactions over pre-established dollar amounts. In addition, the bank prepares periodic reconciliations that compare its cash on hand with its underlying accounting records to identify and resolve any discrepancies.

Serving all Stakeholders

In addition to her entrepreneurial ventures, Contreras-Sweet has also served her community in various other capacities. For example, she served in President Barack Obama's cabinet as the 24th Administrator of the United States Small Business Administration. She also was a founding member of a nonprofit organization called Hispanas Organized for Political Equality (HOPE). The organization seeks to empower its communities "through advocacy, Latina leadership training, and increasing knowledge on the contributions Latinas have made to advance the status of women." ∎

Sources: www.contrerassweet.com, https://smallbiztrends.com/2019/10/successful-hispanic-entrepreneurs.html, http://www.hispaniclifestyle.com/articles/latina-of-influence-maria-contreras-sweet/, https://www.latinas.org/hope-leadership.

Data Analytics Exercise available in Connect to complement this chapter

lighthouse image: Martin73/Shutterstock; big data image: INGARA/Shutterstock

What Is Managerial Accounting?

The prologue explains why managerial accounting is important to the future careers of all business students. It begins by answering two questions: (1) What is managerial accounting? and (2) Why does managerial accounting matter to your career? It concludes by discussing seven topics—Big Data; ethics; strategy; enterprise risk management; environmental, social, and governance (ESG) responsibilities; process management; and leadership—that define the business context within which managerial accounting operates.

Many students enrolled in this course will have recently completed an introductory *financial accounting* course. **Financial accounting** is concerned with reporting financial information to external parties, such as stockholders, creditors, and regulators. **Managerial accounting** is concerned with providing information to people within an organization, such as senior managers, middle managers, and front-line employees. Exhibit P–1 summarizes six key differences between financial and managerial accounting. It recognizes the fundamental difference between financial and managerial accounting is that financial accounting serves the needs of those *outside* the organization, whereas managerial accounting serves the needs of people employed *inside* the organization. Because of this fundamental difference in users, financial accounting emphasizes mandatory reporting in compliance with rules, such as generally accepted

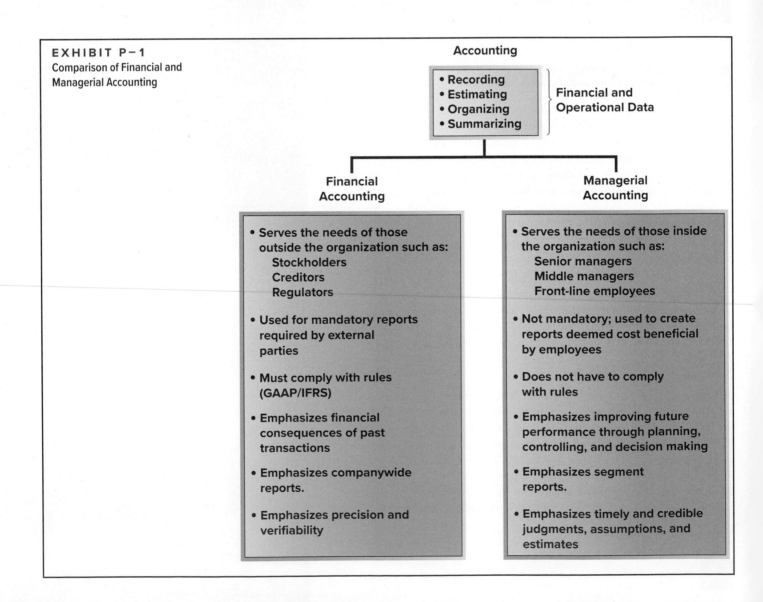

EXHIBIT P–1
Comparison of Financial and Managerial Accounting

Accounting

- Recording
- Estimating
- Organizing
- Summarizing

Financial and Operational Data

Financial Accounting

Managerial Accounting

- Serves the needs of those outside the organization such as:
  - Stockholders
  - Creditors
  - Regulators

- Used for mandatory reports required by external parties

- Must comply with rules (GAAP/IFRS)

- Emphasizes financial consequences of past transactions

- Emphasizes companywide reports.

- Emphasizes precision and verifiability

- Serves the needs of those inside the organization such as:
  - Senior managers
  - Middle managers
  - Front-line employees

- Not mandatory; used to create reports deemed cost beneficial by employees

- Does not have to comply with rules

- Emphasizes improving future performance through planning, controlling, and decision making

- Emphasizes segment reports.

- Emphasizes timely and credible judgments, assumptions, and estimates accounting principles (GAAP) and international financial reporting standards (IFRS), whereas managerial accounting is not mandatory or bound by rules. Financial accounting focuses on reporting companywide historical performance, whereas managerial accounting focuses on managing business *segments* to improve future performance. A **segment** is a part or activity of an organization about which managers would like cost, revenue, or profit data. Examples of business segments include product lines, customer groups (segmented by age, ethnicity, gender, volume of purchases, etc.), geographic territories, divisions, plants, and departments. Finally, financial accounting stresses precision and verifiability, while managerial accounting relies on timely and credible judgments, assumptions, and estimates.

As mentioned in Exhibit P–1, managerial accounting focuses on improving future performance through three vital activities—*planning, controlling,* and *decision making.* **Planning** involves establishing goals and specifying how to achieve them. **Controlling** involves gathering feedback to ensure the plan is being properly executed or modified as circumstances change. **Decision making** involves selecting a course of action from competing alternatives. Now let's take a closer look at these three pillars of managerial accounting.

Planning

Assume you work for Procter & Gamble (P&G) and are in charge of the company's campus recruiting for all undergraduate business majors. In this example, your planning process would begin by establishing a goal such as: our goal is to recruit the "best and brightest" college graduates. The next stage of the planning process would require specifying how to achieve this goal by answering numerous questions such as:

- How many students do we need to hire in total and from each major?
- What schools do we plan to include in our recruiting efforts?
- Which of our employees will be involved in each school's recruiting activities?
- When will we conduct our interviews?
- How will we compare students to one another to decide who will be extended job offers?
- What salary will we offer our new hires? Will the salaries differ by major?
- How much money can we spend on our recruiting efforts?

As you can see, there are many questions that need to be answered as part of the planning process. Plans are often accompanied by a *budget.* A **budget** is a plan for the future expressed in formal quantitative terms. As the head of recruiting at P&G, your budget would include two key components. First, you would have to work with other senior managers inside the company to establish a budgeted amount of total salaries that can be offered to all new hires. Second, you would have to create a budget that quantifies how much you intend to spend on your campus recruiting activities.

LABOR VS. EQUIPMENT: AN IMPORTANT PLANNING DECISION

As e-commerce companies such as Amazon.com continue to thrive, brick-and-mortar retailers are looking for ways to improve customer satisfaction by eliminating the hassle of long checkout lines. For example, Tesco PLC, one of the world's largest supermarket operators, is experimenting with cashierless stores. Its automated process relies on 150 ceiling-mounted cameras to detect what customers buy and then automatically charges them for their groceries as they exit the store. Numerous other companies, such as Carrefour SA, Walmart, and Kroger, are also exploring ways to deliver what Tesco describes as "frictionless shopping" for their customers. While each company's approach to streamlining the shopping process may be unique, they all have important planning and budgeting implications with respect to investing in labor versus equipment.

Source: Parmy Olson, "Grocers Swap Cashiers for Cameras," *The Wall Street Journal,* July 8, 2019, pp. B1–B2.

Controlling

Once you established P&G's recruiting plan, you would transition to the control process. This process involves gathering, evaluating, and responding to feedback to ensure this year's recruiting process meets expectations and next year's recruiting campaign goes even more smoothly. The control process would involve answering questions such as:

- Did we succeed in hiring the planned number of students within each major and at each school?
- Did we lose too many exceptional candidates to competitors?
- Did each of our employees involved in the recruiting process perform satisfactorily?
- Is our method of comparing students to one another working?
- Did the on-campus and office interviews run smoothly?
- Did we stay within our budget in terms of total salary commitments to new hires?
- Did we stay within our budget regarding spending on recruiting activities?

As you can see, there are many questions that arised as part of the control process. When answering these questions, you would go beyond simple yes or no answers to find the underlying reasons why performance exceeded or failed to meet expectations. Part of the control process includes preparing *performance reports*. A **performance report** compares budgeted data to actual data to identify and learn from excellent performance and identify and eliminate sources of unsatisfactory performance. Performance reports can also be used as one of many inputs to help evaluate and reward employees.

Although this example focused on P&G's campus recruiting efforts, we could have described how planning enables FedEx to deliver packages across the globe overnight or how it helps Apple develop and market successive generations of the iPhone. We could have discussed how the control process helps Pfizer, Eli Lilly, and Abbott Laboratories ensure that their pharmaceutical drugs are produced in conformance with rigorous quality standards, or how Publix relies on the control process to keep its grocery shelves stocked. We also could have looked at planning and control failures such as Takata's recall of more than 30 million defective driver-side air bags installed by a variety of automakers such as Honda, Ford, Toyota, and Subaru. In short, all managers (and that probably includes you someday) perform planning and controlling activities.

Decision Making

Perhaps the most basic managerial skill is the ability to make intelligent, data-driven decisions. Broadly speaking, many of those decisions revolve around the following three questions: *What* should we be selling? *Who* should we be serving? *How* should we execute? Exhibit P–2 provides examples of decisions pertaining to each of these three categories.

EXHIBIT P–2
Examples of Decisions

What should we be selling?	Who should we be serving?	How should we execute?
What products and services should be the focus of our marketing efforts?	Who should be the focus of our marketing efforts?	How should we supply our parts and services?
What new products and services should we offer?	Who should we start serving?	How should we expand our capacity?
What prices should we charge for our products and services?	Who should pay price premiums or receive price discounts?	How should we reduce our capacity?
What products and services should we discontinue?	Who should we stop serving?	How should we improve our efficiency and effectiveness?

The left-hand column of Exhibit P–2 suggests all companies make decisions related to the products and services they sell. For example, each year Procter & Gamble decides how to allocate its marketing budget across numerous brands that each generates over $1 billion in sales as well as other brands that have promising growth potential. Mattel decides what new toys to introduce to the market. Southwest Airlines decides what ticket prices to establish for each of its thousands of flights per day. Hyundai decides whether to discontinue certain models of automobiles.

The middle column of Exhibit P–2 indicates that all companies make decisions related to the customers they serve. For example, Duluth Trading Company decides how to allocate its marketing budget between products that tend to appeal to male versus female customers. FedEx decides whether to expand its services into new markets across the globe. HP decides what price discounts to offer corporate clients who purchase large volumes of its products. A bank decides whether to discontinue customers who may be unprofitable.

The right-hand column of Exhibit P–2 says companies also make decisions related to how they execute. For example, Boeing decides whether to rely on outside vendors such as Goodrich, Saab, and Rolls-Royce to manufacture many of the parts used to make its airplanes. Cintas decides whether to expand its laundering and cleaning capacity in a given geographic region by adding square footage to an existing facility or constructing an entirely new facility. In an economic downturn, a manufacturer might have to decide whether to eliminate one 8-hour shift at three plants or to close one plant. Finally, all companies have to decide among competing improvement opportunities. For example, a company may have to decide whether to implement a new software system, to upgrade a piece of equipment, or to provide extra training to its employees.

This portion of the prologue explained the three pillars of managerial accounting—planning, controlling, and decision making. This book prepares you to become an effective manager by explaining how to make intelligent data-driven decisions, how to create financial plans for the future, and how to continually make progress toward achieving goals by obtaining, evaluating, and responding to feedback.

Why Does Managerial Accounting Matter to Your Career?

Many students feel anxious about choosing a major because they are unsure if it will provide a fulfilling career. To reduce these anxieties, we recommend deemphasizing what you cannot control about the future; instead, focus on what you can control right now. More specifically, concentrate on answering the following question: What can you do now to prepare for success in an unknown future career? The best answer is to learn skills that make it easier for you to adapt to an uncertain future. You need to become adaptable!

Whether you end up working in the United States or abroad, for a large corporation, a small entrepreneurial company, a nonprofit organization, or a governmental entity, you'll need to know how to plan for the future, make progress toward achieving goals, and make intelligent decisions. In other words, managerial accounting skills are useful in just about any career, organization, and industry. If you commit energy to this course, you'll be making a smart investment in your future—even though you cannot clearly envision it. Next, we elaborate on this point by explaining how managerial accounting relates to the future careers of business majors and accounting majors.

Business Majors

Exhibit P–3 provides examples of how planning, controlling, and decision making affect three majors other than accounting—marketing, supply chain management, and human resource management.

The left-hand column of Exhibit P–3 says marketing managers make planning decisions related to allocating advertising dollars across various communication mediums

EXHIBIT P-3
Relating Managerial Accounting to Three Business Majors

	Marketing	Supply Chain Management	Human Resource Management
Planning	How much should we budget for TV, print, and internet advertising?	How many units should we plan to produce next period?	How much should we plan to spend for occupational safety training?
	How many salespeople should we plan to hire to serve a new territory?	How much should we budget for next period's utility expense?	How much should we plan to spend on employee recruitment advertising?
Controlling	Is the budgeted price cut increasing unit sales as expected?	Did we spend more or less than expected for the units we actually produced?	Is our employee retention rate exceeding our goals?
	Are we accumulating too much inventory during the holiday shopping season?	Are we achieving our goal of reducing the number of defective units produced?	Are we meeting our goal of completing timely performance appraisals?
Decision Making	Should we sell our services as one bundle or sell them separately?	Should we transfer production of a component part to an overseas supplier?	Should we hire an on-site medical staff to lower our health care costs?
	Should we sell directly to customers or use a distributor?	Should we redesign our manufacturing process to lower inventory levels?	Should we hire temporary workers or full-time employees?

and to staffing new sales territories. From a control standpoint, they closely track sales data to see if a budgeted price cut is generating an anticipated increase in unit sales, or they study inventory levels during the holiday shopping season to adjust prices as needed to optimize sales. Marketing managers also make many important decisions, such as whether to bundle services together and sell them for one price or to sell each service separately. They may also decide whether to sell products directly to the customer or to a distributor, who sells to the end consumer.

The middle column of Exhibit P–3 says supply chain managers plan how many units to produce to satisfy anticipated customer demand. They also budget for operating expenses such as utilities, supplies, and labor costs. In terms of control, they monitor actual spending relative to the budget, and closely watch operational measures such as the number of defects produced relative to the plan. Supply chain managers make numerous decisions, such as deciding whether to transfer production of a component part to an overseas supplier, or choosing whether to redesign a manufacturing process to reduce inventory levels.

The right-hand column of Exhibit P–3 explains how human resource managers make a variety of planning decisions, such as budgeting spending for occupational safety training and employee recruitment advertising. They monitor feedback related to numerous management concerns, such as employee retention rates and the timely completion of employee performance appraisals. They also make many important decisions, such as whether to hire on-site medical staff in an effort to lower health care costs and whether to hire temporary workers or full-time employees in an uncertain economy.

For brevity, Exhibit P–3 does not include all business majors, such as finance, information technology, and economics. Can you explain how planning, controlling, and decision-making activities would relate to these majors?

Accounting Majors

Many accounting graduates begin their careers working for public accounting firms that provide a variety of valuable services for their clients. Some of these graduates will build successful and fulfilling careers in the public accounting industry; however, most leave public accounting at some point to work in other organizations.

The public accounting profession has a strong financial accounting orientation. Its most important function is to protect investors and other external parties by assuring them companies are reporting historical financial results that comply with applicable accounting rules. Managerial accountants also have strong financial accounting skills. For example, they play an important role in helping their organizations design and maintain financial reporting systems that generate reliable financial disclosures. However, the primary role of managerial accountants is to partner with their co-workers within the organization to improve performance.

If you are an accounting major, there is a high likelihood your future will involve working for a nonpublic accounting employer. This employer will expect you to have strong financial accounting skills, but more importantly, it will expect you to help improve organizational performance by applying the planning, controlling, and decision-making skills that are the foundation of managerial accounting.

IN BUSINESS

A NETWORKING OPPORTUNITY

The Institute of Management Accountants (IMA) is a network of more than 100,000 accounting and finance professionals from over 140 countries. Every year the IMA hosts a student leadership conference that attracts 300 students from over 50 colleges and universities. Guest speakers at past conferences have discussed topics such as leadership, advice for a successful career, how to market yourself in a difficult economy, and excelling in today's multigenerational workforce. One student who attended the conference said, "I liked that I was able to interact with professionals who are in fields that could be potential career paths for me." For more information on this worthwhile networking opportunity, contact the IMA at the phone number shown below or visit https://www.imanet.org/events/imas-student-leadership-conferences?ssopc=1.

The Institute of Management Accountants

Source: Conversation with Jodi Ryan, the Institute of Management Accountants' Director, Student & Academic Relations. She can be contacted at (201) 474-1556.

Professional Certification—A Smart Investment If you plan to become an accounting major, the Certified Management Accountant (CMA), Certified in Strategy and Competitive Analysis (CSCA), and Chartered Global Management Accountant (CGMA) designations are globally respected credentials that will increase your credibility, upward mobility, and compensation.

The CMA exam is sponsored by the IMA in Montvale, New Jersey. To become a CMA requires membership in the IMA, a bachelor's degree from an accredited college or university, two continuous years of relevant professional experience, and passage of the CMA exam. Exhibit P–4 summarizes the topics covered in the IMA's two-part CMA exam. For brevity, we are not going to define all the terms included in this exhibit. Its purpose is simply to emphasize that the CMA exam focuses on the planning, controlling, and decision-making skills that are critically important to all managers. Information about becoming a CMA is available on the IMA's website (www.imanet.org) or by calling 1-800-638-4427.

The IMA also sponsors the CSCA exam, which is a three-hour exam that includes 60 multiple-choice questions and one case study. The exam covers three content areas: strategic analysis, creating competitive advantage, and strategy implementation and performance evaluation. It is intended for people who have earned the CMA designation and hold positions ranging from staff accountant to chief financial officer (CFO).

EXHIBIT P–4
CMA Exam Content Specifications

Part 1	*Financial Planning, Performance, and Analytics*
	External financial reporting decisions
	Planning, budgeting, and forecasting
	Performance management
	Cost management
	Internal controls
	Technology and Analytics
Part 2	*Strategic Financial Management*
	Financial statement analysis
	Corporate finance
	Decision analysis
	Risk management
	Investment decisions
	Professional ethics

The CGMA designation is co-sponsored by the American Institute of Certified Public Accountants (AICPA) and the Chartered Institute of Management Accountants (CIMA), each of whom provides a distinct pathway to becoming a CGMA. The AICPA pathway requires a bachelor's degree in accounting (accompanied by a total of 150 college credit-hours), passage of the Certified Public Accountant (CPA) exam, membership in the AICPA, three years of relevant management accounting work experience, and passage of the CGMA exam—which is a case-based exam that focuses on technical skills, business skills, leadership skills, people skills, and ethics, integrity, and professionalism. Notice the AICPA's pathway to becoming a CGMA requires passage of the multi-part CPA exam, which emphasizes rule-based compliance—assurance standards, financial accounting standards, business law, and the tax code. Information on becoming a CGMA is available at www.cgma.org.

IN BUSINESS

HOW'S THE PAY?

The Institute of Management Accountants has created the following table that allows individuals to estimate what their salary would be as a management accountant.

			Your Calculation
Start with this base amount............................		$63,835	$63,835
If you are top-level management......................	ADD	$64,786	
OR, if you are senior-level management..............	ADD	$56,064	
OR, if you are middle-level management.............	ADD	$22,587	
If you have an advanced degree.....................	ADD	$15,490	
If you hold the CMA.................................	ADD	$13,151	
If you hold the CPA.................................	ADD	$16,990	
Your estimated salary level...........................			

For example, if you make it to top-level management in 10 years and have an advanced degree and a CMA, your estimated salary would be $140,702 [$48,722 + $50,462 + (10 × $968) + $16,050 + $15,788].

Source: Shannon Charles, "IMA's Global Salary Survey," *Strategic Finance*, March 2019, pp. 29–39.

Managerial Accounting: Understanding the Broader Context

Exhibit P–5 summarizes how each chapter of the book teaches measurement skills that managers use on the job every day. For example, Chapter 8 teaches you the measurement skills managers use to answer the question: How should I create a financial plan for next year? Chapters 9 and 10 teach you the measurement skills managers use to answer the question: How well am I performing relative to my plan? Chapter 7 teaches you measurement skills related to product, service, and customer profitability. However, it is vitally important you also understand managers need to apply these measurement skills in a broader business context to enable intelligent planning, control, and decision making. This context includes topics such as Big Data; ethics; strategy; enterprise risk management; and environmental, social, and governance (ESG) responsibilities, as well as process management and leadership.

Big Data

Experts estimate every second of every day, we are creating 1.7 megabytes of new information per person. Given our global population of more than 7.5 billion people, this is a truly astonishing rate of data generation. However, less than 0.5% of this data is currently being analyzed and used to support decision making,[1] thereby suggesting business managers have an extraordinary opportunity to harness what is known as the *Big Data* phenomenon. **Big Data** refers to large collections of data gathered from inside or outside a company to provide

Chapter Number	The Key Question from a Manager's Perspective
Chapter 1	What cost classifications do I use for different management purposes?
Chapter 2	How much does it cost us to manufacture customized jobs for each of our customers?
Chapters 3 & 4	What is the value of our ending inventory and cost of goods sold for external reporting purposes?
Chapter 5	How will my profits change if I change my selling price, unit sales, or costs?
Chapter 6	How should the income statement be presented?
Chapter 7	How profitable is each of our products, services, and customers?
Chapter 8	How should I create a financial plan for next year?
Chapters 9 & 10	How well am I performing relative to my plan?
Chapters 11 & 12	How should I implement a performance measurement system to help ensure that we achieve our strategic goals?
Chapter 13	How do I quantify the financial impact of pursuing one course of action versus another?
Chapter 14	How do I make long-term capital investment decisions?
Chapter 15	What cash inflows and outflows explain the change in our cash balance?
Chapter 16	How can we analyze our financial statements to better understand our performance?

EXHIBIT P–5
Measurement Skills: A Manager's Perspective

---

[1] Source: Bernard Marr, "Big Data: 20 Mind-Boggling Facts Everyone Must Read," *Forbes*, September 30, 2015.

opportunities for ongoing reporting and analysis.[2] Big Data can be both "structured," such as memos and reports, and "unstructured," such as videos, pictures, audio, and other digital forms.

Big Data is often discussed in terms of five Vs. The first three of those Vs—variety, volume, velocity—refine the definition of Big Data. *Variety* refers to the data formats in which information is stored. This includes traditional forms and digital formats, including social media, as well as click-streams on a webpage, sensor-enabled feedback, and internet-based audio/video files. *Volume* refers to the continuously expanding quantity of data companies must gather, cleanse, organize, and analyze. For larger companies, this can be hundreds of petabytes of data (where one petabyte equals one million gigabytes). *Velocity* speaks to the rate at which data is received and acted on by organizations. This is particularly important where the data has a limited shelf-life. For example, retailers can better match supply with demand if they are receiving and responding to sales data in seconds or minutes rather than days or weeks.

The remaining Vs—value and veracity—define users' expectations with respect to Big Data. The concept of *Value* implies the time and money organizations expend to analyze Big Data need to result in insights that are valued by stakeholders. For example, shareholders expect Big Data analysis to translate into financial benefits, such as rising sales, increased return on investment, and a higher stock price. *Veracity* means users expect their data to be accurate and trustworthy. For accounting professionals, veracity may be the most important of the "five Vs" because their analysis and opinions, which are relied on by numerous stakeholders (such as managers, investors, and regulators), must be supported by verifiable data.

From a managerial accounting standpoint, the goal for managers is to use *data analytics* to derive value from big data. **Data analytics** refers to the process of analyzing data with the aid of specialized systems and software to draw conclusions about the information they contain.[3] Managers often communicate the findings from their data analysis to others through the use of *data visualization* techniques, such as graphs, charts, maps, and diagrams.

Data analytics can be used for descriptive, diagnostic, predictive, and prescriptive purposes. *Descriptive analytics* answer the question: What happened? For example, managers may use them to better understand historical trends in revenues and expenses. *Diagnostic analytics* answer the question: Why did it happen? For example, managers may analyze economic indicators, such as changes in the unemployment rate, to help explain why sales increased or decreased. *Predictive analytics* answer the question: What will happen? For example, managers can use predictive techniques, such as regression analysis, to estimate sales or expenses for the next month, quarter, or year. Finally, *prescriptive analytics* answer the question: What should I do? For example, managers may use prescriptive analytics to decide which products should be promoted, deemphasized, or discontinued.[4]

IN BUSINESS

LuckyImages/Shutterstock

THE ROLE OF MANAGERIAL ACCOUNTING

"Creating value through values" is the credo of today's management accountant. It means that management accountants should maintain an unwavering commitment to ethical values while using their knowledge and skills to influence decisions that create value for organizational stakeholders. These skills include managing risks and implementing strategy through planning; budgeting and forecasting; and data science, including advanced analytics, visualization, and story-telling. Management accountants are strategic business partners who understand the financial, operational, and market-facing perspectives of the business. They report and analyze financial as well as nonfinancial measures of performance relating to profits (financial statements), processes (customer focus and satisfaction), people (employee learning and satisfaction), and the planet (environmental stewardship).

Source: Conversation with Jeff Thomson, president and CEO of the Institute of Management Accountants.

---

[2] Source: Lisa Arthur, "What Is Big Data," *Forbes,* August 15, 2013.

[3] Source: https://searchdatamanagement.techtarget.com/definition/data-analytics.

[4] Source: Jake Frankenfield, "Data Analytics," published by Investopedia and available at the following link: https://www.investopedia.com/terms/d/data-analytics.asp.

Ethics

Ethical behavior is the lubricant that keeps the economy running. Without that lubricant, the economy would operate much less efficiently—less would be available to consumers, quality would be lower, and prices would be higher. In other words, without fundamental trust in the integrity of business, the economy would operate much less efficiently. Thus, for the good of everyone—including profit-making companies—it is vitally important that business be conducted within an ethical framework that builds and sustains trust.

Code of Conduct for Management Accountants   The Institute of Management Accountants (IMA) has adopted an ethical code called the *Statement of Ethical Professional Practice* that describes in some detail the ethical responsibilities of management accountants. Even though the standards were developed specifically for management accountants, they have much broader applications. The standards consist of two parts, presented in Exhibit P–6. The first part provides general guidelines for ethical behavior. In a nutshell, a management accountant has ethical responsibilities in four broad areas: first, to maintain a high level of professional competence; second, to treat sensitive matters with confidentiality; third, to maintain personal integrity; and fourth, to disclose information in a credible fashion. The second part of the standards specifies what should be done if an individual finds evidence of ethical misconduct.

The ethical standards provide sound, practical advice for management accountants and managers. Most of the rules in the ethical standards are motivated by a very practical consideration—if these rules were not followed in business, then the economy and all of us would suffer. Consider the following examples of the consequences of not abiding by the standards:

- Suppose employees could not be trusted with confidential information. Then top managers would be reluctant to distribute such information within the company and, as a result, decisions would be based on incomplete information and operations would deteriorate.
- Suppose employees accepted bribes from suppliers. Then contracts would tend to go to the suppliers who pay the highest bribes rather than to the most competent suppliers. Would you like to fly in aircraft whose wings were made by the subcontractor who paid the highest bribe? Would you fly as often? What would happen to the airline industry if its safety record deteriorated due to shoddy workmanship on contracted parts and subassemblies?
- Suppose the presidents of companies routinely lied in their annual reports and financial statements. If investors could not rely on the basic integrity of a company's financial statements, they would have little basis for making informed decisions. Suspecting the worst, rational investors would pay less for stocks issued by companies and may not be willing to invest at all. As a consequence, companies would have less money for productive investments—leading to slower economic growth, fewer goods and services, and higher prices.

Not only is ethical behavior the lubricant for our economy, it is the foundation of managerial accounting. The numbers managers rely on for planning, controlling, and decision making are meaningless unless they have been competently, objectively, and honestly gathered, analyzed, and reported. As your career unfolds, you will inevitably face decisions with ethical implications. Before making such decisions, consider performing the following steps. First, define your alternative courses of action. Second, identify all of the parties affected by your decision. Third, define how each course of action will favorably or unfavorably impact each affected party. Once you have a complete understanding of the decision context, seek guidance from external sources such as the IMA Statement of Ethical Professional Practice (see Exhibit P–6), the IMA Ethics Helpline at (800) 245-1383, or a trusted confidant. Before executing your decision, ask yourself one final question: Would I be comfortable disclosing my chosen course of action on the front page of *The Wall Street Journal?*

EXHIBIT P–6
Institute of Management Accountants (IMA) Statement of Ethical Professional Practice

Members of IMA shall behave ethically. A commitment to ethical professional practice includes: overarching principles that express our values, and standards that guide our conduct.

PRINCIPLES

IMA's overarching ethical principles include: Honesty, Fairness, Objectivity, and Responsibility. Members shall act in accordance with these principles and shall encourage others within their organizations to adhere to them.

STANDARDS

IMA members have a responsibility to comply with and uphold the standards of Competence, Confidentiality, Integrity, and Credibility. Failure to comply may result in disciplinary action.

I. COMPETENCE

1.   Maintain an appropriate level of professional leadership and expertise by enhancing knowledge and skills.
2.   Perform professional duties in accordance with relevant laws, regulations, and technical standards.
3.   Provide decision support information and recommendations that are accurate, clear, concise, and timely. Recognize and help manage risk.

II. CONFIDENTIALITY

1.   Keep information confidential except when disclosure is authorized or legally required.
2.   Inform all relevant parties regarding appropriate use of confidential information. Monitor to ensure compliance.
3.   Refrain from using confidential information for unethical or illegal advantage.

III. INTEGRITY

1.   Mitigate actual conflicts of interest. Regularly communicate with business associates to avoid apparent conflicts of interest. Advise all parties of any potential conflicts of interest.
2.   Refrain from engaging in any conduct that would prejudice carrying out duties ethically.
3.   Abstain from engaging in or supporting any activity that might discredit the profession.
4.   Contribute to a positive ethical culture and place integrity of the profession above personal interests.

IV. CREDIBILITY

1.   Communicate information fairly and objectively.
2.   Provide all relevant information that could reasonably be expected to influence an intended user's understanding of the reports, analyses, or recommendations.
3.   Report any delays or deficiencies in information, timeliness, processing, or internal controls in conformance with organization policy and/or applicable law.
4.   Communicate professional limitations or other constraints that would preclude responsible judgment or successful performance of an activity.

RESOLVING ETHICAL ISSUES

In applying the Standards of Ethical Professional Practice, the member may encounter unethical issues or behavior. In these situations, the member should not ignore them, but rather should actively seek resolution of the issue. In determining which steps to follow, the member should consider all risks involved and whether protections exist against retaliation.

When faced with unethical issues, the member should follow the established policies of his or her organization, including use of an anonymous reporting system if available.

If the organization does not have established policies, the member should consider the following courses of action:

*   The resolution process could include a discussion with the member's immediate supervisor. If the supervisor appears to be involved, the issue could be presented to the next level of management.
*   IMA offers an anonymous helpline that the member may call to request how key elements of the *IMA Statement of Ethical Professional Practice* could be applied to the ethical issue.
*   The member should consider consulting his or her own attorney to learn of any legal obligations, rights, and risks concerning the issue.

If resolution efforts are not successful, the member may wish to consider disassociating from the organization.

Institute of Management Accountants, Inc.

Strategy

Companies do not succeed by sheer luck; instead, they need to develop a *strategy* that defines how they intend to succeed in the marketplace. A **strategy** is a "game plan" that is difficult to replicate and differentiates a company from its competitors in ways that attract and retain customers. These sources of differentiation or what are more formally called *customer value propositions*, fall into three broad categories—*customer intimacy, operational excellence,* and *product leadership.*

Companies differentiating themselves in terms of *customer intimacy* are, in essence, saying to their customers, "You should choose us because we customize our products and services to meet your individual needs better than our competitors." Ritz-Carlton, Nordstrom, and Charles Schwab rely primarily on a customer intimacy value proposition for their success. Companies pursuing the second customer value proposition, called *operational excellence,* are saying to their target customers, "You should choose us because we deliver products and services faster, more conveniently, and at a lower price than our competitors." Southwest Airlines, Walmart, and Google are examples of companies that succeed first and foremost because of their operational excellence. Companies pursuing the third customer value proposition, called *product leadership,* are saying to their target customers, "You should choose us because we offer higher quality products than our competitors." Apple, Cisco Systems, and W.L. Gore (the creator of GORE-TEX® fabrics) are examples of companies succeeding because of their product leadership.[5]

The plans managers set forth, the variables they seek to control, and the decisions they make are all influenced by their company's strategy. For example, Walmart would not make plans to build ultra-expensive clothing boutiques because it would conflict with the company's strategy of operational excellence and "everyday low prices." Apple would not seek to control its operations by selecting performance measures that focus solely on cost-cutting because those measures would conflict with its product leadership customer value proposition. Finally, it is unlikely that Rolex would decide to implement drastic price reductions for its watches even if a financial analysis indicated that establishing a lower price might boost short-run profits. Rolex would oppose this course of action because it diminishes the luxury brand underlying the company's product leadership customer value proposition.

Enterprise Risk Management

Every strategy, plan, and decision involves risks. **Enterprise risk management** is a process used by a company to identify those risks and develop responses to them that enable it to be reasonably assured of meeting its goals. The left-hand column of Exhibit P–7 provides 10 examples of the types of business risks companies face. They range from risks relating to the weather to risks associated with computer hackers, complying with the law, supplier strikes, and products harming customers. The right-hand column of Exhibit P–7 provides an example of a control that reduces each of the risks in the left-hand column.[6] Although these types of controls cannot completely eliminate risks, they enable companies to proactively manage their risks rather than passively reacting to unfortunate events that have already occurred.

In managerial accounting, companies use controls to reduce the risk their plans will not be achieved. For example, if a company plans to build a new manufacturing facility within a predefined budget and time frame, it will establish and monitor control measures to ensure the project is concluded on time and within the budget. Risk management is

---

[5] These three customer value propositions were defined by Michael Treacy and Fred Wiersema in "Customer Intimacy and Other Value Disciplines," *Harvard Business Review,* Volume 71, Issue 1, pp. 84–93.

[6] Besides using controls to reduce risks, companies can also choose other risk responses, such as accepting or avoiding a risk.

EXHIBIT P–7
Identifying and Controlling
Business Risks

Examples of Business Risks	Examples of Controls to Reduce Business Risks
• Intellectual assets being stolen from computer files	• Create firewalls that prohibit computer hackers from corrupting or stealing intellectual property
• Products harming customers	• Develop a formal and rigorous new product testing program
• Losing market share due to the unforeseen actions of competitors	• Develop an approach for legally gathering information about competitors' plans and practices
• Poor weather conditions shutting down operations	• Develop contingency plans for overcoming weather-related disruptions
• A website malfunctioning	• Thoroughly test the website before going "live" on the internet
• A supplier strike halting the flow of raw materials	• Establish a relationship with two companies capable of providing needed raw materials
• A poorly designed incentive compensation system causing employees to make bad decisions	• Create a balanced set of performance measures that motivate the desired behavior
• Poor environmental stewardship causing reputational and financial damage	• Create a reporting system that tracks key environmental performance indicators
• Inaccurate budget estimates causing excessive or insufficient production	• Implement a rigorous budget review process
• Failing to comply with equal employment opportunity laws	• Create a report that tracks key metrics related to compliance with the laws

also a critically important aspect of decision making. For example, when a company quantifies the labor cost savings it can realize by sending jobs overseas, it should complement its financial analysis with a prudent assessment of the accompanying risks. Will the overseas manufacturer use child labor? Will the product's quality decline, thereby leading to more warranty repairs, customer complaints, and lawsuits? Will the elapsed time from customer order to delivery dramatically increase? Will terminating domestic employees diminish morale within the company and harm perceptions within the community? These are the types of risks managers should incorporate into their decision-making processes.

Companies also use controls in financial accounting to safeguard assets and minimize the risk of financial reporting errors. Exhibit P–8 describes seven types of controls companies use to safeguard their assets and reduce their financial reporting risks. Each item in the exhibit is labeled as a *preventive control* and/or a *detective control*. A **preventive control** deters undesirable events from occurring. A **detective control** detects undesirable events that have already occurred.

As shown in Exhibit P–8, requiring *authorizations* for certain types of transactions is a preventive control. For example, companies frequently require a specific senior manager sign all checks above a particular dollar amount to reduce the risk of an inappropriate cash disbursement. *Reconciliations* are a detective control. If you have ever compared a bank statement to your checkbook to resolve any discrepancies, then you have performed a type of reconciliation known as a bank reconciliation. This is a detective control because you are seeking to identify any mistakes already made by the bank or existing mistakes in your own records. Another type of reconciliation occurs when a company performs a physical count of its inventory. The value of the physical inventory on hand is compared to the accounting records so any discrepancies can be identified and resolved.

EXHIBIT P–8
Types of Internal Controls for
Financial Reporting

Type of Control	Classification	Description
Authorizations	Preventive	Requiring management to formally approve certain types of transactions.
Reconciliations	Detective	Relating data sets to one another to identify and resolve discrepancies.
Segregation of duties	Preventive	Separating responsibilities related to authorizing transactions, recording transactions, and maintaining custody of the related assets.
Physical safeguards	Preventive	Using cameras, locks, and physical barriers to protect assets.
Performance reviews	Detective	Comparing actual performance to various benchmarks to identify unexpected results.
Maintaining records	Detective	Maintaining written and/or electronic evidence to support transactions.
Information systems security	Preventive/ Detective	Using controls such as passwords and access logs to ensure appropriate data restrictions.

Exhibit P–8 also mentions *segregation of duties,* which is a preventive control separating responsibilities for authorizing transactions, recording transactions, and maintaining custody of the related assets. For example, the same employee should not have the ability to authorize inventory purchases, account for those purchases, and manage the inventory storeroom. *Physical safeguards* prevent unauthorized employees from having access to assets such as inventories and computer equipment. *Performance reviews* are a detective control performed by employees in supervisory positions to ensure actual results are reasonable when compared to relevant benchmarks. If actual results unexpectedly deviate from expectations, then it triggers further analysis to determine the root cause of the deviation. Companies *maintain records* to provide evidence supporting each transaction. For example, companies use serially numbered checks (a detective control) so they can readily track all of their cash disbursements. Finally, companies maintain *information systems security* by using passwords (a preventive control) and access logs (a detective control) to restrict electronic data access as appropriate.

It bears reemphasizing these types of controls help a company reduce its risks, but they cannot guarantee a company will achieve its objectives. For example, two or more employees may collude to circumvent the control system, or a company's senior leaders may manipulate financial results by intentionally overriding prescribed policies and procedures. This reality highlights the importance of having senior leaders (including the chief executive officer and the chief financial officer) who are committed to creating an ethical "tone at the top" of the organization.

IN BUSINESS

TARGET'S CHECK-OUT LANES GRIND TO A HALT

When a glitch during routine computer maintenance shut down all of Target's check-out lanes for a two-hour span, many disgruntled customers took to Twitter to complain using the hashtag #TargetDown. Notice that this computer outage not only inconvenienced numerous customers within Target's stores, but it also created additional reputational damage through social media–enabled "word-of-mouth." This experience highlights why companies invest heavily in enterprise risk management to prevent adverse events such as this from occurring.

Source: Khadeeja Safdar, "Outage Paralyzes Shopping at Target," *The Wall Street Journal,* June 17, 2019, p. B3.

QualityHD/Shutterstock

Environmental, Social, and Governance (ESG) Responsibilities

Perhaps today more than ever, a company's stakeholders—such as investors, customers, employees, suppliers, communities, and environmental and human rights advocates—expect it to deliver strong financial results while conscientiously attending to its *environmental, social, and governance (ESG)* responsibilities. **Environmental, social, and governance (ESG)** are three criteria used by stakeholders for gauging the sustainability and ethical impacts of a company. ESG extends beyond legal compliance to include voluntary actions that satisfy stakeholder expectations. Numerous companies, such as Pirelli, 3M, Eli Lilly and Company, Gildan Activewear, Microsoft, Johnson & Johnson, Baxter International, Abbott Laboratories, REI, PNC Bank, Deloitte, Timberland, Unilever, and Caterpillar, prominently describe their ESG performance on their websites.

Exhibit P–9 presents 33 examples of ESG responsibilities of interest to many organizational stakeholders.[7] Notice five of the examples contain a parenthetical (–) indicating "less is more" in the eyes of stakeholders. The remaining 28 examples contain a parenthetical (+) indicating "more is better" from the stakeholders' standpoint. If a company fails to meet its ESG responsibilities, it can adversely affect stakeholder perceptions and profits. For example, if a company fails to provide safe and humane working conditions for its employees, a stakeholder backlash could cause the company's customers to defect and its "best and brightest" job candidates to apply elsewhere—both of which are likely to eventually harm financial performance. Scenarios like these are why, in managerial accounting, a manager must consider all stakeholders when establishing plans, implementing controls, and making decisions.

IN BUSINESS

THE ENVIRONMENTAL IMPACTS OF FAST FASHION

McKinsey & Co. estimates that, over a 14-year span, the number of times people wore a clothing item before discarding it declined by 36 percent. Given that 53 million metric tons of fiber—less than 13 percent of which is recycled—is annually used in clothing, this trend presents a worrisome environmental problem. More specifically, McKinsey estimates that by 2030 our annual global clothing consumption will use 118 billion cubic meters of water. It will also produce 2.79 billion tons of carbon dioxide and 148 million tons of waste, most of which is landfilled or incinerated. In an effort to tackle this problem, some companies such as Inditex SA and Lenzing AG are investing in recycling technologies, while others such as JCPenney and Macy's are starting to sell secondhand clothing.

Source: Saabira Chaudhuri, "Fast Fashion Leads to New Recycling Effort," *The Wall Street Journal*, October 13, 2019, pp. B1–B2.

EXHIBIT P–9
Examples of Environmental, Social, and Governance (ESG) Responsibilities

Environmental	Social	Governance
• Carbon emissions (–)	• Child labor transparency (+)	• Board of directors' diversity (+)
• Product carbon footprint (–)	• Employee health and safety (+)	• Executive pay transparency (+)
• Toxic emissions and waste (–)	• Customer data privacy (+)	• Tax transparency (+)
• Water usage (–)	• Fair employee compensation (+)	• Ethical decision making (+)
• Packaging material waste (–)	• Community investments (+)	• Enterprise risk transparency (+)
• Green new construction (+)	• Employee training (+)	• Reliable financial reports (+)
• Renewable energy usage (+)	• Cooperative supplier relations (+)	• Clear purpose and priorities (+)
• Responsible materials sourcing (+)	• Policies against harassment (+)	• Corporate culture alignment (+)
• End-of-product life plan (+)	• Consumer protection (+)	• Stakeholder needs awareness (+)
• Responsible production (+)	• Fair pricing (+)	• Responsible supply chain support (+)
• Recycling and reuse strategies (+)	• Policies against discrimination (+)	• ESG impact transparency (+)

---

[7] Many of the examples in Exhibit P–9 were drawn from PwC's website. You can view more examples by visiting https://www.pwc.com/sk/en/environmental-social-and-corporate-governance-esg/esg-reporting.html.

Process Management Perspective

Most companies organize themselves by functional departments, such as the Marketing Department, the Research and Development Department, and the Accounting Department. These departments have a clearly defined "chain of command" specifying superior and subordinate relationships. However, effective managers understand *business processes,* more so than functional departments, serve the needs of a company's most important stakeholders—its customers. A **business process** is a series of steps followed in order to carry out some task in a business. These steps often span departmental boundaries, thereby requiring managers to cooperate across functional departments. The term *value chain* is often used to describe how an organization's functional departments interact with one another to form business processes. A **value chain,** as shown in Exhibit P–10, consists of the major business functions adding value to a company's products and services.

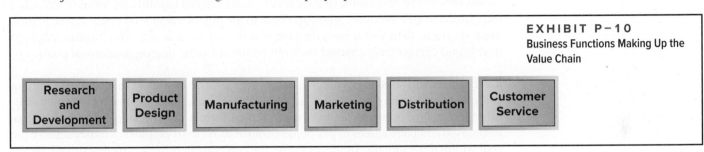

EXHIBIT P–10
Business Functions Making Up the Value Chain

Managers need to understand the value chain for planning, control, and decision making. For example, if a company's engineers plan to design a new product, they must communicate with the Manufacturing Department to ensure the product can actually be produced, the Marketing Department to ensure customers will buy the product, the Distribution Department to ensure large volumes of the product can be cost-effectively transported to customers, and the Accounting Department to ensure the product will increase profits. From a control and decision-making standpoint, managers also need to focus on process excellence instead of functional performance. For example, if the Purchasing Department focuses solely on minimizing the cost of purchased materials, this narrowly focused attempt at cost reduction may lead to greater scrap and rework in the Manufacturing Department, more complaints in the Customer Service Department, and greater challenges in the Marketing Department because dissatisfied customers are turning their attention to competitors.

Managers frequently use a process management method known as *lean resource management,* or what is called *Lean Production* in the manufacturing sector. **Lean Production** is a management approach that organizes resources such as people and machines around the flow of business processes and only produces units in response to customer orders. It is often called *just-in-time* production (or *JIT*) because products are only manufactured in response to customer orders and they are completed just-in-time to be shipped to customers. Lean Production differs from traditional manufacturing methods that organize work departmentally and encourage departments to maximize their output even if it exceeds customer demand and bloats inventories. Because Lean Production only allows production in response to customer orders, the number of units produced equals the number of units sold, thereby resulting in minimal inventory. The lean approach also results in fewer defects, less wasted effort, and quicker customer response times than traditional production methods.

Leadership

An organization's employees bring diverse needs, beliefs, and goals to the workplace. Therefore, an important role for organizational leaders is to unite the behaviors of their fellow employees around two common themes—pursuing strategic goals and making optimal decisions. To fulfill this responsibility, leaders need to understand how *intrinsic motivation, extrinsic incentives,* and *cognitive bias* influence human behavior.

Intrinsic Motivation Intrinsic motivation refers to motivation coming from within us. Stop for a moment and identify the greatest accomplishment of your life. Then ask yourself what motivated you to achieve this goal? In all likelihood, you achieved it because you wanted to, not because someone forced you to do it. In other words, you were intrinsically motivated. Similarly, an organization is more likely to prosper when its employees are intrinsically motivated to pursue its interests. A leader, who employees perceive as *credible* and *respectful* of their value to the organization, can increase the extent to which those employees are intrinsically motivated to pursue strategic goals. As your career evolves, to be perceived as a credible leader, you'll need to possess three attributes—technical competence (that spans the value chain), personal integrity (in terms of work ethic and honesty), and strong communication skills (including oral presentation skills and writing skills). To be perceived as a leader who is respectful of your co-workers' value to the organization, you'll need to possess three more attributes—strong mentoring skills (to help others realize their potential), strong listening skills (to learn from your co-workers and be responsive to their needs), and personal humility (in terms of deferring recognition to all employees who contribute to the organization's success). If you possess these six traits, then you'll have the potential to become a leader who inspires others to readily and energetically channel their efforts toward achieving organizational goals.

Extrinsic Incentives   Many organizations use *extrinsic incentives* to highlight important goals and to motivate employees to achieve them. For example, assume a company establishes the goal of reducing the time needed to perform a task by 20 percent. In addition, assume the company agrees to pay bonus compensation to its employees if they achieve the goal within three months. In this example, the company is using a type of extrinsic incentive known as a bonus to highlight a particular goal and to presumably motivate employees to achieve it.

While proponents of extrinsic incentives rightly assert these types of rewards can have a powerful influence on employee behavior, many critics warn they can also produce dysfunctional consequences. For example, suppose the employees mentioned above earned their bonuses by achieving the 20 percent time reduction goal within three months. However, let's also assume during those three months the quality of the employees' output plummeted, thereby causing a spike in the company's repair costs, product returns, and customer defections. In this instance, did the extrinsic incentive work properly? The answer is yes and no. The bonus system did motivate employees to attain the time reduction goal; however, it also had the unintended consequences of causing employees to neglect product quality, thereby increasing repair costs, product returns, and customer defections. In other words, what may have seemed like a well-intended extrinsic incentive actually produced dysfunctional results for the company. This example highlights an important leadership challenge you are likely to face someday—designing financial compensation systems that fairly reward employees for their efforts without inadvertently creating extrinsic incentives motivating them to take actions that harm the company.

Cognitive Bias   Leaders need to understand all people (including themselves) possess *cognitive biases,* or distorted thought processes, that can adversely affect planning, controlling, and decision making. To illustrate how cognitive bias works, let's consider the scenario of a television "infomercial" where someone is selling a product with a proclaimed value of $200 for $19.99 if viewers call within the next 30 minutes. Why do you think the seller claims the product has a $200 value? The seller is relying on a cognitive bias called *anchoring bias* in an effort to convince viewers that a $180 discount is simply too good to pass up. The "anchor" is the false assertion the product is actually worth $200. If viewers erroneously attach credibility to this contrived piece of information, their distorted analysis of the situation may cause them to spend $19.99 on an item whose true economic value is much less than that amount.

While cognitive biases cannot be eliminated, effective leaders should take two steps to reduce their negative impacts. First, they should acknowledge their own susceptibility to cognitive bias. For example, a leader's judgment might be clouded by optimism bias (being overly optimistic in assessing the likelihood of future outcomes) or self-enhancement bias (overestimating one's strengths and underestimating one's weaknesses relative to, those of others). Second, they should acknowledge the presence of cognitive bias in others and introduce techniques to minimize their adverse consequences. For example, to reduce the risks of confirmation bias (a bias where people pay greater attention to information that confirms their preconceived notions, while devaluing information that contradicts them) or groupthink bias (a bias where some group members support a course of action solely because other group members do), a leader may routinely appoint independent teams of employees to assess the credibility of recommendations set forth by other individuals and groups.

A BROADER VIEW OF THE MANAGEMENT ACCOUNTING PROFESSION

The Institute of Management Accountants (IMA) has established a competency framework to describe the breadth of skills that it believes management accountants need to be successful in the marketplace. The centerpiece of the framework is *Leadership,* which refers to the competencies that are required to collaborate with others and inspire teams to achieve organizational goals. The framework's foundation is *Professional Ethics & Values* and its four remaining competencies include *Strategy, Planning & Performance, Reporting & Control, Technology & Analytics,* and *Business Acumen & Operations.*

   This framework expands upon the pillars of planning, controlling, and decision making described earlier in the prologue. The IMA has defined this expanded set of competencies to guide accounting professionals in developing their own skills and to help them mentor co-workers who are also interested in career advancement.

Source: The 44-page document that provides a detailed description of this framework is available at https://www.imanet.org /career-resources/management-accounting-competencies.

Institute of Management Accountants

Summary

The prologue defined managerial accounting and explained why it is relevant to business and accounting majors. It also discussed seven topics—Big Data; ethics; strategic management; enterprise risk management; environmental, social, and governance (ESG) responsibilities; process management; and leadership—that define the context for applying the quantitative aspects of managerial accounting. The most important goal of the prologue was to help you understand that managerial accounting matters to your future career regardless of your major. Accounting is the language of business, and you'll need to speak it to communicate effectively with and influence fellow managers.

Glossary

Big Data Large collections of data gathered from inside or outside a company to provide opportunities for ongoing reporting and analysis. (p. 9)

Budget A plan for the future expressed in formal quantitative terms. (p. 3)

Business process A series of steps followed in order to carry out some task in a business. (p. 17)

Controlling The process of gathering feedback to ensure a plan is being properly executed or modified as circumstances change. (p. 3)

Data analytics The process of analyzing data with the aid of specialized systems and software to draw conclusions about the information they contain. (p. 10)

Decision making Selecting a course of action from competing alternatives. (p. 3)

Detective control A control that detects undesirable events that have already occurred. (p. 14)

Enterprise risk management A process used by a company to identify its risks and develop responses to them that enable it to be reasonably assured of meeting its goals. (p. 13)

Environmental, Social, and Governance (ESG) Three criteria used by stakeholders for gauging the sustainability and ethical impacts of a company. (p. 16)

Financial accounting The phase of accounting concerned with reporting historical financial information to external parties, such as stockholders, creditors, and regulators. (p. 2)

Lean Production A management approach that organizes resources such as people and machines around the flow of business processes and only produces units in response to customer orders. (p. 17)

Managerial accounting The phase of accounting concerned with providing information to people within an organization, such as senior managers, middle managers, and front-line employees. (p. 2)

Performance report A report comparing budgeted data to actual data to highlight instances of excellent and unsatisfactory performance. (p. 4)

Planning The process of establishing goals and specifying how to achieve them. (p. 3)

Preventive control A control that deters undesirable events from occurring. (p. 14)

Segment Any part or activity of an organization about which managers seek cost, revenue, or profit data. (p. 3)

Strategy A "game plan" that is difficult to replicate and differentiates a company from its competitors in ways that attract and retain customers. (p. 11)

Value chain The major business functions adding value to a company's products and services, such as research and development, product design, manufacturing, marketing, distribution, and customer service. (p. 17)

Questions

P–1 How does managerial accounting differ from financial accounting?

P–2 Pick any major television network and describe some planning and control activities its managers would engage in,

P–3 If you had to decide whether to make a component part or buy it from an overseas supplier, what quantitative and qualitative factors would influence your decision?

P–4 Why do companies prepare budgets?

P–5 Why is managerial accounting relevant to business majors and their future careers?

P–6 Why is managerial accounting relevant to accounting majors and their future careers?

P–7 Pick any large company and describe its strategy using one of the three customer value propositions defined in the prologue.

P–8 Why do management accountants need to understand their company's strategy?

P–9 Pick any large company and describe three risks it faces and how it responds to those risks.

P–10 Pick three industries and describe how the risks faced by companies within those industries can influence their planning, controlling, and decision-making activities.

P–11 Pick any large company and explain three ways it could segment its companywide performance.

P–12 Locate any company whose website discusses its environmental, social, and governance (ESG) responsibilities. Describe three ESG responsibilities mentioned by the company. Why do you think companies pay attention to their ESG responsibilities?

P–13 Why do companies using Lean Production have minimal inventories?

P–14 Why are leadership skills important to managers?

P–15 Why is ethical behavior important to business?

P–16 If you were a restaurant owner, what internal controls would you implement to maintain control of your cash?

P–17 As a form of internal control, what documents would you review before paying an invoice received from a supplier?

P–18 What internal controls would you implement to maintain control of your credit sales and accounts receivable?

P–19 Why do companies take a physical count of their inventory on hand at least once per year?

P–20 Why do companies use sequential prenumbering for documents such as checks, sales invoices, and purchase orders?

 Exercises

EXERCISE P–1 Planning and Control

Assume you are a sales manager working with your boss to create a sales budget for next year. Once the sales budget is established, it will influence how other departments within your company plan to deploy their resources. For example, the manufacturing manager will plan to produce enough units to meet the budgeted unit sales. If the sales budget is too high, it will result in excess inventories, and if it is too low, it will result in lost sales.

You have studied all of the pertinent data and concluded that the "most likely" outcome is estimated sales of $1,000,000. You also believe if the sales team works extra hard and has a terrific year, it has a modest chance of achieving an "optimistic" sales forecast of $1,200,000. Conversely, if the economy sours, you believe your sales team can still achieve a "pessimistic" sales forecast of $900,000.

Required:

1. Assume your company uses its sales budget for only one purpose—to match the supply of manufactured products with customer demand, thereby minimizing inventories and lost sales. What sales forecast would you provide to your boss?

2. Assume your company also uses its sales budget as a motivational tool to help employees strive for "stretch goals" and exceptional results. What sales forecast would you provide to your boss?

3. Assume your company's sales budget is also used for a third purpose—to determine your pay raise, bonus, and potential for promotion. If actual sales exceed the sales budget, it bodes well for your career. If actual sales are less than budgeted sales, it will diminish your financial compensation and potential for promotion. What sales forecast would you provide to your boss?

4. Are your answers to the first three questions the same or different? Why? If you know from past experience your boss usually adds 5–10% to your forecast, how would this affect your answers to the first three questions?

5. Do you think it would be appropriate for your boss to establish the sales budget without any input from you? Why?

6. Do you think the company would allow you to establish the sales budget without any input from your boss? Why?

EXERCISE P–2 Controlling

Assume you work for an airline unloading luggage from airplanes. Your boss has said on average, each airplane contains 100 pieces of luggage. Furthermore, your boss has stated you should be able to unload 100 pieces of luggage from an airplane in 10 minutes. Today an airplane arrived with 150 pieces of luggage and you unloaded all of it in 13 minutes. After finishing with the 150 pieces of luggage, your boss yelled at you for exceeding the 10-minute allowance for unloading luggage from an airplane.

Required:

How would you feel about being yelled at for taking 13 minutes to unload 150 pieces of luggage? How does this scenario relate to the larger issue of how companies design control systems?

EXERCISE P–3 Decision Making

Exhibit P–2 from within the prologue includes 12 questions related to 12 types of decisions companies often face. In the prologue, these 12 decisions were discussed within the context of for-profit companies; however, they are also readily applicable to nonprofit organizations. To illustrate this point, assume you are a senior leader, such as a president, provost, or dean, in a university setting.

Required:

For each of the 12 decisions in Exhibit P–2, provide an example of how it might be applicable to a university setting.

EXERCISE P–4 Ethics and the Manager

Richmond, Inc., operates a chain of 44 department stores. Two years ago, the board of directors of Richmond approved a large-scale remodeling of its stores to attract a more upscale clientele.

Before finalizing these plans, two stores were remodeled as a test. Linda Perlman, assistant controller, was asked to oversee the financial reporting for these test stores, and she and other management personnel were offered bonuses based on the sales growth and profitability of these stores. While completing the financial reports, Perlman discovered a sizable inventory of outdated goods that should have been discounted for sale or returned to the manufacturer. She discussed the situation with her management colleagues; the consensus was to ignore reporting this inventory as obsolete because reporting it would lower profits and their bonuses.

Required:

1. According to the IMA's Statement of Ethical Professional Practice, would it be ethical for Perlman *not* to report the inventory as obsolete?
2. Would it be easy for Perlman to take the ethical action in this situation?

(CMA, adapted)

EXERCISE P–5 Strategy

The table below contains the names of six companies.

Required:

For each company, categorize its strategy as pursuing differentiation through customer intimacy, operational excellence, or product leadership. If you wish to improve your understanding of each company's customer value proposition before completing the exercise, review its most recent annual report. To obtain electronic access to this information, perform an internet search on each company's name followed by the words "annual report."

	Company	Strategy
1.	Deere	?
2.	FedEx	?
3.	State Farm Insurance	?
4.	BMW	?
5.	Amazon.com	?
6.	Charles Schwab	?

EXERCISE P–6 Enterprise Risk Management

The table below refers to seven industries.

Required:

For each industry, provide an example of a business risk faced by companies competing within that industry. Then, describe an example of a control that reduces the business risk you identified.

Industry	Example of Business Risk	Example of Control to Reduce the Business Risk
1. Airlines (e.g., Delta Airlines)		
2. Pharmaceutical drugs (e.g., Merck)		
3. Package delivery (e.g., United Parcel Service)		
4. Banking (e.g., Bank of America)		
5. Oil & gas (e.g., ExxonMobil)		
6. E-commerce (e.g., eBay)		
7. Automotive (e.g., Toyota)		

EXERCISE P–7 Ethics in Business

Consumers and attorneys general in more than 40 states accused a prominent nationwide chain of auto repair shops of misleading customers and selling them unnecessary parts and services, from brake jobs to front-end alignments. Lynn Sharpe Paine reported the situation as follows in "Managing for Organizational Integrity," *Harvard Business Review,* Volume 72, Issue 3:

> In the face of declining revenues, shrinking market share, and an increasingly competitive market . . . management attempted to spur performance of its auto centers. . . . The

automotive service advisers were given product-specific sales quotas—sell so many springs, shock absorbers, alignments, or brake jobs per shift—and paid a commission based on sales. . . . [F]ailure to meet quotas could lead to a transfer or a reduction in work hours. Some employees spoke of the "pressure, pressure, pressure" to bring in sales.

> This pressure-cooker atmosphere created conditions under which employees felt that the only way to satisfy top management was by selling products and services to customers that they didn't really need.

Suppose all automotive repair businesses routinely followed the practice of attempting to sell customers unnecessary parts and services.

Required:
1. How would this behavior affect customers? How might customers attempt to protect themselves against this behavior?
2. How would this behavior probably affect profits and employment in the automotive service industry?

EXERCISE P–8 Cognitive Bias
In the 1970s, one million college-bound students were asked to compare themselves to their peers. Some of the key findings were as follows:
a. 70% of the students rated themselves as above average in leadership ability, while only 2% rated themselves as below average in this regard.
b. With respect to athletic skills, 60% of the students rated their skills as above the median and only 6% rated themselves as below the median.
c. 60% of the students rated themselves in the top 10% in terms of their ability to get along with others, while 25% of the students felt that they were in the top 1% in terms of this interpersonal skill.

Required:
1. What type of cognitive bias reveals itself in the data mentioned above?
2. How might this cognitive bias adversely influence a manager's planning, controlling, and decision-making activities?
3. What steps could managers take to reduce the possibility this cognitive bias would adversely influence their actions?

Source: Dan Lovallo and Daniel Kahneman, "Delusions of Success: How Optimism Undermines Executives' Decisions," *Harvard Business Review,* July 2003, pp. 56–63.

EXERCISE P–9 Ethics and Decision Making

Assume you are the chair of the Department of Accountancy at Mountain State University. One of the accounting professors in your department, Dr. Candler, has been consistently and uniformly regarded by students as an awful teacher for more than 10 years. Other accounting professors within your department have observed Dr. Candler's classroom teaching and they concur his teaching skills are very poor. However, Dr. Candler was granted tenure 12 years ago, thereby ensuring him life-long job security at Mountain State University.

Much to your surprise, today you received a phone call from an accounting professor at Oregon Coastal University. During this phone call you are informed Oregon Coastal University is on the verge of making a job offer to Dr. Candler. However, before extending the job offer, the faculty at Oregon Coastal wants your input regarding Dr. Candler's teaching effectiveness.

Required:
How would you respond to the professor from Oregon Coastal University? What would you say about Dr. Candler's teaching ability? Would you describe your answer to this inquiry as being ethical? Why?

EXERCISE P–10 Environmental, Social, and Governance (ESG) Responsibilities

In his book *Capitalism and Freedom,* economist Milton Friedman wrote on page 133: "There is one and only one social responsibility of business—to use its resources and engage in activities designed to increase its profits so long as it . . . engages in open and free competition, without deception or fraud."

Required:
Explain why you agree or disagree with this quote.

EXERCISE P–11 Intrinsic Motivation and Extrinsic Incentives

In a *Harvard Business Review* article titled "Why Incentive Plans Cannot Work" (Volume 71, Issue 5), author Alfie Kohn wrote: "Research suggests that, by and large, rewards succeed at securing one thing only: temporary compliance. When it comes to producing lasting change in attitudes and behavior, however, rewards, like punishment, are strikingly ineffective. Once the rewards run out, people revert to their old behaviors. . . . Incentives, a version of what psychologists call extrinsic motivators, do not alter the attitudes that underlie our behaviors. They do not create an enduring *commitment* to any value or action. Rather, incentives merely—and temporarily—change what we do."

Required:
1. Do you agree with this quote? Why?
2. As a manager, how would you seek to motivate your employees?
3. As a manager, would you use financial incentives to compensate your employees? If so, what would be the keys to using them effectively? If not, then how would you compensate your employees?

EXERCISE P–12 Cognitive Bias and Decision Making

During World War II, the U.S. military was studying its combat-tested fighter planes to determine the parts of the plane most vulnerable to enemy fire so it could reinforce those sections to improve pilot safety and airplane durability. The data it gathered showed certain sections of its combat-tested fighter planes were consistently hit more often with enemy fire than other sections of the plane.

Required:
1. Would you recommend reinforcing the sections of the plane that were hit most often by enemy fire, or would you reinforce the sections that were hit less frequently by enemy fire? Why?
2. Do you think cognitive bias had the potential to influence the U.S. military's decision-making process with respect to reinforcing its fighter planes?

Source: Jerker Denrell, "Selection Bias and the Perils of Benchmarking," *Harvard Business Review,* Volume 83, Issue 4, pp. 114–119.

EXERCISE P–13 Ethics and Decision Making

Assume you just completed a December weekend vacation to a casino within the United States. During your trip you won $10,000 gambling. When the casino exchanged your chips for cash, it did not record any personal information, such as your driver's license number or social security number. Four months later while preparing your tax returns for the prior year, you stop to contemplate the fact that the Internal Revenue Service requires taxpayers to report all gambling winnings on Form 1040.

Required:
Would you report your gambling winnings to the Internal Revenue Service so you could pay federal income taxes on those winnings? Do you believe your actions are ethical? Why?

Managerial Accounting and Cost Concepts

Mary Altaffer/AP Photo

ENTREPRENEUR SPOTLIGHT

Coss Marte is a former prison inmate who lost 70 pounds during six months of incarceration. He accomplished this remarkable transformation without any gym equipment or a personal trainer—just the walls and floor in his 9' by 6' prison cell. After his release, Marte started a company called CONBODY that provides military-style bodyweight training for its customers. The company offers more than 50 online, on-demand exercise classes as well as live virtual workout opportunities.

Applying Managerial Accounting

In managing his company, Marte has numerous opportunities to apply managerial accounting cost concepts. For example, when preparing a budget, he'd need to distinguish between variable costs (such as instructor labor costs that vary with respect to the number of classes taught) and fixed costs (such as his monthly website maintenance costs). He'd also need to separate relevant costs from irrelevant costs when deciding whether to add a new class or discontinue an existing class.

Serving All Stakeholders

CONBODY's mission "is to bridge a gap between two communities: young professionals and formerly incarcerated individuals." The company also partners with nonprofit organizations to provide former inmates educational resources, mentorship, housing, and employment opportunities. To date, Marte has hired over 40 former inmates as fitness instructors with an astonishing zero percent recidivism rate. ■

Source: www.conbody.com

lighthouse image: Martin73/Shutterstock;
big data image: INGARA/Shutterstock

LEARNING OBJECTIVES

After studying Chapter 1, you should be able to:

LO1–1 Understand cost classifications used for assigning costs to cost objects: direct costs and indirect costs.

LO1–2 Identify and give examples of each of the three basic manufacturing cost categories.

LO1–3 Understand cost classifications used to prepare financial statements: product costs and period costs.

LO1–4 Understand cost classifications used to predict cost behavior: variable costs, fixed costs, and mixed costs.

LO1–5 Understand cost classifications used in making decisions: relevant costs and irrelevant costs.

LO1–6 Prepare income statements for a merchandising company using the traditional and contribution formats.

 Data Analytics Exercise available in Connect to complement this chapter

In accounting, costs can be classified differently depending on the needs of management. For example, the prologue mentioned **financial accounting** reports financial information to external parties, such as stockholders, creditors, and regulators. In this context, costs are classified in accordance with externally imposed rules to enable the preparation of financial statements. Conversely, **managerial accounting** provides information to employees within an organization so they can formulate plans, control operations, and make decisions. In these contexts, costs are classified in diverse ways, enabling managers to predict future costs, compare actual costs to budgeted costs, assign costs to segments of the business (such as product lines, geographic regions, and distribution channels), and contrast costs associated with competing alternatives.

The notion of *different cost classifications for different purposes* is the most important unifying theme of this chapter and one of the key foundational concepts of the entire textbook. Exhibit 1–1 summarizes five types of cost classifications used throughout the textbook, namely cost classifications for (1) assigning costs to cost objects, (2) accounting for costs in manufacturing companies, (3) preparing financial statements, (4) predicting cost behavior, and (5) making decisions. As we begin defining the cost terminology related to each of these cost classifications, refer back to this exhibit to improve your understanding of the overall organization of the chapter.

Cost Classifications for Assigning Costs to Cost Objects

LO1–1
Understand cost classifications used for assigning costs to cost objects: direct costs and indirect costs.

Costs are assigned to cost objects for a variety of purposes, including pricing, preparing profitability studies, and controlling spending. A **cost object** is anything for which cost data are desired—including products, customers, plants, office locations, and departments. For purposes of assigning costs to cost objects, costs are classified as either *direct* or *indirect*.

EXHIBIT 1–1
Summary of Cost Classifications

Purpose of Cost Classification	Cost Classifications
Assigning costs to cost objects	• Direct costs (can be easily traced) • Indirect costs (cannot be easily traced)

Accounting for costs in manufacturing companies	• Manufacturing costs
	  • Direct materials
	  • Direct labor
	  • Manufacturing overhead
	• Nonmanufacturing costs
	  • Selling costs
	  • Administrative costs

Preparing financial statements	• Product costs (inventoriable) • Period costs (expensed)
Predicting cost behavior in response to changes in activity	• Variable costs (proportional to activity) • Fixed costs (constant in total) • Mixed costs (have variable and fixed elements)
Making decisions	• Relevant costs (differ between alternatives) • Irrelevant costs (should be ignored)

Direct Cost

A **direct cost** can be easily traced to a specified cost object. For example, if Adidas is assigning costs to its various regional and national sales offices, then the salary of the sales manager in its Tokyo office would be a direct cost of that office. If a printing company made 10,000 brochures for a specific customer, then the cost of the paper used to make the brochures would be a direct cost of that customer.

Indirect Cost

An **indirect cost** cannot be easily traced to a specified cost object. For example, Amy's Kitchen may produce a variety of organic soups in one factory. The factory manager's salary would be an indirect cost of a particular variety, such as chunky vegetable soup, because it is incurred to run the entire factory—not to produce a specific flavor of soup. *To be traced to a cost object such as a particular product, the cost must be caused by the cost object.* The factory manager's salary is called a *common cost* of producing the various products of the factory. A **common cost** is a cost incurred to support a number of cost objects but cannot be traced to them individually. A common cost is a type of indirect cost.

A particular cost may be direct or indirect, depending on the cost object. While the Amy's Kitchen factory manager's salary is an *indirect* cost of manufacturing chunky vegetable soup, it is a *direct* cost of the manufacturing department. In the first case, the cost object is chunky vegetable soup. In the second case, the cost object is the entire manufacturing department.

Cost Classifications for Manufacturing Companies

Manufacturing companies such as Samtec, Mack Trucks, and 3M separate their costs into two broad categories—manufacturing and nonmanufacturing costs.

LO1–2
Identify and give examples of each of the three basic manufacturing cost categories.

Manufacturing Costs

Most manufacturing companies further separate their manufacturing costs into two direct cost categories, direct materials and direct labor, and one indirect cost category, manufacturing overhead. A discussion of these three categories follows.

Direct Materials Materials used in the final product are called **raw materials.** This term is somewhat misleading because it implies unprocessed natural resources like wood pulp or iron ore. Actually, raw materials refer to any materials used in the final product; and the finished product of one company can become the raw materials of another company. For example, the plastics produced by DuPont are a raw material used by HP in its personal computers.

Direct materials refers to raw materials whose costs can be easily traced to finished products. Examples include the seats Airbus purchases from subcontractors to install in its commercial aircraft, the electronic components Samsung uses in its cell phones, and the doors Whirlpool installs on its refrigerators.

Direct Labor   **Direct labor** includes labor costs easily traceable to finished products. Direct labor is sometimes called *touch labor* because direct labor workers typically touch the products being made. Examples of direct labor include assembly-line workers at Tesla, carpenters at the home builder KB Home, and electricians who install equipment on aircraft at Bombardier Learjet.

Managers occasionally refer to direct manufacturing costs as *prime costs*. **Prime cost** is the sum of direct materials cost and direct labor cost.

Manufacturing Overhead   **Manufacturing overhead,** the third manufacturing cost category, includes all manufacturing costs except direct materials and direct labor. From a product costing standpoint, manufacturing overhead costs are indirect costs because they cannot be readily traced to specific products. For example, manufacturing overhead includes a portion of raw materials known as *indirect materials* as well as *indirect labor.* **Indirect materials** are raw materials, such as the solder used to make electrical connections in a Toshiba HDTV and the glue used to assemble an Ethan Allen chair, whose costs cannot be easily traced to finished products. **Indirect labor** refers to employees, such as janitors, supervisors, materials handlers, maintenance workers, and night security guards, who play an essential role in running a manufacturing facility; however, the cost of compensating these people cannot be easily traced to finished products. Because indirect materials and indirect labor are difficult to trace to specific products, their costs are included in manufacturing overhead.

Manufacturing overhead also includes other production costs, such as depreciation of manufacturing equipment and the utility costs, property taxes, and insurance premiums incurred to operate a manufacturing facility. Although companies also incur depreciation, utility costs, property taxes, and insurance premiums to sustain their non-manufacturing operations, these costs are not included as part of manufacturing overhead. Only those indirect costs associated with *operating the factory* are included in manufacturing overhead.

In practice, managers use various names for manufacturing overhead, such as *indirect manufacturing cost, factory overhead,* and *factory burden.* All of these terms are synonyms for manufacturing overhead. Another term managers frequently use is *conversion cost.* **Conversion cost** is the sum of direct labor and manufacturing overhead, which are the two costs incurred to *convert* direct materials into finished products.

Nonmanufacturing Costs

Nonmanufacturing costs are often divided into two categories: (1) *selling costs* and (2) *administrative costs.* **Selling costs** include all costs incurred to secure customer orders and get the finished product to the customer. These costs are sometimes called *order-getting* and *order-filling costs.* Examples of selling costs include advertising, shipping, sales travel, sales commissions, sales salaries, and costs of finished goods warehouses. Selling costs can be either direct or indirect costs. For example, the cost of an advertising campaign dedicated to one specific product is a direct cost of that product, whereas the salary of a marketing manager who oversees numerous products is an indirect cost with respect to individual products.

Administrative costs include all costs associated with the *general management* of an organization rather than with manufacturing or selling. Examples of administrative costs include executive compensation, general accounting, legal counsel, secretarial, public relations, and similar costs involved in the administration of the organization *as a whole.* Administrative costs can be either direct or indirect costs. For example, the salary of an accounting manager in charge of accounts receivable collections in the East region is a direct cost of that region, whereas the salary of a chief financial officer who oversees all of a company's regions is an indirect cost with respect to individual regions.

Nonmanufacturing costs are also often called selling, general, and administrative (SG&A) costs or just selling and administrative costs.

Cost Classifications for Preparing Financial Statements

When preparing a balance sheet and an income statement, companies need to classify their costs as *product costs* or *period costs*. To understand the difference between product costs and period costs, we must first discuss the matching principle from financial accounting.

Generally, costs are recognized as expenses on the income statement in the period benefitting from the cost. For example, if a company pays for liability insurance in advance for two years, the entire amount is not an expense of the year when the payment is made. Instead, one-half of the cost would be recognized as an expense each year. The reason is both years—not just the first year—benefit from the insurance payment. The unexpensed portion of the insurance payment is reported on the balance sheet as an asset called prepaid insurance.

The *matching principle* is based on the *accrual* concept that *costs incurred to generate a particular revenue should be recognized as expenses in the same period the revenue is recognized.* This means if a cost is incurred to acquire or make something that will eventually be sold, then the cost should be recognized as an expense only when the sale takes place—that is, when the benefit occurs. Such costs are called *product costs*.

LO1–3
Understand cost classifications used to prepare financial statements: product costs and period costs.

Product Costs

For financial accounting purposes, **product costs** include all costs involved in acquiring or making a product. Product costs "attach" to products as they are purchased or manufactured and they remain attached to those products while in inventory awaiting sale. Once sold, their costs are released from inventory as expenses (typically called cost of goods sold) and matched against sales on the income statement. Because product costs are initially assigned to inventories, they are also known as **inventoriable costs.**

For manufacturing companies, product costs include direct materials, direct labor, and manufacturing overhead.[1] A manufacturer's product costs flow through three inventory accounts on the balance sheet—*Raw Materials, Work in Process,* and *Finished Goods*—prior to being recorded in cost of goods sold on the income statement. Raw materials include any materials used in the final product. **Work in process** includes units of product that are only partially complete and will require further work before they are ready for sale to the customer. **Finished goods** consist of completed units of product that have not been sold to customers.

When direct materials are used in production, their costs are transferred from Raw Materials to Work in Process. Direct labor and manufacturing overhead costs are added to Work in Process to convert direct materials into finished goods. Once units of product are completed, their costs are transferred from Work in Process to Finished Goods. When a manufacturer sells its finished goods to customers, the costs are transferred from Finished Goods to Cost of Goods Sold.

We want to emphasize product costs are not necessarily recorded as expenses on the income statement in the period incurred. Rather, as explained above, they are recorded as expenses when the related products *are sold.*

Period Costs

Period costs include all the costs that are not product costs. *All selling and administrative expenses are treated as period costs.* For example, sales commissions, advertising, executive salaries, public relations, and the rental costs of administrative offices are all period costs. Period costs are not included in inventory; instead, they are expensed on the income statement in the period incurred using the usual rules of accrual accounting.

---

[1] For internal management purposes, product costs may exclude some manufacturing costs. For example, see Appendix 2B and the discussion in Chapter 6.

EXHIBIT 1–2
Cost Flows and Classifications in a Manufacturing Company

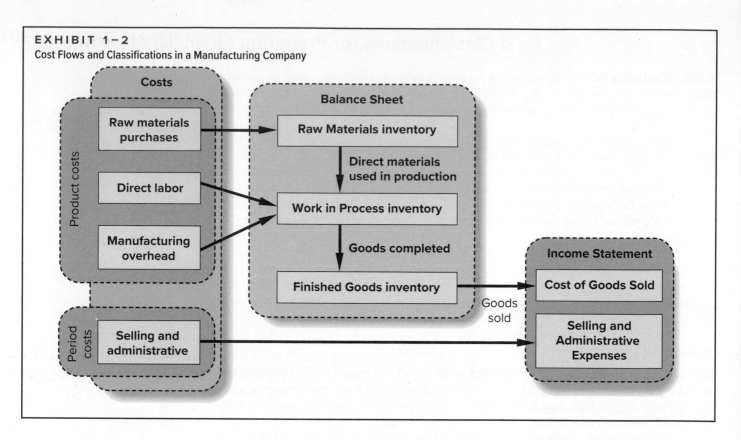

Keep in mind the period incurred is not necessarily the same period cash changes hands. For example, as discussed earlier, the cost of liability insurance is spread across the periods benefitting from the insurance—regardless of when the insurance premium is paid.

Exhibit 1–2 summarizes the product and period cost flows for manufacturers. Notice product costs flow through three inventory accounts on the balance sheet before being recognized as cost of goods sold in the income statement. Conversely, period costs do not flow through inventory on the balance sheet and are not included in cost of goods sold in the income statement. Instead, they are recorded as selling and administrative expenses in the income statement during the period incurred.

IN BUSINESS

THE ADMINISTRATIVE COSTS OF REDESIGNING THE OFFICE

Deliris/Shutterstock

For decades American companies sought to "cram workers into tighter spaces with few separations between colleagues . . . [spending] millions of dollars . . . to create rows of open desks, intimate conference rooms, and elaborate communal gathering areas." However, in the post-COVID-19 era companies are incurring additional administrative costs as they reexamine and redesign their office spaces. For example, HP welcomed back each employee to one of its offices with a kit containing three new office essentials—hand sanitizer, a mask, and gloves. McCann Worldgroup's New York office has closed its cafeteria and ordered dozens of refrigerators and microwaves so employees can bring their lunches to work. Discover Financial Services is considering seating its employees at every other workstation, whereas WeWork is removing 30,000 conference-room chairs from its global offices to enable proper social distancing.

Source: Chip Cutter and Suzanne Vranica, "Offices Revamp to Keep Germs at Bay," *The Wall Street Journal*, May 12, 2020, pp. B1 and B5.

Cost Classifications for Predicting Cost Behavior

For planning purposes, managers need to predict *cost behavior*. **Cost behavior** refers to how a cost reacts to changes in the level of activity. This section defines three types of cost behavior—*variable, fixed,* and *mixed.* The relative proportion of each type of cost in an organization is known as its **cost structure.** For example, an organization might have many fixed costs but few variable or mixed costs. Alternatively, it might have many variable costs but few fixed or mixed costs.

LO1–4
Understand cost classifications used to predict cost behavior: variable costs, fixed costs, and mixed costs.

Variable Cost

A **variable cost** varies, in total, in direct proportion to changes in the level of activity. Common examples of variable costs include cost of goods sold for a merchandising company; direct materials; direct labor; variable elements of manufacturing overhead, such as indirect materials, supplies, and power; and variable elements of selling and administrative expenses, such as commissions and shipping costs.[2]

For a cost to be variable, it must vary *with respect to something.* That "something" is its *activity base.* An **activity base** is a measure of whatever causes the incurrence of a variable cost. An activity base is sometimes referred to as a *cost driver.* Some of the most common activity bases are direct labor-hours, machine-hours, units produced, and units sold. Other examples of activity bases (cost drivers) include the number of miles driven by salespersons, the number of pounds of laundry cleaned by a hotel, the number of calls handled by technical support staff at a software company, and the number of beds occupied in a hospital. *While there are many activity bases within organizations, throughout this textbook, unless stated otherwise, you should assume the activity base under consideration is the total volume of goods and services provided by the organization. We will specify the activity base only when it differs from total output.*

To provide an example of a variable cost, consider Nooksack Expeditions, a small company that provides daylong whitewater rafting excursions on rivers in the North Cascade Mountains. The company provides all of the necessary equipment and experienced guides, and it serves gourmet meals to its guests. The meals are purchased from a caterer for $30 a person for a daylong excursion. The behavior of this variable cost, on both a per-unit and a total basis, is shown below:

Number of Guests	Cost of Meals per Guest	Total Cost of Meals
250	$30	$7,500
500	$30	$15,000
750	$30	$22,500
1,000	$30	$30,000

While total variable costs change as the activity level changes, a variable cost is constant if expressed on a *per-unit* basis. For example, the per-unit cost of the meals remains constant at $30 even though the total cost of the meals increases and decreases with activity. The graph on the left-hand side of Exhibit 1–3 illustrates how total variable cost rises and falls as the activity level rises and falls. At an activity level of 250 guests, the total meal cost is $7,500. At an activity level of 1,000 guests, the total meal cost rises to $30,000.

---

[2] Direct labor costs often can be fixed instead of variable for a variety of reasons. For example, in some countries, such as France, Germany, and Japan, labor regulations and cultural norms may limit management's ability to adjust the labor force in response to changes in activity. In this textbook, always assume direct labor is a variable cost unless you are explicitly told otherwise.

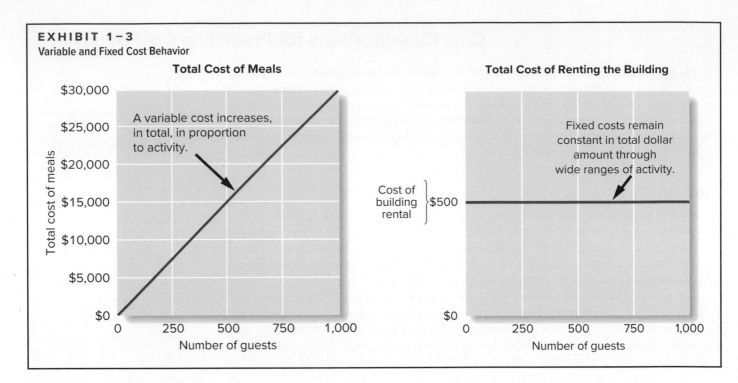

EXHIBIT 1–3
Variable and Fixed Cost Behavior

Total Cost of Meals

A variable cost increases, in total, in proportion to activity.

Total cost of meals (y-axis: $0, $5,000, $10,000, $15,000, $20,000, $25,000, $30,000)

Number of guests (x-axis: 0, 250, 500, 750, 1,000)

Total Cost of Renting the Building

Fixed costs remain constant in total dollar amount through wide ranges of activity.

Cost of building rental $500

Number of guests (x-axis: 0, 250, 500, 750, 1,000)

IN BUSINESS

VDWI Automotive/Alamy Stock Photo

AUTOMOTIVE INDUSTRY'S RELIANCE ON COMPUTER CHIPS GROWS

Pat Geisinger, Intel's chief executive officer (CEO), claims semiconductors will comprise 20 percent of the direct materials cost for premium automobiles by 2030, up from 4 percent in 2019. Given this evolutionary trend, automakers are no longer relying on parts vendors to source their computer chips, instead choosing to create direct ties with semiconductor manufacturers, such as Intel, Qualcomm, and Nvidia. Qualcomm's CEO, Cristiano Amon, says, "the deployment of superfast 5G communications networks would help enable new car features, including the deployment of self-driving cars." Qualcomm also plans to provide chips to support infotainment systems in Renault SA's new electric cars and digital-cockpit and driver-assisted features in General Motors' vehicles.

Source: Asa Fitch, "Chip Shortage Drives Tech and Car Industries Closer," *The Wall Street Journal* September 13, 2021, p. B3.

Fixed Cost

A **fixed cost** remains constant, in total, regardless of changes in the level of activity. Manufacturing overhead usually includes various fixed costs such as depreciation, insurance, property taxes, rent, and supervisory salaries. Similarly, selling and administrative costs often include fixed costs such as administrative salaries, advertising, and depreciation of nonmanufacturing assets. Unlike variable costs, fixed costs are not affected by changes in activity. Consequently, as the activity level rises and falls, total fixed costs remain constant unless influenced by some outside force, such as a landlord increasing your monthly rent. To continue the Nooksack Expeditions example, assume the company rents a building for $500 per month to store its equipment. The total amount of rent paid is the same regardless of the number of guests the company takes on its expeditions during any given month. The concept of a fixed cost is shown graphically on the right-hand side of Exhibit 1–3.

Because total fixed costs remain constant for large variations in the level of activity, the average fixed cost *per unit* becomes progressively smaller as the level of activity increases. If Nooksack Expeditions has only 250 guests in a month, the $500 fixed rental cost would amount to an average of $2 per guest. If there are 1,000 guests, the fixed rental cost would average only 50 cents per guest. The table below illustrates this aspect of the behavior of fixed costs. Note as the number of guests increases, the average fixed cost per guest drops.

Monthly Rental Cost	Number of Guests	Average Cost per Guest
$500	250	$2.00
$500	500	$1.00
$500	750	$0.67
$500	1,000	$0.50

As a general rule, *we caution against expressing fixed costs on an average per-unit basis in internal reports because it creates the false impression fixed costs are like variable costs and actually change as the level of activity changes.*

For planning purposes, fixed costs can be viewed as either *committed* or *discretionary*. **Committed fixed costs** represent organizational investments with a *multiyear* planning horizon that can't be significantly reduced even for short periods of time without making fundamental changes. Examples include investments in facilities and equipment, as well as real estate taxes, insurance premiums, and salaries of top management. Even if operations are interrupted or cut back, committed fixed costs remain largely unchanged in the short term because the costs of restoring them later are likely to be far greater than any short-run savings that might be realized. **Discretionary fixed costs** (often referred to as *managed fixed costs*) usually arise from *annual* decisions by management to spend on certain fixed cost items. Examples of discretionary fixed costs include advertising, research, public relations, management development programs, and internships for students. Discretionary fixed costs can be cut for short periods of time with minimal damage to the long-run goals of the organization.

The Linearity Assumption and the Relevant Range

Management accountants ordinarily assume costs are strictly linear; that is, the relation between cost on the one hand and activity on the other can be represented by a straight line within a narrow band of activity known as the *relevant range*. The **relevant range** is the range of activity within which the assumption that cost behavior is strictly linear is reasonably valid.

The concept of the relevant range is important in understanding fixed costs. For example, suppose the Mayo Clinic rents a machine for $20,000 per month that tests blood samples for the presence of leukemia cells. Furthermore, suppose the capacity of the leukemia diagnostic machine is 3,000 tests per month. The assumption the rent for the diagnostic machine is $20,000 per month is only valid within the relevant range of 0 to 3,000 tests per month. If the Mayo Clinic needed to test 5,000 blood samples per month, then it would need to rent another machine for an additional $20,000 per month. It would be difficult to rent half a diagnostic machine; therefore, the step pattern depicted in Exhibit 1–4 is typical for such costs. This exhibit shows the fixed rental cost is $20,000 for a relevant range of 0 to 3,000 tests. It increases to $40,000 within the relevant range of 3,001 to 6,000 tests. The rental cost increases in discrete steps or increments of 3,000 tests, rather than increasing in a linear fashion per test.

This step-oriented cost behavior pattern can also be used to describe other costs, such as some labor costs. For example, the cost of compensating salaried employees can be characterized using a step pattern. Salaried employees are paid a fixed amount, such as $40,000 per year, for providing the capacity to work a prespecified amount of time, such as 40 hours per week for 50 weeks a year (= 2,000 hours per year). In this example, the total salary cost is $40,000 within a relevant range of 0 to 2,000 hours of work.

EXHIBIT 1–4
Fixed Costs and the Relevant Range

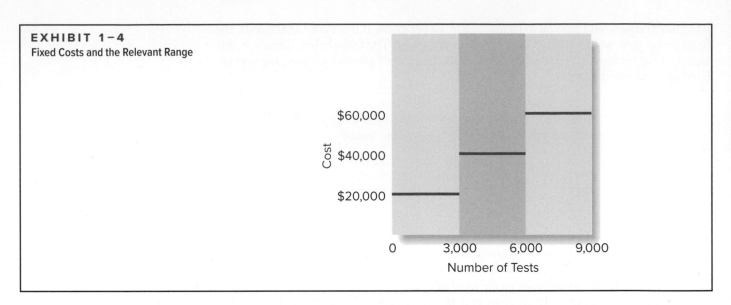

The total salary cost increases to $80,000 (or two employees) if the organization's work requirements expand to a relevant range of 2,001 to 4,000 hours of work. Cost behavior patterns, such as salaried employees, are often called *step-variable costs*. Step-variable costs can often be adjusted quickly as conditions change. Furthermore, the width of step-variable costs is generally so narrow these costs can be treated as variable costs for most purposes. The width of step-fixed costs, on the other hand, is so wide these costs should be treated as entirely fixed within the relevant range.

Exhibit 1–5 summarizes four key concepts related to variable and fixed costs.

EXHIBIT 1–5
Summary of Variable and Fixed Cost Behavior

| | Behavior of the Cost (within the relevant range) | |
Cost	In Total	Per Unit
Variable cost	Total variable cost increases and decreases in proportion to changes in the activity level.	Variable cost per unit remains constant.
Fixed cost	Total fixed cost is not affected by changes in the activity level within the relevant range.	Average fixed cost per unit decreases as the activity level rises and increases as the activity level falls.

IN BUSINESS

HOW MANY GUIDES?

Majestic Ocean Kayaking, of Ucluelet, British Columbia, is owned and operated by Tracy Morben-Eeftink. The company offers a number of guided kayaking excursions ranging from three-hour tours of the Ucluelet harbor to six-day kayaking and camping trips in Clayoquot Sound. One of the company's excursions is a four-day kayaking and camping trip to The Broken Group Islands in the Pacific Rim National Park. Special regulations apply to trips in the park—including a requirement that one certified guide must be assigned for every five guests or fraction thereof. For example, a trip with 12 guests must have at least three certified guides. Guides are not salaried and are paid on a per-day basis. Therefore, the cost to the company of the guides for a trip is a step-variable cost rather than a fixed cost or a strictly variable cost. One guide is needed for 1 to 5 guests, two guides for 6 to 10 guests, three guides for 11 to 15 guests, and so on.

Mixed Costs

A **mixed cost** contains both variable and fixed cost elements. Mixed costs are also known as semivariable costs. To continue the Nooksack Expeditions example, the company incurs a mixed cost called *fees paid to the state*. It includes a license fee of $25,000 per year plus $3 per rafting party paid to the state's Department of Natural Resources. If the company runs 1,000 rafting parties this year, then the total fees paid to the state would be $28,000, made up of $25,000 in fixed cost plus $3,000 in variable cost. Exhibit 1–6 depicts the behavior of this mixed cost.

Even if Nooksack fails to attract any customers, the company will still have to pay the license fee of $25,000. This is why the cost line in Exhibit 1–6 intersects the vertical cost axis at the $25,000 point. For each rafting party the company organizes, the total cost of the state fees will increase by $3. Therefore, the total cost line slopes upward as the variable cost of $3 per party is added to the fixed cost of $25,000 per year.

Because the mixed cost in Exhibit 1–6 is represented by a straight line, the following equation for a straight line can be used to express the relationship between a mixed cost and the level of activity:

$$Y = a + bX$$

In this equation,

Y = The total mixed cost

a = The total fixed cost (the vertical intercept of the line)

b = The variable cost per unit of activity (the slope of the line)

X = The level of activity

Because the variable cost per unit equals the slope of the straight line, the steeper the slope, the higher the variable cost per unit.

In the case of the state fees paid by Nooksack Expeditions, the equation is written as follows:

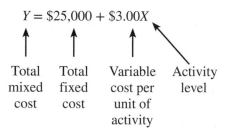

$$Y = \$25{,}000 + \$3.00X$$

Total mixed cost — Total fixed cost — Variable cost per unit of activity — Activity level

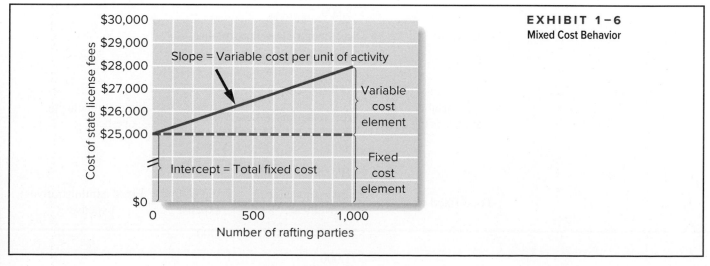

EXHIBIT 1–6
Mixed Cost Behavior

This equation makes it easy to calculate the total mixed cost for any activity level within the relevant range. For example, suppose the company expects to organize 800 rafting parties next year. The total state fees would be calculated as follows:

$$Y = \$25,000 + (\$3.00 \text{ per rafting party} \times 800 \text{ rafting parties})$$
$$= \$27,400$$

Cost Terminology—A Closer Look

To improve your understanding of the definitions and concepts introduced so far, consider the following costs and expenses for the most recent month:

Direct materials		$69,000
Direct labor		$35,000
Variable manufacturing overhead	$15,000	
Fixed manufacturing overhead	28,000	
Total manufacturing overhead		$43,000
Variable selling expense	$12,000	
Fixed selling expense	18,000	
Total selling expense		$30,000
Variable administrative expense	$ 4,000	
Fixed administrative expense	25,000	
Total administrative expense		$29,000

These costs and expenses can be categorized in a number of ways, some of which are shown below:

Product cost   = Direct materials + Direct labor + Manufacturing overhead

= $69,000 + $35,000 + $43,000

= $147,000

Period cost   = Selling expense + Administrative expense

= $30,000 + $29,000

= $59,000

Conversion cost   = Direct labor + Manufacturing overhead

= $35,000 + $43,000

= $78,000

Prime cost   = Direct materials + Direct labor

= $69,000 + $35,000

= $104,000

Variable manufacturing cost   = Direct materials + Direct labor + Variable manufacturing overhead

= $69,000 + $35,000 + $15,000

= $119,000

Total fixed cost   = Fixed manufacturing overhead + Fixed selling expense + Fixed administrative expense

= $28,000 + $18,000 + $25,000

= $71,000

Cost Classifications for Decision Making

Every decision involves choosing from among at least two alternatives. The key to choosing among alternatives is distinguishing between *relevant* and *irrelevant* costs and benefits. **Relevant costs** and **relevant benefits** should be considered when making decisions and irrelevant costs and benefits should be ignored. The remainder of this section expands on these concepts by defining the terms *differential cost* and *revenue, incremental cost, opportunity cost,* and *sunk cost.*

LO1–5
Understand cost classifications used in making decisions: relevant costs and irrelevant costs.

Differential Cost and Revenue

A future cost that differs between any two alternatives is known as a **differential cost.** Differential costs are always relevant costs. Future revenue that differs between any two alternatives is known as **differential revenue.** Differential revenue is an example of a relevant benefit. Any future cost or benefit that does not differ between the alternatives is irrelevant and should be ignored.

A differential cost is also known as an **incremental cost,** although technically an incremental cost should refer only to an increase in cost from one alternative to another, whereas decreases in cost should be referred to as *decremental costs.* Differential cost is a broader term, encompassing both cost increases (incremental costs) and cost decreases (decremental costs) between alternatives.

The accountant's differential cost concept can be compared to the economist's marginal cost concept. In speaking of changes in cost and revenue, the economist uses the terms *marginal cost* and *marginal revenue.* The revenue obtained from selling one more unit of product is called marginal revenue, and the cost involved in producing one more unit is called marginal cost. The economist's marginal concept is basically the same as the accountant's differential concept applied to a single unit of output.

Differential costs can be either fixed or variable. To illustrate, assume that Natural Cosmetics, Inc., is thinking about changing its marketing method from distribution through retailers to distribution by a network of neighborhood sales representatives. Present costs and revenues are compared to projected costs and revenues in the following table:

	Retailer Distribution (present)	Sales Representatives (proposed)	Differential Costs and Revenues
Sales (*variable*)	$700,000	$800,000	$100,000
Cost of goods sold (*variable*)	350,000	400,000	50,000
Advertising (*fixed*)	80,000	45,000	(35,000)
Commissions (*variable*)	0	40,000	40,000
Warehouse rent (*fixed*)	50,000	80,000	30,000
Other expenses (*fixed*)	60,000	60,000	0
Total expenses	540,000	625,000	85,000
Net operating income	$160,000	$175,000	$ 15,000

According to the above analysis, the differential revenue is $100,000 and the differential costs total $85,000, leaving a positive differential net operating income of $15,000 in favor of using sales representatives.

In general, only the differences between alternatives are relevant in decisions. Those items that are the same under all alternatives can be ignored. For example, in the Natural Cosmetics, Inc., example above, the "Other expenses" category, which is $60,000 under both alternatives, can be ignored because it has no effect on the decision. If it were removed from the calculations, the sales representatives would still be preferred by $15,000. This is an extremely important principle in management accounting that we will revisit in later chapters.

COMMUNICATING WITH DATA VISUALIZATIONS

Prescriptive analytics answer the question: What should I do? In the case of Natural Cosmetics, Inc., the company was choosing between two marketing methods—retail distribution or sales representatives. A differential analysis showed that the company should choose to employ sales representatives because it increases profits by $15,000. The waterfall chart shown below could be used to communicate this conclusion throughout the organization.

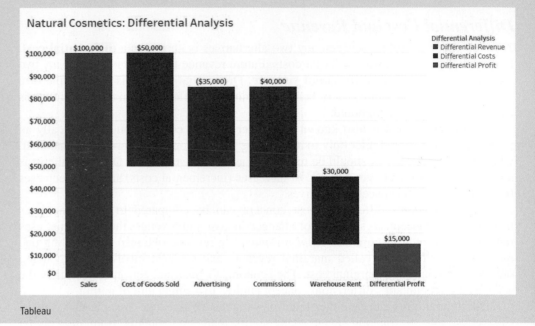

Tableau

Opportunity Cost and Sunk Cost

Opportunity cost is the potential benefit given up when one alternative is selected over another. For example, assume you have a part-time job while attending college paying $200 per week. If you spend one week at the beach during spring break without pay, then the $200 in lost wages would be an opportunity cost of taking the week off to be at the beach. Opportunity costs are not usually found in accounting records, but they are relevant costs that must be explicitly considered in every decision a manager makes. Virtually every alternative involves an opportunity cost.

A **sunk cost** *has already been incurred* and cannot be changed by any decision made now or in the future. Because sunk costs cannot be changed by any decision, they are not differential costs. And because only differential costs are relevant in a decision, sunk costs are irrelevant and should always be ignored.

To illustrate a sunk cost, assume a company paid $50,000 several years ago for a special-purpose machine. The machine was used to make a product that is now obsolete and no longer being sold. Even though in hindsight purchasing the machine may have been unwise, the $50,000 cost has already been incurred and cannot be undone. It would be folly to continue making the obsolete product in a misguided attempt to "recover" the original cost of the machine. In short, the $50,000 originally paid for the machine is a sunk cost that should be ignored in current decisions.

Before moving to the next section, we want to emphasize managers can use cost classifications for other purposes besides those described thus far. For example, managers may wish to classify costs as controllable or uncontrollable for employee performance evaluation purposes. A *controllable cost* can be influenced by the manager being evaluated. An *uncontrollable cost* cannot be influenced by the manager being evaluated. A company's managers may also wish to classify costs as value-added or non-value-added for process improvement purposes. A *value-added cost* increases the value of products and services provided to the company's stakeholders, whereas a *non-value-added cost* does not provide any benefit to the company's stakeholders. The overarching theme of the chapter is to first identify the needs of management and then classify costs accordingly.

IN BUSINESS

RETAILERS ADD MENTAL-HEALTH COUNSELING

In response to the mental-health challenges caused by the COVID-19 pandemic, some retailers started offering counseling services to their customers. For example, CVS hired licensed clinical social workers, who are also trained in cognitive behavioral therapy, to meet with customers at 34 of its store locations. "A mental-health assessment costs $129; a 30-minute counseling session is $69. Based on the assessment results, a customer could return for a few therapy sessions, or they might get a referral for extensive services from a family doctor, psychiatrist, or another local resource." Cara McNulty, president of behavioral health for CVS-owned Aetna Inc., says when you "democratize access to care by putting mental-health support in a retail setting, it makes access easier for people." Presumably, retailers such as CVS are also attracted to this new customer service because its incremental revenues exceed its incremental costs, thereby increasing profits.

Source: Sharon Terlep, "Mental-Health Counseling Comes to Retail Locations," *The Wall Street Journal* August 30, 2021, p. B3.

Using Different Cost Classifications for Different Purposes

This section discusses how to prepare traditional and contribution format income statements for a merchandising company.[3] Merchandising companies do not manufacture the products they sell to customers. For example, Lowe's and Home Depot are merchandising companies because they buy finished products from manufacturers and then resell them to end consumers.

LO1–6
Prepare income statements for a merchandising company using the traditional and contribution formats.

Contrasting these two types of income statements enables us to illustrate the chapter's unifying theme of *different cost classifications for different purposes*. Traditional income statements are prepared primarily for *external reporting purposes*. They rely on cost classifications for preparing financial statements (product and period costs) to depict the financial consequences of *past* transactions. Contribution format income statements are prepared for *internal management purposes*. They use cost classifications for predicting cost behavior (variable and fixed costs) to better inform decisions affecting the *future*.

The two different purposes served by these income statements highlight what is arguably the most important difference between financial accounting and managerial accounting—an emphasis on recording past performance versus an emphasis on making predictions and decisions affecting future performance.

The Traditional Format Income Statement

The left-hand side of Exhibit 1–7 shows a traditional income statement format for merchandising companies. This type of income statement organizes costs into two categories—cost of goods sold and selling and administrative expenses. Sales minus cost of goods sold equals the *gross margin*. The gross margin minus selling and administrative expenses equals net operating income.

The cost of goods sold reports the *product costs* attached to the merchandise sold during the period. The selling and administrative expenses report all *period costs* expensed as incurred. The cost of goods sold for a merchandising company can be computed directly by multiplying the number of units sold by their unit cost or indirectly using the equation below:

$$\text{Cost of goods sold} = \begin{matrix}\text{Beginning}\\\text{merchandise}\\\text{inventory}\end{matrix} + \text{Purchases} - \begin{matrix}\text{Ending}\\\text{merchandise}\\\text{inventory}\end{matrix}$$

---

[3] Subsequent chapters compare the income statement formats for manufacturing companies.

EXHIBIT 1–7
Comparing Traditional and Contribution Format Income Statements for Merchandising Companies (all numbers are given)

Traditional Format			Contribution Format		
Sales		$12,000	Sales		$12,000
Cost of goods sold*		6,000	Variable expenses:		
Gross margin		6,000	Cost of goods sold	$6,000	
Selling and administrative expenses:			Variable selling	600	
Selling	$3,100		Variable administrative	400	7,000
Administrative	1,900	5,000	Contribution margin		5,000
Net operating income		$ 1,000	Fixed expenses:		
			Fixed selling	$2,500	
			Fixed administrative	1,500	4,000
			Net operating income		$ 1,000

*For a manufacturing company, the cost of goods sold would include some variable costs, such as direct materials, direct labor, and variable overhead, and some fixed costs, such as fixed manufacturing overhead. Income statement formats for manufacturing companies will be explored in greater detail in a subsequent chapter.

For example, let's assume the company depicted in Exhibit 1–7 purchased $3,000 of merchandise inventory during the period and had beginning and ending merchandise inventory balances of $7,000 and $4,000, respectively. The equation on the previous page could be used to compute the cost of goods sold as follows:

$$\begin{array}{ccc} \text{Cost of} \\ \text{goods sold} \end{array} = \begin{array}{c} \text{Beginning} \\ \text{merchandise} \\ \text{inventory} \end{array} + \text{Purchases} - \begin{array}{c} \text{Ending} \\ \text{merchandise} \\ \text{inventory} \end{array}$$

$$= \quad \$7,000 \quad + \quad \$3,000 \quad - \quad \$4,000$$

$$= \quad \$6,000$$

Although the traditional income statement is useful for external reporting purposes, it has serious limitations when used for internal purposes. It does not distinguish between fixed and variable costs. For example, under the heading "Selling and administrative expenses," both variable administrative costs ($400) and fixed administrative costs ($1,500) are lumped together ($1,900). Internally, managers need cost data organized by cost behavior to aid in planning, controlling, and decision making. The contribution format income statement has been developed in response to these needs.

The Contribution Format Income Statement

The right-hand side of Exhibit 1–7 shows a contribution format income statement for merchandising companies. The **contribution approach** separates costs into fixed and variable categories, first deducting all variable expenses from sales to obtain the *contribution margin*. For a merchandising company, cost of goods sold is a variable cost that gets included in the "Variable expenses" portion of the contribution format income statement. The **contribution margin** is the amount remaining from sales revenues after all variable expenses have been deducted. This amount *contributes* toward covering fixed expenses and then toward profits. The contribution margin can also be stated on a per-unit basis. For example, if the company depicted in Exhibit 1–7 sold 500 units, then its contribution margin per unit would be $10 per unit (= $5,000 ÷ 500 units).

The contribution format income statement is used as an internal planning and decision-making tool. Its emphasis on cost behavior aids cost-volume-profit analysis, management performance appraisals, and budgeting. Moreover, the contribution approach helps managers organize data pertinent to numerous decisions such as product-line analysis, pricing, use of scarce resources, and make or buy analysis. All of these topics are covered in later chapters.

Summary

This chapter discusses ways managers classify costs. How the costs will be used—for assigning costs to cost objects, preparing external reports, predicting cost behavior, or decision making—dictates how they are classified.

For purposes of assigning costs to cost objects such as products or departments, costs are classified as direct or indirect. Direct costs can be easily traced to cost objects, whereas indirect costs cannot.

For external reporting purposes, costs are classified as either product costs or period costs. Product costs are assigned to inventories and are considered assets until the products are sold. At the point of sale, product costs become cost of goods sold on the income statement. In contrast, period costs are taken directly to the income statement as expenses in the period in which they are incurred.

For purposes of predicting cost behavior, costs are classified into three categories—variable, fixed, and mixed. Variable costs, in total, are strictly proportional to activity. The variable cost per unit is constant. Fixed costs, in total, remain the same as the activity level changes within the relevant range. The average fixed cost per unit decreases as the activity level increases. Mixed costs have variable and fixed elements and can be expressed in equation form as $Y = a + bX$, where Y is the total mixed cost, a is the total fixed cost, b is the variable cost per unit of activity, and X is the activity level.

When making decisions, managers distinguish between relevant and irrelevant costs and benefits. Differential costs and revenues are relevant because they differ between alternatives. Opportunity costs are also relevant because they consider the benefits of the forgone alternative. Sunk costs are irrelevant because they have already occurred in the past and cannot be altered.

Different cost classifications for different purposes is the unifying theme of this chapter, and it can be highlighted by contrasting traditional and contribution format income statements. The traditional income statement format is used primarily for external reporting purposes. It organizes costs using product and period cost classifications. The contribution format income statement aids decision making because it organizes costs using variable and fixed cost classifications.

 Data Analytics Exercise available in Connect to complement this chapter

Review Problem 1: Cost Terms

Porter Company manufactures furniture, including tables. Selected costs are given below:
1. The tables are made of wood that costs $100 per table.
2. The tables are assembled by workers at a wage cost of $40 per table.
3. Workers assembling the tables are supervised by a factory supervisor who is paid $45,000 per year.
4. Electrical costs are $2 per machine-hour. Four machine-hours are required to produce a table.
5. The depreciation on the machines used to make the tables totals $10,000 per year. The machines have no resale value and do not wear out through use.
6. The salary of the president of the company is $200,000 per year.
7. The company spends $250,000 per year to advertise its products.
8. Salespersons are paid a commission of $30 for each table sold.
9. Instead of producing the tables, the company could rent its factory space for $50,000 per year.

Required:
Classify these costs according to the various cost terms used in the chapter. The terms *variable cost* and *fixed cost* refer to how costs behave with respect to the number of tables produced in a year.

Solution to Review Problem 1

	Variable Cost	Fixed Cost	Period (Selling and Administrative) Cost	Direct Materials	Direct Labor	Manufacturing Overhead	Sunk Cost	Opportunity Cost
1. Wood used in a table ($100 per table)	X			X				
2. Labor cost to assemble a table ($40 per table)	X				X			
3. Salary of the factory supervisor ($45,000 per year)		X				X		
4. Cost of electricity to produce tables ($2 per machine-hour)	X					X		
5. Depreciation of machines used to produce tables ($10,000 per year)		X				X	X*	
6. Salary of the company president ($200,000 per year)		X	X					
7. Advertising expense ($250,000 per year)		X	X					
8. Commissions paid to salespersons ($30 per table sold)	X		X					
9. Rental income forgone on factory space ($50,000 per year)								X†

* This is a sunk cost because the outlay for the equipment was made in a previous period.

† This is an opportunity cost because it represents the potential benefit sacrificed when using the factory space to produce tables. Opportunity cost is a special category of cost not ordinarily recorded in an organization's accounting records. To avoid possible confusion with other costs, we will not attempt to classify this cost in any other way except as an opportunity cost.

Review Problem 2: Income Statement Formats

McFarland, Inc., is a merchandiser that provided the following information:

	Amount
Number of units sold	35,000
Selling price per unit	$40
Variable selling expense per unit	$3
Variable administrative expense per unit ..	$1
Total fixed selling expense	$45,000
Total fixed administrative expense	$28,000
Beginning merchandise inventory	$21,000
Ending merchandise inventory	$35,000
Merchandise purchases	$805,000

Required:

1. Prepare a traditional income statement.
2. Prepare a contribution format income statement.

Solution to Review Problem 2

1. Traditional income statement

McFarland, Inc. Traditional Income Statement		
Sales ($40 per unit × 35,000 units)		$1,400,000
Cost of goods sold ($21,000 + $805,000 − $35,000)		791,000
Gross margin		609,000
Selling and administrative expenses:		
Selling expense (($3 per unit × 35,000 units) + $45,000)	$150,000	
Administrative expense (($1 per unit × 35,000 units) + $28,000)	63,000	213,000
Net operating income		$ 396,000

2. Contribution format income statement

McFarland, Inc. Contribution Format Income Statement		
Sales		$1,400,000
Variable expenses:		
Cost of goods sold ($21,000 + $805,000 − $35,000)	$791,000	
Selling expense ($3 per unit × 35,000 units)	105,000	
Administrative expense ($1 per unit × 35,000 units)	35,000	931,000
Contribution margin		469,000
Fixed expenses:		
Selling expense	45,000	
Administrative expense	28,000	73,000
Net operating income		$ 396,000

Glossary

Activity base A measure of whatever causes the incurrence of a variable cost. For example, the total cost of surgical gloves in a hospital will increase as the number of surgeries increases. Therefore, the number of surgeries is the activity base that explains the total cost of surgical gloves. (p. 31)

Administrative costs All executive, organizational, and clerical costs associated with the general management of an organization rather than with manufacturing or selling. (p. 28)

Committed fixed costs Investments in facilities, equipment, and basic organizational structure that can't be significantly reduced even for short periods of time without making fundamental changes. (p. 33)

Common cost A cost incurred to support a number of cost objects that cannot be traced to them individually. For example, the wage cost of the pilot of a 747 airliner is a common cost of all of the passengers on the aircraft. Without the pilot, there would be no flight and no passengers. But no part of the pilot's wage is caused by any one passenger taking the flight. (p. 27)

Contribution approach An income statement format that organizes costs by their behavior. Costs are separated into variable and fixed categories rather than being separated into product and period costs for external reporting purposes. (p. 40)

Contribution margin The amount remaining from sales revenues after all variable expenses have been deducted. (p. 40)

Conversion cost Direct labor cost plus manufacturing overhead cost. (p. 28)

Cost behavior The way in which a cost reacts to changes in the level of activity. (p. 31)

Cost object Anything for which cost data are desired. Examples of cost objects are products, customers, geographic regions, and parts of the organization such as departments or divisions. (p. 26)

Cost structure The relative proportion of fixed, variable, and mixed costs in an organization. (p. 31)

Differential cost A future cost that differs between any two alternatives. (p. 37)

Differential revenue Future revenue that differs between any two alternatives. (p. 37)

Direct cost A cost easily traced to a specified cost object. (p. 27)

Direct labor Factory labor costs easily traced to specific products. Also called *touch labor*. (p. 28)

Direct materials Materials that become an integral part of a finished product and whose costs can be conveniently traced to it. (p. 27)

Discretionary fixed costs Fixed costs that arise from annual decisions by management to spend on certain fixed cost items, such as advertising and research. (p. 33)

Financial accounting The phase of accounting that reports historical financial information to external parties, such as stockholders, creditors, and regulators. (p. 26)

Finished goods Units of product that have been completed but not yet sold to customers. (p. 29)

Fixed cost A cost that remains constant, in total, regardless of changes in the level of activity within the relevant range. If a fixed cost is expressed on a per-unit basis, it varies inversely with the level of activity. (p. 32)

Incremental cost An increase in cost between two alternatives. (p. 37)

Indirect cost A cost that cannot be easily traced to a specified cost object. (p. 27)

Indirect labor The labor costs of janitors, supervisors, materials handlers, and other factory workers that cannot be easily traced to particular products. (p. 28)

Indirect materials Small items of material such as glue and nails that may be an integral part of a finished product, but whose costs cannot be easily traced to it. (p. 28)

Inventoriable costs Synonym for product costs. (p. 29)

Managerial accounting The phase of accounting that provides information to managers for use within the organization. (p. 26)

Manufacturing overhead All manufacturing costs except direct materials and direct labor. (p. 28)

Mixed cost A cost with variable and fixed cost elements. (p. 35)

Opportunity cost The potential benefit given up when one alternative is selected over another. (p. 38)

Period costs Costs taken directly to the income statement as expenses in the period incurred or accrued. (p. 29)

Prime cost Direct materials cost plus direct labor cost. (p. 28)

Product costs All costs involved in acquiring or making a product. In the case of manufactured goods, these costs consist of direct materials, direct labor, and manufacturing overhead. Also see *Inventoriable costs*. (p. 29)

Raw materials Any materials going into the final product. (p. 27)

Relevant benefit A benefit that should be considered when making decisions. (p. 37)

Relevant cost A cost that should be considered when making decisions. (p. 37)

Relevant range The range of activity within which assumptions about variable and fixed cost behavior are valid. (p. 33)

Selling costs All costs incurred to secure customer orders and get the finished product or service into the hands of the customer. (p. 28)

Sunk cost A cost already incurred that cannot be changed by any decision made now or in the future. (p. 38)

Variable cost A cost that varies, in total, in direct proportion to changes in the level of activity. A variable cost is constant per unit. (p. 31)

Work in process Partially complete units of product requiring further work before they are ready for sale to the customer. (p. 29)

Questions

1–1   What are the three major types of product costs in a manufacturing company?

1–2   Define the following: (*a*) direct materials, (*b*) indirect materials, (*c*) direct labor, (*d*) indirect labor, and (*e*) manufacturing overhead.

1–3   Explain the difference between a product cost and a period cost.

1–4   Distinguish between (*a*) a variable cost, (*b*) a fixed cost, and (*c*) a mixed cost.

1–5   What effect does an increase in the activity level have on:
a.   average fixed costs per unit?
b.   variable costs per unit?
c.   total fixed costs?
d.   total variable costs?

1–6   Define the following terms: (*a*) cost behavior and (*b*) relevant range.

1–7   What is meant by an *activity base* when dealing with variable costs? Give several examples of activity bases.

1–8   Managers often assume a strictly linear relationship between cost and the level of activity. Under what conditions would this be a valid or invalid assumption?

1–9   Distinguish between discretionary fixed costs and committed fixed costs.

1–10   Does the concept of the relevant range apply to fixed costs? Explain.

1–11   What is the difference between a traditional format income statement and a contribution format income statement?

1–12   What is the contribution margin?

1–13   Define the following terms: (*a*) differential cost, (*b*) sunk cost, and (*c*) opportunity cost.

1–14   Only variable costs can be differential costs. Do you agree? Explain.

McGraw Hill connect   **Applying Excel**

This Excel worksheet relates to Exhibit 1–7. The workbook, and instructions on how to complete the file, can be found in Connect.   **LO1–6**

	A	B	C	D
1	Chapter 1: Applying Excel			
2				
3	**Data**			
4	Sales	$12,000		
5	Variable costs:			
6	Cost of goods sold	$6,000		
7	Variable selling	$600		
8	Variable administrative	$400		
9	Fixed costs:			
10	Fixed selling	$2,500		
11	Fixed administrative	$1,500		
12				
13	*Enter a formula into each of the cells marked with a ? below*			
14	**Exhibit 1-7**			
15				
16	**Traditional Format Income Statement**			
17	Sales		?	
18	Cost of goods sold		?	
19	Gross margin		?	
20	Selling and administrative expenses:			
21	Selling	?		
22	Administrative	?	?	
23	Net operating income		?	
24				
25	**Contribution Format Income Statement**			
26	Sales		?	
27	Variable expenses:			
28	Cost of goods sold	?		
29	Variable selling	?		
30	Variable administrative	?	?	
31	Contribution margin		?	
32	Fixed expenses:			
33	Fixed selling	?		
34	Fixed administrative	?	?	
35	Net operating income		?	
36				

◄◄ ►► Chapter 1 Form   Filled in Chapter 1 Form

Microsoft Excel

Required:

1. Check your worksheet by changing the variable selling cost in the Data area to $900, keeping all of the other data the same as in Exhibit 1–7. If your worksheet is operating properly, the net operating income under the traditional format income statement and under the contribution format income statement should now be $700 and the contribution margin should now be $4,700. If you do not get these answers, find the errors in your worksheet and correct them.
   How much is the gross margin? Did it change? Why or why not?

2. Suppose that sales are 10% higher as shown below:

Sales	$13,200
Variable costs:	
Cost of goods sold	$6,600
Variable selling	$660
Variable administrative	$440
Fixed costs:	
Fixed selling	$2,500
Fixed administrative	$1,500

Enter these new data into your worksheet. Make sure you change all of the data that are different—not just the sales. Print or copy the income statements from your worksheet.
   What happened to the variable costs and to the fixed costs when sales increased by 10%? Why? Did the contribution margin increase by 10%? Why or why not? Did the net operating income increase by 10%? Why or why not?

The Foundational 15   Mc Graw Hill connect

LO1–1, LO1–2, LO1–3, LO1–4, LO1–5, LO1–6

Martinez Company's relevant range of production is 7,500 units to 12,500 units. When it produces and sells 10,000 units, its average costs per unit are as follows:

	Average Cost per Unit
Direct materials	$6.00
Direct labor	$3.50
Variable manufacturing overhead	$1.50
Fixed manufacturing overhead	$4.00
Fixed selling expense	$3.00
Fixed administrative expense	$2.00
Sales commissions	$1.00
Variable administrative expense	$0.50

Required:

1. For financial accounting purposes, what is the total product cost incurred to make 10,000 units?
2. For financial accounting purposes, what is the total period cost incurred to sell 10,000 units?
3. If 8,000 units are produced and sold, what is the variable cost per unit produced and sold?
4. If 12,500 units are produced and sold, what is the variable cost per unit produced and sold?
5. If 8,000 units are produced and sold, what is the total variable cost of the units produced and sold?
6. If 12,500 units are produced and sold, what is the total variable cost of the units produced and sold?
7. If 8,000 units are produced, what is the average fixed manufacturing cost per unit produced?
8. If 12,500 units are produced, what is the average fixed manufacturing cost per unit produced?
9. If 8,000 units are produced, what is the total fixed manufacturing cost incurred to support this level of production?
10. If 12,500 units are produced, what is the total fixed manufacturing cost incurred to support this level of production?
11. If 8,000 units are produced, what is the total manufacturing overhead cost incurred to support this level of production? What is this total amount expressed on a per-unit basis?

12. If 12,500 units are produced, what is the total manufacturing overhead cost incurred to support this level of production? What is this total amount expressed on a per-unit basis?

13. If the selling price is $22 per unit, what is the contribution margin per unit?

14. If 11,000 units are produced, what are the total direct and indirect manufacturing costs incurred to support this level of production?

15. What incremental manufacturing cost will Martinez incur if it increases production from 10,000 to 10,001 units?

connect **Exercises**

EXERCISE 1–1 Identifying Direct and Indirect Costs LO1–1

Northwest Hospital is a full-service hospital providing everything from major surgery and emergency room care to outpatient clinics.

Required:

For each cost incurred at Northwest Hospital, indicate whether it would most likely be a direct cost or an indirect cost of the specified cost object by placing an X in the appropriate column.

Cost	Cost Object	Direct Cost	Indirect Cost
Ex. Catered food served to patients	A particular patient	X	
1. The wages of pediatric nurses	The pediatric department		
2. Prescription drugs	A particular patient		
3. Heating the hospital	The pediatric department		
4. The salary of the head of pediatrics	The pediatric department		
5. The salary of the head of pediatrics	A particular pediatric patient		
6. Hospital chaplain's salary	A particular patient		
7. Lab tests by outside contractor	A particular patient		
8. Lab tests by outside contractor	A particular department		

EXERCISE 1–2 Classifying Manufacturing Costs LO1–2

The PC Works assembles custom computers from components supplied by various manufacturers. The company is very small and its assembly shop and retail sales store are housed in a single facility in a Redmond, Washington, industrial park. Listed below are some of the costs the company incurs.

Required:

For each cost, indicate whether it would most likely be classified as direct materials, direct labor, manufacturing overhead, selling, or an administrative cost.

1. The cost of a hard drive installed in a computer.
2. The cost of advertising in the *Puget Sound Computer User* newspaper.
3. The wages of employees who assemble computers from components.
4. Sales commissions paid to the company's salespeople.
5. The salary of the assembly shop's supervisor.
6. The salary of the company's accountant.
7. Depreciation on equipment used to test assembled computers before release to customers.
8. Rent on the facility in the industrial park.

EXERCISE 1–3 Classifying Costs as Product or Period Costs LO1–3

Issac Aircams manufactures sophisticated spy cameras for remote-controlled military reconnaissance aircraft. It has approached a bank for a loan to finance its growth. The bank requires financial statements before approving the loan.

Required:

Classify each cost listed below as either a product cost or a period cost for the purpose of preparing financial statements.

1. Depreciation on salespersons' cars.
2. Rent on equipment used in the factory.

3. Lubricants used for machine maintenance.
4. Salaries of personnel who work in the finished goods warehouse.
5. Soap and paper towels used by factory workers at the end of a shift.
6. Factory supervisors' salaries.
7. Heat, water, and power consumed in the factory.
8. Materials used for boxing products for shipment overseas. (Units are not normally boxed.)
9. Advertising costs.
10. Workers' compensation insurance for factory employees.
11. Depreciation on chairs and tables in the factory lunchroom.
12. The wages of the receptionist in the administrative offices.
13. Cost of leasing the corporate jet used by the company's executives.
14. The cost of renting rooms at a Florida resort for the annual sales conference.
15. The cost of packaging the company's product.

EXERCISE 1–4 Fixed and Variable Cost Behavior LO1–4

Espresso Express operates a number of espresso coffee stands in busy suburban malls. The fixed weekly expense of a coffee stand is $1,200 and the variable cost per cup of coffee served is $0.22.

Required:

1. Fill in the following table with your estimates of the company's total cost and average cost per cup of coffee at the indicated levels of activity. Round off the average cost per cup of coffee to the nearest tenth of a cent.

	Cups of Coffee Served in a Week		
	2,000	2,100	2,200
Fixed cost	?	?	?
Variable cost	?	?	?
Total cost	?	?	?
Average cost per cup of coffee served	?	?	?

2. Does the average cost per cup of coffee served increase, decrease, or remain the same as the number of cups of coffee served in a week increases? Explain.

EXERCISE 1–5 Differential, Sunk, and Opportunity Costs LO1–5

Northeast Hospital's Radiology Department is considering replacing an old inefficient X-ray machine with a state-of-the-art digital X-ray machine. The new machine would provide higher quality X-rays in less time and at a lower cost per X-ray. It also requires less power and would use a color laser printer to produce easily readable X-ray images. Instead of investing the funds in the new X-ray machine, the Laboratory Department is lobbying the hospital's management to buy a new DNA analyzer.

Required:

For each item below, indicate by placing an X in the appropriate column whether it should be considered a differential cost, a sunk cost, or an opportunity cost in the decision to replace the old X-ray machine with a new machine. If none of the categories apply for a particular item, leave all columns blank.

Item	Differential Cost	Sunk Cost	Opportunity Cost
Ex. Cost of X-ray film used in the old machine	X		
1. Cost of the old X-ray machine			
2. The salary of the head of the Radiology Department ...			
3. The salary of the head of the Laboratory Department ...			
4. Cost of the new color laser printer			
5. Rent on the space occupied by Radiology			
6. The cost of maintaining the old machine			
7. Benefits from a new DNA analyzer			
8. Cost of electricity to run the X-ray machines			

EXERCISE 1–6 Traditional and Contribution Format Income Statements LO1–6

Cherokee Inc. is a merchandiser that provided the following information:

	Amount
Number of units sold	20,000
Selling price per unit	$30
Variable selling expense per unit	$4
Variable administrative expense per unit	$2
Total fixed selling expense	$40,000
Total fixed administrative expense	$30,000
Beginning merchandise inventory	$24,000
Ending merchandise inventory	$44,000
Merchandise purchases	$180,000

Required:

1. Prepare a traditional income statement.
2. Prepare a contribution format income statement.

EXERCISE 1–7 Direct and Indirect Costs LO1–1

Kubin Company's relevant range of production is 18,000 to 22,000 units. When it produces and sells 20,000 units, its average costs per unit are as follows:

	Average Cost per Unit
Direct materials	$7.00
Direct labor	$4.00
Variable manufacturing overhead	$1.50
Fixed manufacturing overhead	$5.00
Fixed selling expense	$3.50
Fixed administrative expense	$2.50
Sales commissions	$1.00
Variable administrative expense	$0.50

Required:

1. Assume the cost object is units of production:
   a. What is the total direct manufacturing cost incurred to make 20,000 units?
   b. What is the total indirect manufacturing cost incurred to make 20,000 units?
2. Assume the cost object is the Manufacturing Department and its total output is 20,000 units.
   a. How much total manufacturing cost is directly traceable to the Manufacturing Department?
   b. How much total manufacturing cost is an indirect cost that cannot be easily traced to the Manufacturing Department?
3. Assume the cost object is the company's various sales representatives. Furthermore, assume the company spent $50,000 of its total fixed selling expense on advertising and the remainder of the total fixed selling expense comprised the fixed portion of the company's sales representatives' compensation.
   a. When the company sells 20,000 units, what is the total direct selling expense readily traceable to individual sales representatives?
   b. When the company sells 20,000 units, what is the total indirect selling expense that cannot be readily traced to individual sales representatives?
4. Are Kubin's administrative expenses always going to be treated as indirect costs in its internal management reports?

EXERCISE 1–8 Product Costs and Period Costs; Variable and Fixed Costs LO1–3, LO1–4

Refer to the data given in Exercise 1–7. Answer all questions independently.

Required:

1. For financial accounting purposes, what is the total product cost incurred to make 20,000 units?
2. For financial accounting purposes, what is the total period cost incurred to sell 20,000 units?

3. For financial accounting purposes, what is the total product cost incurred to make 22,000 units?
4. For financial accounting purposes, what is the total period cost incurred to sell 18,000 units?

EXERCISE 1–9 Fixed, Variable, and Mixed Costs LO1–4
Refer to the data given in Exercise 1–7. Answer all questions independently.

Required:
1. If 18,000 units are produced and sold, what is the variable cost per unit produced and sold?
2. If 22,000 units are produced and sold, what is the variable cost per unit produced and sold?
3. If 18,000 units are produced and sold, what is the total variable cost related to the units produced and sold?
4. If 22,000 units are produced and sold, what is the total variable cost related to the units produced and sold?
5. If 18,000 units are produced, what is the average fixed manufacturing cost per unit produced?
6. If 22,000 units are produced, what is the average fixed manufacturing cost per unit produced?
7. If 18,000 units are produced, what is the total fixed manufacturing overhead incurred to support this level of production?
8. If 22,000 units are produced, what is the total fixed manufacturing overhead incurred to support this level of production?

EXERCISE 1–10 Differential Costs and Sunk Costs LO1–5
Refer to the data given in Exercise 1–7. Answer all questions independently.

Required:
1. What is the incremental manufacturing cost incurred if the company increases production from 20,000 to 20,001 units?
2. What is the incremental cost incurred if the company increases production *and* sales from 20,000 to 20,001 units?
3. Assume Kubin Company produced 20,000 units and expects to sell 19,800 of them. If a new customer unexpectedly emerges and expresses interest in buying the 200 extra units that have been produced by the company and would otherwise remain unsold, what is the incremental manufacturing cost per unit incurred to sell these units to the customer?
4. Assume Kubin Company produced 20,000 units and expects to sell 19,800 of them. If a new customer unexpectedly emerges and expresses interest in buying the 200 extra units that have been produced by the company and would otherwise remain unsold, what incremental selling and administrative cost per unit is incurred to sell these units to the customer?

EXERCISE 1–11 Cost Behavior; Contribution Format Income Statement LO1–4, LO1–6
Harris Company manufactures and sells a single product. A partially completed schedule of the company's total costs and costs per unit over the relevant range of 30,000 to 50,000 units is given below:

	Units Produced and Sold		
	30,000	40,000	50,000
Total costs:			
Variable cost	$180,000	?	?
Fixed cost	300,000	?	?
Total cost	$480,000	?	?
Costs per unit:			
Variable cost	?	?	?
Fixed cost	?	?	?
Total cost per unit	?	?	?

Required:
1. Complete the above schedule of the company's total costs and costs per unit.
2. Assume the company produces and sells 45,000 units during the year at a selling price of $16 per unit. Prepare a contribution format income statement for the year.

EXERCISE 1–12 Product and Period Cost Flows LO1–3

The Devon Motor Company produces automobiles. On April 1st the company had no beginning inventories and it purchased 8,000 batteries at a cost of $80 per battery. It withdrew 7,600 batteries from the storeroom during the month. Of these, 100 were used to replace batteries in cars used by the company's traveling sales staff. The remaining 7,500 batteries withdrawn from the storeroom were placed in cars being produced by the company. Of the cars in production during April, 90% were completed and transferred from work in process to finished goods. Of the cars completed during the month, 30% were unsold at April 30th.

Required:
1. Determine the cost of batteries appearing in each of the following accounts on April 30th:
   a. Raw Materials
   b. Work in Process
   c. Finished Goods
   d. Cost of Goods Sold
   e. Selling Expense
2. Specify whether each of the above accounts would appear on the balance sheet or on the income statement.

EXERCISE 1–13 Variable and Fixed Cost Behavior LO1–4

Munchak Company's relevant range of production is between 9,000 and 11,000 units. Last month the company produced 10,000 units. Its total manufacturing cost per unit produced was $70. At this level of activity, the company's variable manufacturing costs are 40% of its total manufacturing costs.

Required:
Assume that next month Munchak produces 10,050 units and its cost behavior patterns remain unchanged. Label each of the following statements as true or false with respect to next month. Do not use a calculator to answer items 1 through 6. You can use a calculator to answer items 7 through 12. Record your answers by placing an X under the appropriate heading.

	True	False
1. The variable manufacturing cost per unit will remain the same as last month.		
2. The total fixed manufacturing cost will be greater than last month.		
3. The total manufacturing cost will be greater than last month.		
4. The average fixed manufacturing cost per unit will be less than last month.		
5. The total variable manufacturing cost will be less than last month.		
6. The total manufacturing cost per unit will be greater than last month.		
7. The variable manufacturing cost per unit will equal $28.		
8. The total fixed manufacturing cost will equal $422,100.		
9. The total manufacturing cost will equal $701,400.		
10. The average fixed manufacturing cost per unit (rounded to the nearest cent) will equal $41.79.		
11. The total variable manufacturing cost will equal $280,000.		
12. The total manufacturing cost per unit (rounded to the nearest cent) will equal $69.79.		

EXERCISE 1–14 Cost Classification LO1–2, LO1–3, LO1–4, LO1–5

Wollogong Group Ltd. of New South Wales, Australia, acquired its factory building 10 years ago. For several years, the company has rented out a small annex attached to the rear of the building for $30,000 per year. The renter's lease will expire soon, and rather than renewing the lease, the company has decided to use the annex to manufacture a new product.

Direct materials cost for the new product is $80 per unit. To have a place to store its finished goods, the company will rent a small warehouse for $500 per month. In addition, the company must rent equipment for $4,000 per month to produce the new product. Direct laborers will be hired and paid $60 per unit to manufacture the new product. As in prior years, the space in the annex will continue to be depreciated at $8,000 per year.

The annual advertising cost for the new product will be $50,000. A supervisor will be hired and paid $3,500 per month to oversee production. Electricity for operating machines will be $1.20 per unit. The cost of shipping the new product to customers will be $9 per unit.

To provide funds to purchase materials, meet payrolls, and so forth, the company will have to liquidate some temporary investments. These investments are presently earning a return of $3,000 per year.

Required:

Using the table shown below, describe each of the costs associated with the new product decision in four ways. In terms of cost classifications for predicting cost behavior (column 1), indicate whether the cost is fixed or variable. With respect to cost classifications for manufacturers (column 2), if the item is a manufacturing cost, indicate whether it is direct materials, direct labor, or manufacturing overhead. If it is a nonmanufacturing cost, then select "none" as your answer. With respect to cost classifications for preparing financial statements (column 3), indicate whether the item is a product cost or period cost. Finally, in terms of cost classifications for decision making (column 4), identify any items that are sunk costs or opportunity costs. If you identify an item as an opportunity cost, then select "none" as your answer in columns 1–3.

	Cost Classifications for:			
Cost Item	(1) Predicting Cost Behavior	(2) Manufacturers	(3) Preparing Financial Statements	(4) Decision Making

EXERCISE 1–15 Traditional and Contribution Format Income Statements LO1–6

The Alpine House, Inc., is a large retailer of snow skis. The company assembled the information shown below for the quarter ended March 31st:

	Amount
Sales	$150,000
Selling price per pair of skis	$750
Variable selling expense per pair of skis	$50
Variable administrative expense per pair of skis ...	$10
Total fixed selling expense	$20,000
Total fixed administrative expense	$20,000
Beginning merchandise inventory	$30,000
Ending merchandise inventory	$40,000
Merchandise purchases	$100,000

Required:

1. Prepare a traditional income statement for the quarter ended March 31st.
2. Prepare a contribution format income statement for the quarter ended March 31st.
3. What was the contribution margin per unit?

EXERCISE 1–16 Cost Classifications for Decision Making LO1–5

Warner Corporation purchased a machine seven years ago for $319,000 when it launched product P50. Unfortunately, this machine has broken down and cannot be repaired. The machine could be replaced by a new model 300 machine costing $313,000 or by a new model 200 machine costing $275,000. Management has decided to buy the model 200 machine. It has less capacity than the model 300 machine, but its capacity is sufficient to continue making product P50. Management also considered, but rejected, the alternative of dropping product P50 and not replacing the old machine. If that were done, the $275,000 invested in the new machine could instead have been invested in a project that would have returned a total of $374,000.

Required:

1. What is the total differential cost regarding the decision to buy the model 200 machine rather than the model 300 machine?
2. What is the total sunk cost regarding the decision to buy the model 200 machine rather than the model 300 machine?
3. What is the total opportunity cost regarding the decision to invest in the model 200 machine?

EXERCISE 1–17 Classifying Variable and Fixed Costs and Product and Period Costs LO1–3, LO1–4

Below are listed various costs that are found in organizations.
1. Hamburger buns in a Wendy's restaurant.
2. Advertising by a dental office.
3. Apples processed and canned by Del Monte.
4. Shipping canned apples from a Del Monte plant to customers.
5. Insurance on a Bausch & Lomb factory producing contact lenses.
6. Insurance on Nucor's corporate headquarters.

7. Salary of a supervisor overseeing production of printers at Ricoh.
8. Commissions paid to automobile salespersons.
9. Depreciation of factory lunchroom facilities at a General Electric plant.
10. Steering wheels installed in Tesla electric vehicles.

Required:

Using the table shown below, describe each of the costs mentioned above in two ways. In terms of cost classifications for predicting cost behavior (column 1), indicate whether the cost is fixed or variable with respect to the number of units produced and sold. With respect to cost classifications for preparing financial statements (column 2), indicate whether the item is a product cost or period cost (selling and administrative cost).

	Cost Classifications for:	
	(1)	(2)
	Predicting	Preparing
Cost Item	Cost Behavior	Financial Statements

McGraw Hill connect   **Problems**

PROBLEM 1–18 Direct and Indirect Costs; Variable Costs LO1–1, LO1–4

The following cost data pertain to the operations of Montgomery Department Stores, Inc., for the month of July.

Corporate legal office salaries	$56,000
Apparel Department cost of sales—Evendale Store	$90,000
Corporate headquarters building lease	$48,000
Store manager's salary—Evendale Store	$12,000
Apparel Department sales commission—Evendale Store	$7,000
Store utilities—Evendale Store	$11,000
Apparel Department manager's salary—Evendale Store	$8,000
Central warehouse lease cost	$15,000
Janitorial costs—Evendale Store	$9,000

The Evendale Store is one of many stores owned and operated by the company. The Apparel Department is one of many departments at the Evendale Store. The central warehouse serves all of the company's stores.

Required:

1. What are the total direct costs of the Apparel Department?
2. What are the total direct costs of the Evendale Store?
3. Of the Apparel Department's direct costs, how much are variable with respect to total departmental sales?

PROBLEM 1–19 Traditional and Contribution Format Income Statements LO1–6

Todrick Company is a merchandiser that reported the following information based on 1,000 units sold:

Sales	$300,000
Beginning merchandise inventory	$20,000
Purchases	$200,000
Ending merchandise inventory	$7,000
Fixed selling expense	?
Fixed administrative expense	$12,000
Variable selling expense	$15,000
Variable administrative expense	?
Contribution margin	$60,000
Net operating income	$18,000

Required:

1. Prepare a contribution format income statement.
2. Prepare a traditional format income statement.

3. Calculate the selling price per unit.
4. Calculate the variable cost per unit.
5. Calculate the contribution margin per unit.
6. Which income statement format (traditional format or contribution format) would be more useful to managers in estimating how net operating income will change in response to changes in unit sales? Why?

PROBLEM 1–20 Variable and Fixed Costs; Subtleties of Direct and Indirect Costs LO1–1, LO1–4

Madison Seniors Care Center is a nonprofit organization providing a variety of health services to the elderly. The center is organized into a number of departments, one of which is the Meals on Wheels program that delivers hot meals to seniors in their homes on a daily basis. Below are listed a number of costs of the center and the Meals on Wheels program.

example The cost of groceries used in meal preparation.

a. The cost of leasing the Meals on Wheels van.
b. The cost of incidental supplies such as salt, pepper, napkins, and so on.
c. The cost of gasoline consumed by the Meals on Wheels van.
d. The rent on the facility that houses Madison Seniors Care Center, including the Meals on Wheels program.
e. The salary of the part-time manager of the Meals on Wheels program.
f. Depreciation on the kitchen equipment used in the Meals on Wheels program.
g. The hourly wages of the caregiver who drives the van and delivers the meals.
h. The costs of complying with health safety regulations in the kitchen.
i. The costs of mailing letters soliciting donations to the Meals on Wheels program.

Required:

For each cost listed above, indicate whether it is a direct or indirect cost of the Meals on Wheels program, whether it is a direct or indirect cost of particular seniors served by the program, and whether it is variable or fixed with respect to the number of seniors served. Use the form below for your answer.

Item	Description	Direct or Indirect Cost of the Meals on Wheels Program		Direct or Indirect Cost of Particular Seniors Served by the Meals on Wheels Program		Variable or Fixed with Respect to the Number of Seniors Served by the Meals on Wheels Program	
		Direct	Indirect	Direct	Indirect	Variable	Fixed
Example	The cost of groceries used in meal preparation . . .	X			X		X

PROBLEM 1–21 Traditional and Contribution Format Income Statements LO1–6

Marwick's Pianos, Inc., purchases pianos from a manufacturer for an average cost of $2,450 per unit and then sells them to retail customers for an average price of $3,125 each. The company's selling and administrative costs for a typical month are presented below:

Costs	Cost Formula
Selling:	
Advertising	$700 per month
Sales salaries and commissions	$950 per month, plus 8% of sales
Delivery of pianos to customers	$30 per piano sold
Utilities	$350 per month
Depreciation of sales facilities	$800 per month
Administrative:	
Executive salaries	$2,500 per month
Insurance	$400 per month
Clerical	$1,000 per month, plus $20 per piano sold
Depreciation of office equipment. . . .	$300 per month

During August, Marwick's Pianos, Inc., sold and delivered 40 pianos.

Required:

1. Prepare a traditional format income statement for August.
2. Prepare a contribution format income statement for August. Show costs and revenues on both a total and a per-unit basis down through contribution margin.
3. Refer to the income statement you prepared in (2) above. Why might it be misleading to show the fixed costs on a per-unit basis?

PROBLEM 1–22 Cost Terminology; Contribution Format Income Statement LO1–2, LO1–4, LO1–6

Miller Company's total sales are $120,000. The company's direct labor cost is $15,000, which represents 30% of its total conversion cost and 40% of its total prime cost. Its total selling and administrative expense is $18,000 and its only variable selling and administrative expense is a sales commission of 5% of sales. The company maintains no beginning or ending inventories and its manufacturing overhead costs are entirely fixed costs.

Required:

1. What is the total manufacturing overhead cost?
2. What is the total direct materials cost?
3. What is the total manufacturing cost?
4. What is the total variable selling and administrative cost?
5. What is the total variable cost?
6. What is the total fixed cost?
7. What is the total contribution margin?

PROBLEM 1–23 Cost Classification LO1–1, LO1–3, LO1–4

Listed below are costs found in various organizations.

1. Property taxes, factory.
2. Boxes used for packaging detergent produced by the company.
3. Salespersons' commissions.
4. Supervisor's salary, factory.
5. Depreciation, executive autos.
6. Wages of workers assembling computers.
7. Insurance, finished goods warehouses.
8. Lubricants for production equipment.
9. Advertising costs.
10. Microchips used in producing calculators.
11. Shipping costs on merchandise sold.
12. Magazine subscriptions, factory lunchroom.
13. Thread in a garment factory.
14. Executive life insurance.
15. Ink used in textbook production.
16. Fringe benefits, materials handling workers.
17. Yarn used in sweater production.
18. Wages of receptionist, executive offices.

Required:

Prepare an answer sheet with column headings as shown below. For each cost item, indicate whether it would be variable or fixed with respect to the number of units produced and sold; and then whether it would be a selling cost, an administrative cost, or a manufacturing cost. If it is a manufacturing cost, indicate whether it is a direct cost or an indirect cost with respect to units of product. Three sample answers are provided for illustration.

Cost Item	Variable or Fixed	Selling Cost	Administrative Cost	Manufacturing (Product) Cost Direct	Manufacturing (Product) Cost Indirect
Direct labor	V			X	
Executive salaries	F		X		
Factory rent	F				X

PROBLEM 1–24 Different Cost Classifications for Different Purposes LO1–1, LO1–2, LO1–3, LO1–4, LO1–5

Dozier Company produced and sold 1,000 units during its first month of operations. It reported the following costs and expenses for the month:

Direct materials		$69,000
Direct labor		$35,000
Variable manufacturing overhead	$15,000	
Fixed manufacturing overhead	28,000	
Total manufacturing overhead		$43,000
Variable selling expense	$12,000	
Fixed selling expense	18,000	
Total selling expense		$30,000
Variable administrative expense	$ 4,000	
Fixed administrative expense	25,000	
Total administrative expense		$29,000

Required:

1. With respect to cost classifications for preparing financial statements:
    a. What is the total product cost?
    b. What is the total period cost?
2. With respect to cost classifications for assigning costs to cost objects:
    a. What is the total direct manufacturing cost?
    b. What is the total indirect manufacturing cost?
3. With respect to cost classifications for manufacturers:
    a. What is the total manufacturing cost?
    b. What is the total nonmanufacturing cost?
    c. What are the total conversion cost and prime cost?
4. With respect to cost classifications for predicting cost behavior:
    a. What is the total variable manufacturing cost?
    b. What is the total fixed cost for the company as a whole?
    c. What is the variable cost per unit produced and sold?
5. With respect to cost classifications for decision making:
    a. If Dozier had produced 1,001 units instead of 1,000 units, how much incremental manufacturing cost would it have incurred to make the additional unit?

PROBLEM 1–25 Traditional and Contribution Format Income Statements LO1–6

Milden Company is a merchandiser planning to sell 12,000 units next quarter at a selling price of $100 per unit. The company also gathered the following cost estimates for the next quarter:

Cost	Cost Formula
Cost of goods sold	$35 per unit sold
Advertising expense	$210,000 per quarter
Sales commissions	6% of sales
Shipping expense	$28,000 per quarter + $9.10 per unit sold
Administrative salaries	$145,000 per quarter
Insurance expense	$9,000 per quarter
Depreciation expense	$76,000 per quarter

Required:

1. Prepare a contribution format income statement for the next quarter.
2. Prepare a traditional format income statement for the next quarter.

Select cases are available in Connect.

CASE 1–26 Cost Classification and Cost Behavior LO1–1, LO1–2, LO1–3, LO1–4

The Dorilane Company produces a set of wood patio furniture consisting of a table and four chairs. The company has enough customer demand to justify producing its full capacity of 2,000 sets per year. Annual cost data at full capacity follow:

Direct labor	$118,000
Advertising	$50,000
Factory supervision	$40,000
Property taxes, factory building	$3,500
Sales commissions	$80,000
Insurance, factory	$2,500
Depreciation, administrative office equipment	$4,000
Lease cost, factory equipment	$12,000
Indirect materials, factory	$6,000
Depreciation, factory building	$10,000
Administrative office supplies (billing)	$3,000
Administrative office salaries	$60,000
Direct materials used (wood, bolts, etc.)	$94,000
Utilities, factory	$20,000

Required:

1. Prepare an answer sheet with the column headings shown below. Enter each cost item on your answer sheet, placing the dollar amount under the appropriate headings. As examples, this has been done already for the first two items in the list above. Note that each cost item is classified in two ways: first, as variable or fixed with respect to the number of units produced and sold; and second, as a selling and administrative cost or a product cost. (If the item is a product cost, it should also be classified as either direct or indirect as shown.)

	Cost Behavior		Period (Selling or Administrative) Cost	Product Cost	
Cost Item	Variable	Fixed		Direct	Indirect*
Direct labor	$118,000			$118,000	
Advertising		$50,000	$50,000		

*To units of product.

2. Total the dollar amounts in each of the columns in (1) above. Compute the average product cost of one patio set.
3. Assume production drops to only 1,000 sets annually. Would you expect the average product cost per set to increase, decrease, or remain unchanged? Explain. No computations are necessary.
4. Refer to the original data. The president's brother-in-law considered making himself a patio set and priced the necessary materials at a building supply store. The brother-in-law asked the president if he could purchase a patio set from the Dorilane Company "at cost," and the president agreed to let him do so.
   a. Would you expect any disagreement between the two men over the price the brother-in-law should pay? Explain. What price does the president probably have in mind? The brother-in-law?
   b. Because the company is operating at full capacity, what cost term used in the chapter might justify the president charging the full, regular price to the brother-in-law and still be selling "at cost"?

CASE 1–27 Ethics and the Manager LO1–3

M. K. Gallant is president of Kranbrack Corporation, a company whose stock is traded on a national exchange. In a meeting with investment analysts at the beginning of the year, Gallant predicted the company's earnings would grow by 20% this year. Unfortunately, sales have been less than expected for the year, and Gallant concluded within two weeks of the end of the fiscal year it would be impossible to report an increase in earnings as large as predicted unless some drastic action was taken. Accordingly, Gallant ordered wherever possible, expenditures should be postponed to the new year—including canceling or postponing orders with suppliers, delaying planned maintenance and training, and cutting back on end-of-year advertising and travel. Additionally, Gallant ordered the company's controller to carefully scrutinize all costs currently classified as period costs and reclassify as many as possible as product costs. The company is expected to have substantial inventories at the end of the year.

Required:

1. Why would reclassifying period costs as product costs increase this period's reported earnings?
2. Do you believe Gallant's actions are ethical? Why or why not?

Job-Order Costing: Calculating Unit Product Costs

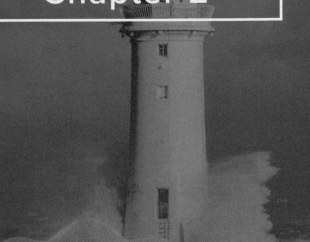

lighthouse image: Martin73/Shutterstock;
big data image: INGARA/Shutterstock

Dmytro Amanzholov/Shutterstock

ENTREPRENEUR SPOTLIGHT

When Spencer Kelly was 14 years old, his bike was stolen—and it ended up changing his life for the better! His father bought him a replacement bike on the condition that he figure out how to repay his dad by the end of the summer. While in the shower early that summer, Spencer had the thought—why can't I make a better soap?—and his company, Expedition Soaps, was born. Today the company produces over 130 products. Every one of the company's soap bars "begins with 5 skin-loving plant oils to delight your skin, including coconut oil, olive oil, corn oil, soybean oil, and sunflower oil."

Applying Managerial Accounting

Expedition Soaps sells its products at numerous craft shows throughout the state of Michigan. In 2020, most of those shows were canceled due to the coronavirus pandemic. However, as the craft shows resume, Spencer can use the principles of job-order costing to decide which craft shows to attend. He would view each craft show as a job and record its sales and costs (e.g., materials cost, labor cost, registration cost). After calculating the profitability of each show (or job), Spencer could retain profitable shows on his calendar while possibly discontinuing his company's presence at unprofitable shows.

Serving All Stakeholders

Expedition Soaps is an avid supporter of the autism community. For example, each year the company donates to OU CARES, an autism support program at Oakland University. It also makes annual contributions to USAutism.org to support the nonprofit organization's College Autism Project. Through a separate fundraising website, Expedition Soaps also makes its products available to local nonprofit organizations to support their fundraising efforts. In fact, Spencer's company contributes about 40 percent of its fundraising revenues back to the local partnering organization. ■

Sources: https://expeditionsoaps.com/, https://expeditionsoapsfundraising.com/.

LEARNING OBJECTIVES

After studying Chapter 2, you should be able to:

LO2–1 Compute a predetermined overhead rate.

LO2–2 Apply overhead cost to jobs using a predetermined overhead rate.

LO2–3 Compute the total cost and unit product cost of a job using a plantwide predetermined overhead rate.

LO2–4 Compute the total cost and unit product cost of a job using multiple predetermined overhead rates

LO2–5 Use job cost sheets to calculate ending inventories and cost of goods sold.

LO2–6 (Appendix 2A) Use activity-based absorption costing to compute unit product costs.

LO2–7 (Appendix 2B) Understand the implications of basing the predetermined overhead rate on activity at capacity rather than on estimated activity for the period.

Data Analytics Exercise available in Connect to complement this chapter

Companies usually assign costs to their products and services for two main reasons. First, it helps them with planning, controlling, and decision making. For example, a company may use product cost information to better understand each product's profitability or to establish each product's selling price. Second, it helps them value ending inventories and cost of goods sold for external reporting purposes. The costs attached to products that have not been sold are included in ending inventories on the balance sheet, whereas the costs attached to units that have been sold are included in cost of goods sold on the income statement.

It is very common for external financial reporting requirements to heavily influence how companies assign costs to their products and services. Because most countries (including the United States) require some form of *absorption costing* for external financial reports, many companies use some form of absorption costing for product costing purposes. In **absorption costing,** all manufacturing costs, both fixed and variable, are assigned to units of product—units are said to *fully absorb manufacturing costs.* *Conversely*, all nonmanufacturing costs are treated as period costs and not assigned to products.

This chapter and the next explain a common type of absorption costing system known as *job-order costing.* In this chapter, we'll discuss the role of job-order costing systems in planning, control, and decision making. Our focus will be on assigning manufacturing costs to individual jobs. In the next chapter, we will explain how job-order costing systems can be used to prepare the schedules of cost of goods manufactured and cost of goods sold and an income statement for external reporting purposes.

Job-Order Costing—An Overview

Job-order costing is used by companies that make many *different* products, each with unique features. For example, a Diesel clothing factory would typically make many different types of jeans for both men and women. A particular order might consist of 1,000 boot-cut men's blue denim jeans, style number A312. This order of 1,000 jeans is called a *job.* In a job-order costing system, costs are traced and allocated to jobs and then the costs of the job are divided by the number of units in the job to arrive at an average cost per unit, also called the *unit product cost.*

Other examples where job-order costing would be used include large-scale construction projects managed by Bechtel International; commercial aircraft produced by Boeing; business cards designed, printed, and shipped by Vistaprint; and airline meals prepared by LSG SkyChefs. All of these companies have diverse outputs. Each Bechtel project is unique and different from every other—the company may be simultaneously constructing a dam in Nigeria and a bridge in Indonesia. Likewise, each airline orders a different type of meal from LSG SkyChefs' catering service.

Job-order costing is also used extensively in service industries. For example, hospitals, law firms, movie studios, accounting firms, advertising agencies, and repair shops all use a variation of job-order costing to accumulate costs. Although the example of job-order costing provided in the following section deals with a manufacturing company, the same procedures are used by many service organizations.

IS THIS REALLY A JOB?

VBT Bicycling Vacations of Bristol, Vermont, offers deluxe bicycling vacations in the United States, Canada, Europe, and other locations throughout the world. For example, the company offers a 10-day tour of the Puglia region of Italy—the "heel of the boot." The tour price includes international airfare, 10 nights of lodging, most meals, use of a bicycle, and ground transportation as needed. Each tour is led by at least two local tour leaders, one of whom rides with the guests along the tour route. The other tour leader drives a "sag wagon" that carries extra water, snacks, and bicycle repair equipment and is available for a shuttle back to the hotel or up a hill. The sag wagon also transports guests' luggage from one hotel to another.

Each specific tour can be considered a job. For example, Giuliano Astore and Debora Trippetti, two natives of Puglia, led a VBT tour with 17 guests over 10 days in late April. At the end of the tour, Giuliano submitted a report to VBT headquarters. This report detailed the on-the-ground costs incurred for this specific tour, including fuel and operating costs for the van, lodging costs for the guests, the costs of meals provided to guests, the costs of snacks, the cost of hiring additional ground transportation as needed, and the wages of the tour leaders. In addition to these costs, some costs are paid directly by VBT in Vermont to vendors. The total cost incurred for the tour is then compared to the total revenue collected from guests to determine the gross profit for the tour.

Sources: Giuliano Astore and Gregg Marston, President, VBT Bicycling Vacations. For more information about VBT, see www.vbt.com.

Joerg Boethling/Alamy Stock Photo

Sandee Noreen

Job-Order Costing—An Example

To introduce job-order costing, we will follow a specific job as it progresses through the manufacturing process. This job consists of two experimental couplings that Yost Precision Machining has agreed to produce for Loops Unlimited, a manufacturer of roller coasters. Couplings connect the cars on the roller coaster and are a critical component in the performance and safety of the ride. Before we begin our discussion, it bears reemphasizing that companies generally classify manufacturing costs into three broad categories: (1) direct materials, (2) direct labor, and (3) manufacturing overhead. As we study the operation of a job-order costing system, we will see how each of these three types of product costs is assigned to jobs for computing unit product costs.

Yost Precision Machining is a small company in Michigan specializing in fabricating precision metal parts used in a variety of applications ranging from deep-sea exploration vehicles to the inertial triggers in automobile air bags. The company's top managers gather every morning in the company's conference room for the daily planning meeting. Attending the meeting this morning are Jean Yost, the company's president; David Cheung, the marketing manager; Debbie Turner, the production manager; and Marc White, the company controller. The president opened the meeting:

Jean: The production schedule indicates we'll be starting Job 2B47 today. Isn't that the special order for experimental couplings, David?

David: Yes. That's the order from Loops Unlimited for two couplings for their new roller coaster ride for Magic Mountain.

Debbie: Why only two couplings? Don't they need a coupling for every car?

David: Yes. But this is a completely new roller coaster. The cars will go faster and will be subjected to more twists, turns, drops, and loops than on any other existing roller coaster. To hold up under these stresses, Loops Unlimited's engineers completely redesigned the cars and couplings. They want us to make just two of these new couplings for testing purposes. If the design works, then we'll have the inside track on the order to supply couplings for the whole ride.

MANAGERIAL
ACCOUNTING IN ACTION
THE ISSUE

YOST
Precision Machining

Jean: We agreed to take on this initial order at our cost to get our foot in the door. Marc, will there be any problem documenting our cost so we can get paid?

Marc: No problem. The contract with Loops stipulates they will pay us based on each coupling's unit product cost as determined by our job-order costing system. I can finalize each coupling's direct materials, direct labor, and manufacturing overhead costs on the day the job is completed.

Jean: Good. Is there anything else we should discuss about this job? No? Well then, let's move on to the next item of business.

Measuring Direct Materials Cost

The blueprints submitted by Loops Unlimited indicate each experimental coupling requires three parts classified as *direct materials:* two G7 Connectors and one M46 Housing. Because each coupling requires two connectors and one housing, the production of two couplings requires four connectors and two housings. This is a custom product being made for the first time, but if this were one of the company's standard products, it would have an established *bill of materials.* A **bill of materials** is a document that lists the quantity of each type of direct material needed to complete a unit of product.

When agreement has been reached with the customer concerning the quantities, prices, and shipment date for the order, a *production order* is issued. The Production Department then prepares a *materials requisition form* similar to the form in Exhibit 2–1. The **materials requisition form** specifies the type and quantity of materials to be drawn from the storeroom and identifies the job charged for the cost of the materials. The form is used to control the flow of materials into production and also for making journal entries in the accounting records (as will be demonstrated in the next chapter).

The Yost Precision Machining materials requisition form in Exhibit 2–1 shows the company's Milling Department requisitioned two M46 Housings and four G7 Connectors for the Loops Unlimited job, which is designated as Job 2B47.

EXHIBIT 2–1
Materials Requisition Form

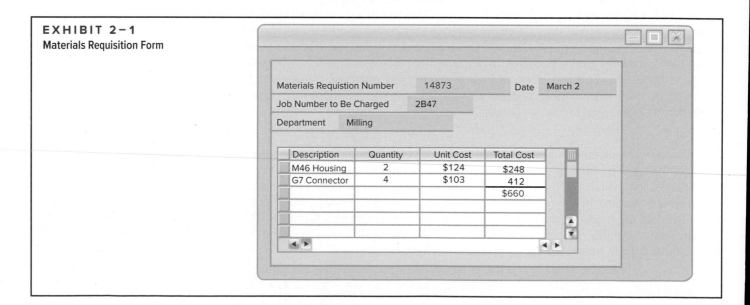

| Materials Requisition Number | 14873 | Date | March 2 |

| Job Number to Be Charged | 2B47 |

| Department | Milling |

Description	Quantity	Unit Cost	Total Cost
M46 Housing	2	$124	$248
G7 Connector	4	$103	412
			$660

Job Cost Sheet

After a production order is issued, the Accounting Department's job-order costing software automatically generates a *job cost sheet* like the one shown in Exhibit 2–2. A **job cost sheet** records the materials, labor, and manufacturing overhead costs charged to that job.

After direct materials are issued, the cost of these materials are automatically recorded on the job cost sheet. Note from Exhibit 2–2, for example, the $660 cost for direct materials shown earlier on the materials requisition form has been charged to Job 2B47 on its job cost sheet. The requisition number 14873 from the materials requisition

JOB COST SHEET

Job Number	2B47		Date Initiated	March 2
Department	Milling		Date Completed	
Item	Special order coupling		Units Completed	
For Stock				

Direct Materials		Direct Labor			Manufacturing Overhead		
Req. No.	Amount	Ticket	Hours	Amount	Hours	Rate	Amount
14873	$660	843	5	$90			

Cost Summary		Units Shipped		
Direct Materials	$	Date	Number	Balance
Direct Labor	$			
Manufacturing Overhead	$			
Total Product Cost	$			
Unit Product Cost	$			

EXHIBIT 2–2
Job Cost Sheet

form appears on the job cost sheet to make it easier to identify the source document for the direct materials charge.

Measuring Direct Labor Cost

As the name implies, direct labor costs can be directly traced to particular jobs. Most companies tabulate labor costs using computerized employee *time tickets*. A **time ticket** provides an hour-by-hour summary of the employee's activities throughout the day. For example, Exhibit 2–3 shows an employee time ticket that assigns $90 of direct labor cost to Job 2B47.

EXHIBIT 2–3
Employee Time Ticket

| Time Ticket No. | 843 | | Date | March 3 |
| Employee | Mary Holden | | Station | 4 |

Started	Ended	Time Completed	Rate	Amount	Job Number
7:00	12:00	5.0	$18	$90	2B47
12:30	2:30	2.0	18	36	2B50
2:30	3:30	1.0	18	18	Maintenance
Totals		8.0		$144	

The company's computerized system automatically posts this labor charge to Job 2B47's job cost sheet, as shown in Exhibit 2–2. The time ticket in Exhibit 2–3 also shows $18 of indirect labor cost related to performing maintenance. This cost is treated as part of manufacturing overhead and does not get directly posted on a job cost sheet.

LO2–1

Compute a predetermined overhead rate.

Computing Predetermined Overhead Rates

Recall that, in absorption costing, product costs include manufacturing overhead as well as direct materials and direct labor. Therefore, manufacturing overhead also needs to be recorded on the job cost sheet. However, assigning manufacturing overhead to a specific job is complicated by three circumstances:

1. Manufacturing overhead is an *indirect cost*. This means it is either impossible or difficult to trace these costs to a particular product or job.
2. Manufacturing overhead consists of many different costs ranging from the grease used in machines to the annual salary of the production manager. Some of these costs are *variable overhead costs* because they vary in direct proportion to changes in the level of production (e.g., indirect materials, indirect labor, supplies, and power) and some are *fixed overhead costs* because they remain constant as the level of production fluctuates (e.g., heat and light, property taxes, and insurance).
3. Many companies have large amounts of fixed manufacturing overhead. Therefore, their total manufacturing overhead costs tend to remain relatively constant from one period to the next even though the number of units they produce can fluctuate widely. Consequently, the average cost per unit varies from one period to the next.

Given these circumstances, companies use one or more allocation bases to assign overhead costs to products. An **allocation base** is a measure, such as direct labor-hours (DLH) or machine-hours (MH), that is common to all products and used to assign overhead costs to them. The most widely used allocation bases in manufacturing are direct labor-hours, direct labor cost, machine-hours, and (where a company has only a single product) units of product.

Manufacturing overhead is commonly allocated to products using a *predetermined overhead rate*. The **predetermined overhead rate** is computed by dividing the total estimated manufacturing overhead cost for the period by the estimated total amount of the allocation base as follows:

$$\text{Predetermined overhead rate} = \frac{\text{Estimated total manufacturing overhead cost}}{\text{Estimated total amount of the allocation base}}$$

The predetermined overhead rate is computed before the period begins using a four-step process. The first step is to estimate the total amount of the allocation base (the denominator) required for next period's estimated level of production. The second step is to estimate the total fixed manufacturing overhead cost for the coming period and the variable manufacturing overhead cost per unit of the allocation base. The third step is to use the cost formula shown below to estimate the total manufacturing overhead cost (the numerator) for the coming period:

$$Y = a + bX$$

where:

Y = The estimated total manufacturing overhead cost
a = The estimated total fixed manufacturing overhead cost
b = The estimated variable manufacturing overhead cost per unit of the allocation base
X = The estimated total amount of the allocation base

The fourth step is to compute the predetermined overhead rate. Notice, the estimated amount of the allocation base is determined before estimating the total manufacturing overhead cost. This needs to be done because total manufacturing overhead cost includes variable overhead costs that depend on the amount of the allocation base.

Applying Manufacturing Overhead

The predetermined overhead rate is computed *before* the period begins and is used to apply overhead cost to jobs throughout the period. The process of assigning overhead cost to jobs is called **overhead application**. The formula for determining the amount of overhead cost to apply to a particular job is:

$$\text{Overhead applied to a particular job} = \text{Predetermined overhead rate} \times \text{Amount of the allocation base incurred by the job}$$

For example, if the predetermined overhead rate is $20 per direct labor-hour, then $20 of overhead cost is *applied* to a job for each direct labor-hour incurred on the job. When the allocation base is direct labor-hours, the formula becomes:

$$\text{Overhead applied to a particular job} = \text{Predetermined overhead rate} \times \text{Actual direct labor-hours worked on the job}$$

Note the amount of overhead applied to a particular job is not the actual amount of overhead caused by the job. Actual overhead costs are not assigned to jobs—if that could be done, the costs would be direct costs, not overhead. The overhead allocated to the job is simply a share of the total overhead estimated at the beginning of the year. This approach to overhead application is known as *normal costing*. A **normal cost system** applies overhead costs to jobs by multiplying a predetermined overhead rate by the actual amount of the allocation base incurred by the jobs.

Manufacturing Overhead—A Closer Look

To illustrate the steps involved in computing and using a predetermined overhead rate, let's return to Yost Precision Machining and make the following assumptions. In step one, the company estimated 40,000 direct labor-hours would be required to support the production planned for the year. In step two, it estimated $640,000 of total fixed manufacturing overhead cost for the coming year and $4.00 of variable manufacturing overhead cost

LO2–2

Apply overhead cost to jobs using a predetermined overhead rate.

per direct labor-hour. Given these assumptions, in step three the company used the cost formula shown below to estimate its total manufacturing overhead cost for the year:

$$Y = a + bX$$

$$Y = \$640,000 + (\$4.00 \text{ per direct labor-hour} \times 40,000 \text{ direct labor-hours})$$

$$Y = \$640,000 + \$160,000$$

$$Y = \$800,000$$

In step four, Yost Precision Machining computed its predetermined overhead rate for the year of $20 per direct labor-hour as shown below:

$$\text{Predetermined overhead rate} = \frac{\text{Estimated total manufacturing overhead cost}}{\text{Estimated total amount of the allocation base}}$$

$$= \frac{\$800,000}{40,000 \text{ direct labor-hours}}$$

$$= \$20 \text{ per direct labor-hour}$$

The job cost sheet in Exhibit 2–4 indicates that 27 direct labor-hours (i.e., DLHs) were charged to Job 2B47. Therefore, a total of $540 of manufacturing overhead cost would be applied to the job:

$$\begin{array}{c} \text{Overhead applied to} \\ \text{Job 2B47} \end{array} = \begin{array}{c} \text{Predetermined} \\ \text{overhead rate} \end{array} \times \begin{array}{c} \text{Actual direct labor-hours} \\ \text{charged to Job 2B47} \end{array}$$

$$= \$20 \text{ per DLH} \times 27 \text{ DLHs}$$

$$= \$540 \text{ of overhead applied to Job 2B47}$$

This amount of overhead has been entered on the job cost sheet in Exhibit 2–4.

The Need for a Predetermined Rate

Instead of using a predetermined rate based on estimates, it may be tempting to suggest companies should use the *actual* total manufacturing overhead cost and the *actual* total amount of the allocation base to compute their overhead rates on a monthly, quarterly, or annual basis. However, if an actual rate is computed monthly or quarterly, seasonal factors in overhead costs or in the allocation base can produce fluctuations in the overhead rate. For example, the costs of heating and cooling a factory in Illinois will be highest in the winter and summer months and lowest in the spring and fall. If the overhead rate is recomputed at the end of each month or each quarter based on actual costs and activity, the overhead rate would go up in the winter and summer and down in the spring and fall. As a result, two identical jobs, one completed in the winter and one completed in the spring, would be assigned different manufacturing overhead costs.

To avoid such confusing fluctuations, companies could compute actual overhead rates on an annual basis. However, with this approach, the manufacturing overhead assigned to any particular job would not be known until the end of the year. For example, the cost of Job 2B47 at Yost Precision Machining would not be known until the end of the year, even though the job will be completed and shipped to the customer in March. For these reasons, most companies use predetermined overhead rates rather than actual overhead rates in their cost accounting systems.

LO2–3

Compute the total cost and unit product cost of a job using a plantwide predetermined overhead rate.

Computation of Total Job Costs and Unit Product Costs

With the application of Yost Precision Machining's $540 of manufacturing overhead to the job cost sheet in Exhibit 2–4, the job cost sheet is complete except for two final steps. First, the totals for direct materials, direct labor, and manufacturing overhead are transferred to the Cost Summary section of the job cost sheet and added together to obtain the

EXHIBIT 2–4
A Completed Job Cost Sheet

JOB COST SHEET

Job Number	2B47
Department	Milling
Item	Special order coupling
For Stock	

Date Initiated	March 2
Date Completed	March 8
Units Completed	2

Direct Materials		Direct Labor			Manufacturing Overhead		
Req. No.	Amount	Ticket	Hours	Amount	Hours	Rate	Amount
14873	$ 660	843	5	$ 90	27	$20/DLH	$540
14875	506	846	8	136			
14912	238	850	4	60			
	$1,404	851	10	160			
			27	$446			

Cost Summary		Units Shipped		
Direct Materials	$ 1,404	Date	Number	Balance
Direct Labor	446	March 8	—	2
Manufacturing Overhead	540			
Total Product Cost	$ 2,390			
Unit Product Cost	$ 1,195*			

*$2,390 ÷ 2 units = $1,195 per unit.

total cost for the job.[1] Then, the total product cost ($2,390) is divided by the number of units (2) to obtain the unit product cost ($1,195). As indicated earlier, *this unit product cost is an average cost and should not be interpreted as the cost that would actually be incurred if another unit were produced.* The incremental cost of an additional unit is something less than the average unit cost of $1,195 because much of the actual overhead costs would not change if another unit were produced.

MANAGERIAL
ACCOUNTING IN ACTION
THE WRAP-UP

In the daily planning meeting on March 9, Jean Yost, the president of Yost Precision Machining, once again drew attention to Job 2B47, the experimental couplings:

Jean: I see Job 2B47 is completed. Let's get those couplings shipped immediately to Loops Unlimited so they can get their testing program under way. Marc, how much are we going to bill Loops for those two units?

Marc: Because we agreed to sell the experimental couplings at cost, we are charging Loops Unlimited just $1,195 a unit.

Jean: Fine. Let's hope the couplings work and we make some money on the big order later.

YOST
Precision Machining

---

[1] Notice, we are assuming that Job 2B47 required direct materials and direct labor beyond the charges shown in Exhibits 2–1 and 2–3.

JOB-ORDER COSTING IN THE SERVICE INDUSTRY

Accenture is one of the world's largest consulting firms with annual revenues greater than $50 billion. Because the firm does not have any inventory on its balance sheet, it might be tempting to conclude that it does not need a job-order costing system. However, that is not true.

Accenture pays its consultants more than $34 billion per year to provide services for clients. Job-order costing enables the firm to compare each client's revenues to the costs of serving those clients. It also enables the firm to determine what portion of its consulting capacity was billable to clients and what portion was not billed to specific clients.

Source: Accenture 2021 Annual Report.

Job-Order Costing—A Managerial Perspective

Managers use job costs for planning and decision-making purposes. For example, they may rely on job profitability reports to influence sales and production plans. If certain types of jobs, such as low-volume engineering-intensive jobs, seem highly profitable, managers may dedicate future advertising expenditures to growing sales of these types of jobs. Conversely, if other types of jobs, such as high-volume labor-intensive jobs, seem unprofitable, managers may reduce the projected sales and production of these types of jobs.

Managers may also use job costs for pricing decisions. For example, if Job A has a total manufacturing cost of $100, managers often use a predefined markup percentage, say 50%, to establish a markup of $50 (= $100 × 50%) and a selling price of $150 (= $100 + $50). Under this approach, known as cost-plus pricing, the managers establish a markup percentage they believe generates enough revenue to cover all of a job's manufacturing costs and a portion of the company's nonmanufacturing costs, while generating some residual profit.

If a company's job-order costing system does not accurately assign manufacturing costs to jobs, it will adversely influence the types of planning and decision-making scenarios just described. In other words, distorted job cost data may cause managers to use additional advertising dollars to pursue certain types of jobs they believe are profitable, but in actuality, are not. Similarly, inaccurate job costs may cause managers to establish selling prices that are too high or too low relative to the prices established by more savvy competitors.

At this point, you may be wondering, how can this happen? How can a job-order costing system inaccurately assign costs to jobs? The key to answering this question is focusing on *indirect* manufacturing costs, also called manufacturing overhead costs. While job-order costing systems accurately trace *direct* materials and *direct* labor costs to jobs, they often fail to accurately allocate manufacturing overhead costs to jobs. The root cause of these inaccuracies often relates to the choice of an allocation base.

Choosing an Allocation Base—A Key to Job Cost Accuracy

Imagine going to a restaurant with three of your friends. The group orders an extra-large pizza for $20 cut into ten slices. One of your friends eats five slices of pizza, your other two friends eat two slices each, and you eat one slice. When the bill arrives, the friend who ate five slices recommends paying the bill using "number of people seated at the table" as the allocation base, thereby requiring you to contribute $5 (= $20 ÷ 4) toward paying the bill. How would you feel about the accuracy of this cost allocation base? In all likelihood, you'd suggest distributing the bill among the four diners using another allocation base called "number of slices eaten." This approach requires each person to

COMMUNICATING WITH DATA VISUALIZATIONS

Descriptive analytics answer the question: What happened? The visualization shown below relates to a hypothetical company that produces numerous jobs, eight of which are contained in the visualization. The blue bars describe "what happened" by summarizing the gross margins earned by each of the eight jobs. Five of these jobs earned positive gross margins and three of them earned negative gross margins.

Diagnostic analytics answer the question: Why did it happen? The red line in the visualization shows that labor intensity (which is defined as each job's direct labor cost divided by its sales) varies inversely with gross margin. Assuming the company uses plantwide overhead allocation based on direct labor-hours, this inverse relationship would alert management to the possibility its cost system is overcosting labor-intensive jobs and undercosting jobs that are less labor-intensive.

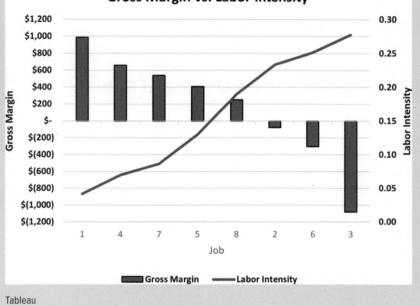

Tableau

pay $2 (= \$20 \div 10$) per slice consumed, thereby requiring you to contribute $2 toward paying the bill. While the distortion caused by using "number of people seated at the table" as the allocation base seems obvious, job-order costing systems often make the same error—they use allocation bases that do not reflect how jobs actually use overhead resources.

To improve job cost accuracy, the allocation base in the predetermined overhead rate should *drive* the overhead cost. A **cost driver** is a factor, such as machine-hours, beds occupied, computer time, or flight-hours, that causes overhead costs. If the base in the predetermined overhead rate does not "drive" overhead costs, it will not accurately measure the cost of overhead resources used by each job. Many companies use job-order costing systems that assume direct labor-hours (or direct labor cost) is the only manufacturing overhead cost driver. They use a single predetermined overhead rate, or what is called a **plantwide overhead rate**, to allocate all manufacturing overhead costs to jobs based on their usage of direct-labor hours. However, while direct labor-hours may "drive" some of a company's manufacturing overhead costs, it is often incorrect to assume that direct-labor hours is a company's *only* manufacturing overhead cost driver. When companies can identify more than one overhead cost driver, they can improve job cost accuracy by using *multiple predetermined overhead rates*.

UNIVERSITY TEES: SERVING OVER 150 CAMPUSES NATIONWIDE

University Tees was founded in 2003 by two Miami University college students to provide screen-printing, embroidery, and promotional products for fraternities, sororities, and student organizations. Today, the company is headquartered in Cleveland, Ohio, and employs as many as four Campus Managers on each of over 150 college campuses across America.

Accurately calculating the cost of each potential customer order is critically important to University Tees because the company needs to be sure the sales price exceeds the cost associated with satisfying the order. The costs include the cost of the blank T-shirts themselves, printing costs (which vary depending on the quantity of shirts produced and the number of colors per shirt), screen costs (which also vary depending on the number of colors included in a design), shipping costs, and the artwork needed to create a design. The company also takes into account its competitors' pricing strategies when developing its own prices.

Source: Conversation with Joe Haddad, cofounder of University Tees.

Job-Order Costing Using Multiple Predetermined Overhead Rates

LO2–4

Compute the total cost and unit product cost of a job using multiple predetermined overhead rates.

A cost system with **multiple predetermined overhead rates** uses more than one overhead rate to apply overhead costs to jobs. For example, a company may choose to use a predetermined overhead rate for each of its production departments. Such a system, while more complex, is more accurate because it reflects differences across departments in terms of how jobs consume overhead costs. For example, in labor-intensive departments, their overhead costs might be applied to jobs based on direct labor-hours. However, in machine-intensive departments, their overhead costs might be applied to jobs using machine-hours.

Multiple Predetermined Overhead Rates—A Departmental Approach

Dickson Company has two production departments, Milling and Assembly. The company uses a job-order costing system and computes a predetermined overhead rate in each department. The predetermined overhead rate in the Milling Department is based on machine-hours, and in the Assembly Department, it is based on direct labor-hours. The company uses *cost-plus pricing* to establish selling prices for its products. **Cost-plus pricing** is a pricing method in which a predetermined markup is applied to a cost base to determine the target selling price. In this instance, Dickson Company uses a markup percentage of 75% of total manufacturing cost to establish selling prices for all of its jobs. At the beginning of the year, the company made the following estimates:

	Department	
	Milling	Assembly
Machine-hours	60,000	3,000
Direct labor-hours	8,000	80,000
Total fixed manufacturing overhead cost	$390,000	$500,000
Variable manufacturing overhead per machine-hour	$2.00	—
Variable manufacturing overhead per direct labor-hour	—	$3.75

During the current month, the company started and completed Job 407. It wants to use its predetermined departmental overhead rates and the information pertaining to Job 407 shown below to establish a selling price for this job:

	Department	
Job 407	Milling	Assembly
Machine-hours	90	4
Direct labor-hours	5	20
Direct materials	$800	$370
Direct labor cost	$70	$280

Exhibit 2–5 explains how Dickson would compute a selling price for Job 407 using a five-step process, the first of which is to calculate the estimated total manufacturing overhead cost in each department using the equation

$$Y = a + bX$$

where:

Y = The estimated total manufacturing overhead cost

a = The estimated total fixed manufacturing overhead cost

b = The estimated variable manufacturing overhead cost per unit of the allocation base

X = The estimated total amount of the allocation base

As shown in step 1 in Exhibit 2–5, this equation provides the Milling Department's estimated total manufacturing overhead cost of $510,000 and the Assembly Department's estimated total overhead cost of $800,000.

The second step is to calculate the predetermined overhead rate for each department using the following formula:

$$\text{Predetermined overhead rate} = \frac{\text{Estimated total manufacturing overhead cost}}{\text{Estimated total amount of the allocation base}}$$

Per step 2 in Exhibit 2–5, this formula results in predetermined overhead rates in the Milling and Assembly Departments of $8.50 per machine-hour and $10.00 per direct labor-hour, respectively.

The third step is to use the general equation shown below to calculate the amount of overhead applied from each department to Job 407.

$$\begin{matrix} \text{Overhead applied to} \\ \text{Job 407} \end{matrix} = \begin{matrix} \text{Predetermined} \\ \text{overhead rate} \end{matrix} \times \begin{matrix} \text{Actual amount of the allocation} \\ \text{base used by Job 407} \end{matrix}$$

As depicted in the middle of Exhibit 2–5, $765 of manufacturing overhead is applied from the Milling Department to Job 407, whereas $200 is applied from the Assembly Department to this same job.

Finally, Exhibit 2–5 summarizes steps 4 and 5, which calculate the total job cost for Job 407 ($2,485) and the selling price of Job 407 ($4,348.75) using the markup percentage of 75%.

It is important to emphasize using a departmental approach to overhead application results in a different selling price for Job 407 than would have been derived using a plantwide overhead rate based on either direct labor-hours or machine-hours. The appeal of using predetermined departmental overhead rates is they presumably provide a more accurate accounting of the costs caused by jobs, which, in turn, should enhance management planning and decision making.

EXHIBIT 2–5
Dickson Company: An Example Using Multiple Predetermined Overhead Rates

Step 1: Calculate the estimated total manufacturing overhead cost for each department.

Milling Department Overhead Cost (Y):	Assembly Department Overhead Cost (Y):
= $390,000 + ($2.00 per MH × 60,000 MHs)	= $500,000 + ($3.75 per DLH × 80,000 DLHs)
= $390,000 + $120,000	= $500,000 + $300,000
= $510,000	= $800,000

Step 2: Calculate the predetermined overhead rate in each department.

Milling Department Overhead Rate:	Assembly Department Overhead Rate:
$= \dfrac{\$510,000}{60,000 \text{ machine-hours}}$	$= \dfrac{\$800,000}{80,000 \text{ direct labor-hours}}$
= $8.50 per machine-hour	= $10.00 per direct labor-hour

Step 3: Calculate the amount of overhead applied from both departments to Job 407.

Milling Department: Overhead Applied to Job 407	Assembly Department: Overhead Applied to Job 407
= $8.50 per MH × 90 MHs	= $10.00 per DLH × 20 DLHs
= $765	= $200

Step 4: Calculate the total job cost for Job 407.

	Milling	Assembly	Total
Direct materials	$800	$370	$1,170
Direct labor	$70	$280	350
Manufacturing overhead applied	$765	$200	965
Total cost of Job 407			$2,485

Step 5: Calculate the selling price for Job 407.

Total cost of Job 407	$2,485.00
Markup ($2,485 × 75%)	1,863.75
Selling price of Job 407	$4,348.75

Multiple Predetermined Overhead Rates—An Activity-Based Approach

Using departmental overhead rates is one approach to creating a job-order costing system with multiple predetermined overhead rates. Another approach is to create overhead rates related to the activities performed within departments. This approach usually results in more overhead rates than a departmental approach because each department may perform more than one activity. When a company creates overhead rates based on the activities it performs, it is employing an approach called *activity-based costing*.

For now, our goal is to simply introduce you to the idea of activity-based costing—an alternative approach to developing multiple predetermined overhead rates. Managers use activity-based costing systems to more accurately measure the demands that jobs, products, customers, and other cost objects make on overhead resources. Appendix 2A provides an in-depth discussion of activity-based absorption costing and contrasts it with the plantwide approach described earlier in this chapter. Chapter 7 describes a more refined approach to activity-based costing that better serves the needs of management than the activity-based absorption costing approach discussed in Appendix 2A.

CLOTHING DESIGNERS EMBRACE ON-DEMAND MANUFACTURING

Resonance Companies Inc. uses on-demand manufacturing to produce clothing for apparel retailers in response to specific orders placed by their customers. Resonance prints fabric digitally, cuts it robotically, uses direct labor to sew the pieces together, and then ships the completed garments directly to the retailers' customers in the appropriate branded packaging. Every clothing item "is stamped with a QR code that shows how much fabric dye, water and other materials were used in production, the amount of power consumed, as well as who made it and where."

The switch to on-demand manufacturing, or what might be described as job-order production, replaces industry norms requiring clothing retailers to (1) place high-volume production orders up to a year in advance, (2) pay suppliers for inventory purchases months before making the merchandise available for sale, (3) spend on advertising to liquidate unpopular items and sizes at discounted prices, and (4) discard unsold merchandise that eventually ends up in local landfills.

Source: Suzanne Kapner, "Designers Sell Clothes First, Make Them Later to Cut Cost," *The Wall Street Journal,* September 27, 2021, pp. B1–B2.

Job-Order Costing—An External Reporting Perspective

This chapter focuses on using job-order costing systems to compute unit product costs for internal management purposes. However, job-order costing systems are also often used to create a balance sheet and income statement for external parties, such as shareholders and lenders. In this section, we explain how a company's job cost sheets provide a subsidiary ledger that summarizes the specific jobs that comprise the amounts reported in *Work-in-Process* and *Finished Goods* on the balance sheet as well as *Cost of Goods Sold* on the income statement.

To illustrate, assume Dixon Company worked on six jobs during May: Jobs A, B, C, D, E, and F. At the end of May, the job cost sheets for these six jobs contained the following data:

LO2–5
Use job cost sheets to calculate ending inventories and cost of goods sold.

	Job A	Job B	Job C	Job D	Job E	Job F
Beginning balance	$64	$50	$110	$100	$116	$132
Charged to the jobs during May:						
Direct materials	$100	$88	$142	$106	$180	$160
Direct labor	$80	$60	$90	$70	$120	$100
Manufacturing overhead applied	$96	$72	$108	$84	$144	$120
Units completed	0	0	100	60	200	160
Units in process at the end of May	90	70	0	0	0	0
Units sold during May	0	0	80	60	200	40

Jobs C, D, E, and F were completed during May. Jobs A and B were incomplete at the end of May. There was no finished goods inventory on May 1, and the company's total manufacturing overhead applied equals its total actual manufacturing overhead.

Given this information, the job cost sheets can be used to calculate *Work in Process* for the May 31 balance sheet by identifying the jobs that still have units in process at the end of the month (Jobs A and B) and summing their total job costs as follows:

	Job A	Job B	Total
Beginning balance	$ 64	$ 50	
Direct materials	100	88	
Direct labor	80	60	
Manufacturing overhead applied	96	72	
Cost of ending work in process inventory	$ 340	$ 270	$610

The job cost sheets can also be used to calculate *Cost of Goods Sold* for May's income statement using a two-step process. First, calculate the unit product costs for all jobs completed during May (Jobs C, D, E, and F) as follows:

	Job C	Job D	Job E	Job F
Beginning balance	$ 110	$ 100	$ 116	$ 132
Direct materials	142	106	180	160
Direct labor	90	70	120	100
Manufacturing overhead applied	108	84	144	120
Total job cost (a)	$ 450	$ 360	$ 560	$ 512
Units completed (b)	100	60	200	160
Unit product cost (a) ÷ (b)	$4.50	$6.00	$2.80	$3.20

Next, calculate the *Cost of Goods Sold* by multiplying each job's unit product cost by the number of units sold:

	Job C	Job D	Job E	Job F	Total
Unit product cost (a)	$4.50	$6.00	$2.80	$3.20	
Units sold (b)	80	60	200	40	
Cost of goods sold (a) × (b)	$ 360	$ 360	$ 560	$ 128	$1,408

The *Finished Goods* inventory for the May 31 balance sheet can also be calculated using a two-step process. First, calculate the number of units in ending finished goods inventory:

	Job C	Job D	Job E	Job F
Units completed (a)	100	60	200	160
Units sold (b)	80	60	200	40
Units in finished goods inventory (a) − (b)	20	0	0	120

Second, multiply the units in finished goods inventory by each job's respective unit product cost:

	Job C	Job D	Job E	Job F	Total
Units in finished goods inventory (a)	20	0	0	120	
Unit product cost (b)	$4.50	$6.00	$2.80	$3.20	
Cost of ending finished goods inventory (a) × (b)	$90	$0	$0	$ 384	$474

Overhead Application and the Income Statement

For simplicity, the example we just completed assumes Dixon Company's total manufacturing overhead applied equals its total actual manufacturing overhead. However, in reality, when a company uses predetermined overhead rates to apply overhead cost to jobs, it is almost a certainty that the amount of overhead applied to all jobs will differ from the actual amount of overhead cost. When a company applies less overhead to production than it actually incurs, it creates what is known as *underapplied overhead*. When it applies more overhead to production than it actually incurs, it results in *overapplied overhead*.

The existence of underapplied or overapplied overhead has implications for how a company prepares its financial statements. For example, the cost of goods sold reported on a company's income statement must be adjusted to reflect underapplied or overapplied overhead. The adjustment for underapplied overhead increases cost of goods sold and decreases net operating income, whereas the adjustment for overapplied overhead decreases cost of goods sold and increases net operating income. Nonetheless, all forthcoming exercises and problems pertaining to this learning objective will assume the amounts of applied and actual overhead are the same.

Job-Order Costing in Service Companies

This chapter focused on manufacturing companies; however, job-order costing is also used in service organizations, such as law firms, movie studios, hospitals, and repair shops. In a law firm, for example, each client is a "job," and the costs of that job are accumulated day by day on a job cost sheet as the client's case is handled by the firm. Legal forms and similar inputs represent the direct materials for the job; the time expended by attorneys is direct labor; and the costs of secretaries and legal aids, rent, depreciation, and so forth, represent the overhead.

In a movie studio such as Columbia Pictures, each film produced by the studio is a "job," and costs of direct materials (costumes and props) and direct labor (actors, directors, and extras) are charged to each film's job cost sheet. A share of the studio's overhead costs, such as utilities, depreciation of equipment, wages of maintenance workers, and so forth, is also charged to each film.

In summary, job-order costing is a versatile and widely used costing method that may be encountered in virtually any organization that provides diverse products or services.

Summary

Job-order costing is used when organizations offer many different products or services, such as in furniture manufacturing, hospitals, and legal firms. When used in a manufacturing context, job-order costing systems accumulate a job's direct materials, direct labor, and manufacturing overhead costs on a job cost sheet. Selling and administrative costs are not assigned to jobs because they are treated as period costs.

Job-order costing systems use materials requisition forms and labor time tickets to trace direct materials and direct labor costs to jobs. Because manufacturing overhead costs are indirect costs, they must be allocated to jobs. Ideally, the allocation base used to allocate overhead costs to jobs should be a cost driver—it should cause the consumption of overhead costs. The most frequently used allocation bases in job-order costing systems are direct labor-hours and machine-hours.

Normal costing systems allocate overhead costs to jobs using predetermined overhead rates estimated before the period begins. A predetermined overhead rate is computed by dividing the estimated total manufacturing overhead cost for the period by the estimated total amount of the allocation base. Job-order costing systems can use only one predetermined overhead rate (also called a plantwide rate) or multiple predetermined overhead rates.

Throughout the period, overhead is applied to jobs by multiplying the predetermined overhead rate by the actual amount of the allocation base recorded for each job. The total manufacturing costs assigned to a job (including direct materials, direct labor, and applied overhead) divided by the number of units within that job equals the unit product cost.

A company's job cost sheets form a subsidiary ledger that can be used to summarize the amounts of work in process and finished goods on the balance sheet and the cost of goods sold in the income statement.

 Data Analytics Exercise available in Connect to complement this chapter

Review Problem: Calculating Unit Product Costs

Redhawk Company has two manufacturing departments—Assembly and Fabrication. The company considers all of its manufacturing overhead costs to be fixed costs. The first set of data shown below is based on estimates made at the beginning of the year for the expected total output. The second set of data relates to one job completed during the year—Job A200.

Estimated Data	Assembly	Fabrication	Total
Manufacturing overhead costs.........	$300,000	$400,000	$700,000
Direct labor-hours...................	25,000	15,000	40,000
Machine-hours.....................	10,000	50,000	60,000

Job A200	Assembly	Fabrication	Total
Direct materials....................	$110	$50	$160
Direct labor.......................	$70	$45	$115
Direct labor-hours..................	10 hours	2 hours	12 hours
Machine-hours.....................	1 hour	7 hours	8 hours

Required:

1. If Redhawk uses a predetermined plantwide overhead rate with direct labor-hours as the allocation base, how much manufacturing overhead would be applied to Job A200?
2. If Redhawk uses predetermined departmental overhead rates with direct labor-hours as the allocation base in Assembly and machine-hours as the allocation base in Fabrication, how much total manufacturing overhead cost would be applied to Job A200?
3. Assume Redhawk uses the departmental overhead rates mentioned in requirement 2 and Job A200 includes 50 units. What is the unit product cost for Job A200?

Solution to Review Problem

1. The predetermined plantwide overhead rate is computed as follows:

$$\text{Predetermined overhead rate} = \frac{\text{Estimated total manufacturing overhead cost}}{\text{Estimated total amount of the allocation base}}$$

$$= \frac{\$700,000}{40,000 \text{ direct labor-hours}}$$

$$= \$17.50 \text{ per direct labor-hour}$$

The manufacturing overhead applied to Job A200 is computed as follows:

$$\text{Overhead applied to Job A200} = \frac{\text{Predetermined}}{\text{overhead rate}} \times \frac{\text{Actual direct labor-hours}}{\text{charged to Job A200}}$$

$$= \$17.50 \text{ per DLH} \times 12 \text{ DLHs}$$

$$= \$210 \text{ of overhead applied to Job A200}$$

2. The predetermined departmental overhead rates are computed as follows:

Assembly Department:

$$\text{Predetermined overhead rate} = \frac{\text{Estimated total manufacturing overhead cost}}{\text{Estimated total amount of the allocation base}}$$

$$= \frac{\$300,000}{25,000 \text{ direct labor-hours}}$$

$$= \$12 \text{ per direct labor-hour}$$

Fabrication Department:

$$\text{Predetermined overhead rate} = \frac{\text{Estimated total manufacturing overhead cost}}{\text{Estimated total amount of the allocation base}}$$

$$= \frac{\$400,000}{50,000 \text{ machine-hours}}$$

$$= \$8.00 \text{ per machine-hour}$$

The manufacturing overhead applied to Job A200 is computed as follows:

Job A200	(1) Overhead Rate	(2) Actual Hours Used	Applied Overhead (1) × (2)
Assembly Department	$12 per DLH	10 hours	$ 120
Fabrication Department	$8 per MH	7 hours	56
Total applied overhead.			$ 176

3. The unit product cost for Job A200 is computed as follows:

Job A200	Assembly	Fabrication	Total
Direct materials	$110	$50	$ 160
Direct labor.	$70	$45	115
Applied overhead	$120	$56	176
Total job cost (a).			$ 451
Number of units in Job A200 (b)			50
Unit product cost (a) ÷ (b).			$9.02

Glossary

Absorption costing A costing method that includes all manufacturing costs—direct materials, direct labor, and both variable and fixed manufacturing overhead—in unit product costs. (p. 60)

Allocation base A measure of activity such as direct labor-hours or machine-hours used to assign costs to cost objects. (p. 64)

Bill of materials A document showing the quantity of each type of direct material required to make a product. (p. 62)

Cost driver A factor, such as machine-hours, beds occupied, computer time, or flight-hours, that causes overhead costs. (p. 69)

Cost-plus pricing A pricing method in which a predetermined markup is applied to a cost base to determine the target selling price. (p. 70)

Job cost sheet A form that records the direct materials, direct labor, and manufacturing overhead cost charged to a job. (p. 62)

Job-order costing A costing system used in situations where many different products, jobs, or services are produced each period. (p. 60)

Materials requisition form A document specifying the type and quantity of materials to be drawn from the storeroom and the job charged for the cost of those materials. (p. 62)

Multiple predetermined overhead rates A costing system with multiple overhead cost pools and a different predetermined overhead rate for each cost pool, rather than a single predetermined overhead rate for the entire company. Each production department may be treated as a separate overhead cost pool. (p. 70)

Normal cost system A costing system that applies overhead costs to jobs by multiplying a predetermined overhead rate by the actual amount of the allocation base incurred by the job. (p. 65)

Overhead application The process of assigning overhead cost to specific jobs. (p. 65)

Plantwide overhead rate A single predetermined overhead rate used throughout a plant. (p. 69)

Predetermined overhead rate A rate used to charge manufacturing overhead cost to jobs that is established in advance for each period. It is computed by dividing the estimated total manufacturing overhead cost for the period by the estimated total amount of the allocation base. (p. 70)

Time ticket A document that records the amount of time an employee spends on various activities. (p. 63)

Questions

2–1 What is job-order costing?
2–2 What is absorption costing?
2–3 What is normal costing?
2–4 How is the unit product cost of a job calculated?
2–5 Explain the four-step process used to compute a predetermined overhead rate.
2–6 What is the purpose of the job cost sheet in a job-order costing system?
2–7 Explain why some production costs must be assigned to products through an allocation process.
2–8 Why do companies use predetermined overhead rates rather than actual manufacturing overhead costs to apply overhead to jobs?
2–9 What factors should be considered in selecting an allocation base to be used in computing a predetermined overhead rate?
2–10 If a company fully allocates all of its overhead costs to jobs, does it guarantee the company will earn a profit for the period?
2–11 Would you expect the amount of applied overhead for a period to equal the actual overhead costs of the period? Why or why not?
2–12 What is underapplied overhead? Overapplied overhead?
2–13 What is a plantwide overhead rate? Why are multiple overhead rates, rather than a plantwide overhead rate, used in some companies?

Applying Excel   Mc Graw Hill connect

LO2–1, LO2–2, LO2–3, LO2–4

This Excel worksheet relates to the Dickson Company example summarized in Exhibit 2–5. The workbook, and instructions on how to complete the file, can be found in Connect.

	A	B	C	D	E
1	Chapter 2: Applying Excel				
2					
3	Data				
4	Markup on job cost	75%			
5					
6		Department			
7		Milling	Assembly		
8	Machine-hours	60,000	3,000		
9	Direct labor-hours	8,000	80,000		
10	Total fixed manufacturing overhead cost	$390,000	$500,000		
11	Variable manufacturing overhead per machine-hour	$2.00			
12	Variable manufacturing overhead per direct labor-hour		$3.75		
13					
14	Cost summary for Job 407	Department			
15		Milling	Assembly		
16	Machine-hours	90	4		
17	Direct labor-hours	5	20		
18	Direct materials	$800	$370		
19	Direct labor cost	$70	$280		
20					
21	Enter a formula into each of the cells marked with a ? below				
22					
23	Step 1: Calculate the estimated total manufacturing overhead cost for each department				
24		Milling	Assembly		
25	Total fixed manufacturing overhead cost	?	?		
26	Variable manufacturing overhead per machine-hour or direct labor-hour	?	?		
27	Total machine-hours or direct labor-hours	?	?		
28	Total variable manufacturing overhead	?	?		
29	Total manufacturing overhead	?	?		
30					
31	Step 2: Calculate the predetermined overhead rate in each department				
32		Milling	Assembly		
33	Total manufacturing overhead	?	?		
34	Total machine-hours or direct labor-hours	?	?		
35	Predetermined overhead rate per machine-hour or direct labor-hour	?	?		
36					
37	Step 3: Calculate the amount of overhead applied from both departments to Job 407				
38		Milling	Assembly		
39	Predetermined overhead rate per machine-hour or direct labor-hour	?	?		
40	Machine-hours or direct labor-hours for the job	?	?		
41	Manufacturing overhead applied	?	?		
42					
43	Step 4: Calculate the total job cost for Job 407				
44		Milling	Assembly	Total	
45	Direct materials	?	?	?	
46	Direct labor cost	?	?	?	
47	Manufacturing overhead applied	?	?	?	
48	Total cost of Job 407			?	
49					
50	Step 5: Calculate the selling price for Job 407				
51	Total cost of Job 407			?	
52	Markup			?	
53	Selling price of Job 407			?	
54					

Chapter 2 Form   Filled in Chapter 2 Form

Microsoft Excel

You should proceed to the requirements below only after completing your worksheet.

Required:

1. Check your worksheet by changing the total fixed manufacturing overhead cost for the Milling Department in the Data area to $300,000, keeping all of the other data the same as in the original example. If your worksheet is operating properly, the total cost of Job 407 should now be $2,350. If you do not get this answer, find the errors in your worksheet and correct them.

    How much is the selling price of Job 407? Did it change? Why or why not?

2. Change the total fixed manufacturing overhead cost for the Milling Department in the Data area back to $390,000, keeping all of the other data the same as in the original example. Determine the selling price for a new job, Job 408, with the following characteristics. You need not bother changing the job number from 407 to 408 in the worksheet.

Cost summary for Job 408	Department	
	Milling	Assembly
Machine-hours	40	10
Direct labor-hours	2	6
Direct materials	$700	$360
Direct labor cost	$50	$150

3. What happens to the selling price for Job 408 if the total number of machine-hours in the Assembly Department increases from 3,000 machine-hours to 6,000 machine-hours? Does it increase, decrease, or stay the same as in part 2 above? Why?

4. Restore the total number of machine-hours in the Assembly Department to 3,000 machine-hours. What happens to the selling price for Job 408 if the total number of direct labor-hours in the Assembly Department decreases from 80,000 direct labor-hours to 50,000 direct labor-hours? Does it increase, decrease, or stay the same as in part 2 above? Why?

The Foundational 15   Mc Graw Hill connect

LO2–1, LO2–2, LO2–3, LO2–4

Sweeten Company had no jobs in progress at the beginning of the year and no beginning inventories. It started, completed, and sold only two jobs during the year—Job P and Job Q. The company uses a plantwide predetermined overhead rate based on machine-hours. At the beginning of the year, it estimated 4,000 machine-hours would be required for the period's estimated level of production. Sweeten also estimated $25,000 of fixed manufacturing overhead cost for the coming period and variable manufacturing overhead of $1.70 per machine-hour.

Because Sweeten has two manufacturing departments—Molding and Fabrication—it is considering replacing its plantwide overhead rate with departmental rates that would also be based on machine-hours. The company gathered the following additional information to enable calculating departmental overhead rates:

	Molding	Fabrication	Total
Estimated total machine-hours used	2,500	1,500	4,000
Estimated total fixed manufacturing overhead	$10,000	$15,000	$25,000
Estimated variable manufacturing overhead per machine-hour	$1.40	$2.20	

The direct materials cost, direct labor cost, and machine-hours used for Jobs P and Q are as follows:

	Job P	Job Q
Direct materials	$13,000	$8,000
Direct labor cost	$21,000	$7,500
Actual machine-hours used:		
Molding	1,700	800
Fabrication	600	900
Total	2,300	1,700

Sweeten Company had no overapplied or underapplied manufacturing overhead costs during the year.

Required:

For questions 1–8, assume Sweeten Company uses a plantwide predetermined overhead rate with machine-hours as the allocation base. For questions 9–15, assume the company uses predetermined departmental overhead rates with machine-hours as the allocation base in both departments.

1. What is the company's plantwide predetermined overhead rate?
2. How much manufacturing overhead was applied to Job P, and how much was applied to Job Q?

3. What is the total manufacturing cost assigned to Job P?
4. If Job P includes 20 units, what is its unit product cost?
5. What is the total manufacturing cost assigned to Job Q?
6. If Job Q includes 30 units, what is its unit product cost?
7. Assume Sweeten Company uses cost-plus pricing (and a markup percentage of 80% of total manufacturing cost) to establish selling prices for all of its jobs. What selling price would the company establish for Jobs P and Q? What are the selling prices for both jobs when stated on a per-unit basis?
8. What is Sweeten Company's cost of goods sold for the year?
9. What are the company's predetermined overhead rates in the Molding Department and the Fabrication Department?
10. How much manufacturing overhead was applied from the Molding Department to Job P, and how much was applied to Job Q?
11. How much manufacturing overhead was applied from the Fabrication Department to Job P, and how much was applied to Job Q?
12. If Job P includes 20 units, what is its unit product cost?
13. If Job Q includes 30 units, what is its unit product cost?
14. Assume Sweeten Company uses cost-plus pricing (and a markup percentage of 80% of total manufacturing cost) to establish selling prices for all of its jobs. What selling price would the company establish for Jobs P and Q? What are the selling prices for both jobs when stated on a per-unit basis?
15. What is Sweeten Company's cost of goods sold for the year?

Mc Graw Hill connect   **Exercises**

EXERCISES 2–1 Compute a Predetermined Overhead Rate LO2–1
Harris Fabrics computes its plantwide predetermined overhead rate annually based on direct labor-hours. At the beginning of the year, it estimated 20,000 direct labor-hours would be required for the period's estimated level of production. The company also estimated $94,000 of fixed manufacturing overhead cost for the coming period and variable manufacturing overhead of $2.00 per direct labor-hour. Harris's actual manufacturing overhead cost for the year was $123,900 and its actual total direct labor was 21,000 hours.

Required:
Compute the company's plantwide predetermined overhead rate.

EXERCISE 2–2 Apply Overhead Cost to Jobs LO2–2
Luthan Company uses a plantwide predetermined overhead rate of $23.40 per direct labor-hour. This predetermined rate is based on a cost formula that estimated $257,400 of total manufacturing overhead cost for an estimated activity level of 11,000 direct labor-hours.

The company incurred actual total manufacturing overhead cost of $249,000 and 10,800 total direct labor-hours.

Required:
Calculate the manufacturing overhead cost applied to all jobs.

EXERCISE 2–3 Computing Total Job Costs and Unit Product Costs Using a Plantwide Predetermined Overhead Rate LO2–3
Mickley Company's plantwide predetermined overhead rate is $14.00 per direct labor-hour and its direct labor wage rate is $17.00 per hour. The following information pertains to Job A-500:

Direct materials	$231
Direct labor	$153

Required:
1. What is the total manufacturing cost assigned to Job A-500?
2. If Job A-500 consists of 40 units, what is its unit product cost?

EXERCISE 2–4 Computing Total Job Costs and Unit Product Costs Using Multiple Predetermined Overhead Rates LO2–4

Fickel Company has two manufacturing departments—Assembly and Testing & Packaging. The predetermined overhead rates in Assembly and Testing & Packaging are $16.00 per direct labor-hour and $12.00 per direct labor-hour, respectively. The company's direct labor wage rate is $20.00 per hour. The following information pertains to Job N-60:

	Assembly	Testing & Packaging
Direct materials	$340	$25
Direct labor	$180	$40

Required:
1. What is the total manufacturing cost assigned to Job N-60?
2. If Job N-60 consists of 10 units, what is its unit product cost?

EXERCISE 2–5 Calculating Ending Inventories and Cost of Goods Sold LO2–5

Morrow Corporation had only one job in process during May—Job X32Z—and had no finished goods inventory on May 1. Job X32Z was started in April and finished during May. Data concerning that job appear below:

	Job X32Z
Beginning balance	$5,000
Charged to the job during May:	
Direct materials	$8,000
Direct labor	$2,000
Manufacturing overhead applied	$4,000
Units completed	100
Units in process at the end of May	0
Units sold during May	40

The company's total manufacturing overhead applied always equals its total actual manufacturing overhead.

Required:
1. What is the cost of goods sold for May?
2. What is the total value of the finished goods inventory at the end of May?
3. What is the total value of the work in process inventory at the end of May?

EXERCISE 2–6 Computing Total Job Costs and Unit Product Costs Using Multiple Predetermined Overhead Rates LO2–4

Braverman Company has two manufacturing departments—Finishing and Fabrication. The predetermined overhead rates in Finishing and Fabrication are $18.00 per direct labor-hour and 110% of direct materials cost, respectively. The company's direct labor wage rate is $16.00 per hour. The following information pertains to Job 700:

	Finishing	Fabrication
Direct materials	$410	$60
Direct labor	$128	$48

Required:
1. What is the total manufacturing cost assigned to Job 700?
2. If Job 700 consists of 15 units, what is its unit product cost?

EXERCISE 2–7 Job-Order Costing for a Service Company LO2–1, LO2–2, LO2–3

Tech Solutions is a consulting firm that uses job-order costing. Its direct materials consist of hardware and software it purchases and installs on behalf of its clients. The firm's direct labor includes salaries of consultants who work at the client's job site, and its overhead consists of costs such as depreciation, utilities, and insurance related to the office headquarters as well as the office supplies consumed serving clients.

Tech Solutions computes its predetermined overhead rate annually based on direct labor-hours. At the beginning of the year, it estimated 80,000 direct labor-hours would be required for the period's estimated level of client service. The company also estimated $680,000 of fixed overhead cost for the coming period and variable overhead of $0.50 per direct labor-hour. The firm's actual overhead cost for the year was $692,000 and its actual total direct labor was 83,000 hours.

Required:

1. Compute the predetermined overhead rate.
2. During the year, Tech Solutions started and completed the Xavier Company engagement. The following information was available for this job:

Direct materials	$38,000
Direct labor cost	$21,000
Direct labor-hours worked	280

Compute the total job cost for Xavier Company.

EXERCISE 2–8 Job-Order Costing; Working Backwards LO2–1, LO2–2, LO2–3

Hahn Company uses job-order costing. Its plantwide predetermined overhead rate uses direct labor-hours as the allocation base. The company pays its direct laborers $15 per hour. During the year, the company started and completed only two jobs—Job Alpha, which used 54,500 direct labor-hours, and Job Omega. The job cost sheets for these two jobs are shown below:

Job Alpha	
Direct materials	?
Direct labor	?
Manufacturing overhead applied	?
Total job cost	$1,533,500

Job Omega	
Direct materials	$235,000
Direct labor	345,000
Manufacturing overhead applied	184,000
Total job cost	$764,000

Required:

1. Calculate the plantwide predetermined overhead rate.
2. Complete the job cost sheet for Job Alpha.

EXERCISE 2–9 Applying Overhead Cost; Computing Unit Product Cost LO2–2, LO2–3

Newhard Company applies overhead cost to jobs on the basis of 125% of direct labor cost. Job 313 includes 1,000 units and its job cost sheet contains $10,000 in direct materials and $12,000 in direct labor.

Required:

What is the total manufacturing cost applied to Job 313? What is this job's unit product cost?

EXERCISE 2–10 Job-Order Costing and Decision Making LO2–1, LO2–2, LO2–3

Taveras Corporation currently operates at 50% of its available manufacturing capacity. It uses job-order costing with a plantwide predetermined overhead rate based on machine-hours. At the beginning of the year, the company made the following estimates:

Machine-hours required to support estimated production	165,000
Fixed manufacturing overhead cost	$1,980,000
Variable manufacturing overhead cost per machine hour	$2.00

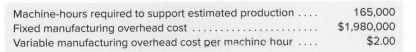

Required:

1. Compute the plantwide predetermined overhead rate.
2. During the year, Job P90 was started, completed, and sold to the customer for $2,500. The following information pertains to this job:

Direct materials	$1,150
Direct labor cost	$830
Machine-hours used	72

Compute the total manufacturing cost assigned to Job P90.

3. Upon comparing Job P90's sales revenue to its total manufacturing cost, the company's chief financial officer said, "If this exact same opportunity walked through our front door tomorrow, I'd turn it down rather than making it and selling it for $2,500."
   a. Construct an argument (supported by numerical analysis) refuting the chief financial officer's assertion.
   b. Construct an argument (accompanied by numerical analysis) supporting the chief financial officer's assertion.

EXERCISE 2–11 Applying Overhead; Calculating Ending Inventories and Cost of Goods Sold LO2–2, LO2–5

Heritage Company uses a job-order costing system to assign costs to jobs. It had no work in process or finished goods inventories on hand at the beginning of May. The table below provides data concerning the only three jobs worked on in May.

	Job X	Job Y	Job Z
Direct labor-hours	200	80	120
Direct materials.	$4,800	$1,800	$3,600
Direct labor	$2,400	$1,000	$1,500

Jobs X and Y were completed in May; however, only 150 of the 200 units included in Job X were sold in May, whereas all 100 of Job Y's units were sold in May. Job Z was not completed by the end of the month.

Overhead costs are applied to jobs based on direct labor-hours, and the predetermined overhead rate is $45 per direct labor-hour. The company's total applied overhead always equals its total actual overhead.

Required:

1. Compute the amount of overhead cost applied to each job during May.
2. Compute the work in process inventory reported in the company's May 31 balance sheet.
3. Compute the finished goods inventory reported in the company's May 31 balance sheet.
4. Compute the cost of goods sold reported in the company's income statement for May.

EXERCISE 2–12 Applying Overhead Cost to a Job LO2–2

Sigma Corporation applies overhead cost to jobs based on direct labor cost. Job V, which was started and completed during the current period, shows charges of $5,000 for direct materials, $8,000 for direct labor, and $6,000 for overhead on its job cost sheet. Job W, which is still in process at year-end, shows charges of $2,500 for direct materials and $4,000 for direct labor.

Required:

1. Should any overhead cost be applied to Job W at year-end? If so, how much? Explain.
2. How will the costs included in Job W's job cost sheet be reported within Sigma Corporation's financial statements at the end of the year?

EXERCISE 2–13 Varying Plantwide Predetermined Overhead Rates LO2–1, LO2–2, LO2–3

Kingsport Container Company makes a single product with wide seasonal variations in demand. The company uses a job-order costing system and computes plantwide predetermined overhead

rates on a quarterly basis using the number of units to be produced as the allocation base. Its estimated costs, by quarter, for the coming year are given below:

	Quarter			
	First	Second	Third	Fourth
Direct materials	$240,000	$120,000	$ 60,000	$180,000
Direct labor	128,000	64,000	32,000	96,000
Manufacturing overhead	300,000	220,000	180,000	?
Total manufacturing costs (a)	$668,000	$404,000	$272,000	$?
Number of units to be produced (b)	80,000	40,000	20,000	60,000
Estimated unit product cost (a) ÷ (b)	$8.35	$10.10	$13.60	?

Management finds the variation in quarterly unit product costs to be confusing. Accordingly, you have been asked to find a more appropriate way of applying manufacturing overhead cost to units of product.

Required:
1. Assuming the estimated variable manufacturing overhead cost per unit is $2.00, what must be the estimated total fixed manufacturing overhead cost per quarter?
2. Assuming the assumptions about cost behavior from the first three quarters hold constant, what is the estimated unit product cost for the fourth quarter?
3. What is causing the estimated unit product cost to fluctuate from one quarter to the next?
4. How would you recommend stabilizing the company's unit product cost? Support your answer with computations.

EXERCISE 2–14 Computing Predetermined Overhead Rates and Job Costs LO2–1, LO2–2, LO2–3
Moody Corporation uses a job-order costing system with a plantwide predetermined overhead rate based on machine-hours. At the beginning of the year, the company made the following estimates:

Machine-hours required to support estimated production	100,000
Fixed manufacturing overhead cost	$650,000
Variable manufacturing overhead cost per machine-hour	$3.00

Required:
1. Compute the plantwide predetermined overhead rate.
2. During the year, Job 400 was started and completed. The following information pertains to this job:

Direct materials	$450
Direct labor cost	$210
Machine-hours used	40

Compute the total manufacturing cost assigned to Job 400.
3. If Job 400 includes 52 units, what is its unit product cost?
4. If Moody uses a markup percentage of 120% of its total manufacturing cost, what selling price per unit would it establish for Job 400?
5. If Moody hired you as a consultant to critique its pricing methodology, what would you say?

EXERCISE 2–15 Departmental Predetermined Overhead Rates LO2–1, LO2–2, LO2–4
White Company has two departments, Cutting and Finishing. The company uses job-order costing and computes a predetermined overhead rate in each department. The Cutting Department bases its rate on machine-hours, and the Finishing Department bases its rate on direct labor-hours. At the beginning of the year, the company made the following estimates:

	Department	
	Cutting	Finishing
Direct labor-hours	6,000	30,000
Machine-hours	48,000	5,000
Total fixed manufacturing overhead cost	$264,000	$366,000
Variable manufacturing overhead per machine-hour	$2.00	—
Variable manufacturing overhead per direct labor-hour ...	—	$4.00

Required:

1. Compute the predetermined overhead rate for each department.
2. The job cost sheet for Job 203, which was started and completed during the year, showed the following:

	Department	
	Cutting	Finishing
Direct labor-hours	6	20
Machine-hours	80	4
Direct materials	$500	$310
Direct labor cost	$108	$360

Using the predetermined overhead rates you computed in (1) above, compute the total manufacturing cost assigned to Job 203.

3. Would you expect substantially different amounts of overhead cost to be assigned to some jobs if the company used a plantwide predetermined overhead rate based on direct labor-hours, rather than using departmental rates? Explain. No computations are necessary.

EXERCISE 2–16 Job-Order Costing for a Service Company LO2–1, LO2–2, LO2–3

Yancey Productions is a film studio that uses job-order costing. The company's direct materials include costumes and props. Its direct labor includes each film's actors, directors, and extras. The company's overhead costs include items such as utilities, depreciation of equipment, senior management salaries, and wages of maintenance workers. Yancey applies its overhead cost to films based on direct labor-dollars.

At the beginning of the year, Yancey made the following estimates:

Direct labor-dollars to support all productions	$8,000,000
Fixed overhead cost	$4,800,000
Variable overhead cost per direct labor-dollar	$0.05

Required:

1. Compute the predetermined overhead rate.
2. During the year, Yancey produced a film titled *You Can Say That Again* that incurred the following costs:

Direct materials	$1,259,000
Direct labor cost	$2,400,000

Compute the total job cost for this particular film.

EXERCISE 2–17 Plantwide and Departmental Predetermined Overhead Rates; Job Costs LO2–1, LO2–2, LO2–3, LO2–4

Delph Company uses job-order costing with a plantwide predetermined overhead rate based on machine-hours. At the beginning of the year, the company estimated that 50,000 machine-hours would be required for the period's estimated level of production. It also estimated $910,000 of fixed manufacturing overhead cost for the coming period and variable manufacturing overhead of $1.80 per machine-hour.

Because Delph has two manufacturing departments—Molding and Fabrication—it is considering replacing its plantwide overhead rate with departmental rates that would also be based on machine-hours. The company gathered the following information to enable calculating departmental overhead rates:

	Molding	Fabrication	Total
Machine-hours	20,000	30,000	50,000
Fixed manufacturing overhead cost	$700,000	$210,000	$910,000
Variable manufacturing overhead cost per machine-hour ...	$3.00	$1.00	

During the year, the company had no beginning or ending inventories and it started, completed, and sold only two jobs—Job D-70 and Job C-200. It provided the following information related to those two jobs:

Job D-70	Molding	Fabrication	Total
Direct materials cost	$375,000	$325,000	$700,000
Direct labor cost	$200,000	$160,000	$360,000
Machine-hours	14,000	6,000	20,000

Job C-200	Molding	Fabrication	Total
Direct materials cost	$300,000	$250,000	$550,000
Direct labor cost	$175,000	$225,000	$400,000
Machine-hours	6,000	24,000	30,000

Delph had no underapplied or overapplied manufacturing overhead during the year.

Required:
1. Assume Delph uses a plantwide predetermined overhead rate based on machine-hours.
   a. Compute the plantwide predetermined overhead rate.
   b. Compute the total manufacturing cost assigned to Job D-70 and Job C-200.
   c. If Delph establishes bid prices that are 150% of total manufacturing costs, what bid prices would it have established for Job D-70 and Job C-200?
   d. What is Delph's cost of goods sold for the year?
2. Assume Delph uses departmental predetermined overhead rates based on machine-hours.
   a. Compute the departmental predetermined overhead rates.
   b. Compute the total manufacturing cost assigned to Job D-70 and Job C-200.
   c. If Delph establishes bid prices that are 150% of total manufacturing cost, what bid prices would it have established for Job D-70 and Job C-200?
   d. What is Delph's cost of goods sold for the year?
3. What managerial insights are revealed by the computations that you performed in this problem? (*Hint:* Do the cost of goods sold amounts that you computed in requirements 1 and 2 differ from one another? Do the bid prices that you computed in requirements 1 and 2 differ from one another? Why?)

 connect | **Problems**

PROBLEM 2–18 Plantwide Predetermined Overhead Rates; Pricing LO2–1, LO2–2, LO2–3
Landen Corporation uses job-order costing. At the beginning of the year, it made the following estimates:

Direct labor-hours required to support estimated production	140,000
Machine-hours required to support estimated production	70,000
Fixed manufacturing overhead cost	$784,000
Variable manufacturing overhead cost per direct labor-hour	$2.00
Variable manufacturing overhead cost per machine-hour	$4.00

During the year, Job 550 was started and completed. The following information pertains to this job:

Direct materials	$175
Direct labor cost	$225
Direct labor-hours	15
Machine-hours	5

Required:

1. Assume Landen has historically used a plantwide predetermined overhead rate with direct labor-hours as the allocation base. Under this approach:
    a. Compute the plantwide predetermined overhead rate.
    b. Compute the total manufacturing cost of Job 550.
    c. If Landen uses a markup percentage of 200% of its total manufacturing cost, what selling price would it establish for Job 550?
2. Assume Landen's controller believes that machine-hours is a better allocation base than direct labor-hours. Under this approach:
    a. Compute the plantwide predetermined overhead rate.
    b. Compute the total manufacturing cost of Job 550.
    c. If Landen uses a markup percentage of 200% of its total manufacturing cost, what selling price would it establish for Job 550?
3. Assume Landen's controller is right about machine-hours being a more accurate overhead cost allocation base than direct labor-hours. If the company continues to use direct labor-hours as its only overhead cost allocation base, what implications does this have for pricing jobs such as Job 550?

PROBLEM 2–19 Plantwide and Departmental Predetermined Overhead Rates; Overhead Application LO2–1, LO2–2

Wilmington Company has two manufacturing departments—Assembly and Fabrication. All of its manufacturing overhead costs are fixed costs. The first set of data shown below is based on estimates from the beginning of the year. The second set of data relates to one particular job completed during the year—Job Bravo.

Estimated Data	Assembly	Fabrication	Total
Manufacturing overhead costs	$600,000	$800,000	$1,400,000
Direct labor-hours	50,000	30,000	80,000
Machine-hours	20,000	100,000	120,000

Job Bravo	Assembly	Fabrication	Total
Direct labor-hours	11	3	14
Machine-hours	3	6	9

Required:

1. If Wilmington uses a plantwide predetermined overhead rate based on direct labor-hours, how much manufacturing overhead would be applied to Job Bravo?
2. If Wilmington uses departmental predetermined overhead rates with direct labor-hours as the allocation base in Assembly and machine-hours as the allocation base in Fabrication, how much manufacturing overhead would be applied to Job Bravo?

PROBLEM 2–20 Job-Order Costing for a Service Company LO2–1, LO2–2, LO2–3

Speedy Auto Repairs uses job-order costing. Its direct materials consist of replacement parts installed in customer vehicles, and its direct labor consists of the mechanics' hourly wages. Speedy's overhead costs include various items, such as the shop manager's salary, depreciation of equipment, utilities, insurance, and magazine subscriptions and refreshments for the waiting room.

The company applies all of its overhead costs to jobs based on direct labor-hours. At the beginning of the year, it made the following estimates:

Direct labor-hours required to support estimated output	20,000
Fixed overhead cost	$350,000
Variable overhead cost per direct labor-hour	$1.00

Required:

1. Compute the predetermined overhead rate.
2. During the year, Mr. Wilkes brought in his vehicle to replace his brakes, spark plugs, and tires. The following information pertains to his job:

Direct materials	$590
Direct labor cost	$109
Direct labor-hours used	6

Compute Mr. Wilkes' total job cost.
3. If Speedy establishes selling prices using a markup percentage of 40% of its total job cost, then how much would it have charged Mr. Wilkes?

PROBLEM 2–21 Multiple Predetermined Overhead Rates; Applying Overhead LO2–1, LO2–2, LO2–4
High Desert Potteryworks makes a variety of pottery products that it sells to retailers. The company's job-order costing system uses departmental predetermined overhead rates to apply manufacturing overhead cost to jobs. The predetermined overhead rate in the Molding Department is based on machine-hours, and the rate in the Painting Department is based on direct labor-hours. At the beginning of the year, the company provided the following estimates:

	Department	
	Molding	Painting
Direct labor-hours	12,000	60,000
Machine-hours	70,000	8,000
Fixed manufacturing overhead cost	$497,000	$615,000
Variable manufacturing overhead per machine-hour	$1.50	–
Variable manufacturing overhead per direct labor-hour	–	$2.00

Job 205 was started on August 1 and completed on August 10. The company's cost records show the following information concerning the job:

	Department	
	Molding	Painting
Direct labor-hours	30	84
Machine-hours	110	20
Direct materials	$770	$1,332
Direct labor cost	$525	$1,470

Required:
1. Compute the predetermined overhead rates used in the Molding Department and the Painting Department.
2. Compute the total overhead cost applied to Job 205.
3. What would be the total manufacturing cost recorded for Job 205? If the job contained 50 units, what would be its unit product cost?

PROBLEM 2–22 Plantwide versus Multiple Predetermined Overhead Rates: Service Industry LO2–1, LO2–2, LO2–3, LO2–4
McCullough Hospital uses a job-order costing system to assign costs to its patients. Its direct materials include a variety of items such as pharmaceutical drugs, heart valves, artificial hips, and pacemakers. Its direct labor costs (e.g., surgeons, anesthesiologists, radiologists, and nurses) associated with specific surgical procedures and tests are traced to individual patients. All other costs, such as depreciation of medical equipment, insurance, utilities, incidental medical supplies, and the labor costs associated with around-the-clock monitoring of patients are treated as overhead costs.

Historically, McCullough has used one predetermined overhead rate based on the number of patient-days (each night a patient spends in the hospital counts as one patient-day) to allocate overhead costs to patients. For the most recent period, this predetermined rate was based on three estimates—fixed overhead costs of $17,200,000, variable overhead costs of $110 per patient-day, and a denominator volume of 20,000 patient-days.

Recently a member of the hospital's accounting staff suggested using two predetermined overhead rates (allocated based on the number of patient-days) to improve the accuracy of the costs allocated to patients. The first overhead rate would include all overhead costs within the Intensive Care Unit (ICU) and the second overhead rate would include all Other overhead costs. Information pertaining to these two cost pools and two of the hospital's patients—Patient A and Patient B—is provided below:

	ICU	Other	Total
Estimated number of patient-days ...	2,000	18,000	20,000
Estimated fixed overhead cost	$3,200,000	$14,000,000	$17,200,000
Estimated variable overhead cost			
per patient-day	$236	$96	

	Patient A	Patient B
Direct materials	$4,500	$6,200
Direct labor	$25,000	$36,000
Total number of patient-days (including ICU)	14	21
Number of patient-days spent in ICU	0	7

Required:
1. Assuming McCullough continues to use only one predetermined overhead rate, calculate:
    a.   The predetermined overhead rate.
    b.   The total cost, including direct materials, direct labor, and applied overhead, assigned to Patient A and Patient B.
2. Assuming McCullough calculates two overhead rates as recommended by the staff accountant, calculate:
    a.   The ICU and Other overhead rates.
    b.   The total cost, including direct materials, direct labor, and applied overhead, assigned to Patient A and Patient B.
3. What insights are revealed by the staff accountant's approach?

PROBLEM 2–23 Calculating Ending Inventories and Cost of Goods Sold LO2–5
Techuxia Corporation worked on four jobs during October: Job A256, Job A257, Job A258, and Job A260. At the end of October, the job cost sheets for these jobs contained the following data:

	Job A256	Job A257	Job A258	Job A260
Beginning balance	$1,200	$ 500	$ 0	$ 0
Charged to the jobs during October:				
Direct materials	$2,600	$3,500	$1,400	$3,500
Direct labor.....................	$ 800	$1,000	$ 600	$ 400
Manufacturing overhead applied...	$1,200	$1,500	$ 900	$ 600
Units completed	100	0	200	0
Units in process at the end of October	0	150	0	120
Units sold during October	80	0	40	0

Jobs A256 and A258 were completed during October. The other two jobs were incomplete at the end of October. There was no finished goods inventory on October 1. The company's total manufacturing overhead applied equals its total actual manufacturing overhead.

Required:
1. What is the cost of goods sold for October?
2. What is the total value of the finished goods inventory at the end of October?
3. What is the total value of the work in process inventory at the end of October?

PROBLEM 2–24 Plantwide versus Multiple Predetermined Overhead Rates LO2–1, LO2–2
Mason Company has two manufacturing departments—Machining and Assembly. All of the company's manufacturing overhead costs are fixed costs. It provided the following estimates at the beginning of the year as well as the following information for Jobs A and B:

Estimated Data	Machining	Assembly	Total
Manufacturing overhead	$500,000	$100,000	$600,000
Direct labor-hours	10,000	50,000	60,000
Machine-hours	50,000	5,000	55,000

Job A		Machining	Assembly	Total
Direct labor-hours	....	5	10	15
Machine-hours	....	11	2	13

Job B		Machining	Assembly	Total
Direct labor-hours	....	4	5	9
Machine-hours	....	12	3	15

Required:
1. If Mason Company uses a plantwide predetermined overhead rate with direct labor-hours as the allocation base, how much manufacturing overhead cost would be applied to Job A? Job B?
2. Assume Mason Company uses departmental predetermined overhead rates. The Machining Department is allocated based on machine-hours and the Assembly Department is allocated based on direct labor-hours. How much manufacturing overhead cost would be applied to Job A? Job B?
3. If Mason multiplies its job costs by a markup percentage to establish selling prices, how might plantwide overhead allocation adversely affect the company's pricing decisions?

PROBLEM 2–25 Calculating Ending Inventories and Cost of Goods Sold LO2–5
Expedition Company worked on five jobs during May: Jobs A10, B20, C30, D40, and E50. At the end of May, the job cost sheets for these five jobs contained the following data:

	Job A10	Job B20	Job C30	Job D40	Job E50
Beginning balance.................	$73	$90	$166	$114	$185
Charged to the jobs during May:					
Direct materials	$110	$90	$140	$110	$220
Direct labor	$90	$100	$80	$120	$150
Manufacturing overhead applied ..	$117	$130	$104	$156	$195
Units completed..................	120	0	50	0	150
Units in process at the end of May ...	0	80	0	130	0
Units sold during May	0	0	50	0	100

Jobs A10, C30, and E50 were completed during May. Jobs B20 and D40 were incomplete at the end of May. There was no finished goods inventory on May 1, and the company's total manufacturing overhead applied always equals its total actual manufacturing overhead.

Required:
1. What is the cost of goods sold for May?
2. What is the total value of the finished goods inventory at the end of May?
3. What is the total value of the work in process inventory at the end of May?

 Mc Graw Hill connect   **Case**

Select cases are available in Connect.

CASE 2–26 Plantwide versus Departmental Overhead Rates; Pricing LO2–1, LO2–2, LO2–3, LO2–4
"Blast it!" said David Wilson, president of Teledex Company. "We've just lost the bid on the Koopers job by $2,000. It seems we're either too high to get the job or too low to make any money on half the jobs we bid."

Teledex Company manufactures products to customers' specifications and uses job-order costing. The company uses a plantwide predetermined overhead rate based on direct labor cost to apply manufacturing overhead (assumed to be all fixed) to jobs. The following estimates were made at the beginning of the year:

	Department			
	Fabricating	Machining	Assembly	Total Plant
Manufacturing overhead	$350,000	$400,000	$90,000	$840,000
Direct labor	$200,000	$100,000	$300,000	$600,000

Jobs require varying amounts of work in the three departments. The Koopers job, for example, would have required manufacturing costs in the three departments as follows:

	Department			
	Fabricating	Machining	Assembly	Total Plant
Direct materials	$3,000	$200	$1,400	$4,600
Direct labor	$2,800	$500	$6,200	$9,500
Manufacturing overhead	?	?	?	?

Required:
1. Using the company's plantwide approach:
    a. Compute the plantwide predetermined overhead rate for the current year.
    b. Determine the amount of manufacturing overhead cost applied to the Koopers job.
2. Suppose instead of using a plantwide predetermined overhead rate, the company had used departmental predetermined overhead rates based on direct labor cost. Under these conditions:
    a. Compute the predetermined overhead rate for each department for the current year.
    b. Determine the amount of manufacturing overhead cost applied to the Koopers job.
3. Explain the difference between the manufacturing overhead applied to the Koopers job using the plantwide approach in question 1(b) and using the departmental approach in question 2(b).
4. Assume it is customary in the industry to bid jobs at 150% of total manufacturing cost (direct materials, direct labor, and applied overhead). What was the company's bid price on the Koopers job using a plantwide predetermined overhead rate? What would have been the bid price if departmental predetermined overhead rates were used to apply overhead cost?

Appendix 2A: Activity-Based Absorption Costing

LO2–6
Use activity-based absorption costing to compute unit product costs.

Chapter 2 described how manufacturing companies use traditional absorption costing systems to calculate unit product costs. In this appendix, we contrast traditional absorption costing with an alternative approach called *activity-based absorption costing*. **Activity-based absorption costing** assigns all manufacturing overhead costs to products based on the *activities* performed to make those products. An **activity** is an event causing the consumption of manufacturing overhead resources. Rather than relying on plantwide or departmental cost pools, the activity-based approach accumulates each activity's overhead costs in *activity cost pools*. An **activity cost pool** is a "bucket" that accumulates costs related to a single activity. Each activity cost pool has one *activity measure*. An **activity measure** is an allocation base used as the denominator for an activity cost pool. The costs accumulated in the numerator of an activity cost pool divided by the quantity of the activity measure in its denominator equals an *activity rate*. An activity rate is used to assign costs from an activity cost pool to products.

Activity-based absorption costing differs from traditional absorption costing in two ways. First, the activity-based approach uses more cost pools than a traditional approach. Second, the activity-based approach includes some activities and activity measures that *do not* relate to the volume of units produced, whereas the traditional approach relies exclusively on allocation bases that are driven by the volume of production. For example, the activity-based approach may include *batch-level activities*. A **batch-level activity** is performed each time a batch is handled or processed, regardless of how many units are in the batch. Batch-level activities include tasks such as placing purchase orders, setting up equipment, and transporting batches of component parts. Costs at the batch level depend on the number of batches processed rather than the number of units produced. The activity-based approach may also include *product-level activities*. A **product-level activity** relates to specific products and must be carried out regardless of how many batches are run or units of product are produced. Product-level activities include tasks

EXHIBIT 2A–1
Maxtar Industries' Traditional
Costing System

Basic Data		
Total estimated manufacturing overhead cost	$1,520,000	
Total estimated direct labor-hours	400,000 DLHs	

	Premium	Standard
Direct materials per unit	$40.00	$30.00
Direct labor per unit	$24.00	$18.00
Direct labor-hours per unit	2.0 DLHs	1.5 DLHs
Units produced	50,000 units	200,000 units

Computation of the Plantwide Predetermined Overhead Rate

$$\text{Predetermined overhead rate} = \frac{\text{Total estimated manufacturing overhead}}{\text{Total estimated amount of the allocation base}}$$

$$= \frac{\$1,520,000}{400,000 \text{ DLHs}} = \$3.80 \text{ per DLH}$$

Traditional Unit Product Costs

	Premium	Standard
Direct materials	$40.00	$30.00
Direct labor	24.00	18.00
Manufacturing overhead (2.0 DLHs × $3.80 per DLH; 1.5 DLHs × $3.80 per DLH)	7.60	5.70
Unit product cost	$71.60	$53.70

such as designing a product and making engineering design changes to a product. Costs at the product-level depend on the number of products supported rather than the number of batches run or the number of units produced.

To illustrate the differences between traditional and activity-based absorption costing, we'll use an example focused on Maxtar Industries, a manufacturer of high-quality smoker/barbecue units. The company has two product lines—Premium and Standard. The company has traditionally applied manufacturing overhead costs to these products using a plantwide predetermined overhead rate based on direct labor-hours. Exhibit 2A–1 shows how the company's traditional costing system computes unit product costs for the two products—$71.60 for Premium and $53.70 for Standard.

Maxtar Industries recently experimented with an activity-based absorption costing system with three activity cost pools: (1) supporting direct labor; (2) setting up machines; and (3) parts administration. The top of Exhibit 2A–2 displays data concerning these activity cost pools. Note the total estimated overhead cost in these three costs pools, $1,520,000, agrees with the total estimated overhead cost in the company's traditional costing system. The company's activity-based approach simply provides an alternative way to allocate the company's manufacturing overhead across the two products.

The activity rates for the three activity cost pools are computed in the second table in Exhibit 2A–2. For example, the total cost in the "setting up machines" activity cost pool, $480,000, is divided by the total activity for that cost pool, 800 setups, to determine the activity rate of $600 per setup.

The activity rates are used to allocate overhead costs to the two products in the third table in Exhibit 2A–2. For example, the activity rate for the "setting up machines" activity cost pool, $600 per setup, is multiplied by the Premium product line's 600 setups to determine the $360,000 machine setup cost allocated to the Premium product line.

EXHIBIT 2A–2
Maxtar Industries' Activity-Based
Absorption Costing System

Basic Data

Activity Cost Pools and Activity Measures	Estimated Overhead Cost	Expected Activity		
		Premium	Standard	Total
Supporting direct labor (DLHs)	$ 800,000	100,000	300,000	400,000
Setting up machines (setups)	480,000	600	200	800
Parts administration (part types)	240,000	140	60	200
Total manufacturing overhead cost ...	$1,520,000			

Computation of Activity Rates

Activity Cost Pools	(a) Estimated Overhead Cost	(b) Total Expected Activity	(a) ÷ (b) Activity Rate
Supporting direct labor ...	$800,000	400,000 DLHs	$2 per DLH
Setting up machines	$480,000	800 setups	$600 per setup
Parts administration	$240,000	200 part types	$1,200 per part type

Assigning Overhead Costs to Products

The Premium Product

Activity Cost Pools	(a) Activity Rate	(b) Activity	(a) × (b) ABC Cost
Supporting direct labor ...	$2 per DLH	100,000 DLHs	$200,000
Setting up machines	$600 per setup	600 setups	360,000
Parts administration	$1,200 per part type	140 part types	168,000
Total			$728,000

The Standard Product

Activity Cost Pools	(a) Activity Rate	(b) Activity	(a) × (b) ABC Cost
Supporting direct labor ...	$2 per DLH	300,000 DLHs	$600,000
Setting up machines	$600 per setup	200 setups	120,000
Parts administration	$1,200 per part type	60 part types	72,000
Total			$792,000

Activity-Based Absorption Costing Product Costs

	Premium	Standard
Direct materials	$40.00	$30.00
Direct labor	24.00	18.00
Manufacturing overhead ($728,000 ÷ 50,000 units; $792,000 ÷ 200,000 units)	14.56	3.96
Unit product cost	$78.56	$51.96

The table at the bottom of Exhibit 2A–2 displays the overhead costs per-unit and the activity-based unit product costs. The overhead cost per-unit is determined by dividing the total overhead cost by the number of units produced. For example, the Premium product line's total overhead cost of $728,000 is divided by 50,000 units to determine the $14.56

overhead cost per-unit. Note the unit product costs differ from those computed using the company's traditional costing system in Exhibit 2A–1. Because the activity-based approach contains both batch-level (setting up machines) and product-level (parts administration) activity cost pools, the unit product costs under the activity-based approach follow the usual pattern in which overhead costs are shifted from the high-volume to the low-volume product. The unit product cost of the Standard product, the high-volume product, has gone down from $53.70 under the traditional costing system to $51.96 under activity-based costing. In contrast, the unit product cost of the Premium product, the low-volume product, has increased from $71.60 under the traditional costing system to $78.56 under activity-based costing. Instead of using direct labor-hours (which moves in tandem with the volume of the production) to assign all manufacturing overhead costs to products, the activity-based approach uses a batch-level activity measure and a product-level activity measure to assign the batch-level and product-level activity cost pools to the two products.

Glossary (Appendix 2A)

Activity An event causing the consumption of overhead resources. (p. 92)

Activity cost pool A "bucket" that accumulates costs related to a single activity measure in an activity-based costing system. (p. 92)

Activity measure An allocation base in an activity-based costing system; ideally, a measure of the amount of activity that drives the costs in an activity cost pool. (p. 92)

Activity-based absorption costing A costing method that assigns all manufacturing overhead costs to products based on the *activities* performed to make those products. (p. 92)

Batch-level activity An activity performed each time a batch is handled or processed, regardless of how many units are in the batch. The amount of resources consumed depends on the number of batches run rather than the number of units produced. (p. 92)

Product-level activity An activity related to specific products that is performed regardless of how many batches are run or units produced. (p. 92)

McGraw Hill connect Appendix 2A: Exercises, Problems, and Case

EXERCISE 2A–1 Activity-Based Absorption Costing LO2–6

Fogerty Company makes two products—Hubs and Sprockets. Data regarding the two products follow:

	Direct Labor-Hours per Unit	Annual Production
Hubs	0.80	10,000 units
Sprockets	0.40	40,000 units

Additional information about the company follows:
a. Hubs require $32 in direct materials per unit, and Sprockets require $18.
b. The direct labor wage rate is $15 per hour.
c. Hubs are more complex to manufacture than Sprockets and require special processing.
d. The company's activity-based absorption costing system has the following activity cost pools:

	Estimated Overhead Cost	Expected Activity		
Activity Cost Pool (and Activity Measure)		Hubs	Sprockets	Total
Machine setups (number of setups)	$72,000	100	300	400
Special processing (machine-hours)	$200,000	5,000	0	5,000
General factory (direct labor-hours)	$816,000	8,000	16,000	24,000

Required:
1. Compute the activity rate for each activity cost pool.
2. Compute the unit product cost for Hubs and Sprockets using activity-based absorption costing.

EXERCISE 2A–2 Activity-Based Absorption Costing as an Alternative to Traditional Product Costing LO2–6

Harrison Company makes two products and uses a traditional costing system in which a single plantwide predetermined overhead rate is computed based on direct labor-hours. Data for the two products for the upcoming year follow:

	Rascon	Parcel
Direct materials cost per unit	$13.00	$22.00
Direct labor cost per unit	$6.00	$3.00
Direct labor-hours per unit	0.40	0.20
Number of units produced	20,000	80,000

These products are customized to some degree for specific customers.

Required:
1. The company's estimated manufacturing overhead costs for the year are $576,000. Using the company's traditional costing system, compute the unit product costs for both products.
2. Management is considering an activity-based absorption costing system in which half of the overhead would continue to be allocated based on direct labor-hours and half would be allocated based on the following engineering design times:

	Rascon	Parcel	Total
Engineering design time (in hours)	3,000	3,000	6,000

Compute unit product costs for both products using the proposed activity-based absorption costing system.
3. Explain why the product costs differ between the two systems.

EXERCISE 2A–3 Activity-Based Absorption Costing as an Alternative to Traditional Product Costing LO2–6

Stillicum Corporation makes ultralightweight backpacking tents. Data concerning the company's two product lines appear below:

	Deluxe	Standard
Direct materials per unit	$72.00	$53.00
Direct labor per unit	$19.00	$15.20
Direct labor-hours per unit	1.0 DLHs	0.8 DLH
Estimated annual production	10,000 units	50,000 units

The company's traditional costing system applies manufacturing overhead to products using direct labor-hours and the following estimates:

Estimated total manufacturing overhead	$325,000
Estimated total direct labor-hours	50,000 DLHs

Required:
1. Determine unit product costs for the Deluxe and Standard products under the company's traditional costing system.
2. The company is considering replacing its traditional costing system with an activity-based absorption costing system containing three activity cost pools:

Activity Cost Pools (and Activity Measures)	Estimated Overhead Cost	Expected Activity		
		Deluxe	Standard	Total
Supporting direct labor (direct labor-hours)	$200,000	10,000	40,000	50,000
Batch setups (setups)	75,000	200	100	300
Safety testing (tests)	50,000	30	70	100
Total manufacturing overhead cost	$325,000			

Calculate unit product costs for the Deluxe and Standard products under the activity-based absorption costing system.

PROBLEM 2A–4 Activity-Based Absorption Costing as an Alternative to Traditional Product Costing LO2–6

Ellix Company manufactures two models of ultra-high fidelity speakers—the X200 model and the X99 model. Data regarding the two products follow:

Product	Direct Labor-Hours	Annual Production	Total Direct Labor-Hours
X200	1.8 DLHs per unit	5,000 units	9,000 DLHs
X99	0.9 DLHs per unit	30,000 units	27,000 DLHs
			36,000 DLHs

Additional information about the company follows:
a. Model X200 requires $72 in direct materials per unit, and model X99 requires $50.
b. The direct labor workers are paid $20 per hour.
c. The company has always used direct labor-hours as the allocation base for applying manufacturing overhead cost to products.
d. Model X200 is more complex to manufacture than model X99 and requires special equipment.
e. Because of the special work required in (d) above, the company is considering an activity-based absorption costing system that applies manufacturing overhead cost to products using three activity cost pools:

Activity Cost Pool	Activity Measure	Estimated Total Cost	Estimated Total Activity		
			X200	X99	Total
Machine setups	Number of setups	$ 360,000	50	100	150
Special processing	Machine-hours	180,000	12,000	0	12,000
General factory	Direct labor-hours	1,260,000	9,000	27,000	36,000
		$1,800,000			

Required:
1. Assume the company continues applying overhead costs to products using direct labor-hours.
   a. Compute the plantwide predetermined overhead rate.
   b. Compute each model's unit product cost.

2. Assume the company decides to apply overhead cost to products using activity-based absorption costing.
   a. Compute the activity rate for each activity cost pool and determine the amount of overhead cost applied to each model.
   b. Compute each model's unit product cost.
3. Explain why overhead cost shifted from the high-volume model to the low-volume model under the activity-based approach.

PROBLEM 2A–5 Activity-Based Absorption Costing as an Alternative to Traditional Product Costing LO2–6

Siegel Company manufactures a product available in a deluxe model and a regular model. The company has manufactured the regular model for years. The deluxe model was introduced several years ago to tap a new segment of the market. Since introduction of the deluxe model, the company's profits have steadily declined and management has become increasingly concerned about the accuracy of its costing system. Sales of the deluxe model have been increasing rapidly.

Manufacturing overhead is assigned to products based on direct labor-hours. For the current year, the company estimated it will incur $900,000 in manufacturing overhead cost and produce 5,000 units of the deluxe model and 40,000 units of the regular model. The deluxe model requires two direct labor-hours per unit, and the regular model requires one direct labor-hour. Material and labor costs per-unit are as follows:

	Model	
	Deluxe	Regular
Direct materials	$40	$25
Direct labor	$38	$19

Required:

1. Compute the predetermined overhead rate using direct labor-hours as the allocation base and calculate the unit product cost of each model.
2. Management is considering using activity-based absorption costing to apply manufacturing overhead cost to products. The activity-based system would have four activity cost pools:

Activity Cost Pool	Activity Measure	Estimated Overhead Cost
Purchasing	Purchase orders issued	$204,000
Processing	Machine-hours	182,000
Scrap/rework	Scrap/rework orders issued	379,000
Shipping	Number of shipments	135,000
		$900,000

Activity Measure	Expected Activity		
	Deluxe	Regular	Total
Purchase orders issued	200	400	600
Machine-hours	20,000	15,000	35,000
Scrap/rework orders issued	1,000	1,000	2,000
Number of shipments	250	650	900

   Calculate an activity rate for each of the four activity cost pools.
3. Using the activity rates from part (2):
   a. Compute the total manufacturing overhead cost applied to each model. Also, calculate each model's manufacturing overhead cost per unit.
   b. Compute each model's unit product cost (including direct materials, direct labor, and manufacturing overhead).
4. From the data you developed in parts (1) through (3), explain what may account for the company's declining profits.

CASE 2A–6 Activity-Based Absorption Costing and Pricing LO2–6

Java Source, Inc., (JSI) roasts, blends, and packages coffee beans for resale. Some of JSI's coffees sell in large volumes, while some newer blends sell in very low volumes. JSI prices its coffees at manufacturing cost plus a markup of 25%.

For next year, JSI's budget includes estimated manufacturing overhead cost of $2,200,000. JSI allocates manufacturing overhead to products using direct labor-hours. The expected direct labor cost totals $600,000, which represents 50,000 hours of direct labor time.

The expected direct materials and direct labor costs for one-pound bags of two of the company's coffee blends appear below.

	Kenya Dark	Viet Select
Direct materials	$4.50	$2.90
Direct labor (0.02 hour per bag)	$0.34	$0.34

JSI's controller believes the company's traditional costing system may be providing misleading cost information; therefore, he gathered the following activity-based cost information:

Activity Cost Pool	Activity Measure	Expected Activity for the Year	Expected Cost for the Year
Purchasing	Purchase orders	2,000 orders	$ 560,000
Material handling	Number of setups	1,000 setups	193,000
Quality control	Number of batches	500 batches	90,000
Roasting	Roasting hours	95,000 roasting hours	1,045,000
Blending	Blending hours	32,000 blending hours	192,000
Packaging	Packaging hours	24,000 packaging hours	120,000
Total manufacturing overhead cost			$2,200,000

Data regarding the expected production and sales of Kenya Dark and Viet Select coffee are presented below.

	Kenya Dark	Viet Select
Expected production and sales	80,000 pounds	4,000 pounds
Batch size	5,000 pounds	500 pounds
Setups	2 per batch	2 per batch
Purchase order size	20,000 pounds	500 pounds
Roasting time per 100 pounds	1.5 roasting hours	1.5 roasting hours
Blending time per 100 pounds	0.5 blending hour	0.5 blending hour
Packaging time per 100 pounds	0.3 packaging hour	0.3 packaging hour

Required:

1. Using direct labor-hours as the manufacturing overhead cost allocation base:
   a. Calculate the plantwide predetermined overhead rate.
   b. Calculate the unit product cost of one pound of Kenya Dark and one pound of Viet Select.
2. Using the activity-based absorption costing approach:
   a. Calculate the total manufacturing overhead cost allocated to Kenya Dark and Viet Select.
   b. Using the data developed in (2a) above, compute Kenya Dark's and Viet Select's manufacturing overhead cost per pound.
   c. Calculate the unit product cost of one pound of Kenya Dark and one pound of Viet Select.
3. Write a brief memo to the president of JSI explaining what you found in (1) and (2) above and discussing the implications of using direct labor-hours as the company's only manufacturing overhead cost allocation base.

(CMA, adapted)

Appendix 2B: The Predetermined Overhead Rate and Capacity

LO2–7

Understand the implications of basing the predetermined overhead rate on activity at capacity rather than on estimated activity for the period.

This appendix contrasts two methods of computing predetermined overhead rates. The first method (which was used throughout the chapter) demonstrates the absorption costing approach used for external reporting purposes.[2] It bases the denominator volume for overhead rates on the estimated, or budgeted, amount of the allocation base for the upcoming period. The second method, often used for internal management purposes, bases the denominator volume for overhead rates on the estimated total amount of the allocation base at capacity. To simplify our forthcoming comparison of these two methods, we make two important assumptions that will hold true throughout the entire appendix: (1) all manufacturing overhead costs are fixed and (2) the estimated, or budgeted, fixed manufacturing overhead at the beginning of the period equals the actual fixed manufacturing overhead at the end of the period.

Let's assume Prahad Corporation manufactures DVDs for local production studios. The company's DVD duplicating machine can produce a new DVD every 10 seconds from a master DVD. The company leases the DVD duplicating machine for a fixed cost of $180,000 per year, and this is the company's only estimated (and actual) manufacturing overhead cost. With allowances for setups and maintenance, the machine is theoretically capable of producing up to 900,000 DVDs per year. However, due to a business downturn, Prahad's customers are unlikely to order more than 600,000 DVDs next year. The company uses machine time as the allocation base for applying manufacturing overhead to DVDs. These data are summarized below:

Prahad Corporation Data	
Total estimated and actual manufacturing overhead cost ..	$180,000 per year
Allocation base—machine time per DVD	10 seconds per DVD
Capacity	900,000 DVDs per year
Budgeted output for next year	600,000 DVDs

If Prahad uses the first method mentioned above, which computes predetermined overhead rates using the estimated or budgeted activity for the period, then its predetermined overhead rate for next year would be $0.03 per second of machine time computed as follows:

$$\frac{\text{Predetermined}}{\text{overhead rate}} = \frac{\text{Estimated total manufacturing overhead cost}}{\text{Estimated total amount of the allocation base}}$$

$$= \frac{\$180,000}{600,000 \text{ DVDs} \times 10 \text{ seconds per DVD}}$$

$$= \$0.03 \text{ per second}$$

Because each DVD requires 10 seconds of machine time, each DVD will be allocated $0.30 of overhead cost.

While this absorption approach is commonly used for external reporting purposes, it has two important limitations from a managerial accounting standpoint. First, if predetermined overhead rates are based on budgeted activity and overhead includes significant fixed costs, then the unit product costs will fluctuate depending on the budgeted level of activity for the period. For example, if Prahad's budgeted output for the year was only

---

[2] Statement of Financial Accounting Standards No. 151: *Inventory Costs* and International Accounting Standard 2: *Inventories* require allocating fixed manufacturing overhead costs to products based on normal capacity. Normal capacity reflects the level of output expected to be produced over numerous periods under normal circumstances. This definition mirrors the language used in this book that refers to basing the predetermined overhead rate on the estimated, or budgeted, amount of the allocation base for the upcoming period.

300,000 DVDs (instead of 600,000 DVDs), its predetermined overhead rate would be $0.06 per second of machine time or $0.60 per DVD rather than $0.30 per DVD. Notice as the company's budgeted output falls, its overhead cost per unit increases. This in turn makes it appear the cost of producing DVDs has increased, which may tempt managers to raise prices at the worst possible time—just as demand is falling.

The second limitation of the absorption approach is charging products for resources they don't use. When the fixed costs of capacity are spread over estimated activity, the units produced absorb the costs of any unused capacity. If the level of activity falls, fewer products must absorb a growing share of idle capacity cost that inflates their actual product costs.

Basing the predetermined overhead rate on the estimated total amount of the allocation base at capacity overcomes the two limitations just discussed. It is computed as follows[3]:

$$\text{Predetermined overhead rate based on capacity} = \frac{\text{Estimated total manufacturing overhead cost at capacity}}{\text{Estimated total amount of the allocation base at capacity}}$$

$$= \frac{\$180,000}{900,000 \text{ DVDs} \times 10 \text{ seconds per DVD}}$$

$$= \$0.02 \text{ per second}$$

When Prahad bases its predetermined overhead rate on activity at capacity, its overhead rate is $0.02 per second instead of $0.03 per second as computed under the absorption approach. Consequently, the overhead cost Prahad will apply to each DVD using the capacity-based approach would be $0.20 (= $0.02 × 10 seconds) per unit instead of $0.30 per unit under the absorption method. Notice the capacity-based amounts per second and per unit are lower than the absorption-based amounts. This occurs because the capacity-based approach uses a higher denominator volume that reflects Prahad's capacity to produce DVDs—9,000,000 seconds.

Prahad's capacity-based rate of $0.02 per second will remain constant even if its budgeted level of activity fluctuates from one period to another. So, if the company's estimated level of activity drops from 600,000 DVDs to 300,000 DVDs, its capacity-based rate stays at $0.02 per second. The company's unused capacity cost increases in this situation, but its unit cost to make DVDs stays constant at $0.20 per unit.

Whenever a company operates at less than full capacity and allocates fixed overhead costs using a capacity-based denominator volume, it will report unused capacity cost computed as follows:

$$\text{Cost of unused capacity} = \left(\begin{array}{c} \text{Amount of the allocation} \\ \text{base at capacity} \end{array} - \begin{array}{c} \text{Actual amount of the} \\ \text{allocation base} \end{array} \right) \times \begin{array}{c} \text{Predetermined} \\ \text{overhead rate} \end{array}$$

For example, let's assume Prahad Company actually used 6,000,000 seconds on the DVD duplicating machine to produce 600,000 DVDs. At this level of output, the company would compute its cost of unused capacity as follows:

$$\text{Cost of unused capacity} = \left(\begin{array}{c} \text{Amount of the allocation} \\ \text{base at capacity} \end{array} - \begin{array}{c} \text{Actual amount of the} \\ \text{allocation base} \end{array} \right) \times \begin{array}{c} \text{Predetermined} \\ \text{overhead rate} \end{array}$$

$$\text{Cost of unused capacity} = (9,000,000 \text{ seconds} - 6,000,000 \text{ seconds}) \times \$0.02 \text{ per second}$$

$$\text{Cost of unused capacity} = 3,000,000 \text{ seconds} \times \$0.02 \text{ per second}$$

$$\text{Cost of unused capacity} = \$60,000$$

---

[3] Ordinarily, because of variable overhead costs, the estimated total manufacturing overhead cost at capacity will be larger than the estimated total manufacturing overhead cost at the estimated level of activity. However, for simplicity, we assume in this appendix that all overhead costs are fixed. Then the total manufacturing overhead cost will be the same regardless of the level of activity.

EXHIBIT 2B–1
Prahad Corporation: An Income
Statement That Recognizes the Cost
of Unused Capacity

Prahad Corporation
Income Statement
For the Year Ended December 31

Sales[1]		$1,200,000
Cost of goods sold[2]		1,080,000
Gross margin		120,000
Other expenses:		
Cost of unused capacity	$60,000	
Selling and administrative expenses[3]	90,000	150,000
Net operating loss		$ (30,000)

[1] Assume sales of 600,000 CDs at $2 per CD.
[2] Assume the unit product cost of the CDs is $1.80, including $0.20 for manufacturing overhead.
[3] Assume selling and administrative expenses total $90,000.

Exhibit 2B–1 illustrates how Prahad would disclose this cost of unused capacity ($60,000) within an income statement prepared for internal management purposes. Rather than treating it as a product cost (as is done in the absorption approach), Prahad's capacity-based approach treats this cost as a period expense reported below the gross margin. By separately disclosing the *Cost of unused capacity* as a lump sum of $60,000 on the income statement, instead of burying it in Cost of Goods Sold, the need to effectively manage capacity is highlighted for the company's managers. Generally speaking, a company's managers should respond to large unused capacity costs by either seeking new business opportunities that consume the capacity or cutting costs and shrinking the amount of available capacity.

Appendix 2B: Exercises, Problem, and Case

EXERCISE 2B–1 Overhead Rate Based on Capacity LO2–7
Wixis Cabinets makes custom wooden cabinets for high-end stereo systems from specialty woods. The company uses a job-order costing system. The capacity of the plant is determined by the capacity of its constraint, which is time on the automated bandsaw that makes finely beveled cuts in wood according to the preprogrammed specifications of each cabinet. The bandsaw can operate up to 180 hours per month. The estimated total manufacturing overhead cost at capacity is $14,760 per month. The company bases its predetermined overhead rate on capacity, so its predetermined overhead rate is $82 per hour of bandsaw use.

The results of a recent month's operations appear below:

Sales	$43,740
Beginning inventories	$0
Ending inventories	$0
Direct materials	$5,350
Direct labor	$8,860
Manufacturing overhead incurred	$14,760
Selling and administrative expense	$8,180
Actual hours of bandsaw use	150

Required:
1. Prepare an income statement following the example in Exhibit 2B–1 that records the cost of unused capacity as a period expense.
2. Why do unused capacity costs arise when the predetermined overhead rate is based on capacity?

EXERCISE 2B–2 Overhead Rates and Capacity Issues LO2–1, LO2–2, LO2–7

Security Pension Services helps clients set up and administer pension plans in compliance with tax laws and regulatory requirements. The firm uses a job-order costing system that applies overhead to clients' accounts based on professional staff hours charged to the accounts. Data concerning two recent years appear below:

	Last Year	This Year
Estimated professional staff hours to be charged to clients' accounts	4,600	4,500
Estimated overhead cost	$310,500	$310,500
Professional staff hours available	6,000	6,000

"Professional staff hours available" is a measure of the firm's capacity. Any available hours not charged to clients represent unused capacity. All of the firm's overhead is fixed.

Required:

1. Marta Brinksi is an established client whose pension plan was set up many years ago. In both this year and last year, only 2.5 hours of professional staff time were charged to Ms. Brinksi's account. If the company bases its predetermined overhead rate on the estimated overhead cost and the estimated professional staff hours to be charged to clients, how much overhead cost would have been applied to Ms. Brinksi's account last year? This year?

2. Suppose the company bases its predetermined overhead rate on the estimated overhead cost and the estimated professional staff hours to be charged to clients as in (1) above. Also, suppose the actual professional staff hours charged to clients and the actual overhead costs turn out to be exactly as estimated in both years. How much unused capacity cost would the company report last year? How about for this year?

3. Refer back to the data concerning Ms. Brinksi in (1) above. If the company bases its predetermined overhead rate on the *professional staff hours available,* how much overhead cost would have been applied to Ms. Brinksi's account last year? This year?

4. Suppose the company bases its predetermined overhead rate on the professional staff hours available as in (3) above. Also, suppose the actual professional staff hours charged to clients and the actual overhead costs turn out to be exactly as estimated in both years. How much unused capacity cost would the company report last year? How about for this year?

PROBLEM 2B–3 Predetermined Overhead Rate and Capacity LO2–1, LO2–2, LO2–7

Platinum Web Services designs and maintains websites for small business entrepreneurs. Competition has been intensifying in recent years and the company is losing business to larger web design firms. Summary data concerning the last two years of operations follow:

	Last Year	This Year
Estimated hours of service demanded	1,000	800
Estimated overhead cost	$160,000	$160,000
Actual hours of service provided	750	500
Actual overhead cost incurred	$160,000	$160,000
Hours of service available at capacity	1,600	1,600

The company applies its overhead costs to jobs using the hours of service provided as the allocation base. For example, this year and last year, 40 service-hours were required to maintain the website for a small company called *Verde Consulting.* All of Platinum's overhead costs are fixed, and the actual overhead cost incurred was exactly as estimated at the beginning of the year in last year and this year.

Required:

1. Platinum Web Services computes its predetermined overhead rate at the beginning of each year based on the estimated overhead cost and the estimated hours of service demanded for the year. Using this approach, how much overhead would have been applied to the Verde Consulting job last year? How about this year?

2. The president of Platinum Web Services heard some companies in the industry changed to a system of computing the predetermined overhead rate based on the hours of service available at capacity. He would like to know what effect this method would have on job costs. How much overhead cost would have been applied to the Verde Consulting job last year using this method? How much would have been applied his year?

3. If Platinum computes its predetermined overhead rate based on the hours of service available at capacity as in (2) above, how much unused capacity cost would the company have incurred last year? This year?

4. What business problem is Platinum Web Services facing? Which method of computing the predetermined overhead rate is likely to be more helpful in addressing this problem? Explain.

CASE 2B–4 Ethics; Predetermined Overhead Rate and Capacity LO2–2, LO2–7

Pat Miranda, the new controller of Vault Hard Drives, Inc., just returned from a seminar on the choice of activity level in the predetermined overhead rate. Even though the subject did not sound exciting at first, she found there were some important ideas presented that should get a hearing at her company. After returning from the seminar, she arranged a meeting with the production manager, J. Stevens, and the assistant production manager, Marvin Washington.

Pat: I ran across an idea I wanted to share with both of you. It's about the way we compute predetermined overhead rates.

J.: We're all ears.

Pat: We compute the predetermined overhead rate by dividing the estimated total factory overhead for the coming year, which is all a fixed cost, by the estimated total units produced for the coming year.

Marvin: We've been doing that as long as I've been with the company.

J.: And it has been done that way at every other company I've worked at, except at most places they divide by direct labor-hours.

Pat: We use units because it is simpler and we make one product with minor variations. But there's another way to do it. Instead of basing the overhead rate on the estimated total units produced for the coming year, we could base it on the total units produced at capacity.

Marvin: Oh, the Marketing Department will love that. It will drop the costs on all of our products. They'll go wild cutting prices.

Pat: That is a worry, but I wanted to talk to both of you first before going over to Marketing.

J.: Aren't you always going to have a lot of unused capacity costs?

Pat: That's correct, but let me show you how we would handle it. Here's an example based on our budget for next year.

Budgeted (estimated) production	160,000 units
Budgeted sales	160,000 units
Capacity	200,000 units
Selling price	$60 per unit
Variable manufacturing cost	$15 per unit
Total manufacturing overhead cost (all fixed)	$4,000,000
Selling and administrative expenses (all fixed)	$2,700,000
Beginning inventories	$0

Traditional Approach to Computation of the Predetermined Overhead Rate

$$\frac{\text{Estimated total manufacturing overhead cost, } \$4,000,000}{\text{Estimated total units produced, } 160,000} = \$25 \text{ per unit}$$

Budgeted Income Statement		
Revenue (160,000 units × $60 per unit)		$9,600,000
Cost of goods sold:		
Variable manufacturing (160,000 units × $15 per unit)	$2,400,000	
Manufacturing overhead applied (160,000 units × $25 per unit)	4,000,000	6,400,000
Gross margin		3,200,000
Selling and administrative expenses		2,700,000
Net operating income		$ 500,000

New Approach to Computation of the Predetermined Overhead Rate
Using Capacity in the Denominator

$$\frac{\text{Estimated total manufacturing overhead cost at capacity, \$4,000,000}}{\text{Total units at capacity, 200,000}} = \$20 \text{ per unit}$$

Budgeted Income Statement		
Revenue (160,000 units × $60 per unit)		$9,600,000
Cost of goods sold:		
Variable manufacturing (160,000 units × $15 per unit)	$2,400,000	
Manufacturing overhead applied		
(160,000 units × $20 per unit)	3,200,000	5,600,000
Gross margin		4,000,000
Cost of unused capacity [(200,000 units − 160,000 units)		
× $20 per unit]		800,000
Selling and administrative expenses		2,700,000
Net operating income		$ 500,000

J.: Whoa!! I don't think I like the looks of that "Cost of unused capacity." If that expense shows up on the income statement, someone from headquarters is likely to come down here looking for people to lay off.

Marvin: I'm worried about something else too. What happens when sales don't meet expectations? Can we pull the "hat trick"?

Pat: I'm sorry, I don't understand.

J.: Marvin's talking about something that happens fairly regularly. When sales are down and profits are going to be lower than the president told the owners they were going to be, the president comes down here and asks us to deliver some more profits.

Marvin: And we pull them out of our hat.

J.: Yeah, we just increase production until we get the profits we want.

Pat: I still don't understand. You mean you increase sales?

J.: Nope, we increase production. We're the production managers, not the sales managers.

Pat: I get it. Because you have produced more, the sales force has more units it can sell.

J.: Nope, the marketing people don't do a thing. We just build inventories and that does the trick.

Required:
In all of the questions below, assume the predetermined overhead rate under the traditional method is $25 per unit, and under the new capacity-based method it is $20 per unit.

1. Assume actual sales is 150,000 units and the actual production in units, actual selling price, actual variable manufacturing cost per unit, and actual fixed costs all equal their respective budgeted amounts. Given these assumptions:
   a. Compute net operating income using the traditional income statement format.
   b. Compute net operating income using the new income statement format.
2. What effect does the new capacity-based approach have on the volatility of net operating income?
3. Assume actual sales is 150,000 units and the actual selling price, actual variable manufacturing cost per unit, and actual fixed costs all equal their respective budgeted amounts. Under the traditional approach, how many units would have to be produced to realize net operating income of $500,000?
4. Assume actual sales is 150,000 units and the actual selling price, actual variable manufacturing cost per unit, and actual fixed costs all equal their respective budgeted amounts. Under the new capacity-based approach, how many units would have to be produced to realize net operating income of $500,000?
5. Will the "hat trick" be easier or harder to perform if the new capacity-based method is used?
6. Do you think the "hat trick" is ethical?

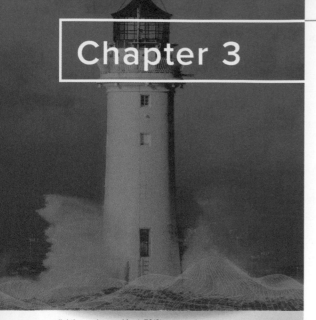

lighthouse image: Martin73/Shutterstock;
big data image: INGARA/Shutterstock

Chapter 3

Job-Order Costing: Cost Flows and External Reporting

LEARNING OBJECTIVES

After studying Chapter 3, you should be able to:

LO3–1 Understand the flow of costs in a job-order costing system and prepare appropriate journal entries to record costs.

LO3–2 Use T-accounts to show the flow of costs in a job-order costing system.

LO3–3 Prepare schedules of cost of goods manufactured and cost of goods sold and an income statement.

LO3–4 Compute underapplied or overapplied overhead cost and prepare the journal entry to close the balance in Manufacturing Overhead to the appropriate accounts.

LO3–5 *(Appendix 3A) Use Microsoft Excel to summarize the flow of costs in a job-order costing system.*

 Data Analytics Exercise available in Connect to complement this chapter

Yvette Freeman

ENTREPRENEUR SPOTLIGHT

After working more than 10 years in nonprofit communications and 11 years in higher education publishing, Yvette Freeman started Red Angle Photography in Hendersonville, North Carolina. Her company specializes in fine art beauty, maternity, family, and high school senior portraiture, as well as corporate headshots and branding. Growing up, Yvette loved taking photos of family and friends and creating albums of her images. Since turning her life-long love of photography into a full-time profession, she has taken 18 award-winning photographs in The Portrait Masters' annual image competition.

Applying Managerial Accounting

At Red Angle Photography every client is unique—much like a job-order production environment. Therefore, Yvette could use job cost sheets to record the costs she incurs serving each client. For example, her direct material costs would include items such as printed images; framed, canvas, or metal prints; and custom photo albums and cards. Her direct labor cost would include the time spent setting up and disassembling before and after a photo shoot, the time consumed taking and editing photographs, plus the round-trip transportation time to her clients' chosen venues. Yvette's overhead would include the costs of her camera and lenses, lighting equipment, and branded cargo trailer that she uses as a "photography studio on wheels."

Serving All Stakeholders

In addition to owning Red Angle Photography, Yvette Freeman also started The Envoy magazine for the purpose of "educating, featuring, and promoting minority and women entrepreneurs, community members, and creative artists across the U.S." Published three times per year, the magazine provides news relevant to minority and women-owned businesses, expert advice for starting and growing a business, and a directory of participating minority and women entrepreneurs and artists." She also started POSITIVELIGHTimages to showcase people of color in the most "positive light" possible. Her goal is "to create beautiful images that dispel stereotypes and misconceptions by featuring people of color from all walks of life, and illustrating their unique, and not-so-unique, life experiences, relationships, talent, and fortitude." ∎

Sources: www.redanglephotography.com; www.theenvoyguide.com.

Chapter 2 discussed how companies use job-order costing to assign manufacturing costs to individual jobs. This chapter describes how companies use job-order costing to prepare a balance sheet and income statement for external reporting purposes.

Exhibit 3–1 summarizes seven vocabulary terms introduced in the previous chapter. Please review these terms, each of which is included in the Glossary at the end of this chapter, because it will help you understand the forthcoming learning objectives.

EXHIBIT 3–1
Summary of Important Vocabulary Terms

Vocabulary Term	Definition
Job-order costing	A costing system used when many different products, jobs, or services are produced each period.
Absorption costing	A costing method that includes all manufacturing costs—direct materials, direct labor, and both variable and fixed manufacturing overhead—in the cost of a product.
Allocation base	A measure of activity such as direct labor-hours or machine-hours used to assign costs to cost objects.
Predetermined overhead rate	A rate used to charge manufacturing overhead cost to jobs established in advance for each period. It is computed using the following equation: $$\text{Predetermined overhead rate} = \frac{\text{Estimated total manufacturing overhead cost}}{\text{Estimated total amount of the allocation base}}$$
Overhead application	The process of assigning overhead costs to specific jobs using the following formula: $$\frac{\text{Overhead applied}}{\text{to a particular job}} = \frac{\text{Predetermined}}{\text{overhead rate}} \times \frac{\text{Amount of the allocation}}{\text{base incurred by the job}}$$
Normal costing	A costing system that applies overhead costs to jobs by multiplying a predetermined overhead rate by the actual amount of the allocation base incurred by the job.
Job cost sheet	A form that records the direct materials, direct labor, and manufacturing overhead cost charged to a job.

Job-Order Costing—The Flow of Costs

In Chapter 1, we used Exhibit 1–2 to illustrate the cost flows and classifications in a manufacturing company. Now we are going to use a similar version of that exhibit, as shown in Exhibit 3–2, to introduce the cost flows and classifications in a manufacturing company that uses job-order costing.

Exhibit 3–2 shows in job-order costing a company's *product costs* flow through three inventory accounts on the balance sheet and then to cost of goods sold in the income statement. More specifically, raw materials purchases are recorded in the *Raw Materials* inventory account. **Raw materials** include any materials that go into the final product.

LO3–1
Understand the flow of costs in a job-order costing system and prepare appropriate journal entries to record costs.

EXHIBIT 3–2
Cost Flows and Classifications in a Manufacturing Company That Uses Job-Order Costing

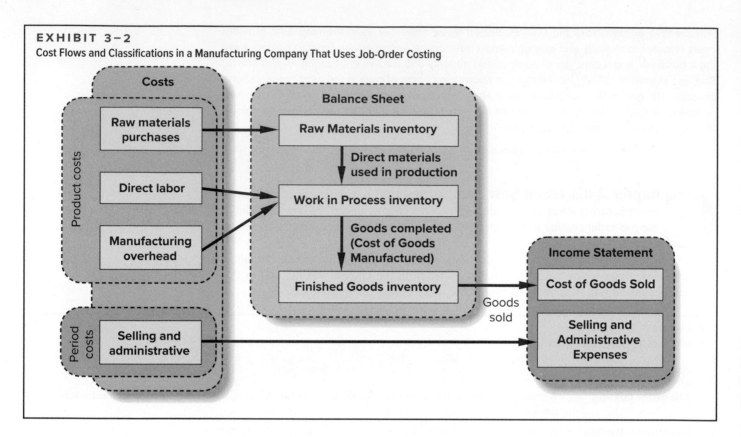

When raw materials are used in production as direct materials, their costs are transferred to *Work in Process* inventory.[1] **Work in process** consists of units of product that are only partially complete and will require further work before they are ready for sale to the customer. To transform direct materials into completed jobs, direct labor cost is added to Work in Process and manufacturing overhead cost is applied to Work in Process by multiplying the predetermined overhead rate by the actual quantity of the allocation base consumed by each job.[2] When jobs are completed, their costs are transferred from Work in Process to *Finished Goods* inventory. **Finished goods** consist of completed units of product that have not yet been sold to customers.

The amount transferred from Work in Process to Finished Goods is referred to as the *cost of goods manufactured*. The **cost of goods manufactured** includes the manufacturing costs associated with units of product finished during the period. As jobs are sold, their costs are transferred from Finished Goods to Cost of Goods Sold. At this point, the various costs attached to each job are finally recorded as an expense on the income statement. Until that point, these costs are in inventory accounts on the balance sheet. Period costs (or selling and administrative expenses) do not flow through inventories on the balance sheet. They are recorded as expenses on the income statement in the period incurred.

To illustrate the cost flows within a job-order costing system, we will record Ruger Corporation's transactions for the month of April. Ruger is a producer of gold and silver commemorative medallions and it worked on only two jobs in April. Job A, a special minting of 1,000 gold medallions commemorating the invention of motion pictures, was started during March and completed in April. As of March 31st, Job A had been assigned $30,000 in manufacturing costs, which corresponds with Ruger's Work in Process balance on April 1st of $30,000. Job B, an order for 10,000 silver medallions commemorating the fall of the Berlin Wall, was started in April and was incomplete at the end of the month.

---

[1] Indirect materials are accounted for as part of manufacturing overhead.

[2] For simplicity, Exhibit 3–2 assumes that Cost of Goods Sold does not need to be adjusted as discussed later in the chapter.

The Purchase and Issue of Materials

On April 1, Ruger Corporation had $7,000 in raw materials on hand. During the month, the company purchased on account an additional $60,000 in raw materials. The purchase is recorded in journal entry (1) below:

(1)

Raw Materials	60,000	
Accounts Payable....................................		60,000

Remember that Raw Materials is an asset account. Thus, when raw materials are purchased, they are initially recorded as an asset—not as an expense.

Issue of Direct and Indirect Materials   During April, *materials requisition forms* were prepared to authorize withdrawing $52,000 in raw materials from the storeroom for use in production. These raw materials included $50,000 of direct and $2,000 of indirect materials. Entry (2) records issuing the materials to the production departments.

(2)

Work in Process	50,000	
Manufacturing Overhead	2,000	
Raw Materials		52,000

The materials charged to Work in Process represent direct materials for specific jobs. These costs are also recorded on the appropriate job cost sheets. This point is illustrated in Exhibit 3–3, where $28,000 of the $50,000 in direct materials is charged to Job A's cost sheet and the remaining $22,000 is charged to Job B's cost sheet. (In this example, all data are presented in summary form and the job cost sheet is abbreviated.)

The $2,000 charged to Manufacturing Overhead in entry (2) is indirect materials. The debit side of the Manufacturing Overhead account always records actual manufacturing overhead costs, such as indirect materials used during the period. The credit side of this account, as you will see in transaction (7), always records manufacturing overhead applied to work in process.

Notice in Exhibit 3–3 Job A has a beginning balance of $30,000. This balance represents the cost of work done during March that has been carried forward to April. Also note the Work in Process account contains the same $30,000 balance. Thus, the Work in Process account summarizes all costs appearing on the job cost sheets for jobs still in process. Job A was the only job in process at the beginning of April, so the beginning balance in the Work in Process account equals Job A's beginning balance of $30,000.

Labor Cost

In April, the employee *time tickets* (which provide hourly summaries of each employee's activities throughout the day) included $60,000 for direct labor and $15,000 for indirect labor. The following entry summarizes these costs:

(3)

Work in Process	60,000	
Manufacturing Overhead	15,000	
Salaries and Wages Payable		75,000

Only the direct labor cost of $60,000 is added to the Work in Process account. At the same time direct labor costs are added to Work in Process, they are also added to individual job cost sheets, as shown in Exhibit 3–4. During April, $40,000 of direct labor was charged to Job A and the remaining $20,000 was charged to Job B.

The $15,000 charged to Manufacturing Overhead represents indirect labor costs, such as supervision, janitorial work, and maintenance.

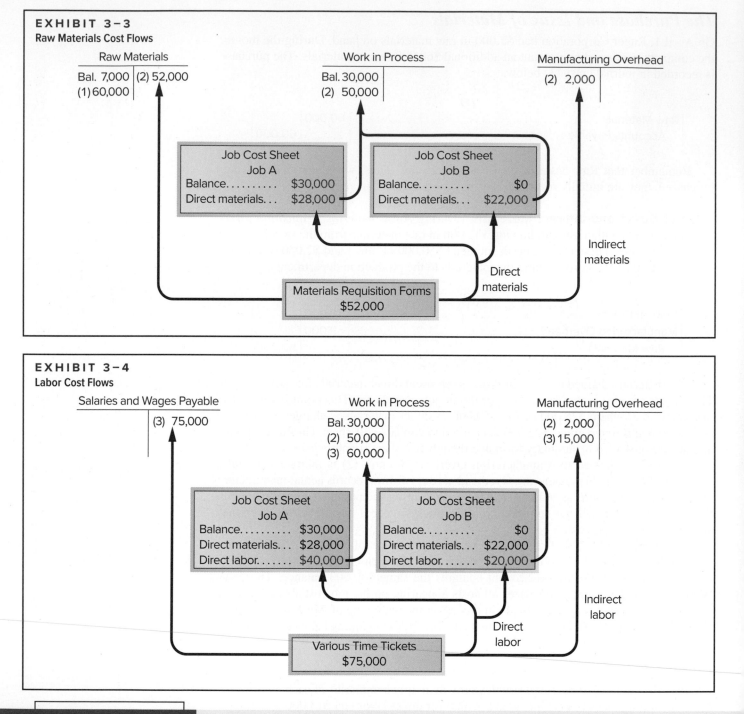

EXHIBIT 3-3
Raw Materials Cost Flows

EXHIBIT 3-4
Labor Cost Flows

VISTAPRINT: A JOB-ORDER PRODUCTION ENVIRONMENT

Most people associate Vistaprint with business cards; however, the company also sells a huge variety of other products such as photo calendars, coffee mugs, pens, invitations, stationery, clothing, car magnets, and trade show banners. Each Vistaprint customer order represents a job. For example, Yelp may buy 1,000 coffee mugs that contain its corporate logo, whereas BDO might purchase 10,000 pens with its distinct logo. Individual customers also design and purchase unique products such as wedding announcements and anniversary party invitations.

Vistaprint's direct material costs can be readily traced to specific jobs. Furthermore, the direct labor cost associated with its design services can also be traced to individual jobs. However, the overhead costs associated with the company's automated production processes would not be readily traceable to particular jobs.

Source: www.vistaprint.com

Manufacturing Overhead Costs

Recall that all manufacturing costs other than direct materials and direct labor are classified as manufacturing overhead costs. These costs are recorded in the Manufacturing Overhead account when incurred. To illustrate, assume Ruger Corporation incurred the following general factory costs during April:

Utilities (heat, water, and power).	$21,000
Rent on factory equipment	16,000
Miscellaneous factory overhead costs	3,000
Total.	$40,000

The following entry records these costs:

(4)

Manufacturing Overhead	40,000	
Accounts Payable*		40,000

*Accounts such as Cash may also be credited

In addition, assume during April, Ruger Corporation recorded $13,000 in accrued property taxes and $7,000 in expired prepaid insurance on factory buildings and equipment as follows:

(5)

Manufacturing Overhead	20,000	
Property Taxes Payable		13,000
Prepaid Insurance		7,000

Finally, assume the company recorded $18,000 in depreciation on factory equipment as follows:

(6)

Manufacturing Overhead	18,000	
Accumulated Depreciation		18,000

In short, all actual manufacturing overhead costs are debited to the Manufacturing Overhead account when incurred.

Applying Manufacturing Overhead

Because actual manufacturing overhead costs are charged to the Manufacturing Overhead account rather than Work in Process, it begs the question how are manufacturing overhead costs assigned to Work in Process? The answer is, they are assigned using a predetermined overhead rate—which is calculated by dividing the estimated total manufacturing overhead cost for the period by the estimated total amount of the allocation base. For example, if we assume machine-hours is the allocation base, then overhead cost would be applied to jobs by multiplying the predetermined overhead rate by the number of machine-hours charged to each job.

To illustrate, assume Ruger Corporation's predetermined overhead rate is $6 per machine-hour. Also assume during April, 10,000 machine-hours were worked on Job A and 5,000 machine-hours were worked on Job B (a total of 15,000 machine-hours). Thus, $90,000 in overhead cost ($6 per machine-hour × 15,000 machine-hours = $90,000) would be applied to Work in Process as follows:

(7)

Work in Process	90,000	
Manufacturing Overhead		90,000

Exhibit 3–5 shows the flow of costs through the Manufacturing Overhead account. The actual overhead costs on the debit side of the Manufacturing Overhead account were recorded in entries (2)–(6), whereas the application of overhead to Work in Process occurs in entry (7).

The Concept of a Clearing Account   The Manufacturing Overhead account operates as a clearing account. Actual manufacturing overhead costs are debited to the account as incurred throughout the year. When jobs are completed (or at the end of an accounting period), overhead cost is applied to the jobs using the predetermined overhead rate—Work in Process is debited and Manufacturing Overhead is credited. This sequence of events is illustrated below:

**Manufacturing Overhead
(a clearing account)**

Actual overhead costs are charged to this account as they are incurred throughout the period.	Overhead is applied to Work in Process using the predetermined overhead rate.

The predetermined overhead rate is based on estimates of what the level of activity and overhead costs are *expected* to be, and it is established before the year begins. As a result, the overhead cost applied during a year will almost certainly differ from the actual overhead cost incurred. For example, notice from Exhibit 3–5 Ruger Corporation's actual overhead costs are $5,000 greater than the overhead cost applied to Work in Process, resulting in a $5,000 debit balance in the Manufacturing Overhead account. We will reserve discussion of what to do with this $5,000 balance until later in the chapter.

EXHIBIT 3–5
The Flow of Costs in Overhead Application

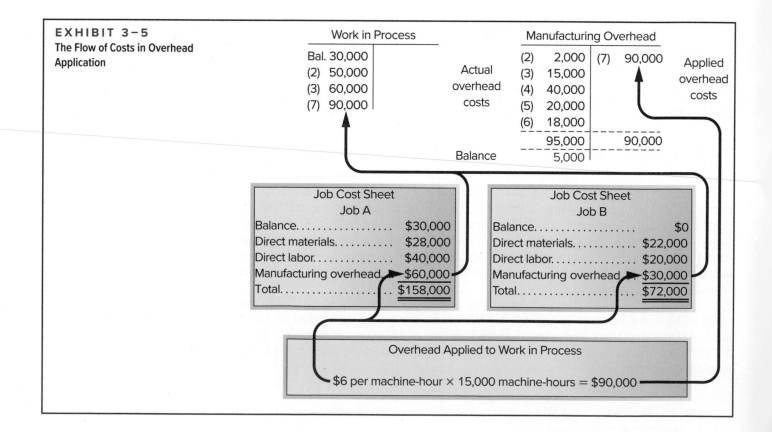

For the moment, we can conclude from Exhibit 3–5 the cost of a completed job includes the actual direct materials cost of the job, the actual direct labor cost of the job, and the manufacturing overhead cost *applied* to the job. Pay particular attention to the following subtle but important point: *Actual overhead costs are not charged to jobs; actual overhead costs do not appear on the job cost sheet, nor do they appear in the Work in Process account. Only the applied overhead cost, based on the predetermined overhead rate, appears on the job cost sheet and in the Work in Process account.*

Nonmanufacturing Costs

In addition to manufacturing costs, companies also incur selling and administrative costs. These costs are treated as period expenses and charged directly to the income statement. *Nonmanufacturing costs should not go into the Manufacturing Overhead account.* To illustrate the correct treatment of nonmanufacturing costs, assume Ruger Corporation incurred $30,000 in selling and administrative salary costs during April. The following entry summarizes the accrual of those salaries:

(8)

Salaries Expense.....................................	30,000	
Salaries and Wages Payable		30,000

Assume depreciation on office equipment during April was $7,000. The entry is as follows:

(9)

Depreciation Expense	7,000	
Accumulated Depreciation		7,000

Notice the difference between this entry and entry (6) where we recorded depreciation on factory equipment. In entry (6), depreciation on factory equipment was debited to Manufacturing Overhead and is therefore a product cost. In entry (9), depreciation on office equipment is debited to Depreciation Expense because it's a period expense rather than a product cost.

Finally, assume advertising was $42,000 and other selling and administrative expenses in April totaled $8,000. The following entry records these items:

(10)

Advertising Expense	42,000	
Other Selling and Administrative Expense..............	8,000	
Accounts Payable*		50,000

*Other accounts such as Cash may also be credited

The amounts in entries (8) through (10) are recorded directly into expense accounts—they have no effect on product costs. The same will be true of any other selling and administrative expenses incurred during April, including sales commissions, depreciation on sales equipment, rent on office facilities, and insurance on office facilities.

Cost of Goods Manufactured

When a job is completed, the finished output is transferred from the production departments to the finished goods warehouse. By this time, the accounting department has charged the job with direct materials and direct labor cost and applied overhead using the predetermined overhead rate. A transfer of costs is made within the costing system that *parallels* the physical transfer of goods to the finished goods warehouse. The costs of the completed job are transferred out of the Work in Process account and into the Finished Goods account. The sum of all amounts transferred between these two accounts represents the *cost of goods manufactured.*

In the case of Ruger Corporation, remember that Job A was completed during April and Job B was incomplete at the end of the month. Thus, the following entry transfers the cost of Job A from Work in Process to Finished Goods:

(11)

Finished Goods	158,000	
Work in Process		158,000

The $158,000, which appears on Job A's cost sheet in Exhibit 3–5, represents the cost of goods manufactured for the month.

Because Job B was not completed by the end of the month, its costs remain in Work in Process and carry over to the next month. If a balance sheet were prepared at the end of April, Job B's cost ($72,000) would appear in the asset account Work in Process.

Cost of Goods Sold

As completed jobs are shipped to customers, their costs are transferred from Finished Goods to Cost of Goods Sold. If an entire job is shipped at one time, then its entire cost is transferred to Cost of Goods Sold. However, sometimes only a portion of the units involved in a particular job will be immediately sold. In these situations, the unit product cost is used to determine how much product cost should be removed from Finished Goods and charged to Cost of Goods Sold.

For Ruger Corporation, we will assume 750 of the 1,000 gold medallions in Job A were shipped to customers by the end of the month for total sales revenue of $225,000. Because 1,000 units were produced and the total cost of the job from the job cost sheet was $158,000, the unit product cost was $158. The following journal entries record the sale (all sales were on account):

(12)

Accounts Receivable	225,000	
Sales		225,000

(13)

Cost of Goods Sold	118,500	
Finished Goods		118,500
(750 units × $158 per unit = $118,500)		

Entry (13) completes the flow of costs through the job-order costing system. To pull the entire Ruger Corporation example together, journal entries (1) through (13) are summarized in Exhibit 3–6. In addition, Exhibit 3–7 presents the flow of costs through the accounts in T-account form.

LO3–2
Use T-accounts to show the flow of costs in a job-order costing system.

EXHIBIT 3–6
Summary of Journal Entries—Ruger Corporation

(1)

Raw Materials	60,000	
Accounts Payable		60,000

(2)

Work in Process	50,000	
Manufacturing Overhead	2,000	
Raw Materials		52,000

(3)

Work in Process	60,000	
Manufacturing Overhead	15,000	
Salaries and Wages Payable		75,000

(4)

Manufacturing Overhead	40,000	
Accounts Payable		40,000

(5)

Manufacturing Overhead	20,000	
Property Taxes Payable		13,000
Prepaid Insurance		7,000

(6)

Manufacturing Overhead	18,000	
Accumulated Depreciation		18,000

(7)

Work in Process	90,000	
Manufacturing Overhead		90,000

(8)

Salaries Expense	30,000	
Salaries and Wages Payable		30,000

(9)

Depreciation Expense	7,000	
Accumulated Depreciation		7,000

(10)

Advertising Expense	42,000	
Other Selling and Administrative Expense	8,000	
Accounts Payable		50,000

(11)

Finished Goods	158,000	
Work in Process		158,000

(12)

Accounts Receivable	225,000	
Sales		225,000

(13)

Cost of Goods Sold	118,500	
Finished Goods		118,500

EXHIBIT 3–7
Summary of Cost Flows—Ruger Corporation

Accounts Receivable			
Bal.	XX		
(12)	225,000		

Prepaid Insurance			
Bal.	XX		
		(5)	7,000

Raw Materials			
Bal.	7,000	(2)	52,000
(1)	60,000		
Bal.	15,000		

Work in Process			
Bal.	30,000	(11)	158,000
(2)	50,000		
(3)	60,000		
(7)	90,000		
Bal.	72,000		

Finished Goods			
Bal.	0	(13)	118,500
(11)	158,000		
Bal.	39,500		

Accumulated Depreciation			
		Bal.	XX
		(6)	18,000
		(9)	7,000

Manufacturing Overhead			
(2)	2,000	(7)	90,000
(3)	15,000		
(4)	40,000		
(5)	20,000		
(6)	18,000		
	95,000		90,000
Bal.	5,000		

Accounts Payable			
		Bal.	XX
		(1)	60,000
		(4)	40,000
		(10)	50,000

Salaries and Wages Payable			
		Bal.	XX
		(3)	75,000
		(8)	30,000

Property Taxes Payable			
		Bal.	XX
		(5)	13,000

Sales			
		(12)	225,000

Cost of Goods Sold			
(13)	118,500		

Salaries Expense			
(8)	30,000		

Depreciation Expense			
(9)	7,000		

Advertising Expense			
(10)	42,000		

Other Selling and Administrative Expense			
(10)	8,000		

Explanation of entries:
 (1) Raw materials purchased.
 (2) Direct and indirect materials issued into production.
 (3) Direct and indirect factory labor cost incurred.
 (4) Utilities and other factory costs incurred.
 (5) Property taxes and insurance incurred on the factory.
 (6) Depreciation recorded on factory assets.
 (7) Overhead cost applied to Work in Process.
 (8) Administrative salaries expense incurred.
 (9) Depreciation recorded on office equipment.
(10) Advertising and other selling and administrative expense incurred.
(11) Cost of goods manufactured transferred to finished goods.
(12) Sale of Job A recorded.
(13) Cost of goods sold recorded for Job A.

Schedules of Cost of Goods Manufactured and Cost of Goods Sold

This section uses the Ruger Corporation example to explain how to prepare schedules of cost of goods manufactured and cost of goods sold as well as an income statement. The **schedule of cost of goods manufactured** contains three elements of product costs—direct materials, direct labor, and manufacturing overhead—and it summarizes the portions of those costs remaining in ending Work in Process inventory and transferred out to Finished Goods. The **schedule of cost of goods sold** also contains three product costs—direct materials, direct labor, and manufacturing overhead—and summarizes the portions of those costs remaining in ending Finished Goods inventory and transferred out to Cost of Goods Sold.

LO3–3
Prepare schedules of cost of goods manufactured and cost of goods sold and an income statement.

Schedule of Cost of Goods Manufactured

Exhibit 3–8 presents Ruger Corporation's schedule of cost of goods manufactured, which is based on three underlying equations. First, as shown in the left-hand column of numbers, the *raw materials used in production* are computed using the following equation:

$$\text{Raw materials used in production} = \text{Beginning raw materials inventory} + \text{Purchases of raw materials} - \text{Ending raw materials inventory}$$

For Ruger Corporation, the beginning raw materials inventory of $7,000 plus the purchases of raw materials of $60,000 minus the ending raw materials inventory of $15,000 equals the raw materials used in production of $52,000. If the company does not use any indirect materials, then the raw materials used in production equals the direct materials used in production. Conversely, if indirect materials are used, they must be subtracted from raw materials used in production to arrive at the direct materials used in production. For Ruger, raw materials used in production of $52,000 minus indirect materials of $2,000 equals direct materials used in production of $50,000. Because indirect materials are part of manufacturing overhead, they must be removed from the calculation of direct materials used in production.

EXHIBIT 3–8
Schedule of Cost of Goods Manufactured

Ruger Corporation Schedule of Cost of Goods Manufactured For the Month Ending April 30			
Beginning work in process inventory...............			$ 30,000
Direct materials:			
Beginning raw materials inventory...............	$ 7,000		
Add: Purchases of raw materials................	60,000		
Total raw materials available	67,000		
Deduct: Ending raw materials inventory	15,000		
Raw materials used in production...............	52,000		
Deduct: Indirect materials used in production	2,000		
Direct materials used in production		50,000	
Direct labor.....................................		60,000	
Manufacturing overhead applied to work in process...		90,000	
Total manufacturing costs added to production.....			200,000
Total manufacturing costs to account for..........			230,000
Deduct: Ending work in process inventory			72,000
Cost of goods manufactured			$158,000

The second equation, shown in the middle column of Exhibit 3–8, calculates *total manufacturing costs added to production* as follows:

$$
\begin{matrix}
\text{Total} \\
\text{manufacturing} \\
\text{costs added to production}
\end{matrix}
=
\begin{matrix}
\text{Direct materials} \\
\text{used in} \\
\text{production}
\end{matrix}
+ \text{Direct labor} +
\begin{matrix}
\text{Manufacturing} \\
\text{overhead applied to} \\
\text{work in process}
\end{matrix}
$$

For Ruger Corporation, the direct materials used in production of $50,000 plus the direct labor of $60,000 plus the manufacturing overhead applied to work in process of $90,000 equals the total manufacturing costs added to production of $200,000. Notice, the direct materials used in production ($50,000) is included in total manufacturing costs added to production instead of raw materials purchases ($60,000). The direct materials used in production usually differs from the raw material purchases whenever the raw materials inventory balance changes or indirect materials are withdrawn from raw materials inventory.

This equation includes manufacturing overhead applied to work in process rather than actual manufacturing overhead costs. For Ruger Corporation, its manufacturing overhead applied to work in process of $90,000 is computed by multiplying the predetermined overhead rate of $6 per machine-hour by the actual amount of the allocation base recorded on all jobs, or 15,000 machine-hours. *The actual manufacturing overhead costs incurred during the period are not added to the Work in Process account.*

The third equation, shown in the right-hand column of Exhibit 3–8, calculates the cost of goods manufactured as follows:

$$
\begin{matrix}
\text{Cost of goods} \\
\text{manufactured}
\end{matrix}
=
\begin{matrix}
\text{Beginning work in} \\
\text{process inventory}
\end{matrix}
+
\begin{matrix}
\text{Total} \\
\text{manufacturing costs} \\
\text{added to production}
\end{matrix}
-
\begin{matrix}
\text{Ending work in} \\
\text{process inventory}
\end{matrix}
$$

For Ruger, the beginning work in process inventory of $30,000 plus the total manufacturing costs added to production of $200,000 minus the ending work in process inventory of $72,000 equals the cost of goods manufactured of $158,000. The cost of goods manufactured represents the cost of the goods completed during the period and transferred from Work in Process to Finished Goods.

Schedule of Cost of Goods Sold

The schedule of cost of goods sold shown in Exhibit 3–9 uses the following equation to compute the unadjusted cost of goods sold:

$$
\begin{matrix}
\text{Unadjusted cost} \\
\text{of goods sold}
\end{matrix}
=
\begin{matrix}
\text{Beginning finished} \\
\text{goods inventory}
\end{matrix}
+
\begin{matrix}
\text{Cost of goods} \\
\text{manufactured}
\end{matrix}
-
\begin{matrix}
\text{Ending finished} \\
\text{goods inventory}
\end{matrix}
$$

The beginning finished goods inventory ($0) plus the cost of goods manufactured ($158,000) equals the cost of goods available for sale ($158,000). The cost of goods available for sale ($158,000) minus the ending finished goods inventory ($39,500) equals the unadjusted cost of goods sold ($118,500). Finally, the unadjusted cost of goods sold ($118,500) plus the underapplied overhead ($5,000) equals adjusted cost of goods sold ($123,500). The next section of the chapter takes a closer look at why cost of goods sold needs to be adjusted for the amount of underapplied or overapplied overhead.

EXHIBIT 3–9
Schedule of Cost of Goods Sold

Ruger Corporation Schedule of Cost of Goods Sold For the Month Ending April 30	
Beginning finished goods inventory	$ 0
Add: Cost of goods manufactured (from Exhibit 3–8)	158,000
Cost of goods available for sale	158,000
Deduct: Ending finished goods inventory	39,500
Unadjusted cost of goods sold	118,500
Add: Underapplied overhead	5,000
Adjusted cost of goods sold	$123,500

*Note underapplied overhead is added to cost of goods sold. If overhead were overapplied, it would be deducted from cost of goods sold.

Income Statement

Exhibit 3–10 presents Ruger Corporation's income statement for April. Notice the cost of goods sold on this statement carries over from Exhibit 3–9. The selling and administrative expenses (which total $87,000) did not flow through the schedules of cost of goods manufactured and cost of goods sold. Journal entries 8–10 show these items were immediately debited to expense accounts rather than inventory accounts.

EXHIBIT 3–10
Income Statement

Ruger Corporation Income Statement For the Month Ending April 30		
Sales		$225,000
Cost of goods sold ($118,500 + $5,000)		123,500
Gross margin		101,500
Selling and administrative expenses:		
Salaries expense	$30,000	
Depreciation expense	7,000	
Advertising expense	42,000	
Other expense	8,000	87,000
Net operating income		$ 14,500

COMMUNICATING WITH DATA VISUALIZATIONS

Diagnostic analytics answer the question: Why did it happen? For example, this visualization introduces some additional data to depict Ruger Corporation's quarter-over-quarter net operating income for the last eight quarters. Notice, the net operating income in Year 2 is less than that in Year 1 for each of the company's four quarters. Diagnostically speaking, the visualization suggests management should focus its attention on expense management more so than revenue management. In fact, the Year 2 sales in quarters one through three are greater than the same quarter's sales in the prior year. The lower quarterly net operating incomes in Year 2 are being driven by much higher expenses than the quarterly results from the previous year.

(Continued)

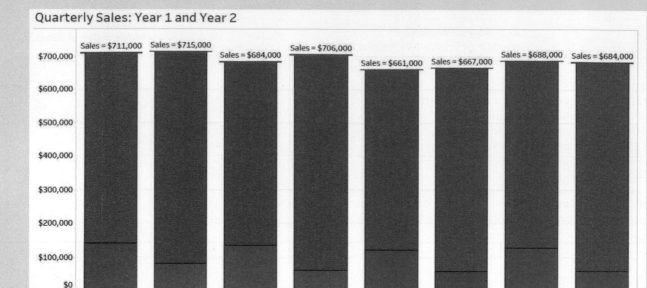

Quarterly Sales: Year 1 and Year 2

| | Sales = $711,000 | Sales = $715,000 | Sales = $684,000 | Sales = $706,000 | Sales = $661,000 | Sales = $667,000 | Sales = $688,000 | Sales = $684,000 |

Category ■ Total Expenses ■ Net Operating Income

Tableau

B.B. BARNS OFFERS LANDSCAPE DESIGN AND INSTALLATION

B. B. Barns describes itself as Asheville, North Carolina's "premiere garden center and landscape service provider." In addition to its four-acre garden center, the company provides custom-designed landscape architectural plans complete with installation and maintenance services. For B. B. Barns, each client represents a job that consumes direct materials, direct labor, and overhead. Examples of direct materials include shrubs, perennial and annual flowers, mulch, hardscaping materials (e.g., bricks and stone), and plant containers. Direct labor costs include the landscape architect who designed the plans as well as the employees responsible for completing the installation. Overhead costs include tools such as shovels and rakes, equipment such as backhoes and dump trucks, and fuel for the equipment.

Source: www.bbbarns.com

Underapplied and Overapplied Overhead—A Closer Look

LO3–4

Compute underapplied or overapplied overhead cost and prepare the journal entry to close the balance in Manufacturing Overhead to the appropriate accounts.

This section explains how to compute underapplied and overapplied overhead and how to dispose of any balance remaining in the Manufacturing Overhead account at the end of a period.

Computing Underapplied and Overapplied Overhead

Because the predetermined overhead rate is established before the period begins and is based entirely on estimated data, the overhead cost applied to Work in Process will generally differ from the amount of overhead cost actually incurred. In the case of Ruger Corporation, for example, the predetermined overhead rate of $6 per machine-hour was used to apply $90,000 of overhead cost to Work in Process, whereas actual overhead costs for April were $95,000 (see Exhibit 3–5). The difference between overhead cost applied to Work in Process and actual overhead costs is called either **underapplied overhead** or **overapplied overhead**. For Ruger Corporation, overhead was underapplied by $5,000 because the applied cost ($90,000) was $5,000 less than the actual cost ($95,000). If the situation had been reversed and the company had applied $95,000 in overhead cost to Work in Process while incurring actual overhead cost of only $90,000, then the overhead would have been overapplied.

What is the cause of underapplied or overapplied overhead? Basically, the method of applying overhead to jobs using a predetermined overhead rate assumes actual overhead costs will be proportional to the actual amount of the allocation base incurred during the period. So, if the predetermined overhead rate is $6 per machine-hour, it is assumed actual overhead costs will equal $6 for every machine-hour actually worked. There are at least two reasons why this may not be true. First, many overhead costs are fixed costs that do not change as the number of machine-hours incurred goes up or down. Second, overhead spending may or may not be under control. If the individuals responsible for overhead costs do a good job, those costs should be less than estimated at the beginning of the period. If they do a poor job, those costs will be more than expected.

To illustrate, suppose two companies—Turbo Crafters and Black & Howell—prepared the following estimates for the coming year:

	Turbo Crafters	Black & Howell
Allocation base	Machine-hours	Direct materials cost
Estimated manufacturing overhead cost (a)............	$300,000	$120,000
Estimated total amount of the allocation base (b).......	75,000 machine-hours	$80,000 direct materials cost
Predetermined overhead rate (a) ÷ (b)	$4 per machine-hour	150% of direct materials cost

Note when the allocation base is dollars (such as direct materials cost in the case of Black & Howell), the predetermined overhead rate is expressed as a percentage of the allocation base. When dollars are divided by dollars, the result is a percentage.

Now assume because of unexpected changes in overhead spending and unit sales, the *actual* overhead cost incurred and the actual amount of the allocation base used during the year in each company are as follows:

	Turbo Crafters	Black & Howell
Actual manufacturing overhead cost....................	$290,000	$130,000
Actual total amount of the allocation base	68,000 machine-hours	$90,000 direct materials cost

Given this actual data and each company's predetermined overhead rate, the manufacturing overhead applied to Work in Process during the year would be computed as follows:

	Turbo Crafters	Black & Howell
Predetermined overhead rate (a)....................	$4 per machine-hour	150% of direct materials cost
Actual total amount of the allocation base (b)	68,000 machine-hours	$90,000 direct materials cost
Manufacturing overhead applied (a) × (b)	$272,000	$135,000

This results in underapplied and overapplied overhead as shown below:

	Turbo Crafters	Black & Howell
Actual manufacturing overhead cost.............	$290,000	$130,000
Manufacturing overhead applied................	272,000	135,000
Underapplied (overapplied) manufacturing overhead	$ 18,000	$ (5,000)

For Turbo Crafters, the overhead cost applied to Work in Process of $272,000 is less than the actual overhead cost for the year of $290,000; therefore, overhead is underapplied by $18,000.

For Black & Howell, the overhead cost applied to Work in Process of $135,000 is greater than the actual overhead cost for the year of $130,000, so overhead is overapplied by $(5,000).

EXHIBIT 3–11
Summary of Overhead Concepts

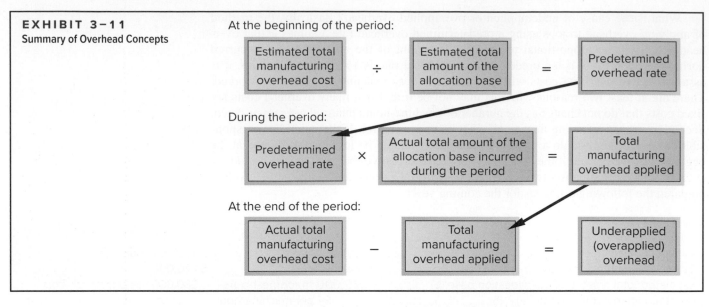

At the beginning of the period:

Estimated total manufacturing overhead cost ÷ Estimated total amount of the allocation base = Predetermined overhead rate

During the period:

Predetermined overhead rate × Actual total amount of the allocation base incurred during the period = Total manufacturing overhead applied

At the end of the period:

Actual total manufacturing overhead cost − Total manufacturing overhead applied = Underapplied (overapplied) overhead

A summary of these concepts is presented in Exhibit 3–11.

Disposition of Underapplied or Overapplied Overhead Balances

The Turbo Crafters and Black & Howell examples show one way to calculate underapplied or overapplied overhead. However, another equivalent method of determining the amount of underapplied or overapplied overhead is to properly analyze the Manufacturing Overhead T-account. Explaining this second method also enables us to discuss the topic of preparing a journal entry to dispose of underapplied or overapplied overhead for financial reporting purposes.

If we return to the Ruger Corporation example and look at the Manufacturing Overhead T-account in Exhibit 3–7, you will see there is a debit balance of $5,000. Remember debit entries to this account represent actual overhead costs, whereas credit entries represent applied overhead costs. In this case, the applied overhead costs (the credits) are less than the actual overhead costs (the debits) by $5,000—hence, manufacturing overhead is underapplied. In other words, if there is a *debit* balance in the Manufacturing Overhead account of X dollars, then the overhead is *underapplied* by X dollars. On the other hand, if there is a *credit* balance in the Manufacturing Overhead account of Y dollars, then the overhead is *overapplied* by Y dollars.

Once we have quantified the underapplied or overapplied overhead, it must be disposed of in one of two ways:

1. It can be closed to Cost of Goods Sold.
2. It can be closed proportionally to Work in Process, Finished Goods, and Cost of Goods Sold.

Closed to Cost of Goods Sold   Closing the balance in Manufacturing Overhead to Cost of Goods Sold is the simpler of the two methods. In the Ruger Corporation example, the entry to close the $5,000 of underapplied overhead to Cost of Goods Sold is:

(14)

Cost of Goods Sold	5,000	
Manufacturing Overhead		5,000

Because the Manufacturing Overhead account has a debit balance, it must be credited to close out the account. This increases April's Cost of Goods Sold by $5,000 as shown below:

Unadjusted cost of goods sold [from entry (13)]	$118,500
Add underapplied overhead [from entry (14)]	5,000
Adjusted cost of goods sold	$123,500

Ruger Corporation's adjusted cost of goods sold of $123,500 as shown here agrees with the company's income statement shown in Exhibit 3–10.

Keep in mind unadjusted cost of goods sold is based on the manufacturing overhead cost applied to jobs, not the amount of actual manufacturing overhead cost incurred. So, when overhead is underapplied it means two things—not enough overhead cost was applied to jobs and the cost of goods sold is understated. Adding the underapplied overhead to the cost of goods sold corrects this understatement.

Closed Proportionally to Work in Process, Finished Goods, and Cost of Goods Sold

Closing underapplied or overapplied overhead proportionally to Work in Process, Finished Goods, and Cost of Goods Sold is more accurate than closing the entire balance into Cost of Goods Sold; however, it is also more complex. We'll explain the proportional allocation of underapplied or overapplied overhead using a three-step process.

The first step is to break the overhead cost applied to production into three pieces—the portion included in ending Work in Process, the portion included in ending Finished Goods, and the portion applied to Cost of Goods Sold during the period. The second step is to state each of these three amounts as a percent of the total overhead cost applied to production. The third step is to derive the amounts needed for the journal entry by multiplying the percentages from step two by the amount of underapplied or overapplied overhead.

Exhibit 3–12 illustrates this three-step process for Ruger Corporation. As you may remember, Ruger worked on only two jobs in April—Job A and Job B. Job A consisted of 1,000 gold medallions, 750 of which were sold to customers and 250 of which remained in Finished Goods at the end of the month. Job B consisted of 10,000 silver medallions and it was incomplete at the end of April.

In step one of Exhibit 3–12, Ruger takes its total manufacturing overhead applied to production from Exhibit 3–5 ($90,000) and splits it between Job A ($60,000) and Job B ($30,000). Because Job B was incomplete at the end of April, all of its applied overhead cost ($30,000) resides in Work in Process at the end of the month, whereas the $60,000 of overhead cost applied to Job A needs to be split into two accounts. A total of 25% of Job A's gold medallions (= 250 ÷ 1,000) were in Finished Goods at the end of April; therefore, 25% of Job A's applied overhead cost, or $15,000 (= $60,000 × 25%), also remains in Finished Goods. Similarly, 75% of Job A's gold medallions (= 750 ÷ 1,000) were sold during April; thus, 75% of Job A's applied overhead cost, or $45,000 (= $60,000 × 75%), is included in Cost of Goods Sold.

In step 2 of Exhibit 3–12, the amounts of applied overhead cost in Work in Process ($30,000), Finished Goods ($15,000), and Cost of Goods Sold ($45,000) are each stated as a percent of the total manufacturing overhead cost applied to production during the ($90,000). In other words, 33.33% of the period's total applied overhead cost resides in Work in Process at the end of April. Similarly, 16.67% of the total remains in Finished Goods and 50% is included in Cost of Goods Sold.

Step 3 from Exhibit 3–12 uses the percentages from step 2 to proportionally allocate the $5,000 of underapplied overhead to Work in Process, Finished Goods, and Cost of Goods Sold. Work in Process is allocated $1,666.50 of underapplied overhead, whereas Finished Goods and Cost of Goods Sold are allocated $833.50 and $2,500, respectively. Using these dollar amounts, the journal entry is recorded as follows:

Work in Process	1,666.50	
Finished Goods	833.50	
Cost of Goods Sold	2,500.00	
Manufacturing Overhead		5,000.00

Note the $5,000 credit to Manufacturing Overhead ensures this account ends the month with a zero balance. Furthermore, it bears emphasizing if Ruger's overhead had been overapplied rather than underapplied, the entry above would have been just the reverse. The Manufacturing Overhead account would have had a credit balance, thus necessitating a reversal of the debits and credits shown above.

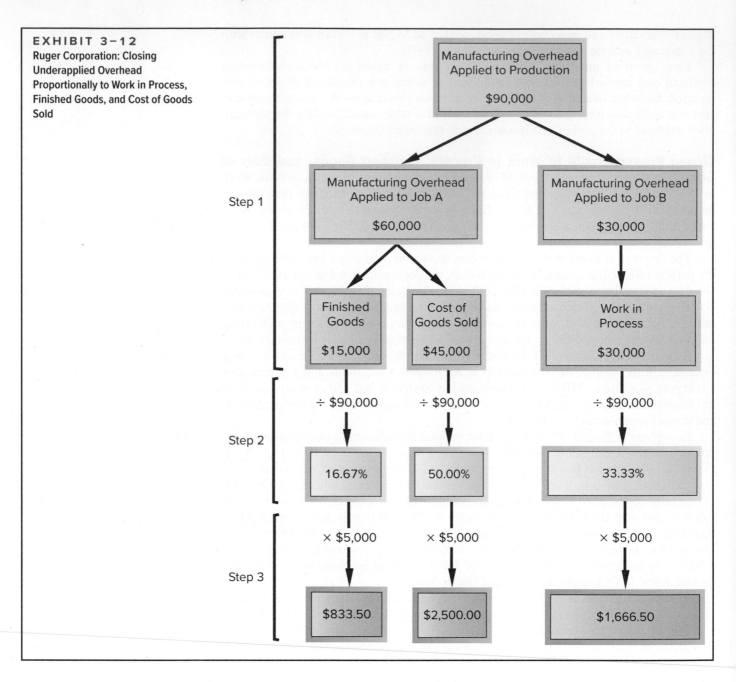

EXHIBIT 3–12
Ruger Corporation: Closing
Underapplied Overhead
Proportionally to Work in Process,
Finished Goods, and Cost of Goods
Sold

Comparing the Two Methods for Disposing of Underapplied or Overapplied Overhead

Closing the underapplied or overapplied overhead to Work in Process, Finished Goods, and Cost of Goods Sold is more accurate than the simpler approach of closing it out to Cost of Goods Sold. For example, the simpler approach overstates Ruger Corporation's Cost of Goods Sold by $2,500 (= $5,000 − $2,500) and understates its net operating income by the same amount.

A General Model of Product Cost Flows

Exhibit 3–13 presents a T-account model of the flow of manufacturing costs in a job-order costing system. This model can be very helpful in understanding how manufacturing costs flow through a normal costing system and finally end up as Cost of Goods Sold on the income statement.

EXHIBIT 3–13
A General Model of Cost Flows (Using Normal Costing)

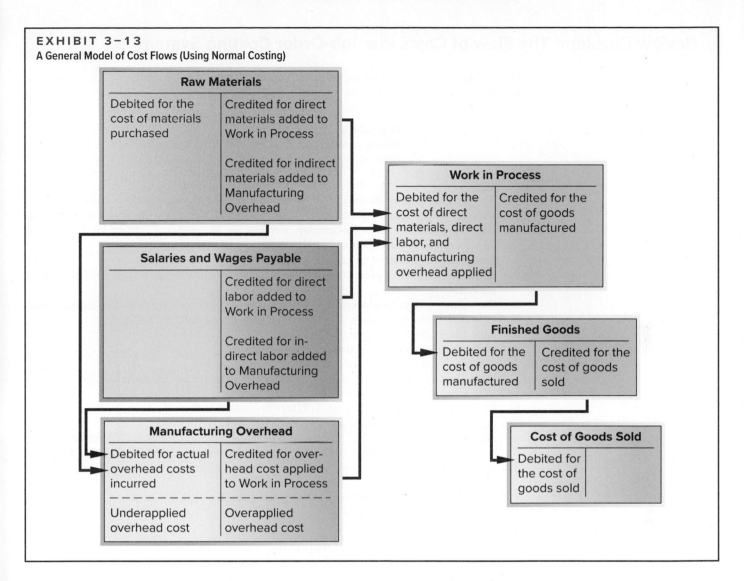

Summary

The most important concept to understand in this chapter is the flow of costs for manufacturers. Raw materials purchased from suppliers are stored in raw materials inventory until requisitioned for use in production. Direct materials are added to work in process along with direct labor and applied overhead. Once units of production are complete, their manufacturing costs are transferred from Work in Process to Finished Goods. When units of production are sold, their associated costs are transferred from Finished Goods to Cost of Goods Sold. Selling and administrative expenses are not attached to units of production. Instead, they are recorded as expenses on the income statement as incurred.

Manufacturing overhead costs are applied to jobs using a predetermined overhead rate. Because the predetermined overhead rate is based on estimates, the actual overhead cost incurred during a period may be more or less than the amount of overhead cost applied to production—resulting in underapplied or overapplied overhead. Underapplied or overapplied overhead can be closed to Cost of Goods Sold or closed proportionally to Work in Process, Finished Goods, and Cost of Goods Sold. When overhead is underapplied, manufacturing overhead costs have been understated and therefore inventories and/or cost of goods sold must be adjusted upwards. When overhead is overapplied, manufacturing overhead costs have been overstated and therefore inventories and/or cost of goods sold must be adjusted downwards.

 Data Analytics Exercise available in Connect to complement this chapter

Review Problem: The Flow of Costs in a Job-Order Costing System

Hogle Corporation is a manufacturer that uses job-order costing. On January 1, the company's inventory balances were as follows:

Raw materials	$20,000
Work in process	$15,000
Finished goods	$30,000

The company applies overhead cost to jobs on the basis of machine-hours worked. For the current year, the company's predetermined overhead rate was based on a cost formula that estimated $450,000 of total manufacturing overhead for an estimated activity level of 75,000 machine-hours. The following transactions were recorded for the year:

a. Raw materials purchased on account, $410,000.
b. Raw materials used in production, $380,000 ($360,000 direct materials and $20,000 indirect materials).
c. The following costs were accrued for employee services: direct labor, $75,000; indirect labor, $110,000; sales commissions, $90,000; and administrative salaries, $200,000.
d. Sales travel costs (on account), $17,000.
e. Utility costs (on account) in the factory, $43,000.
f. Advertising costs (on account), $180,000.
g. Depreciation recorded for the year, $350,000 (80% relates to factory assets and 20% relates to selling and administrative assets).
h. Insurance expired during the year, $10,000 (70% relates to factory operations and the remaining 30% relates to selling and administrative activities).
i. Manufacturing overhead was applied to production. Due to greater than expected demand for its products, the company worked 80,000 machine-hours on all jobs during the year.
j. Jobs costing $900,000 to manufacture according to their job cost sheets were completed during the year.
k. Jobs sold on account to customers during the year, $1,500,000. The jobs cost $870,000 to manufacture according to their job cost sheets.

Required:

1. Prepare journal entries to record the preceding transactions.
2. Post the entries in (1) above to T-accounts (don't forget to enter the beginning balances in the inventory accounts).
3. Is Manufacturing Overhead underapplied or overapplied for the year? Prepare a journal entry to close any balance in the Manufacturing Overhead account to Cost of Goods Sold.
4. Prepare an income statement for the year.

Solution to Review Problem

1.	a.	Raw Materials	410,000	
		Accounts Payable..................................		410,000
	b.	Work in Process	360,000	
		Manufacturing Overhead	20,000	
		Raw Materials		380,000
	c.	Work in Process	75,000	
		Manufacturing Overhead...........................	110,000	
		Sales Commissions Expense	90,000	
		Administrative Salaries Expense	200,000	
		Salaries and Wages Payable........................		475,000
	d.	Sales Travel Expense	17,000	
		Accounts Payable..................................		17,000
	e.	Manufacturing Overhead............................	43,000	
		Accounts Payable..................................		43,000
	f.	Advertising Expense	180,000	
		Accounts Payable..................................		180,000

g. Manufacturing Overhead   280,000
    Depreciation Expense   70,000
        Accumulated Depreciation.   350,000
h. Manufacturing Overhead   7,000
    Insurance Expense   3,000
        Prepaid Insurance.   10,000

i. The predetermined overhead rate for the year is computed as follows:

$$\text{Predetermined overhead rate} = \frac{\text{Estimated total manufacturing overhead cost}}{\text{Estimated total amount of the allocation base}}$$

$$= \frac{\$450,000}{75,000 \text{ machine-hours}}$$

$$= \$6 \text{ per machine-hour}$$

Based on the 80,000 machine-hours actually worked during the year, the company applied $480,000 in overhead cost to production: $6 per machine-hour × 80,000 machine-hours = $480,000. The following entry records this application of overhead cost:

    Work in Process   480,000
        Manufacturing Overhead   480,000
j. Finished Goods   900,000
        Work in Process   900,000
k. Accounts Receivable   1,500,000
        Sales.   1,500,000
    Cost of Goods Sold   870,000
        Finished Goods   870,000

2.

Accounts Receivable

(k)	1,500,000		

Prepaid Insurance

		(h)	10,000

Raw Materials

Bal.	20,000	(b)	380,000
(a)	410,000		
Bal.	50,000		

Work in Process

Bal.	15,000	(j)	900,000
(b)	360,000		
(c)	75,000		
(i)	480,000		
Bal.	30,000		

Finished Goods

Bal.	30,000	(k)	870,000
(j)	900,000		
Bal.	60,000		

Manufacturing Overhead

(b)	20,000	(i)	480,000
(c)	110,000		
(e)	43,000		
(g)	280,000		
(h)	7,000		
	460,000		480,000
		Bal.	20,000

Accumulated Depreciation

		(g)	350,000

Accounts Payable

		(a)	410,000
		(d)	17,000
		(e)	43,000
		(f)	180,000

Salaries and Wages Payable

		(c)	475,000

Sales

		(k)	1,500,000

Cost of Goods Sold

(k)	870,000		

Sales Commissions Expense

(c)	90,000		

Administrative Salaries Expense

(c)	200,000		

Sales Travel Expense

(d)	17,000		

Advertising Expense

(f)	180,000		

Depreciation Expense

(g)	70,000		

Insurance Expense

(h)	3,000		

3. Manufacturing overhead is overapplied for the year. The entry to close it out to Cost of Goods Sold is as follows:

Manufacturing Overhead	20,000	
Cost of Goods Sold		20,000

4.

Hogle Corporation Income Statement For the Year Ended December 31		
Sales		$1,500,000
Cost of goods sold ($870,000 − $20,000)		850,000
Gross margin		650,000
Selling and administrative expenses:		
Sales commissions expense	$ 90,000	
Administrative salaries expense	200,000	
Sales travel expense	17,000	
Advertising expense	180,000	
Depreciation expense	70,000	
Insurance expense	3,000	560,000
Net operating income		$ 90,000

Glossary

Absorption costing A costing method that includes all manufacturing costs—direct materials, direct labor, and both variable and fixed manufacturing overhead—in unit product costs. (p. 107)

Allocation base A measure of activity, such as direct labor-hours or machine-hours, used to assign costs to cost objects. (p. 107)

Cost of goods manufactured The manufacturing costs associated with units of product completed during the period. (p. 108)

Finished goods Units of product completed but not yet sold to customers. (p. 108)

Job cost sheet A form that records the direct materials, direct labor, and manufacturing overhead cost charged to a job. (p. 107

Job-order costing A costing system used when many different products, jobs, or services are produced each period. (p. 107)

Normal costing A costing system that applies overhead to a job by multiplying a predetermined overhead rate by the actual amount of the allocation base used by the job. (p. 107)

Overapplied overhead A credit balance in the Manufacturing Overhead account that occurs when the overhead cost applied to Work in Process is greater than the overhead cost actually incurred during a period. (p. 120)

Overhead application The process of assigning overhead cost to specific jobs. (p. 107)

Predetermined overhead rate A rate used to charge manufacturing overhead cost to jobs established in advance for each period. It is computed by dividing the estimated total manufacturing overhead cost for the period by the estimated total amount of the allocation base. (p. 107)

Raw materials Any materials going into the final product. (p. 107)

Schedule of cost of goods manufactured A schedule containing three product costs—direct materials, direct labor, and manufacturing overhead—that summarizes the portions of those costs remaining in ending Work in Process and transferred out to Finished Goods. (p. 117)

Schedule of cost of goods sold A schedule containing three product costs—direct materials, direct labor, and manufacturing overhead—that summarizes the portions of those costs remaining in ending Finished Goods and transferred out to Cost of Goods Sold. (p. 117)

Underapplied overhead A debit balance in the Manufacturing Overhead account occurring when the overhead cost applied to Work in Process is less than the overhead cost actually incurred. (p. 120)

Work in process Partially complete units of product requiring more work before they are ready for sale to the customer. (p. 108)

Questions

3–1 What link connects the schedule of cost of goods manufactured to the schedule of cost of goods sold?

3–2 What account is credited when overhead is applied to Work in Process? Would you expect each period's applied overhead to equal the actual overhead costs? Why or why not?

3–3 What is underapplied overhead? Overapplied overhead? How do you close these amounts at the end of the period?

3–4 Provide two reasons why overhead might be underapplied.

3–5 What adjustment is made for underapplied overhead on the schedule of cost of goods sold? What adjustment is made for overapplied overhead?

3–6 How do you compute raw materials used in production?

3–7 How do you compute the total manufacturing costs added to production within a schedule of cost of goods manufactured?

3–8 How do you compute cost of goods manufactured?

3–9 How do you compute unadjusted cost of goods sold?

3–10 How do direct labor costs flow through a job-order costing system?

Applying Excel

The Excel worksheet form shown below relates to the Turbo Crafters example from earlier in the chapter. The workbook, and instructions on how to complete the file, can be found in Connect.

LO3–1, LO3–4

	A	B	C	D
1	Chapter 3: Applying Excel			
2				
3	Data			
4	Allocation base	Machine-hours		
5	Estimated manufacturing overhead cost	$300,000		
6	Estimated total amount of the allocation base	75,000 machine-hours		
7	Actual manufacturing overhead cost	$290,000		
8	Actual total amount of the allocation base	68,000 machine-hours		
9				
10	Enter a formula into each of the cells marked with a ? below			
11				
12	Computation of the predetermined overhead rate			
13	Estimated manufacturing overhead cost	?		
14	Estimated total amount of the allocation base	? machine-hours		
15	Predetermined overhead rate	? per machine-hour		
16				
17	Computation of underapplied or overapplied manufacturing overhead			
18	Actual manufacturing overhead cost	?		
19	Manufacturing overhead cost applied to Work in Process during the year:			
20	Predetermined overhead rate	? per machine-hour		
21	Actual total amount of the allocation base	? machine-hours		
22	Manufacturing overhead applied	?		
23	Underapplied (overapplied) manufacturing overhead	?		
24				

Chapter 3 Form / Filled in Chapter 3 Form / Chapter 3 Formulas

Microsoft Excel

You should proceed to the requirements below only after completing your worksheet.

Required:

1. Check your worksheet by changing the estimated total amount of the allocation base in the Data area to 60,000 machine-hours, keeping all of the other data the same as in the original example. If your worksheet is operating properly, the predetermined overhead rate should now be $5.00 per machine-hour. If you do not get this answer, find the errors in your worksheet and correct them.

    How much is the underapplied (overapplied) manufacturing overhead? Did it change? Why or why not?

2. Determine the underapplied (overapplied) manufacturing overhead for a different company with the following data:

Allocation base	Machine-hours
Estimated manufacturing overhead cost	$100,000
Estimated total amount of the allocation base	50,000 machine-hours
Actual manufacturing overhead cost	$90,000
Actual total amount of the allocation base	40,000 machine-hours

3. What happens to the underapplied (overapplied) manufacturing overhead from part (2) if the estimated amount of the allocation base is changed to 40,000 machine-hours and everything else remains the same? Why is the amount of underapplied (overapplied) manufacturing overhead different from part (2)?

4. Change the estimated amount of the allocation base back to 50,000 machine-hours so the data look exactly like they did in part (2). Now change the actual manufacturing overhead cost to $100,000. What is the underapplied (overapplied) manufacturing overhead now? Why is the underapplied (overapplied) manufacturing overhead different from part (2)?

The Foundational 15   Mc Graw Hill connect

LO3–1, LO3–2, LO3–3, LO3–4

Bunnell Corporation is a manufacturer that uses job-order costing. On January 1, the company's inventory balances were as follows:

Raw materials	$40,000
Work in process	$18,000
Finished goods	$35,000

The company applies overhead cost to jobs using direct labor-hours. For this year, the company's predetermined overhead rate of $16.25 per direct labor-hour was based on a cost formula that estimated $650,000 of total manufacturing overhead for an estimated activity level of 40,000 direct labor-hours. The following transactions were recorded this year:

a. Raw materials purchased on account, $510,000.

b. Raw materials used in production, $480,000. All of of the raw materials were used as direct materials.

c. The following costs were accrued for employee services: direct labor, $600,000; indirect labor, $150,000; selling and administrative salaries, $240,000.

d. Incurred various selling and administrative expenses (e.g., advertising, sales travel costs, and finished goods warehousing), $367,000.

e. Incurred various manufacturing overhead costs (e.g., depreciation, insurance, and utilities), $500,000.

f. Manufacturing overhead cost was applied to production. The company actually worked 41,000 direct labor-hours on all jobs during the year.

g. Jobs costing $1,680,000 to manufacture according to their job cost sheets were completed during the year.

h. Jobs were sold on account to customers during the year for a total of $2,800,000. The jobs cost $1,690,000 to manufacture according to their job cost sheets.

Required:

For this year:

1. What is the journal entry to record raw materials used in production?
2. What is the ending balance in Raw Materials?
3. What is the journal entry to record the labor costs?
4. What is the total manufacturing overhead applied to production?

5. What is the total manufacturing cost added to Work in Process?
6. What is the journal entry to record the transfer of completed jobs referred to in item g above?
7. What is the ending balance in Work in Process?
8. What is the total actual manufacturing overhead cost incurred?
9. Is manufacturing overhead underapplied or overapplied? By how much?
10. What is the cost of goods available for sale?
11. What is the journal entry to record the cost of goods sold referred to in item h above?
12. What is the ending balance in Finished Goods?
13. Assuming the company closes its underapplied or overapplied overhead to Cost of Goods Sold, what is the adjusted cost of goods sold?
14. What is the gross margin?
15. What is the net operating income?

Mc Graw Hill **connect**   **Exercises**

EXERCISE 3–1 Prepare Journal Entries LO3–1
Larned Corporation recorded the following transactions for the just completed month.
a. Purchased $80,000 of raw materials on account.
b. $71,000 in raw materials were used in production. Of this amount, $62,000 was direct materials and the remainder was indirect materials.
c. Paid employees $112,000 cash. Of this amount, $101,000 was direct labor and the remainder was indirect labor.
d. Depreciation of $175,000 was incurred on factory equipment.

Required:
Record the above transactions in journal entries.

EXERCISE 3–2 Prepare T-Accounts LO3–2, LO3–4
Jurvin Enterprises is a manufacturing company with no beginning inventories. A subset of the transactions it recorded during a recent month is shown below.
a. Purchased $94,000 in raw materials for cash.
b. $89,000 in raw materials were used in production. Of this amount, $78,000 was direct materials and the remainder was indirect materials.
c. Paid employees $132,000 cash. Of this amount, $112,000 was direct labor and the remainder was indirect labor.
d. Paid $143,000 for additional manufacturing overhead costs.
e. Applied manufacturing overhead of $152,000 to production using the company's predetermined overhead rate.
f. All of the jobs in process at the end of the month were completed.
g. All of the completed jobs were shipped to customers.
h. Any underapplied or overapplied overhead was closed to Cost of Goods Sold.

Required:
1. Post the above transactions to T-accounts.
2. Calculate the adjusted cost of goods sold for the period.

EXERCISE 3–3 Schedules of Cost of Goods Manufactured and Cost of Goods Sold LO3–3
Primare Corporation provided the following data for last month's manufacturing operations.

Purchases of raw materials	$30,000
Indirect materials used in production	$5,000
Direct labor	$58,000
Manufacturing overhead applied to work in process	$87,000
Underapplied overhead	$4,000

Inventories	Beginning	Ending
Raw materials	$12,000	$18,000
Work in process	$56,000	$65,000
Finished goods	$35,000	$42,000

Required:
1. Prepare a schedule of cost of goods manufactured.
2. Prepare a schedule of cost of goods sold. Assume the underapplied or overapplied overhead is closed to Cost of Goods Sold.

EXERCISE 3–4 Underapplied and Overapplied Overhead LO3–4

Osborn Manufacturing uses a predetermined overhead rate of $18.20 per direct labor-hour. This predetermined rate was based on a cost formula that estimates $218,400 of total manufacturing overhead for an estimated activity level of 12,000 direct labor-hours.

    The company actually incurred $215,000 of manufacturing overhead and 11,500 direct labor-hours during the period.

Required:
1. Calculate the underapplied or overapplied manufacturing overhead.
2. Assume the company's underapplied or overapplied overhead is closed to Cost of Goods Sold. Would the closing journal entry increase or decrease gross margin? By how much?

EXERCISE 3–5 Journal Entries and T-accounts LO3–1, LO3–2

The Polaris Company uses a job-order costing system. The following transactions occurred in October:
a. Raw materials purchased on account, $210,000.
b. Raw materials used in production, $190,000 ($178,000 direct materials and $12,000 indirect materials).
c. Accrued direct labor cost of $90,000 and indirect labor cost of $110,000.
d. Depreciation recorded on factory equipment, $40,000.
e. Other manufacturing overhead costs accrued during October, $70,000.
f. The company applies manufacturing overhead cost to production using a predetermined rate of $8 per machine-hour. A total of 30,000 machine-hours were used in October.
g. Jobs costing $520,000 were completed and transferred to Finished Goods.
h. Jobs costing $480,000 were shipped to customers. These jobs were sold on account at 25% above cost.

Required:
1. Prepare journal entries to record the transactions given above.
2. Prepare T-accounts for Manufacturing Overhead and Work in Process. Post the relevant transactions from above to each account. Compute the ending balance in each account, assuming Work in Process has a beginning balance of $42,000.

EXERCISE 3–6 Schedules of Cost of Goods Manufactured and Cost of Goods Sold; Income Statement LO3–3

Mason Company provided the following data for this year:

Sales	$524,000
Direct labor cost	$70,000
Raw material purchases.	$118,000
Selling expenses.	$140,000
Administrative expenses	$63,000
Manufacturing overhead applied to work in process. . . .	$90,000
Actual manufacturing overhead costs	$80,000

Inventories	Beginning	Ending
Raw materials	$7,000	$15,000
Work in process	$10,000	$5,000
Finished goods	$20,000	$35,000

Required:
1. Prepare a schedule of cost of goods manufactured. Assume all raw materials used in production were direct materials.
2. Prepare a schedule of cost of goods sold. Assume the company's underapplied or overapplied overhead is closed to Cost of Goods Sold.
3. Prepare an income statement.

EXERCISE 3–7 Applying Overhead; Cost of Goods Manufactured LO3–3, LO3–4

Chang Company provided the following data for this year:

Manufacturing overhead costs incurred:	
Indirect materials	$ 15,000
Indirect labor	130,000
Property taxes, factory	8,000
Utilities, factory	70,000
Depreciation, factory	240,000
Insurance, factory	10,000
Total actual manufacturing overhead costs incurred	$473,000
Other costs incurred:	
Purchases of raw materials (both direct and indirect)	$400,000
Direct labor cost	$60,000
Inventories:	
Raw materials, beginning	$20,000
Raw materials, ending	$30,000
Work in process, beginning	$40,000
Work in process, ending	$70,000

The company uses a predetermined overhead rate of $25 per machine-hour to apply overhead cost to jobs. A total of 19,400 machine-hours were used during the year.

Required:
1. Compute the underapplied or overapplied overhead cost.
2. Prepare a schedule of cost of goods manufactured.

EXERCISE 3–8 Applying Overhead; Journal Entries; Disposing of Underapplied or Overapplied Overhead LO3–1, LO3–2, LO3–4

Latta Company provided the following T-accounts for this year.

Manufacturing Overhead			
(a)	460,000	(b)	390,000
Bal.	70,000		

Work in Process			
Bal.	15,000	(c)	710,000
	260,000		
	85,000		
(b)	390,000		
Bal.	40,000		

Finished Goods			
Bal.	50,000	(d)	640,000
(c)	710,000		
Bal.	120,000		

Cost of Goods Sold		
(d)	640,000	

The overhead applied to production is distributed among Work in Process, Finished Goods, and Cost of Goods Sold at the end of the year as follows:

Work in Process, ending	$ 19,500
Finished Goods, ending	58,500
Cost of Goods Sold	312,000
Overhead applied	$390,000

For example, of the $40,000 ending balance in Work in Process, $19,500 was applied overhead.

Required:
1. Identify reasons for entries (a) through (d).
2. Assume underapplied or overapplied overhead is closed to Cost of Goods Sold. Prepare the necessary journal entry.
3. Assume underapplied or overapplied overhead is closed proportionally to Work in Process, Finished Goods, and Cost of Goods Sold. Prepare the necessary journal entry.

EXERCISE 3–9 Applying Overhead; T-accounts; Journal Entries LO3–1, LO3–2, LO3–4
Harwood Company's job-order costing system applies overhead cost to jobs based on machine-hours. The predetermined overhead rate of $2.40 per machine-hour was based on a cost formula that estimates $192,000 of total manufacturing overhead for an estimated activity level of 80,000 machine-hours.

Required:
1. Assume during the year the company works only 75,000 machine-hours and incurs the following costs in the Manufacturing Overhead and Work in Process accounts:

	Manufacturing Overhead			Work in Process	
(Maintenance)	21,000	?	(Direct materials)	710,000	
(Indirect materials)	8,000		(Direct labor)	90,000	
(Indirect labor)	60,000		(Overhead)	?	
(Utilities)	32,000				
(Insurance)	7,000				
(Depreciation)	56,000				

Copy the data in the T-accounts above onto your answer sheet. Compute the overhead cost applied to Work in Process for the year and make the entry in your T-accounts.
2. Compute the underapplied or overapplied overhead and show the balance in your Manufacturing Overhead T-account. Prepare a journal entry to close the company's underapplied or overapplied overhead to Cost of Goods Sold.
3. Explain why the manufacturing overhead was underapplied or overapplied.

EXERCISE 3–10 Applying Overhead; Journal Entries; T-accounts LO3–1, LO3–2
Dillon Products manufactures various machined parts to customer specifications. The company uses a job-order costing system and applies overhead cost to jobs based on machine-hours. At the beginning of the year, the company used a cost formula to estimate $4,800,000 in manufacturing overhead cost at an activity level of 240,000 machine-hours.

The company spent the month of January working on a large order for 16,000 custom-made machined parts. The company had no work in process at the beginning of January. Cost data relating to January follow:
a. Raw materials purchased on account, $325,000.
b. Raw materials used in production, $290,000 (80% direct materials and 20% indirect materials).
c. Labor cost accrued in the factory, $180,000 (one-third direct labor and two-thirds indirect labor).
d. Depreciation recorded on factory equipment, $75,000.
e. Other manufacturing overhead costs incurred on account, $62,000.
f. Manufacturing overhead cost was applied to production on the basis of 15,000 machine-hours actually worked.
g. The completed job for 16,000 custom-made machined parts was moved into the finished goods warehouse on January 31 to await delivery to the customer. (In computing the dollar amount for this entry, remember the cost of a completed job consists of direct materials, direct labor, and *applied* overhead.)

Required:
1. Prepare journal entries to record items (a) through (f) above [ignore item (g) for the moment].
2. Prepare T-accounts for Manufacturing Overhead and Work in Process. Post the relevant items from your journal entries to these T-accounts.
3. Prepare a journal entry for item (g) above.
4. If 10,000 of the custom-made machined parts are shipped to the customer in February, how much of this job's cost will be included in cost of goods sold for February?

Mc Graw Hill connect **Problems**

PROBLEM 3–11 T-Account Analysis of Cost Flows LO3–2, LO3–3, LO3–4

Selected T-accounts of Moore Company are given below for the just-completed year:

Raw Materials

Bal. 1/1	15,000	Credits	?
Debits	120,000		
Bal. 12/31	25,000		

Manufacturing Overhead

Debits	230,000	Credits	?

Work in Process

Bal. 1/1	20,000	Credits	470,000
Direct materials	90,000		
Direct labor	150,000		
Overhead	240,000		
Bal. 12/31	?		

Factory Wages Payable

Debits	185,000	Bal. 1/1	9,000
		Credits	180,000
		Bal. 12/31	4,000

Finished Goods

Bal. 1/1	40,000	Credits	?
Debits	?		
Bal. 12/31	60,000		

Cost of Goods Sold

Debits	?	

Required:
1. What was the cost of raw materials used in production?
2. How much of the materials in (1) above consisted of indirect materials?
3. How much of the factory labor cost is indirect labor?
4. What was the cost of goods manufactured?
5. What was the unadjusted cost of goods sold? Do not include any underapplied or overapplied overhead in your answer.
6. If overhead is applied to production based on direct labor cost, what was the predetermined overhead rate?
7. Was manufacturing overhead underapplied or overapplied? By how much?
8. Compute the ending balance in Work in Process. Assume this balance consists entirely of goods started during the year. If $8,000 of this balance is direct labor cost, how much is direct materials cost? Applied overhead cost?

PROBLEM 3–12 Predetermined Overhead Rate; Disposing of Underapplied or Overapplied Overhead LO3–4

Luzadis Company makes furniture using the latest automated technology. The company uses a job-order costing system and applies manufacturing overhead cost to products based on machine-hours. The predetermined overhead rate was based on a cost formula that estimates $900,000 of total manufacturing overhead for an estimated activity level of 75,000 machine-hours.

During the year, a large quantity of furniture on the market caused Luzadis to cut production and build inventories. The company provided the following data for the year:

Machine-hours	60,000
Manufacturing overhead cost	$850,000
Inventories at year-end:	
Raw materials	$30,000
Work in process (includes overhead applied of $36,000)	$100,000
Finished goods (includes overhead applied of $180,000)	$500,000
Cost of goods sold (includes overhead applied of $504,000)	$1,400,000

Required:
1. Compute the underapplied or overapplied overhead.
2. Assume the company closes underapplied or overapplied overhead to Cost of Goods Sold. Prepare the appropriate journal entry.
3. Assume the company allocates underapplied or overapplied overhead proportionally to Work in Process, Finished Goods, and Cost of Goods Sold. Prepare the appropriate journal entry.
4. How much higher or lower will net operating income be if the underapplied or overapplied overhead is allocated to Work in Process, Finished Goods, and Cost of Goods Sold rather than being closed to Cost of Goods Sold?

PROBLEM 3–13 Schedules of Cost of Goods Manufactured and Cost of Goods Sold; Income Statement LO3–3
Superior Company provided the following data for this year (all raw materials are used in production as direct materials):

Selling expenses	$140,000
Purchases of raw materials	$290,000
Direct labor	?
Administrative expenses	$100,000
Manufacturing overhead applied to work in process	$285,000
Actual manufacturing overhead cost	$270,000

Beginning and ending inventory balances were as follows:

	Beginning	Ending
Raw materials	$40,000	$10,000
Work in process	?	$35,000
Finished goods	$50,000	?

The total manufacturing costs added to production for the year were $683,000; the cost of goods available for sale totaled $740,000; the unadjusted cost of goods sold totaled $660,000; and the net operating income was $30,000. The company's underapplied or overapplied overhead is closed to Cost of Goods Sold.

Required:
Prepare schedules of cost of goods manufactured and cost of goods sold and an income statement. (*Hint:* Prepare the income statement and schedule of cost of goods sold first followed by the schedule of cost of goods manufactured.)

PROBLEM 3–14 Schedule of Cost of Goods Manufactured; Overhead Analysis LO3–3, LO3–4
Gitano Products uses job-order costing and applies overhead cost to jobs based on direct materials *used in production* (*not* on the basis of raw materials purchased). Its predetermined overhead rate is based on a cost formula that estimated $800,000 of manufacturing overhead for an estimated

allocation base of $500,000 direct material dollars to be used in production. The company provided the following data for the just-completed year:

Purchase of raw materials	$510,000
Direct labor cost	$90,000
Manufacturing overhead costs:	
Indirect labor	$170,000
Property taxes	$48,000
Depreciation of equipment	$260,000
Maintenance	$95,000
Insurance	$7,000
Rent, building.	$180,000

	Beginning	Ending
Raw Materials	$20,000	$80,000
Work in Process	$150,000	$70,000
Finished Goods	$260,000	$400,000

Required:
1. Compute the predetermined overhead rate.
2. Compute the amount of underapplied or overapplied overhead.
3. Prepare a schedule of cost of goods manufactured. Assume all raw materials are used in production as direct materials.
4. Compute the unadjusted cost of goods sold. Do not include any underapplied or overapplied overhead in your answer. What options are available for disposing of underapplied or overapplied overhead?
5. Assume the $70,000 ending balance in Work in Process includes $24,000 of direct materials. Given this assumption, supply the information missing below:

Direct materials	$24,000
Direct labor.	?
Manufacturing overhead	?
Work in process inventory.	$70,000

PROBLEM 3–15 Journal Entries; T-Accounts; Financial Statements LO3–1, LO3–2, LO3–3, LO3–4
Froya Fabrikker A/S of Bergen, Norway, manufactures specialty heavy equipment for use in North Sea oil fields. The company uses a job-order costing system that applies manufacturing overhead cost to jobs based on direct labor-hours. Its predetermined overhead rate was based on a cost formula that estimated $360,000 of manufacturing overhead for an estimated allocation base of 900 direct labor-hours. The following transactions occurred during the year:
a. Raw materials purchased on account, $200,000.
b. Raw materials used in production (all direct materials), $185,000.
c. Utility bills incurred on account, $70,000 (90% related to factory operations, and the remainder related to selling and administrative activities).
d. Accrued salary and wage costs:

Direct labor (975 hours).	$230,000
Indirect labor	$90,000
Selling and administrative salaries	$110,000

e. Maintenance costs incurred on account in the factory, $54,000.
f. Advertising costs incurred on account, $136,000.
g. Depreciation recorded for the year, $95,000 (80% related to factory equipment, and the remainder related to selling and administrative equipment).
h. Rental cost incurred on account, $120,000 (85% related to factory facilities, and the remainder related to selling and administrative facilities).
i. Manufacturing overhead cost applied to jobs, $___?___.

j.   Cost of goods manufactured, $770,000.
k.   Sales (all on account) totaled $1,200,000. These goods cost $800,000 according to their job
     cost sheets.
     The beginning balances in the inventory accounts were:

Raw Materials	$30,000
Work in Process	$21,000
Finished Goods	$60,000

Required:
1.   Prepare journal entries to record the preceding transactions.
2.   Post your entries to T-accounts. (Don't forget to enter the beginning inventory balances
     above.) Determine the ending balances in the inventory accounts and in the Manufacturing
     Overhead account.
3.   Prepare a schedule of cost of goods manufactured.
4.   Prepare a journal entry to close any balance in the Manufacturing Overhead account to Cost
     of Goods Sold. Prepare a schedule of cost of goods sold.
5.   Prepare an income statement.

PROBLEM 3–16 Comprehensive Problem LO3–1, LO3–2, LO3–4
Gold Nest Company of Guandong, China, makes birdcages for the South China market. The company sells its birdcages through an extensive network of street vendors who receive commissions
on their sales.
     The company uses a job-order costing system that applies overhead to jobs based on direct
labor cost. Its predetermined overhead rate is based on a cost formula that estimated $330,000 of
manufacturing overhead for an estimated activity level of $200,000 direct labor dollars. The begin-
ning inventory balances were as follows:

Raw materials	$25,000
Work in process	$10,000
Finished goods	$40,000

     During the year, the following transactions occured:
a.   Raw materials purchased on account, $275,000.
b.   Raw materials used in production, $280,000 (materials costing $220,000 were charged
     directly to jobs; the remaining materials were indirect).
c.   Cash paid to employees:

Direct labor	$180,000
Indirect labor	$72,000
Sales commissions	$63,000
Administrative salaries	$90,000

d.   Rent for the year, $18,000 ($13,000 related to factory operations, and the remainder related to
     selling and administrative activities).
e.   Utility costs incurred in the factory, $57,000.
f.   Advertising costs incurred, $140,000.
g.   Depreciation on equipment, $100,000 ($88,000 related to equipment used in factory opera-
     tions; the remaining $12,000 related to equipment used in selling and administrative activities).
h.   Manufacturing overhead cost applied to jobs, $? .
i.   Completed goods costing $675,000 to manufacture.
j.   Sales for the year (all paid in cash) totaled $1,250,000. The manufacturing cost of these goods
     was $700,000.

Required:
1.   Prepare journal entries to record the transactions for the year.
2.   Prepare T-accounts for each inventory account, Manufacturing Overhead, and Cost of
     Goods Sold. Post relevant data from your journal entries to these T-accounts (don't forget
     to enter the beginning balances in your inventory accounts). Compute an ending balance in
     each account.

3. Is Manufacturing Overhead underapplied or overapplied? Prepare a journal entry to close Manufacturing Overhead to Cost of Goods Sold.
4. Prepare an income statement. (Do not prepare a schedule of cost of goods manufactured; all of the information needed for the income statement is available in the journal entries and T-accounts you have prepared.)

PROBLEM 3–17 Cost Flows; T-Accounts; Income Statement LO3–2, LO3–3, LO3–4

Supreme Videos, Inc., produces short musical videos for sale to retail outlets. The company's balance sheet accounts as of January 1 are given below.

Supreme Videos, Inc. Balance Sheet January 1		
Assets		
Current assets:		
Cash		$ 63,000
Accounts receivable		102,000
Inventories:		
Raw materials (film, costumes)	$ 30,000	
Videos in process..........................	45,000	
Finished videos awaiting sale	81,000	156,000
Prepaid insurance		9,000
Total current assets		330,000
Studio and equipment	730,000	
Less accumulated depreciation	210,000	520,000
Total assets		$850,000
Liabilities and Stockholders' Equity		
Accounts payable		$160,000
Capital stock	$420,000	
Retained earnings	270,000	690,000
Total liabilities and stockholders' equity		$850,000

Because the videos differ in length and complexity of production, the company uses a job-order costing system to determine the cost of each video produced. Studio (manufacturing) overhead is charged to videos based on camera-hours of activity. The company's predetermined overhead rate for the year is based on a cost formula that estimated $280,000 in manufacturing overhead for an estimated allocation base of 7,000 camera-hours. The following transactions occurred during the year:

a. Film, costumes, and similar raw materials purchased on account, $185,000.
b. Film, costumes, and other raw materials used in production, $200,000 (85% of this material was direct to the videos in production, and the other 15% was indirect).
c. Utility costs incurred in the production studio, $72,000.
d. Depreciation on the studio, cameras, and other equipment, $84,000. Three-fourths of this depreciation related to production of the videos, and the remainder related to equipment used in marketing and administration.
e. Advertising expense incurred, $130,000.
f. Costs for salaries and wages were incurred as follows:

Direct labor (actors and directors)	$82,000
Indirect labor (carpenters to build sets, costume designers, and so forth)	$110,000
Administrative salaries	$95,000

g. Prepaid insurance expired during the year, $7,000 (80% related to production of videos, and 20% related to marketing and administrative activities).
h. Miscellaneous marketing and administrative expenses incurred, $8,600.
i. Studio (manufacturing) overhead was applied to videos in production. The company used 7,250 camera-hours during the year.

j.   Videos costing $550,000 to produce were transferred to the finished videos warehouse.
k.   Sales for the year totaled $925,000 and were all on account. The total cost to produce these videos was $600,000.
l.   Collections from customers during the year, $850,000.
m.   Payments to suppliers on account during the year, $500,000; payments to employees for salaries and wages, $285,000.

Required:

1.   Prepare a T-account for each account on the company's balance sheet and enter the beginning balances.
2.   Record the transactions in the T-accounts. Prepare new T-accounts as needed. Key your entries to the letters (a) through (m) above. Compute the ending balance in each account.
3.   Is the Studio (manufacturing) Overhead account underapplied or overapplied? Make an entry in the T-accounts to close the Studio Overhead account to Cost of Goods Sold.
4.   Prepare a schedule of cost of goods manufactured. If done correctly, the cost of goods manufactured should agree with which of the above transactions?
5.   Prepare a schedule of cost of goods sold. If done correctly, the unadjusted cost of goods sold should agree with which of the above transactions?
6.   Prepare an income statement.

Case Mc Graw Hill connect

Select cases are available in Connect.

CASE 3–18 Ethics and the Manager LO3-4

Terri Ronsin was recently transferred to the Home Security Systems Division of National Home Products. Shortly after taking over her new position as divisional controller, she was asked to develop the division's predetermined overhead rate for the upcoming year. The accuracy of the rate is important because it is used throughout the year and any underapplied or overapplied overhead is closed out to Cost of Goods Sold at the end of the year. National Home Products uses direct labor-hours in all of its divisions as the allocation base for manufacturing overhead.

To compute the predetermined overhead rate, Terri divided her estimated total manufacturing overhead by the production manager's estimate of the total direct labor-hours for the coming year. She took her computations to the division's general manager for approval but was quite surprised when he suggested a modification in the allocation base. Her conversation with the general manager of the Home Security Systems Division, Harry Irving, went like this:

Ronsin: Here are my calculations for next year's predetermined overhead rate. If you approve, we can enter the rate into the computer on January 1 and be up and running in the job-order costing system right away this year.

Irving: Thanks for coming up with the calculations so quickly, and they look just fine. There is, however, one slight modification I would like to see. Your estimate of the total direct labor-hours for the year is 440,000 hours. How about cutting that to about 420,000 hours?

Ronsin: I don't know if I can do that. The production manager says she will need about 440,000 direct labor-hours to meet the sales projections. Besides, there are going to be over 430,000 direct labor-hours during the current year and sales are projected to be higher next year.

Irving: Teri, I know all of that. I would still like to reduce the direct labor-hours in the allocation base to something like 420,000 hours. You probably don't know I had an agreement with your predecessor as divisional controller to shave 5% off the estimated direct labor-hours every year. That way, we kept a reserve to boost net operating income at the end of the year. We called it our Christmas bonus. Corporate headquarters always seemed pleased we could pull off such a miracle at the end of the year. This system has worked well for many years, and I don't want to change it now.

Required:

1.   Explain how shaving 5% off the estimated direct labor-hours in the allocation base for the predetermined overhead rate boosts net operating income at the end of the year.
2.   Should Terri Ronsin go along with the general manager's request?

Appendix 3A: Job-Order Costing: A Microsoft Excel–Based Approach

In this appendix, we use Microsoft Excel to show how the transactions in a job-order costing system impact a company's balance sheet. While the main body of the chapter focused on using journal entries to record transactions, the approach shown here will help you develop a new and valuable managerial skill—analyzing how transactions affect the balance sheet without having to prepare formal journal entries.

To set the stage for the forthcoming example, we need to review two fundamental accounting equations and specify three important assumptions.

Fundamental Accounting Equations

A balance sheet is based on the following accounting equation:

$$\text{Assets} = \text{Liabilities} + \text{Stockholders' Equity}$$

In the Excel spreadsheets we'll be using in this appendix, one column will always be populated with an "=" sign. The accounts on the left-hand side of the "=" sign will be asset accounts and the accounts on the right-hand side will be liability and stockholders' equity accounts. After we record every transaction, the amounts on the left-hand side of the "=" sign must equal the amounts on the right-hand side.

The second foundational equation relates to the Retained Earnings account on a company's balance sheet. The ending balance in retained earnings is computed using the following equation:

$$\begin{array}{c}\text{Ending balance in}\\\text{retained earnings}\end{array} = \begin{array}{c}\text{Beginning balance in}\\\text{retained earnings}\end{array} + \begin{array}{c}\text{Net}\\\text{operating}\\\text{income}\end{array} - \text{Dividends}$$

This equation highlights the connection between the balance sheet and income statement. It recognizes that net operating income from the income statement is embedded within retained earnings on the balance sheet. Thus, in our Microsoft Excel–based approach, any transactions involving sales or expenses will be recorded in the Retained Earnings column of the balance sheet.

Three Key Assumptions

The first assumption in the appendix is we will always use only one predetermined overhead rate. In other words, we are going to use the same approach demonstrated in the main body of this chapter. This requires using an account titled Manufacturing Overhead within our Microsoft Excel spreadsheets that serves the same purpose as the Manufacturing Overhead clearing account discussed earlier in the chapter.

The second assumption is underapplied or overapplied manufacturing overhead will always be closed to Cost of Goods Sold. Because the income statement is embedded in the Retained Earnings account on the balance sheet, we will always close underapplied or overapplied overhead to Retained Earnings.

Our third assumption is we'll record transactions within Microsoft Excel by using positive numbers to increase balance sheet accounts and negative numbers (shown in parentheses) to decrease those accounts. This is a slightly different approach than we used in the main body of the chapter where all transactions were depicted using the language of debits and credits—in journal entry form and in T-account form. This appendix replaces the language of debits and credits with an equivalent alternative. Instead, it identifies the balance sheet accounts affected by each transaction and determines if those account balances should increase or decrease.

Sapphire Company–Setting the Stage

Sapphire Company uses a job-order costing system to assign manufacturing costs to jobs. Its balance sheet on January 1 is as follows[3]:

Sapphire Company Balance Sheet January 1		
Assets		
Cash		$ 15,000
Raw materials	$8,000	
Work in process	5,000	
Finished goods	13,000	26,000
Prepaid expenses		3,000
Property, plant, and equipment (net)		240,000
Total assets		$284,000
Liabilities and Stockholders' Equity		
Accounts payable		$ 4,000
Retained earnings		280,000
Total liabilities and stockholders' equity		$284,000

Exhibit 3A–1 contains a Microsoft Excel spreadsheet that includes the beginning balances shown in the balance sheet above. Notice column "J" of the spreadsheet contains "=" signs (see cells J5 and J6). This means after we record each of the forthcoming transactions, the amounts on the left-hand side of column "J" will always need to equal the amounts on the right-hand side of column "J."

Also, notice the spreadsheet contains all of the accounts shown in the January 1 balance sheet plus an account called Manufacturing Overhead. As discussed earlier in the chapter, Manufacturing Overhead is a clearing account that always has a beginning and ending balance of zero. This account is used to record two things—all actual overhead costs and the manufacturing overhead applied to production using the predetermined overhead rate. The difference between the actual overhead cost and the overhead applied to production is the underapplied or overapplied overhead.

Finally, to conserve space, the Excel spreadsheet abbreviates Property, Plant, and Equipment (net) as PP&E (net). The term *net* implies the acquisition cost of property, plant, and equipment is reported *net* of accumulated depreciation.

Sapphire Company–Transaction Analysis

The remainder of the appendix proceeds in three steps. First, it lists Sapphire Company's transactions for the month of January. Second, it explains how each of these transactions is recorded in the Microsoft Excel spreadsheet. Finally, it explains how to use the

EXHIBIT 3A–1
Sapphire Company: Transaction Analysis

	A	B	C	D	E	F	G	H	I	J	K	L
1						Sapphire Company						
2						Transaction Analysis						
3						For the Month Ended January 31						
5	Transactions		Cash	Raw Materials	Work in Process	Finished Goods	Manufacturing Overhead	Prepaid Expenses	PP&E (net)	=	Accounts Payable	Retained Earnings
6	Beginning balances @ 1/1		$ 15,000	$ 8,000	$ 5,000	$ 13,000	$ -	$ 3,000	$240,000	=	$ 4,000	$280,000
7												

Exhibit 3A-1 / Exhibit 3A-2 / Exhibit 3A-3 / Exhibit 3A-4 / Exhibit 3A-5

Microsoft Excel

---

[3] To reduce the width of the Excel spreadsheets in this appendix, all examples, exercises, and problems, exclude a Common Stock account.

information depicted in the spreadsheet to prepare a schedule of cost of goods manufactured, a schedule of cost of goods sold, and an income statement for the month of January.

To begin our illustration, let's assume Sapphire Company has a predetermined overhead rate of $25 per direct labor-hour based on a cost formula that estimated $100,000 in manufacturing overhead cost for an estimated allocation base of 4,000 direct labor-hours. During January, the company completed the following transactions:

a. Purchased raw materials on account, $80,000.
b. Raw materials used in production, $78,000 ($70,000 was direct materials and $8,000 indirect materials).
c. Paid $135,000 of salaries and wages in cash ($68,000 was direct labor, $45,000 indirect labor, and $22,000 related to employees responsible for selling and administration).
d. Utility costs incurred (on account) to support production, $15,000.
e. Depreciation on property, plant, and equipment, $40,000 (70% related to manufacturing equipment and 30% related to assets that support selling and administration).
f. Advertising expenses paid in cash, $18,000.
g. Prepaid insurance expired during the month, $1,000 (80% related to production, and 20% related to selling and administration).
h. Manufacturing overhead applied to production, $102,500. This amount was computed by multiplying 4,100 direct labor-hours worked in January by the predetermined overhead rate of $25 per direct labor-hour.
i. Cost of goods manufactured, $235,000.
j. Cash sales, $320,000.
k. Cost of goods sold, $245,000.
l. Cash payments to creditors, $92,000.
m. Close overapplied overhead of $5,700 to cost of goods sold.

Exhibit 3A–2 summarizes how each of the transactions would be recorded in the Microsoft Excel spreadsheet. The underlying explanations for each transaction are as follows (each transaction includes a parenthetical reference to its row within the Microsoft Excel spreadsheet):

a. (row 7) Purchasing raw materials on account for $80,000 will increase Raw Materials and Accounts Payable by $80,000.
b. (row 8) When raw materials are used in production, it decreases Raw Materials by $78,000. The direct materials of $70,000 are added to Work in Process, whereas the

---

EXHIBIT 3A–2

Sapphire Company: Completed Transaction Analysis

	A	B	C	D	E	F	G	H	I	J	K	L
1						Sapphire Company						
2						Transaction Analysis						
3						For the Month Ended January 31						
				Raw	Work in	Finished	Manufacturing	Prepaid			Accounts	Retained
5	Transactions		Cash	Materials	Process	Goods	Overhead	Expenses	PP&E (net)	=	Payable	Earnings
6		Beginning balances @ 1/1	$ 15,000	$ 8,000	$ 5,000	$ 13,000	$ -	$ 3,000	$240,000	=	$ 4,000	$280,000
7	(a)	Raw material purchases		80,000						=	80,000	
8	(b)	Raw materials used in production		(78,000)	70,000		8,000			=		
9	(c)	Salaries and wages	(135,000)		68,000		45,000			=		(22,000)
10	(d)	Utility costs					15,000			=	15,000	
11	(e)	Depreciation					28,000		(40,000)	=		(12,000)
12	(f)	Advertising	(18,000)							=		(18,000)
13	(g)	Expiration of prepaid insurance					800	(1,000)		=		(200)
14	(h)	Manufacturing overhead applied			102,500		(102,500)			=		
15	(i)	Cost of goods manufactured			(235,000)	235,000				=		
16	(j)	Sales	320,000							=		320,000
17	(k)	Cost of goods sold				(245,000)				=		(245,000)
18	(l)	Payments to creditors	(92,000)							=	(92,000)	
19	(m)	Overapplied overhead					5,700			=		5,700
20		Ending balances @ 1/31	$ 90,000	$ 10,000	$ 10,500	$ 3,000	$ -	$ 2,000	$200,000	=	$ 7,000	$308,500
21												

Exhibit 3A-1 **Exhibit 3A-2** Exhibit 3A-3 Exhibit 3A-4 Exhibit 3A-5

Microsoft Excel

indirect materials of $8,000 are added to Manufacturing Overhead. Notice actual manufacturing overhead costs, such as the $8,000 of indirect materials, *are not added to* Work in Process. As you will see in a later transaction, manufacturing overhead is applied to Work in Process using the predetermined overhead rate.

c. (*row 9*) The salaries and wages decrease Cash by $135,000. The direct labor cost of $68,000 increases Work in Process, whereas the indirect labor cost of $45,000 increases Manufacturing Overhead. The $22,000 paid to employees working in selling and administrative roles is a period cost recorded on January's income statement. Because the income statement is embedded in Retained Earnings, we decrease Retained Earnings by $22,000.

d. (*row 10*) The utility costs support production, so they are treated as a product cost rather than a period cost. Thus, Manufacturing Overhead increases by $15,000 and Accounts Payable increases by the same amount.

e. (*row 11*) The depreciation reduces Property, Plant, and Equipment (net) by $40,000. This is equivalent to recording accumulated depreciation of $40,000. The depreciation on manufacturing equipment of $28,000 (a product cost) increases Manufacturing Overhead, whereas the depreciation on selling and administrative assets of $12,000 (a period cost) decreases Retained Earnings.

f. (*row 12*) Advertising is a period cost so Cash and Retained Earnings decrease by $18,000.

g. (*row 13*) The expired insurance coverage decreases Prepaid Expenses by $1,000. The insurance related to production (a product cost) increases Manufacturing Overhead by $800. The insurance related to selling and administration of $200 (a period cost) decreases Retained Earnings by $200.

h. (*row 14*) The manufacturing overhead applied increases Work in Process and decreases Manufacturing Overhead by $102,500. Notice manufacturing overhead is applied to Work in Process using the predetermined overhead rate. Actual manufacturing overhead costs are not recorded in Work in Process. In a later transaction, the actual overhead costs will be compared to the applied overhead to determine the underapplied or overapplied overhead.

i. (*row 15*) The cost of goods manufactured refers to the cost of the goods transferred from work in process to finished goods. This transaction decreases Work in Process by $235,000 and increases Finished Goods by the same amount.

j. (*row 16*) The sales will increase Cash by $320,000, and given that sales appear on the income statement, Retained Earnings will increase by the same amount.

k. (*row 17*) The cost of goods sold must be removed from finished goods; therefore, Finished Goods decreases by $245,000. Because cost of goods sold appears on the income statement, Retained Earnings decreases by the same amount.

l. (*row 18*) The cash payments to creditors decrease Cash and Accounts Payable by $92,000.

m. (*row 19*) The manufacturing overhead applied of $102,500 is $5,700 greater than the actual overhead costs of $96,800 (= $8,000 + $45,000 + $15,000 + $28,000 + $800). Therefore, manufacturing overhead is overapplied by $5,700. We record this transaction by increasing Manufacturing Overhead by $5,700 and increasing Retained Earnings by the same amount. The increase in Retained Earnings means we are decreasing Cost of Goods Sold (which increases net operating income).

Once we have recorded all transactions, the company's balance sheet at January 31 can be derived by summing each column in the spreadsheet (see row 20 for the ending balances reported on Sapphire Company's balance sheet at January 31).

Sapphire Company–Schedules of Cost of Goods Manufactured and Cost of Goods Sold

The transactions recorded in Exhibit 3A–2 can be used to create schedules of cost of goods manufactured and cost of goods sold. Exhibit 3A–3 shows Sapphire Company's schedule of cost of goods manufactured. Each row heading in this exhibit contains a cell reference indicating where the number appears in Exhibit 3A–2.

EXHIBIT 3A–3

Sapphire Company: Schedule of Cost of Goods Manufactured

	A	B	C	D
1	**Sapphire Company**			
2	**Schedule of Cost of Goods Manufactured**			
3	**For the Month Ended January 31**			
5	Beginning work in process inventory (E6)			$ 5,000
6	Direct materials:			
7	Beginning raw materials inventory (D6)	$ 8,000		
8	Add: Purchases of raw materials (D7)	80,000		
9	Total raw materials available	88,000		
10	Deduct: Ending raw materials inventory (D20)	10,000		
11	Raw materials used in production	78,000		
12	Deduct: Indirect materials included in manufacturing overhead (G8)	8,000		
13	Direct materials used in production		$ 70,000	
14	Direct labor (E9)		68,000	
15	Manufacturing overhead applied to work in process (E14)		102,500	
16	Total manufacturing costs added to production			240,500
17	Total manufacturing costs to account for			245,500
18	Deduct: Ending work in process inventory (E20)			10,500
19	Cost of goods manufactured			$ 235,000
20				

Exhibit 3A-1 | Exhibit 3A-2 | **Exhibit 3A-3** ...

Microsoft Excel

Notice the cost of goods manufactured of $235,000 from Exhibit 3A–3 equals the cost of goods manufactured mentioned in transaction "i" and recorded in row 15 of Exhibit 3A–2.

Exhibit 3A–4 shows Sapphire Company's schedule of cost of goods sold. Each row heading in this exhibit contains a cell reference indicating where the number appears in Exhibit 3A–2.

	A	B
1	**Sapphire Company**	
2	**Schedule of Cost of Goods Sold**	
3	**For the Month Ended January 31**	
5	Beginning finished goods inventory (F6)	$ 13,000
6	Add: Cost of goods manufactured (F15)	235,000
7	Cost of goods available for sale	248,000
8	Deduct: Ending finished goods inventory (F20)	3,000
9	Unadjusted cost of goods sold	245,000
10	Deduct: Overapplied overhead (G19)	5,700
11	Adjusted cost of goods sold	$ 239,300
12		

Exhibit 3A-1 / Exhibit 3A-2 / Exhibit 3A-3 / **Exhibit 3A-4** / Exhibit 3A-5

Microsoft Excel

EXHIBIT 3A–4

Sapphire Company: Schedule of Cost of Goods Sold

In the schedule of cost of goods sold, we subtract overapplied overhead of $5,700 from unadjusted cost of goods sold because overapplied overhead means too much overhead was added to production during the period, and hence, the cost of goods sold was overstated. In Exhibit 3A–2, we add overapplied overhead to retained earnings (see row 19) because lowering cost of goods sold increases net operating income, which in turn increases retained earnings.

Sapphire Company–Income Statement

Exhibit 3A–5 shows Sapphire Company's income statement for the month of January. The sales and selling and administrative expenses come from the transaction analysis in Exhibit 3A–2 and they each contain a corresponding parenthetical cell reference. The cost of goods sold ($239,300) is carried over from the schedule of cost of goods sold in Exhibit 3A–4.

EXHIBIT 3A–5
Sapphire Company: Income Statement

	A	B	C
1	**Sapphire Company**		
2	**Income Statement**		
3	**For the Month Ended January 31**		
5	Sales (L16)		$ 320,000
6	Cost of goods sold		239,300
7	Gross margin		80,700
8	Selling and administrative expenses:		
9	Salaries expense (L9)	$ 22,000	
10	Depreciation expense (L11)	12,000	
11	Advertising expense (L12)	18,000	
12	Insurance expense (L13)	200	52,200
13	Net operating income		$ 28,500
14			

Exhibit 3A-1 Exhibit 3A-2 Exhibit 3A-3 Exhibit 3A-4 **Exhibit 3A-5**

Microsoft Excel

Appendix 3A: Exercises and Problems   Mc Graw Hill connect

EXERCISE 3A–1 Transaction Analysis LO3–5
Carmen Company is a manufacturer who completed numerous transactions during the month, some of which are shown below:
a. Raw materials used in production as direct materials, $56,000.
b. Paid direct laborers $40,000 in cash for their work on various jobs.
c. Applied $35,000 of manufacturing overhead to production.
d. Various jobs costing $110,000 were completed and transferred to Finished Goods.
e. Various completed jobs costing $90,000 were sold to customers.
f. Cash sales, $160,000.
g. Selling and administrative expenses paid in cash, $18,000.

Required:
The table shown below includes a subset of Carmen Company's balance sheet accounts. Record each of the above transactions using the given accounts. If a transaction increases an account balance, record the amount as a positive number. If it decreases an account balance, record the amount in parentheses.

Transaction	Cash	Raw Materials	Work in Process	Finished Goods	Manufacturing Overhead		Retained Earnings
a.						=	
b.						=	
c.						=	
d.						=	
e.						=	
f.						=	
g.						=	

EXERCISE 3A–2 Transaction Analysis LO3–5

Adams Company is a manufacturer who completed numerous transactions during the month, some of which are shown below:

a.   Manufacturing overhead costs incurred on account, $80,000.

b.   Depreciation of assets, $35,000 (80% related to factory equipment, and the remainder related to selling and administrative equipment).

c.   Prepaid insurance expired, $2,500 (75% related to production, and 25% related to selling and administration).

d.   Applied $115,000 of manufacturing overhead to production.

e.   Closed $5,125 of overapplied overhead to cost of goods sold.

Required:

The table shown below includes a subset of Adams Company's balance sheet accounts. Record each of the above transactions using the given accounts. If a transaction increases an account balance, record the amount as a positive number. If it decreases an account balance, record the amount in parentheses.

Transaction	Work in Process	Manufacturing Overhead	Prepaid Expenses	PP&E (net)		Accounts Payable	Retained Earnings
a.					=		
b.					=		
c.					=		
d.					=		
e.					=		

EXERCISE 3A–3 Transaction Analysis LO3–5

Dixon Company is a manufacturer who completed numerous transactions during the month, some of which are shown below:

a.   Raw materials purchased on account, $100,000.

b.   Raw materials used in production, $78,000 direct materials and $16,000 indirect materials.

c.   Sales commissions paid in cash, $45,000.

d.   Depreciation of assets, $60,000 (65% related to factory equipment, and the remainder related to selling and administrative equipment).

e.   Sales, $450,000 (70% cash sales and the remainder were sales on account).

f.   Factory utilities paid in cash, $12,000.

g.   Applied $138,000 of manufacturing overhead to production.

h.   Various jobs costing $190,000 were completed and transferred to Finished Goods.

i.   Cash receipts from customers who had previously purchased on credit, $115,000.

j.   Various completed jobs costing $220,000 were sold to customers.

k.   Cash paid to raw material suppliers, $90,000.

Required:

The table shown below includes only one account from Dixon Company's balance sheet—Retained Earnings. For each of the above transactions, select "No" if it does not affect Retained Earnings. Conversely, if the transaction does affect Retained Earnings, then record the amount of the increase or (decrease) to this account under the "Yes" column.

	Retained Earnings	
Transaction	Yes	No
a.		
b.		
c.		
d.		
e.		
f.		
g.		
h.		
i.		
j.		
k.		

PROBLEM 3A–4 Transaction Analysis LO3–5

Morrison Company uses job-order costing to assign manufacturing costs to jobs. Its balance sheet on January 1 is as follows:

Morrison Company
Balance Sheet
January 1

Assets

Cash		$ 32,000
Raw materials	$ 9,000	
Work in process	4,000	
Finished goods	17,000	30,000
Prepaid expenses		2,000
Property, plant, and equipment (net)		190,000
Total assets		$254,000

Liabilities and Stockholders' Equity

Accounts payable		$ 7,000
Retained earnings		247,000
Total liabilities and stockholders' equity		$254,000

During January the company completed the following transactions:
a. Purchased raw materials on account, $74,000.
b. Raw materials used in production, $77,000 ($67,000 was direct materials and $10,000 was indirect materials).
c. Paid $167,000 of salaries and wages in cash ($95,000 was direct labor, $35,000 was indirect labor, and $37,000 was related to employees responsible for selling and administration).
d. Various manufacturing overhead costs incurred (on account) to support production, $33,000.
e. Depreciation recorded on property, plant, and equipment, $90,000 (70% related to manufacturing equipment and 30% related to assets that support selling and administration).
f. Various selling expenses paid in cash, $27,000.
g. Prepaid insurance expired, $1,200 (80% related to production, and 20% related to selling and administration).
h. Manufacturing overhead applied to production, $132,000.
i. Cost of goods manufactured, $288,000.
j. Cash sales to customers, $395,000.
k. Cost of goods sold (unadjusted), $285,000.
l. Cash payments to creditors, $62,000.
m. Underapplied or overapplied overhead, $? .

Required:
1. Calculate the ending balances on the company's balance sheet on January 31. You can derive your answers using Microsoft Excel and Exhibit 3A–2 as your guide, or you can use paper, pencil, and a calculator. (Hint: Be sure to calculate the underapplied or overapplied overhead and then account for its affect on the balance sheet.)
2. What is Morrison Company's net operating income for January?

PROBLEM 3A–5 Transaction Analysis LO3–5

Star Videos, Inc., produces short musical videos for sale to retail outlets. The company's balance sheet accounts as of January 1 are given below.

Star Videos, Inc. Balance Sheet January 1		
Assets		
Cash		$ 73,000
Accounts receivable		96,000
Inventories:		
Raw materials (film, costumes)	$33,000	
Videos in process................................	47,000	
Finished videos awaiting sale	78,000	158,000
Prepaid insurance		8,000
Studio and equipment (net)		530,000
Total assets		$865,000
Liabilities and Stockholders' Equity		
Accounts payable		$150,000
Retained earnings		715,000
Total liabilities and stockholders' equity		$865,000

Because the videos differ in length and complexity of production, the company uses a job-order costing system to determine the cost of each video produced. Studio (manufacturing) overhead is charged to videos based on camera-hours of activity. The company's predetermined overhead rate for the year ($40 per camera-hour) is based on a cost formula that estimated $280,000 in manufacturing overhead for an estimated allocation base of 7,000 camera-hours. Underapplied or overapplied overhead is closed to cost of goods sold. The following transactions were recorded for the year:

a. Film, costumes, and similar raw materials purchased on account, $183,000.
b. Film, costumes, and other raw materials issued to production, $210,000 (85% of this material was direct to the videos in production, and the other 15% was indirect).
c. Utility costs incurred (on account) in the production studio, $78,000.
d. Depreciation on the studio, cameras, and other equipment, $82,000. Three-fourths of this depreciation related to actual production of the videos, and the remainder related to equipment used in marketing and administration.
e. Advertising expense incurred (on account), $131,000.
f. Salaries and wages paid in cash as follows:

Direct labor (actors and directors)	$84,000
Indirect labor (carpenters to build sets, costume designers, and so forth).........................	$105,000
Administrative salaries	$95,000

g. Prepaid insurance expired, $7,000 (70% related to production of videos, and 30% related to marketing and administrative activities).
h. Miscellaneous marketing and administrative expenses incurred (on account), $9,600.
i. Studio (manufacturing) overhead was applied to videos in production. The company recorded 7,250 camera-hours of activity.
j. Videos costing $565,000 were transferred to the finished videos warehouse.
k. Sales for the year totaled $930,000 and were all on account.
l. The total cost to produce the videos that were sold was $610,000.
m. Collections from customers totaled $880,000.
n. Payments to suppliers on account, $515,000.
o. Underapplied or overapplied overhead, $___?___.

Required:

1. Using Exhibit 3A–2 as your guide, prepare a transaction analysis that records all of the above transactions. Calculate the ending balances at December 31 for all balance sheet accounts.
2. Using Exhibit 3A–3 as your guide, prepare a schedule of cost of goods manufactured. If done correctly, your cost of goods manufactured should equal what amount mentioned in the transactions above?
3. Using Exhibit 3A–4 as your guide, prepare a schedule of cost of goods sold. If done correctly, your unadjusted cost of goods sold should equal what amount mentioned in the transactions above?
4. Using Exhibit 3A–5 as your guide, prepare an income statement.

PROBLEM 3A–6 Transaction Analysis LO3–5

Brooks Corporation uses job-order costing to assign manufacturing costs to jobs. The company closes its underapplied or overapplied overhead to cost of goods sold. Its balance sheet on March 1 is as follows:

Brooks Corporation
Balance Sheet
March 1

Assets

Cash		$ 83,000
Raw materials	$18,000	
Work in process	14,000	
Finished goods	22,000	54,000
Prepaid expenses		1,800
Property, plant, and equipment (net)		175,000
Total assets		$313,800

Liabilities and Stockholders' Equity

Accounts payable	$ 12,000
Retained earnings	301,800
Total liabilities and stockholders' equity	$313,800

During March the company completed the following transactions:
a. Purchased raw materials for cash, $69,000.
b. Raw materials used in production, $77,000 ($67,000 was direct materials and $10,000 was indirect materials).
c. Paid $178,000 of salaries and wages in cash ($102,000 was direct labor, $23,000 was indirect labor, and $53,000 was related to employees responsible for selling and administration).
d. Various manufacturing overhead costs paid in cash to support production, $41,000.
e. Depreciation on property, plant, and equipment, $35,000 (85% related to manufacturing equipment and 15% related to assets that support selling and administration).
f. Various selling expenses incurred on account, $27,000.
g. Prepaid insurance expired, $450 (60% related to production, and 40% related to selling and administration).
h. Manufacturing overhead applied to production, $101,000.
i. Cost of goods manufactured, $__?__. (Hint: The Work in Process balance on March 31 is $5,000.)
j. Cash sales to customers, $429,000.
k. Cost of goods sold (unadjusted), $__?__. (Hint: The Finished Goods balance at March 31 is $6,000.)
l. Cash payments to creditors, $35,000.
m. Underapplied or overapplied overhead, $__?__.

Required:

For March:

1. Calculate the ending balances reported on the company's balance sheet. You can derive your answers using Microsoft Excel and Exhibit 3A–2 as your guide, or you can use paper, pencil, and a calculator. (Hint: Be sure to calculate the underapplied or overapplied overhead and then account for its affect on the balance sheet.)

2. Prepare Brooks Corporation's schedule of cost of goods manufactured. You can derive your answers using Microsoft Excel and Exhibit 3A–3 as your guide, or you can use paper, pencil, and a calculator.

3. Prepare Brooks Corporation's schedule of cost of goods sold. You can derive your answers using Microsoft Excel and Exhibit 3A–4 as your guide, or you can use paper, pencil, and a calculator.

4. Prepare Brooks Corporation's income statement. You can derive your answers using Microsoft Excel and Exhibit 3A–5 as your guide, or you can use paper, pencil, and a calculator.

Chapter 4

Process Costing

Rob Kim/Getty Images for NYCWFF

lighthouse image: Martin73/Shutterstock;
big data image: INGARA/Shutterstock

LEARNING OBJECTIVES

After studying Chapter 4, you should be able to:

LO4–1 Record the flow of materials, labor, and overhead through a process costing system.

LO4–2 Compute the equivalent units of production using the weighted-average method.

LO4–3 Compute the cost per equivalent unit using the weighted-average method.

LO4–4 Assign costs to units using the weighted-average method.

LO4–5 Prepare a cost reconciliation report using the weighted-average method.

LO4–6 *(Appendix 4A) Compute the equivalent units of production using the FIFO method.*

LO4–7 *(Appendix 4A) Compute the cost per equivalent unit using the FIFO method.*

LO4–8 *(Appendix 4A) Assign costs to units using the FIFO method.*

LO4–9 *(Appendix 4A) Prepare a cost reconciliation report using the FIFO method.*

LO4–10 *(Appendix 4B) Allocate service department costs to operating departments using the direct method.*

LO4–11 *(Appendix 4B) Allocate service department costs to operating departments using the step-down method.*

 Data Analytics Exercise available in Connect to complement this chapter

ENTREPRENEUR SPOTLIGHT

Formed by sisters Robin McBride and Andrea McBride-John, the McBride Sisters Collection is the largest Black- and women-owned vineyard to produce and distribute its own wines in the United States. The sisters, who share a father, grew up worlds apart—Robin in Monterey, CA, and Andrea in Marlborough, New Zealand. Being unaware of each other's existence until they reached adulthood, the two women quickly bonded around a shared passion for wine. Today, their most sought-after wines, which combine "old world elegance with new world finesse," can be found in Target, Kroger, and Total Wines stores nationwide.

Applying Managerial Accounting

The McBride sisters could use process costing to calculate unit product costs. For example, the company might define its departments as Harvesting, Crushing and Pressing, Fermenting, Clarifying, and finally Aging and Bottling. In the Fermenting Department, the company could calculate the equivalent units of production and the cost per equivalent unit. This cost information could then be used to calculate the cost of ending work in process inventory within the Fermenting Department and the cost of the units completed and transferred to the Clarifying Department.

Serving All Stakeholders

California has more than 4,000 wineries, but women own only four percent of them. To help fix this gender inequity, as well as similar disparities in the finance and hospitality industries, the McBride sisters started the SHE CAN Professional Development Fund. The fund's mission is "to close the gender and race gap in leadership positions in [the] wine & spirits, hospitality, and finance industries by providing professional development scholarships to emerging women leaders." Some of the fund's past grant recipients include Daphne Hill (owner of Daphne's Bridal Boutique), Sherille D. Barber (owner of Barber Therapy & Associates), and Johanne P. Pradel (founder and chief creative director, COOL Creative Inc.). ∎

Sources: https://money.yahoo.com/mcbride-sisters-collection-inc-announces-141800920.html, https://www.winespectator.com /articles/wines-dynamo-sister-team, http://www.ecolovewine.com/mcbridesisters, https://www.cpajournal.com/2018/11/19/from-the -vine-to-the-bottle/, https://www.mcbridesisters.com/Our-Story/SHE-CAN, https://www.mcbridesistersfund.org/.

Job-order costing and process costing are two common methods for determining unit product costs. As explained in previous chapters, job-order costing is used when many different jobs or products are worked on each period. Examples of industries using job-order costing include furniture manufacturing, special-order printing, shipbuilding, and many types of service organizations.

By contrast, **process costing** is used in industries that convert raw materials into homogeneous (i.e., uniform) products, such as bricks, soda, or paper, on a continuous basis. Examples of companies using process costing include Reynolds Consumer Products (aluminum ingots), Scott Paper (paper towels), General Mills (flours), ExxonMobil (gasoline and lubricating oils), Coppertone (sunscreens), and Kellogg's (breakfast cereals). In addition, process costing is sometimes used in companies with assembly operations. A form of process costing may also be used in utilities that produce gas, water, and electricity.

Our purpose in this chapter is to explain how product costing works in a process costing system.

Comparison of Job-Order and Process Costing

In this section, we discuss three similarities and three differences between job-order and process costing.

Similarities between Job-Order and Process Costing

Much of what you learned in previous chapters about job-order costing applies to process costing. For example:

1. Both systems have the same purposes—to assign material, labor, and manufacturing overhead costs to products for computing unit product costs.
2. Both systems use the same manufacturing accounts, including Manufacturing Overhead, Raw Materials, Work in Process, and Finished Goods.
3. The flow of costs through the manufacturing accounts is basically the same in both systems.

Differences between Job-Order and Process Costing

Exhibit 4–1 summarizes three differences between job-order and process costing. First, job-order costing is used when a company produces many different jobs having unique production requirements. Process costing is used when a company produces a continuous

	Job-Order Costing	Process Costing
EXHIBIT 4–1 Differences between Job-Order and Process Costing	1. Many different jobs are worked on during each period, with each job having unique production requirements. 2. Costs are accumulated by individual job. 3. Unit costs are computed *by job* on the job cost sheet.	1. A single product is produced either on a continuous basis or for long periods of time. All units of product are identical. 2. Costs are accumulated by department. 3. Unit costs are computed *by department.*

flow of identical units. Second, job-order costing uses job cost sheets to accumulate costs for individual jobs. Process costing accumulates costs by department (rather than by job) and assigns these costs uniformly to all identical units passing through the department. Third, job-order costing uses job cost sheets to compute unit costs for each job. Process costing systems compute unit costs by department.

Cost Flows in Process Costing

This section overviews how manufacturing costs flow through a process costing system.

Processing Departments

A **processing department** is an organizational unit where work is performed on a product and where materials, labor, or overhead costs are added to the product. For example, a Nalley's potato chip factory might have three processing departments—one for preparing potatoes, one for cooking, and one for inspecting and packaging. A brick factory might have two processing departments—one for mixing and molding clay into bricks and one for firing the molded bricks. Regardless of the number of processing departments, they all have two essential features. First, the activity in the processing department is performed uniformly on all units passing through it. Second, the processing department's output is homogeneous; in other words, all of the units produced are identical.

Products in a process costing environment, such as bricks or potato chips, typically flow in sequence from one department to another as in Exhibit 4–2.

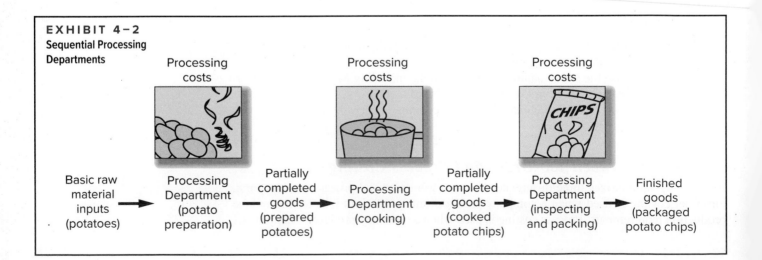

EXHIBIT 4–2
Sequential Processing Departments

FOOD MANUFACTURERS ARE USING ROBOTS WITH LASER VISION

Cognex Corporation makes vision sensors for robots that food manufacturers are using to replace direct laborers and increase efficiency. For example, "at a sausage factory, more powerful cameras and quicker processors enable robots to detect the twisted point between two cylindrical wieners fast enough that they can be cut apart at the rate of 200 a minute." Robots with laser vision and artificial intelligence are also replacing human beings in other food processing tasks such as precisely slicing chicken cutlets and inspecting toppings on machine-made pizzas.

Yole Développement, a market research firm, estimates that the demand for robots with sensing and imaging capabilities will grow by 10-fold in the near future. Accordingly, many companies are investing heavily in these emerging technologies. For example, Intel Corporation bought Mobileye NV for $15.3 billion to obtain access to the Israeli company's vision-based driver-assistance technology.

Source: Natasha Khan, "Robots Gain a New Sense: Sight," *The Wall Street Journal,* September 12, 2018, p. B3.

Kinwun/Getty Images

The Flow of Materials, Labor, and Overhead Costs

Cost accumulation is simpler in process costing than in job-order costing. In a process costing system, instead of having to assign costs to hundreds of different jobs, costs are assigned to only a few processing departments.

Exhibit 4–3 shows a T-account model of materials, labor, and overhead cost flows in a process costing system. Several key points should be noted from this exhibit. First, a separate Work in Process account is maintained for *each processing department.*

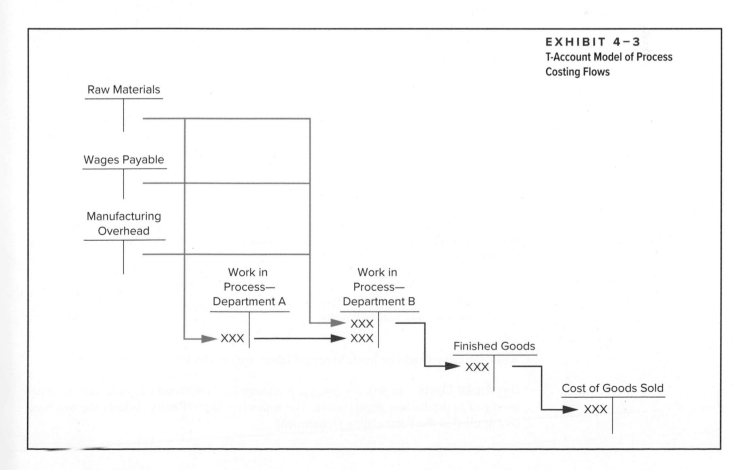

EXHIBIT 4–3
T-Account Model of Process Costing Flows

In contrast, in a job-order costing system, the entire company may have only one Work in Process account. Second, the completed production of the first processing department (Department A in the exhibit) is transferred to the Work in Process account of the second processing department (Department B). After further work in Department B, the completed units are transferred to Finished Goods. (In Exhibit 4–3, we show only two processing departments, but a company can have many processing departments.)

Finally, materials, labor, and overhead costs can be added in *any* processing department—not just the first. Costs in Department B's Work in Process account consist of the materials, labor, and overhead costs incurred in Department B plus the costs assigned to units transferred in from Department A (called transferred-in costs).

Materials, Labor, and Overhead Cost Entries

LO4–1
Record the flow of materials, labor, and overhead through a process costing system.

To complete our discussion of cost flows in a process costing system, in this section we show journal entries relating to materials, labor, and overhead costs at Megan's Classic Cream Soda, a company that has two processing departments—Formulating and Bottling. In the Formulating Department, ingredients are checked for quality and then mixed and injected with carbon dioxide to create bulk cream soda. In the Bottling Department, bottles are checked for defects, filled with cream soda, capped, visually inspected again for defects, and then packed for shipping.

Materials Costs As in job-order costing, materials are drawn from the storeroom using a materials requisition form. Materials can be added in any processing department, although it is not unusual for materials to be added only in the first processing department, with subsequent departments adding only labor and overhead costs.

At Megan's Classic Cream Soda, some materials (i.e., water, flavors, sugar, and carbon dioxide) are added in the Formulating Department and some materials (i.e., bottles, caps, and packing materials) are added in the Bottling Department. The journal entry to record the materials used in the Formulating Department is as follows:

Work in Process—Formulating	XXX	
Raw Materials.		XXX

The journal entry to record the materials used in the Bottling Department is as follows:

Work in Process—Bottling	XXX	
Raw Materials.		XXX

Labor Costs In process costing, labor costs are traced to departments—not to individual jobs. The following journal entry records the labor costs in the Formulating Department:

Work in Process—Formulating	XXX	
Salaries and Wages Payable.		XXX

A similar entry would be made to record labor costs in the Bottling Department.

Overhead Costs In process costing, predetermined overhead rates are used to apply overhead to production departments. The following journal entry records the overhead cost applied in the Formulating Department:

| Work in Process—Formulating | XXX | |
| Manufacturing Overhead | | XXX |

A similar entry would be made to apply manufacturing overhead cost in the Bottling Department.

Completing the Cost Flows   Once processing has been completed in a department, the units are transferred to the next department for further processing, as illustrated in the T-accounts in Exhibit 4–3. The following journal entry transfers the cost of completed units within the Formulating Department to the Bottling Department:

| Work in Process—Bottling | XXX | |
| Work in Process—Formulating | | XXX |

After processing is finished in the Bottling Department, the costs of the completed units are transferred to the Finished Goods inventory account:

| Finished Goods | XXX | |
| Work in Process—Bottling | | XXX |

Finally, when a customer's order is filled and units are sold, the cost of the units is transferred to Cost of Goods Sold:

| Cost of Goods Sold | XXX | |
| Finished Goods | | XXX |

To summarize, the cost flows between accounts are basically the same in process costing as they are in job-order costing. The only difference at this point is process costing systems maintain separate Work in Process accounts for each department.

Process Costing Computations: Three Key Concepts

In process costing, each department needs to calculate two numbers for financial reporting purposes—the cost of ending work in process inventory and the cost of completed units transferred to the next stage of the production process. The key to deriving these two numbers is calculating *unit costs* within each department. On the surface, these departmental unit cost calculations may seem very straightforward—simply divide the department's costs (the numerator) by its units produced (the denominator). However, to set the stage for correctly performing this seemingly simple computation, you need to understand three key foundational concepts.

Key Concept #1

There is more than one way to calculate departmental unit costs. This chapter explains two methods for performing these calculations, the *weighted-average method* and the *FIFO method*. The **weighted-average method** of process costing, which is explained in the main body of the chapter, calculates unit costs by combining costs and outputs from the current and prior periods. The **FIFO method** of process costing, which is covered in Appendix 4A, calculates unit costs based solely on the costs and outputs from the current period.

Key Concept #2

Each department needs to calculate a separate unit cost for each type of manufacturing cost that it incurs. For example, if a given department adds materials cost, labor cost, and overhead cost to the production process it needs to compute a unit cost for each of these three cost categories. To simplify things, companies often consolidate these three cost categories into two groups by combining labor and overhead costs into a category called *conversion costs* (or conversion for short). **Conversion cost** is direct labor cost plus manufacturing overhead cost.

Key Concept #3

Quantifying each department's number of units produced during a period is complicated by the fact most departments usually have some partially completed units on hand at the end of the period. These partially completed units are translated into an *equivalent* number of fully completed units using the following formula:

$$\text{Equivalent units} = \text{Number of partially completed units} \times \text{Percentage completion}$$

Equivalent units is the product of the number of partially completed units and the percentage completion of those units with respect to the processing in the department. Roughly speaking, equivalent units is the number of complete units that could have been obtained from the materials and effort that went into the partially completed units.

For example, suppose Department A has 500 units in its ending work in process inventory that are 60 percent complete with respect to processing in the department. These 500 partially completed units are equivalent to 300 fully complete units ($500 \times 60\% = 300$). Therefore, Department A's ending work in process inventory would contain 300 equivalent units.

COMMUNICATING WITH DATA VISUALIZATIONS

This visualization could be used to describe how the weighted-average and FIFO methods of computing equivalent units of production differ from one another. It highlights the only difference between the two methods, which relates to accounting for beginning work in process inventory. The weighted-average method combines the units completed in the prior and current months when calculating the equivalent units of production, whereas the FIFO method only includes the units completed in the current month when calculating the equivalent units of production.

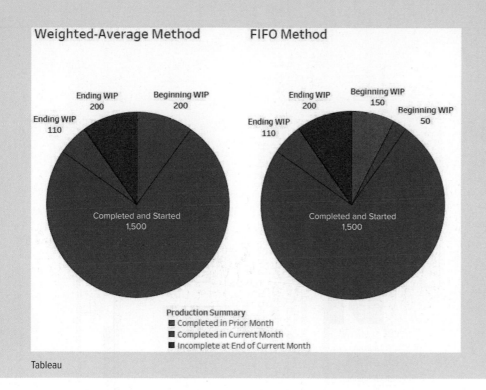

Weighted-Average Method   FIFO Method

Ending WIP 200   Beginning WIP 200

Ending WIP 110

Ending WIP 200   Beginning WIP 150

Beginning WIP 50

Ending WIP 110

Completed and Started 1,500

Completed and Started 1,500

Production Summary
- ■ Completed in Prior Month
- ■ Completed in Current Month
- ■ Incomplete at End of Current Month

Tableau

The Weighted-Average Method: An Example

We now turn our attention to Double Diamond Skis, a company that manufactures a high-performance deep-powder ski, and that uses process costing to determine its unit product costs. The company's production process is illustrated in Exhibit 4–4. Skis go through a sequence of five processing departments, starting with the Shaping and Milling Department and ending with the Finishing and Pairing Department.

We will use the Double Diamond Skis example to explain the weighted-average method of process costing in four steps:

Step 1: Compute the equivalent units of production.
Step 2: Compute the cost per equivalent unit.
Step 3: Assign costs to units.
Step 4: Prepare a cost reconciliation report.

Step 1: Compute the Equivalent Units of Production

The *equivalent units of production* is the name we use for the denominator in unit cost calculations. Each processing department calculates the equivalent units of production for each of its manufacturing cost categories. In the weighted-average method, the **equivalent units of production** for a department is the number of completed units transferred to the next department (or to finished goods) plus the equivalent units in the department's ending work in process inventory. This definition in equation form is as follows:

Weighted–Average Method
(a separate calculation is made for each cost category in each processing department)

$$\text{Equivalent units of production} = \text{Units transferred to the next department or to finished goods} + \text{Equivalent units in ending work in process inventory}$$

LO4–2
Compute the equivalent units of production using the weighted-average method.

EXHIBIT 4–4
The Production Process at Double Diamond Skis*

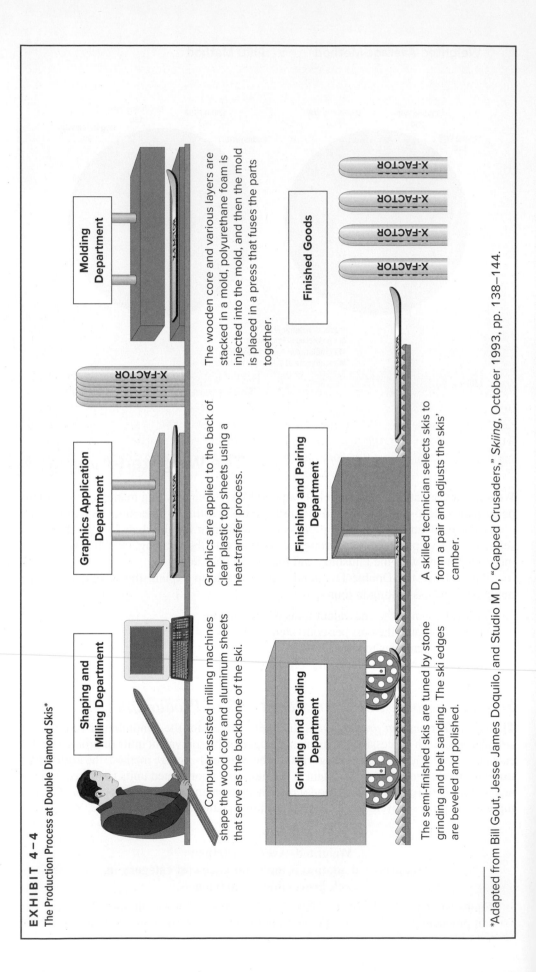

Shaping and Milling Department

Computer-assisted milling machines shape the wood core and aluminum sheets that serve as the backbone of the ski.

Graphics Application Department

Graphics are applied to the back of clear plastic top sheets using a heat-transfer process.

Molding Department

The wooden core and various layers are stacked in a mold, polyurethane foam is injected into the mold, and then the mold is placed in a press that fuses the parts together.

Grinding and Sanding Department

The semi-finished skis are tuned by stone grinding and belt sanding. The ski edges are beveled and polished.

Finishing and Pairing Department

A skilled technician selects skis to form a pair and adjusts the skis' camber.

Finished Goods

*Adapted from Bill Gout, Jesse James Doquilo, and Studio M D, "Capped Crusaders," *Skiing*, October 1993, pp. 138–144.

To better understand this formula, consider the Shaping and Milling Department at Double Diamond Skis. This department uses computerized milling machines to precisely shape the wooden core and metal sheets used to form the backbone of the ski. Exhibit 4–5 summarizes the Shaping and Milling Department's production data for the month of May for its two manufacturing cost categories, materials and conversion.

Shaping and Milling Department	Units	Percent Complete	
		Materials	Conversion
Beginning work in process inventory......	200	55%	30%
Units started into production during May	5,000		
Units completed during May and transferred to the next department......	4,800	100%*	100%*
Ending work in process inventory.........	400	40%	25%

*We always assume that units transferred out of a department are 100% complete with respect to the processing done in that department.

EXHIBIT 4–5
Shaping and Milling Department
Production Data for May

The first thing to note about Exhibit 4–5 is the flow of units through the department (focus on the data under the Units heading). The department started with 200 units in beginning work in process inventory. During May, 5,000 units were started into production. This made a total of 5,200 units. Of this total, 4,800 units were completed during May and transferred to the next department and 400 units were still in the department's ending work in process inventory. In general, the units in beginning work in process inventory plus the units started into production must equal the units in ending work in process inventory plus the units completed and transferred out. In equation form, this is:

$$\begin{matrix} \text{Units in beginning} \\ \text{work in process} \\ \text{inventory} \end{matrix} + \begin{matrix} \text{Units started} \\ \text{into production} \\ \text{or transferred in} \end{matrix} = \begin{matrix} \text{Units in ending} \\ \text{work in process} \\ \text{inventory} \end{matrix} + \begin{matrix} \text{Units completed} \\ \text{and transferred out} \end{matrix}$$

A second point worth mentioning about Exhibit 4–5 is its beginning work in process inventory was 55 percent complete with respect to materials and 30 percent complete with respect to conversion. This means 55 percent of the materials cost required to complete the units in beginning work in process inventory had already been incurred. Likewise, 30 percent of the conversion costs required to complete the units in beginning work in process inventory had already been incurred. However, when using the weighted-average method to compute equivalent units of production, these two completion percentages pertaining to the beginning work in process inventory (55% for materials and 30% for conversion) will be ignored.

The third point to highlight from Exhibit 4–5 is the Shaping and Milling Department's ending work in process inventory is 40 percent complete with respect to materials and 25 percent complete with respect to conversion. This means 40 percent of the materials cost and 25 percent of the conversion costs required to complete the units in ending work in process inventory have already been incurred. Under the weighted-average method, these two completion percentages pertaining to the ending work in process inventory (40% for materials and 25% for conversion) will be included in the computation of equivalent units of production.

Exhibit 4–6 summarizes the equivalent units of production calculations within the Shaping and Milling Department for materials and conversion. Notice these calculations ignore the fact the units in the beginning work in process inventory were partially complete with respect to materials and conversion. For example, the 200 units in beginning inventory were already 30 percent complete with respect to conversion costs. However, the

EXHIBIT 4–6
Equivalent Units of Production:
Weighted-Average Method

Shaping and Milling Department	Materials	Conversion
Units transferred to the next department	4,800	4,800
Equivalent units in ending work in process inventory:		
Materials: 400 units × 40% complete	160	
Conversion: 400 units × 25% complete		100
Equivalent units of production	4,960	4,900

weighted-average method is concerned only with the 100 equivalent units in ending inventories and the 4,800 units transferred to the next department (for a total of 4,900 equivalent units of production); it ignores the fact the beginning work in process inventory was already partially complete. In other words, the 4,900 equivalent units of production computed using the weighted-average method include work accomplished in the prior period. This is a key point concerning the weighted-average method and it is easy to overlook.

Exhibit 4–7 provides another way of looking at the computation of equivalent units of production. It depicts the computations for conversion costs.

EXHIBIT 4–7
Visual Perspective of Equivalent
Units of Production

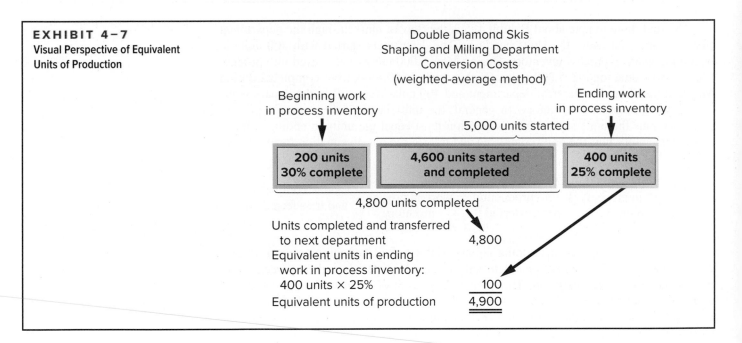

Step 2: Compute the Cost per Equivalent Unit

LO4–3
Compute the cost per
equivalent unit using the
weighted-average method.

In step 2 we determine the total cost to include in the numerator and then divide it by the equivalent units of production from step 1 to derive the cost per equivalent unit for materials and conversion. To help us with this step, Exhibit 4–8 displays the Shaping and Milling Department's cost data for the Month of May.

EXHIBIT 4–8
Shaping and Milling Department
Cost Data for May

	Materials	Conversion	Total
Cost of beginning work in process inventory	$ 9,600	$ 5,575	$ 15,175
Costs added during the period	368,600	350,900	719,500
Total cost	$378,200	$ 356,475	$734,675

Given this cost data, we can compute the Shaping and Milling Department's cost per equivalent unit for materials and conversion using the following equation:

Weighted-Average Method
(a separate calculation is made for each cost category
in each processing department)

$$\text{Cost per equivalent unit} = \frac{\text{Cost of beginning work in process inventory} + \text{Cost added during the period}}{\text{Equivalent units of production}}$$

Note the numerator is the sum of the cost of beginning work in process inventory and the cost added during the period. Thus, the weighted-average method averages together costs and outputs from the prior and current periods.

Using this equation, the Shaping and Milling Department's costs per equivalent unit for materials and conversion for May are computed as follows:

Shaping and Milling Department Costs per Equivalent Unit	Materials	Conversion
Cost of beginning work in process inventory	$ 9,600	$ 5,575
Costs added during the period	368,600	350,900
Total cost (a)	$378,200	$ 356,475
Equivalent units of production (see Exhibit 4–6) (b)	4,960	4,900
Cost per equivalent unit (a) ÷ (b)	$76.25	$72.75

Step 3: Assign Costs to Units

In step 3 we use the costs per equivalent unit to value the equivalent units in ending inventory and the completed units transferred to the next department. For example, each unit transferred out of Double Diamond's Shaping and Milling Department to the Graphics Application Department, as depicted in Exhibit 4–4, carries a cost of $149.00 ($76.25 for materials and $72.75 for conversion). Because 4,800 units were transferred to the next department (see Exhibit 4–5), the total cost assigned to those units is $715,200 (= 4,800 units × $149.00 per unit).

A complete accounting of the costs of ending work in process inventory and the units completed and transferred out appears below:

LO4–4
Assign costs to units using the weighted-average method.

Shaping and Milling Department Costs of Ending Work in Process Inventory and the Units Transferred Out	Materials	Conversion	Total
Ending work in process inventory:			
Equivalent units (see Exhibit 4–6) (a)	160	100	
Cost per equivalent unit (b)	$76.25	$72.75	
Cost of ending work in process inventory (a) × (b)	$12,200	$7,275	$19,475
Units completed and transferred out:			
Units transferred to the next department (see Exhibit 4–6) (a)	4,800	4,800	
Cost per equivalent unit (b)	$76.25	$72.75	
Cost of units transferred out (a) × (b)	$366,000	$349,200	$715,200

For materials and conversion, the equivalent units in ending work in process inventory and the completed units transferred to the next department are multiplied by the cost per equivalent unit to determine the cost assigned to the units. For example, the 100 equivalent units of conversion in ending work in process inventory are multiplied by the cost per equivalent unit of $72.75 to determine the conversion costs included in ending work in process inventory of $7,275. Similarly, the 4,800 units completed and transferred out are multiplied by the conversion cost per equivalent unit of $72.75 to determine the conversion costs attached to the completed units transferred out of $349,200.

Step 4: Prepare a Cost Reconciliation Report

LO4–5

Prepare a cost reconciliation report using the weighted-average method.

The costs assigned to the equivalent units in ending work in process inventory and the completed units transferred out reconcile with the costs we started with in Exhibit 4–8 as shown below:

Shaping and Milling Department Cost Reconciliation	
Costs to be accounted for:	
Cost of beginning work in process inventory (Exhibit 4–8)	$ 15,175
Costs added to production during the period (Exhibit 4–8)	719,500
Total cost to be accounted for....................................	$734,675
Costs accounted for:	
Cost of ending work in process inventory (see above)	$ 19,475
Cost of units transferred out (see above)	715,200
Total cost accounted for	$734,675

The $715,200 cost of the units transferred to the next department, Graphics Application, will be accounted for in that department as "costs transferred in." It will be treated in the process costing system as just another category of costs like materials or conversion costs. The only difference is the costs transferred in will always be 100 percent complete with respect to the work done in the Shaping and Milling Department. Costs are passed on from one department to the next in this fashion, until they reach the last processing department, Finishing and Pairing. When the products are completed in this last department, their costs are transferred to finished goods.

Operation Costing

Job-order costing and process costing represent two ends of a continuum. On one end is job-order costing, which is used by companies producing many different products. On the other end is process costing, which is used by companies producing larger quantities of homogeneous products. Between these two extremes are many hybrid systems that include characteristics of both job-order and process costing. One of these hybrids is called *operation costing.*

Operation costing is used when products have some common characteristics and some individual characteristics. Shoes, for example, have common characteristics because all styles involve cutting and sewing done on a repetitive basis, using the same equipment. Shoes also have individual characteristics—some are made of expensive leathers and others use inexpensive synthetic materials.

Products are typically processed in batches when operation costing is used, with each batch charged for its own specific materials. In this sense, operation costing is similar to job-order costing. However, labor and overhead costs are accumulated by operation or by department, and these costs are assigned to units as in process costing. If shoes are being produced, each shoe is charged for its specific materials and the same per-unit conversion cost, regardless of the style involved. Thus, the company distinguishes between styles in terms of materials but employs the simplicity of process costing for labor and overhead costs.

Examples of other products suitable for operation costing include electronic equipment (such as semiconductors), textiles, clothing, and jewelry. These products are produced in batches, but they vary considerably from model to model or style to style in terms of materials cost.

CORONAVIRUS PRESENTS CHALLENGES AND OPPORTUNITIES FOR MANUFACTURERS

Ardisam Inc. encountered an unexpected spike in demand for its fishing and gardening equipment when people responded to the COVID-19 lockdown by turning their attention to outdoor recreational activities. However, the company was unable to satisfy much of this demand because it could not acquire enough raw materials from its suppliers in China. Honey-Can-Do International's overhead costs increased when it reconfigured its processes to maintain social distance. For instance, now the company only allows one worker instead of two to unload shipping containers, thereby doubling the amount of time needed for this procurement activity.

In addition to the challenges just described, the impacts of COVID-19 have also created unexpected opportunities for some American manufacturers. For example, Littlestown Foundry, a Pennsylvania-based producer of aluminum-cast components, received additional sales of $350,000 from a customer that wanted to shift its raw material purchases from Chinese providers to suppliers located in the United States.

Source: Bob Tita and Austen Hufford, "Supply Snafus, New Costs Hobble Factories," *The Wall Street Journal,* June 5, 2020, pp. B1–B2.

Summary

Process costing is used when homogeneous products or services are produced on a continuous basis. Costs flow through the manufacturing accounts in basically the same way in process costing as in job-order costing. However, costs are accumulated by department rather than by job in process costing.

In process costing, the equivalent units of production is determined for each cost category in each department. Under the weighted-average method, the equivalent units of production equals the number of completed units transferred out to the next department or to finished goods plus the equivalent units in ending work in process inventory. The equivalent units in ending work in process inventory equals the product of the number of partially completed units and the percentage completion of those units with respect to the specific cost category.

Under the weighted-average method, the cost per equivalent unit for a specific cost category is computed by combining the cost of beginning work in process inventory and the cost added during the period and then dividing this sum by the equivalent units of production. The cost per equivalent unit is used to value ending work in process inventory and the units transferred to the next department or to finished goods.

The cost reconciliation report reconciles the cost of beginning inventory and the costs added to production with the cost of ending inventory and the cost of units transferred out.

Costs are transferred from one department to the next until the last processing department. At that point, the cost of completed units is transferred to finished goods.

Data Analytics Exercise available in Connect to complement this chapter

Review Problem: Process Cost Flows and Costing Units

Luxguard Home Paint Company produces exterior latex paint sold in one-gallon containers. The company has two processing departments—Base Fab and Finishing. White paint, which is used as a base for all the company's paints, is mixed from raw ingredients in the Base Fab Department. Pigments are then added to the basic white paint, the pigmented paint is squirted under pressure into one-gallon containers, and the containers are labeled and packed for shipping in the Finishing Department. Information relating to the company's operations for April follows:

a. Raw materials used in production: Base Fab Department, $851,000; and Finishing Department, $629,000.

b. Direct labor costs: Base Fab Department, $330,000; and Finishing Department, $270,000.

c. Applied manufacturing overhead cost: Base Fab Department, $665,000; and Finishing Department, $405,000.

d. Transferred basic white paint from the Base Fab Department to the Finishing Department, $1,850,000.

e. Transferred paint from the Finishing Department to Finished Goods, $3,200,000.

Required:

1. Prepare journal entries to record items (a) through (e) above.

2. Post the journal entries from (1) above to T-accounts. The balance in the Base Fab Department's Work in Process account on April 1 was $150,000; the beginning balance in the Finishing Department's Work in Process account was $70,000. After posting entries to the T-accounts, find the ending balance in each department's Work in Process account.

3. Compute the Base Fab Department's cost of ending work in process inventory for materials, labor, overhead, and in total for April. Also, compute the Base Fab Department's cost of the completed units transferred to the next department for materials, labor, overhead, and in total for April. The following additional information is available regarding production in the Base Fab Department during April:

Production data:	
Units (gallons) in process, April 1: materials 100% complete;	
labor and overhead 60% complete	30,000
Units (gallons) started into production during April	420,000
Units (gallons) completed and transferred to the Finishing Department	370,000
Units (gallons) in process, April 30: materials 50% complete;	
labor and overhead 25% complete	80,000
Cost data:	
Work in process inventory, April 1:	
Materials	$ 92,000
Labor	21,000
Overhead	37,000
Total cost of work in process inventory	$ 150,000
Cost added during April:	
Materials	$ 851,000
Labor	330,000
Overhead	665,000
Total cost added during April	$1,846,000

4. Prepare a cost reconciliation report for April.

Solution to Review Problem

1.	a.	Work in Process—Base Fab Department	851,000	
		Work in Process—Finishing Department	629,000	
		Raw Materials		1,480,000
	b.	Work in Process—Base Fab Department	330,000	
		Work in Process—Finishing Department	270,000	
		Salaries and Wages Payable		600,000

c. Work in Process—Base Fab Department 665,000
    Work in Process—Finishing Department 405,000
      Manufacturing Overhead   1,070,000

d. Work in Process—Finishing Department 1,850,000
    Work in Process—Base Fab Department   1,850,000

e. Finished Goods 3,200,000
    Work in Process—Finishing Department   3,200,000

2.

Raw Materials			
Bal.	XXX	(a)	1,480,000

Salaries and Wages Payable		
	(b)	600,000

Work in Process—Base Fab Department

Bal.	150,000	(d)	1,850,000
(a)	851,000		
(b)	330,000		
(c)	665,000		
Bal.	146,000		

Manufacturing Overhead

(Various actual costs)		(c)	1,070,000

Work in Process—Finishing Department

Bal.	70,000	(e)	3,200,000
(a)	629,000		
(b)	270,000		
(c)	405,000		
(d)	1,850,000		
Bal.	24,000		

Finished Goods

Bal.	XXX	
(e)	3,200,000	

3. First, we compute the equivalent units of production for each cost category:

Base Fab Department Equivalent Units of Production			
	Materials	Labor	Overhead
Units transferred to the next department	370,000	370,000	370,000
Equivalent units in ending work in process inventory (materials: 80,000 units × 50% complete; labor: 80,000 units × 25% complete; overhead: 80,000 units × 25% complete)	40,000	20,000	20,000
Equivalent units of production	410,000	390,000	390,000

Then we compute the cost per equivalent unit for each cost category:

Base Fab Department Costs per Equivalent Unit			
	Materials	Labor	Overhead
Costs:			
Cost of beginning work in process inventory	$ 92,000	$ 21,000	$ 37,000
Costs added during the period	851,000	330,000	665,000
Total cost (a)	$943,000	$351,000	$702,000
Equivalent units of production (b)	410,000	390,000	390,000
Cost per equivalent unit (a) ÷ (b)	$2.30	$0.90	$1.80

The costs per equivalent unit are assigned to the units in ending work in process inventory and the units transferred out as follows:

Base Fab Department Costs of Ending Work in Process Inventory and the Units Transferred Out				
	Materials	Labor	Overhead	Total
Ending work in process inventory:				
Equivalent units (a)...........................	40,000	20,000	20,000	
Cost per equivalent unit (b)	$2.30	$0.90	$1.80	
Cost of ending work in process inventory (a) × (b)	$92,000	$18,000	$36,000	$146,000
Units completed and transferred out:				
Units transferred to the next department (a)......	370,000	370,000	370,000	
Cost per equivalent unit (b)	$2.30	$0.90	$1.80	
Cost of units completed and transferred out (a) × (b)..	$851,000	$333,000	$666,000	$1,850,000

4.

Base Fab Department Cost Reconciliation	
Costs to be accounted for:	
Cost of beginning work in process inventory	$ 150,000
Costs added to production during the period	1,846,000
Total cost to be accounted for	$1,996,000
Costs accounted for as follows:	
Cost of ending work in process inventory	$ 146,000
Cost of units transferred out	1,850,000
Total cost accounted for	$1,996,000

Glossary

Conversion cost Direct labor cost plus manufacturing overhead cost. (p. 158)

Equivalent units The product of the number of partially completed units and their percentage of completion with respect to a particular cost. Equivalent units are the number of complete whole units that could be obtained from the materials and effort contained in partially completed units. (p. 158)

Equivalent units of production (weighted-average method) The units transferred to the next department (or to finished goods) during the period plus the equivalent units in the department's ending work in process inventory. (p. 159)

FIFO method A process costing method that calculates unit costs based solely on the costs and outputs from the current period. (p. 158)

Operation costing A hybrid costing system used when products have some common characteristics and some individual characteristics. (p. 164)

Process costing A costing method used when homogeneous products are produced on a continuous basis. (p. 153)

Processing department An organizational unit where work is performed on a product and where materials, labor, or overhead costs are added to the product. (p. 154)

Weighted-average method A process costing method that calculates unit costs by combining costs and outputs from the current and prior periods. (p. 158)

Questions

4–1 Under what conditions is it appropriate to use process costing?

4–2 In what ways are job-order and process costing similar?

4–3 Why is cost accumulation simpler in a process costing system than in a job-order costing system?

4–4 How many Work in Process accounts are maintained in a company that uses process costing?

4–5 Assume a company has two processing departments—Mixing followed by Firing. Prepare a journal entry to show a transfer of work in process from the Mixing Department to the Firing Department.

4–6   Assume a company has two processing departments —Mixing followed by Firing. Explain what costs might be added to the Firing Department's Work in Process account.

4–7   What is meant by *equivalent units of production* when the weighted-average method is used?

4–8   Watkins Trophies, Inc., produces thousands of medallions made of bronze, silver, and gold. The medallions are identical except for the materials used in their manufacture. What costing system would you advise the company to use?

Mc Graw Hill connect   **Applying Excel**

This exercise relates to the Double Diamond Skis' Shaping and Milling Department that was discussed earlier in the chapter. The Excel worksheet shown below consolidates data from Exhibits 4–5 and 4–8. The workbook, and instructions on how to complete the file, can be found in Connect.

LO4–2, LO4–3, LO4–4, LO4–5

	A	B	C	D
1	Chapter 4: Applying Excel			
2				
3	Data			
4	Beginning work in process inventory:			
5	Units in process	200		
6	Completion with respect to materials	55%		
7	Completion with respect to conversion	30%		
8	Costs in the beginning work in process inventory:			
9	Materials cost	$9,600		
10	Conversion cost	$5,575		
11	Units started into production during the period	5,000		
12	Costs added to production during the period:			
13	Materials cost	$368,600		
14	Conversion cost	$350,900		
15	Ending work in process inventory:			
16	Units in process	400		
17	Completion with respect to materials	40%		
18	Completion with respect to conversion	25%		
19				
20	*Enter a formula into each of the cells marked with a ? below*			
21				
22	**Weighted-Average Method:**			
23				
24	**Equivalent Units of Production**			
25		Materials	Conversion	
26	Units transferred to the next department	?	?	
27	Ending work in process inventory:			
28	Materials	?		
29	Conversion		?	
30	Equivalent units of production	?	?	
31				
32	**Costs per Equivalent Unit**			
33		Materials	Conversion	
34	Cost of beginning work in process inventory	?	?	
35	Costs added during the period	?	?	
36	Total cost	?	?	
37	Equivalent units of production	?	?	
38	Cost per equivalent unit	?	?	
39				
40	**Costs of Ending Work in Process Inventory and the Units Transferred Out**			
41		Materials	Conversion	Total
42	Ending work in process inventory:			
43	Equivalent units of production	?	?	
44	Cost per equivalent unit	?	?	
45	Cost of ending work in process inventory	?	?	?
46				
47	Units completed and transferred out:			
48	Units transferred to the next department	?	?	
49	Cost per equivalent unit	?	?	
50	Cost of units transferred out	?	?	?
51				
52	**Cost Reconciliation**			
53	Costs to be accounted for:			
54	Cost of beginning work in process inventory	?		
55	Costs added to production during the period	?		
56	Total cost to be accounted for	?		
57	Costs accounted for as follows:			
58	Cost of ending work in process inventory	?		
59	Cost of units transferred out	?		
60	Total cost accounted for	?		

Chapter 4 Form   Chapter 4 Formulas   Chapte

Microsoft Excel

You should proceed to the requirements below only after completing your worksheet.

Required:

1.   Check your worksheet by changing the beginning work in process inventory to 100 units, the units started into production during the period to 2,500 units, and the units in ending work in process inventory to 200 units, keeping all other data the same as in the original example. If your worksheet is operating properly, the cost per equivalent unit for materials should now be $152.50 and the cost per equivalent unit for conversion should be $145.50. If you do not get these answers, find the errors in your worksheet and correct them.

How much is the total cost of the units transferred out? Did it change? Why or why not?

2.   Change all numbers in the Data area of your worksheet so that it looks like this:

Beginning work in process inventory:	
Units in process	200
Completion with respect to materials	100%
Completion with respect to conversion	20%
Costs in the beginning work in process inventory:	
Materials cost	$2,000
Conversion cost	$800
Units started into production during the period	1,800
Costs added to production during the period:	
Materials cost	$18,400
Conversion cost	$38,765
Ending work in process inventory:	
Units in process	100
Completion with respect to materials	100%
Completion with respect to conversion	30%

What is the cost of the units transferred out?

3.   What happens to the cost of the units transferred out in part (2) above if the percentage completion with respect to conversion for the beginning inventory is changed from 20% to 40% and everything else remains the same? What happens to the cost per equivalent unit for conversion? Explain.

The Foundational 15   Mc Graw Hill connect

L04–1, L04–2, L04–3, L04–4, L04–5

Clopack Company manufactures one product that goes through one processing department called Mixing. All raw materials are introduced at the start of work in the Mixing Department. The company uses the weighted-average method of process costing. Its Work in Process T-account for the Mixing Department for June follows (all forthcoming questions pertain to June):

Work in Process—Mixing Department

June 1 balance	28,000	Completed and transferred to Finished Goods	?
Materials	120,000		
Direct labor	79,500		
Overhead	97,000		
June 30 balance	?		

The June 1 work in process inventory includes 5,000 units with $16,000 in materials cost and $12,000 in conversion cost. The June 1 work in process inventory was 100% complete with respect to materials and 50% complete with respect to conversion. During June, 37,500 units were started into production. The June 30 work in process inventory consisted of 8,000 units 100% complete with respect to materials and 40% complete with respect to conversion.

Required:
1. Prepare the journal entries to record the raw materials used in production and the direct labor cost incurred.
2. Prepare the journal entry to record the overhead cost applied to production.
3. How many units were completed and transferred to finished goods?
4. Compute the equivalent units of production for materials.
5. Compute the equivalent units of production for conversion.
6. What is the cost of beginning work in process inventory plus the cost added during the period for materials?
7. What is the cost of beginning work in process inventory plus the cost added during the period for conversion?
8. What is the cost per equivalent unit for materials?
9. What is the cost per equivalent unit for conversion?
10. What is the cost of ending work in process inventory for materials?
11. What is the cost of ending work in process inventory for conversion?
12. What is the cost of materials transferred to finished goods?
13. What is the amount of conversion cost transferred to finished goods?
14. Prepare the journal entry to record the transfer of costs from Work in Process to Finished Goods.
15. What is the total cost to be accounted for? What is the total cost accounted for?

Mc Graw Hill connect   **Exercises**

EXERCISE 4–1 Process Costing Journal Entries LO4–1

Quality Brick Company produces bricks in two processing departments—Molding and Firing. Information relating to the company's operations in March follows:
a. Raw materials used in production: Molding Department, $23,000; and Firing Department, $8,000.
b. Direct labor costs: Molding Department, $12,000; and Firing Department, $7,000.
c. Manufacturing overhead was applied: Molding Department, $25,000; and Firing Department, $37,000.
d. Unfired, molded bricks were transferred from the Molding Department to the Firing Department. The cost of the unfired, molded bricks was $57,000.
e. Finished bricks were transferred from the Firing Department to the finished goods warehouse. The cost of the finished bricks was $103,000.
f. Finished bricks were sold to customers. The cost of the finished bricks sold was $101,000.

Required:
Prepare journal entries to record items (a) through (f) above.

EXERCISE 4–2 Equivalent Units of Production—Weighted-Average Method LO4–2

Clonex Labs, Inc., uses the weighted-average method of process costing. The following data are available for one department for October:

	Units	Percent Completed	
		Materials	Conversion
Work in process, October 1	30,000	65%	30%
Work in process, October 31	15,000	80%	40%

The department started 175,000 units into production during the month and transferred 190,000 completed units to the next department.

Required:
Compute the equivalent units of production for October.

EXERCISE 4–3 Cost per Equivalent Unit—Weighted-Average Method LO4–3

Superior Micro Products uses the weighted-average method of process costing. Data for the Assembly Department for May appear below:

	Materials	Labor	Overhead
Work in process, May 1	$18,000	$5,500	$27,500
Cost added during May	$238,900	$80,300	$401,500
Equivalent units of production	35,000	33,000	33,000

Required:

Compute the cost per equivalent unit for materials, labor, overhead, and in total.

EXERCISE 4–4 Assigning Costs to Units—Weighted-Average Method LO4–4

Data concerning a recent period's activity in the Prep Department, the first processing department in a company that uses process costing, appear below:

	Materials	Conversion
Equivalent units in ending work in process inventory	2,000	800
Cost per equivalent unit	$13.86	$4.43

A total of 20,100 units were completed and transferred to the next processing department during the period.

Required:

1. Compute the cost of ending work in process inventory for materials, conversion, and in total.
2. Compute the cost of the units completed and transferred out for materials, conversion, and in total.

EXERCISE 4–5 Cost Reconciliation Report—Weighted-Average Method LO4–5

Maria Am Corporation uses the weighted-average method of process costing. The Baking Department is one of the processing departments in its strudel manufacturing facility. In June in the Baking Department, the cost of beginning work in process inventory was $3,570, the cost of ending work in process inventory was $2,860, and the cost added to production was $43,120.

Required:

Prepare a cost reconciliation report for the Baking Department for June.

EXERCISE 4–6 Equivalent Units of Production—Weighted-Average Method LO4–2

Highlands Company uses the weighted-average method of process costing. It processes wood pulp for various manufacturers of paper products. Data relating to tons of pulp processed during June are provided below:

		Percent Completed	
	Tons of Pulp	Materials	Labor and Overhead
Work in process, June 1	20,000	90%	80%
Work in process, June 30	30,000	60%	40%
Started into production during June	190,000		

Required:

1. Compute the number of tons of pulp completed and transferred out during June.
2. Compute the equivalent units of production for materials and for labor and overhead for June.

EXERCISE 4–7 Process Costing Journal Entries LO4–1

Chocolaterie de Geneve, SA, is located in a French-speaking canton in Switzerland. The company makes chocolate truffles that are sold in popular embossed tins. The company has two processing departments—Cooking and Molding. In the Cooking Department, the raw ingredients for the truffles are mixed and then cooked in special candy-making vats. In the Molding Department, the melted chocolate and other ingredients from the Cooking Department are carefully poured into molds and decorative flourishes are applied by hand. After cooling, the truffles are packed for sale.

The company uses a process costing system. The T-accounts below show the flow of costs through the two departments in April:

Work in Process—Cooking

Balance 4/1	8,000	Transferred out	160,000
Direct materials	42,000		
Direct labor	50,000		
Overhead	75,000		

Work in Process—Molding

Balance 4/1	4,000	Transferred out	240,000
Transferred in	160,000		
Direct labor	36,000		
Overhead	45,000		

Required:

Prepare journal entries showing the flow of costs through the two processing departments.

EXERCISE 4–8 Equivalent Units; Cost per Equivalent Unit; Assigning Costs to Units—Weighted-Average Method LO4–2, LO4–3, LO4–4

Helix Corporation uses the weighted-average method of process costing. It produces prefabricated flooring in a series of steps carried out in production departments. All of the material used in the first production department is added at the beginning of processing in that department. Data for May for the first production department follow:

	Units	Percent Complete	
		Materials	Conversion
Work in process inventory, May 1	5,000	100%	40%
Work in process inventory, May 31	10,000	100%	30%
Materials cost in work in process inventory, May 1		$1,500	
Conversion cost in work in process inventory, May 1		$4,000	
Units started into production		180,000	
Units transferred to the next production department		175,000	
Materials cost added during May		$54,000	
Conversion cost added during May		$352,000	

Required:

For May:

1. Calculate the first production department's equivalent units of production for materials and conversion.
2. Compute the first production department's cost per equivalent unit for materials and conversion.
3. Compute the first production department's cost of ending work in process inventory for materials, conversion, and in total.
4. Compute the first production department's cost of the units transferred to the next production department for materials, conversion, and in total.

EXERCISE 4–9 Equivalent Units and Cost per Equivalent Unit—Weighted-Average Method LO4–2, LO4–3

Pureform, Inc., uses the weighted-average method of process costing. It manufactures a product passing through two departments. Data for a recent month for the first department follow:

	Units	Materials	Labor	Overhead
Work in process inventory, beginning	5,000	$4,320	$1,040	$1,790
Units started in process	45,000			
Units transferred out	42,000			
Work in process inventory, ending	8,000			
Cost added during the month		$52,800	$21,500	$32,250

The beginning work in process inventory was 80% complete for materials and 60% complete for labor and overhead. The ending work in process inventory was 75% complete for materials and 50% complete for labor and overhead.

Required:

1. Compute the first department's equivalent units of production for materials, labor, and overhead for the month.
2. Determine the first department's cost per equivalent unit for materials, labor, and overhead for the month.

EXERCISE 4–10 Equivalent Units of Production—Weighted-Average Method LO4–2

Alaskan Fisheries, Inc., processes salmon for various distributors and uses the weighted-average method of process costing. The company has two processing departments—Cleaning and Packing. Data relating to pounds of salmon processed in the Cleaning Department during July are presented below:

		Percent Completed	
	Pounds of Salmon	Materials	Labor and Overhead
Work in process inventory, July 1	20,000	100%	30%
Work in process inventory, July 31	25,000	100%	60%

A total of 380,000 pounds of salmon were started into processing during July. All materials are added at the beginning of processing in the Cleaning Department.

Required:

Compute the Cleaning Department's equivalent units of production for materials and labor and overhead in the month of July.

EXERCISE 4–11 Comprehensive Exercise; Second Production Department—Weighted-Average Method LO4–2, LO4–3, LO4–4, LO4–5

Scribners Corporation produces fine papers in three production departments—Pulping, Drying, and Finishing. In the Pulping Department, raw materials such as wood fiber and rag cotton are mechanically and chemically treated to separate their fibers. The result is a thick slurry of fibers. In the Drying Department, the wet fibers transferred from the Pulping Department are laid down on porous webs, pressed to remove excess liquid, and dried in ovens. In the Finishing Department, the dried paper is coated, cut, and spooled onto reels. The company uses the weighted-average method in its process costing system. Data for March for the Drying Department follow:

		Percent Completed	
	Units	Pulping	Conversion
Work in process inventory, March 1	5,000	100%	20%
Work in process inventory, March 31	8,000	100%	25%
Pulping cost in work in process inventory, March 1			$4,800
Conversion cost in work in process inventory, March 1			$500
Units transferred to the next production department			157,000
Pulping cost added during March			$102,450
Conversion cost added during March			$31,300

No materials are added in the Drying Department. Pulping cost represents the costs of the wet fibers transferred in from the Pulping Department. Wet fiber is processed in the Drying Department in batches; each unit in the above table is a batch, and one batch of wet fibers produces a set amount of dried paper that is passed on to the Finishing Department.

Required:

For March:

1. Compute the Drying Department's equivalent units of production for pulping and conversion.
2. Compute the Drying Department's cost per equivalent unit for pulping and conversion.
3. Compute the Drying Department's cost of ending work in process inventory for pulping, conversion, and in total.

4. Compute the Drying Department's cost of units transferred out to the Finishing Department for pulping, conversion, and in total.
5. Prepare a cost reconciliation report for the Drying Department.

EXERCISE 4–12 Equivalent Units; Assigning Costs; Cost Reconciliation—Weighted-Average Method LO4–2, LO4–4, LO4–5

Superior Micro Products uses the weighted-average method of process costing. During January, the Assembly Department completed its processing of 25,000 units and transferred them to the next department. The cost of beginning work in process inventory and the costs added during January totaled $599,780. The ending work in process inventory in January consisted of 3,000 units, which were 80% complete for materials and 60% complete for labor and overhead. The costs per equivalent unit for the month were as follows:

	Materials	Labor	Overhead
Cost per equivalent unit	$12.50	$3.20	$6.40

Required:

For January:

1. Compute the equivalent units of materials, labor, and overhead in the ending work in process inventory.
2. Compute the cost of ending work in process inventory for materials, labor, overhead, and in total.
3. Compute the cost of the units transferred to the next department for materials, labor, overhead, and in total.
4. Prepare a cost reconciliation report. (Note: You will not be able to break the cost to be accounted for into the cost of beginning work in process inventory and costs added during the month.)

Mc Graw Hill connect   **Problems**

PROBLEM 4–13 Comprehensive Problem; Second Production Department—Weighted-Average Method LO4–2, LO4–3, LO4–4, LO4–5

Old Country Links, Inc., produces sausages in three production departments—Mixing, Casing and Curing, and Packaging. In the Mixing Department, meats are prepared, ground, and mixed with spices. The spiced meat mixture is transferred to the Casing and Curing Department, where the mixture is force-fed into casings and hung and cured in climate-controlled smoking chambers. In the Packaging Department, the cured sausages are sorted, packed, and labeled. The company uses the weighted-average method of process costing. Data for September for the Casing and Curing Department follow:

	Units	Percent Completed		
		Mixing	Materials	Conversion
Work in process inventory, September 1	1	100%	90%	80%
Work in process inventory, September 30	1	100%	80%	70%

	Mixing	Materials	Conversion
Work in process inventory, September 1	$1,670	$90	$605
Cost added during September	$81,460	$6,006	$42,490

Mixing cost represents the costs of the spiced meat mixture transferred in from the Mixing Department. The spiced meat mixture is processed in the Casing and Curing Department in batches; each unit in the above table is a batch, and one batch of spiced meat mixture produces a set amount of sausages that are passed on to the Packaging Department. During September, 50 batches (i.e., units) were completed and transferred to the Packaging Department.

Required:

For September:

1. Determine the Casing and Curing Department's equivalent units of production for mixing, materials, and conversion.
2. Compute the Casing and Curing Department's cost per equivalent unit for mixing, materials, and conversion.
3. Compute the Casing and Curing Department's cost of ending work in process inventory for mixing, materials, conversion, and in total.
4. Compute the Casing and Curing Department's cost of units transferred out to the Packaging Department for mixing, materials, conversion, and in total.
5. Prepare a cost reconciliation report for the Casing and Curing Department.

PROBLEM 4–14 Analysis of Work in Process T-account—Weighted-Average Method LO4–1, LO4–2, LO4–3, LO4–4

Weston Products manufactures an industrial cleaning compound that goes through three processing departments—Grinding, Mixing, and Cooking. All raw materials are introduced at the start of work in the Grinding Department. The Work in Process T-account for the Grinding Department for May is given below:

Work in Process—Grinding Department

Inventory, May 1	21,800	Completed and transferred to the Mixing Department	?
Materials	133,400		
Conversion	225,500		
Inventory, May 31	?		

The May 1 work in process inventory had 18,000 pounds with $14,600 in materials cost and $7,200 in conversion cost. The May 1 work in process inventory was 100% complete for materials and 30% complete for conversion. During May, 167,000 pounds were started into production. The May 31 inventory consisted of 15,000 pounds that were 100% complete for materials and 60% complete for conversion. The company uses the weighted-average method of process costing.

Required:

For May:

1. Compute the Grinding Department's equivalent units of production for materials and conversion.
2. Compute the Grinding Department's costs per equivalent unit for materials and conversion.
3. Compute the Grinding Department's cost of ending work in process inventory for materials, conversion, and in total.
4. Compute the Grinding Department's cost of units transferred out to the Mixing Department for materials, conversion, and in total.

PROBLEM 4–15 Comprehensive Problem—Weighted-Average Method LO4–2, LO4–3, LO4–4, LO4–5

Sunspot Beverages, Ltd., of Fiji uses the weighted-average method of process costing. It makes blended tropical fruit drinks in two stages. Fruit juices are extracted from fresh fruits and then blended in the Blending Department. The blended juices are bottled and packed for shipping in the Bottling Department. The following information pertains to the operations of the Blending Department for June.

		Percent Completed	
	Units	Materials	Conversion
Work in process, beginning	20,000	100%	75%
Started into production	180,000		
Completed and transferred out	160,000		
Work in process, ending	40,000	100%	25%
		Materials	Conversion
Work in process, beginning		$25,200	$24,800
Cost added during June		$334,800	$238,700

Required:

For June:

1. Calculate the Blending Department's equivalent units of production for materials and conversion.
2. Calculate the Blending Department's cost per equivalent unit for materials and conversion.
3. Calculate the Blending Department's cost of ending work in process inventory for materials, conversion, and in total.
4. Calculate the Blending Department's cost of units transferred out to the Bottling Department for materials, conversion, and in total.
5. Prepare a cost reconciliation report for the Blending Department.

PROBLEM 4–16 Comprehensive Problem—Weighted-Average Method LO4–2, LO4–3, LO4–4, LO4–5

Builder Products, Inc., uses the weighted-average method of process costing. It manufactures a caulking compound that goes through three processing stages prior to completion. Information on work in the first department, Cooking, is given below for May:

Production data:	
Pounds in process, May 1; materials 100% complete; conversion 80% complete	10,000
Pounds started into production during May	100,000
Pounds completed and transferred out	?
Pounds in process, May 31; materials 60% complete; conversion 20% complete	15,000
Cost data:	
Work in process inventory, May 1:	
Materials cost	$1,500
Conversion cost	$7,200
Cost added during May:	
Materials cost	$154,500
Conversion cost	$90,800

Required:

For May:

1. Compute the equivalent units of production for materials and conversion.
2. Compute the cost per equivalent unit for materials and conversion.
3. Compute the cost of ending work in process inventory for materials, conversion, and in total.
4. Compute the cost of units transferred out to the next department for materials, conversion, and in total.
5. Prepare a cost reconciliation report.

PROBLEM 4–17 Cost Flows LO4–1

Lubricants, Inc., produces a special kind of grease widely used by race car drivers. The grease is produced in two processing departments—Refining and Blending. Raw materials are introduced at various points in the Refining Department.

The following incomplete Work in Process account is available for the Refining Department for March:

Work in Process—Refining Department

March 1 balance	38,000	Completed and transferred to Blending	?
Materials	495,000		
Direct labor	72,000		
Overhead	181,000		
March 31 balance	?		

The March 1 work in process inventory in the Refining Department includes materials, $25,000; direct labor, $4,000; and overhead, $9,000.

Costs incurred during March in the Blending Department were materials used, $115,000; direct labor, $18,000; and overhead cost applied to production, $42,000.

Required:

1. Prepare journal entries to record the costs incurred in both the Refining Department and Blending Department during March. Key your entries to the items (a) through (g) below.

    a. Raw materials used in production.

    b. Direct labor costs incurred.

    c. Manufacturing overhead costs incurred for the entire factory, $225,000. (Credit Accounts Payable.)

    d. Manufacturing overhead was applied to production using a predetermined overhead rate.

    e. Units completed in the Refining Department were transferred to the Blending Department, $740,000.

    f. Units completed in the Blending Department were transferred to Finished Goods, $950,000.

    g. Completed units were sold on account, $1,500,000. The Cost of Goods Sold was $900,000.

2. Post the journal entries from (1) above to T-accounts. The following account balances existed at the beginning of March. (The beginning balance in the Refining Department's Work in Process is given in the T-account shown above.)

Raw Materials	$618,000
Work in Process—Blending Department	$65,000
Finished Goods	$20,000

After posting the entries to the T-accounts, find the ending balance in the inventory accounts and the Manufacturing Overhead account.

PROBLEM 4–18 Interpreting a Report—Weighted-Average Method LO4–2, LO4–3, LO4–4

Cooperative San José of southern Sonora state in Mexico makes a unique syrup using cane sugar and local herbs. The syrup is sold in small bottles and prized as a flavoring for drinks and desserts. The bottles are sold for $12 each. The first stage in the production process occurs in the Mixing Department, which removes foreign matter from the raw materials and mixes them in the proper proportions in large vats. The company uses the weighted-average method of process costing.

A hastily prepared report for the Mixing Department for April appears below:

Units to be accounted for:	
Work in process, April 1 (materials 90% complete;	
conversion 80% complete)	30,000
Started into production	200,000
Total units to be accounted for	230,000
Units accounted for as follows:	
Transferred to next department	190,000
Work in process, April 30 (materials 75% complete;	
conversion 60% complete)	40,000
Total units accounted for	230,000
Cost Reconciliation	
Cost to be accounted for:	
Work in process, April 1	$ 98,000
Cost added during the month	827,000
Total cost to be accounted for	$925,000
Cost accounted for as follows:	
Work in process, April 30	$119,400
Transferred to next department	805,600
Total cost accounted for	$925,000

Management would like some additional information about Cooperative San José's operations.

Required:

1. What were the Mixing Department's equivalent units of production for materials and conversion for April?

2. What were the Mixing Department's costs per equivalent unit for materials and conversion for April? The beginning inventory included materials, $67,800; and conversion cost, $30,200. The costs added during the month consisted of materials, $579,000; and conversion cost, $248,000.
3. How many of the units transferred out of the Mixing Department in April were started and completed during that month?
4. The manager of the Mixing Department stated, "Materials prices jumped from about $2.50 per unit in March to $3 per unit in April, but due to good cost control I was able to hold our materials cost to less than $3 per unit for the month." Should this manager be rewarded for good cost control? Explain.

Mc Graw Hill **connect**   **Cases**

Select cases are available in Connect.

CASE 4–19 Second Department—Weighted-Average Method LO4–2, LO4–3, LO4–4

"I think we goofed by hiring the new assistant controller," said Ruth Scarpino, president of Provost Industries. "Just look at this report he prepared for last month for the Finishing Department. I can't understand it."

Finishing Department costs:	
Work in process inventory, April 1, 450 units; materials	
100% complete; conversion 60% complete	$ 8,208*
Costs transferred in during the month from the	
preceding department, 1,950 units	17,940
Materials cost added during the month	6,210
Conversion costs incurred during the month	13,920
Total departmental costs	$46,278
Finishing Department costs assigned to:	
Units completed and transferred to finished goods,	
1,800 units at $25.71 per unit..	$46,278
Work in process inventory, April 30, 600 units;	
materials 0% complete; conversion 35% complete	0
Total departmental costs assigned	$46,278

*Consists of cost transferred in, $4,068; materials cost, $1,980; and conversion cost, $2,160.

"He's struggling to learn our system," replied Frank Harrop, the operations manager. "The problem is he's been away from process costing for a long time, and it's coming back slowly."

"It's not just the format of his report I'm concerned about. Look at that $25.71 unit cost he's come up with for April. Doesn't that seem high to you?" said Ms. Scarpino.

"Yes, it does seem high; but on the other hand, I know we had an increase in materials prices during April, and that may be the explanation," replied Mr. Harrop. "I'll get someone else to redo this report and then we can see what's going on."

Provost Industries manufactures a ceramic product that goes through two processing departments—Molding and Finishing. The company uses the weighted-average method of process costing.

Required:

1. Prepare a report for the Finishing Department showing how much cost should have been assigned to the units completed and transferred to finished goods, and how much cost should have been assigned to ending work in process inventory in the Finishing Department.
2. Explain to the president why the unit cost on the new assistant controller's report is so high.

CASE 4–20 Ethics and the Manager, Understanding the Impact of Percentage Completion on Profit— Weighted-Average Method LO4–2, LO4–3, LO4–4

Gary Stevens and Mary James are production managers in the Consumer Electronics Division of General Electronics Company, which has several dozen plants scattered throughout the world. Mary manages the plant located in Des Moines, Iowa, while Gary manages the plant in El Segundo, California. Production managers are paid a salary plus a bonus equal to 5% of their base salary if

the entire division meets or exceeds its target profits for the year. The bonus is determined in March after the company's annual report has been prepared and issued to stockholders.

Shortly after the beginning of the new year, Mary received a phone call from Gary that went like this:

Gary: I just got the preliminary profit figures for the division for last year and we are within $200,000 of making the year's target profits. All we have to do is pull a few strings, and we'll be over the top!

Mary: What do you mean?

Gary: Well, one thing that would be easy to change is your estimate of the percentage completion of your ending work in process inventories.

Mary: I don't know if I can do that, Gary. Those percentage completion figures are supplied by Tom Winthrop, my lead supervisor, who I have always trusted to provide us with good estimates. Besides, I have already sent the percentage completion figures to corporate headquarters.

Gary: You can always tell them there was a mistake. Think about it, Mary. All of us managers are doing as much as we can to pull this bonus out of the hat. You may not want the bonus check, but the rest of us sure could use it.

The final processing department in Mary's production facility began the year with no work in process inventory. During the year, 210,000 units were transferred in from the prior processing department and 200,000 units were completed and sold. Costs transferred in from the prior department totaled $39,375,000. No materials are added in the final processing department. A total of $20,807,500 of conversion cost was incurred in the final processing department during the year.

Required:

1. Tom Winthrop estimated the units in ending work in process inventory in the final processing department were 30% complete for conversion costs. If this estimate of the percentage completion is used, what would be the cost of goods sold for the year?
2. Does Gary Stevens want the estimated percentage completion to be increased or decreased? Explain why.
3. What percentage completion would increase net operating income by $200,000 over the net operating income based on Winthrop's original estimates?
4. Do you think Mary James should alter estimates of the percentage completion? Why or why not?

Appendix 4A: FIFO Method

The FIFO method of process costing is more accurate than the weighted-average method, but it is more complex. It calculates unit costs using only the costs and outputs from the current period, whereas the weighted-average method calculates unit costs using costs and outputs from the current and prior periods.

We will illustrate the FIFO method using the data from Exhibits 4–5 and 4–8 pertaining to Double Diamond Skis' Shaping and Milling Department. We will also organize our explanation using the same four-step process used for the weighted-average method.

Step 1: Compute the Equivalent Units of Production

LO4–6

Compute the equivalent units of production using the FIFO method.

The computation of equivalent units of production using the FIFO method differs from the weighted-average method in two ways.

First, the "units transferred out" is divided into two parts. One part consists of the units from beginning inventory that were completed and transferred out, and the other part includes the units *started* and *completed* during the current period.

Second, under the FIFO method, both beginning and ending work in process inventories are converted to equivalent units. For the beginning inventory, the equivalent units represent the work done to *complete* the units; for the ending inventory, the equivalent units represent the work done to bring the units to a stage of partial completion at the end of the period (the same as with the weighted-average method).

The formula for computing the equivalent units of production under the FIFO method is more complex than under the weighted-average method:

**FIFO Method
(a separate calculation is made for each cost category
in each processing department)**

Equivalent units of production = Equivalent units to complete beginning work in process inventory*

+ Units started and completed during the period

+ Equivalent units in ending work in process inventory

$$\begin{matrix}\text{*Equivalent units to} & \text{Units in beginning} & & \left(\text{Percentage completion}\right) \\ \text{complete beginning work} = & \text{work in process} & \times & \left(100\% - \text{of beginning work in}\right) \\ \text{in process inventory} & \text{inventory} & & \left(\text{process inventory}\right)\end{matrix}$$

Or the equivalent units of production can also be determined as follows:

$$\begin{matrix}\text{Equivalent} & \text{Units} & \text{Equivalent units} & \text{Equivalent units in} \\ \text{units of} = & \text{transferred} + & \text{in ending work in} - & \text{beginning work in} \\ \text{production} & \text{out} & \text{process inventory} & \text{process inventory}\end{matrix}$$

To illustrate the FIFO method, refer again to the data in Exhibit 4–5 for the Shaping and Milling Department at Double Diamond Skis. The department completed and transferred 4,800 units to the Graphics Application Department during May. Because 200 of these units came from the beginning inventory, the Shaping and Milling Department must have started and completed 4,600 units during May. The 200 units in the beginning inventory were 55% complete with respect to materials and 30% complete with respect to conversion costs when the month started. Thus, to complete these units the department must have added another 45% of materials costs (100% − 55% = 45%) and another 70% of conversion costs (100% − 30% = 70%). Following this line of reasoning, the equivalent units of production for the Shaping and Milling Department for May would be computed as shown in Exhibit 4A–1.

	Materials	Conversion
Equivalent units needed to complete beginning work in process inventory:		
Materials: 200 units × (100% − 55%)*	90	
Conversion: 200 units × (100% − 30%)*		140
Units started and completed during the period	4,600[†]	4,600[†]
Equivalent units in ending work in process inventory:		
Materials: 400 units × 40% complete	160	
Conversion: 400 units × 25% complete		100
Equivalent units of production	4,850	4,840

EXHIBIT 4A–1
Equivalent Units of Production: FIFO Method

*This is the work needed to complete the units in beginning inventory.
[†]5,000 units started − 400 units in ending work in process = 4,600 units started and completed. This can also be computed as 4,800 units completed and transferred to the next department − 200 units in beginning work in process inventory. The FIFO method assumes the units in beginning inventory are finished first.

Stop at this point and compare the data in Exhibit 4A–1 with the data in Exhibit 4–6, which shows the computation of equivalent units of production under the weighted-average method. Also refer to Exhibit 4A–2, which compares the two methods.

The essential difference between the two methods is the weighted-average method blends costs and outputs from the current period with costs and outputs from the prior period, whereas the FIFO method separates the two periods. To see this more clearly, consider the following reconciliation of the two calculations of equivalent units of production:

Shaping and Milling Department	Materials	Conversion
Equivalent units of production—weighted-average method	4,960	4,900
Less equivalent units in beginning work in process inventory:		
200 units × 55%	110	
200 units × 30%		60
Equivalent units of production—FIFO method	4,850	4,840

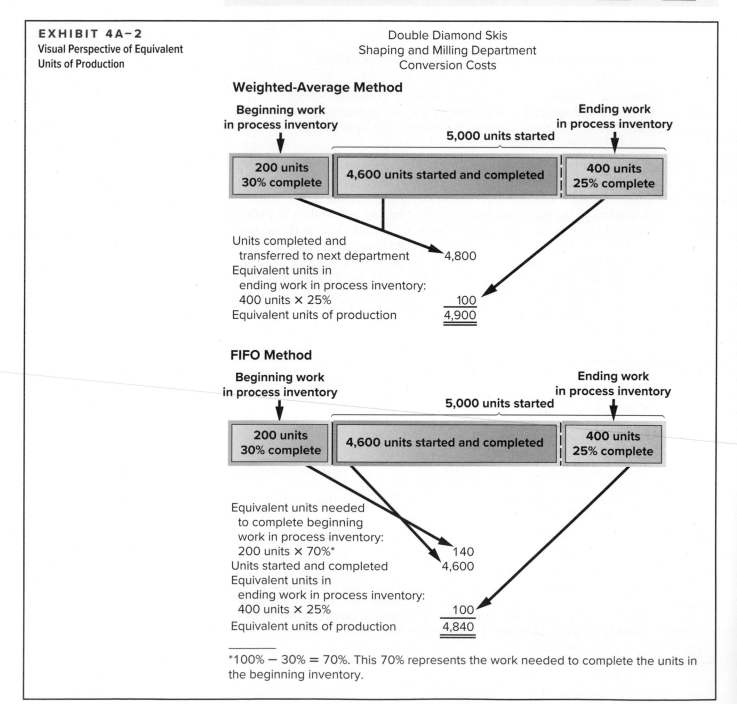

EXHIBIT 4A–2
Visual Perspective of Equivalent Units of Production

Double Diamond Skis
Shaping and Milling Department
Conversion Costs

Weighted-Average Method

Beginning work in process inventory → **200 units 30% complete**

5,000 units started

4,600 units started and completed

Ending work in process inventory → **400 units 25% complete**

Units completed and transferred to next department   4,800
Equivalent units in ending work in process inventory:
  400 units × 25%   100
Equivalent units of production   4,900

FIFO Method

Beginning work in process inventory → **200 units 30% complete**

5,000 units started

4,600 units started and completed

Ending work in process inventory → **400 units 25% complete**

Equivalent units needed to complete beginning work in process inventory:
  200 units × 70%*   140
Units started and completed   4,600
Equivalent units in ending work in process inventory:
  400 units × 25%   100
Equivalent units of production   4,840

*100% − 30% = 70%. This 70% represents the work needed to complete the units in the beginning inventory.

As shown in the reconciliation of the two costing methods, the FIFO method removes the equivalent units already in beginning inventory from the equivalent units of production as defined using the weighted-average method. Thus, the FIFO method isolates the equivalent units of production due to work performed during the current period. The weighted-average method blends together the equivalent units already in beginning inventory with the work performed in the current period.

Step 2: Compute the Cost per Equivalent Unit

In the FIFO method, the cost per equivalent unit is computed as follows:

LO4–7
Compute the cost per equivalent unit using the FIFO method.

FIFO Method
(a separate calculation is made for each cost category
in each processing department)

$$\text{Cost per equivalent unit} = \frac{\text{Cost added during the period}}{\text{Equivalent units of production}}$$

Unlike the weighted-average method, FIFO method's cost per equivalent unit is based only on the costs incurred in the current period.

By incorporating cost data from Exhibit 4–8, the Shaping and Milling Department's costs per equivalent unit for materials and for conversion for May are computed below:

Shaping and Milling Department Costs per Equivalent Unit—FIFO method	Materials	Conversion
Cost added during the period (see Exhibit 4–8) (a)	$368,600	$350,900
Equivalent units of production (see above) (b)	4,850	4,840
Cost per equivalent unit (a) ÷ (b)	$76.00	$72.50

Step 3: Assign Costs to Units

The costs per equivalent unit are used to value (1) the equivalent units needed to complete beginning work in process inventory, (2) the equivalent units in ending work in process inventory, and (3) the units started and completed during the period. For example, each unit started, completed, and transferred out of the Shaping and Milling Department to the Graphics Application Department will carry with it a cost of $148.50—$76.00 for materials and $72.50 for conversion. Because 4,600 units were started, completed, and transferred out in May to the next department (see Exhibit 4A–1), the total cost assigned to those units would be $683,100 (4,600 units × $148.50 per unit).

LO4–8
Assign costs to units using the FIFO method.

A complete accounting of the costs assigned to the units in ending work in process inventory and the units transferred out appears below. It is more complicated than the weighted-average method. This is because the cost of the units transferred out consists of three separate components: (1) the cost in beginning work in process inventory; (2) the cost to complete the units in beginning work in process inventory; and (3) the cost of units started and completed during the period. Notice the cost in beginning work in process inventory ($15,175) is *excluded* in the numerator of the FIFO method's computation of the cost per equivalent unit. However, it is *included* in the numerator of the weighted-average method's computation of the cost per equivalent unit. This is a major difference between the FIFO and weighted-average methods.

Shaping and Milling Department Costs of Ending Work in Process Inventory and Units Transferred Out—FIFO Method			
	Materials	Conversion	Total
Ending work in process inventory:			
Equivalent units in ending work in process inventory (see Exhibit 4A–1) (a)	160	100	
Cost per equivalent unit (b)	$76.00	$72.50	
Cost of ending work in process inventory (a) × (b)	$12,160	$7,250	$19,410
Units transferred out:			
Cost in beginning work in process inventory	$9,600	$5,575	$15,175
Cost to complete the units in beginning work in process inventory:			
Equivalent units needed to complete beginning work in process inventory (see Exhibit 4A–1) (a)	90	140	
Cost per equivalent unit (b)	$76.00	$72.50	
Cost to complete the units in beginning work in process inventory (a) × (b)	$6,840	$10,150	$16,990
Cost of units started and completed this period:			
Units started and completed this period (see Exhibit 4A–1) (a)	4,600	4,600	
Cost per equivalent unit (b)	$76.00	$72.50	
Cost of units started and completed this period (a) × (b)	$349,600	$333,500	$683,100
Total cost of units transferred out			$715,265

Step 4: Prepare a Cost Reconciliation Report

LO4–9

Prepare a cost reconciliation report using the FIFO method.

The costs assigned to ending work in process inventory and the units transferred out reconcile with the costs we started with in Exhibit 4–8 as shown below:

Shaping and Milling Department Cost Reconciliation	
Costs to be accounted for:	
Cost of beginning work in process inventory (Exhibit 4–8)	$ 15,175
Costs added to production during the period (Exhibit 4–8)	719,500
Total cost to be accounted for	$734,675
Costs accounted for as follows:	
Cost of ending work in process inventory (see above)	$ 19,410
Cost of units transferred out (see above)	715,265
Total cost accounted for	$734,675

The $715,265 cost of the units transferred to the next department, Graphics Application, is accounted for in that department as "costs transferred in." As in the weighted-average method, this cost is treated as just another category of costs, like materials or conversion costs. The only difference is the costs transferred in will always be 100% complete with respect to the work done in the Shaping and Milling Department. Costs are passed on from one department to the next in this fashion, until they reach the last processing department, Finishing and Pairing. When the products are completed in this last department, their costs are transferred to finished goods.

A Comparison of Costing Methods

In most situations, the weighted-average and FIFO methods will produce very similar unit costs. If there never are any ending inventories, the two methods will produce identical results. Without any ending inventories, no costs can be carried forward to the next period; thus, the weighted-average method bases unit costs on just the current period's costs—as done in the FIFO method. If there *are* ending inventories, either erratic input prices or erratic production levels would be required to generate much of a difference in unit costs under the two methods. This is because the weighted-average method blends the unit costs from the prior period with the unit costs of the current period. Unless these unit costs differ greatly, the blending will not make much difference.

Nevertheless, from the standpoint of cost control, the FIFO method is better than the weighted-average method. Current performance should be evaluated based on costs of the current period only, but the weighted-average method mixes costs of the current period with costs of the prior period. Thus, under the weighted-average method, the manager's performance in the current period is influenced by what happened in the prior period. This problem does not arise under the FIFO method because it separates the prior period's costs from the current period. For the same reason, the FIFO method also provides more up-to-date cost data for decision-making purposes.

▣ connect   Appendix 4A: Exercises, Problems, and Case

EXERCISE 4A–1 Computation of Equivalent Units of Production—FIFO Method LO4–6
Refer to the data for Clonex Labs, Inc., in Exercise 4–2.

Required:
Assuming the company uses the FIFO method, compute the equivalent units of production for materials and conversion for October.

EXERCISE 4A–2 Cost per Equivalent Unit—FIFO Method LO4–7
Superior Micro Products uses the FIFO method of process costing. Data for the Assembly Department for May appear below:

	Materials	Labor	Overhead
Cost added during May	$193,320	$62,000	$310,000
Equivalent units of production	27,000	25,000	25,000

Required:
Compute the cost per equivalent unit for materials, labor, overhead, and in total.

EXERCISE 4A–3 Assigning Costs to Units—FIFO Method LO4–8
Data concerning a recent period's activity in the Assembly Department, the first processing department in a company using the FIFO method of process costing, appear below:

	Materials	Conversion
Cost of work in process inventory at the beginning of the period ...	$3,200	$650
Equivalent units in the ending work in process inventory	400	200
Equivalent units required to complete the beginning work in process inventory	600	1,200
Cost per equivalent unit for the period	$2.32	$0.75

A total of 26,000 units were completed and transferred to the next processing department during the period. Beginning work in process inventory had 2,000 units and ending work in process inventory had 1,000 units.

Required:
1. Compute the Assembly Department's cost of ending work in process inventory for materials, conversion, and in total for the period.
2. Compute the Assembly Department's cost of units transferred out to the next department for materials, conversion, and in total for the period.

EXERCISE 4A–4 Cost Reconciliation Report—FIFO Method LO4–9
Schroeder Baking Corporation uses process costing in its large-scale baking operations. In the Mixing Department in July, the cost of beginning work in process inventory was $1,460, the cost of ending work in process inventory was $3,120, and the cost added to production was $36,540.

Required:
Prepare a cost reconciliation report for the Mixing Department for July.

EXERCISE 4A–5 Computation of Equivalent Units of Production—FIFO Method LO4–6
MediSecure, Inc., uses the FIFO method of process costing. It produces clear plastic containers for pharmacies in a process that starts in the Molding Department. Data concerning that department's operations in the most recent period appear below:

Beginning work in process:	
Units in process	500
Completion with respect to materials	80%
Completion with respect to conversion	40%
Units started into production during the month	153,600
Units completed and transferred out	153,700
Ending work in process:	
Units in process	400
Completion with respect to materials	75%
Completion with respect to conversion	20%

Required:
Compute the Molding Department's equivalent units of production for materials and conversion for the period.

EXERCISE 4A–6 Equivalent Units of Production—FIFO Method LO4–6
Refer to the data for Alaskan Fisheries, Inc., in Exercise 4–10.

Required:
Compute the Cleaning Department's equivalent units of production for materials and for labor and overhead for July.

EXERCISE 4A–7 Equivalent Units of Production and Cost per Equivalent Unit—FIFO Method LO4–6, LO4–7
Refer to the data for Pureform, Inc., in Exercise 4–9.

Required:
Assume the company uses the FIFO method of process costing.
1. Compute the first department's equivalent units of production for materials, labor, and overhead for the month.
2. Compute the first department's cost per equivalent unit for materials, labor, overhead, and in total for the month.

EXERCISE 4A–8 Equivalent Units of Production—FIFO Method LO4–6
Refer to the data for Highlands Company in Exercise 4–6. Assume the company uses the FIFO method of process costing.

Required:
1. Compute the number of tons of pulp completed and transferred out during June.
2. Compute the equivalent units of production for materials and for labor and overhead for June.

EXERCISE 4A–9 Equivalent Units; Equivalent Units of Production; Assigning Costs—FIFO Method LO4–6, LO4–7, LO4–8

Jarvene Corporation uses the FIFO method of process costing. The following data are for the most recent month of operations in one of the company's processing departments:

Units in beginning inventory	400
Units started into production	3,000
Units in ending inventory	300
Units transferred to the next department	3,100

	Materials	Conversion
Percentage completion of beginning inventory	80%	40%
Percentage completion of ending inventory	70%	60%

The cost of beginning inventory was $11,040, of which $8,120 was for materials and the remainder was for conversion cost. The costs added during the month equaled $132,730. The costs per equivalent unit for the month were:

	Materials	Conversion
Cost per equivalent unit	$25.40	$18.20

Required:

For the month:
1. Compute the total cost per equivalent unit.
2. Compute the equivalent units of material and conversion in the ending inventory.
3. Compute the equivalent units of material and conversion required to complete the beginning inventory.
4. Compute the number of units started and completed.
5. Compute the cost of ending work in process inventory for materials, conversion, and in total.
6. Compute the cost of the units transferred to the next department for materials, conversion, and in total.

PROBLEM 4A–10 Equivalent Units of Production; Assigning Costs; Cost Reconciliation Report—FIFO Method LO4–6, LO4–7, LO4–8, LO4–9

Selzik Company makes cake mixes that go through two processing departments—Blending and Packaging. The following activity was recorded in the Blending Department during July:

Production data:	
Units in process, July 1 (materials 100% complete; conversion 30% complete)	10,000
Units started into production	170,000
Units in process, July 31 (materials 100% complete; conversion 40% complete) . . .	20,000
Cost data:	
Work in process inventory, July 1:	
Materials cost	$8,500
Conversion cost	$4,900
Cost added during the month:	
Materials cost	$139,400
Conversion cost	$244,200

All materials are added at the beginning of work in the Blending Department. The company uses the FIFO method of process costing.

Required:

For July:
1. Calculate the Blending Department's equivalent units of production for materials and conversion.
2. Calculate the Blending Department's cost per equivalent unit for materials and conversion.

3. Calculate the Blending Department's cost of ending work in process inventory for materials, conversion, and in total.
4. Calculate the Blending Department's cost of units transferred out to the next department for materials, conversion, and in total.
5. Prepare a cost reconciliation report for the Blending Department.

PROBLEM 4A–11 Equivalent Units of Production; Cost per Equivalent Unit; Assigning Costs—FIFO Method LO4–6, LO4–7, LO4–8, LO4–9

Refer to the data for the Blending Department of Sunspots Beverages, Ltd., in Problem 4–15. Assume the company uses the FIFO method of process costing.

Required:

For June:

1. Compute the Blending Department's equivalent units of production for materials and conversion.
2. Compute the Blending Department's cost per equivalent unit for materials and conversion.
3. Calculate the Blending Department's cost of ending work in process inventory for materials, conversion, and in total.
4. Calculate the Blending Department's cost of units transferred out to the next department for materials, conversion, and in total.
5. Prepare a cost reconciliation report for the Blending Department.

CASE 4A–12 Second Department—FIFO Method LO4–6, LO4–7, LO4–8

Refer to the data for Provost Industries in Case 4–19. Assume the company uses the FIFO method of process costing.

Required:

1. Prepare a report for the Finishing Department for April showing how much cost should have been assigned to the units completed and transferred to finished goods and how much cost should have been assigned to the ending work in process inventory.
2. As stated in the case, the company experienced an increase in materials prices during April. Would the effects of this price increase show up more under the weighted-average method or the FIFO method? Why?

Appendix 4B: Service Department Cost Allocations

Most large organizations have *operating departments* and *service departments.* The central purposes of the organization are performed in the operating departments. In contrast, service departments do not directly engage in operating activities. Instead, they provide services or assistance to the operating departments. Examples of operating departments include the Surgery Department at Mt. Sinai Hospital, the Geography Department at the University of Washington, the Marketing Department at Allstate Insurance Company, and production departments at manufacturers such as Mitsubishi, HP, and Michelin. In process costing, the processing departments are all operating departments. Examples of service departments include Cafeteria, Internal Auditing, Human Resources, Cost Accounting, and Purchasing.

Companies allocate service department costs to operating departments for various reasons such as motivating and evaluating their managers, encouraging efficient use of service department resources, and calculating unit costs. Chapter 11 discusses service department cost allocations for the first two reasons mentioned above—motivating and evaluating managers and encouraging efficient use of service department resources. This appendix focuses on allocating service department costs to operating departments for calculating unit costs.

For example, a manufacturer may incur service department costs that need to be included in the unit product cost calculations for valuing inventories and cost of goods sold for external reporting purposes. Service companies also incur service department costs they may wish to incorporate into their operating departments' unit cost calculations. For example, hospitals often calculate unit costs such as the cost per patient-day or the cost per laboratory test. Allocating service department costs to the operating departments serving patients or performing laboratory tests provides a more comprehensive understanding of the hospital's various unit costs.

This appendix illustrates two methods used to allocate service department costs to other departments: the direct method and the step-down method.[1] However, before getting into the details of these two methods, we need to explain the concept of *interdepartmental services*.

Interdepartmental Services   Many service departments provide services to each other, as well as to operating departments. For example, the Cafeteria Department provides meals for all employees, including those working in other service departments, as well as those working in operating departments. In turn, the Cafeteria Department may receive services from other service departments, such as from Custodial Services or from Personnel. Services provided between service departments are known as *interdepartmental* or *reciprocal services*.

Direct Method

The *direct method* is simpler than the step-down method because it ignores any services provided by one service department to another service department (e.g., interdepartmental services). Even if a service department (such as Personnel) provides a large amount of service to another service department (such as the Cafeteria), the direct method does not allow for any cost allocations between these two departments. Rather, the direct method allocates all service department costs *directly* to the operating departments, bypassing the other service departments; hence, the term *direct method*.

For an example of the direct method, consider Mountain View Hospital, which has two service departments and two operating departments as shown below. The hospital allocates its Hospital Administration costs based on employee-hours and its Custodial Services costs based on square feet occupied.

> **LO4–10**
> Allocate service department costs to operating departments using the direct method.

	Service Departments		Operating Departments		
	Hospital Administration	Custodial Services	Laboratory	Patient Care	Total
Departmental costs before allocation	$360,000	$90,000	$261,000	$689,000	$1,400,000
Employee-hours.....	12,000	6,000	18,000	30,000	66,000
Space occupied— square feet	10,000	200	5,000	45,000	60,200

The direct method of allocating the hospital's service department costs to the operating departments is shown in Exhibit 4B–1. Several things should be noted in this exhibit. First, the employee-hours of the Hospital Administration Department and the Custodial Services Department are ignored when allocating the costs of Hospital Administration. *Under the direct method, any of the allocation base attributable to the service departments themselves is ignored; only the amount of the allocation base attributable to the*

---

[1]   The reciprocal method can also be used to allocate service department costs to operating departments. However, this method requires the use of simultaneous linear equations that are beyond the scope of this book.

EXHIBIT 4B-1
Direct Method of Allocation

	Service Departments		Operating Departments		
	Hospital Administration	Custodial Services	Laboratory	Patient Care	Total
Departmental costs before allocation	$360,000	$90,000	$ 261,000	$689,000	$1,400,000
Allocation:					
Hospital Administration costs ($^{18}/_{48}$, $^{30}/_{48}$)*	(360,000)		135,000	225,000	
Custodial Services costs ($^{5}/_{50}$, $^{45}/_{50}$)†		(90,000)	9,000	81,000	
Total cost after allocation	$ 0	$ 0	$ 405,000	$995,000	$1,400,000

*Based on the employee-hours in the two operating departments, which are 18,000 hours + 30,000 hours = 48,000 hours.
†Based on the square feet occupied by the two operating departments, which is 5,000 square feet + 45,000 square feet = 50,000 square feet.

operating departments is used in the allocation. Note the same rule is used when allocating the costs of the Custodial Services Department. Even though the Hospital Administration and Custodial Services departments occupy some space, this is ignored when the Custodial Services costs are allocated. Finally, note after all allocations are complete, all service department costs are contained in the two operating departments.

Step-Down Method

LO4–11

Allocate service department costs to operating departments using the step-down method.

Unlike the direct method, the *step-down method* provides for allocation of a service department's costs to other service departments, as well as to operating departments. The step-down method is sequential. The sequence typically begins with the department providing the greatest amount of service to other service departments. After its costs have been allocated, the process continues, step-by-step, ending with the department providing the least amount of services to other service departments. This step procedure is illustrated in Exhibit 4B–2.

EXHIBIT 4B-2
Graphic Illustration—Step-Down Method

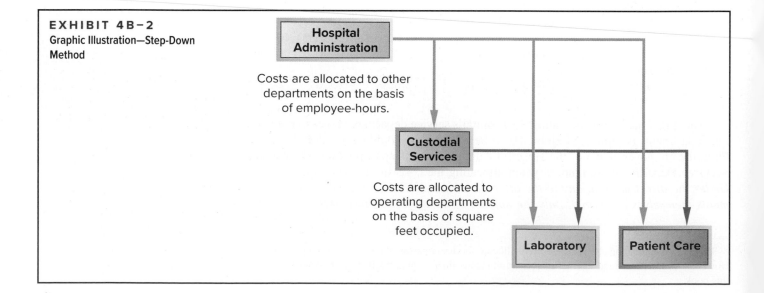

EXHIBIT 4B-3
Step-Down Method of Allocation

	Service Departments		Operating Departments		
	Hospital Administration	Custodial Services	Laboratory	Patient Care	Total
Departmental costs before allocation	$360,000	$ 90,000	$261,000	$ 689,000	$1,400,000
Allocation:					
Hospital Administration costs (6/54, 18/54, 30/54)*	(360,000)	40,000	120,000	200,000	
Custodial Services costs (5/50, 45/50)†		(130,000)	13,000	117,000	
Total cost after allocation	$ 0	$ 0	$394,000	$1,006,000	$1,400,000

*Based on the employee-hours in Custodial Services and the two operating departments, which are 6,000 hours + 18,000 hours + 30,000 hours = 54,000 hours.
†As in Exhibit 4B–1, this allocation is based on the square feet occupied by the two operating departments.

Exhibit 4B–3 shows the details of the step-down method. Note the following three key points about these allocations. First, under the Allocation heading in Exhibit 4B–3, you see two allocations, or steps. In the first step, the costs of Hospital Administration are allocated to another service department (Custodial Services) as well as to the operating departments. In contrast to the direct method, the allocation base for Hospital Administration costs now includes the employee-hours for Custodial Services as well as for the operating departments. However, the allocation base still excludes the employee-hours for Hospital Administration itself. *In both the direct and step-down methods, any amount of the allocation base attributable to the service department whose cost is being allocated is always ignored.*

Second, looking again at Exhibit 4B–3, note in the second step under the Allocation heading, the cost of Custodial Services is allocated to the two operating departments, and none of the cost is allocated to Hospital Administration even though Hospital Administration occupies space in the building. *In the step-down method, any amount of the allocation base attributable to a service department whose cost has already been allocated is ignored.* After a service department's costs have been allocated, costs of other service departments are not reallocated back to it. Third, note the cost of Custodial Services allocated to other departments in the second step ($130,000) includes the costs of Hospital Administration allocated to Custodial Services in the first step.

Appendix 4B: Exercises, Problems, and Case

EXERCISE 4B–1 Direct Method LO4–10
Seattle Western University provided the following data for its service department cost allocations:

	Service Departments		Operating Departments	
	Administration	Facility Services	Undergraduate Programs	Graduate Programs
Departmental costs before allocations	$2,400,000	$1,600,000	$26,800,000	$5,700,000
Student credit-hours			20,000	5,000
Space occupied—square feet	25,000	10,000	70,000	30,000

Required:

Using the direct method, allocate the costs of the service departments to the two operating departments. Allocate the Administration cost based on student credit-hours and the Facility Services cost based on space occupied.

EXERCISE 4B–2 Step-Down Method LO4–11

Madison Park Co-op, a whole foods grocery and gift shop, provided the following data for its service department cost allocations:

	Service Departments		Operating Departments	
	Administration	Janitorial	Groceries	Gifts
Departmental costs before allocations	$150,000	$40,000	$2,320,000	$950,000
Employee-hours.........................	320	160	3,100	740
Space occupied—square feet	250	100	4,000	1,000

Required:

Using the step-down method, allocate the costs of the service departments to the two operating departments. Allocate Administration first on the basis of employee-hours and then Janitorial based on space occupied.

EXERCISE 4B–3 Step-Down Method LO4–11

The Ferre Publishing Company provided the following data for its three service departments and two operating departments.

	Service Departments			Operating Departments		
	Administration	Janitorial	Maintenance	Binding	Printing	Total
Costs	$140,000	$105,000	$48,000	$275,000	$430,000	$998,000
Number of employees	60	35	140	315	210	760
Square feet of space occupied	15,000	10,000	20,000	40,000	100,000	185,000
Hours of press time				30,000	60,000	90,000

The company uses the step-down method to allocate service department costs in the following order: Administration (number of employees), Janitorial (space occupied), and Maintenance (hours of press time).

Required:

Using the step-down method, allocate the service department costs to the operating departments.

EXERCISE 4B–4 Direct Method LO4–10

Refer to the data for the Ferre Publishing Company in Exercise 4B–3.

Required:

Assuming the company uses the direct method rather than the step-down method, how much cost would be assigned to each operating department?

PROBLEM 4B–5 Step-Down Method LO4–11

Woodbury Hospital provided the following data for its three service departments and three operating departments.

	Service Departments			Operating Departments			
	Housekeeping Services	Food Services	Admin. Services	Laboratory	Radiology	General Hospital	Total
Total cost	$87,000	$301,060	$249,020	$405,900	$520,500	$475,800	$2,039,280
Meals served			800	2,000	1,000	68,000	71,800
Square feet of space	5,000	13,000	6,500	10,000	7,500	108,000	150,000
Files processed				14,000	7,000	25,000	46,000

The costs of the service departments are allocated by the step-down method using the allocation bases and in the order shown in the following table:

Service Department	Allocation Bases
Housekeeping Services	Square feet of space
Food Services	Meals served
Administrative Services	Files processed

All billing in the hospital is done through Laboratory, Radiology, or General Hospital. The hospital's administrator wants the costs of the three service departments allocated to these three billing centers.

Required:

Using the step-down method, prepare the cost allocation desired by the hospital administrator. Include under each billing center the direct costs of the center, as well as the costs allocated from the service departments.

CASE 4B–6 Step-Down Method versus Direct Method LO4–10, LO4–11

"This is really an odd situation," said Jim Carter, general manager of Highland Publishing Company. "We get most of the jobs we bid on that require a lot of press time in the Printing Department, yet profits on those jobs are never as high as they ought to be. On the other hand, we lose most of the jobs we bid on that require a lot of time in the Binding Department. I would be inclined to think that the problem is with our overhead rates, but we're already computing separate overhead rates for each department. So what else could be wrong?"

Highland Publishing Company is a large organization offering a variety of printing and binding work. The Printing and Binding departments are supported by three service departments. The costs of these service departments are allocated to other departments in the order listed below. The Personnel cost is allocated based on number of employees. The Custodial Services cost is allocated based on square feet of space occupied and the Maintenance cost is allocated based on machine-hours.

Department	Total Labor-Hours	Square Feet of Space Occupied	Number of Employees	Machine-Hours	Direct Labor-Hours
Personnel	20,000	4,000	10		
Custodial Services	30,000	6,000	15		
Maintenance	50,000	20,000	25		
Printing	90,000	80,000	40	150,000	60,000
Binding	260,000	40,000	120	30,000	175,000
	450,000	150,000	210	180,000	235,000

Budgeted overhead costs in each department for the current year are shown below:

Personnel	$ 360,000
Custodial Services	141,000
Maintenance	201,000
Printing	525,000
Binding	373,500
Total budgeted cost	$1,600,500

Because of its simplicity, the company has always used the direct method to allocate service department costs to the two operating departments.

Required:

1. Using the step-down method, allocate the service department costs to the consuming departments. Then compute predetermined overhead rates in the two operating departments. Use machine-hours as the allocation base in the Printing Department and direct labor-hours as the allocation base in the Binding Department.

2. Repeat (1) above, this time using the direct method. Again compute predetermined overhead rates in the Printing and Binding departments.

3. Assume during the current year the company bids on a job requiring machine and labor time as follows:

	Machine-Hours	Direct Labor-Hours
Printing Department................	15,400	900
Binding Department................	800	2,000
Total hours	16,200	2,900

   a. Calculate the overhead cost assigned to the job if the company used the overhead rates developed in (1) above. Then calculate the overhead cost assigned to the job if the company used the overhead rates developed in (2) above.

   b. Explain to Mr. Carter, the general manager, why the step-down method provides a better basis for computing predetermined overhead rates than the direct method.

Cost-Volume-Profit Relationships

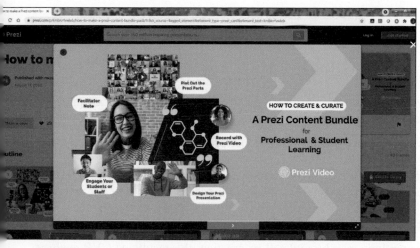

littlenySTOCK/Shutterstock

lighthouse image: Martin73/Shutterstock;
big data image: INGARA/Shutterstock

ENTREPRENEUR SPOTLIGHT

Peter Arvai is the cofounder of Prezi, a state-of-the-art presentation software company. His company's products help oral presenters better organize and deliver their thoughts, thereby enabling the audience to reach "that 'ah-hah' moment faster." Today, Prezi supports over 100 million users who have made more than 360 million presentations. The company's website cites user-based research claiming Prezi is 12.5 percent more organized, 16.4 percent more engaging, 21.9 percent more persuasive, and 25.3 percent more effective than PowerPoint.

Applying Managerial Accounting

Prezi sells three main product lines (Prezi Present, Prezi Video, and Prezi Design) on one software platform in standard, plus, and premium packages to three customer segments: individual; students and educators; and business. As the company considers what prices to charge for its various software packages across its three customer segments, it would use cost-volume-profit (CVP) analysis to answer the question: What will be the impact on profits of implementing one pricing plan versus another? If the company raises its prices, it will likely cause unit sales to decline, and vice versa—lowering its prices will likely cause unit sales to increase. CVP analysis can help the company find the price points it believes will maximize profits.

Serving all Stakeholders

Peter Arvai played an instrumental role in founding WeAreOpen—a nonprofit entity promoting diversity and inclusion in the workplace. The organization's core belief is a company's employees and its business partners should be "judged solely on the basis of their actions and their work performance, and without regard for their sex, age, sexual orientation, national or ethnic background, political convictions, physical abilities, or other characteristics." To date, more than 1,000 companies have publicly joined and supported the WeAreOpen mission. Arvai has also founded another nonprofit called BridgeBudapest "to encourage young Hungarians to believe that global success can happen from Hungary." ■

Sources: www.prezi.com, https://nyitottakvagyunk.hu/en/about-us/, https://bridgebudapest.org/.

LEARNING OBJECTIVES

After studying Chapter 5, you should be able to:

LO5–1 Calculate the variable expense ratio and the contribution margin ratio.

LO5–2 Explain how changes in unit sales affect contribution margin and net operating income.

LO5–3 Compute the degree of operating leverage at a particular level of sales and explain how it can be used to predict changes in net operating income.

LO5–4 Calculate the break-even point.

LO5–5 Compute the margin of safety and explain its significance.

LO5–6 Calculate the level of sales needed to achieve a desired target profit.

LO5–7 Show the effects on net operating income of changes in unit sales, selling price, variable cost per unit, and total fixed costs.

LO5–8 Prepare and interpret a cost-volume-profit (CVP) graph and a profit graph.

LO5–9 Compute the break-even point for a multiproduct company and explain the effects of shifts in the sales mix on contribution margin and the break-even point.

LO5–10 *(Appendix 5A) Analyze a mixed cost using a scattergraph plot and the high-low method.*

LO5–11 *(Appendix 5A) Analyze a mixed cost using a scattergraph plot and the least-squares regression method.*

 Data Analytics Exercise available in Connect to complement this chapter

Cost-volume-profit (CVP) analysis helps managers make many important decisions such as what products and services to offer, what prices to charge, and what marketing strategy to use. Its primary purpose is to estimate how profits are affected by the following five factors:

1. Selling prices.
2. Unit sales (also called sales volume).
3. Unit variable costs.
4. Total fixed costs.
5. Mix of products sold.

To simplify CVP calculations, managers typically adopt the following assumptions with respect to these factors[1]:

1. Selling price is constant. The price of a product or service will not change as unit sales change.
2. Costs are linear and can be accurately divided into variable and fixed components. The variable costs per unit and total fixed costs are constant over the entire relevant range.
3. In multiproduct companies, the mix of products sold remains constant.

While these assumptions may be violated in practice, the results of CVP analysis are often "good enough" to be quite useful. Perhaps the greatest danger lies in relying on simple CVP analysis when a manager is contemplating a large change in unit sales that lies outside the relevant range. However, even in these situations the CVP model can be adjusted to account for anticipated changes in selling prices, variable costs per unit, total fixed costs, and the sales mix that arise when the estimated unit sales fall outside the relevant range.

To help explain the role of CVP analysis in business decisions, we'll turn our attention to Acoustic Concepts, Inc., a company founded by Prem Narayan.

MANAGERIAL ACCOUNTING IN ACTION
THE ISSUE

ACOUSTIC
concepts
inc

Prem started Acoustic Concepts, Inc., to market a new speaker he designed for automobile sound systems. The speaker, called the Sonic Blaster, uses an advanced microprocessor and proprietary software to boost amplification to awesome levels. Prem contracted with a Taiwanese electronics manufacturer to produce the speaker. With seed money provided by his family, Prem placed an order with the manufacturer and ran advertisements in auto magazines.

The Sonic Blaster's immediate success enabled Prem to move the company's headquarters out of his apartment and into a nearby industrial park. He also hired a receptionist, an accountant, a sales manager, and a small sales staff to sell the speakers to retail stores. The accountant, Bob Luchinni, had worked for several small companies where he acted as a business advisor and bookkeeper. The following discussion occurred soon after Bob was hired:

Prem: Bob, I have a lot of questions about the company's finances that I hope you can answer.
Bob: We're in great shape. The loan from your family will be paid off within a few months.

---

[1]   One additional assumption often used in manufacturing companies is that inventories do not change. The number of units produced equals the number of units sold.

Prem: I know, but I am worried about the risks I've taken on by expanding operations. What would happen if a competitor entered the market and our sales slipped? How far could sales drop without putting us into the red? Another question I've been trying to resolve is how much our sales would have to increase to justify the big marketing campaign the sales staff is pushing for.

Bob: Marketing always wants more money for advertising.

Prem: And they are always pushing me to drop the speaker's selling price to boost unit sales, but I'm not sure the increased volume will offset the loss in revenue from the lower price.

Bob: These questions are all related to the relationships among our selling prices, costs, and unit sales. I shouldn't have a problem coming up with some answers.

Prem: Can we meet again in a couple of days to see what you have come up with?

Bob: Sounds good. By then I'll have some preliminary answers for you as well as some Microsoft Excel modeling tools you can use for data visualization purposes.

CVP Analysis: The Foundational Tools

To prepare for his meeting with Prem, Bob turned his attention to three foundational tools he'll use to demonstrate the power of CVP analysis: (1) the contribution approach income statement, (2) the variable expense and contribution margin ratios, and (3) the profit equations.

The Contribution Approach Income Statement

Because CVP analysis relies on an understanding of cost behavior, Bob prepared a *contribution approach* income statement for the month of June (see Exhibit 5–1). The **contribution approach** separates costs into variable and fixed categories, first deducting all variable expenses from sales to obtain the *contribution margin*. The **contribution margin** is the amount remaining from sales after all variable expenses have been deducted. Acoustic Concepts' income statement, which is based on four data inputs—unit sales of 400 units, selling price per unit of $250, variable expenses per unit of $150, and total fixed expenses of $35,000—shows sales of $100,000, variable expenses of $60,000, and net operating income of $5,000. The contribution margin per unit (also called Unit CM) is $100.

Acoustic Concepts, Inc. Contribution Income Statement For the Month of June	Total	Per Unit	Percent of Sales
Sales (400 speakers)	$100,000	$250	100%
Variable expenses.	60,000	150	60%
Contribution margin	40,000	$100	40%
Fixed expenses	35,000		
Net operating income.	$ 5,000		

EXHIBIT 5–1
Acoustic Concepts, Contribution Income Statement

Variable Expense Ratio and the Contribution Margin Ratio (CM Ratio)

Exhibit 5–1 includes Acoustic Concepts' *variable expense ratio* (60%) and the *contribution margin ratio* (40%). The **variable expense ratio** expresses variable expenses as a percentage of sales and is computed as follows:

$$\text{Variable expense ratio} = \frac{\text{Variable expenses}}{\text{Sales}}$$

For Acoustic Concepts, the computations are:

$$\text{Variable expense ratio} = \frac{\text{Total variable expenses}}{\text{Total sales}} = \frac{\$60,000}{\$100,000} = 60\%$$

Because Acoustic Concepts has only one product, the variable expense ratio can also be computed on a per-unit basis as follows:

$$\text{Variable expense ratio} = \frac{\text{Variable expense per unit}}{\text{Unit selling price}} = \frac{\$150}{\$250} = 60\%$$

Similarly, the **contribution margin ratio (CM ratio)** expresses contribution margin as a percentage of sales and is computed as follows:

$$\text{CM ratio} = \frac{\text{Contribution margin}}{\text{Sales}}$$

For Acoustic Concepts, the computations are:

$$\text{CM ratio} = \frac{\text{Total contribution margin}}{\text{Total sales}} = \frac{\$40,000}{\$100,000} = 40\%$$

The CM ratio can also be computed on a per-unit basis as follows:

$$\text{CM ratio} = \frac{\text{Unit contribution margin}}{\text{Unit selling price}} = \frac{\$100}{\$250} = 40\%$$

The CM ratio quantifies the portion of each sales dollar that helps cover fixed expenses. Once all fixed expenses have been covered, the CM ratio defines the portion of each sales dollar contributing to profits. For Acoustic Concepts, 40 cents of each sales dollar contributes towards covering fixed expenses and providing a profit. The variable expense ratio and CM ratio always add up to 1.0. In the case of Acoustic Concepts, if you were only given the company's variable expense ratio (60%), you could compute its CM ratio as follows:

$$\text{CM ratio} = 1 - \text{Variable expense ratio}$$
$$= 1 - 60\%$$
$$= 40\%$$

The Profit Equations

The foundation for Bob's profit equations is the contribution format income statement, which can be expressed mathematically as follows (for brevity we use the term profit instead of net operating income):

$$\text{Profit} = (\text{Sales} - \text{Variable expenses}) - \text{Fixed expenses}$$

This equation can in turn be refined in various ways to model CVP relationships. In Bob's case, he decided to introduce Prem to three equivalent profit equations.

Profit Equation #1 Because Acoustic Concepts has *only one product,* Bob's first profit equation splits sales into two variables—selling price per unit (P) and quantity of units sold (Q). It also splits variable expenses into two variables—variable expenses per unit (V) and quantity of units sold (Q). Mathematically, this profit equation is depicted as follows:

$$\text{Sales} = \text{Selling price per unit} \times \text{Quantity sold} = P \times Q$$

$$\text{Variable expenses} = \text{Variable expenses per unit} \times \text{Quantity sold} = V \times Q$$

$$\text{Profit} = (P \times Q - V \times Q) - \text{Fixed expenses}$$

Using this equation, we can summarize Acoustic Concepts' income statement from Exhibit 5–1 as follows:

$$
\begin{aligned}
\text{Profit} &= (P \times Q - V \times Q) - \text{Fixed expenses} \\
&= (\$250 \times 400 - \$150 \times 400) - \$35{,}000 \\
&= (\$250 - \$150) \times 400 - \$35{,}000 \\
&= \$100 \times 400 - \$35{,}000 \\
&= \$40{,}000 - \$35{,}000 \\
&= \$5{,}000
\end{aligned}
$$

Profit Equation #2 Bob's second profit equation streamlines his first profit equation by combining the selling price per unit (P) minus the variable expenses per unit (V) into one number, the Unit CM:

$$\text{Profit} = \text{Unit CM} \times Q - \text{Fixed expenses}$$

Using this equation, we can summarize Acoustic Concepts' income statement from Exhibit 5–1 as follows:

$$
\begin{aligned}
\text{Profit} &= \text{Unit CM} \times Q - \text{Fixed expenses} \\
&= \$100 \times 400 - \$35{,}000 \\
&= \$40{,}000 - \$35{,}000 \\
&= \$5{,}000
\end{aligned}
$$

Profit Equation #3 Bob's third equation uses the CM ratio to model profits as follows:

$$\text{Profit} = \text{CM ratio} \times \text{Sales} - \text{Fixed expenses}$$

Using this equation we can summarize Acoustic Concepts' income statement from Exhibit 5–1 as follows:

$$
\begin{aligned}
\text{Profit} &= \text{CM ratio} \times \text{Sales} - \text{Fixed expenses} \\
&= 0.40 \times \$100{,}000 - \$35{,}000 \\
&= \$40{,}000 - \$35{,}000 \\
&= \$5{,}000
\end{aligned}
$$

With these foundational tools in place, Bob was ready to show Prem how to analyze his company's CVP relationships.

CVP Analysis: Focusing on Unit Sales

As a first step, Bob decided to illustrate how CVP analysis could answer five questions related to Acoustic Concepts' unit sales that would be of interest to Prem. These five questions are as follows:

1. If unit sales increase or decrease, how will it affect profits?
2. If unit sales change by a certain percent, by what percent will profits change?
3. What is the break-even point in unit sales?
4. How far can unit sales fall before hitting the break-even point?
5. How many units must be sold to attain a target profit?

LO5–2

Explain how changes in unit sales affect contribution margin and net operating income.

What if Unit Sales Increase or Decrease?

It's one of the most basic questions managers can ask: If unit sales increase or decrease, how will it affect profits? In the context of Acoustic Concepts, Prem Narayan might phrase the question this way: If monthly unit sales increase from the 400 units we sold in June to 450 units, what will be my monthly profits? To answer this question, let's remind ourselves of Acoustic Concepts' data from Exhibit 5–1:

Selling price per unit.	$250
Variable expenses per unit	$150
Contribution margin per unit.	$100
Contribution margin ratio.	40%
Fixed expenses	$35,000

Given those data, Bob could use his profit equations to answer Prem's question three ways.

Profit Equation #1 This equation explicitly includes the selling price per unit ($250) and variable expenses per unit ($150). It computes a revised profit of $10,000 as follows:

$$\text{Profit} = (P \times Q - V \times Q) - \text{Fixed expenses}$$
$$= (\$250 \times 450 - \$150 \times 450) - \$35,000$$
$$= (\$250 - \$150) \times 450 - \$35,000$$
$$= \$100 \times 450 - \$35,000$$
$$= \$45,000 - \$35,000$$
$$= \$10,000$$

Notice, the selling price per unit (P), variable expenses per unit (V), and fixed expenses hold constant. The only variable being adjusted is the quantity of units sold (Q), which increases from 400 to 450.

Profit Equation #2   This equation combines the selling price per unit (P) minus the variable expenses per unit (V) into one number, the Unit CM ($100). It computes a revised profit of $10,000 as follows:

$$\text{Profit} = \text{Unit CM} \times Q - \text{Fixed expenses}$$
$$= \$100 \times 450 - \$35,000$$
$$= \$45,000 - \$35,000$$
$$= \$10,000$$

Profit Equation #3   This equation calculates the revised sales of $112,500 (= $250 × 450 units) and uses the contribution margin ratio (40%) to compute the revised profit of $10,000:

$$\text{Profit} = \text{CM ratio} \times \text{Sales} - \text{Fixed expenses}$$
$$= 0.40 \times \$112,500 - \$35,000$$
$$= \$45,000 - \$35,000$$
$$= \$10,000$$

If we slightly adjust Prem's question to ask—If monthly unit sales increase from the 400 units we sold in June to 450 units, how much will my profits increase?—we can use the CM ratio within the following equation to quantify the *change* in profit:

$$\text{Change in profit} = \text{CM ratio} \times \text{Change in sales} - \text{Change in fixed expenses}$$

Given that June's sales of $100,000 (= $250 × 400 units) would increase to $112,500 (= $250 × 450 units) and fixed expenses hold constant, the answer to Prem's question would be derived as follows:

$$\text{Change in profit} = \text{CM ratio} \times \text{Change in sales} - \text{Change in fixed expenses}$$
$$= 0.40 \times \$12,500 - \$0$$
$$= \$5,000$$

When Acoustic Concepts sells 400 units, it earns a profit of $5,000, whereas when it sells 450 units, it earns a profit of $10,000; hence, the change in profit is an increase of $5,000.

Operating Leverage

Another way for Bob and Prem to analyze the profit impact of increasing unit sales from 400 to 450 units is to do so in percentage terms. Given an increase of 50 units translates to a 12.5 percent (= 50/400) increase in unit sales, Prem could rephrase his question as follows: If unit sales increase by 12.5 percent, by what percent will my profits increase? To answer this question, Bob needs to explain *operating leverage* to Prem. **Operating leverage** is a measure of how sensitive net operating income is to a given percentage change in unit sales. Operating leverage acts as a multiplier. If operating leverage is high, a small percentage increase in unit sales can produce a much larger percentage increase in net operating income.

The **degree of operating leverage** is a measure, at a given level of sales, of how a percentage change in unit sales will affect profits. It is calculated using the following formula:

$$\text{Degree of operating leverage} = \frac{\text{Contribution margin}}{\text{Net operating income}}$$

LO5–3
Compute the degree of operating leverage at a particular level of sales and explain how it can be used to predict changes in net operating income.

Given Exhibit 5–1 shows Acoustic Concepts' contribution margin and net operating income in June were $40,000 and $5,000, respectively, the degree of operating leverage would be computed as follows:

$$\text{Degree of operating leverage} = \frac{\$40,000}{\$5,000} = 8$$

Because Acoustic Concepts' degree of operating leverage is 8, its net operating income grows eight times as fast as its sales. Thus, if the unit sales increase by 12.5 percent, Acoustic Concepts' net operating income will increase by eight times this amount, or 100 percent. In other words, June's net operating income of $5,000 will increase by 100% to a profit of $10,000. In general, this relation between the percentage change in unit sales and the percentage change in net operating income is given by the following formula:

$$\frac{\text{Percentage change in}}{\text{net operating income}} = \frac{\text{Degree of}}{\text{operating leverage}} \times \frac{\text{Percentage}}{\text{change in sales}}$$

Acoustic Concepts: Percentage change in net operating income $= 8 \times 12.5\% = 100\%$

The degree of operating leverage is not constant; it is greatest at the sales level corresponding with zero profits and decreases as sales and profits rise. It quickly estimates what impact various percentage changes in unit sales will have on profits, without the necessity of preparing contribution format income statements. If a company's profits are near zero, a small percentage increase in unit sales can cause a huge percentage increase in profits. *This explains why management often works very hard for only a small increase in sales volume.* If the degree of operating leverage is 5, then a 6 percent increase in unit sales would translate into a 30 percent increase in profits.

If two companies have the same total revenue and total expenses but different proportions of fixed and variable costs, then the company with the higher proportion of fixed costs will have higher operating leverage. When sales are growing, the company with the higher operating leverage will see its profits grow faster than the company with lower operating leverage. Conversely, if sales plummet, the company with higher operating leverage will experience a sharper drop in profits because its fixed costs remain constant in the face of declining sales.

Break-Even Analysis

LO5–4
Calculate the break-even point.

Most managers, including Prem, have a keen interest in a very important question: What is my *break-even point* in unit sales? The **break-even point** is the level of sales at which profit is zero. To calculate the break-even point (in unit sales and dollar sales), managers can use the equation method or the formula method. We'll demonstrate both approaches using Acoustic Concepts' data from Exhibit 5–1:

Selling price per unit..................................	$250
Variable expenses per unit	$150
Contribution margin per unit.........................	$100
Contribution margin ratio.............................	40%
Fixed expenses	$35,000

The Equation Method   Because Acoustic Concepts has only one product, Bob could use the first of his three profit equations to calculate the break-even point in unit sales. The key to this approach is inserting $0 for the profit and then solving for unit sales (Q) as follows:

$$\text{Profit} = (P \times Q - V \times Q) - \text{Fixed expenses}$$
$$\$0 = (\$250 \times Q - \$150 \times Q) - \$35,000$$
$$\$0 = \$100 \times Q - \$35,000$$
$$\$100 \times Q = \$0 + \$35,000$$
$$Q = \$35,000 \div 100$$
$$Q = 350$$

Thus, Acoustic Concepts will break even (or earn zero profit) if it sells 350 speakers per month.

The Formula Method   The formula method is a shortcut version of the equation method. It centers on the idea discussed earlier in the chapter that each unit sold provides a certain amount of contribution margin toward covering fixed expenses. In a single product situation, the formula for computing the unit sales to break even is:

$$\text{Unit sales to break even} = \frac{\text{Fixed expenses}}{\text{Unit CM}}$$

For Acoustic Concepts, the unit sales to break even is computed as follows:

$$\text{Unit sales to break even} = \frac{\text{Fixed expenses}}{\text{Unit CM}}$$
$$= \frac{\$35,000}{\$100}$$
$$= 350$$

Notice 350 units is the same answer we got with the equation method. This will always be the case because the formula method and equation method are mathematically equivalent. The formula method simply skips a few steps in the equation method.

Break-Even Point in Dollar Sales   In addition to finding the break-even point in unit sales, we can also find the break-even point in dollar sales using three methods. First, we could solve for the break-even point in *unit* sales using the equation method or formula method and then multiply the result by the selling price. For Acoustic Concepts, the break-even point in dollar sales using this approach would be computed as 350 speakers × $250 per speaker, or $87,500 in total sales.

Second, we can use one of Bob's profit equations to compute the break-even point in dollar sales. Remembering Acoustic Concepts' contribution margin ratio is 40 percent and its fixed expenses are $35,000, this equation calculates the break-even point in dollar sales as follows:

$$\text{Profit} = \text{CM ratio} \times \text{Sales} - \text{Fixed expenses}$$
$$\$0 = 0.40 \times \text{Sales} - \$35,000$$
$$0.40 \times \text{Sales} = \$0 + \$35,000$$
$$\text{Sales} = \$35,000 \div 0.40$$
$$\text{Sales} = \$87,500$$

Third, we can use the formula method to compute the dollar sales to break even as shown below:

$$\text{Dollar sales to break even} = \frac{\text{Fixed expenses}}{\text{CM ratio}}$$

In the case of Acoustic Concepts, the computations are performed as follows:

$$\text{Dollar sales to break even} = \frac{\text{Fixed expenses}}{\text{CM ratio}}$$
$$= \frac{\$35,000}{0.40}$$
$$= \$87,500$$

Again, you'll notice the break-even point in dollar sales ($87,500) is the same under all three methods. This will always be the case because these methods are mathematically equivalent.

Margin of Safety

LO5–5

Compute the margin of safety and explain its significance.

Once Bob has shown Prem how to compute the company's break-even point of 350 units, or $87,500 in dollar sales, he can illustrate how to use the *margin of safety* to answer a question Prem asked earlier: How far could June's sales of $100,000 drop before hitting our break-even point? The **margin of safety** equals total budgeted (or actual) sales minus break-even sales. It is the amount sales can drop before losses are incurred. The higher the margin of safety, the lower the risk of not breaking even and incurring a loss. In equation form, the margin of safety is:

$$\text{Margin of safety in dollars} = \text{Total budgeted (or actual) sales} - \text{Break-even sales}$$

The margin of safety also can be expressed in percentage form by dividing the margin of safety in dollars by total dollar sales:

$$\text{Margin of safety percentage} = \frac{\text{Margin of safety in dollars}}{\text{Total budgeted (or actual) sales in dollars}}$$

The calculation of the margin of safety for Acoustic Concepts is:

Sales (at the current volume of 400 speakers) (a)	$100,000
Break-even sales (at 350 speakers)	87,500
Margin of safety in dollars (b)	$ 12,500
Margin of safety percentage, (b) ÷ (a)	12.5%

This margin of safety means at the current level of sales and with the company's current prices and cost structure, a reduction in sales of $12,500, or 12.5 percent, would result in just breaking even.

In a single-product company like Acoustic Concepts, the margin of safety also can be expressed in terms of the number of units sold by dividing the margin of safety in dollars by the selling price per unit. In this case, the margin of safety is 50 speakers ($12,500 ÷ $250 per speaker = 50 speakers).

COMMUNICATING WITH DATA VISUALIZATIONS

Predictive analytics answer the question: What will happen? This visualization predicts Acoustic Concepts' margin of safety for any sales volume between 0 and 900 units. For any sales volume less than or equal to 350 units, the company would have no margin of safety because it would be operating at or below the break-even point. For each unit sold above the break-even point (350 units), the margin of safety would increase by $250. For example, if Acoustic Concepts sells 352 units, its margin of safety would be $500 (= 2 units × $250). When the company sells 400 units, its margin of safety is $12,500 (= 50 units × $250).

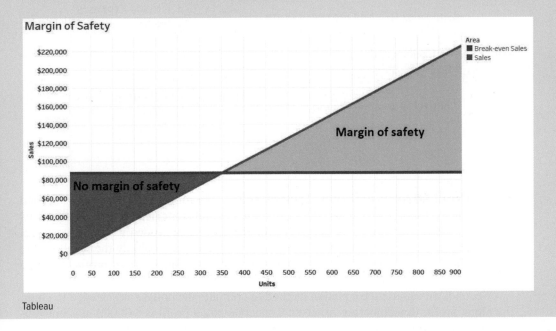

Tableau

Target Profit Analysis

Target profit analysis answers the question: How many units must be sold to attain a target profit? It is similar to break-even analysis except we are changing the profit to some number greater than zero. In **target profit analysis,** we estimate the level of unit sales and dollar sales needed to achieve a target profit. For example, suppose Bob and Prem would like to estimate the sales needed to attain a target profit of $40,000 per month.

LO5–6

Calculate the level of sales needed to achieve a desired target profit.

To calculate the answer in unit sales and dollar sales, they could use the equation method or the formula method.

The Equation Method   To compute the unit sales needed to achieve a target profit of $40,000 per month, Acoustic Concepts can use the same profit equation used for its break-even analysis. Remembering the company's contribution margin per unit is $100 and its total fixed expenses are $35,000, the answer is computed as follows:

$$\text{Profit} = \text{Unit } CM \times Q - \text{Fixed expense}$$
$$\$40,000 = \$100 \times Q - \$35,000$$
$$\$100 \times Q = \$40,000 + \$35,000$$
$$Q = \$75,000 \div \$100$$
$$Q = 750$$

Thus, the target profit can be achieved by selling 750 speakers per month. Notice the only difference between this equation and the equation used for Acoustic Concepts' break-even calculation is the profit figure. In the break-even scenario, the profit is $0, whereas in the target profit scenario the profit is $40,000.

The Formula Method   In a single-product situation, we can compute the unit sales required to attain a specific target profit using the following formula:

$$\text{Unit sales to attain the target profit} = \frac{\text{Target profit} + \text{Fixed expenses}}{\text{Unit CM}}$$

For Acoustic Concepts, the unit sales needed to attain a target profit of $40,000 is computed as follows:

$$\text{Unit sales to attain the target profit} = \frac{\text{Target profit} + \text{Fixed expenses}}{\text{Unit CM}}$$
$$= \frac{\$40,000 + \$35,000}{\$100}$$
$$= 750$$

Target Profit Analysis in Terms of Dollar Sales   To compute the dollar sales needed to attain a target profit, we can use the same three methods for calculating the dollar sales needed to break even. First, we can solve for the *unit* sales needed to attain the target profit using the equation method or formula method and then multiply the result by the selling price. For Acoustic Concepts, the dollar sales to attain its target profit would be computed as 750 speakers × $250 per speaker, or $187,500 in total sales.

Second, we can use the equation method to compute the dollar sales needed to attain the target profit. Remembering Acoustic Concepts' target profit is $40,000, its contribution margin ratio is 40 percent, and its fixed expenses are $35,000, the equation method calculates the answer as follows:

$$\text{Profit} = \text{CM ratio} \times \text{Sales} - \text{Fixed expenses}$$
$$\$40,000 = 0.40 \times \text{Sales} - \$35,000$$
$$0.40 \times \text{Sales} = \$40,000 + \$35,000$$
$$\text{Sales} = \$75,000 \div 0.40$$
$$\text{Sales} = \$187,500$$

Third, we can use the formula method to compute the dollar sales needed to attain the target profit as shown below:

$$\text{Dollar sales to attain the target profit} = \frac{\text{Target profit} + \text{Fixed expenses}}{\text{CM ratio}}$$

For Acoustic Concepts, the computations would be:

$$\text{Dollar sales to attain the target profit} = \frac{\text{Target profit} + \text{Fixed expenses}}{\text{CM ratio}}$$

$$= \frac{\$40,000 + \$35,000}{0.40}$$

$$= \$187,500$$

Again, the answers are the same regardless of which method we use. This is because all of the methods discussed are simply different roads to the same destination.

ROUNDUP: A HERBICIDE MAKING HEADLINES

Bayer AG sells Roundup—a herbicide containing a chemical called glyphosate. While the U.S. Environmental Protection Agency and the European Chemicals Agency have deemed glyphosate as "safe to use," the World Health Organization's International Agency for Research on Cancer has labeled glyphosate a "probable human carcinogen." Furthermore, two juries have found that Roundup caused the plaintiff's cancer, and 11,000 more lawsuits filed by farmers, landscapers, and gardeners claim the same.

In spite of these lawsuits, U.S. farmers continue to apply almost 300 million pounds of glyphosate to their crops every year—in part because its lower cost raises their contribution margin per acre. They also use glyphosate because it is less toxic and breaks down within the soil more quickly than competing alternatives, such as paraquat and atrazine. Karen Williams, who raises crops, cattle, and sheep in New Zealand, says, "if you take glyphosate out of the toolbox we would have to completely redesign our farming system."

Tada Images/Shutterstock

Source: Jacob Bunge, "Farmers Stay with Bayer Herbicide," *The Wall Street Journal*, March 22, 2019, p. B1.

CVP Analysis: Expanding Our Focus to Four Profit Levers

To this point in the chapter, we have focused on analyzing unit sales and its relationship to profits, the break-even point, the margin of safety, and a target profit. However, managers often want to quantify the impact on profits of changes not only to unit sales, but also to selling price per unit, variable costs per unit, and total fixed costs. In this section, we'll use the data from Acoustic Concepts to provide five independent examples of how to calculate the impact on profits of changing one or more of the selling price per unit, unit sales, variable expenses per unit, and total fixed expenses. For each of the five examples, we'll illustrate two methods for deriving the solution.

As a starting point, let's remind ourselves Acoustic Concepts sold 400 speakers in June and its net operating income for the month was $5,000. Additional pertinent data for the company are as follows:

LO5–7

Show the effects on net operating income of changes in unit sales, selling price, variable costs per unit, and total fixed costs.

Selling price per unit.	$250
Variable expenses per unit	$150
Contribution margin per unit.	$100
Contribution margin ratio.	40%
Fixed expenses	$35,000

Example 1: Change in Fixed Costs and Unit Sales

Acoustic Concepts' sales manager would like to increase the monthly advertising budget by $10,000, which in turn would raise monthly fixed costs from $35,000 to $45,000. She believes the additional advertising would increase monthly unit sales from 400 units to

520 units, thereby growing sales by $30,000. Should the advertising budget be increased? Bob could use the following profit equation to answer this question:

$$\begin{aligned}
\text{Profit} &= (P \times Q - V \times Q) - \text{Fixed expenses} \\
&= (\$250 \times 520 - \$150 \times 520) - \$45,000 \\
&= (\$250 - \$150) \times 520 - \$45,000 \\
&= \$100 \times 520 - \$45,000 \\
&= \$52,000 - \$45,000 \\
&= \$7,000
\end{aligned}$$

Because the sales manager's proposal would increase monthly net operating income from $5,000 to $7,000, Prem should approve this proposal. As an alternative, Bob could also use *incremental analysis* to derive the same answer. **Incremental analysis** includes only the costs and revenues that will change if the proposal is implemented. While the methodology for evaluating the proposal differs, the answer is the same—the additional advertising would increase net operating income by $2,000:

Incremental contribution margin:	
$30,000 × 40% CM ratio..........................	$12,000
Less incremental advertising expense	10,000
Increased net operating income.......................	$ 2,000

Because the proposal increases sales by $30,000, the CM ratio of 40 percent can be used to translate the growth in sales to the incremental increase in contribution margin of $12,000. The additional contribution margin of $12,000 exceeds the incremental fixed cost of $10,000, which increases profits by $2,000.

Example 2: Change in Variable Costs and Unit Sales

Refer to the original data. Prem is considering using higher-quality components, which would increase the variable costs per unit by $10, from $150 per unit to $160 per unit. However, the sales manager estimates the higher-quality components would increase sales from 400 speakers per month to 480 speakers. Should the higher-quality components be used? The following profit equation answers this question:

$$\begin{aligned}
\text{Profit} &= (P \times Q - V \times Q) - \text{Fixed expenses} \\
&= (\$250 \times 480 - \$160 \times 480) - \$35,000 \\
&= (\$250 - \$160) \times 480 - \$35,000 \\
&= \$90 \times 480 - \$35,000 \\
&= \$43,200 - \$35,000 \\
&= \$8,200
\end{aligned}$$

Because the sales manager's proposal increases monthly net operating income from $5,000 to $8,200, Prem should approve the higher-quality components. The $3,200 increase in net operating income could also be computed as follows:

Expected total contribution margin	
with higher-quality components:	
480 speakers × $90 per speaker	$43,200
Present total contribution margin:	
400 speakers × $100 per speaker	40,000
Increase in total contribution margin...................	$ 3,200

This approach compares the expected total contribution margin with the higher-quality components ($43,200) to the present total contribution margin ($40,000) to quantify the $3,200 increase in total contribution margin.

Example 3: Change in Fixed Costs, Selling Price, and Unit Sales

Refer to the original data. The sales manager would like to cut the selling price by $20 per unit, from $250 per unit to $230 per unit, and increase the advertising budget by $15,000 per month, thereby increasing fixed costs from $35,000 to $50,000. She believes these two steps will increase unit sales by 50 percent (i.e., they will raise monthly sales from 400 units to 600 units). Should the changes be made? The following profit equation indicates that this proposal should be rejected:

$$\text{Profit} = (P \times Q - V \times Q) - \text{Fixed expenses}$$
$$= (\$230 \times 600 - \$150 \times 600) - \$50,000$$
$$= (\$230 - \$150) \times 600 - \$50,000$$
$$= \$80 \times 600 - \$50,000$$
$$= \$48,000 - \$50,000$$
$$= \$(2,000)$$

This proposal decreases monthly net operating income from $5,000 to $(2,000). The $7,000 decrease in net operating income could also be computed as follows:

Expected total contribution margin with lower selling price:	
600 speakers × $80 per speaker	$48,000
Present total contribution margin:	
400 speakers × $100 per speaker	40,000
Incremental contribution margin	8,000
Change in fixed expenses:	
Less incremental advertising expense	15,000
Reduction in net operating income	$ (7,000)

This approach proceeds in two steps. First, it shows the expected total contribution margin with the lower selling price of $48,000 exceeds the present total contribution margin of $40,000 by $8,000. However, the second step shows the $8,000 increase in contribution margin is not enough to offset the $15,000 increase in fixed costs, thus reducing net operating income by $7,000.

Example 4: Change in Variable Costs, Fixed Costs, and Unit Sales

Refer to the original data. The sales manager would like to pay salespersons a sales commission of $15 per speaker sold, rather than the flat salaries now totaling $6,000 per month. This change would increase variable costs per unit from $150 to $165 and decrease fixed costs from $35,000 to $29,000. She is confident this change in compensation scheme would increase monthly unit sales by 15 percent (i.e., it would increase unit sales from 400 units to 460 units). Should the changes be made? The following profit equation indicates this proposal should be accepted:

$$\text{Profit} = (P \times Q - V \times Q) - \text{Fixed expenses}$$
$$= (\$250 \times 460 - \$165 \times 460) - \$29,000$$
$$= (\$250 - \$165) \times 460 - \$29,000$$
$$= \$85 \times 460 - \$29,000$$
$$= \$39,100 - \$29,000$$
$$= \$10,100$$

This proposal increases monthly net operating income from $5,000 to $10,100. The $5,100 increase in net operating income could also be computed as follows:

Expected total contribution margin with sales staff on commissions:	
460 speakers × $85 per speaker	$39,100
Present total contribution margin:	
400 speakers × $100 per speaker	40,000
Decrease in total contribution margin...................	(900)
Change in fixed expenses:	
Add salaries avoided if a commission is paid	6,000
Increase in net operating income.....................	$ 5,100

This approach proceeds in two steps. First, it shows the expected total contribution margin with sales staff on commissions of $39,100 is less than the present total contribution margin of $40,000 by $(900). However, the second step shows the $(900) decrease in contribution margin is more than offset by the avoided salaries of $6,000, thus increasing net operating income by $5,100.

Example 5: Change in Selling Price

Refer to the original data. The company has an opportunity to make a bulk sale of 150 speakers to a wholesaler if an acceptable price can be negotiated. This sale would not alter the company's regular sales or affect the company's total fixed costs. What price per speaker should be quoted to the wholesaler if Acoustic Concepts wants a profit of $3,000 on the bulk sale? The following profit equation focuses on the *incremental* effects of accepting the wholesale opportunity; hence, it defines incremental target profit of $3,000, incremental unit sales (Q) of 150 units, and incremental fixed expenses of $0.

$$\text{Profit} = (P \times Q - V \times Q) - \text{Fixed expenses}$$
$$\$3,000 = (P \times 150 - \$150 \times 150) - \$0$$
$$\$3,000 = (P \times 150) - \$22,500 - \$0$$
$$P \times 150 = \$25,500 - \$0$$
$$P = \$25,500 \div 150$$
$$P = \$170$$

If Acoustic Concepts sets a price of $170 per unit, it will provide a target profit of $3,000. The selling price of $170 per unit can also be computed as follows:

Variable cost per speaker	$150
Desired profit per speaker	
$3,000 ÷ 150 speakers....................	20
Quoted price per speaker...................	$170

This approach starts with the incremental variable cost per speaker of $150 and adds the desired profit per speaker of $20 to arrive at the quoted price per speaker of $170.

BLUE APRON'S MEAL KIT SALES SPIKE DURING PANDEMIC

During the coronavirus lockdown, monthly meal kit sales in the United States jumped from $50 million to $100 million. This dramatic increase in customer demand was good news for Blue Apron Holdings, a meal kit seller that had seen its stock market valuation drop from $2 billion in 2017 to $90 million just before the pandemic. To translate its unexpected jump in sales to higher contribution margin and profits, the company reduced the size of its menu and simplified its ingredient lists. Blue Apron also increased its marketing budget (a fixed cost) in an effort to retain its newly acquired customers.

Source: Jaewon Kang and Heather Haddon, "Meal Kits Thrive in a Lockdown," *The Wall Street Journal,* May 4, 2020, p. B5.

Scott Eisen/Stringer/Getty Images

Using Microsoft Excel to Prepare CVP and Profit Graphs

Bob's final topic of discussion with Prem started by explaining how to use Microsoft Excel and the data in Exhibit 5–2 to model CVP relationships with a cost-*volume-profit (CVP) graph.* A **cost-volume-profit (CVP) graph** highlights the relationships among sales, cost, and profit over a wide range of unit sales. In a CVP graph, unit sales are depicted on the horizontal (*X*) axis and dollars on the vertical (*Y*) axis. Preparing a CVP graph in Microsoft Excel involves four steps using the data in rows 20 and 21 of Exhibit 5–2.

LO5–8

Prepare and interpret a cost-volume-profit (CVP) graph and a profit graph.

Step 1. Define two levels of unit sales. In Exhibit 5–2, Bob defined unit sales of 0 units and 600 units (see cells B20 and B21). He also changed cell B6 to 600 units to agree with his choice in cell B21.

Step 2. Calculate the total sales dollars earned at the levels of unit sales chosen in step 1. For Acoustic Concepts, the total sales dollars at each sales volume are $0 (0 units × $250 per unit) and $150,000 (600 × $250 per unit). These amounts are shown in cells C20 and C21.

EXHIBIT 5–2

Preparing CVP and Profit Graphs

	A	B	C	D	E	F
1		Acoustic Concepts, Inc.				
2		Contribution Income Statement				
3		For the Month of June				
4						
5	Data Inputs:					
6	Unit sales (Q)	600				
7	Selling price per unit (P)	$ 250				
8	Variable expenses per unit (V)	$ 150				
9	Total fixed expenses	$ 35,000				
10						
11		Total	Per Unit	Percent of Sales		
12	Sales	$ 150,000	$ 250	100%		
13	Variable expenses	90,000	$ 150	60%		
14	Contribution margin	60,000	$ 100	40%		
15	Fixed expenses	35,000				
16	Net operating income	$ 25,000				
17						
18	CVP Graph Information					
19			Sales Dollars	Fixed Expenses	Total Expenses	
20	Data Points	-	$ -	$ 35,000	$ 35,000	
21		600	$ 150,000	$ 35,000	$ 125,000	
22						
23	Profit Graph Information					
24			Profit			
25	Data Points	-	$ (35,000)			
26		600	$ 25,000			
27						

Exhibit 5-2   Exhibit 5-3   Exhibit 5-4 ... ⊕

Microsoft Excel

Step 3. Calculate the total fixed expenses incurred at the levels of unit sales chosen in step 1. For Acoustic Concepts, the total fixed expenses at each sales volume are $35,000 (as shown in cells D20 and D21). By definition, total fixed costs remain constant within the relevant range.

Step 4. Calculate the total expenses (fixed plus variable) incurred at the levels of unit sales chosen in step 1. For Acoustic Concepts, the total expenses at each sales volume are $35,000 (= $35,000 + [0 units × $150 per unit]) and $125,000 (= $35,000 + [600 units × $150 per unit]). These amounts are shown in cells E20 and E21.

Exhibit 5–3 shows a CVP graph created using these data inputs. It was created by:

- Selecting cells B19:E21
- Going to the Insert tab; clicking on the Scatter Plot drop-down menu; choosing the Scatter with Smooth Lines option
- Clicking on the Switch Row/Column button within the Chart Tools ribbon
- Clicking on Add Chart Element within the Chart Tools ribbon; selecting Axis Titles and then Primary Horizontal; editing the X-axis label to say Unit Sales
- Editing the chart title to say CVP Graph

When interpreting this CVP graph, the anticipated profit or loss at any given level of unit sales is measured by the vertical distance between the total sales and total expense lines. The break-even point is where the total sales and total expense lines cross. The break-even point of 350 speakers in Exhibit 5–3 agrees with the break-even point computed earlier.

When sales are below the break-even point—in this case, 350 units—the company incurs a loss. Note the loss (represented by the vertical distance between the total expense and total sales lines) gets bigger as sales decline. When sales are above the break-even point, the company earns a profit, and the size of the profit (represented by the vertical distance between the total sales and total expense lines) increases as sales increase.

EXHIBIT 5–3
Acoustics Concepts: CVP Graph

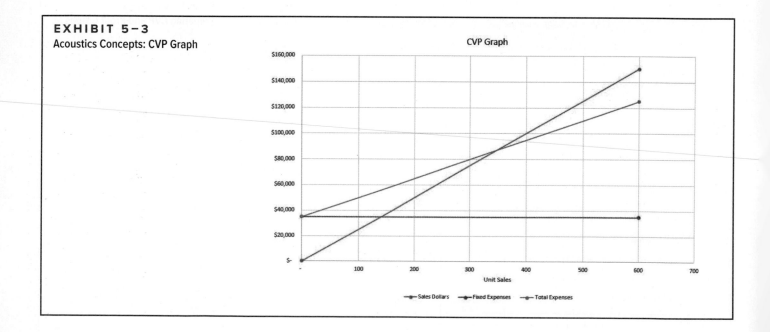

An even simpler form of the CVP graph is called a *profit graph,* which can be prepared in Microsoft Excel using the two-step process shown in rows 25 and 26 in Exhibit 5–2.

Step 1. Define two levels of unit sales. In Exhibit 5–2, Bob defined unit sales of 0 units and 600 units (see cells B25 and B26).

Step 2. Calculate the profit earned at the levels of unit sales chosen in step 1. To calculate the profit when unit sales are zero, Bob used the formula (-B15) to derive an answer of $(35,000). To calculate the profit when unit sales are 600 units, Bob set cell C26 equal to the net operating income in cell B16. To confirm your understanding of how these profits are calculated, let's use the following profit equation introduced earlier in the chapter:

$$\text{Profit} = \text{Unit CM} \times Q - \text{Fixed expenses}$$

At sales of 0 units, the profit (in cell C25) is calculated as follows:

$$\text{Profit} = \text{Unit CM} \times Q - \text{Fixed expenses}$$
$$\text{Profit} = \$100 \times 0 - \$35,000$$
$$\text{Profit} = \$(35,000)$$

At sales of 600 units, the profit (in cell C26) is calculated as follows:

$$\text{Profit} = \text{Unit CM} \times Q - \text{Fixed expenses}$$
$$\text{Profit} = \$100 \times 600 - \$35,000$$
$$\text{Profit} = \$60,000 - \$35,000$$
$$\text{Profit} = \$25,000$$

Exhibit 5–4 shows a profit graph created using these data inputs. It was created by:

- Selecting cells B24:C26
- Going to the Insert tab; clicking on the Scatter Plot drop-down menu; choosing the Scatter with Smooth Lines option
- Clicking on Add Chart Element within the Chart Tools ribbon; selecting Axis Titles and then Primary Vertical; editing the Y-axis label to say Profit
- Clicking on Add Chart Element within the Chart Tools ribbon; selecting Axis Titles and then Primary Horizontal; editing the X-axis label to say Unit Sales
- Clicking on the unit sales figures as currently shown; under Format Axis going to the Labels section; changing Label Position to Low
- Editing the chart title to say Profit Graph

The profit graph shows a break-even point of 350 units. The profit steadily increases to the right of the break-even point as unit sales increase, and it steadily decreases to the left of the break-even point as unit sales decrease. When unit sales are zero, the loss of $(35,000) equals Acoustic Concepts' total fixed expenses.

Once the Excel spreadsheet has been set up correctly, Prem could adjust any of three data inputs (selling price per unit, variable costs per unit, and total fixed costs) and the CVP and profit graphs would automatically update to reflect his changes.

MANAGERIAL
ACCOUNTING IN ACTION
THE WRAP-UP

Prem and Bob met to discuss the results of Bob's analysis.

Prem: Bob, everything you have shown me is pretty clear. I can see what impact the sales manager's suggestions would have on our profits. Some of those suggestions are quite good and others are not. I am concerned our margin of safety is only 50 speakers. What can we do to increase this number?

Bob: Well, we have to increase total sales or decrease the break-even point or both.

Prem: And to decrease the break-even point, we have to either decrease our fixed expenses or increase our unit contribution margin?

Bob: Exactly.

EXHIBIT 5–4
Acoustic Concepts: Profit Graph

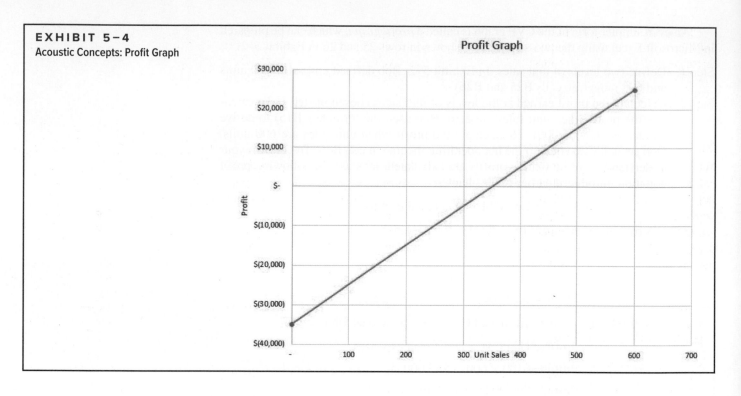

Prem: And to increase our unit contribution margin, we must either increase our selling price or decrease the variable cost per unit?

Bob: Correct.

Prem: So what do you suggest?

Bob: Well, the analysis doesn't tell us which of these to do, but it does indicate we have a potential problem here.

Prem: If you don't have any immediate suggestions, I would like to call a meeting next week to discuss increasing the margin of safety. I think everyone will be concerned about how vulnerable we are to small downturns in sales.

Bob: And with your new Excel spreadsheet in hand, you can quickly prepare CVP and profit graphs to visualize the financial scenarios discussed during your meeting.

Multiproduct Break-Even Analysis

LO5–9

Compute the break-even point for a multiproduct company and explain the effects of shifts in the sales mix on contribution margin and the break-even point.

To this point in the chapter, all our examples with Acoustic Concepts were based on the assumption the company makes only one product. However, it is very common for companies to make more than product. Therefore, the purpose of this section is to explain (1) how multiproduct companies compute their break-even point in sales dollars and (2) how shifts in the sales mix affect total contribution margin and the break-even point.

The Definition of Sales Mix

The term **sales mix** refers to the relative proportions in which a company's products are sold. The goal is to achieve the combination, or mix, that yields the greatest profits. If high-margin rather than low-margin products make up a relatively large proportion of total sales, profits will be greater.

Changes in the sales mix can cause perplexing variations in a company's profits. A shift in the sales mix from high-margin to low-margin products can cause total profits to decrease even though total sales may increase. Conversely, a shift in the sales mix from low-margin to high-margin products can cause the reverse—total profits may increase even though total sales decrease.

Sales Mix and Break-Even Analysis

When a company sells more than one product, each of these products will have different selling prices, costs, and contribution margins. Consequently, the break-even point depends on the mix in which the products are sold. To illustrate, consider Virtual Journeys Unlimited, a small company that sells two DVDs: the Monuments DVD, a tour of the United States' most popular National Monuments; and the Parks DVD, which tours the United States' National Parks. The company's September sales, expenses, and break-even point are shown in Exhibit 5–5.

EXHIBIT 5–5
Multiproduct Break-Even Analysis

Virtual Journeys Unlimited
Contribution Income Statement
For the Month of September

	Monuments DVD		Parks DVD		Total	
	Amount	Percent	Amount	Percent	Amount	Percent
Sales	$20,000	100%	$80,000	100%	$100,000	100%
Variable expenses	15,000	75%	40,000	50%	55,000	55%
Contribution margin	$ 5,000	25%	$40,000	50%	45,000	45%
Fixed expenses					27,000	
Net operating income					$ 18,000	

Computation of the break-even point:

$$\frac{\text{Fixed expenses}}{\text{Overall CM ratio}} = \frac{\$27,000}{0.45} = \$60,000$$

Verification of the break-even point:

	Monuments DVD	Parks DVD	Total
Current dollar sales	$20,000	$80,000	$100,000
Percentage of total dollar sales	20%	80%	100%
Sales at the break-even point	$12,000	$48,000	$60,000

	Monuments DVD		Parks DVD		Total	
	Amount	Percent	Amount	Percent	Amount	Percent
Sales	$12,000	100%	$48,000	100%	$ 60,000	100%
Variable expenses	9,000	75%	24,000	50%	33,000	55%
Contribution margin	$ 3,000	25%	$24,000	50%	27,000	45%
Fixed expenses					27,000	
Net operating income					$ 0	

As shown in the exhibit, the break-even point is $60,000 in sales, which was computed by dividing the company's fixed expenses of $27,000 by its overall CM ratio of 45 percent. However, this is the break-even point only if the company's sales mix does not change. Currently, the Monuments DVD is responsible for 20 percent of the company's dollar sales and the Parks DVD for 80 percent. Assuming this sales mix does not change, if total sales are $60,000, the sales of the Monuments DVD would be $12,000 (20% of $60,000) and the sales of the Parks DVD would be $48,000 (80% of $60,000). As shown in Exhibit 5–5, at these levels of sales, the company would indeed break even. But $60,000 in sales represents the break-even point only if the sales mix does not change. *If the sales mix changes, then the break-even point will also usually change.* This is illustrated by the results for October in which the sales mix shifted away from the more profitable Parks DVD (which has a 50% CM ratio) toward the less profitable Monuments DVD (which has a 25% CM ratio). These results appear in Exhibit 5–6.

Although sales have remained unchanged at $100,000, the sales mix is exactly the reverse of what it was in Exhibit 5–5, with the bulk of the sales now coming from the less profitable Monuments DVD. Notice this shift in the sales mix caused both the overall CM ratio and total profits to drop sharply from the prior month even though total sales are the same. The overall CM ratio dropped from 45 percent in September to 30 percent in October, and net operating income dropped from $18,000 to $3,000. In addition, with the drop in the overall CM ratio, the company's break-even point is no longer $60,000 in sales. Because the company is now realizing less average contribution margin per dollar of sales, it takes more sales to cover the same amount of fixed costs. Thus, the break-even point has increased from $60,000 to $90,000 in sales per year.

In preparing a break-even analysis, an assumption must be made concerning the sales mix. Usually the assumption is it will not change. However, if the sales mix is expected to change, then this must be explicitly considered in any CVP computations.

EXHIBIT 5–6
Multiproduct Break-Even Analysis: A Shift in Sales Mix (see Exhibit 5–5)

Virtual Journeys Unlimited
Contribution Income Statement
For the Month of October

	Monuments DVD		Parks DVD		Total	
	Amount	Percent	Amount	Percent	Amount	Percent
Sales	$80,000	100%	$20,000	100%	$100,000	100%
Variable expenses................	60,000	75%	10,000	50%	70,000	70%
Contribution margin	$20,000	25%	$10,000	50%	30,000	30%
Fixed expenses					27,000	
Net operating income					$ 3,000	

Computation of the break-even point:

$$\frac{\text{Fixed expenses}}{\text{Overall CM ratio}} = \frac{\$27,000}{0.30} = \$90,000$$

IN BUSINESS

FOOD COMPANIES CHALLENGED BY RISING COSTS

Food companies, such as General Mills, J.M. Smucker, Campbell Soup, and Conagra Brands, are paying more for ingredients and packaging materials as well as freight, fuel, and labor. The critical question these companies face is: To what extent should they pass these cost increases on to their customers through higher prices? From a cost-volume-profit standpoint, the challenge is estimating how various price points (P) will affect the quantity of units sold (Q). Given a company's customers, have competing alternatives when it comes to spending their money, if the company attempts to pass all cost increases on to customers, it may depress unit sales and suboptimize profits. Conversely, if the company does not pass on any cost increases to its customers, profits may plummet when total sales are unable to offset higher variable and fixed costs.

Source: Jesse Newman and Dave Sebastian, "General Mills Says Costs Keep Rising," *The Wall Street Journal,* September 23, 2021, p. B3.

Summary

CVP analysis is based on three foundational tools: the contribution income statement, the contribution margin and variable expense ratios, and the profit equations. It can be used to estimate how profits respond to changes in the selling price per unit, unit sales, variable expenses per unit, and total fixed expenses.

The degree of operating leverage allows quick estimation of what impact a given percentage change in unit sales would have on the company's net operating income. The higher the degree of operating leverage, the greater is the impact on the company's profits. The degree of operating leverage is not constant—it depends on the company's current level of sales.

Break-even analysis is used to estimate the sales needed to break even. The unit sales required to break even can be estimated by dividing the fixed expenses by the unit contribution margin. The margin of safety is the amount by which the company's budgeted (or actual) sales exceed break-even sales.

Target profit analysis is used to estimate the sales needed to attain a specified target profit. The unit sales required to attain the target profit can be estimated by dividing the sum of the target profit and fixed expense by the unit contribution margin.

A CVP graph depicts the relationships between unit sales on the one hand and fixed expenses, variable expenses, total expenses, total sales, and profits on the other hand. The profit graph is simpler than the CVP graph and shows how profits depend on sales. The CVP and profit graphs are useful for visualizing how costs and profits respond to changes in sales.

The profits of a multiproduct company are affected by its sales mix. Changes in the sales mix can affect the break-even point, margin of safety, and other critical factors.

 Data Analytics Exercise available in Connect to complement this chapter

Review Problem: CVP Relationships

Voltar Company manufactures and sells a specialized cordless telephone for high electromagnetic radiation environments. The company's contribution format income statement for the most recent year is given below:

	Total	Per Unit	Percent of Sales
Sales (20,000 units)	$1,200,000	$60	100%
Variable expenses.	900,000	45	? %
Contribution margin	300,000	$15	? %
Fixed expenses	240,000		
Net operating income.	$ 60,000		

Required:

1. Compute the company's CM ratio and variable expense ratio.
2. Compute the company's break-even point in unit sales and dollar sales. Use the equation method.
3. Assume an increase in unit sales causes total sales to increase by $400,000 next year. If cost behavior patterns remain unchanged, by how much will the company's net operating income increase? Use the CM ratio to compute your answer.
4. Refer to the original data. Assume next year management wants the company to earn a profit of at least $90,000. How many units will have to be sold to earn this target profit?
5. Refer to the original data. Compute the company's margin of safety in dollar and percentage form.
6. a. Compute the company's degree of operating leverage at the present level of sales.
   b. Assume through a more intense effort by the sales staff, the company's unit sales increase by 8% next year. By what percentage would you expect net operating income to increase? Use the degree of operating leverage to obtain your answer.
   c. Verify your answer to (b) by preparing a new contribution format income statement showing an 8% increase in unit sales.
7. Refer to the original data. In an effort to increase sales and profits, management is considering the use of a higher-quality speaker. The higher-quality speaker would increase variable costs by $3 per unit, but management could eliminate one quality inspector who is paid a salary of $30,000 per year. The sales manager estimates the higher-quality speaker would increase annual unit sales by at least 20%.
   a. Assuming changes are made as described above, prepare a projected contribution format income statement for next year. Show data on a total, per-unit, and percentage basis.
   b. Compute the company's new break-even point in unit sales and dollar sales. Use the formula method.
   c. Would you recommend the changes be made?

Solution to Review Problem

1.
$$\text{CM ratio} = \frac{\text{Unit contribution margin}}{\text{Unit selling price}} = \frac{\$15}{\$60} = 25\%$$

$$\text{Variable expense ratio} = \frac{\text{Variable expense}}{\text{Selling price}} = \frac{\$45}{\$60} = 75\%$$

2.
$$\text{Profit} = \text{Unit CM} \times Q - \text{Fixed expenses}$$
$$\$0 = \$15 \times Q - \$240,000$$
$$\$15Q = \$240,000$$
$$Q = \$240,000 \div \$15$$
$$Q = 16,000 \text{ units; or, at } \$60 \text{ per unit, } \$960,000$$

3.

Increase in sales	$400,000
Contribution margin ratio	× 25%
Expected increase in contribution margin	$100,000

Because the fixed expenses are not expected to change, net operating income will increase by the entire $100,000 increase in contribution margin computed above.

4. Equation method:

$$\text{Profit} = \text{Unit CM} \times Q - \text{Fixed expenses}$$
$$\$90,000 = \$15 \times Q - \$240,000$$
$$\$15Q = \$90,000 + \$240,000$$
$$Q = \$330,000 \div \$15$$
$$Q = 22,000 \text{ units}$$

Formula method:

$$\frac{\text{Unit sales to attain}}{\text{the target profit}} = \frac{\text{Target profit} + \text{Fixed expenses}}{\text{Contribution margin per unit}} = \frac{\$90,000 + \$240,000}{\$15 \text{ per unit}} = 22,000 \text{ units}$$

5.   Margin of safety in dollars = Total sales − Break-even sales

$$= \$1{,}200{,}000 - \$960{,}000 = \$240{,}000$$

$$\text{Margin of safety percentage} = \frac{\text{Margin of safety in dollars}}{\text{Total sales}} = \frac{\$240{,}000}{\$1{,}200{,}000} = 20\%$$

6. a. should be Degree of operating leverage = Contribution margin/Net operating income
        =$300,000/$60,000 = 5

    b.

Expected increase in sales	8%
Degree of operating leverage	× 5
Expected increase in net operating income.	40%

    c. If unit sales increase by 8%, then 21,600 units (20,000 × 1.08 = 21,600) will be sold next
        year. The new contribution format income statement would be as follows:

	Total	Per Unit	Percent of Sales
Sales (21,600 units)	$1,296,000	$60	100%
Variable expenses	972,000	45	75%
Contribution margin	324,000	$15	25%
Fixed expenses	240,000		
Net operating income	$ 84,000		

        Thus, the $84,000 expected net operating income for next year represents a 40% increase
        over the $60,000 net operating income earned during the current year:

$$\frac{\$84{,}000 - \$60{,}000}{\$60{,}000} = \frac{\$24{,}000}{\$60{,}000} = 40\% \text{ increase}$$

        Note the increase in sales from 20,000 to 21,600 units has increased *both* total sales and
        total variable expenses.

7. a. A 20% increase in unit sales would result in 24,000 units being sold next year: 20,000
        units × 1.20 = 24,000 units.

	Total	Per Unit	Percent of Sales
Sales (24,000 units)	$1,440,000	$60	100%
Variable expenses.	1,152,000	48*	80%
Contribution margin	288,000	$12	20%
Fixed expenses	210,000†		
Net operating income.	$ 78,000		

        *$45 + $3 = $48; $48 ÷ $60 = 80%.
        †$240,000 − $30,000 = $210,000.

        Note the change in per-unit variable expenses results in a change in both the per-unit
        contribution margin and the CM ratio.

    b.
$$\text{Unit sales to break even} = \frac{\text{Fixed expenses}}{\text{Unit contribution margin}}$$

$$= \frac{\$210{,}000}{\$12 \text{ per unit}} = 17{,}500 \text{ units}$$

$$\text{Dollar sales to break even} = \frac{\text{Fixed expenses}}{\text{CM ratio}}$$

$$= \frac{\$210{,}000}{0.20} - \$1{,}050{,}000$$

c. Yes, based on these data, the changes should be made. The changes increase the company's net operating income from the present $60,000 to $78,000 per year. Although the changes also result in a higher break-even point (17,500 units as compared to the present 16,000 units), the company's margin of safety actually becomes greater than before:

$$\text{Margin of safety in dollars} = \text{Total sales} - \text{Break-even sales}$$
$$= \$1,440,000 - \$1,050,000 = \$390,000$$

As shown in (5), the company's present margin of safety is only $240,000. Thus, several benefits will result from the proposed changes.

Glossary

Break-even point The level of sales at which profit is zero. (p. 203)

Contribution approach An income statement that separates costs into variable and fixed categories, first deducting all variable expenses from sales to obtain the contribution margin. (p. 197)

Contribution margin The amount remaining from sales after all variable expenses have been deducted. (p. 197)

Contribution margin ratio (CM ratio) A ratio that divides contribution margin by sales. (p. 198)

Cost-volume-profit (CVP) graph A graphical representation of the relationships between an organization's revenues, costs, and profits on the one hand and its sales volume on the other hand. (p. 211)

Degree of operating leverage A measure, at a given level of sales, of how a percentage change in sales volume will affect profits. The degree of operating leverage is computed by dividing contribution margin by net operating income. (p. 201)

Incremental analysis An analytical approach focusing only on the costs and revenues that change as a result of a decision. (p. 208)

Margin of safety The excess of budgeted or actual dollar sales over the break-even dollar sales. (p. 204)

Operating leverage A measure of how sensitive net operating income is to a given percentage change in unit sales. (p. 201)

Sales mix The relative proportions in which a company's products are sold. Sales mix expresses the sales of each product as a percentage of total sales. (p. 214)

Target profit analysis Estimating the level of sales needed to achieve a desired target profit. (p. 205)

Variable expense ratio A ratio computed by dividing variable expenses by sales. (p. 198)

Questions

5–1 What is the meaning of *contribution margin ratio?* How is this ratio useful in planning business operations?

5–2 What is an *incremental analysis?*

5–3 In all respects, Company A and Company B are identical except Company A's costs are mostly variable, whereas Company B's costs are mostly fixed. When sales increase, which company will realize the greater increase in profits? Explain.

5–4 What is *operating leverage?*

5–5 What is the *break-even point?*

5–6 Explain how the lines on a CVP graph and the break-even point would change if (*a*) the selling price per unit decreased, (*b*) fixed cost increased throughout the entire range of activity portrayed on the graph, and (*c*) variable cost per unit increased.

5–7 What is the *margin of safety?*

5–8 What is meant by *sales mix?* What assumption is usually made concerning sales mix in CVP analysis?

5–9 Explain how a shift in the sales mix could result in both a higher break-even point and lower net operating income.

The Excel worksheet appearing below recreates portions of the Review Problem relating to Voltar Company. The workbook, and instructions on how to complete the file, can be found in Connect.

LO5–3, LO5–4, LO5–5, LO5–7

	A	B	C	D
1	Chapter 5: Applying Excel			
2				
3	Data			
4	Unit sales	20,000	units	
5	Selling price per unit	$60	per unit	
6	Variable expenses per unit	$45	per unit	
7	Fixed expenses	$240,000		
8				
9	*Enter a formula into each of the cells marked with a ? below*			
10	**Review Problem: CVP Relationships**			
11				
12	*Compute the CM ratio and variable expense ratio*			
13	Selling price per unit	?	per unit	
14	Variable expenses per unit	?	per unit	
15	Contribution margin per unit	?	per unit	
16				
17	CM ratio	?		
18	Variable expense ratio	?		
19				
20	*Compute the break-even point*			
21	Break-even in unit sales	?	units	
22	Break-even in dollar sales	?		
23				
24	*Compute the margin of safety*			
25	Margin of safety in dollars	?		
26	Margin of safety percentage	?		
27				
28	*Compute the degree of operating leverage*			
29	Sales	?		
30	Variable expenses	?		
31	Contribution margin	?		
32	Fixed expenses	?		
33	Net operating income	?		
34				
35	Degree of operating leverage	?		
36				

Chapter 5 Form / Filled in Chapter 5 Form

Microsoft Excel

You should proceed to the requirements below only after completing your worksheet.

Required:

1. Check your worksheet by changing the fixed expenses to $270,000. If your worksheet is operating properly, the degree of operating leverage should be 10. If you do not get this answer, find the errors in your worksheet and correct them. How much is the margin of safety percentage? Did it change? Why or why not?

2. Enter the following data from a different company into your worksheet:

Unit sales	10,000
Selling price per unit........................	$120
Variable expenses per unit	$72
Fixed expenses	$420,000

What is the margin of safety percentage? What is the degree of operating leverage?

3. Using the degree of operating leverage and without changing anything in your worksheet, calculate the percentage change in net operating income if unit sales increase by 15%.

4. Confirm the calculations you made in part (3) above by increasing the unit sales in your worksheet by 15%. What is the new net operating income and by what percentage did it increase?

5. Thad Morgan, a motorcycle enthusiast, has been exploring the possibility of relaunching the Western Hombre brand of cycle that was popular in the 1930s. The retro-look cycle would be sold for $10,000, and at that price, Thad estimates he could sell 600 units each year. The variable cost to produce and sell the cycles would be $7,500 per unit. The annual fixed cost would be $1,200,000.

   a. Using your worksheet, what would be the unit sales to break even, the margin of safety in dollars, and the degree of operating leverage?

   b. Thad is worried about the selling price. Rumors are circulating that other retro brands of cycles may be revived. If so, the selling price for the Western Hombre would have to be reduced to $9,000 to compete effectively. In that event, Thad also would reduce fixed expenses by $300,000 by reducing advertising expenses, but he still hopes to sell 600 units per year. Do you think this is a good plan? Explain. Also, explain the degree of operating leverage that appears on your worksheet.

The Foundational 15   Mc Graw Hill connect

LO5–1, LO5–2, LO5–3, LO5–4, LO5–5, LO5–6, LO5–7

Oslo Company prepared the following contribution format income statement based on a sales volume of 1,000 units (the relevant range of production is 500 units to 1,500 units):

Sales	$20,000
Variable expenses............................	12,000
Contribution margin	8,000
Fixed expenses	6,000
Net operating income........................	$ 2,000

Required:

(Answer each question independently and always refer to the original data unless instructed otherwise.)

1. What is the contribution margin per unit?
2. What is the contribution margin ratio?
3. What is the variable expense ratio?
4. If sales increase to 1,001 units, what would be the increase in net operating income?
5. If sales decline to 900 units, what would be the net operating income?
6. If the selling price increases by $2 per unit and the sales volume decreases by 100 units, what would be the net operating income?
7. If the variable cost per unit increases by $1, spending on advertising increases by $1,500, and unit sales increase by 250 units, what would be the net operating income?
8. What is the break-even point in unit sales?
9. What is the break-even point in dollar sales?
10. How many units must be sold to achieve a target profit of $5,000?
11. What is the margin of safety in dollars? What is the margin of safety percentage?
12. What is the degree of operating leverage?

13. Using the degree of operating leverage, what is the estimated percent increase in net operating income that would result from a 5% increase in unit sales?

14. Assume the amounts of the company's total variable expenses and total fixed expenses were reversed. In other words, assume the total variable expenses are $6,000 and the total fixed expenses are $12,000. Under this scenario and assuming total sales remain the same, what is the degree of operating leverage?

15. Using the degree of operating leverage you computed in the previous question, what is the estimated percent increase in net operating income that would result from a 5% increase in unit sales?

McGraw Hill connect   **Exercises**

EXERCISE 5–1 Computing the CM Ratio and Variable Expense Ratio LO5–1

Last month when Holiday Creations, Inc., sold 50,000 units, its sales, variable expenses, and fixed expenses were $200,000, $120,000, and $65,000, respectively.

Required:
1. What is the company's contribution margin (CM) ratio?
2. What is the company's variable expense ratio?

EXERCISE 5–2 The Effect of Changes in Unit Sales on Net Operating Income LO5–2

Whirly Corporation's contribution format income statement for the most recent month is shown below:

	Total	Per Unit
Sales (10,000 units)	$350,000	$ 35.00
Variable expenses	200,000	20.00
Contribution margin	150,000	$ 15.00
Fixed expenses	135,000	
Net operating income	$ 15,000	

Required:
(Consider each case independently):
1. What would be the revised net operating income per month if the sales volume increases by 100 units?
2. What would be the revised net operating income per month if the sales volume decreases by 100 units?
3. What would be the revised net operating income per month if the sales volume is 9,000 units?

EXERCISE 5–3 Compute and Use the Degree of Operating Leverage LO5–3

Engberg Company installs lawn sod in home yards. The company's most recent monthly contribution format income statement follows:

	Amount	Percent of Sales
Sales	$80,000	100%
Variable expenses	32,000	40%
Contribution margin	48,000	60%
Fixed expenses	38,000	
Net operating income	$10,000	

Required:
1. What is the company's degree of operating leverage?
2. Using the degree of operating leverage, estimate the impact on net operating income of a 5% increase in unit sales.
3. Verify your estimate from part (2) above by constructing a new contribution format income statement for the company assuming a 5% increase in unit sales.

EXERCISE 5–4 Break-Even Analysis LO5–4

Mauro Products sells a woven basket for $15 per unit. Its variable expense is $12 per unit and the company's monthly fixed expense is $4,200.

Required:
1. Calculate the company's break-even point in unit sales.
2. Calculate the company's break-even point in dollar sales.
3. If the company's fixed expenses increase by $600, what would become the new break-even point in unit sales? In dollar sales?

EXERCISE 5–5 Compute the Margin of Safety LO5–5

Molander Corporation is a distributor of a sun umbrella used at resort hotels. Data concerning the next month's budget appear below:

Selling price per unit.	$30
Variable expense per unit	$20
Fixed expense per month	$7,500
Unit sales per month.	1,000

Required:
1. What is the company's margin of safety?
2. What is the company's margin of safety as a percentage of its sales?

EXERCISE 5–6 Target Profit Analysis LO5–6

Lin Corporation has a single product whose selling price is $120 per unit and whose variable expense is $80 per unit. The company's monthly fixed expense is $50,000.

Required:
1. Calculate the unit sales needed to attain a target profit of $10,000.
2. Calculate the dollar sales needed to attain a target profit of $15,000.

EXERCISE 5–7 Changes in Variable Costs, Fixed Costs, Selling Price, and Unit Sales LO5–7

Data for Hermann Corporation are shown below:

	Per Unit	Percent of Sales
Selling price	$90	100%
Variable expenses.	63	70
Contribution margin	$27	30%

Fixed expenses are $30,000 per month and the company is selling 2,000 units per month.

Required:
1. How much will net operating income increase (decrease) per month if the monthly advertising budget increases by $5,000, the monthly sales volume increases by 100 units, and the total monthly sales increase by $9,000?
2. Refer to the original data. How much will net operating income increase (decrease) per month if the company uses higher-quality components that increase the variable expense by $2 per unit and increase unit sales by 10%.

EXERCISE 5–8 Prepare a Cost-Volume-Profit (CVP) Graph LO5–8

Karlik Enterprises distributes a single product whose selling price is $24 per unit and whose variable expense is $18 per unit. The company's monthly fixed expense is $24,000.

Required:
1. Prepare a cost-volume-profit graph for the company using sales volumes of zero units and 8,000 units.
2. Estimate the company's break-even point in unit sales using your cost-volume-profit graph.

EXERCISE 5–9 Prepare a Profit Graph LO5–8

Jaffre Enterprises distributes a single product whose selling price is $16 per unit and whose variable expense is $11 per unit. The company's fixed expense is $16,000 per month.

Required:
1. Prepare a profit graph for the company using sales volumes of zero units and 4,000 units.
2. Estimate the company's break-even point in unit sales using your profit graph.

EXERCISE 5–10 Multiproduct Break-Even Analysis LO5–9

Lucido Products markets two computer games: Claimjumper and Makeover. A contribution format income statement for a recent month for the two games appears below:

	Claimjumper	Makeover	Total
Sales	$30,000	$70,000	$100,000
Variable expenses................	20,000	50,000	70,000
Contribution margin	$10,000	$20,000	30,000
Fixed expenses			24,000
Net operating income.............			$ 6,000

Required:
1. What is the company's overall contribution margin (CM) ratio?
2. What is the company's overall break-even point in dollar sales?
3. Verify the overall break-even point by constructing a contribution format income statement showing the appropriate levels of sales for the two products.

EXERCISE 5–11 Missing Data; Basic CVP Concepts LO5–2, LO5–9

Fill in the missing amounts in each of the eight cases below. Each case is independent of the others. (*Hint:* One way to find the missing amounts would be to prepare a contribution format income statement for each case, enter the known data, and then compute the missing items.)

a. Assume only one product is being sold in each of the four following case situations:

Case	Units Sold	Sales	Variable Expenses	Contribution Margin per Unit	Fixed Expenses	Net Operating Income (Loss)
1...........	15,000	$180,000	$120,000	?	$50,000	?
2...........	?	$100,000	?	$10	$32,000	$8,000
3...........	10,000	?	$70,000	$13	?	$12,000
4...........	6,000	$300,000	?	?	$100,000	$(10,000)

b. Assume more than one product is being sold in each of the four following case situations:

Case	Sales	Variable Expenses	Average Contribution Margin Ratio	Fixed Expenses	Net Operating Income (Loss)
1.....................	$500,000	?	20%	?	$7,000
2.....................	$400,000	$260,000	?	$100,000	?
3.....................	?	?	60%	$130,000	$20,000
4.....................	$600,000	$420,000	?	?	$(5,000)

EXERCISE 5–12 Multiproduct Break-Even Analysis LO5–9

Olongapo Sports Corporation distributes two premium golf balls—Flight Dynamic and Sure Shot. Monthly sales and the contribution margin ratios for the two products follow:

	Product		
	Flight Dynamic	Sure Shot	Total
Sales	$150,000	$250,000	$400,000
CM ratio	80%	36%	?

Fixed expenses total $183,750 per month.

Chapter 5

Required:
1. Prepare a contribution format income statement for the company as a whole.
2. What is the company's break-even point in dollar sales based on the current sales mix?
3. If sales increase by $100,000 a month, by how much would monthly net operating income increase? What are your assumptions?

EXERCISE 5–13 Changes in Selling Price, Unit Sales, Variable Cost per Unit, and Total Fixed Costs LO5–2, LO5–3, LO5–7

Miller Company's contribution format income statement for the most recent month is shown below:

	Total	Per Unit
Sales (20,000 units)	$300,000	$15.00
Variable expenses	180,000	9.00
Contribution margin	120,000	$ 6.00
Fixed expenses	70,000	
Net operating income	$ 50,000	

Required:
Consider each of the four requirements independently:
1. Assume the sales volume increases by 3,000 units:
   a. What is the revised net operating income?
   b. What is the percent increase in unit sales?
   c. Using the most recent month's degree of operating leverage, what is the percent increase in net operating income?
2. What is the revised net operating income if the selling price decreases by $1.50 per unit and the number of units sold increases by 25%?
3. What is the revised net operating income if the selling price increases by $1.50 per unit, fixed expenses increase by $20,000, and the number of units sold decreases by 5%?
4. What is the revised net operating income if the selling price per unit increases by 12%, variable expenses increase by 60 cents per unit, and the number of units sold decreases by 10%?

EXERCISE 5–14 Break-Even and Target Profit Analysis LO5–1, LO5–4, LO5–6, LO5–7

Lindon Company is the exclusive distributor for an automotive product selling for $40 per unit with a CM ratio of 30%. The company's fixed expenses are $180,000 per year and it plans to sell 16,000 units this year.

Required:
1. What are the variable expenses per unit?
2. What is the break-even point in unit sales and in dollar sales?
3. What amount of unit sales and dollar sales is required to attain a target profit of $60,000 per year?
4. Assume by using a more efficient shipper, the company can reduce its variable expenses by $4 per unit. What is the company's new break-even point in unit sales and dollar sales? What dollar sales are required to attain a target profit of $60,000?

EXERCISE 5–15 Operating Leverage LO5–2, LO5–3

Magic Realm, Inc., developed a new fantasy board game and sold 15,000 units last year at a selling price of $20 per game. Fixed expenses associated with the game are $182,000 per year, and variable expenses are $6 per game. Production of the game was outsourced to a printing contractor, so variable expenses consist mostly of payments to this contractor.

Required:
1. Prepare a contribution format income statement for the game last year and compute the degree of operating leverage.
2. Management is confident the company can sell 18,000 games next year (an increase of 3,000 games, or 20%, over last year). Given this assumption:
   a. What is the expected percentage increase in net operating income for next year?
   b. What is the expected amount of net operating income for next year? (Do not prepare an income statement; use the degree of operating leverage to compute your answer.)

EXERCISE 5–16 Break-Even Analysis and CVP Graphing LO5–4, LO5–7, LO5–8

The Hartford Symphony Guild is planning its annual dinner-dance and assembled the following expected costs for the event:

Dinner (per person)...	$18
Favors and program (per person)...........................	$2
Band	$2,800
Rental of ballroom...	$900
Professional entertainment during intermission	$1,000
Tickets and advertising	$1,300

The expected ticket price is $35 per person.

Required:
1. What is the break-even point for the dinner-dance (in terms of the number of persons who must attend)?
2. Assume only 300 persons attended the dinner-dance last year. If the same number attend this year, what price per ticket must be charged to break even?
3. Refer to the original data ($35 ticket price per person). Prepare a CVP graph for the dinner-dance from zero tickets up to 600 tickets sold.

EXERCISE 5–17 Break-Even and Target Profit Analysis LO5–4, LO5–6, LO5–7

Outback Outfitters sells a small camp stove for $50 per unit. Variable expenses are $32 per unit, and fixed expenses total $108,000 per month.

Required:
1. What is the break-even point in unit sales and in dollar sales?
2. If the variable expenses per stove increase as a percentage of the selling price, will it result in a higher or a lower break-even point? Why? (Assume the fixed expenses remain unchanged.)
3. At present, the company is selling 8,000 stoves per month. The sales manager is convinced a 10% reduction in the selling price would result in a 25% increase in unit sales. Prepare two contribution format income statements, one under present operating conditions, and one as operations would appear after the proposed changes. Show both total and per-unit data on your statements.
4. Refer to the data in (3) above. How many stoves would have to be sold at the new selling price to attain a target profit of $35,000 per month?

EXERCISE 5–18 Break-Even and Target Profit Analysis; Margin of Safety; CM Ratio LO5–1, LO5–2, LO5–4, LO5–5, LO5–6

Menlo Company distributes a single product. The company's sales and expenses for last month follow:

	Total	Per Unit
Sales	$450,000	$30
Variable expenses..............................	180,000	12
Contribution margin	270,000	$18
Fixed expenses	216,000	
Net operating income..........................	$ 54,000	

Required:
1. What is the monthly break-even point in unit sales and in dollar sales?
2. Without resorting to computations, what is the total contribution margin at the break-even point?
3. How many units would have to be sold each month to attain a target profit of $90,000? Verify your answer by preparing a contribution format income statement at the target sales level.
4. Refer to the original data. Compute the company's margin of safety in dollar and percentage terms.
5. What is the company's CM ratio? If the company can sell more units, thereby increasing sales by $50,000 per month, and there is no change in fixed expenses, by how much would you expect monthly net operating income to increase?

Problems   Mc Graw Hill connect

PROBLEM 5–19 Break-Even Analysis; Pricing LO5–2, LO5–4, LO5–7

Last year Minden Company introduced a new product and sold 15,000 units at a price of $70 per unit. The product's variable expenses are $40 per unit and its fixed expenses are $540,000 per year.

Required:

1. What was this product's net operating income (loss) last year?
2. What is the product's break-even point in unit sales and dollar sales?
3. Assume the company conducted a marketing study that estimates it can increase annual sales of this product by 5,000 units for each $2 reduction in its selling price. If the company will only consider price reductions in increments of $2 (e.g., $68, $66, etc.), what is the maximum annual profit it can earn on this product? What sales volume and selling price per unit generate the maximum profit?
4. What would be the break-even point in unit sales and dollar sales using the selling price you calculated in requirement 3? Why is this break-even point different from the break-even point you computed in requirement 2?

PROBLEM 5–20 CVP Applications: Break-Even Analysis; Cost Structure; Target Sales LO5–1, LO5–2, LO5–3, LO5–4, LO5–6, LO5–7

Northwood Company manufactures a basketball selling for $25 per unit in a small plant heavily relying on direct labor workers. Thus, variable expenses are high, totaling $15 per ball, of which 60% is direct labor cost.

Last year, the company sold 30,000 balls, with the following results:

Sales (30,000 balls)	$750,000
Variable expenses	450,000
Contribution margin	300,000
Fixed expenses	210,000
Net operating income	$ 90,000

Required:

1. Compute (a) last year's CM ratio and the break-even point in balls and (b) the degree of operating leverage at last year's sales level.
2. Due to an increase in labor rates, the company estimates next year's variable expenses will increase by $3 per ball. If this change takes place and the selling price per ball remains constant at $25, what will be next year's CM ratio and the break-even point in balls?
3. Refer to the data in (2) above. If the expected change in variable expenses takes place, how many balls will have to be sold next year to earn the same net operating income, $90,000, as last year?
4. Refer again to the data in (2) above. The president feels the company must raise the selling price of its basketballs. If Northwood Company wants to maintain the same CM ratio as last year (as computed in requirement 1a), what selling price per ball must it charge next year to cover the increased labor costs?
5. Refer to the original data. The company is discussing the construction of a new, automated manufacturing plant. The new plant would slash variable expenses per ball by 40%, but it would cause fixed expenses per year to double. If the new plant is built, what would be the company's new CM ratio and new break-even point in balls?
6. Refer to the data in (5) above.
   a. If the new plant is built, how many balls will have to be sold next year to earn the same net operating income, $90,000, as last year?
   b. Assume the new plant is built and next year the company manufactures and sells 30,000 balls (the same number as sold last year). Prepare a contribution format income statement and compute the degree of operating leverage.
   c. If you were a member of top management, would you support constructing the new plant? Explain.

PROBLEM 5–21 Sales Mix; Multiproduct Break-Even Analysis LO5–9

Gold Star Rice, Ltd., of Thailand exports Thai rice throughout Asia. The company grows three varieties of rice—White, Fragrant, and Loonzain. Budgeted sales by product and in total for the coming month are shown below:

	Product						Total	
	White		Fragrant		Loonzain		Total	
Percentage of total sales....................	20%		52%		28%		100%	
Sales	$150,000	100%	$390,000	100%	$210,000	100%	$750,000	100%
Variable expenses..........................	108,000	72%	78,000	20%	84,000	40%	270,000	36%
Contribution margin	$42,000	28%	$312,000	80%	$126,000	60%	480,000	64%
Fixed expenses							449,280	
Net operating income......................							$30,720	

$$\text{Dollar sales to break-even} = \frac{\text{Fixed expenses}}{\text{CM ratio}} = \frac{\$449,280}{0.64} = \$702,000$$

As shown by these data, net operating income is budgeted at $30,720 for the month and the estimated break-even sales is $702,000.

Assume actual sales for the month total $750,000 as planned; however, actual sales by product are White, $300,000; Fragrant, $180,000; and Loonzain, $270,000.

Required:

1. Prepare a contribution format income statement for the month based on the actual sales data. Present the income statement in the format shown above.
2. Compute the break-even point in dollar sales for the month based on your actual data.
3. Considering the company met its $750,000 sales budget for the month, the president is shocked at the results shown on your income statement in (1) above. Prepare a brief memo for the president explaining why the net operating income (loss) and the break-even point in dollar sales are different from what was budgeted.

PROBLEM 5–22 CVP Applications; Contribution Margin Ratio; Break-Even Analysis; Cost Structure LO5–1, LO5–2, LO5–4, LO5–6, LO5–7

PEM, Inc., is experiencing financial difficulty due to erratic sales of its only product, a high-capacity battery for laptop computers. The company's contribution format income statement for the most recent month is given below:

Sales (19,500 units × $30 per unit)........................	$585,000
Variable expenses.......................................	409,500
Contribution margin	175,500
Fixed expenses	180,000
Net operating loss.......................................	$ (4,500)

Required:

1. Compute the company's CM ratio and its break-even point in unit sales and dollar sales.
2. The president believes a $16,000 increase in the monthly advertising budget, combined with an intensified effort by the sales staff, will increase unit sales and the total sales by $80,000 per month. If the president is right, what will be the increase (decrease) in the company's monthly net operating income?
3. Refer to the original data. The sales manager is convinced a 10% reduction in the selling price, combined with an increase of $60,000 in the monthly advertising budget, will double unit sales. If the sales manager is right, what will be the revised net operating income (loss)?
4. Refer to the original data. The Marketing Department thinks a fancy new package for the laptop computer battery would grow sales. The new package would increase variable costs by 75 cents per unit. Assuming no other changes, how many units would have to be sold each month to attain a target profit of $9,750?

5. Refer to the original data. By automating, the company could reduce variable expenses by $3 per unit. However, fixed expenses would increase by $72,000 each month.
    a. Compute the new CM ratio and the new break-even point in unit sales and dollar sales.
    b. Assume the company expects to sell 26,000 units next month. Prepare two contribution format income statements, one assuming operations are not automated and one assuming they are. (Show data on a per-unit and percentage basis, as well as in total, for each alternative.)
    c. Would you recommend the company automate its operations? Explain.

PROBLEM 5–23 CVP Applications; Contribution Margin Ratio: Degree of Operating Leverage LO5–1, LO5–2, LO5–3, LO5–4, LO5–7

Feather Friends, Inc., distributes a high-quality wooden birdhouse that sells for $20 per unit. Variable expenses are $8 per unit, and fixed expenses total $180,000 per year. Its operating results for last year were as follows:

Sales	$400,000
Variable expenses	160,000
Contribution margin	240,000
Fixed expenses	180,000
Net operating income	$ 60,000

Required:

Answer each question independently based on the original data:
1. What is the product's CM ratio?
2. Use the CM ratio to determine the break-even point in dollar sales.
3. Assume this year's unit sales and total sales increase by 3,750 units and $75,000, respectively. If the fixed expenses do not change, how much will net operating income increase?
4. a. What is the degree of operating leverage based on last year's sales?
    b. Assume the president expects this year's unit sales to increase by 20%. Using the degree of operating leverage from last year, what percentage increase in net operating income will the company realize this year?
5. The sales manager is convinced a 10% reduction in the selling price, combined with a $30,000 increase in advertising, would increase this year's unit sales by 25%. If the sales manager is right, what would be this year's net operating income if his ideas are implemented? Do you recommend implementing the sales manager's suggestions? Why?
6. The president does not want to change the selling price. Instead, he wants to increase the sales commission by $1 per unit. He thinks this move, combined with some increase in advertising, would increase this year's unit sales by 25%. How much could the president increase this year's advertising expense and still earn the same $60,000 net operating income as last year?

PROBLEM 5–24 Break-Even and Target Profit Analysis LO5–4, LO5–6

The Shirt Works sells a large variety of tee shirts and sweatshirts. Steve Hooper, the owner, is thinking of expanding his sales by hiring high school students, on a commission basis, to sell sweatshirts bearing the name and mascot of the local high school.

These sweatshirts would have to be ordered from the manufacturer six weeks in advance and could not be returned because of the unique printing required. The sweatshirts would cost Hooper $8 each with a minimum order of 75 sweatshirts. Any additional sweatshirts would have to be ordered in increments of 75.

Because Hooper's plan would not require any additional facilities, the only costs associated with the project would be the costs of the sweatshirts and the costs of the sales commissions. The selling price of the sweatshirts would be $13.50 each. Hooper would pay the students a commission of $1.50 for each shirt sold.

Required:

1. What level of unit sales and dollar sales is needed to attain a target profit of $1,200?
2. Assume Hooper places an initial order for 75 sweatshirts. What is his break-even point in unit sales and dollar sales?
3. How many sweatshirts would Hooper need to sell to earn a target profit of $1,320?

PROBLEM 5–25 Changes in Fixed and Variable Costs; Break-Even and Target Profit Analysis LO5–4, LO5–6, LO5–7

Neptune Company has developed a small inflatable toy it is anxious to introduce to its customers. The company's Marketing Department estimates demand for the new toy will range between 15,000 units and 35,000 units per month. The new toy will sell for $3 per unit. Enough capacity exists in the company's plant to produce 18,000 units of the toy each month. Variable expenses to manufacture and sell one unit would be $1.00, and incremental fixed expenses associated with the toy would total $22,000 per month.

Neptune has also identified an outside supplier who could produce the toy for a price of $1.75 per unit plus a fixed fee of $15,000 per month for any production volume up to 20,000 units. For a production volume between 20,001 and 40,000 units, the fixed fee would increase to a total of $30,000 per month.

Required:

1. Calculate the break-even point in unit sales assuming Neptune does not hire the outside supplier.
2. How much profit will Neptune earn assuming:
   a. It produces and sells 18,000 units?
   b. It does not produce any units and instead outsources the production of 18,000 units to the outside supplier and then sells those units to its customers?
3. Calculate the break-even point in unit sales assuming Neptune plans to use all of its production capacity to produce the first 18,000 units it sells and also commits to hiring the outside supplier to produce up to 17,000 additional units.
4. Assume Neptune plans to use all of its production capacity to produce the first 18,000 units it sells and also commits to hiring the outside supplier to produce up to 17,000 additional units.
   a. What total unit sales would Neptune need to achieve to equal the profit earned in requirement 2a?
   b. What total unit sales would Neptune need to achieve to attain a target profit of $16,500 per month?
   c. How much profit will Neptune earn if it sells 35,000 units per month?
   d. How much profit will Neptune earn if it sells 35,000 units per month and agrees to pay its marketing manager a bonus of 10 cents for each unit sold above the break-even point from requirement 3?
5. If Neptune outsources all production to the outside supplier, how much profit will the company earn if it sells 35,000 units?

PROBLEM 5–26 CVP Applications; Break-Even Analysis; Graphing LO5–2, LO5–4, LO5–7, LO5–8

The Fashion Shoe Company operates a chain of women's shoe shops carrying many styles of shoes all sold for $30 per pair. Sales personnel in the shops are paid a sales commission on each pair of shoes sold plus a small base salary.

The following data pertain to Shop 48 and are typical of the company's many outlets:

	Per Pair of Shoes
Selling price	$30.00
Variable expenses:	
Invoice cost	$13.50
Sales commission	4.50
Total variable expenses	$18.00

	Annual
Fixed expenses:	
Advertising	$ 30,000
Rent	20,000
Salaries	100,000
Total fixed expenses	$150,000

Required:

1. What is Shop 48's annual break-even point in unit sales and dollar sales?
2. Prepare a CVP graph showing cost and revenue data for Shop 48 from zero shoes up to 17,000 pairs of shoes sold each year. Clearly indicate the break-even point on the graph.
3. If 12,000 pairs of shoes are sold in a year, what would be Shop 48's net operating income (loss)?
4. The company is considering paying the Shop 48 store manager an incentive commission of 75 cents per pair of shoes (in addition to the salesperson's commission). If this change is made, what will be the new break-even point in unit sales and dollar sales?
5. Refer to the original data. As an alternative to (4) above, the company is considering paying the Shop 48 store manager 50 cents commission on each pair of shoes sold in excess of the break-even point. If this change is made, what will be Shop 48's net operating income (loss) if 15,000 pairs of shoes are sold?
6. Refer to the original data. The company is considering eliminating sales commissions entirely in its shops and increasing fixed salaries by $31,500 annually. If this change is made, what will be Shop 48's new break-even point in unit sales and dollar sales? Would you recommend this change be made? Explain.

PROBLEM 5–27 Sales Mix; Break-Even Analysis; Margin of Safety LO5–5, LO5–9

Island Novelties, Inc., of Palau makes two products—Hawaiian Fantasy and Tahitian Joy. Each product's selling price, variable expense per unit, and annual unit sales are as follows:

	Hawaiian Fantasy	Tahitian Joy
Selling price per unit.	$15	$100
Variable expense per unit	$9	$20
Number of units sold annually	20,000	5,000

Fixed expenses total $475,800 per year.

Required:

1. Assuming the sales mix given above:
   a. Prepare a contribution format income statement showing both dollar and percent columns for each product and for the company as a whole.
   b. Compute the company's break-even point in dollar sales. Also, compute its margin of safety in dollars and its margin of safety percentage.
2. The company has developed a new product called Samoan Delight that sells for $45 each and has variable expenses of $36 per unit. If the company can sell 10,000 units of Samoan Delight without incurring any additional fixed expenses:
   a. Prepare a revised contribution format income statement that includes Samoan Delight. Assume sales of the other two products do not change.
   b. Compute the company's revised break-even point in dollar sales. Also, compute its revised margin of safety in dollars and margin of safety percentage.
3. The president of the company examines your figures and says, "There's something strange here. Our fixed expenses haven't changed and you show greater total contribution margin if we add the new product, but you also show our break-even point going up. With greater contribution margin, the break-even point should go down, not up. You've made a mistake somewhere." Explain to the president what happened.

PROBLEM 5–28 Sales Mix; Multiproduct Break-Even Analysis LO5–9

Topper Sports, Inc., produces high-quality sports equipment. The company's Racket Division manufactures three tennis rackets—Standard, Deluxe, and Pro—widely used in amateur play. Selected information on the rackets is given below:

	Standard	Deluxe	Pro
Selling price per racket	$40.00	$60.00	$90.00
Variable expenses per racket:			
Production	$22.00	$27.00	$31.50
Selling (5% of selling price)	$2.00	$3.00	$4.50

All sales are made through the company's own retail outlets. The Racket Division has the following fixed costs:

	Per Month
Fixed production costs...............	$120,000
Advertising expense.................	100,000
Administrative salaries...............	50,000
Total......................	$270,000

Sales, in units, over the past two months were as follows:

	Standard	Deluxe	Pro	Total
April........	2,000	1,000	5,000	8,000
May	8,000	1,000	3,000	12,000

Required:
1. Prepare contribution format income statements for April and May. Use the following headings:

Standard		Deluxe		Pro		Total	
Amount	Percent	Amount	Percent	Amount	Percent	Amount	Percent
Sales							
Etc.							

Place the fixed expenses only in the Total column. Do not show percentages for the fixed expenses.

2. Upon seeing the income statements in (1) above, the president stated, "I can't believe this! We sold 50% more rackets in May than in April, yet profits went down. It's obvious costs are out of control in that division." What other explanation can you give for the drop in net operating income?

3. Compute the Racket Division's break-even point in dollar sales for April.

4. Without doing any calculations, explain whether the break-even point would be higher or lower with May's sales mix than with April's sales mix.

5. Assume sales of the Standard racket increase by $20,000. What would be the effect on net operating income? What would be the effect if Pro racket sales increased by $20,000? Do not prepare income statements; use the incremental analysis approach in determining your answer.

PROBLEM 5–29 Changes in Cost Structure; Break-Even Analysis; Operating Leverage; Margin of Safety LO5–3, LO5–4, LO5–5, LO5–7

Morton Company's contribution format income statement for last month is given below:

Sales (15,000 units × $30 per unit).............	$450,000
Variable expenses...........................	315,000
Contribution margin	135,000
Fixed expenses	90,000
Net operating income.......................	$ 45,000

The industry in which Morton Company operates is quite sensitive to cyclical movements in the economy. Thus, profits vary considerably from year to year according to general economic conditions. The company has a large amount of unused capacity and is studying ways of improving profits.

Required:
1. New equipment has come onto the market that would allow Morton Company to automate a portion of its operations. Variable expenses would be reduced by $9 per unit. However, fixed expenses would increase to a total of $225,000 each month. Prepare two contribution format income statements, one showing present operations and one showing how operations would

appear if the new equipment is purchased. Show an Amount column, a Per Unit column, and a Percent column on each statement. Do not show percentages for the fixed expenses.

2. Refer to the income statements in (1). For the present operations and the proposed new operations, compute (a) the degree of operating leverage, (b) the break-even point in dollar sales, and (c) the margin of safety in dollars and the margin of safety percentage.

3. Refer again to the data in (1). As a manager, what factor would be critical in deciding whether to purchase the new equipment? (Assume enough funds are available to make the purchase.)

4. Refer to the original data. Rather than purchase new equipment, the marketing manager argues the company's marketing strategy should be changed. Rather than pay sales commissions, which are currently included in variable expenses, the company would pay salespersons fixed salaries and would invest heavily in advertising. The marketing manager claims this new approach would increase unit sales by 30% without any change in selling price; the company's new monthly fixed expenses would be $180,000; and its net operating income would increase by 20%. Compute the company's break-even point in dollar sales under the new marketing strategy. Do you support the marketing manager's proposal?

PROBLEM 5–30 Graphing; Incremental Analysis; Operating Leverage LO5–3, LO5–4, LO5–6, LO5–7, LO5–8

Angie Silva recently opened The Sandal Shop in Brisbane, Australia, a store specializing in fashionable sandals. In time, she hopes to open a chain of sandal shops. As a first step, she gathered the following data for her new store:

Sales price per pair of sandals	$40
Variable expenses per pair of sandals	16
Contribution margin per pair of sandals	$24
Fixed expenses per year:	
Building rental	$15,000
Equipment depreciation	7,000
Selling	20,000
Administrative	18,000
Total fixed expenses	$60,000

Required:

1. What is the break-even point in unit sales and dollar sales?

2. Prepare a CVP graph or a profit graph for the store from zero pairs up to 4,000 pairs of sandals sold each year. Indicate the break-even point on your graph.

3. Angie decided she must earn a profit of $18,000 the first year to justify her time and effort. How many pairs of sandals must be sold to attain this target profit?

4. Angie now has two salespersons working in the store—one full time and one part time. It will cost her an additional $8,000 per year to convert the part-time position to a full-time position. Angie believes the change would increase annual sales by $25,000. Should she convert the position? Use the incremental approach. (Do not prepare an income statement.)

5. Refer to the original data. During the first year, the store sold only 3,000 pairs of sandals and reported the following operating results:

Sales (3,000 pairs)	$120,000
Variable expenses	48,000
Contribution margin	72,000
Fixed expenses	60,000
Net operating income	$ 12,000

a. What is the store's degree of operating leverage?

b. Angie is confident a more intense sales effort and a more creative advertising program will increase unit sales by 50% next year. Using the degree of operating leverage, what would be the expected percentage increase in net operating income if Angie is able to increase unit sales by 50%?

PROBLEM 5–31 Interpretive Questions on the CVP Graph LO5–4, LO5–8

A CVP graph such as the one shown below is a useful technique for showing relationships among an organization's costs, volume, and profits.

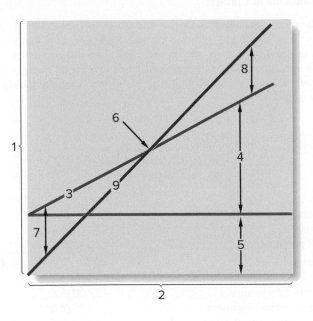

Required:
1. Identify the numbered components in the CVP graph.
2. State the effect of each of the following actions on line 3, line 9, and the break-even point. For line 3 and line 9, state whether the action will cause the line to:
   Remain unchanged.
   Shift upward.
   Shift downward.
   Have a steeper slope (i.e., rotate upward).
   Have a flatter slope (i.e., rotate downward).
   Shift upward *and* have a steeper slope.
   Shift upward *and* have a flatter slope.
   Shift downward *and* have a steeper slope.
   Shift downward *and* have a flatter slope.

   In the case of the break-even point, state whether the action will cause the break-even point to:
   Remain unchanged.
   Increase.
   Decrease.
   Probably change, but the direction is uncertain.

   Treat each case independently.

   x.   *Example.*   Fixed expenses are reduced by $5,000 per period.
        Answer (see choices above):   Line 3:   Shift downward.
                                               Line 9:   Remain unchanged.
                                               Break-even point: Decrease.

   a.   The unit selling price is increased from $18 to $20.
   b.   Unit variable expenses are decreased from $12 to $10.
   c.   Fixed expenses are increased by $3,000 per period.
   d.   Two thousand more units are sold during the period than were budgeted.
   e.   Due to paying salespersons a commission rather than a flat salary, fixed expenses are reduced by $8,000 per period and unit variable expenses are increased by $3.
   f.   Due to an increase in the cost of materials, both unit variable expenses and the selling price are increased by $2.
   g.   Advertising costs are increased by $10,000 per period, resulting in a 10% increase in the number of units sold.
   h.   Due to automating an operation previously done by workers, fixed expenses are increased by $12,000 per period and unit variable expenses are reduced by $4.

Case   Mc Graw Hill connect®

Select cases are available in Connect.

CASE 5–32 Cost Structure; Break-Even and Target Profit Analysis LO5–4, LO5–6, LO5–7

Pittman Company is a small but growing manufacturer of telecommunications equipment. The company has no sales force of its own; rather, it relies on independent sales agents to market its products. These agents are paid a sales commission of 15% for all items sold.

Barbara Cheney, Pittman's controller, just prepared the company's budgeted income statement for next year as follows:

Pittman Company Budgeted Income Statement For the Year Ended December 31		
Sales		$16,000,000
Manufacturing expenses:		
Variable..............................	$7,200,000	
Fixed overhead	2,340,000	9,540,000
Gross margin		6,460,000
Selling and administrative expenses:		
Commissions to agents	2,400,000	
Fixed marketing expenses...............	120,000*	
Fixed administrative expenses	1,800,000	4,320,000
Net operating income.....................		2,140,000
Fixed interest expenses...................		540,000
Income before income taxes...............		1,600,000
Income taxes (30%).......................		480,000
Net income..............................		$ 1,120,000

*Primarily depreciation on storage facilities.

As Barbara handed the statement to Karl Vecci, Pittman's president, she commented, "I went ahead and used the agents' 15% commission rate in completing these statements, but we've just learned they refuse to handle our products next year unless we increase the commission rate to 20%."

"That's the last straw," Karl replied angrily. "Those agents have been demanding more and more, and this time they've gone too far. How can they possibly defend a 20% commission rate?"

"They claim after paying for advertising, travel, and the other costs of promotion, there's nothing left over for profit," replied Barbara.

"That's ridiculous," retorted Karl. "And I also say it's time we dumped those guys and got our own sales force. Can you get your people to work up some cost figures for us to look at?"

"We've already worked them up," said Barbara. "Several companies we know of pay a 7.5% commission to their own salespeople, along with a small salary. Of course, we would have to handle all promotion costs, too. We figure our fixed expenses would increase by $2,400,000 per year, but that would be more than offset by the $3,200,000 (20% × $16,000,000) we would avoid on agents' commissions."

The breakdown of the $2,400,000 cost follows:

Salaries:	
Sales manager.......................................	$ 100,000
Salespersons..	600,000
Travel and entertainment................................	400,000
Advertising...	1,300,000
Total..	$2,400,000

"Super," replied Karl. "And I noticed the $2,400,000 equals what we're paying the agents under the old 15% commission rate."

"It's even better than that," explained Barbara. "We can actually save $75,000 a year because that's what we're paying our auditors to check out the agents' reports. So our overall administrative expenses would be less."

"Pull all of these numbers together and we'll show them to the executive committee tomorrow," said Karl. "With the approval of the committee, we can move on the matter immediately."

Required:

1. Compute Pittman Company's break-even point in dollar sales for next year assuming:
   a. The agents' commission rate remains unchanged at 15%.
   b. The agents' commission rate is increased to 20%.
   c. The company employs its own sales force.
2. Assume Pittman Company decides to continue selling through agents and pays the 20% commission rate. Calculate the dollar sales required to generate the same net income as contained in the budgeted income statement for next year.
3. Calculate the dollar sales at which net income would be equal regardless of whether Pittman Company sells through agents (at a 20% commission rate) or employs its own sales force.
4. Compute the degree of operating leverage the company would expect to have at the end of next year assuming:
   a. The agents' commission rate remains unchanged at 15%.
   b. The agents' commission rate is increased to 20%.
   c. The company employs its own sales force.
   Use income *before* income taxes in your operating leverage computation.
5. Based on the data in (1) through (4) above, make a recommendation whether the company should continue to use sales agents (at a 20% commission rate) or employ its own sales force. Give reasons for your answer.

(CMA, adapted)

Appendix 5A: Analyzing Mixed Costs

The main body of Chapter 5 assumed all costs could be readily classified as variable or fixed. In reality, many costs contain both variable *and* fixed components—they are *mixed costs.* This appendix describes various methods companies can use to separate mixed costs into their variable and fixed components, thereby enabling cost-volume-profit (CVP) analysis.

Mixed costs are very common in most organizations. For example, the overall cost of performing surgeries for patients at the Harvard Medical School Hospital is a mixed cost. The costs of equipment depreciation and surgeons' and nurses' salaries are fixed, but the costs of surgical gloves, power, and other supplies are variable. At Southwest Airlines, maintenance costs are a mixed cost. The company incurs fixed costs for renting maintenance facilities and for keeping skilled mechanics on the payroll, but the costs of replacement parts, lubricating oils, tires, and so forth, are variable with respect to how often and how far the company's aircraft are flown.

The fixed portion of a mixed cost represents the minimum cost of having a service *ready and available* for use. The variable portion represents the cost incurred for *actual consumption* of the service, thus it varies in proportion to the amount of service actually consumed.

Managers can use a variety of methods to estimate the fixed and variable components of a mixed cost such as *account analysis,* the *engineering approach,* the *high-low method,* and *least-squares regression analysis.* In **account analysis,** an account is classified as either variable or fixed based on the analyst's prior knowledge of how the cost in the account behaves. For example, direct materials would be classified as variable and a building lease cost would be classified as fixed because of the nature of those costs.

The **engineering approach** to cost analysis involves a detailed analysis of what cost behavior should be, based on an industrial engineer's evaluation of the production methods to be used, the materials specifications, labor requirements, equipment usage, production efficiency, power consumption, and so on.

The high-low method and least-squares regression method estimate the fixed and variable elements of a mixed cost by analyzing past records of cost and activity data. Throughout the remainder of this appendix, we will define these two cost estimation methods and use an example from Brentline Hospital to illustrate how they each derive their respective fixed and variable cost estimates. The least-squares regression computations will be explained using Microsoft Excel because it can perform the underlying mathematics much faster than using a pencil and a calculator.

Diagnosing Cost Behavior with a Scattergraph Plot

LO5–10

Analyze a mixed cost using a scattergraph plot and the high-low method.

Assume Brentline Hospital wants to predict future monthly maintenance costs for budgeting purposes. The senior management team believes maintenance cost is a mixed cost and the variable portion of this cost is driven by the number of patient-days. Each day a patient is in the hospital counts as one patient-day. The hospital's chief financial officer gathered the following data for the most recent seven-month period:

Month	Activity Level: Patient-Days	Maintenance Cost Incurred
January	5,600	$7,900
February	7,100	$8,500
March	5,000	$7,400
April	6,500	$8,200
May	7,300	$9,100
June	8,000	$9,800
July	6,200	$7,800

The first step in applying the high-low method or the least-squares regression method is to diagnose cost behavior with a scattergraph plot. The scattergraph plot of maintenance costs versus patient-days at Brentline Hospital is shown in Exhibit 5A–1. Two things should be noted about this scattergraph:

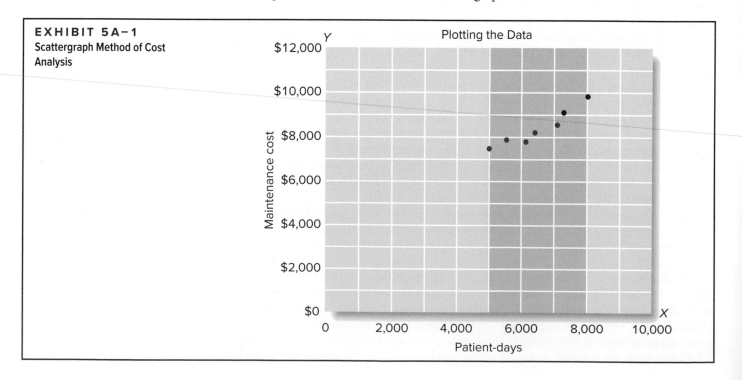

EXHIBIT 5A–1
Scattergraph Method of Cost Analysis

1. The total maintenance cost, *Y*, is plotted on the vertical axis. Cost is known as the **dependent variable** because the amount of cost incurred during a period depends on the level of activity for the period. (That is, as the level of activity increases, total cost also will ordinarily increase.)
2. The activity, *X* (patient-days in this case), is plotted on the horizontal axis. Activity is known as the **independent variable** because it causes variations in the cost.

From the scattergraph plot, it is evident maintenance costs do increase with the number of patient-days in an approximately *linear* fashion. In other words, the points lie more or less along a straight line that slopes upward and to the right. **Linear cost behavior** exists whenever a straight line is a reasonable approximation for the relation between cost and activity.

Plotting the data on a scattergraph is an essential diagnostic step that should be performed before performing the high-low or least-squares regression calculations. If the scattergraph plot reveals linear cost behavior, then it makes sense to perform the high-low or least-squares regression calculations to separate the mixed cost into its variable and fixed components. If the scattergraph plot does not depict linear cost behavior, then it makes no sense to proceed any further in analyzing the data.

Once we determine the dependent and independent variables have a linear relationship, the high-low and least-squares regression methods both rely on the following equation for a straight line (as introduced in Chapter 1) to express the relationship between a mixed cost and the level of activity:

$$Y = a + bX$$

In this equation,

Y = The total mixed cost
a = The total fixed cost (the vertical intercept of the line)
b = The variable cost per unit of activity (the slope of the line)
X = The level of activity

The High-Low Method

The high-low method is based on the rise-over-run formula for the slope of a straight line. Assuming the relation between cost and activity can be represented by a straight line, then the slope of the straight line is equal to the variable cost per unit of activity. Consequently, the following formula can be used to estimate the variable cost:

$$\text{Variable cost} = \text{Slope of the line} = \frac{\text{Rise}}{\text{Run}} = \frac{Y_2 - Y_1}{X_2 - X_1}$$

To analyze mixed costs with the **high-low method,** begin by identifying the period with the lowest level of activity and the period with the highest level of activity. The period with the lowest activity is selected as the first point in the above formula and the period with the highest activity is selected as the second point. Consequently, the formula becomes:

$$\text{Variable cost} = \frac{Y_2 - Y_1}{X_2 - X_1} = \frac{\text{Cost at the high activity level} - \text{Cost at the low activity level}}{\text{High activity level} - \text{Low activity level}}$$

or

$$\text{Variable cost} = \frac{\text{Change in cost}}{\text{Change in activity}}$$

Therefore, when the high-low method is used, the variable cost is estimated by dividing the difference in cost between the high and low levels of activity by the change in activity between those two points.

To return to the Brentline Hospital example, using the high-low method, we first identify the periods with the highest and lowest *activity* —in this case, June and March.

We then use the activity and cost data from these two periods to estimate the variable cost component as follows:

	Patient-Days	Maintenance Cost Incurred
High activity level (June)	8,000	$9,800
Low activity level (March).	5,000	7,400
Change	3,000	$2,400

$$\text{Variable cost} = \frac{\text{Change in cost}}{\text{Change in activity}} = \frac{\$2,400}{3,000 \text{ patient-days}} = \$0.80 \text{ per patient-day}$$

Having determined the variable maintenance cost is 80 cents per patient-day, we can now calculate the amount of fixed cost. This is done by taking the total cost at *either* the high or the low activity level and deducting the variable cost element. In the computation below, total cost at the high activity level is used in computing the fixed cost element:

$$\text{Fixed cost element} = \text{Total cost} - \text{Varable cost element}$$
$$= \$9,800 - (\$0.80 \text{ per patient-day} \times 8,000 \text{ patient-days})$$
$$= \$3,400$$

Given that we have estimated the variable and fixed cost elements, the maintenance cost can now be expressed as $3,400 per month plus 80 cents per patient-day, or as:

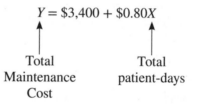

$$Y = \$3,400 + \$0.80X$$

Total
Maintenance
Cost

Total
patient-days

The data used in this illustration are shown graphically in Exhibit 5A–2. Notice a straight line has been drawn through the points corresponding to the low and high levels of activity. In essence, that is what the high-low method does—it draws a straight line through those two points.

Sometimes the high and low levels of activity don't coincide with the high and low amounts of cost. For example, the period with the highest level of activity may not have the highest amount of cost. Nevertheless, the costs at the highest and lowest levels of *activity* are always used to analyze a mixed cost under the high-low method. The reason is that the analyst would like to use data that reflect the greatest possible variation in activity.

The high-low method is very simple to apply, but it suffers from a major (and sometimes critical) defect—it utilizes only two data points. Generally, two data points are not enough to produce accurate estimates. Additionally, the periods with the highest and lowest activity tend to be unusual. A cost formula estimated solely using data from these unusual periods may misrepresent the true cost behavior during normal periods. Such a distortion is evident in Exhibit 5A–2. The straight line should probably be shifted down somewhat so it is closer to more of the data points. For these reasons, least-squares regression will generally be more accurate than the high-low method.

LO5–11

Analyze a mixed cost using a scattergraph plot and the least-squares regression method.

The Least-Squares Regression Method

The **least-squares regression method,** unlike the high-low method, uses all of the data to separate a mixed cost into its fixed and variable components. A *regression line* of the form $Y = a + bX$ is fitted to the data, where a (the intercept) represents the

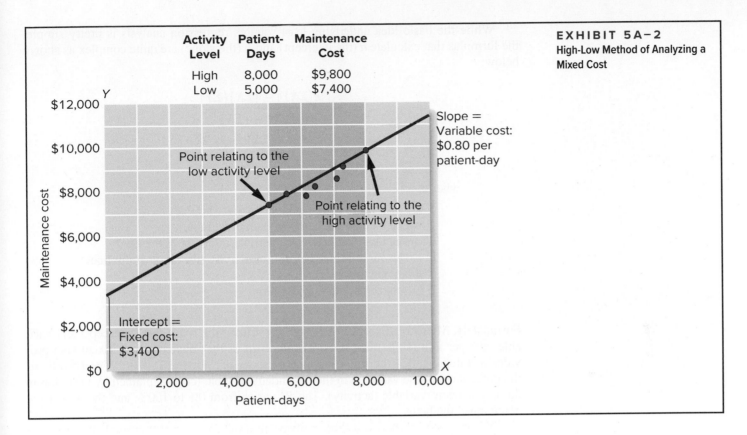

Activity Level	Patient-Days	Maintenance Cost
High	8,000	$9,800
Low	5,000	$7,400

EXHIBIT 5A–2
High-Low Method of Analyzing a Mixed Cost

total fixed cost and *b* (the slope) represents the variable cost per unit of activity. The basic idea underlying the least-squares regression method is illustrated in Exhibit 5A–3 using hypothetical data points. Notice how the deviations from the plotted points to the regression line are measured vertically on the graph. These vertical deviations are called the regression errors. There is nothing mysterious about the least-squares regression method. It simply computes the regression line that minimizes the sum of these squared errors.

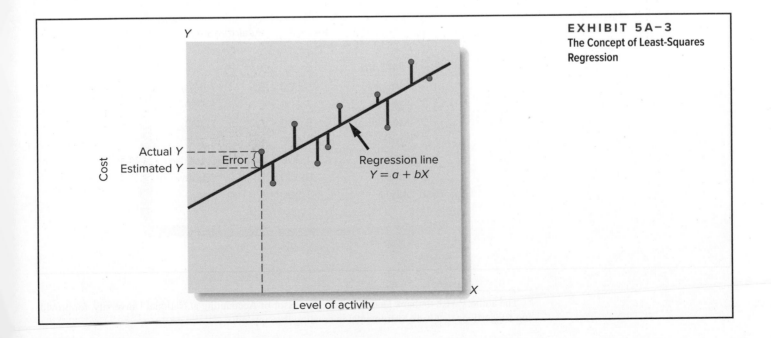

EXHIBIT 5A–3
The Concept of Least-Squares Regression

While the basic idea underlying least-squares regression analysis is pretty simple, the formulas that calculate a (the intercept) and b (the slope) are quite complex as shown below:

$$b = \frac{n(\Sigma XY) - (\Sigma X)(\Sigma Y)}{n(\Sigma X^2) - (\Sigma X)^2}$$

$$a = \frac{(\Sigma Y) - b(\Sigma X)}{n}$$

where:

X = The level of activity (independent variable)
Y = The total mixed cost (dependent variable)
a = The total fixed cost (the vertical intercept of the line)
b = The variable cost per unit of activity (the slope of the line)
n = Number of observations
Σ = Sum across all n observations

Fortunately, Microsoft Excel can be used to estimate the fixed cost (intercept) and variable cost per unit (slope) that minimize the sum of the squared errors. Excel also provides a statistic called the R^2, which is a measure of "goodness of fit." The **R^2** tells us the percentage of the variation in the dependent variable (cost) explained by variation in the independent variable (activity). The R^2 varies from 0% to 100%, and the higher the percentage, the better.

As mentioned earlier, you should always plot the data in a scattergraph, but it is particularly important to check the data visually when the R^2 is low. A quick look at the scattergraph can reveal there is little relation between the cost and the activity or the relation is something other than a simple straight line. In such cases, additional analysis would be required.

Exhibit 5A–4 uses Excel to depict the Brentline Hospital data we used earlier to illustrate the high-low method. We'll be using this same data set to illustrate how Excel can be used to create a scattergraph plot and to calculate the intercept a, the slope b, and the R^2 using least-squares regression.[2]

EXHIBIT 5A–4
The Least-Squares Regression Worksheet for Brentline Hospital

	A	B	C
1		Patient	Maintenance
2		Days	Cost
3	Month	X	Y
4	January	5,600	$ 7,900
5	February	7,100	$ 8,500
6	March	5,000	$ 7,400
7	April	6,500	$ 8,200
8	May	7,300	$ 9,100
9	June	8,000	$ 9,800
10	July	6,200	$ 7,800
11			

Least-squares regression

Microsoft Excel

[2] The authors wish to thank Don Schwartz, Professor of Accounting at National University, for providing suggestions that were instrumental in creating this appendix.

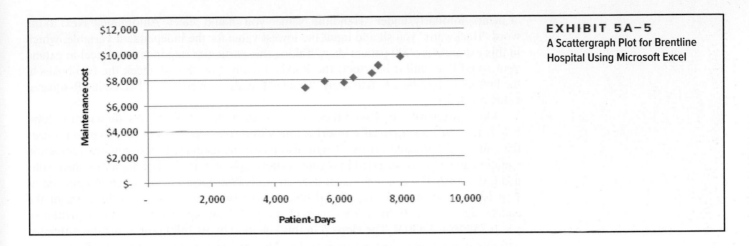

EXHIBIT 5A–5
A Scattergraph Plot for Brentline Hospital Using Microsoft Excel

To prepare a scattergraph plot in Excel, begin by highlighting the data in cells B4 through C10 (as shown in Exhibit 5A–4). From the Charts group within the Insert tab, select the "Scatter" subgroup and then click on the choice that has no lines connecting the data points. This should produce a scattergraph plot similar to the one shown in Exhibit 5A–5. Notice the number of patient-days is plotted on the X-axis and the maintenance cost is plotted on the Y-axis.[3] As we saw verified earlier in Exhibit 5A–1, the data is approximately linear, so it makes sense to proceed with estimating a regression equation that minimizes the sum of the squared errors.

To determine the intercept a, the slope b, and the R^2, begin by right-clicking on any data point in the scattergraph plot and selecting "Add Trendline." This should produce the screen shown in Exhibit 5A–6. Notice under "Trendline Options" you should select

EXHIBIT 5A–6
Trendline Options in Microsoft Excel

Format Trendline

Trendline Options ∨

◢ Trendline Options

- Exponential
- ● Linear
- Logarithmic
- Polynomial   Order   2
- Power
- Moving Average   Period 2

Trendline Name

- ● Automatic   Linear (Series1)
- Custom

Forecast

Forward   0.0   periods
Backward   5000.0   periods

☐ Set Intercept   0.0
☑ Display Equation on chart
☑ Display R-squared value on chart

Microsoft Excel

---

[3] To insert labels for the X-axis and Y-axis, go to the Layout tab in Excel. Then, within the Labels group, select Axis Titles.

"Linear." Similarly, under "Trendline Name" you should select "Automatic." Next to the word "Backward" you should input the lowest value for the independent variable, which in this example is 5000 patient-days. Taking this particular step instructs Excel to extend your fitted line until it intersects the Y-axis. Finally, you should check the two boxes at the bottom of Exhibit 5A–6 that say "Display Equation on chart" and "Display R-squared value on chart."

Once you have established these settings, then click "Close." As shown in Exhibit 5A–7, this will automatically insert a line within the scattergraph plot that minimizes the sum of the squared errors. It will also cause the estimated least-squares regression equation and R^2 to be inserted into your scattergraph plot. Instead of depicting the results using the form $Y = a + bX$, Excel uses an equivalent form of the equation depicted as $Y = bX + a$. In other words, Excel reverses the two terms shown to the right of the equals sign. So, in Exhibit 5A–7, Excel shows a least-squares regression equation of $y = 0.7589x + 3,430.9$. The slope b in this equation of $0.7589 represents the estimated variable maintenance cost per patient-day. The intercept a in this equation of $3,430.90 (or approximately $3,431) represents the estimated fixed monthly maintenance cost. Note that the R^2 is approximately 0.90, which is quite good and indicates that 90 percent of the variation in maintenance cost is explained by the variation in patient-days.

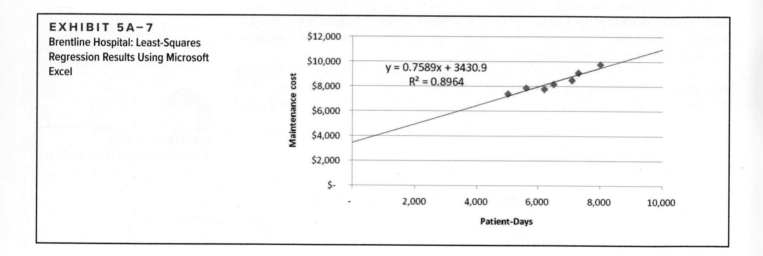

EXHIBIT 5A–7
Brentline Hospital: Least-Squares Regression Results Using Microsoft Excel

Comparing the High-Low and Least-Squares Regression Methods

The table below compares Brentline Hospital's cost estimates using the high-low method and the least-squares regression method:

	High-Low Method	Least-Squares Regression Method
Variable cost estimate per patient-day	$0.800	$0.759
Fixed cost estimate per month	$3,400	$3,431

When Brentline uses the least-squares regression method to create a straight line that minimizes the sum of the squared errors, it results in estimated fixed costs that are $31 higher than the amount derived using the high-low method. It also decreases the slope of the straight line, resulting in a lower variable cost estimate of $0.759 per patient-day rather than $0.80 per patient-day as derived using the high-low method.

Glossary (Appendix 5A)

Account analysis A method that classifies accounts as either variable or fixed based on the analyst's prior knowledge of how the cost in the account behaves. (p. 237)

Dependent variable A variable that responds to some causal factor; total cost is the dependent variable, as represented by the letter Y, in the equation $Y = a + bX$. (p. 239)

Engineering approach A detailed analysis of cost behavior based on an industrial engineer's evaluation of the inputs required to carry out a particular activity and of the prices of those inputs. (p. 238)

High-low method A method of separating a mixed cost into its fixed and variable elements by analyzing the change in cost between the high and low activity levels. (p. 239)

Independent variable A variable that acts as a causal factor; activity is the independent variable, as represented by the letter X, in the equation $Y = a + bX$. (p. 239)

Least-squares regression method A method of separating a mixed cost into its fixed and variable elements by fitting a regression line that minimizes the sum of the squared errors. (p. 240)

Linear cost behavior Cost behavior is said to be linear whenever a straight line is a reasonable approximation for the relation between cost and activity. (p. 239)

R^2 A measure of goodness of fit in least-squares regression analysis. It is the percentage of variation in the dependent variable explained by variation in the independent variable. (p. 248)

 **Appendix 5A: Exercises, Problems, and Case**

EXERCISE 5A–1 High-Low Method LO5–10

The Cheyenne Hotel in Big Sky, Montana, recorded its total electrical costs and number of occupancy-days over the last year. An occupancy-day represents a room rented for one day. The hotel's business is highly seasonal, with peaks occurring during the ski season and in the summer.

Month	Occupancy-Days	Electrical Costs
January	1,736	$4,127
February	1,904	$4,207
March	2,356	$5,083
April	960	$2,857
May	360	$1,871
June	744	$2,696
July	2,108	$4,670
August	2,406	$5,148
September	840	$2,691
October	124	$1,588
November	720	$2,454
December	1,364	$3,529

Required:

1. Using the high-low method, estimate the fixed cost of electricity per month and the variable cost of electricity per occupancy-day. Round off the fixed cost to the nearest whole dollar and the variable cost to the nearest whole cent.

2. What other factors in addition to occupancy-days are likely to affect the variation in electrical costs from month to month?

EXERCISE 5A–2 Least-Squares Regression LO5–11

Bargain Rental Car wants to better understand the variable and fixed portions of its car washing costs. The company operates its own car wash facility that cleans each rental car before releasing it to another customer. Management believes the variable portion of its car washing costs relates to the number of rental returns. Accordingly, the following data have been compiled:

Month	Rental Returns	Car Wash Costs
January	2,380	$10,825
February	2,421	$11,865
March	2,586	$11,332
April	2,725	$12,422
May	2,968	$13,850
June.	3,281	$14,419
July	3,353	$14,935
August.	3,489	$15,738
September	3,057	$13,563
October.	2,876	$11,889
November.	2,735	$12,683
December.	2,983	$13,796

Required:

1. Prepare a scattergraph plot. (Place car wash costs on the vertical axis and rental returns on the horizontal axis.)
2. Using least-squares regression, estimate the variable cost per rental return and the monthly fixed cost incurred to wash cars. The total fixed cost should be estimated to the nearest dollar and the variable cost per rental return to the nearest cent.

EXERCISE 5A–3 Cost Behavior; High-Low Method LO5–10

Hoi Chong Transport, Ltd., operates a fleet of delivery trucks in Singapore. The company knows if a truck is driven 105,000 kilometers during a year, the average operating cost is 11.4 cents per kilometer. If a truck is driven only 70,000 kilometers during a year, the average operating cost increases to 13.4 cents per kilometer.

Required:

1. Using the high-low method, estimate the variable operating cost per kilometer and the annual fixed operating cost associated with the fleet of trucks.
2. Express the variable and fixed costs in the form $Y = a + bX$.
3. If a truck were driven 80,000 kilometers during a year, what total operating cost would you expect to be incurred?

EXERCISE 5A–4 High-Low Method; Scattergraph Analysis LO5–10

Archer Company is a wholesaler of custom-built air-conditioning units for commercial buildings. It gathered the following monthly data relating to units shipped and total shipping expense:

Month	Units Shipped	Total Shipping Expense
January	3	$1,800
February	6	$2,300
March	4	$1,700
April	5	$2,000
May	7	$2,300
June.	8	$2,700
July	2	$1,200

Required:

1. Prepare a scattergraph using the data given above. Plot cost on the vertical axis and activity on the horizontal axis. Is there an approximately linear relationship between shipping expense and the number of units shipped?

2. Using the high-low method, estimate the cost formula for shipping expense. Draw a straight line through the high and low data points shown in the scattergraph you prepared in requirement (1). Make sure your line intersects the Y-axis.

3. Comment on the accuracy of your high-low estimates assuming a least-squares regression analysis estimated the total fixed costs to be $910.71 per month and the variable cost to be $217.86 per unit. How would the straight line you drew in requirement 2 differ from a straight line that minimizes the sum of the squared errors?

4. What factors, other than the number of units shipped, likely affect the company's shipping expense? Explain.

EXERCISE 5A–5 Least-Squares Regression LO5–11
George Caloz & Frères, located in Grenchen, Switzerland, makes luxury custom watches in small lots. One of the company's products, a platinum diving watch, goes through an etching process. The company has recorded etching costs as follows over the last six weeks:

Week	Units	Total Etching Cost
1...........................	4	$ 18
2...........................	3	17
3...........................	8	25
4...........................	6	20
5...........................	7	24
6...........................	2	16
	30	$120

For planning purposes, management wants to know the variable etching cost per unit and the total fixed etching cost per week.

Required:
1. Prepare a scattergraph plot. (Plot etching costs on the vertical axis and units on the horizontal axis.)
2. Using the least-squares regression method, estimate the variable etching cost per unit and the total fixed etching cost per week. Express these estimates in the form $Y = a + bX$.
3. If the company processes five units next week, what would be the expected total etching cost? (Round your answer to the nearest cent.)

PROBLEM 5A–6 Least-Squares Regression; Scattergraph; Comparison of Activity Bases LO5–11
The Hard Rock Mining Company wants to separate its utilities cost into variable and fixed elements for planning purposes. The controller believes tons mined might be a good base for developing a cost formula. The production superintendent disagrees; she thinks direct labor-hours would be a better base. Quarterly data for tons mined, direct labor-hours, and utilities cost are as follows:

Quarter	Tons Mined	Direct Labor-Hours	Utilities Cost
Year 1:			
First	15,000	5,000	$50,000
Second	11,000	3,000	$45,000
Third	21,000	4,000	$60,000
Fourth	12,000	6,000	$75,000
Year 2:			
First	18,000	10,000	$100,000
Second	25,000	9,000	$105,000
Third	30,000	8,000	$85,000
Fourth	28,000	11,000	$120,000

Required:
1. Using tons mined as the independent variable, prepare a scattergraph that plots tons mined on the horizontal axis and utilities cost on the vertical axis. Using the least-squares regression method, estimate the variable utilities cost per ton mined and the total fixed utilities cost per quarter. Express these estimates in the form $Y = a + bX$.
2. Using direct labor-hours as the independent variable, prepare a scattergraph that plots direct labor-hours on the horizontal axis and utilities cost on the vertical axis. Using the least-squares regression method, estimate the variable utilities cost per direct labor-hour and the total fixed utilities cost per quarter. Express these estimates in the form $Y = a + bX$.
3. Would you recommend the company use tons mined or direct labor-hours as a base for planning utilities cost?

PROBLEM 5A–7 Cost Behavior; High-Low Method; Contribution Format Income Statement LO5–10
Morrisey & Brown, Ltd., is the sole distributor of a product with growing sales. Its income statements for the three most recent months follow:

Morrisey & Brown, Ltd.			
Income Statements			
For the Three Months Ended September 30			
	July	August	September
Sales in units	4,000	4,500	5,000
Sales	$400,000	$450,000	$500,000
Cost of goods sold	240,000	270,000	300,000
Gross margin	160,000	180,000	200,000
Selling and administrative expenses:			
Advertising expense	21,000	21,000	21,000
Shipping expense	34,000	36,000	38,000
Salaries and commissions	78,000	84,000	90,000
Insurance expense	6,000	6,000	6,000
Depreciation expense	15,000	15,000	15,000
Total selling and administrative expenses	154,000	162,000	170,000
Net operating income	$ 6,000	$ 18,000	$ 30,000

Required:
1. By analyzing data from the company's income statements, classify each of its expenses (including cost of goods sold) as either variable, fixed, or mixed.
2. Using the high-low method, separate each mixed expense into variable and fixed elements. Express the variable and fixed portions of each mixed expense in the form $Y = a + bX$.
3. Redo the company's income statement at the 5,000-unit level of activity using the contribution format.

PROBLEM 5A–8 High-Low Method; Predicting Cost LO5–10
Nova Company's total overhead cost at various levels of activity are presented below:

Month	Machine-Hours	Total Overhead Cost
April	70,000	$198,000
May	60,000	$174,000
June	80,000	$222,000
July	90,000	$246,000

Assume the total overhead cost above consists of utilities, supervisory salaries, and maintenance. The breakdown of these costs at the 60,000 machine-hour level of activity is:

Utilities (variable)............................	$ 48,000
Supervisory salaries (fixed)	21,000
Maintenance (mixed)........................	105,000
Total overhead cost	$174,000

Nova Company's management wants to break down the maintenance cost into its variable and fixed cost elements.

Required:
1. Estimate how much of the $246,000 of overhead cost in July was maintenance cost. (*Hint:* To do this, it may be helpful to first determine how much of the $246,000 consisted of utilities and supervisory salaries. Think about the behavior of variable and fixed costs.)
2. Using the high-low method, estimate a cost formula for maintenance in the form $Y = a + bX$.
3. Express the company's *total* overhead cost in the form $Y = a + bX$.
4. What *total* overhead cost would you expect at an activity level of 75,000 machine-hours?

PROBLEM 5A–9 High-Low Method; Contribution Format Income Statement LO5–10
Milden Company is a distributor that wants to start using a contribution format income statement for planning purposes. The company analyzed its expenses and developed the following cost formulas:

Cost	Cost Formula
Cost of good sold	$35 per unit sold
Advertising expense............	$210,000 per quarter
Sales commissions	6% of sales
Shipping expense..............	?
Administrative salaries..........	$145,000 per quarter
Insurance expense.............	$9,000 per quarter
Depreciation expense	$76,000 per quarter

Because shipping expense is a mixed cost, the company needs to estimate the variable shipping expense per unit sold and the fixed shipping expense per quarter using the following data:

Quarter	Units Sold	Shipping Expense
Year 1:		
First	10,000	$119,000
Second	16,000	$175,000
Third	18,000	$190,000
Fourth	15,000	$164,000
Year 2:		
First	11,000	$130,000
Second	17,000	$185,000
Third	20,000	$210,000
Fourth	13,000	$147,000

Required:
1. Using the high-low method, estimate a cost formula for shipping expense in the form $Y = a + bX$.
2. In the first quarter of Year 3, the company plans to sell 12,000 units at a selling price of $100 per unit. Prepare a contribution format income statement for the quarter.

PROBLEM 5A–10 Least-Squares Regression Method; Scattergraph; Cost Behavior LO5–11

Professor John Morton has just been appointed chairperson of the Finance Department at Westland University. In reviewing the department's cost records, Professor Morton found the following total cost associated with Finance 101 over the last five terms:

Term	Number of Sections Offered	Total Cost
Fall, last year	4	$10,000
Winter, last year.....	6	$14,000
Summer, last year ...	2	$7,000
Fall, this year	5	$13,000
Winter, this year.....	3	$9,500

Professor Morton knows there are some variable costs, such as amounts paid to graduate assistants, associated with the course. He would like to have the variable and fixed costs separated for planning purposes.

Required:
1. Prepare a scattergraph plot. (Plot total cost on the vertical axis and number of sections offered on the horizontal axis.)
2. Using the least-squares regression method, estimate the variable cost per section and the total fixed cost per term for Finance 101. Express these estimates in the form $Y = a + bX$.
3. Assume because of the small number of sections offered during the Winter Term this year, Professor Morton will have to offer eight sections of Finance 101 during the Fall Term. Compute the expected total cost for Finance 101. Can you see any problem with using the cost formula from (2) above to derive this total cost figure? Explain.

CASE 5A–11 Mixed Cost Analysis and the Relevant Range LO5–10

Ramon Company wants to develop a cost formula to estimate the variable and fixed components of its monthly manufacturing overhead costs. The company is using machine-hours as its measure of activity and gathered the data below for this year and last year:

Month	Last Year Machine-Hours	Last Year Overhead Costs	This Year Machine-Hours	This Year Overhead Costs
January................	21,000	$84,000	21,000	$86,000
February..............	25,000	$99,000	24,000	$93,000
March	22,000	$89,500	23,000	$93,000
April.................	23,000	$90,000	22,000	$87,000
May	20,500	$81,500	20,000	$80,000
June..................	19,000	$75,500	18,000	$76,500
July	14,000	$70,500	12,000	$67,500
August................	10,000	$64,500	13,000	$71,000
September	12,000	$69,000	15,000	$73,500
October...............	17,000	$75,000	17,000	$72,500
November..............	16,000	$71,500	15,000	$71,000
December.............	19,000	$78,000	18,000	$75,000

The company leases all of its manufacturing equipment. The lease arrangement calls for a flat monthly fee up to 19,500 machine-hours. If the machine-hours used exceed 19,500, then the fee becomes strictly variable with respect to the total number of machine-hours consumed during the month. Lease expense is a major element of overhead cost.

Required:

1. Using the high-low method, estimate a manufacturing overhead cost formula in the form $Y = a + bX$.

2. Prepare a scattergraph using all of the data for the two-year period. Fit a straight line or lines to the plotted points using a ruler. Describe the cost behavior pattern revealed by your scattergraph plot.

3. Assume a least-squares regression analysis using all of the given data points estimated the total fixed cost to be $40,102 and the variable cost to be $2.13 per machine-hour. Do you have any concerns about the accuracy of these estimates or the high-low estimates you computed?

4. Assume the company consumes 22,500 machine-hours during a month. Using the high-low method, estimate the total overhead cost at this level of activity. Be sure to consider only the data points contained in the relevant range of activity when performing your computations.

5. Comment on the accuracy of your high-low estimates assuming a least-squares regression analysis using only the data points in the relevant range of activity estimated the total fixed cost to be $10,090 and the variable cost to be $3.53 per machine-hour.

CASE 5A–12 Analysis of Mixed Costs in a Pricing Decision LO5–11

Maria Chavez owns a catering company that serves food and beverages at parties and business functions. Chavez's business is seasonal, with a heavy schedule during the summer months and holidays and a lighter schedule at other times.

One of the major events Chavez's customers request is a cocktail party. She offers a standard cocktail party and has estimated the cost per guest as follows:

Food and beverages	$15.00
Labor (0.5 hr. @ $10.00/hr.)	5.00
Overhead (0.5 hr. @ $13.98/hr.)	6.99
Total cost per guest	$26.99

The standard cocktail party lasts three hours and Chavez hires one worker for every six guests, so that works out to one-half hour of labor per guest. These workers are hired only as needed and are paid only for the hours they actually work.

When bidding on cocktail parties, Chavez adds a 15% markup to yield a price of $31 per guest. She is confident about her estimates of the costs of food and beverages and labor but is not as comfortable with the estimate of overhead cost. The $13.98 overhead cost per labor-hour was determined by dividing total overhead expenses for the last 12 months by total labor-hours for the same period. Monthly data concerning overhead costs and labor-hours follow:

Month	Labor-Hours	Overhead Expenses
January	2,500	$ 55,000
February	2,800	59,000
March	3,000	60,000
April	4,200	64,000
May	4,500	67,000
June	5,500	71,000
July	6,500	74,000
August	7,500	77,000
September	7,000	75,000
October	4,500	68,000
November	3,100	62,000
December	6,500	73,000
Total	57,600	$805,000

Chavez has received a request to bid on a 180-guest fundraising cocktail party to be given next month by an important local charity. (The party would last the usual three hours.) She would like to win this contract because the guest list for this charity event includes many prominent individuals whom she would like to secure as future clients. Maria is confident that these potential customers would be favorably impressed by her company's services at the charity event.

Required:
1. Prepare a scattergraph plot that puts labor-hours on the X-axis and overhead expenses on the Y-axis. What insights are revealed by your scattergraph?
2. Use the least-squares regression method to estimate the fixed and variable components of overhead expenses. Express these estimates in the form $Y = a + bX$.
3. If Chavez charges $31 per guest for the 180-guest cocktail party, how much contribution margin will she earn serving this event?
4. How low could Chavez bid for the charity event in terms of a price per guest and still break even on the event?
5. The individual organizing the charity's fundraising event mentioned he already received a bid under $30 from another catering company. Do you think Chavez should bid below her normal $31 per guest price for the charity event? Why or why not?

(CMA, adapted)

Variable Costing and Segment Reporting: Tools for Management

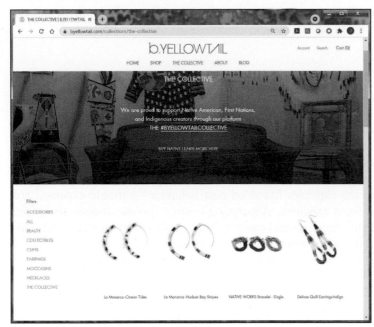

B.YELLOWTAIL

ENTREPRENEUR SPOTLIGHT

Bethany Yellowtail is a graduate of the Fashion Institute of Design and Merchandising. She "started her fashion career at the BCBG Max Ariza Group, moving on to become a lead pattern maker for several private label companies before launching her own brand." She is currently the CEO of B. Yellowtail and the B. Yellowtail Collective, which sell and promote "handmade, heirloom-quality jewelry, textiles and accessories crafted by carefully selected indigenous artists from all corners of North America." The company's product lines include dresses, cuffs, earrings, moccasins, necklaces, scarves, and skirts.

Applying Managerial Accounting

B. Yellowtail can segment its sales by product line. For example, it could break its total sales into product lines such as those mentioned above—dresses, cuffs, earrings, moccasins, necklaces, scarves, and skirts. Furthermore, it could divide its earring sales into segments, such as horsehair tassel earrings, mosaic stud earrings, and Cheyanne Symone Pearl Direction earrings. The company also has other product segments such as lotions, soaps, candles, and stationery.

Serving All Stakeholders

At B. Yellowtail, for each face mask the company sells, it donates one face mask to the indigenous communities most affected by COVID-19. To date, the company has donated more than 25,000 face masks to Orenda Tribe to be distributed to indigenous people in the Southwest portion of the United States. Navajo Nation was hit hard by COVID-19 with more than 8,500 confirmed cases and more than 400 deaths. ■

Source: www.byellowtail.com

LEARNING OBJECTIVES

After studying Chapter 6, you should be able to:

LO6–1 Explain how variable costing differs from absorption costing and compute unit product costs under each method.

LO6–2 Prepare income statements using both variable and absorption costing.

LO6–3 Reconcile variable costing and absorption costing net operating incomes and explain why the two amounts differ.

LO6–4 Prepare a segmented income statement that differentiates traceable fixed costs from common fixed costs and use it to make decisions.

LO6–5 Compute companywide and segment break-even points for a company with traceable fixed costs.

LO6–6 *(Appendix 6A) Prepare an income statement using super-variable costing and reconcile this approach with variable costing.*

 Data Analytics Exercise available in Connect to complement this chapter

This chapter explains how manufacturing companies prepare *variable costing* income statements, which rely on the contribution format, for internal decision-making purposes. The variable costing approach will be contrasted with *absorption costing* income statements, which are generally used for external reports. It also explains how the contribution format can be used to prepare *segmented* income statements. A **segment** is a part or activity of an organization, such as divisions, individual stores, geographic regions, customers, and product lines, about which managers would like cost, revenue, or profit data.

Overview of Variable and Absorption Costing

As you read about variable and absorption costing income statements in the coming pages, focus your attention on three key concepts. First, both income statement formats include product costs and period costs, although they define these cost classifications differently. Second, variable costing income statements are grounded in the contribution format. They categorize expenses based on cost behavior—variable expenses are reported separately from fixed expenses. Absorption costing income statements ignore variable and fixed cost distinctions, instead categorizing costs as manufacturing and nonmanufacturing. Third, variable and absorption costing net operating incomes often differ from one another. The reason for the difference always relates to the fact that variable costing and absorption costing income statements account for fixed manufacturing overhead differently. *Pay very close attention to the two different ways that variable costing and absorption costing account for fixed manufacturing overhead.*

Variable Costing

Under **variable costing**, only those manufacturing costs that vary with output are treated as product costs. This would usually include direct materials, direct labor, and the variable portion of manufacturing overhead. Fixed manufacturing overhead is not treated as a product cost under this method. Rather, fixed manufacturing overhead is treated as a period cost and, like selling and administrative expenses, it is reported as an expense on the income statement in its entirety each period. Consequently, variable costing unit product costs do not include any fixed manufacturing overhead cost. Variable costing is sometimes referred to as *direct costing* or *marginal costing*.

Absorption Costing

Absorption costing treats *all* manufacturing costs as product costs, regardless of whether they are variable or fixed. Absorption costing unit product costs include direct materials, direct labor, and *both* variable and fixed manufacturing overhead. Thus, absorption costing allocates a portion of fixed manufacturing overhead cost to each unit of product, along with the variable manufacturing costs. Because absorption costing includes all manufacturing costs in product costs, it is frequently referred to as the *full cost* method.

Selling and Administrative Expenses

Selling and administrative expenses are never treated as product costs, regardless of the costing method. Thus, under absorption and variable costing, variable and fixed selling and administrative expenses are always treated as period costs and are reported as expenses on the income statement as incurred.

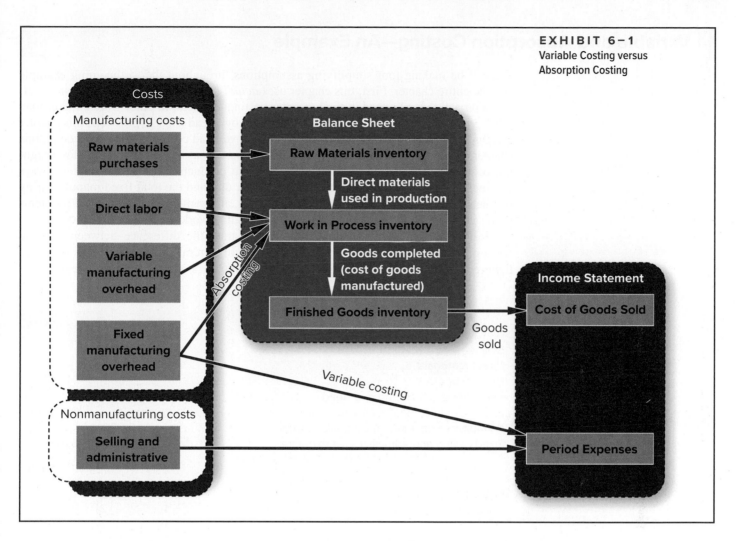

EXHIBIT 6–1
Variable Costing versus
Absorption Costing

Summary of Differences   The reason variable costing and absorption costing often report different net operating incomes, as illustrated in Exhibit 6–1, is because the two methods account for fixed manufacturing overhead costs differently—all other costs have the same affect on net operating income under the two methods. In absorption costing, fixed manufacturing overhead costs are included in work in process inventory. When units are completed, these costs are transferred to finished goods, and only when the units are sold do these costs flow through to the income statement as part of cost of goods sold. In variable costing, fixed manufacturing overhead costs are period costs—just like selling and administrative costs—and taken immediately to the income statement as period expenses.[1]

---

[1]   Variable costing advocates believe fixed manufacturing costs provide the capacity to make products but are not part of the cost of making individual units of product and will be incurred even if nothing is made during the period. Thus, the matching principle suggests treating fixed manufacturing costs as period costs. Absorption costing advocates believe all manufacturing costs are required to make individual units of product, thus the matching principle dictates treating fixed manufacturing costs as product costs.

Variable and Absorption Costing—An Example

We will be making four simplifying assumptions throughout the forthcoming example and the entire chapter. First, this chapter uses *actual costing* rather than the *normal costing* approach that was used in the job-order costing chapters. In other words, rather than relying on predetermined overhead rates to apply overhead costs to products, this chapter assigns *actual* variable and fixed manufacturing overhead costs to products. Second, this chapter always uses the actual *number of units produced* as the allocation base for assigning actual fixed manufacturing overhead costs to products. Third, this chapter always assumes that the variable manufacturing costs per unit and the total fixed manufacturing overhead cost per period remain constant. Fourth, all examples, exercises, and problems in this chapter assume there is no beginning or ending work in process inventory.

Having stated those assumptions, let's illustrate the difference between variable costing and absorption costing using Weber Light Aircraft, a company that produces light recreational aircraft. Data concerning the company's operations appear below:

	Per Aircraft	Per Month
Selling price	$100,000	
Direct materials	$19,000	
Direct labor	$5,000	
Variable manufacturing overhead	$1,000	
Fixed manufacturing overhead		$70,000
Variable selling and administrative expense	$10,000	
Fixed selling and administrative expense		$20,000

	January	February	March
Beginning inventory	0	0	1
Units produced	1	2	4
Units sold	1	1	5
Ending inventory	0	1	0

As you review the data above, it is important to notice the months of January, February, and March have the same selling price per aircraft, variable costs per aircraft, and total monthly fixed expenses. The only data that change from one month to the next are the number of units produced (January = 1 unit produced; February = 2 units produced; March = 4 units produced) and the number of units sold (January = 1 unit sold; February = 1 unit sold; March = 5 units sold).

Variable Costing Contribution Format Income Statement

LO6–2
Prepare income statements using both variable and absorption costing.

To prepare the company's variable costing income statements for January, February, and March, we begin by computing the unit product cost. Under variable costing, the unit product cost consists solely of variable production costs as shown below:

Variable Costing Unit Product Cost	
Direct materials	$19,000
Direct labor	5,000
Variable manufacturing overhead	1,000
Unit product cost	$25,000

Because each month's unit product cost is $25,000 per aircraft, the variable costing cost of goods sold for all three months can be computed as follows:

Variable Costing Cost of Goods Sold			
	January	February	March
Unit product cost (a)	$25,000	$25,000	$25,000
Units sold (b)	1	1	5
Variable cost of goods sold (a) × (b)	$25,000	$25,000	$125,000

And the company's total selling and administrative expense would be calculated as follows:

Selling and Administrative Expenses			
	January	February	March
Variable selling and administrative expense (@ $10,000 per unit sold)	$10,000	$10,000	$50,000
Fixed selling and administrative expense	20,000	20,000	20,000
Total selling and administrative expense	$30,000	$30,000	$70,000

Putting it all together, Exhibit 6–2 shows the variable costing income statements for each month. Notice, the contribution format is used in these income statements. Also, the monthly fixed manufacturing overhead cost ($70,000) is recorded as a monthly period expense.

Variable Costing Contribution Format Income Statements			
	January	February	March
Sales	$100,000	$100,000	$500,000
Variable expenses:			
Variable cost of goods sold	25,000	25,000	125,000
Variable selling and administrative expense	10,000	10,000	50,000
Total variable expenses	35,000	35,000	175,000
Contribution margin	65,000	65,000	325,000
Fixed expenses:			
Fixed manufacturing overhead	70,000	70,000	70,000
Fixed selling and administrative expense . . .	20,000	20,000	20,000
Total fixed expenses	90,000	90,000	90,000
Net operating income (loss)	$ (25,000)	$ (25,000)	$235,000

EXHIBIT 6–2
Variable Costing Income Statements

A simple method for understanding how Weber Light Aircraft computed its variable costing net operating income for each month is to focus on the contribution margin per aircraft sold, which is computed as follows:

Contribution Margin per Aircraft Sold		
Selling price per aircraft		$100,000
Variable cost of goods sold per aircraft	$25,000	
Variable selling and administrative expense per aircraft	10,000	35,000
Contribution margin per aircraft		$ 65,000

The variable costing net operating income for each period can always be computed by multiplying the number of units sold by the contribution margin per unit and then subtracting total fixed expenses. For Weber Light Aircraft, these computations would appear as follows:

	January	February	March
Number of aircraft sold	1	1	5
Contribution margin per aircraft	× $ 65,000	× $ 65,000	× $ 65,000
Total contribution margin	$ 65,000	$ 65,000	$325,000
Total fixed expenses	90,000	90,000	90,000
Net operating income (loss)	$(25,000)	$(25,000)	$235,000

Notice, January and February have the same net operating loss. This occurs because one aircraft was sold in each month and, as previously mentioned, the selling price per aircraft, variable costs per aircraft, and total monthly fixed expenses remain constant.

Absorption Costing Income Statement

To prepare the company's absorption costing income statements for January, February, and March, we begin by computing each month's unit product cost. Under absorption costing, the unit product costs include variable production costs and fixed manufacturing overhead costs as shown below:

Absorption Costing Unit Product Cost			
	January	February	March
Direct materials	$19,000	$19,000	$19,000
Direct labor	5,000	5,000	5,000
Variable manufacturing overhead	1,000	1,000	1,000
Fixed manufacturing overhead ($70,000 ÷ 1 unit produced in January; $70,000 ÷ 2 units produced in February; $70,000 ÷ 4 units produced in March) ...	70,000	35,000	17,500
Unit product cost	$95,000	$60,000	$42,500

Notice in each month, Weber's fixed manufacturing overhead cost of $70,000 is divided by the number of units produced to determine the fixed manufacturing overhead cost per unit.

Given these unit product costs, the company's absorption costing net operating income in each month would be determined as shown in Exhibit 6–3.

EXHIBIT 6–3
Absorption Costing Income Statements

Absorption Costing Income Statements			
	January	February	March
Sales	$100,000	$100,000	$500,000
Cost of goods sold ($95,000 × 1 unit; $60,000 × 1 unit; $60,000 × 1 unit + $42,500 × 4 units) ...	95,000	60,000	230,000
Gross margin	5,000	40,000	270,000
Selling and administrative expenses	30,000	30,000	70,000
Net operating income (loss)	$ (25,000)	$ 10,000	$200,000

The sales for all three months in Exhibit 6–3 are the same as the sales shown in the variable costing income statements. The January cost of goods sold includes one unit produced in January at a cost of $95,000. The February cost of goods sold includes one unit produced in February at a cost of $60,000. The March cost of goods sold ($230,000) includes one unit produced in February at a cost of $60,000 plus four units produced in March with a total cost of $170,000 (= 4 units produced × $42,500 per unit). The selling and administrative expenses equal the amounts reported in the variable costing income statements; however, they are reported as one amount rather than being separated into variable and fixed components.

Note that even though sales were exactly the same in January and February and the cost structure did not change, the absorption net operating income was $35,000 higher in February than in January. This occurs because one aircraft produced in February is not sold until March. This aircraft has $35,000 of fixed manufacturing overhead attached to it that was incurred in February but will not be included in cost of goods sold until March.

Reconciliation of Variable Costing with Absorption Costing Income

LO6–3
Reconcile variable costing and absorption costing net operating incomes and explain why the two amounts differ.

As noted earlier, variable costing and absorption costing net operating incomes may not be the same. In the case of Weber Light Aircraft, the net operating incomes are the same in January but differ in the other two months. These differences occur because under absorption costing some fixed manufacturing overhead is capitalized in inventories (i.e., included in product costs) rather than being immediately expensed on the income statement. If inventories increase during a period, under absorption costing some of the fixed manufacturing overhead of the current period will be *deferred* in ending inventories. For example, in February two aircraft were produced, and each carried with it $35,000 (= $70,000 ÷ 2 aircraft produced) in fixed manufacturing overhead. Because only one aircraft was sold, $35,000 of this fixed manufacturing overhead was on February's absorption costing income statement as part of cost of goods sold, whereas the other $35,000 attached to the unsold aircraft would be included in February's ending finished goods inventory on the balance sheet. In contrast, under variable costing, *all* of the $70,000 of fixed manufacturing overhead appeared on the February income statement as a period expense. Consequently, February's net operating income was $35,000 higher under absorption costing than under variable costing. This was reversed in March when four units were produced, but five were sold. In March, under absorption costing, $105,000 of fixed manufacturing overhead was included in cost of goods sold ($35,000 for the unit *released* from February's ending inventory plus $17,500 for each of the four units produced and sold in March), but only $70,000 was recognized as a period expense under variable costing. Hence, March's net operating income was $35,000 lower under absorption costing than under variable costing.

These differences in variable and absorption costing net operating income can be explained using a two-step process. The first step uses the equation shown below to calculate each month's fixed manufacturing overhead deferred in (released from) inventories:

$$
\begin{array}{ccc}
\text{Fixed manufacturing overhead} & \text{Fixed manufacturing} & \text{Fixed manufacturing} \\
\text{deferred in} & = \quad \text{overhead in} \quad - & \text{overhead in} \\
\text{(released from) inventory} & \text{ending inventories} & \text{beginning inventories}
\end{array}
$$

These calculations for Weber Light Aircarft are as follows:

Fixed Manufacturing Overhead Deferred in, or Released from, Inventories under Absorption Costing			
	January	February	March
Fixed manufacturing overhead in ending inventories	$0	$ 35,000	$ 0
Deduct: Fixed manufacturing overhead in beginning inventories	0	0	35,000
Fixed manufacturing overhead deferred in (released from) inventories	$0	$ 35,000	$(35,000)

The second step is to use the equation shown below to reconcile the variable and absorption costing net operating incomes:

$$\begin{matrix} \text{Absorption costing} \\ \text{net operating} \\ \text{income (loss)} \end{matrix} = \begin{matrix} \text{Variable costing} \\ \text{net operating} \\ \text{income (loss)} \end{matrix} + \begin{matrix} \text{Fixed manufacturing} \\ \text{overhead deferred in} \\ \text{(released from) inventories} \end{matrix}$$

Exhibit 6–4 shows these calculations for Weber Light Aircraft.

EXHIBIT 6–4
Reconciliation of Variable Costing and Absorption Costing Net Operating Incomes

Reconciliation of Variable Costing and Absorption Costing Net Operating Incomes			
	January	February	March
Variable costing net operating income (loss).....	$(25,000)	$(25,000)	$235,000
Add fixed manufacturing overhead deferred in (released from) inventory under absorption costing	0	35,000	(35,000)
Absorption costing net operating income (loss) ...	$(25,000)	$ 10,000	$200,000

Exhibit 6–5 summarizes the reasons why variable costing and absorption costing net operating incomes differ from one another. When the units produced equal the units sold, which is the goal of lean production, inventories do not change; therefore, absorption costing net operating income equals variable costing net operating income. This occurs because both methods include *only* the current period's fixed manufacturing overhead in cost of goods sold. When the units produced exceed the units sold, inventories increase; therefore, absorption costing net operating income will exceed variable costing net operating income. This occurs because absorption costing defers some of the current period's fixed manufacturing overhead in ending inventories, whereas variable costing includes all of the current period's fixed manufacturing overhead in cost of goods sold. When the units produced are less than the units sold, inventories decrease; therefore, absorption costing net operating income will be less than variable costing net operating income. This occurs because absorption cost of goods sold includes all of the current period's

Relation between Production and Sales for the Period	Effect on Inventories	Relation between Absorption and Variable Costing Net Operating Incomes
Units produced = Units sold	No change in inventories	Absorption costing net operating income = Variable costing net operating income
Units produced > Units sold	Inventories increase	Absorption costing net operating income > Variable costing net operating income*
Units produced < Units sold	Inventories decrease	Absorption costing net operating income < Variable costing net operating income†

*Net operating income is higher under absorption costing because fixed manufacturing overhead cost is *deferred* in inventory under absorption costing as inventories increase.
†Net operating income is lower under absorption costing because fixed manufacturing overhead cost is *released* from inventory under absorption costing as inventories decrease.

EXHIBIT 6–5
Comparative Income Effects—
Absorption and Variable Costing

fixed manufacturing overhead plus some fixed overhead released from the prior period's ending inventory, whereas variable cost of goods sold includes only the current period's fixed manufacturing overhead.[2]

IN BUSINESS

SUPPLY CHAIN'S CHAIN REACTION

The COVID-19 pandemic caused raw materials procurement challenges, bloating inventories for many automobile manufacturers and suppliers. For example, a semiconductor shortage caused General Motors and Ford to pause their production lines, leading to thousands of unfinished vehicles being stored at abandoned racetracks and airport parking lots awaiting computer chips. These disruptions in production triggered a chain reaction that left many "upstream" automotive suppliers such as Howmet Aerospace with excess inventories of aluminum truck wheels stacked up on its factory floors.

Source: Bob Tita, "Products Wait Unfinished for Parts," *The Wall Street Journal,* August 31, 2021, https://www.wsj.com/articles/unfinished-tractors-pickup-trucks-pile-up-as-components-run-short-11630321200.

Jeffrey Scott Dean/Bloomberg via Getty Images

Advantages of Variable Costing and the Contribution Approach

Variable costing, together with the contribution approach, offers appealing advantages for internal reports that do not exist under absorption costing. This section discusses three of those advantages.

---

[2] These general statements about the relation between variable costing and absorption costing net operating income assume LIFO is used to value inventories. Even when LIFO is not used, the general statements tend to be correct. Although U.S. GAAP allows LIFO and FIFO inventory flow assumptions, International Financial Reporting Standards do not allow a LIFO inventory flow assumption.

Enabling CVP Analysis

Variable costing income statements enable cost-volume-profit (CVP) analysis because they categorize costs as variable and fixed. For example, let's suppose Weber Light Aircraft is interested in computing the sales needed to attain a target profit of $235,000. A CVP analysis based on the January variable costing income statement from Exhibit 6–2 would proceed as follows:

Sales (a)	$100,000
Contribution margin (b)	$65,000
Contribution margin ratio (b) ÷ (a)	65%
Total fixed expenses	$90,000

$$\text{Dollar sales to attain target profit} = \frac{\text{Target profit} + \text{Fixed expenses}}{\text{CM ratio}}$$

$$= \frac{\$235,000 + \$90,000}{0.65} = \$500,000$$

Thus, a CVP analysis based on the January variable costing income statement predicts that sales of $500,000 are needed to attain a target profit of $235,000. And indeed, the month of March shows that when sales are $500,000, the variable costing net operating income *is* $235,000. Conversely, March's absorption costing income is *not* $235,000. This counter-intuitive result arises because absorption costing income is influenced by unit sales *and* changes in inventories. In March, inventories decreased, so some of the fixed manufacturing overhead that had been deferred in February's ending inventories was released to the March income statement, resulting in a net operating income that is $35,000 lower than the $235,000 predicted by CVP analysis.

Explaining Changes in Net Operating Income

Under variable costing the number of units produced does not affect net operating income; therefore, when sales go up or down, profits move in the same direction. When sales are constant, net operating income is constant. So, in the months of January and February, when sales hold steady at $100,000, the net operating loss of $(25,000) remains the same too. This intuitive relationship between sales and profits does not exist in absorption costing. So, even though January and February sales are the same, the absorption income in February is $35,000 higher than in January. This occurs because in January one unit is produced and sold, so all of that month's fixed overhead ($70,000) is included in cost of goods sold. In February, two units are produced and one is sold, so half of that month's fixed overhead ($35,000) is deferred in ending inventories rather than being included in cost of goods sold.

Absorption costing income statements can be confusing and are easily misinterpreted. Look again at the absorption costing income statements in Exhibit 6–3. A manager might wonder why net operating income went up from January to February even though sales were exactly the same. Was it a result of lower selling costs, more efficient operations, or some other factor? In fact, it was simply because the number of units produced exceeded the number of units sold in February, and so some of the fixed manufacturing overhead costs were deferred in inventories in that month. These costs have not gone away—they will eventually flow through the income statement in a later period when inventories go down. There is no way to tell this from the absorption costing income statements.

Supporting Decision Making

Variable costing correctly identifies the additional variable costs incurred to make one more unit. It also emphasizes the impact of fixed costs on profits. The total amount of fixed manufacturing costs appears explicitly on the income statement, highlighting that the whole amount of fixed manufacturing costs must be covered for the company to be truly profitable. In the Weber Light Aircraft example, the variable costing income statements correctly report that the cost of producing another unit is $25,000 and they explicitly recognize that $70,000 of fixed manufacturing overhead must be covered to earn a profit.

Under absorption costing, fixed manufacturing overhead costs appear to be variable with respect to the number of units sold, but they are not. For example, in January, the absorption unit product cost at Weber Light Aircraft is $95,000, but the variable portion of this cost is only $25,000. The fixed overhead costs of $70,000 are commingled with variable production costs, thereby tempting, managers to mistakenly believe if another unit is produced, it will cost the company $95,000.

Segmented Income Statements and the Contribution Approach

In the remainder of the chapter, we'll learn how to use the contribution approach to create segmented income statements that are useful for analyzing the profitability of segments, making decisions, and measuring the performance of segment managers.

Traceable and Common Fixed Costs and the Segment Margin

This section defines three new terms needed to prepare segmented income statements using the contribution approach—*traceable fixed cost, common fixed cost,* and *segment margin.*

A **traceable fixed cost** is a fixed cost incurred because of the existence of a segment—if the segment had never existed, the fixed cost would not have been incurred; and if the segment is eliminated, the fixed cost will disappear. Examples of traceable fixed costs include the following:

- The salary of the Fritos product manager at PepsiCo is a *traceable* fixed cost of the Fritos business segment of PepsiCo.
- The maintenance cost for the building in which Boeing 747s are assembled is a *traceable* fixed cost of the 747 business segment of Boeing.
- The liability insurance at Disney World is a *traceable* fixed cost of the Disney World business segment of The Walt Disney Corporation.

A **common fixed cost** is a fixed cost that supports the operations of more than one segment but is not traceable in whole or in part to any one segment. Even if a segment is entirely eliminated, the common fixed costs will not change. For example:

- The salary of the CEO of General Motors is a *common* fixed cost of the various divisions of General Motors.
- The cost of heating a Safeway or Kroger grocery store is a *common* fixed cost of the store's various departments—groceries, produce, bakery, meat, and so forth.
- The cost of the receptionist's salary at an office shared by a number of doctors is a *common* fixed cost of the doctors. The cost is traceable to the office, but not to individual doctors.

To prepare a segmented income statement, each segment's variable expenses are deducted from its sales to determine its contribution margin. The contribution margin tells us what happens to profits as unit sales change—holding a segment's capacity and fixed costs constant. The contribution margin is especially useful in decisions involving temporary uses of capacity such as special orders. These types of decisions often involve only sales and variable costs—the two components of contribution margin.

The **segment margin** is obtained by deducting each segment's traceable fixed costs from its contribution margin. It represents the margin available after a segment has covered all of its own costs. *The segment margin is the best gauge of the long-run profitability of a segment* because it includes only those costs that are caused by the segment. If a segment can't cover its own costs, then that segment probably should be dropped (unless it has important side effects on other segments). Notice, common fixed costs are not allocated to segments.

Identifying Traceable Fixed Costs

The distinction between traceable and common fixed costs is crucial in segment reporting because traceable fixed costs are charged to segments and common fixed costs are not. The general guideline is to treat as traceable costs *only those costs that would disappear over time if the segment itself disappeared.* For example, if one division within a company were sold or discontinued, it would no longer be necessary to pay that division manager's salary. Therefore, the division manager's salary would be classified as a traceable fixed cost of the division. On the other hand, the president of the company undoubtedly would continue to be paid even if one of many divisions was dropped. Therefore, the president's salary is common to the company's divisions and should not be charged to them. *Any allocation of common costs (such as depreciation of corporate facilities) to segments reduces the value of the segment margin as a measure of long-run segment profitability and segment performance.*

Traceable Fixed Costs Can Become Common Fixed Costs

Fixed costs that are traceable to one segment may be a common cost of another segment. For example, United Airlines might want a segmented income statement that shows the segment margin for a particular flight from Chicago to Paris further broken down into first-class, business-class, and economy-class segment margins. The fixed landing fee paid to Charles deGaulle Airport in Paris is a traceable cost of the flight, but it is a common cost of the first-class, business-class, and economy-class segments. Even if the first-class cabin is empty, the entire landing fee must be paid. So the landing fee is not a traceable cost of the first-class cabin. But on the other hand, paying the fee is necessary in order to have any first-class, business-class, or economy-class passengers. So the landing fee is a common cost of these three classes.

Vail Valley Foundation

SEGMENT REPORTING AT THE VILAR PERFORMING ARTS CENTER

The Vilar Performing Arts Center is a 535-seat theater located in Beaver Creek, Colorado, that presents an unusually wide variety of performances categorized into six business segments—Family Series, Broadway Series, Theatre/Comedy Series, Dance Series, Classical Series, and Concert Series. The executive director of the Vilar, Kris Sabel, must decide which shows to book, what financial terms to offer to the artists, what contributions are likely from underwriters (i.e., donors), and what prices to charge for tickets. He evaluates the profitability of the segments using segmented income statements that include traceable costs (such as the costs of transporting, lodging, and feeding the artists) and exclude common costs (such as his salary, the salaries of his staff, depreciation on the theater, and general marketing expenses).

Data concerning the Classical Series segment for one season appears below:

Number of shows		4
Number of seats budgeted		863
Number of seats sold		655
Average seats sold per show		164
Ticket sales	$46,800	
Underwriting (donors)...............	65,000	
Total revenue.......................		$111,800
Artists' fees........................	$78,870	
Other traceable expenses............	11,231	
Total expenses		90,101
Classical Series segment margin		$ 21,699

Although the Classical Series sold an average of only 164 seats per show, its overall segment margin ($21,699) is positive thanks to $65,000 of underwriting revenues from donors. Had common costs been allocated to the Classical Series, it may have appeared unprofitable and been discontinued—resulting in fewer shows during the season; less diverse programming; disappointment among a small, but dedicated, number of fans; and lower overall income for the Vilar due to the loss of its Classical Series segment margin.

Segmented Income Statements—An Example

ProphetMax, Inc., is a rapidly growing computer software company. Exhibit 6–6 shows its variable costing income statement for the most recent month. As the company has grown, its senior managers have asked for segmented income statements that could be used to make decisions and evaluate managerial performance. ProphetMax's controller responded by creating examples of contribution format income statements segmented by the company's divisions, product lines, and sales channels. She created Exhibit 6–7 to explain that ProphetMax's profits can be segmented into its two divisions—the Business Products Division and the Consumer Products Division. The Consumer Products Division's profits can be further segmented into the Clip Art and Computer Games product lines. Finally, the Computer Games product line's profits (within the Consumer Products Division) can be segmented into the Online Sales and Retail Stores sales channels.

EXHIBIT 6–6
ProphetMax, Inc.: Variable Costing
Income Statement

ProphetMax, Inc. Variable Costing Income Statement	
Sales	$ 500,000
Variable expenses:	
Variable cost of goods sold................	180,000
Other variable expenses	50,000
Total variable expenses	230,000
Contribution margin	270,000
Fixed expenses	256,500
Net operating income	$ 13,500

EXHIBIT 6–7
ProphetMax, Inc.: Examples of
Business Segments

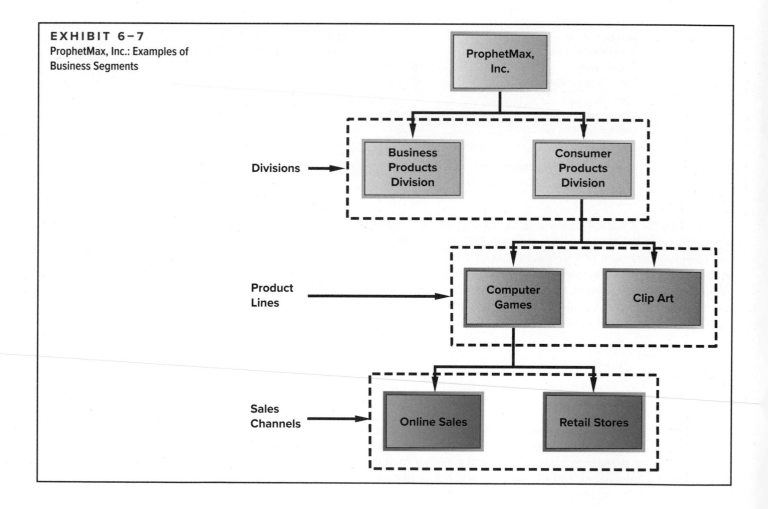

Levels of Segmented Income Statements

Exhibit 6–8 contains the controller's segmented income statements for the segments depicted in Exhibit 6–7. The contribution format income statement for the entire company appears at the very top of the exhibit under the column labeled Total Company. Notice the net operating income shown in this column ($13,500) is the same as the net operating income shown in Exhibit 6–6. Immediately to the right of the Total Company

EXHIBIT 6−8
ProphetMax, Inc.: Segmented
Income Statements in the
Contribution Format

Segments Defined as Divisions

	Total Company	Divisions Business Products Division	Divisions Consumer Products Division
Sales	$500,000	$300,000	$200,000
Variable expenses:			
Variable cost of goods sold	180,000	120,000	60,000
Other variable expenses	50,000	30,000	20,000
Total variable expenses	230,000	150,000	80,000
Contribution margin	270,000	150,000	120,000
Traceable fixed expenses	171,000	90,000	81,000
Divisional segment margin	99,000	$ 60,000	$ 39,000
Common fixed expenses not traceable to individual divisions	85,500		
Net operating income	$ 13,500		

Segments Defined as Product Lines of the Consumer Products Division

	Consumer Products Division	Product Line Clip Art	Product Line Computer Games
Sales	$200,000	$75,000	$125,000
Variable expenses:			
Variable cost of goods sold	60,000	20,000	40,000
Other variable expenses	20,000	5,000	15,000
Total variable expenses	80,000	25,000	55,000
Contribution margin	120,000	50,000	70,000
Traceable fixed expenses	70,000	30,000	40,000
Product-line segment margin	50,000	$20,000	$ 30,000
Common fixed expenses not traceable to individual product lines	11,000		
Divisional segment margin	$ 39,000		

Segments Defined as Sales Channels for One Product Line, Computer Games, of the Consumer Products Division

	Computer Games	Sales Channels Online Sales	Sales Channels Retail Stores
Sales	$125,000	$100,000	$25,000
Variable expenses:			
Variable cost of goods sold	40,000	32,000	8,000
Other variable expenses	15,000	5,000	10,000
Total variable expenses	55,000	37,000	18,000
Contribution margin	70,000	63,000	7,000
Traceable fixed expenses	25,000	15,000	10,000
Sales-channel segment margin	45,000	$ 48,000	$ (3,000)
Common fixed expenses not traceable to individual sales channels	15,000		
Product-line segment margin	$ 30,000		

column are two columns—one for each of the two divisions. We can see that the Business Products Division's traceable fixed expenses are $90,000 and the Consumer Products Division's are $81,000. These $171,000 of traceable fixed expenses (as shown in the Total Company column) plus the $85,500 of common fixed expenses not traceable to individual divisions equals ProphetMax's total fixed expenses ($256,500) as shown in Exhibit 6–6. We can also see that the Business Products Division's segment margin is $60,000 and the Consumer Products Division's is $39,000. These segment margins show the company's divisional managers how much each of their divisions is contributing to the company's profits.

The middle portion of Exhibit 6–8 further segments the Consumer Products Division into its two product lines—Clip Art and Computer Games. The dual nature of some fixed costs can be seen in this portion of the exhibit. Notice, in the top portion of Exhibit 6–8 when segments are defined as divisions, the Consumer Products Division has $81,000 in traceable fixed expenses. However, when we drill down to the product lines (in the middle portion of the exhibit), only $70,000 of the $81,000 expense that was traceable to the Consumer Products Division is traceable to the product lines. The other $11,000 becomes a common fixed expense of the two product lines of the Consumer Products Division.

Why would $11,000 of traceable fixed expense become a common fixed expense when the division is divided into product lines? The $11,000 is the monthly depreciation expense on a machine used to encase products in tamper-proof packages for the consumer market. The depreciation expense is a traceable cost of the Consumer Products Division as a whole, but it is a common cost of the division's two product lines. Even if one of the product lines were discontinued entirely, the machine would still be used to wrap the remaining products. Therefore, none of the depreciation expense can be traced to individual products. Conversely, the $70,000 traceable fixed expense can be traced to the individual product lines because it consists of the costs of product-specific advertising. A total of $30,000 was spent on advertising clip art and $40,000 was spent on advertising computer programs.

The bottom portion of Exhibit 6–8 further segments the Computer Games product line into two sales channels—Online Sales and Retail Stores. The dual nature of some fixed costs can also be seen in this portion of the exhibit. In the middle portion of Exhibit 6–8 when segments are defined as product lines, the Computer Games product line has $40,000 in traceable fixed expenses. However, when we look at the sales channels in the bottom portion of the exhibit, only $25,000 of the $40,000 that was traceable to Computer Games is traceable to the sales channels. The other $15,000 becomes a common fixed expense of the two sales channels for the Computer Games product line.

COMMUNICATING WITH DATA VISUALIZATIONS

Descriptive analytics answer the question: What happened? This visualization is based on Exhibit 6–8, and it depicts ProphetMax's sales by business segments. The first bar splits the company's total sales ($500,000) into the Business Products Division ($300,000) and Consumer Products Division ($200,000). The second bar splits the Consumer Products Division ($200,000) into its product lines—Clip Art ($75,000) and Computer Games ($125,000). The third bar splits Computer Games ($125,000) into two sales channels—Online Sales ($100,000) and Retail Stores ($25,000).

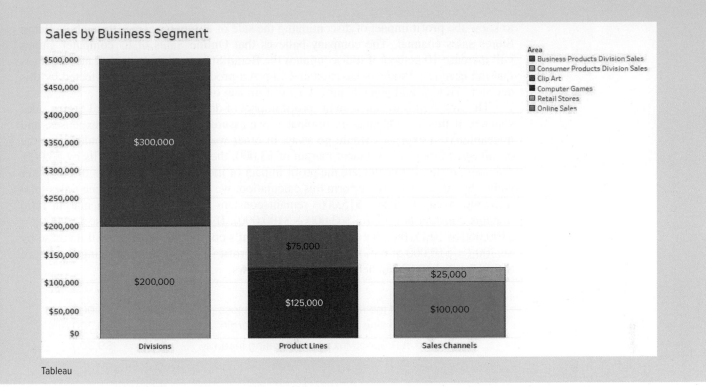

Sales by Business Segment

Area
- Business Products Division Sales
- Consumer Products Division Sales
- Clip Art
- Computer Games
- Retail Stores
- Online Sales

Tableau

IN BUSINESS

ZARA MAKES POST-PANDEMIC SHIFT TO ONLINE SALES

Inditex SA announced that its post-pandemic future includes closing 1,200 of its more than 7,400 retail store locations worldwide. The closures will "affect as many as 100 of Inditex's Zara, Massimo Dutti, Pull & Bear and other stores in the Americas . . . [that] currently account for between 5 percent and 6 percent in sales." Inditex plans to spend $1.13 billion on digital investments with the goal of boosting online sales from 14 percent to 25 percent of total sales. The company's accelerated shift from brick-and-mortar store locations to online sales punctuates "a yearslong reckoning brought about by a boom in online shopping."

Source: Saabira Chaudhuri, "Zara Owner to Shut 1,200 Stores in Online Push," *The Wall Street Journal,* June 11, 2020, p. B3.

Segmented Income Statements—Decision Making and Break-Even Analysis

Once a company prepares contribution format segmented income statements, it can use those statements to make decisions and perform break-even analysis.

Decision Making

Let's refer again to the bottom portion of Exhibit 6–8 to illustrate how segmented income statements support decision making. Notice Online Sales has a segment margin of $48,000 and Retail Stores has a segment margin of $(3,000). Let's assume that ProphetMax wants to know the profit impact of discontinuing the sale of computer games through its Retail Stores sales channel. The company believes that Online Sales of its computer games will increase 10 percent if it discontinues the Retail Stores sales channel. It also believes that the Business Products Division and Clip Art product line will be unaffected by this decision. How would you compute the profit impact of this decision?

The first step is to calculate the profit impact of discontinuing the Retail Stores sales channel. If this sales channel is eliminated, we assume its sales, variable expenses, and traceable fixed expenses would go away. In other words, the company could avoid the Retail Stores' negative segment margin of $3,000, thereby increasing profits by $3,000. The second step is to calculate the profit impact of increasing Online Sales of computer games by 10 percent. To perform this calculation, we assume that the Online Sales total traceable fixed expenses ($15,000) remain constant and its contribution margin ratio remains constant at 63% (= $63,000 ÷ $100,000). If Online Sales increase $10,000 (= $100,000 × 10%), then the Online Sales segment's contribution margin will increase by $6,300 (= $10,000 × 63%). Thus, the overall profit impact of discontinuing the Retail Stores sales channel can be summarized as follows:

Avoidance of the Retail Stores' segment loss	$3,000
Increase in Online Sales contribution margin	6,300
Increase in ProphetMax's net operating income	$9,300

LO6–5

Compute companywide and segment break-even points for a company with traceable fixed costs.

Break-Even Analysis

In Chapter 5, we learned how to compute a companywide break-even point for a multi-product company with no traceable fixed expenses. Now we are going to use the Prophet-Max, Inc., data in Exhibit 6–8 to explain how to compute companywide and segment break-even points for a company with traceable fixed expenses. Beginning with the companywide perspective, the formula for computing the break-even point for a multiproduct company with traceable fixed expenses is as follows:

$$\frac{\text{Dollar sales for company}}{\text{to break even}} = \frac{\text{Traceable fixed expenses} + \text{Common fixed expenses}}{\text{Overall CM ratio}}$$

In the case of ProphetMax, we should begin by reviewing the information in the Total Company column in the top portion of Exhibit 6–8. This column of data indicates that ProphetMax's total traceable fixed expenses are $171,000 and its total common fixed expenses are $85,500. Furthermore, the company's overall contribution margin of $270,000 divided by its total sales of $500,000 equals its overall CM ratio of 0.54. Given this information, ProphetMax's companywide break-even point is computed as follows:

$$\frac{\text{Dollar sales for company}}{\text{to break even}} = \frac{\text{Traceable fixed expenses} + \text{Common fixed expenses}}{\text{Overall CM ratio}}$$

$$= \frac{\$171,000 + \$85,500}{0.54}$$

$$= \frac{\$256,500}{0.54}$$

$$= \$475,000$$

This computation assumes a constant sales mix. In other words, it assumes 60 percent of the total sales ($300,000 ÷ $500,000) will always come from the Business Products Division and 40 percent ($200,000 ÷ $500,000) will always come from the Consumer Products Division.

To compute the break-even point for a business segment, the formula is as follows:

$$\text{Dollar sales for a segment to break even} = \frac{\text{Segment traceable fixed expenses}}{\text{Segment CM ratio}}$$

Exhibit 6–8 shows the Business Products Division's traceable fixed expenses are $90,000 and its CM ratio is 0.50 ($150,000 ÷ $300,000). Given this information, the Business Products Division's break-even point is computed as follows:

$$\text{Dollar sales for a segment to break even} = \frac{\text{Segment traceable fixed expenses}}{\text{Segment CM ratio}}$$

$$= \frac{\$90,000}{0.50}$$

$$= \$180,000$$

Similarly, Exhibit 6–8 shows the Consumer Products Division's traceable fixed expenses are $81,000 and its CM ratio is 0.60 ($120,000 ÷ $200,000); therefore, its break-even point is computed as follows:

$$\text{Dollar sales for a segment to break even} = \frac{\text{Segment traceable fixed expenses}}{\text{Segment CM ratio}}$$

$$= \frac{\$81,000}{0.60}$$

$$= \$135,000$$

Notice the sum of the segment break-even sales figures of $315,000 ($180,000 + $135,000) is less than the companywide break-even point of $475,000. This occurs because the segment break-even calculations *do not include the company's common fixed expenses,* which can be verified by preparing income statements based on each segment's break-even dollar sales:

	Total Company	Business Products Division	Consumer Products Division
Sales	$315,000	$180,000	$135,000
Variable expenses	144,000	90,000	54,000
Contribution margin	171,000	90,000	81,000
Traceable fixed expenses	171,000	90,000	81,000
Segment margin	0	$ 0	$ 0
Common fixed expenses	85,500		
Net operating loss	$ (85,500)		

When each segment achieves its break-even point, the company's overall net operating loss of $85,500 equals its common fixed expenses of $85,500. This reality can often lead managers astray when making decisions. In an attempt to "cover the company's common fixed expenses," managers often allocate common fixed expenses to business segments when performing break-even calculations and making decisions. *This is a mistake!* Allocating common fixed expenses to business segments artificially inflates each segment's break-even point. This may cause managers to erroneously discontinue business segments where the inflated break-even point appears unobtainable. The decision to retain or discontinue a business segment should be based on the sales and expenses that would disappear if the segment were dropped. Because common fixed expenses *will persist even if a business segment is dropped,* they should not be allocated to business segments when making decisions.

MICROSOFT SHIFTS ITS ATTENTION TO CLOUD COMPUTING

For decades Microsoft Corporation and its iconic franchise Windows were synonymous. Even today, more than 1.5 billion devices still use some version of Windows software. Nonetheless, the company has diversified beyond Windows given the industry's "irreversible migration from personal computing to mobile devices and the web." Now Microsoft is placing greater emphasis on Azure, its cloud computing operation, as well as its Office 365 and Dynamics business-software services segments.

While Microsoft's personal computing business, which includes Windows, still accounts for 42 percent of the company's total revenue, the revenue growth rate in this segment is only 2 percent. Conversely, Azure's revenue has jumped by 98 percent, and Office 365's sales have grown by 41 percent.

Source: Jay Greene, "Microsoft Looks Beyond Windows," *The Wall Street Journal,* March 30, 2018, pp. B1–B2.

Segmented Income Statements—Common Mistakes

All of the costs attributable to a segment—and only those costs—should be assigned to the segment. Unfortunately, companies often make mistakes when assigning costs to segments. They omit some costs, inappropriately assign traceable fixed costs, and arbitrarily allocate common fixed costs.

Omission of Costs

The costs assigned to a segment should include all costs attributable to that segment from the company's entire value chain. However, when companies use absorption costing for internal management purposes, they *only* assign manufacturing costs to their products, thereby overlooking "upstream" costs in the value chain, such as research and development and product design, and "downstream" costs, such as marketing, distribution, and customer service. These nonmanufacturing costs are just as essential in measuring product profitability as are the manufacturing costs, yet the absorption costing approach ignores them—causing managers to unwittingly develop and maintain undercosted products that result in losses.

Inappropriate Methods for Assigning Traceable Costs among Segments

In addition to omitting costs, many companies do not correctly report traceable fixed expenses on segmented income statements. They do not trace fixed expenses to segments even when it is feasible to do so and they use inappropriate allocation bases to assign traceable fixed expenses to segments.

Failure to Trace Costs Directly   Costs that can be traced directly to segments should be charged directly to them and not allocated to other segments. For example, the rent for a branch office of an insurance company should be charged directly to the branch office rather than included in a companywide overhead pool that spreads the cost throughout the company.

Inappropriate Allocation Base   Some companies use arbitrary allocation bases to allocate costs to segments. For example, they allocate selling and administrative expenses on the basis of sales revenues. Thus, if a segment generates 20 percent of total company sales, it is allocated 20 percent of the company's selling and administrative expenses. Sales should only be used to allocate selling and administrative expenses to segments if a 10 percent increase in their sales will result in a 10 percent increase in selling and administrative expenses. To the extent these expenses are not driven by sales volume, they will be improperly allocated—with a disproportionately high percentage of the selling and administrative expenses assigned to the segments with the largest sales.

Arbitrarily Dividing Common Costs among Segments

The third business practice causing distorted segment costs is assigning nontraceable costs to segments. For example, some companies allocate the common costs of the corporate headquarters building to their products. However, in a multiproduct company, no single product is responsible for any significant amount of this cost. Even if a product were eliminated entirely, there would usually be no significant effect on any of the costs of the corporate headquarters building. In short, there is no cause-and-effect relationship between the cost of the corporate headquarters building and the existence of any one product. Consequently, arbitrarily allocating these common fixed costs to products artificially raises their costs and increases the possibility that truly profitable products may be erroneously discontinued. Furthermore, allocating common fixed costs to managers attempts to hold those managers accountable for costs they cannot control.

IN BUSINESS

AIRPORTS DIVERSIFY REVENUES THROUGH LAND DEVELOPMENT

The Pittsburgh International Airport has historically derived most of its revenue from providing aeronautical services to airline companies. However, the airport plans to change that by using 200 of its 3,000 acres to develop a new business segment—a campus for companies that use 3-D printing in their manufacturing. In fact, airport officials have already signed Arencibia, a "company that supplies and recycles gases for 3-D printing," as their first anchor tenant.

Other American airports are pursuing similar plans to diversify their revenues. For example, the Cincinnati/Northern Kentucky International Airport hopes to develop a 350-acre campus that will lure logistics providers such as Deutsche Post AG's DHL Americas. Airports in Asia, Europe, and the Middle East are also building mini-cities around their core facilities that include exhibition spaces, apartments, and office buildings.

Source: Keiko Morris, "Pittsburgh Airport Ramps Up Side Gig as Land Developer," *The Wall Street Journal,* December 18, 2019, p. B6.

Anne Kitzman/Shutterstock

Summary

Variable and absorption costing are alternative methods of determining unit product costs. Under variable costing, only those manufacturing costs that vary with output are treated as product costs. This includes direct materials, variable overhead, and ordinarily direct labor. Fixed manufacturing overhead is treated as a period cost and is expensed on the income statement as incurred. By contrast, absorption costing treats fixed manufacturing overhead as a product cost, along with direct materials, direct labor, and variable overhead. Under both costing methods, selling and administrative expenses are treated as period costs and are expensed on the income statement as incurred.

Because absorption costing treats fixed manufacturing overhead as a product cost, a portion of fixed manufacturing overhead is assigned to each unit as it is produced. If units of product are unsold at the end of a period, then the fixed manufacturing overhead cost attached to those units is carried in ending inventory on the balance sheet rather than being recognized as an expense within cost of goods sold on the income statement. When these units are sold in a subsequent period, the fixed manufacturing overhead cost attached to them is released from the inventory account and recorded as part of cost of goods sold. Thus, under absorption costing, it is possible to defer a portion of the fixed manufacturing overhead cost from one period to a future period through the inventory account.

Unfortunately, this shifting of fixed manufacturing overhead cost between periods can cause erratic fluctuations in net operating income and can result in confusion and unwise decisions. To guard against mistakes when they interpret income statement data, managers should be alert to changes in inventory levels or unit product costs during the period.

Segmented income statements provide information for evaluating the profitability and performance of divisions, product lines, sales territories, and other segments of a company. Under the contribution approach, variable costs and fixed costs are clearly distinguished from each other and only those costs that are traceable to a segment are assigned to the segment. A cost is considered traceable to a segment only if the cost is caused by the segment and could be avoided by eliminating the segment. Fixed common costs are not allocated to segments. The segment margin consists of sales, less variable expenses, and less traceable fixed expenses of the segment.

   The dollar sales required for a segment to break even is computed by dividing the segment's traceable fixed expenses by its contribution margin ratio. A company's common fixed expenses should not be allocated to segments when performing break-even calculations because they will not change in response to segment-level decisions.

 Data Analytics Exercise available in Connect to complement this chapter

Review Problem 1: Contrasting Variable and Absorption Costing

Dexter Corporation produces and sells a single product, a wooden hand loom for weaving small items such as scarves. Selected cost and operating data relating to the product for two years are given below:

Selling price per unit	$50
Manufacturing costs:	
Variable manufacturing cost per unit produced:	
Direct materials.....................................	$11
Direct labor	$6
Variable manufacturing overhead	$3
Fixed manufacturing overhead per year	$120,000
Selling and administrative expenses:	
Variable selling and administrative per unit sold	$4
Fixed selling and administrative per year.............	$70,000

	Year 1	Year 2
Units in beginning inventory.......................	0	2,000
Units produced during the year	10,000	6,000
Units sold during the year	8,000	8,000
Units in ending inventory	2,000	0

Required:
1. Assume the company uses absorption costing.
    a. Compute the unit product cost in each year.
    b. Prepare an income statement for each year.
2. Assume the company uses variable costing.
    a. Compute the unit product cost in each year.
    b. Prepare an income statement for each year.
3. Reconcile the variable costing and absorption costing net operating incomes.

Solution to Review Problem 1

1. a. Under absorption costing, all manufacturing costs, variable and fixed, are included in unit product costs:

	Year 1	Year 2
Direct materials	$11	$11
Direct labor	6	6
Variable manufacturing overhead	3	3
Fixed manufacturing overhead		
($120,000 ÷ 10,000 units)	12	
($120,000 ÷ 6,000 units)................		20
Unit product cost	$32	$40

b. The absorption costing income statements follow:

	Year 1	Year 2
Sales (8,000 units × $50 per unit)	$400,000	$400,000
Cost of goods sold (8,000 units × $32 per unit);		
[(2,000 units × $32 per unit) +		
(6,000 units × $40 per unit)]	256,000	304,000
Gross margin	144,000	96,000
Selling and administrative expenses		
(8,000 units × $4 per unit + $70,000)	102,000	102,000
Net operating income (loss)	$ 42,000	$ (6,000)

2. a. Under variable costing, only the variable manufacturing costs are included in unit product costs:

	Year 1	Year 2
Direct materials	$11	$11
Direct labor	6	6
Variable manufacturing overhead	3	3
Unit product cost	$20	$20

b. The variable costing income statements follow:

	Year 1		Year 2	
Sales (8,000 units × $50 per unit)		$400,000		$400,000
Variable expenses:				
Variable cost of goods sold				
(8,000 units × $20 per unit)	$160,000		$160,000	
Variable selling and administrative				
expenses (8,000 units × $4 per unit)	32,000	192,000	32,000	192,000
Contribution margin		208,000		208,000
Fixed expenses:				
Fixed manufacturing overhead.	$120,000		$120,000	
Fixed selling and administrative				
expenses	70,000	190,000	70,000	190,000
Net operating income		$ 18,000		$ 18,000

3. The reconciliation of the variable and absorption costing net operating incomes follows:

	Year 1	Year 2
Fixed manufacturing overhead in ending inventories		
(2,000 units × $12 per unit; 0 units × $20 per unit)	$24,000	$ 0
Deduct: Fixed manufacturing overhead in beginning		
inventories (0; 2,000 units × $12 per unit).	0	24,000
Fixed manufacturing overhead deferred in		
(released from) inventories	$24,000	$ (24,000)

	Year 1	Year 2
Variable costing net operating income	$18,000	$ 18,000
Add: Fixed manufacturing overhead costs deferred		
in inventory under absorption costing		
(2,000 units × $12 per unit)	24,000	
Deduct: Fixed manufacturing overhead costs released		
from inventory under absorption costing		
(2,000 units × $12 per unit)		(24,000)
Absorption costing net operating income (loss)	$ 42,000	$ (6,000)

Review Problem 2: Segmented Income Statements

The business staff of the law firm Frampton, Davis & Smythe has constructed the following report that breaks down the firm's overall results for last month into two business segments—family law and commercial law:

	Company Total	Family Law	Commercial Law
Revenues from clients	$1,000,000	$400,000	$600,000
Variable expenses	220,000	100,000	120,000
Contribution margin	780,000	300,000	480,000
Traceable fixed expenses	670,000	280,000	390,000
Segment margin	110,000	20,000	90,000
Common fixed expenses.	60,000	24,000	36,000
Net operating income (loss)	$ 50,000	$ (4,000)	$ 54,000

However, this report is not quite correct. The common fixed expenses such as the managing partner's salary, general administrative expenses, and general firm advertising have been allocated to the two segments based on revenues from clients.

Required:

1. Redo the segment report, eliminating the allocation of common fixed expenses. Would the firm be better off financially if the family law segment were dropped? (Note: Many of the firm's commercial law clients also use the firm for their family law requirements such as drawing up wills.)

2. The firm's advertising agency has proposed an ad campaign targeted at boosting the revenues of the family law segment. The ad campaign would cost $20,000, and the advertising agency claims it would increase family law revenues by $100,000. The managing partner of Frampton, Davis & Smythe believes this increase in business could be accommodated without any increase in fixed expenses. Estimate the effect this ad campaign would have on the family law segment margin and on the firm's overall net operating income.

3. Compute the companywide break-even point in dollar sales and the dollar sales required for each business segment to break even.

Solution to Review Problem 2

1. The corrected segmented income statement appears below:

	Company Total	Family Law	Commercial Law
Revenues from clients	$1,000,000	$400,000	$600,000
Variable expenses	220,000	100,000	120,000
Contribution margin	780,000	300,000	480,000
Traceable fixed expenses	670,000	280,000	390,000
Segment margin	110,000	$ 20,000	$ 90,000
Common fixed expenses.	60,000		
Net operating income	$ 50,000		

No, the firm would not be better off financially if the family law practice were dropped. The family law segment is covering all of its own costs and is contributing $20,000 per month to covering the common fixed expenses of the firm. While the segment margin for family law is much lower than for commercial law, it is still profitable. Moreover, family law may be a service the firm must provide to its commercial clients in order to remain competitive.

2. The ad campaign would increase the family law segment margin by $55,000 as follows:

Increased revenues from clients	$100,000
Family law contribution margin ratio ($300,000 ÷ $400,000)	× 75%
Increased contribution margin	$ 75,000
Less cost of the ad campaign	20,000
Increased segment margin	$ 55,000

Because there would be no increase in fixed expenses (including common fixed expenses), the increase in overall net operating income is also $55,000.

3. The companywide break-even point is computed as follows:

$$\text{Dollar sales for company to break even} = \frac{\text{Traceable fixed expenses} + \text{Common fixed expenses}}{\text{Overall CM ratio}}$$

$$= \frac{\$670,000 + \$60,000}{0.78}$$

$$= \frac{\$730,000}{0.78}$$

$$= \$935,897 \text{ (rounded)}$$

The break-even point for the family law segment is computed as follows:

$$\text{Dollar sales for a segment to break even} = \frac{\text{Segment traceable fixed expenses}}{\text{Segment CM ratio}}$$

$$= \frac{\$280,000}{0.75}$$

$$= \$373,333 \text{ (rounded)}$$

The break-even point for the commercial law segment is computed as follows:

$$\text{Dollar sales for a segment to break even} = \frac{\text{Segment traceable fixed expenses}}{\text{Segment CM ratio}}$$

$$= \frac{\$390,000}{0.80}$$

$$= \$487,500$$

Glossary

Absorption costing A costing method that includes all manufacturing costs—direct materials, direct labor, and both variable and fixed manufacturing overhead—in unit product costs. (p. 254)

Common fixed cost A fixed cost supporting more than one business segment, but not traceable in whole or in part to any of those segments. (p. 263)

Segment Any part or activity of an organization about which managers seek cost, revenue, or profit data. (p. 254)

Segment margin A segment's contribution margin less its traceable fixed costs. It represents the margin available after a segment has covered all of its own traceable costs. (p. 263)

Traceable fixed cost A fixed cost incurred because of the existence of a particular business segment that would be eliminated if the segment were eliminated. (p. 263)

Variable costing A costing method that includes only variable manufacturing costs—direct materials, direct labor, and variable manufacturing overhead—in unit product costs. (p. 254)

Questions

6–1 What is the difference between absorption costing and variable costing?

6–2 Are selling and administrative expenses treated as product costs or as period costs under variable costing?

6–3 Explain how fixed manufacturing overhead costs are shifted from one period to another under absorption costing.

6–4 What are the arguments in favor of treating fixed manufacturing overhead costs as product costs?

6–5 What are the arguments in favor of treating fixed manufacturing overhead costs as period costs?

6–6 If the units produced equals the units sold, which method would you expect to show the higher net operating income, variable costing or absorption costing? Why?

6–7 If the units produced exceed the units sold, which method would you expect to show the higher net operating income, variable costing or absorption costing? Why?

6–8 If fixed manufacturing overhead costs are released from inventory under absorption costing, what does this tell you about the level of production in relation to the level of unit sales?

6–9 Under absorption costing, how is it possible to increase net operating income without increasing sales?

6–10 How does Lean Production reduce or eliminate the difference in reported net operating income between absorption and variable costing?

6–11 What is a segment of an organization? Give several examples of segments.

6–12 What costs are assigned to a segment under the contribution approach?

6–13 Distinguish between a traceable fixed cost and a common fixed cost. Give several examples of each.

6–14 Explain how the contribution margin differs from the segment margin.

6–15 Why aren't common fixed costs allocated to segments under the contribution approach?

6–16 How is it possible for a fixed cost that is traceable to a segment to become a common fixed cost if the segment is divided into further segments?

6–17 Should a company allocate its common fixed costs to business segments when computing the break-even point for those segments? Why?

Applying Excel   connect

LO6–2

The Excel worksheet shown below recreates portions of Review Problem 1 relating to Dexter Corporation. The workbook, and instructions on how to complete the file, can be found in Connect.

	A	B	C	D	E	F
1	Chapter 6: Applying Excel					
2						
3	Data					
4	Selling price per unit	$50				
5	Manufacturing costs:					
6	Variable per unit produced:					
7	Direct materials	$11				
8	Direct labor	$6				
9	Variable manufacturing overhead	$3				
10	Fixed manufacturing overhead per year	$120,000				
11	Selling and administrative expenses:					
12	Variable per unit sold	$4				
13	Fixed per year	$70,000				
14						
15		Year 1	Year 2			
16	Units in beginning inventory	0				
17	Units produced during the year	10,000	6,000			
18	Units sold during the year	8,000	8,000			
19						
20	Enter a formula into each of the cells marked with a ? below					
21	Review Problem 1: Contrasting Variable and Absorption Costing					
22						
23	Compute the Ending Inventory					
24		Year 1	Year 2			
25	Units in beginning inventory	0	?			
26	Units produced during the year	?	?			
27	Units sold during the year	?	?			
28	Units in ending inventory	?	?			
29						
30	Compute the Absorption Costing Unit Product Cost					
31		Year 1	Year 2			
32	Direct materials	?	?			
33	Direct labor	?	?			
34	Variable manufacturing overhead	?	?			
35	Fixed manufacturing overhead	?	?			
36	Absorption costing unit product cost	?	?			
37						
38	Construct the Absorption Costing Income Statement					
39		Year 1	Year 2			
40	Sales	?	?			
41	Cost of goods sold	?	?			
42	Gross margin	?	?			
43	Selling and administrative expenses	?	?			
44	Net operating income	?	?			
45						
46	Compute the Variable Costing Unit Product Cost					
47		Year 1	Year 2			
48	Direct materials	?	?			
49	Direct labor	?	?			
50	Variable manufacturing overhead	?	?			
51	Variable costing unit product cost	?	?			
52						
53	Construct the Variable Costing Income Statement					
54		Year 1			Year 2	
55	Sales		?			?
56	Variable expenses:					
57	Variable cost of goods sold	?			?	
58	Variable selling and administrative expenses	?	?		?	?
59	Contribution margin		?			?
60	Fixed expenses:					
61	Fixed manufacturing overhead	?			?	
62	Fixed selling and administrative expenses	?	?		?	?
63	Net operating income		?			?
64						

Chapter 6 Form / Filled in Chapter 6 Form / Chapter 6

Microsoft Excel

You should proceed to the requirements below only after completing your worksheet. The LIFO inventory flow assumption is used throughout this problem.

Required:

1. Check your worksheet by changing the units sold in the Data to 6,000 for Year 2. The cost of goods sold under absorption costing for Year 2 should now be $240,000. If it isn't, check cell C41. The formula in this cell should be =IF(C26< C27,C26*C36+(C27–C26)*B36,C27*C36). If your worksheet is operating properly, the net operating income under both absorption costing and variable costing should be $(34,000) for Year 2. That is, the loss in Year 2 is $34,000 under both methods. If you do not get these answers, find the errors in your worksheet and correct them.

   Why is the absorption costing net operating income now equal to the variable costing net operating income in Year 2?

2. Enter the following data from a different company into your worksheet:

Data		
Selling price per unit	$75	
Manufacturing costs:		
Variable per unit produced:		
Direct materials	$12	
Direct labor.....................................	$5	
Variable manufacturing overhead	$7	
Fixed manufacturing overhead per year...........	$150,000	
Selling and administrative expenses:		
Variable per unit sold	$1	
Fixed per year	$60,000	
	Year 1	Year 2
Units in beginning inventory.......................	0	
Units produced during the year	15,000	10,000
Units sold during the year	12,000	12,000

   Is the net operating income under variable costing different in Year 1 and Year 2? Why or why not? Explain the relation between the net operating income under absorption costing and variable costing in Year 1. Explain the relation between the net operating income under absorption costing and variable costing in Year 2.

3. At the end of Year 1, the company's board of directors set a target for Year 2 net operating income of $500,000 under absorption costing. If this target is met, a large bonus would be paid to the CEO of the company. Keeping everything else the same from part (2) above, change the units produced in Year 2 to 50,000 units. Would this change result in a bonus being paid to the CEO? Do you think this change would be in the best interests of the company? What is likely to happen in Year 3 to the absorption costing net operating income if sales remain constant at 12,000 units per year?

The Foundational 15   Mc Graw Hill **connect**

LO6–1, LO6–2, LO6–3, LO6–4, LO6–5

Diego Company manufactures one product that is sold for $80 per unit in two geographic regions— East and West. The following information pertains to the company's first year of operations in which it produced 40,000 units and sold 35,000 units.

Variable costs per unit:	
Manufacturing:	
Direct materials	$24
Direct labor	$14
Variable manufacturing overhead	$2
Variable selling and administrative	$4
Fixed costs per year:	
Fixed manufacturing overhead	$800,000
Fixed selling and administrative expense	$496,000

The company sold 25,000 units in the East region and 10,000 units in the West region. It determined $250,000 of its fixed selling and administrative expense is traceable to the West region, $150,000 is traceable to the East region, and the remaining $96,000 is a common fixed expense. The company will continue to incur the total amount of its fixed manufacturing overhead costs as long as it continues to produce any amount of its only product.

Required:

Answer each question independently based on the original data unless instructed otherwise. You do not need to prepare a segmented income statement until question 13.

1. What is the unit product cost under variable costing?
2. What is the unit product cost under absorption costing?
3. What is the company's total contribution margin under variable costing?
4. What is the company's net operating income under variable costing?
5. What is the company's total gross margin under absorption costing?
6. What is the company's net operating income under absorption costing?
7. What is the difference between the variable costing and absorption costing net operating incomes? What is the cause of this difference?
8. What is the company's break-even point in unit sales? Is it above or below the actual unit sales? Compare the break-even point in unit sales to your answer for question 6 and comment.
9. If the sales volumes in the East and West regions had been reversed, what would be the company's overall break-even point in unit sales?
10. What would have been the company's variable costing net operating income if it had produced and sold 35,000 units? You do not need to perform any calculations to answer this question.
11. What would have been the company's absorption costing net operating income if it had produced and sold 35,000 units? You do not need to perform any calculations to answer this question.
12. If the company produces 5,000 fewer units than it sells in its second year of operations, will absorption costing net operating income be higher or lower than variable costing net operating income in Year 2? Why? No calculations are necessary.
13. Prepare a contribution format segmented income statement that includes a Total column and columns for the East and West regions.
14. Diego is considering eliminating the West region because an internally generated report suggests the region's total *gross margin* in the first year of operations was $50,000 less than its traceable fixed selling and administrative expenses. Diego believes if it drops the West region, the East region's sales will grow by 5% in Year 2. Using the contribution approach for analyzing segment profitability and assuming all else remains constant in Year 2, what would be the profit impact of dropping the West region in Year 2?
15. Assume the West region invests $30,000 in a new advertising campaign in Year 2 that increases its unit sales by 20%. If all else remains constant, what would be the profit impact of pursuing the advertising campaign?

Mc Graw Hill connect   **Exercises**

EXERCISE 6–1 Variable and Absorption Costing Unit Product Costs LO6–1

Ida Company produces a handcrafted musical instrument called a gamelan that is similar to a xylophone. The gamelans are sold for $850. Selected data for the company's operations last year follow:

Units in beginning inventory	0
Units produced	250
Units sold	225
Units in ending inventory	25
Variable costs per unit:	
Direct materials	$100
Direct labor	$320
Variable manufacturing overhead	$40
Variable selling and administrative	$20
Fixed costs:	
Fixed manufacturing overhead	$60,000
Fixed selling and administrative	$20,000

Required:

1.   Assume the company uses absorption costing. Compute the unit product cost for one gamelan.
2.   Assume the company uses variable costing. Compute the unit product cost for one gamelan.

EXERCISE 6–2 Variable Costing Income Statement; Explanation of Difference in Net Operating Income LO6–2

Refer to the data in Exercise 6–1 for Ida Company. The absorption costing income statement prepared by the company's accountant for last year appears as shown:

Sales	$191,250
Cost of goods sold	157,500
Gross margin	33,750
Selling and administrative expense	24,500
Net operating income	$ 9,250

Required:

1.   Under absorption costing, how much fixed manufacturing overhead cost is included in the company's inventory at the end of last year?
2.   Prepare an income statement for last year using variable costing. Explain the difference in net operating income between the two costing methods.

EXERCISE 6–3 Reconciliation of Absorption and Variable Costing Net Operating Incomes LO6–3

Jorgansen Lighting, Inc., manufactures heavy-duty street lighting systems for municipalities. The company uses variable costing for internal management reports and absorption costing for external reports. The company provided the following data:

	Year 1	Year 2	Year 3
Inventories:			
Beginning (units)	200	170	180
Ending (units)	170	180	220
Variable costing net operating income	$1,080,400	$1,032,400	$996,400

The company's fixed manufacturing overhead per unit was constant at $560 for all three years.

Required:

1.   Calculate each year's absorption costing net operating income. Present your answer in the form of a reconciliation report.
2.   Assume in Year 4 the company's variable costing net operating income was $984,400 and its absorption costing net operating income was $1,012,400.
     a.   Did inventories increase or decrease during Year 4?
     b.   How much fixed manufacturing overhead cost was deferred or released from inventory during Year 4?

EXERCISE 6–4 Basic Segmented Income Statement LO6–4

Royal Lawncare Company produces and sells two packaged products—Weedban and Greengrow. Revenue and cost information relating to the products follow:

	Product	
	Weedban	Greengrow
Selling price per unit	$6.00	$7.50
Variable expenses per unit	$2.40	$5.25
Traceable fixed expenses per year	$45,000	$21,000

Last year the company produced and sold 15,000 units of Weedban and 28,000 units of Greengrow. Its annual common fixed expenses are $33,000.

Required:
Prepare a contribution format income statement segmented by product lines.

EXERCISE 6–5 Companywide and Segment Break-Even Analysis LO6–5

Piedmont Company segments its business into two regions—North and South. The company prepared the contribution format segmented income statement as shown below:

	Total Company	North	South
Sales	$600,000	$400,000	$200,000
Variable expenses	360,000	280,000	80,000
Contribution margin	240,000	120,000	120,000
Traceable fixed expenses	120,000	60,000	60,000
Segment margin	120,000	$ 60,000	$ 60,000
Common fixed expenses	50,000		
Net operating income	$ 70,000		

Required:
1. Compute the companywide break-even point in dollar sales.
2. Compute the break-even point in dollar sales for the North region.
3. Compute the break-even point in dollar sales for the South region.

EXERCISE 6–6 Variable and Absorption Costing Unit Product Costs and Income Statements LO6–1, LO6–2

Lynch Company manufactures and sells a single product. The following costs were incurred during the company's first year of operations:

Variable costs per unit:	
Manufacturing:	
Direct materials	$6
Direct labor	$9
Variable manufacturing overhead	$3
Variable selling and administrative	$4
Fixed costs per year:	
Fixed manufacturing overhead	$300,000
Fixed selling and administrative	$190,000

During the year, the company produced 25,000 units and sold 20,000 units. The selling price of the company's product is $50 per unit.

Required:
1. Assume the company uses absorption costing:
   a. Compute the unit product cost.
   b. Prepare an income statement for the year.
2. Assume the company uses variable costing:
   a. Compute the unit product cost.
   b. Prepare an income statement for the year.

EXERCISE 6–7 Segmented Income Statement LO6–4

Shannon Company segments its income statement into North and South Divisions. The company's overall sales, contribution margin ratio, and net operating income are $500,000, 46%, and $10,000, respectively. The North Division's contribution margin and contribution margin ratio are $150,000 and 50%, respectively. The South Division's segment margin is $30,000. The company has $90,000 of common fixed expenses that cannot be traced to either division.

Required:

Prepare a segmented income statement for Shannon Company using the contribution format. For the company as a whole and for each division, show each item on the segmented income statements as a percent of sales.

EXERCISE 6–8 Deducing Changes in Inventories LO6–3

Parker Products, Inc., is a manufacturer whose absorption costing income statement reported sales of $123 million and a net operating loss of $18 million. According to a CVP analysis prepared for management, the company's break-even point is $115 million in sales.

Required:

Assuming the CVP analysis is correct, is it likely the company's inventory level increased, decreased, or remained unchanged during the year? Explain.

EXERCISE 6–9 Variable and Absorption Costing Unit Product Costs and Income Statements LO6–1, LO6–2, LO6–3

Walsh Company manufactures and sells one product. The following information pertains to each of the company's first two years of operations:

Variable costs per unit:	
Manufacturing:	
Direct materials	$25
Direct labor	$15
Variable manufacturing overhead	$5
Variable selling and administrative	$2
Fixed costs per year:	
Fixed manufacturing overhead	$250,000
Fixed selling and administrative expenses	$80,000

During its first year of operations, Walsh produced 50,000 units and sold 40,000 units. During its second year of operations, it produced 40,000 units and sold 50,000 units. The selling price of the company's product is $60 per unit.

Required:

1. Assume the company uses variable costing:
   a. Compute the unit product cost for Year 1 and Year 2.
   b. Prepare an income statement for Year 1 and Year 2.
2. Assume the company uses absorption costing:
   a. Compute the unit product cost for Year 1 and Year 2.
   b. Prepare an income statement for Year 1 and Year 2.
3. Explain the difference between variable costing and absorption costing net operating income in Year 1. Also, explain why the two net operating incomes differ in Year 2.

EXERCISE 6–10 Companywide and Segment Break-Even Analysis LO6–5

Crossfire Company segments its business into two regions—East and West. The company prepared a contribution format segmented income statement as shown below:

	Total Company	East	West
Sales	$900,000	$600,000	$300,000
Variable expenses	675,000	480,000	195,000
Contribution margin	225,000	120,000	105,000
Traceable fixed expenses	141,000	50,000	91,000
Segment margin	84,000	$ 70,000	$ 14,000
Common fixed expenses	59,000		
Net operating income	$ 25,000		

Required:

1. Compute the companywide break-even point in dollar sales.
2. Compute the break-even point in dollar sales for the East region.
3. Compute the break-even point in dollar sales for the West region.
4. Prepare a new segmented income statement based on the break-even dollar sales you computed in requirements 2 and 3. Use the same format as shown above. What is Crossfire's net operating income (loss) in your new segmented income statement?
5. Do you think Crossfire should allocate its common fixed expenses to the East and West regions when computing the break-even points for each region? Why?

EXERCISE 6–11 Segmented Income Statement LO6–4

Wingate Company, a wholesale distributor of electronic equipment, has been experiencing losses as shown by its most recent monthly contribution format income statement:

Sales	$1,000,000
Variable expenses	390,000
Contribution margin	610,000
Fixed expenses..........................	625,000
Net operating income (loss)	$ (15,000)

In an effort to resolve the problem, the company wants to prepare an income statement segmented by division. Accordingly, the Accounting Department provided the following information:

	Division		
	East	Central	West
Sales	$250,000	$400,000	$350,000
Variable expenses as a percentage of sales	52%	30%	40%
Traceable fixed expenses	$160,000	$200,000	$175,000

Required:

1. Prepare a contribution format income statement segmented by divisions.
2. The Marketing Department believes increasing the West Division's monthly advertising by $15,000 will increase that division's sales by 20%. Assuming these estimates are accurate, how much would the company's net operating income increase (decrease) if the proposal is implemented?

EXERCISE 6–12 Variable Costing Income Statement; Reconciliation LO6–2, LO6–3

Whitman Company has just completed its first year of operations. The company's absorption costing income statement for the year follows:

Whitman Company Income Statement	
Sales (35,000 units × $25 per unit).....................	$875,000
Cost of goods sold (35,000 units × $16 per unit)..........	560,000
Gross margin	315,000
Selling and administrative expenses	280,000
Net operating income	$ 35,000

The company's selling and administrative expenses consist of $210,000 per year in fixed expenses and $2 per unit sold in variable expenses. The $16 unit product cost given above is computed as follows:

Direct materials	$ 5
Direct labor	6
Variable manufacturing overhead	1
Fixed manufacturing overhead ($160,000 ÷ 40,000 units)........	4
Absorption costing unit product cost	$16

Required:

1. Redo the company's income statement in the contribution format using variable costing.
2. Reconcile any difference between the net operating income on your variable costing income statement and the net operating income on the absorption costing income statement above.

EXERCISE 6–13 Inferring Costing Method; Unit Product Cost LO6–1

Sierra Company incurs the following costs to produce and sell its only product.

Variable costs per unit:	
Direct materials	$9
Direct labor	$10
Variable manufacturing overhead	$5
Variable selling and administrative expenses	$3
Fixed costs per year:	
Fixed manufacturing overhead	$150,000
Fixed selling and administrative expenses	$400,000

During this year, 25,000 units were produced and 22,000 units were sold. The Finished Goods inventory account at the end of this year shows a balance of $72,000 for the 3,000 unsold units.

Required:

1. Calculate this year's ending balance in Finished Goods inventory two ways—using variable costing and using absorption costing. Does it appear the company is using variable costing or absorption costing to assign costs to the 3,000 units in its Finished Goods inventory?
2. Assume the company wishes to prepare this year's financial statements for its stockholders.
   a. Is Finished Goods inventory of $72,000 the correct amount to include on the balance sheet for external reporting purposes? Explain.
   b. What balance should be reported in the Finished Goods inventory account for external reporting purposes?

EXERCISE 6–14 Variable Costing Unit Product Cost and Income Statement; Break-Even Analysis LO6–1, LO6–2

Chuck Wagon Grills, Inc., makes a barbecue grill it sells for $210. Data for last year's operations follow:

Units in beginning inventory	0
Units produced	20,000
Units sold	19,000
Units in ending inventory	1,000
Variable costs per unit:	
Direct materials	$ 50
Direct labor	80
Variable manufacturing overhead	20
Variable selling and administrative	10
Total variable cost per unit	$160
Fixed costs:	
Fixed manufacturing overhead	$700,000
Fixed selling and administrative	285,000
Total fixed costs	$985,000

Required:

1. Assume the company uses variable costing. Compute the unit product cost for one barbecue grill.
2. Assume the company uses variable costing. Prepare a contribution format income statement for last year.
3. How many barbecue grills must be sold to break even?

EXERCISE 6–15 Absorption Costing Unit Product Cost and Income Statement LO6–1, LO6–2

Refer to the data in Exercise 6–14 for Chuck Wagon Grills. Assume in this exercise the company uses absorption costing.

Required:

1. Compute the unit product cost for one barbecue grill.
2. Prepare an income statement for last year.

EXERCISE 6–16 Working with a Segmented Income Statement; Break-Even Analysis LO6–4, LO6–5

Raner, Harris & Chan is a consulting firm specializing in information systems for medical and dental clinics. The firm has two offices—one in Chicago and one in Minneapolis. It classifies the direct costs of consulting jobs as variable costs. A contribution format segmented income statement for the company's most recent year is given below:

	Total Company		Office Chicago		Minneapolis	
Sales	$450,000	100%	$150,000	100%	$300,000	100%
Variable expenses	225,000	50%	45,000	30%	180,000	60%
Contribution margin	225,000	50%	105,000	70%	120,000	40%
Traceable fixed expenses	126,000	28%	78,000	52%	48,000	16%
Office segment margin	99,000	22%	$ 27,000	18%	$ 72,000	24%
Common fixed expenses not traceable to offices	63,000	14%				
Net operating income	$ 36,000	8%				

Required:

1. Compute the companywide break-even point in dollar sales. Also, compute the break-even point for the Chicago office and for the Minneapolis office. Is the companywide break-even point greater than, less than, or equal to the sum of the Chicago and Minneapolis break-even points? Why?
2. How much would the company's net operating income increase if Minneapolis increased its sales by $75,000 per year? Assume no change in cost behavior patterns.
3. Refer to the original data. Assume sales in Chicago increase by $50,000 next year and sales in Minneapolis and all fixed costs remain unchanged.
   a. Prepare a new segmented income statement for the company using the above format. Show both amounts and percentages.
   b. Compare the income statement you prepared in requirement 3a to the original data. Did the Chicago office's contribution margin ratio change? Why? Did its segment margin ratio change? Why?

EXERCISE 6–17 Working with a Segmented Income Statement LO6–4

Refer to the data in Exercise 6–16. Assume Minneapolis's sales by major market are:

	Minneapolis		Market Medical		Dental	
Sales	$300,000	100%	$200,000	100%	$100,000	100%
Variable expenses	180,000	60%	128,000	64%	52,000	52%
Contribution margin	120,000	40%	72,000	36%	48,000	48%
Traceable fixed expenses	33,000	11%	12,000	6%	21,000	21%
Market segment margin	87,000	29%	$ 60,000	30%	$ 27,000	27%
Common fixed expenses not traceable to markets	15,000	5%				
Office segment margin	$ 72,000	24%				

The company is planning a $5,000 advertising campaign next month in either the Medical or Dental market. Marketing studies indicate this campaign would increase Medical market sales by $40,000 or Dental market sales by $35,000.

Required:

1. How much would the company's profits increase (decrease) if it advertised in the Medical market?
2. How much would the company's profits increase (decrease) if it advertised in the Dental market?
3. Should the company advertise in the Medical or Dental market?
4. In Exercise 6–16, Minneapolis shows $48,000 in traceable fixed expenses. What happened to the $48,000 in this exercise?

Problems Mc Graw Hill connect

PROBLEM 6–18 Variable and Absorption Costing Unit Product Costs and Income Statements LO6–1, LO6–2

Haas Company manufactures and sells one product. The following information pertains to each of the company's first three years of operations:

Variable costs per unit:	
Manufacturing:	
Direct materials	$20
Direct labor	$12
Variable manufacturing overhead	$4
Variable selling and administrative	$2
Fixed costs per year:	
Fixed manufacturing overhead	$960,000
Fixed selling and administrative expenses	$240,000

During its first year of operations, Haas produced 60,000 units and sold 60,000 units. During its second year of operations, it produced 75,000 units and sold 50,000 units. In its third year, Haas produced 40,000 units and sold 65,000 units. The selling price of the company's product is $58 per unit.

Required:

1. Compute the company's break-even point in unit sales.
2. Assume the company uses variable costing:
   a. Compute the unit product cost for Year 1, Year 2, and Year 3.
   b. Prepare an income statement for Year 1, Year 2, and Year 3.
3. Assume the company uses absorption costing:
   a. Compute the unit product cost for Year 1, Year 2, and Year 3.
   b. Prepare an income statement for Year 1, Year 2, and Year 3.
4. Compare the net operating incomes you computed in requirements 2 and 3 to the break-even point in unit sales you computed in requirement 1. Which net operating income figures (variable costing or absorption costing) seem counterintuitive? Why?

PROBLEM 6–19 Variable Costing Income Statement; Reconciliation LO6–1, LO6–2, LO6–3

During Heaton Company's first two years of operations, it reported absorption costing net operating income as follows:

	Year 1	Year 2
Sales (@ $25 per unit)	$1,000,000	$1,250,000
Cost of goods sold (@ $18 per unit)	720,000	900,000
Gross margin	280,000	350,000
Selling and administrative expenses*	210,000	230,000
Net operating income	$ 70,000	$ 120,000

*$2 per unit variable; $130,000 fixed each year.

The company's $18 unit product cost is computed as follows:

Direct materials	$ 4
Direct labor	7
Variable manufacturing overhead	1
Fixed manufacturing overhead ($270,000 ÷ 45,000 units)	6
Absorption costing unit product cost	$18

Production and cost data for the first two years of operations are:

	Year 1	Year 2
Units produced	45,000	45,000
Units sold	40,000	50,000

Required:
1. Using variable costing, what is the unit product cost for both years?
2. What is the variable costing net operating income in Year 1 and in Year 2?
3. Reconcile the absorption costing and the variable costing net operating income figures for each year.

PROBLEM 6–20 Variable and Absorption Costing Unit Product Costs and Income Statements; Explanation of Difference in Net Operating Income LO6–1, LO6–2, LO6–3

High Country, Inc., produces and sells many recreational products. The company just opened a new plant to produce a folding camp cot that will be marketed throughout the United States. The following cost and revenue data relate to May, the first month of the plant's operation:

Beginning inventory	0
Units produced	10,000
Units sold	8,000
Selling price per unit	$75
Selling and administrative expenses:	
Variable per unit	$6
Fixed (per month)	$200,000
Manufacturing costs:	
Direct materials cost per unit	$20
Direct labor cost per unit	$8
Variable manufacturing overhead cost per unit	$2
Fixed manufacturing overhead cost (per month)	$100,000

Required:
1. Assume the company uses absorption costing.
   a. Calculate the camp cot's unit product cost.
   b. Prepare an income statement for May.
2. Assume the company uses variable costing.
   a. Calculate the camp cot's unit product cost.
   b. Prepare a contribution format income statement for May.
3. Explain the reason for any difference in the ending inventory balances under the two costing methods and the impact of this difference on reported net operating income.

PROBLEM 6–21 Segment Reporting and Decision Making LO6–4

Vulcan Company's contribution format income statement for June is as follows:

Vulcan Company Income Statement For the Month Ended June 30	
Sales	$750,000
Variable expenses	336,000
Contribution margin	414,000
Fixed expenses	378,000
Net operating income	$ 36,000

Management wants to improve profits and gathered the following data:

a. The company is divided into two sales territories—Northern and Southern. The Northern territory recorded $300,000 in sales and $156,000 in variable expenses during June; the remaining sales and variable expenses were recorded in the Southern territory. Fixed expenses of $120,000 and $108,000 are traceable to the Northern and Southern territories, respectively. The rest of the fixed expenses are common to the two territories.

b. The company is the exclusive distributor for two products—Paks and Tibs. Sales of Paks and Tibs totaled $50,000 and $250,000, respectively, in the Northern territory during June. Variable expenses are 22% of the selling price for Paks and 58% for Tibs. Cost records show $30,000 of the Northern territory's fixed expenses are traceable to Paks and $40,000 to Tibs, with the remainder common to the two products.

Required:

1. Prepare contribution format income statements showing the total company segmented by sales territories and then the Northern territory segmented by product line. Show each item on these segmented income statements as a percent of sales.
2. What insights would you share with management about the Northern and Southern territories?
3. What insights would you share with management about Paks and Tibs?

PROBLEM 6–22 Variable Costing Income Statements; Income Reconciliation LO6–1, LO6–2, LO6–3

Denton Company manufactures and sells a single product. Cost data for the product are given:

Variable costs per unit:	
Direct materials	$ 7
Direct labor	10
Variable manufacturing overhead	5
Variable selling and administrative	3
Total variable cost per unit	$25
Fixed costs per month:	
Fixed manufacturing overhead...................	$315,000
Fixed selling and administrative.................	245,000
Total fixed cost per month.......................	$560,000

The product sells for $60 per unit. Production and sales data for July and August, the first two months of operations, follow:

	Units Produced	Units Sold
July	17,500	15,000
August	17,500	20,000

The company's Accounting Department prepared the following absorption costing income statements for July and August:

	July	August
Sales	$900,000	$1,200,000
Cost of goods sold	600,000	800,000
Gross margin	300,000	400,000
Selling and administrative expenses	290,000	305,000
Net operating income	$ 10,000	$ 95,000

Required:
1. Determine the unit product cost under:
   a. Absorption costing.
   b. Variable costing.
2. Prepare variable costing income statements for July and August.
3. Reconcile the variable costing and absorption costing net operating incomes.
4. The Accounting Department determined the company's break-even point is 16,000 units per month, computed as follows:

$$\frac{\text{Fixed cost per month}}{\text{Unit contribution margin}} = \frac{\$560,000}{\$35 \text{ per unit}} = 16,000 \text{ units}$$

"I'm confused," said the president. "The accountants say our break-even point is 16,000 units per month, but we sold only 15,000 units in July, and the income statement they prepared shows a $10,000 profit for that month. Either the income statement is wrong or the break-even point is wrong." Prepare a brief memo for the president, explaining what happened on the July absorption costing income statement.

PROBLEM 6–23 Absorption and Variable Costing; Production Constant, Sales Fluctuate LO6–1, LO6–2, LO6–3

Tami Tyler opened Tami's Creations, Inc., a small manufacturing company, at the beginning of the year. Getting the company through its first quarter of operations placed a considerable strain on Ms. Tyler's personal finances. The following income statement for the first quarter was prepared by a friend who just completed a course in managerial accounting at State University.

Tami's Creations, Inc. Income Statement For the Quarter Ended March 31		
Sales (28,000 units)		$1,120,000
Variable expenses:		
Variable cost of goods sold......................	$462,000	
Variable selling and administrative	168,000	630,000
Contribution margin		490,000
Fixed expenses:		
Fixed manufacturing overhead....................	$300,000	
Fixed selling and administrative...................	200,000	500,000
Net operating loss		$ (10,000)

Ms. Tyler is discouraged over the loss shown for the quarter, particularly because she hoped to use the statement as support for a bank loan. Another friend, a CPA, insists the company should be using absorption costing rather than variable costing and claims if absorption costing had been used, the company probably would have reported a profit for the quarter.

At this point, Ms. Tyler makes only one product—a swimsuit. Production and cost data for the first quarter follow:

Units produced	30,000
Units sold	28,000
Variable costs per unit:	
Direct materials	$3.50
Direct labor	$12.00
Variable manufacturing overhead	$1.00
Variable selling and administrative	$6.00

Required:

1. Complete the following:
    a. Compute the unit product cost under absorption costing.
    b. What is the company's absorption costing net operating income (loss) for the quarter?
    c. Reconcile the variable and absorption costing net operating income (loss) figures.
2. Was the CPA correct in suggesting the company earned a "profit" for the quarter? Explain.
3. During the second quarter of operations, the company again produced 30,000 units but sold 32,000 units. (Assume no change in total fixed costs.)
    a. What is the company's variable costing net operating income (loss) for the second quarter?
    b. What is the company's absorption costing net operating income (loss) for the second quarter?
    c. Reconcile the variable costing and absorption costing net operating incomes for the second quarter.

PROBLEM 6–24 Companywide and Segment Break-Even Analysis; Decision Making LO6–4, LO6–5
Toxaway Company is a merchandiser with two divisions—Commercial and Residential. The company's accounting intern was asked to prepare segmented income statements the company's divisional managers could use to calculate their break-even points and make decisions. She took the prior month's companywide income statement and prepared the absorption format segmented income statement shown below:

	Total Company	Commercial	Residential
Sales	$750,000	$250,000	$500,000
Cost of goods sold	500,000	140,000	360,000
Gross margin	250,000	110,000	140,000
Selling and administrative expenses...........	240,000	104,000	136,000
Net operating income	$ 10,000	$ 6,000	$ 4,000

In preparing these statements, the intern determined Toxaway's only variable selling and administrative expense is a 10% sales commission on all sales. The company's total fixed expenses include $72,000 of common fixed expenses that will continue even if the Commercial or Residential segment is discontinued, $55,000 of fixed expenses that will disappear if the Commericial segment is dropped, and $38,000 of fixed expenses that will disappear if the Residential segment is dropped.

Required:

1. Do you agree with the intern's decision to use an absorption format for her segmented income statement? Why?
2. Based on a review of the intern's segmented income statement:
   a. How much of the company's common fixed expenses did she allocate to the Commercial and Residential segments?
   b. Which of the following three allocation bases did she most likely use to allocate common fixed expenses to the Commercial and Residential segments: (a) sales, (b) cost of goods sold, or (c) gross margin?
3. Do you agree with the intern's decision to allocate common fixed expenses to the Commercial and Residential segments? Why?
4. Redo the intern's segmented income statement using the contribution format.
5. Compute the companywide break-even point in dollar sales.
6. Compute the break-even point in dollar sales for the Commercial Division and for the Residential Division.
7. Assume the company decided to pay its sales representatives in the Commercial and Residential Divisions a total monthly salary of $15,000 and $30,000, respectively, and to lower its companywide sales commission percentage from 10% to 5%. Calculate the new break-even point in dollar sales for the Commercial Division and the Residential Division.

PROBLEM 6–25 Prepare and Interpret Income Statements; Changes in Both Sales and Production; Lean Production LO6–1, LO6–2, LO6–3

Starfax, Inc., manufactures a small part widely used in various electronic products. Results for the first three years of operations were as follows (absorption costing basis):

	Year 1	Year 2	Year 3
Sales	$800,000	$640,000	$800,000
Cost of goods sold	580,000	400,000	620,000
Gross margin	220,000	240,000	180,000
Selling and administrative expenses...............	190,000	180,000	190,000
Net operating income (loss)	$ 30,000	$ 60,000	$ (10,000)

In the latter part of Year 2, a competitor went out of business and dumped a large number of units on the market. As a result, Starfax's sales dropped by 20% during Year 2 even though production increased during the year. Management had expected sales to remain constant at 50,000 units; the increased production was designed to provide a buffer of protection against unexpected spurts in demand. By the start of Year 3, management had excess inventory and realized growth in demand was unlikely; thus, it cut back production throughout the year as shown below:

	Year 1	Year 2	Year 3
Production in units	50,000	60,000	40,000
Sales in units	50,000	40,000	50,000

Additional information about the company follows:

a. The company's plant is highly automated. Variable manufacturing expenses (direct materials, direct labor, and variable manufacturing overhead) total only $2 per unit, and fixed manufacturing overhead expenses total $480,000 per year.
b. A new fixed manufacturing overhead rate is computed each year based on that year's actual fixed manufacturing overhead costs divided by the actual number of units produced.
c. Variable selling and administrative expenses were $1 per unit sold in each year. Fixed selling and administrative expenses totaled $140,000 per year.
d. The company uses a FIFO inventory flow assumption. (FIFO means first-in first-out. In other words, it assumes the oldest units in inventory are sold first.)

Starfax's management can't understand why profits doubled during Year 2 when sales dropped by 20% and why a loss was incurred during Year 3 when sales recovered to previous levels.

Required:
1. Prepare a variable costing income statement for each year.
2. Refer to the absorption costing income statements above.
   a. Compute the unit product cost in each year under absorption costing. Show how much of this cost is variable and how much is fixed.
   b. Reconcile the variable costing and absorption costing net operating income figures for each year.
3. Refer again to the absorption costing income statements. Explain why net operating income was higher in Year 2 than Year 1 under the absorption approach, even though fewer units were sold in Year 2 than Year 1.
4. Refer again to the absorption costing income statements. Explain why the company suffered a loss in Year 3 but reported a profit in Year 1 although the same number of units was sold in each year.
5. a. Explain how operations would have differed in Year 2 and Year 3 if the company had been using Lean Production.
   b. If Lean Production had been used during Year 2 and Year 3, what would the company's net operating income (or loss) have been in each year under absorption costing? No computations are necessary.

PROBLEM 6–26 Restructuring a Segmented Income Statement LO6–4
Millard Corporation is a wholesale distributor of office products. It purchases office products from manufacturers and distributes them in the West, Central, and East regions. Each of these regions is about the same size, and each has its own manager and sales staff.

The company has been experiencing losses for many months. In an effort to improve profits, management prepared the segmented income statement for May as shown below.

	Sales Region		
	West	Central	East
Sales	$450,000	$800,000	$ 750,000
Regional expenses (traceable):			
Cost of goods sold	162,900	280,000	376,500
Advertising.......................................	108,000	200,000	210,000
Salaries..	90,000	88,000	135,000
Utilities	13,500	12,000	15,000
Depreciation	27,000	28,000	30,000
Shipping expense	17,100	32,000	28,500
Total regional expenses	418,500	640,000	795,000
Regional income (loss) before corporate expenses	31,500	160,000	(45,000)
Corporate expenses:			
Advertising (general)	18,000	32,000	30,000
General administrative expense	50,000	50,000	50,000
Total corporate expenses	68,000	82,000	80,000
Net operating income (loss)	$ (36,500)	$ 78,000	$(125,000)

The cost of goods sold and shipping expense are both variable. All other costs are fixed.

Required:
1. List any weaknesses that you see in the company's segmented income statement given above.
2. What allocation base is the company using to assign corporate expenses to the regions? Do you agree with this approach?

3. Prepare a new contribution format segmented income statement for May. Show a Total column and a column for each region. Show each item on the segmented income statement as a percent of the sales within its column.
4. Analyze the statement you prepared in part (3) above. What insights would you bring to management's attention?

PROBLEM 6–27 Incentives Created by Absorption Costing; Ethics and the Manager LO6–2

Carlos Cavalas, the manager of Echo Products' Brazilian Division, is setting the production schedule for the last quarter of the year. The Brazilian Division planned to sell 3,600 units during the year, but by September 30 only the following activity had been reported:

	Units
Inventory, January 1	0
Production	2,400
Sales	2,000
Inventory, September 30	400

The division can rent warehouse space to store up to 1,000 units. The minimum inventory level the division should carry is 50 units. The minimum production must be at least 200 units per quarter to retain a nucleus of key employees. Maximum production capacity is 1,500 units per quarter.

The sales forecast for the last quarter is only 600 units and fixed manufacturing overhead is a major element of product cost.

Required:

1. Assume the division is using variable costing. How many units should be scheduled for production during the last quarter of the year? (The basic formula for computing the required production for the quarter is Required production = Expected sales + Desired ending inventory − Beginning inventory.) Show computations and explain your answer. Will the number of units scheduled for production affect the division's reported income or loss for the year? Explain.
2. Assume the division is using absorption costing and the divisional manager is given an annual bonus based on divisional operating income. If Mr. Cavalas wants to maximize his division's operating income for the year, how many units should be scheduled for production during the last quarter? [See the formula in (1) above.] Explain.
3. Identify the ethical issues involved in the decision Mr. Cavalas must make about the level of production for the last quarter of the year.

PROBLEM 6–28 Companywide and Segment Break-Even Analysis LO6–5

Piedmont Fasteners Corporation makes three different clothing fasteners in its manufacturing facility in North Carolina. All three products are sold in highly competitive markets, so the company is unable to raise prices without losing an unacceptable number of customers. Data from the most recent period concerning these products appear below:

	Velcro	Metal	Nylon
Annual sales volume	100,000	200,000	400,000
Unit selling price	$1.65	$1.50	$0.85
Variable expense per unit	$1.25	$0.70	$0.25
Contribution margin per unit	$0.40	$0.80	$0.60

Total fixed expenses are $400,000 per period. Of the total fixed expenses, $20,000 could be avoided if the Velcro product is dropped, $80,000 if the Metal product is dropped, and $60,000 if the Nylon product is dropped. The remaining fixed expenses of $240,000 consist of common fixed expenses such as administrative salaries and rent on the factory building that could be avoided only by going out of business.

The company's managers would like to compute the break-even point in dollar sales for the company as a whole, and the break-even point in unit sales for each product. They are considering two methods for computing each product's break-even point in unit sales:

Method #1: Include each product's traceable fixed costs and an allocated share of the common fixed costs in the numerator of each break-even calculation. The common fixed costs would be allocated to the three products using sales dollars as the allocation base.

Method #2: Only include each product's traceable fixed costs in the numerator of each break-even calculation.

Required:

1. Using data from the most recent period, prepare a contribution format segmented income statement. What is the net operating income?
2. What is the company's over all break-even point in dollar sales?
3. Using method 1:
   a. Calculate the break-even point in unit sales for each product.
   b. What will be the company's overall profit if it sells exactly the break-even quantity of each product?
4. Using method 2:
   a. Calculate the break-even point in unit sales for each product.
   b. What will be the company's overall profit if it sells exactly the break-even quantity of each product?
5. Which method should the company use to calculate each product's break-even point in unit sales? Why?

Cases   Mc Graw Hill connect

Select cases are available in Connect.

CASE 6–29 Variable and Absorption Costing Unit Product Costs and Income Statements LO6–1, LO6–2

O'Brien Company manufactures and sells one product. The following information pertains to each of the company's first three years of operations:

Variable costs per unit:	
Manufacturing:	
Direct materials	$32
Direct labor	$20
Variable manufacturing overhead	$4
Variable selling and administrative	$3
Fixed costs per year:	
Fixed manufacturing overhead	$660,000
Fixed selling and administrative expenses	$120,000

During its first year of operations, O'Brien produced 100,000 units and sold 80,000 units. During its second year of operations, it produced 75,000 units and sold 90,000 units. In its third year, O'Brien produced 80,000 units and sold 75,000 units. The selling price of the company's product is $75 per unit.

Required:

1. Assume the company uses variable costing and a FIFO inventory flow assumption (FIFO means first-in first-out; in other words, it assumes the oldest units in inventory are sold first):
   a. Compute the unit product cost for Year 1, Year 2, and Year 3.
   b. Prepare an income statement for Year 1, Year 2, and Year 3.
2. Assume the company uses variable costing and a LIFO inventory flow assumption (LIFO means last-in first-out; in other words, it assumes the newest units in inventory are sold first):
   a. Compute the unit product cost for Year 1, Year 2, and Year 3.
   b. Prepare an income statement for Year 1, Year 2, and Year 3.

3. Assume the company uses absorption costing and a FIFO inventory flow assumption (FIFO means first-in first-out; in other words, it assumes the oldest units in inventory are sold first):
   a. Compute the unit product cost for Year 1, Year 2, and Year 3.
   b. Prepare an income statement for Year 1, Year 2, and Year 3.
4. Assume the company uses absorption costing and a LIFO inventory flow assumption (LIFO means last-in first-out; in other words, it assumes the newest units in inventory are sold first):
   a. Compute the unit product cost for Year 1, Year 2, and Year 3.
   b. Prepare an income statement for Year 1, Year 2, and Year 3.

CASE 6–30 Service Organization; Segment Reporting LO6–4

Music Teachers, Inc., is an educational association for music teachers with 20,000 members. The association operates from a central headquarters but has local membership chapters throughout the United States. Monthly meetings are held by the local chapters to discuss recent developments on topics of interest to music teachers. The association's magazine, *Teachers' Forum,* is issued monthly with features about recent developments in the field. The association publishes books and reports and also sponsors professional courses that qualify for continuing professional education credit. The association's statement of revenues and expenses for the current year is presented below.

Music Teachers, Inc. Statement of Revenues and Expenses For the Year Ended November 30	
Revenues	$3,275,000
Expenses:	
Salaries	920,000
Personnel costs	230,000
Occupancy costs	280,000
Reimbursement of member costs to local chapters	600,000
Other membership services	500,000
Printing and paper	320,000
Postage and shipping	176,000
Instructors' fees	80,000
General and administrative	38,000
Total expenses	3,144,000
Excess of revenues over expenses	$ 131,000

The board of directors of Music Teachers, Inc., wants a segmented income state showing the contribution of each segment to the association. The association has four divisions—Membership, Magazine Subscriptions, Books and Reports, and Continuing Education—and gathered the following data:

a. The 20,000 members of the association pay dues of $100 per year, of which $20 covers a one-year subscription to the *Teachers' Forum.* Other benefits include membership in the association and chapter affiliation. The portion of the dues covering the magazine subscription ($20) should be assigned to the Magazine Subscriptions Division.

b. A total of 2,500 one-year subscriptions to *Teachers' Forum* were also sold last year to nonmembers and libraries at $30 per subscription. In addition to subscriptions, the journal generated $100,000 in advertising revenues.

c. The costs to produce the *Teachers' Forum* magazine included $7 per subscription for printing and paper and $4 per subscription for postage and shipping.

d. A total of 28,000 technical reports and professional texts were sold by the Books and Reports Division at an average selling price per unit of $25. Average costs per publication were $4 for printing and paper and $2 for postage and shipping.

e. The association offers a variety of continuing education courses to both members and nonmembers. The one-day courses had a tuition cost of $75 each and were attended by 2,400 students. A total of 1,760 students took two-day courses at a tuition cost of $125 for each student. Outside instructors were paid to teach some courses.

f.   Salary costs and space occupied by division follow:

	Salaries	Space Occupied (square feet)
Membership......................	$210,000	2,000
Magazine Subscriptions	150,000	2,000
Books and Reports	300,000	3,000
Continuing Education	180,000	2,000
Corporate staff	80,000	1,000
Total............................	$920,000	10,000

Personnel costs are 25% of salaries in the separate divisions as well as for the corporate staff. The $280,000 in occupancy costs (which can be allocated to segments based on their square feet occupied) includes $50,000 in rental cost for a warehouse used by the Books and Reports Division for storage purposes.

g.   Printing and paper costs other than for magazine subscriptions and for books and reports relate to the Continuing Education Division.

h.   General and administrative expenses include costs relating to the administration of the association as a whole. The company's corporate staff does some mailing of materials for general administrative purposes.

The expenses traced or assigned to the corporate staff, as well as any other expenses not traceable to the segments, will be treated as common costs. It is not necessary to distinguish between variable and fixed costs.

Required:

1.   Prepare a segmented income statement for Music Teachers, Inc., that shows the segment margin for each division as well as results for the association as a whole.

2.   Give arguments for and against allocating all costs of the association to the four divisions.

(CMA, adapted)

Appendix 6A: Super-Variable Costing

LO6–6

Prepare an income statement using super-variable costing and reconcile this approach with variable costing.

In the discussion of variable costing in this chapter, we assumed direct labor and a portion of manufacturing overhead are variable costs that attach to products. However, these assumptions about cost behavior may not be true. For example, it may be easier and more accurate to assume *all* manufacturing overhead costs are fixed costs because the variable portion of these costs is insignificant or too difficult to estimate. Furthermore, many companies' labor costs (including direct and indirect labor) are more fixed than variable due to labor regulations, labor contracts, or management policy. In countries such as France, Germany, Spain, and Japan, management often has little flexibility in adjusting the labor force to changes in business activity. Even in countries such as the United States and the United Kingdom, where management usually has greater latitude to adjust the size of its labor force, many managers choose to view labor as a fixed cost. They make this choice because the cost savings from terminating or laying off employees during a short-term business downturn may be swamped by the negative effects on employee morale and the costs of later finding and training suitable replacements. Moreover, treating employees as variable costs subtly fosters the attitude that employees are expendable and replaceable like materials rather than unique, difficult-to-replace assets.

Super-variable costing is a variation on variable costing in which direct labor and manufacturing overhead costs are considered to be fixed. **Super-variable costing** classifies all direct labor and manufacturing overhead costs as fixed period costs and *only direct materials as a variable product cost*. To simplify, in this appendix we also assume that selling and administrative expenses are entirely fixed.

Super-Variable Costing and Variable Costing—An Example

To illustrate the difference between treating direct labor as a fixed cost (as in super-variable costing) and treating direct labor as a variable cost (as in variable costing), we will use a modified version of the Weber Light Aircraft example from the main body of the chapter. Data concerning the company's operations appear below:

	Per Aircraft	Per Month
Selling price	$100,000	
Direct materials	$19,000	
Direct labor		$20,000
Fixed manufacturing overhead.		$74,000
Fixed selling and administrative expense		$40,000

	January	February	March
Beginning inventory	0	0	1
Units produced	2	2	2
Units sold	2	1	3
Ending inventory	0	1	0

Notice in this example direct labor is a fixed cost—$20,000 per month. Also, Weber Light Aircraft has no variable manufacturing overhead costs and no variable selling and administrative expenses. For the months of January, February, and March, the company's selling price per aircraft, variable cost per aircraft, monthly production in units, and total monthly fixed expenses never change. The only thing that changes in this example is the number of units sold (January = 2 units sold; February = 1 unit sold; March = 3 units sold).

We first will construct the company's super-variable costing income statements for January, February, and March. Then we will show how the company's net operating income would be calculated for the same months using variable costing if it were incorrectly assumed that direct labor is a variable cost. As you'll see, both income statements rely on the contribution format.

Super-Variable Costing Income Statements

To prepare the company's super-variable costing income statements for each month, we follow four steps. First, we compute sales by multiplying the number of units sold by the selling price per unit, which in this example is $100,000 per unit. Second, we compute the variable cost of goods sold by multiplying the number of units sold by the unit product cost, which in this example is the direct materials cost of $19,000 per unit. Third, we compute the contribution margin by subtracting variable cost of goods sold from sales. Fourth, we compute net operating income by subtracting total fixed expenses, which in this example is $134,000 per month (= $20,000 + $74,000 + $40,000), from the contribution margin.

Using these four steps, Weber's super-variable costing income statements for each month would appear as shown in Exhibit 6A–1. Notice the only variable expense is variable cost of goods sold, which is the $19,000 of direct materials per unit sold. For example, in March, the unit product cost of $19,000 is multiplied by three units sold to obtain the variable cost of goods sold of $57,000. The total monthly fixed manufacturing expenses of $94,000 include $20,000 of direct labor and $74,000 of fixed manufacturing overhead.

Variable Costing Income Statements

The variable costing income statements in this example differ from the super-variable costing income statements in one important respect—we will assume direct labor is incorrectly classified as a variable cost and included in unit product costs. Because the monthly direct labor cost is $20,000 and two aircraft are produced each month, if direct labor costs are included in unit product costs, then Weber Light Aircraft will assign

EXHIBIT 6A–1
Super-Variable Costing Income Statements

	January	February	March
Sales (@ $100,000 per unit)	$200,000	$100,000	$300,000
Variable cost of goods sold (@ $19,000 per unit)	38,000	19,000	57,000
Contribution margin	162,000	81,000	243,000
Fixed expenses:			
Fixed manufacturing expenses	94,000	94,000	94,000
Fixed selling and administrative expenses	40,000	40,000	40,000
Total fixed expenses	134,000	134,000	134,000
Net operating income (loss)	$ 28,000	$ (53,000)	$109,000

$10,000 of direct labor cost to each aircraft it produces. Thus, the company's unit product costs under variable costing are computed as follows:

	January	February	March
Direct materials	$19,000	$19,000	$19,000
Direct labor	10,000	10,000	10,000
Unit product cost	$29,000	$29,000	$29,000

Given these unit product cost figures, the company's variable costing income statements are computed as shown in Exhibit 6A–2. For example, in March, the unit product cost of $29,000 is multiplied by three units sold to obtain the variable cost of goods sold of $87,000. The total fixed manufacturing overhead of $74,000 and total fixed selling and administrative expenses of $40,000 are both recorded as period expenses.

Reconciliation of Super-Variable Costing and Variable Costing Income

The super-variable costing and variable costing net operating incomes are both $28,000 in January. However, in February, the super-variable costing income is $10,000 lower than the variable costing income, and the opposite holds true in March. In other words, the super-variable costing income in March is $10,000 higher than the variable costing income.

EXHIBIT 6A–2
Variable Costing Income Statements

	January	February	March
Sales (@ $100,000 per unit)	$200,000	$100,000	$300,000
Variable cost of goods sold (@ $29,000 per unit)	58,000	29,000	87,000
Contribution margin	142,000	71,000	213,000
Fixed expenses:			
Fixed manufacturing overhead	74,000	74,000	74,000
Fixed selling and administrative expenses	40,000	40,000	40,000
Total fixed expenses	114,000	114,000	114,000
Net operating income (loss)	$ 28,000	$ (43,000)	$ 99,000

Why do these two costing methods produce different net operating incomes? The answer can be found in the accounting for direct labor costs. Super-variable costing treats direct labor as a fixed period expense, whereas variable costing treats direct labor as a variable product cost. In other words, super-variable costing records the entire direct labor cost of $20,000 as an expense on each month's income statement. Conversely, variable costing assigns $10,000 of direct labor cost to each unit produced. The $10,000 assigned to each unit produced remains in inventory on the balance sheet until the unit is sold—at which point the $10,000 assigned to it is transferred to variable cost of goods sold on the income statement. Given this background, the super-variable costing and variable costing incomes for each month can be reconciled as follows:

	January	February	March
Direct labor cost in ending inventory (@ $10,000 per unit)...................	$ 0	$10,000	$ 0
Deduct: Direct labor cost in beginning inventory (@ $10,000 per unit).....................	0	0	10,000
Direct labor cost deferred in (released from) inventory	$ 0	$10,000	$(10,000)

	January	February	March
Super-variable costing net operating income (loss)	$28,000	$(53,000)	$109,000
Direct labor deferred in (released from) inventory................................	0	10,000	(10,000)
Variable costing net operating income (loss)....	$28,000	$(43,000)	$ 99,000

In January, both costing methods report the same net operating income ($28,000). This occurs because the unit produced in January was also sold in January and, as a result, both methods expense $20,000 of direct labor in the income statement. In February, two units are produced, but only one unit is sold; therefore, super-variable costing income is $10,000 less than variable costing income. This difference arises because super-variable costing expenses $20,000 of direct labor in the income statement, whereas variable costing expenses only $10,000 of direct labor in the income statement ($10,000 per unit × 1 unit sold) while deferring the other $10,000 of direct labor in inventory ($10,000 per unit × 1 unit produced but not sold). In March, two units are produced and three units are sold; hence, super-variable costing income is $10,000 greater than variable costing income. This difference arises because super-variable costing expenses $20,000 of direct labor on the income statement, whereas variable costing expenses $30,000 of direct labor on the income statement ($10,000 per unit × 3 units sold). Notice one of the units sold in March was actually produced in February. Under variable costing, the $10,000 of direct labor attached to the unit produced in February is released from inventory and included in variable cost of goods sold for March.

In summary, the key issue considered in this appendix is how a company treats direct labor costs. If a company treats direct labor as a variable cost, the cost system may encourage managers to treat labor costs as an expense to be minimized when sales decline, and this may result in reduced morale and eventual problems when business picks up. Second, in practice, management may have little ability to adjust the direct labor force even if it wanted to, meaning direct labor costs are in fact fixed. In either case, treating direct labor costs as variable can lead to bad decisions. The super-variable costing approach overcomes this problem by treating labor costs as fixed costs.

Glossary (Appendix 6A)

Super-variable costing A costing method that classifies all direct labor and manufacturing overhead costs as fixed period costs and *only direct materials as a variable product cost.* (p. 298)

Appendix 6A: Exercises and Problems

EXERCISE 6A–1 Super-Variable Costing Income Statement LO6–6
Zola Company manufactures and sells one product. The following information pertains to the company's first year of operations:

Variable cost per unit:	
Direct materials	$18
Fixed costs per year:	
Direct labor	$200,000
Fixed manufacturing overhead.	$250,000
Fixed selling and administrative expenses	$80,000

The company does not incur any variable manufacturing overhead costs or variable selling and administrative expenses. During its first year of operations, Zola produced 25,000 units and sold 20,000 units. The selling price of the company's product is $50 per unit.

Required:
1. Assume the company uses super-variable costing:
   a. Compute the unit product cost for the year.
   b. Prepare an income statement for the year.

EXERCISE 6A–2 Super-Variable Costing and Variable Costing Unit Product Costs and Income Statements LO6–2, LO6–6
Lyons Company manufactures and sells one product. The following information pertains to the company's first year of operations:

Variable cost per unit:	
Direct materials	$13
Fixed costs per year:	
Direct labor	$750,000
Fixed manufacturing overhead	$420,000
Fixed selling and administrative expenses	$110,000

The company does not incur any variable manufacturing overhead costs or variable selling and administrative expenses. During its first year of operations, Lyons produced 60,000 units and sold 52,000 units. The selling price of the company's product is $40 per unit.

Required:
1. Assume the company uses super-variable costing:
   a. Compute the unit product cost for the year.
   b. Prepare an income statement for the year.
2. Assume the company uses a variable costing system that assigns $12.50 of direct labor cost to each unit produced:
   a. Compute the unit product cost for the year.
   b. Prepare an income statement for the year.
3. Prepare a reconciliation explaining the difference between the super-variable costing and variable costing net operating incomes.

EXERCISE 6A–3 Super-Variable Costing and Variable Costing Unit Product Costs and Income Statements LO6–2, LO6–6

Kelly Company manufactures and sells one product. The following information pertains to each of the company's first two years of operations:

Variable cost per unit:	
Direct materials	$12
Fixed costs per year:	
Direct labor	$500,000
Fixed manufacturing overhead	$450,000
Fixed selling and administrative expenses	$180,000

The company does not incur any variable manufacturing overhead costs or variable selling and administrative expenses. During its first year of operations, Kelly produced 50,000 units and sold 40,000 units. During its second year of operations, it produced 50,000 units and sold 60,000 units. The selling price of the company's product is $50 per unit.

Required:
1. Assume the company uses super-variable costing:
   a. Compute the unit product cost for Year 1 and Year 2.
   b. Prepare an income statement for Year 1 and Year 2.
2. Assume the company uses a variable costing system that assigns $10 of direct labor cost to each unit produced:
   a. Compute the unit product cost for Year 1 and Year 2.
   b. Prepare an income statement for Year 1 and Year 2.
3. Prepare a reconciliation explaining the difference between the super-variable costing and variable costing net operating incomes in Years 1 and 2.

PROBLEM 6A–4 Super-Variable Costing and Variable Costing Unit Product Costs and Income Statements LO6–2, LO6–6

Ogilvy Company manufactures and sells one product. The following information pertains to each of the company's first three years of operations:

Variable cost per unit:	
Direct materials	$16
Fixed costs per year:	
Direct labor	$540,000
Fixed manufacturing overhead	$822,000
Fixed selling and administrative expenses	$370,000

The company does not incur any variable manufacturing overhead costs or variable selling and administrative expenses. During its first year of operations, Ogilvy produced 60,000 units and sold 60,000 units. During its second year of operations, it produced 60,000 units and sold 55,000 units. In its third year, Ogilvy produced 60,000 units and sold 65,000 units. The selling price of the company's product is $45 per unit.

Required:
1. Assume the company uses super-variable costing:
   a. Compute the unit product cost for Year 1, Year 2, and Year 3.
   b. Prepare an income statement for Year 1, Year 2, and Year 3.
2. Assume the company uses a variable costing system that assigns $9 of direct labor cost to each unit produced:
   a. Compute the unit product cost for Year 1, Year 2, and Year 3.
   b. Prepare an income statement for Year 1, Year 2, and Year 3.
3. Prepare a reconciliation explaining the difference between the super-variable costing and variable costing net operating incomes in Years 1, 2, and 3.

PROBLEM 6A–5 Super-Variable Costing, Variable Costing, and Absorption Costing Income Statements LO6–2, LO6–6

Bracey Company manufactures and sells one product. The following information pertains to the company's first year of operations:

Variable cost per unit:	
Direct materials	$19
Fixed costs per year:	
Direct labor	$250,000
Fixed manufacturing overhead	$300,000
Fixed selling and administrative expenses.	$90,000

The company does not incur any variable manufacturing overhead costs or variable selling and administrative expenses. During its first year of operations, Bracey produced 20,000 units and sold 18,000 units. The selling price of the company's product is $55 per unit.

Required:
1. Assume the company uses super-variable costing:
   a. Compute the unit product cost for the year.
   b. Prepare an income statement for the year.
2. Assume the company uses a variable costing system that assigns $12.50 of direct labor cost to each unit produced:
   a. Compute the unit product cost for the year.
   b. Prepare an income statement for the year.
3. Assume the company uses an absorption costing system that assigns $12.50 of direct labor cost and $15.00 of fixed manufacturing overhead cost to each unit produced:
   a. Compute the unit product cost for the year.
   b. Prepare an income statement for the year.
4. Prepare a reconciliation explaining the difference between the super-variable costing and variable costing net operating incomes. Prepare another reconciliation explaining the difference between the super-variable costing and absorption costing net operating incomes.

Activity-Based Costing: A Tool to Aid Decision Making

Paul Morigi/Invision for Intuit/AP Images

ENTREPRENEUR SPOTLIGHT

Kavita Shukla is the founder of Fresh Paper—a company that sells patented paper sheets that extend the life of perishable foods. Her paper sheets are stocked by large retailers, such as Whole Foods and Walmart, and are purchased by farmers and families throughout the world. Not only does Kavita hold four patents, but she also "is the youngest woman ever to receive the biennial INDEX Design to Improve Life Award." In fact, her accomplishments caught the attention of Hollywood director Bryce Dallas Howard, who created a short film to tell her story of "simple beginnings, belief, and empowerment."

Applying Managerial Accounting

In addition to selling its products to wholesale customers, Fresh Paper also welcomes online orders from its retail customers. Its website offers a variety of purchase options, including starter packs, value packs, and monthly subscriptions. The company could use activity-based costing to quantify the cost of its order-processing activities and the profitability of its various wholesale and retail customers. It could implement pricing and marketing strategies that motivate these customers to place orders that maximize revenues earned relative to the batch-level costs associated with fulfilling them.

LEARNING OBJECTIVES

After studying Chapter 7, you should be able to:

LO7–1 Understand activity-based costing and how it differs from a traditional costing system.

LO7–2 Assign costs to cost pools using a first-stage allocation.

LO7–3 Compute activity rates for cost pools.

LO7–4 Assign costs to a cost object using a second-stage allocation.

LO7–5 Use activity-based costing to compute product and customer margins.

LO7–6 *(Appendix 7A) Use time-driven activity-based costing to assign costs to cost objects.*

LO7–7 *(Appendix 7A) Use time-driven activity-based costing to analyze capacity.*

 Data Analytics Exercise available in Connect to complement this chapter

Serving All Stakeholders

Kavita Shukla founded her company to help tackle the global challenge of reducing food waste. Her company's website offers three statistics that define the magnitude of the problem and the immense benefits that can be realized by solving it. First, one-third of all food produced across the globe is wasted, costing the global economy about $940 billion per year. Second, in spite of this immense waste, 793 million people throughout the world do not have enough food to eat. Third, if 25 percent of our wasted food could be salvaged, it would feed 870 million under-nourished people. ■

Sources: https://freshpaper.com.au, https://freshpaper.com.au/food-wastage, https://www.kavitashukla.com.

This chapter explains how organizations use activity-based costing, rather than traditional absorption costing, to calculate unit product costs for internal decision-making purposes. **Activity-based costing (ABC)** is a costing method that provides managers with cost information for strategic and other decisions that potentially affect capacity, and therefore "fixed" as well as variable costs. Chapter 6 focused on using variable costing to aid decisions that do not affect fixed costs. This chapter extends that idea by showing how activity-based costing is used to aid decisions that potentially affect fixed costs as well as variable costs.

Activity-Based Costing: An Overview

LO7–1
Understand activity-based costing and how it differs from a traditional costing system.

Traditional absorption costing is designed to provide data for external financial reports. It has three limitations when used for internal management purposes. First, it only assigns manufacturing costs to products—ignoring any nonmanufacturing costs that may be consumed by products. Second, it assigns *all* manufacturing costs to products even if those products do not consume those costs. Third, it relies on a limited number of overhead cost pools that always use allocation bases correlated with the volume of output. This ignores any non-volume-related cost drivers that exist in organizations, thereby allocating too much overhead cost to high-volume products and too little overhead to low-volume products.

In contrast, activity-based costing is designed for internal management purposes; therefore, it overcomes the limitations of traditional cost systems in three ways:

1. Nonmanufacturing as well as manufacturing costs may be assigned to products, but only on a cause-and-effect basis.
2. Some manufacturing costs may be excluded from product costs.
3. Numerous overhead cost pools are used, each of which is allocated to products and other cost objects using its own unique measure of activity.

Each of these departures from traditional absorption costing will be discussed in turn.

Nonmanufacturing Costs and Activity-Based Costing

In traditional absorption costing, manufacturing costs are assigned to products and non-manufacturing costs are not assigned to products. Conversely, activity-based costing recognizes many nonmanufacturing costs are incurred to sell, distribute, and service specific products. Thus, ABC includes manufacturing *and* nonmanufacturing costs when measuring product profitability. More specifically, ABC systems trace all direct nonmanufacturing costs to products. Commissions paid to salespersons, shipping costs, and warranty repair costs are examples of nonmanufacturing costs that can be directly traced to individual products. They also allocate indirect nonmanufacturing costs to products whenever the products have presumably caused the costs to be incurred. In this chapter, we emphasize this point by expanding the definition of *overhead* to include all indirect costs—manufacturing and nonmanufacturing.

Manufacturing Costs and Activity-Based Costing

Traditional absorption costing systems assign *all* manufacturing costs to products—even if they are not caused by the products. For example, in Chapters 2 and 3 we learned that a predetermined plantwide overhead rate is computed by dividing *all* budgeted manufacturing overhead costs by the budgeted amount of the allocation base. This approach ensures *all* manufacturing overhead costs are allocated to products based on their direct labor-hour usage. In contrast, activity-based costing systems purposely do not assign two types of manufacturing overhead costs to products—*organization-sustaining costs* and *unused capacity costs* (also called idle capacity costs).

Organization-sustaining costs include costs such as the factory security guard's wages, the plant controller's salary, and the cost of supplies used by the plant manager's secretary. Absorption costing systems allocate these types of manufacturing overhead costs to products even though they are unaffected by which products are made during a period. Conversely, activity-based costing systems treat organization-sustaining costs as period expenses rather than arbitrarily assigning them to products.

Absorption costing systems also allocate the cost of unused capacity to products. If the budgeted level of activity declines, the overhead rate and unit product costs rise, thereby ensuring that the shrinking volume of output absorbs the increasing cost of idle capacity. In contrast, activity-based costing systems charge products only for the cost of the capacity they use—not for the cost of the capacity they don't use.[1]

Exhibit 7–1 summarizes the two departures from traditional absorption costing that we have discussed thus far. The top portion of the exhibit shows that absorption costing treats all manufacturing costs as product costs and all nonmanufacturing costs as period costs. The bottom portion of the exhibit shows that activity-based costing expands the definition of *overhead* to include all indirect costs—manufacturing and nonmanufacturing. The overhead costs caused by products are allocated to them, whereas any overhead costs not caused by products are treated as period costs. It also shows that ABC treats direct nonmanufacturing costs as product costs rather than period costs.

Cost Pools, Allocation Bases, and Activity-Based Costing

Traditional cost systems use a limited number of overhead cost pools and rely exclusively on volume-related allocation bases—such as direct labor-hours, machine-hours, or number of units produced. For companies whose overhead costs highly correlate with their volume of output, these design features may provide managers with reasonably accurate cost data for internal decision making. However, when a company's operations include numerous non-volume-related cost drivers, a traditional cost system will most likely allocate too much overhead to its high-volume products and not enough to its low-volume products. Activity-based costing can help correct these cost distortions by using more cost pools and including volume-related and non-volume-related allocation bases.

In activity-based costing, an **activity** is any event that causes the consumption of overhead resources. An **activity cost pool** is a "bucket" in which costs are accumulated that relate to a single activity measure in the ABC system. An **activity measure** is an allocation base in an activity-based costing system. The term *cost driver* is also used to refer to an activity measure because the activity measure should "drive" the cost being allocated. The two most common types of activity measures are *transaction drivers* and *duration drivers*. **Transaction drivers** are simple counts of the number of times an activity occurs, such as the number of bills sent out to customers. **Duration drivers** measure the amount of time required to perform an activity, such as the time spent preparing individual bills for customers.

---

[1] Appendix 2B discusses how the cost of unused capacity can be accounted for as a period cost in an income statement. This treatment highlights the cost of unused capacity rather than burying it in inventory and cost of goods sold. The procedures laid out in this chapter for activity-based costing have the same end effect.

EXHIBIT 7–1

Differences between Traditional Absorption Costing and Activity-Based Costing

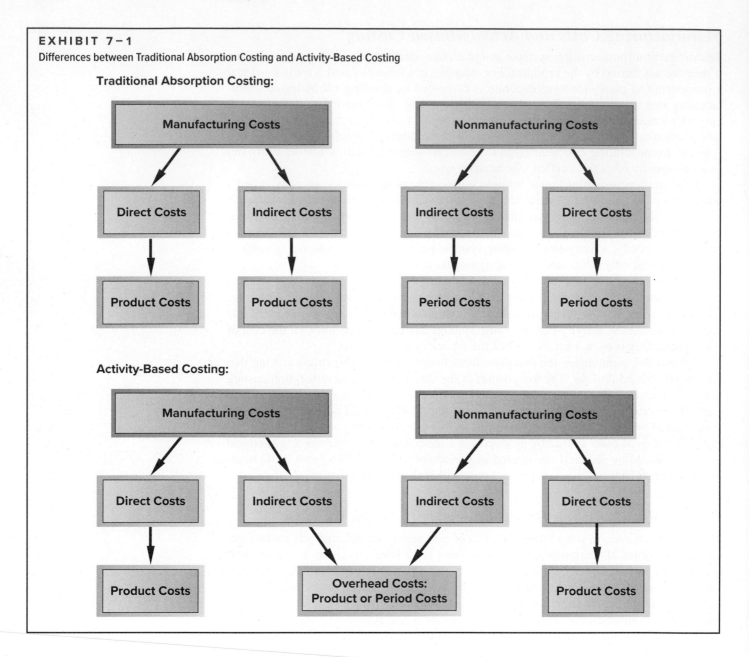

Traditional cost systems recognize only one level of activity—the volume of production. In contrast, activity-based costing defines five levels of activity—unit-level, batch-level, product-level, customer-level, and organization-sustaining—that largely do *not* relate to the volume of units produced. The costs and corresponding activity measures for unit-level activities do relate to the volume of units produced; however, the remaining categories do not. These levels are described as follows:[2]

1. **Unit-level activities** are performed each time a unit is produced. The costs of unit-level activities should be proportional to the number of units produced. For example, providing power to run processing equipment would be a unit-level activity because power tends to be consumed in proportion to the number of units produced.
2. **Batch-level activities** are performed each time a batch is handled or processed, regardless of how many units are in the batch. Placing purchase orders, setting up equipment, and arranging for shipments to customers are examples of batch-level activities. Costs

---

[2] Robin Cooper, "Cost Classification in Unit-Based and Activity-Based Manufacturing Cost Systems," *Journal of Cost Management,* Fall 1990, pp. 4–14.

at the batch level depend on the number of batches processed rather than on the number of units produced, the number of units sold, or other measures of volume.

3. **Product-level activities** are performed for specific products regardless of how many batches are run or units produced. Designing a product, advertising a product, and maintaining a product manager and staff are examples of product-level activities.

4. **Customer-level activities** are performed for specific customers and do not relate to specific products. Sales calls, catalog mailings, customer meetings, and general technical support are examples of customer-level activities.

5. **Organization-sustaining activities** are performed regardless of which customers are served, which products are produced, how many batches are run, or how many units are made. Examples include heating the factory, cleaning executive offices, providing a computer network, arranging for loans, and preparing annual reports to shareholders.

IN BUSINESS

DINING IN THE CANYON

Western River Expeditions (www.westernriver.com) runs river rafting trips on the Colorado, Green, and Salmon rivers. One of its most popular trips is a six-day trip down the Grand Canyon, which features famous rapids such as Crystal and Lava Falls as well as the awesome scenery accessible only from the bottom of the Grand Canyon. The company runs trips of one or two rafts, each of which carries two guides and up to 18 guests. The company provides all meals on the trip, which are prepared by the guides.

In terms of the hierarchy of activities, a guest can be considered as a unit and a raft as a batch. In that context, the wages paid to the guides are a batch-level cost because each raft requires two guides regardless of the number of guests in the raft. Each guest is given a mug to use during the trip and to take home at the end of the trip as a souvenir. The cost of the mug is a unit-level cost because the number of mugs given away is strictly proportional to the number of guests on a trip.

What about the costs of food served to guests and guides—is this a unit-level cost, a batch-level cost, a product-level cost, or an organization-sustaining cost? At first glance, it might be thought that food costs are a unit-level cost—the greater the number of guests, the higher the food costs. However, that is not quite correct. Standard menus have been created for each day of the trip. For example, the first night's menu might consist of shrimp cocktail, steak, cornbread, salad, and cheesecake. The day before a trip begins, all of the food needed for the trip is taken from the central warehouse and packed in modular containers. It isn't practical to finely adjust the amount of food for the actual number of guests planned to be on a trip—most of the food comes prepackaged in large lots. For example, the shrimp cocktail menu may call for two large bags of frozen shrimp per raft and that many bags will be packed regardless of how many guests are expected on the raft. Consequently, the costs of food are not a unit-level cost that varies with the number of guests actually on a trip. Instead, the costs of food are a batch-level cost.

Source: Sandee Noreen

Activity-Based Costing: An Example

Classic Brass, Inc., makes two main product lines for luxury yachts—standard stanchions and custom compass housings. The president of the company, John Towers, recently attended a management conference at which activity-based costing was discussed. Following the conference, he called a meeting of the company's top managers to discuss what he had learned. Attending the meeting were production manager Susan Richter, marketing manager Tom Olafson, and accounting manager Mary Goodman. He began the conference by distributing the company's income statement that Mary Goodman had prepared a few hours earlier (see Exhibit 7–2):

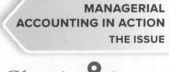

MANAGERIAL ACCOUNTING IN ACTION
THE ISSUE

Classic Brass Inc.

John: Well, it's official. Our company has sunk into the red for the first time in its history—a loss of $1,250.

Tom: I don't know what else we can do! Given our successful efforts to grow sales of the custom compass housings, I was expecting to see a boost to our bottom line, not

EXHIBIT 7–2
Classic Brass Income Statement

	Classic Brass Income Statement For the Year Ended December 31		
Sales			$3,200,000
Cost of goods sold:			
Direct materials		$ 975,000	
Direct labor.		351,250	
Manufacturing overhead*		1,000,000	2,326,250
Gross margin			873,750
Selling and administrative expenses:			
Shipping expense		65,000	
General administrative expense..............		510,000	
Marketing expense..........................		300,000	875,000
Net operating loss............................			$ (1,250)

*The company's traditional cost system allocates manufacturing overhead to products using a plantwide overhead rate and machine-hours as the allocation base. Inventory levels did not change during the year.

a net loss. Granted, we have been losing even more bids than usual for standard stanchions because of our recent price increase, but . . .

John: Do you think our prices for standard stanchions are too high?

Tom: No, I don't think our prices are too high. I think our competitors' prices are too low. In fact, I'll bet they are pricing below their cost.

Susan: Why would our competitors price below their cost?

Tom: They are out to grab market share.

Susan: What good is more market share if they are losing money on every unit sold?

John: I think Susan has a point. Mary, what is your take on this?

Mary: If our competitors are pricing standard stanchions below cost, shouldn't they be losing money rather than us? If our company is the one using accurate information to make informed decisions while our competitors are supposedly clueless, then why is our "bottom line" taking a beating? Unfortunately, I think we may be the ones relying on distorted cost data, not our competitors.

John: Based on what I heard at the conference that I just attended, I am inclined to agree. One of the presentations at the conference dealt with activity-based costing. As the speaker began describing the usual insights revealed by activity-based costing systems, I was sitting in the audience getting an ill feeling in my stomach.

Mary: Honestly John, I have been claiming for years that our existing cost system is okay for external reporting, but it is dangerous to use it for internal decision making. It sounds like you are on board now, right?

John: Yes.

Mary: Well then, how about if all of you commit the time and energy to help me build a fairly simple activity-based costing system that may shed some light on the problems we are facing?

John: Let's do it. I want each of you to appoint one of your top people to a special "ABC team" to investigate how we cost products.

Once the ABC team was assembled, it broke down the implementation into five steps:

1. Define activities, activity cost pools, and activity measures.
2. Assign overhead costs to activity cost pools.
3. Calculate activity rates.
4. Assign overhead costs to cost objects.
5. Prepare management reports.

Step 1: Define Activities, Activity Cost Pools, and Activity Measures

To complete step one of its implementation plan, the team met with employees who work in overhead departments and asked them to describe their major activities and then select an activity measure for each one of those activities. After extensive discussions with numerous employees, the implementation team identified five activities and activity measures as follows:

Activity Cost Pools at Classic Brass	
Activity Cost Pool	Activity Measure
Customer orders	Number of customer orders
Product design	Number of product designs
Order size	Machine-hours
Customer relations	Number of active customers
Other	Not applicable

The *Customer Orders* activity includes the cost of all resources used to take customer orders and set up machines to process those orders. This is a batch-level activity because each order costs the same regardless of whether the customer is buying one unit or 1,000 units. The activity measure for this cost pool is the number of customer orders received.

The *Product Design* activity includes the cost of all resources used to design new products. This is a product-level activity because the amount of design work on a new product does not depend on the number of units ultimately ordered or batches ultimately run. The activity measure for this cost pool is the number of product designs.

The *Order Size* activity includes the costs consumed making individual units of product, such as factory supplies, electricity to run machines, and equipment depreciation. This is a unit-level activity because each unit requires some of these resources. The activity measure for this cost pool is machine-hours.

The *Customer Relations* activity includes the costs consumed managing customer relationships, such as completing sales calls and entertaining customers. It is a customer-level activity and its activity measure is the number of customers the company has on its active customer list.

The *Other* activity includes all overhead costs that are not associated with customer orders, product design, the size of the orders, or customer relations. These costs mainly consist of organization-sustaining costs and the costs of unused, idle capacity. These costs *will not* be assigned to products because they represent resources that are *not* consumed by products.

IN VOGUE, ON DEMAND

It may seem logical to conclude fashion designers would prefer ordering their garments from suppliers in large batch sizes to lower the average production cost per unit. However, the downsides of ordering clothes in huge batches—often as much as a year in advance—are the designers cannot customize production to meet individual customer preferences and they cannot adjust inventories in response to emerging fashion trends.

Spencer Fung, manager of supply chain management company Li & Fung Ltd., says, "Just look at the average size of orders—it's been going down for years. It went from hundreds of thousands to tens of thousands. And it will keep going down until it approaches a unit of one." Enter fashion designer Rebecca Minkoff, who believes no inventory is the best inventory; hence, not a stitch of her "sustainably made" clothes are produced until a customer orders them. Numerous other companies such as Gap Inc., Kohl's Corp., and Amazon have also taken steps to better match supply with demand by shrinking batch sizes and shortening lead times.

Sources: Suzanne Kapner, "Designers Try Selling Clothes First, Making Them Later," *The Wall Street Journal*, September 25, 2021, https://www.wsj.com/articles/designers-try-selling-clothes-first-making-them-later-11632562202, and Natasha Khan, "Tech Puts Fast Fashion on Steroids," *The Wall Street Journal*, April 10, 2018, p. B7.

LO7–2
Assign costs to cost pools using a first-stage allocation.

Step 2: Assign Overhead Costs to Activity Cost Pools

Exhibit 7–3 shows the annual overhead costs (both manufacturing and nonmanufacturing) that Classic Brass intends to assign to its activity cost pools. Notice the data in the exhibit are organized by department (e.g., Production, General Administrative, and Marketing). This is because the data have been extracted from the company's general ledger. General ledgers usually classify costs within the departments where the costs are incurred. For example, salaries, supplies, rent, and so forth incurred in the marketing department are charged to that department. The functional orientation of the general ledger mirrors the presentation of costs in the absorption income statement in Exhibit 7–2. In fact, you'll notice the total costs for the Production Department in Exhibit 7–3 ($1,000,000) equal the total manufacturing overhead costs from the income statement in Exhibit 7–2. Similarly, the total costs for the General Administrative and Marketing Departments in Exhibit 7–3 ($510,000 and $300,000) equal the marketing and general and administrative expenses shown in Exhibit 7–2.

Three costs included in the income statement in Exhibit 7–2—direct materials, direct labor, and shipping expenses—are excluded from the costs shown in Exhibit 7–3. The ABC team purposely excluded these costs from Exhibit 7–3 because the existing cost system can accurately trace direct materials, direct labor, and shipping costs to products. There is no need to incorporate these direct costs in the activity-based allocations of indirect costs.

The ABC implementation relied on employees from the company's overhead departments to complete the *first-stage allocation*. The **first-stage allocation** in an ABC system is the process of assigning functionally organized overhead costs derived from a company's general ledger to the activity cost pools.

Exhibit 7–4 shows the employees' estimated percentages used to allocate departmental overhead costs to the five activities included in the ABC cost model. For example, the overhead employees estimated their indirect factory wages were consumed by activities as follows: Customer Orders (25%), Product Design (40%), Order Size (20%), Customer Relations (10%), and Other (5%). They also estimated the factory equipment depreciation should be distributed 20% to Customer Orders, 60% to Order Size, and 20% to the Other cost pool. As one final example, the ABC implementation team also decided to treat the entire cost of the factory building lease as an organization-sustaining cost because there is no way to avoid even a portion of this cost if a particular product or customer were dropped.

Exhibit 7–5 shows how the ABC implementation team used the percentage distributions from Exhibit 7–4 to allocate departmental overhead costs to activities. For example, the indirect factory wages of $500,000 are multiplied by the 25 percent entry under

EXHIBIT 7–3 Annual Overhead Costs (Both Manufacturing and Nonmanufacturing) at Classic Brass			
Production Department:			
Indirect factory wages		$500,000	
Factory equipment depreciation		300,000	
Factory utilities.................................		120,000	
Factory building lease		80,000	$1,000,000
General Administrative Department:			
Administrative wages and salaries................		400,000	
Office equipment depreciation...................		50,000	
Administrative building lease		60,000	510,000
Marketing Department:			
Marketing wages and salaries		250,000	
Selling expenses................................		50,000	300,000
Total overhead cost			$1,810,000

EXHIBIT 7-4
Results of Interviews: Distribution of Resource Consumption across Activity Cost Pools

	A	B	C	D	E	F	G	H
1		*Activity Cost Pools*						
2		*Customer Orders*	*Product Design*	*Order Size*	*Customer Relations*	*Other*	*Totals*	
4	Production Department:							
5	Indirect factory wages	25%	40%	20%	10%	5%	100%	
6	Factory equipment depreciation	20%	0%	60%	0%	20%	100%	
7	Factory utilities	0%	10%	50%	0%	40%	100%	
8	Factory building lease	0%	0%	0%	0%	100%	100%	
10	General Administrative Department:							
11	Administrative wages and salaries	15%	5%	10%	30%	40%	100%	
12	Office equipment depreciation	30%	0%	0%	25%	45%	100%	
13	Administrative building lease	0%	0%	0%	0%	100%	100%	
15	Marketing Department:							
16	Marketing wages and salaries	22%	8%	0%	60%	10%	100%	
17	Selling expenses	10%	0%	0%	70%	20%	100%	
18								

Exhibit 7-4 | Exhibit 7-5 | Exhibit 7-6 | Exhibit 7-8 | Exhibit 7-9 | Exhibit 7-10 | ... ⊕

Microsoft Excel

EXHIBIT 7-5
First-Stage Allocations to Activity Cost Pools

	A	B	C	D	E	F	G	H
1		*Activity Cost Pools*						
2		*Customer Orders*	*Product Design*	*Order Size*	*Customer Relations*	*Other*	*Totals*	
4	Production Department:							
5	Indirect factory wages	$ 125,000	$ 200,000	$ 100,000	$ 50,000	$ 25,000	$ 500,000	
6	Factory equipment depreciation	60,000	0	180,000	0	60,000	300,000	
7	Factory utilities	0	12,000	60,000	0	48,000	120,000	
8	Factory building lease	0	0	0	0	80,000	80,000	
10	General Administrative Department:							
11	Administrative wages and salaries	60,000	20,000	40,000	120,000	160,000	400,000	
12	Office equipment depreciation	15,000	0	0	12,500	22,500	50,000	
13	Administrative building lease	0	0	0	0	60,000	60,000	
15	Marketing Department:							
16	Marketing wages and salaries	55,000	20,000	0	150,000	25,000	250,000	
17	Selling expenses	5,000	0	0	35,000	10,000	50,000	
19	Total	$ 320,000	$ 252,000	$ 380,000	$ 367,500	$ 490,500	$ 1,810,000	
20								

Exhibit 7-4 | Exhibit 7-5 | Exhibit 7-6 | Exhibit 7-8 | Exhibit 7-9 | Exhibit 7-10 | ... ⊕

Microsoft Excel

Exhibit 7-4 shows that Customer Orders consume 25% of the resources represented by the $500,000 of indirect factory wages.

25% × $500,000 = $125,000

Other entries in the table are computed in a similar fashion.

Customer Orders in Exhibit 7–4 to arrive at the $125,000 entry under Customer Orders in Exhibit 7–5. Similarly, the indirect factory wages of $500,000 are multiplied by the 40 percent entry under Product Design in Exhibit 7–4 to arrive at the $200,000 entry under Product Design in Exhibit 7–5. All of the entries in Exhibit 7–5 are computed in this way.

Now that the first-stage allocations to the activity cost pools have been completed, the next step is to compute the activity rates.

Step 3: Calculate Activity Rates

LO7–3
Compute activity rates for cost pools.

Exhibit 7–6 shows how the implementation team computed the activity rates used for assigning overhead costs to products and customers. Each of these rates represents the *average* cost per unit of the activity measure—they do not represent avoidable costs. For example, the $320,000 total annual cost for the Customer Orders cost pool (which was computed in Exhibit 7–5) is divided by the total of 1,000 customer orders per year to arrive at the activity rate of $320 per customer order. Similarly, the $252,000 *total* cost for the Product Design cost pool is divided by the *total* of 400 product designs per year to determine the activity rate of $630 per design. Note that an activity rate is not computed for the Other category of costs. This is because the *Other* cost pool consists of organization-sustaining costs and unused capacity costs that are not allocated to products and customers.

Exhibit 7–7 provides a visual perspective of the implementation team's activity-based cost model. Note the Other category, which contains organization-sustaining costs and unused capacity costs, is not allocated to products or customers.

Step 4: Assign Overhead Costs to Cost Objects

LO7–4
Assign costs to a cost object using a second-stage allocation.

Next, the implementation team turned its attention to *second-stage allocation*. In **second-stage allocation**, activity rates are used to apply overhead costs to products and customers. First, we illustrate how to assign costs to products, followed by an example of how to assign costs to customers.

EXHIBIT 7–6
Computation of Activity Rates

	A	B	C	D	E	F	G
		(a)	(b)		(a) ÷ (b)		
1	*Activity Cost Pools*	*Total Cost**	*Total Activity*		*Activity Rate*		
2	Customer orders	$320,000	1,000	orders	$320	per order	
3	Product design	$252,000	400	designs	$630	per design	
4	Order size	$380,000	20,000	MHs	$19	per MH	
5	Customer relations	$367,500	250	customers	$1,470	per customer	
6	Other	$490,500	Not applicable		Not applicable		
8	*From Exhibit 7–5.						
9							

Exhibit 7-4 | Exhibit 7-5 | **Exhibit 7-6** | Exhibit 7-8 | Exhibit 7-9 | ... ⊕

Microsoft Excel

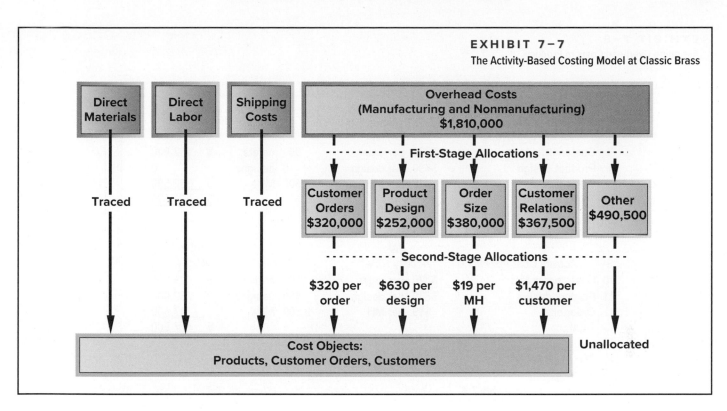

EXHIBIT 7–7
The Activity-Based Costing Model at Classic Brass

The data needed by the ABC team to assign overhead costs to Classic Brass's two products—standard stanchions and custom compass housings—are as follows:

Standard Stanchions

1. This product line does not require any new product design resources.
2. 30,000 units were ordered during the year, comprising 600 separate orders.
3. Each stanchion requires 35 minutes of machine time for a total of 17,500 machine-hours.

Custom Compass Housings

1. This is a custom product that requires new product design resources.
2. There were 400 orders for custom compass housings. Orders for this product are placed separately from orders for standard stanchions.
3. There were 400 custom designs prepared. One custom design was prepared for each order.
4. Because some orders were for more than one unit, a total of 1,250 custom compass housings were produced during the year. A custom compass housing requires an average of 2 machine-hours for a total of 2,500 machine-hours.

Notice, 600 customer orders were placed for standard stanchions and 400 customer orders were placed for custom compass housings, for a total of 1,000 customer orders. All 400 product designs related to custom compass housings; none related to standard stanchions. Producing 30,000 standard stanchions required 17,500 machine-hours and producing 1,250 custom compass housings required 2,500 machine-hours, for a total of 20,000 machine-hours.

EXHIBIT 7–8
Assigning Overhead Costs to Products

	A	B	C	D	E	F
1	**Overhead Cost for the Standard Stanchions**					
2	*Activity Cost Pools*	*(a) Activity Rate**		*(b) Activity*		*(a) × (b) ABC Cost*
3	Customer orders	$320	per order	600	orders	$ 192,000
4	Product design	$630	per design	0	designs	0
5	Order size	$19	per MH	17,500	MHs	332,500
6	Total					$ 524,500
7						
8	**Overhead Cost for the Custom Compass Housing**					
9	*Activity Cost Pools*	*(a) Activity Rate**		*(b) Activity*		*(a) × (b) ABC Cost*
10	Customer orders	$320	per order	400	orders	$ 128,000
11	Product design	$630	per design	400	designs	252,000
12	Order size	$19	per MH	2,500	MHs	47,500
13	Total					$ 427,500
14						
15	*From Exhibit 7-6.					
16						

◄   ►   …   **Exhibit 7-8**   Exhibit 7-9   Exhibit 7-10   Skip This Tab   …   ⊕

Microsoft Excel

Exhibit 7–8 shows the overhead cost allocations to standard stanchions and custom compass housings. For example, the exhibit shows that $192,000 of overhead costs are assigned from the Customer Orders activity cost pool to the standard stanchions ($320 per order × 600 orders). Similarly, $128,000 of overhead costs are assigned from the Customer Orders activity cost pool to the custom compass housings ($320 per order × 400 orders). The Customer Orders cost pool contained a total of $320,000 (see Exhibit 7–5 or 7–6), and this total amount has been assigned to the two products ($192,000 + $128,000 = $320,000).

Exhibit 7–8 shows a total of $952,000 of overhead costs is assigned to Classic Brass's two product lines—$524,500 to standard stanchions and $427,500 to custom compass housings. This amount is less than the $1,810,000 of overhead costs included in the ABC system. Why? The total amount of overhead assigned to products does not match the total amount of overhead cost in the ABC system because the ABC team purposely did not assign the $367,500 of Customer Relations and $490,500 of Other costs to products. The Customer Relations activity is a customer-level activity and the Other activity is an organization-sustaining activity—neither activity is caused by products. As shown below, when the Customer Relations and Other activity costs are added to the $952,000 of overhead costs assigned to products, the total is $1,810,000.

	Standard Stanchions	Custom Compass Housings	Total
Overhead Costs Assigned to Products			
Customer orders	$ 192,000	$128,000	$ 320,000
Product design	0	252,000	252,000
Order size...........................	332,500	47,500	380,000
Subtotal (a).........................	$ 524,500	$427,500	952,000
Overhead Costs Not Assigned to Products			
Customer relations			367,500
Other...............................			490,500
Subtotal (b)			858,000
Total overhead cost (a) + (b)			$1,810,000

Next, we describe another example of second-stage allocation—assigning activity costs to customers. The data needed by Classic Brass to assign overhead costs to one of its customers—Windward Yachts—are as follows:

Windward Yachts

1. The company placed a total of three orders.
   a. Two orders were for 150 standard stanchions per order.
   b. One order was for a single custom compass housing unit.
2. A total of 177 machine-hours were used to fulfill the three customer orders.
   a. The 300 standard stanchions required 175 machine-hours.
   b. The custom compass housing required 2 machine-hours.
3. Windward Yachts is one of 250 customers served by Classic Brass.

Exhibit 7–9 shows the ABC system assigned $6,423 of overhead costs to Windward Yachts. This includes $960 ($320 per order × 3 orders) of overhead costs from the Customer Orders activity cost pool; $630 ($630 per design × 1 design) from the Product Design cost pool; $3,363 ($19 per machine-hour × 177 machine-hours) from the Order Size cost pool; and $1,470 ($1,470 per customer × 1 customer) from the Customer Relations cost pool.

With second-stage allocations complete, the ABC design team was ready to turn its attention to creating reports that would help explain the company's first-ever net operating loss.

EXHIBIT 7–9
Assigning Overhead Costs to Customers

	A	B	C	D	E	F
1	**Overhead Cost for Windward Yachts**					
2						
3	*Activity Cost Pools*	*(a)* *Activity Rate**		*(b)* *Activity*		*(a) × (b)* *ABC Cost*
4	Customer orders	$320	per order	3	orders	$ 960
5	Product design	$630	per design	1	designs	630
6	Order size	$19	per MH	177	MHs	3,363
7	Customer relations	$1,470	per customer	1	customer	1,470
8	Total overhead cost assigned to customer					$ 6,423
9						
10	*From Exhibit 7-6.					
11						

Exhibit 7-9 | Exhibit 7-10 | Skip This Tab | Exhibit 7-11 | Exhibit ...

Microsoft Excel

LO7–5

Use activity-based costing to compute product and customer margins.

Step 5: Prepare Management Reports

The most common management reports prepared with ABC data are product and customer profitability reports. These reports help companies channel their resources to their most profitable growth opportunities while at the same time highlighting products and customers that drain profits. We begin by illustrating a product profitability report followed by a customer profitability report.

The Classic Brass ABC team realized that the profit from a product, also called the *product margin,* is a function of the product's sales and the direct and indirect costs that the product causes. The ABC cost allocations shown in Exhibit 7–8 only summarize each product's indirect (i.e., overhead) costs. Therefore, to compute a product's profit (i.e., product margin), the design team needed to gather each product's sales and direct costs in addition to the overhead costs previously computed. The pertinent sales and direct cost data for each product are shown below. Notice the numbers in the total column agree with the income statement in Exhibit 7–2.

	Standard Stanchions	Custom Compass Housings	Total
Sales	$2,660,000	$540,000	$3,200,000
Direct costs:			
Direct materials	$905,500	$69,500	$975,000
Direct labor.	$263,750	$87,500	$351,250
Shipping	$60,000	$5,000	$65,000

Having gathered the above data, the design team created the product profitability report shown in Exhibit 7–10. The report revealed that standard stanchions are profitable, with a positive product margin of $906,250, whereas the custom compass housings are unprofitable, with a negative product margin of $49,500. Keep in mind that the product profitability report purposely does not include the costs in the Customer Relations and Other activity cost pools. These costs, which total $858,000, were excluded from the report because they are not caused by the products. Customer Relations costs are caused by customers, not products. The Other costs are organization-sustaining costs and unused capacity costs that are not caused by any particular product.

EXHIBIT 7–10
Product Margins—Activity-Based Costing

⊿	A	B	C	D	E	F	C
1	**Product Margins—Activity-Based Costing**						
2			*Standard Stanchions*			*Custom Compass Housings*	
3	Sales		$ 2,660,000			$ 540,000	
4	Costs:						
5	Direct materials	$ 905,500			$ 69,500		
6	Direct labor	263,750			87,500		
7	Shipping	60,000			5,000		
8	Customer orders (from Exhibit 7-8)	192,000			128,000		
9	Product design (from Exhibit 7-8)	-			252,000		
10	Order size (from Exhibit 7-8)	332,500			47,500		
11	Total cost		1,753,750			589,500	
12	Product margin		$ 906,250			$ (49,500)	
13							

Exhibit 7-10   Skip This Tab   Exhibit 7-11   Exhibit 7-12   Exhibit 7-13 ...

Microsoft Excel

The product margins can be reconciled with the company's net operating loss as follows:

	Standard Stanchions	Custom Compass Housings	Total
Sales (See Exhibit 7–10)	$2,660,000	$540,000	$3,200,000
Total costs (See Exhibit 7–10)............	1,753,750	589,500	2,343,250
Product margins (See Exhibit 7–10)	$ 906,250	$ (49,500)	856,750
Overhead costs not assigned to products:			
Customer relations			367,500
Other.........................			490,500
Total........................			858,000
Net operating loss......................			$ (1,250)

Next, the design team created a customer profitability report for Windward Yachts. Similar to the product profitability report, the design team needed to gather data concerning sales to Windward Yachts and the direct material, direct labor, and shipping costs associated with those sales. Those data are presented below:

	Windward Yachts
Sales	$11,350
Direct costs:	
Direct materials	$ 2,123
Direct labor......................	$ 1,900
Shipping	$ 205

Using these data and the data from Exhibit 7–9, the design team created the customer profitability report shown in Exhibit 7–11. The report revealed the customer margin for Windward Yachts is $699. A similar report could be prepared for each of Classic Brass's 250 customers, thereby enabling the company to cultivate relationships with its most profitable customers, while taking steps to reduce the negative impact of unprofitable customers.

EXHIBIT 7–11
Customer Margin—Activity-Based Costing

	A	B	C	D
1	**Customer Margin—Activity-Based Costing**			
2			*Windward Yachts*	
3	Sales		$11,350	
4	Costs:			
5	Direct materials	$ 2,123		
6	Direct labor	1,900		
7	Shipping	205		
8	Customer orders (from Exhibit 7–9)	960		
9	Product design (from Exhibit 7–9)	630		
10	Order size (from Exhibit 7–9)	3,363		
11	Customer relations (from Exhibit 7–9)	1,470	10,651	
12	Customer margin		$ 699	
13				

| ◄ ► ... | Exhibit 7-8 | Exhibit 7-9 | Exhibit 7-10 | Skip Thi ... ⊕ |

Microsoft Excel

USING ACTIVITY-BASED COSTING TO LOWER HEALTH-CARE COSTS

Researchers at Duke University, Harvard University, and Massachusetts General Hospital used activity-based costing to explore an interesting question: If hospital nurses call patients after they are discharged from the hospital, will it lower the hospital's overall operating cost? To answer this question, the researchers needed to compare the cost of performing the post-discharge phone calls to the savings realized from reducing the number of patients that return to the Emergency Department (ED).

The researchers took the process of conducting post-discharge phone calls and broke it into five activities: (1) reviewing the chart, (2) providing discharge instructions to the patient, (3) asking for and receiving patient feedback about their encounter, (4) helping patients with follow-up problems, and (5) documenting the encounter. They concluded that this five-step process costs $243.14 per avoided trip to the ED. However, given that the average cost per ED visit is $378.03, the phone calls produced a savings of $134.89 per avoided ED visit.

Source: Yingna Liu, Ines Luciani-McGillivray, Mary Fran Hughes, Ali S. Raja, Robert S. Kaplan, and Brian J. Yun, "Time-Driven Activity-Based Costing of Emergency Department Postdischarge Nurse Calls," *Journal of Healthcare Management,* November–December 2020, pp. 419–428.

Comparison of Traditional and ABC Product Costs

The ABC team used a two-step process to compare its traditional and ABC product costs. First, the team reviewed the product margins reported by the traditional cost system. Then, it contrasted the differences between the traditional and ABC product margins.

Product Margins Computed Using the Traditional Cost System

Exhibit 7–12 shows the traditional cost system's product margins for Standard Stanchions ($615,750) and Custom Compass Housings ($258,000). Each product's sales, direct materials, and direct labor equal the amounts used in Exhibit 7–10 to calculate the ABC product margins. In other words, the traditional cost system and the ABC system treat these three pieces of revenue and cost data identically.

The manufacturing overhead allocated to each product is based on a plantwide rate of $50 per machine-hour, calculated as follows:

$$\text{Plantwide overhead rate} = \frac{\text{Total estimated manufacturing overhead}}{\text{Total estimated machine-hours}}$$

$$= \frac{\$1,000,000}{20,000 \text{ machine-hours}}$$

$$= \$50 \text{ per machine-hour}$$

The total estimated manufacturing overhead used in the numerator of this rate ($1,000,000) agrees with the total manufacturing overhead shown in the income statement in Exhibit 7–2. The 20,000 machine-hours used in the denominator of the plantwide rate agrees with the total machine-hours used to compute the Order Size activity rate in Exhibit 7–6.

Because 17,500 machine-hours were worked on standard stanchions, this product line is assigned $875,000 (17,500 machine-hours × $50 per machine-hour) of manufacturing overhead cost. Similarly, the custom compass housings required 2,500 machine-hours, so this product line is assigned $125,000 (2,500 machine-hours × $50 per machine-hour) of manufacturing overhead cost.

EXHIBIT 7–12
Product Margins—Traditional Cost System

	A	B	C	D	E	F	G	H	I	J
1	**Product Margins—Traditional Cost System**									
2			*Standard Stanchions*		*Custom Compass Housings*				*Total*	
3	Sales		$ 2,660,000		$ 540,000				$3,200,000	
4	Cost of goods sold:									
5	Direct materials	$ 905,500			$ 69,500			$ 975,000		
6	Direct labor	263,750			87,500			351,250		
7	Manufacturing overhead	875,000	2,044,250		125,000	282,000		1,000,000	2,326,250	
8	Product margin		$ 615,750			$ 258,000			873,750	
9	Selling and administrative								875,000	
10	Net operating loss								$ (1,250)	
11										

Microsoft Excel

Notice, the net operating loss of $1,250 shown in Exhibit 7–12 agrees with the loss reported in the income statement in Exhibit 7–2 and with the loss shown in the table beneath Exhibit 7–10. The company's *total* sales, *total* costs, and resulting net operating loss are the same regardless of whether you are looking at the absorption income statement in Exhibit 7–2, the ABC product profitability analysis, or the traditional product profitability analysis in Exhibit 7–12. Although the "total pie" remains constant across the traditional and ABC systems, what differs is how the pie is divided between the two product lines. The traditional product margin calculations suggest that standard stanchions are generating a product margin of $615,750 and the custom compass housings a product margin of $258,000. However, these product margins differ from the ABC product margins reported in Exhibit 7–10. Indeed, the traditional cost system is sending misleading signals to Classic Brass's managers about each product's profitability. Let's explain why.

The Differences between ABC and Traditional Product Costs

The changes in product margins caused by switching from the traditional cost system to the activity-based costing system are shown below:

	Standard Stanchions	Custom Compass Housings
Product margins—traditional...............	$615,750	$ 258,000
Product margins—ABC....................	906,250	(49,500)
Change in reported product margins	$290,500	$(307,500)

The traditional cost system overcosts the standard stanchions and consequently reports an artificially low product margin for this product. The switch to an activity-based view of product profitability increases the product margin on standard stanchions by $290,500. In contrast, the traditional cost system undercosts the custom compass housings and reports an artificially high product margin for this product. The switch to activity-based costing decreases the product margin on custom compass housings by $307,500.

EXHIBIT 7–13
A Comparison of Traditional and Activity-Based Cost Assignments

⊿	A	B	C	D	E	F	G	H	I
1			*Standard Stanchions*			*Custom Compass Housings*			
2	**Traditional Cost System**		(a) Amount	(a) ÷ (c) %		(b) Amount	(b) ÷ (c) %		(c) Total
3	Direct materials		$ 905,500	92.9%		$ 69,500	7.1%		$ 975,000
4	Direct labor		263,750	75.1%		87,500	24.9%		351,250
5	Manufacturing overhead		875,000	87.5%		125,000	12.5%		1,000,000
6	Total cost assigned to products		$ 2,044,250			$ 282,000			2,326,250
7	Selling and administrative								875,000
8	Total cost								$ 3,201,250
9									
10	**Activity-Based Costing System**								
11	Direct costs:								
12	Direct materials		$ 905,500	92.9%		$ 69,500	7.1%		$ 975,000
13	Direct labor		263,750	75.1%		87,500	24.9%		351,250
14	Shipping		60,000	92.3%		5,000	7.7%		65,000
15	Indirect costs:								
16	Customer orders		192,000	60.0%		128,000	40.0%		320,000
17	Product design		-	0.0%		252,000	100.0%		252,000
18	Order size		332,500	87.5%		47,500	12.5%		380,000
19	Total cost assigned to products		$ 1,753,750			$ 589,500			2,343,250
20	Costs not assigned to products:								
21	Customer relations								367,500
22	Other								490,500
23	Total cost								$ 3,201,250
24									

◄ ►   ... | Exhibit 7-12 | **Exhibit 7-13** | ⊕

Microsoft Excel

Exhibit 7–13 explains why the traditional product margins differ from the ABC product margins. Rows 3–8 summarize the traditional margins previously calculated in Exhibit 7–12 and rows 12–19 depict the ABC margins previously calculated in Exhibit 7–10. The only new information in Exhibit 7–13 is the two columns of percentages. The first of these two columns shows the percentage of each cost assigned to standard stanchions. For example, the $905,500 of direct materials cost traced to standard stanchions is 92.9 percent of the company's total direct materials cost of $975,000. The second column of percentages does the same thing for custom compass housings.

There are three reasons why the traditional and activity-based costing systems report different product margins. First, Classic Brass's traditional cost system allocates all manufacturing overhead costs to products even if those products did not cause those costs. Conversely, ABC assigns to products only the costs they have caused; therefore, the manufacturing overhead costs included in the Customer Relations and Other activity cost pools are purposely not allocated to products. The Customer Relations costs are caused by customers, not products, and the Other activity includes organization-sustaining and unused capacity costs—neither of which is caused by products.

Second, the company's traditional cost system uses one volume-related allocation base (machine-hours) to allocate 87.5 percent of manufacturing overhead to standard stanchions and 12.5 percent to custom compass housings. However, the ABC system revealed standard stanchions caused only 60 percent of the Customer Orders cost, while the custom compass housings caused 40% of these costs. It also showed standard stanchions caused 0% of the Product Design costs, whereas 100% of those costs were caused by custom compass housings. By overlooking the batch-level (Customer Orders) and product-level (Product Design) activity costs, the traditional system's exclusive reliance on volume-based overhead allocation assigns too much overhead to standard stanchions (the high-volume product) and too little to custom compass housings (the low-volume product).

The third reason product margins differ between the two cost systems is because traditional cost systems ignore nonmanufacturing costs caused by products and ABC systems include nonmanufacturing costs on a cause-and-effect basis. In the case of Classic Brass, its ABC system directly traces shipping costs to products and includes nonmanufacturing overhead costs caused by products within its activity cost pools.

**MANAGERIAL
ACCOUNTING IN ACTION
THE WRAP-UP**

Classic Brass

The ABC design team presented the results of its work in a meeting attended by all of the top managers of Classic Brass, including president John Towers, production manager Susan Richter, marketing manager Tom Olafson, and accounting manager Mary Goodman. The ABC team brought copies of the chart showing the ABC design (Exhibit 7–7), and the table comparing the traditional and ABC cost assignments (Exhibit 7–13). After the formal presentation by the ABC team, the following discussion took place:

John: According to the ABC analysis, we had it all backwards. We are losing money on the custom products and making a fistful on the standard products.

Mary: I had no idea the Product Design work for custom compass housings was so expensive! I knew burying these costs in our plantwide overhead rate was penalizing standard stanchions, but I didn't understand the magnitude of the problem.

Susan: I never did believe we were making a lot of money on the custom jobs. You ought to see all of the problems they create for us in production.

Tom: The custom jobs always seem to give us headaches in marketing, too.

John: If we are losing money on custom compass housings, why not suggest to our customers they go elsewhere for that kind of work?

Tom: Wait a minute, we would lose a lot of sales.

Susan: So what, we would save a lot more costs.

Mary: Maybe yes, maybe no. Some of the costs would not disappear if we were to drop the custom business.

Tom: Like what?

Mary: Well Tom, I believe you said about 10 percent of your time is spent dealing with new products. As a consequence, 10 percent of your salary was allocated to the Product Design cost pool. If we were to drop all of the products requiring design work, would you be willing to take a 10 percent pay cut?

Tom: I trust you're joking.

Mary: Do you see the problem? Just because 10 percent of your time is spent on custom products doesn't mean the company would save 10 percent of your salary if the custom products were dropped. Before we take a drastic action like dropping the custom products, we should identify which costs are really relevant.

John: We wouldn't want to drop a lot of products only to find our costs really haven't changed much. It is true that dropping the products would free up resources like Tom's time, but we had better be sure we have some good use for those resources *before* we take such an action.

COMMUNICATING WITH DATA VISUALIZATIONS

Diagnostic analytics answer the question: Why did it happen? This visualization is based on Exhibit 7–13, and it compares the traditional and ABC cost allocations for Classic Brass. The company's traditional and ABC systems assigned a total of $2,044,250 and $1,753,750, respectively, to the standard stanchions—suggesting the traditional system overcosted standard stanchions by $290,500. Similarly, the company's traditional and ABC systems assigned a total of $282,000 and $589,500, respectively, to the custom compass housings—suggesting the traditional system undercosted custom compass housings by $307,500.

The biggest reason why the traditional system failed to accurately measure each product's true cost relates to the Product Design (purple) activity. The traditional cost assigned 87.5% of these costs to standard stanchions and 12.5% to custom compass housings. However, the ABC system shows that all of these costs should be allocated to custom compass housings. Notice, there is no purple portion within the standard stanchion's ABC bar, as shown below.

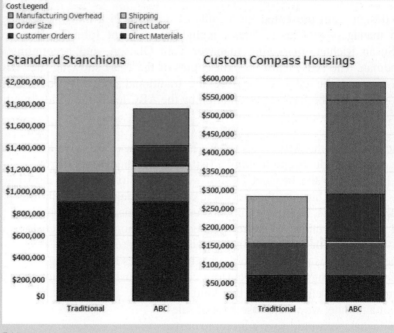

Tableau

USING ACTIVITY-BASED COSTING TO MEASURE PHARMACY COSTS FOR DIABETES MANAGEMENT

According to researchers from Kuwait, the global cost of treating diabetes exceeds $1 trillion per year, or 1.8% of global gross domestic product (GDP). To help better understand these costs, the researchers studied the cost drivers of pharmacy services in a diabetes care institute. Their cost model included the direct costs of diabetes medications plus the pharmacists' labor costs incurred to perform four activities: dispensing medications, pharmacotherapy consulting, inventory management, and compounding. Their findings showed it costs $4,666,633 per year to provide pharmacy services to 3,745 patients—an average annual cost of $1,246 per patient. The researchers noted "more than 12% of patient pharmacy visits to collect medications do not result in actual dispensing. These are non-value-added encounters. Thus, using technologies that screen patient medication eligibility and provide guidance before seeing a pharmacist would significantly reduce pharmacist workloads."

Source: Abdullah Alibrahim, Yousef Abdulsalam, Salma Al Mutawa, Hashem Behbehani, Dari Alhuwail, and Saud Al Jenaaei, "Towards Value-Based Healthcare: Establishing Baseline Pharmacy Care Costs for Diabetes Management," *International Journal of Health Planning & Management,* October 2021.

Activity-Based Costing: Further Considerations

Thus far, we have illustrated how ABC is used to calculate product and customer profitability and contrasted it with traditional absorption costing. However, when companies contemplate implementing ABC, there are a variety of other factors they should consider:

1. An ABC system's activity rates can help organizations identify opportunities for process improvements. When used in this way, activity-based costing is often called *activity-based management.* **Activity-based management** involves focusing on activities to eliminate waste, decrease processing time, reduce defects, and lower costs. For example, looking at the activity rates in Exhibit 7–6, managers at Classic Brass may conclude $320 to process a customer order is far too expensive for this non-value-added activity. As a consequence, they may target their process improvement efforts toward the Customer Orders activity.

   Benchmarking is another way to leverage the information in activity rates. **Benchmarking** is a systematic approach to identifying the activities with the greatest room for improvement. It is based on comparing the performance in an organization with the performance of other, similar organizations known for their outstanding performance. If a particular part of the organization performs far below the world-class standard, managers will likely target that area for improvement.

2. An ABC system usually does not replace the company's cost system used for external reporting purposes. While ABC typically provides more accurate cost data than legacy systems that support external reporting, the benefits of this increased accuracy may not outweigh the costs of maintaining two systems.

3. ABC systems measure how costs are consumed by products and customers. They do not distinguish between relevant and irrelevant costs in specific decision contexts. Before making any significant decisions using ABC data, managers must identify which costs are relevant for the decision at hand. For example, if an ABC system assigns some unavoidable fixed costs to the products that consume them, those costs should be ignored when making decisions, such as whether to keep or drop certain products.

4. ABC systems often fail to be embraced by a company's managers for three reasons. First, they perceive the ABC implementation as an accounting project that is disconnected from their jobs on the operational side of the business. Second, they perceive the ABC system as unimportant because it does not replace the existing cost system that supports external reporting. Third, they feel threatened by ABC profitability data that contradicts historical and cultural norms regarding which products and customers are most profitable. To overcome these hurdles, an ABC system must be visibly and vocally supported by top management, designed by a cross-functional team of influential managers, and linked to the company's performance evaluation and reward system.

Summary

Traditional cost accounting methods suffer from several limitations that can distort costs for decision-making purposes. All manufacturing costs—even those not caused by any specific product—are allocated to products. Nonmanufacturing costs caused by products are not assigned to products. And finally, traditional methods place too much reliance on unit-level allocation bases such as direct labor and machine-hours. This results in overcosting high-volume products and undercosting low-volume products and can lead to poor decisions.

Activity-based costing estimates the costs of the resources consumed by cost objects such as products and customers. The activity-based costing approach assumes cost objects generate activities that in turn consume costly resources. Activities form the link between costs and cost objects. Activity-based costing is concerned with overhead—both manufacturing overhead and selling and administrative overhead. The accounting for direct labor and direct materials is usually the same under traditional and ABC costing methods.

To build an ABC system, companies typically choose a small set of activities that summarize much of the work performed in overhead departments. Associated with each activity is an activity cost pool. To the extent possible, overhead costs are directly traced to these activity cost pools. The remaining overhead costs are allocated to the activity cost pools in the first-stage allocation. Interviews with managers often form the basis for these allocations.

An activity rate is computed for each cost pool by dividing the costs assigned to the cost pool by the activity measure. Activity rates provide useful information to managers concerning the costs of performing overhead activities. A particularly high cost for an activity may trigger efforts to improve the way the activity is performed.

In the second-stage allocation, activity rates are used to apply costs to cost objects such as products and customers. The costs computed under activity-based costing are often quite different from the costs generated by a company's traditional cost accounting system. While the ABC system is almost certainly more accurate, managers should nevertheless exercise caution before making decisions based on the ABC data. Some of the costs may not be avoidable and hence would not be relevant.

 Data Analytics Exercise available in Connect to complement this chapter

Review Problem: Activity-Based Costing

Ferris Corporation makes a single product—a fire-resistant commercial filing cabinet—that it sells to office furniture distributors. The company has an ABC system it uses for internal decision making. The company has two overhead departments whose costs are as follows:

Manufacturing overhead	$500,000
Selling and administrative overhead	300,000
Total overhead costs	$800,000

The company's ABC system has the following activity cost pools and activity measures:

Activity Cost Pool	Activity Measure
Assembling units	Number of units
Processing orders	Number of orders
Supporting customers	Number of customers
Other	Not applicable

Costs assigned to the "Other" activity cost pool have no activity measure; they consist of organization-sustaining costs and unused capacity costs—neither of which are assigned to orders, customers, or the product.

Ferris Corporation distributes the costs of manufacturing overhead and selling and administrative overhead to the activity cost pools based on employee interviews, the results of which are reported below:

	Assembling Units	Processing Orders	Supporting Customers	Other	Total
Manufacturing overhead	50%	35%	5%	10%	100%
Selling and administrative overhead	10%	45%	25%	20%	100%
Total activity	1,000 units	250 orders	100 customers		

Required:
1. Perform the first-stage allocation of overhead costs to the activity cost pools as in Exhibit 7–5.
2. Compute activity rates for the activity cost pools as in Exhibit 7–6.
3. OfficeMart is one of Ferris Corporation's customers. Last year, OfficeMart ordered filing cabinets four different times. OfficeMart ordered a total of 80 filing cabinets during the year. Construct a table as in Exhibit 7–9 showing the overhead costs attributable to OfficeMart.
4. The selling price of a filing cabinet is $595. The cost of direct materials is $180 per filing cabinet, and direct labor is $50 per filing cabinet. What is the customer margin of OfficeMart? See Exhibit 7–11 for an example of how to complete this report.

Solution to Review Problem

1. The first-stage allocation of costs to the activity cost pools appears below:

	Activity Cost Pools				
	Assembling Units	Processing Orders	Supporting Customers	Other	Total
Manufacturing overhead	$250,000	$175,000	$ 25,000	$ 50,000	$500,000
Selling and administrative overhead	30,000	135,000	75,000	60,000	300,000
Total cost.	$280,000	$310,000	$100,000	$110,000	$800,000

2. The activity rates for the activity cost pools are:

Activity Cost Pools	(a) Total Cost	(b) Total Activity	(a) ÷ (b) Activity Rate
Assembling units.	$280,000	1,000 units	$280 per unit
Processing orders.	$310,000	250 orders	$1,240 per order
Supporting customers	$100,000	100 customers	$1,000 per customer

3. The overhead costs attributable to OfficeMart are computed as follows:

Activity Cost Pools	(a) Activity Rate	(b) Activity	(a) × (b) ABC Cost
Assembling units.	$280 per unit	80 units	$22,400
Processing orders.	$1,240 per order	4 orders	$4,960
Supporting customers	$1,000 per customer	1 customer	$1,000

4. The customer margin is computed as follows:

Sales ($595 per unit × 80 units)		$47,600
Costs:		
Direct materials ($180 per unit × 80 units)	$14,400	
Direct labor ($50 per unit × 80 units)	4,000	
Assembling units (above)	22,400	
Processing orders (above)	4,960	
Supporting customers (above)	1,000	46,760
Customer margin		$ 840

Glossary

Activity An event causing the consumption of overhead resources. (p. 307)

Activity cost pool A "bucket" that accumulates costs related to a single activity measure in an activity-based costing system. (p. 307)

Activity measure An allocation base in an activity-based costing system; ideally, a measure of the amount of activity that drives the costs in an activity cost pool. (p. 307)

Activity-based costing (ABC) A costing method based on activities that provides managers with cost information for strategic and other decisions potentially affecting capacity and therefore fixed as well as variable costs. (p. 306)

Activity-based management (ABM) A management approach focusing on managing activities as a way of eliminating waste and reducing delays and defects. (p. 325)

Batch-level activities Activities performed each time a batch of goods is handled or processed, regardless of how many units are in the batch. The amount of resource consumed depends on the number of batches run rather than the number of units in the batch. (p. 308)

Benchmarking A systematic approach to identifying the activities with the greatest potential for improvement. (p. 325)

Customer-level activities Activities carried out to support customers that are unrelated to specific products. (p. 309)

Duration driver A measure of the time required to perform an activity. (p. 307)

First-stage allocation The process of assigning overhead costs to activity cost pools in an activity-based costing system. (p. 312)

Organization-sustaining activities Activities that are carried out regardless of which customers are served, which products are produced, how many batches are run, or how many units are made. (p. 309)

Product-level activities Activities related to specific products that must be performed regardless of how many units are produced and sold or batches run. (p. 309)

Second-stage allocation Using activity rates to apply costs to products and customers in activity-based costing. (p. 314)

Transaction driver A count of the number of times an activity occurs. (p. 307)

Unit-level activities Activities performed each time a unit is produced. (p. 308)

Questions

7–1 How does activity-based costing differ from traditional absorption costing?

7–2 Why does relying exclusively on volume-related overhead allocation bases distort product costs?

7–3 What steps can an organization take to reduce its managers' resistance to activity-based costing?

7–4 What are unit-level, batch-level, product-level, customer-level, and organization-sustaining activities?

7–5 What types of costs should not be assigned to products in an activity-based costing system?

7–6 What are the two stages of allocation in activity-based costing?

7–7 Do activity rates measure avoidable costs? Explain.

7–8 When activity-based costing is used, why do manufacturing overhead costs often shift from high-volume products to low-volume products?

7–9 How can the activity rates (i.e., cost per activity) for the various activities be used to target process improvements?

7–10 The differences between traditional and activity-based product margins are primarily caused by a company's unit-level activities. Do you agree?

Applying Excel   Mc Graw Hill connect

LO7–1, LO7–2, LO7–3, LO7–4, LO7–5

The Excel worksheet shown below recreates the Review Problem pertaining to Ferris Corporation. The workbook, and instructions on how to complete the file, can be found in Connect.

You should proceed to the requirements below only after completing your worksheet.

Required:

1. Check your worksheet by doubling the units ordered in cell B16 to 160. The customer margin under activity-based costing should now be $7,640 and the traditional costing product margin should be $(21,600). If you do not get these results, find the errors in your worksheet and correct them.

   a. Why has the customer margin under activity-based costing more than doubled when the number of units ordered is doubled?

   b. Why has the traditional costing product margin exactly doubled from a loss of $10,800 to a loss of $21,600?

   c. Which costing system, activity-based costing or traditional costing, provides a more accurate picture of what happens to profits as the number of units ordered increases? Explain.

	A	B	C	D	E	F	G
1	Chapter 7: Applying Excel						
2							
3	**Data**						
4	Manufacturing overhead	$500,000					
5	Selling and administrative overhead	$300,000					
6							
7		Assembling Units	Processing Orders	Supporting Customers	Other		
8	Manufacturing overhead	50%	35%	5%	10%		
9	Selling and administrative overhead	10%	45%	25%	20%		
10	Total activity	1,000	250	100			
11		units	orders	customers			
12							
13	OfficeMart orders:						
14	Customers	1	customer				
15	Orders	4	orders				
16	Number of filing cabinets ordered in total	80	units				
17	Selling price	$595					
18	Direct materials	$180					
19	Direct labor	$50					
20							
21	Enter a formula into each of the cells marked with a ? below						
22	**Review Problem: Activity-Based Costing**						
23							
24	*Perform the first stage allocations*						
25		Assembling Units	Processing Orders	Supporting Customers	Other	Total	
26	Manufacturing overhead	?	?	?	?	?	
27	Selling and administrative overhead	?	?	?	?	?	
28	Total cost	?	?	?	?	?	
29							
30	*Compute the activity rates*						
31	Activity Cost Pools	Total Cost	Total Activity		Activity Rate		
32	Assembling units	?	? units		? per unit		
33	Processing orders	?	? orders		? per order		
34	Supporting customers	?	? customers		? per customer		
35							
36	*Compute the overhead cost attributable to the OfficeMart orders*						
37	Activity Cost Pools	Activity Rate		Activity	ABC Cost		
38	Assembling units	? per unit		? units	?		
39	Processing orders	? per order		? orders	?		
40	Supporting customers	? per customer		? customer	?		
41							
42	*Determine the customer margin for the OfficeMart orders under Activity-Based Costing*						
43	Sales		?				
44	Costs:						
45	Direct materials	?					
46	Direct labor	?					
47	Unit-related overhead	?					
48	Order-related overhead	?					
49	Customer-related overhead	?	?				
50	Customer margin		?				
51							
52	*Determine the product margin for the OfficeMart orders under a traditional cost system*						
53	Manufacturing overhead	?					
54	Total activity	? units					
55	Manufacturing overhead per unit	? per unit					
56							
57	Sales		?				
58	Costs:						
59	Direct materials	?					
60	Direct labor	?					
61	Manufacturing overhead	?	?				
62	Traditional costing product margin		?				
63							

H ◀ ▶ H | **Chapter 7 Form** | Filled in Chapter 7 Form | Chapter 7 Formulas |

Microsoft Excel

2. Let's assume OfficeMart places different orders next year, purchasing higher-end filing cabinets more frequently, but in smaller quantities per order. Enter the following data into your worksheet:

Data				
Manufacturing overhead	$500,000			
Selling and administrative overhead	$300,000			
	Assembling Units	Processing Orders	Supporting Customers	Other
Manufacturing overhead	50%	35%	5%	10%
Selling and administrative overhead	10%	45%	25%	20%
Total activity	1,000 units	250 orders	100 customers	
OfficeMart orders:				
Customers	1 customer			
Orders.	20 orders			
Total number of filing cabinets ordered	80 units			
Selling price	$795			
Direct materials	$185			
Direct labor.	$ 90			

a. What is the customer margin under activity-based costing?
b. What is the product margin under the traditional cost system?
c. Explain why the profitability picture looks much different now than it did when OfficeMart was ordering less expensive filing cabinets less frequently, but in larger quantities per order.

3. Using the data you entered in part (2), change the percentage of selling and administrative overhead attributable to processing orders from 45% to 30% and the percentage attributable to supporting customers from 25% to 40%. That portion of the worksheet should look like this:

	Assembling Units	Processing Orders	Supporting Customers	Other
Manufacturing overhead	50%	35%	5%	10%
Selling and administrative overhead	10%	30%	40%	20%
Total activity	1,000 units	250 orders	100 customers	

a. Relative to the results from part (2), what has happened to the customer margin under activity-based costing? Why?
b. Relative to the results from part (2), what has happened to the product margin under the traditional cost system? Why?

The Foundational 15   Mc Graw Hill connect

LO7-1, LO7-3, LO7-4

Hickory Company manufactures two products—14,000 units of Product Y and 6,000 units of Product Z. The company uses a plantwide overhead rate based on direct labor-hours. It is considering implementing an activity-based costing (ABC) system that allocates all $684,000 of its manufacturing overhead to four cost pools. The following additional information is available for the company as a whole and for Products Y and Z:

Activity Cost Pool	Activity Measure	Estimated Overhead Cost	Expected Activity
Machining	Machine-hours	$200,000	10,000 MHs
Machine setups	Number of setups	$100,000	200 setups
Product design	Number of products	$84,000	2 products
General factory	Direct labor-hours	$300,000	12,000 DLHs

Activity Measure	Product Y	Product Z
Machine-hours	7,000	3,000
Number of setups	50	150
Number of products	1	1
Direct labor-hours	8,000	4,000

Required:

1. What is the company's plantwide overhead rate?
2. Using the plantwide overhead rate, how much manufacturing overhead cost is allocated to Product Y? How much is allocated to Product Z?
3. What is the activity rate for the Machining activity cost pool?
4. What is the activity rate for the Machine Setups activity cost pool?
5. What is the activity rate for the Product Design activity cost pool?
6. What is the activity rate for the General Factory activity cost pool?
7. Which of the four activities is a batch-level activity? Why?
8. Which of the four activities is a product-level activity? Why?
9. Using the ABC system, how much total manufacturing overhead cost is assigned to Product Y?
10. Using the ABC system, how much total manufacturing overhead cost is assigned to Product Z?
11. Using the plantwide overhead rate, what percentage of the total overhead cost is allocated to Product Y? What percentage is allocated to Product Z?
12. Using the ABC system, what percentage of the Machining costs is assigned to Product Y? What percentage is assigned to Product Z? Are these percentages similar to those obtained in requirement 11? Why?
13. Using the ABC system, what percentage of Machine Setups cost is assigned to Product Y? What percentage is assigned to Product Z? Are these percentages similar to those obtained in requirement 11? Why?
14. Using the ABC system, what percentage of the Product Design cost is assigned to Product Y? What percentage is assigned to Product Z? Are these percentages similar to those obtained in requirement 11? Why?
15. Using the ABC system, what percentage of the General Factory cost is assigned to Product Y? What percentage is assigned to Product Z? Are these percentages similar to those obtained in requirement 11? Why?

Mc Graw Hill connect **Exercises**

EXERCISE 7–1 ABC Cost Hierarchy LO7–1

The following activities occur at Greenwich Corporation, a company that manufactures a variety of products.
a. Receive raw materials from suppliers.
b. Manage parts inventories.
c. Do rough milling work on products.
d. Interview and process new employees in the personnel department.
e. Design new products.
f. Perform periodic preventive maintenance on general-use equipment.
g. Use the general factory building.
h. Issue purchase orders for a job.

Required:
Classify each of the activities above as either a unit-level, batch-level, product-level, or organization-sustaining activity.

EXERCISE 7–2 First Stage Allocation LO7–2

SecuriCorp operates a fleet of armored cars that make scheduled pickups and deliveries in the Los Angeles area. The company is implementing an activity-based costing system with four activity cost pools: Travel, Pickup and Delivery, Customer Service, and Other. The activity measures are miles for the Travel cost pool, number of pickups and deliveries for the Pickup and Delivery cost pool, and number of customers for the Customer Service cost pool. The Other cost pool has no activity measure because it is an organization-sustaining activity. The following costs will be assigned using the activity-based costing system:

Driver and guard wages	$ 720,000
Vehicle operating expense	280,000
Vehicle depreciation	120,000
Customer representative salaries and expenses	160,000
Office expenses	30,000
Administrative expenses	320,000
Total cost	$1,630,000

The distribution of resource consumption across the activity cost pools is as follows:

	Travel	Pickup and Delivery	Customer Service	Other	Totals
Driver and guard wages	50%	35%	10%	5%	100%
Vehicle operating expense	70%	5%	0%	25%	100%
Vehicle depreciation	60%	15%	0%	25%	100%
Customer representative salaries and expenses	0%	0%	90%	10%	100%
Office expenses	0%	20%	30%	50%	100%
Administrative expenses	0%	5%	60%	35%	100%

Required:
Complete the first stage allocations of costs to activity cost pools as illustrated in Exhibit 7–5.

EXERCISE 7–3 Compute Activity Rates LO7–3
Green Thumb Gardening is a small gardening service using activity-based costing to estimate costs for pricing and other purposes. The owner of the company believes costs are driven primarily by the size of customer lawns, the size of customer garden beds, the distance to travel to customers, and the number of customers. In addition, the costs of maintaining garden beds depend on whether the beds are low-maintenance beds (mainly ordinary trees and shrubs) or high-maintenance beds (mainly flowers and exotic plants). Accordingly, the company uses the five activity cost pools listed below:

Activity Cost Pool	Activity Measure
Caring for lawn	Square feet of lawn
Caring for garden beds–low maintenance	Square feet of low-maintenance beds
Caring for garden beds–high maintenance	Square feet of high-maintenance beds
Travel to jobs	Miles
Customer billing and service	Number of customers

The company completed its first-stage cost allocations and summarized its annual costs and activity as follows:

Activity Cost Pool	Estimated Overhead Cost	Expected Activity
Caring for lawn	$72,000	150,000 square feet of lawn
Caring for garden beds–low maintenance	$26,400	20,000 square feet of low-maintenance beds
Caring for garden beds–high maintenance	$41,400	15,000 square feet of high-maintenance beds
Travel to jobs	$3,250	12,500 miles
Customer billing and service	$8,750	25 customers

Required:

Compute the activity rate for each of the activity cost pools.

EXERCISE 7–4 Second-Stage Allocation LO7–4

Klumper Corporation is a diversified manufacturer of industrial goods. The company's activity-based costing system contains the following six activity cost pools and activity rates:

Activity Cost Pool	Activity Rate
Supporting direct labor	$6 per direct labor-hour
Machine processing	$4 per machine-hour
Machine setups	$50 per setup
Production orders	$90 per order
Shipments	$14 per shipment
Product sustaining	$840 per product

Activity data have been supplied for the following two products:

	Total Expected Activity	
	K425	M67
Number of units produced per year	200	2,000
Direct labor-hours	80	500
Machine-hours	100	1,500
Machine setups	1	4
Production orders	1	4
Shipments	1	10
Product sustaining	1	1

Required:

How much total overhead cost would be assigned to K425 and M67 using the activity-based costing system?

EXERCISE 7–5 Product and Customer Profitability Analysis LO7–4, LO7–5

Thermal Rising, Inc., makes paragliders for sale through specialty sporting goods stores. The company has a standard paraglider model, but also makes custom-designed paragliders. Management designed an activity-based costing system with the following activity cost pools and activity rates:

Activity Cost Pool	Activity Rate
Supporting direct labor	$26 per direct labor-hour
Order processing	$284 per order
Custom design processing	$186 per custom design
Customer service	$379 per customer

Management wants to calculate the profitability of a particular customer, Big Sky Outfitters, which ordered the following products over the last 12 months:

	Standard Model	Custom Design
Number of gliders	20	3
Number of orders	1	3
Number of custom designs	0	3
Direct labor-hours per glider	26.35	28.00
Selling price per glider	$1,850	$2,400
Direct materials cost per glider	$564	$634

The company's direct labor rate is $19.50 per hour.

Required:

Using the company's activity-based costing system, compute the customer margin of Big Sky Outfitters.

EXERCISE 7–6 Cost Hierarchy LO7–1

Flash Express purchases USB flash drives from suppliers and then applies corporate logos to the exterior of those flash drives for its customers. The company maintains a dedicated piece of equipment for each type of product that it processes, such as "top hat" flash drives, credit card flash drives, swing flash drives, and wristband flash drives. The company defines its batches based on customer orders. For example, if one customer places an order for 1,000 credit card flash drives, then that order is processed and shipped as one batch. If another customer places an order for 100 "top hat" flash drives, 100 swing flash drives, and 100 wrist band flash drives, then that order is processed as three batches and shipped as one batch.

A number of activities carried out at Flash Express are listed below.
a. Sales representatives' periodic visits to customers to keep them informed about the company's existing products and its new product introductions.
b. Engaging in price negotiations with the company's supplier of credit card flash drives.
c. Programming and calibrating the "top hat" logo application machine so it properly applies the logo for a specific customer's production run.
d. Visually inspecting each flash drive produced to ensure the logo has been applied in a defect-free manner.
e. Preparing shipping documents and packaging for a customer order.
f. Periodic maintenance of the equipment used to process wristband flash drives.
g. Lighting and heating the company's production facility.
h. Preparation of the company's quarterly financial reports.

Required:

Classify each of the activities above as either a unit-level, batch-level, product-level, customer-level, or organization-sustaining activity.

EXERCISE 7–7 First-Stage Allocations LO7–2

The operations vice president of Security Home Bank is investigating the efficiency of the bank's operations. She is concerned about the costs of handling routine transactions at the bank and would like to compare these costs at the bank's various branches. If the branches with the most efficient operations can be identified, their methods can be studied and replicated elsewhere. While the bank maintains meticulous records of wages and other costs, there has been no attempt to show how those costs are related to the various services provided by the bank. The operations vice president has asked for your help in conducting an activity-based costing study of bank operations. In particular, she would like to know the cost of opening an account, the cost of processing deposits and withdrawals, and the cost of processing other customer transactions.

The Westfield branch of Security Home Bank submitted the following cost data for last year:

Teller wages..	$160,000
Assistant branch manager salary............................	75,000
Branch manager salary	80,000
Total...	$315,000

Virtually all other costs of the branch—rent, depreciation, utilities, and so on—are organization-sustaining costs that cannot be meaningfully assigned to individual customer transactions such as depositing checks.

In addition to the cost data above, the employees of the Westfield branch were interviewed concerning how their time was distributed last year across the activities included in the activity-based costing study. The results of those interviews appear below:

	Opening Accounts	Processing Deposits and Withdrawals	Processing Other Customer Transactions	Other Activities	Total
Teller wages	5%	65%	20%	10%	100%
Assistant branch manager salary	15%	5%	30%	50%	100%
Branch manager salary	5%	0%	10%	85%	100%

Required:

Prepare the first-stage allocation for the activity-based costing study. (See Exhibit 7–5 for an example of a first-stage allocation.)

EXERCISE 7–8 Computing and Interpreting Activity Rates LO7–3

(This exercise is a continuation of Exercise 7–7; it should be assigned *only* if Exercise 7–7 also is assigned.) The manager of the Westfield branch of Security Home Bank provided the following data concerning the branch's transactions during the past year:

Activity	Total Activity at the Westfield Branch
Opening accounts	500 new accounts opened
Processing deposits and withdrawals	100,000 deposits and withdrawals processed
Processing other customer transactions	5,000 other customer transactions processed

The lowest costs reported by other branches for these activities are displayed below:

Activity	Lowest Cost among All Security Home Bank Branches
Opening accounts	$26.75 per new account
Processing deposits and withdrawals	$1.24 per deposit or withdrawal
Processing other customer transactions	$11.86 per other customer transaction

Required:

1. Using the first-stage allocation from Exercise 7–7 and the above data, compute the activity rates for the activity-based costing system. (Use Exhibit 7–6 as a guide.)
2. What do these results suggest to you concerning operations at the Westfield branch?

EXERCISE 7–9 Second-Stage Allocation to an Order LO7–4

Durban Metal Products makes specialty metal parts and uses activity-based costing for internal decision-making purposes. The company has four activity cost pools as follows:

Activity Cost Pool	Activity Measure	Activity Rate
Order size	Number of direct labor-hours	$16.85 per direct labor-hour
Customer orders	Number of customer orders	$320.00 per customer order
Product testing	Number of testing hours	$89.00 per testing hour
Selling	Number of sales calls	$1,090.00 per sales call

The company's owner wants to know the cost of a customer order requiring 200 direct labor-hours, 4 hours of product testing, and 2 sales calls.

Required:

What is the total overhead cost assigned to this order?

EXERCISE 7–10 Customer Profitability Analysis LO7–3, LO7–4, LO7–5

Worley Company buys surgical supplies from a variety of manufacturers and then resells and delivers these supplies to hundreds of hospitals. Worley sets its prices for all hospitals by marking up its cost of goods sold to those hospitals by 5%. For example, if a hospital buys supplies from Worley that cost Worley $100 to buy from manufacturers, Worley would charge the hospital $105 to purchase these supplies.

For years, Worley believed the 5% markup covered its selling and administrative expenses and provided a reasonable profit. However, in the face of declining profits, Worley decided to implement an activity-based costing system to improve its understanding of customer profitability. The company broke its selling and administrative expenses into five activities as shown:

Activity Cost Pool (Activity Measure)	Total Cost	Total Activity
Customer deliveries (Number of deliveries)	$ 500,000	5,000 deliveries
Manual order processing (Number of manual orders)	248,000	4,000 orders
Electronic order processing (Number of electronic orders)	200,000	12,500 orders
Line item picking (Number of line items picked)	450,000	450,000 line items
Other organization-sustaining costs (None)	602,000	
Total selling and administrative expenses	$2,000,000	

Worley gathered the data below for two of the many hospitals it serves—University and Memorial (each hospital purchased medical supplies that cost Worley $30,000 to buy from manufacturers):

	Activity	
Activity Measure	University	Memorial
Number of deliveries	10	25
Number of manual orders	0	30
Number of electronic orders	15	0
Number of line items picked	120	250

Required:
1. Compute the total revenue Worley would receive from University and Memorial.
2. Compute the activity rate for each activity cost pool.
3. Compute the total activity costs assigned to University and Memorial.
4. Compute Worley's customer margin for University and Memorial. (*Hint:* Do not overlook the $30,000 cost of goods sold that Worley incurred serving each hospital.)
5. Describe the purchasing behaviors likely to characterize Worley's least profitable customers.

EXERCISE 7–11 Second-Stage Allocation and Margin Calculations LO7–4, LO7–5
Foam Products, Inc., makes foam seat cushions for the automotive and aerospace industries. The company's activity-based costing system has four activity cost pools, which are listed below along with their activity measures and activity rates:

Activity Cost Pool	Activity Measure	Activity Rate
Supporting direct labor	Number of direct labor-hours	$5.55 per direct labor-hour
Batch processing	Number of batches	$107.00 per batch
Order processing	Number of orders	$275.00 per order
Customer service	Number of customers	$2,463.00 per customer

The company just completed a single order from Interstate Trucking for 1,000 custom seat cushions. The order was produced in two batches. Each seat cushion required 0.25 direct labor-hour. The selling price was $20 per unit, the direct materials cost was $8.50 per unit, and the direct labor cost was $6.00 per unit. This was Interstate Trucking's only order during the year.

Required:
Using Exhibit 7–11 as a guide, calculate the customer margin for Interstate Trucking.

EXERCISE 7–12 Activity Measures LO7–1

Various activities at Ming Corporation, a manufacturing company, are listed below. Each activity has been classified as a unit-level, batch-level, product-level, or customer-level activity.

Activity	Level of Activity	Examples of Activity Measures
a. Direct labor workers assemble a product...............	Unit	
b. Products are designed by engineers	Product	
c. Equipment is set up	Batch	
d. Machines are used to shape and cut materials	Unit	
e. Monthly bills are sent out to regular customers	Customer	
f. Materials are moved from the receiving dock to production lines	Batch	
g. All completed units are inspected for defects	Unit	

Required:

Complete the table by providing an example of an activity measure for each activity.

EXERCISE 7–13 Computing ABC Product Costs LO7–3, LO7–4

Fogerty Company makes two products—titanium Hubs and Sprockets. Data regarding the two products follow:

	Direct Labor-Hours per Unit	Annual Production
Hubs	0.80	10,000 units
Sprockets	0.40	40,000 units

Additional information about the company follows:
a. Hubs require $32 in direct materials per unit, and Sprockets require $18.
b. The direct labor wage rate is $15 per hour.
c. Hubs require special equipment and are more complex to manufacture than Sprockets.
d. The ABC system has the following activity cost pools:

Activity Cost Pool (Activity Measure)	Estimated Overhead Cost	Activity		
		Hubs	Sprockets	Total
Machine setups (number of setups)	$72,000	100	300	400
Special processing (machine-hours)	$200,000	5,000	0	5,000
General factory (organization-sustaining)	$816,000	NA	NA	NA

Required:

1. Compute the activity rate for each activity cost pool. Did you compute an activity rate for all of the activity cost pools? Why?
2. Determine the unit product cost of each product according to the ABC system.

EXERCISE 7–14 Calculating and Interpreting Activity-Based Costing Data LO7–3, LO7–4

Hiram's Lakeside is a popular restaurant located on Lake Washington in Seattle. The restaurant's owner wants to better understand his costs and hired a student intern to conduct an activity-based costing study. The intern identified three activities, completed the first-stage cost allocations and gathered the activity measure data shown below.

Activity Cost Pool	Activity Measure	Total Cost	Total Activity
Serving a party of diners	Number of parties served	$33,000	6,000 parties
Serving a diner..................	Number of diners served	$138,000	15,000 diners
Serving drinks	Number of drinks ordered	$24,000	10,000 drinks

The above costs exclude organization-sustaining costs such as rent, property taxes, and top-management salaries.

Some costs, such as the cost of cleaning the linens that cover the restaurant's tables, vary with the number of parties served. Other costs, such as washing plates and glasses, depend on the number of diners served or the number of drinks served.

Prior to the activity-based costing study, the owner knew very little about the restaurant's costs. He only knew the total cost for the month (including organization-sustaining costs) was $240,000 and 15,000 diners had been served. Therefore, the average cost per diner was $16.

Required:
1. According to the activity-based costing system, what is the total cost of serving each of the following parties of diners?
   a. A party of four diners who order three drinks in total.
   b. A party of two diners who do not order any drinks.
   c. A party of one diner who orders two drinks.
2. Convert the total costs you computed in (1) above to costs per diner. In other words, what is the average cost per diner for serving each of the following parties?
   a. A party of four diners who order three drinks in total.
   b. A party of two diners who do not order any drinks.
   c. A party of one diner who orders two drinks.
3. Why do the costs per diner for the three different parties differ from each other and from the overall average cost of $16 per diner?

EXERCISE 7–15 Comprehensive Activity-Based Costing Exercise LO7–2, LO7–3, LO7–4, LO7–5
Advanced Products Corporation supplied the following data from its activity-based costing system:

Overhead Costs	
Wages and salaries......................	$300,000
Other overhead costs...................	100,000
Total overhead costs...................	$400,000

Activity Cost Pool	Activity Measure	Total Activity for the Year
Supporting direct labor	Number of direct labor-hours	20,000 DLHs
Order processing	Number of customer orders	400 orders
Customer support	Number of customers	200 customers
Other	This is an organization-sustaining activity	Not applicable

Distribution of Resource Consumption Across Activities	Supporting Direct Labor	Order Processing	Customer Support	Other	Total
Wages and salaries..............	40%	30%	20%	10%	100%
Other overhead costs............	30%	10%	20%	40%	100%

During the year, Advanced Products completed one order for a new customer, Shenzhen Enterprises. This customer did not order any other products during the year. Data concerning that order follow:

Data concerning the Shenzhen Enterprises Order	
Units ordered............................	10 units
Direct labor-hours........................	2 DLHs per unit
Selling price.............................	$300 per unit
Direct materials	$180 per unit
Direct labor..............................	$50 per unit

Required:

1. Using Exhibit 7–5 as a guide, prepare a report showing the first-stage allocations of overhead costs to the activity cost pools.
2. Using Exhibit 7–6 as a guide, compute the activity rates for the activity cost pools.
3. Calculate the total overhead costs for the order from Shenzhen Enterprises including customer support costs.
4. Using Exhibit 7–11 as a guide, calculate the customer margin for Shenzhen Enterprises.

Mc Graw Hill connect   Problems

PROBLEM 7–16 Comparing Traditional and Activity-Based Product Margins LO7–1, LO7–3, LO7–4, LO7–5

Hi-Tek Manufacturing, Inc., makes two industrial component parts—B300 and T500. An absorption costing income statement for the most recent period is shown below:

Hi-Tek Manufacturing, Inc. Income Statement	
Sales	$2,100,000
Cost of goods sold	1,600,000
Gross margin	500,000
Selling and administrative expenses	550,000
Net operating loss	$ (50,000)

Hi-Tek produced and sold 70,000 units of B300 at a price of $20 per unit and 17,500 units of T500 at a price of $40 per unit. The company's traditional cost system allocates manufacturing overhead to products using a plantwide overhead rate and direct labor dollars as the allocation base. Additional information relating to the company's two product lines is shown below:

	B300	T500	Total
Direct materials	$436,300	$251,700	$ 688,000
Direct labor	$200,000	$104,000	304,000
Manufacturing overhead			608,000
Cost of goods sold			$1,600,000

The company created an activity-based costing system to evaluate the profitability of its products. Hi-Tek's ABC implementation team concluded that $50,000 and $100,000 of the company's advertising expenses could be directly traced to B300 and T500, respectively. The remainder of the selling and administrative expenses was organization-sustaining in nature. The ABC team also distributed the company's manufacturing overhead to four activities as shown:

	Manufacturing	Activity		
Activity Cost Pool (and Activity Measure)	Overhead	B300	T500	Total
Machining (machine-hours)	$213,500	90,000	62,500	152,500
Setups (setup hours)	157,500	75	300	375
Product-sustaining (number of products)	120,000	1	1	2
Other (organization-sustaining costs)	117,000	NA	NA	NA
Total manufacturing overhead cost	$608,000			

Required:

1. Using Exhibit 7–12 as a guide, compute the product margins for B300 and T500 under the company's traditional costing system.
2. Using Exhibit 7–10 as a guide, compute the product margins for B300 and T500 under the activity-based costing system.
3. Using Exhibit 7–13 as a guide, prepare a quantitative comparison of the traditional and activity-based cost assignments. Explain why the traditional and activity-based cost assignments differ.

PROBLEM 7–17 Comparing Traditional and Activity-Based Product Margins LO7–1, LO7–3, LO7–4, LO7–5

Smoky Mountain Corporation makes two types of hiking boots—Xtreme and Pathfinder. Data concerning these two product lines appear below:

	Xtreme	Pathfinder
Selling price per unit	$140.00	$99.00
Direct materials per unit	$72.00	$53.00
Direct labor per unit	$24.00	$12.00
Direct labor-hours per unit	2.0 DLHs	1.0 DLH
Estimated annual production and sales	20,000 units	80,000 units

The company has a traditional costing system that applies manufacturing overhead to units based on direct labor-hours. Data concerning manufacturing overhead and direct labor-hours for the upcoming year appear below:

Estimated total manufacturing overhead	$1,980,000
Estimated total direct labor-hours	120,000 DLHs

Required:

1. Using Exhibit 7–12 as a guide, compute the product margins for Xtreme and Pathfinder under the company's traditional costing system.
2. The company is considering replacing its traditional costing system with an activity-based costing system that would assign its manufacturing overhead to the following four activity cost pools (the Other cost pool includes organization-sustaining costs and idle capacity costs):

Activities and (Activity Measures)	Estimated Overhead Cost	Expected Activity		
		Xtreme	Pathfinder	Total
Supporting direct labor (direct labor-hours) ...	$ 783,600	40,000	80,000	120,000
Batch setups (setups)	495,000	200	100	300
Product sustaining (number of products)	602,400	1	1	2
Other	99,000	NA	NA	NA
Total manufacturing overhead cost	$1,980,000			

Using Exhibit 7–10 as a guide, compute the product margins for Xtreme and Pathfinder under the activity-based costing system.
3. Using Exhibit 7–13 as a guide, prepare a quantitative comparison of the traditional and activity-based cost assignments. Explain why the traditional and activity-based cost assignments differ.

PROBLEM 7–18 Activity-Based Costing and Bidding on Jobs LO7–2, LO7–3, LO7–4

Mercer Asbestos Removal Company removes potentially toxic asbestos insulation from buildings. There has been a long-simmering dispute between the company's estimator and the work supervisors. The on-site supervisors claim the estimators do not adequately distinguish between routine work, such as removing asbestos insulation around heating pipes in older homes, and nonroutine work, such as removing asbestos-contaminated ceiling plaster in industrial buildings.

The on-site supervisors believe nonroutine work is far more expensive than routine work and should bear higher customer charges. The estimator sums up his position in this way: "My job is to measure the area to be cleared of asbestos. As directed by top management, I simply multiply the square footage by $2.50 to determine the bid price. Because our average cost is only $2.175 per square foot, that leaves enough cushion to take care of the additional costs of nonroutine work. Besides, it is difficult to know what is routine or not routine until you actually start tearing things apart."

To shed light on this controversy, the company gathered the following activity-based costing data:

Activity Cost Pool	Activity Measure	Total Activity
Removing asbestos	Thousands of square feet	800 thousand square feet
Estimating and job setup	Number of jobs	500 jobs
Working on nonroutine jobs	Number of nonroutine jobs	100 nonroutine jobs
Other (organization-sustaining costs and idle capacity costs)	None	

Note: The 100 nonroutine jobs are included in the total of 500 jobs. Both nonroutine jobs and routine jobs require estimating and setup.

Costs for the Year	
Wages and salaries	$ 300,000
Disposal fees	700,000
Equipment depreciation	90,000
On-site supplies	50,000
Office expenses	200,000
Licensing and insurance	400,000
Total cost	$1,740,000

Distribution of Resource Consumption Across Activities

	Removing Asbestos	Estimating and Job Setup	Working on Nonroutine Jobs	Other	Total
Wages and salaries	50%	10%	30%	10%	100%
Disposal fees	60%	0%	40%	0%	100%
Equipment depreciation	40%	5%	20%	35%	100%
On-site supplies	60%	30%	10%	0%	100%
Office expenses	10%	35%	25%	30%	100%
Licensing and insurance	30%	0%	50%	20%	100%

Required:

1. Using Exhibit 7–5 as a guide, perform the first-stage allocation of costs to the activity cost pools.
2. Using Exhibit 7–6 as a guide, compute the activity rates for the activity cost pools.
3. Calculate the total cost and the average cost per thousand square feet of each of the following jobs according to the activity-based costing system.
   a. A routine 1,000-square-foot asbestos removal job.
   b. A routine 2,000-square-foot asbestos removal job.
   c. A nonroutine 2,000-square-foot asbestos removal job.
4. Given the results you obtained in (3) above, do you agree with the estimator that the company's present policy for bidding on jobs is adequate?

PROBLEM 7–19 Second-Stage Allocations and Product Margins LO7–4, LO7–5

Pixel Studio, Inc., creates computer-generated animations for films and television. Much of the company's work consists of short commercials for television, but the company also does realistic computer animations for special effects in movies.

The company's owners created an activity-based costing system to better understand their costs in the face of growing competition. It includes three activities: animation concept, animation production, and contract administration. The animation concept activity is carried out at the contract proposal stage when the company bids on projects. This is an intensive activity involving individuals from all parts of the company in creating story boards and prototype stills to be shown to the prospective client. Once a project is accepted by the client, the animation goes into production and contract administration begins. Almost all of the work involved in animation production is done by the technical staff, whereas the administrative staff is largely responsible for contract administration. The activity cost pools and their activity measures are listed below:

Activity Cost Pool	Activity Measure	Activity Rate
Animation concept	Number of proposals	$6,040 per proposal
Animation production	Minutes of completed animation	$7,725 per minute
Contract administration	Number of contracts	$6,800 per contract

These activity rates include all of the company's costs, except for its organization-sustaining costs and idle capacity costs. There are no direct labor or direct materials costs.

Preliminary analysis using these activity rates indicates the local commercial segment of the market may be unprofitable. Producers of local commercials usually ask three or four companies like Pixel Studio to bid, which results in an unusually low ratio of accepted contracts to bids. Furthermore, the animation sequences are shorter for local commercials than for other work. Because animation work is billed at fairly standard rates according to the running time of the completed animation, this means the revenues from these short projects tend to be below average. Activity data concerning the local commercial market appear below:

Activity Measure	Local Commercials
Number of proposals	25
Minutes of completed animation	5
Number of contracts	10

The total sales from the 10 contracts for local commercials was $180,000.

Required:

1. Calculate the cost of serving the local commercial market.
2. Calculate the margin earned serving the local commercial market. (Remember, this company has no direct materials or direct labor costs.)
3. What would you recommend to management concerning the local commercial market?

PROBLEM 7–20 Evaluating the Profitability of Services LO7–2, LO7–3, LO7–4, LO7–5

Gallatin Carpet Cleaning has always charged a flat fee per hundred square feet of carpet cleaned. The current fee is $28 per hundred square feet. However, there is some question about whether the company is making a profit on jobs requiring considerable travel time. The owner's daughter suggested answering this question by designing an activity-based costing system using the information shown below:

Activity Cost Pool	Activity Measure	Activity for the Year
Cleaning carpets	Square feet cleaned (00s)	20,000 hundred square feet
Travel to jobs	Miles driven	60,000 miles
Job support	Number of jobs	2,000 jobs
Other (organization-sustaining costs and idle capacity costs) ...	None	Not applicable

The total cost of operating the company for the year is $430,000, which includes the following costs:

Wages	$150,000
Cleaning supplies	40,000
Cleaning equipment depreciation	20,000
Vehicle expenses	80,000
Office expenses	60,000
President's compensation	80,000
Total cost	$430,000

She distributed these operating costs across her four activities as follows:

	Cleaning Carpets	Travel to Jobs	Job Support	Other	Total
Wages	70%	20%	0%	10%	100%
Cleaning supplies	100%	0%	0%	0%	100%
Cleaning equipment depreciation	80%	0%	0%	20%	100%
Vehicle expenses	0%	60%	0%	40%	100%
Office expenses	0%	0%	45%	55%	100%
President's compensation	0%	0%	40%	60%	100%

Job support consists of receiving calls from potential customers at the home office, scheduling jobs, billing, resolving issues, and so on.

Required:
1. Using Exhibit 7–5 as a guide, prepare the first-stage allocation of costs to the activity cost pools.
2. Using Exhibit 7–6 as a guide, compute the activity rates for the activity cost pools.
3. The company recently completed a 500-square-foot carpet-cleaning job at the Flying N Ranch—a 75-mile round-trip from the company's home office. Compute the cost of this job using the activity-based costing system.
4. The revenue from the Flying N Ranch was $140 (500 square feet @ $28 per hundred square feet). Using Exhibit 7–11 as a guide, calculate the customer margin earned on this job.
5. What do you conclude concerning the profitability of the Flying N Ranch job? Explain.
6. What advice would you give the president concerning pricing jobs in the future?

Appendix 7A: Time-Driven Activity-Based Costing: A Microsoft Excel–Based Approach

This appendix introduces you to *time-driven activity-based costing* (TDABC), which overcomes two limitations of the activity-based costing (ABC) model described in the main body of the chapter. First, TDABC does not require extensive interviews with employees (as depicted in Exhibit 7–4) to perform stage-one allocations. For a company employing thousands of people, these interviews can be very time-consuming—which limits a company's ability to frequently update its cost model. Second, the ABC model depicted in Exhibits 7–4 and 7–5 assumes employees will self-report their own idle time within the "Other" cost pool. In reality, most employees are very averse to reporting their own idle time because it may signal to management that the size of the labor force can be reduced.

This appendix demonstrates how TDABC can be used to assign indirect costs to cost objects such as products and customers. We'll also explain how TDABC can be used for capacity analysis purposes. For simplicity, we limit the scope of this appendix to focus solely on labor costs. While TDABC systems can include other types of indirect costs such as equipment costs and utility costs, we purposely omit these kinds of costs to simplify our capacity analysis discussion.

Ridley Company: An Example

Ridley Company would like to improve its understanding of customer profitability and capacity utilization. As an initial pilot project, the company decided to use TDABC to analyze its Customer Service Department labor costs. The goals of the project are to obtain a better understanding of how customer service labor costs are used by individual customers and to obtain a more informed basis for making employee staffing decisions within the department. In the past, the company relied on "educated guesses" to make staffing decisions, which often resulted in an imbalance between the number of employees on the payroll and the number of employees needed to serve customers. Ridley hopes that TDABC will enable it to estimate the financial implications of better aligning its labor capacity with its customer demand.

The Data Inputs

Exhibit 7A–1 summarizes three types of data inputs for Ridley's TDABC model— resource data, activity data, and cost object data. The resource data includes the number of employees in the Customer Service Department (30), the average salary per employee ($29,952), the number of weeks in a year (52), the minutes available per week (2,400), and the practical capacity percentage (80%). The practical capacity percentage acknowledges that employees are not serving customers 100 percent of their available minutes. They spend some of their available time on vacation, on breaks, in training, attending to personal needs, etc. Thus, Ridley estimates that 80 percent of an employee's available minutes are spent actually serving customers.

The activity data contained in Exhibit 7A–1 specifies three activities within the Customer Service Department, namely order processing (cell B13), query resolution (cell C13), and credit reviews (cell D13). It also states the average number of minutes required to perform each activity one time. For example, on average it takes 10 minutes to process one order, 30 minutes to resolve one query from a customer, and 40 minutes to review one customer's credit worthiness.[3] The cost object data shown in Exhibit 7A–1 provide activity data for customers A, B, and C as well as all customers served by the Customer Service Department during the year. For example, customers A, B, and C placed 30, 18, and 7 orders, respectively. A total of 200,000 orders were placed by all of Ridley's customers during the year.

---

[3] For simplicity, we assume that all orders, queries, and credit reviews consume the same amount of minutes per unit of the activity.

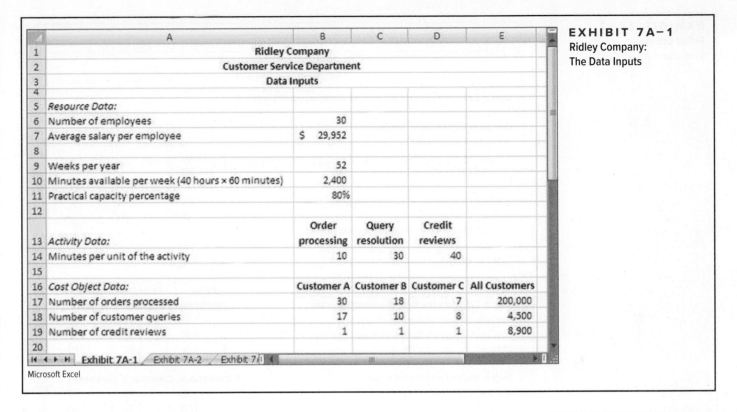

Customer Cost Analysis

LO7-6
Use time-driven activity-based costing to assign costs to cost objects.

Exhibit 7A–2 summarizes the three-step TDABC process that Ridley Company uses to assign Customer Service Department labor costs to customers A, B, and C. The first step is to divide the total cost of the resources supplied in cell B10 ($898,560) by the practical capacity of the resources supplied in cell B14 (2,995,200 minutes) to obtain the cost per minute of the resource supplied in cell B16 ($0.30). Notice that cell B12 shows a practical capacity per employee of 99,840 minutes. This amount is obtained by multiplying together three cells from the data inputs tab shown in Exhibit 7A–1—cell B9 (52 weeks), cell B10 (2,400 minutes per week), and cell B11 (80%).

The second step in Exhibit 7A–2 is to calculate the time-driven activity rate for each of the three activities. For example, the time-driven activity rate for the order processing activity of $3.00 per order (cell B21) is derived by multiplying 10 minutes per unit of the activity (cell B19) by the cost per minute of the resource supplied of $0.30 (cell B20). Similarly, the time-driven activity rate for the query resolution activity of $9.00 per query (cell C21) is derived by multiplying 30 minutes per unit of the activity (cell C19) by the cost per minute of the resource supplied of $0.30 (cell C20).

The third step in Exhibit 7A–2 is to assign customer service labor costs to customers A, B, and C. For example, the total customer service costs assigned to Customer A of $255 (cell B36) is the sum of the order processing costs of $90 (cell B26), the query resolution costs of $153 (cell B30), and the credit review costs of $12 (cell B34). Notice that the number of orders processed in cell B24 (30), the number of customer queries in cell B28 (17), and the number of credit reviews in cell B32 (1) are linked to cells B17 through B19 in the data inputs tab shown in Exhibit 7A–1.

The type of cost assignments summarized in Exhibit 7A–2 could be useful to Ridley Company in larger initiatives, such as measuring customer profitability and managing its customer mix based on those insights. Furthermore, the cost assignments shown in Exhibit 7A–2 were performed without having to interview the 30 employees within the Customer Service Department. Instead, Ridley Company only needed to make a reasonable estimate regarding its practical capacity percentage (80%) and to estimate the amount of time required to perform each activity one time in order to compute its time-driven activity rates.

EXHIBIT 7A–2
Ridley Company:
Customer Cost Analysis

	A	B	C	D
1	Ridley Company			
2	Customer Service Department			
3	Customer Cost Analysis			
4				
5	Step 1: Calculate the cost per minute of the resource supplied			
6				
7	*Customer Service Department:*			
8	Number of employees (a)	30		
9	Average salary per employee (b)	$ 29,952		
10	Total cost of resources supplied (a) × (b)	$ 898,560		
11				
12	Practical capacity per employee (in minutes) (a)	99,840		
13	Number of employees (b)	30		
14	Practical capacity of resources supplied (in minutes) (a) × (b)	2,995,200		
15				
16	Cost per minute of the resource supplied	$ 0.30		
17				
18	**Step 2: Calculate the time-driven activity rate**	**Order processing**	**Query resolution**	**Credit reviews**
19	Minutes per unit of the activity (a)	10	30	40
20	Cost per minute of the resource supplied (b)	$ 0.30	$ 0.30	$ 0.30
21	Time-driven activity rate (a) × (b)	$ 3.00	$ 9.00	$ 12.00
22				
23	**Step 3: Assign costs to cost objects**	**Customer A**	**Customer B**	**Customer C**
24	Number of orders processed (a)	30	18	7
25	Time-driven activity rate (b)	$ 3.00	$ 3.00	$ 3.00
26	Order processing costs assigned (a) × (b)	$ 90.00	$ 54.00	$ 21.00
27				
28	Number of customer queries (a)	17	10	8
29	Time-driven activity rate (b)	$ 9.00	$ 9.00	$ 9.00
30	Query resolution costs assigned (a) × (b)	$ 153.00	$ 90.00	$ 72.00
31				
32	Number of credit checks (a)	1	1	1
33	Time-driven activity rate (b)	$ 12.00	$ 12.00	$ 12.00
34	Credit review costs assigned (a) × (b)	$ 12.00	$ 12.00	$ 12.00
35				
36	Total customer service costs assigned	$ 255.00	$ 156.00	$ 105.00
37				

Exhibit 7A-1 | **Exhibit 7A-2** | Exhibit

Microsoft Excel

However, the data in Exhibit 7A–2 does not help Ridley quantify and manage its used and unused capacity costs, nor does it enable the company to estimate the number of customer service department employees that it would need to meet future customer demand. To glean these types of insights from Ridley's TDABC system, we turn our attention to the topic of capacity analysis.

LO7–7
Use time-driven activity-based costing to analyze capacity.

Capacity Analysis

Exhibit 7A–3 shows the four-step process that Ridley Company uses for capacity management purposes. It focuses on *all* of Ridley's customers rather than just customers A, B, and C. The first step is to calculate the total used capacity in minutes of 2,491,000 (= 2,000,000 + 135,000 + 356,000). The second step is to take the total minutes available of 2,995,200 from cell B11 (and as previously computed in cell B14 in Exhibit 7A–2) minus the minutes used of 2,491,000 (from cell B12) to derive the 504,200 minutes of unused capacity shown in cell B13.

The third step translates the unused capacity in minutes to unused capacity in terms of employees. We perform this calculation because customer service employees are a

	A	B	C	D	E
1	Ridley Company				
2	Customer Service Department				
3	Capacity Analysis				
4					
5	Step 1: Calculate the used capacity in minutes	Order processing	Query resolution	Credit reviews	Total
6	Customer demand for each activity (a)	200,000	4,500	8,900	
7	Customer service minutes required per unit of each activity (b)	10	30	40	
8	Customer service minutes used to meet demand (a) × (b)	2,000,000	135,000	356,000	2,491,000
9					
10	Step 2: Calculate the unused capacity in minutes				
11	Total customer service minutes available to meet demand (a)	2,995,200			
12	Total customer service minutes used to meet demand (b)	2,491,000			
13	Unused capacity in minutes (a) – (b)	504,200			
14					
15	Step 3: Calculate the unused capacity in number of employees				
16	Unused capacity in minutes (a)	504,200			
17	Practical capacity per employee (in minutes) (b)	99,840			
18	Unused capacity in number of employees (a) ÷ (b)	5.05			
19					
20	Step 4: Calculate the financial impact of matching capacity with demand				
21	Potential adjustment in number of employees (rounded) (a)	(5.00)			
22	Average salary per employee (b)	$ 29,952			
23	Impact on expenses of matching capacity with demand (a) × (b)	$(149,760)			
24					
25	Note: Cell B21 uses the formula =If(B18>0,rounddown(-B18,0),roundup(-B18,0))				
26					

Exhibit 7A-2 | **Exhibit 7A-3** | Exhibit 7A-4 | Exhi

Microsoft Excel

EXHIBIT 7A–3
Ridley Company:
Capacity Analysis

step-fixed cost rather than a variable cost. In other words, Ridley does not purchase customer service capacity by the minute. Instead, it hires individual employees who each provides 99,840 minutes of practical capacity per year. Because the unused capacity in minutes is 504,200 and the practical capacity of one employee is 99,840 minutes, the total unused capacity equates with 5.05 employees (= 504,200 ÷ 99,840).

The fourth step calculates the financial impact of matching capacity with demand. The key to this step is the formula in cell B21 of Exhibit 7A–3, which rounds the value reported in cell B18 to a whole number. We perform this rounding function because Ridley alters its step-fixed employee headcount in terms of whole employees, not portions of an employee. So, for example, cell B18 shows an unused capacity of 5.05 employees; however, Ridley cannot eliminate .05 employee. It could possibly eliminate five or six employees, but nothing in between. Because eliminating six employees would leave the Customer Service Department a little short-handed, we round down to five employees. Given the average salary per employee of $29,952, the impact on expenses of matching labor capacity with demand is a savings of $149,760 (= 5.00 × $29,952).

"What-If" Analysis

The data inputs in Exhibit 7A–1 also enable Ridley to answer some interesting "what if" questions. For example, what if the company was able to lower its credit review time from 40 minutes to 30 minutes? How would this affect the costs assigned to customers A, B, and C? To answer this question, we would change cell D14 in Exhibit 7A–1 from 40 minutes to 30 minutes. The revised customer cost analysis that would be instantly generated is shown in Exhibit 7A–4.

Notice cell D19 shows 30 minutes per credit review instead of the 40 minutes shown in the same cell in Exhibit 7A–2. This in turn lowers the cost per credit review to $9.00 (as shown in cell D21) rather than the $12.00 shown in the same cell in Exhibit 7A–2. The lower time-driven activity rate of $9.00 carries forward to cells B33 through D33 and

EXHIBIT 7A–4

Ridley Company's Customer Cost Analysis: A "What If" Analysis

	A	B	C	D
1		Ridley Company		
2		Customer Service Department		
3		Customer Cost Analysis		
4				
5	Step 1: Calculate the cost per minute of the resource supplied			
6				
7	*Customer Service Department:*			
8	Number of employees (a)	30		
9	Average salary per employee (b)	$ 29,952		
10	Total cost of resources supplied (a) × (b)	$ 898,560		
11				
12	Practical capacity per employee (in minutes) (a)	99,840		
13	Number of employees (b)	30		
14	Practical capacity of resources supplied (in minutes) (a) × (b)	2,995,200		
15				
16	Cost per minute of the resource supplied	$ 0.30		
17				
18	Step 2: Calculate the time-driven activity rate	Order processing	Query resolution	Credit reviews
19	Minutes per unit of the activity (a)	10	30	30
20	Cost per minute of the resource supplied (b)	$ 0.30	$ 0.30	$ 0.30
21	Time-driven activity rate (a) × (b)	$ 3.00	$ 9.00	$ 9.00
22				
23	Step 3: Assign costs to cost objects	Customer A	Customer B	Customer C
24	Number of orders processed (a)	30	18	7
25	Time-driven activity rate (b)	$ 3.00	$ 3.00	$ 3.00
26	Order processing costs assigned (a) × (b)	$ 90.00	$ 54.00	$ 21.00
27				
28	Number of customer queries (a)	17	10	8
29	Time-driven activity rate (b)	$ 9.00	$ 9.00	$ 9.00
30	Query resolution costs assigned (a) × (b)	$ 153.00	$ 90.00	$ 72.00
31				
32	Number of credit checks (a)	1	1	1
33	Time-driven activity rate (b)	$ 9.00	$ 9.00	$ 9.00
34	Credit review costs assigned (a) × (b)	$ 9.00	$ 9.00	$ 9.00
35				
36	Total customer service costs assigned	$ 252.00	$ 153.00	$ 102.00
37				

◄ ◄ ► ►   **Exhibit 7A-4** / Exhibit 7A-5 / Exerci ◄

Microsoft Excel

in turn lowers each customer's total customer service costs by $3. For example, customer A's total customer service cost is $252 in cell B36 of Exhibit 7A–4, whereas the corresponding total in cell B36 of Exhibit 7A–2 is $255.

Let's further assume Ridley Company wants to answer the question: What if we also increase the number of orders processed from 200,000 (as shown in cell E17 in Exhibit 7A–1) to 265,000? How would the projected increase in the number of orders processed affect our staffing needs in the Customer Service Department? After making the appropriate change in cell E17 of Exhibit 7A–1, Exhibit 7A–5 provides the answer to this question—Ridley Company would need to hire one more employee at an estimated cost of $29,952.

To understand how this answer is derived, let's start with Step 1 within Exhibit 7A–5, which shows 265,000 orders processed in cell B6. This increase in the number of orders processed increases the number of customer service minutes needed to meet customer demand to 3,052,000 (cell E8). Step 2 shows that the total customer service minutes available of 2,995,200 (cell B11) is now less than the number of minutes used

EXHIBIT 7A–5
Ridley Company's Capacity Analysis: A "What If" Analysis

	A	B	C	D	E
1	**Ridley Company**				
2	**Customer Service Department**				
3	**Capacity Analysis**				
4					
5	**Step 1: Calculate the used capacity in minutes**	**Order processing**	**Query resolution**	**Credit reviews**	**Total**
6	Customer demand for each activity (a)	265,000	4,500	8,900	
7	Customer service minutes required per unit of each activity (b)	10	30	30	
8	Customer service minutes used to meet demand (a) × (b)	2,650,000	135,000	267,000	3,052,000
9					
10	**Step 2: Calculate the unused capacity in minutes**				
11	Total customer service minutes available to meet demand (a)	2,995,200			
12	Total customer service minutes used to meet demand (b)	3,052,000			
13	Unused capacity in minutes (a) − (b)	(56,800)			
14					
15	**Step 3: Calculate the unused capacity in number of employees**				
16	Unused capacity in minutes (a)	(56,800)			
17	Practical capacity per employee (in minutes) (b)	99,840			
18	Unused capacity in number of employees (a) ÷ (b)	(0.57)			
19					
20	**Step 4: Calculate the financial impact of matching capacity with demand**				
21	Potential adjustment in number of employees (rounded) (a)	1.00			
22	Average salary per employee (b)	$ 29,952			
23	Impact on expenses of matching capacity with demand (a) × (b)	$ 29,952			
24					
25	Note: Cell B21 uses the formula =If(B18>0,rounddown(-B18,0),roundup(-B18,0))				
26					

Exhibit 7A-4 | **Exhibit 7A-5** | Exercise 7A-1 Inputs

Microsoft Excel

to meet demand of 3,052,000 (cell B12), which results in unused capacity of (56,800) minutes as shown in cell B13. Because the unused capacity is a negative number, it implies Ridley does not have enough capacity available to satisfy the estimated customer demand. Step 3 in Exhibit 7A–5 translates the shortage in minutes to a shortfall stated in terms of number of employees—or (0.57) employee as shown in cell B18. Given that Ridley cannot hire slightly more than one-half of an employee, cell B21 rounds this number to 1.00 and then cell B23 translates the estimated cost of hiring one additional employee to $29,952.

This concludes our introduction to TDABC. The strengths of this methodology include (1) it is easy to update because it does not require employee interviews, (2) it quantifies unused capacity costs in an objective fashion that does not require employees to self-report their own idle time, and (3) it helps companies estimate the financial impact of aligning capacity with demand, particularly with respect to step-fixed resources such as the customer service employees in the Ridley Company example.

Appendix 7A: Exercises and Problems   Mc Graw Hill connect

EXERCISE 7A–1 Time-Driven Activity-Based Costing LO 7–6

Saratoga Company manufactures jobs to customer specifications. The company is conducting a time-driven activity-based costing study in its Purchasing Department to better understand how Purchasing Department labor costs are consumed by individual jobs. To aid the study, the company provided the following data regarding its Purchasing Department and three of its many jobs:

Number of employees	12
Average salary per employee	$28,000
Weeks of employment per year	52
Hours worked per week	40
Practical capacity percentage	85%

	Requisition Processing	Bid Evaluation	Inspection
Minutes per unit of the activity	15	45	30

	Job X	Job Y	Job Z
Number of requisitions processed	8	5	4
Number of bid evaluations	3	2	4
Number of inspections	6	2	6

Required:
1. Calculate the cost per minute of the resource supplied in the Purchasing Department.
2. Calculate the time-driven activity rate for each of Saratoga's three activities.
3. Calculate the total purchasing labor costs assigned to Job X, Job Y, and Job Z.

EXERCISE 7A–2 Time-Driven Activity-Based Costing LO 7–7

Refer to the data in Exercise 7A–1. In addition, assume Saratoga Company provided the following activity data for *all* jobs produced during the year:

	Requisition Processing	Bid Evaluation	Inspection
Activity demands for all jobs	7,000	9,400	10,000

Required:
1. Calculate Saratoga's used capacity in minutes.
2. Calculate Saratoga's unused capacity in minutes.
3. Calculate Saratoga's unused capacity in number of employees. (Do not round your answer to a whole number.)
4. Calculate the impact on expenses of matching capacity with demand. (Be sure to round your potential adjustment in the number of employees to a whole number.)

EXERCISE 7A–3 Time-Driven Activity-Based Costing LO 7–6, LO 7–7

Refer to the data in Exercises 7A–1 and 7A–2. Now assume Saratoga Company would like to answer the following "what if" question using its time-driven activity-based costing system: Assuming our estimated activity demands for all jobs in the next period will be as shown below, how will this affect our job costs and our staffing levels within the Purchasing Department?

	Requisition Processing	Bid Evaluation	Inspection
Activity demands for all jobs	7,600	9,900	11,000

Required:

1. How will these revised activity demands affect the total Purchasing Department labor costs assigned to Job X, Job Y, and Job Z? No calculations are necessary.
2. Using the revised activity demands, calculate Saratoga's used capacity in minutes.
3. Using the revised activity demands, calculate Saratoga's unused capacity in minutes.
4. Using the revised activity demands, calculate Saratoga's unused capacity in number of employees. (Do not round your answer to a whole number.)
5. Based on the revised activity demands, calculate the impact on expenses of matching capacity with demand. (Be sure to round your potential adjustment in the number of employees to a whole number.)

PROBLEM 7A–4 Time-Driven Activity-Based Costing LO 7–6, LO 7–7

Stahl Company is conducting a time-driven activity-based costing study in its Shipping Department. To aid the study, the company provided the following data regarding its Shipping Department and the customers served by the department:

Number of employees	34			
Average salary per employee	$34,000			
Weeks of employment per year	52			
Hours worked per week	40			
Practical capacity percentage	80%			

	Line-Item Picking	Packaging	Loading Deliveries	
Minutes per unit of the activity	5	15	30	

	Customer L	Customer M	Customer N	All Customers
Number of line items picked	280	160	90	335,000
Number of boxes packaged	50	20	15	46,800
Number of deliveries loaded	6	2	10	12,100

Required:

1. Using the customer cost analysis shown in Exhibit 7A–2 as your guide, compute the following:
   a. The cost per minute of the resource supplied in the Shipping Department.
   b. The time-driven activity rate for each of Stahl's three activities.
   c. The total labor costs consumed by Customer L, Customer M, and Customer N.
2. Using the capacity analysis shown in Exhibit 7A–3 as your guide, compute the following:
   a. The used capacity in minutes.
   b. The unused capacity in minutes.
   c. The unused capacity in number of employees. (Do not round your answer to a whole number.)
   d. The impact on expenses of matching capacity with demand. (Be sure to round your potential adjustment in the number of employees to a whole number.)

PROBLEM 7A–5 Time-Driven Activity-Based Costing LO 7–6, LO 7–7

Athens Company is conducting a time-driven activity-based costing study in its Engineering Department. To aid the study, the company provided the following data regarding its Engineering Department and the customers served by the department:

Number of employees.	10
Average salary per employee	$90,000
Weeks of employment per year	52
Hours worked per week	40
Practical capacity percentage	85%

	New Product Design	Engineering Change Orders	Product Testing
Hours per unit of the activity	40	20	8

	Customer A	Customer B	Customer C	All Customers
Number of new products designed	3	2	4	180
Number of engineering change orders	5	2	2	250
Number of products tested	8	4	6	160

Required:

1. Using the customer cost analysis shown in Exhibit 7A–2 as your guide, compute the following:
   a. The cost per hour of the resource supplied in the Engineering Department.
   b. The time-driven activity rate per hour for each of Athens' three activities.
   c. The total engineering costs consumed by Customer A, Customer B, and Customer C.
2. Using the capacity analysis shown in Exhibit 7A–3 as your guide, compute the following:
   a. The used capacity in hours.
   b. The unused capacity in hours.
   c. The unused capacity in number of employees. (Do not round your answer to a whole number.)
   d. The impact on expenses of matching capacity with demand. (Be sure to round your potential adjustment in the number of employees to a whole number.)
3. Assume Athens is considering expanding its business such that the estimated number of new products designed would increase to 250, the number of engineering change orders would jump to 320, and the number of products tested would rise to 240. Using these revised figures, calculate the following:
   a. The used capacity in hours.
   b. The unused capacity in hours.
   c. The unused capacity in number of employees. (Do not round your answer to a whole number.)
   d. The impact on expenses of matching capacity with demand. (Be sure to round your potential adjustment in the number of employees to a whole number.)

Master Budgeting

Chapter 8

rh2010/123RF

ENTREPRENEUR SPOTLIGHT

Trinity Heavenz came from an impoverished neighborhood of Uganda to found era92—a tech company that provides a range of services for its clients including web and mobile design; landing page design; brand identity design; magazine and brochure design; and print, packaging, and merchandise design. To date, the company has developed more than 300 websites. Its client list includes Stanbic Bank, Impact Nations, The Remnant Generation, The Institute for Social Transformation, and Fields of Life.

Applying Managerial Accounting

To aid in its annual planning process, era92 could create a master budget. The budget could be broken down into various business segments. For example, Merline Ulysse, who is in charge of Business Development in the United Kingdom, could have her own budget. Similarly, Brenda Nassali (Digital Projects Manager) and Shamir Kwizera (Photography & Film) could also rely on their own budgets to execute their responsibilities. All of these individual budgets would roll up into the companywide budget Trinity would use to coordinate and allocate resources across the organization.

Serving All Stakeholders

Heavenz believes that "talent is equally distributed but the opportunity is not." To address this problem, he started era92's Elevate program, which provides "a new pathway for youth in education, employment, and empowerment, proving that by learning and improving digital skills, one can increase their chances of becoming employed or starting their own business or freelance career in Uganda." He also started a nonprofit organization called 92hands.org that serves its communities through five programs—One Child Education, US4 Women, Feeding Kosovo, The Wise Builders, and Kids Back to School. ∎

Sources: https://era92.com/our-story, https://era92elevate.org/elevate/, https://92hands.org/about-us.

lighthouse image: Martin73/Shutterstock; big data image: INGARA/Shutterstock

LEARNING OBJECTIVES

After studying Chapter 8, you should be able to:

LO8–1   Understand why organizations budget and the processes they use to create budgets.

LO8–2   Prepare a sales budget, including a schedule of expected cash collections.

LO8–3   Prepare a production budget.

LO8–4   Prepare a direct materials budget, including a schedule of expected cash disbursements for purchases of materials.

LO8–5   Prepare a direct labor budget.

LO8–6   Prepare a manufacturing overhead budget.

LO8–7   Prepare a selling and administrative expense budget.

LO8–8   Prepare a cash budget.

LO8–9   Prepare a budgeted income statement.

LO8–10   Prepare a budgeted balance sheet.

 Data Analytics Exercise available in Connect to complement this chapter

In this chapter, we describe how organizations strive to achieve their financial goals by preparing *budgets*. A **budget** is a plan for the future expressed in quantitative terms. A company's budget ordinarily covers a one-year period corresponding to its fiscal year, and it is often broken down into quarterly and monthly budgets. Some companies also use a *perpetual budget,* which is a 12-month budget that continuously rolls forward one month (or quarter) at a time as the current month (or quarter) is completed. This approach keeps managers continually focused one year ahead.

Why and How Do Organizations Create Budgets?

LO8-1
Understand why organizations budget and the processes they use to create budgets.

Budgets are used for two purposes—*planning* and *control*. **Planning** involves developing goals and preparing various budgets to achieve those goals. **Control** involves gathering feedback to ensure that the plan is being properly executed or modified as circumstances change. To be effective, a good budgeting system must provide for both planning and control.

Why Do Organizations Create Budgets?

From a planning standpoint, organizations use budgets to:

1. Encourage managers to *think about* and *plan* for the future.
2. *Communicate* financial goals throughout the organization.
3. *Allocate resources* within the organization where they can be used most effectively.
4. *Coordinate* the plans and activities of departmental managers.
5. Uncover potential *bottlenecks* before they occur.

From a control standpoint, organizations compare their budgets to actual results to:

1. *Improve* the efficiency and effectiveness of operations.
2. *Evaluate* and *reward* employees.

IN BUSINESS

skodonnell/Shutterstock

AMAZON EXPANDS ITS TRAINING BUDGET

Amazon.com is spending $700 million over six years to retrain its workforce. Beth Galetti, the company's senior vice president of worldwide HR, says, "The most consistent thing we see that's changing is the need for some level of technical skills in any job." For example, the company's fulfillment center employees need to learn how to work with a variety of automated tools, whereas its software engineers need to acquire more advanced skills, such as machine learning. Amazon has also seen a 500 percent growth rate in job openings for data scientists as well as networking and security engineers, all of whom need continuous training to update their technical skills.

Source: Chip Cutter, "Amazon Retrains More of Its Staff for Digital Future," *The Wall Street Journal,* December 11, 2019, p. B4.

How Do Organizations Create Budgets?

Companies usually create budgets by relying on some combination of top-down budgeting and *self-imposed budgeting.* A **self-imposed budget** or **participative budget** is a budget prepared with the full cooperation and participation of managers at all levels.

With a top-down approach, top-level managers initiate the budgeting process by issuing profit targets. Lower-level managers are directed to prepare budgets that meet those targets. This approach often demoralizes lower-level managers because it ignores their knowledge and opinions. Furthermore, the targets imposed by top-level managers, who may possess strategic vision while lacking operational knowledge, may be unrealistically high or unknowingly too low. If the targets are too high and top-level managers penalize lower-level managers for not meeting them, it will generate resentment rather than cooperation and commitment.

Given these complications, many companies choose to involve lower-level managers in the budgeting process because:

1. It shows respect for their opinions.
2. It leverages their knowledge to provide more accurate estimates than those imposed by top-level managers who have less intimate knowledge of day-to-day operations.
3. It increases their motivation to achieve their own self-imposed goals.
4. It empowers them to take ownership of the budget and to be accountable for deviations from it.

While it may be tempting to conclude that companies should rely entirely on self-imposed budgets, this approach has two important limitations. First, lower-level managers may make suboptimal budgeting estimates if they lack the broad strategic perspective possessed by top managers. Second, if the budget is used to reward employees, then lower-level managers may create too much *budgetary slack* to ensure their actual results exceed the plan. For these reasons, most companies use a combination of inputs from top-level managers and lower-level managers when creating their budgets. The budget estimates prepared by lower-level managers are usually reviewed by higher levels of management. Without such a review, self-imposed budgets may fail to support the organization's strategy or may be too slack, resulting in suboptimal performance.

When managers throughout the organization work collaboratively to prepare a budget, they often strive to establish challenging but "highly achievable" targets. Highly achievable goals are likely to build a lower-level manager's confidence and commitment to the budget while also reducing the likelihood they will engage in undesirable behavior to secure their desired compensation. Finally, top-level managers should not pressure lower-level managers to take extreme measures to "meet the budget." Creating this type of budgeting environment breeds hostility, tension, and mistrust rather than a cooperative pursuit of continuous process improvement.

The Master Budget: An Overview

The remainder of the chapter illustrates a type of integrated business plan known as a *master budget*. The **master budget** includes a number of separate but interdependent budgets that interrelate the company's sales, production, and financial goals. The master budget culminates in a cash budget, a budgeted income statement, and a budgeted balance sheet. Exhibit 8–1 summarizes the various parts of the master budget and how they are related.

The first step in the budgeting process is preparing a **sales budget**, which is a schedule showing the expected sales for the budget period. An accurate sales budget is the key to the entire budgeting process. As illustrated in Exhibit 8–1, all other parts of the master budget depend on the sales budget. If the sales budget is inaccurate, the rest of the budget will be inaccurate. The sales budget is based on the company's sales forecast, which may require the use of sophisticated mathematical models and statistical tools that are beyond the scope of this course.

The sales budget influences the variable portion of the selling and administrative expense budget and feeds into the production budget, which estimates how many units to produce during the budget period. The production budget in turn is used to prepare the

EXHIBIT 8–1
The Master Budget
Interrelationships

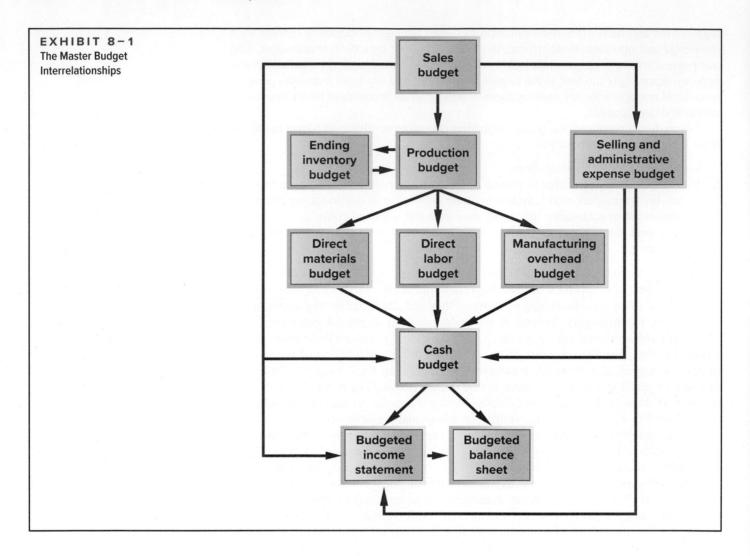

direct materials, direct labor, and manufacturing overhead budgets. Once a company has prepared these three manufacturing cost budgets, it can prepare the ending finished goods inventory budget.

The master budget concludes with the preparation of a cash budget, income statement, and balance sheet. Information from the sales budget, selling and administrative expense budget, and manufacturing cost budget all influence the preparation of the *cash budget*. A **cash budget** is a schedule that estimates how cash will be acquired and used. The budgeted income statement estimates net income for the budget period and relies on information from the sales budget, ending finished goods inventory budget, selling and administrative expense budget, and cash budget. The final schedule of the master budget is the balance sheet, which estimates a company's assets, liabilities, and stockholders' equity at the end of a budget period.

Seeing the Big Picture

The 10 schedules contained in a master budget can be overwhelming; therefore, it is important to see the big picture in two respects. First, a master budget for a manufacturing company is designed to answer 10 key questions, as follows:

1.   How much sales will we earn?
2.   How much cash will we collect from customers?

3. How many units of finished goods do we need to produce?
4. How much raw material will we need to purchase?
5. How much conversion cost (direct labor and manufacturing overhead) will we incur?
6. How much cash will we pay to our suppliers and our direct laborers, and how much will we pay for manufacturing overhead resources?
7. How much selling and administrative expense will we incur, and how much cash will we pay related to those expenses?
8. How will our cash balance and financing needs change?
9. How much net income will we earn?
10. What will our balance sheet look like at the end of the budget period?

Second, it is important to understand that many of the schedules in a master budget hinge on a variety of estimates and assumptions. Exhibit 8–2 summarizes the questions underlying these estimates and assumptions for seven of the schedules included in a master budget. As you study the forthcoming budget schedules, keep these two "big picture" insights in mind—the budget is designed to answer 10 key questions and it is based on various estimates and assumptions—because they will help you understand *why* and *how* a master budget is created.

EXHIBIT 8–2
Estimates and Assumptions for a Master Budget

Sales budget:
1. What are the budgeted unit sales?
2. What is the budgeted selling price per unit?
3. What percentage of accounts receivable will be collected in the current and subsequent periods?

Production budget:
1. What percentage of next period's unit sales needs to be maintained in ending finished goods inventory?

Direct materials budget:
1. How many units of raw materials are needed to make one unit of finished goods?
2. What is the budgeted cost for one unit of raw material?
3. What percentage of next period's production needs should be maintained in ending raw materials inventory?
4. What percentage of raw materials purchases will be paid in the current and subsequent periods?

Direct labor budget:
1. How many direct labor-hours are required per unit of finished goods?
2. What is the budgeted direct labor wage rate per hour?

Manufacturing overhead budget:
1. What is the budgeted variable overhead cost per unit of the allocation base?
2. What is the total budgeted fixed overhead cost per period?
3. What is the budgeted depreciation expense on factory assets per period?

Selling and administrative expense budget:
1. What is the budgeted variable selling and administrative expense per unit sold?
2. What is the total budgeted fixed selling and administrative expense per period?
3. What is the budgeted depreciation expense on nonfactory assets per period?

Cash budget:
1. What is the budgeted minimum cash balance?
2. What are our estimated expenditures for noncurrent asset purchases and dividends?
3. What is the estimated interest rate on borrowed funds?

Preparing the Master Budget

Tom Wills is the majority stockholder and chief executive officer of Hampton Freeze, Inc., a company he started two years ago. The company makes premium popsicles using natural ingredients and featuring exotic flavors such as tangy tangerine and minty mango. The company's business is highly seasonal, with most of the sales occurring in spring and summer.

In the company's second year of operations, a major cash crunch in the first and second quarters almost forced it into bankruptcy. In spite of this cash crunch, the year turned out to be a very successful year in terms of cash flow and net income. Partly as a result of that harrowing experience, Tom decided to hire a professional financial manager. He interviewed several promising candidates for the job and chose Larry Giano, who had considerable experience in the packaged foods industry. In the job interview, Tom questioned Larry about the steps he would take to prevent a recurrence of this year's cash crunch:

Tom: As I mentioned earlier, we are going to end this year with a very nice profit. What you may not know is that we had some very big financial problems this year.

Larry: Let me guess. You ran out of cash sometime in the first or second quarter.

Tom: How did you know?

Larry: Most of your sales are in the second and third quarter, right?

Tom: Sure, everyone wants to buy popsicles in the spring and summer, but nobody wants them when the weather turns cold.

Larry: So you don't have many sales in the first quarter?

Tom: Right.

Larry: And in the second quarter, which is the spring, you are producing like crazy to fill orders?

Tom: Sure.

Larry: So in the first quarter, you don't have many sales. In the second quarter, you are producing like crazy, which eats up cash, but you aren't paid by the grocery stores that sell your popsicles until long after you have paid your employees and suppliers. No wonder you had a cash problem.

Tom: So what can we do about it?

Larry: The first step is to predict the cash shortfall before it occurs and then approach a bank to arrange a line of credit.

Tom: How can we predict the cash shortfall?

Larry: You create a cash budget. In fact, while you're at it, you might as well do a master budget. You'll find it well worth the effort because we can use a master budget to estimate the financial statement implications of numerous "what if" questions. For example, with the click of a mouse, we can answer questions such as: If unit sales are 10 percent less than our original forecast, what will be the impact on profits? Or what if we increase our selling price by 15 percent and unit sales drop by 5 percent? What will be the impact on profits?

Tom: That sounds great, Larry! Not only do we need a cash budget, but I would love to have a master budget that could answer the types of "what if" questions that you just described. Let's get started.

Larry's master budget for next year included 10 schedules:

1. A sales budget, including a schedule of expected cash collections.
2. A production budget (a merchandise purchases budget would be used in a merchandising company).
3. A direct materials budget, including a schedule of expected cash disbursements for purchases of materials.
4. A direct labor budget.
5. A manufacturing overhead budget.
6. An ending finished goods inventory budget.

7. A selling and administrative expense budget.
8. A cash budget.
9. A budgeted income statement.
10. A budgeted balance sheet.

The Beginning Balance Sheet

Exhibit 8–3 shows the first tab included in Larry's Microsoft Excel master budget file. It contains Hampton Freeze's beginning balance sheet for next year. Larry included this balance sheet in his master budget file so he could link some of these data to subsequent schedules. For example, as you'll eventually see, he used cell references within Excel to link the beginning accounts receivable balance of $90,000 to the schedule of expected cash collections. He also used cell references to link the beginning cash balance of $42,500 to the cash budget.

The Budgeting Assumptions

Exhibit 8–4 shows the second tab included in Larry's master budget file. It is labeled Budgeting Assumptions and contains all of the estimates and assumptions needed for Hampton Freeze's entire master budget. Beginning with the estimates used for the sales budget, Exhibit 8–4 shows that Hampton Freeze's budgeted quarterly unit sales are 10,000, 30,000, 40,000, and 20,000 cases. Its budgeted selling price is $20 per case. The company expects to collect 70 percent of its credit sales in the quarter of sale, and the remaining 30 percent in the quarter after sale. The company's bad debts are negligible.

Exhibit 8–4 also shows the production budget assumes Hampton Freeze will maintain ending finished goods inventory equal to 20 percent of the next quarter's unit sales. In terms of the company's only direct material, high fructose sugar, it budgets 15 pounds

EXHIBIT 8–3
Hampton Freeze: The Beginning Balance Sheet

	A	B	C
1	Hampton Freeze, Inc.		
2	Balance Sheet		
3	December 31 of This Year		
4			
5	Assets		
6	Current assets:		
7	Cash	$ 42,500	
8	Accounts receivable	90,000	
9	Raw materials inventory (21,000 pounds)	4,200	
10	Finished goods inventory (2,000 cases)	26,000	
11	Total current assets		$ 162,700
12	Plant and equipment:		
13	Land	80,000	
14	Buildings and equipment	700,000	
15	Accumulated depreciation	(292,000)	
16	Plant and equipment, net		488,000
17	Total assets		$ 650,700
18			
19	Liabilities and Stockholders' Equity		
20	Current liabilities:		
21	Accounts payable		$ 25,800
22	Stockholders' equity:		
23	Common stock	$ 175,000	
24	Retained earnings	449,900	
25	Total stockholders' equity		624,900
26	Total liabilities and stockholders' equity		$ 650,700

Beginning Balance Sheet

Microsoft Excel

EXHIBIT 8–4
Hampton Freeze: Budgeting Assumptions*

	A	B	C	D	E	F
		Hampton Freeze, Inc.				
1		Budgeting Assumptions				
2		For the Year Ended December 31 of Next Year				
3						
4						
5		All 4 Quarters		Quarter		
6	Sales Budget		1	2	3	4
7	Budgeted sales in cases		10,000	30,000	40,000	20,000
8	Selling price per case	$ 20.00				
9	Percentage of sales collected in the quarter of sale	70%				
10	Percentage of sales collected in the quarter after sale	30%				
11						
12	Production Budget					
13	Percentage of next quarter's sales in ending finished goods inventory	20%				
14						
15	Direct Materials Budget					
16	Pounds of sugar per case	15				
17	Cost per pound of sugar	$ 0.20				
18	Percentage of next quarter's production needs in ending inventory	10%				
19	Percentage of purchases paid in the quarter purchased	50%				
20	Percentage of purchases paid in the quarter after purchase	50%				
21						
22	Direct Labor Budget					
23	Direct labor-hours required per case	0.40				
24	Direct labor cost per hour	$ 15.00				
25						
26	Manufacturing Overhead Budget					
27	Variable manufacturing overhead per direct labor-hour	$ 4.00				
28	Fixed manufacturing overhead per quarter	$ 60,600				
29	Depreciation per quarter	$ 15,000				
30						
31						
32	Selling and Administrative Expense Budget					
33	Variable selling and administrative expense per case	$ 1.80				
34	Fixed selling and administrative expense per quarter:					
35	Advertising	$ 20,000				
36	Executive salaries	$ 55,000				
37	Insurance	$ 10,000				
38	Property tax	$ 4,000				
39	Depreciation	$ 10,000				
40						
41	Cash Budget					
42	Minimum cash balance	$ 30,000				
43	Equipment purchases		$ 50,000	$ 40,000	$ 20,000	$ 20,000
44	Dividends	$ 8,000				
45	Simple interest rate per quarter	3%				
46						

| ◄ ► | | **Budgeting Assumptions** | Schedule : | ◄ | | ► |

Microsoft Excel

---

*For simplicity, we assume that all quarterly estimates, except quarterly unit sales and equipment purchases, will be the same for all four quarters.

of sugar per case of popsicles at a cost of $0.20 per pound.[1] It expects to maintain ending raw materials inventory equal to 10 percent of the raw materials needed to satisfy the following quarter's production. In addition, the company plans to pay for 50 percent of its material purchases within the quarter of purchase and the remaining 50 percent in the following quarter.

Continuing with a summary of Exhibit 8–4, the two key assumptions underlying the direct labor budget are that 0.40 direct labor-hours is required per case of popsicles and the direct labor cost per hour is $15. The manufacturing overhead budget is based on three underlying assumptions—the variable overhead cost per direct labor-hour is $4.00, the total fixed overhead per quarter is $60,600, and the quarterly depreciation on factory assets is $15,000. Exhibit 8–4 also shows that the budgeted variable selling and administrative expense per case of popsicles is $1.80 and the fixed selling and administrative expenses per quarter include advertising ($20,000), executive salaries ($55,000), insurance ($10,000), property tax ($4,000), and depreciation expense ($10,000). The remaining budget assumptions depicted in Exhibit 8–4 pertain to the cash budget. The company expects to maintain a minimum cash balance each quarter of $30,000; it plans to make quarterly equipment purchases of $50,000, $40,000, $20,000, and $20,000;[2] it plans to pay quarterly dividends of $8,000; and it expects to pay simple interest on borrowed money of 3 percent per quarter.

The Budgeting Assumptions tab in Exhibit 8–4 simplifies the process of using a master budget to answer "what if" questions. For example, assume that Larry wanted to answer the question: If we increase the selling price per unit by $2 and quarterly sales drop by 1,000 units, what would be the impact on profits? With a properly constructed Budgeting Assumptions tab, Larry would only need to make a few adjustments to the data within this tab and the formulas embedded in each of the budget schedules would automatically update the projected financial results. This is much simpler than attempting to adjust data inputs within each of the master budget schedules.

The Sales Budget

Schedule 1 contains Hampton Freeze's sales budget for next year. As you study this schedule, keep in mind that all of its numbers are derived from cell references to the Budgeting Assumptions tab and formulas—none of the numbers appearing in the schedule were actually keyed into their respective cells. Furthermore, it bears emphasizing that all remaining schedules in the master budget are prepared in the same fashion—they rely almost exclusively on cell references and formulas.

For the year, Hampton Freeze expects to sell 100,000 cases of popsicles at a price of $20 per case for total budgeted sales of $2,000,000. The budgeted unit sales for each quarter (10,000, 30,000, 40,000, and 20,000) come from cells C7 through F7 in the Budgeting Assumptions tab shown in Exhibit 8–4, and the selling price per case ($20.00) comes from cell B8 in the Budgeting Assumptions tab. Schedule 1 also shows next year's expected cash collections are $1,970,000. The accounts receivable balance of $90,000 collected in the first quarter comes from cell B8 of the beginning balance sheet in Exhibit 8–3. All other cash collections rely on the estimated cash collection percentages from cells B9 and B10 of the Budgeting Assumptions tab. For example, Schedule 1 shows the budgeted sales for the first quarter equal $200,000. In the first quarter, Hampton Freeze expects to collect 70 percent of this amount, or $140,000. In the second quarter, the company expects to collect the remaining 30 percent of this amount, or $60,000.

---

[1] While popsicle manufacturing is likely to involve other raw materials, such as popsicle sticks and packaging materials, for simplicity, we have limited our scope to high fructose sugar.

[2] For simplicity, we assume that depreciation on these newly acquired assets is included in the quarterly depreciation estimates included in the Budgeting Assumptions tab.

SCHEDULE 1

	A	B	C	D	E	F
1		Hampton Freeze, Inc.				
2		Sales Budget				
3		For the Year Ended December 31 of Next Year				
4						
5				Quarter		
6		1	2	3	4	Year
7	Budgeted unit sales (in cases)	10,000	30,000	40,000	20,000	100,000
8	Selling price per unit	$ 20.00	$ 20.00	$ 20.00	$ 20.00	$ 20.00
9	Total sales	$200,000	$600,000	$800,000	$400,000	$2,000,000
10						
11		70%	30%			
12		Schedule of Expected Cash Collections				
13	Beginning accounts receivable[1]	$ 90,000				$ 90,000
14	First-quarter sales[2]	140,000	$ 60,000			200,000
15	Second-quarter sales[3]		420,000	$180,000		600,000
16	Third-quarter sales[4]			560,000	$240,000	800,000
17	Fourth-quarter sales[5]	-	-	-	280,000	280,000
18	Total cash collections[6]	$230,000	$480,000	$740,000	$520,000	$1,970,000
19						
20						

◄ ► … **Schedule 1** Schedule … ⊕ ⁝ ◄

Microsoft Excel

---

[1]Cash collections from last year's fourth-quarter sales. See the beginning balance sheet in Exhibit 8–3.
[2]$200,000 × 70%; $200,000 × 30%.
[3]$600,000 × 70%; $600,000 × 30%.
[4]$800,000 × 70%; $800,000 × 30%.
[5]$400,000 × 70%.
[6]Uncollected fourth-quarter sales ($120,000) appear as accounts receivable on the company's end-of-year budgeted balance sheet (see Schedule 10).

IN BUSINESS

BUDGETING FOR HOLIDAY RETURNS

In addition to preparing sales budgets, companies need to budget for the expense of managing sales returns. B-Stock Solutions, which runs online liquidation sites for major retailers, estimates that customers return more than $90 billion worth of merchandise purchased during the holiday season. The National Retail Federation estimates that 80 percent of shoppers prefer in-store returns rather than returning items through carriers, such as UPS and FedEx. Given this reality, many e-commerce merchants are providing ways for customers to return digital purchases to physical locations. For example, Amazon offers free returns at more than 18,000 drop-off locations.

Source: Jennifer Smith, "Retailers Brace for Holiday Returns," *The Wall Street Journal*, December 20, 2019, p. B2.

The Production Budget

The *production budget* is prepared after the sales budget. The **production budget** estimates the number of units that must be produced to fulfill sales and provide the desired
ending finished goods inventory. Production needs are calculated as follows:

LO8–3
Prepare a production budget.

Budgeted unit sales	XXX
Add desired units of ending finished goods inventory.	XXX
Total needs	XXX
Less units of beginning finished goods inventory.	XXX
Required production in units.	XXX

Schedule 2 contains the production budget for Hampton Freeze. The budgeted sales
data come from cells B7 through E7 of the sales budget. The desired ending finished
goods inventory for the first quarter of 6,000 cases is computed by multiplying budgeted
sales from the second quarter (30,000 cases) by the desired ending finished goods inventory percentage (20%) in cell B13 of the Budgeting Assumptions tab. The total needs for
the first quarter (16,000 cases) are determined by adding together the budgeted sales of
10,000 cases for the quarter and the desired ending inventory of 6,000 cases. Because the
company already has 2,000 cases in beginning finished goods inventory (as shown in
the beginning balance sheet in Exhibit 8–3), only 14,000 cases need to be produced in the
first quarter.

Pay particular attention to the Year column (Column F) in the production budget. In
some instances (e.g., budgeted unit sales and required production in units), the amounts
in the column are the sum of the quarterly amounts. In other cells, (e.g., desired units of
ending finished goods inventory and units of beginning finished goods inventory), the
amounts are not the sum of the quarterly figures. From the standpoint of the entire year,
the ending finished goods inventory, which Larry Giano assumed to be 3,000 units, is the

SCHEDULE 2

Hampton Freeze, Inc.
Production Budget
For the Year Ended December 31 of Next Year
(in cases)

	1	2	3	4	Year
Budgeted unit sales (Schedule 1)	10,000	30,000	40,000	20,000	100,000
Add desired units of ending finished goods inventory*	6,000	8,000	4,000	3,000	3,000
Total needs	16,000	38,000	44,000	23,000	103,000
Less units of beginning finished goods inventory†	2,000	6,000	8,000	4,000	2,000
Required production in units	14,000	32,000	36,000	19,000	101,000

* Twenty percent of next quarter's sales. For example, the second-quarter sales are 30,000 cases. Therefore, the desired
ending inventory of finished goods for the first quarter would be 20% × 30,000 cases = 6,000 cases.
†The beginning inventory in each quarter is the same as the prior quarter's ending inventory.

same as the ending finished goods inventory for the fourth quarter—it is *not* the sum of the ending finished goods inventories for all four quarters. Similarly, from the standpoint of the entire year, the beginning finished goods inventory (2,000 units) is the same as the beginning finished goods inventory for the first quarter—it is *not* the sum of the beginning finished goods inventories for all four quarters.

Inventory Purchases—Merchandising Company

Hampton Freeze prepares a production budget because it is a *manufacturing* company. If it were a *merchandising* company, it would prepare a **merchandise purchases budget** showing the amount of goods to be purchased from suppliers during the period.

The format of the merchandise purchases budget is shown below:

Budgeted cost of goods sold	XXX
Add desired ending merchandise inventory	XXX
Total needs.	XXX
Less beginning merchandise inventory	XXX
Required purchases	XXX

A merchandising company prepares a merchandise purchases budget, such as the one above, for each item carried in stock. It can be expressed in dollars (using the headings shown above) or in units. The top line of a merchandise purchases budget based on units would say Budgeted unit sales instead of Budgeted cost of goods sold.

A merchandise purchases budget is usually accompanied by a schedule of expected cash disbursements for merchandise purchases. The format of this schedule mirrors the schedule of expected cash disbursements for purchases of materials shown at the bottom of Schedule 3.

The Direct Materials Budget

LO8–4
Prepare a direct materials budget, including a schedule of expected cash disbursements for purchases of materials.

A *direct materials budget* is prepared after the production budget. The **direct materials budget** estimates the raw materials purchases needed to fulfill the production budget and provide for adequate inventories. The required purchases of raw materials are computed as follows:

Required production in units of finished goods.	XXX
Units of raw materials needed per unit of finished goods	XXX
Units of raw materials needed to meet production.	XXX
Add desired units of ending raw materials inventory	XXX
Total units of raw materials needed	XXX
Less units of beginning raw materials inventory	XXX
Units of raw materials to be purchased	XXX
Unit cost of raw materials	XXX
Cost of raw materials to be purchased	XXX

The direct materials budget (as shown in Schedule 3) begins with the quarterly required production as computed in cells B14 through E14 of the production budget (Schedule 2). The second line of the direct materials budget recognizes that 15 pounds of sugar (see cell B16 from the Budgeting Assumptions tab) are required to make one case of popsicles. The third line of the budget presents the raw materials needed to meet production. For example, in the first quarter, the required production of 14,000 cases is multiplied by 15 pounds to equal 210,000 pounds of sugar needed to meet production. The fourth line shows the desired units of ending raw materials inventory. For the first

SCHEDULE 3

	A	B	C	D	E	F
3		Hampton Freeze, Inc.				
4		Direct Materials Budget				
5		For the Year Ended December 31 of Next Year				
6						Assumed
7		Quarter				
8		1	2	3	4	Year
9	Required production in cases (Schedule 2)	14,000	32,000	36,000	19,000	101,000
10	Units of raw materials needed per case	15	15	15	15	15
11	Units of raw materials needed to meet production	210,000	480,000	540,000	285,000	1,515,000
12	Add desired units of ending raw materials inventory[1]	48,000 10%	54,000 10%	28,500 10%	22,500	22,500
13	Total units of raw materials needed	258,000	534,000	568,500	307,500	1,537,500
14	Less units of beginning raw materials Inventory	21,000	48,000	54,000	28,500	21,000
15	Units of raw materials to be purchased	237,000	486,000	514,500	279,000	1,516,500
16	Cost of raw materials per pound	$ 0.20	$ 0.20	$ 0.20	$ 0.20	$ 0.20
17	Cost of raw materials to be purchased	$ 47,400	$ 97,200	$ 102,900	$ 55,800	$ 303,300
18						
19		50%	50%			
20	Schedule of Expected Cash Disbursements for Purchases of Materials					
21						
22	Beginning accounts payable[2]	$ 25,800				$ 25,800
23	First-quarter purchases[3]	23,700	$ 23,700			47,400
24	Second-quarter purchases[4]		48,600	$ 48,600		97,200
25	Third-quarter purchases[5]			51,450	$ 51,450	102,900
26	Fourth-quarter purchases[6]	-	-	-	27,900	27,900
27	Total cash disbursements for materials	$ 49,500	$ 72,300	$ 100,050	$ 79,350	$ 301,200
28						

Schedule 1 Schedule 2 **Schedule 3** Schedule 4 Sch ... ⊕

Microsoft Excel

[1]Ten percent of the next quarter's production needs. For example, the second-quarter production needs are 480,000 pounds. Therefore, the desired ending inventory for the first quarter would be 10% × 480,000 pounds = 48,000 pounds. The desired ending inventory for quarter 4 (22,500 pounds) assumes the first quarter production needs in the following year are 225,000 pounds (225,000 pounds × 10% = 22,500 pounds).
[2]Cash payments for last year's fourth-quarter purchases. See the beginning-of-year balance sheet in Exhibit 8–3.
[3]$47,400 × 50%; $47,400 × 50%.
[4]$97,200 × 50%; $97,200 × 50%.
[5]$102,900 × 50%; $102,900 × 50%.
[6]$55,800 × 50%. Unpaid fourth-quarter purchases ($27,900) appear as accounts payable on the company's end-of-year budgeted balance sheet (see Schedule 10).

quarter, this amount is computed by multiplying the raw materials needed to meet production in the second quarter of 480,000 pounds by the desired ending inventory percentage of 10 percent as shown in cell B18 of the Budgeting Assumptions tab. The desired units of ending raw materials inventory of 48,000 pounds are added to 210,000 pounds to provide the total units of raw materials needed of 258,000 pounds. However, because the company already has 21,000 pounds of sugar in beginning inventory (as shown in cell A9 in the beginning balance sheet in Exhibit 8–3), only 237,000 pounds of sugar need to be purchased in the first quarter. Because the budgeted cost of raw materials per pound is $0.20 (see cell B17 from the Budgeting Assumptions tab), the cost of raw material to be purchased in the first quarter is $47,400. For the entire year, the company plans to purchase $303,300 of raw materials.

Schedule 3 also shows next year's expected cash disbursements for material purchases are $301,200. The accounts payable balance of $25,800 paid in the first quarter comes from cell C21 of the beginning balance sheet in Exhibit 8–3. All other cash disbursements use the estimated cash payment percentages (both of which are 50%) from cells B19 and

B20 of the Budgeting Assumptions tab. For example, Schedule 3 shows budgeted raw material purchases in the first quarter of $47,400. In the first quarter, Hampton Freeze expects to pay 50 percent of this amount, or $23,700. In the second quarter, the company expects to pay the remaining 50 percent, or $23,700.

IN BUSINESS

BUILDERS' BUDGETS FEELING THE SQUEEZE

The COVID-19 pandemic highlighted the need for companies to be nimble when adjusting their budgets to unexpected marketplace changes. For home builders, their direct materials budgets required major adjustments as supply chain shortages forced them to choose new materials and suppliers to meet their construction deadlines. Builders often absorbed substantially higher costs for these new materials because the alternative—waiting months for their usual materials to restock—would have caused excessive lost sales or rent revenues. Home builders' direct labor budgets also fluctuated during the pandemic, with initial layoffs followed by an abrupt pivot to handle unanticipated surges in demand.

Dan Reynolds Photography/Getty Images

Source: Lydia O'Neal, "Builders Seek Alternatives to Scarce Construction Materials," *The Wall Street Journal*, October 7, 2021, https://www.wsj.com/articles/builders-hunt-for-alternatives-to-materials-in-short-supply-11633512601.

The Direct Labor Budget

LO8–5

Prepare a direct labor budget.

The **direct labor budget** estimates the direct labor-hours required to satisfy the production budget. Companies that neglect direct labor budgeting run the risk of facing labor shortages or having to hire and lay off workers at awkward times, which in turn diminishes employee moral and operational efficiency.

The first line of Hampton Freeze's direct labor budget in Schedule 4 shows the required production for each quarter, which is taken from cells B14 through E14 of the production budget (Schedule 2). The direct labor-hours needed for each quarter is

SCHEDULE 4

	A	B	C	D	E	F
1		Hampton Freeze, Inc.				
2		Direct Labor Budget				
3		For the Year Ended December 31 of Next Year				
4						
5				Quarter		
6		*1*	*2*	*3*	*4*	*Year*
7	Required production in cases (Schedule 2)	14,000	32,000	36,000	19,000	101,000
8	Direct labor-hours per case	0.40	0.40	0.40	0.40	0.40
9	Total direct labor-hours needed	5,600	12,800	14,400	7,600	40,400
10	Direct labor cost per hour	$ 15.00	$ 15.00	$ 15.00	$ 15.00	$ 15.00
11	Total direct labor cost	$ 84,000	$ 192,000	$ 216,000	$ 114,000	$ 606,000
12						

Schedule 1 | Schedule 2 | Schedule 3 | **Schedule 4** | Sch ... ⊕

Microsoft Excel

*This schedule assumes that the direct labor workforce will be fully adjusted to the total direct labor-hours needed each quarter.

computed by multiplying the number of units to be produced by 0.40 direct labor-hour per unit (see cell B23 from the Budgeting Assumptions tab). For example, 14,000 cases will be produced in the first quarter, each requiring 0.40 direct labor-hour, so a total of 5,600 direct labor-hours (14,000 cases × 0.40 direct labor-hour per case) are needed in that quarter. Direct labor-hours are translated into direct labor costs by multiplying the direct labor-hour requirements by the direct labor rate of $15 per hour (see cell B24 from the Budgeting Assumptions tab). For example, the direct labor cost in the first quarter is $84,000 (5,600 direct labor-hours × $15 per direct labor-hour).[3]

WILL CHECKOUT COUNTERS BECOME OBSOLETE?

Most retailers continue to rely heavily on cashiers to tally a customer's amount due and to process the corresponding payment. However, Amazon.com's new Amazon Go stores use computer technology to replace cashiers and to eliminate the need for any type of barcode-scanning checkout process. The company's innovative new stores rely on "computer vision and machine-learning algorithms to track shoppers and charge them for what they select, thereby eliminating checkout counters. . . . A customer entering [a] store scans his or her phone and then becomes represented as a 3-D object to the system." While the Amazon Go model holds much promise for future development, the company currently has no plans to use this technology within its Whole Foods Market grocery stores.

MariaX/Shutterstock

Source: Laura Stevens, "Amazon's Cashierless 'Go' Convenience Store Set to Open," *The Wall Street Journal,* January 20, 2018.

The Manufacturing Overhead Budget

The **manufacturing overhead budget** estimates all production costs other than direct materials and direct labor. At Hampton Freeze, manufacturing overhead is separated into variable and fixed components (see Schedule 5). As shown in the Budgeting Assumptions tab (Exhibit 8–4), the variable component is $4 per direct labor-hour and the fixed component is $60,600 per quarter. Because the variable component depends on direct labor, the manufacturing overhead budget begins with the budgeted quarterly direct labor-hours from cells B9 through E9 of the direct labor budget (Schedule 4). These amounts are multiplied by the variable overhead rate to determine the variable component of manufacturing overhead. For example, the variable manufacturing overhead for the first quarter is $22,400 (5,600 direct labor-hours × $4.00 per direct labor-hour). This is added to the fixed manufacturing overhead to determine the total manufacturing overhead for the quarter of $83,000 ($22,400 + $60,600).

The last line of Schedule 5 shows the budgeted cash disbursements for manufacturing overhead. Because some of the overhead costs are not cash outflows, the total budgeted manufacturing overhead costs must be adjusted to determine the cash disbursements for manufacturing overhead. At Hampton Freeze, the only significant noncash manufacturing overhead cost is depreciation, which is $15,000 per quarter (see cell B29 in the Budgeting Assumptions tab). These noncash depreciation charges are deducted from the total budgeted manufacturing overhead to determine each quarter's expected cash disbursements. Hampton Freeze pays all overhead costs involving cash disbursements in the quarter incurred. Note the company's predetermined overhead rate for the year is $10 per direct labor-hour, which is calculated by dividing the total budgeted manufacturing overhead ($404,000) by the budgeted direct labor-hours (40,400).

LO8–6
Prepare a manufacturing overhead budget.

---

[3] Many companies have employment policies or contracts requiring to pay overtime premiums and preventing them from laying off and rehiring workers as needed. The costs associated with the idle time and overtime resulting from these policies are usually treated as part of manufacturing overhead. In this chapter, for simplicity, we bypass these considerations by always assuming the direct labor workforce is adjusted as needed to match the budgeted production needs.

SCHEDULE 5

	A	B	C	D	E	F
1		Hampton Freeze, Inc.				
2		Manufacturing Overhead Budget				
3		For the Year Ended December 31 of Next Year				
4						
5		Quarter				
6		1	2	3	4	Year
7	Budgeted direct labor-hours (Schedule 4)	5,600	12,800	14,400	7,600	40,400
8	Variable manufacturing overhead rate	$ 4.00	$ 4.00	$ 4.00	$ 4.00	$ 4.00
9	Variable manufacturing overhead	$ 22,400	$ 51,200	$ 57,600	$ 30,400	$ 161,600
10	Fixed manufacturing overhead	60,600	60,600	60,600	60,600	242,400
11	Total manufacturing overhead	83,000	111,800	118,200	91,000	404,000
12	Less depreciation	15,000	15,000	15,000	15,000	60,000
13	Cash disbursements for manufacturing overhead	$ 68,000	$ 96,800	$ 103,200	$ 76,000	$ 344,000
14						
15	Total manufacturing overhead (a)					$ 404,000
16	Budgeted direct labor-hours (b)					40,400
17	Predetermined overhead rate for the year (a) ÷ (b)					$10.00

◄ ► Schedule 3 | Schedule 4 | **Schedule 5** | Schedule 6 | ... ⊕ : ◄

Microsoft Excel

The Ending Finished Goods Inventory Budget

After completing Schedules 1–5, Larry Giano had the data needed to prepare the **ending finished goods inventory budget**[4], shown in Schedule 6. The absorption unit product cost is $13 per case of popsicles—consisting of $3 of direct materials, $6 of direct labor, and $4 of manufacturing overhead. Manufacturing overhead is applied to units of product using the rate of $10 per direct labor-hour from cell F17 of the Manufacturing Overhead budget. The budgeted cost of ending inventory is $39,000.

The Selling and Administrative Expense Budget

LO8–7

Prepare a selling and administrative expense budget.

Schedule 7 contains the *selling and administrative expense budget* for Hampton Freeze. The **selling and administrative expense budget** estimates a company's nonmanufacturing expenses and it is divided into variable and fixed components. The schedule begins with quarterly unit sales from cells B7 through E7 of the sales budget (Schedule 1). The budgeted variable selling and administrative expenses are estimated by multiplying the budgeted unit sales by the variable selling and administrative expense of $1.80 per case (see cell B33 from the Budgeting Assumptions tab). For example, the budgeted variable selling and administrative expense for the first quarter is $18,000 (10,000 cases × $1.80 per case). The fixed selling and administrative expenses of $99,000 per quarter (see cells B35 through B39 from the Budgeting Assumptions tab) are then added to the variable selling and administrative expenses to arrive at the total budgeted selling and administrative expenses. Finally, to determine the cash disbursements for selling and administrative

---

[4] For simplicity, the beginning balance sheet and the ending finished goods inventory budget both report a unit product cost of $13. For purposes of answering "what if" questions, this schedule would assume a FIFO inventory flow. In other words, the ending inventory would consist solely of units produced during the budget year.

SCHEDULE 6

	A	B	C	D	E	F	G	H
1				Hampton Freeze, Inc.				
2				Ending Finished Goods Inventory Budget				
3				(absorption costing basis)				
4				For the Year Ended December 31 of Next Year				
5								
6	Item	Quantity			Cost			Total
7	Production cost per case:							
8	Direct materials	15.00	pounds		$ 0.20	per pound		$ 3.00
9	Direct labor	0.40	hours		$15.00	per hour		6.00
10	Manufacturing overhead	0.40	hours		$10.00	per hour		4.00
11	Unit product cost							$ 13.00
12								
13	Budgeted finished goods inventory:							
14	Ending finished goods inventory in cases (Schedule 2)							3,000
15	Unit product cost (see above)							$ 13.00
16	Ending finished goods inventory in dollars							$ 39,000

... | Schedule 5 | **Schedule 6** | Sch ... (+)

Microsoft Excel

SCHEDULE 7

	A	B	C	D	E	F
1			Hampton Freeze, Inc.			
2			Selling and Administrative Expense Budget			
3			For the Year Ended December 31 of Next Year			
4						
5				Quarter		
6		1	2	3	4	Year
7	Budgeted unit sales (Schedule 1)	10,000	30,000	40,000	20,000	100,000
8	Variable selling and administrative expense per case	$ 1.80	$ 1.80	$ 1.80	$ 1.80	$ 1.80
9	Variable selling and administrative expense	$ 18,000	$ 54,000	$ 72,000	$ 36,000	$180,000
10	Fixed selling and administrative expenses:					
11	Advertising	20,000	20,000	20,000	20,000	80,000
12	Executive salaries	55,000	55,000	55,000	55,000	220,000
13	Insurance	10,000	10,000	10,000	10,000	40,000
14	Property taxes	4,000	4,000	4,000	4,000	16,000
15	Depreciation	10,000	10,000	10,000	10,000	40,000
16	Total fixed selling and administrative expenses	99,000	99,000	99,000	99,000	396,000
17	Total selling and administrative expenses	117,000	153,000	171,000	135,000	576,000
18	Less depreciation	10,000	10,000	10,000	10,000	40,000
19	Cash disbursements for selling and administrative expenses	$107,000	$143,000	$161,000	$125,000	$536,000

... | Schedule 5 | Schedule 6 | **Schedule 7** | ... (+)

Microsoft Excel

items, the total budgeted selling and administrative expense is adjusted by subtracting noncash selling and administrative expenses (in this case, just depreciation).[5]

The Cash Budget

The cash budget has four main sections:

1. The cash receipts section.
2. The cash disbursements section.
3. The cash excess or deficiency section.
4. The financing section.

The receipts section lists all cash inflows except borrowed money. Generally, the major source of receipts is from sales. The disbursements section includes all cash payments except principal and interest repayments. Examples of these payments include raw materials purchases, direct labor and manufacturing overhead payments, equipment purchases, and dividends.

The cash excess or deficiency section is computed as follows:

Beginning cash balance	XXX
Add cash receipts	XXX
Total cash available	XXX
Less cash disbursements	XXX
Excess (deficiency) of cash available over disbursements	XXX

If a cash deficiency exists during any budget period or if there is a cash excess less than the minimum required cash balance, the company will need to borrow money. Conversely, when there is excess cash greater than the minimum required cash balance, the company can repay principal and interest to lenders.

---

[5] Other adjustments might need to be made for differences between cash flows on the one hand and revenues and expenses on the other hand. For example, if property taxes are paid twice a year in installments of $8,000 each, the expense for property tax would have to be "backed out" of the total budgeted selling and administrative expenses and the cash installment payments added to the appropriate quarters to determine the cash disbursements. Similar adjustments might also need to be made in the manufacturing overhead budget. We generally ignore these complications in this chapter.

IN BUSINESS

MISMATCHED CASH FLOWS—CLIMBING THE HILLS AND VALLEYS

Eric W. Noreen

The Washington Trails Association (WTA) is a private, nonprofit organization primarily concerned with protecting and maintaining hiking trails in the state of Washington. Some 2,000 WTA volunteer workers donate more than 80,000 hours per year maintaining trails in rugged landscapes on federal, state, and private lands. The organization is supported by membership dues, voluntary contributions, grants, and some contract work for the government.

The organization's income and expenses are erratic—although somewhat predictable—over the course of the year, as shown in the following chart. Expenses tend to be highest in the spring and summer when most of the trail maintenance work is done. However, income spikes in December well after the expenses have been incurred. With cash outflows running ahead of cash inflows for much of the year, it is very important for the WTA to carefully plan its cash budget and to maintain adequate cash reserves to be able to pay its bills.

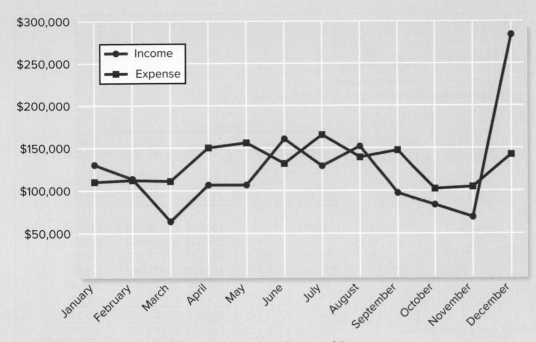

$300,000

$250,000

$200,000

$150,000

$100,000

$50,000

● Income
■ Expense

January February March April May June July August September October November December

Note: Total income and total expense are approximately equal over the course of the year.

Sources: Conversation with Elizabeth Lunney, president of the Washington Trails Association; WTA documents; and the WTA website www.wta.org.

The financing section of the cash budget summarizes estimated borrowings and principal and interest repayments. *In this chapter unless explicitly stated otherwise, we assume all borrowings take place on the first day of the borrowing period and all repayments take place on the last day of the final period included in the cash budget.* To calculate borrowings and interest payments, you'll need to pay attention to the company's desired minimum cash balance and to the terms of the company's loan agreement with the bank. For example, Hampton Freeze's desired minimum cash balance is $30,000 (see cell B42 in the Budgeting Assumptions tab). Furthermore, *we'll assume Hampton Freeze's loan agreement requires borrowing money in increments of $10,000* and charges simple interest of 3 percent per quarter (as shown in cell B45 in Exhibit 8–4).[6]

The beginning cash balance in the first quarter of $42,500 (shown in Schedule 8) agrees with cell B7 of the beginning balance sheet in Exhibit 8–3. Each quarter's collections from customers come from cells B18 through E18 of the schedule of expected cash collections in Schedule 1. Each quarter's beginning cash balance plus the collections from customers equals the total cash available. For example, in the first quarter, the beginning cash balance of $42,500 plus the collections from customers of $230,000 equals the total cash available of $272,500.

Each quarter's cash disbursements for direct materials come from cells B27 through E27 of the schedule of expected cash disbursements for materials (see Schedule 3). The quarterly cash payments for direct labor were calculated in cells B11 through E11 of the direct labor budget (see Schedule 4), whereas the quarterly cash payments related to manufacturing overhead were calculated in cells B13 through E13 of the manufacturing overhead budget (see Schedule 5). The quarterly cash payments for selling and

---

[6] We use simple interest rather than compound interest throughout the chapter for simplicity.

SCHEDULE 8

Hampton Freeze, Inc.
Cash Budget
For the Year Ended December 31 of Next Year

	Schedule	Quarter 1	Quarter 2	Quarter 3	Quarter 4	Year
Beginning cash balance		$42,500	$36,000	$33,900	$165,650	$42,500
Add cash receipts:						
Collections from customers	1	230,000	480,000	740,000	520,000	1,970,000
Total cash available		272,500	516,000	773,900	685,650	2,012,500
Less cash disbursements:						
Direct materials	3	49,500	72,300	100,050	79,350	301,200
Direct labor	4	84,000	192,000	216,000	114,000	606,000
Manufacturing overhead	5	68,000	96,800	103,200	76,000	344,000
Selling and administrative	7	107,000	143,000	161,000	125,000	536,000
Equipment purchases		50,000	40,000	20,000	20,000	130,000
Dividends		8,000	8,000	8,000	8,000	32,000
Total cash disbursements		366,500	552,100	608,250	422,350	1,949,200
Excess (deficiency) of cash available over disbursements		(94,000)	(36,100)	165,650	263,300	63,300
Financing:						
Borrowings (at the beginnings of quarters)		130,000	70,000	-	-	200,000
Repayments (at end of the year)		-	-	-	(200,000)	(200,000)
Interest		-	-	-	(21,900)	(21,900)
Total financing		130,000	70,000	-	(221,900)	(21,900)
Ending cash balance		$36,000	$33,900	$165,650	$41,400	$41,400

Schedule 5 | Schedule 6 | Schedule 7 | **Schedule 8** | S... ...

Microsoft Excel

administrative expenses come from cells B19 through E19 of the selling and administrative expense budget (see Schedule 7). So putting it all together, in the first quarter, the cash disbursements for direct materials ($49,500), direct labor ($84,000), manufacturing overhead ($68,000), selling and administrative expenses ($107,000), equipment purchases ($50,000), and the dividend ($8,000) (see cells C43 and B44 in Exhibit 8–4) equal the total cash disbursements of $366,500.

Each quarter's total cash available minus its total disbursements equals the excess (deficiency) of cash available over disbursements. For example, in the first quarter, the total cash available of $272,500 minus the total disbursements of $366,500 results in a cash deficiency of $94,000. Given the company's minimum required cash balance of $30,000, its minimum required borrowings for the first quarter would be computed as follows:

Required Borrowings at the Beginning of the First Quarter:	
Desired ending cash balance	$ 30,000
Plus deficiency of cash available over disbursements	94,000
Minimum required borrowings	$124,000

Recall the bank loans in increments of $10,000; therefore. Hampton Freeze will have to borrow $130,000.

In next year's second quarter, Hampton Freeze estimates it will have another cash deficiency of $36,100 (see cell D19); therefore, the company's minimum required borrowings at the beginning of the second quarter would be computed as follows:

Required Borrowings at the Beginning of the Second Quarter:
Desired ending cash balance	$30,000
Plus deficiency of cash available over disbursements	36,100
Minimum required borrowings	$66,100

Given the bank's lending terms, Hampton Freeze will have to borrow $70,000 on the first day of the second quarter.

In the third and fourth quarters, Hampton Freeze has an excess of cash available over disbursements greater than $30,000, so it will not need to borrow money. In the third quarter, Hampton Freeze has excess cash of $165,650, yet the cash budget does not include any principal or interest repayments during this quarter. This occurs because, unless stated otherwise, we always assume the company will repay any principal and interest on the *last day of the final period* included in the cash budget. On the last day of the fourth quarter, Hampton Freeze has excess cash of $263,300, so it can repay the $200,000 it borrowed from the lender plus $21,900 of interest, computed as follows:

Interest on the $130,000 borrowed at the beginning of the first quarter:	
$130,000 × 0.03 per quarter × 4 quarters*	$15,600
Interest on the $70,000 borrowed at the beginning of the second quarter:	
$70,000 × 0.03 per quarter × 3 quarters*	6,300
Total interest accrued to the end of the fourth quarter	$21,900

*Simple, rather than compounded, interest is assumed for simplicity

The ending cash balance for each period is computed by taking the excess (deficiency) of cash available over disbursements plus the total financing. For example, in the first quarter, Hampton Freeze's cash deficiency of $(94,000) plus its total financing of $130,000 equals its ending cash balance of $36,000. The ending cash balance for each quarter then becomes the beginning cash balance for the next quarter. Also, the amounts under the Year column in the cash budget are not always the sum of the amounts for the four quarters. In particular, the beginning cash balance for the year is the same as the beginning cash balance for the first quarter and the ending cash balance for the year is the same as the ending cash balance for the fourth quarter.

COMMUNICATING WITH DATA VISUALIZATIONS

Predictive analytics answer the question: What will happen? This visualization is based on Hampton Freeze's cash budget (Schedule 8) and depicts the seasonal nature of the company's business. The company has negative operating cash flows (defined as total cash receipts minus total cash disbursements) in each of the first two quarters; hence, it will need to borrow money during these quarters ($130,000 + $70,000) to prepare for the busy summer selling season. It will be able to repay all principal and interest on its borrowings ($221,900) by the end of the fourth quarter.

(Continued)

Cash Budget

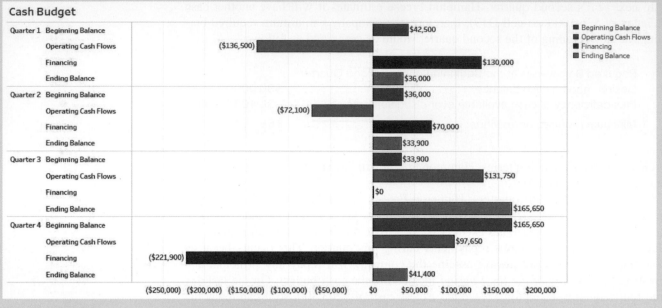

Tableau

The Budgeted Income Statement

LO8–9

Prepare a budgeted income statement.

Schedule 9 contains the budgeted income statement for Hampton Freeze. All of its sales and expenses come from the data in the beginning balance sheet and the data developed in Schedules 1–8. The sales of $2,000,000 come from cell F9 of the sales budget (Schedule 1). Given that the unit product cost of the year's beginning inventory and the year's production both equal $13 per unit, the cost of goods sold of $1,300,000 can be computed by multiplying 100,000 units sold (see cell F7 from Schedule 1) by the unit product cost of $13 per unit (see cell H11 in Schedule 6).[7] The selling and administrative expenses of $576,000 come from cell F17 of the selling and administrative expenses budget (Schedule 7). Finally, the interest expense of $21,900 comes from cell G23 of the cash budget (Schedule 8).

Because Larry Giano created a Budgeting Assumptions tab in his Excel file (see Exhibit 8–4) and linked all of his budget schedules together using properly constructed Excel formulas, he can make changes to his underlying budgeting assumptions and instantly see the impact on net income. For example, if Larry wanted to estimate the profit impact if fourth quarter sales are 18,000 cases instead of 20,000 cases, he would change the 20,000 cases shown in cell F7 of his Budgeting Assumptions tab to 18,000 cases. The revised net income of $87,045 would instantly appear in cell C12 of the budgeted income statement.

---

[7] Cost of goods sold can also be computed using equations introduced in earlier chapters. Manufacturing companies can use the equation Cost of goods sold = Beginning finished goods inventory + Cost of goods manufactured − Ending finished goods inventory. Merchandising companies can use the equation Cost of goods sold = Beginning merchandise inventory + purchases − Ending merchandise inventory.

SCHEDULE 9

	A	B	C
1	**Hampton Freeze, Inc.**		
2	**Budgeted Income Statement**		
3	**For the Year Ended December 31 of Next Year**		
4			
5		*Schedules*	
6	Sales	1	$ 2,000,000
7	Cost of goods sold	1, 6	1,300,000
8	Gross margin		700,000
9	Selling and administrative expenses	7	576,000
10	Net operating Income		124,000
11	Interest expense	8	21,900
12	Net Income		$ 102,100

Schedule 9 | Schedule 10 | (+)

Microsoft Excel

The Budgeted Balance Sheet

Hampton Freeze's budgeted balance sheet, accompanied by explanations of how the numbers were derived, is presented in Schedule 10. It was created using data from the beginning balance sheet (Exhibit 8–3) and Schedules 1–9.

After completing the master budget, Larry Giano took the documents to Tom Wills, chief executive officer of Hampton Freeze, for his review.

LO8–10
Prepare a budgeted balance sheet.

MANAGERIAL
ACCOUNTING IN ACTION
THE WRAP-UP

Larry: Here's the budget. Overall, the income is excellent, and the net cash flow for the entire year is positive.

Tom: Yes, but the cash budget shows we have the same negative cash flows in the first and second quarters that we had this year.

Larry: That's true. I don't see any way around that problem. However, if you take this budget to the bank today, they'll probably approve an open line of credit so you can borrow enough money to make it through the first two quarters without any problem.

Tom: Sounds good.

Larry: Also, keep in mind the master budget contains all the embedded formulas you'll need to answer the types of "what if" questions we discussed earlier. If you want to calculate the financial impact of changing any of your master budget's underlying estimates or assumptions, you can do it with the click of a mouse!

Tom: This sounds fabulous, Larry. Thanks for all of your work on this project.

SCHEDULE 10

	A	B	C	D	E
1	Hampton Freeze, Inc.				
2	Budgeted Balance Sheet				
3	December 31 of Next Year				
4					
5	*Assets*				
6	Current assets:				
7	Cash	$ 41,400	(a)		
8	Accounts receivable	120,000	(b)		
9	Raw materials inventory	4,500	(c)		
10	Finished goods inventory	39,000	(d)		
11	Total current assets			$ 204,900	
12	Plant and equipment:				
13	Land	80,000	(e)		
14	Buildings and equipment	830,000	(f)		
15	Accumulated depreciation	(392,000)	(g)		
16	Plant and equipment, net			518,000	
17	Total assets			$ 722,900	
18					
19	*Liabilities and Stockholders' Equity*				
20	Current liabilities:				
21	Accounts payable (raw materials)			$ 27,900	(h)
22	Stockholders' equity:				
23	Common stock, no par	$ 175,000	(i)		
24	Retained earnings	520,000	(j)		
25	Total stockholders' equity			695,000	
26	Total liabilities and stockholders' equity			$ 722,900	
27					

◄ ► ... e 9 | **Schedule 10** | ⊕ | ⋮ | ◄ | ► |

Microsoft Excel

Explanations of December 31 budgeted balance sheet figures:
(a) From cell G25 of the cash budget (Schedule 8).
(b) Thirty percent of fourth-quarter sales, from Schedule 1 ($400,000 × 30% = $120,000).
(c) From the direct materials budget (Schedule 3). Cell E12 multiplied by cell E16. In other words, 22,500 pounds × $0.20 per pound = $4,500.
(d) From cell H16 of the ending finished goods inventory budget (Schedule 6).
(e) From cell B13 of the beginning balance sheet (Exhibit 8–3).
(f) Cell B14 of the beginning balance sheet (Exhibit 8–3) plus cell G16 from the cash budget (Schedule 8). In other words, $700,000 + $130,000 = $830,000.
(g) The beginning balance of $292,000 (from cell B15 of the beginning balance sheet in Exhibit 8–3) plus the depreciation of $60,000 included in cell F12 of the manufacturing overhead budget (Schedule 5) plus depreciation expense of $40,000 included in cell F18 in the selling and administrative expense budget (Schedule 7). In other words, $292,000 + $60,000 + $40,000 = $392,000.
(h) One-half of fourth-quarter raw materials purchases, from Schedule 3 ($55,800 × 50% = $27,900).
(i) From cell B23 of the beginning balance sheet (Exhibit 8–3).
(j)

Beginning balance, from cell B24 of Exhibit 8–3	$449,900
Add net income, from cell C12 of Schedule 9..................	102,100
	552,000
Deduct dividends paid, from cell G17 of Schedule 8............	32,000
Ending balance	$520,000

Summary

This chapter describes the budgeting process and shows how the various operating budgets relate to each other. The sales budget is the foundation for a master budget. Once the sales budget has been set, the production budget and the selling and administrative expense budget can be prepared because they depend on how many units are to be sold. The production budget determines how many units are to be produced, so after it is prepared, the various manufacturing cost budgets can be prepared. All of these budgets feed into the cash budget and the budgeted income statement and balance sheet. The parts of the master budget are connected in many ways. For example, the schedule of expected cash collections, which is completed in connection with the sales budget, provides data for both the cash budget and the budgeted balance sheet.

 Data Analytics Exercise available in Connect to complement this chapter

Review Problem: Budget Schedules

Mynor Corporation manufactures and sells a seasonal product with peak sales in the third quarter. The following information concerns operations for Year 2—the coming year—and for the first two quarters of Year 3:

a. The company's single product sells for $8 per unit. Budgeted unit sales for the next six quarters are as follows (all sales are on credit):

	Year 2 Quarter				Year 3 Quarter	
	1	2	3	4	1	2
Budgeted unit sales	40,000	60,000	100,000	50,000	70,000	80,000

b. Sales are collected in the following pattern: 75 percent in the quarter the sales are made, and the remaining 25 percent in the following quarter. On January 1, Year 2, the company's balance sheet showed $65,000 in accounts receivable, all of which will be collected in the first quarter of the year. Bad debts are negligible and can be ignored.

c. The company desires an ending finished goods inventory at the end of each quarter equal to 30 percent of the budgeted unit sales for the next quarter. On December 31, Year 1, the company had 12,000 units on hand.

d. Five pounds of raw materials are required to complete one unit of product. The company requires ending raw materials inventory at the end of each quarter equal to 10 percent of the following quarter's production needs. On December 31, Year 1, the company had 23,000 pounds of raw materials on hand.

e. The raw material costs $0.80 per pound. Raw material purchases are paid for in the following pattern: 60 percent paid in the quarter the purchases are made, and the remaining 40 percent paid in the following quarter. On January 1, Year 2, the company's balance sheet showed $81,500 in accounts payable for raw material purchases, all of which will be paid for in the first quarter of the year.

Required:
Prepare the following budgets and schedules for the year, showing both quarterly and total figures:
1. A sales budget and a schedule of expected cash collections.
2. A production budget.
3. A direct materials budget and a schedule of expected cash payments for purchases of materials.

Solution to Review Problem

1. The sales budget is prepared as follows:

	Year 2 Quarter				
	1	2	3	4	Year 2
Budgeted unit sales	40,000	60,000	100,000	50,000	250,000
Selling price per unit	× $8	× $8	× $8	× $8	× $8
Total sales	$320,000	$480,000	$800,000	$400,000	$2,000,000

Based on the budgeted sales above, the schedule of expected cash collections is prepared as follows:

	Year 2 Quarter				Year 2
	1	2	3	4	
Beginning accounts receivable	$ 65,000				$ 65,000
First-quarter sales ($320,000 × 75%, 25%)	240,000	$ 80,000			320,000
Second-quarter sales ($480,000 × 75%, 25%)		360,000	$120,000		480,000
Third-quarter sales ($800,000 × 75%, 25%)			600,000	$200,000	800,000
Fourth-quarter sales ($400,000 × 75%)				300,000	300,000
Total cash collections	$305,000	$440,000	$720,000	$500,000	$1,965,000

2. Based on the sales budget in units, the production budget is prepared as follows:

	Year 2 Quarter				Year 2	Year 3 Quarter	
	1	2	3	4	Year 2	1	2
Budgeted unit sales	40,000	60,000	100,000	50,000	250,000	70,000	80,000
Add desired ending finished goods inventory*	18,000	30,000	15,000	21,000†	21,000	24,000	
Total needs	58,000	90,000	115,000	71,000	271,000	94,000	
Less beginning finished goods inventory	12,000	18,000	30,000	15,000	12,000	21,000	
Required production	46,000	72,000	85,000	56,000	259,000	73,000	

*30% of the following quarter's budgeted unit sales.
†30% of the budgeted Year 3 first-quarter sales.

3. Based on the production budget, raw materials will need to be purchased during the year as follows:

	Year 2 Quarter				Year 2	Year 3 Quarter
	1	2	3	4	Year 2	1
Required production in units of finished goods.........	46,000	72,000	85,000	56,000	259,000	73,000
Units of raw materials needed per unit of finished goods	× 5	× 5	× 5	× 5	× 5	× 5
Units of raw materials needed to meet production	230,000	360,000	425,000	280,000	1,295,000	365,000
Add desired units of ending raw materials inventory* ...	36,000	42,500	28,000	36,500†	36,500	
Total units of raw materials needed	266,000	402,500	453,000	316,500	1,331,500	
Less units of beginning raw materials inventory	23,000	36,000	42,500	28,000	23,000	
Units of raw materials to be purchased	243,000	366,500	410,500	288,500	1,308,500	
Unit cost of raw materials	× $0.80	× $0.80	× $0.80	× $0.80	× $0.80	
Cost of raw materials to be purchased	$194,400	$293,200	$328,400	$230,800	$1,046,800	

*10% of the following quarter's production needs in pounds.
†10% of the Year 3 first-quarter production needs in pounds.

Based on the raw material purchases above, expected cash payments are computed as follows:

	Year 2 Quarter				Year 2
	1	2	3	4	
Beginning accounts payable	$ 81,500				$ 81,500
First-quarter purchases ($194,400 × 60%, 40%)	116,640	$ 77,760			194,400
Second-quarter purchases ($293,200 × 60%, 40%)		175,920	$117,280		293,200
Third-quarter purchases ($328,400 × 60%, 40%)			197,040	$131,360	328,400
Fourth-quarter purchases ($230,800 × 60%)				138,480	138,480
Total cash disbursements	$198,140	$253,680	$314,320	$269,840	$1,035,980

Glossary

Budget A plan for the future expressed in quantitative terms. (p. 354)

Cash budget A schedule estimating how cash will be acquired and used over a specific time period. (p. 356)

Control The process of gathering feedback to ensure a plan is being properly executed or modified as circumstances change. (p. 354)

Direct labor budget A plan showing the direct labor-hours required to fulfill the production budget. (p. 366)

Direct materials budget A plan showing the amount of raw materials that must be purchased to fulfill the production budget and provide adequate inventories. (p. 364)

Ending finished goods inventory budget A budget showing the dollar amount of unsold finished goods inventory appearing on the ending balance sheet. (p. 368)

Manufacturing overhead budget A plan showing the production costs, other than direct materials and direct labor, that will be incurred over a specified time period. (p. 367)

Master budget A number of separate but interdependent budgets quantifying the company's sales, production, and financial goals and culminating in a cash budget, budgeted income statement, and budgeted balance sheet. (p. 355)

Merchandise purchases budget A plan used by a merchandising company showing the amount of goods to be purchased from suppliers during the period. (p. 364)

Participative budget See *Self-imposed budget.* (p. 354)

Planning The process of establishing goals and specifying how to achieve them. (p. 354)

Production budget A plan showing the number of units that must be produced during a period to satisfy both sales and inventory needs. (p. 363)

Sales budget A schedule showing expected sales in dollars and units. (p. 355)

Self-imposed budget A method of preparing budgets in which managers prepare their own budgets. These budgets are then reviewed by higher-level managers, and any issues are resolved by mutual agreement. (p. 354)

Selling and administrative expense budget A schedule of planned nonmanufacturing expenses. (p. 368)

Questions

8–1 What is a budget? What is budgetary control?

8–2 Why do companies prepare budgets.

8–3 What is a perpetual budget?

8–4 What is a master budget, and what schedules comprise it?

8–5 Why is the sales forecast the starting point in budgeting?

8–6 Do planning and control mean the same thing?

8–7 Why is it a good idea to create a "Budgeting Assumptions" tab when creating a master budget in Microsoft Excel?

8–8 What is a self-imposed budget? What are the major advantages of self-imposed budgets? What caution must be exercised in their use?

8–9 How can budgeting assist a company in planning its workforce staffing levels?

8–10 "The principal purpose of the cash budget is to see how much cash the company will have in the bank at the end of the year." Do you agree? Explain.

Mc Graw Hill connect Applying Excel

LO8–2, LO8–3, LO8–4

The Excel worksheet shown below recreates the Review Problem related to Mynor Corporation. The workbook, and instructions on how to complete the file, can be found in Connect.

	A	B	C	D	E	F	G	H	I
1	**Chapter 8: Applying Excel**								
2									
3	**Data**			*Year 2 Quarter*			*Year 3 Quarter*		
4			*1*	*2*	*3*	*4*	*1*	*2*	
5	Budgeted unit sales		40,000	60,000	100,000	50,000	70,000	80,000	
6									
7	• Selling price per unit	$8	per unit						
8	• Accounts receivable, beginning balance	$65,000							
9	• Sales collected in the quarter sales are made	75%							
10	• Sales collected in the quarter after sales are made	25%							
11	• Desired ending finished goods inventory is	30%	of the budgeted unit sales of the next quarter						
12	• Finished goods inventory, beginning	12,000	units						
13	• Raw materials required to produce one unit	5	pounds						
14	• Desired ending inventory of raw materials is	10%	of the next quarter's production needs						
15	• Raw materials inventory, beginning	23,000	pounds						
16	• Raw material costs	$0.80	per pound						
17	• Raw materials purchases are paid	60%	in the quarter the purchases are made						
18	and	40%	in the quarter following purchase						
19	• Accounts payable for raw materials, beginning balance	$81,500							
20									
21	*Enter a formula into each of the cells marked with a ? below*								
22	**Review Problem: Budget Schedules**								
23									
24	*Construct the sales budget*			*Year 2 Quarter*			*Year 3 Quarter*		
25			*1*	*2*	*3*	*4*	*1*	*2*	
26	Budgeted unit sales		?	?	?	?	?	?	
27	Selling price per unit		?	?	?	?	?	?	
28	Total sales		?	?	?	?	?	?	
29									
30	*Construct the schedule of expected cash coll*			*Year 2 Quarter*					
31			*1*	*2*	*3*	*4*	*Year*		
32	Accounts receivable, beginning balance		?				?		
33	First-quarter sales		?	?			?		
34	Second-quarter sales			?	?		?		
35	Third-quarter sales				?	?	?		
36	Fourth-quarter sales					?	?		
37	Total cash collections		?	?	?	?	?		
38									
39	*Construct the production budget*			*Year 2 Quarter*				*Year 3 Quarter*	
40			*1*	*2*	*3*	*4*	*Year*	*1*	*2*
41	Budgeted unit sales		?	?	?	?	?	?	?
42	Add desired finished goods inventory		?	?	?	?	?	?	
43	Total needs		?	?	?	?	?	?	
44	Less beginning inventory		?	?	?	?	?	?	
45	Required production		?	?	?	?	?	?	
46									
47	*Construct the raw materials purchases budget*			*Year 2 Quarter*				*Year 3 Quarter*	
48			*1*	*2*	*3*	*4*	*Year*	*1*	
49	Required production (units)		?	?	?	?	?	?	
50	Raw materials required to produce one unit		?	?	?	?	?	?	
51	Production needs (pounds)		?	?	?	?	?	?	
52	Add desired ending inventory of raw materials (pounds)		?	?	?	?	?		
53	Total needs (pounds)		?	?	?	?	?		
54	Less beginning inventory of raw materials (pounds)		?	?	?	?	?		
55	Raw materials to be purchased		?	?	?	?	?		
56	Cost of raw materials per pound		?	?	?	?	?		
57	Cost of raw materials to be purchased		?	?	?	?	?		
58									
59	*Construct the schedule of expected cash paym*			*Year 2 Quarter*					
60			*1*	*2*	*3*	*4*	*Year*		
61	Accounts payable, beginning balance		?				?		
62	First-quarter purchases		?	?			?		
63	Second-quarter purchases			?	?		?		
64	Third-quarter purchases				?	?	?		
65	Fourth-quarter purchases					?	?		
66	Total cash disbursements		?	?	?	?	?		
67									

Chapter 8 Form   (+)

Microsoft Excel

You should proceed to the requirements below only after completing your worksheet.

Required:

1. Check your worksheet by changing the budgeted unit sales in Quarter 2 of Year 2 in cell C5 to 75,000 units. The total expected cash collections for the year should now be $2,085,000. The required production for the year should be 274,000 units. The cost of raw materials to be purchased for the year should be $1,106,800, whereas the total cash disbursements for the year should be $1,095,980. If you do not get these answers, find the errors in your worksheet and correct them. Why have the total cash disbursements for raw materials increased?
2. The company just hired a new marketing manager who insists unit sales can be dramatically increased by dropping the selling price from $8 to $7. The marketing manager would like to use the following projections in the budget:

	Year 2 Quarter				Year 3 Quarter	
	1	2	3	4	1	2
Budgeted unit sales	50,000	70,000	120,000	80,000	90,000	100,000
Selling price per unit	$7					

a. What are the total expected cash collections for the year under this revised budget?
b. What is the total required production for the year under this revised budget?
c. What is the total cost of raw materials to be purchased for the year under this revised budget?
d. What are the total expected cash disbursements for raw materials for the year under this revised budget?
e. After seeing this revised budget, the production manager cautioned that due to the limited availability of a complex milling machine, the plant can produce no more than 90,000 units in any one quarter. Is this a potential problem? If so, what can be done about it?

Mc Graw Hill connect   The Foundational 15

Morganton Company makes one product and provided the following information to help prepare its master budget:

a. The budgeted selling price per unit is $70. Budgeted unit sales for June, July, August, and September are 8,400, 10,000, 12,000, and 13,000 units, respectively. All sales are on credit.
b. Forty percent of credit sales are collected in the month of the sale and 60% in the following month.
c. The ending finished goods inventory equals 20% of the following month's unit sales.
d. The ending raw materials inventory equals 10% of the following month's raw materials production needs. Each unit of finished goods requires 5 pounds of raw materials. The raw materials cost $2.00 per pound.
e. Thirty percent of raw materials purchases are paid for in the month of purchase and 70% in the following month.
f. The direct labor wage rate is $15 per hour. Each unit of finished goods requires two direct labor-hours.
g. The variable selling and administrative expense per unit sold is $1.80. The fixed selling and administrative expense per month is $60,000.

LO8–2, LO8–3, LO8–4, LO8–5, LO8–7, LO8–9, LO8–10

Required:

For July:

1. What are the budgeted sales?
2. What are the expected cash collections?
3. What is the ending accounts receivable balance?
4. What is the estimated production in units?
5. Assume 61,000 pounds of raw materials are needed to meet production in August. How many pounds of raw materials should be purchased?
6. What is the estimated cost of raw materials purchases?
7. What are the total estimated cash disbursements for raw materials purchases? Assume the cost of raw material purchases in June is $88,880.

8. What is the estimated ending accounts payable balance?
9. What is the estimated ending raw materials inventory balance?
10. What is the total estimated direct labor cost?
11. If we assume there is no fixed manufacturing overhead and the variable manufacturing overhead is $10 per direct labor-hour, what is the estimated unit product cost?
12. What is the estimated ending finished goods inventory balance?
13. What are the estimated cost of goods sold and gross margin?
14. What is the estimated total selling and administrative expense?
15. What is the estimated net operating income?

Exercises

EXERCISE 8–1 Schedule of Expected Cash Collections LO8–2

Silver Company makes a product with peak sales in May of each year. Its sales budget for the second quarter is given below:

	April	May	June	Total
Budgeted sales (all on account).........	$300,000	$500,000	$200,000	$1,000,000

The company estimates 20% of a month's sales are collected in the month of sale, another 70% are collected in the month following sale, and the remaining 10% are collected in the second month following sale. Bad debts are negligible and can be ignored. February sales totaled $230,000, and March sales totaled $260,000.

Required:

1. Using Schedule 1 as your guide, prepare a schedule of expected cash collections from sales, by month and in total, for the second quarter.
2. What is the accounts receivable balance on June 30th?

EXERCISE 8–2 Production Budget LO8–3

Down Under Products' sales budget for the next four months is as follows:

	Unit Sales
April.................	50,000
May	75,000
June	90,000
July	80,000

The company wants its ending inventory levels to equal 10% of the following month's unit sales. The inventory at the end of March was 5,000 units.

Required:

Using Schedule 2 as your guide, prepare a production budget, by month and in total, for the second quarter.

EXERCISE 8–3 Direct Materials Budget LO8–4

Three grams of musk oil are required for each bottle of Mink Caress, a popular perfume made by a company in western Siberia. The cost of the musk oil is $1.50 per gram. Budgeted quarterly production of Mink Caress is given below for Year 2 and the first quarter of Year 3:

	Year 2				Year 3
	First	Second	Third	Fourth	First
Budgeted production, in bottles	60,000	90,000	150,000	100,000	70,000

The inventory of musk oil at the end of a quarter must equal 20% of the following quarter's production needs. A total of 36,000 grams of musk oil will be on hand to start the first quarter of Year 2.

Required:

Using Schedule 3 as your guide, prepare a direct materials budget for musk oil, by quarter and in total, for Year 2.

EXERCISE 8–4 Direct Labor Budget LO8–5

The production manager of Rordan Corporation prepared the following quarterly production forecast for next year:

	1st Quarter	2nd Quarter	3rd Quarter	4th Quarter
Units to be produced	8,000	6,500	7,000	7,500

Each unit requires 0.35 direct labor-hour, and direct laborers are paid $15.00 per hour.

Required:

Using Schedule 4 as your guide, prepare a direct labor budget for next year.

EXERCISE 8–5 Manufacturing Overhead Budget LO8–6

Yuvwell Corporation's direct labor budget for next year contained the following information:

	1st Quarter	2nd Quarter	3rd Quarter	4th Quarter
Budgeted direct labor-hours	8,000	8,200	8,500	7,800

The company uses direct labor-hours as its overhead allocation base. The variable portion of its predetermined manufacturing overhead rate is $3.25 per direct labor-hour and its total fixed manufacturing overhead is $48,000 per quarter. The only noncash item included in fixed manufacturing overhead is depreciation of $16,000 per quarter.

Required:

1. Using Schedule 5 as your guide, prepare the company's manufacturing overhead budget for next year.
2. Compute the company's predetermined overhead rate (including both variable and fixed manufacturing overhead) for next year.

EXERCISE 8–6 Selling and Administrative Expense Budget LO8–7

Weller Company's budgeted unit sales for next year are provided below:

	1st Quarter	2nd Quarter	3rd Quarter	4th Quarter
Budgeted unit sales	15,000	16,000	14,000	13,000

The company's variable selling and administrative expense per unit is $2.50. Fixed selling and administrative expenses include advertising expenses of $8,000 per quarter, executive salaries of $35,000 per quarter, and depreciation of $20,000 per quarter. In addition, the company will make insurance payments of $5,000 in the first quarter and $5,000 in the third quarter. Finally, property taxes of $8,000 will be paid in the second quarter.

Required:

Using Schedule 7 as your guide, prepare the company's selling and administrative expense budget for next year.

EXERCISE 8–7 Cash Budget LO8–8

Garden Depot is a retailer that provided the following budgeted cash flows for next year:

	1st Quarter	2nd Quarter	3rd Quarter	4th Quarter
Total cash receipts	$180,000	$330,000	$210,000	$230,000
Total cash disbursements	$260,000	$230,000	$220,000	$240,000

The company's beginning cash balance for next year will be $20,000. The company requires a minimum cash balance of $10,000 and may borrow money at the beginning of any quarter and may repay any part of its loans at the end of any quarter. Interest payments, based on a quarterly interest rate of 3%, are due on any principal at the time it is repaid. For simplicity, assume interest is not compounded.

Required:
Using Schedule 8 as your guide, prepare the company's cash budget for next year.

EXERCISE 8–8 Budgeted Income Statement LO8–9
Gig Harbor Boating is the wholesale distributor of a recreational sailboat. Management provided the following data for budgeting purposes:

Budgeted unit sales	460
Selling price per unit	$1,950
Cost per unit	$1,575
Variable selling and administrative expense (per unit)	$75
Fixed selling and administrative expense (per year)	$105,000
Interest expense for the year	$14,000

Required:
Using Schedule 9 as your guide, prepare a budgeted income statement for the year.

EXERCISE 8–9 Budgeted Balance Sheet LO8–10
Mecca Copy, a photocopying center located on University Avenue, provided the following data to prepare a budgeted balance sheet for next year:

	Ending Balances
Cash	?
Accounts receivable	$8,100
Supplies inventory	$3,200
Equipment	$34,000
Accumulated depreciation	$16,000
Accounts payable	$1,800
Common stock	$5,000
Retained earnings	?

The beginning balance of retained earnings was $28,000, budgeted net income is $11,500, and budgeted dividends are $4,800.

Required:
Prepare the company's budgeted balance sheet.

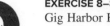

EXERCISE 8–10 Production and Direct Materials Budgets LO8–3, LO8–4
Pearl Products Limited of Shenzhen, China, manufactures and distributes toys throughout Southeast Asia. Three cubic centimeters (cc) of solvent H300 are required to manufacture each unit of Supermix, one of the company's products. The company is planning its raw materials needs for the third quarter, the quarter in which peak sales of Supermix occur. To keep production and sales moving smoothly, the company has the following inventory requirements:

a.   The finished goods inventory on hand at the end of each month must equal 3,000 units of Supermix plus 20% of the next month's sales. The finished goods inventory on June 30 is budgeted to be 10,000 units.

b.   The raw materials inventory on hand at the end of each month must equal one-half of the following month's production needs for raw materials. The raw materials inventory on June 30 is budgeted to be 54,000 cc of solvent H300.

c. The company maintains no work in process inventories.

A monthly sales budget for Supermix for the third and fourth quarters of the year follows:

	Budgeted Unit Sales
July	35,000
August	40,000
September	50,000
October	30,000
November	20,000
December	10,000

Required:

1. Prepare a production budget for Supermix for the months July, August, September, and October.

2. Examine the production budget you prepared in (1) above. Why will the company produce more units than it sells in July and August, and fewer units than it sells in September and October?

3. Prepare a direct materials budget showing the quantity of solvent H300 to be purchased for July, August, and September, and for the quarter in total.

EXERCISE 8–11 Cash Budget Analysis LO8–8

A cash budget, by quarters, is given below for a retail company (000 omitted). The company requires a minimum cash balance of $5,000 to start each quarter.

	Quarter				
	1	2	3	4	Year
Cash balance, beginning	$ 6	$?	$?	$?	$?
Add collections from customers	?	?	96	?	323
Total cash available	71	?	?	?	?
Less disbursements:					
Purchase of inventory	35	45	?	35	?
Selling and administrative expenses	?	30	30	?	113
Equipment purchases	8	8	10	?	36
Dividends	2	2	2	2	?
Total disbursements	?	85	?	?	?
Excess (deficiency) of cash available over disbursements	(2)	?	11	?	?
Financing:					
Borrowings	?	15	—	—	?
Repayments (including interest)*	—	—	(?)	(17)	(?)
Total financing	?	?	?	?	?
Cash balance, ending	$?	$?	$?	$?	$?

*Interest will total $1,000 for the year.

Required:

Fill in the missing amounts in the above table.

EXERCISE 8–12 Schedules of Expected Cash Collections and Disbursements; Income Statement; Balance Sheet LO8–2, LO8–4, LO8–9, LO8–10

Beech Corporation is a merchandising company that is preparing a master budget for the third quarter. The company's balance sheet as of June 30th is shown below:

Beech Corporation Balance Sheet June 30	
Assets	
Cash	$ 90,000
Accounts receivable	136,000
Inventory	62,000
Plant and equipment, net of depreciation	210,000
Total assets	$498,000
Liabilities and Stockholders' Equity	
Accounts payable	$ 71,100
Common stock	327,000
Retained earnings	99,900
Total liabilities and stockholders' equity	$498,000

Beech's managers made the following additional assumptions and estimates:

1. Estimated sales for July, August, September, and October will be $210,000, $230,000, $220,000, and $240,000, respectively.
2. All sales are on credit and all credit sales are collected. Each month's credit sales are collected 35% in the month of sale and 65% in the month following the sale. All of the accounts receivable at June 30 will be collected in July.
3. Each month's ending inventory must equal 30% of the cost of next month's sales. The cost of goods sold is 60% of sales. The company pays for 40% of its merchandise purchases in the month of the purchase and the remaining 60% in the month following the purchase. All of the accounts payable at June 30 will be paid in July.
4. Monthly selling and administrative expenses are always $60,000. Each month $5,000 of this total amount is depreciation expense and the remaining $55,000 relates to expenses that are paid in the month they are incurred.
5. The company does not plan to borrow money or pay or declare dividends during the quarter ended September 30. The company does not plan to issue any common stock or repurchase its own stock during the quarter ended September 30.

Required:

1. Prepare a schedule of expected cash collections for July, August, and September. Also, compute total cash collections for the quarter ended September 30.
2. a. Prepare a merchandise purchases budget for July, August, and September. Also, compute total merchandise purchases for the quarter ended September 30.
   b. Prepare a schedule of expected cash disbursements for merchandise purchases for July, August, and September. Also, compute total cash disbursements for merchandise purchases for the quarter ended September 30.
3. Using Schedule 9 as your guide, prepare an income statement for the quarter ended September 30.
4. Prepare a balance sheet as of September 30.

EXERCISE 8–13 Schedules of Expected Cash Collections and Disbursements; Income Statement; Balance Sheet LO8–2, LO8–4, LO8–9, LO8–10

Refer to the data for Beech Corporation in Exercise 8–12. The company is considering making the following changes to the assumptions underlying its master budget:

1. Each month's credit sales are collected 45% in the month of sale and 55% in the month following the sale.
2. Each month's ending inventory must equal 20% of the cost of next month's sales.
3. The company pays for 30% of its merchandise purchases in the month of the purchase and the remaining 70% in the month following the purchase.

All other information from Exercise 8–12 not mentioned above remains the same.

Required:

Using the new assumptions described above, complete the following requirements:

1. Prepare a schedule of expected cash collections for July, August, and September. Also, compute total cash collections for the quarter ended September 30.
2. a. Prepare a merchandise purchases budget for July, August, and September. Also, compute total merchandise purchases for the quarter ended September 30.
   b. Prepare a schedule of expected cash disbursements for merchandise purchases for July, August, and September. Also, compute total cash disbursements for merchandise purchases for the quarter ended September 30.
3. Using Schedule 9 as your guide, prepare an income statement for the quarter ended September 30.
4. Prepare a balance sheet as of September 30.

EXERCISE 8–14 Sales and Production Budgets LO8–2, LO8–3

The marketing department of Jessi Corporation submitted the following sales forecast for next year (all sales are on account):

	1st Quarter	2nd Quarter	3rd Quarter	4th Quarter
Budgeted unit sales	11,000	12,000	14,000	13,000

The selling price of the company's product is $18.00 per unit. Management expects to collect 65% of sales in the quarter in which the sales are made and 30% in the following quarter; 5% of sales are expected to be uncollectible. The beginning balance of accounts receivable, all of which is expected to be collected in the first quarter, is $70,200.

The company expects to start the first quarter with 1,650 units in finished goods inventory. Management desires an ending finished goods inventory in each quarter equal to 15% of the next quarter's budgeted sales. The desired ending finished goods inventory for the fourth quarter is 1,850 units.

Required:

1. Calculate the estimated sales for each quarter and for the year as a whole. (Hint: Refer to Schedule 1 for guidance.)
2. Calculate the expected cash collections for each quarter and for the year as a whole. (Hint: Refer to Schedule 1 for guidance.)
3. Calculate the required production in units of finished goods for each quarter and for the year as a whole. (Hint: Refer to Schedule 2 for guidance.)

EXERCISE 8–15 Direct Labor and Manufacturing Overhead Budgets LO8–5, LO8–6

Hruska Corporation's production budget for next year contained the following estimates:

	1st Quarter	2nd Quarter	3rd Quarter	4th Quarter
Units to be produced	12,000	10,000	13,000	14,000

Each unit requires 0.2 direct labor-hour and direct laborers are paid $16.00 per hour.

In addition, the variable manufacturing overhead rate is $1.75 per direct labor-hour. The fixed manufacturing overhead is $86,000 per quarter. The only noncash element of manufacturing overhead is depreciation of $23,000 per quarter.

Required:

1. Calculate the company's total estimated direct labor cost for each quarter and for the year as a whole. (Hint: Refer to Schedule 4 for guidance.)
2. Calculate the company's total estimated manufacturing overhead cost for each quarter and for the year as a whole. (Hint: Refer to Schedule 5 for guidance.)
3. Calculate the company's cash disbursements for manufacturing overhead for each quarter and for the year as a whole. (Hint: Refer to Schedule 5 for guidance.)

EXERCISE 8–16 Direct Materials and Direct Labor Budgets LO8–4, LO8–5

Zan Corporation's production budget for next year contains the following estimates:

	1st Quarter	2nd Quarter	3rd Quarter	4th Quarter
Units to be produced	5,000	8,000	7,000	6,000

In addition, 6,000 grams of raw materials inventory is on hand at the start of the 1st Quarter and the beginning accounts payable for the 1st Quarter is $2,880.

Each unit requires 8 grams of raw materials that cost $1.20 per gram. Management desires to end each quarter with an inventory of raw materials equal to 25% of the following quarter's production needs. The desired ending inventory for the 4th Quarter is 8,000 grams. Management plans to pay for 60% of raw materials purchases in the quarter acquired and 40% in the following quarter. Each unit requires 0.20 direct labor-hour and direct laborers are paid $15 per hour.

Required:
1. Calculate the estimated grams of raw materials that need to be purchased each quarter and for the year as a whole. (Hint: Refer to Schedule 3 for guidance.)
2. Calculate the cost of raw materials purchases for each quarter and for the year as a whole. (Hint: Refer to Schedule 3 for guidance.)
3. Calculate the expected cash disbursements for purchases of materials for each quarter and for the year as a whole. (Hint: Refer to Schedule 3 for guidance.)
4. Calculate the estimated direct labor cost for each quarter and for the year as a whole. (Hint: Refer to Schedule 4 for guidance.)

EXERCISE 8–17 Cash Flows; Budgeted Income Statement and Balance Sheet LO 8–2, LO 8–3, LO 8–4, LO8–9, LO8–10

Wheeling Company is a merchandiser that provided a balance sheet as of September 30 as shown below:

	Wheeling Company Balance Sheet September 30	
Assets		
Cash		$ 59,000
Accounts receivable		90,000
Inventory		32,400
Buildings and equipment, net of depreciation		214,000
Total assets		$395,400
Liabilities and Stockholders' Equity		
Accounts payable		$ 73,000
Common stock		216,000
Retained earnings		106,400
Total liabilities and stockholders' equity		$395,400

The company is in the process of preparing a budget for October and assembled the following data:
1. Sales are budgeted at $240,000 for October and $250,000 for November. Of these sales, 35% will be for cash; the remainder will be credit sales. Forty percent of a month's credit sales are collected in the month the sales are made, and the remaining 60% are collected in the following month. All of the September 30 accounts receivable will be collected in October.
2. The budgeted cost of goods sold is always 45% of sales and the ending merchandise inventory is always 30% of the following month's cost of goods sold.
3. All merchandise purchases are on account. Thirty percent of all purchases are paid for in the month of purchase and 70% are paid for in the following month. All of the September 30 accounts payable to suppliers will be paid during October.
4. Selling and administrative expenses for October are budgeted at $78,000, exclusive of depreciation. These expenses will be paid in cash. Depreciation is budgeted at $2,000 for the month.

Required:
1. Using the information provided, calculate or prepare the following for October:
   a. The budgeted cash collections.
   b. The budgeted merchandise purchases.
   c. The budgeted cash disbursements for merchandise purchases.
   d. The budgeted net operating income.
   e. An end-of-month budgeted balance sheet.

2. Assume the following changes to the underlying budgeting assumptions: (1) 50% of a month's credit sales are collected in the month the sales are made and the remaining 50% are collected in the following month, (2) the ending merchandise inventory is always 10% of the following month's cost of goods sold, and (3) 20% of all purchases are paid for in the month of purchase and 80% are paid for in the following month. Using these new assumptions, calculate or prepare the following for October:
   a. The budgeted cash collections.
   b. The budgeted merchandise purchases.
   c. The budgeted cash disbursements for merchandise purchases.
   d. Net operating income.
   e. An end-of-month budgeted balance sheet.
3. Compare your answers in requirements 1 and 2. If Wheeling Company is able to achieve the budgeted projections described in requirement 2, will it improve the company's financial performance relative to the projections you derived in requirement 1?

EXERCISE 8–18 Cash Flows; Budgeted Income Statement and Balance Sheet LO 8–2, LO 8–3, LO8–9, LO8–10

Wolfpack Company is a merchandising company that is preparing a budget for the month of July. It provided the following information:

Wolfpack Company Balance Sheet June 30	
Assets	
Cash	$ 75,000
Accounts receivable	50,000
Inventory	30,000
Buildings and equipment, net of depreciation	150,000
Total assets	$305,000
Liabilities and Stockholders' Equity	
Accounts payable	$ 35,300
Common stock	100,000
Retained earnings..............................	169,700
Total liabilities and stockholders' equity	$305,000

Budgeting Assumptions:
1. All sales are on account. Thirty percent of the credit sales are collected in the month of sale and the remaining 70% are collected in the month subsequent to the sale. The accounts receivable at June 30 will be collected in July.
2. All merchandise purchases are on account. Twenty percent of merchandise inventory purchases are paid in the month of the purchase and the remaining 80% are paid in the month after the purchase.
3. The budgeted inventory balance at July 31 is $22,000.
4. Depreciation expense is $3,000 per month. All other selling and administrative expenses are paid in full in the month the expense is incurred.
5. The company's cash budget for July shows expected cash collections of $77,000, expected cash disbursements for merchandise purchases of $44,500, and cash paid for selling and administrative expenses of $15,000.

Required:
1. For the month of July, calculate the following:
   a. Budgeted sales
   b. Budgeted merchandise purchases
   c. Budgeted cost of goods sold
   d. Budgeted net operating income
2. Prepare a budgeted balance sheet as of July 31.

Problems   Mc Graw Hill connect

PROBLEM 8–19 Cash Budget; Income Statement; Balance Sheet LO8–2, LO8–4, LO8–8, LO8–9, LO8–10

Minden Company is a wholesale distributor of premium European chocolates. The company's balance sheet as of April 30 is given below:

Minden Company Balance Sheet April 30	
Assets	
Cash	$ 9,000
Accounts receivable	54,000
Inventory	30,000
Buildings and equipment, net of depreciation	207,000
Total assets	$300,000
Liabilities and Stockholders' Equity	
Accounts payable	$ 63,000
Note payable	14,500
Common stock	180,000
Retained earnings	42,500
Total liabilities and stockholders' equity	$300,000

The company is in the process of preparing a budget for May and assembled the following data:

a. Sales are budgeted at $200,000 for May. Of these sales, $60,000 will be for cash; the remainder will be credit sales. One-half of a month's credit sales are collected in the month the sales are made, and the remainder are collected in the following month. All of the April 30 accounts receivable will be collected in May.

b. Purchases of inventory are expected to total $120,000 during May. These purchases will all be on account. Forty percent of all purchases are paid for in the month of purchase; the remainder are paid in the following month. All of the April 30 accounts payable to suppliers will be paid during May.

c. The May 31 inventory balance is budgeted at $40,000.

d. Selling and administrative expenses for May are budgeted at $72,000, exclusive of depreciation. These expenses will be paid in cash. Depreciation is budgeted at $2,000 for the month.

e. The note payable on the April 30 balance sheet will be paid during May, with $100 in interest. (All of the interest relates to May.)

f. New refrigerating equipment costing $6,500 will be purchased for cash during May.

g. During May, the company will borrow $20,000 from its bank by giving a new note payable to the bank for that amount. The new note will be due in one year.

Required:

For May:

1. Calculate the expected cash collections from customers.
2. Calculate the expected cash disbursements for merchandise purchases.
3. Prepare a cash budget.
4. Using Schedule 9 as your guide, prepare a budgeted income statement.
5. Prepare an end-of-month budgeted balance sheet.

PROBLEM 8–20 Cash Budget; Income Statement; Balance Sheet; Changing Assumptions LO8–2, LO8–4, LO8–8, LO8–9, LO8–10

Refer to the data for Minden Company in Problem 8–19. The company is considering making the following changes to the assumptions underlying its master budget:

1. Sales are budgeted for $220,000 for May.
2. Each month's credit sales are collected 60% in the month of sale and 40% in the month following the sale.

3. The company pays for 50% of its merchandise purchases in the month of the purchase and the remaining 50% in the month following the purchase.

All other information from Problem 8–19 not mentioned above remains the same.

Required:
Using the new assumptions described above, complete the following requirements for May:
1. Calculate the expected cash collections.
2. Calculate the expected cash disbursements for merchandise purchases.
3. Prepare a cash budget.
4. Using Schedule 9 as your guide, prepare a budgeted income statement.
5. Prepare an end-of-month budgeted balance sheet.

PROBLEM 8–21 Schedules of Expected Cash Collections and Disbursements LO8–2, LO8–4, LO8–8

Ashton Company, a distributor of exercise equipment, is preparing a cash budget for December. It provided the following information:
a. The cash balance on December 1 is $40,000.
b. Actual sales for October and November and expected sales for December are as follows:

	October	November	December
Cash sales	$65,000	$70,000	$83,000
Sales on account	$400,000	$525,000	$600,000

Sales on account are collected over a three-month period as follows: 20% collected in the month of sale, 60% collected in the month following sale, and 18% collected in the second month following sale. The remaining 2% are uncollectible.

c. Purchases of inventory will total $280,000 for December. Thirty percent of a month's inventory purchases are paid during the month of purchase. The accounts payable remaining from November's inventory purchases total $161,000, all of which will be paid in December.

d. Selling and administrative expenses are budgeted at $430,000 for December. Of this amount, $50,000 is for depreciation.

e. A new web server for the Marketing Department costing $76,000 will be purchased for cash during December, and dividends totaling $9,000 will be paid during the month.

f. The company maintains a minimum cash balance of $20,000. An open line of credit is available from the company's bank to increase its cash balance as needed.

Required:
For December:
1. Calculate the expected cash collections.
2. Calculate the expected cash disbursements for merchandise purchases.
3. Prepare a cash budget. Indicate in the financing section any borrowing needed during the month. Assume any interest will not be paid until the following month.

PROBLEM 8–22 Evaluating a Company's Budget Procedures LO8–1
Springfield Corporation's annual budgeting process begins in late August, when the president establishes targets for next year's total sales dollars and net operating income.

The sales target is given to the marketing manager, who formulates a sales budget by product line. From this budget, sales quotas by product line are established for each of the corporation's sales districts.

The marketing manager also estimates a marketing expense budget to support the target sales volume.

The executive vice president uses the sales and profit targets, the sales budget by product line, and the marketing expense budget to estimate the manufacturing and corporate office expense budgets.

The production manager meets with the factory managers to develop a manufacturing plan that achieves the production budget while abiding by the executive vice president's cost constraints. The budgeting process usually comes to a halt at this point because the production and factory managers do not consider their allocated financial resources to be adequate.

When this standstill occurs, the vice president of finance, executive vice president, marketing manager, and production manager meet to determine the final budgets for each of the areas. This normally results in a modest increase in the total amount available for manufacturing costs, while the marketing expense and corporate office expense budgets are cut. The total sales and net operating income figures proposed by the president are seldom changed. Although the participants are seldom pleased with the compromise, these budgets are final. Each executive then develops a new detailed budget for the operations in their area.

None of the areas achieved its budget in recent years. Sales often run below the target. When budgeted sales are not achieved, each area is expected to cut costs so the president's profit target can still be met. However, the profit target is seldom met because costs are not cut enough. In fact, costs often run above the original budget in all functional areas. The president is disturbed that Springfield has not been able to meet the sales and profit targets. He hired a consultant with considerable relevant industry experience. The consultant reviewed the budgets for the past four years. He concluded the product-line sales budgets were reasonable and the cost and expense budgets were adequate for the budgeted sales and production levels.

Required:

1. Discuss how Springfield Corporation's budgeting process contributes to its failure to achieve the president's sales and profit targets.
2. Suggest how Springfield Corporation's budgeting process could be revised to correct the problem.
3. Should the functional areas be expected to cut their costs when sales volume falls below budget? Explain your answer.

(CMA, adapted)

PROBLEM 8–23 Schedule of Expected Cash Collections; Cash Budget LO8–2, LO8–8

Prime Products hopes to borrow $30,000 on April 1 and repay it plus interest of $1,200 on June 30. The following data are available for the months April through June, during which the loan will be used:

a. On April 1, the start of the loan period, the cash balance will be $24,000. Accounts receivable on April 1 will total $140,000, of which $120,000 will be collected during April and $16,000 will be collected during May. The remainder will be uncollectible.

b. The company estimates 30% of a month's sales are collected in the month of sale, 60% in the month following sale, and 8% in the second month following sale. The other 2% are bad debts that are never collected. Budgeted sales and expenses for the three-month period follow:

	April	May	June
Sales (all on account)	$300,000	$400,000	$250,000
Merchandise purchases	$210,000	$160,000	$130,000
Payroll	$20,000	$20,000	$18,000
Lease payments	$22,000	$22,000	$22,000
Advertising	$60,000	$60,000	$50,000
Equipment purchases	—	—	$65,000
Depreciation	$15,000	$15,000	$15,000

c. Merchandise purchases are paid in full during the month following purchase. Accounts payable for merchandise purchases during March, which will be paid in April, total $140,000.

Required:

1. Calculate the expected cash collections for April, May, and June, and for the three months in total.
2. Prepare a cash budget, by month and in total, for the three-month period. Assume the $30,000 loan is made on April 1 and repaid with interest on June 30.
3. If the company needs a minimum cash balance of $20,000 to start each month, can the loan be repaid as planned? Explain.

PROBLEM 8–24 Cash Budget with Supporting Schedules LO8–2, LO8–4, LO8–8

Garden Sales, Inc., usually has to borrow money during the second quarter to support peak sales of lawn care equipment during May. It gathered the following information to prepare a cash budget for the quarter:

a.   Budgeted monthly absorption costing income statements for April–July are:

	April	May	June	July
Sales	$600,000	$900,000	$500,000	$400,000
Cost of goods sold	420,000	630,000	350,000	280,000
Gross margin	180,000	270,000	150,000	120,000
Selling and administrative expenses:				
Selling expense	79,000	120,000	62,000	51,000
Administrative expense*	45,000	52,000	41,000	38,000
Total selling and administrative expenses . . .	124,000	172,000	103,000	89,000
Net operating income	$ 56,000	$ 98,000	$ 47,000	$ 31,000

*Includes $20,000 of depreciation each month.

b.   Sales are 20% for cash and 80% on account.
c.   Sales on account are collected over a three-month period with 10% collected in the month of sale, 70% collected in the first month following the month of sale, and the remaining 20% collected in the second month following the month of sale. February's sales totaled $200,000, and March's sales totaled $300,000.
d.   Inventory purchases are paid for within 15 days. Therefore, 50% of a month's inventory purchases are paid for in the month of purchase. The remaining 50% are paid in the following month. Accounts payable at March 31 for inventory purchases during March total $126,000.
e.   Each month's ending inventory must equal 20% of the cost of the merchandise to be sold in the following month. The merchandise inventory at March 31 is $84,000.
f.   Dividends of $49,000 will be declared and paid in April.
g.   Land costing $16,000 will be purchased for cash in May.
h.   The cash balance at March 31 is $52,000; the company must maintain a cash balance of at least $40,000 at the end of each month.
i.   The company has an agreement with a local bank that allows the company to borrow in increments of $1,000 at the beginning of each month, up to a total loan balance of $200,000. The interest rate on these loans is 1% per month, and for simplicity we will assume interest is not compounded. The company would, as far as it is able, repay the loan plus accumulated interest at the end of the quarter.

Required:

1.   Prepare a schedule of expected cash collections for April, May, and June, and for the quarter in total.
2.   Prepare the following for merchandise inventory:
  a.   A merchandise purchases budget for April, May, and June.
  b.   A schedule of expected cash disbursements for merchandise purchases for April, May, and June, and for the quarter in total.
3.   Prepare a cash budget for April, May, and June as well as in total for the quarter.

PROBLEM 8–25 Cash Budget with Supporting Schedules; Changing Assumptions LO8–2, LO8–4, LO8–8

Refer to the data for Garden Sales, Inc., in Problem 8–24. The company's president is interested in knowing how reducing inventory levels and collecting accounts receivable sooner will impact the cash budget. He revises the cash collection and ending inventory assumptions as follows:

1.   Sales continue to be 20% for cash and 80% on credit. However, credit sales from April, May, and June are collected over a three-month period with 25% collected in the month of sale, 65%

collected in the month following sale, and 10% in the second month following sale. Credit sales from February and March are collected during the second quarter using the collection percentages specified in Problem 8–24.

2. The company maintains its ending inventory levels for April, May, and June at 15% of the cost of merchandise to be sold in the following month. The merchandise inventory at March 31 remains $84,000 and accounts payable for inventory purchases at March 31 remains $126,000.

All other information from Problem 8–24 not referred to above remains the same.

Required:

1. Using the president's new assumptions in (1) above, prepare a schedule of expected cash collections for April, May, and June and for the quarter in total.
2. Using the president's new assumptions in (2) above, prepare the following for merchandise inventory:
    a. A merchandise purchases budget for April, May, and June.
    b. A schedule of expected cash disbursements for merchandise purchases for April, May, and June and for the quarter in total.
3. Using the president's new assumptions, prepare a cash budget for April, May, and June, and for the quarter in total.
4. Prepare a brief memorandum for the president explaining how his revised assumptions affect the cash budget.

PROBLEM 8–26 Behavioral Aspects of Budgeting; Ethics and the Manager LO8–1

Norton Company, a manufacturer of infant furniture and carriages, is preparing a master budget for next year. Scott Ford has recently joined Norton's accounting staff and wants to learn as much as possible about the company's budgeting process. During a recent lunch with Marge Atkins, sales manager, and Pete Granger, production manager, Ford initiated the following conversation.

Ford: Because I'm new around here and am going to be involved with the preparation of the annual budget, I'd be interested to learn how the two of you estimate sales and production numbers.

Atkins: We start out very methodically by looking at recent history, discussing what we know about current accounts, potential customers, and the general state of consumer spending. Then, we add that usual dose of intuition to come up with the best forecast we can.

Granger: I usually take the sales projections as the basis for my projections. Of course, we have to make an estimate of what this year's ending inventories will be, which is sometimes difficult.

Ford: Why does that present a problem? There must have been an estimate of ending inventories in the budget for the current year.

Granger: Those numbers aren't always reliable because Marge makes some adjustments to the sales numbers before passing them on to me.

Ford: What kind of adjustments?

Atkins: Well, we don't want to fall short of the sales projections, so we generally give ourselves a little breathing room by lowering the initial sales projection anywhere from 5% to 10%.

Granger: So, you can see why this year's budget is not a very reliable starting point. We always have to adjust the projected production rates as the year progresses and, of course, this changes the ending inventory estimates. By the way, we make similar adjustments to expenses by adding at least 10% to the estimates; I think everyone around here does the same thing.

Required:

1. Marge Atkins and Pete Granger have described the use of what is sometimes called *budgetary slack.*
    a. Explain why Atkins and Granger behave in this manner and describe the benefits they expect to realize from the use of budgetary slack.
    b. Explain how the use of budgetary slack can adversely affect Atkins and Granger.
2. As a management accountant, Scott Ford believes the behavior described by Marge Atkins and Pete Granger may be unethical. By referring to the IMA's Statement of Ethical Professional Practice in the Prologue, explain why the use of budgetary slack may be unethical.

(CMA, adapted)

PROBLEM 8–27 Cash Collections; Cash Disbursements; Budgeted Balance Sheet LO8–2, LO8–3, LO8–4, 8–10

Deacon Company is a merchandising company that is preparing a budget for the three-month period ended June 30. The following information is available:

Deacon Company Balance Sheet March 31	
Assets	
Cash	$ 55,000
Accounts receivable	36,000
Inventory	40,000
Buildings and equipment, net of depreciation	100,000
Total assets	$231,000
Liabilities and Stockholders' Equity	
Accounts payable	$ 51,300
Common Stock	70,000
Retained earnings	109,700
Total liabilities and stockholders' equity	$231,000

Budgeted Income Statements	April	May	June
Sales	$100,000	$110,000	$130,000
Cost of goods sold	60,000	66,000	78,000
Gross margin	40,000	44,000	52,000
Selling and administrative expenses......	15,000	16,500	19,500
Net operating income..................	$ 25,000	$ 27,500	$ 32,500

Budgeting Assumptions:
1. Sixty percent of sales are cash sales and 40% of sales are credit sales. Twenty percent of all credit sales are collected in the month of sale and the remaining 80% are collected in the month subsequent to the sale.
2. Budgeted sales for July are $140,000.
3. Ten percent of merchandise inventory purchases are paid in cash at the time of the purchase. The remaining 90% of purchases are credit purchases. All purchases on credit are paid in the month subsequent to the purchase.
4. Each month's ending merchandise inventory should equal $10,000 plus 50% of the next month's cost of goods sold.
5. Depreciation expense is $1,000 per month. All other selling and administrative expenses are paid in full in the month the expense is incurred.

Required:
1. Calculate the expected cash collections for April, May, and June.
2. Calculate the budgeted merchandise purchases for April, May, and June.
3. Calculate the expected cash disbursements for merchandise purchases for April, May, and June.
4. Prepare a budgeted balance sheet at June 30. (Hint: You need to calculate the cash paid for selling and administrative expenses during April, May, and June to determine the cash balance in your June 30 balance sheet.)

PROBLEM 8–28 Cash Budget with Supporting Schedules LO8–2, LO8–4, LO8–7, LO8–8

Westex Products is a wholesale distributor of industrial cleaning products. When the treasurer of Westex Products approached the company's bank late in the current year seeking short-term financing, he was told money was very tight and any borrowing over the next year would have to be supported by a detailed statement of cash collections and disbursements. The treasurer also was told it would be very helpful to the bank if borrowers would indicate the quarters in which they need funds, as well as the amounts needed, and the quarters in which repayments could be made.

Because the treasurer is unsure as to the particular quarters in which bank financing will be needed, he assembled the following information to assist in preparing a detailed cash budget:

a. Budgeted sales and merchandise purchases for next year, as well as actual sales and purchases for the last quarter of the current year, are:

	Sales	Merchandise Purchases
Current Year:		
Fourth quarter actual	$200,000	$126,000
Next Year:		
First quarter estimated	$300,000	$186,000
Second quarter estimated	$400,000	$246,000
Third quarter estimated	$500,000	$305,000
Fourth quarter estimated	$200,000	$126,000

b. All sales are on account. The company normally collects 65% of a quarter's sales before the quarter ends and another 33% in the following quarter. The remainder is uncollectible. This pattern of collections is now being experienced in the current year's fourth-quarter actual data.

c. Eighty percent of a quarter's merchandise purchases are paid for within the quarter. The remainder is paid for in the following quarter.

d. Selling and administrative expenses for next year are budgeted at $50,000 per quarter plus 15% of sales. Of the fixed amount, $20,000 each quarter is depreciation.

e. The company will pay $10,000 in dividends each quarter.

f. Land purchases of $75,000 will be made in the second quarter, and purchases of $48,000 will be made in the third quarter. These purchases will be for cash.

g. The Cash account contained $10,000 at the end of the current year. The treasurer feels that this represents a minimum balance that must be maintained.

h. The company's bank allows borrowing in increments of $1,000 at the beginning of each quarter, up to a total loan balance of $100,000. The interest rate on these loans is 2.5% per quarter and, for simplicity, we will assume interest is not compounded. The company would, as far as it is able, repay the loan plus accumulated interest at the end of the year.

i. At present, the company has no loans outstanding.

Required:

1. Calculate the expected cash collections by quarter and in total for next year.
2. Calculate the expected cash disbursements for merchandise purchases by quarter and in total for next year.
3. Calculate the expected cash disbursements for selling and administrative expenses, by quarter and in total for next year.
4. Prepare a cash budget by quarter and in total for next year.

PROBLEM 8–29 Completing a Master Budget LO8–2, LO8–4, LO8–7, LO8–8, LO8–9, LO8–10

The following data relate to the operations of Shilow Company, a wholesale distributor of consumer goods:

Current assets as of March 31:	
Cash	$8,000
Accounts receivable	$20,000
Inventory	$36,000
Building and equipment, net	$120,000
Accounts payable	$21,750
Common stock	$150,000
Retained earnings	$12,250

a. The gross margin is 25% of sales.
b. Actual and budgeted sales data:

March (actual)	$50,000
April	$60,000
May	$72,000
June	$90,000
July	$48,000

c. Sales are 60% for cash and 40% on credit. Credit sales are collected in the month following sale. The accounts receivable at March 31 are a result of March credit sales.
d. Each month's ending inventory should equal 80% of the following month's budgeted cost of goods sold.
e. One-half of a month's inventory purchases is paid for in the month of purchase; the other half is paid for in the following month. The accounts payable at March 31 are the result of March purchases of inventory.
f. Monthly expenses are as follows: commissions, 12% of sales; rent, $2,500 per month; other expenses (excluding depreciation), 6% of sales. Assume these expenses are paid monthly. Depreciation is $900 per month (includes depreciation on new assets).
g. Equipment costing $1,500 will be purchased for cash in April.
h. Management would like to maintain a minimum cash balance of at least $4,000 at the end of each month. The company has an agreement with a local bank allowing it to borrow in increments of $1,000 at the beginning of each month, up to a total loan balance of $20,000. The interest rate on these loans is 1% per month and, for simplicity, we will assume interest is not compounded. The company would, as far as it is able, repay the loan plus accumulated interest at the end of the quarter.

Required:
Using the preceding data:
1. Complete the following schedule:

Schedule of Expected Cash Collections	April	May	June	Quarter
Cash sales	$36,000			
Credit sales	20,000	___	___	___
Total collections	$56,000			

2. Complete the following:

Merchandise Purchases Budget	April	May	June	Quarter
Budgeted cost of goods sold	$45,000*	$54,000		
Add desired ending inventory	43,200†			
Total needs	88,200			
Less beginning inventory	36,000	___	___	___
Required purchases	$52,200			

*For April sales: $60,000 sales × 75% cost ratio = $45,000.
†$54,000 × 80% = $43,200

Schedule of Expected Cash Disbursements—Merchandise Purchases	April	May	June	Quarter
March purchases	$21,750			$21,750
April purchases	26,100	$26,100		52,200
May purchases				
June purchases				
Total disbursements	$47,850			

3. Complete the following cash budget:

Cash Budget	April	May	June	Quarter
Beginning cash balance	$ 8,000			
Add cash collections	56,000			
Total cash available	64,000			
Less cash disbursements:				
For inventory	47,850			
For expenses.........................	13,300			
For equipment	1,500			
Total cash disbursements	62,650			
Excess (deficiency) of cash	1,350			
Financing:				
Etc.				

4. Using Schedule 9 as your guide, prepare an absorption costing income statement for the quarter ended June 30.
5. Prepare a balance sheet as of June 30.

PROBLEM 8–30 Integration of the Sales, Production, and Direct Materials Budgets LO8–2, LO8–3, LO8–4

Milo Company manufactures beach umbrellas. The company is preparing budgets for the third quarter and assembled the following information:

a. The Marketing Department estimated unit sales as follows for the remainder of the year:

July	30,000	October	20,000
August	70,000	November	10,000
September	50,000	December	10,000

The selling price of the beach umbrellas is $12 per unit.

b. All sales are on account. Based on past experience, sales are collected in the following pattern:

> 30% in the month of sale
> 65% in the month following sale
> 5% uncollectible

Sales for June totaled $300,000.

c. The company maintains finished goods inventories equal to 15% of the following month's sales. This requirement will be met at the end of June.

d. Each beach umbrella requires 4 feet of Gilden, a material that is sometimes hard to acquire. Therefore, the company requires ending inventory of Gilden equal to 50% of the following month's production needs. The inventory of Gilden on hand at the beginning and end of the quarter will be:

June 30	72,000 feet
September 30	? feet

e. Gilden costs $0.80 per foot. One-half of a month's purchases of Gilden is paid for in the month of purchase; the remainder is paid for in the following month. The accounts payable on July 1 for purchases of Gilden during June will be $76,000.

Required:

1. Calculate the estimated sales, by month and in total, for the third quarter. (Hint: Refer to Schedule 1 for guidance.)
2. Calculate the expected cash collections, by month and in total, for the third quarter. (Hint: Refer to Schedule 1 for guidance.)

3. Calculate the estimated quantity of beach umbrellas that need to be produced in July, August, September, and October. (Hint: Refer to Schedule 2 for guidance.)

4. Calculate the quantity of Gilden (in feet) that needs to be purchased by month and in total, for the third quarter. (Hint: Refer to Schedule 3 for guidance.)

5. Calculate the cost of the raw material (Gilden) purchases by month and in total, for the third quarter. (Hint: Refer to Schedule 3 for guidance.)

6. Calculate the expected cash disbursements for raw material (Gilden) purchases, by month and in total, for the third quarter. (Hint: Refer to Schedule 3 for guidance.)

PROBLEM 8–31 Completing a Master Budget LO8–2, LO8–4, LO8–7, LO8–8, LO8–9, LO8–10

Hillyard Company, an office supplies specialty store, gathered the following information to prepare its master budget for the first quarter of the year:

a. As of December 31 (the end of the prior quarter), the company's general ledger showed the following account balances:

	Debits	Credits
Cash	$ 48,000	
Accounts receivable	224,000	
Inventory	60,000	
Buildings and equipment (net)	370,000	
Accounts payable		$ 93,000
Common stock		500,000
Retained earnings		109,000
	$702,000	$702,000

b. Actual sales for December and budgeted sales for the next four months are as follows:

December (actual)	$280,000
January.......................	$400,000
February......................	$600,000
March	$300,000
April.........................	$200,000

c. Sales are 20% for cash and 80% on credit. All payments on credit sales are collected in the month following sale. The accounts receivable at December 31 are a result of December credit sales.

d. The company's gross margin is 40% of sales. (In other words, cost of goods sold is 60% of sales.)

e. Monthly expenses are budgeted as follows: salaries and wages, $27,000 per month; advertising, $70,000 per month; shipping, 5% of sales; other expenses, 3% of sales. Depreciation, including depreciation on new assets acquired during the quarter, will be $42,000 for the quarter.

f. Each month's ending inventory should equal 25% of the following month's cost of goods sold.

g. One-half of a month's inventory purchases is paid for in the month of purchase; the other half is paid in the following month.

h. During February, the company will purchase a new copy machine for $1,700 cash. During March, other equipment will be purchased for cash at a cost of $84,500.

i. During January, the company will declare and pay $45,000 in cash dividends.

j. Management wants to maintain a minimum cash balance of $30,000. The company has an agreement with a local bank allowing it to borrow in increments of $1,000 at the beginning of each month. The interest rate on these loans is 1% per month, and, for simplicity, we will assume interest is not compounded. The company would, as far as it is able, repay the loan plus accumulated interest at the end of the quarter.

Required:
Using the data above, complete the following statements and schedules for the first quarter:
1.   Schedule of expected cash collections:

	January	February	March	Quarter
Cash sales	$ 80,000			
Credit sales	224,000			
Total cash collections	$304,000			

2.   a.   Merchandise purchases budget:

	January	February	March	Quarter
Budgeted cost of goods sold	$240,000*	$360,000		
Add desired ending inventory	90,000†			
Total needs	330,000			
Less beginning inventory	60,000			
Required purchases	$270,000			

*$400,000 sales × 60% cost ratio = $240,000.
†$360,000 × 25% = $90,000.

b.   Schedule of expected cash disbursements for merchandise purchases:

	January	February	March	Quarter
December purchases	$ 93,000			$ 93,000
January purchases	135,000	135,000		270,000
February purchases	—			
March purchases	—			
Total cash disbursements				
for purchases	$228,000			

3.   Cash budget:

	January	February	March	Quarter
Beginning cash balance	$ 48,000			
Add cash collections	304,000			
Total cash available	352,000			
Less cash disbursements:				
Inventory purchases	228,000			
Selling and administrative expenses	129,000			
Equipment purchases	—			
Cash dividends	45,000			
Total cash disbursements	402,000			
Excess (deficiency) of cash	(50,000)			
Financing:				
Etc.				

4.   Using Schedule 9 as your guide, prepare an absorption costing income statement for the quarter ending March 31.
5.   Prepare a balance sheet as of March 31.

Select cases are available in Connect.

CASE 8–32 Evaluating a Company's Budget Procedures LO8–1

Tom Emory and Jim Morris strolled back to their plant from the administrative offices of Ferguson & Son Manufacturing Company. Tom is manager of the machine shop in the company's factory; Jim is manager of the equipment maintenance department.

The men had just attended the monthly performance evaluation meeting for plant department heads. These meetings had been held on the third Tuesday of each month since Robert Ferguson Jr., the president's son, had become plant manager a year earlier.

As they were walking, Tom Emory spoke: "Boy, I hate those meetings! I never know whether my department's accounting reports will show good or bad performance. I'm beginning to expect the worst. If the accountants say I saved the company a dollar, I'm called 'Sir,' but if I spend even a little too much—boy, do I get in trouble. I don't know if I can hold on until I retire."

Tom had just been given the worst evaluation he had ever received in his long career with Ferguson & Son. He was the most respected of the experienced machinists in the company. He had been with Ferguson & Son for many years and was promoted to supervisor of the machine shop when the company expanded and moved to its present location. The president (Robert Ferguson Sr.) often stated the company's success was due to the high-quality work of machinists like Tom. As supervisor, Tom stressed the importance of craftsmanship and told his workers he wanted no sloppy work coming from his department.

When Robert Ferguson Jr. became the plant manager, he required monthly performance comparisons between actual and budgeted costs for each department. The departmental budgets were intended to encourage the supervisors to reduce inefficiencies and seek cost reduction opportunities. The company controller was instructed to have his staff "tighten" the budget slightly whenever a department attained its budget in a given month; this was done to reinforce the plant manager's desire to reduce costs. The young plant manager often stressed the importance of continued progress toward attaining the budget; he also made it known that he kept a file of these performance reports for future reference when he succeeded his father.

Tom Emory's conversation with Jim Morris continued as follows:

Emory: I really don't understand. We've worked so hard to meet the budget, and the minute we do so, they tighten it on us. We can't work any faster and still maintain quality. I think my men are ready to quit trying. Besides, those reports don't tell the whole story. We always seem to be interrupting the big jobs for all those small rush orders. All that setup and machine adjustment time is killing us. And quite frankly, Jim, you were no help. When our hydraulic press broke down last month, your people were nowhere to be found. We had to take it apart ourselves and got stuck with all that idle time.

Morris: I'm sorry about that, Tom, but you know my department has had trouble making budget, too. We were running well behind at the time of that problem, and if we'd spent a day on that old machine, we would never have made it up. Instead, we made the scheduled inspections of the forklift trucks because we knew we could do those in less than the budgeted time.

Emory: Well, Jim, at least you have some options. I'm locked into what the scheduling department assigns to me, and you know they're being harassed by sales for those special orders. Incidentally, why didn't your report show all the supplies you guys wasted last month when you were working in Bill's department?

Morris: We're not out of the woods on that deal yet. We charged the maximum we could to other work and haven't even reported some of it yet.

Emory: Well, I'm glad you have a way of getting out of the pressure. The accountants seem to know everything happening in my department, sometimes even before I do. I thought all that budget and accounting stuff was supposed to help, but it just gets me into trouble. It's all a big pain. I'm trying to put out quality work; they're trying to save pennies.

Required:

1. Identify the problems with Ferguson & Son Manufacturing Company's budgetary control system and explain how the problems are likely to reduce the effectiveness of the system.
2. Explain how Ferguson & Son Manufacturing Company's budgetary control system could be revised to improve its effectiveness.

(CMA, adapted)

CASE 8–33 Master Budget with Supporting Schedules LO8–2, LO8–4, LO8–8, LO8–9, LO8–10

You have just been hired as a new management trainee by Earrings Unlimited, a distributor of earrings to various retail outlets located in shopping malls across the country. In the past, the company has done very little in the way of budgeting and, at certain times of the year, has experienced a shortage of cash. Because you are well trained in budgeting, you have decided to prepare a master budget for the upcoming second quarter. To this end, you have worked with accounting and other areas to gather the information assembled below.

The company sells many styles of earrings, but all are sold for the same price—$10 per pair. Actual sales of earrings for the last three months and budgeted sales for the next six months follow (in pairs of earrings):

January (actual)	20,000	June (budget)	50,000
February (actual)	26,000	July (budget)	30,000
March (actual)	40,000	August (budget)	28,000
April (budget)	65,000	September (budget)	25,000
May (budget)	100,000		

The concentration of sales before and during May is due to Mother's Day. Sufficient inventory should be on hand at the end of each month to supply 40% of the earrings sold in the following month.

Suppliers are paid $4 for a pair of earrings. One-half of a month's purchases is paid for in the month of purchase; the other half is paid for in the following month. All sales are on credit. Only 20% of a month's sales are collected in the month of sale. An additional 70% are collected in the following month, and the remaining 10% are collected in the second month following sale. Bad debts have been negligible.

Monthly operating expenses for the company are given below:

Variable:	
Sales commissions	4% of sales
Fixed:	
Advertising	$200,000
Rent	$18,000
Salaries	$106,000
Utilities	$7,000
Insurance	$3,000
Depreciation	$14,000

Insurance is paid on an annual basis, in November of each year.

The company plans to purchase $16,000 in new equipment during May and $40,000 in new equipment during June; both purchases will be for cash. The company declares dividends of $15,000 each quarter, payable in the first month of the following quarter.

The company's balance sheet as of March 31 is given below:

Assets	
Cash	$ 74,000
Accounts receivable ($26,000 February sales; $320,000 March sales)	346,000
Inventory	104,000
Prepaid insurance	21,000
Property and equipment (net)	950,000
Total assets	$1,495,000

Liabilities and Stockholders' Equity	
Accounts payable	$ 100,000
Dividends payable	15,000
Common stock	800,000
Retained earnings	580,000
Total liabilities and stockholders' equity	$1,495,000

The company maintains a minimum cash balance of $50,000. All borrowing is done at the beginning of a month; any repayments are made at the end of a month.

The company has an agreement with a bank that allows the company to borrow in increments of $1,000 at the beginning of each month. The interest rate on these loans is 1% per month, and, for simplicity, we will assume interest is not compounded. At the end of the quarter, the company would pay the bank all of the accumulated interest on the loan and as much of the loan as possible (in increments of $1,000), while still retaining at least $50,000 in cash.

Required:

Prepare a master budget for the three-month period ending June 30. Include the following detailed schedules:

1. a. A sales budget, by month and in total.
    b. A schedule of expected cash collections, by month and in total.
    c. A merchandise purchases budget in units and in dollars. Show the budget by month and in total.
    d. A schedule of expected cash disbursements for merchandise purchases, by month and in total.

2. A cash budget. Show the budget by month and in total. Determine any borrowing that would be needed to maintain the minimum cash balance of $50,000.

3. A budgeted income statement for the three-month period ending June 30. Use the contribution approach.

4. A budgeted balance sheet as of June 30.

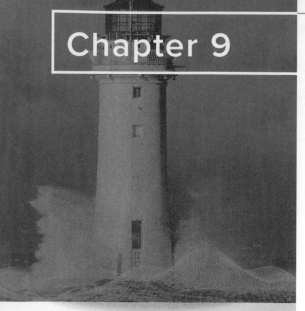

lighthouse image: Martin73/Shutterstock;
big data image: INGARA/Shutterstock

LEARNING OBJECTIVES

After studying Chapter 9, you should be able to:

LO9–1 Prepare a planning budget and a flexible budget with one cost driver.

LO9–2 Calculate and interpret activity variances.

LO9–3 Calculate and interpret revenue and spending variances.

LO9–4 Prepare a performance report with one cost driver that combines activity variances and revenue and spending variances.

LO9–5 Prepare a planning budget and a flexible budget with more than one cost driver.

LO9–6 Prepare a performance report with more than one cost driver that combines activity variances and revenue and spending variances.

 Data Analytics Exercise available in Connect to complement this chapter

Flexible Budgets and Performance Analysis

Craig Barritt/Getty Images

ENTREPRENEUR SPOTLIGHT

Taraji Henson has had an interest in hair care her entire life. Eventually, she turned that passion into a new business called TPH by Taraji. Her company's scalp-first approach to hair care "creates the optimal environment for healthy hair no matter the style." Its product categories include scalp care, cleanse, intense moisture, and repair for coily, curly, wavy, and straight hair. Taraji's products are sold at Amazon.com and Target, as well as through her own website at www.tphbytaraji.com. Her business venture caught the attention of *Entrepreneur's Handbook,* which named her one of seven "entrepreneurs to watch in 2021."

Applying Managerial Accounting

TPH by Taraji launched in January 2020—a couple months before the COVID-19 pandemic began crippling the economy. Any budgeted expectations the company may have had in January 2020 needed to be flexed throughout the year to adjust for the pandemic's impact on sales. For example, as millions of Americans lost their jobs or were furloughed, it lowered their disposable incomes, which quite possibly reduced the amount of money they could spend on hair care products.

Serving All Stakeholders

Taraji Henson founded the Boris Henson Foundation to change "the perception of mental illness in the African-American community by encouraging those who suffer with this debilitating illness to get the help they need." Taraji named the organization in honor of her father, who suffered from mental health issues following his service in the Vietnam War. The Boris Henson Foundation supports numerous initiatives, such as increasing mental health resources in urban schools, reducing prison recidivism rates, and increasing the number of African American therapists. ∎

Sources: https://entrepreneurshandbook.co/7-entrepreneurs-to-watch-in-2021-6a3ca4da3d0, https://tphbytaraji.com/pages/about-us, https://borislhensonfoundation.org/.

The last chapter explored how budgets are developed before a period begins. In this chapter, we explain how those budgets can be adjusted and compared to actual results to improve performance. For example, should a manager be penalized for spending 10 percent more than budgeted for a variable expense like direct materials if unit sales are 10 percent higher than budgeted? Of course not because an organization's actual expenses will naturally differ from its budgeted expenses when the actual level of activity (such as unit sales) differs from the budgeted activity. After studying this chapter, you'll know how to adjust a budget to draw meaningful comparisons between actual results and what should have happened given the actual level of activity.

The Variance Analysis Cycle

Companies use the *variance analysis cycle,* as illustrated in Exhibit 9–1, to evaluate and improve performance. The cycle begins by preparing performance reports that highlight variances, which are the differences between actual results and what should have occurred according to the budget. The variances raise questions. Why did this variance occur? Why is this variance larger than it was last period? The significant variances are investigated so their root causes can be either replicated or eliminated. Then, after next period's operations, the cycle begins again with the preparation of a new performance report. The emphasis should be on highlighting superior and unsatisfactory results, finding the root causes of these outcomes, and then replicating the sources of superior achievement and eliminating the sources of unsatisfactory performance. The variance analysis cycle should not be used to assign blame for poor performance.

Managers frequently use the concept of *management by exception* in conjunction with the variance analysis cycle. **Management by exception** is a management system that compares actual results to a budget so significant deviations can be flagged as exceptions and investigated. This approach enables managers to focus on the most important variances while bypassing trivial discrepancies between the budget and actual results. For example, a variance of $5 is probably not big enough to warrant attention, whereas a variance of $5,000 might be worth further study. Another clue is the size of the variance relative to the amount of spending. A variance that is only 0.1 percent of spending on an item is probably caused by random factors. On the other hand, a variance of 10 percent of spending is much more likely to be a signal that something is wrong. In addition to watching for unusually large variances, the pattern of the variances should be monitored. For example, a run of steadily mounting variances should trigger an investigation even though none of the variances is large enough by itself to warrant investigation.

Next, we explain how organizations use flexible budgets to compare actual results to what should have occurred according to the budget.

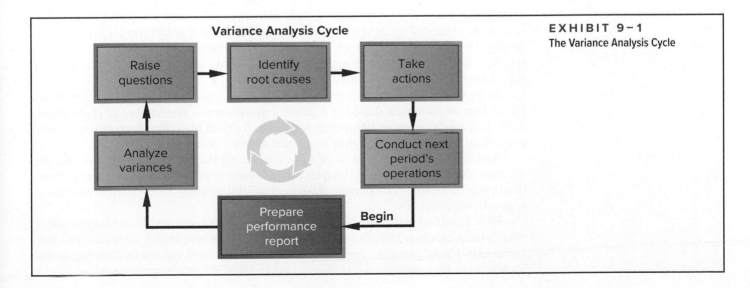

Variance Analysis Cycle

EXHIBIT 9–1
The Variance Analysis Cycle

Preparing Planning Budgets and Flexible Budgets with One Cost Driver

LO9–1

Prepare a planning budget and a flexible budget with one cost driver.

Characteristics of a Flexible Budget

The budgets we explored in the last chapter were *planning budgets*. A **planning budget** is prepared before the period begins and is valid for only the planned level of activity. A static planning budget is suitable for planning but is inappropriate for evaluating how well costs are controlled. If the actual level of activity differs from what was planned, it would be misleading to compare actual costs to the static, unchanged planning budget. If activity is higher than expected, variable costs should be higher than expected; and if activity is lower than expected, variable costs should be lower than expected.

Flexible budgets take into account how the actual level of activity should affect costs. A **flexible budget** shows what revenues and costs should have been, given the actual level of activity. When a flexible budget is used in performance evaluation, actual costs are compared to what the costs *should have been for the actual level of activity* rather than the static planning budget. This is a very important distinction. If adjustments for the level of activity are not made, it is very difficult to interpret discrepancies between budgeted and actual costs.

IN BUSINESS

Michael Sears/MCT/Newscom

WHY DO COMPANIES NEED FLEXIBLE BUDGETS?

The difficulty of accurately predicting future financial performance can be readily understood by reading the annual report of any publicly traded company. For example, Nucor Corporation, a steel manufacturer headquartered in Charlotte, North Carolina, cites numerous reasons why its actual results may differ from expectations, including the following: (1) changes in the supply and cost of raw materials, (2) changes in the availability and cost of electricity and natural gas, (3) changes in the market demand for steel products, (4) fluctuations in currency conversion rates, (5) significant changes in laws or government regulations, and (6) the cyclical nature of the steel industry.

Source: Nucor Corporation 2020 Annual Report.

Deficiencies of the Static Planning Budget

To illustrate the difference between a static planning budget and a flexible budget, consider Rick's Hairstyling, an upscale hairstyling salon located in Beverly Hills owned and managed by Rick Manzi. Recently Rick has been attempting to get better control of his revenues and costs, and at the urging of his accounting and business adviser, Victoria Kho, he started to prepare monthly budgets.

At the end of February, Rick prepared the March budget in Exhibit 9–2. Rick believes the number of customers served in a month (also known as the number of client-visits) is the best way to measure the overall level of activity in his salon. Each customer who comes into the salon for hairstyling is counted as one client-visit.

Note that the term *revenue* is used in the planning budget rather than *sales*. We use the term *revenue* throughout the chapter because some organizations have sources of revenue other than sales. For example, donations, as well as sales, are counted as revenue in nonprofit organizations.

Rick identified eight categories of costs—wages and salaries, hairstyling supplies, client gratuities, electricity, rent, liability insurance, employee health insurance, and miscellaneous. Client gratuities consist of flowers, candies, and glasses of champagne that Rick gives to his customers while they are in the salon.

Rick's Hairstyling Planning Budget For the Month Ended March 31		**EXHIBIT 9-2** Planning Budget
Budgeted client-visits (q)	1,000	
Revenue ($180.00q)	$180,000	
Expenses:		
Wages and salaries ($65,000 + $37.00q)	102,000	
Hairstyling supplies ($1.50q)	1,500	
Client gratuities ($4.10q)	4,100	
Electricity ($1,500 + $0.10q)	1,600	
Rent ($28,500)	28,500	
Liability insurance ($2,800)	2,800	
Employee health insurance ($21,300)	21,300	
Miscellaneous ($1,200 + $0.20q)	1,400	
Total expenses	163,200	
Net operating income	$ 16,800	

Working with Victoria, Rick estimated a cost formula for each cost. For example, the cost formula for electricity is $1,500 + $0.10q, where q equals the number of client-visits. In other words, electricity is a mixed cost with a $1,500 fixed element and a $0.10 per client-visit variable element. Once the budgeted level of activity was set at 1,000 client-visits, Rick computed the budgeted amount for each line item in the budget. For example, using the cost formula, he set the budgeted cost for electricity at $1,600 (= $1,500 + $0.10 × 1,000). To finalize his budget, Rick computed his expected net operating income for March of $16,800.

At the end of March, Rick prepared the income statement in Exhibit 9–3, which shows 1,100 clients actually visited his salon in March and his actual net operating income for the month was $21,230. It is important to realize the actual results are *not* determined by plugging the actual number of client-visits into the revenue and cost formulas. The formulas are *estimates* of what the revenues and costs should be for a given level of activity. What actually happens usually differs from what is supposed to happen.

The first thing Rick noticed when comparing Exhibits 9–2 and 9–3 is the actual profit of $21,230 (from Exhibit 9–3) was substantially higher than the budgeted profit of $16,800 (from Exhibit 9–2). While this was good news, Rick wanted to know more. Business was up by 10 percent—the salon had 1,100 client-visits instead of the budgeted 1,000 client-visits. Could this alone explain the higher net operating income? The answer is no. An increase in net operating income of 10 percent would have resulted in net operating income of only $18,480 (= 1.1 × $16,800), not the $21,230 actually earned during the month. What is responsible for this better outcome? Higher prices? Lower costs? Something else? Whatever the cause, Rick would like to know the answer and then hopefully repeat the same performance next month.

In an attempt to analyze what happened in March, Rick prepared the report comparing actual to budgeted costs in Exhibit 9–4. Note most of the variances in this report are labeled unfavorable (U) rather than favorable (F) even though net operating income was actually higher than expected. For example, wages and salaries show an unfavorable variance of $4,900 because the actual wages and salaries expense was $106,900, whereas the budget estimated wages and salaries of $102,000. The problem with the report, as Rick

EXHIBIT 9–3
Actual Results—Income Statement

Rick's Hairstyling Income Statement For the Month Ended March 31	
Actual client-visits	1,100
Revenue	$194,200
Expenses:	
Wages and salaries	106,900
Hairstyling supplies	1,620
Client gratuities	6,870
Electricity	1,550
Rent	28,500
Liability insurance	2,800
Employee health insurance	22,600
Miscellaneous	2,130
Total expenses	172,970
Net operating income	$ 21,230

EXHIBIT 9–4
Comparison of Actual Results to the Static Planning Budget

Rick's Hairstyling Comparison of Actual Results to the Planning Budget For the Month Ended March 31			
	Actual Results	Planning Budget	Variances*
Client-visits	1,100	1,000	
Revenue	$194,200	$180,000	$14,200 F
Expenses:			
Wages and salaries	106,900	102,000	4,900 U
Hairstyling supplies	1,620	1,500	120 U
Client gratuities	6,870	4,100	2,770 U
Electricity	1,550	1,600	50 F
Rent	28,500	28,500	0
Liability insurance	2,800	2,800	0
Employee health insurance	22,600	21,300	1,300 U
Miscellaneous	2,130	1,400	730 U
Total expenses	172,970	163,200	9,770 U
Net operating income	$ 21,230	$ 16,800	$ 4,430 F

*The revenue variance is labeled favorable (unfavorable) when the actual revenue is greater than (less than) the planning budget. The expense variances are labeled favorable (unfavorable) when the actual expense is less than (greater than) the planning budget.

immediately realized, is that it compares revenues and costs at one level of activity (1,000 client-visits) to revenues and costs at a different level of activity (1,100 client-visits). This is like comparing apples to oranges. Because Rick had 100 more client-visits than expected, some of his costs should be higher than budgeted. From Rick's standpoint, the increase in activity was good; however, it's having a negative impact on most of the costs in the report. Rick knew something would have to be done to make the report more meaningful, but he was unsure what to do. So, he made an appointment with Victoria Kho to discuss the next step.

Victoria: How is the budgeting going?
Rick: Pretty well. I created a budget for March and compared it to the actual results, but that report isn't helping me.
Victoria: Because your actual level of activity didn't match your budgeted activity?
Rick: Right. I know the level of activity shouldn't affect my fixed costs, but we had more client-visits than I had expected, which had to affect my other costs.
Victoria: So you want to know whether the higher actual costs are justified by the higher level of activity?
Rick: Precisely.
Victoria: If you leave your reports and data with me, I'll create a report to share with you tomorrow.

MANAGERIAL
ACCOUNTING IN ACTION
THE ISSUE

RICK'S
Hairstyling Salon

How a Flexible Budget Works

A flexible budget shows what costs *should be* for the actual level of activity. To illustrate how flexible budgets work, Victoria prepared the report in Exhibit 9–5 showing what the *revenues and costs should have been given the actual level of activity* in March. The cost formula for each cost is used to estimate what the cost should have been for 1,100 client-visits—the actual level of activity for March. For example, using the cost formula $1,500 + $0.10q, the cost of electricity in March *should have been* $1,610 (= $1,500 + $0.10 × 1,100). Also, notice the amounts of rent ($28,500), liability insurance ($2,800), and employee health insurance ($21,300) in the flexible budget equal the corresponding amounts in the planning budget (see Exhibit 9–2). This occurs because fixed costs are not affected by the activity level.

Rick's Hairstyling Flexible Budget For the Month Ended March 31	
Actual client-visits (q)	1,100
Revenue ($180.00)q	$198,000
Expenses:	
Wages and salaries ($65,000 + $37.00q)	105,700
Hairstyling supplies ($1.50q)	1,650
Client gratuities ($4.10q)	4,510
Electricity ($1,500 + $0.10q)	1,610
Rent ($28,500)	28,500
Liability insurance ($2,800)	2,800
Employee health insurance ($21,300)	21,300
Miscellaneous ($1,200 + $0.20q)	1,420
Total expenses	167,490
Net operating income	$ 30,510

EXHIBIT 9–5
Flexible Budget Based on
Actual Activity

We can see from the flexible budget the net operating income in March *should have been* $30,510, but recall from Exhibit 9–3 the net operating income was actually only $21,230.

To summarize to this point, Rick budgeted for a profit of $16,800. The actual profit was quite a bit higher—$21,230. However, Victoria's flexible budget shows profit should have been even higher—$30,510.

Flexible Budget Variances

To explain the discrepancies between budgeted and actual results, Victoria broke down the variances in Exhibit 9–4 into two types of variances—activity variances and revenue and spending variances. We explain how she did it in the next two sections.

LO9–2
Calculate and interpret activity variances.

Activity Variances

Victoria prepared the report in Exhibit 9–6 comparing the flexible budget to the planning budget. The flexible budget shows what should have happened at the actual level of activity, whereas the planning budget shows what should have happened at the budgeted level of activity. Each resulting variance highlights the portion of the difference between the planning budget and the actual results caused solely because the actual level of activity differed from what had been expected.

For example, the flexible budget based on 1,100 client-visits shows revenue of $198,000 (= $180 per client-visit × 1,100 client-visits). The planning budget based on 1,000 client-visits shows revenue of $180,000 (= $180 per client-visit × 1,000 client-visits). Because the salon had 100 more client-visits than anticipated in the planning budget, actual revenue should have been higher than planned revenue by $18,000

EXHIBIT 9–6
Activity Variances from Comparing the Flexible Budget Based on Actual Activity to the Planning Budget

	Rick's Hairstyling Activity Variances For the Month Ended March 31		
	Flexible Budget	Planning Budget	Activity Variances*
Client-visits	1,100	1,000	
Revenue ($180.00q)	$198,000	$180,000	$18,000 F
Expenses:			
Wages and salaries ($65,000 + $37.00q)	105,700	102,000	3,700 U
Hairstyling supplies ($1.50q)	1,650	1,500	150 U
Client gratuities ($4.10q)	4,510	4,100	410 U
Electricity ($1,500 + $0.10q)	1,610	1,600	10 U
Rent ($28,500)	28,500	28,500	0
Liability insurance ($2,800)	2,800	2,800	0
Employee health insurance ($21,300) ..	21,300	21,300	0
Miscellaneous ($1,200 + $0.20q)	1,420	1,400	20 U
Total expenses	167,490	163,200	4,290 U
Net operating income	$ 30,510	$ 16,800	$13,710 F

*The revenue variance is labeled favorable (unfavorable) when the revenue in the flexible budget is greater than (less than) the planning budget. The expense variances are labeled favorable (unfavorable) when the expense in the flexible budget is less than (greater than) the planning budget.

(= \$198,000 − \$180,000). This activity variance is shown on the report as \$18,000 F (favorable). Similarly, the flexible budget based on 1,100 client-visits shows electricity cost of \$1,610 (= \$1,500 + \$0.10 per client-visit × 1,100 client-visits). The planning budget based on 1,000 client-visits shows electricity cost of \$1,600 (= \$1,500 + \$0.10 per client-visit × 1,000 client-visits). Because the salon had 100 more client-visits than anticipated in the planning budget, the actual electricity cost should have been higher than the planned cost by \$10 (= \$1,610 − \$1,600). The activity variance for electricity is shown on the report as \$10 U (unfavorable). Note in this case, the label "unfavorable" may be a little misleading. The electricity cost *should* be \$10 higher because business was up by 100 client-visits; therefore, it would be misleading to describe this variance in negative terms given it was a necessary cost of serving more customers. For reasons such as this, we would like to caution you against assuming that unfavorable variances always indicate bad performance and favorable variances always indicate good performance.

Because all of these variances are solely due to the difference between the actual and budgeted levels of activity, they are called **activity variances.** For example, the activity variance for revenue is \$18,000 F, the activity variance for electricity is \$10 U, and so on. The most important activity variance appears at the very bottom of the report; namely, the \$13,710 F (favorable) variance for net operating income. This variance says the higher level of activity should cause net operating income to be \$13,710 higher than the planning budget.

Notice activity was up by 10 percent, suggesting the flexible budget's net operating income should be 10 percent higher than the planned profit of \$16,800, or \$18,480 (= 1.1 × \$16,800). However, the flexible budget shows much higher net operating income of \$30,510. Why? The short answer is: Because of fixed costs. Applying the 10 percent increase to the budgeted net operating income to estimate the profit at the higher level of activity implicitly assumes the revenues and *all* of the costs increase by 10 percent. But they do not. Three of the costs—rent, liability insurance, and employee health insurance—do not increase at all because they are fixed costs. So while sales do increase by 10 percent, these costs do not increase, causing net operating income to increase by more than 10 percent. A similar effect occurs with the mixed costs, which contain fixed cost elements—wages and salaries, electricity, and miscellaneous. While sales increase by 10 percent, these mixed costs increase by less than 10 percent, resulting in an overall increase in net operating income of more than 10 percent. Because of the fixed costs, percentage changes in net operating income are ordinarily larger than the percentage increases in activity.

Revenue and Spending Variances

LO9–3
Calculate and interpret revenue and spending variances.

The last section answered the question "What impact did the change in activity have on revenues, costs, and profit?" In this section, we answer the question "How well did we control our revenues, costs, and profit?"

Exhibit 9–7 shows how Victoria compared actual results to the flexible budget—in essence comparing what actually happened to what should have happened given the actual level of activity.

Focusing first on revenue, the actual revenue totaled \$194,200. However, the flexible budget indicates revenue should have been \$198,000. Consequently, revenue was \$3,800 less than it should have been, given the actual number of client-visits for the month. This discrepancy is labeled as a \$3,800 U (unfavorable) variance and is called a *revenue variance*. A **revenue variance** is the difference between the actual revenue and what the revenue should have been, given the actual level of activity. If actual revenue exceeds what the revenue should have been, the variance is labeled favorable. If actual revenue is less than what the revenue should have been, the variance is labeled unfavorable. Why would actual revenue differ from the flexible budget? Basically, the revenue variance is favorable if the average selling price is greater than expected; it is unfavorable if the average selling price is less than expected. This could happen for a variety of reasons including a change in selling price, a different mix of products sold, a change in the amount of discounts given, poor accounting controls, and so on.

EXHIBIT 9–7
Revenue and Spending Variances from Comparing Actual Results to the Flexible Budget

Rick's Hairstyling Revenue and Spending Variances For the Month Ended March 31	Actual Results	Flexible Budget	Revenue and Spending Variances*
Client-visits	1,100	1,100	
Revenue ($180.00q)	$194,200	$198,000	$3,800 U
Expenses:			
Wages and salaries ($65,000 + $37.00q)	106,900	105,700	1,200 U
Hairstyling supplies ($1.50q)	1,620	1,650	30 F
Client gratuities ($4.10q)	6,870	4,510	2,360 U
Electricity ($1,500 + $0.10q)	1,550	1,610	60 F
Rent ($28,500)	28,500	28,500	0
Liability insurance ($2,800)	2,800	2,800	0
Employee health insurance ($21,300)	22,600	21,300	1,300 U
Miscellaneous ($1,200 + $0.20q)	2,130	1,420	710 U
Total expenses	172,970	167,490	5,480 U
Net operating income	$ 21,230	$ 30,510	$9,280 U

*The revenue variance is labeled favorable (unfavorable) when the actual revenue is greater than (less than) the flexible budget. The expense variances are labeled favorable (unfavorable) when the actual expense is less than (greater than) the flexible budget.

IN BUSINESS

Ingram Publishing/Alamy Stock Photo

PANDEMIC CAUSES SHIFT IN BEER SALES

A company's actual results can differ from its plans for many unanticipated reasons. For example, the coronavirus lockdown "reversed the trajectory of long-declining beers such as Bud Light, Miller Lite, and Coors Light" by shifting consumer purchases "from tap rooms to grocery store aisles." As many people lost their jobs and bars, tap rooms, and restaurants closed, beer drinkers dropped their usual higher-priced craft beers in favor of cheaper national brands bought at grocery stores and big box stores. They also bought beer in 24- and 30-packs to reduce the number of trips to those stores. At the same time, retailers and distributors decided to simplify their supply chains by reducing the number of craft brands they carried. Collectively, these market dynamics increased pandemic-period sales of mainstream beers like Coors Light and Miller Lite by 10.7 percent compared to the same period from the prior year, which stands in stark contrast to the 3.1 percent decline in sales these same brands experienced throughout 2019.

Source: Jennifer Maloney, "Pandemic Boosts Big Beer Brands," *The Wall Street Journal,* May 19, 2020, p. B3.

Focusing next on costs, the actual electricity cost was $1,550; however, the flexible budget indicates electricity costs should have been $1,610 for the 1,100 client-visits in March. Because the cost was $60 less than expected, it is labeled as a favorable variance, $60 F. This is an example of a *spending variance*. A **spending variance** is the difference between the actual amount of the cost and how much a cost should have been, given the actual level of activity. If the actual cost is greater than expected, the variance is labeled as unfavorable. If the actual cost is less than expected, the variance is labeled as favorable. Why would a cost have a favorable or unfavorable variance? There are many possible explanations including paying a higher price for inputs than should have been paid, using too many inputs for the actual level of activity, a change in technology, and so on. In the next chapter we will explore these types of explanations in greater detail.

Note from Exhibit 9–7 the overall net operating income variance is $9,280 U (unfavorable). This means given the actual level of activity for the period, the net operating income was $9,280 lower than it should have been. There are a number of reasons for this. The most prominent is the unfavorable revenue variance of $3,800. Next in line is the $2,360 unfavorable variance for client gratuities. Looking at this in another way, client gratuities were more than 50 percent larger than they should have been according to the flexible budget. This is a variance that Rick would almost certainly want to investigate further. He may find this unfavorable variance is not necessarily a bad thing. It is possible, for example, that more lavish use of gratuities led to the 10 percent increase in client-visits.

Exhibit 9–7 also includes a $1,300 unfavorable variance related to employee health insurance, thereby highlighting how a fixed cost can have a spending variance. While fixed costs do not depend on the level of activity, the actual amount of a fixed cost can differ from the flexible budget. For example, perhaps Rick's employee health insurance premiums unexpectedly increased by $1,300 during March.

A Performance Report Combining Activity and Revenue and Spending Variances

LO9–4
Prepare a performance report with one cost driver that combines activity variances and revenue and spending variances.

Exhibit 9–8 displays Victoria's performance report combining the activity variances (from Exhibit 9–6) with the revenue and spending variances (from Exhibit 9–7). The format of this report is a bit different from the previous reports because the variances appear between the amounts being compared rather than after them. For example, the activity

EXHIBIT 9–8
Performance Report Combining Activity Variances with Revenue and Spending Variances

Rick's Hairstyling
Flexible Budget Performance Report
For the Month Ended March 31

	(1) Actual Results	Revenue and Spending Variances (1) – (2)	(2) Flexible Budget	Activity Variances (2) – (3)	(3) Planning Budget
Client-visits	1,100		1,100		1,000
Revenue ($180.00q)	$194,200	$3,800 U	$198,000	$18,000 F	$180,000
Expenses:					
Wages and salaries ($65,000 + $37.00q)	106,900	1,200 U	105,700	3,700 U	102,000
Hairstyling supplies ($1.50q)	1,620	30 F	1,650	150 U	1,500
Client gratuities ($4.10q)	6,870	2,360 U	4,510	410 U	4,100
Electricity ($1,500 + $0.10q)	1,550	60 F	1,610	10 U	1,600
Rent ($28,500)	28,500	0	28,500	0	28,500
Liability insurance ($2,800)	2,800	0	2,800	0	2,800
Employee health insurance ($21,300)	22,600	1,300 U	21,300	0	21,300
Miscellaneous ($1,200 + $0.20q)	2,130	710 U	1,420	20 U	1,400
Total expenses	172,970	5,480 U	167,490	4,290 U	163,200
Net operating income	$ 21,230	$9,280 U	$ 30,510	$13,710 F	$ 16,800

variances appear between the flexible budget and the planning budget. In Exhibit 9–6, the activity variances appeared after the flexible budget and the planning budget.

Note two numbers in particular in the performance report—the activity variance for net operating income of $13,710 F (favorable) and the overall revenue and spending variance for net operating income of $9,280 U (unfavorable). It is worth repeating what those two numbers mean. The $13,710 favorable activity variance occurred because actual activity (1,100 client-visits) was greater than the budgeted level of activity (1,000 client-visits). The $9,280 unfavorable overall revenue and spending variance occurred because the profit was not as large as it should have been for the actual level of activity. These two different variances mean very different things and call for different types of actions. To generate a favorable activity variance for net operating income, managers must take actions to increase client-visits. To generate a favorable overall revenue and spending variance, managers must take actions to protect selling prices, increase operating efficiency, and reduce the prices of inputs.

The performance report in Exhibit 9–8 provides better information to managers than a simple comparison of the planning budget with actual results as shown in Exhibit 9–4. In Exhibit 9–4, the effects of changes in activity were jumbled together with the effects of how well prices were controlled and operations were managed. The performance report in Exhibit 9–8 clearly separates these effects, allowing managers to better evaluate operational performance.

For example, Exhibit 9–4 calculates a hairstyling supplies variance of $120 U by comparing the planning budget ($1,500) to the flexible budget ($1,620). However, this is like comparing apples to oranges because these two budgets are based on different levels of activity. Exhibit 9–8 overcomes this limitation by showing how this $120 U variance is composed of two different variances—a favorable spending variance of $30 and an unfavorable activity variance of $150. The favorable spending variance occurred because less was spent on hairstyling supplies than expected for the actual level of activity. The activity variance occurs because activity was greater than anticipated in the planning budget, which naturally increased the expected cost of hairstyling supplies.

Once Victoria completed Exhibit 9–8, she met with Rick to explain it to him.

COMMUNICATING WITH DATA VISUALIZATIONS

Diagnostic analytics answer the question Why did it happen? This visualization shows the spending variances for Rick's Hairstyling (see Exhibit 9–8). The upper-left quadrant includes variances that are larger in dollar terms but lower in percentage terms. The lower-right quadrant shows the variances that are larger in percentage terms but lower in dollar terms. The upper-right quadrant highlights the variances that are concerning in terms of dollars *and* percentages. Rick would investigate the root cause of any variances that exceed predetermined dollar or percentage thresholds to understand why his actual profit differed from what he expected based on the actual level of activity.

The client gratuities spending variance is the largest in dollar and percentage terms. The wages and salaries spending variance is greater than $1,000 but only represents 1.1 percent of the amount in the flexible budget. On the other hand, the miscellaneous spending variance of $700 is smaller in terms of dollars but represents 50 percent of the amount in the flexible budget.

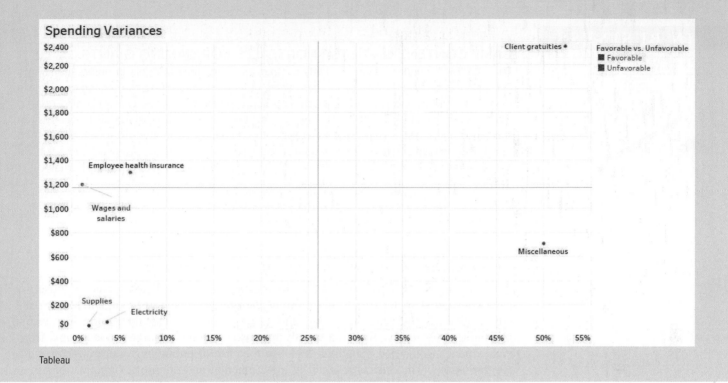

Spending Variances

Tableau

Victoria: Let me show you what I've got. (Victoria shows Rick the flexible budget performance report in Exhibit 9–8.) I used the cost formulas to create a flexible budget that allowed me to benchmark what your costs should have been.

Rick: That's what you labeled the "flexible budget based on 1,100 client-visits?"

Victoria: That's right. Your original budget was based on 1,000 client-visits, so it understated what some of the costs should have been when you actually served 1,100 customers.

Rick: That's clear enough. These spending variances aren't quite as shocking as the variances on my first report.

Victoria: Yes, but you still have an unfavorable variance of $2,360 for client gratuities.

Rick: I know how that happened. In March there was a big political fundraising dinner that unexpectedly increased our number of client-visits. Because we had less time to spend with our regular customers, I compensated by ordering lots of flowers, which I gave away by the bunch.

Victoria: With the prices you charge, Rick, I am sure the gesture was appreciated.

Rick: One thing bothers me about the report. When we discussed my costs before, you called rent, liability insurance, and employee health insurance fixed costs. How can I have a variance for a fixed cost? Doesn't fixed mean that it doesn't change?

Victoria: We call these costs *fixed* because they shouldn't be affected by *changes in the level of activity.* However, they can change for other reasons. Also, the term *fixed* suggests the cost can't be controlled, but that isn't true. It is often easier to control fixed costs than variable costs. For example, it would be fairly easy for you to change your insurance bill by adjusting the amount of insurance you carry. It would be much more difficult for you to significantly reduce your spending on hairstyling supplies— a variable cost that is a necessary part of serving customers.

Rick: I think I understand, but it *is* confusing.

Victoria: Just remember variable costs are proportional to activity and fixed costs do not depend on the level of activity. However, fixed costs can change for reasons unrelated to changes in the level of activity. And controllability has little to do with whether a cost is variable or fixed. Fixed costs are often more controllable than variable costs.

MANAGERIAL
ACCOUNTING IN ACTION
THE WRAP-UP

RICK'S
Hairstyling Salon

GAME CONTENT OFFSETS SHORTFALLS FOR GAMING GIANTS

The COVID-19 pandemic caused many companies to flex their budgets in unforeseen ways. For instance, Sony reduced its projected sales of its PlayStation 5 gaming consoles by more than three million units due to unanticipated supply chain difficulties. Nintendo also revised down expected sales of its Switch gaming consoles by one million units due to component shortages and logistics issues. Fortunately, both companies benefitted from well-established user bases, whose purchases of new games and online content—neither of which were subject to the hardware production constraints—helped to offset the companies' budget shortfalls.

Source: Jacky Wong, "For Sony and Nintendo, Supply Chain Pile-Up is Just a Speed Bump," *The Wall Street Journal*, February 7, 2022, https://www.wsj.com/articles/for-sony-and-nintendo-the-supply-chain-pile-up-is-just-a-speed-bump-11643972945.

Performance Reports in Nonprofit Organizations

The performance reports in nonprofit organizations are basically the same as those we have considered so far—with one prominent difference. Nonprofit organizations usually receive a significant amount of funding from sources other than sales. For example, universities receive their funding from sales (i.e., tuition charged to students), from endowment income and donations, and—in the case of public universities—from state appropriations. This means revenue in governmental and nonprofit organizations may consist of both fixed and variable elements. For example, the Seattle Opera Company's revenue in a recent year consisted of grants and donations of $12,719,000 and ticket sales of $8,125,000 (or about $75.35 per ticket sold). Consequently, the revenue formula for the opera company can be written as:

$$\text{Revenue} = \$12,719,000 + \$75.35q$$

where q is the number of tickets sold. In other respects, the performance report for the Seattle Opera and other nonprofit organizations would be similar to the performance report in Exhibit 9–8.

Performance Reports in Cost Centers

Performance reports can also be prepared for departments that do not sell anything to outsiders, such as production departments in manufacturing companies. These reports would look similar to Exhibit 9–8—except revenue, and consequently net operating income, would not appear on the report. Because the managers in these departments are responsible for costs, but not revenues, they are often called *cost centers.*

Preparing Planning Budgets and Flexible Budgets with Multiple Cost Drivers

LO9–5
Prepare a planning budget and a flexible budget with more than one cost driver.

At Rick's Hairstyling, we thus far assumed there is only one cost driver—the number of client-visits. However, in the activity-based costing chapter, we found more than one cost driver might be needed to adequately explain all of the costs in an organization. For example, some of the costs at Rick's Hairstyling probably depend more on the number of hours the salon is open for business than the number of client-visits. Specifically, most of Rick's employees are paid salaries, but some are paid on an hourly basis. None of the employees is paid based on the number of customers actually served. Consequently, the cost formula for wages and salaries would be more accurate if it were stated in terms of the hours of operation rather than the number of client-visits. The cost of electricity is even more complex. Some of the cost is fixed—the heat must be kept at some minimum level even at night when the salon is closed. Some of the cost depends on the number of client-visits—the power consumed by hair dryers depends on the number of customers served. Some of the cost depends on the number of hours the salon is open—the costs of lighting the salon and heating it to a comfortable temperature. Consequently, the cost formula for electricity would be more accurate if it were stated in terms of both the number of client-visits and the hours of operation rather than just in terms of the number of client-visits.

Exhibit 9–9 shows a planning budget incorporating these changes. It includes two cost drivers—client-visits and hours of operation—where q_1 refers to client-visits and q_2 refers to hours of operation. The budgeted number of client visits is 1,000 and the budgeted hours of operation is 190.

As expected, the planning budget using two cost drivers differs from the planning budget based on one cost driver that is shown in Exhibit 9–2. For example, the revised cost formula for wages and salaries, which is $65,000 + $220q_2$, now depends on the hours of operation rather than the number of client-visits. Because the salon is expected to operate for 190 hours, the planning budget includes wages and salaries of $106,800 (= $65,000 + 220×190). The electricity cost depends on both client-visits and hours of operation, and its cost formula is $390 + $0.10q_1 + $6.00q_2$. Because the planned number of client-visits was 1,000 and the salon expected to operate for 190 hours, the planning budget includes electricity expense of $1,630 (= $390 + $0.10 \times 1,000 + 6.00×190). Notice the net operating income in the planning budget based on two cost drivers is $11,970, whereas the net operating income in the planning budget based on one cost driver (see Exhibit 9–2) is $16,800. These two amounts differ because the planning budget based on two cost drivers is more accurate than the planning budget based on one driver.

If we assume Rick's salon actually had 1,100 client-visits during the month and actually operated for the budgeted amount of 190 hours, the cost formulas shown in Exhibit 9–9 can also be used to create the flexible budget shown in Exhibit 9–10. The flexible budget based on two cost drivers differs from the flexible budget based on one cost driver shown in Exhibit 9–5. For example, the wages and salaries in Exhibit 9–10 are $106,800, whereas the wages and salaries in Exhibit 9–5 are $105,700. The difference arises because the variable portion of this expense is driven by the hours of operation in Exhibit 9–10; however, it is assumed to be a function of client-visits in Exhibit 9–5. The flexible budgets in these two exhibits also report different net operating incomes. The flexible budget in Exhibit 9–5, which is based on one cost driver, shows net operating

Rick's Hairstyling Planning Budget For the Month Ended March 31		EXHIBIT 9–9 Planning Budget Based on More Than One Cost Driver
Budgeted client-visits (q_1)	1,000	
Budgeted hours of operation (q_2)	190	
Revenue ($180.00q_1$)	$180,000	
Expenses:		
Wages and salaries ($65,000 + $220q_2$)	106,800	
Hairstyling supplies ($1.50q_1$)	1,500	
Client gratuities ($4.10q_1$).................................	4,100	
Electricity ($390 + $0.10q_1 + $6.00q_2$)	1,630	
Rent ($28,500)	28,500	
Liability insurance ($2,800)................................	2,800	
Employee health insurance ($21,300)	21,300	
Miscellaneous ($1,200 + $0.20q_1$)	1,400	
Total expenses	168,030	
Net operating income	$ 11,970	

EXHIBIT 9-10
Flexible Budget Based on More Than One Cost Driver

Rick's Hairstyling Flexible Budget For the Month Ended March 31	
Actual client-visits (q_1)	1,100
Actual hours of operation (q_2)	190
Revenue (180.00q_1$)	$198,000
Expenses:	
Wages and salaries ($65,000 + 220q_2$)	106,800
Hairstyling supplies (1.50q_1$)	1,650
Client gratuities (4.10q_1$)	4,510
Electricity ($390 + 0.10q_1$ + 6.00q_2$)	1,640
Rent ($28,500)	28,500
Liability insurance ($2,800)	2,800
Employee health insurance ($21,300)	21,300
Miscellaneous ($1,200 + 0.20q_1$)	1,420
Total expenses	168,620
Net operating income	$ 29,380

LO9-6

Prepare a performance report with more than one cost driver that combines activity variances and revenue and spending variances.

income of $30,510. The flexible budget in Exhibit 9–10, which is based on two cost drivers, shows net operating income of $29,380.

The revised flexible budget based on both client-visits and hours of operation can be used to create the performance report shown in Exhibit 9–11. The difference between this performance report and the one in Exhibit 9–8 is the cost formulas based on more than one cost driver are more accurate than the cost formulas based on just one cost driver; hence, the variances will also be more accurate. For example, the spending variance for

EXHIBIT 9-11
Performance Report with More Than One Cost Driver That Combines Activity Variances with Revenue and Spending Variances

Rick's Hairstyling
Flexible Budget Performance Report
For the Month Ended March 31

	Actual Results	Revenue and Spending Variances	Flexible Budget	Activity Variances	Planning Budget
Client-visits (q_1)	1,100		1,100		1,000
Hours of operation (q_2)	190		190		190
Revenue (180.00q_1$)	$194,200	$3,800 U	$198,000	$ 18,000 F	$180,000
Expenses:					
Wages and salaries ($65,000 + 220.00q_2$) . .	106,900	100 U	106,800	0	106,800
Hairstyling supplies (1.50q_1$)	1,620	30 F	1,650	150 U	1,500
Client gratuities (4.10q_1$)	6,870	2,360 U	4,510	410 U	4,100
Electricity ($390 + 0.10q_1$ + 6.00q_2$)	1,550	90 F	1,640	10 U	1,630
Rent ($28,500)	28,500	0	28,500	0	28,500
Liability insurance ($2,800)	2,800	0	2,800	0	2,800
Employee health insurance ($21,300)	22,600	1,300 U	21,300	0	21,300
Miscellaneous ($1,200 + 0.20q_1$)	2,130	710 U	1,420	20 U	1,400
Total expenses	172,970	4,350 U	168,620	590 U	168,030
Net operating income	$ 21,230	$8,150 U	$ 29,380	$ 17,410 F	$ 11,970

electricity is $60 F when the flexible budget is based on one cost driver (see Exhibit 9–8), but it is $90 F when using two cost drivers (see Exhibit 9–11).

PANDEMIC LOCKDOWNS CAUSE PELOTON SALES TO SURGE

When the COVID-19 pandemic caused nationwide lockdowns, many companies saw their sales plummet. However, this was not the case for Peloton Interactive. The company's number of subscribers doubled to 886,100 while its number of online workouts spiked from 24 million to 44 million—causing quarterly sales to jump by 66 percent. From a flexible budgeting standpoint, Peloton's actual levels of activity far exceeded its budget. These huge jumps in the number of subscribers and the number of workouts would have to be considered in order to make meaningful comparisons between actual results and the plan.

Source: Micah Maidenberg, "Lockdowns Power Peloton Sales Surge," *The Wall Street Journal*, May 7, 2020, p. B4.

Scott Heins/Getty Images

Summary

Directly comparing actual revenues and costs to static planning budget revenues and costs can easily lead to erroneous conclusions. Actual revenues and costs differ from budgeted revenues and costs for a variety of reasons, but one of the biggest is a change in the level of activity. One would expect actual revenues and costs to increase or decrease as the activity level increases or decreases. Flexible budgets enable managers to isolate the various causes of the differences between budgeted and actual revenues and costs.

A flexible budget is a budget that is adjusted to the actual level of activity. It is the best estimate of what revenues and costs should have been, given the actual level of activity. The flexible budget can be compared to the budget from the beginning of the period or to the actual results.

Activity variances arise by comparing the flexible budget to the planning budget. They show how a revenue or cost should have changed in response to the difference between actual and planned activity.

Revenue and spending variances arise when comparing actual results to the flexible budget. A favorable revenue variance indicates revenue was larger than expected, given the actual level of activity. An unfavorable revenue variance indicates revenue was less than expected, given the actual level of activity. A favorable spending variance indicates the cost was less than expected, given the actual level of activity. An unfavorable spending variance indicates the cost was greater than expected, given the actual level of activity. A flexible budget performance report combines activity variances and revenue and spending variances.

Planning budgets, flexible budgets, and flexible budget performance reports can be prepared using more than one cost driver. When a company uses multiple cost drivers to compare its actual results to the budget, it should provide more accurate and insightful variances than those computed using only one cost driver.

Data Analytics Exercise available in Connect to complement this chapter

Review Problem: Variance Analysis Using a Flexible Budget

Harrald's Fish House is a family-owned restaurant specializing in Scandinavian-style seafood. Data concerning the restaurant's monthly revenues and costs appear below (q refers to the number of meals served):

	Formula
Revenue	$16.50q
Cost of ingredients	$6.25q
Wages and salaries	$10,400
Utilities	$800 + $0.20q
Rent	$2,200
Miscellaneous	$600 + $0.80q

Required:

1. Prepare the restaurant's planning budget for April assuming 1,800 meals are served.
2. Assume 1,700 meals were actually served in April. Prepare a flexible budget for this level of activity.
3. The actual results for April appear below. Prepare a flexible budget performance report for the restaurant for April.

Revenue	$27,920
Cost of ingredients	$11,110
Wages and salaries	$10,130
Utilities	$1,080
Rent	$2,200
Miscellaneous	$2,240

Solution to Review Problem

1. The planning budget for April appears below:

Harrald's Fish House Planning Budget For the Month Ended April 30	
Budgeted meals served (q)	1,800
Revenue ($16.50q)	$29,700
Expenses:	
Cost of ingredients ($6.25q)	11,250
Wages and salaries ($10,400)	10,400
Utilities ($800 + $0.20q)	1,160
Rent ($2,200)	2,200
Miscellaneous ($600 + $0.80q)	2,040
Total expenses	27,050
Net operating income	$ 2,650

2. The flexible budget for April appears below:

Harrald's Fish House Flexible Budget For the Month Ended April 30	
Actual meals served (q)	1,700
Revenue ($16.50q)	$28,050
Expenses:	
Cost of ingredients ($6.25q)	10,625
Wages and salaries ($10,400)	10,400
Utilities ($800 + $0.20q)	1,140
Rent ($2,200)	2,200
Miscellaneous ($600 + $0.80q)	1,960
Total expenses	26,325
Net operating income	$ 1,725

3.   The flexible budget performance report for April appears below:

	(1) Actual Results	Revenue and Spending Variances (1) – (2)	(2) Flexible Budget	Activity Variances (2) – (3)	(3) Planning Budget
Meals served	1,700		1,700		1,800
Revenue ($16.50q)	$27,920	$130 U	$28,050	$1,650 U	$29,700
Expenses:					
Cost of ingredients ($6.25q)	11,110	485 U	10,625	625 F	11,250
Wages and salaries ($10,400)	10,130	270 F	10,400	0	10,400
Utilities ($800 + $0.20q)	1,080	60 F	1,140	20 F	1,160
Rent ($2,200)	2,200	0	2,200	0	2,200
Miscellaneous ($600 + $0.80q)	2,240	280 U	1,960	80 F	2,040
Total expenses	26,760	435 U	26,325	725 F	27,050
Net operating income	$ 1,160	$565 U	$ 1,725	$ 925 U	$ 2,650

Harrald's Fish House
Flexible Budget Performance Report
For the Month Ended April 30

Glossary

Activity variance The difference between the amount of revenue or expense in the flexible budget and the planning budget. It is caused solely by the difference between the actual and planned levels of activity. (p. 411)

Flexible budget A budget showing what revenues and costs should have been, given the actual level of activity. (p. 406)

Management by exception A management system that compares actual results to a budget so significant deviations can be flagged as exceptions and investigated. (p. 405)

Planning budget A budget created before the period begins that is valid only for the planned level of activity. (p. 406)

Revenue variance The difference between the actual amount of revenue and how much it should have been, given the actual level of activity. A favorable (unfavorable) revenue variance occurs because the revenue is higher (lower) than expected, given the actual level of activity. (p. 411)

Spending variance The difference between the actual amount of a cost and how much it should have been, given the actual level of activity. A favorable (unfavorable) spending variance occurs because the cost is lower (higher) than expected, given the actual level of activity. (p. 412)

Questions

9–1   What is a static planning budget?
9–2   What is a flexible budget and how does it differ from a static planning budget?
9–3   What are some of the possible reasons actual results may differ from what had been budgeted at the beginning of a period?
9–4   Why is it difficult to interpret a difference between how much expense was budgeted and how much was actually spent?
9–5   What is an activity variance and what does it mean?
9–6   If the actual level of activity is greater than the planned level of activity, would you expect the activity variances for variable expenses to be favorable, unfavorable, or a combination of the two?
9–7   What is a revenue variance and what does it mean?
9–8   What is a spending variance and what does it mean?
9–9   What does a flexible budget performance report do that a simple comparison of budgeted to actual results does not do?
9–10   How does a flexible budget based on two cost drivers differ from a flexible budget based on one cost driver?

Applying Excel McGraw Hill **connect**

LO9–1, LO9–2, LO9–3, LO9–4

The Excel worksheet shown below recreates the Review Problem relating to Harrald's Fish House. The workbook, and instructions on how to complete the file, can be found in Connect.

You should proceed to the requirements below only after completing your worksheet.

Required:

1. Check your worksheet by changing the revenue in cell D4 to $16.00; the cost of ingredients in cell D5 to $6.50; and the wages and salaries in cell B6 to $10,000. The activity variance for net operating income should now be $850 U and the spending variance for total expenses should be $410 U. If you do not get these answers, find the errors in your worksheet and correct them.

   a. What is the activity variance for revenue? Explain this variance.
   b. What is the spending variance for the cost of ingredients? Explain this variance.

	A	B	C	D	E	F	G	H
1	Chapter 9: Applying Excel							
2								
3	**Data**							
4	Revenue			$16.50 q				
5	Cost of ingredients			$6.25 q				
6	Wages and salaries	$10,400						
7	Utilities	$800	+	$0.20 q				
8	Rent	$2,200						
9	Miscellaneous	$600	+	$0.80 q				
10								
11	Actual results:							
12	Revenue	$27,920						
13	Cost of ingredients	$11,110						
14	Wages and salaries	$10,130						
15	Utilities	$1,080						
16	Rent	$2,200						
17	Miscellaneous	$2,240						
18								
19	Planning budget activity	1,800 meals served						
20	Actual activity	1,700 meals served						
21								
22	*Enter a formula into each of the cells marked with a ? below*							
23	**Review Problem: Variance Analysis Using a Flexible Budget**							
24								
25	*Construct a flexible budget performance report*							
26			Revenue					
27			and					
28		Actual	Spending		Flexible	Activity		Planning
29		Results	Variances		Budget	Variances		Budget
30	Meals served	?			?			?
31	Revenue	?	?		?	?		?
32	Expenses:							
33	Cost of ingredients	?	?		?	?		?
34	Wages and salaries	?	?		?	?		?
35	Utilities	?	?		?	?		?
36	Rent	?	?		?	?		?
37	Miscellaneous	?	?		?	?		?
38	Total expenses	?	?		?	?		?
39	Net operating income	?	?		?	?		?
40								

I◄ ◄ ► ►I   **Chapter 9 Form** / Filled in Chapter 9 Form / Chapter 9 Form ◄

Microsoft Excel

2. Revise the data in your worksheet to reflect the results for the following year:

Data		
Revenue		$16.50q
Cost of ingredients		$6.25q
Wages and salaries	$10,400	
Utilities	$800 +	$0.20q
Rent	$2,200	
Miscellaneous	$600 +	$0.80q
Actual results:		
Revenue	$28,900	
Cost of ingredients	$11,300	
Wages and salaries	$10,300	
Utilities	$1,120	
Rent	$2,300	
Miscellaneous	$2,020	
Planning budget activity	1,700 meals served	
Actual activity	1,800 meals served	

Using the flexible budget performance report, briefly evaluate the company's performance for the year and indicate where attention should be focused.

Mc Graw Hill **connect** **The Foundational 15**

LO9–1, LO9–2, LO9–3

Adger Corporation is a service company that measures its output based on the number of customers served. The company provided the following fixed and variable cost estimates for budgeting purposes and the actual results for May as shown below:

	Fixed Element per Month	Variable Element per Customer Served	Actual Total for May
Revenue		$5,000	$160,000
Employee salaries and wages	$50,000	$1,100	$88,000
Travel expenses		$600	$19,000
Other expenses	$36,000		$34,500

When preparing its planning budget, the company estimated it would serve 30 customers per month; however, during May the company actually served 35 customers.

Required (all computations pertain to the month of May):
1. What amount of revenue would be included in Adger's flexible budget?
2. What amount of employee salaries and wages would be included in Adger's flexible budget?
3. What amount of travel expenses would be included in Adger's flexible budget?
4. What amount of other expenses would be included in Adger's flexible budget?
5. What net operating income would appear in Adger's flexible budget?
6. What is Adger's revenue variance?
7. What is Adger's employee salaries and wages spending variance?
8. What is Adger's travel expenses spending variance?
9. What is Adger's other expenses spending variance?
10. What amount of revenue would be included in Adger's planning budget?
11. What amount of employee salaries and wages would be included in Adger's planning budget?
12. What amount of travel expenses would be included in Adger's planning budget?
13. What amount of other expenses would be included in Adger's planning budget?
14. What activity variance would Adger report with respect to its revenue?
15. What activity variances would Adger report with respect to each of its expenses?

Exercises   McGraw Hill connect

EXERCISE 9–1 Prepare a Flexible Budget LO9–1
Puget Sound Divers provides diving services, such as underwater ship repairs, to its clients. The company's planning budget for May appears below:

Puget Sound Divers Planning Budget For the Month Ended May 31	
Budgeted diving-hours (q)	100
Revenue (365.00q$)	$36,500
Expenses:	
Wages and salaries ($8,000 + 125.00q$)	20,500
Supplies (3.00q$)	300
Equipment rental ($1,800 + 32.00q$)	5,000
Insurance ($3,400)	3,400
Miscellaneous ($630 + 1.80q$)	810
Total expenses	30,010
Net operating income	$ 6,490

During May, the company's actual activity was 105 diving-hours.

Required:
Using Exhibit 9–5 as your guide, prepare a flexible budget for May.

EXERCISE 9–2 Activity Variances LO9–2
Flight Café prepares in-flight meals for airlines and its planning budget for July appears below:

Flight Café Planning Budget For the Month Ended July 31	
Budgeted meals (q)	18,000
Revenue (4.50q$)	$81,000
Expenses:	
Raw materials (2.40q$)	43,200
Wages and salaries ($5,200 + 0.30q$)	10,600
Utilities ($2,400 + 0.05q$)	3,300
Facility rent ($4,300)	4,300
Insurance ($2,300)	2,300
Miscellaneous ($680 + 0.10q$)	2,480
Total expenses	66,180
Net operating income	$14,820

In July, 17,800 meals were actually served. The company's flexible budget for this level of activity appears below:

Flight Café Flexible Budget For the Month Ended July 31	
Budgeted meals (q)	17,800
Revenue (4.50q$)	$80,100
Expenses:	
Raw materials (2.40q$)	42,720
Wages and salaries ($5,200 + 0.30q$)	10,540
Utilities ($2,400 + 0.05q$)	3,290
Facility rent ($4,300)	4,300
Insurance ($2,300)	2,300
Miscellaneous ($680 + 0.10q$)	2,460
Total expenses	65,610
Net operating income	$14,490

Required:

1. Calculate the company's activity variances for July. (Hint: Refer to Exhibit 9–6.)
2. Which of the activity variances should be of concern to management? Explain.

EXERCISE 9–3 Revenue and Spending Variances LO9–3

Quilcene Oysteria farms and sells oysters in the Pacific Northwest. The company harvested and sold 8,000 pounds of oysters in August. The company's flexible budget for August appears below:

Quilcene Oysteria Flexible Budget For the Month Ended August 31	
Actual pounds (q)	8,000
Revenue ($4.00q)	$ 32,000
Expenses:	
Packing supplies ($0.50q)	4,000
Oyster bed maintenance ($3,200)	3,200
Wages and salaries ($2,900 + $0.30q)	5,300
Shipping ($0.80q)	6,400
Utilities ($830)	830
Other ($450 + $0.05q)	850
Total expenses	20,580
Net operating income	$ 11,420

The actual results for August were as follows:

Quilcene Oysteria Income Statement For the Month Ended August 31	
Actual pounds	8,000
Revenue	$35,200
Expenses:	
Packing supplies	4,200
Oyster bed maintenance	3,100
Wages and salaries	5,640
Shipping	6,950
Utilities	810
Other	980
Total expenses	21,680
Net operating income	$13,520

Required:

Calculate the company's revenue and spending variances for August. (Hint: Refer to Exhibit 9–7.)

EXERCISE 9–4 Prepare a Flexible Budget Performance Report LO9–4

Vulcan Flyovers offers scenic overflights of Mount St. Helens. Data concerning the company's operations in July appear below:

	Vulcan Flyovers Operating Data For the Month Ended July 31		
	Actual Results	Flexible Budget	Planning Budget
Flights (q)	48	48	50
Revenue ($320.00q)	$13,650	$15,360	$16,000
Expenses:			
Wages and salaries ($4,000 + $82.00q)	8,430	7,936	8,100
Fuel ($23.00q)	1,260	1,104	1,150
Airport fees ($650 + $38.00q)	2,350	2,474	2,550
Aircraft depreciation ($7.00q)	336	336	350
Office expenses ($190 + $2.00q)	460	286	290
Total expenses	12,836	12,136	12,440
Net operating income	$ 814	$ 3,224	$ 3,560

The company measures its activity in terms of flights. Customers can buy individual tickets for overflights or hire an entire plane at a discount.

Required:
1. Using Exhibit 9–8 as your guide, prepare a flexible budget performance report for July.
2. Which of the variances should be of concern to management? Explain.

EXERCISE 9–5 Prepare a Flexible Budget with More Than One Cost Driver LO9–5
Alyeski Tours operates day tours of coastal glaciers in Alaska on its tour boat *The Blue Glacier*. Management identified two cost drivers for budgeting purposes—the number of cruises and the number of passengers. The company publishes a schedule of day cruises that it may supplement with special sailings if there is sufficient demand. Up to 80 passengers can be accommodated on the tour boat. Data concerning the company's cost formulas appear below:

	Fixed Cost per Month	Cost per Cruise	Cost per Passenger
Vessel operating costs	$5,200	$480.00	$2.00
Advertising	$1,700		
Administrative costs	$4,300	$24.00	$1.00
Insurance	$2,900		

For example, vessel operating costs should be $5,200 per month plus $480 per cruise plus $2 per passenger. The company's sales should average $25 per passenger. In July, the company provided 24 cruises for a total of 1,400 passengers.

Required:
Using Exhibit 9–10 as your guide, prepare the company's flexible budget for July.

EXERCISE 9–6 Working with More Than One Cost Driver LO9–2, LO9–3, LO9–5, LO9–6
The Gourmand Cooking School runs short cooking courses at its small campus. Management has identified two cost drivers it uses for budgeting purposes—the number of courses and the total number of students. For example, the school might run two courses in a month and have a total of 50 students enrolled in those two courses. Data concerning the company's cost formulas appear below:

	Fixed Cost per Month	Cost per Course	Cost per Student
Instructor wages		$3,080	
Classroom supplies			$260
Utilities	$870	$130	
Campus rent	$4,200		
Insurance	$1,890		
Administrative expenses	$3,270	$15	$4

For example, administrative expenses should be $3,270 per month plus $15 per course plus $4 per student. The company's sales should average $800 per student.

The company planned to run three courses with a total of 45 students; however, it actually ran three courses with a total of only 42 students. The actual operating results for September were as follows:

	Actual
Revenue	$32,400
Instructor wages	$9,080
Classroom supplies	$8,540
Utilities	$1,530
Campus rent	$4,200
Insurance	$1,890
Administrative expenses	$3,790

Required:
Using Exhibit 9–11 as your guide, prepare a flexible budget performance report for September.

EXERCISE 9–7 Flexible Budgets and Activity Variances LO9–1, LO9–2
Jake's Roof Repair provided the following data concerning its costs:

	Fixed Cost per Month	Cost per Repair-Hour
Wages and salaries	$23,200	$16.30
Parts and supplies		$8.60
Equipment depreciation	$1,600	$0.40
Truck operating expenses	$6,400	$1.70
Rent	$3,480	
Administrative expenses	$4,500	$0.80

For example, wages and salaries should be $23,200 plus $16.30 per repair hour. The company expected to work 2,800 repair-hours in May but actually worked 2,900 repair-hours. The company expects its sales to be $44.50 per repair-hour.

Required:
Compute the company's activity variances for May. (Hint: Refer to Exhibit 9–6.)

EXERCISE 9–8 Planning Budget LO9–1
Wyckam Manufacturing Inc. provided the following cost formulas for its manufacturing costs:

	Fixed Cost per Month	Cost per Machine-Hour
Direct materials		$4.25
Direct labor	$36,800	
Supplies		$0.30
Utilities	$1,400	$0.05
Depreciation	$16,700	
Insurance	$12,700	

For example, utilities should be $1,400 per month plus $0.05 per machine-hour. The company expects to work 5,000 machine-hours in June. Note the company's direct labor is a fixed cost.

Required:
Using Exhibit 9–2 as your guide, prepare the company's planning budget for June.

EXERCISE 9–9 Planning Budget LO9–1
Lavage Rapide owns and operates a large automatic car wash facility near Montreal. The following table provides estimates concerning the company's costs:

	Fixed Cost per Month	Cost per Car Washed
Cleaning supplies		$0.80
Electricity	$1,200	$0.15
Maintenance		$0.20
Wages and salaries	$5,000	$0.30
Depreciation	$6,000	
Rent	$8,000	
Administrative expenses	$4,000	$0.10

For example, electricity costs should be $1,200 per month plus $0.15 per car washed. The company expects to wash 9,000 cars in August and to collect an average of $4.90 per car washed.

Required:

Using Exhibit 9–2 as your guide, prepare the company's planning budget for August.

EXERCISE 9–10 Flexible Budget LO9–1

Refer to the data for Lavage Rapide in Exercise 9–9. The company actually washed 8,800 cars in August.

Required:

Using Exhibit 9–5 as your guide, prepare the company's flexible budget for August.

EXERCISE 9–11 Activity Variances LO9–2

Refer to the data for Lavage Rapide in Exercise 9–9. The company actually washed 8,800 cars in August.

Required:

Calculate the company's activity variances for August. (Hint: Refer to Exhibit 9–6.)

EXERCISE 9–12 Revenue and Spending Variances LO9–3

Refer to the data for Lavage Rapide in Exercise 9–9. Also assume the company's actual operating results for August are as follows:

Lavage Rapide Income Statement For the Month Ended August 31	
Actual cars washed	8,800
Revenue	$43,080
Expenses:	
Cleaning supplies	7,560
Electricity	2,670
Maintenance	2,260
Wages and salaries	8,500
Depreciation	6,000
Rent	8,000
Administrative expenses	4,950
Total expenses	39,940
Net operating income	$ 3,140

Required:

Calculate the company's revenue and spending variances for August. (Hint: Refer to Exhibit 9–7.)

EXERCISE 9–13 Prepare a Flexible Budget Performance Report LO9–4

Refer to the data for Lavage Rapide in Exercises 9–9 and 9–12.

Required:

Using Exhibit 9–8 as your guide, prepare a flexible budget performance report for August.

EXERCISE 9–14 Flexible Budget Performance Report in a Cost Center LO9–1, LO9–2, LO9–3, LO9–4

Packaging Solutions Corporation manufactures and sells a wide variety of packaging products. Its Production Department's planning budget and flexible budget are based on the following formulas, where q is the number of labor-hours worked in a month:

	Cost Formulas
Direct labor	$15.80q
Indirect labor	$8,200 + $1.60q
Utilities	$6,400 + $0.80q
Supplies	$1,100 + $0.40q
Equipment depreciation	$23,000 + $3.70q
Factory rent	$8,400
Property taxes	$2,100
Factory administration	$11,700 + $1.90q

The Production Department planned to work 8,000 labor-hours in March; however, it actually worked 8,400 labor-hours during the month. Its actual costs incurred in March are listed below:

	Actual Cost Incurred in March
Direct labor	$134,730
Indirect labor	$19,860
Utilities	$14,570
Supplies	$4,980
Equipment depreciation	$54,080
Factory rent	$8,700
Property taxes	$2,100
Factory administration	$26,470

Required:

1. Using Exhibit 9–2 as your guide, prepare the Production Department's planning budget for the month.
2. Using Exhibit 9–5 as your guide, prepare the Production Department's flexible budget for the month.
3. Using Exhibit 9–8 as your guide, prepare the Production Department's flexible budget performance report for March.
4. Which variances in the flexible budget performance report should be brought to management's attention? Explain.

EXERCISE 9–15 Flexible Budgets and Revenue and Spending Variances LO9–1, LO9–3

Via Gelato, a popular neighborhood gelato shop, provided the following cost formulas and actual results for the month of June:

	Fixed Element per Month	Variable Element per Liter	Actual Total for June
Revenue		$12.00	$71,540
Raw materials		$4.65	$29,230
Wages	$5,600	$1.40	$13,860
Utilities	$1,630	$0.20	$3,270
Rent	$2,600		$2,600
Insurance	$1,350		$1,350
Miscellaneous	$650	$0.35	$2,590

While gelato is sold by the cone or cup, the shop measures its activity in terms of the total number of liters of gelato sold. For example, wages should be $5,600 plus $1.40 per liter of gelato sold and the actual wages for June were $13,860. Via Gelato expected to sell 6,000 liters in June but actually sold 6,200 liters.

Required:

Calculate Via Gelato's revenue and spending variances for June. (Hint: Refer to Exhibit 9–7.)

EXERCISE 9–16 Flexible Budget Performance Report LO9–1, LO9–2, LO9–3, LO9–4
AirQual Test Corporation provides on-site air quality testing services. The company provided the following cost formulas and actual results for the month of February:

	Fixed Component per Month	Variable Component per Job	Actual Total for February
Revenue		$360	$18,950
Technician wages	$6,400		$6,450
Mobile lab operating expenses	$2,900	$35	$4,530
Office expenses	$2,600	$2	$3,050
Advertising expenses	$970		$995
Insurance	$1,680		$1,680
Miscellaneous expenses	$500	$3	$465

The company uses the number of jobs as its measure of activity. For example, mobile lab operating expenses should be $2,900 plus $35 per job, and the actual mobile lab operating expenses for February were $4,530. The company expected to work 50 jobs in February but actually worked 52 jobs.

Required:
Using Exhibit 9–8 as your guide, prepare a flexible budget performance report for February.

Problems   Mc Graw Hill connect

PROBLEM 9–17: Flexible Budget Performance Reports; Working Backwards LO9–1, LO9–2, LO9–3, LO9–4
Ray Company provided the following excerpts from its Production Department's flexible budget performance report:

Ray Company Production Department Flexible Budget Performance Report For the Month Ended August 31					
	Actual Results	Spending Variances	Flexible Budget	Activity Variances	Planning Budget
Labor-hours (q)	9,480		?		9,000
Direct labor ($?q)	$134,730	$?	$132,720	$?	$?
Indirect labor ($? + $1.50q)	?	1,780 F	21,640	?	?
Utilities ($6,500 + $?q)	?	1,450 U	?	336 U	12,800
Supplies ($? + $?q)	4,940	?	4,444	?	4,300
Equipment depreciation ($78,400)	?	0	?	?	?
Factory administration ($18,700 + $1.90q)	?	?	?	?	?
Total expenses	$288,088	$?	$?	$?	$?

Required:
Complete the Production Department's Flexible Budget Performance Report by filling in all the question marks.

PROBLEM 9–18 Activity and Spending Variances LO9–1, LO9–2, LO9–3
You have just been hired by FAB Corporation, the manufacturer of a revolutionary new garage door opening device. The president asked you to review the company's costing system and "do what you can to help us get better control of our manufacturing overhead costs." You find the company has never used a flexible budget, and you suggest preparing such a budget would be an excellent first step in overhead planning and control.

After much effort and analysis, you estimated the following cost formulas and gathered the following actual cost data for March:

	Cost Formula	Actual Cost in March
Utilities	$20,600 + $0.10 per machine-hour	$24,200
Maintenance	$40,000 + $1.60 per machine-hour	$78,100
Supplies	$0.30 per machine-hour	$8,400
Indirect labor	$130,000 + $0.70 per machine-hour	$149,600
Depreciation	$70,000	$71,500

During March, the company worked 26,000 machine-hours and produced 15,000 units. The company originally planned to work 30,000 machine-hours during March.

Required:
1. Calculate the activity variances for March. (Hint: Refer to Exhibit 9–6.) Explain what these variances mean.
2. Calculate the spending variances for March. (Hint: Refer to Exhibit 9–7.) Explain what these variances mean.

PROBLEM 9–19 More Than One Cost Driver LO9–2, LO9–3, LO9–5, LO9–6

Milano Pizza has a small area for in-store dining as well as offers take-out and free home delivery services. The pizzeria's owner determined the shop has two major cost drivers—the number of pizzas sold and the number of deliveries made.

The pizzeria's cost formulas appear below:

	Fixed Cost per Month	Cost per Pizza	Cost per Delivery
Pizza ingredients		$3.80	
Kitchen staff	$5,220		
Utilities	$630	$0.05	
Delivery person			$3.50
Delivery vehicle	$540		$1.50
Equipment depreciation	$275		
Rent	$1,830		
Miscellaneous	$820	$0.15	

In November, the pizzeria budgeted for 1,200 pizzas at an average selling price of $13.50 per pizza and for 180 deliveries.

Data concerning the pizzeria's actual results in November were as follows:

	Actual Results
Pizzas	1,240
Deliveries	174
Revenue	$17,420
Pizza ingredients	$4,985
Kitchen staff	$5,281
Utilities	$984
Delivery person	$609
Delivery vehicle	$655
Equipment depreciation	$275
Rent	$1,830
Miscellaneous	$954

Required:
1. Using Exhibit 9–11 as your guide, prepare a flexible budget performance report for November.
2. Explain the activity variances.

PROBLEM 9–20 Critique a Report; Prepare a Performance Report LO9–1, LO9–2, LO9–3, LO9–4

TipTop Flight School offers flying lessons at a small municipal airport. The school's owner and manager attempted to evaluate performance and control costs using a variance report comparing the planning budget to actual results. A recent variance report appears below:

TipTop Flight School Variance Report For the Month Ended July 31	Actual Results	Planning Budget	Variances	
Lessons	155	150		
Revenue	$33,900	$33,000	$900	F
Expenses:				
Instructor wages	9,870	9,750	120	U
Aircraft depreciation	5,890	5,700	190	U
Fuel	2,750	2,250	500	U
Maintenance	2,450	2,330	120	U
Ground facility expenses	1,540	1,550	10	F
Administration	3,320	3,390	70	F
Total expenses	25,820	24,970	850	U
Net operating income	$ 8,080	$ 8,030	$ 50	F

After several months of using these reports, the owner has become frustrated. For example, she is confident instructor wages were very tightly controlled in July, but the report shows an unfavorable variance.

She developed the planning budget using the following formulas, where q is the number of lessons sold:

	Cost Formulas
Revenue	$220q$
Instructor wages	$65q$
Aircraft depreciation	$38q$
Fuel	$15q$
Maintenance	$530 + $12q$
Ground facility expenses	$1,250 + $2q$
Administration	$3,240 + $1q$

Required:
1. Should the owner feel frustrated with the variance reports? Explain.
2. Using Exhibit 9–8 as your guide, prepare a flexible budget performance report for the school for July.
3. Evaluate the school's performance for July.

PROBLEM 9–21 Performance Report for a Nonprofit Organization LO9–1, LO9–2, LO9–3, LO9–4

The St. Lucia Blood Bank, a private charity partly supported by government grants, is located on the Caribbean island of St. Lucia. The blood bank just finished its operations for September, which was a very busy month because a powerful hurricane caused many injuries on neighboring islands. The hurricane largely bypassed St. Lucia, but residents of St. Lucia willingly donated their blood to help people on other islands. As a consequence, the blood bank collected over 20 percent more blood than originally planned for the month.

A report prepared by a government official comparing actual costs to budgeted costs for the blood bank appears below. Continued support from the government depends on the blood bank's ability to demonstrate control over its costs.

St. Lucia Blood Bank Cost Control Report For the Month Ended September 30			
	Actual Results	Planning Budget	Variances
Liters of blood collected	620	500	
Medical supplies	$ 9,250	$ 7,500	$1,750 U
Lab tests	6,180	6,000	180 U
Equipment depreciation	2,800	2,500	300 U
Rent	1,000	1,000	0
Utilities	570	500	70 U
Administration	11,740	11,250	490 U
Total expense	$31,540	$28,750	$2,790 U

The managing director of the blood bank was very unhappy with the unfavorable variances in this report, claiming his costs were higher than expected due to the emergency on the neighboring islands. He also pointed out the additional costs had been fully covered by payments from grateful recipients on the other islands. The government official who prepared the report countered that all figures had already been submitted by the blood bank to the government; he was just pointing out actual costs were a lot higher than promised in the budget.

The following cost formulas were used to prepare the planning budget:

	Cost Formulas
Medical supplies	$15.00q
Lab tests	$12.00q
Equipment depreciation	$2,500
Rent	$1,000
Utilities	$500
Administration	$10,000 + $2.50q

Required:
1. Using Exhibit 9–8 as your guide, prepare a flexible budget performance report for September.
2. Do you think any of the variances in the report you prepared should be investigated? Why?

PROBLEM 9–22 Critiquing a Variance Report; Preparing a Performance Report LO9–1, LO9–2, LO9–3, LO9–4

Westmont Corporation uses a comprehensive budgeting system for planning and control purposes. While departmental supervisors are happy with the system, the factory manager is not.

A report for the company's Assembly Department for March follows:

Assembly Department Cost Report For the Month Ended March 31			
	Actual Results	Planning Budget	Variances
Machine-hours	35,000	40,000	
Variable costs:			
Supplies	$ 29,700	$ 32,000	$2,300 F
Scrap	19,500	20,000	500 F
Indirect materials	51,800	56,000	4,200 F
Fixed costs:			
Wages and salaries	79,200	80,000	800 F
Equipment depreciation	60,000	60,000	—
Total cost	$240,200	$248,000	$7,800 F

After receiving this report, the supervisor of the Assembly Department stated, "These reports are super. It makes me feel good to see how well things are going in my department. I can't understand why those people upstairs complain so much about the reports."

For the last several years, the company's marketing department chronically failed to meet the sales goals expressed in the company's monthly budgets.

Required:
1. The company's president is uneasy about the cost reports and would like you to evaluate their usefulness.
2. What changes, if any, should be made in the reports to give better insight into how well departmental supervisors are controlling costs?
3. Using Exhibit 9–8 as your guide, prepare a new performance report for the quarter, incorporating any changes you suggested in question (2) above.
4. How well were costs controlled in the Assembly Department in March?

PROBLEM 9–23 Critiquing a Cost Report; Preparing a Performance Report LO9–1, LO9–2, LO9–3, LO9–4
Frank Weston, supervisor of the Freemont Corporation's Machining Department, was upset after being reprimanded for his department's poor performance over the prior month. The department's cost control report is given below:

Freemont Corporation–Machining Department Cost Control Report For the Month Ended June 30	Actual Results	Planning Budget	Variances
Machine-hours	38,000	35,000	
Direct labor wages	$ 86,100	$ 80,500	$ 5,600 U
Supplies	23,100	21,000	2,100 U
Maintenance	137,300	134,000	3,300 U
Utilities	15,700	15,200	500 U
Supervision	38,000	38,000	0
Depreciation	80,000	80,000	0
Total	$380,200	$368,700	$11,500 U

"I just can't understand all of these unfavorable variances," Weston complained to the supervisor of another department. "When the boss called me in, I thought he was going to give me a pat on the back because I know my department worked more efficiently last month than ever before. Instead, he tore me apart. I thought for a minute it might be over the supplies that were stolen out of our warehouse last month. But they only amounted to a couple of hundred dollars, and just look at this report. Everything is unfavorable."

Direct labor wages and supplies are variable costs; supervision and depreciation are fixed costs; and maintenance and utilities are mixed costs. The fixed component of the budgeted maintenance cost is $92,000; the fixed component of the budgeted utilities cost is $11,700.

Required:
1. Evaluate the company's cost control report and explain why the variances were all unfavorable.
2. Using Exhibit 9–8 as your guide, prepare a performance report that will help Mr. Weston's superiors assess how well costs were controlled in the Machining Department.

Cases 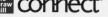 connect

Select cases are available in Connect.

CASE 9–24 Ethics and the Manager LO9–3
Tom Kemper is the controller of the Wichita manufacturing facility of Prudhom Enterprises, Inc.

The annual cost control report is one of the many reports filed with corporate headquarters and is due shortly after the beginning of the new year. Kemper does not like putting work off to the last minute, so just before Christmas he prepared a preliminary draft of the cost control report. Some adjustments would later be required for transactions that occur between Christmas and New Year's Day. A copy of the preliminary draft report, which Kemper completed on December 21, follows:

Wichita Manufacturing Facility Cost Control Report December 21 Preliminary Draft	Actual Results	Flexible Budget	Spending Variances
Labor-hours	18,000	18,000	
Direct labor	$ 326,000	$ 324,000	$ 2,000 U
Power	19,750	18,000	1,750 U
Supplies	105,000	99,000	6,000 U
Equipment depreciation	343,000	332,000	11,000 U
Supervisory salaries	273,000	275,000	2,000 F
Insurance	37,000	37,000	0
Industrial engineering	189,000	210,000	21,000 F
Factory building lease	60,000	60,000	0
Total expenses	$1,352,750	$1,355,000	$ 2,250 F

Melissa Ilianovitch, the general manager at the Wichita facility, asked to see a copy of the report, at which point the following discussion took place:

Ilianovitch: Wow! Almost all of the variances on the report are unfavorable. The only favorable variances are for supervisory salaries and industrial engineering. How did we have an unfavorable variance for depreciation?

Kemper: Do you remember that milling machine that broke down because the wrong lubricant was used by the machine operator?

Ilianovitch: Yes.

Kemper: We couldn't fix it. We had to scrap the machine and buy a new one.

Ilianovitch: This report doesn't look good. I was raked over the coals last year when we had just a few unfavorable variances.

Kemper: I'm afraid the final report is going to look even worse.

Ilianovitch: Oh?

Kemper: The line item for industrial engineering on the report is for work we hired Ferguson Engineering to do for us. The original contract was for $210,000, but we asked them to do some additional work not in the contract. We have to reimburse Ferguson Engineering for the costs of that additional work. The $189,000 in actual costs appearing on the preliminary draft report reflects only their billings up through December 21. The last bill they sent us was on November 28, and they completed the project just last week. Yesterday I got a call from Laura Sunder over at Ferguson and she said they would be sending us a final bill for the project before the end of the year. The total bill, including the reimbursements for the additional work, is going to be . . .

Ilianovitch: I am not sure I want to hear this.

Kemper: $225,000

Ilianovitch: Ouch!

Kemper: The additional work added $15,000 to the cost of the project.

Ilianovitch: I can't turn in a report with an overall unfavorable variance! They'll kill me at corporate headquarters. Call up Laura at Ferguson and ask her not to send the bill until after the first of the year. We have to have that $21,000 favorable variance for industrial engineering on the report.

Required:

What should Tom Kemper do? Explain.

CASE 9–25 Critiquing a Report; Calculating Spending Variances LO9–3, LO9–5

Boyne University offers an extensive continuing education program in numerous cities. For the convenience of its faculty and administrative staff and to save costs, the university operates a motor pool. The motor pool's monthly planning budget is based on operating 20 vehicles; however, for the month of March, the university purchased one additional vehicle. The motor pool furnishes gasoline, oil, and other supplies for its automobiles. A mechanic does routine maintenance and minor repairs. Major repairs are performed at a nearby commercial garage.

The following cost control report shows actual operating costs for March compared to that month's planning budget.

Boyne University Motor Pool			
Cost Control Report			
For the Month Ended March 31			
	March Actual	Planning Budget	(Over) Under Budget
Miles	63,000	50,000	
Autos	21	20	
Gasoline	$ 9,350	$ 7,500	$(1,850)
Oil, minor repairs, parts	2,360	2,000	(360)
Outside repairs	1,420	1,500	80
Insurance	2,120	2,000	(120)
Salaries and benefits	7,540	7,540	0
Vehicle depreciation	5,250	5,000	(250)
Total	$28,040	$25,540	$(2,500)

The planning budget was based on the following assumptions:
a. $0.15 per mile for gasoline.
b. $0.04 per mile for oil, minor repairs, and parts.
c. $75 per automobile per month for outside repairs.
d. $100 per automobile per month for insurance.
e. $7,540 per month for salaries and benefits.
f. $250 per automobile per month for depreciation.

The supervisor of the motor pool is unhappy with the report, claiming it paints an unfair picture of the motor pool's performance.

Required:
1. Calculate the spending variances for March. (Hint: Refer to Exhibit 9–7.)
2. What are the deficiencies in the original cost control report? How do your calculations in part (1) above overcome these deficiencies?
    (CMA, adapted)

CASE 9–26 Performance Report with More Than One Cost Driver LO9–2, LO9–3, LO9–5, LO9–6
The Little Theatre is a nonprofit organization that stages plays for children. The theater has a very small full-time professional administrative staff. Through a special arrangement with the actors' union, actors and directors rehearse without pay and are paid only for actual performances.

The Little Theatre planned to put on six different productions with a total of 108 performances. For example, one of the productions was *Peter Rabbit,* which had a six-week run with three performances on each weekend. The costs from the current year's planning budget appear below:

The Little Theatre	
Costs from the Planning Budget	
For the Year Ended December 31	
Budgeted number of productions	6
Budgeted number of performances	108
Actors and directors wages	$216,000
Stagehands wages	32,400
Ticket booth personnel and ushers wages	16,200
Scenery, costumes, and props	108,000
Theater hall rent	54,000
Printed programs	27,000
Publicity	12,000
Administrative expenses	43,200
Total	$508,800

Some of the costs vary with the number of productions, some vary with the number of performances, and some are fixed. The costs of scenery, costumes, props, and publicity vary with the number of productions. It doesn't make any difference how many times *Peter Rabbit* is performed, the cost of the scenery is the same. Likewise, the cost of publicizing a play with posters and radio commercials is the same whether there are 10, 20, or 30 performances. On the other hand, the wages of the actors, directors, stagehands, ticket booth personnel, and ushers vary with the number of performances. Similarly, the costs of renting the hall and printing the programs vary with the number of performances. For administrative expenses, 75 percent of the budgeted costs are fixed, 15 percent depend on the number of productions staged, and the remaining 10 percent depend on the number of performances.

After the beginning of the year, the theater's board of directors authorized expanding the theater's program to seven productions and a total of 168 performances. Not surprisingly, actual costs were considerably higher than the planning budget. (Grants from donors and ticket sales were also correspondingly higher but are not shown here.) Data concerning the actual costs were as follows:

The Little Theatre Actual Costs For the Year Ended December 31	
Actual number of productions	7
Actual number of performances	168
Actors and directors wages	$341,800
Stagehands wages	49,700
Ticket booth personnel and ushers wages	25,900
Scenery, costumes, and props	130,600
Theater hall rent	78,000
Printed programs	38,300
Publicity	15,100
Administrative expenses	47,500
Total	$726,900

Required:

1. Using Exhibit 9–11 as your guide, prepare a flexible budget performance report for the year.
2. If you were on the board of directors, would you be pleased with how well costs were controlled during the year? Why, or why not?
3. The cost formulas provide figures for the average cost per production and average cost per performance. How accurate do you think these figures would be for predicting the cost of a new production or an additional performance of an existing production?

Chapter 10

lighthouse image: Martin73/Shutterstock;
big data image: INGARA/Shutterstock

LEARNING OBJECTIVES

After studying Chapter 10, you should be able to:

LO10–1 Compute the direct materials price and quantity variances and explain their significance.

LO10–2 Compute the direct labor rate and efficiency variances and explain their significance.

LO10–3 Compute the variable manufacturing overhead rate and efficiency variances and explain their significance.

LO10–4 (Appendix 10A) Compute and interpret the fixed overhead budget and volume variances.

LO10–5 (Appendix 10B) Prepare an income statement using a standard cost system.

 Data Analytics Exercise available in Connect to complement this chapter

Standard Costs and Variances

Johnny Nunez/WireImage/Getty Images

ENTREPRENEUR SPOTLIGHT

After completing a 12-year career as a professional basketball player, Ulysses "Junior" Bridgeman and two colleagues started Bridgeman Foods by purchasing five underperforming Wendy's restaurants. Eventually, the Bridgeman Hospitality Group grew to more than 300 restaurants including various brands, such as Wendy's, Chili's, Perkins, and Fazoli's. In 2017, Bridgeman divested his ownership stake in the Bridgeman Hospitality Group and became the President and CEO of Coca-Cola Heartland, which owns a production facility in Lenexa, Kansas, and 18 regional distribution centers.

Applying Managerial Accounting

Restaurant owners pay very close attention to ingredient (materials) quantity standards. For example, if Wendy's beef patties are too large, it will cause cost overruns that lower profits, whereas if the patties are too small, it will lead to dissatisfied customers, which in turn lowers sales and profits. Managing the purchase price of ingredients also requires managerial attention. While it may be tempting to conclude that lower purchase prices always lead to higher profits, that is not true. An excessive focus on driving down the price of ingredients may lower product quality, increase storage costs, and increase spoilage, all of which adversely affect profits.

Serving All Stakeholders

Coca-Cola Heartland's website says, "our culture is built around putting people first, and that starts with continuing to embrace and serve our local community." The company focuses its philanthropic efforts in four areas: education, health and well-being, diversity, and the environment. It supports numerous organizations such as Boys & Girls Clubs of America, Susan G. Komen, Special Olympics Illinois, the Negro League's Baseball Museum, and the Veterans Community Project. ∎

Sources: Jack Dougherty, "Junior Bridgeman Used Fast Food to Become One of the 5 Richest Former Athletes in the World," *Sportscasting,* April 21, 2020; https://www.celebritynetworth.com/richest-athletes/nba/junior-bridgeman-net-worth/; https://bfcompanies.com/bridgemanhospitality/#!company; https://www.heartlandcocacola.com/community

In the last chapter, we studied how flexible budget variances help organizations compare actual results to the budget. The net operating income activity variance explains how changes in the level of activity affect profits. The revenue and spending variances indicate how well revenues and costs were controlled given the actual level of activity. However, with regard to spending variances, we can often get even more detail about how well costs were controlled. For example, at Rick's Hairstyling, an unfavorable spending variance for hairstyling supplies could be due to paying too much for the supplies or using too many supplies, or some combination of the two. In this chapter, we use standard costs to decompose spending variances into two parts—a part focused on acquisition prices and a part focused on efficient resource usage.

Standard Costs—Setting the Stage

A *standard* is a benchmark for measuring performance. For example, auto service centers like Firestone and Midas often set labor time standards for the completion of certain tasks, such as installing a carburetor or doing a valve job. Fast-food outlets such as McDonald's and Subway have exacting standards for the price and quantity of meat going into a sandwich. Your doctor evaluates your weight using standards for individuals of your age, height, and gender. The buildings we live in conform to standards set in building codes.

Standards are also used in managerial accounting where they relate to the *quantity* and acquisition *price* of inputs used in manufacturing goods or providing services. *Quantity standards* specify how much of an input should be used to make a product or provide a service. *Price standards* specify how much should be paid for each unit of the input. If either the quantity or acquisition price of an input departs significantly from the standard, managers investigate the discrepancy to find the cause of the problem and eliminate it.

Next we'll demonstrate how companies establish quantity and price standards for direct materials, direct labor, and variable manufacturing overhead, and then we'll discuss how those standards are used to calculate variances and manage operations.

> **MANAGERIAL ACCOUNTING IN ACTION**
> **THE WRAP-UP**
>
> Colonial Pewter Company

The Colonial Pewter Company makes only one product—an elaborate reproduction of an 18th century pewter statue. The statue is made largely by hand, using traditional metalworking tools. Consequently, the manufacturing process is labor intensive and requires a high level of skill.

Colonial Pewter recently expanded its workforce to take advantage of unexpected demand for the statue as a gift. The company started with a small cadre of experienced pewter workers but had to hire less experienced workers as a result of the expansion. The president of the company, J. D. Wriston, called a meeting to discuss production problems. Attending the meeting are Tom Kuchel, the production manager; Janet Warner, the purchasing manager; and Terry Sherman, the corporate controller.

J. D.: I've got a feeling we aren't getting the production we should out of our new people.

Tom: Give us a chance. Some of the new people have been with the company for less than a month.

Janet: Let me add production seems to be wasting an awful lot of material—particularly pewter. That stuff is very expensive.

Tom: What about the shipment of defective pewter you bought—the one with the iron contamination? That caused us major problems.

Janet: How was I to know it was off-grade? Besides, it was a great deal.

J. D.: Calm down, everybody. Let's get the facts before we start attacking each other.

Tom: I agree. The more facts the better.

J. D.: Okay, Terry, it's your turn. Facts are the controller's department.

Terry: I'm afraid I can't provide the answers off the top of my head, but if you give me a week I can set up a system that answers questions relating to worker productivity, material waste, and input prices.

J. D.: Let's mark it on our calendars.

Setting Direct Materials Standards

Terry Sherman's first task was to prepare quantity and price standards for the company's only significant raw material, pewter ingots. The **standard quantity per unit** defines the amount of direct materials that should be used for each unit of finished product, including an allowance for normal inefficiencies, such as scrap and spoilage.[1] After consulting with the production manager, Tom Kuchel, Terry set the quantity standard for pewter at 3.0 pounds per statue.

The **standard price per unit** defines the price that should be paid for each unit of direct materials, and it should reflect the final, delivered cost of those materials. After consulting with purchasing manager Janet Warner, Terry set the standard price of pewter at $4.00 per pound.

Once Terry established the quantity and price standards, he computed the standard direct materials cost per statue as follows:

$$3.0 \text{ pounds per statue} \times \$4.00 \text{ per pound} = \$12.00 \text{ per statue}$$

IN BUSINESS

Fabrice Dimier/Bloomberg/Getty Images

MANAGING MATERIALS AND LABOR

Schneider Electric's Oxford, Ohio, plant manufactures *busways* that transport electricity from its point of entry into a building to remote locations throughout the building. The plant's managers pay close attention to direct material costs because they are more than half of the plant's total manufacturing costs. To help control scrap rates for direct materials such as copper, steel, and aluminum, the accounting department prepares direct materials quantity variances. These variances compare the amount of direct materials that were actually used to the standard quantity of direct materials that should have been used to make a product (according to computations by the plant's engineers). Keeping a close eye on these differences helps to identify and deal with the causes of excessive scrap, such as an inadequately trained machine operator, poor-quality raw material inputs, or a malfunctioning machine.

Because direct labor is also a significant component of the plant's total manufacturing costs, the management team daily monitors the direct labor efficiency variance. This variance compares the actual amount of labor time used to the standard amount of labor time allowed to make a product. When idle workers cause an unfavorable labor efficiency variance, managers temporarily move workers from departments with slack to departments with a backlog of work to be done.

Source: Author's conversation with Doug Taylor, plant controller, Schneider Electric's Oxford, Ohio, plant.

Setting Direct Labor Standards

Direct labor quantity and price standards are expressed in terms of labor-hours or a labor rate. The **standard hours per unit** defines the amount of direct labor-hours that should be used to produce one unit of finished goods. One approach used to determine this

---

[1] Although companies often create "practical" rather than "ideal" materials quantity standards that include allowances for normal inefficiencies such as scrap, spoilage, and rejects, this practice is often criticized because it contradicts the zero defects goal that underlies many process improvement programs. If these types of allowances are built into materials quantity standards, they should be periodically reviewed and reduced over time to reflect improved processes, better training, and better equipment.

standard is for an industrial engineer to do a time and motion study, actually clocking the time required for each task. Throughout the chapter, we'll assume that "tight but attainable" labor standards are used rather than "ideal" standards that can only be attained by the most skilled and efficient employees working at peak effort 100 percent of the time. Therefore, after consulting with the production manager and considering reasonable allowances for breaks, personal needs of employees, cleanup, and machine downtime, Terry set the standard hours per unit at 0.50 direct labor-hour per statue.

The **standard rate per hour** defines the company's expected direct labor wage rate per hour, including employment taxes and fringe benefits. Using wage records and in consultation with the production manager, Terry Sherman established a standard rate per hour of $22.00. This standard rate reflects the expected "mix" of workers, even though the actual hourly wage rates may vary somewhat from individual to individual due to differing skills or seniority.

Once Terry established the time and rate standards, he computed the standard direct labor cost per statue as follows:

0.50 direct labor-hour per statue × $22.00 per direct labor-hour = $11.00 per statue

Setting Variable Manufacturing Overhead Standards

As with direct labor, the quantity and price standards for variable manufacturing overhead are expressed in terms of hours and a rate. The *standard hours per unit* for variable overhead measures the amount of the allocation base from a company's predetermined overhead rate required to produce one unit of finished goods. In the case of Colonial Pewter, we will assume the company uses direct labor-hours as the allocation base in its predetermined overhead rate. Therefore, the standard hours per unit for variable overhead is exactly the same as the standard hours per unit for direct labor—0.50 direct labor-hour per statue.

The *standard rate per unit* that a company expects to pay for variable overhead equals *the variable portion of the predetermined overhead rate*. At Colonial Pewter, the variable portion of the predetermined overhead rate is $6.00 per direct labor-hour. Therefore, Terry computed the standard variable manufacturing overhead cost per statue as follows:

0.50 direct labor-hour per statue × $6.00 per direct-labor hour = $3.00 per statue

This $3.00 per unit cost for variable manufacturing overhead appears along with direct materials ($12 per unit) and direct labor ($11 per unit) on the *standard cost card* in Exhibit 10–1. A **standard cost card** shows the standard quantity (or hours) and standard price (or rate) of the inputs required to produce a unit of a specific product. The **standard cost per unit** for all three variable manufacturing costs is computed the same way. The standard quantity (or hours) per unit is multiplied by the standard price (or rate) per unit to obtain the standard cost per unit.

Inputs	(1) Standard Quantity or Hours	(2) Standard Price or Rate	Standard Cost (1) × (2)
Direct materials	3.0 pounds	$4.00 per pound	$12.00
Direct labor	0.50 hour	$22.00 per hour	11.00
Variable manufacturing overhead	0.50 hour	$6.00 per hour	3.00
Total standard cost per unit			$26.00

EXHIBIT 10–1
Standard Cost Card—Variable Manufacturing Costs

Using Standards in Flexible Budgets

Once Terry Sherman created the standard cost card in Exhibit 10–1, he gathered the following data for the month of June to enable calculating his variances:

Planned output in June	2,100 statues
Actual output in June	2,000 statues
Actual direct materials cost in June*	$24,700
Actual direct labor cost in June	$22,680
Actual variable manufacturing overhead cost in June	$7,140

*There were no beginning or ending inventories of raw materials in June; all materials purchased were used.

Using the above data and the standard cost data from Exhibit 10–1, Terry computed the spending and activity variances shown in Exhibit 10–2. Notice the actual results and flexible budget columns are each based on the actual output of 2,000 statues. The planning budget column is based on the planned output of 2,100 statues. The standard costs of $12.00 per unit for materials, $11.00 per unit for direct labor, and $3.00 per unit for variable manufacturing overhead are each multiplied by the actual output of 2,000 statues to compute the amounts in the flexible budget column. For example, the standard direct labor cost per unit of $11.00 multiplied by 2,000 statues equals the direct labor flexible budget of $22,000. Similarly, the three standard variable cost figures are multiplied by 2,100 statues to compute the amounts in the planning budget column. For example, the direct labor cost for the planning budget is $23,100 (= $11.00 per unit × 2,100 units).

The spending variances in Exhibit 10–2 are computed by taking actual results minus the flexible budget. For all three variable manufacturing costs, this computation results in a positive number because the actual cost incurred to produce 2,000 statues exceeds the standard cost allowed for 2,000 statues. Because, in all three instances, the actual cost incurred exceeds the standard cost allowed for the actual level of output, the variance is labeled unfavorable (U). Had any of the actual costs incurred been less than the standard cost allowed, the corresponding variances would have been labeled favorable (F).

The activity variances shown in the exhibit are computed by taking the flexible budget minus the planning budget. For all three variable manufacturing costs, these computations result in negative numbers and what are labeled as favorable (F) variances. The label favorable is used in these instances because the standard cost allowed for the actual output is less than the standard cost allowed for the planned output. Had the actual level of activity been greater than the planned level of activity, all computations would have resulted in positive numbers and unfavorable (U) activity variances.

EXHIBIT 10–2

Flexible Budget Performance Report for Variable Manufacturing Costs

Colonial Pewter
Flexible Budget Performance Report—Variable Manufacturing Costs
For the Month Ended June 30

	Actual Results	Spending Variances	Flexible Budget	Activity Variances	Planning Budget
Statues produced (q)	2,000		2,000		2,100
Direct materials ($12.00q)......................	$24,700	$700 U	$24,000	$1,200 F	$25,200
Direct labor ($11.00q)	$22,680	$680 U	$22,000	$1,100 F	$23,100
Variable manufacturing overhead ($3.00q)	$7,140	$1,140 U	$6,000	$300 F	$6,300

While the performance report in Exhibit 10–2 is useful, it would be more useful if the spending variances could be broken down into their price-related and quantity-related components. For example, the direct materials spending variance in the report is $700 unfavorable. This means that, given the actual level of production, direct materials costs were too high by $700—at least according to the standard costs. Was this due to higher-than-expected prices for materials, or using too much material?

A General Model for Standard Cost Variance Analysis

Standard cost variance analysis decomposes spending variances from the flexible budget into two elements—one due to the price paid for the input and the other due to the amount of the input used. A **price variance** is the difference between the actual amount paid for an input and the standard amount that should have been paid, multiplied by the actual amount of the input purchased. A **quantity variance** is the difference between how much of an input was actually used and how much should have been used for the actual level of output and is stated in dollar terms using the standard price of the input.

Exhibit 10–3 presents a general model that decomposes the spending variance for a variable cost into a *price variance* and a *quantity variance*.[2] Column (1) corresponds with the Actual Results column in Exhibit 10–2. Column (3) corresponds with the Flexible Budget column in Exhibit 10–2. Column (2) has been inserted into Exhibit 10–3 to separate the spending variance into a price variance and a quantity variance.

Three things should be noted from Exhibit 10–3. First, it can be used to compute a price variance and a quantity variance for each of the three variable cost elements—direct materials, direct labor, and variable manufacturing overhead—even though the variances have different names. A price variance is called a *materials price variance* in the case of direct materials, a *labor rate variance* in the case of direct labor, and a *variable overhead*

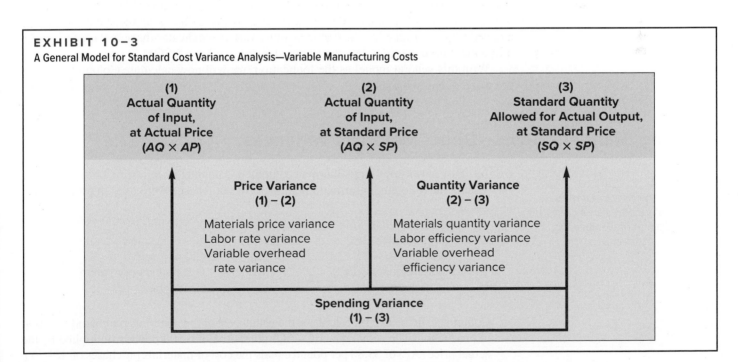

EXHIBIT 10–3
A General Model for Standard Cost Variance Analysis—Variable Manufacturing Costs

---

[2] This general model can always be used to compute direct labor and variable manufacturing overhead variances. However, it can be used to compute direct materials variances only when the actual quantity of materials purchased equals the actual quantity of materials used in production. Later in the chapter, we will explain how to compute direct materials variances when these quantities differ.

rate variance in the case of variable manufacturing overhead. A quantity variance is called a *materials quantity variance* in the case of direct materials, a *labor efficiency variance* in the case of direct labor, and a *variable overhead efficiency variance* in the case of variable manufacturing overhead.

Second, all three columns in the exhibit are based on the *actual amount of output* produced during the period. Even the flexible budget column (column 3) shows the standard cost allowed for the *actual amount of output* produced during the period. The key to understanding the flexible budget column in Exhibit 10–3 is to grasp the meaning of the term *standard quantity allowed (SQ)*. The **standard quantity allowed** (when computing direct materials variances) or **standard hours allowed** (when computing direct labor and variable manufacturing overhead variances) refers to the amount of an input *that should have been used* to manufacture the actual output. It is computed by multiplying the actual output by the standard quantity (or hours) per unit. The standard quantity (or hours) allowed is then multiplied by the standard price (or rate) to obtain the total cost according to the flexible budget. For example, if a company actually produced 100 units and its standard quantity of direct materials per unit is 5 pounds, then its *standard quantity allowed (SQ)* would be 500 pounds (= 100 units × 5 pounds per unit). If the company's standard cost per pound is $2.00, then the direct materials cost in its flexible budget would be $1,000 (= 500 pounds × $2.00 per pound).

Third, the spending, price, and quantity variances—regardless of what they are called—are computed exactly the same way regardless of whether one is dealing with direct materials, direct labor, or variable manufacturing overhead. The spending variance takes the cost in column (1) and subtracts the cost in column (3). The price variance takes the cost in column (1) and subtracts the cost in column (2). The quantity variance takes the cost in column (2) and subtracts the cost in column (3). In all of these calculations, a positive number is labeled unfavorable (U) and a negative number is labeled favorable (F). An unfavorable price variance indicates the actual price (AP) per unit of the input was greater than the standard price (SP). A favorable price variance indicates the actual price (AP) of the input was less than the standard price (SP). An unfavorable quantity variance indicates the actual quantity (AQ) of the input used was greater than the standard quantity allowed (SQ). Conversely, a favorable quantity variance indicates the actual quantity (AQ) of the input used was less than the standard quantity allowed (SQ).

With this general model as the foundation, we will now calculate Colonial Pewter's price and quantity variances.

Using Standard Costs—Direct Materials Variances

LO10–1

Compute the direct materials price and quantity variances and explain their significance.

Exhibit 10–4 shows how Terry Sherman computed Colonial Pewter's direct materials variances using the following information (all materials purchased were used in production)[3]:

Actual output in June	2,000 statues
Standard price (SP)	$4.00 per pound
Actual price (AP)	$3.80 per pound
Standard quantity (SQ)	3.00 pounds per statue
Actual quantity (AQ)	6,500 pounds

- Column (1) in the exhibit calculates the actual cost of the materials purchased and used in production. The actual quantity (AQ) purchased of 6,500 pounds multiplied by the actual price (AP) of $3.80 per pound equals the cost of materials purchases of $24,700.

---

[3] Throughout this section, we assume zero beginning and ending inventories of materials and that all materials purchased during the period are used during that period. The more general case in which there are beginning and ending inventories of materials and materials are not necessarily used during the period in which they are purchased is considered later in the chapter.

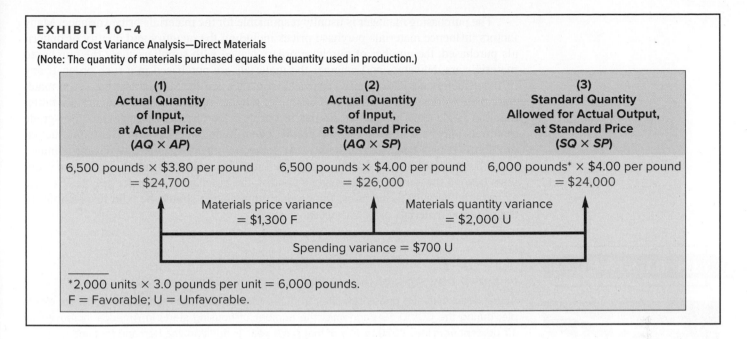

EXHIBIT 10–4
Standard Cost Variance Analysis—Direct Materials
(Note: The quantity of materials purchased equals the quantity used in production.)

(1) Actual Quantity of Input, at Actual Price (AQ × AP)	(2) Actual Quantity of Input, at Standard Price (AQ × SP)	(3) Standard Quantity Allowed for Actual Output, at Standard Price (SQ × SP)
6,500 pounds × $3.80 per pound = $24,700	6,500 pounds × $4.00 per pound = $26,000	6,000 pounds* × $4.00 per pound = $24,000

Materials price variance = $1,300 F

Materials quantity variance = $2,000 U

Spending variance = $700 U

*2,000 units × 3.0 pounds per unit = 6,000 pounds.
F = Favorable; U = Unfavorable.

- Column (2) calculates the amount that should have been paid for the actual quantity purchased. The actual quantity (AQ) purchased of 6,500 pounds multiplied by the standard price (SP) of $4.00 per pound equals the total cost of $26,000.
- Column (3) uses a two-step process to calculate the standard cost allowed for the actual number of statues produced. The first step calculates the standard quantity allowed (SQ) using the following equation:

Standard quantity allowed = Actual output × Standard quantity per unit

- The actual output of 2,000 statues multiplied by the standard quantity per unit of 3.00 pounds equals the standard quantity allowed (SQ) of 6,000 pounds. The second step multiplies the standard quantity allowed (SQ) of 6,000 pounds by the standard price (SP) of $4.00 per pound to obtain the standard cost allowed for the actual output of $24,000.
- The difference between the $24,700 actually spent (column 1) and the $24,000 that should have been spent (column 3) is the spending variance of $700 U. This variance is unfavorable (denoted by U) because the amount actually spent exceeds what should have been spent for materials purchases. Also, note this variance agrees with the direct materials spending variance in Exhibit 10–2.
- Calculating materials price and quantity variances will help Colonial Pewter better understand the portions of its $700 U spending variance caused by deviating from its price and quantity standards.

Materials Price Variance

The difference between the $24,700 in column (1) and the $26,000 in column (2) is the *materials price variance* of $1,300 F. A **materials price variance** measures the difference between a direct material's actual price per unit and its standard price per unit, multiplied by the actual quantity purchased. In this instance, the materials price variance is favorable (denoted by F) because the actual price of $3.80 per pound is $0.20 less than the standard price of $4.00. Because 6,500 pounds were purchased, the total amount of the variance is $1,300 (= $0.20 per pound × 6,500 pounds). If the actual purchase price per pound had exceeded the standard price, the materials price variance would have been unfavorable (U).

The purchasing manager is usually responsible for the materials price variance. Many factors influence materials purchase prices including the quantity and quality of materials purchased, the number of purchase orders placed with suppliers, how the purchased materials are delivered, and whether the materials are purchased in a rush order. If any of these factors deviates from what was assumed when the standards were set, a materials price variance will arise. For example, purchasing second-grade materials rather than top-grade materials may result in a favorable price variance because the lower-grade materials may be less costly. However, the lower-grade materials may create production problems. It also bears emphasizing that someone other than the purchasing manager could be responsible for a materials price variance. For example, due to production problems beyond the purchasing manager's control, the purchasing manager may have to use express delivery. In these cases, the production manager should be held responsible for the resulting materials price variances.

IN BUSINESS

Steven Belanger/Shutterstock

LUMBER PRICES SOAR DURING THE COVID-19 PANDEMIC

Actual direct materials prices can differ from their standard prices for many reasons. For example, during the COVID-19 pandemic, the number of housing starts in America increased by 17 percent from May 2020 to July of that same year. In addition, the demand for lumber further increased as home-bound "do-it-yourselfers" and restaurant owners began buying lumber for construction projects, such as building outdoor decks and dining areas. Consequently, the price of lumber soared by 130 percent, which in turn raised the price of a newly constructed single-family home by more than $16,000.

Source: Michael Flood, "Why Strong Demand and Tight Supply Have Caused Lumber Prices to Soar," New England Building Supply, https://nebldgsupply.com/strong-demand-and-tight-supply-have-caused-lumber-prices-to-soar/.

Materials Quantity Variance

Referring again to Exhibit 10–4, the difference between the $26,000 in column (2) and the $24,000 in column (3) is the *materials quantity variance* of $2,000 U. The **materials quantity variance** measures the difference between the actual quantity of materials used in production and the standard quantity of materials allowed for the actual output, multiplied by the standard price per unit of materials. In this instance, the materials quantity variance is unfavorable (denoted by U) because the actual quantity of 6,500 pounds is 500 pounds greater than the standard quantity allowed of 6,000 pounds. Because the standard price is $4.00 per pound, the total amount of the variance is $2,000 (= 500 pounds × $4.00 per pound). If the actual quantity used had been less than the standard quantity allowed, the variance would have been favorable (F).

Why is the standard price of pewter, rather than the actual price, used in this calculation? The production manager is ordinarily responsible for the materials quantity variance. If the actual price were used in the calculation of the materials quantity variance, the production manager's performance evaluation would be unfairly influenced by the efficiency or inefficiency of the purchasing manager.

Excessive materials usage can result from many factors, including faulty machines, inferior materials quality, untrained workers, and poor supervision. Generally speaking, it is the responsibility of the production manager to see that material usage is kept in line with standards. There may be times, however, when the *purchasing* manager is responsible for an unfavorable materials quantity variance. For example, if the purchasing manager buys inferior materials at a lower price, the materials may be unsuitable for use and may result in excessive waste. Thus, the purchasing manager rather than the production manager would be responsible for the materials quantity variance.

Exhibit 10–5 shows an alternative method for computing Colonial Pewter's direct materials variances using the equations-based approach.

Materials Price Variance:

Materials price variance = $(AQ \times AP) - (AQ \times SP)$
Materials price variance = $AQ(AP - SP)$
Materials price variance = 6,500 pounds ($3.80 per pound − $4.00 per pound)
Materials price variance = $1,300 F

Materials Quantity Variance:

Materials quantity variance = $(AQ \times SP) - (SQ \times SP)$
Materials quantity variance = $SP(AQ - SQ)$
Materials quantity variance = $4.00 per pound (6,500 pounds − 6,000 pounds)
Materials quantity variance = $2,000 U

where:
AQ = Actual quantity of inputs purchased and used in production
SQ = Standard quantity of inputs allowed for the actual output
AP = Actual price per unit of the input
SP = Standard price per unit of the input

EXHIBIT 10−5
Direct Materials Variances:
The Equations-Based Approach

COMMUNICATING WITH DATA VISUALIZATIONS

Diagnostic analytics answer the question: Why did it happen? This visualization is based on Exhibit 10–4 and explains why Colonial Pewter's actual raw material purchases ($24,700) differed from the amount allowed for the actual output ($24,000). The company paid $3.80 per pound, which is $0.20 less than the standard price of $4.00. Because the company purchased 6,500 pounds, its materials price variance is $1,300 F (= $0.20 × 6,500 pounds), or 5.0 percent of the amount that should have been paid according to the standard price (= $1,300 ÷ $26,000).

Referring again to Exhibit 10–4, the company used 6,500 pounds in production, which is 500 more pounds than the standard allowance of 6,000 pounds. Because the company's standard price per pound is $4.00, its materials quantity variance is $2,000 U (= 500 pounds × $4.00 per pound), or 8.3 percent of the amount that should have been paid according to the standard price (= $2,000 ÷ $24,000).

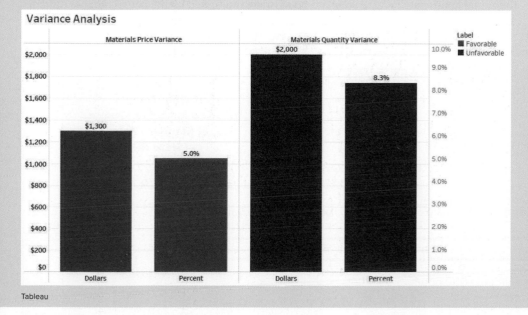

Variance Analysis

Tableau

Using Standard Costs—Direct Labor Variances

LO10–2

Compute the direct labor rate and efficiency variances and explain their significance.

Exhibit 10–6 shows how Terry Sherman computed Colonial Pewter's direct labor variances using the following information:

Actual output in June.....................	2,000 statues
Standard rate (SR)	$22.00 per hour
Actual rate (AR).........................	$21.60 per hour
Standard hours (SH).....................	0.50 hour per statue
Actual hours (AH).......................	1,050 hours

- Column (1) in the exhibit calculates the actual labor cost applied to production. The actual hours (AH) used of 1,050 hours multiplied by the actual rate (AR) of $21.60 per hour equals the actual labor cost of $22,680.
- Column (2) calculates the amount that should have been paid for the actual hours worked. The actual hours (AH) used of 1,050 hours multiplied by the standard rate (SR) of $22.00 per hour equals the total cost of $23,100.
- Column (3) uses a two-step process to calculate the standard cost allowed for the actual number of statues produced. The first step calculates the standard hours allowed (SH) using the following equation:

$$\text{Standard hours allowed} = \text{Actual output} \times \text{Standard hours per unit}$$

The actual output of 2,000 statues multiplied by the standard hours per unit of 0.50 hour equals the standard hours allowed (SH) of 1,000 hours. The second step multiplies the standard hours allowed (SH) of 1,000 hours by the standard rate (SR) of $22.00 per hour to obtain the standard cost allowed for the actual output of $22,000.

- The difference between the $22,680 actually paid (column 1) and the $22,000 that should have been paid (column 3) is the spending variance of $680 U. This variance is unfavorable (denoted by U) because the amount actually paid to direct laborers exceeds what should have been paid to them. Also, note this variance agrees with the direct labor spending variance in Exhibit 10–2.

Labor Rate Variance

The difference between the $22,680 in column (1) and the $23,100 in column (2) is the *labor rate variance* of $420 F. The **labor rate variance** measures the difference between the actual hourly rate and the standard hourly rate, multiplied by the actual number of hours

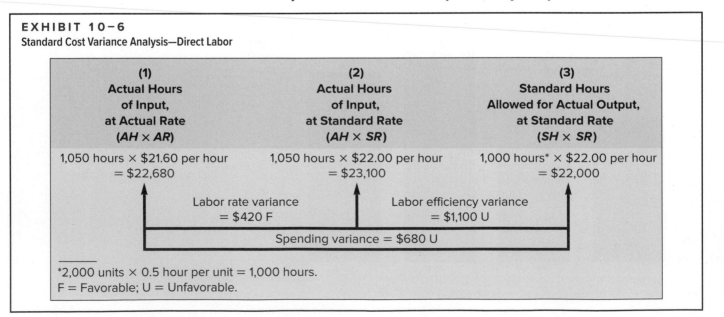

EXHIBIT 10–6
Standard Cost Variance Analysis—Direct Labor

(1) Actual Hours of Input, at Actual Rate (AH × AR)	(2) Actual Hours of Input, at Standard Rate (AH × SR)	(3) Standard Hours Allowed for Actual Output, at Standard Rate (SH × SR)
1,050 hours × $21.60 per hour = $22,680	1,050 hours × $22.00 per hour = $23,100	1,000 hours* × $22.00 per hour = $22,000

Labor rate variance = $420 F

Labor efficiency variance = $1,100 U

Spending variance = $680 U

*2,000 units × 0.5 hour per unit = 1,000 hours.
F = Favorable; U = Unfavorable.

worked during the period. In this case, the labor rate variance is favorable (denoted by F) because the actual hourly rate of $21.60 is $0.40 less than the standard hourly rate of $22.00. Because 1,050 hours were worked, the total amount of the variance is $420 (= $0.40 per hour × 1,050 hours). If the actual hourly rate had been greater than the standard hourly rate, the variance would have been labeled unfavorable (U).

Labor rate variances can arise based on how production supervisors use their direct labor workers. Skilled workers paid high hourly rates may be given duties readily performed by less skilled workers. This will cause an unfavorable labor rate variance because the actual hourly rate of pay will exceed the standard rate specified for the particular task. In contrast, a favorable rate variance would result when workers who are paid at a rate lower than specified in the standard are assigned to the task. However, the lower-paid workers may not be as efficient. Finally, overtime work at premium rates will cause an unfavorable labor rate variance if the overtime premium is charged to the direct labor account.

IN BUSINESS

MANUFACTURERS FACE STIFF COMPETITION FOR WORKERS

During the COVID-19 pandemic, Michigan-based furniture manufacturer Haworth Inc. could not hire enough people to staff its assembly lines at a standard wage rate of $14 per hour. The pandemic-induced labor shortage drastically increased competition for workers, thereby eliminating Haworth's historic wage advantage over service and retail employers. Consequently, the company was losing prospective workers to the likes of Wendy's, who was offering less-demanding work for the same money. In an effort to attract more employees, Haworth raised its compensation to $15 per hour, plus another dollar for the night shift, and added amenities such as a 24-hour gym and holiday gift giveaways.

Source: Austin Hufford and Nora Naughton, "Factory Jobs Go Begging as Wages Fail to Keep Up," *The Wall Street Journal*, June 23, 2021, https://www.wsj.com/articles/wage-gains-at-factories-fall-behind-growth-in-fast-food-11624354200.

Labor Efficiency Variance

Referring back to Exhibit 10–6, the difference between the $23,100 in column (2) and the $22,000 in column (3) is the *labor efficiency variance* of $1,100 U. The **labor efficiency variance** measures the difference between the actual labor-hours used and the standard hours allowed for the actual output, multiplied by the standard hourly rate. For Colonial Pewter, the labor efficiency variance is unfavorable (denoted by U) because the actual hours used of 1,050 hours is 50 hours greater than the standard hours allowed of 1,000 hours. Because the standard hourly rate is $22.00, the total amount of the variance is $1,100 (= 50 hours × $22.00). If the actual hours used were less than the standard hours allowed, the labor efficiency variance would have been favorable.

Possible causes of an unfavorable labor efficiency variance include poorly trained or motivated workers; poor-quality materials, requiring more labor time; faulty equipment, causing breakdowns and work interruptions; and poor supervision of workers. The managers in charge of production would usually be responsible for the labor efficiency variance. However, the purchasing manager could be held responsible if the purchase of poor-quality materials resulted in excessive labor processing time.

Another important cause of an unfavorable labor efficiency variance may be insufficient demand for the company's products. Managers in some companies argue that it is difficult, and perhaps unwise, to constantly adjust the workforce in response to changes in the amount of work to be done. In such companies, the direct labor workforce is essentially fixed in the short run. If demand is insufficient to keep everyone busy, workers are not laid off, which in turn creates an unfavorable labor efficiency variance.

If customer orders are insufficient to keep the workers busy, the work center manager has two options—either accept an unfavorable labor efficiency variance or build inventory. A central lesson of Lean Production is that building inventory with no immediate prospect

EXHIBIT 10–7
Direct Labor Variances:
The Equations-Based Approach

Labor Rate Variance:

Labor rate variance = $(AH \times AR) - (AH \times SR)$
Labor rate variance = $AH(AR - SR)$
Labor rate variance = 1,050 hours ($21.60 per hour − $22.00 per hour)
Labor rate variance = $420 F

Labor Efficiency Variance:

Labor efficiency variance = $(AH \times SR) - (SH \times SR)$
Labor efficiency variance = $SR(AH - SH)$
Labor efficiency variance = $22.00 per hour (1,050 hours − 1,000 hours)
Labor efficiency variance = $1,100 U

where:
AH = Actual quantity of labor-hours used in production
SH = Standard quantity of labor-hours allowed for the actual output
AR = Actual rate per direct labor-hour
SR = Standard rate per direct labor-hour

of sale is a bad idea. Excessive inventory—particularly work in process inventory—leads to high defect rates, obsolete goods, and inefficient operations. As a consequence, when the workforce is fixed in the short term, managers must be cautious about how labor efficiency variances are used. Some experts advocate eliminating labor efficiency variances in such situations—at least for the purposes of motivating and controlling workers on the shop floor.

Exhibit 10–7 shows an alternative method for computing Colonial Pewter's direct labor variances using the equations-based approach.

IN BUSINESS

DEERE SETTLES FIRST LABOR STRIKE IN 35 YEARS

There are numerous reasons why a company's materials and labor standards change over time. For example, when Deere & Company settled its first labor strike in 35 years, it agreed to a 10 percent pay raise and $8,500 bonus for each union employee as well as pay raises for its non-union employees. Analysts estimate that labor accounts for 15 percent of Deere's cost of goods sold and the results of its settlement will lower Deere's operating margin by about 1 percent. The settlement will also increase the company's standard hourly labor rate and the standard manufacturing cost incurred to make its John Deere–branded agricultural equipment.

Source: Bob Tita, "Deere Puts Effort into Rebuilding Inventory," *The Wall Street Journal*, November 23, 2021, pp. B1–B2.

Using Standard Costs—Variable Manufacturing Overhead Variances

LO10–3
Compute the variable manufacturing overhead rate and efficiency variances and explain their significance.

Exhibit 10–8 shows how Terry Sherman computed Colonial Pewter's variable manufacturing variances using the following information (the company's predetermined overhead rate uses direct labor-hours as the allocation base):

Actual output in June	2,000 statues
Standard rate (SR)	$6.00 per hour
Standard hours (SH)	0.50 hour per statue
Actual hours (AH)	1,050 hours
Actual variable manufacturing overhead	$7,140

EXHIBIT 10–8
Standard Cost Variance Analysis—Variable Manufacturing Overhead

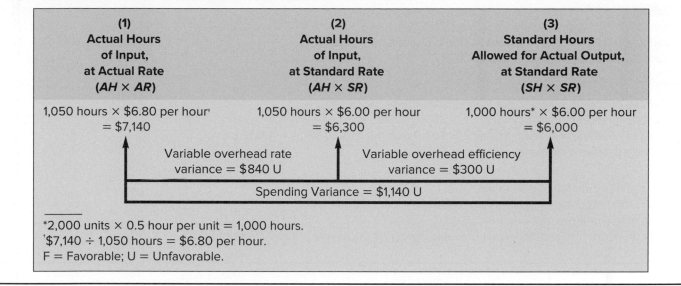

(1) Actual Hours of Input, at Actual Rate (AH × AR)	(2) Actual Hours of Input, at Standard Rate (AH × SR)	(3) Standard Hours Allowed for Actual Output, at Standard Rate (SH × SR)
1,050 hours × $6.80 per hour† = $7,140	1,050 hours × $6.00 per hour = $6,300	1,000 hours* × $6.00 per hour = $6,000

Variable overhead rate variance = $840 U

Variable overhead efficiency variance = $300 U

Spending Variance = $1,140 U

*2,000 units × 0.5 hour per unit = 1,000 hours.
†$7,140 ÷ 1,050 hours = $6.80 per hour.
F = Favorable; U = Unfavorable.

- Column (1) in the exhibit shows the actual variable manufacturing overhead cost for the month of $7,140. This amount divided by the actual labor-hours (AH) of 1,050 hours equals the actual variable manufacturing overhead cost per labor-hour of $6.80.
- Column (2) calculates the variable overhead cost that should have been incurred for the actual hours worked. The actual hours (AH) used of 1,050 hours multiplied by the standard rate (SR) of $6.00 per hour equals the total cost of $6,300.
- Column (3) uses a two-step process to calculate the standard cost allowed for the actual number of statues produced. The first step calculates the standard hours allowed (SH) using the following equation:

$$\text{Standard hours allowed} = \text{Actual output} \times \text{Standard hours per unit}$$

The actual output of 2,000 statues multiplied by the standard hours per unit of 0.50 hour equals the standard hours allowed (SH) of 1,000 hours. The second step multiplies the standard hours allowed (SH) of 1,000 hours by the standard rate (SR) of $6.00 per hour to obtain the standard cost allowed for the actual output of $6,000.
- The difference between the $7,140 actually incurred (column 1) and the $6,000 that should have been incurred (column 3) is the spending variance of $1,140 U. This variance is unfavorable (denoted by U) because the actual variable overhead cost exceeds what should have been incurred. Also, note this variance agrees with the variable manufacturing spending variance in Exhibit 10–2.

Variable Manufacturing Overhead Rate and Efficiency Variances

The difference between the $7,140 in column (1) and the $6,300 in column (2) is the *variable overhead rate variance* of $840 U. The **variable overhead rate variance** measures the difference between the actual variable overhead cost incurred and the standard cost that should have been incurred based on the actual activity. The difference between the $6,300 in column (2) and the $6,000 in column (3) is the *variable overhead efficiency variance* of $300 U. The **variable overhead efficiency variance** measures the difference between the actual level of activity and the standard activity allowed for the actual output, multiplied by the variable part of the predetermined overhead rate.

For Colonial Pewter the variable overhead efficiency variance is unfavorable (denoted by U) because the actual hours used of 1,050 hours is 50 hours greater than the standard

EXHIBIT 10-9
Variable Manufacturing Overhead Variances: The Equations-Based Approach

Variable Overhead Rate Variance:

Variable overhead rate variance = $(AH \times AR) - (AH \times SR)$
Variable overhead rate variance = $AH(AR - SR)$
Variable overhead rate variance = 1,050 hours ($6.80 - $6.00)
Variable overhead rate variance = $840 U

Variable Overhead Efficiency Variance:

Variable overhead efficiency variance = $(AH \times SR) - (SH \times SR)$
Variable overhead efficiency variance = $SR(AH - SH)$
Variable overhead efficiency variance = $6.00 per hour (1,050 hours − 1,000 hours)
Variable overhead efficiency variance = $300 U

where:
AH = Actual quantity of labor-hours used in production
SH = Standard quantity of labor-hours allowed for the actual output
AR = Actual rate per labor-hour
SR = Standard rate per labor-hour (Variable portion of the predetermined overhead rate)

hours allowed of 1,000 hours. Because the standard hourly rate is $6.00, the total amount of the variance is $300 (= 50 hours × $6.00). If the actual hours used were less than the standard hours allowed, the variable overhead efficiency variance would have been favorable.

The variable overhead efficiency variance is calculated the same way as the direct labor efficiency variance except for one detail—the rate used to translate the variance into dollars. In both cases, the variance is the difference between the actual hours worked and the standard hours allowed for the actual output. In the case of the direct labor efficiency variance, this difference is multiplied by the standard direct labor rate. In the case of the variable overhead efficiency variance, this difference is multiplied by the variable portion of the predetermined overhead rate. So when direct labor is used as the overhead allocation base, whenever the direct labor efficiency variance is favorable, the variable overhead efficiency variance will also be favorable. And whenever the direct labor efficiency variance is unfavorable, the variable overhead efficiency variance will be unfavorable. Indeed, the variable overhead efficiency variance really doesn't tell us anything about how efficiently overhead resources were used. It depends solely on how efficiently direct labor was used.

Exhibit 10–9 shows how to compute Colonial Pewter's variable overhead variances using the equations-based approach.

In preparation for the scheduled meeting to discuss his analysis of Colonial Pewter's standard costs and variances, Terry summarized his manufacturing cost variances as follows:

Materials price variance	$ 1,300 F
Materials quantity variance	2,000 U
Labor rate variance	420 F
Labor efficiency variance	1,100 U
Variable overhead rate variance	840 U
Variable overhead efficiency variance	300 U
Total of the variances	$2,520 U

MANAGERIAL ACCOUNTING IN ACTION THE WRAP-UP

Colonial Pewter Company

He distributed these results to the management group of Colonial Pewter, which included J. D. Wriston, the president of the company; Tom Kuchel, the production manager; and Janet Warner, the purchasing manager. J. D. Wriston opened the meeting with the following question:

J. D.:   Terry, would you mind summarizing what you found?
Terry: As you can see, the biggest problems are the unfavorable materials quantity variance of $2,000 and the unfavorable labor efficiency variance of $1,100.

J. D.:　Tom, you're the production boss. What do you think is causing the unfavorable labor efficiency variance?

Tom:　It has to be the inexperience of our new production workers. My plan is to pair up each of the new guys with one of our old-timers and have them work together for a while. It would slow down our older guys a bit, but I'll bet the unfavorable variance disappears and our new workers would learn a lot.

J. D.:　Sounds good. Now, what about that $2,000 unfavorable materials quantity variance?

Terry:　Tom, are the new workers generating a lot of scrap?

Tom:　Yes, I think so. I can watch the scrap closely for a few days to see where it's being generated. If it is the new workers, I can have the old-timers work with them on the problem when I team them up.

J. D.:　Janet, the favorable materials price variance of $1,300 isn't helping us if it is contributing to the unfavorable materials quantity and labor efficiency variances. Let's make sure that our raw material purchases conform to our quality standards.

Janet:　Will do.

J. D.:　Good. Let's reconvene in a few weeks to revisit these variances.

An Important Subtlety in the Materials Variances

Most companies use the *quantity of materials purchased* to compute the materials price variance and the *quantity of materials used* in production to compute the materials quantity variance. There are two reasons for this practice. First, delaying the computation of the price variance until the materials are used would result in less timely variance reports. Second, computing the price variance when the materials are purchased allows materials to be carried in the inventory accounts at their standard cost. This greatly simplifies bookkeeping.

When we computed materials price and quantity variances for Colonial Pewter in Exhibit 10–4, we assumed 6,500 pounds of materials were purchased and used in production. However, it is very common for a company's quantity of materials purchased to differ from its quantity used in production. When this happens, the materials price variance is computed using the *quantity of materials purchased,* whereas the materials quantity variance is computed using the *quantity of materials used* in production.

To illustrate, assume the following information for Colonial Pewter in June:

Actual output in June	2,000 statues
Standard price (SP)	$4.00 per pound
Actual price (AP)	$3.80 per pound
Standard quantity (SQ)	3.00 pounds per statue
Actual quantity purchased (AQ)	7,000 pounds
Actual quantity used (AQ)	6,500 pounds

Exhibit 10–10 shows how to compute the company's materials price and quantity variances using the above information.

- Column (1) in the exhibit calculates the actual cost of materials purchases. The actual quantity (AQ) purchased of 7,000 pounds multiplied by the actual price (AP) of $3.80 per pound equals the total cost of $26,600.
- Column (2) has one set of numbers for calculating the price variance and another set for calculating the quantity variance. The actual quantity (AQ) *purchased* of 7,000 pounds multiplied by the standard price (SP) of $4.00 per pound equals $28,000—the amount that should have been spent for the actual quantity *purchased.* The actual quantity (AQ) *used* of 6,500 pounds multiplied by the standard price (SP) of $4.00 per pound equals $26,000—the amount that should have been spent for the actual quantity *used.*

EXHIBIT 10–10
Standard Cost Variance Analysis—Direct Materials
(Note: The quantity of materials purchased does not equal the quantity used in production.)

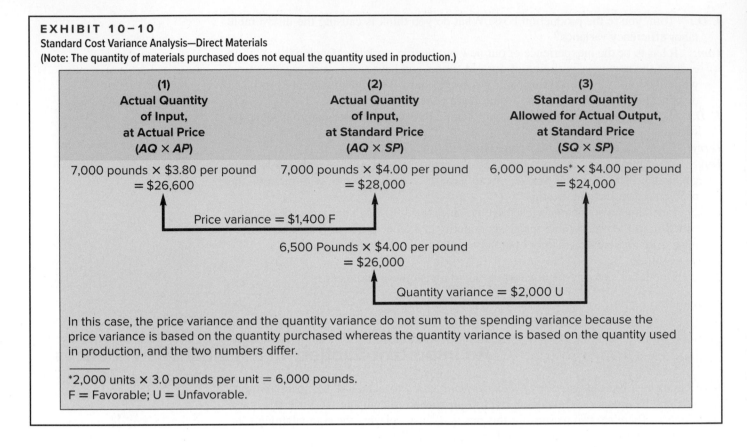

(1)	(2)	(3)
Actual Quantity of Input, at Actual Price $(AQ \times AP)$	**Actual Quantity of Input, at Standard Price** $(AQ \times SP)$	**Standard Quantity Allowed for Actual Output, at Standard Price** $(SQ \times SP)$
7,000 pounds × $3.80 per pound = $26,600	7,000 pounds × $4.00 per pound = $28,000	6,000 pounds* × $4.00 per pound = $24,000

Price variance = $1,400 F

6,500 Pounds × $4.00 per pound = $26,000

Quantity variance = $2,000 U

In this case, the price variance and the quantity variance do not sum to the spending variance because the price variance is based on the quantity purchased whereas the quantity variance is based on the quantity used in production, and the two numbers differ.

———
*2,000 units × 3.0 pounds per unit = 6,000 pounds.
F = Favorable; U = Unfavorable.

- Column (3) uses a two-step process to calculate the standard cost allowed for the actual number of statues produced. The first step calculates the standard quantity allowed (SQ) using the following equation:

  Standard quantity allowed = Actual output × Standard quantity per unit

  The actual output of 2,000 statues multiplied by the standard quantity per unit of 3.00 pounds equals the standard quantity allowed (SQ) of 6,000 pounds. The second step multiplies the standard quantity allowed (SQ) of 6,000 pounds by the standard price (SP) of $4.00 per pound to obtain the standard cost allowed for the actual output of $24,000.

  The materials price variance of $1,400 F arises because the actual price of $3.80 per pound is $0.20 less than the standard price of $4.00. Because 7,000 pounds were purchased, the total amount of the variance is $1,400 (= $0.20 × 7,000 pounds). The materials quantity variance of $2,000 U arises because the actual pounds used of 6,500 pounds is 500 pounds greater that the standard pounds allowed of 6,000 pounds. Because the standard price is $4.00 per pound, the total amount of the variance is $2,000 (= 500 pounds × $4.00 per pound).

  Because the price variance is based on the amount purchased and the quantity variance is based on the amount used, the two variances do not generally sum to the spending variance from the flexible budget, which is wholly based on the amount used. We would also like to emphasize that the variances depicted in Exhibit 10–10 can also be computed using the equations shown in Exhibit 10–11. The approaches shown in *Exhibits 10–10 and 10–11 can always be used to compute direct materials variances. However, Exhibits 10–4 and 10–5 can only be used in the special case when the quantity of materials purchased equals the quantity of materials used.*

Materials Price Variance:	EXHIBIT 10-11
	Direct Materials Variances: The Equations-Based Approach (when the quantity of materials purchased does not equal the quantity used in production)

Materials price variance = $(AQ \times AP) - (AQ \times SP)$
Materials price variance = $AQ(AP - SP)$
Materials price variance = 7,000 pounds ($3.80 per pound − $4.00 per pound)
Materials price variance = $1,400 F

where:
AQ = Actual quantity of inputs *purchased*
AP = Actual price per unit of the input
SP = Standard price per unit of the input

Materials Quantity Variance:

Materials quantity variance = $(AQ \times SP) - (SQ \times SP)$
Materials quantity variance = $SP(AQ - SQ)$
Materials quantity variance = $4.00 per pound (6,500 pounds − 6,000 pounds)
Materials quantity variance = $2,000 U

where:
AQ = Actual quantity of inputs *used in production*
SQ = Standard quantity of inputs allowed for the actual output
SP = Standard price per unit of the input

Standard Costs—Managerial Implications

Advantages of Standard Costs

Standard cost systems have a number of advantages.

1. Standard costs are a key element in a management by exception approach as defined in the previous chapter. If costs conform to the standards, managers can focus on other issues. When costs significantly deviate from the standards, managers are alerted problems may exist that require attention. This approach helps managers focus on important issues.
2. Standards provide benchmarks that employees can use to evaluate and improve their own performance.
3. Standard costs can greatly simplify bookkeeping. Instead of recording actual costs for each job, the standard costs for direct materials, direct labor, and overhead can be charged to jobs.
4. Standard costs fit naturally in an integrated system of "responsibility accounting." The standards establish what costs should be, who should be responsible for them, and whether actual costs are under control.

Potential Problems with Standard Costs

The improper use of standard costs can present a number of potential problems.

1. Standard cost variance reports are usually prepared on a monthly basis and often are released days or even weeks after the end of the month. As a consequence, the information in the reports may be outdated and useless. To address this concern, some companies report variances and other key operating data daily or even more frequently.
2. If managers use variances only to assign blame and punish subordinates, morale may suffer. Furthermore, subordinates may be tempted to cover up unfavorable variances or take actions not in the best interests of the company to make sure the variances are favorable.
3. Labor-hour standards and efficiency variances make two important assumptions. First, they assume the production process is labor-paced; if labor works faster, output will go up. However, output in many companies is not determined by how fast labor works; rather, it is determined by the processing speed of machines. Second,

the computations assume labor is a variable cost. However, direct labor can often be a fixed cost. If labor is fixed, then an undue emphasis on labor efficiency variances creates pressure to build excess inventories.

4. In some cases, a "favorable" variance can be worse than an "unfavorable" variance. For example, Hardee's has a standard for the amount of hamburger meat in a beef patty. A "favorable" variance would mean less meat was used than the standard specifies, resulting in substandard hamburgers and dissatisfied customers.

5. Too much emphasis on meeting the standards may overshadow other important objectives such as maintaining and improving quality, on-time delivery, and customer satisfaction. This tendency can be reduced by using supplemental performance measures focusing on these other objectives.

6. Just meeting standards is not sufficient because companies need to continually improve to remain competitive. For this reason, some companies focus on the trends in their standard cost variances—aiming for continual improvement rather than just meeting the standards. In other companies, engineered standards are replaced either by a rolling average of actual costs, which is expected to decline, or by very challenging target costs.

IN BUSINESS

Foodcollection/StockFood

STANDARD COSTS APPLY TO SERVICE COMPANIES TOO

Many manufacturers use standard cost systems; however, service companies can also use price and quantity standards for management control purposes. For example, the average cost of a burger sold at American restaurants is $1.86, consisting of $1.05 for the beef patty, $0.52 for the bun, $0.12 for lettuce, $0.07 for the tomato, and $0.10 for onion, mayonnaise, ketchup, and mustard.

At restaurants such as McDonald's, Burger King, Five Guys, and Steak 'n Shake, managers can use price and quantity standards to control their ingredient costs. If the average amount of beef being used in each burger exceeds the quantity standard, thereby shrinking the profit margin per burger sold, managers can solve the problem by reducing the amount of beef in a patty. Conversely, if the average portion of meat being used in each burger is less than the standard quantity, thereby leading to dissatisfied customers and lost sales, managers can resolve the issue by "beefing-up" the size of their burgers.

Source: Julie Jargon, "Diners Lose Taste for Pricey Burgers," *The Wall Street Journal,* June 1, 2017, pp. B1–B2.

Summary

A standard is a benchmark for measuring performance. Standards are set for both the quantity and the cost of inputs needed to manufacture goods or to provide services. Quantity standards indicate how much of an input, such as labor time or raw materials, should be used to make a product or provide a service. Cost standards indicate what the cost per unit of the input should be.

When standards are compared to actual performance, the difference is referred to as a *variance.* Variances are computed and reported to management on a regular basis for both the quantity and the price elements of direct materials, direct labor, and variable overhead. Price variances are computed by taking the difference between actual and standard prices and multiplying the result by the amount of input purchased. Quantity variances are computed by taking the difference between the actual amount of the input used and the amount of input allowed for the actual output, and then multiplying the result by the standard price per unit.

Standard cost systems provide companies with a number of advantages, such as supporting the management by exception approach, simplifying bookkeeping, and providing a benchmark employees can use to judge their own performance. However, critics of standard cost systems argue they provide outdated information, motivate employees to make poor decisions in an effort to generate favorable variances, and fail to embrace the mindset of continuous process improvement.

Traditional standard cost variance reports are often supplemented with other performance measures focused on critical areas such as product quality, inventory levels, and on-time delivery.

 Data Analytics Exercise available in Connect to complement this chapter

Review Problem: Standard Costs

Xavier Company produces a single product. Variable manufacturing overhead is applied to products on the basis of direct labor-hours. The standard cost card for one unit of product is as follows:

Inputs	(1) Standard Quantity or Hours	(2) Standard Price or Rate	Standard Cost (1) × (2)
Direct materials	6 ounces	$0.50 per ounce	$ 3.00
Direct labor	0.6 hour	$30.00 per hour	18.00
Variable manufacturing overhead ...	0.6 hour	$10.00 per hour	6.00
Total standard cost per unit			$27.00

During June, 2,000 units were produced. The costs associated with June's operations were as follows:

Material purchased: 18,000 ounces at $0.60 per ounce	$10,800
Material used in production: 14,000 ounces	—
Direct labor: 1,100 hours at $30.50 per hour	$33,550
Variable manufacturing overhead costs incurred	$12,980

Required:
Compute the direct materials, direct labor, and variable manufacturing overhead variances.

Solution to Review Problem

Direct Materials Variances

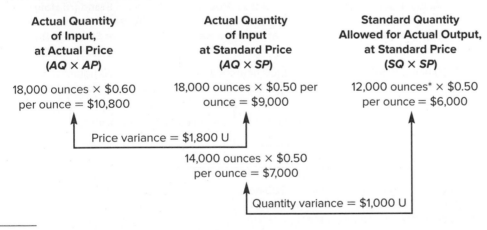

Actual Quantity of Input, at Actual Price (*AQ* × *AP*)	Actual Quantity of Input at Standard Price (*AQ* × *SP*)	Standard Quantity Allowed for Actual Output, at Standard Price (*SQ* × *SP*)
18,000 ounces × $0.60 per ounce = $10,800	18,000 ounces × $0.50 per ounce = $9,000	12,000 ounces* × $0.50 per ounce = $6,000

Price variance = $1,800 U

14,000 ounces × $0.50 per ounce = $7,000

Quantity variance = $1,000 U

*2,000 units × 6 ounces per unit = 12,000 ounces.
F = Favorable; U = Unfavorable.

Using formulas, the same variances are computed as follows:

$$\text{Materials price variance} = (AQ \times AP) - (AQ \times SP)$$
$$= AQ(AP - SP)$$
$$= 18{,}000 \text{ ounces } (\$0.60 \text{ per ounce} - \$0.50 \text{ per ounce})$$
$$= \$1{,}800 \text{ U}$$
$$\text{Materials quantity variance} = (AQ \times SP) - (SQ \times SP)$$
$$= SP(AQ - SQ)$$
$$= \$0.50 \text{ per ounce } (14{,}000 \text{ ounces} - 12{,}000 \text{ ounces})$$
$$= \$1{,}000 \text{ U}$$

Direct Labor Variances

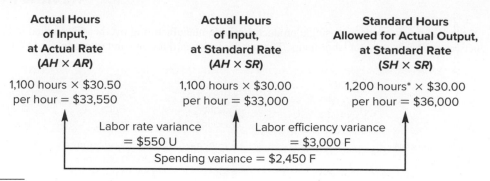

Actual Hours of Input, at Actual Rate ($AH \times AR$)	Actual Hours of Input, at Standard Rate ($AH \times SR$)	Standard Hours Allowed for Actual Output, at Standard Rate ($SH \times SR$)
1,100 hours × $30.50 per hour = $33,550	1,100 hours × $30.00 per hour = $33,000	1,200 hours* × $30.00 per hour = $36,000

Labor rate variance = $550 U

Labor efficiency variance = $3,000 F

Spending variance = $2,450 F

---

*2,000 units × 0.6 hour per unit = 1,200 hours.
F = Favorable; U = Unfavorable.

Using formulas, the same variances are computed as follows:

$$\text{Labor rate variance} = (AH \times AR) - (AH \times SR)$$
$$= AH(AR - SR)$$
$$= 1,100 \text{ hours } (\$30.50 \text{ per hour} - \$30.00 \text{ per hour})$$
$$= \$550 \text{ U}$$
$$\text{Labor efficiency variance} = (AH \times SR) - (SH \times SR)$$
$$= SR(AH - SH)$$
$$= \$30.00 \text{ per hour } (1,100 \text{ hours} - 1,200 \text{ hours})$$
$$= \$3,000 \text{ F}$$

Variable Manufacturing Overhead Variances

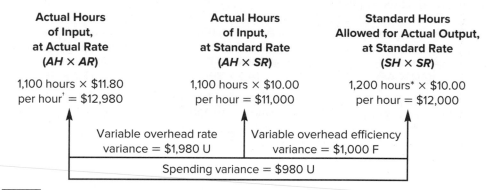

Actual Hours of Input, at Actual Rate ($AH \times AR$)	Actual Hours of Input, at Standard Rate ($AH \times SR$)	Standard Hours Allowed for Actual Output, at Standard Rate ($SH \times SR$)
1,100 hours × $11.80 per hour† = $12,980	1,100 hours × $10.00 per hour = $11,000	1,200 hours* × $10.00 per hour = $12,000

Variable overhead rate variance = $1,980 U

Variable overhead efficiency variance = $1,000 F

Spending variance = $980 U

---

*2,000 units × 0.6 hour per unit = 1,200 hours.
†$12,980 ÷ 1,100 hours = $11.80 per hour.
F = Favorable; U = Unfavorable.

Using formulas, the same variances are computed as follows:

Variable overhead rate variance
$$= (AH \times AR) - (AH \times SR)$$
$$= AH(AR - SR)$$
$$= 1,100 \text{ hours } (\$11.80 \text{ per hour} - \$10.00 \text{ per hour})$$
$$= \$1,980 \text{ U}$$

Variable overhead efficiency variance
$$= (AH \times SR) - (SH \times SR)$$
$$= SR(AH - SH)$$
$$= \$10.00 \text{ per hour } (1,100 \text{ hours} - 1,200 \text{ hours})$$
$$= \$1,000 \text{ F}$$

Glossary

Labor efficiency variance The difference between the actual labor-hours taken to complete a task and the standard hours allowed for the actual output, multiplied by the standard hourly labor rate. (p. 449)

Labor rate variance The difference between the actual hourly labor rate and the standard rate, multiplied by the actual hours worked. (p. 448)

Materials price variance The difference between a direct material's actual price per unit and its standard price per unit, multiplied by the quantity purchased. (p. 445)

Materials quantity variance The difference between the actual quantity of materials used in production and the standard quantity allowed for the actual output, multiplied by the standard price per unit. (p. 446)

Price variance A variance computed by taking the difference between the actual price and the standard price and multiplying the result by the actual quantity of the input. (p. 443)

Quantity variance A variance computed by taking the difference between the actual quantity of the input used and the amount of the input that should have been used for the actual level of output and multiplying the result by the standard price of the input. (p. 443)

Standard cost card A detailed listing of the standard amounts of inputs and their costs required to produce one unit of a specific product. (p. 441)

Standard cost per unit The standard quantity allowed of an input per unit of a specific product, multiplied by the standard price of the input. (p. 441)

Standard hours allowed The time that should have been taken to complete the period's output. It is computed by multiplying the actual number of units produced by the standard hours per unit. (p. 444)

Standard hours per unit The amount of direct labor time allowed to complete a single unit of product, including allowances for breaks, machine downtime, cleanup, rejects, and other normal inefficiencies. (p. 440)

Standard price per unit The price that should be paid for each unit of direct materials. It should reflect the final, delivered cost of those materials. (p. 440)

Standard quantity allowed The amount of direct materials that should have been used to complete the period's actual output. It is computed by multiplying the actual number of units produced by the standard quantity per unit. (p. 444)

Standard quantity per unit The amount of direct materials allowed for each unit of finished product, including an allowance for normal inefficiencies, such as scrap and spoilage. (p. 440)

Standard rate per hour The labor rate allowed per hour of labor time, including employment taxes and fringe benefits. (p. 441)

Variable overhead efficiency variance The difference between the actual level of activity and the standard activity allowed, multiplied by the variable part of the predetermined overhead rate. (p. 451)

Variable overhead rate variance The difference between the actual variable overhead cost incurred and the standard cost allowed for the actual activity. (p. 451)

Questions

10–1 What is a quantity standard? What is a price standard?

10–2 Why are separate price and quantity variances computed?

10–3 Who is responsible for the materials price variance? The materials quantity variance? The labor efficiency variance?

10–4 The materials price variance can be computed at what two different points in time? Which point is better? Why?

10–5 If the materials price variance is favorable, but the materials quantity variance is unfavorable, what might this indicate?

10–6 Should standards be used to identify who to blame for problems?

10–7 "Our workers are all under labor contracts; therefore, our labor rate variance is bound to be zero." Discuss.

10–8 What effect, if any, would you expect poor-quality materials to have on direct labor variances?

10–9   If variable manufacturing overhead is applied to production on the basis of direct labor-hours and the direct labor efficiency variance is unfavorable, will the variable overhead efficiency variance be favorable or unfavorable, or could it be either? Explain.

10–10 Why can undue emphasis on labor efficiency variances lead to excess work in process inventories?

Applying Excel   Mc Graw Hill **connect**

LO10–1, LO10–2, LO10–3

The Excel worksheet shown below recreates the example in the text pertaining to Colonial Pewter Company. The workbook, and instructions on how to complete the file, can be found in Connect. You should proceed to the requirements below only after completing your worksheet.

Required:

1. Check your worksheet by changing the direct materials standard quantity in cell B6 to 2.9 pounds, the direct labor standard quantity in cell B7 to 0.6 hours, and the variable manufacturing overhead in cell B8 to 0.6 hours. The materials spending variance should now be $1,500 U, the labor spending variance should now be $3,720 F, and the variable overhead spending variance should now be $60 F. If you do not get these answers, find the errors in your worksheet and correct them.

    a.   What is the materials quantity variance? Explain this variance.

    b.   What is the labor rate variance? Explain this variance.

	A	B	C	D	E	F	G
1	Chapter 10: Applying Excel						
2							
3	**Data**						
4	*Exhibit 10-1: Standard Cost Card*						
5	Inputs	Standard Quantity		Standard Price			
6	Direct materials	3.0 pounds		$4.00 per pound			
7	Direct labor	0.50 hours		$22.00 per hour			
8	Variable manufacturing overhead	0.50 hours		$6.00 per hour			
9							
10	Actual results:						
11	Actual output	2,000 units					
12	Actual variable manufacturing overhead cost	$7,140					
13		Actual Quantity		Actual price			
14	Actual direct materials cost	6,500 pounds		$3.80 per pound			
15	Actual direct labor cost	1,050 hours		$21.60 per hour			
16							
17	*Enter a formula into each of the cells marked with a ? below*						
18	**Main Example: Chapter 10**						
19							
20	*Exhibit 10-4: Standard Cost Variance Analysis–Direct Materials*						
21	Actual Quantity of Input, at Actual Price	? pounds ×		? per pound =		?	
22	Actual Quantity of Input, at Standard Price	? pounds ×		? per pound =		?	
23	Standard Quantity Allowed for the Actual Output, at Standard Price	? pounds ×		? per pound =		?	
24	Direct materials variances:						
25	Materials price variance	?					
26	Materials quantity variance	?					
27	Materials spending variance	?					
28							
29	*Exhibit 10-6: Standard Cost Variance Analysis–Direct Labor*						
30	Actual Hours of Input, at Actual Rate	? hours ×		? per hour =		?	
31	Actual Hours of Input, at Standard Rate	? hours ×		? per hour =		?	
32	Standard Hours Allowed for the Actual Output, at Standard Rate	? hours ×		? per hour =		?	
33	Direct labor variances:						
34	Labor rate variance	?					
35	Labor efficiency variance	?					
36	Labor spending variance	?					
37							
38	*Exhibit 10-8: Standard Cost Variance Analysis–Variable Manufacturing Overhead*						
39	Actual Hours of Input, at Actual Rate	? hours ×		? per hour =		?	
40	Actual Hours of Input, at Standard Rate	? hours ×		? per hour =		?	
41	Standard Hours Allowed for the Actual Output, at Standard Rate	? hours ×		? per hour =		?	
42	Variable overhead variances:						
43	Variable overhead rate variance	?					
44	Variable overhead efficiency variance	?					
45	Variable overhead spending variance	?					
46							
	◄ ◄ ► ►	**Chapter 10 Form**	Filled in Chapter 10 Form	Chapter 10 Formulas			

Microsoft Excel

2. Revise the data in your worksheet to reflect the results for the subsequent period:

Data		
Exhibit 10–1: Standard Cost Card		
Inputs	Standard Quantity	Standard Price
Direct materials	3.0 pounds	$4.00 per pound
Direct labor	0.50 hours	$22.00 per hour
Variable manufacturing overhead	0.50 hours	$6.00 per hour
Actual results:		
Actual output	2,100 units	
Actual variable manufacturing overhead cost ...	$5,100	
	Actual Quantity	Actual price
Actual direct materials cost	6,350 pounds	$4.10 per pound
Actual direct labor cost	1,020 hours	$22.10 per hour

  a.   What is the materials quantity variance? What is the materials price variance?
  b.   What is the labor efficiency variance? What is the labor rate variance?
  c.   What is the variable overhead efficiency variance? What is the variable overhead rate variance?

Mc Graw Hill connect   **The Foundational 15**

Preble Company manufactures one product. Its variable manufacturing overhead is applied to production based on direct labor-hours and its standard cost card per unit is as follows:

LO10–1, LO10–2, LO10–3

Inputs	(1) Standard Quantity or Hours	(2) Standard Price or Rate	Standard Cost (1) × (2)
Direct materials	5 pounds	$8.00 per pound	$40.00
Direct labor	2 hours	$14 per hour	28.00
Variable overhead	2 hours	$5 per hour	10.00
Total standard cost per unit			$78.00

The planning budget for March was based on producing and selling 25,000 units. However, during March the company actually produced and sold 30,000 units and incurred the following costs:
  a.   Purchased 160,000 pounds of raw materials at a cost of $7.50 per pound. All of this material was used in production.
  b.   Direct laborers worked 55,000 hours at a rate of $15.00 per hour.
  c.   Total variable manufacturing overhead for the month was $280,500.

Required:
For March:

  1.   What raw materials cost would be included in the company's planning budget?
  2.   What raw materials cost would be included in the company's flexible budget?
  3.   What is the materials price variance?
  4.   What is the materials quantity variance?
  5.   If Preble had purchased 170,000 pounds of materials at $7.50 per pound and used 160,000 pounds in production, what would be the materials price variance?
  6.   If Preble had purchased 170,000 pounds of materials at $7.50 per pound and used 160,000 pounds in production, what would be the materials quantity variance?
  7.   What direct labor cost would be included in the company's planning budget?
  8.   What direct labor cost would be included in the company's flexible budget?
  9.   What is the labor rate variance?
  10. What is the labor efficiency variance?
  11. What is the labor spending variance?
  12. What variable manufacturing overhead cost would be included in the company's planning budget?

13. What variable manufacturing overhead cost would be included in the company's flexible budget?
14. What is the variable overhead rate variance?
15. What is the variable overhead efficiency variance?

Exercises

EXERCISE 10–1 Direct Materials Variances LO10–1

Bandar Industries manufactures sporting equipment. One of the company's products is a football helmet that requires special plastic. During the quarter ending June 30, the company manufactured 35,000 helmets, using 22,500 kilograms of plastic. The plastic cost the company $171,000.

According to the standard cost card, each helmet should require 0.6 kilogram of plastic, at a cost of $8 per kilogram.

Required:

1. What is the standard quantity of kilograms of plastic (SQ) that is allowed to make 35,000 helmets?
2. What is the standard materials cost allowed (SQ × SP) to make 35,000 helmets?
3. What is the materials spending variance?
4. What are the materials price variance and the materials quantity variance?

EXERCISE 10–2 Direct Labor Variances LO10–2

SkyChefs, Inc., prepares in-flight meals for a number of major airlines. One of the company's products is grilled salmon with mixed vegetables. During the most recent week, the company prepared 4,000 of these meals using 960 direct labor-hours. The company paid its direct labor workers a total of $19,200 for this work, or $20.00 per hour.

According to the standard cost card for this meal, it should require 0.25 direct labor-hour at a cost of $19.75 per hour.

Required:

1. What is the standard labor-hours allowed (SH) to prepare 4,000 meals?
2. What is the standard labor cost allowed (SH × SR) to prepare 4,000 meals?
3. What is the labor spending variance?
4. What are the labor rate variance and the labor efficiency variance?

EXERCISE 10–3 Variable Overhead Variances LO10–3

Logistics Solutions maintains warehouses that stock items carried by its dot.com clients. When a client receives an order from a customer, the order is forwarded to Logistics Solutions, which pulls the item from storage, packs it, and ships it to the customer. The company uses a predetermined variable overhead rate based on direct labor-hours.

In the most recent month, 120,000 items were shipped to customers using 2,300 direct labor-hours. The company incurred a total of $7,360 in variable overhead costs.

According to the company's standards, 0.02 direct labor-hour is required to fulfill an order for one item and the variable overhead rate is $3.25 per direct labor-hour.

Required:

1. What is the standard labor-hours allowed (SH) to ship 120,000 items to customers?
2. What is the standard variable overhead cost allowed (SH × SR) to ship 120,000 items to customers?
3. What is the variable overhead spending variance?
4. What are the variable overhead rate variance and the variable overhead efficiency variance?

EXERCISE 10–4 Direct Labor and Variable Manufacturing Overhead Variances LO10–2, LO10–3

Erie Company manufactures a mobile fitness device called the Jogging Mate. The company's labor standards for one Jogging Mate are as follows:

Standard Hours	Standard Rate per Hour	Standard Cost
18 minutes	$17.00	$5.10

During August, 5,750 hours of direct labor time were needed to make 20,000 units of the Jogging Mate. The direct labor cost totaled $102,350 for the month.

Required:
1. What is the standard labor-hours allowed (SH) to make 20,000 Jogging Mates?
2. What is the standard labor cost allowed (SH × SR) to make 20,000 Jogging Mates?
3. What is the labor spending variance?
4. What are the labor rate variance and the labor efficiency variance?
5. The budgeted variable manufacturing overhead rate is $4 per direct labor-hour. During August, the company incurred $21,850 in variable manufacturing overhead cost. Compute the variable overhead rate and efficiency variances for the month.

EXERCISE 10–5 Working Backwards from Labor Variances LO10–2

Quality Motor Company established the standard labor cost for a motor tune-up shown below:

	Standard Hours	Standard Rate	Standard Cost
Motor tune-up	2.5	$25.00	$62.50

The record showing the time spent in the shop last week on motor tune-ups has been misplaced. However, the shop supervisor recalls 50 tune-ups were completed during the week, and the controller recalls the following variance data relating to tune-ups:

Labor rate variance.	$150 F
Labor spending variance	$200 U

Required:
1. Determine the number of actual labor-hours spent on tune-ups during the week.
2. Determine the actual hourly pay rate for tune-ups last week. (Round your answer to the nearest cent.)

(*Hint:* A useful way to proceed would be to work from known to unknown data either by using the variance formulas in Exhibit 10–7 or by using the columnar format shown in Exhibit 10–6.)

EXERCISE 10–6 Direct Materials and Direct Labor Variances LO10–1, LO10–2

Huron Company produces a cleaning compound known as Zoom. The direct materials and direct labor standards for one unit of Zoom are given below:

	Standard Quantity or Hours	Standard Price or Rate	Standard Cost
Direct materials	4.6 pounds	$2.50 per pound	$11.50
Direct labor	0.2 hour	$18.00 per hour	$3.60

During the most recent month, the following activity was recorded:
 a. Twenty thousand pounds of material were purchased at a cost of $2.35 per pound.
 b. All of the material purchased was used to produce 4,000 units of Zoom.
 c. 750 hours of direct labor time were recorded at a total labor cost of $14,925.

Required:
1. Compute the materials price and quantity variances for the month.
2. Compute the labor rate and efficiency variances for the month.

EXERCISE 10–7 Direct Materials Variances LO10–1

Refer to the data in Exhibit 10–6. Assume instead of producing 4,000 units during the month, the company produced only 3,000 units, using 14,750 pounds of material. (The rest of the material purchased remained in raw materials inventory.)

Required:
Compute the materials price and quantity variances for the month.

EXERCISE 10–8 Direct Materials and Direct Labor Variances LO10–1, LO10–2

Dawson Toys, Ltd., produces a toy called the Maze with the following standards:

> Direct materials: 6 microns per toy at $1.50 per micron
> Direct labor: 1.3 hours per toy at $21 per hour

During July, the company produced 3,000 Maze toys. The toy's production data for the month are as follows:

Direct materials: 25,000 microns were purchased at a cost of $1.48 per micron. 5,000 of these microns were still in inventory at the end of the month.

Direct labor: 4,000 direct labor-hours were worked at a cost of $88,000.

Required:
1. Compute the following variances for July:
    a. The materials price and quantity variances.
    b. The labor rate and efficiency variances.
2. Explain the possible causes of each variance.

Problems   **connect**

PROBLEM 10–9 Comprehensive Variance Analysis LO10–1, LO10–2, LO10–3

Marvel Parts, Inc., manufactures auto accessories including a set of seat covers that can be adjusted to fit most cars. According to its standards, the factory should work 2,850 hours each month to produce 1,900 sets of seat covers. The standard costs associated with this level of production are:

	Total	Per Set of Covers
Direct materials	$42,560	$22.40
Direct labor	$51,300	27.00
Variable manufacturing overhead		
(based on direct labor-hours)	$6,840	3.60
		$53.00

During August, the factory worked 2,800 direct labor-hours and produced 2,000 sets of covers. The following actual costs were recorded during the month:

	Total	Per Set of Covers
Direct materials (12,000 yards)	$45,600	$22.80
Direct labor	$49,000	24.50
Variable manufacturing overhead	$7,000	3.50
		$50.80

At standard, each set of covers should require 5.6 yards of material. All of the materials purchased during the month were used in production.

Required:
Compute the following variances for August:
1. The materials price and quantity variances.
2. The labor rate and efficiency variances.
3. The variable overhead rate and efficiency variances.

PROBLEM 10–10 Multiple Products, Materials, and Processes LO10–1, LO10–2

Mickley Corporation produces two products, Alpha6s and Zeta7s, which pass through two operations, Sintering and Finishing. Each of the products uses two raw materials—X442 and Y661. The standards for each product (on a per-unit basis) are as follows:

Product	Raw Material		Standard Labor Time	
	X442	Y661	Sintering	Finishing
Alpha6	1.8 kilos	2.0 liters	0.20 hour	0.80 hour
Zeta7	3.0 kilos	4.5 liters	0.35 hour	0.90 hour

Information relating to materials purchased and used in production during May follows:

Material	Purchases	Purchase Cost	Standard Price	Used in Production
X442	14,500 kilos	$52,200	$3.50 per kilo	8,500 kilos
Y661	15,500 liters	$20,925	$1.40 per liter	13,000 liters

The following additional information is available:
a. The company recognizes price variances when materials are purchased.
b. The standard labor rate is $19.80 per hour in Sintering and $19.20 per hour in Finishing.
c. During May, 1,200 direct labor-hours were worked in Sintering at a total labor cost of $27,000, and 2,850 direct labor-hours were worked in Finishing at a total labor cost of $59,850.
d. Production during May was 1,500 Alpha6s and 2,000 Zeta7s.

Required:
1. Prepare a standard cost card for each product, showing the standard cost of direct materials and direct labor.
2. Compute the materials price and quantity variances for each material.
3. Compute the labor rate and efficiency variances for each operation.

PROBLEM 10–11 Direct Materials and Direct Labor Variances; Computations from Incomplete Data LO10–1, LO10–2
Sharp Company manufactures a product with the following standards:

	Standard Quantity or Hours	Standard Price or Rate	Standard Cost
Direct materials	3 feet	$11 per foot	$33
Direct labor	? hours	? per hour	?

During March, the company purchased direct materials for $111,300, all of which were used in the production of 3,200 units. In addition, 4,900 direct labor-hours were worked on the product during the month. The cost of this labor time was $95,550. The following variances have been computed for the month:

Materials quantity variance	$4,400 U
Labor spending variance	$450 F
Labor efficiency variance	$2,000 U

Required:
1. For direct materials:
   a. Compute the actual cost per foot of materials for March.
   b. Compute the price variance and the spending variance.
2. For direct labor:
   a. Compute the standard direct labor rate per hour.
   b. Compute the standard hours allowed for the month's production.
   c. Compute the standard hours allowed per unit of product.
(*Hint:* In completing the problem, it may be helpful to move from known to unknown data either by using the columnar format shown in Exhibits 10–4 and 10–6 or by using the variance formulas in Exhibits 10–5 and 10–7.)

PROBLEM 10–12 Variance Analysis in a Hospital LO10–1, LO10–2, LO10–3
John Fleming, chief administrator for Valley View Hospital, is concerned about the costs for tests in the hospital's lab. Charges for lab tests are consistently higher at Valley View than other hospitals and have resulted in many complaints. Also, because of strict regulations on amounts reimbursed for lab tests, payments received from insurance companies and governmental units have not been high enough to cover lab costs.

Mr. Fleming asked you to evaluate costs in the hospital's lab for the past month. The following information is available:

a. Two types of tests are performed in the lab—blood tests and smears. During the past month, 1,800 blood tests and 2,400 smears were performed in the lab.

b. Small glass plates are used in both types of tests. During the past month, the hospital purchased 12,000 plates at a cost of $56,400. 1,500 of these plates were unused at the end of the month; no plates were on hand at the beginning of the month.

c. During the past month, 1,150 hours of labor time were recorded in the lab at a cost of $21,850.

d. The lab's variable overhead cost last month totaled $7,820.

Valley View Hospital has never used standard costs. By searching industry literature, however, you determined the following nationwide averages for hospital labs:

Plates: Two plates are required per lab test. These plates cost $5.00 each and are disposed of after the test is completed.

Labor: Each blood test should require 0.3 hour to complete, and each smear should require 0.15 hour to complete. The average cost of this lab time is $20 per hour.

Overhead: Overhead cost is based on direct labor-hours. The average rate for variable overhead is $6 per hour.

Required:

1. Compute a materials price variance for the plates purchased last month and a materials quantity variance for the plates used last month.

2. For labor cost in the lab:
   a. Compute a labor rate variance and a labor efficiency variance.
   b. In most hospitals, one-half of the workers in the lab are senior technicians and one-half are assistants. In an effort to reduce costs, Valley View Hospital employs only one-fourth senior technicians and three-fourths assistants. Would you recommend this policy be continued? Explain.

3. Compute the variable overhead rate and efficiency variances. Is there any relation between the variable overhead efficiency variance and the labor efficiency variance? Explain.

PROBLEM 10–13 Basic Variance Analysis; the Impact of Variances on Unit Costs LO10–1, LO10–2, LO10–3

Koontz Company manufactures a number of products. The standards relating to one of these products are shown below, along with actual cost data for May.

	Standard Cost per Unit	Actual Cost per Unit
Direct materials:		
Standard: 1.80 feet at $3.00 per foot	$ 5.40	
Actual: 1.80 feet at $3.30 per foot		$ 5.94
Direct labor:		
Standard: 0.90 hour at $18.00 per hour	16.20	
Actual: 0.92 hour at $17.50 per hour		16.10
Variable overhead:		
Standard: 0.90 hour at $5.00 per hour	4.50	
Actual: 0.92 hour at $4.50 per hour		4.14
Total cost per unit	$26.10	$26.18
Excess of actual cost over standard cost per unit		$0.08

The production superintendent was pleased when he saw this report and commented: "This $0.08 excess cost is well within the 2% limit management has set for acceptable variances. It's obvious there's not much to worry about with this product."

Actual production for the month was 12,000 units. Variable overhead cost is assigned to products based on direct labor-hours. There were no beginning or ending inventories of materials.

Required:

1. Compute the following variances for May:
   a. Materials price and quantity variances.
   b. Labor rate and efficiency variances.
   c. Variable overhead rate and efficiency variances.

2. How much of the $0.08 excess unit cost is traceable to each of the variances computed in (1) above.
3. How much of the $0.08 excess unit cost is traceable to apparent inefficient use of labor time?
4. Do you agree the excess unit cost is not of concern?

PROBLEM 10–14 Basic Variance Analysis LO10–1, LO10–2, LO10–3

Becton Labs, Inc., produces various chemical compounds for industrial use. One compound, called Fludex, has the following standard cost per unit:

	Standard Quantity or Hours	Standard Price or Rate	Standard Cost
Direct materials	2.5 ounces	$20.00 per ounce	$50.00
Direct labor	1.4 hours	$22.50 per hour	31.50
Variable manufacturing overhead	1.4 hours	$3.50 per hour	4.90
Total standard cost per unit			$86.40

During November, the following activity was recorded related to the production of Fludex:

a. Materials purchased, 12,000 ounces at a cost of $225,000.
b. There was no beginning inventory of materials; however, at the end of the month, 2,500 ounces of material remained in ending inventory.
c. The company employs 35 lab technicians to work on the production of Fludex. During November, they each worked an average of 160 hours at an average pay rate of $22 per hour.
d. Variable manufacturing overhead is assigned to Fludex on the basis of direct labor-hours. Variable manufacturing overhead costs during November totaled $18,200.
e. During November, the company produced 3,750 units of Fludex.

Required:
1. For direct materials:
    a. Compute the price and quantity variances.
    b. The materials were purchased from a new supplier who is anxious to enter into a long-term purchase contract. Would you recommend the company sign the contract? Explain.
2. For direct labor:
    a. Compute the rate and efficiency variances.
    b. In the past, the 35 technicians employed in the production of Fludex consisted of 20 senior technicians and 15 assistants. During November, the company experimented with fewer senior technicians and more assistants in order to reduce labor costs. Would you recommend the new labor mix be continued? Explain.
3. Compute the variable overhead rate and efficiency variances. What relation do you see between this efficiency variance and the labor efficiency variance?

PROBLEM 10–15 Comprehensive Variance Analysis LO10–1, LO10–2, LO10–3

Miller Toy Company manufactures a plastic swimming pool at its Westwood Plant. The plant is experiencing problems as shown by its June contribution format income statement below:

	Flexible Budget	Actual
Sales (15,000 pools)	$675,000	$675,000
Variable expenses:		
Variable cost of goods sold*	435,000	461,890
Variable selling expenses	20,000	20,000
Total variable expenses	455,000	481,890
Contribution margin	220,000	193,110
Fixed expenses:		
Manufacturing overhead	130,000	130,000
Selling and administrative	84,000	84,000
Total fixed expenses	214,000	214,000
Net operating income (loss)	$ 6,000	$ (20,890)

*Contains direct materials, direct labor, and variable manufacturing overhead.

Janet Dunn, who has just been appointed general manager of the Westwood Plant, has been given instructions to "get things under control." Upon reviewing the plant's income statement, Ms. Dunn concluded the major problem lies in the variable cost of goods sold. She has been provided with the following standard cost per swimming pool:

	Standard Quantity or Hours	Standard Price or Rate	Standard Cost
Direct materials	3.0 pounds	$5.00 per pound	$15.00
Direct labor	0.8 hour	$16.00 per hour	12.80
Variable manufacturing overhead	0.4 hour*	$3.00 per hour	1.20
Total standard cost per unit			$29.00

*Based on machine-hours.

During June the plant produced 15,000 pools and incurred the following costs:
a. Purchased 60,000 pounds of materials at a cost of $4.95 per pound.
b. Used 49,200 pounds of materials in production. (Finished goods and work in process inventories are insignificant and can be ignored.)
c. Worked 11,800 direct labor-hours at a cost of $17.00 per hour.
d. Incurred variable manufacturing overhead cost totaling $18,290 for the month. A total of 5,900 machine-hours was recorded.
It is the company's policy to close all variances to cost of goods sold on a monthly basis.

Required:
1. Compute the following variances for June:
   a. Materials price and quantity variances.
   b. Labor rate and efficiency variances.
   c. Variable overhead rate and efficiency variances.
2. Summarize the variances you computed in (1) above by showing the net overall favorable or unfavorable variance for the month. What impact did this figure have on the company's income statement? Show computations.
3. Pick out the two most significant variances you computed in (1) above. Explain to Ms. Dunn possible causes of these variances.

PROBLEM 10–16 Comprehensive Variance Analysis LO10–1, LO10–2, LO10–3
Highland Company produces a lightweight backpack popular with college students. Standard variable costs relating to a single backpack are given below:

	Standard Quantity or Hours	Standard Price or Rate	Standard Cost
Direct materials	?	$6 per yard	$?
Direct labor	?	?	?
Variable manufacturing overhead	?	$3 per direct labor-hour	?
Total standard cost per unit			$?

Overhead is applied to production based on direct labor-hours. During March, 1,000 backpacks were manufactured and sold. Selected information relating to the month's production is given below:

	Materials Used	Direct Labor	Variable Manufacturing Overhead
Total standard cost allowed*	$16,800	$21,000	$4,200
Actual costs incurred	$15,000	?	$3,600
Materials price variance	?		
Materials quantity variance	$1,200 U		
Labor rate variance		?	
Labor efficiency variance		?	
Variable overhead rate variance			?
Variable overhead efficiency variance			?

*For the month's production.

The following additional information is available for March's production:

Actual direct labor-hours	1,500
Difference between standard and actual cost	
per backpack produced during March	$0.15 F

Required: (Hint: It may be helpful to complete a general model diagram for direct materials, direct labor, and variable manufacturing overhead before attempting to answer any of the requirements.)
1. What is the standard cost of a single backpack?
2. What was the actual cost per backpack produced during March?
3. How many yards of material are required at standard per backpack?
4. What was the materials price variance for March if there were no beginning or ending inventories of materials?
5. What is the standard direct labor rate per hour?
6. What was the labor rate variance for March? The labor efficiency variance?
7. What was the variable overhead rate variance for March? The variable overhead efficiency variance?
8. Prepare a standard cost card for one backpack.

Mc Graw Hill **connect**   **Case**

Select cases are available in Connect.

CASE 10–17 Working Backwards from Variance Data LO10–1, LO10–2, LO10–3
Vitex, Inc., manufactures a popular consumer product and it provided the following data from its standard cost system:

Inputs	(1) Standard Quantity or Hours	(2) Standard Price or Rate	Standard Cost (1) × (2)
Direct materials	6 pounds	$3 per pound	$18.00
Direct labor	0.8 hour	$15 per hour	12.00
Variable manufacturing overhead	0.8 hour	$3 per hour	2.40
Total standard cost per unit			$32.40

	Total Standard Cost*	Variances Reported	
		Price or Rate	Quantity or Efficiency
Direct materials	$405,000	$6,900 F	$9,000 U
Direct labor	$270,000	$14,550 U	$21,000 U
Variable manufacturing overhead	$54,000	$1,300 F	$? U

*Applied to Work in Process during the period.

The company's manufacturing overhead cost is applied to production based on direct labor-hours. All of the materials purchased during the period were used in production. Work in process inventories are insignificant and can be ignored.

Required:
1. How many units were produced last period?
2. How many pounds of direct material were purchased and used in production?
3. What was the actual cost per pound of material?
4. How many actual direct labor-hours were worked during the period?
5. What was the actual rate paid per direct labor-hour?
6. How much actual variable manufacturing overhead cost was incurred during the period?

Appendix 10A: Predetermined Overhead Rates and Overhead Analysis in a Standard Costing System

LO10–4
Compute and interpret the fixed overhead budget and volume variances.

In this appendix, we explain how the predetermined overhead rates discussed in the job-order costing chapters can be used in a standard costing system. Throughout this appendix, we assume absorption costing is used to assign *all* manufacturing costs—both variable and fixed—to products.

MicroDrive Corporation: An Example

Exhibit 10A–1 pertains to MicroDrive Corporation, a company that produces miniature electric motors. The data within this exhibit is divided into three sections. The first section summarizes the budgeted overhead costs and budgeted machine-hours included in the company's planning budget. Note the company's planning budget is based on producing 25,000 motors. Given two machine-hours are allowed per motor, the planning budget allows for 50,000 machine-hours. At this level of activity, the budgeted variable manufacturing overhead is $75,000 and the budgeted fixed manufacturing overhead is $300,000.

The second section includes information MicroDrive uses to apply overhead costs to production. Notice the company actually produced 20,000 motors instead of the 25,000 motors included in the planning budget. Given two machine-hours are allowed per motor, the standard machine-hours allowed for the actual production is 40,000 machine-hours. This is the quantity of machine-hours the company will use to apply variable and fixed overhead costs to production.

The third section summarizes the company's actual variable and fixed manufacturing overhead costs for the period as well as its actual machine-hours used during the period. As we will describe in greater detail shortly, *it is very important to understand in a standard cost system the actual hours (42,000 machine-hours) are not used to apply overhead costs to production. Variable and fixed overhead costs are applied to production using the standard hours allowed for the actual production (40,000 machine-hours).*

EXHIBIT 10A–1
MicroDrive Corporation Data

Budgeted (Planned) Overhead:	
Budgeted variable manufacturing overhead ..	$ 75,000
Budgeted fixed manufacturing overhead	300,000
Total budgeted manufacturing overhead	$375,000
Budgeted production (a)	25,000 motors
Standard machine-hours per motor (b)	2 machine-hours per motor
Budgeted machine-hours (a) × (b)	50,000 machine-hours
Applying Overhead:	
Actual production (a)	20,000 motors
Standard machine-hours per motor (b)	2 machine-hours per motor
Standard machine-hours allowed for the actual production (a) × (b)	40,000 machine-hours
Actual Overhead and Machine-Hours:	
Actual variable manufacturing overhead	$ 71,400
Actual fixed manufacturing overhead	308,000
Total actual manufacturing overhead	$379,400
Actual machine-hours	42,000 machine-hours

Predetermined Overhead Rates

Recall from earlier chapters the following formula is used to establish the predetermined overhead rate at the beginning of the period:

$$\text{Predetermined overhead rate} = \frac{\text{Estimated total manufacturing overhead cost}}{\text{Estimated total amount of the allocation base}}$$

The estimated total amount of the allocation base in the formula for the predetermined overhead rate is called the **denominator activity.**

Once the predetermined overhead rate has been established, it remains unchanged throughout the period, even if the actual level of activity differs from what was estimated. Consequently, the amount of overhead applied to each unit of product is the same regardless of when it is produced during the period.

As alluded to in Exhibit 10A–1, MicroDrive Corporation uses 50,000 budgeted machine-hours as its denominator activity in the predetermined overhead rate. Consequently, the company's predetermined overhead rate is computed as follows:

$$\text{Predetermined overhead rate} = \frac{\$375,000}{50,000 \text{ MHs}} = \$7.50 \text{ per MH}$$

This predetermined overhead rate can be broken down into its variable and fixed components as follows:

$$\text{Variable component of the predetermined overhead rate} = \frac{\$75,000}{50,000 \text{ MHs}} = \$1.50 \text{ per MH}$$

$$\text{Fixed component of the predetermined overhead rate} = \frac{\$300,000}{50,000 \text{ MHs}} = \$6.00 \text{ per MH}$$

For every standard machine-hour recorded, work in process is charged with $7.50 of manufacturing overhead, of which $1.50 is variable manufacturing overhead and $6.00 is fixed manufacturing overhead. In total, MicroDrive Corporation would apply $300,000 of overhead to work in process as shown below:

$$\begin{aligned} \text{Overhead applied} &= \text{Predetermined overhead rate} \times \text{Standard hours allowed for the actual output} \\ &= \$7.50 \text{ per machine-hour} \times 40,000 \text{ machine-hours} \\ &= \$300,000 \end{aligned}$$

Overhead Application in a Standard Cost System

In the job-order costing chapters we applied overhead to work in process on the basis of the actual level of activity (e.g., the actual direct labor-hours worked or the actual machine-hours used). This approach was correct because at the time we were dealing with a normal cost system.[4] However, we are now dealing with a standard cost system where overhead is applied to work in process based on the *standard hours allowed for the actual output of the period* rather than the actual number of hours worked. Exhibit 10A–2 illustrates this point. In a standard cost system, every unit of output is charged with the same amount of overhead cost, regardless of how much time the unit actually requires for processing.

---

[4] Normal cost systems are defined in the Chapters 2 and 3 glossaries.

EXHIBIT 10A–2
Applied Overhead Costs: Normal
Cost System versus Standard Cost
System

Normal Cost System		Standard Cost System	
Manufacturing Overhead		Manufacturing Overhead	
Actual overhead costs incurred.	Applied overhead costs: Actual hours × Pre-determined overhead rate.	Actual overhead costs incurred.	Applied overhead costs: Standard hours allowed for actual output × Pre-determined overhead rate.
Underapplied or overapplied overhead		Underapplied or overapplied overhead	

Budget Variance

Exhibit 10A–3 shows the fixed manufacturing overhead variances computed in a standard costing system—a *budget variance* and a *volume variance*. The **budget variance** is the difference between the actual fixed manufacturing overhead and the budgeted fixed manufacturing overhead for the period. The formula is:

$$\text{Budget variance} = \text{Actual fixed overhead} - \text{Budgeted fixed overhead}$$

If the actual fixed overhead cost exceeds the budgeted fixed overhead, the budget variance is unfavorable. If the actual fixed overhead cost is less than the budgeted fixed overhead, the budget variance is favorable.

Applying the formula to the MicroDrive Corporation data, the budget variance is computed as follows:

$$\text{Budget variance} = \$308{,}000 - \$300{,}000 = \$8{,}000 \text{ U}$$

According to the budget, the fixed manufacturing overhead should have been $300,000, but it was actually $308,000. Because the actual cost exceeds the budget by $8,000, the variance is unfavorable; however, this label does not automatically signal ineffective

EXHIBIT 10A–3
Fixed Overhead Variances

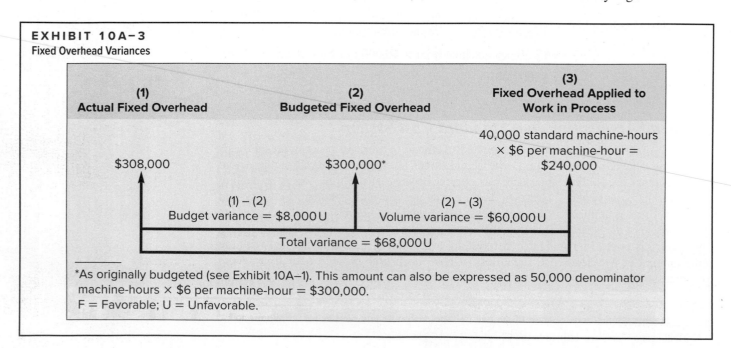

(1) Actual Fixed Overhead	(2) Budgeted Fixed Overhead	(3) Fixed Overhead Applied to Work in Process
		40,000 standard machine-hours × $6 per machine-hour = $240,000
$308,000	$300,000*	$240,000

(1) – (2)
Budget variance = $8,000 U

(2) – (3)
Volume variance = $60,000 U

Total variance = $68,000 U

*As originally budgeted (see Exhibit 10A–1). This amount can also be expressed as 50,000 denominator machine-hours × $6 per machine-hour = $300,000.
F = Favorable; U = Unfavorable.

managerial performance. For example, this variance may result from waste and inefficiency, or it may be due to an unforeseen yet prudent investment in fixed overhead resources that improves product quality or manufacturing cycle efficiency.

Volume Variance

The **volume variance** is defined by the following formula:

$$\text{Volume variance} = \frac{\text{Budgeted fixed}}{\text{overhead}} - \frac{\text{Fixed overhead applied}}{\text{to work in process}}$$

When the budgeted fixed manufacturing overhead exceeds the fixed manufacturing overhead applied to work in process, the volume variance is unfavorable. When the budgeted fixed manufacturing overhead is less than the fixed manufacturing overhead applied to work in process, the volume variance is favorable.

In the case of MicroDrive Corporation, the company produced 20,000 motors and the standard for each motor is 2 machine-hours. Therefore, the standard hours allowed for the actual output is 40,000 machine-hours (= 20,000 motors × 2 machine-hours). As shown in Exhibit 10A–3, the predetermined fixed manufacturing overhead rate of $6.00 per machine-hour is multiplied by the 40,000 standard machine-hours allowed for the actual output to arrive at $240,000 of fixed manufacturing overhead applied to work in process. Given the budgeted fixed overhead of $300,000, the volume variance is computed as follows:

$$\text{Volume variance} = \$300,000 - \$240,000 = \$60,000 \text{ U}$$

The volume variance depends on the difference between the hours used in the denominator to compute the predetermined overhead rate and the standard hours allowed for the actual output of the period. In other words, the volume variance can also be computed using the following formula:

$$\frac{\text{Volume}}{\text{variance}} = \frac{\text{Fixed component of the}}{\text{predetermined overhead rate}} \times \left(\frac{\text{Denominator}}{\text{hours}} - \frac{\text{Standard hours allowed}}{\text{for the actual output}} \right)$$

In the case of MicroDrive Corporation, the volume variance can be computed using this formula as follows:

$$\text{Volume variance} = \frac{\$6.00 \text{ per}}{\text{machine-hour}} \times \left(\frac{50,000}{\text{machine-hours}} - \frac{40,000}{\text{machine-hours}} \right)$$
$$= \$6.00 \text{ per machine-hour} \times 10,000 \text{ machine-hours}$$
$$= \$60,000 \text{ U}$$

Focusing on this new formula, the volume variance is unfavorable if the actual level of activity is less than planned. The volume variance is favorable if the actual level of activity is greater than planned. It is important to note that the volume variance does not measure overspending or underspending. A company should incur the same dollar amount of fixed overhead cost regardless of whether the period's activity was above or below the planned (denominator) level.

The volume variance is often viewed as a measure of the utilization of facilities. If the standard hours allowed for the actual output are greater than (less than) the denominator hours, it signals efficient (inefficient) usage of facilities. However, other measures of utilization—such as the percentage of capacity utilized—are easier to compute and understand.

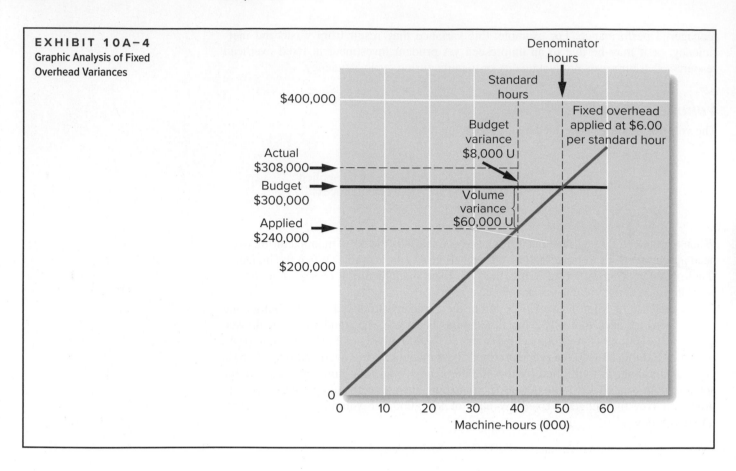

EXHIBIT 10A–4
Graphic Analysis of Fixed
Overhead Variances

Graphic Analysis of Fixed Overhead Variances

Exhibit 10A–4 shows a graphic analysis that offers insights into the fixed overhead budget and volume variances. As shown in the graph, fixed overhead cost is applied to work in process at the predetermined rate of $6.00 for each standard hour of activity. (The applied-cost line is the upward-sloping line on the graph.) Because a denominator level of 50,000 machine-hours was used in computing the $6.00 rate, the applied-cost line crosses the budget-cost line at exactly 50,000 machine-hours. If the denominator hours and the standard hours allowed for the actual output are the same, there is no volume variance. It is only when the standard hours differ from the denominator hours that a volume variance arises.

In MicroDrive's case, the standard hours allowed for the actual output (40,000 hours) are less than the denominator hours (50,000 hours). The result is an unfavorable volume variance because less cost was applied to production than originally budgeted. If the situation had been reversed and the standard hours allowed for the actual output had exceeded the denominator hours, then the volume variance on the graph would have been favorable.

Cautions in Fixed Overhead Analysis

A volume variance arises because we act *as if* the fixed costs are variable when applying fixed overhead to work in process. The graph in Exhibit 10A–4 illustrates this point. Notice fixed overhead costs are applied to work in process at a rate of $6 per hour *as if* they are variable. Treating these costs as if they are variable is necessary for product costing purposes, but it can easily mislead managers into thinking that fixed costs are *in fact* variable. In a sense, the volume variance is the error that occurs by treating fixed costs, which are not proportional to activity, as though they are.

Reconciling Overhead Variances and Underapplied or Overapplied Overhead

In a standard cost system, the underapplied or overapplied overhead for a period equals the sum of the overhead variances. To see this, we will return to the MicroDrive Corporation example.

As discussed earlier, in a standard cost system, overhead is applied to work in process based on the standard hours allowed for the actual output. The following table shows how the underapplied or overapplied overhead for MicroDrive is computed.

Predetermined overhead rate (a)............	$7.50 per machine-hour
Standard machine-hours allowed for the actual production [Exhibit 10A–1] (b)	40,000 machine-hours
Manufacturing overhead applied (a) × (b)	$300,000
Total actual manufacturing overhead [Exhibit 10A–1]	$379,400
Manufacturing overhead underapplied or overapplied.........................	$79,400 underapplied

We previously computed the budget variance and the volume variance for this company. We also need to compute the variable manufacturing overhead variances. The data for these computations are contained in Exhibit 10A–1. Recalling the formulas for the variable manufacturing overhead variances from Exhibit 10–9, we can compute the variable overhead rate and efficiency variances as follows:

$$\text{Variable overhead rate variance} = (AH \times AR) - (AH \times SR)$$
$$= AH(AR - SR)$$
$$= 42,000 \text{ machine-hours} \times \left(\$1.70 \text{ per machine-hour}^4 - \$1.50 \text{ per machine-hour} \right)$$
$$= \$8,400 \text{ U}$$

$$\text{Variable overhead efficiency variance} = (AH \times SR) - (SH \times SR)$$
$$= SR(AH - SH)$$
$$= \$1.50 \text{ per machine-hour} \times \left(42,000 \text{ machine-hours} - 40,000 \text{ per machine-hours} \right)$$
$$= \$3,000 \text{ U}$$

We can now compute the sum of all of the overhead variances as follows:

Variable overhead rate variance	$ 8,400 U
Variable overhead efficiency variance	3,000 U
Fixed overhead budget variance	8,000 U
Fixed overhead volume variance	60,000 U
Total of the overhead variances	$79,400 U

Note the total of the overhead variances is $79,400, which equals the underapplied overhead of $79,400. In general, if the overhead is underapplied, the total of the standard cost overhead variances is unfavorable. If the overhead is overapplied, the total of the standard cost overhead variances is favorable.

---

[5] $AR = \$71,400 \div 42,000$ machine-hours $= \$1.70$ per machine-hour.

Glossary (Appendix 10A)

Budget variance The difference between the actual fixed overhead costs and the budgeted fixed overhead costs for the period. (p. 472)

Denominator activity The level of activity used to compute the predetermined overhead rate. (p. 471)

Volume variance The variance arising when the standard hours allowed for the actual output differ from the denominator activity level used to compute the predetermined overhead rate. It is computed by multiplying the fixed component of the predetermined overhead rate by the difference between the denominator hours and the standard hours allowed for the actual output. (p. 473)

Appendix 10A: Exercises and Problems Mc Graw Hill **connect**

EXERCISE 10A–1 Fixed Overhead Variances LO10–4

Primara Corporation applies overhead to products based on the standard direct labor-hours allowed for the actual output. Data concerning the most recent year appear below:

Total budgeted fixed overhead cost for the year	$250,000
Actual fixed overhead cost for the year	$254,000
Budgeted direct labor-hours (denominator level of activity)	25,000
Actual direct labor-hours	27,000
Standard direct labor-hours allowed for the actual output	26,000

Required:
1. Compute the fixed portion of the predetermined overhead rate for the year.
2. Compute the fixed overhead budget variance and volume variance.

EXERCISE 10A–2 Predetermined Overhead Rate; Overhead Variances LO10–3, LO10–4

Norwall Company's budgeted variable manufacturing overhead cost is $3.00 per machine-hour and its budgeted fixed manufacturing overhead is $300,000 per month.

The following information is available for a recent month:
a. The denominator activity of 60,000 machine-hours is used to compute the predetermined overhead rate.
b. At a denominator activity of 60,000 machine-hours, the company should produce 40,000 units of product.
c. The company's actual operating results were:

Number of units produced	42,000
Actual machine-hours	64,000
Actual variable manufacturing overhead cost	$185,600
Actual fixed manufacturing overhead cost	$302,400

Required:
1. Compute the predetermined overhead rate and break it down into variable and fixed cost elements.
2. Compute the standard hours allowed for the actual production.
3. Compute the variable overhead rate and efficiency variances and the fixed overhead budget and volume variances.

EXERCISE 10A–3 Applying Overhead in a Standard Costing System LO10–4

Privack Corporation applies overhead to products based on the standard direct labor-hours allowed for the actual output. Data concerning the most recent year appear below:

Budgeted variable overhead cost per direct labor-hour	$2
Total budgeted fixed overhead cost per year	$250,000
Budgeted direct labor-hours (denominator level of activity)	40,000
Actual direct labor-hours	39,000
Standard direct labor-hours allowed for the actual output	38,000

Required:

1. Compute the predetermined overhead rate for the year. Be sure to include the total budgeted fixed overhead and the total budgeted variable overhead in the numerator of your rate.
2. Compute the amount of overhead applied to the output of the period.

EXERCISE 10A–4 Fixed Overhead Variances LO10–4

Selected operating information on three different companies for a recent year is given below:

	Company		
	A	B	C
Full-capacity machine-hours	10,000	18,000	20,000
Budgeted machine-hours*	9,000	17,000	20,000
Actual machine-hours	9,000	17,800	19,000
Standard machine-hours allowed			
for actual production	9,500	16,000	20,000

*Denominator activity for computing the predetermined overhead rate.

Required:

For each company, explain why it would have a favorable or unfavorable volume variance.

EXERCISE 10A–5 Using Fixed Overhead Variances LO10–4

The standard cost card for the single product manufactured by Cutter, Inc., is given below:

Inputs	(1) Standard Quantity or Hours	(2) Standard Price or Rate	Standard Cost (1) × (2)
Direct materials	3 yards	$6.00 per yard	$ 18
Direct labor	4 hours	$15.50 per hour	62
Variable overhead	4 hours	$1.50 per hour	6
Fixed overhead	4 hours	$5.00 per hour	20
Total standard cost per unit			$106

Manufacturing overhead is applied to production based on standard direct labor-hours. During the year, the company worked 37,000 hours and manufactured 9,500 units. Selected data relating to the company's fixed manufacturing overhead cost for the year are shown below:

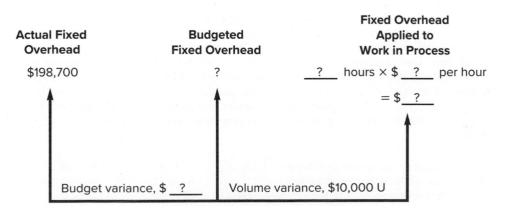

Actual Fixed Overhead	Budgeted Fixed Overhead	Fixed Overhead Applied to Work in Process
$198,700	?	__?__ hours × $__?__ per hour
		= $__?__

Budget variance, $ __?__   Volume variance, $10,000 U

Required:

1. What were the standard hours allowed for the year's production?
2. What was the amount of budgeted fixed overhead cost?
3. What was the fixed overhead budget variance?
4. What denominator activity level did the company use in setting the predetermined overhead rate?

EXERCISE 10A–6 Predetermined Overhead Rate LO10–4

Lasser Company plans to produce 10,000 units next period at a denominator activity of 30,000 direct labor-hours. The direct labor wage rate is $12 per hour. The company's standards allow 2.5 yards of direct materials per unit; the standard material cost is $8.60 per yard. The company's budget includes variable manufacturing overhead of $1.90 per direct labor-hour and fixed manufacturing overhead of $168,000 per period.

Required:

1. Using 30,000 direct labor-hours as the denominator activity, compute the predetermined overhead rate and break it down into variable and fixed elements.
2. Complete the standard cost card below:

Inputs	(1) Standard Quantity or Hours	(2) Standard Price or Rate	Standard Cost (1) × (2)
Direct materials	2.5 yards	$8.60 per yard	$21.50
Direct labor	?	?	?
Variable manufacturing overhead	?	?	?
Fixed manufacturing overhead	?	?	?
Total standard cost per unit			$?

EXERCISE 10A–7 Relations Among Fixed Overhead Variances LO10–4

Selected information relating to Yost Company's operations for the most recent year is given below:

Activity:	
Denominator activity (machine-hours).	45,000
Standard hours allowed per unit	3
Actual number of units produced	14,000
Costs:	
Actual fixed overhead costs incurred	$267,000
Fixed overhead budget variance	$3,000 F

The company applies overhead cost to products based on standard machine-hours.

Required:

1. What were the standard machine-hours allowed for the actual number of units produced?
2. What was the total budgeted fixed overhead cost for the period?
3. What was the fixed portion of the predetermined overhead rate?
4. What was the fixed overhead volume variance?

PROBLEM 10A–8 Applying Overhead; Overhead Variances LO10–3, LO10–4

Lane Company manufactures a single product requiring a great deal of hand labor. Overhead cost is applied based on standard direct labor-hours. The budgeted variable manufacturing overhead is $2 per direct labor-hour and the budgeted fixed manufacturing overhead is $480,000 per year.

The standard quantity of materials is 3 pounds per unit and the standard cost is $7 per pound. The standard direct labor-hours per unit is 1.5 hours and the standard labor rate is $12 per hour.

The company planned to operate at a denominator activity level of 60,000 direct labor-hours and to produce 40,000 units during the most recent year. Actual activity and costs for the year were as follows:

Actual number of units produced	42,000
Actual direct labor-hours worked	65,000
Actual variable manufacturing overhead cost incurred	$123,500
Actual fixed manufacturing overhead cost incurred	$483,000

Required:

1. Compute the predetermined overhead rate for the year. Break the rate down into variable and fixed elements.
2. Prepare a standard cost card for the company's product.

3. Do the following:
   a. Compute the standard direct labor-hours allowed for the year's production.
   b. Complete the following Manufacturing Overhead T-account for the year:

Manufacturing Overhead

?	?
?	?

4. Determine the reason for any underapplied or overapplied overhead for the year by computing the variable overhead rate and efficiency variances and the fixed overhead budget and volume variances.
5. Suppose the company had chosen 65,000 direct labor-hours as the denominator activity rather than 60,000 hours. State which, if any, of the variances computed in (4) above would have changed, and explain how the variance(s) would have changed. No computations are necessary.

PROBLEM 10A–9 Applying Overhead; Overhead Variances LO10–3, LO10–4

Baird Company makes Polish sausage. It applied manufacturing overhead to production based on standard direct labor-hours. According to the company's planning budget, the following manufacturing overhead costs should be incurred at an activity level of 35,000 labor-hours (the denominator activity level):

Variable manufacturing overhead cost.......	$ 87,500
Fixed manufacturing overhead cost	210,000
Total manufacturing overhead cost..........	$297,500

During the most recent year, the following operating results were recorded:

Activity:	
Actual labor-hours worked	30,000
Standard labor-hours allowed for the actual output	32,000
Cost:	
Actual variable manufacturing overhead cost incurred	$78,000
Actual fixed manufacturing overhead cost incurred	$209,400

At the end of the year, the company's Manufacturing Overhead account contained the following data:

Manufacturing Overhead

Actual	287,400	Applied	272,000
	15,400		

Management would like to determine the cause of the $15,400 underapplied overhead.

Required:
1. Compute the predetermined overhead rate. Break the rate down into variable and fixed cost elements.
2. Show how the $272,000 Applied figure in the Manufacturing Overhead account was computed.
3. Break down the $15,400 underapplied overhead into four components: (1) variable overhead rate variance, (2) variable overhead efficiency variance, (3) fixed overhead budget variance, and (4) fixed overhead volume variance.
4. Explain the meaning of each variance computed in (3) above.

PROBLEM 10A–10 Comprehensive Standard Cost Variances LO10–1, LO10–2, LO10–3, LO10–4

"Wonderful! Not only did our salespeople do a good job in meeting the sales budget this year, but our production people did a good job in controlling costs as well," said Kim Clark, president of

Martell Company. "Our $18,300 overall manufacturing cost variance is only 1.2% of the $1,536,000 standard cost of products made during the year. That's well within the 3% parameter set by management for acceptable variances. It looks like everyone will be in line for a bonus this year."

The company produces and sells a single product with a standard cost card as follows:

Inputs	(1) Standard Quantity or Hours	(2) Standard Price or Rate	Standard Cost (1) × (2)
Direct materials	2 feet	$8.45 per foot	$16.90
Direct labor	1.4 hours	$16 per hour	22.40
Variable overhead	1.4 hours	$2.50 per hour	3.50
Fixed overhead	1.4 hours	$6 per hour	8.40
Total standard cost per unit			$51.20

The following additional information is available for the year just completed:

a. The company manufactured 30,000 units during the year.
b. A total of 64,000 feet of material was purchased during the year at a cost of $8.55 per foot. All of this material was used to manufacture the 30,000 units produced. There were no beginning or ending inventories.
c. The company worked 43,500 direct labor-hours at a direct labor cost of $15.80 per hour.
d. Overhead is applied to products based on standard direct labor-hours. Data relating to manufacturing overhead costs follow:

Denominator activity level (direct labor-hours)	35,000
Budgeted fixed overhead costs	$210,000
Actual variable overhead costs incurred	$108,000
Actual fixed overhead costs incurred	$211,800

Required:

1. Compute the materials price and quantity variances.
2. Compute the labor rate and efficiency variances.
3. For manufacturing overhead compute:
   a. The variable overhead rate and efficiency variances.
   b. The fixed overhead budget and volume variances.
4. Total the variances you have computed, and compare the net amount with the $18,300 mentioned by the president. Do you agree bonuses should be given to everyone for good cost control? Explain.

PROBLEM 10A–11 Comprehensive Standard Cost Variances LO10–1, LO10–2, LO10–3, LO10–4
Flandro Company uses a standard cost system and sets its predetermined overhead rate based on direct labor-hours. The following data are taken from the company's planning budget for the current year:

Denominator activity (direct labor-hours)	5,000
Variable manufacturing overhead cost	$25,000
Fixed manufacturing overhead cost	$59,000

The standard cost card for the company's only product is given below:

Inputs	(1) Standard Quantity or Hours	(2) Standard Price or Rate	Standard Cost (1) × (2)
Direct materials	3 yards	$4.40 per yard	$13.20
Direct labor	1 hour	$12 per hour	12.00
Manufacturing overhead	1 hour	$16.80 per hour	16.80
Total standard cost per unit			$42.00

During the year, the company produced 6,000 units and incurred the following actual results:

Materials purchased, 24,000 yards at $4.80 per yard	$115,200
Materials used in production (in yards)	18,500
Direct labor cost incurred, 5,800 hours at $13 per hour	$75,400
Variable manufacturing overhead cost incurred	$29,580
Fixed manufacturing overhead cost incurred	$60,400

Required:

1. Create a new standard cost card that separates the variable manufacturing overhead per unit and the fixed manufacturing overhead per unit.
2. Compute the materials price and quantity variances. Also, compute the labor rate and efficiency variances.
3. Compute the variable overhead rate and efficiency variances. Also, compute the fixed overhead budget and volume variances.
4. What effect, if any, does the choice of a denominator activity level have on unit standard costs? Is the volume variance a controllable variance from a spending point of view? Explain.

PROBLEM 10A–12 Selection of a Denominator; Overhead Analysis; Standard Cost Card LO10–3, LO10–4
Morton Company's budgeted variable manufacturing overhead is $4.50 per direct labor-hour and its budgeted fixed manufacturing overhead is $270,000 per year.

The company manufactures a single product whose standard direct labor-hours per unit is 2 hours. The standard direct labor wage rate is $15 per hour. The standards also allow 4 feet of raw material per unit at a standard cost of $8.75 per foot.

Although normal activity is 30,000 direct labor-hours each year, the company expects to operate 40,000 hours this year.

Required:

1. Assume the company chooses 30,000 direct labor-hours as the denominator level of activity. Compute the predetermined overhead rate, breaking it down into variable and fixed cost elements.
2. Assume the company chooses 40,000 direct labor-hours as the denominator level of activity. Compute the predetermined overhead rate, breaking it down into variable and fixed cost elements.
3. Complete two standard cost cards as outlined below.

Inputs	(1) Standard Quantity or Hours	(2) Standard Price or Rate	Standard Cost (1) × (2)
Denominator Activity: 30,000 Direct Labor-Hours			
Direct materials	4 feet	$8.75 per foot	$35.00
Direct labor	?	?	?
Variable manufacturing overhead	?	?	?
Fixed manufacturing overhead	?	?	?
Total standard cost per unit			$?
Denominator Activity: 40,000 Direct Labor-Hours			
Direct materials	4 feet	$8.75 per foot	$35.00
Direct labor	?	?	?
Variable manufacturing overhead	?	?	?
Fixed manufacturing overhead	?	?	?
Total standard cost per unit			$?

4. Assume the company actually produces 18,000 units and works 38,000 direct labor-hours. Actual manufacturing overhead costs for the year are:

Variable manufacturing overhead cost	$174,800
Fixed manufacturing overhead cost	271,600
Total manufacturing overhead cost	$446,400

Do the following:

a. Compute the standard direct labor-hours allowed for this year's production.

b. Complete the Manufacturing Overhead T-account below. Assume the company uses 30,000 direct labor-hours (normal activity) as the denominator activity in computing predetermined overhead rates, as you have done in (1) above.

Manufacturing Overhead

Actual costs	446,400	Applied costs	?
	?		?

c. Determine the cause of the underapplied or overapplied overhead for the year by computing the variable overhead rate and efficiency variances and the fixed overhead budget and volume variances.

5. Looking at the variances you computed, what appears to be the major disadvantage of using normal activity rather than expected actual activity as a denominator in computing the predetermined overhead rate? What advantages can you see to offset this disadvantage?

Appendix 10B: Standard Cost Systems: A Financial Reporting Perspective Using Microsoft Excel

LO10–5

Prepare an income statement using a standard cost system.

The main body of Chapter 10 and Appendix 10A focused on calculating standard cost variances for management control purposes. This appendix explains how to use a standard cost system to create a balance sheet and an income statement for financial reporting purposes. We purposely use Microsoft Excel to create these two financial statements because it enables us to teach you a valuable managerial skill—how to evaluate a transaction's impact on the balance sheet.

To set the stage for the forthcoming example, we need to review two fundamental accounting equations and specify four important assumptions.

Fundamental Accounting Equations

A company's balance sheet is based on the following accounting equation that is the bedrock of double-entry bookkeeping:

$$\text{Assets} = \text{Liabilities} + \text{Stockholders' Equity}$$

In the Excel spreadsheets we'll use in this appendix, one column will always be populated with an "=" sign. The accounts on the left-hand side of the "=" sign will be asset accounts and the accounts on the right-hand side will be liability and equity accounts. After we record every transaction, the amounts on the left-hand side of the "=" sign must equal the amounts on the right-hand side.

The second foundational equation relates to the Retained Earnings account on a company's balance sheet. The ending balance in retained earnings is computed using the following equation:

$$\begin{array}{c}\text{Ending balance in} \\ \text{retained earnings}\end{array} = \begin{array}{c}\text{Beginning balance in} \\ \text{retained earnings}\end{array} + \begin{array}{c}\text{Net} \\ \text{operating} \\ \text{income}\end{array} - \text{Dividends}$$

This equation highlights the connection between the balance sheet and the income statement. It explicitly recognizes that net operating income from the income statement plugs into Retained Earnings on the balance sheet. In this appendix, we will not include any dividends; therefore, the only transactions recorded in the Retained Earnings account will be transactions affecting net operating income. Any transactions involving the recording of sales or the recognition of expenses will be recorded in the Retained Earnings column of the balance sheet. This approach highlights the critically important idea that a company's income statement is embedded within the Retained Earnings account in its balance sheet.

Four Key Assumptions

The first assumption we use in this appendix is Raw Materials, Work in Process, and Finished Goods are always carried at their *standard cost*. In other words, the standard prices paid for inputs and the standard quantities of inputs allowed for the actual level of production *will be used to flow costs through the inventory accounts*. The actual prices paid for inputs and the actual quantities of inputs used in production *will not affect the costs recorded in the inventory accounts*.

This approach to standard costing greatly simplifies the bookkeeping process. To enable this simplification, we will always close all standard cost variances to Cost of Goods Sold rather than closing them to the various inventory accounts *and* Cost of Goods Sold. When the closing entry increases Cost of Goods Sold, we will decrease Retained Earnings. We do this because increasing Cost of Goods Sold lowers net operating income, which, in turn, lowers Retained Earnings. Conversely, when the closing entry decreases Cost of Goods Sold, we will increase Retained Earnings. We do this because decreasing Cost of Goods Sold increases net operating income, which, in turn, increases Retained Earnings.

The second assumption relates to the *clearing accounts* we use to record standard cost variances. Clearing accounts always begin and end each accounting period with a zero balance. In our Excel spreadsheets, each variance will always have its own clearing account appearing on the right-hand side of the "=" sign. Putting these clearing accounts on the right-hand side of the "=" sign (rather than the left-hand side) enables us to record all favorable variances as *increases* to their respective clearing accounts and all unfavorable variances as *decreases* to their accounts. Once all variances have been recorded, the final transaction of the period will close each clearing account to Cost of Goods Sold and record the resulting change in net operating income within the Retained Earnings account.

The third assumption relates to restricting the number of general ledger accounts used in this appendix. In terms of asset accounts, we will always limit the scope of our accounts to include Cash, Raw Materials, Work in Process, Finished Goods, and Property, Plant, and Equipment, net of accumulated depreciation (which may be abbreviated as PP&E, net). With respect to liability and equity accounts, we will always use only one account—Retained Earnings.[6]

Our fourth assumption is we'll record transactions within Microsoft Excel by using positive numbers to increase accounts and negative numbers (shown in parentheses) to decrease accounts. This is a slightly different approach than relying on the language of debits and credits. Instead of recording debits and credits, we'll identify the accounts affected by each transaction and then record increases or decreases in those accounts.

Standard Cost Systems: An Example

Dylan Corporation manufactures only one product and uses a standard cost system for internal management and financial reporting purposes. The company uses a *plantwide predetermined overhead rate* based on direct labor-hours as the allocation base. All of the

---

[6] Ordinarily we would include a Common Stock account within the Stockholders' Equity section of the balance sheet. However, to minimize the number of columns in our spreadsheets, this appendix omits the Common Stock account and uses the term *Liabilities and Equity* rather than *Liabilities and Stockholders' Equity*.

company's manufacturing overhead costs are fixed—it does not incur any variable manufacturing overhead costs. The predetermined overhead rate is based on a cost formula that estimated $1,875,000 of fixed manufacturing overhead for an estimated allocation base of 75,000 labor-hours.

The company wants to create an ending balance sheet and an income statement for the current year. Its beginning balance sheet is shown in Exhibit 10B–1 (all numbers are in thousands). Work in Process does not appear on the beginning balance sheet because Dylan Corporation does not maintain any beginning or ending work in process inventory. A standard cost card for the company's only product is shown in Exhibit 10B–2.

EXHIBIT 10B–1
Dylan Corporation: Beginning Balance Sheet

	A	B
1	**Dylan Corporation**	
2	**Balance Sheet**	
3	**1/1/XX**	
4	**(dollars in thousands)**	
5		
6	**Assets**	
7	Cash	$ 1,100
8	Raw materials inventory*	400
9	Finished goods inventory**	714
10	Property, plant, and equipment, net	5,200
11	Total assets	$ 7,414
12		
13	**Liabilities and Equity**	
14	Retained earnings	7,414
15	Total liabilities and equity	$ 7,414
16		
17	* 80,000 pounds × $5.00 per pound = $400,000	
18	** 14,000 units × $51.00 per unit = $714,000	
19		

Exhibit 10B-1 / Exhibit 10B-2 / Exhib

Microsoft Excel

EXHIBIT 10B–2
Dylan Corporation: Standard Cost Card

	A	B	C	D	E	F
1		**Dylan Corporation**				
2		**Standard Cost Card**				
3	*Inputs*	(1) Standard Quantity or Hours		(2) Standard Price or Rate		Standard Cost (1) × (2)
4	Direct materials	4.2	pounds	$ 5.00	per pound	$ 21.00
5	Direct labor	0.75	hour	$ 15.00	per hour	11.25
6	Fixed manufacturing overhead	0.75	hour	$ 25.00	per hour	18.75
7	Total standard cost per unit					$ 51.00
8						

Exhibit 10B-1   Exhibit 10B-2 / Exhibit 10B-3 / Exhibit 1

Microsoft Excel

Summary of Transactions

During the year, Dylan completed the following transactions:

a. Purchased 380,000 pounds of raw material for cash at a price of $4.75 per pound.
b. Added 365,000 pounds of raw material to work in process to produce 88,000 units.
c. Assigned direct labor costs to work in process. The direct laborers (who were paid in cash) worked 72,000 hours at an average cost of $14.50 per hour to manufacture 88,000 units.
d. Applied fixed overhead to work in process using the predetermined overhead rate multiplied by the number of labor-hours allowed to manufacture 88,000 units. Actual fixed overhead costs for the year were $1,750,000. Of this total, $900,000 related to items such as insurance, utilities, and indirect labor salaries that were all paid in cash and $850,000 related to depreciation of manufacturing equipment.
e. Transferred 88,000 units from work in process to finished goods.
f. Sold (for cash) 85,000 units to customers at a price of $62.00 per unit.
g. Transferred the standard cost associated with the 85,000 units sold from finished goods to cost of goods sold.
h. Paid $450,000 of selling and administrative expenses.
i. Closed all standard cost variances to cost of goods sold.

Exhibit 10B–3 shows the spreadsheet we'll be using to record Dylan Corporation's transactions. Notice cell A7 depicts the beginning balance for the period (1/1) and cell A17 depicts the ending balance (12/31). In between the beginning and ending balances, rows 8 through 16 will be used to record transactions *a* through *i*. Also, note the beginning balances shown in row 7 of the spreadsheet (in thousands) correspond to the amounts shown in the balance sheet in Exhibit 10B–1. Finally, we want to emphasize columns H through M represent the clearing accounts corresponding to the six variances we'll be

---

EXHIBIT 10B–3
Dylan Corporation: The Transaction Template

	A	B	C	D	E	F	G H	I	J	K	L	M	N
1							Dylan Corporation						
2							Transaction Analysis						
3							For the Year Ended 12/31/XX						
4							(dollars in thousands)						
6		Cash	Raw Materials	Work in Process	Finished Goods	PP&E (net)	= Materials Price Variance	Materials Quantity Variance	Labor Rate Variance	Labor Efficiency Variance	Fixed Overhead Budget Variance	Fixed Overhead Volume Variance	Retained Earnings
7	1/1	$ 1,100	$ 400	$ -	$ 714	$ 5,200	= $ -	$ -	$ -	$ -	$ -	$ -	$ 7,414
8	a.												
9	b.												
10	c.												
11	d.												
12	e.												
13	f.												
14	g.												
15	h.												
16	i.												
17	12/31												
22													

Exhibit 10B-1 | Exhibit 10B-2 | **Exhibit 10B-3** | Exhibit 10B-4 | Exhibit 10B-5

Source: Microsoft Excel

computing shortly. Each variance account in these six columns starts with a beginning balance of zero and concludes the period with an ending balance of zero. They each record a variance for the period and then close that variance to Cost of Goods Sold at the end of the period, thereby ensuring an ending balance of zero.

Now we are ready to demonstrate a three-step process for preparing Dylan Corporation's income statement. First, we are going to compute all six of the company's manufacturing cost variances. Second, we will record transactions *a* through *i*. Finally, we will prepare Dylan's income statement for the year.

Calculating the Variances

For Dylan Corporation, the quantity of materials purchased (380,000 pounds) does not equal the quantity used in production (365,000 pounds); therefore, the materials price variance will be based on the *quantity of materials purchased* and the materials quantity variance will be based on the *quantity of materials used in production*. The computations of these two variances are as follows:

Materials price variance:
Materials price variance $= (AQ \times AP) - (AQ \times SP)$
Materials price variance $= AQ(AP - SP)$
Materials price variance $=$ 380,000 pounds ($4.75 per pound $-$ $5.00 per pound)
Materials price variance $=$ $95,000 F

Materials quantity variance:
Materials quantity variance $= (AQ \times SP) - (SQ \times SP)$
Materials quantity variance $= SP(AQ - SQ)$
Materials quantity variance $=$ $5.00 per pound (365,000 pounds $-$ 369,600 pounds*)
Materials quantity variance $=$ $23,000 F

---
*SQ $=$ 88,000 units produced $\times$ 4.2 pounds per unit $=$ 369,600 pounds

The materials price variance is favorable because the actual price per pound ($4.75) is less than the standard price per pound ($5.00). The materials quantity variance is favorable because the 365,000 pounds used in production are less than the 369,600 pounds (= 88,000 units × 4.2 pounds per unit) the standards allow for the actual level of output.

The direct labor rate and efficiency variances are computed as follows:

Labor rate variance:
Labor rate variance $= (AH \times AR) - (AH \times SR)$
Labor rate variance $= AH(AR - SR)$
Labor rate variance $=$ 72,000 hours ($14.50 per hour $-$ $15.00 per hour)
Labor rate variance $=$ $36,000 F

Labor efficiency variance:
Labor efficiency variance $= (AH \times SR) - (SH \times SR)$
Labor efficiency variance $= SR(AH - SH)$
Labor efficiency variance $=$ $15.00 per hour (72,000 hours $-$ 66,000 hours*)
Labor efficiency variance $=$ $90,000 U

---
*SQ $=$ 88,000 units produced $\times$ 0.75 hour per unit $=$ 66,000 hours

The labor rate variance is favorable because the actual labor rate ($14.50) is less than the standard labor rate ($15.00). The labor efficiency variance is unfavorable because the 72,000 hours actually worked are greater than the 66,000 hours (= 88,000 units × 0.75 hour per unit) the standards allow for the actual level of output.

The fixed overhead budget and volume variances are computed as follows:

Budget variance:

Budget variance = Actual fixed overhead − Budgeted fixed overhead

Budget variance = $1,750,000 − $1,875,000

Budget variance = $125,000 F

Volume variance:

Volume variance = Budgeted fixed overhead − Fixed overhead applied to work in process

Volume variance = $1,875,000 − $1,650,000*

Volume variance = $225,000 U

_____

*Fixed overhead applied to work in process = 66,000 hours allowed for the actual output × $25 per hour = $1,650,000

The fixed overhead budget variance of $125,000 is favorable (F) because the actual amount of fixed overhead ($1,750,000) is less than the budgeted amount of fixed overhead ($1,875,000), whereas the fixed overhead volume variance of $225,000 is unfavorable (U) because the budgeted fixed overhead ($1,875,000) is greater than the fixed overhead applied to work in process ($1,650,000). The fixed overhead applied to work in process is calculated by multiplying the predetermined overhead rate ($25.00) by the *number of direct labor-hours allowed for the actual level of production* (66,000 hours). Fixed overhead is *not* applied to production using the actual direct labor-hours worked!

Recording the Transactions

Exhibit 10B–4 shows how to properly record all of the transactions for Dylan Corporation (all amounts are in thousands). You'll notice all favorable variances (in columns H through M) are recorded without parentheses and all unfavorable variances (in columns H through M) are recorded with parentheses. This occurs because favorable variances increase net operating income (and retained earnings) when they are closed to cost of goods sold and unfavorable variances decrease net operating income (and retained earnings) when they are closed to cost of goods sold. For example, the materials price variance of $95,000 F appears in cell H8 without parentheses. To close this variance, we record $(95,000) in cell H16, thereby bringing the ending balance in the Materials Price Variance clearing account to zero. The $(95,000) in cell H16 is offset by adding $95,000 to Retained Earnings. When all six variances are closed to Cost of Goods Sold, their combined effect is to reduce net operating income and Retained Earnings by the $(36,000) shown in cell N16.

Once all transactions are recorded, Microsoft Excel can quickly compute the ending balances for all balance sheet accounts as shown in row 17 of Exhibit 10B–4. Notice all of the variance accounts (in columns H through M) have an ending balance of zero because they all serve as clearing accounts. Also note the inventory accounts in the ending balance sheet are valued using *standard costs*. For example, the ending balance in Raw Materials ($475,000) consists of 95,000 pounds of materials each carried in inventory at a standard cost of $5.00 per pound. The ending balance in Finished Goods ($867,000) consists of 17,000 units each valued at a standard cost of $51.00 per unit.

EXHIBIT 10B-4
Dylan Corporation: Transaction Analysis

Dylan Corporation
Transaction Analysis
For the Year Ended 12/31/XX
(dollars in thousands)

	Cash	Raw Materials	Work in Process	Finished Goods	PP&E (net)	=	Materials Price Variance	Materials Quantity Variance	Labor Rate Variance	Labor Efficiency Variance	Fixed Overhead Budget Variance	Fixed Overhead Volume Variance	Retained Earnings
1/1	1,100	$ 400	$ -	$ 714	$ 5,200	=	$ -	$ -	$ -	$ -	$ -	$ -	$ 7,414
a.	(1,805)	1,900				=	95						
b.		(1,825)	1,848			=		23					
c.	(1,044)		990			=			36	(90)			
d.	(900)		1,650		(850)	=					125	(225)	
e.			(4,488)	4,488		=							
f.	5,270					=							5,270
g.				(4,335)		=							(4,335)
h.	(450)					=							(450)
i.						=	(95)	(23)	(36)	90	(125)	225	(36)
12/31	2,171	$ 475	$ -	$ 867	$ 4,350	=	$ -	$ -	$ -	$ -	$ -	$ -	$ 7,863

Exhibit 10B-1 / Exhibit 10B-2 / Exhibit 10B-3 / **Exhibit 10B-4** / Exhibit 10B

Microsoft Excel

The explanations for transactions *a* through *i* (as recorded above) are as follows:

a. Cash decreases by the actual cost of the raw materials purchased, which is $AQ \times AP$ (380,000 × $4.75 = $1,805,000). Raw Materials increase by the standard cost of the raw materials purchased, which is $AQ \times SP$ (380,000 × $5 = $1,900,000). The materials price variance is $95,000 F.

b. Raw Materials decrease by the standard cost of the raw materials used in production, which is $AQ \times SP$ (365,000 × $5.00 = $1,825,000). Work in Process increases by the standard cost of the standard quantity of raw materials allowed for the actual output, which is $SQ \times SP$ (369,600 × $5.00 = $1,848,000). The materials quantity variance is $23,000 F.

c. Cash decreases by the actual amount paid to direct laborers, which is $AH \times AR$ (72,000 × $14.50 = $1,044,000). Work in Process increases by the standard cost of the standard amount of hours allowed for the actual output, which is $SH \times SR$ (66,000 × $15.00 = $990,000). The labor rate variance is $36,000 F and the labor efficiency variance is $90,000 U.

d. Cash decreases by the actual amount paid for various fixed overhead costs, which is $900,000. Work in Process increases by the standard amount of hours allowed for the actual output multiplied by the predetermined overhead rate, which is 66,000 hours × $25.00 per hour = $1,650,000. PP&E (net) decreases by the amount of depreciation for the period, which is $850,000. The fixed overhead budget variance is $125,000 F and the fixed overhead volume variance is $225,000 U.

e. Work in process decreases by the number of units transferred to Finished Goods multiplied by the standard cost per unit, which is 88,000 units × $51.00 per unit = $4,488,000. Finished Goods increases by the same amount.

f. Cash increases by the number of units sold multiplied by the selling price per unit, which is 85,000 units sold × $62.00 per unit = $5,270,000. Retained Earnings increases by the same amount.

g. Finished Goods decrease by the number of units sold multiplied by their standard cost per unit, which is 85,000 units sold × $51.00 per unit = $4,335,000. Retained Earnings decreases by the same amount.

h. Cash and Retained Earnings decrease by $450,000 to record the selling and administrative expenses.

i. All variance accounts take their balance to zero as they are closed to Cost of Goods Sold. The net effect of closing all of these variances is to increase Cost of Goods Sold by $36,000. The equation supporting this logic is as follows: $(95,000) + $(23,000) + $(36,000) + $90,000 + $(125,000) + $225,000 = $36,000. Because Cost of Goods Sold increases by $36,000, it lowers net operating income and Retained Earnings by the same amount.

EXHIBIT 10B–5
Dylan Corporation: Income Statement

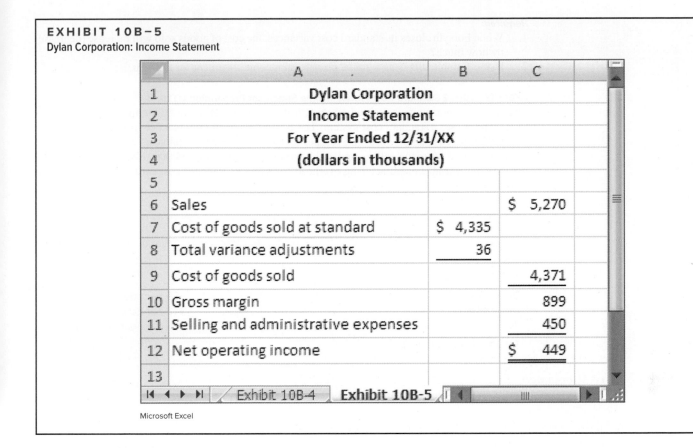

	A	B	C
1	**Dylan Corporation**		
2	**Income Statement**		
3	**For Year Ended 12/31/XX**		
4	**(dollars in thousands)**		
5			
6	Sales		$ 5,270
7	Cost of goods sold at standard	$ 4,335	
8	Total variance adjustments	36	
9	Cost of goods sold		4,371
10	Gross margin		899
11	Selling and administrative expenses		450
12	Net operating income		$ 449
13			

Exhibit 10B-4　**Exhibit 10B-5**

Microsoft Excel

Preparing the Income Statement

Exhibit 10B–5 shows Dylan Corporation's income statement derived from the Retained Earnings column of Exhibit 10B–4. The sales in the income statement of $5,270,000 come from cell N13 in Exhibit 10B–4. The cost of goods sold at standard ($4,335,000) comes from cell N14 of Exhibit 10B–4. Finally, the sum of the variance adjustments ($36,000) and the selling and administrative expenses ($450,000) come from cells N16 and N15, respectively. Although all of the numbers in Exhibit 10B–5 are shown as positive numbers, the cost of goods sold at standard ($4,335,000), the selling and administrative expenses ($450,000), and the variance adjustments ($36,000) are shown as negative numbers in column N of Exhibit 10B–4 to recognize they each reduce retained earnings.

McGraw Hill connect　　**Appendix 10B: Exercises and Problems**

EXERCISE 10B–1 Standard Cost Flows; Income Statement Preparation LO10–5

Forsyth Company manufactures one product, it does not maintain any beginning or ending inventories, and it uses a standard cost system. During the year, the company produced and sold 10,000 units at a price of $135 per unit. Its standard cost per unit produced is $105 and its selling and administrative expenses totaled $235,000. Forsyth does not have any variable manufacturing overhead costs and it recorded the following variances during the year:

Materials price variance..........................	$6,500 F
Materials quantity variance	$10,200 U
Labor rate variance................................	$3,500 U
Labor efficiency variance	$4,400 F
Fixed overhead budget variance	$2,500 F
Fixed overhead volume variance	$12,000 F

Required:

1. When Forsyth closes its standard cost variances, the cost of goods sold will increase (decrease) by how much?
2. Using Exhibit 10B–5 as a guide, prepare an income statement for the year.

EXERCISE 10B–2 Standard Cost Flows; Income Statement Preparation LO10–5

Swain Company manufactures one product, it does not maintain any beginning or ending inventories, and it uses a standard cost system. The company's beginning balance in Retained Earnings is $70,000. It sells one product for $165 per unit and it generated total sales during the period of $577,500 while incurring selling and administrative expenses of $54,000. Swain Company does not have any variable manufacturing overhead costs and its standard cost card for its only product is as follows:

	(1) Standard Quantity or Hours	(2) Standard Price or Rate	Standard Cost (1) × (2)
Direct materials	7.0 pounds	$9 per pound	$ 63
Direct labor	2.5 hours	$12 per hour	30
Fixed manufacturing overhead	2.5 hours	$20 per hour	50
Total standard cost per unit			$143

During the period, Swain recorded the following variances:

Materials price variance...........................	$3,400 U
Materials quantity variance	$9,000 F
Labor rate variance	$3,900 U
Labor efficiency variance	$6,600 U
Fixed overhead budget variance	$1,300 U
Fixed overhead volume variance...................	$5,500 F

Required:

1. When Swain closes its standard cost variances, the cost of goods sold will increase (decrease) by how much?
2. Using Exhibit 10B–5 as a guide, prepare an income statement for the year.
3. What is Swain's ending balance in Retained Earnings?

EXERCISE 10B–3 Standard Cost Flows LO10–5

Bowen Company manufactures one product, it does not maintain any beginning or ending inventories, and it uses a standard cost system. Its predetermined overhead rate includes $1,000,000 of fixed overhead in the numerator and 50,000 direct labor-hours in the denominator. The company purchased (with cash) and used 30,000 yards of raw materials at a cost of $9.80 per yard. Its direct laborers worked 20,000 hours and were paid a total of $290,000. The company started and completed 8,100 units of finished goods during the period. Bowen's standard cost card for its only product is as follows:

Inputs	(1) Standard Quantity or Hours	(2) Standard Price or Rate	Standard Cost (1) × (2)
Direct materials	3.0 yards	$10.00 per yard	$ 30.00
Direct labor..........................	2.4 hours	$14.00 per hour	33.60
Fixed manufacturing overhead	2.4 hours	$20.00 per hour	48.00
Total standard cost per unit			$111.60

Required:

1. When recording the raw material purchases:
   a. The Raw Materials inventory will increase (decrease) by how much?
   b. The Cash will increase (decrease) by how much?
2. When recording the raw materials used in production:
   a. The Raw Materials inventory will increase (decrease) by how much?
   b. The Work in Process inventory will increase (decrease) by how much?
3. When recording the direct labor costs added to production:
   a. The Work in Process inventory will increase (decrease) by how much?
   b. The Cash will increase (decrease) by how much?
4. When applying fixed manufacturing overhead to production, the Work in Process inventory will increase (decrease) by how much?
5. When transferring manufacturing costs from Work in Process to Finished Goods, the Finished Goods inventory will increase (decrease) by how much?

EXERCISE 10B–4 Standard Cost Flows LO10–5

Hartwell Company manufactures one product, it does not maintain any beginning or ending inventories, and it uses a standard cost system. Its predetermined overhead rate includes $1,760,000 of fixed manufacturing overhead in the numerator and 44,000 direct labor-hours in the denominator. The actual fixed manufacturing overhead for the period was $1,780,000.

The company purchased (with cash) and used 60,000 yards of raw materials at a cost of $11.00 per yard. Its direct laborers worked 40,000 hours and were paid a total of $600,000. The company started and completed 28,000 units of finished goods during the period. Hartwell's standard cost card for its only product is as follows:

Inputs	(1) Standard Quantity or Hours	(2) Standard Price or Rate	Standard Cost (1) × (2)
Direct materials	2 yards	$12.00 per yard	$ 24.00
Direct labor	1.5 hours	$15.00 per hour	22.50
Fixed manufacturing overhead	1.5 hours	$40.00 per hour	60.00
Total standard cost per unit			$106.50

Required:

1. When recording the raw material purchases:
   a. The Raw Materials inventory will increase (decrease) by how much?
   b. The Cash will increase (decrease) by how much?
   c. The materials price variance will be favorable or unfavorable and by how much?
2. When recording the raw materials used in production:
   a. The Raw Materials inventory will increase (decrease) by how much?
   b. The Work in Process inventory will increase (decrease) by how much?
   c. The materials quantity variance will be favorable or unfavorable and by how much?
3. When recording the direct labor costs added to production:
   a. The Work in Process inventory will increase (decrease) by how much?
   b. The Cash will increase (decrease) by how much?
   c. The labor rate and efficiency variances will be favorable or unfavorable and by how much?
4. When applying fixed manufacturing overhead to production:
   a. The Work in Process inventory will increase (decrease) by how much?
   b. The fixed overhead budget and volume variances will be favorable or unfavorable and by how much?
5. When transferring costs from Work in Process to Finished Goods, the Finished Goods inventory will increase (decrease) by how much?

PROBLEM 10B–5 Transaction Analysis; Income Statement Preparation LO10–1, LO10–2, LO10–4, LO10–5

Wallis Company manufactures only one product and uses a standard cost system. The company uses a predetermined plantwide overhead rate based on direct labor-hours as the allocation base. All of the company's manufacturing overhead costs are fixed—it does not incur any variable manufacturing overhead costs. The predetermined overhead rate is based on a cost formula that estimated $2,880,000 of fixed manufacturing overhead for an estimated allocation base of 288,000 direct labor-hours. Wallis does not maintain any beginning or ending work in process inventory.

The company's beginning balance sheet is as follows:

Wallis Company Balance Sheet 1/1/XX (dollars in thousands)	
Assets	
Cash	$ 700
Raw materials inventory	150
Finished goods inventory	270
Property, plant, and equipment, net	8,500
Total assets	$9,620
Liabilities and Equity	
Retained earnings	$9,620
Total liabilities and equity	$9,620

The company's standard cost card for its only product is as follows:

Inputs	(1) Standard Quantity or Hours	(2) Standard Price or Rate	Standard Cost (1) × (2)
Direct materials	2 pounds	$30.00 per pound	$ 60.00
Direct labor	3.00 hours	$15.00 per hour	45.00
Fixed manufacturing overhead	3.00 hours	$10.00 per hour	30.00
Total standard cost per unit			$135.00

During the year Wallis completed the following transactions:
a. Purchased (with cash) 230,000 pounds of raw material at a price of $29.50 per pound.
b. Added 215,000 pounds of raw material to work in process to produce 95,000 units.
c. Assigned direct labor costs to work in process. The direct laborers (who were paid in cash) worked 245,000 hours at an average cost of $16.00 per hour to manufacture 95,000 units.
d. Applied fixed overhead to work in process inventory using the predetermined overhead rate multiplied by the number of direct labor-hours allowed to manufacture 95,000 units. Actual fixed overhead costs for the year were $2,740,000. Of this total, $1,340,000 related to items such as insurance, utilities, and salaried indirect laborers that were all paid in cash and $1,400,000 related to depreciation of equipment.
e. Transferred 95,000 units from work in process to finished goods.
f. Sold (for cash) 92,000 units to customers at a price of $170 per unit.
g. Transferred the standard cost associated with the 92,000 units sold from finished goods to cost of goods sold.
h. Paid $2,120,000 of selling and administrative expenses.
i. Closed all standard cost variances to cost of goods sold.

Required:
1. Compute all direct materials, direct labor, and fixed overhead variances for the year.
2. Using Exhibit 10B–3 as a guide, record transactions *a* through *i* for Wallis Company.
3. Compute the ending balances for Wallis Company's balance sheet.
4. Using Exhibit 10B–5 as a guide, prepare Wallis Company's income statement for the year.

PROBLEM 10B–6 Transaction Analysis; Income Statement Preparation LO10–1, LO10–2, LO10–3, LO10–4, LO10–5
Phoenix Company manufactures only one product and uses a standard cost system. The company uses a plantwide predetermined overhead rate based on direct labor-hours as the allocation base. The predetermined overhead rate is based on a cost formula that estimated $2,880,000 of fixed and

variable manufacturing overhead for an estimated allocation base of 240,000 direct labor-hours. Phoenix does not maintain any beginning or ending work in process inventory.

The company's beginning balance sheet is as follows:

Phoenix Company Balance Sheet 1/1/XX (dollars in thousands)	
Assets	
Cash	$ 1,200
Raw materials inventory	300
Finished goods inventory	540
All other assets	12,000
Total assets	$14,040
Liabilities and Equity	
Retained earnings...........................	$14,040
Total liabilities and equity	$14,040

The company's standard cost card for its only product is as follows:

Inputs	(1) Standard Quantity or Hours	(2) Standard Price or Rate	Standard Cost (1) × (2)
Direct materials	3 pounds	$25.00 per pound	$ 75.00
Direct labor	2.00 hours	$16.00 per hour	32.00
Variable manufacturing overhead	2.00 hours	$2.00 per hour	4.00
Fixed manufacturing overhead..........	2.00 hours	$10.00 per hour	20.00
Total standard cost per unit			$131.00

During the year Phoenix completed the following transactions:
a. Purchased (with cash) 460,000 pounds of raw material at a price of $26.50 per pound.
b. Added 430,000 pounds of raw material to work in process to produce 125,000 units.
c. Assigned direct labor costs to work in process. The direct laborers (who were paid in cash) worked 265,000 hours at an average cost of $15.00 per hour to manufacture 125,000 units.
d. Applied variable manufacturing overhead to work in process inventory using the variable portion of the predetermined overhead rate multiplied by the number of direct labor-hours allowed to manufacture 125,000 units. Actual variable manufacturing overhead costs for the year (all paid in cash) were $480,000.
e. Applied fixed manufacturing overhead to work in process inventory using the fixed portion of the predetermined overhead rate multiplied by the number of direct labor-hours allowed to manufacture 125,000 units. Actual fixed manufacturing overhead costs for the year were $2,450,000. Of this total, $1,300,000 related to items such as insurance, utilities, and salaried indirect laborers that were all paid in cash and $1,150,000 related to depreciation of equipment.
f. Transferred 125,000 units from work in process to finished goods.
g. Sold (for cash) 123,000 units to customers at a price of $175 per unit.
h. Transferred the standard cost associated with the 123,000 units sold from finished goods to cost of goods sold.
i. Paid $3,300,000 of selling and administrative expenses.
j. Closed all standard cost variances to cost of goods sold.

Required:
1. Compute all direct materials, direct labor, variable overhead, and fixed overhead variances for the year.
2. Using Exhibit 10B–3 as a guide, record transactions a through j for Phoenix Company.
3. Compute the ending balances for Phoenix Company's balance sheet.
4. Using Exhibit 10B–5 as a guide, prepare Phoenix Company's income statement for the year.

Chapter 11

Responsibility Accounting Systems

JHVEPhoto/Shutterstock

lighthouse image: Martin73/Shutterstock;
big data image: INGARA/Shutterstock

LEARNING OBJECTIVES

After studying Chapter 11, you should be able to:

LO11-1 Compute return on investment (ROI) and show how changes in sales, expenses, and assets affect ROI.

LO11-2 Compute residual income and explain its strengths and weaknesses.

LO11-3 Determine the range, if any, within which a negotiated transfer price should fall.

LO11-4 Charge operating departments for services provided by service departments.

 Data Analytics Exercise available in Connect to complement this chapter

ENTREPRENEUR SPOTLIGHT

Sara Blakely was selling fax machines, had only $5,000 in savings, and had just moved out of her mom's house when she came up with a life-changing idea. While getting dressed for a party, she cut the feet out of some control top pantyhose and wore them beneath her pants. Blakely noted, "I looked fabulous. I felt great. I had no panty lines, I looked thinner and smoother, but they rolled up my legs all night." Eventually, she worked out the kinks and created shapewear by Spanx. Today, Spanx sells shapewear, leggings, clothing, bras, panties, hosiery, activewear, and men's wear in over 50 countries.

Applying Managerial Accounting

Spanx can use responsibility accounting for management control purposes. For example, the company might define its responsibility centers by product line, such as leggings, shapewear, and hosiery. Or it might define responsibility centers by sales channel, such as Spanx retail stores, Spanx partner stores, and e-commerce. It might further divide Spanx partner stores by geographic region. If the managers in charge of the company's responsibility centers had control over costs and revenue, then they would be managing profit centers. If they also had the authority to make investments in operating assets, then they would be managing investment centers.

Serving All Stakeholders

Sara Blakely supports women because she believes it "offers one of the greatest returns on investment." In 2006, she founded the Spanx by Sara Blakely Foundation, which supports numerous initiatives, such as the Red Backpack Fund that has donated $5,000 to each of 1,000 female-owned businesses. Sara also created The Belly Art Project, which donates 100 percent of its proceeds to Every Mother Counts, which works to make pregnancy and childbirth safe for all women. In 2013, she "became the first self-made female billionaire to sign the Melinda and Bill Gates' and Warren Buffett's Giving Pledge, promising to give at least half her wealth to charity." ■

Sources: https://www.inc.com/sara-blakely/how-sara-blakley-started-spanx.html, https://www.spanx.com, https://www.forbes.com/profile/sara-blakely/?sh=4b61b8d276bb, http://www.spanxfoundation.com/about/, http://www.bellyartproject.org/about.

Except in very small organizations, a company's owners and its top managers must delegate decision-making authority to others. When a company's owners (e.g., stockholders) delegate decision-making authority to top managers, they employ *corporate governance systems* to direct and control the actions of those managers. When properly implemented, corporate governance systems provide incentives and feedback mechanisms to help ensure a company's board of directors and top managers pursue goals aligned with the owners' interests.[1] Similarly, when a company's top managers delegate decision-making authority to subordinates, they employ *management control systems* to direct and control the actions of those subordinates. When properly implemented, management control systems provide incentives and feedback mechanisms to help ensure a company's employees pursue goals aligned with its interests.

This chapter explains a variety of performance measures and management controls companies use to align employee and corporate interests. First, it discusses the advantages and disadvantages of decentralization. Next, it provides a brief overview of responsibility accounting systems, followed by a discussion of two performance measures commonly used within those systems—return on investment (ROI) and residual income. The chapter concludes with an overview of transfer pricing and service department charges.

Decentralization in Organizations

In a **decentralized organization,** decision-making authority is spread throughout the organization rather than being confined to a few top executives. Organizations do differ, however, in the extent to which they are decentralized. In strongly centralized organizations, decision-making authority is reluctantly delegated to lower-level managers who have little freedom to make decisions. In strongly decentralized organizations, even the lowest-level managers are empowered to make as many decisions as possible.

Advantages and Disadvantages of Decentralization

The major advantages of decentralization include:

1. By delegating day-to-day problem solving to lower-level managers, top-level managers can concentrate on bigger issues, such as overall strategy.
2. Empowering lower-level managers to make decisions puts the decision-making authority in the hands of those who tend to have the most detailed and up-to-date information about day-to-day operations.
3. By eliminating layers of decision making and approvals, organizations can respond more quickly to customers and changes in the operating environment.
4. Granting decision-making authority helps train lower-level managers for higher-level positions.
5. Empowering lower-level managers to make decisions increases their motivation and job satisfaction.

The major disadvantages of decentralization include:

1. Lower-level managers may make decisions without fully understanding the company's overall strategy.
2. If lower-level managers make their own decisions independently of each other, coordination may be lacking.

---

[1] These comments on corporate governance were adapted from the 2004 report titled OECD Principles of Corporate Governance published by the Organization for Economic Co-Operation and Development.

3. Lower-level managers may have objectives that clash with the objectives of the entire organization.[2] For example, managers may be more interested in increasing the size of their department, leading to more power and prestige, than in increasing the department's effectiveness.

4. Spreading innovative ideas may be difficult in a decentralized organization. Someone in one part of the organization may have a terrific idea that would benefit other parts of the organization, but without strong central direction, the idea may not be adopted by other parts of the organization.

Responsibility Accounting

Many decentralized organizations use *responsibility accounting* systems to link lower-level managers' decision-making authority with accountability for the outcomes of those decisions. The basic idea underlying **responsibility accounting,** is a manager should be held responsible for those items—and *only* those items—the manager can control. Each line item (i.e., revenue or cost) in the budget is the responsibility of a manager who is held responsible for explaining and productively responding to large deviations between the budgeted and actual amounts. In effect, responsibility accounting *personalizes* accounting information by holding individuals responsible for revenues and costs.

The term **responsibility center** is used for any part of an organization whose manager controls cost, profit, or investments. The three primary types of responsibility centers are *cost centers, profit centers,* and *investment centers.*

Cost, Profit, and Investment Centers

Cost Center   The manager of a **cost center** has control over costs, but not revenue or investment funds. Service departments such as accounting, finance, general administration, legal, and personnel are usually classified as cost centers. In addition, manufacturing facilities are often treated as cost centers. The managers of cost centers are expected to minimize costs while providing the level of products and services needed by other parts of the organization. For example, the manager of a manufacturing facility would be evaluated at least in part by comparing actual costs to how much costs should have been for the actual level of output. Flexible budget variances and standard cost variances, such as those discussed in earlier chapters, are often used to evaluate cost center performance.

Profit Center   The manager of a **profit center** has control over both costs and revenue, but not investment funds. For example, the manager in charge of a Six Flags amusement park would be responsible for both the revenues and costs, and hence the profits, of the amusement park but may not have control over major investments in the park. Profit center managers are often evaluated by comparing actual profit to budgeted profit.

Investment Center   The manager of an **investment center** has control over cost, revenue, and investments in operating assets. For example, General Motors' vice president of manufacturing in North America would have a great deal of discretion over investments

---

[2] Similar problems exist with top-level managers as well. The shareholders of the company delegate their decision-making authority to the top managers. Unfortunately, top managers may abuse that trust by rewarding themselves and their friends too generously, spending too much company money on palatial offices, and so on. The issue of how to ensure that top managers act in the best interests of the company's owners continues to challenge experts. To a large extent, the owners rely on performance evaluation using return on investment and residual income measures, as discussed later in the chapter, and on bonuses and stock options. The stock market is also an important disciplining mechanism. If top managers squander the company's resources, the price of the company's stock will almost surely fall—possibly resulting in a loss of prestige, bonuses, and a job. And, of course, particularly outrageous self-dealing may land a CEO in court.

in manufacturing—such as investing in equipment to produce more fuel-efficient engines. Once General Motors' top-level managers and board of directors approve the vice president's investment proposals, that vice president is held responsible for making them pay off. As discussed in the next section, investment center managers are often evaluated using return on investment (ROI) or residual income.

FUEL RETAILERS BENEFIT FROM RECORD MARGINS

Fuel retailers, such as Alimentation Couche-Tard, Murphy USA, and Marathon Petroleum, experienced a steep drop in demand for gasoline during the COVID-19 pandemic. However, this drain on return on investment (ROI) was more than offset by record margins. For example, Couche-Tard recorded a gross profit of $1.2 billion during the quarter ended April 30, 2020—a 50 percent increase over the same quarter a year earlier. Although the company sold 21 percent less fuel in the year-over-year comparison, its margins increased from 19 cents a gallon to 47 cents a gallon.

Source: Rebecca Elliott, "Gasoline Prices Benefit Fuel Retailers," *The Wall Street Journal,* July 6, 2020, p. B2.

89stocker/Shutterstock

Evaluating Investment Center Performance—Return on Investment

Return on investment (ROI) is a financial measure commonly used to evaluate investment center performance. **Return on investment (ROI)** is defined as net operating income divided by average operating assets:

$$\text{ROI} = \frac{\text{Net operating income}}{\text{Average operating assets}}$$

LO11–1
Compute return on investment (ROI) and show how changes in sales, expenses, and assets affect ROI.

The goal is to increase ROI because it indicates more profit is being earned per dollar invested in operating assets.

Net Operating Income and Operating Assets Defined

Note *net operating income,* rather than net income, is used in the ROI formula. **Net operating income** is income before interest and taxes and is sometimes referred to as EBIT (earnings before interest and taxes). Net operating income is used in the formula because the base (i.e., denominator) consists of *operating assets.* To be consistent, we use net operating income in the numerator.

Operating assets include cash, accounts receivable, inventory, plant and equipment, and all other assets held for operating purposes. Examples of assets not included in operating assets (i.e., nonoperating assets) include land held for future use, an investment in another company, or a building rented to someone else. These assets are not held for operating purposes and therefore excluded from operating assets. The operating assets used in the formula are computed as the average of the beginning and ending balances.

Most companies use the net book value (i.e., acquisition cost less accumulated depreciation) of depreciable assets to calculate average operating assets. This approach has drawbacks. An asset's net book value decreases over time as the accumulated depreciation increases. This decreases the denominator in the ROI calculation, thus increasing ROI. Consequently, ROI mechanically increases over time. Moreover, replacing old depreciated equipment with new equipment increases the book value of depreciable assets and decreases ROI. Hence, using net book value in the calculation of average operating assets results in a predictable pattern of increasing ROI over time as accumulated depreciation grows and discourages replacing old equipment with new, updated equipment. An alternative to using net book value is the gross cost of the asset, which ignores accumulated depreciation. Gross cost stays constant over time because depreciation is ignored; therefore, ROI does not grow automatically over time, and replacing a fully depreciated asset with a comparably priced new asset will not adversely affect ROI.

Nevertheless, most companies use the net book value approach to computing average operating assets because it is consistent with their financial reporting practices of recording the net book value of assets on the balance sheet and including depreciation as an operating expense on the income statement. Therefore, we will always use the net book value approach.

Understanding ROI

The equation for ROI can also be expressed in terms of **margin** and **turnover** as follows:

$$ROI = Margin \times Turnover$$

where

$$Margin = \frac{Net\ operating\ income}{Sales}$$

and

$$Turnover = \frac{Sales}{Average\ operating\ assets}$$

Note sales in the margin and turnover formulas cancel out when they are multiplied together, yielding the original formula for ROI.

The margin and turnover formulas help managers better understand how to increase ROI. Margin is ordinarily improved by increasing selling prices, reducing operating expenses, or increasing unit sales. Because of operating leverage, a given percentage increase in unit sales usually leads to an even larger percentage increase in net operating income. Some managers tend to focus too much on margin and ignore turnover. However, turnover incorporates a crucial area of a manager's responsibility—the investment in operating assets. Excessive funds tied up in operating assets depress turnover and lower ROI.

IN BUSINESS

Andrey Armyagov/Shutterstock

HARLEY-DAVIDSON TAKES STEPS TO INCREASE ITS ROI

When the COVID-19 pandemic caused Harley-Davidson's quarterly sales to drop by 27 percent, the company responded by reducing the number of models that it manufactures by one-third. Jochen Zeitz, the company's CEO, said through "years of expansion . . . it was evident to me that we had lost our focus." Reducing the number of models will enable the company to increase its return on investment (ROI) in two ways. First, by discontinuing low-margin models, the company can now pay greater attention to producing and promoting its higher-margin touring-bike models. Second, with less manufacturing complexity, the company hopes to cut expenses by $250 million per year.

Source: Bob Tita, "Harley Sales Decline as It Shifts Strategy," *The Wall Street Journal*, July 29, 2020, p. B8.

Managers can increase ROI by taking a variety of actions that change sales, expenses, and operating assets. For example, a manager may invest in operating assets to reduce operating expenses or increase sales. Whether the net effect is favorable or not is judged in terms of its overall impact on ROI.

For example, suppose the Montvale Burger Grill expects the following operating results next month:

Sales	$100,000
Operating expenses	$90,000
Net operating income	$10,000
Average operating assets	$50,000

The expected return on investment (ROI) for the month is computed as follows:

$$ROI = Margin \times Turnover$$

$$ROI = \frac{Net\ operating\ income}{Sales} \times \frac{Sales}{Average\ operating\ assets}$$

$$= \frac{\$10,000}{\$100,000} \times \frac{\$100,000}{\$50,000}$$

$$= 10\% \times 2 = 20\%$$

Now let's suppose the manager of the Montvale Burger Grill is considering investing $2,000 in a state-of-the-art soft-serve ice cream machine. This new machine would boost sales by $4,000 but would require additional operating expenses of $1,000. Thus, net operating income would increase by $3,000, to $13,000. The new ROI would be:

$$ROI = Margin \times Turnover$$

$$ROI = \frac{Net\ operating\ income}{Sales} \times \frac{Sales}{Average\ operating\ assets}$$

$$= \frac{\$13,000}{\$104,000} \times \frac{\$104,000}{\$52,000}$$

$$= 12.5\% \times 2 = 25\% \text{ (as compared to 20\% originally)}$$

E.I. du Pont de Nemours and Company (better known as DuPont) developed the diagram in Exhibit 11–1 to help managers better understand how to increase ROI. It includes margin and turnover as the components of ROI and provides benchmark data that can be compared to an investment center manager's historical performance, other investment centers in the organization, or other companies in the industry.

IN BUSINESS

SMUCKER'S SALES JUMP BUT MARGINS SHRINK

During the COVID-19 pandemic, J.M. Smucker's sales rose due to higher prices and greater demand, thereby exerting an upward influence on the company's turnover and return on investment (ROI). However, it's gross margin percentage fell to 34.7 percent from 40.2 percent a year earlier because of higher ingredient and packaging costs as well as rising transportation and manufacturing costs, which in turn exerted downward pressure on the company's ROI. Given strong customer demand for its products, Smucker hopes to boost its gross margins by passing along cost inflation to customers through higher prices.

Source: Adriano Marchese, "Higher Prices Boost J.M. Smucker Sales," *The Wall Street Journal,* November 24, 2021, p. B3.

Kristoffer Tripplaar/Alamy Stock Photo

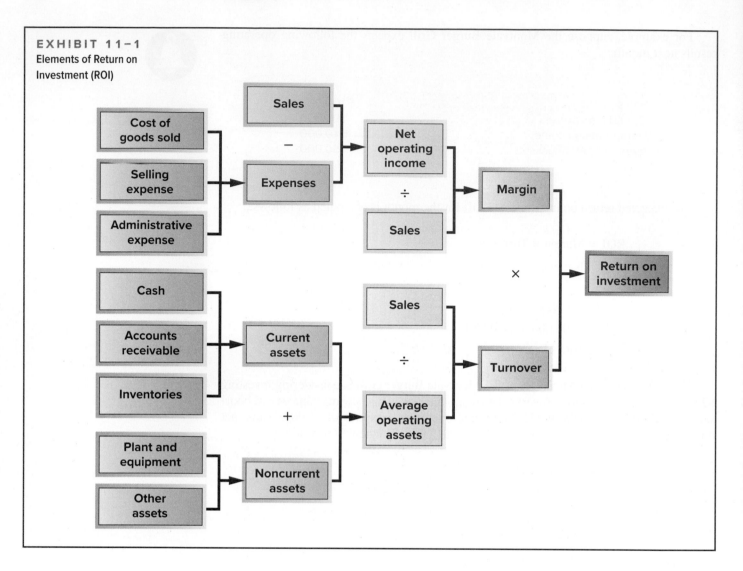

EXHIBIT 11–1
Elements of Return on Investment (ROI)

Criticisms of ROI

Although ROI is widely used in evaluating investment center performance, it has three important limitations:

1. Telling managers to increase ROI while offering no further guidance is insufficient. Managers may not know how to increase ROI; they may increase ROI in ways that contradict the company's strategy; or they may take actions that increase ROI in the short run but harm the company in the long run (such as cutting back on research and development). This is why ROI is best used as part of a balanced scorecard performance measurement system, as discussed in the next chapter.
2. When managers take over an investment center, they inherit many committed costs beyond their control, thus making it difficult to fairly assess their performance based solely on controllable results.
3. Managers evaluated based on ROI may reject investment opportunities that lower their investment center's ROI even though those investments exceed the company's desired return.

Residual Income

Residual income is another approach to measuring an investment center's performance. **Residual income** is the net operating income an investment center earns above the minimum required return on its operating assets. It is calculated as follows[3]:

LO11–2
Compute residual income and explain its strengths and weaknesses.

$$\begin{array}{c} \text{Residual} \\ \text{income} \end{array} = \begin{array}{c} \text{Net operating} \\ \text{income} \end{array} - \left(\begin{array}{c} \text{Average operating} \\ \text{assets} \end{array} \times \begin{array}{c} \text{Minimum required} \\ \text{rate of return} \end{array} \right)$$

When residual income is used to measure performance, the objective is to maximize the total amount of residual income, not to maximize ROI. This is an important distinction. If the objective were to maximize ROI, then every company should divest all of its products except the one with the highest ROI.

To illustrate, consider the following data for an investment center—the Ketchikan Division of Alaskan Marine Services Corporation.

Alaskan Marine Services Corporation Ketchikan Division Basic Data for Performance Evaluation	
Net operating income (a)	$20,000
Average operating assets (b)	$100,000
Return on investment (ROI) (a) ÷ (b)	20%
Minimum required rate of return	15%

The company uses ROI to evaluate its investment center managers and, as shown above, the Ketchikan Division's ROI is 20 percent. The controller of the company favors replacing ROI with residual income and has used the above data to calculate Ketchikan's residual income:

Alaskan Marine Services Corporation Ketchikan Division Residual Income	
Net operating income (a)	$20,000
Minimum required return (15% × $100,000) (b)	15,000
Residual income (a) − (b)	$ 5,000

With $100,000 in operating assets and a 15 percent minimum required rate of return, the company would expect the Ketchikan Division to earn a minimum required return of $15,000 (= $100,000 × 15%). Because the division's net operating income of $20,000 exceeds its minimum required return of $15,000, it has residual income of $5,000. If the controller persuades the company to replace ROI with residual income, the manager of the Ketchikan Division would be evaluated based on the growth in residual income from year to year.

Motivation and Residual Income

The controller wants to switch from ROI to residual income because it will better motivate managers to make investment decisions that align with the company's interests.

---

[3] Economic Value Added (EVA™) is an adaptation of residual income that has been trademarked by Stern Stewart & Company. Under EVA, companies often modify their accounting principles in various ways. For example, funds used for research and development are often treated as investments rather than as expenses. In this text, we will not draw any distinction between residual income and EVA.

To illustrate, suppose the manager of the Ketchikan Division is considering purchasing a computerized diagnostic machine to aid in servicing marine diesel engines. The machine would cost $25,000 and is expected to generate additional operating income of $4,500 a year. From the company's standpoint, this is a good investment because its 18 percent ($4,500 ÷ $25,000) rate of return exceeds the minimum required rate of return of 15 percent.

If the manager of the Ketchikan Division is evaluated based on residual income, she would pursue the investment in the diagnostic machine as shown below:

Alaskan Marine Services Corporation Ketchikan Division Performance Evaluated Using Residual Income			
	Present	New Project	Overall
Average operating assets	$100,000	$25,000	$125,000
Net operating income	$20,000	$4,500	$24,500
Minimum required return	15,000	3,750*	18,750
Residual income	$ 5,000	$ 750	$ 5,750

*$25,000 × 15% = $3,750

The project increases the Ketchikan Division's residual income by $750, so the manager would invest in the new diagnostic machine.

Now suppose the manager is evaluated based on ROI. The effect of the diagnostic machine on the division's ROI is computed below:

Alaskan Marine Services Corporation Ketchikan Division Performance Evaluated Using ROI			
	Present	New Project	Overall
Average operating assets (a)	$100,000	$25,000	$125,000
Net operating income (b)	$20,000	$4,500	$24,500
ROI, (b) ÷ (a)	20%	18%	19.6%

The new project reduces the division's ROI from 20 percent to 19.6 percent. This happens because the 18 percent rate of return on the new diagnostic machine, while above the company's 15 percent minimum required rate of return, is below the division's current ROI of 20 percent. If the manager of the division is evaluated based on ROI, she will be reluctant to propose such an investment even though it would be desirable from the company's standpoint.

Generally, a manager evaluated based on ROI will reject any project whose rate of return is below the division's current ROI even if the project's rate of return is above the company's minimum required rate of return. In contrast, managers evaluated using residual income will pursue any project whose rate of return is above the minimum required rate of return because it increases their residual income. Because it is in the best interests of the company to pursue projects whose rate of return exceeds the minimum required rate of return, managers evaluated based on residual income will make better decisions concerning investment projects than managers evaluated using ROI.[4]

---

[4] The residual income approach has one major disadvantage. Larger divisions often have more residual income than smaller divisions, not necessarily because they are better managed, but simply because they are bigger. Therefore, residual income can't be used to compare the performance of divisions of different sizes.

COMMUNICATING WITH DATA VISUALIZATIONS

Prescriptive analytics answer the question: What should I do? The visualization below is based on the Ketchikan Division of Alaskan Marine Services Corporation. It compares the division's present ROI (20%) and residual income ($5,000) with the ROI (18.0%) and residual income ($5,750) of the new project. It supports the controller's assertion the company should use residual income instead of ROI to evaluate managerial performance. Because the new project earns residual income of $750, its return must exceed the company's minimum required rate of return. Thus, the company would want the divisional manager to pursue the new project. However, if evaluated based on ROI, the manager will bypass the project because its ROI of 18 percent is less than his present ROI of 20 percent.

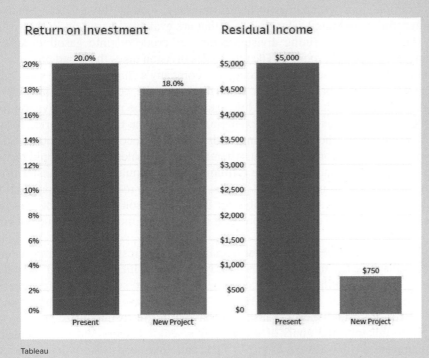

Tableau

IN BUSINESS

SHORTAGES REDUCE OPTIONS FOR CONSUMERS

For manufacturers of everything from lawnmowers and outdoor grills to home appliances and automobiles, supply-chain issues have forced companies to make tough decisions on production to remain profitable. In response to limited availability of labor, supplies, and parts, many businesses have reduced the range of products available to consumers. Companies such as Whirlpool, Weber, and Toro have streamlined their offerings, offsetting increased manufacturing costs by focusing their production efforts on higher-margin products. General Motors has also redirected its assembly efforts, halting production of its Malibu midsize sedan while continuing to run its more profitable upscale SUV lines at full capacity.

Source: Sharon Terlep and Austen Hufford, "Budget Appliances Become Scarcer," *The Wall Street Journal,* October 5, 2021, https://www.wsj.com/articles/why-budget-appliances-tvs-are-in-short-supply-but-premium-models-are-in-stock-11633339801.

Transfer Pricing

A company's profit centers and investment centers often supply goods and services to other responsibility centers within the same company. For example, the truck division of Toyota (an investment center) supplies trucks to other Toyota divisions to use in their operations. When these responsibility centers are evaluated based on their profit, ROI, or residual income, a price must be established for such a transfer—otherwise, the truck division will not recognize any financial benefit related to the transfer and the other divisions will not incur any cost associated with the transfer. The price in such a situation is called a *transfer price*. A **transfer price** is the price charged when one responsibility center provides goods or services to another responsibility center in the same company.

For example, most companies in the oil industry, such as Royal Dutch Shell, have petroleum refining and retail sales divisions that are evaluated based on ROI or residual income. The petroleum refining division processes crude oil into gasoline, kerosene, lubricants, and other end products. The retail sales division takes these end products from the refining division and sells them through the company's chain of service stations.

Creating a transfer price for each product enables the petroleum refining division to recognize revenue on its transfers while also requiring the retail sales division to recognize a corresponding expense. For example, if we assume the transfer price for gasoline is $0.80 a gallon, then the refining division would recognize revenue of $0.80 a gallon on its segment income statement, whereas the retail sales division would record an expense of $0.80 a gallon. Clearly, the refining division would like the transfer price to be as high as possible to maximize its profits, whereas the retailing division would like the transfer price to be as low as possible for the same reason. However, the transaction has no effect on the entire company's profit. It is like taking money out of one pocket and putting it into the other.

Profit center and investment center managers are interested in how transfer prices are set because their financial compensation is directly influenced by their responsibility center's profits. Similarly, a company's senior leaders, such as its chief executive officer (CEO) and chief financial officer (CFO), also have a strong interest in how transfer prices are established because they have a desire to maximize companywide profits. Unfortunately, the goals of a company's senior leaders and its responsibility center managers do not always align. In fact, situations can arise where a responsibility center manager's transfer pricing decisions actually decrease profits for the company as a whole. We refer to this counterproductive scenario as *suboptimization*. **Suboptimization** occurs when responsibility center managers forgo additional companywide profits by making decisions not in the best interests of the company or even their own responsibility center.

The objective in setting transfer prices is to avoid suboptimization by motivating managers to act in the best interests of the company.[5] Three common approaches (each discussed in turn) are used to set transfer prices:

1. Allow the managers involved in the transfer to negotiate the transfer price.
2. Set transfer prices at cost using either variable cost or full (absorption) cost.
3. Set transfer prices at the market price.

While each of these approaches has its strengths and weaknesses, none of them completely eliminates the risk of suboptimization.

---

[5] The dynamics of transfer pricing decisions become more complex with multinational corporations. In this context, the objectives of international transfer pricing expand to include minimizing taxes, duties, and foreign exchange risks, along with enhancing a company's competitive position and improving its relations with foreign governments.

Negotiated Transfer Prices

As the name implies, a *negotiated transfer price* involves a negotiation between two responsibility center managers—a prospective buyer and a seller. If the negotiation is successful, it results in a **negotiated transfer price** agreed to by the buyer and the seller. If the negotiation is unsuccessful, the two parties will not exchange products or services because they failed to agree on a transfer price.

When a company allows responsibility center managers to negotiate their own transfer prices, it provides two benefits. First, it preserves the autonomy of the negotiating parties, which is consistent with the spirit of decentralization. Second, it acknowledges the managers involved in the negotiation are likely to have much better information about the potential costs and benefits of the transfer than others in the company.

However, negotiated transfer prices also have two disadvantages—not all managers understand their own businesses and not all managers are cooperative negotiators. As a result, negotiations often break down even when it would be in the managers' own best interests (and the company's best interest) to come to an agreement. Sometimes failed negotiations arise from the way managers are evaluated and rewarded. If managers are pitted against each other rather than against their own past performance or reasonable benchmarks, a noncooperative negotiating atmosphere is almost guaranteed.

Generally speaking, two responsibility center managers will agree to a transfer price only if it falls within a **range of acceptable transfer prices** that increases both the buyer's and seller's profits. The lower limit for this range of acceptable transfer prices is determined by the seller, whereas the upper limit of this range is determined by the buyer. Next, we'll introduce an example explaining how the range of acceptable transfer prices is calculated.

LO11–3
Determine the range, if any, within which a negotiated transfer price should fall.

Negotiated Transfer Prices: An Example

Harris & Louder, Ltd., owns fast-food restaurants and snack food and beverage manufacturers in the United Kingdom. One of its restaurants, Pizza Maven, serves pizza and a variety of beverages including ginger beer, which it serves on tap. Harris & Louder just purchased a new company, Imperial Beverages, that produces ginger beer. The managing director of Imperial Beverages approached the managing director of Pizza Maven about purchasing Imperial Beverages' ginger beer to sell at Pizza Maven restaurants rather than its usual brand of ginger beer. Because managers at Pizza Maven agree the quality of Imperial Beverages' ginger beer is comparable to the quality of their regular brand, their decision hinges largely on the transfer price they'd pay to Imperial Beverages.

The formulas for computing the range of acceptable transfer prices that will increase both parties' profits will be derived using the following information:

Imperial Beverages:	
Ginger beer production capacity per month	10,000 barrels
Variable cost per barrel of ginger beer	$8 per barrel
Fixed costs per month	$70,000
Selling price of Imperial Beverages' ginger beer	
on the outside market	$20 per barrel
Pizza Maven:	
Purchase price of regular brand of ginger beer	$18 per barrel
Monthly consumption of ginger beer	2,000 barrels

The Selling Division's Lowest Acceptable Transfer Price The selling division, Imperial Beverages, will agree to a transfer price only if it increases divisional profits. Thus, assuming no effect on fixed costs, the transfer price must exceed Imperial Beverages' variable cost per barrel of $8 plus the opportunity cost (or forgone contribution margin), if any, from lost sales to regular customers. This can be expressed in equation form as follows:

Seller's perspective:

$$\frac{\text{Transfer}}{\text{price}} \geq \frac{\text{Variable cost}}{\text{per unit}} + \frac{\text{Total contribution margin on lost sales}}{\text{Number of units transferred}}$$

The Buying Division's Highest Acceptable Transfer Price   The buying division, Pizza Maven, will agree to a transfer price only if it increases divisional profits. Because Pizza Maven has an outside supplier, its decision is simple—buy from the inside supplier if the price is less than or equal to the outside supplier's price.

Buyer's perspective:

$$\text{Transfer price} \leq \text{Cost of buying from outside supplier}$$

Or if an outside supplier does not exist:

$$\text{Transfer price} \leq \text{Profit to be earned per unit sold (not including the transfer price)}$$

Next, we'll compute the range of acceptable transfer prices for three scenarios: (1) the selling division has idle capacity, (2) the selling division has no idle capacity, and (3) the selling division has some idle capacity.

Selling Division Has Idle Capacity   Suppose Imperial Beverages has sufficient idle capacity to satisfy Pizza Maven's demand for ginger beer without sacrificing any sales to its regular customers. To be specific, let's suppose Imperial Beverages is selling only 7,000 barrels of ginger beer a month on the outside market. That leaves unused capacity of 3,000 barrels a month—more than enough to satisfy Pizza Maven's requirement of 2,000 barrels a month. What range of transfer prices, if any, would make both divisions better off with the transfer of 2,000 barrels a month?

1.   The selling division, Imperial Beverages, will be interested in the transfer only if:

$$\frac{\text{Transfer}}{\text{price}} \geq \frac{\text{Variable cost}}{\text{per unit}} + \frac{\text{Total contribution margin on lost sales}}{\text{Number of units transferred}}$$

Because Imperial Beverages has sufficient idle capacity, it will not have to sacrifice any sales to regular customers. Therefore, the variable cost per unit of $8 becomes the lowest acceptable transfer price:

$$\text{Transfer price} \geq \$8 + \frac{\$0}{2,000} = \$8$$

2.   The buying division, Pizza Maven, can buy similar ginger beer from an outside supplier for $18. Therefore, this purchase price is the highest acceptable transfer price:

$$\text{Transfer price} \leq \text{Cost of buying from outside supplier} = \$18$$

3.   Combining the requirements of both the selling division and the buying division, the range of acceptable transfer prices is:

$$\$8 \leq \text{Transfer price} \leq \$18$$

Assuming the managers understand their own businesses and are cooperative, they should be able to agree on a transfer price within this range.

Selling Division Has No Idle Capacity   Suppose Imperial Beverages is selling 10,000 barrels of ginger beer a month on the outside market at $20 per barrel. In this situation, Imperial Beverages has no idle capacity, so it would have to divert 2,000 barrels of ginger beer from its regular customers to fill the order from Pizza Maven. What range of transfer prices, if any, would make both divisions better off transferring the 2,000 barrels within the company?

1. The selling division, Imperial Beverages, will be interested in the transfer only if:

$$\frac{\text{Transfer}}{\text{price}} \geq \frac{\text{Variable cost}}{\text{per unit}} + \frac{\text{Total contribution margin on lost sales}}{\text{Number of units transferred}}$$

Because Imperial Beverages has no idle capacity, there *are* lost outside sales. Given the contribution margin per barrel on these outside sales is \$12 (\$20 − \$8), the lowest acceptable transfer price of \$20 is computed as follows:

$$\text{Transfer price} \geq \$8 + \frac{(\$20 - \$8) \times 2{,}000}{2{,}000} = \$8 + (\$20 - \$8) = \$20$$

From the selling division's standpoint, the transfer price must at least cover the revenue on the lost sales, which is \$20 per barrel. This makes sense because the cost of producing the 2,000 barrels is the same whether they are sold to Pizza Maven or to regular customers. The only difference is Imperial Beverages loses the revenue of \$20 per barrel if it transfers the barrels to Pizza Maven.

2. As before, the buying division, Pizza Maven, can buy similar ginger beer from an outside supplier for \$18. Therefore, this purchase price is the highest acceptable transfer price:

$$\text{Transfer price} \leq \text{Cost of buying from outside supplier} = \$18$$

3. The selling division would insist on a transfer price of at least \$20. But the buying division would refuse any transfer price above \$18. Because there is no range of acceptable transfer prices, the negotiation process will fail and no transfer will take place. Is this good? The answer is yes. From the standpoint of the entire company, the transfer doesn't make sense. Why give up sales of \$20 to save costs of \$18?

The transfer price is a mechanism for dividing between the two divisions any profit the entire company earns as a result of the transfer. If the company as a whole loses money on the transfer, there will be no profit to divide up, and it will be impossible for the two divisions to come to an agreement. On the other hand, if the company makes money on the transfer, there will be a profit to share, and it will always be possible for the two divisions to find a mutually agreeable transfer price that increases the profits of both divisions.

Selling Division Has Some Idle Capacity Suppose Imperial Beverages is selling 9,000 barrels of ginger beer a month on the outside market. Pizza Maven can only sell one kind of ginger beer on tap. It cannot buy 1,000 barrels from Imperial Beverages and 1,000 barrels from its regular supplier; it must buy all of its 2,000 barrels of ginger beer from one source.

To fill the entire 2,000 barrels from Pizza Maven, Imperial Beverages would have to divert 1,000 barrels from its regular customers who are paying \$20 per barrel. The other 1,000 barrels can be made using idle capacity. What range of transfer prices, if any, would make both divisions better off transferring the 2,000 barrels within the company?

1. As before, the selling division, Imperial Beverages, will insist on a transfer price that at least covers its variable cost and opportunity cost:

$$\frac{\text{Transfer}}{\text{price}} \geq \frac{\text{Variable cost}}{\text{per unit}} + \frac{\text{Total contribution margin on lost sales}}{\text{Number of units transferred}}$$

Because Imperial Beverages does not have enough idle capacity to fill the entire order for 2,000 barrels, there *are* lost outside sales. Given the contribution margin per barrel on these outside sales is \$12 (\$20 − \$8), the lowest acceptable transfer price of \$14 is computed as follows:

$$\text{Transfer price} \geq \$8 + \frac{(\$20 - \$8) \times 1,000}{2,000} = \$8 + \$6 = \$14$$

Thus, for the selling division, the transfer price must cover the variable cost of \$8 plus the average opportunity cost of lost sales of \$6.

2. As before, the buying division, Pizza Maven, can buy similar ginger beer from an outside supplier for \$18. Therefore, this purchase price is the highest acceptable transfer price:

$$\text{Transfer price} \leq \text{Cost of buying from outside supplier} = \$18$$

3. Combining the requirements for both the selling and buying divisions, the range of acceptable transfer prices is:

$$\$14 \leq \text{Transfer price} \leq \$18$$

Assuming the managers understand their own businesses and are cooperative, they should be able to agree on a transfer price within this range.

No Outside Supplier   If Pizza Maven has no outside supplier for the ginger beer, the highest price the buying division would be willing to pay depends on how much the buying division expects to make on the transferred units—excluding the transfer price. If, for example, Pizza Maven expects to earn \$30 per barrel of ginger beer after paying its own expenses, then it should be willing to pay up to \$30 per barrel to Imperial Beverages. Remember, however, this assumes Pizza Maven cannot buy ginger beer from other sources.

Evaluation of Negotiated Transfer Prices   As discussed earlier, if an internal transfer results in higher companywide profits, there is always a range of transfer prices that enables the selling and buying divisions to each earn higher profits. Therefore, if the managers understand their own businesses and are cooperative, then they should always be able to agree on a transfer price if it is in the best interests of the company that they do so. However, given the disputes often accompanying the negotiation process, many companies rely on some other means of setting transfer prices, such as cost-based and market-based transfer prices.

Transfers at the Cost to the Selling Division

Many companies set transfer prices at either the variable cost or full (absorption) cost incurred by the selling division. Although this approach is relatively simple to use, it has some major defects.

First, the use of cost—particularly full cost—as a transfer price can lead to suboptimization. Return to the example involving the ginger beer. The full cost of ginger beer can never be less than \$15 per barrel (\$8 per barrel variable cost + \$7 per barrel fixed cost at capacity). What if the cost of buying the ginger beer from an outside supplier is less than \$15—for example, \$14 per barrel? If the transfer price were set at full cost, then Pizza Maven would never want to buy ginger beer from Imperial Beverages because it could buy its ginger beer from an outside supplier at a lower price. However, from the standpoint of the company as a whole, ginger beer should be transferred from Imperial Beverages to Pizza Maven whenever Imperial Beverages has idle capacity. Why? Because when Imperial Beverages has idle capacity, it only costs the company \$8 in variable cost to produce a barrel of ginger beer, but it costs \$14 per barrel to buy from an outside supplier.

Second, if cost is used as the transfer price, the selling division will never show a profit on any internal transfer. The only division showing a profit is the division making the final sale to an outside party.

Third, cost-based prices do not provide incentives to control costs. If the actual costs of one division are simply passed on to the next, there is little incentive for anyone to reduce costs. This problem can be overcome by using budgeted costs or standard costs rather than actual costs for transfer prices.

Despite these shortcomings, cost-based transfer prices are often used in practice. Advocates argue they are easily understood and convenient to use.

Transfers at Market Price

Using a product or service's **market price** (i.e., the price charged for an item on the open market) as a transfer price is possible in situations where there is an *outside market of customers* that routinely purchase the transferred product or service.

When a selling division has no idle capacity, the market price is the optimal transfer price. This is because, from the company's perspective, the real cost of the transfer is the opportunity cost of the lost revenue on the outside sale. Whether the item is transferred internally or sold on the outside market, the production costs are exactly the same. If the market price is used as the transfer price, the selling division manager will not lose any profit by making the transfer, and the buying division manager will get the correct signal about how much it really costs the company for the transfer to take place.

While market-based transfer prices work well when the selling division has no idle capacity, they do not work well when the selling division has idle capacity. Recalling once again the ginger beer example, the outside market price for the ginger beer produced by Imperial Beverages is $20 per barrel. However, Pizza Maven can purchase all of the ginger beer it wants from its own outside supplier for $18 per barrel. Thus, Pizza Maven would never willingly accept a transfer price of $20 from Imperial Beverages when it can buy ginger beer from its own supplier at a price of $18 per barrel. Thus, a market-based transfer price of $20 per barrel would lead to suboptimization. It would motivate Pizza Maven to pay an outside supplier $18 per barrel instead of making the optimal choice from a companywide standpoint, which is choosing to obtain additional barrels of ginger beer from Imperial Beverages at a variable manufacturing cost of $8 per barrel (assuming that Imperial Beverages has idle capacity).

In some market-based transfer pricing schemes, the transfer price would be lowered to $18, the outside supplier's market price. Pizza Maven would be directed to pay Imperial Beverages a transfer price of $18 per barrel as long as Imperial Beverages is willing to sell. This scheme can work reasonably well, but a drawback is managers at Pizza Maven will regard the cost of ginger beer as $18 rather than $8, which is the real cost to the company when the selling division has idle capacity. Consequently, the managers of Pizza Maven will make pricing and other decisions based on an incorrect cost.

Unfortunately, none of the possible solutions to the transfer pricing problem are perfect—not even market-based transfer prices. Next, we discuss service department charges, which can be viewed as transfer prices charged by service departments to operating departments.

Service Department Charges

Most large organizations have both *operating departments* and *service departments.* The central purposes of the organization are carried out in the **operating departments.** In contrast, **service departments** do not directly engage in operating activities. Instead, they provide services to the operating departments. Examples of service departments include Cafeteria, Internal Auditing, Human Resources, Cost Accounting, and Purchasing.

LO11–4
Charge operating departments for services provided by service departments.

Service department costs are charged to operating departments for a variety of reasons, including:

- To encourage operating departments to make wise use of service department resources. If the services were provided for free, operating managers would be inclined to waste these resources.
- To provide operating departments with more complete cost data for making decisions. Actions taken by operating departments have impacts on service department costs. For example, hiring another employee will increase costs in the human resources department. Such service department costs should be charged to the operating departments; otherwise, the operating departments will not take them into account when making decisions.
- To help measure the profitability of operating departments. Charging service department costs to operating departments provides a more complete accounting of the costs incurred as a consequence of activities in the operating departments.
- To create an incentive for service departments to operate efficiently. Charging service department costs to operating departments provides a system of checks and balances because cost-conscious operating departments will take an active interest in keeping service department costs low.

Service Department Charges: Key Concepts

There are two key concepts for calculating service department charges. First, variable and fixed service department costs should be charged to operating departments separately because it provides more useful data for planning and control purposes. Second, a service department's *budgeted costs,* rather than its actual costs, should be charged to operating departments. This prohibits a service department from passing on cost overruns to operating departments. We expand on these concepts below.

Variable Costs

A service department's variable costs should be charged to operating departments according to whatever activity causes the cost. For example, variable costs of a maintenance department caused by the number of machine-hours worked in the operating departments should be charged to the operating departments on the basis of machine-hours. The equation for charging a service department's variable costs to operating departments is as follows:

$$\text{Variable costs charged to operating departments} = \text{Budgeted variable rate} \times \text{Actual level of activity}$$

Notice the service department's *budgeted* variable rate per unit is used in this equation rather than its actual variable rate. This ensures service departments remain solely responsible for explaining any differences between their actual and budgeted variable rate. If service departments could base their charges on the actual variable rate, then operating departments would be unfairly held accountable for cost inefficiencies in the service departments.

Also note the operating department's actual level of activity (rather than its budgeted level of activity) is used in the above equation. This ensures the total amount charged to operating departments varies in direct proportion to their actual usage of service department resources. Conversely, if the operating department's budgeted level of activity were used in the above equation, it would unfairly allow operating departments to exceed their budgeted usage of service department resources free-of-charge.

Fixed Costs

The fixed costs of service departments are charged to operating departments in a three-step process. First, the operating and service department managers agree on the operating department's estimated future usage of the service department's fixed cost resources. In this chapter, this estimated future usage will always be quantified in terms of the operating department's peak-period service needs or its long-run average needs. Second, the service department managers make the fixed cost commitments required to deliver the estimated peak-period or long-run average needs as specified by the operating departments. Third, service departments use the equation below to charge *predetermined lump-sum amounts* of fixed costs to operating departments:

$$\begin{array}{l}\text{Fixed costs}\\\text{charged to operating}\\\text{departments}\end{array} = \text{Budgeted total fixed costs} \times \text{Peak-period capacity required}$$

Notice the service department's *budgeted* total fixed costs are used in this equation rather than its actual total fixed costs. This ensures service departments remain solely responsible for explaining any differences between their actual and budgeted fixed costs.

Also note the service department's budgeted fixed costs are charged to operating departments based on peak-period capacity required rather than a variable allocation base. This ensures the service department's fixed costs are borne by operating departments in proportion to the amount of capacity each operating department requires. The fact that an operating department does not need the peak level of service every period is immaterial; the capacity to deliver this level of service must be available and the budgeted cost of providing that capacity should be charged to operating departments.

Service Department Charges: An Example

Seaboard Airlines has a Maintenance Department that serves two operating departments—the Freight Division and the Passenger Division. The Maintenance Department's variable servicing costs are budgeted at $10 per flight-hour and its total fixed costs are budgeted at $750,000 for the year. The fixed costs are allocated to the operating departments based on their peak-period service needs. Approximately 40 percent of the Maintenance Department's peak-period capacity is used by the Freight Division and 60 percent is used by the Passenger Division.

At the end of the year, the Freight and Passenger Divisions actually logged 8,000 and 17,000 flight-hours, respectively. The Maintenance Department also actually incurred total variable and fixed costs of $260,000 and $780,000, respectively. Given this information, the amount of Maintenance Department cost charged to each division for the year would be computed as follows:

	Actual activity	Division	
		Freight	Passenger
Variable cost charges:			
Budgeted variable rate →	$10 per flight-hour × 8,000 flight-hours ...	$ 80,000	
	$10 per flight-hour × 17,000 flight-hours ...		$170,000
Fixed cost charges:			
Peak-period capacity required →	40% × $750,000	300,000	
	60% × $750,000		450,000
	Total charges	$380,000	$620,000

Budgeted fixed cost

Notice variable servicing costs are charged to the operating divisions based on the budgeted rate ($10 per hour) and the *actual activity* for the year. In contrast, the charges for fixed costs are based entirely on budgeted data. Also note the two operating divisions are *not* charged for the actual costs of the service department, which are influenced by how well the service department is managed. Instead, the service department is held responsible for the actual costs not charged to other departments as shown below:

	Variable	Fixed
Total actual costs incurred	$260,000	$780,000
Total charges to operating departments	250,000*	750,000**
Spending variance—responsibility of the Maintenance Department	$ 10,000	$ 30,000

*$80,000 + $170,000 = $250,000
**$300,000 + $450,000 = $750,000

Some Cautions in Allocating Service Department Costs

Pitfalls in Allocating Fixed Costs

Rather than charge fixed costs to operating departments in predetermined lump-sum amounts, some companies allocate them using a *variable* allocation base that fluctuates from period to period. This practice distorts decisions and creates serious inequities between departments. The inequities arise because the fixed costs allocated to one department are heavily influenced by what happens in *other* departments.

Sales dollars is an example of a variable allocation base often used to allocate fixed costs from service departments to operating departments. Using sales dollars as a base is simple, straightforward, and easy to use. Furthermore, people tend to view sales dollars as a measure of ability to pay, and, hence, as a measure of how readily costs can be absorbed from other parts of the organization.

Unfortunately, sales dollars is often a very poor base for allocating costs because sales dollars vary from period to period, whereas the costs are often largely *fixed*. Therefore, if one department's sales decline, it will shift allocated costs from that department to other departments whose sales have grown or at least held constant. In effect, the departments with growing sales are penalized in the form of higher cost allocations. The result is often resentment on the part of the managers of the better departments.

For example, let's assume a large men's clothing store has one service department and three sales departments—Suits, Shoes, and Accessories. The service department's costs total $60,000 per period and are allocated to the three sales departments according to sales dollars. A recent period showed the following allocation:

	Departments			
	Suits	Shoes	Accessories	Total
Sales by department	$260,000	$40,000	$100,000	$400,000
Percentage of total sales	65%	10%	25%	100%
Allocation of service department costs, based on percentage of total sales	$39,000	$6,000	$15,000	$60,000

In the following period, let's assume the manager of the Suits Department launched a successful program to expand sales in his department by $100,000. Furthermore, let's assume sales in the other two departments remained unchanged, total service department costs remained unchanged, and the sales departments' expected usage of service department resources remained unchanged. Given these assumptions, the service department cost allocations to the sales departments would change as shown below:

	Departments			
	Suits	Shoes	Accessories	Total
Sales by department	$360,000	$40,000	$100,000	$500,000
Percentage of total sales	72%	8%	20%	100%
Allocation of service department costs, based on percentage of total sales	$43,200	$4,800	$12,000	$60,000
Increase (or decrease) from prior allocation	$4,200	$(1,200)	$(3,000)	$0

After seeing these allocations, the manager of the Suits Department is likely to complain because by growing sales in his department, he is being forced to carry a larger share of the service department costs. In essence, this manager is being punished for his outstanding performance by being saddled with a greater proportion of service department costs. On the other hand, the managers of the departments showing no sales growth are being relieved of a portion of the costs they had been carrying. Yet, there was no change in the amount of services provided for any department across the two periods.

This example shows why a variable allocation base such as sales dollars should only be used for allocating costs when service department costs actually vary with the chosen allocation base. When service department costs are fixed, they should be charged to operating departments according to the guidelines mentioned earlier.

Summary

Many companies use responsibility accounting systems that classify their business units as cost centers, profit centers, and investment centers. Responsibility accounting systems personalize accounting information by holding responsibility center managers accountable for their revenues and costs.

Return on investment (ROI) and residual income are widely used to evaluate the performance of investment centers. ROI, which can also be expressed as a function of margin and turnover, suffers from the underinvestment problem—managers are reluctant to invest in projects that exceed the company's required rate of return but decrease their investment center's ROI. The residual income approach solves this problem by giving managers full credit for any profit a project earns in excess of the company's required rate of return.

A transfer price is the price charged when one responsibility center provides goods or services to another responsibility center in the same company. Using a transfer price enables the provider of these goods and services to recognize a financial benefit associated with the transaction while also requiring the recipient to pay for the goods and services received.

Service department charges can be viewed as transfer prices charged for services provided by service departments to operating departments. Variable and fixed service department costs should be charged to operating departments separately. A service department's budgeted costs, rather than its actual costs, should be charged to operating departments. The operating departments should be charged for variable costs based on their actual level of activity rather than their budgeted usage. They should also be charged for fixed costs based on their peak-period requirements.

 Data Analytics Exercise available in Connect to complement this chapter

Review Problem 1: Return on Investment (ROI) and Residual Income

The Magnetic Imaging Division of Medical Diagnostics, Inc., reported the following results for last year's operations:

Sales	$25 million
Net operating income	$3 million
Average operating assets	$10 million

Required:
1. Compute the Magnetic Imaging Division's margin, turnover, and ROI.
2. If Medical Diagnostics, Inc., has a minimum required rate of return of 25%, then what is the Magnetic Imaging Division's residual income?

Solution to Review Problem
1. The required calculations follow:

$$\text{Margin} = \frac{\text{Net operating income}}{\text{Sales}}$$
$$= \frac{\$3,000,000}{\$25,000,000}$$
$$= 12\%$$

$$\text{Turnover} = \frac{\text{Sales}}{\text{Average operating assets}}$$
$$= \frac{\$25,000,000}{\$10,000,000}$$
$$= 2.5$$

$$\text{ROI} = \text{Margin} \times \text{Turnover}$$
$$= 12\% \times 2.5$$
$$= 30\%$$

2.   The Magnetic Imaging Division's residual income is computed as follows:

Average operating assets	$10,000,000
Net operating income	$3,000,000
Minimum required return (25% × $10,000,000)	2,500,000
Residual income	$500,000

Review Problem 2: Transfer Pricing

Situation A

Collyer Products, Inc., has a Valve Division that manufactures and sells a standard valve:

Capacity in units	100,000
Selling price to outside customers	$30
Variable costs per unit	$16
Fixed costs per unit (based on capacity)	$9

The company has a Pump Division that could use this valve in one of its pumps. The Pump Division is currently purchasing 10,000 valves per year from an overseas supplier at a cost of $29 per valve.

Required:
1.   Assume the Valve Division has enough idle capacity to handle all of the Pump Division's needs. What is the range of acceptable transfer prices, if any, for the transfer between the two divisions?
2.   Assume the Valve Division is selling all of the valves it can produce to outside customers. What is the range of acceptable transfer prices, if any, for the transfer between the two divisions?
3.   Assume the Valve Division is selling all of the valves it can produce to outside customers. Also assume that $3 in variable expenses can be avoided on transfers within the company, due to reduced selling costs. What is the range of acceptable transfer prices, if any, for the transfer between the two divisions?

Solution to Situation A

1.   Because the Valve Division has idle capacity, it does not have to give up any outside sales to take on the Pump Division's business. Applying the formula for the lowest acceptable transfer price from the viewpoint of the selling division, we get:

$$\text{Transfer price} \geq \frac{\text{Variable cost}}{\text{per unit}} + \frac{\text{Total contribution margin on lost sales}}{\text{Number of units transferred}}$$

$$\text{Transfer price} \geq \$16 + \frac{\$0}{10,000} = \$16$$

The Pump Division would be unwilling to pay more than $29, the price it is currently paying an outside supplier for its valves. Therefore, the transfer price must fall within the range:

$$\$16 \leq \text{Transfer price} \leq \$29$$

2.   Because the Valve Division has no idle capacity, there *are* lost outside sales. Given that the contribution margin per unit on these outside sales is $14 ($30 − $16), the lowest acceptable transfer price of $30 is computed as follows:

$$\text{Transfer price} \geq \frac{\text{Variable cost}}{\text{per unit}} + \frac{\text{Total contribution margin on lost sales}}{\text{Number of units transferred}}$$

$$\text{Transfer price} \geq \$16 + \frac{(\$30 - \$16) \times 10,000}{10,000} = \$16 + \$14 = \$30$$

Because the Pump Division can purchase valves from an outside supplier at only $29 per unit, no transfers will be made between the two divisions.

3. Applying the formula for the lowest acceptable transfer price from the viewpoint of the selling division, we get:

$$\text{Transfer price} \geq \frac{\text{Variable cost}}{\text{per unit}} + \frac{\text{Total contribution margin on lost sales}}{\text{Number of units transferred}}$$

$$\text{Transfer price} \geq (\$16 - \$3) + \frac{(\$30 - \$16) \times 10{,}000}{10{,}000} = \$13 + \$14 = \$27$$

In this case, the transfer price must fall within the range:

$$\$27 \leq \text{Transfer price} \leq \$29$$

Situation B

Refer to the original data in situation A above. Assume the Pump Division needs 20,000 special high-pressure valves per year. The Valve Division's variable costs to manufacture and ship the special valve would be $20 per unit. To produce these special valves, the Valve Division would have to reduce its production and sales of regular valves from 100,000 units per year to 70,000 units per year.

Required:

From the Valve Division's perspective, what is the lowest acceptable transfer price?

Solution to Situation B

To produce the 20,000 special valves, the Valve Division will have to give up sales of 30,000 regular valves to outside customers. Applying the formula for the lowest acceptable transfer price from the viewpoint of the selling division, we get:

$$\text{Transfer price} \geq \text{Variable cost per unit} + \frac{\text{Total contribution margin on lost sales}}{\text{Number of units transferred}}$$

$$\text{Transfer price} \geq \$20 + \frac{(\$30 - \$16) \times 30{,}000}{20{,}000} = \$20 + \$21 = \$41$$

Glossary

Cost center A business segment whose manager has control over cost but not revenue or investments in operating assets. (p. 496)

Decentralized organization An organization in which decision-making authority is spread throughout the organization rather than being confined to a few top executives. (p. 495)

Investment center A business segment whose manager has control over cost, revenue, and investments in operating assets. (p. 496)

Margin Net operating income divided by sales. (p. 498)

Market price The price charged for an item on the open market. (p. 509)

Negotiated transfer price A transfer price agreed on between buying and selling divisions. (p. 505)

Net operating income Income before interest and income taxes have been deducted. (p. 497)

Operating assets Cash, accounts receivable, inventory, plant and equipment, and all other assets held for operating purposes. (p. 497)

Operating department A department that performs an organization's central purposes. (p. 509)

Profit center A business segment whose manager has control over cost and revenue but not investments in operating assets. (p. 496)

Range of acceptable transfer prices The range of transfer prices that increases profits for the selling and buying divisions. (p. 505)

Residual income The net operating income an investment center earns above the minimum required return on its operating assets. (p. 501)

Responsibility accounting A manager should be held responsible for those items—and *only* those items—that the manager can actually control. (p. 496)

Responsibility center Any business segment whose manager has control over costs, revenues, or investments in operating assets. (p. 496)

Return on investment (ROI) Net operating income divided by average operating assets. It also equals margin multiplied by turnover. (p. 497)

Service department A department that does not perform operating activities; rather, it provides services to operating departments. (p. 509)

Suboptimization An overall profit that is less than a segment or a company is capable of earning. (p. 504)

Transfer price The price charged when one responsibility center provides goods or services to another responsibility center in the same company. (p. 504)

Turnover Sales divided by average operating assets. (p. 498)

Questions

11–1 What is *decentralization?*

11–2 What benefits result from decentralization?

11–3 Distinguish between a cost center, a profit center, and an investment center.

11–4 What are *margin* and *turnover?*

11–5 What is *residual income?*

11–6 How can using ROI to evaluate investment center managers lead to bad decisions? How does the residual income approach overcome this problem?

11–7 What is a transfer price?

11–8 What is *suboptimization?*

11–9 Why should a service department's budgeted costs, rather than its actual costs, be charged to operating departments?

11–10 Why is using sales dollars usually a poor choice for allocating fixed costs to operating departments?

Applying Excel

The Excel worksheet below recreates the Review Problem pertaining to the Magnetic Imaging Division of Medical Diagnostics, Inc. The workbook, and instructions on how to complete the file, can be found in Connect.

LO11–1, LO11–2

	A	B	C	D	E
1	Chapter 11: Applying Excel				
2					
3	Data				
4	Sales	$25,000,000			
5	Net operating income	$3,000,000			
6	Average operating assets	$10,000,000			
7	Minimum required rate of return	25%			
8					
9	Enter a formula into each of the cells marked with a ? below				
10	Review Problem: Return on Investment (ROI) and Residual Income				
11					
12	Compute the ROI				
13	Margin	?			
14	Turnover	?			
15	ROI	?			
16					
17	Compute the residual income				
18	Average operating assets	?			
19	Net operating income	?			
20	Minimum required return	?			
21	Residual income	?			
22					

Chapter 11 Form / Filled in Chapter 11 Form

Microsoft Excel

You should proceed to the requirements below only after completing your worksheet.

Required:

1. Check your worksheet by changing the average operating assets in cell B6 to $8,000,000. The ROI should now be 38% and the residual income should now be $1,000,000. If you do not get these answers, find the errors in your worksheet and correct them.

   Explain why the ROI and the residual income both increase when the average operating assets decrease.

2. Revise the data in your worksheet as follows:

Data	
Sales	$1,200
Net operating income	$72
Average operating assets	$500
Minimum required rate of return	15%

   a. What is the ROI?
   b. What is the residual income?
   c. Explain the relationship between the ROI and the residual income.

The Foundational 15   Mc Graw Hill connect

L011–1, L011–2   Westerville Company reported the following results from last year's operations:

Sales	$1,000,000
Variable expenses	300,000
Contribution margin	700,000
Fixed expenses	500,000
Net operating income	$ 200,000
Average operating assets	$ 625,000

At the beginning of this year, the company has a $120,000 investment opportunity with the following cost and revenue characteristics:

Sales	$200,000
Contribution margin ratio	60% of sales
Fixed expenses	$90,000

The company's minimum required rate of return is 15%.

Required:

1. What is last year's margin?
2. What is last year's turnover?
3. What is last year's return on investment (ROI)?
4. What is the margin related to this year's investment opportunity?
5. What is the turnover related to this year's investment opportunity?
6. What is the ROI related to this year's investment opportunity?
7. If the company pursues the investment opportunity and otherwise performs the same as last year, what margin will it earn this year?
8. If the company pursues the investment opportunity and otherwise performs the same as last year, what turnover will it earn this year?
9. If the company pursues the investment opportunity and otherwise performs the same as last year, what ROI will it earn this year?
10. If Westerville's chief executive officer will earn a bonus only if her ROI from this year exceeds her ROI from last year, would she pursue the investment opportunity? Would the owners of the company want her to pursue the investment opportunity?

11. What is last year's residual income?
12. What is the residual income of this year's investment opportunity?
13. If the company pursues the investment opportunity and otherwise performs the same as last year, what residual income will it earn this year?
14. If Westerville's chief executive officer will earn a bonus only if her residual income from this year exceeds her residual income from last year, would she pursue the investment opportunity?
15. Assume the contribution margin ratio of the investment opportunity was 50% instead of 60%. If Westerville's chief executive officer will earn a bonus only if her residual income from this year exceeds her residual income from last year, would she pursue the investment opportunity? Would the owners of the company want her to pursue the investment opportunity?

Mc Graw Hill connect   **Exercises**

EXERCISE 11–1 Compute the Return on Investment (ROI) LO11–1

Alyeska Services Company, a division of a major oil company, provides various services to the operators of the North Slope oil field in Alaska. Data concerning the most recent year appear below:

Sales	$7,500,000
Net operating income	$600,000
Average operating assets	$5,000,000

Required:
1. Compute the margin.
2. Compute the turnover.
3. Compute the return on investment (ROI).

EXERCISE 11–2 Residual Income LO11–2

Juniper Design provides design services to residential developers. Last year, the company had net operating income of $600,000 on sales of $3,000,000. The company's average operating assets were $2,800,000 and its minimum required rate of return was 18%.

Required:
Compute the company's residual income.

EXERCISE 11–3 Transfer Pricing Basics LO11–3

Sako Company's Audio Division produces a speaker used by manufacturers of various audio products. Sales and cost data on the speaker follow:

Selling price per unit on the intermediate market	$60
Variable costs per unit	$42
Fixed costs per unit (based on capacity)	$8
Capacity in units	25,000

Sako Company has a Hi-Fi Division that could use this speaker in one of its products. The Hi-Fi Division will need 5,000 speakers per year. It has received a quote of $57 per speaker from another manufacturer. Sako Company evaluates division managers on the basis of divisional profits.

Required:
1. Assume the Audio Division sells only 20,000 speakers per year to outside customers.
    a. From the standpoint of the Audio Division, what is the lowest acceptable transfer price for speakers sold to the Hi-Fi Division?
    b. From the standpoint of the Hi-Fi Division, what is the highest acceptable transfer price for speakers acquired from the Audio Division?
    c. What is the range of acceptable transfer prices (if any) between the two divisions? If left free to negotiate without interference, would you expect the division managers to

voluntarily agree to the transfer of 5,000 speakers from the Audio Division to the Hi-Fi Division? Why or why not?

    d.   From the standpoint of the entire company, should the transfer take place? Why or why not?

2.   Assume the Audio Division is selling 22,500 speakers per year to outside customers.

    a.   From the standpoint of the Audio Division, what is the lowest acceptable transfer price for speakers sold to the Hi-Fi Division?

    b.   From the standpoint of the Hi-Fi Division, what is the highest acceptable transfer price for speakers acquired from the Audio Division?

    c.   What is the range of acceptable transfer prices (if any) between the two divisions? If left free to negotiate without interference, would you expect the division managers to voluntarily agree to the transfer of 5,000 speakers from the Audio Division to the Hi-Fi Division? Why or why not?

    d.   From the standpoint of the entire company, should the transfer take place? Why or why not?

3.   Assume the Audio Division is selling 25,000 speakers per year to outside customers.

    a.   From the standpoint of the Audio Division, what is the lowest acceptable transfer price for speakers sold to the Hi-Fi Division?

    b.   From the standpoint of the Hi-Fi Division, what is the highest acceptable transfer price for speakers acquired from the Audio Division?

    c.   What is the range of acceptable transfer prices (if any) between the two divisions? If left free to negotiate without interference, would you expect the division managers to voluntarily agree to the transfer of 5,000 speakers from the Audio Division to the Hi-Fi Division? Why or why not?

    d.   From the standpoint of the entire company, should the transfer take place? Why or why not?

EXERCISE 11–4 Service Department Charges LO11–4

Hannibal Steel Company's Transport Services Department provides trucks to haul ore from the company's mine to its two steel mills—the Northern Plant and the Southern Plant. Budgeted costs for the Transport Services Department total $350,000 per year, consisting of $0.25 per ton variable cost and $300,000 fixed cost. The level of fixed cost is determined by peak-period requirements. During the peak period, the Northern Plant requires 70% of the Transport Services Department's capacity and the Southern Plant requires 30%.

During the year, the Transport Services Department actually hauled 130,000 tons of ore to the Northern Plant and 50,000 tons to the Southern Plant. The Transport Services Department incurred $364,000 in cost during the year, of which $54,000 was variable and $310,000 was fixed.

Required:

1.   How much of the Transport Services Department's variable costs should be charged to each plant?

2.   How much of the Transport Services Department's fixed costs should be charged to each plant?

3.   Should any of the Transport Services Department's actual total cost of $364,000 be treated as a spending variance and not charged to the plants? Explain.

EXERCISE 11–5 Return on Investment (ROI) LO11–1

Provide the missing data in the following table for a distributor of martial arts products:

	Division		
	Alpha	Bravo	Charlie
Sales	$?	$11,500,000	$?
Net operating income	$?	$ 920,000	$210,000
Average operating assets	$800,000	$?	$?
Margin	4%	?	7%
Turnover	5	?	?
Return on investment (ROI)	?	20%	14%

EXERCISE 11–6 Contrasting Return on Investment (ROI) and Residual Income LO11–1, LO11–2

Tan Corporation of Japan has two regional divisions with headquarters in Osaka and Yokohama. Selected data on the two divisions follow:

	Division	
	Osaka	Yokohama
Sales	$3,000,000	$9,000,000
Net operating income	$210,000	$720,000
Average operating assets	$1,000,000	$4,000,000

Required:

1. For each division, compute the margin, turnover, and return on investment (ROI).
2. Compute the residual income for each division assuming the company's minimum required rate of return is 15%.

EXERCISE 11–7 Transfer Pricing from the Viewpoint of the Entire Company LO11–3

Division A manufactures electronic circuit boards that can be sold to Division B of the same company or to outside customers. Last year, the following activity occurred in Division A:

Selling price per circuit board	$125
Variable cost per circuit board	$90
Number of circuit boards:	
Produced during the year	20,000
Sold to outside customers	16,000
Sold to Division B	4,000

Sales to Division B were at the same price as sales to outside customers. The circuit boards purchased by Division B were used in an electronic instrument manufactured by that division (one board per instrument). Division B incurred $100 in additional variable cost per instrument and then sold the instruments for $300 each.

Required:

1. Calculate the net operating incomes earned by Division A, Division B, and the company as a whole.
2. Assume Division A's manufacturing capacity is 20,000 circuit boards. Next year, Division B wants to purchase 5,000 circuit boards from Division A rather than 4,000. (Circuit boards of this type are not available from outside sources.) From the standpoint of the company as a whole, should Division A sell the 1,000 additional circuit boards to Division B or continue selling them to outside customers? Explain.

EXERCISE 11–8 Computing and Interpreting Return on Investment (ROI) LO11–1

Selected operating data for two divisions of Outback Brewing, Ltd., of Australia are given below:

	Division	
	Queensland	New South Wales
Sales	$4,000,000	$7,000,000
Average operating assets	$2,000,000	$2,000,000
Net operating income	$360,000	$420,000
Property, plant, and equipment (net)	$950,000	$800,000

Required:

1. Compute each division's margin, turnover, and return on investment (ROI).
2. Which divisional manager is doing the better job? Why?

EXERCISE 11–9 Return on Investment (ROI) and Residual Income Relations LO11–1, LO11–2

Supply the missing data for three service companies shown in the table below:

	Company		
	A	B	C
Sales	$9,000,000	$7,000,000	$4,500,000
Net operating income	$?	$ 280,000	$?
Average operating assets	$3,000,000	$?	$1,800,000
Return on investment (ROI)	18%	14%	?
Minimum required rate of return:			
Percentage	16%	?	15%
Dollar amount	$?	$ 320,000	$?
Residual income	$?	$?	$ 90,000

EXERCISE 11–10 Sales Dollars as an Allocation Base for Fixed Costs LO11–4

Konig Enterprises owns and operates three restaurants. The company allocates its fixed administrative expenses to those restaurants based on sales dollars. Last year the fixed administrative expenses totaled $2,000,000 and were allocated as follows:

	Restaurants			
	Rick's Harborside	Imperial Garden	Ginger Wok	Total
Total sales—Last Year	$16,000,000	$15,000,000	$9,000,000	$40,000,000
Percentage of total sales ...	40%	37.5%	22.5%	100%
Allocation (based on the above percentages)	$800,000	$750,000	$450,000	$2,000,000

This year Imperial Garden increased its sales by $10 million. The sales levels in the other two restaurants remained unchanged. The company's sales data for this year were as follows:

	Restaurants			
	Rick's Harborside	Imperial Garden	Ginger Wok	Total
Total sales—This Year	$16,000,000	$25,000,000	$9,000,000	$50,000,000
Percentage of total sales ...	32%	50%	18%	100%

Fixed administrative expenses for this year remained unchanged at $2,000,000.

Required:

1. Using sales dollars as an allocation base, show the allocation of the fixed administrative expenses among the three restaurants for this year.
2. Calculate the change in each restaurant's allocated cost from last year to this year. As the manager of the Imperial Garden, how would you feel about the amount charged to you for this year?
3. Comment on the usefulness of sales dollars as an allocation base.

EXERCISE 11–11 Cost-Volume-Profit Analysis and Return on Investment (ROI) LO11–1

Posters.com is an Internet retailer of high-quality posters. The company has $1,000,000 in operating assets and fixed expenses of $150,000 per year. With this level of operating assets and fixed expenses, the company can support sales of up to $3,000,000 per year. The company's contribution margin ratio is 25%, which means an additional dollar of sales results in additional contribution margin, and net operating income, of 25 cents.

Required:
1. Complete the following table showing the relation between sales and return on investment (ROI).

Sales	Net Operating Income	Average Operating Assets	ROI
$2,500,000	$475,000	$1,000,000	?
$2,600,000	$?	$1,000,000	?
$2,700,000	$?	$1,000,000	?
$2,800,000	$?	$1,000,000	?
$2,900,000	$?	$1,000,000	?
$3,000,000	$?	$1,000,000	?

2. What happens to the company's return on investment (ROI) as sales increase? Explain.

EXERCISE 11–12 Effects of Changes in Profits and Assets on Return on Investment (ROI) LO11–1
Fitness Fanatics is a regional chain of health clubs that evaluates its club managers based on return on investment (ROI). The company's Springfield Club reported the following results for the past year:

Sales	$1,400,000
Net operating income	$70,000
Average operating assets	$350,000

Required:
The following questions are to be considered independently.
1. Compute the Springfield club's return on investment (ROI).
2. Assume the club manager can increase sales by $70,000 and net operating income by $18,200. Further assume this is possible without any increase in average operating assets. What would be the club's return on investment (ROI)?
3. Assume the club manager can reduce expenses by $14,000 without any change in sales or average operating assets. What would be the club's return on investment (ROI)?
4. Assume the club manager can reduce average operating assets by $70,000 without any change in sales or net operating income. What would be the club's return on investment (ROI)?

EXERCISE 11–13 Transfer Pricing Situations LO11–3
In each of the cases below, assume Division X has a product that can be sold to outside customers or to Division Y of the same company. The managers of the divisions are evaluated based on their divisional profits.

	Case	
	A	B
Division X:		
Capacity in units	200,000	200,000
Number of units being sold to outside customers	200,000	160,000
Selling price per unit to outside customers	$90	$75
Variable costs per unit	$70	$60
Fixed costs per unit (based on capacity)	$13	$8
Division Y:		
Number of units needed for production	40,000	40,000
Purchase price per unit now being paid		
to an outside supplierr	$86	$74

Required:

1. Refer to the data in case A above. Assume in this case $3 per unit in variable selling costs can be avoided on intracompany sales.
   a. What is the lowest acceptable transfer price from the perspective of the selling division?
   b. What is the highest acceptable transfer price from the perspective of the buying division?
   c. What is the range of acceptable transfer prices (if any) between the two divisions? If the managers are free to negotiate and make decisions on their own, will a transfer probably take place? Explain.

2. Refer to the data in case B above. In this case, there will be no savings in variable selling costs on intracompany sales.
   a. What is the lowest acceptable transfer price from the perspective of the selling division?
   b. What is the highest acceptable transfer price from the perspective of the buying division?
   c. What is the range of acceptable transfer prices (if any) between the two divisions? If the managers are free to negotiate and make decisions on their own, will a transfer probably take place? Explain.

EXERCISE 11–14 Evaluating New Investments Using Return on Investment (ROI) and Residual Income LO11–1, LO11–2

Selected sales and operating data for three divisions of different structural engineering firms are given below:

	Division A	Division B	Division C
Sales	$12,000,000	$14,000,000	$25,000,000
Average operating assets	$3,000,000	$7,000,000	$5,000,000
Net operating income	$600,000	$560,000	$800,000
Minimum required rate of return	14%	10%	16%

Required:

1. Compute each division's margin, turnover, and return on investment (ROI).
2. Compute each division's residual income.
3. Assume each division is presented with an investment opportunity yielding a 15% rate of return.
   a. If performance is being measured by ROI, which division or divisions will accept the opportunity? Reject? Why?
   b. If performance is being measured by residual income, which division or divisions will accept the opportunity? Reject? Why?

EXERCISE 11–15 Service Department Charges LO11–4

Korvanis Corporation operates a Medical Services Department that charges its variable costs to operating departments based on the actual number of employees in each department. It charges fixed costs to operating departments based on the long-run average number of employees.

The Medical Services Department's variable costs are budgeted at $80 per employee and its fixed costs are budgeted at $400,000 per year. Actual Medical Services Department costs for the most recent year were $41,000 for variable costs and $408,000 for fixed costs. Data concerning employees in the three operating departments follow:

	Cutting	Milling	Assembly
Budgeted number of employees	170	100	280
Actual number of employees for the			
most recent year	150	80	270
Long-run average number of employees	180	120	300

Required:

1. Calculate the Medical Services Department charges to each of the operating departments—Cutting, Milling, and Assembly.
2. How much, if any, of the Medical Services Department's actual costs should be treated as a spending variance and not charged to operating departments?

EXERCISE 11–16 Effects of Changes in Sales, Expenses, and Assets on ROI LO11–1
CommercialServices.com provides business-to-business services on the Internet. Data concerning the most recent year appear below:

Sales	$3,000,000
Net operating income	$150,000
Average operating assets	$750,000

Required:
Consider each question independently.
1. Compute the company's return on investment (ROI).
2. The entrepreneur who founded the company is convinced sales will increase next year by 50% and net operating income will increase by 200%, with no increase in average operating assets. What would be the company's ROI?
3. The company's chief financial officer believes a more realistic scenario would be a $1,000,000 increase in sales, requiring a $250,000 increase in average operating assets, with a resulting $200,000 increase in net operating income. What would be the company's ROI in this scenario?

Mc Graw Hill **connect**   **Problems**

PROBLEM 11–17 Return on Investment (ROI) and Residual Income LO11–1, LO11–2
Financial data for Joel de Paris, Inc., for last year follow:

Joel de Paris, Inc. Balance Sheet	Beginning Balance	Ending Balance
Assets		
Cash	$ 140,000	$ 120,000
Accounts receivable	450,000	530,000
Inventory	320,000	380,000
Plant and equipment, net	680,000	620,000
Investment in Buisson, S.A.	250,000	280,000
Land (undeveloped)	180,000	170,000
Total assets	$2,020,000	$2,100,000
Liabilities and Stockholders' Equity		
Accounts payable	$ 360,000	$ 310,000
Long-term debt	1,500,000	1,500,000
Stockholders' equity	160,000	290,000
Total liabilities and stockholders' equity	$2,020,000	$2,100,000

Joel de Paris, Inc. Income Statement		
Sales		$4,050,000
Operating expenses		3,645,000
Net operating income		405,000
Interest and taxes:		
Interest expense	$150,000	
Tax expense	110,000	260,000
Net income		$ 145,000

The company paid dividends of $15,000 last year. The "Investment in Buisson, S.A.," on the balance sheet represents an investment in the stock of another company. The company's minimum required rate of return is 15%.

Required:
1. Compute the company's average operating assets for last year.
2. Compute the company's margin, turnover, and return on investment (ROI) for last year.
   (Hint: Should you use net income or net operating income in your calculations?)
3. What was the company's residual income last year?

PROBLEM 11–18 Service Department Charges LO11–4
Tasman Products has a Maintenance Department that services equipment in the company's Forming Department and Assembly Department. The cost of this servicing is charged to the operating departments based on machine-hours.

Data for the Maintenance Department follow:

	Budget	Actual
Variable costs for lubricants	$96,000*	$110,000
Fixed costs for salaries and other	$150,000	$153,000

*Budgeted at $0.40 per machine-hour.

Data for the Forming and Assembly Departments follow:

	Percentage of Peak-Period Capacity Required	Machine-Hours	
		Budget	Actual
Forming Department	70%	160,000	190,000
Assembly Department	30%	80,000	70,000
Total	100%	240,000	260,000

The amount of fixed costs in the Maintenance Department is determined by peak-period requirements.

Required:
1. How much Maintenance Department cost should be charged to the Forming Department and to the Assembly Department?
2. How much, if any, of the Maintenance Department's actual costs should be treated as a spending variance and not charged to the Forming and Assembly departments? Explain.

PROBLEM 11–19 Comparison of Performance Using Return on Investment (ROI) LO11–1
Comparative data on three companies in the same service industry are given below:

	Company		
	A	B	C
Sales	$600,000	$500,000	$?
Net operating income	$ 84,000	$ 70,000	$?
Average operating assets	$300,000	$?	$1,000,000
Margin	?	?	3.5%
Turnover	?	?	2
ROI	?	7%	?

Required:
1. What advantages are there to breaking down ROI into margin and turnover?
2. Fill in the missing information above, and comment on the relative performance of the three companies. Make *specific recommendations* about how to improve the ROI.

(Adapted from National Association of Accountants,
Research Report No. 35, p. 34)

PROBLEM 11–20 Transfer Price with an Outside Market LO11–3

Hrubec Products, Inc., operates a Pulp Division that manufactures wood pulp for use in the production of various paper goods. Revenue and costs associated with a ton of pulp follow:

Selling price		$70
Expenses:		
Variable	$42	
Fixed (based on a capacity of 50,000 tons per year)	18	60
Net operating income		$10

Hrubec Products has just acquired a small company that manufactures paper cartons. Hrubec plans to treat its newly acquired Carton Division as a profit center. The manager of the Carton Division is currently purchasing 5,000 tons of pulp per year from a supplier at a cost of $63 per ton. Hrubec's president is anxious for the Carton Division to begin purchasing its pulp from the Pulp Division if the managers of the two divisions can negotiate an acceptable transfer price.

Required:

For (1) and (2) below, assume the Pulp Division can sell all of its pulp to outside customers for $70 per ton.

1. What is the Pulp Division's lowest acceptable transfer price? What is the Carton Division's highest acceptable transfer price? What is the range of acceptable transfer prices (if any) between the two divisions? Are the managers of the Carton and Pulp Divisions likely to agree to a transfer price for 5,000 tons of pulp next year? Why or why not?
2. If the Pulp Division meets the price the Carton Division is currently paying to its supplier and sells 5,000 tons of pulp to the Carton Division each year, what will be the effect on the profits of the Pulp Division, the Carton Division, and the company as a whole?

For (3)–(6) below, assume the Pulp Division is currently selling only 30,000 tons of pulp each year to outside customers at the stated $70 price.

3. What is the Pulp Division's lowest acceptable transfer price? What is the Carton Division's highest acceptable transfer price? What is the range of acceptable transfer prices (if any) between the two divisions? Are the managers of the Carton and Pulp Divisions likely to agree to a transfer price for 5,000 tons of pulp next year? Why or why not?
4. Suppose the Carton Division's outside supplier drops its price to only $59 per ton. Should the Pulp Division meet this price? Explain. If the Pulp Division does *not* meet the $59 price, what will be the effect on the company's profits?
5. Refer to (4) above. If the Pulp Division refuses to meet the $59 price, should the Carton Division be required to purchase from the Pulp Division at a higher price for the good of the company?
6. Refer to (4) above. Assume due to inflexible management policies, the Carton Division is required to purchase 5,000 tons of pulp each year from the Pulp Division at $70 per ton. What will be the effect on the company's profits?

PROBLEM 11–21 Return on Investment (ROI) and Residual Income LO11–1, LO11–2

"I know headquarters wants us to add that new product line," said Dell Havasi, manager of Billings Company's Office Products Division. "But I want to see the numbers before I make a decision. Our division's return on investment (ROI) has led the company for three years, and I don't want any letdown."

Billings Company is a decentralized wholesaler with five autonomous divisions. The divisions are evaluated using ROI, with year-end bonuses given to the divisional managers who have the highest ROIs. Operating results for the company's Office Products Division for this year are given below:

Sales	$10,000,000
Variable expenses	6,000,000
Contribution margin	4,000,000
Fixed expenses	3,200,000
Net operating income	$ 800,000
Divisional average operating assets	$ 4,000,000

The company had an overall return on investment (ROI) of 15% this year (considering all divisions). Next year the Office Products Division has an opportunity to add a new product requiring $1,000,000 of additional average operating assets. The annual cost and revenue estimates for the new product would be:

Sales	$2,000,000
Variable expenses	60% of sales
Fixed expenses	$640,000

Required:

1. Compute the Office Products Division's margin, turnover, and ROI for this year.
2. Compute the Office Products Division's margin, turnover, and ROI for the new product by itself.
3. Compute the Office Products Division's margin, turnover, and ROI for next year assuming it performs the same as this year and adds the new product.
4. If you were in Dell Havasi's position, would you accept or reject the new product? Explain.
5. Why do you suppose headquarters is anxious for the Office Products Division to add the new product?
6. Suppose the company's minimum required rate of return on operating assets is 12% and performance is evaluated using residual income.
   a. Compute the Office Products Division's residual income for this year.
   b. Compute the Office Products Division's residual income for the new product by itself.
   c. Compute the Office Products Division's residual income for next year assuming it performs the same as this year and adds the new product.
   d. Using the residual income approach, if you were in Dell Havasi's position, would you accept or reject the new product? Explain.

PROBLEM 11–22 Service Department Charges LO11–4

Sharp Motor Company has a cafeteria that serves two operating divisions—an Auto Division and a Truck Division. The costs of operating the cafeteria are budgeted at $40,000 per month plus $3 per meal served.

The fixed costs of the cafeteria are determined by peak-period requirements. The Auto Division is responsible for 65% of the peak-period requirements, and the Truck Division is responsible for the other 35%.

For June, the Auto Division estimated it would need 35,000 meals, and the Truck Division estimated it would need 20,000 meals. However, due to unexpected layoffs of employees during the month, only 20,000 meals were served to the Auto Division. Another 20,000 meals were served to the Truck Division as planned.

The cafeteria's actual fixed costs for June totaled $42,000 and its actual meal costs totaled $128,000.

Required:

1. How much cafeteria cost should be charged to each division for June?
2. Assume the company follows the practice of allocating *all* cafeteria costs to the divisions based on the number of meals served. On this basis, how much cost would be allocated to each division for June?
3. What criticisms can you make of the allocation method used in part (2) above?
4. If managers of operating departments know fixed service costs are going to be allocated based on peak-period requirements, what will be their probable strategy when estimating their peak-period requirements for the company's budget committee? As a member of top management, what would you do to neutralize such strategies?

PROBLEM 11–23 Market-Based Transfer Price LO11–3

Stavos Company's Screen Division manufactures a standard screen for high-definition televisions (HDTVs). The cost per screen is:

Variable cost per screen	$ 70
Fixed cost per screen	30*
Total cost per screen	$100

*Based on a capacity of 10,000 screens per year.

Part of the Screen Division's output is sold to outside manufacturers of HDTVs and part is sold to Stavos Company's Quark Division, which produces an HDTV under its own name. The Screen Division charges $140 per screen for all sales.

The net operating income associated with the Quark Division's HDTV is computed as follows:

Selling price per unit		$480
Variable cost per unit:		
Cost of the screen	$140	
Variable cost of electronic parts	210	
Total variable cost		350
Contribution margin		130
Fixed costs per unit		80*
Net operating income per unit		$ 50

*Based on a capacity of 3,000 units per year.

The Quark Division has an order from an overseas source for 1,000 HDTVs. The overseas source wants to pay only $340 per unit.

Required:
1. Assume the Quark Division has enough idle capacity to fill the 1,000-unit order. Is the division likely to accept the $340 price or to reject it? Explain.
2. Assume both the Screen Division and the Quark Division have idle capacity. Under these conditions, what is the financial advantage (disadvantage) for the company as a whole (on a per-unit basis) if the Quark Division *rejects* the $340 price?
3. Assume the Quark Division has idle capacity but the Screen Division is operating at capacity and could sell all of its screens to outside manufacturers. Under these conditions, what is the financial advantage (disadvantage) for the company as a whole (on a per-unit basis) if the Quark Division *accepts* the $340 unit price?
4. What conclusions do you draw concerning the use of market price as a transfer price in intracompany transactions?

PROBLEM 11–24 Return on Investment (ROI) Analysis LO11–1
Last year's contribution format income statement for Huerra Company is given below:

	Total	Unit
Sales	$4,000,000	$80.00
Variable expenses	2,800,000	56.00
Contribution margin	1,200,000	24.00
Fixed expenses	840,000	16.80
Net operating income	360,000	7.20
Income taxes @ 30%	108,000	2.16
Net income	$ 252,000	$ 5.04

The company had average operating assets of $2,000,000 during the year.

Required:
1. Compute last year's margin, turnover, and return on investment (ROI).
   For each of the following questions, indicate whether last year's margin and turnover will increase, decrease, or remain unchanged as a result of the events described, and then compute the new ROI. Consider each question separately.
2. Using Lean Production, the company is able to reduce the average level of inventory by $400,000.
3. The company achieves a cost savings of $32,000 per year by using less costly materials.
4. The company purchases machinery and equipment that increase average operating assets by $500,000. Sales remain unchanged. The new, more efficient equipment reduces production costs by $20,000 per year.

5. As a result of a more intense effort by salespeople, sales are increased by 20%; operating assets remain unchanged.

6. At the beginning of the year, obsolete inventory is scrapped, thereby lowering net operating income by $40,000.

7. At the beginning of the year, the company uses $200,000 of cash (received on accounts receivable) to repurchase some of its common stock.

PROBLEM 11–25 Basic Transfer Pricing LO11–3

Alpha and Beta are divisions within the same company. The managers of both divisions are evaluated based on their return on investment (ROI). Assume the following information for the two divisions:

	Case			
	1	2	3	4
Alpha Division:				
Capacity in units	80,000	400,000	150,000	300,000
Number of units now being sold to outside customers	80,000	400,000	100,000	300,000
Selling price per unit to outside customers	$30	$90	$75	$50
Variable costs per unit	$18	$65	$40	$26
Fixed costs per unit (based on capacity)	$6	$15	$20	$9
Beta Division:				
Number of units needed annually	5,000	30,000	20,000	120,000
Purchase price now being paid to an outside supplier	$27	$89	$75*	—

*Before any purchase discount.

Required:

1. Refer to case 1 shown above. Alpha Division can avoid $2 per unit in commissions on any sales to Beta Division.
   a. What is Alpha Division's lowest acceptable transfer price?
   b. What is Beta Division's highest acceptable transfer price?
   c. What is the range of acceptable transfer prices (if any) between the two divisions? Will the managers agree to a transfer? Explain.

2. Refer to case 2 shown above. A study indicates Alpha Division can avoid $5 per unit in shipping costs on any sales to Beta Division.
   a. What is Alpha Division's lowest acceptable transfer price?
   b. What is Beta Division's highest acceptable transfer price?
   c. What is the range of acceptable transfer prices (if any) between the two divisions? Would you expect any disagreement between the two divisional managers over what the exact transfer price should be? Explain.
   d. Assume Alpha Division offers to sell 30,000 units to Beta Division for $88 per unit and Beta Division refuses this price. What will be the company's loss in potential profits?

3. Refer to case 3 shown above. Assume Beta Division is now receiving an 8% price discount from the outside supplier.
   a. What is Alpha Division's lowest acceptable transfer price?
   b. What is Beta Division's highest acceptable transfer price?
   c. What is the range of acceptable transfer prices (if any) between the two divisions? Will the managers agree to a transfer? Explain.
   d. Assume Beta Division offers to purchase 20,000 units from Alpha Division at $60 per unit. If Alpha Division accepts this price, would you expect its ROI to increase, decrease, or remain unchanged? Why?

4. Refer to case 4 shown above. Assume Beta Division wants Alpha Division to provide it with 120,000 units of a *different* product from the one Alpha Division is producing now. The new product would require $21 per unit in variable costs and would require Alpha Division to cut back production of its present product by 45,000 units annually. What is Alpha Division's lowest acceptable transfer price?

Select cases are available in Connect.

CASE 11–26 Transfer Pricing; Divisional Performance LO11–3

Weller Industries has six divisions. Its Electrical Division (which is operating at capacity) produces a variety of electrical items, including an X52 electrical fitting that it sells to regular customers for $7.50 each. The fitting has a variable manufacturing cost of $4.25.

The company's Brake Division wants the Electrical Division to provide a large quantity of X52 fittings for $5 each. The Brake Division, which is operating at 50% of capacity, will put the fitting into a brake unit it produces and sells to an airplane manufacturer. The cost of the brake unit being built by the Brake Division follows:

Purchased parts (from outside vendors).............	$22.50
Electrical fitting X52	5.00
Other variable costs	14.00
Fixed overhead and administration	8.00
Total cost per brake unit..........................	$49.50

Although the Brake Division's proposed price of $5 for the X52 fitting is well below the Electrical Division's regular price of $7.50, the manager of the Brake Division believes the price concession is necessary for his division to win the contract for the airplane brake units. He has heard "through the grapevine" the airplane manufacturer will reject his bid if it is more than $50 per brake unit. Thus, if the Brake Division is forced to pay the regular $7.50 price for the X52 fitting, it will either not get the contract or suffer a substantial loss. The manager of the Brake Division believes the price concession benefits his division and the company as a whole.

Weller Industries uses return on investment (ROI) to measure divisional performance.

Required:
1. What is the Electrical Division's lowest acceptable transfer price? If you were the manager of the Electrical Division, would you supply the X52 fitting to the Brake Division for $5 each as requested? Why or why not?
2. Assuming the airplane brakes can be sold for $50, what is the financial advantage (disadvantage) for the company (on a per-unit basis) if the Electrical Division supplies fittings to the Brake Division? Explain your answer.
3. What is the Brake Division's highest acceptable transfer price? Should the two divisional managers be able to agree on a transfer price in this particular situation?
4. Discuss the organizational behavior problems, if any, inherent in this situation. What would you advise the company's president to do?

(CMA, adapted)

lighthouse image: Martin73/Shutterstock;
big data image: INGARA/Shutterstock

LEARNING OBJECTIVES

After studying Chapter 12, you should be able to:

LO12–1 Identify examples of performance measures appropriate for each of the four balanced scorecard categories.

LO12–2 Identify four types of quality costs and use them to create a quality cost report.

LO12–3 Calculate throughput (manufacturing cycle) time, delivery cycle time, manufacturing cycle efficiency (MCE), and overall equipment effectiveness (OEE).

LO12–4 Understand how to construct and use a balanced scorecard.

 Data Analytics Exercise available in Connect to complement this chapter

Strategic Performance Measurement

Hillary Kladke/Moment/Getty Images

ENTREPRENEUR SPOTLIGHT

Collette DiVitto developed a passion for baking while attending high school. After experimenting with numerous recipes, she created a cinnamon chocolate chip cookie her friends and family described as amazing! After completing Clemson University's LIFE program, she founded Collettey's Cookies (www.colletteys.com), which sells "The Amazing Cookie" as well as other tempting treats, such as oatmeal raisin cookies, peanut butter cookies, and gluten-free cinnamon chocolate chip cookies. In addition to internet sales, Collette's products are sold in nine stores across three states.

Applying Managerial Accounting

Collettey's Cookies maintains a strategic performance measurement dashboard on its website that separates its goals into three phases (https://www.colletteys.com/company-growth/). Some of its goals across these phases include "move to a commercial kitchen" (100% achieved), "build corporate accounts" (27% achieved), "create PR strategy" (82% achieved), and "design and launch merchandise" (62% achieved).

Serving All Stakeholders

Collettey's Cookies' mission includes creating jobs for people with special needs, changing the public's perception of this population's capabilities, and advocating for tax incentives for employers that hire workers with special needs. Her website notes, "Eighty-two percent of people with a disability are unemployed. Many of them want to work, have valuable skills to contribute, and ache for the chance to prove themselves and earn a living." Her dashboard includes numerous measures that support the company's mission, such as "open the world's eye to see abilities" (65% achieved), "develop workshops for others struggling with employment" (85% achieved), and "visit and speak at schools" (78% achieved). ■

Source: www.colletteys.com

A

company uses performance measures for a variety of reasons such as guiding employees in executing its strategy and then influencing their rewards for doing so. The centerpiece of this chapter is a performance measurement system called a *balanced scorecard*. A **balanced scorecard** consists of an integrated set of performance measures derived from a company's strategy.

The Balanced Scorecard: An Overview

Exhibit 12–1 highlights four key concepts related to the balanced scorecard. First, as shown on the left side of the exhibit, a company's balanced scorecard emanates from its vision and *strategy* for succeeding in the marketplace. A **strategy** is a "game plan" that is difficult to replicate and differentiates a company from its competitors in ways that attract and retain customers. These sources of differentiation, or what are more formally called *customer value propositions,* are the essence of strategy.

As discussed in the Prologue, customer value propositions fall into three broad categories—*customer intimacy, operational excellence,* and *product leadership.* Companies differentiating themselves in terms of *customer intimacy* are, in essence, saying to their customers, "You should choose us because we customize our products and services to meet your individual needs better than our competitors." Companies pursuing the second customer value proposition, called *operational excellence,* are saying to their target customers, "You should choose us because we deliver products and services faster, more conveniently, and at a lower price than our competitors." Companies pursuing the third customer value proposition, called *product leadership,* are saying to their target

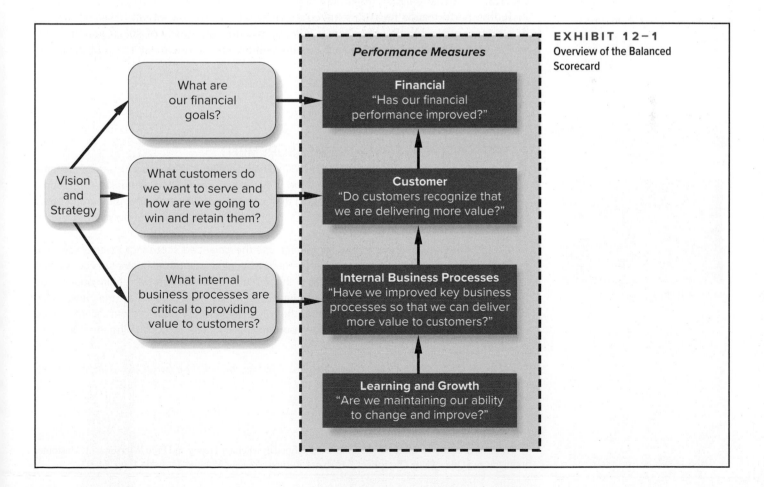

EXHIBIT 12–1
Overview of the Balanced Scorecard

customers, "You should choose us because we offer more innovative and higher quality products than our competitors."[1]

The second key point from Exhibit 12–1 is the measures included in a balanced scorecard usually fall into four categories: learning and growth, internal business processes, customer, and financial. Internal business processes are what the company does in an attempt to satisfy customers. For example, in a manufacturing company, assembling a product is an internal business process. In an airline, handling baggage is an internal business process. Some of the measures included in these categories may be financial while others may be nonfinancial in nature.

The third insight from Exhibit 12–1 is a company's strategy has an important influence on the measures it will include in the four categories of its balanced scorecard. For example, a company focused on product leadership might create learning and growth measures related to its engineering training program, internal business process measures related to its research and development process, customer measures related to their perceptions of product innovation, and financial measures related to sales growth from new products. All of these measures have a shared emphasis on new product development, which is very important to a company pursuing a product leadership customer value proposition.

The fourth key idea related to the balanced scorecard (as indicated by the vertical arrows in Exhibit 12–1) is the four categories of measures are linked to one another in a cause-and-effect fashion as follows: a company's employees need to continuously learn in order to improve internal business processes; improving business processes is necessary to improve customer satisfaction; and improving customer satisfaction is necessary to improve financial results.

The remainder of the chapter is organized in three main sections. The first section describes a variety of performance measures for each of the four balanced scorecard categories. Next, the chapter illustrates how a company can build a complete scorecard, including performance measures linked together on a cause-and-effect basis, to support its strategic goals. Finally, the chapter concludes with a summary of social and environmental performance measures because many companies include these types of measures within their balanced scorecards.

IN BUSINESS

SAUL LOEB/AFP/Getty Images

RETHINKING PERFORMANCE MEASUREMENT

As restaurants started reopening during the COVID-19 pandemic, "service with safety" became an imperative. Restaurant staff were retrained in numerous ways, such as ripping up "disposable menus in front of customers after taking their orders to assure them that they aren't being reused" and limiting contact with diners by "uncorking a bottle of wine and setting it on the table instead of filling their glasses."

In this chapter, you'll learn how companies use the balanced scorecard to organize their performance measures into four categories—financial, customer, internal business process, and learning and growth. The intuitive appeal of these four categories can be readily understood through the eyes of post–COVID-19 restaurant owners as they confronted the new reality that their financial success was going to be heavily influenced by their customers' intensified attention to cleanliness, which in turn had important implications for redesigning their business processes and training their employees.

Source: Te-Ping Chen and Heather Haddon, "Rules Press Restaurant Staff," *The Wall Street Journal,* June 15, 2020, pp. B1–B2.

---

[1]   These three customer value propositions were defined by Michael Treacy and Fred Wiersema in "Customer Intimacy and Other Value Disciplines," *Harvard Business Review,* Volume 71, Issue 1, pp. 84–93.

Learning and Growth Measures

Business leaders and consultants often say a company's employees are its most important asset. This axiom is grounded in the belief that if a company with a viable strategy enables its employees to continuously learn and expand their capabilities, it should ultimately improve financial performance.

Exhibit 12–2 contains 15 examples of learning and growth measures organizations might include in their balanced scorecards. The measures are organized under six headings that influence employee learning and growth—recruiting, skills development, compensation and advancement, wellness/safety, job satisfaction, and retention. Each measure contains a parenthetical + or − to indicate if the goal is to increase or decrease the measure. For example, the measure *percent of "outstanding" interview candidates that accepted our job offer* has a parenthetical + sign because it would be expected to increase over time.

Each measure included in the learning and growth section of a balanced scorecard should influence other measures within the scorecard. For example, a company may hypothesize increasing its *average training hours per employee* will lead to process improvements such as fewer errors. Or it may hypothesize lowering its employee turnover percentage will lead to greater loyalty from customers who appreciate working with a "familiar face."

LO12–1
Identify examples of performance measures appropriate for each of the four balanced scorecard categories.

IN BUSINESS

TOUGHER INTERVIEWS INCREASE JOB ACCEPTANCE RATES

Research from Glassdoor suggests that job acceptance rates from candidates between the ages of 25 and 34 rise by 3.1 percent when they perceive job interviews to be increasingly difficult. Glassdoor's senior economist Daniel Zhao said, "job seekers, especially younger ones, want the chance to perform and be assessed for the unique skills they bring to the table. . . [therefore,] having candidates complete skills tests as part of the vetting process raises acceptance rates by 2.5 percentage points." On the contrary, when these same job applicants are asked to take a personality test, it decreases their job acceptance rate by 2.3 percent.

From a balanced scorecard perspective, a company's job offer acceptance rate is an important learning and growth measure that can eventually drive improvements in other measures related to internal business process performance, customer satisfaction, and profits.

Source: Kathryn Dill, "Tough Interview Process Is Linked to a Higher Job-Acceptance Rate," *The Wall Street Journal*, February 27, 2020, p. B4

EXHIBIT 12–2
Examples of Learning and Growth Performance Measures

Recruiting:

- Percent of "outstanding" interview candidates that accepted our job offer (+)
- Recruiting expenditures per hired employee (−)

Skills development:

- Percent of employees that strongly agree with the statement "I am consistently given the resources that I need to do my job." (+)
- Average mentorship hours per employee (+)
- Average training hours per employee (+)

Compensation and advancement:

- Percent of leadership positions filled with internal candidates (+)
- Percent of workforce promoted within the last three years (+)
- Average pay raise percentage per employee (+)

Wellness/Safety:

- Absenteeism rate (−)
- Average number of workplace accidents per employee (−)

Job satisfaction:

- Percent of employees that strongly agree with the statement "This is a great place to work." (+)
- Percent of employees that strongly agree with the statement "My contribution to the company is recognized and respected by my co-workers." (+)
- Number of process improvement suggestions per employee (+)

Retention:

- Employee turnover percentage (−)
- Average years of tenure per employee (+)

Internal Business Process Measures

Effective managers understand *business processes,* rather than functional departments, serve the needs of a company's most important stakeholders—its customers. A **business process** is a series of steps followed in order to complete some task in a business. These steps often span departmental boundaries, thereby requiring managers to cooperate to improve internal business process performance measures.

Exhibit 12–3 contains 18 examples of internal business process measures organizations might include in their balanced scorecards. The measures are organized under six dimensions of business process performance—innovation, product and service quality, agility (which refers to a company's ability to adapt or change quickly), cost, time, and lean resource management (as described in the Prologue). Each measure contains a parenthetical + or − to indicate if the goal is to increase or decrease the measure.

As mentioned earlier, each company's internal business process measures will vary depending on its strategy. A company focused on product leadership may choose business process measures related to innovation and product quality. A company differentiating itself from competitors based on operational excellence may select process measures related to cost and time. Finally, a company with a customer intimacy strategy may focus on service quality and agility measures.

EXHIBIT 12–3
Examples of Internal Business Process Measures

Innovation:

- Number of new products designed (+)
- Number of patents approved (+)
- Percentage of previously designed parts used in new products (+)

Product and service quality:

- Number of warranty claims (−)
- Defect-free units as a percentage of completed units (+)
- Percent of customer complaints settled on first contact (+)

Agility:

- Number of modular product designs (+)
- Percent of suppliers with long-term contracts (+)
- Average batch size (−)

Cost:

- Cost of quality (−)
- Non-value-added activity costs (−)
- Lost sales due to out-of-stock merchandise (−)

Time:

- Delivery cycle time (−)
- Throughput (Manufacturing cycle) time (−)
- Manufacturing cycle efficiency (MCE) (+)

Lean Resource Management:

- Overall equipment effectiveness (OEE) (+)
- WIP Inventory as a percent of sales (+)
- Workstation cleanliness score (+)

Customer Measures

Exhibit 12–4 contains 18 examples of customer measures organizations might include in their balanced scorecards. The measures are organized under six headings—customer satisfaction, customer acquisition/retention, customer lifetime value, customer loyalty, customer service, and customer value proposition.

If a company improves its learning and growth and internal business process measures, these improvements should ultimately have a positive influence on its customer measures. If this cause-and-effect relationship does not materialize, it suggests the company does not have a complete understanding of the performance attributes shaping its customers' perceptions and behaviors.

EXHIBIT 12–4
Example of Customer Measures

Customer satisfaction:

- Percent of customers that strongly agree with the statement "I would readily recommend your company to someone else." (+)
- Number of customer referrals (+)

Customer acquisition/retention:

- Market share percentage (+)
- Customer defection rate (–)
- Average customer acquisition cost (–)
- Percent of customer leads that generate a sale (+)

Customer lifetime value:

- Average revenue per order (+)
- Average gross margin per order (+)
- Average time between purchases (–)

Customer loyalty:

- Percent of a customer's overall spending committed to our company (also called "share of wallet") (+)
- Number of collaborative customer-driven product innovations (+)

Customer service:

- Percent of customers that strongly agree with the statement "My order was delivered on time." (+)
- Percent of customers that strongly agree with the statement "My problem was resolved quickly." (+)
- Percent of customers that strongly agree with the statement "Your website was easy to use." (+)
- Percent of customers that strongly agree with the statement "Your employees treated me courteously." (+)

Customer value proposition:

- Customer perception of our product leadership (+)
- Customer perception of our operational excellence (+)
- Customer perception of our customer intimacy (+)

IN BUSINESS

AMAZON'S CUSTOMER SATISFACTION DROPS, BUT ITS SALES GROW

Usually, companies expect to see a correlation between customer satisfaction and sales—as customer satisfaction grows, so do sales. However, during the COVID-19 pandemic, this was not the case at Amazon.com. Research conducted by RBC Capital Markets showed a "sharp rise in the number of Amazon customers who made at least two to three purchases a month, as well as the number of those who claim to have spent $200 or more on Amazon over past 90 days." Conversely, the number of customers who were "very satisfied or extremely satisfied" with Amazon dipped from 73 percent the prior year to 64 percent. Given that investors expect Amazon's sales to grow 18 percent per year, the company will be working hard to reverse its decline in customer satisfaction.

Source: Dan Gallagher, "Amazon Doesn't Need No Satisfaction," *The Wall Street Journal*, June 9, 2020, p. B12.

Miami Herald/Getty Images

Financial Measures

Exhibit 12–5 includes 20 examples of financial measures organized under six headings—sales, profits, profitability ratios, trend performance, cash flows, and market performance. Although we are not going to explain how to calculate these measures within this chapter, it bears emphasizing Chapter 16 discusses profitability ratios, trend performance, and market performance; Chapter 15 is dedicated to cash flows; and earlier chapters explained how to calculate profits using the traditional (absorption) and contribution methods.

The balanced scorecard framework rejects the notion improving process-oriented measures automatically leads to financial success. On the contrary, the scorecard includes a financial perspective for the express purpose of holding organizations accountable for translating improvements in nonfinancial performance to "bottom-line" results. If favorable trends in a company's learning and growth, internal business processes, and customer measures do not translate to financial results, the balanced scorecard forces the organization to re-examine its strategy for differentiating itself from competitors.

EXHIBIT 12-5
Examples of Financial Measures

Sales:

- Sales from new customers (+)
- Sales from products less than three years old (+)
- Patent-protected sales (+)

Profitability ratios:

- Gross margin percentage (+)
- Net profit margin percentage (+)
- Return on assets (ROA) (+)
- Return on equity (ROE) (+)

Cash flows:

- Net cash flow from operating activities (+)
- Net cash flow from operating activities ÷ average operating assets (+)
- Net cash flow from operating activities ÷ sales (+)

Profits:

- Contribution margin (+)
- Net operating income (+)
- Residual income (+)

Trend performance:

- Sales growth rate (+)
- Contribution margin growth rate (+)
- Net operating income growth rate (+)
- Net cash flow from operating activities growth rate (+)

Market performance:

- Stock price (+)
- Earnings-per-share (EPS) (+)
- Price-earnings ratio (+)

Cost of Quality: A Closer Look

This section takes a closer look at one of the internal business process measures included in Exhibit 12–3—the cost of quality. It defines four types of quality costs and explains how to compute the cost of quality.

Cost of Quality

LO12-2

Identify four types of quality costs and use them to create a quality cost report.

A defect-free product meeting or exceeding its design specifications has a high **quality of conformance.** Preventing, detecting, and dealing with defects that lower the quality of conformance causes the incurrence of four types of quality costs—*prevention costs, appraisal costs, internal failure costs,* and *external failure costs.* **Prevention costs** are incurred to prevent defects from occurring. **Appraisal costs**, are incurred to identify production defects *before* shipping them to customers. **Internal failure costs** result from identifying defects before they are shipped to customers. **External failure costs** result when a defective product is delivered to customers. Exhibit 12–6 contains examples of costs within each of these four categories.

The sum of these four types of costs is called the **cost of quality**. A company's goal is to lower its cost of quality over time. The key to accomplishing this goal is recognizing the following distinction—prevention costs and appraisal costs are incurred to keep production defects from shipping to customers, whereas internal failure costs and external failure costs are incurred because defects occur despite efforts to prevent them. Thus, the objective of an effective quality management program is to make additional investments in prevention and appraisal that are more than offset by reductions in internal and external failure costs. Preventing defects from occurring is preferable to detecting them after they have occurred.

A company can prepare a *quality cost report* to measure its progress in lowering its overall cost of quality. A **quality cost report** details the prevention costs, appraisal costs, and the costs of internal and external failures arising from the company's current

EXHIBIT 12–6
Examples of Quality Costs

Prevention Costs:
Systems development
Quality engineering
Quality training
Quality circles
Statistical process control activities
Supervision of prevention activities
Quality data gathering, analysis, and reporting
Quality improvement projects
Technical support provided to suppliers
Audits of the effectiveness of the quality system

Appraisal Costs:

Test and inspection of incoming materials
Test and inspection of in-process goods
Final product testing and inspection
Supplies used in testing and inspection
Supervision of testing and inspection activities
Depreciation of test equipment
Maintenance of test equipment
Plant utilities in the inspection area
Field testing and appraisal at customer site

Internal Failure Costs:
Net cost of scrap
Net cost of spoilage
Rework labor and overhead
Reinspection of reworked products
Retesting of reworked products
Downtime caused by quality problems
Disposal of production defects
Analysis of the cause of defects in production
Re-entering data because of keying errors
Debugging software errors

External Failure Costs:

Cost of field servicing and handling complaints
Warranty repairs and replacements
Repairs and replacements beyond the warranty period
Product recalls
Liability arising from production defects
Returns and allowances arising from quality problems
Lost sales arising from a reputation for poor quality

quality management efforts. Exhibit 12–7 contains an example of a quality cost report for Ventura Company.

Several things should be noted from the data in the exhibit. First, Ventura Company's quality costs are poorly distributed in both years, with most of the costs due to either internal failure or external failure. The external failure costs are particularly high in Year 1 in comparison to other costs.

Second, note the company increased its spending on prevention and appraisal activities in Year 2. As a result, internal failure costs went up in that year (from $2 million in Year 1 to $3 million in Year 2), but external failure costs dropped sharply (from $5.15 million in Year 1 to only $2 million in Year 2). Because of the increase in appraisal activity in Year 2, more defects were caught inside the company before being shipped to customers. This resulted in more cost for scrap, rework, and so forth, but saved huge amounts in warranty repairs, warranty replacements, and other external failure costs.

Third, note as a result of greater emphasis on prevention and appraisal, *total* quality cost decreased in Year 2. As continued emphasis is placed on prevention and appraisal in future years, total quality cost should continue to decrease. That is, future increases in prevention and appraisal costs should be more than offset by decreases in failure costs. Moreover, appraisal costs should also decrease over time as more effort is placed into prevention.

Quality Cost Reports: Strengths and Limitations

A quality cost report has several uses. First, quality cost information helps managers see the financial significance of defects. Managers usually are not aware of the magnitude of their quality costs because these costs cut across departmental lines and are not normally tracked and accumulated by the cost system. Thus, when first presented with a quality cost report, managers often are surprised by the high costs of poor quality.

Second, quality cost information helps managers identify the relative importance of the quality problems faced by their companies. For example, the quality cost report may show scrap is a major quality problem or the company is incurring huge warranty costs. With this information, managers have a better idea of where to focus their efforts.

EXHIBIT 12-7
Quality Cost Report

	Ventura Company Quality Cost Report For Years 1 and 2			
	Year 1		Year 2	
	Amount	Percent*	Amount	Percent*
Prevention costs:				
Systems development	$ 270,000	0.54%	$ 400,000	0.80%
Quality training	130,000	0.26%	210,000	0.42%
Supervision of prevention activities	40,000	0.08%	70,000	0.14%
Quality improvement projects	210,000	0.42%	320,000	0.64%
Total prevention cost	650,000	1.30%	1,000,000	2.00%
Appraisal costs:				
Inspection	560,000	1.12%	600,000	1.20%
Reliability testing	420,000	0.84%	580,000	1.16%
Supervision of testing and inspection	80,000	0.16%	120,000	0.24%
Depreciation of test equipment	140,000	0.28%	200,000	0.40%
Total appraisal cost	1,200,000	2.40%	1,500,000	3.00%
Internal failure costs:				
Net cost of scrap	750,000	1.50%	900,000	1.80%
Rework labor and overhead	810,000	1.62%	1,430,000	2.86%
Downtime due to defects in quality	100,000	0.20%	170,000	0.34%
Disposal of production defects	340,000	0.68%	500,000	1.00%
Total internal failure cost	2,000,000	4.00%	3,000,000	6.00%
External failure costs:				
Warranty repairs	900,000	1.80%	400,000	0.80%
Warranty replacements	2,300,000	4.60%	870,000	1.74%
Allowances	630,000	1.26%	130,000	0.26%
Cost of field servicing	1,320,000	2.64%	600,000	1.20%
Total external failure cost	5,150,000	10.30%	2,000,000	4.00%
Total quality cost	$9,000,000	18.00%	$7,500,000	15.00%

*As a percentage of total sales. In each year, sales totaled $50,000,000.

Third, quality cost information helps managers see whether their quality costs are poorly distributed. In general, quality costs should be distributed more toward prevention and appraisal activities and less toward failures.

Counterbalancing these uses, quality cost information has three limitations. First, simply measuring and reporting quality costs does not solve quality problems. Problems can be solved only by taking action. Second, results usually lag behind quality improvement programs. Initially, total quality cost may even increase as quality control systems are designed and installed. Decreases in quality costs may not occur until the quality program has been in effect for some time. And third, the most important quality cost, lost sales arising from customer ill will, is usually omitted from the quality cost report because it is difficult to estimate.

Operating Performance Measures: A Closer Look

This section takes a closer look at four of the internal business process measures included in Exhibit 12–3—throughput (manufacturing cycle) time, delivery cycle time, manufacturing cycle efficiency (MCE), and overall equipment effectiveness (OEE).

Throughput (Manufacturing Cycle) Time

LO12–3
Calculate throughput (manufacturing cycle) time, delivery cycle time, manufacturing cycle efficiency (MCE), and overall equipment effectiveness (OEE).

The elapsed time from when production is started until finished goods are shipped to customers is called **throughput time,** or *manufacturing cycle time.* The goal is to continuously reduce this measure and the formula for computing it is as follows:

$$\text{Throughput (manufacturing cycle) time} =$$
$$\text{Process time} + \text{Inspection time} + \text{Move time} + \text{Queue time}$$

Process time includes the amount of time work is actually done on the product. *Inspection time* includes the time spent ensuring the product is not defective. *Move time* is the time required to move materials or partially completed products from workstation to workstation. *Queue time* includes the time a product spends waiting to be worked on, moved, inspected, or shipped. Only one of these four activities adds value to the product—process time. The other three activities—inspecting, moving, and queuing—add no value and should be reduced as much as possible.

Delivery Cycle Time

The elapsed time from when a customer order is received until the finished goods are shipped is called **delivery cycle time.** The goal is to reduce this measure; the formula for computing it is as follows:

$$\text{Delivery cycle time} = \text{Wait time} + \text{Throughput time}$$

Wait time is the elapsed time from when a customer order is received until production of the order is started. This is a non-value-added activity that should be reduced or eliminated. When companies succeed in drastically reducing or eliminating wait time plus the non-value-added components of throughput time, it often enables them to increase customer satisfaction and profits. The relation between throughput (manufacturing cycle) time and delivery cycle time is illustrated in Exhibit 12–8.

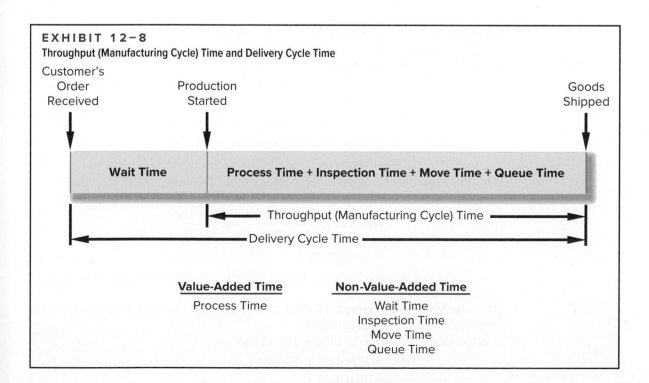

EXHIBIT 12–8
Throughput (Manufacturing Cycle) Time and Delivery Cycle Time

Value-Added Time	Non-Value-Added Time
Process Time	Wait Time
	Inspection Time
	Move Time
	Queue Time

Manufacturing Cycle Efficiency (MCE)

Throughput time, which is a key measure in delivery performance, can be put into better perspective by computing the **manufacturing cycle efficiency (MCE).** The MCE is computed by relating the value-added time to the throughput time. The goal is to increase this measure; the formula for computing it is as follows:

$$MCE = \frac{\text{Value-added time (Process time)}}{\text{Throughput (manufacturing cycle) time}}$$

Any non-value-added time results in an MCE of less than 1. An MCE of 0.5, for example, would mean half of the total production time consists of inspection, moving, and similar non-value-added activities. In many manufacturing companies, the MCE is less than 0.1 (10%), which means 90 percent of the time a unit is in process is spent on non-value-added activities. Monitoring MCE helps companies reduce non-value-added activities and deliver products to customers faster at lower cost.

Example   During a recent quarter, Novex Company recorded the following average times per order:

	Days
Wait time	17.0
Inspection time	0.4
Process time	2.0
Move time	0.6
Queue time	5.0

Goods are shipped when production is completed.

Required:
1. Compute the throughput (manufacturing cycle) time.
2. Compute the manufacturing cycle efficiency (MCE).
3. What percentage of the production time is spent in non-value-added activities?
4. Compute the delivery cycle time.

Solution
1. Throughput time = Process time + Inspection time + Move time + Queue time

    = 2.0 days + 0.4 day + 0.6 day + 5.0 days

    = 8.0 days
2. Only process time represents value-added time; therefore, MCE is computed as follows:

    $$MCE = \frac{\text{Value-added time}}{\text{Throughput time}} = \frac{2.0 \text{ days}}{8.0 \text{ days}}$$

    = 0.25

    Thus, once put into production, a typical order is actually being worked on only 25 percent of the time.
3. Because MCE is 25 percent, 75 percent (100% − 25%) of total production time is spent in non-value-added activities.
4. Delivery cycle time = Wait time + Throughput time

    = 17.0 days + 8.0 days

    = 25.0 days

Overall Equipment Effectiveness (OEE)

Overall equipment effectiveness (OEE) is a performance measure used by many lean manufacturers. **Overall equipment effectiveness** measures the productivity of a piece of equipment along three dimensions—utilization, efficiency, and quality. The equation for calculating OEE is as follows:

$$\text{OEE} = \text{Utilization rate} \times \text{Efficiency rate} \times \text{Quality rate}$$

where:

$$\text{Utilization rate} = \text{Actual run time} \div \text{Machine time available}$$
$$\text{Efficiency rate} = \text{Actual run rate} \div \text{Ideal run rate}$$
$$\text{Quality rate} = \text{Defect-free output} \div \text{Total output}$$

The keys to increasing the utilization rate include avoiding machine breakdowns and minimizing average setup times. The efficiency rate is maximized by avoiding minor work stoppages and by retaining and properly training operators to run and regularly maintain the machine. The quality rate is improved by reducing the number of defective units produced as a percent of the total output.

Example Jayson Company's customer demand for its only product exceeds its manufacturing capacity. The company provided the following information for a machine whose limited capacity is prohibiting the company from producing and selling additional units:

Actual run time this week.	4,550 minutes
Machine time available per week	6,500 minutes
Actual run rate this week	3.8 units per minute
Ideal run rate.	4.0 units per minute
Defect-free output this week	16,000 units
Total output this week (including defects)	17,290 units

Calculate the machine's OEE:

Utilization rate $=$ Actual run time $\div$ Machine time available
$=$ 4,550 minutes $\div$ 6,500 minutes
$=$ 0.70

Efficiency rate $=$ Actual run rate $\div$ Ideal run rate
$=$ 3.8 units per minute $\div$ 4.0 units per minute
$=$ 0.95

Quality rate $=$ Defect-free output $\div$ Total output
$=$ 16,000 units $\div$ 17,290 units
$=$ 0.925

OEE $=$ Utilization rate $\times$ Efficiency rate $\times$ Quality rate
$=$ .70 $\times$ .95 $\times$ .925
$=$ 0.615

The overall equipment effectiveness can also be analyzed in terms of units produced as follows:

Maximum possible output (6,500 × 4.0) (a).		26,000
Utilization loss [(6,500 − 4,550) × 4.0].	7,800	
Efficiency loss [(4.0 − 3.8) × 4,550]	910	
Quality loss (17,290 − 16,000)	1,290	10,000
Defect-free output (b)		16,000
OEE (b) ÷ (a).		0.615

This analysis reveals Jayson Company sacrificed 10,000 units of production (due to utilization, efficiency, and quality losses) that could have been sold to customers.

COMMUNICATING WITH DATA VISUALIZATIONS

Diagnostic analytics answer the question: Why did it happen? This visualization explains why Jayson Company had only 16,000 units of defect-free output compared to 26,000 units of available capacity. It lost 7,800 units because 30 percent of the available machine-minutes were unused. It lost 910 units because the machine's actual run rate was 5 percent less than its ideal run rate. It lost 1,290 units because 7.5 percent of the total output was defective.

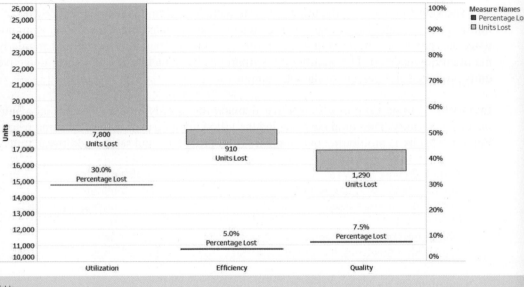

Tableau

Constructing a Balanced Scorecard

LO12–4

Understand how to construct and use a balanced scorecard.

Earlier in the chapter, we introduced more than 70 examples of measures companies might include in their balanced scorecards. Now we are shifting our focus to assembling these measures into a complete balanced scorecard. Our discussion will proceed in two steps. First, we'll demonstrate how companies select strategy-driven measures and link them together in a series of testable if-then hypothesis statements. Second, we'll discuss some important issues related to using balanced scorecard measures to evaluate and reward employees.

Selecting Balanced Scorecard Measures

At the beginning of the chapter, we mentioned the four categories of a balanced score-card are interrelated to one another. Those interrelationships were depicted by the vertical arrows in Exhibit 12–1—a company's employees need to continuously learn and grow to improve internal business processes; improving business processes is necessary to improve customer satisfaction; and improving customer satisfaction is necessary to improve financial results.

To illustrate these interrelationships, let's suppose Jaguar's strategy is to offer distinctive, richly finished luxury automobiles to wealthy individuals who prize hand-crafted, individualized products. To deliver this customer intimacy value proposition to its wealthy target customers, Jaguar might create such a large number of options for details, such as leather seats, interior and exterior color combinations, and wooden dashboards, that each car becomes virtually one of a kind. Instead of just offering tan or blue leather seats in standard cowhide, the company may offer customers the choice of an almost infinite palette of colors in numerous exotic leathers. For such a system to succeed, Jaguar would have to deliver completely customized cars within a reasonable amount of time—and without incurring more cost for this customization than the customer is willing to pay.

Exhibit 12–9 suggests how Jaguar might reflect this strategy in its balanced scorecard. Each measure contains a parenthetical + or − indicating if the goal is to increase or decrease the measure. The exhibit also contains arrows linking the measures together on a cause-and-effect basis. Each link can be read as a hypothesis in the form "If we improve this measure, then this other performance measure should also improve." Starting from the bottom of Exhibit 12–9, we can read the links between performance measures as follows.

If we increase our employee retention rate and our average training hours per employee, then it will increase the number of options available while decreasing the average number of errors per vehicle and the average time to install an option. If we increase the number of options available, decrease the average number of errors per vehicle, and decrease the average time to install an option, then it will increase our customers' satisfaction with the number of options available, which in turn will increase our market share percentage in the luxury car market.

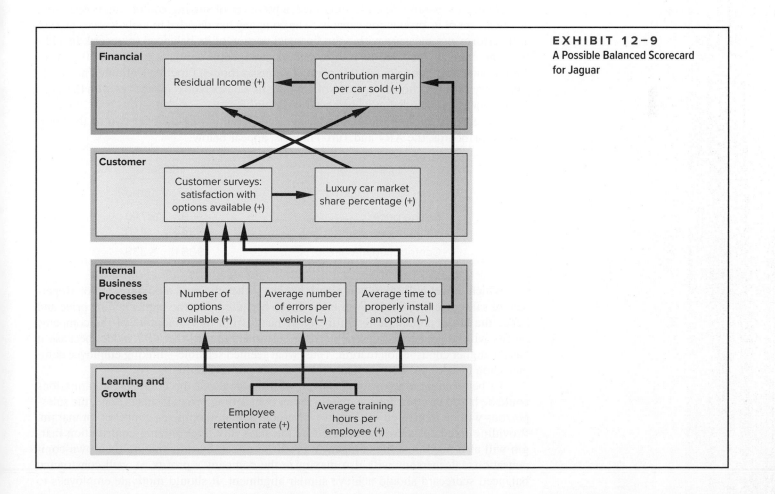

EXHIBIT 12–9
A Possible Balanced Scorecard for Jaguar

Continuing up Exhibit 12–9, if we increase our customers' satisfaction with the number of options available and decrease the average time to install an option, it will increase our contribution margin per car sold. Finally, if we increase our market share percentage in the luxury car market and our contribution margin per car sold, it will increase our residual income.

In essence, the balanced scorecard describes a theory of how the company can take concrete actions to attain its desired outcomes (financial, in this case). The strategy defined in Exhibit 12–9 seems plausible, but it should be regarded as only a theory. For example, if the company succeeds in increasing the number of options available and in decreasing its average number of errors per vehicle and its average time to install an option and yet there is no increase in customer satisfaction, the market share percentage, the contribution margin per car, or residual income, the strategy would have to be reconsidered. One of the advantages of the balanced scorecard is it continually tests the theories underlying management's strategy. If a strategy is not working, it should become evident when some of the predicted effects (i.e., higher residual income) don't occur. Without this feedback, an organization may drift on indefinitely with an ineffective strategy based on faulty assumptions.

Tying Compensation to the Balanced Scorecard

Incentive compensation for employees, such as bonuses, can, and probably should, be tied to balanced scorecard performance measures. However, this should be done only after the organization has been successfully managed with the scorecard for some time—perhaps a year or more. Managers must be confident the performance measures are reliable, sensible, understood by those who are being evaluated, and not easily manipulated.

While selecting measures for a balanced scorecard and then using those measures to reward employees may seem pretty straight forward, too often organizations use performance measures to reward employees in ways that cause suboptimal results. To illustrate this point, let's assume Pipeline Unlimited, a producer of surfing equipment, is operating at 75 percent of its production capacity. The company has decided to include sales growth as a performance measure within the financial portion of its balanced scorecard. In addition, the company decided to compensate its salespeople by paying them a 10 percent commission based on sales. At this point, it seems as though Pipeline Unlimited has made some very sensible choices in terms of aligning its salespersons' incentives with the sales growth measure included in its balanced scorecard.

However, to explore the matter further, let's assume that data for two of the company's surfboards, the XR7 and Turbo models, appear below:

	Model	
	XR7	Turbo
Selling price	$695	$749
Variable expenses	344	410
Contribution margin	$351	$339

Which model will salespeople push hardest if they are paid a commission of 10 percent of sales revenue? The answer is the Turbo because it has the higher selling price and hence the larger commission. On the other hand, from the standpoint of the company, profits will be greater if salespeople steer customers toward the XR7 model because it has the higher contribution margin. Thus, what seemed sensible—linking employee compensation to sales growth—is likely to cause suboptimal results.

To better align employee incentives with the goals of the company, commissions could be based on contribution margin rather than selling price. If this is done, the salespersons will be motivated sell the mix of products that maximizes contribution margin. Providing fixed costs are not affected by the sales mix, maximizing contribution margin will also maximize the company's profit. In effect, by maximizing their own compensation, salespersons will also maximize the company's profits. A well-constructed balanced scorecard should achieve similar alignment. It should motivate employees to choose actions aligned with the company's overall strategic goals and properly reward them for doing so.

STARBUCKS ATTENDS TO ITS SOCIAL RESPONSIBILITIES

Starbucks is setting ambitious goals for reducing its impact on the environment. The company is looking at numerous opportunities such as reducing food and packaging waste, expanding the use of reusable coffee cups, adding plant-based options to its menu, improving the energy efficiency of newly constructed stores, and improving its suppliers' environmental practices. Kevin Johnson, the company's CEO, said, "the journey we undertake is not only the right one for Starbuck's responsibility as a corporate citizen of the world but is also fundamental to our brand relevance." In terms of measurable goals, by 2030, the company plans to reduce its carbon emissions and the waste it sends to landfills by 50 percent.

Source: Heather Haddon, "Starbucks Pledges to Slash Water Use, Waste, Emissions," *The Wall Street Journal*, January 22, 2020, p. B7.

Andrew Balcombe/Shutterstock

Environmental, Social, and Governance (ESG): An Expanded Set of Responsibilities

A company's stakeholders—including investors, customers, employees, suppliers, regulators, communities, and environmental and human rights advocates—expect it to deliver strong financial results while conscientiously attending to its *environmental, social, and governance* (ESG) responsibilities. In this section, we take a closer look at the meaning of these responsibilities and why companies attend to them. We also discuss ESG reporting practices and provide examples of ESG performance measures.

ESG Responsibilities: A Closer Look

Environmental, social, and governance (ESG) are three criteria used by stakeholders for gauging the sustainability and ethical impacts of a company. *Environmental* sustainability includes topics such as emissions, carbon footprint, and toxic waste management; water and energy usage; biodiversity preservation; materials sourcing; recycling and reuse planning; and product packaging. *Social* considerations include providing employees with adequate training and fair wages as well as a safe, harassment-free workplace that is committed to diversity, equity, and inclusion (DEI). They also include protecting customers' private data while investing in their communities and selling them safe, properly labeled products at fair prices. Senior leaders provide effective *governance* by defining policies and strategies that promote environmental stewardship, social performance, ethical decision making, and transparent reporting throughout the supply chain.

While many companies proactively embrace their ESG responsibilities based on the moral imperative of "doing the right thing," these same companies also understand that attending to these responsibilities can expand sales opportunities and reduce risk exposures. For example, General Motors, Ford Motor Company, Toyota, and Audi now sell hybrid or fully electric vehicles in response to societal concerns about auto emissions and fossil fuels depletion. Timberland uses recycled plastic from millions of water bottles to manufacture its increasingly popular Earthkeepers® footwear. Similarly, the shoe company Allbirds has built its entire brand around sustainability—using selective sourcing of natural and recyclable materials, close collaboration with supply chain partners, and responsible manufacturing processes to differentiate itself from competitors.

From a risk management standpoint, most companies realize overlooking their ESG responsibilities will damage their reputations. For example, if a company discharges lethal pollutants into the environment, purchases products from an overseas supplier that employs child labor, or systematically discriminates against a group of its employees, it will eventually cause negative publicity. This, in turn, will trigger undesirable after-effects such as customer boycotts or defections, a decline in job applications from top-notch candidates, and increase in employee turnover, disenchanted investors, and possibly even lawsuits and government-imposed fines. To reduce these kinds of risks, many companies incorporate ESG considerations in their planning and control processes. For example, Starbucks uses a program called the Coffee and Farmers Equity (C.A.F.E.) Practices to continuously monitor the economic, social, and environmental impacts of its network of more than 400,000 coffee growers in 30 countries

ESG Reporting Practices

Most of the world's largest companies prepare ESG performance reports (also called sustainability reports) for their external stakeholders. While a growing percentage of these companies also hire public accounting firms to provide assurance services that add credibility to their ESG disclosures, there is little consensus regarding the standards for preparing and reviewing these reports, particularly across industries. A number of organizations have created their own ESG data collection and reporting standards, including the Global Reporting Initiative (GRI), the Sustainability Accounting Standards Board (SASB), the United Nations' Principles for Responsible Investment (PRI), and the World Economic Forum and International Business Council's collaborative Stakeholder Capitalism Metrics initiative. Each of these standard-setters retains its own metrics for evaluating specific impacts, thereby creating challenges for companies and public accounting firms seeking generally accepted reporting guidelines.[2]

From an internal reporting perspective, the balanced scorecard provides a useful framework for organizing ESG performance measures. Exhibit 12–10 provides 31 examples of ESG performance measures across the four balanced scorecard categories. Each measure is coded with a parenthetical + or − to indicate if the goal is to increase or decrease the measure. While some companies incorporate these types of measures into their existing balanced scorecards, others choose to implement a variety of adaptations. For example, some companies add a fifth category to their scorecards that purposely focuses on an expanded set of stakeholders. Other companies establish separate scorecards dedicated to their own and/or their suppliers' ESG performance. Regardless of these diverse formatting choices, a company should always connect its scorecard measures to one another using if-then hypothesis statements. Individual measures are of limited value unless they ultimately drive the attainment of larger strategic goals. Furthermore, a company's scorecard measures should be linked to how its senior leaders and managers are evaluated and rewarded. Otherwise, a company's proclaimed commitment to fulfilling its ESG responsibilities may not lead to corresponding actions and results.

IN BUSINESS

WATER SCARCITY LEADS TO NEW STRATEGIES

Analysts have suggested water usage could soon have more impact on the food-and-beverage industry's bottom line than carbon-reduction initiatives. In response, PepsiCo has announced its intention to be "net water positive" by 2030, meaning it plans to provide more water back into the community than it uses. This involves initiatives such as returning water into aquifers in areas of scarcity as well as conservation projects that reduce runoff and increase rainwater absorption into the ground. The company also plans to tighten its water efficiency standards at over 1,000 company-owned and third-party facilities. PepsiCo says these measures will reduce its usage in water-stressed areas by nearly 11 billion litres by 2030—a 50 percent reduction in usage compared to 2015.

Source: Dieter Holger, "PepsiCo Sets Plan to Cut Its Water Use," *The Wall Street Journal*, August 18, 2021, https://www.wsj.com/articles/pepsico-aims-to-replenish-more-water-than-it-uses-11629201601.

---

[2] In tandem with standardizing ESG reporting, there is growing movement toward *impact-weighted financial accounting* (IWFA), which assigns a dollar value to a company's ESG impact on its financial statements. For more information, see https://impacteconomyfoundation.org/impactweightedaccounts framework/.

EXHIBIT 12-10

Examples of Environmental, Social, and Governance (ESG) Measures for the Balanced Scorecard

	Environmental	Social	Governance
Learning and growth	• Number of LEED-certified facilities (+) • Number of product engineers trained in eco-conscious product design (+)	• Number of occupational injuries/accidents (−) • Average compensation for female employees ÷ average compensation for male employees (+) • Percent of job applicants from under-represented groups that are hired (+) • Average community service hours per employee (+)	• Number of female directors ÷ number of male directors (+) • Number of board members receiving ESG training (+) • Percent of employees that strongly agree with the statement "My company has a supportive and inclusive corporate culture." (+)
Internal business processes	• Average water consumed per unit produced (−) • Percent of raw material inputs that have been recycled (+) • Pounds of waste produced (−) • Average carbon emissions per unit produced (−)	• Number of product warranty claims ÷ sales revenue (−) • Total cost of quality ÷ sales (−)	• Number of certified diverse suppliers (+) • Number of suppliers having third-party verification of child labor law compliance (+)
Customer	• Percent of customers that strongly agree with the statement "Your company is committed to environmental stewardship." (+) • Percent of customers buying eco-conscious products (+)	• Percent of customers that strongly agree with the statement "Your company cares about the communities where it operates." (+) • Percent of customers that strongly agree with the statement "Your company has a superior commitment to product safety." (+)	• Percent of customers that strongly agree with the statement "Your company provides me the information I need to assess its environmental and social performance." (+) • Percent of customers that strongly agree with the statement "Your company conducts itself in an ethical manner." (+)
Financial	• Percent of revenue from eco-conscious products (+) • Average fuel cost per sales dollar (−) • Capital expenditures on "green" products and processes (+)	• Total workers' compensation costs (−) • Dollars invested in data security ÷ cost of data breaches (+)	• Total tax dollars saved via environmental tax incentives (+) • CEO compensation ÷ average employee compensation (−) • Percent of investors that strongly agree with the statement "This company provides timely and transparent financial disclosures." (+)

Summary

The centerpiece of this chapter is the balanced scorecard, which is an integrated set of performance measures derived from a company's strategy. Performance measures used in balanced scorecards fall into four categories—learning and growth, internal business processes, customer, and financial.

A company's internal business process measures can include the cost of quality, which quantifies the sum of prevention costs, appraisal costs, internal failure costs, and external failure costs. Generally speaking, management should focus its attention on preventing defects because small investments in prevention can lead to dramatic reductions in appraisal costs as well as internal and external failure costs. The costs of quality are often summarized in a quality cost report that helps managers understand the importance of quality costs, spot problem areas, and assess the way in which the quality costs are distributed.

Internal business process measures can also include time-based measures such as throughput time, delivery cycle time, and manufacturing cycle efficiency, as well as overall equipment effectiveness—which considers machine utilization, efficiency, and quality. The goals are to decrease throughput time and delivery cycle time while increasing manufacturing cycle efficiency (MCE) and overall equipment effectiveness (OEE).

An organization begins creating a balanced scorecard by defining its strategy. Then, it translates this strategy into accompanying performance measures that track its progress in executing the strategy. These performance measures should be linked together in a cause-and-effect manner. One of the advantages of the balanced scorecard is it continually tests the theories underlying management's strategy. If a strategy is not working, it should become evident when some of the predicted if-then relationships don't occur. The measures contained in a balanced scorecard should also be linked to how employees are evaluated and rewarded; otherwise, the measures are likely to be ignored.

Environmental, social, and governance (ESG) are three criteria used by stakeholders for gauging the sustainability and ethical impacts of a company. While many companies proactively embrace their ESG responsibilities based on the moral imperative of "doing the right thing," these same companies also understand that attending to these responsibilities can expand sales opportunities and reduce risk exposures. From an external reporting standpoint, most of the world's largest companies prepare ESG performance reports for their external stakeholders. From an internal reporting perspective, the balanced scorecard provides a useful framework for organizing ESG performance measures.

 Data Analytics Exercise available in Connect to complement this chapter

Review Problem: Operating Performance Measures

Codington Corporation records the time required to fill customer orders. It recorded the following data for a particular order:

	Hours
Wait time	20.8
Process time	2.2
Inspection time	0.2
Move time	4.8
Queue time	18.6

Required:

1. Calculate the throughput (manufacturing cycle) time.
2. Calculate the manufacturing cycle efficiency (MCE).
3. Calculate the delivery cycle time.

Solution to Review Problem

1. The throughput time is computed as follows:

    Throughput time = Process time + Inspection time + Move time + Queue time
    Throughput time = 2.2 hours + 0.2 hour + 4.8 hours + 18.6 hours
    Throughput time = 25.8 hours

2. The manufacturing cycle efficiency (MCE) is computed as follows:

    MCE = Value-added time (Process time)/Throughput time
    MCE = 2.2 hours/25.8 hours
    MCE = 0.09 (rounded)

3. The delivery cycle time is computed as follows:

    Delivery cycle time = Wait time + Throughput time
    Delivery cycle time = 20.8 hours + 25.8 hours
    Delivery cycle time = 46.6 hours

Glossary

Appraisal costs Costs incurred to identify production defects before they are shipped to customers. (p. 538)

Balanced scorecard An integrated set of performance measures derived from the organization's strategy. (p. 533)

Business process A series of steps followed in order to complete some task in a business. (p. 536)

Cost of quality The sum of prevention costs, appraisal costs, internal failure costs, and external failure costs. (p. 538)

Delivery cycle time The elapsed time from when a customer order is received until the finished goods are shipped. (p. 541)

Environmental, social, and goverance (ESG) Three criteria used by stakeholders for gauging the sustainability and ethical impacts of a company. (p. 547)

External failure costs Costs incurred when a defective product or service is delivered to a customer. (p. 538)

Internal failure costs Costs incurred when production defects are identified before shipment to customers. (p. 538)

Manufacturing cycle efficiency (MCE) Process (value-added) time as a percentage of throughput time. (p. 542)

Overall equipment effectiveness A ratio measuring the productivity of a piece of equipment. (p. 543)

Prevention costs Costs incurred to prevent defects. (p. 538)

Quality cost report A report summarizing prevention costs, appraisal costs, and the costs of internal and external failures. (p. 538)

Quality of conformance The degree to which a product or service meets or exceeds its design specifications and is free of defects. (p. 538)

Strategy A "game plan" that is difficult to replicate and differentiates a company from its competitors in ways that attract and retain customers. (p. 533)

Throughput time The elapsed time from when production is started until finished goods are shipped. (p. 541)

Questions

12–1 What are the four categories of measures in a balanced scorecard?

12–2 What are the four types of costs summarized in a quality cost report? How do companies seek to lower their cost of quality?

12–3 What is the difference between delivery cycle time and throughput time? What four elements make up throughput time? What elements of throughput time are value-added and what elements are non-value-added?

12–4   What does a manufacturing cycle efficiency (MCE) of less than 1 mean? How would you interpret an MCE of 0.40?

12–5   Why do the measures used in a balanced scorecard differ from company to company?

12–6   Why should the measures included in a balanced scorecard be linked together using if-then hypothesis statements?

12–7   Why does the balanced scorecard include financial performance measures as well as internal business processes measures?

12–8   Why should companies link their balanced scorecard measures to their employee reward systems?

12–9   Why do companies measure their corporate social responsibility performance?

12–10   What is the Global Reporting Initiative?

Applying Excel   Mc Graw Hill connect

LO12–3

The Excel worksheet below recreates the Review Problem pertaining to Codington Corporation. The workbook, and instructions on how to complete the file, can be found in Connect.

	A	B	C
1	**Chapter 12: Applying Excel**		
2			
3	**Data**		
4	Wait time	20.8	hours
5	Process time	2.2	hours
6	Inspection time	0.2	hours
7	Move time	4.8	hours
8	Queue time	18.6	hours
9			
10	*Enter a formula into each of the cells marked with a ? below*		
11	**Review Problem: Operating Performance Measures**		
12			
13	***Compute the Following Operating Performance Measures:***		
14	Throughput time	?	hours
15	Manufacturing cycle efficiency (MCE)	?	
16	Delivery cycle time	?	hours
17			
18			

Chapter 12 Form   Filled in Chapter 12 Form   Chapter 12 Form ...

Microsoft Excel

You should proceed to the requirements below only after completing your worksheet.

Required:

1. Check your worksheet by changing the wait time in cell B4 to 5.8 hours and the queue time in cell B8 to 8.6 hours. The throughput time should now be 15.8 hours. The manufacturing cycle efficiency (MCE) should now be 0.14, and the delivery cycle time should now be 21.6 hours. If you do not get these answers, find the errors in your worksheet and correct them.

    Explain why the throughput time and delivery cycle time both decreased. Why did the manufacturing cycle efficiency (MCE) increase?

2. Revise the data in your worksheet as follows:

Data	
Wait time	1.0 hours
Process time	2.2 hours
Inspection time	0.2 hours
Move time	0.8 hours
Queue time	0.6 hours

a. What is the throughput time?
b. What is the manufacturing cycle efficiency (MCE)?
c. What is the delivery cycle time?

 **Exercises**

EXERCISE 12–1 Examples of Balanced Scorecard Performance Measures LO12–1

Reid Company is implementing a balanced scorecard performance measurement system. Its senior management team assembled the measures shown below for possible inclusion in its scorecard.

Required:

For each measure, indicate by placing an *X* in the appropriate column whether it would most likely be classified in the learning and growth, internal business process, customer, or financial category of the company's balanced scorecard.

Item	Learning & Growth	Internal Business Process	Customer	Financial
Ex. Employee absenteeism rate	X			
1. Sales from new customers				
2. Customer defection rate				
3. Average fuel cost per sales dollar				
4. Average number of workplace accidents per employee				
5. Delivery cycle time				
6. Average training hours per employee				
7. Number of job applicants from under-represented groups				
8. Percent of customers that strongly agree with the statement "Your employees treated me courteously."				
9. Return on assets				
10. Percent of customers that strongly agree with the statement "Your company has a superior commitment to product safety."				
11. Number of modular product designs				
12. Lost sales due to out-of-stock merchandise				
13. Pounds of waste produced				
14. Number of customer referrals				
15. Residual income				
16. Average mentorship hours per employee				

EXERCISE 12–2 Classification of Quality Costs LO12–2

A number of activities that are part of a company's quality control system are listed below:
a. Product testing.
b. Product recalls.
c. Rework labor and overhead.
d. Quality circles.
e. Downtime caused by defects.
f. Cost of field servicing.
g. Inspection of goods.
h. Quality engineering.
i. Warranty repairs.
j. Statistical process control.
k. Net cost of scrap.
l. Depreciation of test equipment.
m. Returns and allowances arising from poor quality.
n. Disposal of production defects.
o. Technical support to suppliers.
p. Systems development.
q. Warranty replacements.
r. Field testing at customer site.
s. Quality training.

Required:

1. Classify the costs associated with each of these activities into one of the following categories: prevention cost, appraisal cost, internal failure cost, or external failure cost.
2. Which of the four types of costs in (1) above are incurred to keep poor quality of conformance from occurring? Which of the four types of costs in (1) above are incurred because poor quality of conformance has occurred?

EXERCISE 12–3 Measures of Internal Business Process Performance LO12–3

Management of Mittel Company wants to reduce the elapsed time from when a customer places an order to when it is shipped. It provided the following data for a recent quarter:

Inspection time	0.3 day
Wait time (from order to start of production)	14.0 days
Process time	2.7 days
Move time	1.0 day
Queue time	5.0 days

Required:

1. Compute the throughput time.
2. Compute the manufacturing cycle efficiency (MCE) for the quarter.
3. What percentage of the throughput time was spent in non-value-added activities?
4. Compute the delivery cycle time.
5. If using Lean Production eliminates all queue time, what will be the new MCE?

EXERCISE 12–4 Building a Balanced Scorecard LO12–4

Lost Peak ski resort, a family-owned resort serving day skiers from nearby towns, was recently acquired by Western Resorts, a major ski resort operator. The new owners plan to upgrade the resort into a destination resort for vacationers. As part of this plan, the new owners intend to make major improvements in the Powder 8 Lodge, the resort's on-the-hill cafeteria. The menu at the lodge is very limited—hamburgers, hot dogs, chili, pizzas, french fries, and packaged snacks. With little competition on the mountain, the previous owners felt no urgency to upgrade the menu or service quality.

As part of the deal when acquiring Lost Peak, Western Resorts agreed to retain all of the current resort employees. The manager of the lodge, while hardworking and enthusiastic, has very little experience in the restaurant business. The manager is responsible for selecting the menu, recruiting and training employees, and overseeing daily operations. The kitchen staff prepare food and wash dishes. The dining room staff take orders, serve as cashiers, and clean the dining room area.

Shortly after taking over Lost Peak, management of Western Resorts held a day-long meeting with all Powder 8 Lodge employees to discuss its future plans for the lodge. At the end of this meeting, management and lodge employees selected the following performance measures to be used in creating a balanced scorecard:

a. Weekly Powder 8 Lodge sales
b. Weekly Powder 8 Lodge profit
c. Number of menu items
d. Dining area cleanliness as rated by a representative from Western Resorts management
e. Customer satisfaction with menu choices as measured by customer surveys
f. Customer satisfaction with service as measured by customer surveys
g. Average time to take an order
h. Average time to prepare an order
i. Percentage of kitchen staff completing a reimbursed cooking course at the local community college
j. Percentage of dining room staff completing a reimbursed hospitality course at the local community college

Required:

1. Using the above performance measures, construct a balanced scorecard for the Powder 8 Lodge. Use Exhibit 12–9 as a guide. Use arrows to show causal links and indicate with a + or − whether the performance measure should increase or decrease.
2. What hypotheses are built into the balanced scorecard for the Powder 8 Lodge? Which of these hypotheses do you believe are most questionable? Why?
3. How will management know if one of the hypotheses underlying the balanced scorecard is false?

EXERCISE 12–5 Overall Equipment Effectiveness LO12–3

Jefferson Company's demand for its only product exceeds its manufacturing capacity. The company provided the following information for the machine whose limited capacity is prohibiting the company from producing and selling additional units.

Actual run time this week	4,900 minutes
Machine time available per week	7,000 minutes
Actual run rate this week	3.8 units per minute
Ideal run rate	4.0 units per minute
Defect-free output this week	15,827 units
Total output this week (including defects)	18,620 units

Required:

1. Compute the utilization rate.
2. Compute the efficiency rate
3. Compute the quality rate
4. Compute the overall equipment effectiveness (OEE).

EXERCISE 12–6 Defining Balanced Scorecard Measures LO12–1, LO12–4

Askew Company is creating a balanced scorecard and just completed a brainstorming activity to define areas where it needs to improve regarding learning and growth, internal business process performance, customer satisfaction, and financial results. The results of its brainstorming session are summarized below:

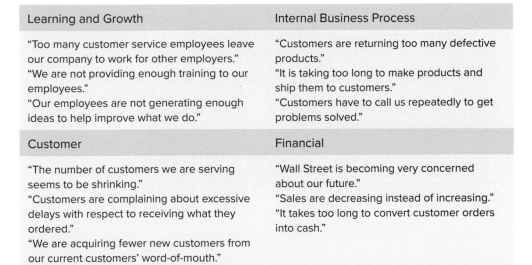

Learning and Growth	Internal Business Process
"Too many customer service employees leave our company to work for other employers." "We are not providing enough training to our employees." "Our employees are not generating enough ideas to help improve what we do."	"Customers are returning too many defective products." "It is taking too long to make products and ship them to customers." "Customers have to call us repeatedly to get problems solved."
Customer	**Financial**
"The number of customers we are serving seems to be shrinking." "Customers are complaining about excessive delays with respect to receiving what they ordered." "We are acquiring fewer new customers from our current customers' word-of-mouth."	"Wall Street is becoming very concerned about our future." "Sales are decreasing instead of increasing." "It takes too long to convert customer orders into cash."

The company asked you to guide its balanced scorecard implementation process from this point forward.

Required:

1. Provide one example of a plausible performance measure for each comment raised during the company's brainstorming session.
2. Choose a strategy for the company based on its brainstorming goals (either product leadership, operational excellence, or customer intimacy) and define three plausible if-then hypothesis statements using some of your measures from requirement 1. Use a + or − to indicate whether each performance measure should increase or decrease.

EXERCISE 12–7 If-Then Hypothesis Statements LO12–4

The table below contains five measures under the column heading If and five measures under the column heading Then:

If	Then
Employee turnover percentage	⟶ Number of warranty claims
Customer defection rate	⟶ Sales growth rate
Number of new products designed	⟶ Percent of a customer's overall spending committed to our company
Non-value-added activity costs	⟶ Net operating income
Number of process improvement suggestions per employee	⟶ Non-value-added activity costs

Required:

1. For each row in the table, write an if-then hypothesis statement connecting the two measures. Indicate whether each measure should increase or decrease.
2. For each row in the table, provide one reason why a company that improves each of the five "if" measures may not see the expected improvement in its associated "then" measure.

EXERCISE 12–8 Cost of Quality   LO12-2

Walton Company measured its quality costs for the past two years and summarized those costs using the four categories shown below:

	Last Year	This Year
Prevention costs	$357,000	$650,000
Appraisal costs	$445,000	$545,000
Internal failure costs	$790,000	$500,000
External failure costs	$1,100,000	$680,000

Required:

1. Calculate the total cost of quality last year and this year.
2. For last year, calculate the cost in each of the four categories as a percent of the total cost of quality.
3. For this year, calculate the cost in each of the four categories as a percent of the total cost of quality.
4. Discuss the company's efforts to manage its costs of quality over the two-year period. Is performance trending in a favorable or unfavorable direction? Why?

EXERCISE 12–9 Balanced Scorecard Performance Measures LO12–1, LO12–4

The table shown below contains four performance measures for four different companies. Each set of performance measures contains one measure for each of the four perspectives of the balanced scorecard.

Company A:

Average years of tenure per employee
Sales from products less than three years old
Market share percentage
Number of new products designed

Company B:

Customer perception of our product leadership
Percent of "outstanding" interview candidates that accepted our job offer
Number of patents approved
Patent-protected sales

Company C:

Pounds of waste produced
Percent of revenue from eco-conscious products
Number of process improvement suggestions per employee
Percent of customers that strongly agree with the statement "Your company is committed to environmental stewardship."

Company D:

Net operating income growth rate
Manufacturing cycle efficiency
Percent of customers that strongly agree with the statement "My order was delivered on time."
Average training hours per employee

Required:

1. For each of companies A, B, C, and D:
    a. Label each of the four measures as Learning & Growth, Internal Business Process, Customer, or Financial perspectives. Indicate whether each measure should increase or decrease.
    b. Create three if-then hypothesis statements that link (1) the Learning & Growth measure with the Internal Business Process measure, (2) the Internal Business Process measure to the Customer measure, and (3) the Customer measure to the Financial measure.
2. For each of companies A, B, C, and D, describe whether its set of four measures reflects an operational excellence, customer intimacy, or product leadership customer value proposition. Why?

EXERCISE 12–10 Internal Business Process Measures and Customer Value Propositions LO12–1

The table below contains performance measures companies might use as internal business process measures in their balanced scorecards. Each measure is accompanied by a + or − to indicate whether the performance measure should increase or decrease over time.

Required:

For each measure, place an X in one of the first three columns indicating whether the measure would be adopted by a company pursuing a strategy focused on operational excellence, product leadership, or customer intimacy. In the fourth column, provide an explanation for your answer.

Item	Operational Excellence	Product Leadership	Customer Intimacy	Explanation
Ex. Number of patents approved		X		Patents often provide the foundation for delivering new and innovative products to customers.
1. Delivery cycle time (−)				
2. Number of new products designed (+)				
3. Average contact hours per customer (+)				
4. Non-value-added activity costs (−)				
5. Percent of suppliers with long-term contracts (+)				
6. Number of modular product designs (+)				
7. Number of customized products co-designed with customers (+)				
8. Defect-free units as a percentage of completed units (+)				
9. Number of options available for customers to choose from (+)				

EXERCISE 12–11 Using If-Then Hypothesis Statements to Connect Balanced Scorecard Performance Measures LO12–4

The table shown below contains three performance measures for each of the four perspectives of the balanced scorecard:

Learning and Growth:

Percent of employees that strongly agree with the statement "I am consistently given the resources that I need to do my job."
Absenteeism rate
Percent of employees that strongly agree with the statement "I would say that this is a great place to work."

Internal Business Process:

Throughput time
Percent of customer complaints settled on first contact
Cost of quality

Customer:

Average gross margin per order
Customer perception of operational excellence
Percent of customers that strongly agree with the statement "My problem was resolved quickly."

Financial:

Net cash flow from operating activities
Gross margin percentage
Net profit margin percentage

Required:

1.   Choose one of the three learning and growth measures and write an if-then hypothesis statement connecting it to one of the three internal business process measures. Then create an if-then hypothesis statement connecting your internal business process measure to one of the three customer measures. Finally, write an if-then hypothesis statement connecting your customer measure to one of the three financial measures. Indicate whether each measure should increase or decrease.

2.   Choose one of the two remaining learning and growth measures and write an if-then hypothesis statement connecting it to one of the two remaining internal business process measures. Then create an if-then hypothesis statement connecting your internal business process measure to one of the two remaining customer measures. Finally, write an if-then hypothesis statement connecting your customer measure to one of the two remaining financial measures. Indicate whether each measure should increase or decrease.

3.   Write an if-then hypothesis statement connecting your remaining learning and growth measure to your remaining internal business process measure. Then create an if-then hypothesis statement connecting your remaining internal business process measure to your remaining customer measure. Finally, write an if-then hypothesis statement connecting your remaining customer measure to your remaining financial measure. Indicate whether each measure should increase or decrease.

Problems  connect

PROBLEM 12–12 Overall Equipment Effectiveness LO12–3

Kilmer Company's customer demand for its only product exceeds its manufacturing capacity. The company provided the following information for the machine whose limited capacity is prohibiting the company from producing and selling additional units:

Actual run time this week	6,600 minutes
Machine time available per week	11,000 minutes
Actual run rate this week	5.1 units per minute
Ideal run rate	6.0 units per minute
Defect-free output this week	23,562 units
Total output this week (including defects)	33,660 units

Required:

1.   With respect to the company's overall equipment effectiveness, calculate the following:
    a.   The utilization rate.
    b.   The efficiency rate.
    c.   The quality rate
    d.   The overall equipment effectiveness (OEE).
2.   With respect to the company's overall equipment effectiveness, calculate the following:
    a.   The utilization loss in units during the week.
    b.   The efficiency loss in units during the week.
    c.   The quality loss in units during the week.

PROBLEM 12–13 Creating Balanced Scorecards That Support Different Strategies LO12–4

The Midwest Consulting Group (MCG) helps companies build balanced scorecards. As part of its marketing efforts, MCG conducts an annual balanced scorecard workshop for prospective clients. As MCG's newest employee, your boss asked you to participate in this year's workshop by explaining to attendees how a company's strategy determines the appropriate measures for its balanced scorecard. Your boss provided you with the excerpts below from the annual reports of two current MCG clients. She asked you to use these excerpts in your portion of the workshop.

Excerpt from Applied Pharmaceuticals' annual report:

> The keys to our business are consistent and timely new product introductions and manufacturing process integrity. The new product introduction side of the equation is a function of research and development (R&D) yield (e.g., the number of marketable drug compounds created relative to the total number of potential compounds pursued). We optimize our R&D yield and first-to-market capability by investing in state-of-the-art technology, hiring the

highest possible percentage of the "best and the brightest" engineers that we pursue, and providing world-class training to those engineers. Manufacturing process integrity is all about establishing world-class quality specifications and then relentlessly engaging in prevention and appraisal activities to minimize defect rates. Our customers must have an awareness of and respect for our brand image of being "first to market and first in quality." If we deliver on this pledge to our customers, then our financial goal of increasing our return on stockholders' equity should take care of itself.

Excerpt from Destination Resorts International's annual report:

Our business succeeds or fails based on the quality of the service our front-line employees provide to customers. Therefore, it is imperative we strive to maintain high employee morale and minimize employee turnover. In addition, it is critical we train our employees to use technology to create one seamless worldwide experience for our repeat customers. Once an employee enters a customer preference (e.g., provide two extra pillows in the room, deliver fresh brewed coffee to the room at 8:00 A.M., etc.) into our database, our worldwide work-force strives to ensure a customer will never need to repeat it at any of our destination resorts. If we properly train and retain a motivated workforce, we should see continuous improve-ment in our percentage of error-free repeat customer check-ins, the time taken to resolve cus-tomer complaints, and our independently assessed room cleanliness. This in turn should drive improvement in our customer retention, which is the key to meeting our revenue growth goals.

Required:

1. Based on the excerpts above, compare and contrast the strategies of Applied Pharmaceuticals and Destination Resorts International.
2. Select balanced scorecard measures for each company and link them together using the frame-work from Exhibit 12–9. Use arrows to show the causal links between the performance mea-sures and show whether the performance measure should increase or decrease over time. Feel free to create measures not be specifically mentioned in the chapter if they make sense given the strategic goals of each company.
3. What hypotheses are built into each balanced scorecard? Why do the hypotheses differ between the two companies?

PROBLEM 12–14 Dysfunctional Effects of Some Performance Measures LO12–1

There is often more than one way to improve a performance measure. Unfortunately, some of the actions taken by managers to make their performance look better may actually harm the organiza-tion. For example, suppose the marketing department is held responsible only for increasing the performance measure "total revenues." Increases in total revenues may be achieved by working harder and smarter, but they can also usually be achieved by simply cutting prices. The increase in volume from cutting prices almost always results in greater total revenues; however, it does not always lead to greater total profits. Those who design performance measurement systems need to keep in mind managers who are under pressure to perform may take actions to improve perfor-mance measures that have negative consequences elsewhere.

Required:

For each of the following situations, describe actions managers might take to improve the perfor-mance measure in ways detrimental to the organization:

1. Concerned with the slow rate at which new products are brought to market, top management of a consumer electronics company introduces a new performance measure—speed-to-market. The research and development department is given responsibility for this performance mea-sure, which measures the average amount of time a product is in development before it is released to the market for sale.
2. The CEO of an airline company is dissatisfied with the amount of time her ground crews take to unload luggage from airplanes. To solve the problem, she decides to measure the average elapsed time from when an airplane parks at the gate to when all pieces of luggage are unloaded from the airplane. For each month an airport's ground crew can lower its "average elapsed time" relative to the prior month, the CEO pays a lump-sum bonus to be split equally among members of the crew.
3. A manufacturing company is struggling to ship orders to customers by the promised date. To solve this problem, the production manager has been given the responsibility of increasing the percentage of orders shipped on time. When a customer calls in an order, the production manager and the customer agree to a delivery date. If the order is not completed by that date, it is counted as a late shipment.
4. Concerned with employee productivity, the board of directors of a large corporation decided to hold each subsidiary's manager responsible for increasing revenue per employee.

PROBLEM 12–15 Internal Business Process Performance Measures LO12–3

Tombro Industries is automating one of its plants and developing a flexible manufacturing system. In an effort to revise its performance measurement system, the company gathered the following data for the last four months:

	Month			
	1	2	3	4
Quality control measures:				
Number of defects	185	163	124	91
Number of warranty claims	46	39	30	27
Number of customer complaints	102	96	79	58
Material control measures:				
Purchase order lead time	8 days	7 days	5 days	4 days
Scrap as a percent of total cost	1%	1%	2%	3%
Machine performance measures:				
Machine downtime as a percentage of availability	3%	4%	4%	6%
Use as a percentage of availability	95%	92%	89%	85%
Setup time (hours)	8	10	11	12
Delivery performance measures:				
Throughput time	?	?	?	?
Manufacturing cycle efficiency (MCE)	?	?	?	?
Delivery cycle time	?	?	?	?
Percentage of on-time deliveries	96%	95%	92%	89%

The president read in industry journals that throughput time, MCE, and delivery cycle time are important measures of performance, but no one is sure how to compute them. You have been asked to assist the company and gathered the following data:

	Average per Month (in days)			
	1	2	3	4
Wait time per order before start				
of production	9.0	11.5	12.0	14.0
Inspection time per unit	0.8	0.7	0.7	0.7
Process time per unit	2.1	2.0	1.9	1.8
Queue time per unit	2.8	4.4	6.0	7.0
Move time per unit	0.3	0.4	0.4	0.5

Required:

1. For each month, compute the following:
   a. Throughput time.
   b. MCE.
   c. Delivery cycle time.
2. Using the performance measures given in the main body of the problem and the performance measures computed in (1) above, do the following:
   a. Identify areas where the company seems to be improving.
   b. Identify areas where the company seems to be deteriorating.
3. Refer to the inspection time, process time, and so forth, given for month 4.
   a. Assume in month 5 the inspection time, process time, and so forth are the same as for month 4, except the company is able to completely eliminate the queue time using Lean Production. Compute the new throughput time and MCE.
   b. Assume in month 6 the inspection time, process time, and so forth are the same as in month 4, except the company is able to eliminate the queue time and inspection time using Lean Production. Compute the new throughput time and MCE.

PROBLEM 12–16 Creating a Balanced Scorecard LO12–4

Mason Paper Company (MPC) manufactures commodity grade papers for use in computer printers and photocopiers. MPC reported net operating losses for the last two years due to intense price pressure from larger competitors. The MPC management team—including Kristen Townsend

(CEO), Mike Martinez (VP of Manufacturing), Tom Andrews (VP of Marketing), and Wendy Chen (CFO)—is contemplating a change in strategy to save the company from impending bankruptcy. Excerpts from a recent management team meeting are shown below:

Townsend: As we all know, the commodity paper manufacturing business is all about economies of scale. The largest competitors with the lowest cost per unit win. The limited capacity of our older machines prohibits us from competing in the high-volume commodity paper grades. Furthermore, expanding capacity by buying a new paper-making machine is out of the question given the high price tag. Therefore, I propose we abandon cost reduction as a strategic goal and pursue manufacturing flexibility as the key to our future success.

Chen: Manufacturing flexibility? What does that mean?

Martinez: It means we have to abandon our "crank out as many tons of paper as possible" mentality. Instead, we need to pursue the low-volume business opportunities that exist in the nonstandard, specialized paper grades. To succeed in this regard, we'll need to improve our flexibility in three ways. First, we must improve our ability to switch between paper grades. Right now, we require an average of four hours to change over to another paper grade. Timely customer deliveries are a function of changeover performance. Second, we need to expand the range of paper grades we can manufacture. Currently, we can only manufacture three paper grades. Our customers must perceive we are a "one-stop shop" that can meet all of their paper grade needs. Third, we need to improve our yields (e.g., tons of acceptable output relative to total tons processed) in the nonstandard paper grades. Our percentage of waste within these grades will be unacceptably high unless we do something to improve our processes. Our variable costs will go through the roof if we cannot increase our yields!

Chen: Wait just a minute! These changes are going to destroy our equipment utilization numbers!

Andrews: You're right, Wendy; however, equipment utilization is not the goal when competing in terms of flexibility. Our customers don't care about our equipment utilization. Instead, as Mike just alluded to, they want just-in-time delivery of smaller quantities of a full range of paper grades. If we can shrink the elapsed time from order placement to order delivery and expand our product offerings, it will increase sales from current customers and bring in new customers. Furthermore, we will be able to charge a premium price because of the limited competition within this niche from our cost-focused larger competitors. Our contribution margin per ton should drastically improve!

Martinez: Of course, executing the change in strategy will not be easy. We'll need to make a substantial investment in training because ultimately it is our people who create our flexible manufacturing capabilities.

Chen: If we adopt this new strategy, it is definitely going to impact how we measure performance. We'll need to create measures that motivate employees to make decisions that support our flexibility goals.

Townsend: Wendy, you hit the nail right on the head. For our next meeting, could you pull together some potential measures that support our new strategy?

Required:
1. Contrast MPC's previous manufacturing strategy with its new manufacturing strategy.
2. Generally speaking, why would a company that changes its strategic goals need to change its performance measurement system as well? What are some examples of measures that would have been appropriate for MPC prior to its change in strategy? Why would those measures fail to support MPC's new strategy?
3. Construct a balanced scorecard supporting MPC's new manufacturing strategy. Use arrows to show the causal links between the performance measures and show whether the performance measure should increase or decrease over time. Feel free to create measures that are not mentioned in the chapter, but nonetheless make sense given the strategic goals of the company.
4. What hypotheses are built into MPC's balanced scorecard? Which of these hypotheses do you believe are most questionable and why?

PROBLEM 12–17 Analyzing a Quality Cost Report LO12–2

Mercury, Inc., produces cell phones at its plant in Texas. A year ago, a consumer survey ranked the company's cell phones low in product quality. Shocked by this result, Jorge Gomez, Mercury's president, set up a task force to implement a formal quality improvement program. Included on this task force were representatives from the Engineering, Marketing, Customer Service, Production, and Accounting departments. After working together for a year, the task force prepared the quality cost report shown below:

Mercury, Inc. Quality Cost Report (in thousands)	Last Year	This Year
Prevention costs:		
Machine maintenance	$ 70	$ 120
Training suppliers	0	10
Quality circles	0	20
Total prevention cost	70	150
Appraisal costs:		
Incoming inspection	20	40
Final testing	80	90
Total appraisal cost.	100	130
Internal failure costs:		
Rework	50	130
Scrap.	40	70
Total internal failure cost	90	200
External failure costs:		
Warranty repairs	90	30
Customer returns	320	80
Total external failure cost	410	110
Total quality cost	$ 670	$ 590
Total production cost	$4,200	$4,800

Required:

1. Expand the company's quality cost report by showing the costs in both years as percentages of both total production cost and total quality cost.
2. Has Mercury, Inc.'s quality improvement program been successful? Explain.
3. How could Mercury, Inc., measure the cost of *not* implementing the quality improvement program.

(CMA, adapted)

PROBLEM 12–18 Creating a Balanced Scorecard LO12–4

Ariel Tax Services prepares tax returns for individual and corporate clients. As the company gradually expanded to 10 offices, founder Max Jacobs started losing control of operations. In response, he decided to implement a performance measurement system to control operations and facilitate eventual expansion to 20 offices.

Jacobs describes the keys to the success of his business as follows:

"Our only real asset is our people. We must keep our employees highly motivated and we must hire the 'cream of the crop.' Interestingly, employee morale and recruiting success are both driven by the same two factors—compensation and career advancement. In other words, providing superior compensation relative to the industry average coupled with fast-track career advancement opportunities keeps morale high and makes us a very attractive place to work. It drives a high rate of job offer acceptances relative to job offers tendered.

Hiring highly qualified people and keeping them energized ensures operational success, which in our business is a function of productivity, efficiency, and effectiveness. Productivity boils down to employees being billable rather than idle. Efficiency relates to the time required to complete a tax return. Finally, effectiveness is critical to our business because we cannot tolerate errors. Completing a tax return quickly is meaningless if the return contains errors.

Our growth depends on acquiring new customers through word-of-mouth from satisfied repeat customers. We believe our customers come back year after year because they value error-free, timely, and courteous tax return preparation. Common courtesy is an important aspect of our business! We call it service quality, and it all ties back to employee morale because happy employees treat their clients with care and concern.

While sales growth is obviously important to our future plans, growth without a corresponding increase in profitability is useless. Therefore, we understand increasing our profit margin is a function of cost-efficiency and sales growth. Given payroll is our biggest expense, we must maintain an optimal balance between staffing levels and the revenue being generated. As I alluded to earlier, the key to maintaining this balance is employee productivity. If we can achieve cost-efficient sales growth, we should eventually have 20 profitable offices!"

Required:

1. Create a balanced scorecard for Ariel Tax Services. Link your scorecard measures using the framework from Exhibit 12–9. Indicate whether each measure should increase or decrease. Feel free to create measures not mentioned in the chapter if they make sense given the strategic goals of the company.
2. What hypotheses are built into the balanced scorecard for Ariel Tax Services? Which of these hypotheses do you believe are most questionable and why?
3. Discuss the potential advantages and disadvantages of implementing an internal business process measure called *total dollar amount of tax refunds generated*. Would you recommend using this measure in Ariel's balanced scorecard?
4. Would it be beneficial to measure each office's individual performance with respect to the scorecard measures you created? Why or why not?

PROBLEM 12–19 Quality Cost Report LO12–2

In response to intense foreign competition, Florex Company has taken steps to improve the quality of its products. A summary of its quality costs (in thousands) over the past two years is given below:

	Costs (in thousands)	
	Last Year	This Year
Inspection....................................	$750	$900
Quality engineering	$420	$570
Depreciation of test equipment	$210	$240
Rework labor	$1,050	$1,500
Statistical process control	$0	$180
Cost of field servicing.......................	$1,200	$900
Supplies used in testing	$30	$60
Systems development	$480	$750
Warranty repairs	$3,600	$1,050
Net cost of scrap...........................	$630	$1,125
Product testing	$810	$1,200
Product recalls	$2,100	$750
Disposal of production defects...............	$720	$975

Sales have been flat over the past few years, at $75,000,000 per year.

Required:

1. Prepare a quality cost report for this year and last year. Carry percentage computations to two decimal places.
2. Prepare a written evaluation that discusses the distribution of quality costs, changes in the distribution from last year to this year, and reasons for those changes.

PROBLEM 12–20 Measures of Internal Business Process Performance LO12–3

DataSpan, Inc. implemented Lean Production and would like to redesign its performance measures accordingly. It has provided the following data sets:

	Month			
	1	2	3	4
Percentage of on-time deliveries	91%	86%	83%	79%
Total sales (units)	3,210	3,072	2,915	2,806

	Average per Month (in days)			
	1	2	3	4
Move time per unit	0.4	0.3	0.4	0.4
Process time per unit	2.1	2.0	1.9	1.8
Wait time per order before start of production	16.0	17.5	19.0	20.5
Queue time per unit	4.3	5.0	5.8	6.7
Inspection time per unit	0.6	0.7	0.7	0.6

Required:

1. For each month, compute:
   a. The throughput time.
   b. The delivery cycle time.
   c. The manufacturing cycle efficiency (MCE).
2. Evaluate the company's performance over the last four months.
3. Refer to the data for month 4.
   a. Assume in month 5 the company uses Lean Production to completely eliminate the queue time, and all else remains the same as month 4. Compute the new throughput time and MCE.
   b. Assume in month 6 the company eliminates all queue time and inspection time, and all else remains the same as month 4. Compute the new throughput time and MCE.

Case

Select cases are available in Connect.

CASE 12–21 Balanced Scorecard LO12–4

Haglund Department Store is facing increasing competition from large national chains. In an effort to grow profits, the company is designing a balanced scorecard that addresses two problems. First, customers are taking too long to pay bills incurred using the department store's credit card. Furthermore, the company's bad debts greatly exceed industry norms. An investigation revealed the late payments and unpaid bills are caused by customers disputing incorrect charges on their bills. These incorrect charges usually occur because salesclerks incorrectly enter data on the charge account slip. Second, the company has excess unsold seasonal apparel that must be liquidated at a huge loss.

The company's managers suggested the following measures for possible inclusion in the balanced scorecard:

a. Percentage of charge account bills containing errors.
b. Percentage of salesclerks trained to correctly enter data on charge account slips.
c. Average age of accounts receivable.
d. Profit per employee.
e. Customer satisfaction with accuracy of charge account bills from monthly customer survey.
f. Total sales revenue.
g. Sales per employee.
h. Travel expenses for buyers for trips to fashion shows.
i. Unsold inventory at the end of the season as a percentage of total cost of sales.
j. Courtesy shown by junior staff members to senior staff members based on surveys of senior staff.
k. Percentage of suppliers making just-in-time deliveries.
l. Sales per square foot of floor space.
m. Written-off accounts receivable (bad debts) as a percentage of sales.
n. Quality of food in the staff cafeteria based on staff surveys.
o. Percentage of employees who have attended the city's cultural diversity workshop.
p. Total profit.

Required:

1. Construct a balanced scorecard for the company using some of the measures suggested by its managers. You do not have to use all of the suggested performance measures, but your balanced scorecard should reveal a strategy for dealing with the accounts receivable and unsold merchandise problems. Use arrows to show the causal links between performance measures within your balanced scorecard and explain whether the performance measures should show increases or decreases.

2. Assume the company adopts your balanced scorecard. After operating for a year, some performance measures show improvements, but not others. What should management do next?

3. a. Suppose customers express greater satisfaction with the accuracy of their charge account bills, but the performance measures for the average age of accounts receivable and for bad debts do not improve. Explain why this might happen.

    b. Suppose the performance measures for the average age of accounts receivable, bad debts, and unsold inventory improve, but total profits do not. Explain why this might happen. Assume in your answer the explanation lies within the company.

Chapter 13

Differential Analysis: The Key to Decision Making

Interim Archives/Contributor/Getty Images

lighthouse image: Martin73/Shutterstock;
big data image: INGARA/Shutterstock

LEARNING OBJECTIVES

After studying Chapter 13, you should be able to:

LO13–1 Identify relevant and irrelevant costs and benefits in a decision.

LO13–2 Prepare an analysis showing whether a product line or other business segment should be added or dropped.

LO13–3 Identify relevant costs and benefits associated with sourcing decisions.

LO13–4 Prepare an analysis showing whether a special order should be accepted.

LO13–5 Determine the most profitable use of a constrained resource.

LO13–6 Determine the value of obtaining more of the constrained resource.

LO13–7 Prepare an analysis showing whether joint products should be sold at the split-off point or processed further.

LO13–8 *(Appendix 13A) Compute the selling price of a product using the absorption costing approach to cost-plus pricing.*

LO13–9 *(Appendix 13A) Understand how customers' sensitivity to changes in price should influence pricing decisions.*

LO13–10 *(Appendix 13A) Analyze pricing decisions using value-based pricing.*

LO13–11 *(Appendix 13A) Compute the target cost for a new product or service.*

 Data Analytics Exercise available in Connect to complement this chapter

ENTREPRENEUR SPOTLIGHT

Neil Blumenthal and Dave Gilboa co-founded Warby Parker to solve what they saw as a simple problem—the price of eyeglasses was too high. By designing their own glasses and interacting directly with customers, they were able "to provide high quality, better-looking prescription eyewear at a fraction of the going price." Today the company is valued at $3 billion with more than 130 retail locations across the United States accompanied by a market-leading online sales portal. In 2015, *Fast Company* named Warby Parker the most innovative company in the world.

Applying Managerial Accounting

With more than 130 retail locations throughout the United States, Warby Parker can use differential analysis when deciding to add a new store or to discontinue an existing location. For example, when contemplating closing a store, the company would compare the lost revenue with the avoidable costs. If the avoidable costs exceeded the forgone revenue, it would suggest closing the store. The financial analysis would purposely exclude any costs that would remain unchanged whether the store remains open or closes.

Serving All Stakeholders

Warby Parker says that one billion people across the globe lack access to glasses. To help fix this problem, the company "partners with non-profits like VisionSpring to ensure that for every pair of glasses sold, a pair is distributed to someone in need." The company also prepares an annual *Impact Report* that measures its corporate social responsibility performance along four dimensions: (1) customers, (2) employees, (3) community, and (4) sustainability. In addition, Warby Parker has also published a *Racial Equity Strategy* supported by ten goals, such as increasing "Black representation in the field of optometry and in the technology sector." ■

Sources: www.warbyparker.com/history, https://www.axios.com/warby-parker-3-billion-valuation-03f53fcc-f18c-4f20-8bf3-1a6fc4f378fb.html, www.warbyparker.com/dave-gilboa, www.warbyparker.com/impact-report-racial-equity-strategy

This chapter discusses what may be a manager's most important responsibility—making decisions. Examples of decisions include deciding what products to sell, whether to make or buy component parts, what prices to charge, what channels of distribution to use, and whether to accept special orders at special prices. Making such decisions is often a difficult task complicated by numerous alternatives and massive amounts of data; however, in this chapter you will learn how to narrow your focus to the information that matters.

Decision Making: Six Key Concepts

There are six key concepts you need to understand to make intelligent decisions. This section discusses each of those concepts and then concludes by introducing some additional terminology created to help you solve the exercises and problems at the end of the chapter.

LO13–1
Identify relevant and irrelevant costs and benefits in a decision.

Key Concept #1

Every decision involves choosing from among at least two alternatives. Therefore, the first step in decision making is defining the alternatives. For example, if a company is deciding whether to make a component part or buy it from an outside supplier, the alternatives are *make* or *buy* the component part. Similarly, if a company is considering discontinuing a particular product, the alternatives are to *keep* or *drop* the product.

Key Concept #2

Once you have defined the alternatives, you need to distinguish between *relevant* and *irrelevant* costs and benefits. **Relevant costs** and **relevant benefits** should be considered when making decisions, whereas *irrelevant costs* and *irrelevant benefits* should be ignored. This is an important concept for two reasons. First, ignoring irrelevant data saves decision makers tremendous amounts of time and effort. Second, erroneously including irrelevant costs and benefits when analyzing alternatives can lead to bad decisions.

Key Concept #3

The key to effective decision making is *differential analysis*—focusing on future costs and benefits that differ between the alternatives. Everything else is irrelevant and should be ignored. A future cost that differs between any two alternatives is known as a **differential cost.** Differential costs are always relevant costs. Future revenue that differs between any two alternatives is known as **differential revenue.** Differential revenue is an example of a relevant benefit.

The terms *incremental cost* and *avoidable cost* are often used to describe differential costs. An **incremental cost** is an increase in cost between two alternatives. For example, if you are choosing between buying the standard model or deluxe model of your favorite automobile, the costs of the upgrades in the deluxe model are incremental costs. An **avoidable cost** can be eliminated by choosing one alternative over another. For example, assume you have decided to watch a movie tonight; however, you are trying to choose between two alternatives—going to the movie theater or renting a movie. The cost of the movie ticket is an avoidable cost. You would avoid this cost by renting a movie. Similarly, the movie rental fee is an avoidable cost because you could avoid it by going to the movie theater. Avoidable costs (and incremental costs) are always relevant costs.

Differential costs and benefits can be qualitative or quantitative. While qualitative differences between alternatives can have an important impact on decisions and, therefore, should not be ignored, our goal in this chapter is to hone your quantitative analysis skills. Therefore, our primary focus will be on analyzing quantitative differential costs and benefits—those having readily measurable impacts on future cash flows.

Key Concept #4

Sunk costs are always irrelevant when choosing among alternatives. A **sunk cost** has already been incurred and cannot be changed regardless of what a manager decides to do. Sunk costs have no impact on future cash flows and remain the same no matter what alternatives are being considered; therefore, they are irrelevant and should be ignored when making decisions.

For example, suppose a company purchased a five-year-old truck for $12,000. The amount paid for the truck is a sunk cost because it has already been incurred and the transaction cannot be undone. The $12,000 paid for the truck is irrelevant in making decisions such as whether to keep, sell, or replace the truck. Furthermore, any accounting depreciation expense related to the truck is irrelevant in making decisions. This is true because accounting depreciation is a noncash expense that has no effect on future cash flows. It simply spreads the sunk cost of the truck over its useful life.[1]

Key Concept #5

Future costs and benefits that *do not differ between alternatives* are irrelevant to the decision-making process. Continuing with the movie example, assume you plan to buy a Domino's pizza after watching a movie. If you are going to buy the same pizza regardless of your movie-watching venue, the cost of the pizza is irrelevant when choosing between the theater and the rental. The cost of the pizza is *not* a sunk cost because it has not yet been incurred. Nonetheless, the cost of the pizza is irrelevant to the choice of venue because it is a future cost that does not differ between the alternatives.

Key Concept #6

Opportunity costs also need to be considered when making decisions. An **opportunity cost** is the potential benefit given up when one alternative is selected over another. For example, if you gave up a high-paying summer job to travel overseas, the forgone wages would be an opportunity cost of traveling abroad. Opportunity costs are not usually found in accounting records, but they are a differential cost that must be explicitly considered in every decision a manager makes.

This chapter covers various decision contexts, such as keep or drop decisions, make or buy decisions, special order decisions, and sell or process further decisions. While tackling these diverse decision contexts may seem a bit overwhelming, keep in mind they all share a unifying theme—choosing between alternatives based on their differential costs and benefits. To emphasize this common theme, many end-of-chapter exercises and problems that span a variety of learning objectives will often use the same terminology— financial advantage (disadvantage)—when asking you to choose between alternatives. For example, they will ask questions such as:

1. What is the financial advantage (disadvantage) of closing the store?
2. What is the financial advantage (disadvantage) of buying the component part from a supplier rather than making it?
3. What is the financial advantage (disadvantage) of accepting the special order?
4. What is the financial advantage (disadvantage) of further processing the intermediate product?

In all of these various contexts, a financial advantage exists if pursuing an alternative, such as closing a store or accepting a special order, passes the cost/benefit test. In other words, it exists if the alternative's differential benefits (i.e., its future cash inflows) exceed

---

[1] See Appendix 14C for a discussion of how depreciation expense impacts decisions when tax implications are considered.

its differential costs (i.e., its future cash outflows). Conversely, a financial (disadvantage) exists when an alternative fails the cost/benefit test—its differential benefits are less than its differential costs.[2]

IN BUSINESS

DON'T RETURN THAT!

U.S. retailers annually send six billion pounds of merchandise returned by online customers to landfills. The reason? Restocking returned merchandise costs an average $10 to $20 per item, whereas choosing to discard the returns costs much less. As Amanda Mull from *The Atlantic* magazine notes, "perfectly good stuff gets thrown away . . . all the time, simply because the financial math of doing anything else doesn't work out." To reduce their returns, some companies are offering extra discounts that entice customers to withdraw their return requests. Amazon, Target, and Walmart have begun using artificial intelligence to determine the total cost of a return and whether it makes financial sense to have a customer relinquish the item. In the case of inexpensive or bulky items, these companies often choose to issue a full refund while allowing their customers to keep the merchandise.

Sources: Suzanne Kapner and Paul Ziobro, "Retailers Say Skip Returns of Unwanted Items," *The Wall Street Journal*, January 11, 2021, https://www.wsj.com/articles/amazon-walmart-tell-consumers-to-skip-returns-of-unwanted-items-11610274600, and Amanda Mull, "Unhappy Returns," *The Atlantic*, November 2021, https://www.theatlantic.com/magazine/archive/2021/11/free-returns-online-shopping/620169/.

Identifying Relevant Costs and Benefits: An Example

Oak Harbor Woodworks is contemplating renting a new labor-saving machine for $3,000 per year. The machine will be used on the company's butcher block production line. Data concerning the company's annual sales and costs of butcher blocks with and without the new machine are shown below:

	Without the New Machine	With the New Machine
Units produced and sold	5,000	5,000
Selling price per unit	$40	$40
Direct materials cost per unit	$14	$14
Direct labor cost per unit	$8	$5
Variable overhead cost per unit	$2	$2
Fixed expenses, other	$62,000	$62,000
Fixed expenses, rental of new machine	—	$3,000

Exhibit 13–1 uses the *total cost approach* to compute the net operating income for both alternatives. The net operating income without the new machine is $18,000, and with the new machine it is $30,000. The difference in the net operating incomes in these two columns indicates a $12,000 (= $30,000 − $18,000) financial advantage associated with renting the new machine. The irrelevant items (which includes sales, direct materials, variable overhead, and fixed expenses, other) appear in both columns, so they cancel each other out when isolating the $12,000 difference in favor of renting the machine.

---

[2] Over the life of a company, cumulative net cash flows equal cumulative net income. Therefore, if a decision maximizes future net cash flows, it will also maximize future cumulative net income. However, because of accruals, in any particular period net income will usually be different from net cash flow. A decision based on maximizing future net cash flows might, in the short run, reduce net income, but in the long run cumulative net income will be higher than it otherwise would have been.

EXHIBIT 13–1
Total and Differential Costs

	Without the New Machine	With New Machine	Differential Costs and Benefits
Sales (5,000 units × $40 per unit)	$200,000	$200,000	$　0
Variable expenses:			
Direct materials (5,000 units × $14 per unit)	70,000	70,000	0
Direct labor (5,000 units × $8 per unit; 5,000 units × $5 per unit)	40,000	25,000	15,000
Variable overhead (5,000 units × $2 per unit).	10,000	10,000	0
Total variable expenses	120,000	105,000	
Contribution margin	80,000	95,000	
Fixed expenses:			
Other.	62,000	62,000	0
Rental of new machine	0	3,000	(3,000)
Total fixed expenses	62,000	65,000	
Net operating income	$　18,000	$　30,000	$12,000

The third column in Exhibit 13–1 uses the *differential cost approach* to derive the same financial advantage of $12,000 (= $15,000 + $(3,000)) associated with renting the new machine. A positive number in the Differential Costs and Benefits column indicates the difference between the alternatives favors the new machine; a negative number indicates it favors the current situation. A zero in the third column means the total amount is the same for both alternatives. If we properly account for the costs and benefits that do not differ between the alternatives, they will cancel out when comparing alternatives; hence, they can be ignored.

Rather than setting up comparative income statements, we could have arrived at the same solution much more quickly by ignoring the irrelevant costs and benefits.

- The selling price per unit and the number of units sold do not differ between the alternatives. Therefore, the total sales revenues are the same for the two alternatives, as shown in Exhibit 13–1. Because the sales revenues are exactly the same, they have no effect on the difference in net operating income between the two alternatives. That is shown in the last column in Exhibit 13–1, which shows a $0 differential benefit.
- The direct materials cost per unit, the variable overhead cost per unit, and the number of units produced and sold do not differ between the alternatives. Consequently, the total direct materials cost and the total variable overhead cost are the same for both alternatives and can be ignored.
- The "other" fixed expenses do not differ between the alternatives, so they can be ignored as well.

Indeed, the only costs that differ between the alternatives are direct labor costs and the fixed rental cost of the new machine. Therefore, the two alternatives can be compared based only on these relevant costs:

Financial Advantage of Renting the New Machine	
Decrease in direct labor costs (5,000 units at a cost savings of $3 per unit)	$15,000
Increase in fixed expenses	(3,000)
Financial advantage of renting the new machine	$12,000

Focusing solely on the relevant costs and benefits provides the same answer ($12,000 in favor of renting the new machine) as when we listed all costs and benefits in Exhibit 13–1. We get the same answer because the only costs and benefits relevant to the decision are those that differ between the alternatives and, hence, are not zero in the last column of Exhibit 13–1.

Why Isolate Relevant Costs?

In the preceding example, we used the total cost approach and the differential cost approach to calculate the same answer. Thus, it would be natural to ask, "Why bother to isolate relevant costs when total costs will do the job just as well?" Isolating relevant costs is desirable for at least two reasons.

First, rarely will enough information be available to prepare an income statement for both alternatives. Assume, for example, you are making a decision relating to a portion of a business process in a multidepartment, multiproduct company. Under these circumstances, it would be impossible to prepare an income statement, thus necessitating the differential cost approach.

Second, commingling irrelevant and relevant costs creates a risk that an irrelevant piece of data may be used improperly, resulting in an incorrect decision.

Adding and Dropping Product Lines and Other Segments

Exhibit 13–2 shows income statements Discount Drug Company prepared for its three product lines—drugs, cosmetics, and housewares. Based on housewares' net operating loss of $(8,000), the company is tempted to *drop* this particular product line. While the company's income statement acknowledges dropping housewares will sacrifice $20,000 in contribution margin, it also suggests dropping housewares will reduce fixed expenses by $28,000, thereby increasing profits by $8,000. However, before reaching the premature conclusion that housewares should be dropped, the company needs to take a closer look at its fixed expenses. More specifically, it needs to determine which fixed expenses can be avoided if housewares is dropped and which are unavoidable and therefore irrelevant to the keep or drop decision. After further analysis of its fixed expenses, the company determined the following:

LO13–2
Prepare an analysis showing whether a product line or other business segment should be added or dropped.

1. The salaries expense is avoidable because the salaries are paid to employees working directly on the product. All of the employees working in housewares would be discharged if the product line is dropped.
2. The advertising expense is avoidable because the advertisements are specific to each product line and would disappear if the line is dropped.
3. The utilities expense is unavoidable because its a companywide utility bill that will remain the same if housewares is dropped. The amount charged to housewares in the income statement is an arbitrary allocation of common fixed costs based on square feet occupied.

EXHIBIT 13–2
Discount Drug Company
Product Lines

	Total	Product Line		
		Drugs	Cosmetics	House-wares
Sales	$250,000	$125,000	$75,000	$50,000
Variable expenses	105,000	50,000	25,000	30,000
Contribution margin	145,000	75,000	50,000	20,000
Fixed expenses:				
Salaries	50,000	29,500	12,500	8,000
Advertising	15,000	1,000	7,500	6,500
Utilities	2,000	500	500	1,000
Depreciation—fixtures	5,000	1,000	2,000	2,000
Rent	20,000	10,000	6,000	4,000
Insurance	3,000	2,000	500	500
General administrative	30,000	15,000	9,000	6,000
Total fixed expenses	125,000	59,000	38,000	28,000
Net operating income (loss)	$ 20,000	$ 16,000	$12,000	$ (8,000)

4. While the depreciation expense is traceable to housewares, it is irrelevant to the keep or drop decision because depreciation is a noncash expense related to previously purchased fixtures that has no impact on future cash flows. Although the fixtures are nearly new, they are custom-built and will have no resale value if the housewares line is dropped.

5. The rent expense is unavoidable because it is paid to occupy the entire building housing the company. If housewares is dropped, the company will still pay rent of $20,000 per month. The amount charged to housewares in the income statement is an arbitrary allocation of common fixed costs based on sales dollars.

6. The insurance expense is avoidable because it relates to inventories specific to the housewares product line. If housewares is dropped, the related inventories will be liquidated and the insurance premiums will decrease proportionately.

7. The general administrative expense is unavoidable because it represents the costs of accounting, purchasing, and general management that will persist even if housewares is dropped. The amount charged to housewares in the income statement is an arbitrary allocation of common fixed costs based on sales dollars.

In summary, $15,000 of the fixed expenses associated with the housewares product line are avoidable and $13,000 are not:

Fixed Expenses	Total Cost Assigned to Housewares	Not Avoidable*	Avoidable
Salaries	$ 8,000		$ 8,000
Advertising	6,500		6,500
Utilities	1,000	$ 1,000	
Depreciation—fixtures	2,000	2,000	
Rent	4,000	4,000	
Insurance	500		500
General administrative	6,000	6,000	
Total	$28,000	$13,000	$15,000

*These fixed costs represent either sunk costs or future costs that will not change whether the housewares line is retained or discontinued.

As stated earlier, if the housewares product line is dropped, the company will lose its contribution margin of $20,000 but avoid only $15,000 of fixed expenses. Therefore, the financial disadvantage of dropping the housewares product line is $(5,000), as shown below:

Contribution margin lost if the housewares product line is discontinued (see Exhibit 13–2)...	$(20,000)
Fixed expenses that can be avoided if the housewares product line is discontinued (see above)..	15,000
Financial (disadvantage) of dropping the housewares product line	$ (5,000)

Although a misguided look at Exhibit 13–2 tempted management to drop the housewares product line, a correct analysis of the relevant costs reveals the company should retain it.

Sourcing Decisions

LO13–3
Identify relevant costs and benefits associated with sourcing decisions.

Providing a product or service to a customer involves many steps. For example, consider all of the steps necessary to develop and sell a product such as a Fitbit fitness watch. First, engineers need to develop the underlying electronics that provide customers with capabilities such as real-time GPS tracking, heart rate monitoring, and activity monitoring. In addition, they need to design a wrist watch that not only houses the electronic circuitry, but also meets the customers' needs in terms of aesthetics, durability, and functionality. Second, the watches need to be assembled, tested, individually packaged, and boxed in larger quantities to enable shipping. Third, the finished goods need to be transported to retail sales locations and eventually sold to customers. Finally, the company needs to provide after-sale services such as Internet and phone-based help lines, warranty claims, and product returns. All of these activities, from development, to production, to after-sales service, are called a *value chain.*

Separate companies may carry out each of the activities in the value chain, or a single company may carry out several. When a company is involved in more than one activity in the entire value chain, it is **vertically integrated.** Some companies control all of the activities in the value chain from producing basic raw materials through final distribution of finished goods and provision of after-sales service. Other companies are content to integrate on a smaller scale by purchasing many of the parts and materials that go into their finished products. A decision to carry out one of the activities in the value chain internally, rather than buying from an external supplier, is called a **sourcing decision.** Quite often these decisions involve whether to make a component part or buy it from a supplier. They also include whether to perform various organizational activities (such as after-sales customer service, payroll, accounting, human resource management, and marketing) or outsource them to an external provider.

Strategic Aspects of Sourcing Decisions

Vertical integration provides certain advantages. An integrated company is less dependent on its suppliers and may be able to ensure a smoother flow of parts and materials for production than a nonintegrated company. Also, some companies feel they can control quality better by producing their own parts rather than relying on the quality control standards of outside suppliers. In addition, an integrated company realizes profits from the parts it "makes" rather than "buys."

The advantages of vertical integration are counterbalanced by the advantages of using external suppliers. By pooling demand from a number of companies, a supplier may enjoy economies of scale that result in higher quality and lower costs than would be possible if the company attempted to make the parts or provide the service on its own. A company must be careful, however, to retain control over activities that are essential to maintaining its competitive position. For example, HP controls the software for laser printers that it makes in cooperation with Canon Inc. of Japan.

An Example of a Sourcing Decision

Mountain Goat Cycles currently makes the heavy-duty gear shifters it installs on its most popular line of mountain bikes. The company's Accounting Department reports the following costs of making 8,000 shifters each year:

	Per Unit	8,000 Units
Direct materials	$ 6	$ 48,000
Direct labor	4	32,000
Variable overhead	1	8,000
Supervisor's salary	3	24,000
Depreciation of special equipment	2	16,000
Allocated general overhead	5	40,000
Total cost	$21	$168,000

An outside supplier offered to sell 8,000 shifters a year to Mountain Goat Cycles for a price of only $19 each, or a total of $152,000 (= 8,000 shifters × $19 each). Should the company stop making the shifters internally and buy them from the outside supplier? As always, the decision depends on the relevant costs—those that differ between the alternatives. If the costs that can be avoided by buying the shifters from the outside supplier are less than $152,000, then the company should continue to make its own shifters. On the other hand, if the avoidable costs are greater than $152,000, the outside supplier's offer should be accepted.

Exhibit 13–3 contains the relevant cost analysis of the sourcing decision related to the gear shifters. The total amount paid to the supplier of $152,000 is the only relevant cash flow shown in the Buy column. The Make column includes direct materials ($48,000), direct labor ($32,000), and variable overhead ($8,000). All of these costs are relevant to the decision because they could be avoided by purchasing the shifters from the outside supplier. In other words, Mountain Goat Cycles would no longer incur these variable manufacturing costs if it stopped making the shifters. The Make column also includes the supervisor's salary of $24,000. This is a relevant cost because the supervisor of the gear shifter manufacturing process would not be retained if the company stops making the shifters.[3]

The depreciation of special equipment of $16,000 (as shown in the original data) is an irrelevant cost because the equipment has already been purchased; thus, the cost

---

[3] Many companies adhere to a "no layoffs" policy because they believe it improves employee morale, organizational learning, customer satisfaction, and financial results. Furthermore, in some countries, such as France, Germany, and Japan, labor regulations and cultural norms may limit management's ability to reduce the size of the labor force. In these contexts, it would be incorrect to assume that direct labor and supervision are automatically avoidable costs in sourcing decisions. Nonetheless, for the sake of consistency, within this chapter you should assume that direct labor and supervisory salaries are avoidable costs when analyzing sourcing decisions unless you are explicitly told otherwise.

	Total Relevant Costs—8,000 units		
	Make	Buy	
Outside purchase price		$152,000	
Direct materials (8,000 units × $6 per unit)	$ 48,000		
Direct labor (8,000 units × $4 per unit)	32,000		
Variable overhead (8,000 units × $1 per unit)	8,000		
Supervisor's salary	24,000		
Depreciation of special equipment (not relevant)			
Allocated general overhead (not relevant)			
Total cost.	$112,000	$152,000	
Financial advantage of making the gear shifters		$40,000	

EXHIBIT 13-3
Mountain Goat Cycles' Sourcing Decision

incurred to buy the equipment is a sunk cost. The depreciation charge of $16,000 simply spreads this sunk cost over the equipment's useful life. If the equipment could be sold, its salvage value would be relevant. Or if the equipment could be used to make other products, this could be relevant as well. However, we will assume the equipment has no salvage value and no other use except making the heavy-duty gear shifters.

The allocated general overhead of $40,000 (as shown in the original data) is also irrelevant because it represents allocated common costs that will continue unchanged even if the shifters are bought from an outside supplier. Throughout this chapter, you should assume these types of allocated common costs are irrelevant to the decision unless you are explicitly told otherwise. If you are explicitly told a portion of allocated common costs can be avoided by choosing one alternative over another, then, by all means, treat the explicitly identified avoidable costs as relevant costs. Otherwise, err on the side of ignoring allocated common costs when choosing between alternatives.

Because the avoidable costs related to making the shifters are $40,000 less than the total amount that would be paid to the outside supplier, Mountain Goat Cycles should reject the outside supplier's offer. However, the company may wish to consider one additional factor before coming to a final decision—the opportunity cost of the space currently used to produce the shifters.

Opportunity Cost

If the space now being used to produce the shifters *would otherwise be idle,* then Mountain Goat Cycles should continue making its own shifters because idle space has an opportunity cost of zero.

But what if the space now being used to make shifters could be used for some other purpose? In that case, the space would have an opportunity cost equal to the segment margin that could be derived from the best alternative use of the space.

To illustrate, assume the space now being used to make shifters could be used to produce a new cross-country bike that would generate a segment margin of $60,000 per year. Under these conditions, Mountain Goat Cycles would be $20,000 better off buying the shifters from the outside supplier and using the newly available space to produce the cross-country bike:

	Make	Buy
Total annual cost (see Exhibit 13–3)	$112,000	$152,000
Opportunity cost—segment margin forgone on a potential new product line	60,000	
Total cost	$172,000	$152,000
Financial advantage of buying the gear shifters from the outside supplier		$20,000

Special Order Decisions

Managers must often evaluate whether a *special order* should be accepted. A **special order** is a one-time order that is not part of the company's normal ongoing business. To illustrate, Mountain Goat Cycles has just received a request from the Seattle Police Department to produce 100 specially modified mountain bikes at a price of $558 each. Mountain Goat Cycles can easily modify its City Cruiser model to fit the specifications of the Seattle Police. The normal selling price of the City Cruiser bike is $698, and its unit product cost is $564 as shown below:

Direct materials	$372
Direct labor	90
Manufacturing overhead	102
Unit product cost	$564

The variable portion of the above manufacturing overhead is $12 per unit. The order would have no effect on the company's total fixed manufacturing overhead costs.

The modifications requested by the Seattle Police Department include welded brackets to hold radios, nightsticks, and other gear that add $34 in incremental variable costs. In addition, the company would have to pay a graphics design studio $2,400 to design and cut stencils for spray painting the Seattle Police Department's logo on the bikes. The company's managers believe this order will have no effect on its other sales and can be produced without disrupting any regularly scheduled production.

To quantify the financial advantage (disadvantage) of accepting the Seattle Police Department's order, Mountain Goat Cycles should focus its attention on the incremental costs and benefits associated with the order. Because the existing fixed manufacturing overhead costs would not be affected by the order, they are not relevant. The financial advantage (disadvantage) of the special order would be computed as follows:

	Per Unit	Total 100 Bikes
Incremental revenue (a)	$558	$55,800
Less incremental costs:		
Variable costs:		
Direct materials	372	37,200
Direct labor	90	9,000
Variable manufacturing overhead	12	1,200
Special modifications	34	3,400
Total variable cost	$508	50,800
Fixed cost:		
Purchase of stencils		2,400
Total incremental cost (b)		53,200
Financial advantage of accepting the order (a) − (b)		$ 2,600

Therefore, even though the $558 price on the special order is below the normal $564 unit product cost and the order would require additional costs, the company is still better off accepting the order. In general, a special order should be accepted if its incremental revenue exceeds its incremental costs. However, it is important to make sure there is idle capacity and the special order does not reduce normal unit sales or undercut prices on normal sales. For example, if the company was operating at capacity, opportunity costs would have to be added to the analysis above.

Volume Trade-Off Decisions

Companies are forced to make *volume trade-off decisions* when they do not have enough capacity to produce all the products and sales volumes demanded by their customers. In these situations, companies must trade off or sacrifice production of some products in favor of others in an effort to maximize profits. The key questions become: How should companies manage those trade-offs? Which products should they produce and sell and which sales opportunities should they intentionally bypass?

To answer these questions, our discussion of volume trade-off decisions will proceed in three steps. First, we'll define the meaning of a constraint. Second, we'll explain how to determine the most profitable use of a constrained resource. Third, we'll discuss how to determine the value of obtaining more of a constrained resource and how to manage constraints to increase profits.

What Is a Constraint?

A **constraint** is anything preventing you from getting more of what you want. Every individual and every organization face at least one constraint, so it is not difficult to find examples of constraints.[4] You may not have enough time to study thoroughly for every subject *and* to go out with your friends on the weekend, so time is your constraint. United Airlines has only a limited number of loading gates available at its busy Chicago O'Hare hub, so its constraint is loading gates. Vail Resorts has only a limited amount of land to develop as homesites and commercial lots at its ski areas, so its constraint is land.

As an example, long waiting periods for surgery are a chronic problem in the National Health Service (NHS), the government-funded provider of health care in the United Kingdom. The diagram in Exhibit 13–4 illustrates a simplified version of the steps followed by a surgery patient. The number of patients who can be processed through each step in a day is indicated in the exhibit. For example, appointments for outpatient visits can be made for as many as 100 referrals from general practitioners in a day.

The constraint, or **bottleneck,** in the system is determined by the step that limits total output because it has the smallest capacity—in this case, surgery. The total number of patients processed through the entire system cannot exceed 15 per day—the maximum number of patients who can be treated in surgery. No matter how hard managers, doctors, and nurses try to improve the processing rate elsewhere in the system, they will never succeed in driving down wait lists until the capacity of surgery is increased. In fact, improvements elsewhere in the system—particularly before the constraint—are likely to result in even longer waiting times and more frustrated patients and health care providers. Thus, to be effective, improvement efforts must be focused on the constraint. A business process, such as the process for serving surgery patients, is like a chain. If you want to increase the strength of a chain, you should focus on strengthening the weakest link.

The procedure to follow to strengthen the chain is clear. First, identify the weakest link, which is the constraint. In the case of the NHS, the constraint is surgery. Second, do not place a greater strain on the system than the weakest link can handle—if you do, the chain will break. In the case of the NHS, more referrals than surgery can accommodate lead to unacceptably long waiting lists. Third, concentrate improvement efforts on strengthening the weakest link. In the case of the NHS, this means finding ways to increase the number of surgeries that can be performed in a day. Fourth, if the improvement efforts are successful, eventually the weakest link will improve to the point where it

---

[4]   The exercises and problems at the end of this chapter always assume the company has only one constraint. When companies have more than one constraint, the optimal production mix can be found using a quantitative method known as linear programming, which is available within Microsoft Excel using a feature called Solver. For an introduction to product mix decision making in the presence of more than one constraint, see the Excel Analytics, Applying Tableau, and Applying Power BI exercises that accompany this chapter within Connect.

EXHIBIT 13–4
Processing Surgery Patients at an NHS Facility (simplified)*

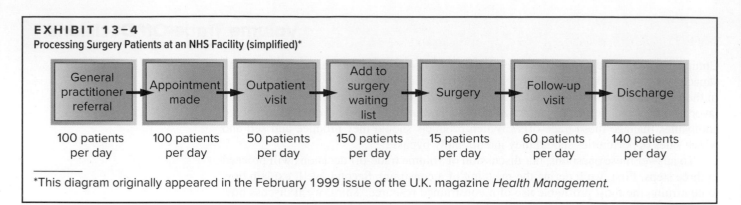

General practitioner referral	Appointment made	Outpatient visit	Add to surgery waiting list	Surgery	Follow-up visit	Discharge
100 patients per day	100 patients per day	50 patients per day	150 patients per day	15 patients per day	60 patients per day	140 patients per day

*This diagram originally appeared in the February 1999 issue of the U.K. magazine *Health Management*.

is no longer the weakest link. At that point, the new weakest link (i.e., the new constraint) must be identified, and improvement efforts shifted over to that link. This simple sequential process provides a powerful strategy for optimizing business processes.

Utilizing a Constrained Resource to Maximize Profits

LO13–5
Determine the most profitable use of a constrained resource.

Managers routinely face the challenge of managing constrained resources in a manner that maximizes profits. A department store, for example, has a limited amount of floor space and therefore cannot stock every available product. A manufacturer has a limited number of machine-hours and a limited number of direct labor-hours at its disposal. When companies face these types of constraints, their managers must decide which products or services make the most profitable use of those limited resources. Because fixed costs remain the same regardless of how a constrained resource is used, managers should ignore them when making volume trade-off decisions and instead focus their attention on identifying the mix of products that maximizes the total contribution margin.

Given some products must be cut back when a constraint exists, the key to maximizing the total contribution margin may seem obvious—favor the products with the highest unit contribution margins. Unfortunately, that is not correct. Rather, the correct solution is to favor the products providing the highest *contribution margin per unit of the constrained resource*. To illustrate, in addition to its other products, Mountain Goat Cycles makes saddlebags for bicycles called *panniers* that come in two models—a touring model and a mountain model. Cost and revenue data for these models follow:

	Mountain Pannier	Touring Pannier
Selling price per unit.	$25	$30
Variable cost per unit	10	18
Contribution margin per unit	$15	$12
Contribution margin (CM) ratio	60%	40%

The mountain pannier appears to be more profitable than the touring pannier. It has a $15 contribution margin per unit as compared to only $12 per unit for the touring model, and it has a 60 percent CM ratio as compared to only 40 percent for the touring model.

But now let's let us add one more piece of information—the plant making the panniers is operating at capacity. At Mountain Goat Cycles, the bottleneck limiting capacity is a stitching machine. The mountain pannier requires two minutes of stitching time per unit, and the touring pannier requires one minute of stitching time per unit. The stitching machine is available for 12,000 minutes per month, and the company can sell up to 4,000 mountain panniers and 7,000 touring panniers per month. Producing up to this demand for both products would require 15,000 minutes, as shown below:

	Mountain Pannier	Touring Pannier	Total
Monthly demand (a)	4,000 units	7,000 units	
Stitching machine time required to produce one unit (b).	2 minutes	1 minute	
Total stitching time required (a) × (b)	8,000 minutes	7,000 minutes	15,000 minutes

Producing up to demand would require 15,000 minutes, but only 12,000 minutes are available—confirming the stitching machine is the bottleneck. Because the stitching machine does not have enough capacity to satisfy the demand for both panniers, some orders will have to be turned down. When choosing which orders to accept or decline, managers should focus on each product's contribution margin per unit of the constrained resource. This figure is computed by dividing a product's contribution margin per unit by the amount of the constrained resource required to make one unit. These calculations are shown below for the mountain and touring panniers:

	Mountain Pannier	Touring Pannier
Contribution margin per unit (a)	$15.00	$12.00
Stitching machine time required to produce one unit (b)	2 minutes	1 minute
Contribution margin per unit of the constrained resource (a) ÷ (b)	$7.50 per minute	$12.00 per minute

Each minute on the stitching machine devoted to the touring pannier increases contribution margin and profits by $12.00. The comparable figure for the mountain pannier is only $7.50 per minute. Therefore, even though the mountain model has the larger contribution margin per unit and the larger CM ratio, the touring model should be produced first because it provides the larger contribution margin per unit of the constrained resource.

To verify the touring model is the more profitable product, suppose an hour of additional stitching time is available and unfilled orders exist for both products. The additional hour on the stitching machine could be used to make either 30 mountain panniers (60 minutes ÷ 2 minutes per mountain pannier) or 60 touring panniers (60 minutes ÷ 1 minute per touring pannier), with the following profit implications:

	Mountain Pannier	Touring Pannier
Contribution margin per unit (a)	$ 15	$ 12
Additional units that can be processed in one hour (b)	30	60
Additional contribution margin (a) × (b)	$450	$720

Because the touring panniers' additional contribution margin of $720 exceeds the mountain panniers' contribution margin of $450, the touring panniers make the most profitable use of the company's constrained resource—the stitching machine. To maximize profits, the company should produce all of the touring panniers the market demands (7,000 units) and use any remaining capacity to produce mountain panniers. The computations to determine how many mountain panniers can be produced are as follows:

Monthly demand for touring panniers (a)	7,000 units
Stitching machine time required to produce one touring pannier (b).	1 minute
Total stitching time required to produce touring panniers (a) × (b)	7,000 minutes
Remaining stitching time available (12,000 minutes − 7,000 minutes) (c).	5,000 minutes
Stitching machine time required to produce one mountain pannier (d).	2 minutes
Production of mountain panniers (c) ÷ (d)	2,500 units

With this product mix of 7,000 touring panniers and 2,500 mountain panniers, the company can earn a total contribution margin of $121,500, computed as follows:

	Mountain Pannier	Touring Pannier	Total
Contribution margin per unit (a)	$15	$12	
Number of units produced (b).	2,500	7,000	
Contribution margin (a) × (b)	$37,500	$84,000	$121,500

COMMUNICATING WITH DATA VISUALIZATIONS

Prescriptive analytics answer the question: What should I do? This visualization shows Mountain Goat Cycles how to optimize its constraining resource—the stitching machine. The company will maximize its profits by using the first 7,000 minutes of stitching machine time to make touring panniers and the remaining 5,000 minutes to make mountain panniers. The touring panniers and mountain panniers will earn contribution margins of $84,000 and $37,500, respectively, for a total contribution margin of $121,500.

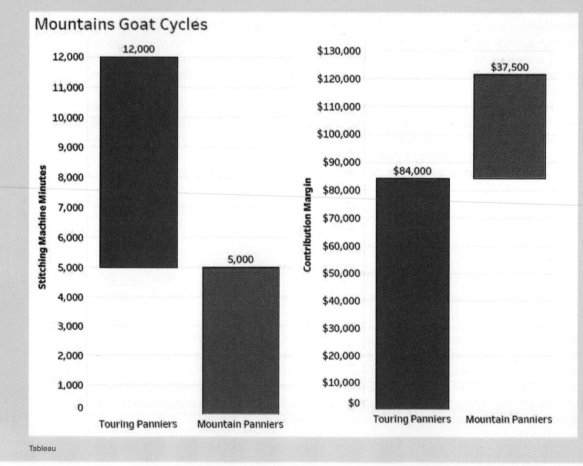

Tableau

Managing Constraints

When a constraint exists, managers can increase profits by making the products with the highest contribution margin per unit of the constrained resource. However, they can also increase profits by increasing the capacity of the bottleneck. When a manager increases the capacity of a bottleneck, it is called **relaxing (or elevating) the constraint.** The benefits from relaxing the constraint are often enormous and can be easily quantified using each product's contribution margin per unit of the constrained resource.

To illustrate, assume Mountain Goat Cycles currently works one eight-hour shift per day. To relax its constraint on the stitching machine, the company is considering paying the stitching machine operator to work overtime. No other employees would have to work overtime because all other operations involved in making panniers have excess capacity. The question for Mountain Goat Cycles is: Up to how much overtime premium per hour can we pay the stitching machine operator and still increase profits? To help answer this question, the table below translates the mountain and touring panniers' contribution margins per minute on the stitching machine to their contribution margins per hour.

LO13–6
Determine the value of obtaining more of the constrained resource.

	Mountain Pannier	Touring Pannier
Contribution margin per minute of the constrained resource (a)	\$7.50 per minute	\$12.00 per minute
Minutes per hour (b)	60 minutes	60 minutes
Contribution margin per hour of the constrained resource (a) × (b)	\$450 per hour	\$720 per hour

Mountain Goat Cycle's first step when calculating the value of relaxing the constraint is determining which product the stitching machine operator would make during the overtime period. Because the company can meet its entire monthly demand of 7,000 touring panniers during the regular eight-hour shifts, its overtime hours would be dedicated to making more mountain panniers. In other words, the company has 4,000 units of demand for mountain panniers, but, after satisfying demand for touring panniers, it can only make 2,500 units with the capacity available during its eight-hour shifts. So, if Mountain Goat Cycles decides to pay the stitching machine operator to work overtime, the machine operator will focus on making 1,500 additional mountain panniers (= 4,000 − 2,500).

Because mountain panniers earn \$450 of contribution margin per hour on the stitching machine, the company could pay an overtime premium up to \$450 per hour and still increase profits. If we assume Mountain Goat Cycles agrees to pay the stitching machine operator an overtime premium of \$10 per hour (in addition to the regular hourly rate of \$20), the company can increase profits by \$440 (= \$450 − \$10) for every overtime hour worked.

These calculations show how a company can greatly benefit from relaxing the constraint in its manufacturing process. They also highlight the importance of efficiently using constrained resources. In the case of Mountain Goat Cycles, if the stitching machine breaks down, depending on the magnitude of the outage, it will cost the company between \$450 and \$720 per hour of downtime. In contrast, there is no forgone contribution margin if time is lost on a machine that is not the bottleneck—such machines have excess capacity anyway. Given the profit implications of effectively managing their constrained resources, most companies work hard to elevate their constraints using one or more of the following methods:

- Working overtime on the bottleneck.
- Subcontracting some of the processing that would ordinarily be done at the bottleneck.
- Investing in additional machines at the bottleneck.
- Shifting workers from processes that are not bottlenecks to the process that is the bottleneck.
- Focusing business process improvement efforts on the bottleneck.
- Reducing defective units. Each defective unit that is processed through the bottleneck and subsequently scrapped takes the place of a good unit that could have been sold.

The last three bullet points are particularly attractive because they are essentially free and may even yield additional cost savings.

AS CHECKOUT LINES GROW, MORE CUSTOMERS BUY ONLINE

Have you ever walked into a large retail store and noticed that only three or four of the dozens of checkout lanes are open? To make matters worse, each open checkout lane has numerous customers standing in line waiting to pay for their purchases. In essence, these checkout lanes represent a constraint that does not exist at online retailers, such as **Amazon.com**.

A survey conducted by Ayden estimates that 86 percent of shoppers have walked out of a retail store location in the last 12 months due to long checkout lines, thereby costing brick-and-mortar retailers $37.7 billion in lost sales. As retailers such as **Macy's, J.C. Penney, Kohl's, Target**, and **Nordstrom** seek to cut costs by reducing headcount, they are losing sales to customers who would rather stay home, save time, avoid the hassles, and shop online.

Source: Suzanne Kapner, "Stores Slash Staffs and Watch Lines Grow," *The Wall Street Journal,* May 1, 2018, pp. B1, B2.

Joint Product Costs and Sell or Process Further Decisions

LO13–7
Prepare an analysis showing whether joint products should be sold at the split-off point or processed further.

In some industries, two or more products, known as **joint products,** are produced from a single raw material input. For example, in the petroleum refining industry, a large number of joint products are extracted from crude oil, including gasoline, jet fuel, home heating oil, lubricants, asphalt, and various organic chemicals. The point in a manufacturing process where joint products (such as gasoline and jet fuel) can be recognized as separate products is referred to as the **split-off point.**

Quite often, joint products can be sold at the split-off point or processed further and sold for a higher price. Deciding whether to sell a joint product at the split-off point or process it further is known as a **sell or process further decision.** To make these decisions, managers follow a three-step process. First, they ignore all **joint costs** incurred up to the split-off point. These costs are ignored because they are sunk costs that cannot be changed regardless of whether the manager chooses to sell a joint product at the split-off point or process it further.

Second, they calculate the incremental revenue earned by further processing the joint product. This computation is performed by taking the revenue earned after further processing the joint product and subtracting the revenue that could be earned by selling the joint product at the split-off point.

Third, they take the incremental revenue from step two and subtract the incremental costs associated with processing the joint product beyond the split-off point. If the resulting answer is positive, then the joint product should be processed further and sold for a higher price. If the answer is negative, then the joint product should be sold at the split-off point without any further processing.

Santa Maria Wool Cooperative: An Example

Santa Maria Wool Cooperative buys raw wool from local sheepherders, separates the wool into three grades—coarse, fine, and superfine—and then dyes the wool using pigments from local materials. Exhibit 13–5 diagrams the company's production process.

The company's joint costs include $200,000 for the raw wool and $40,000 for separating the raw wool into three intermediate products. The three types of undyed wool are called intermediate products because they are not finished at this point. Nevertheless, a market does exist for undyed wool—although at a significantly lower price than finished, dyed wool. More specifically and as shown in Exhibit 13–5, the undyed coarse wool, undyed fine wool, and undyed superfine wool each can be sold at the split-off point for $120,000, $150,000, and $60,000 respectively.

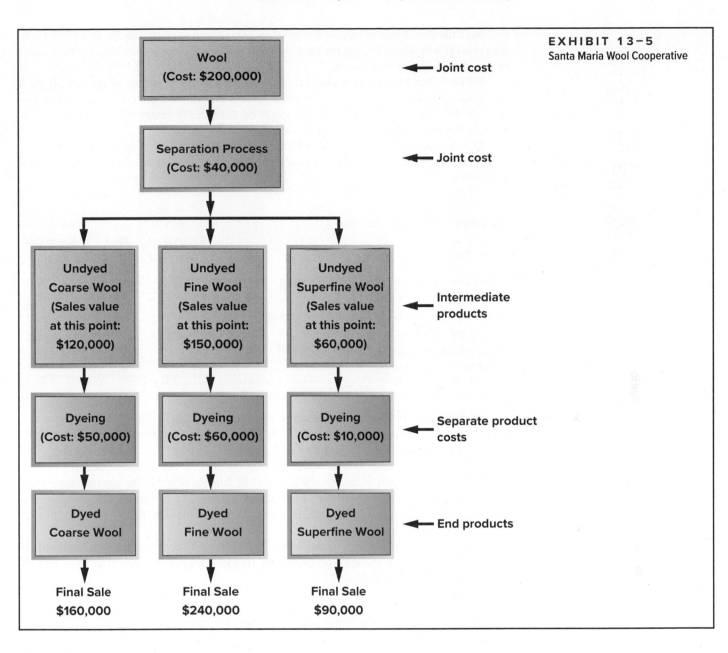

EXHIBIT 13–5
Santa Maria Wool Cooperative

Exhibit 13–5 also shows the cost of further processing the undyed coarse wool, undyed fine wool, and undyed superfine wool is $50,000, $60,000, and $10,000 respectively. Furthermore, the sales values of dyed coarse wool, dyed fine wool, and dyed superfine wool are $160,000, $240,000, and $90,000, respectively.

If Santa Maria Wool Cooperative chooses to further process all three of its intermediate products, it will earn a profit of $130,000, as shown below:

Analysis of the profitability of the overall operation:		
Combined final sales value		
($160,000 + $240,000 + $90,000)		$490,000
Less costs of producing the end products:		
Cost of wool.....................................	$200,000	
Cost of separating wool.........................	40,000	
Combined costs of dyeing		
($50,000 + $60,000 + $10,000)................	120,000	360,000
Profit		$130,000

Note the joint costs of buying the wool ($200,000) and separating the wool ($40,000) are relevant when considering the profitability of the *entire operation* because they could be avoided if it were shut down.

While Santa Maria can make a profit of $130,000 if it further processes all three products, the questions we want to explore further are: Should the company further process all three products? Could the company be financially better off by selling one or more of the three products at the split-off point?

The appropriate way to answer these sell-or-process-further questions is to compare the incremental revenues and incremental costs for each of the joint products as follows:

Analysis of sell or process further:	Coarse Wool	Fine Wool	Superfine Wool
Final sales value after further processing	$160,000	$240,000	$90,000
Less sales value at the split-off point	120,000	150,000	60,000
Incremental revenue from further processing	40,000	90,000	30,000
Less cost of further processing (dyeing)	50,000	60,000	10,000
Financial advantage (disadvantage) of further processing	$ (10,000)	$ 30,000	$20,000

As this analysis shows, the company would be better off selling the undyed coarse wool at the split-off point rather than processing it further. The other two products should be processed further and dyed before selling them.

Note the joint costs of the wool ($200,000) and of the wool separation process ($40,000) are irrelevant in the decision to sell or further process the intermediate products. While these costs are relevant when deciding whether to run the *entire operation,* they are irrelevant when deciding whether to sell the intermediate products at the split-off point or further process them.

Finally, we can recompute Santa Maria's overall profitability if it chooses to sell the undyed coarse wool at the split-off point and further process the dyed fine wool and the dyed superfine wool as follows:

Analysis of the profitability of the overall operation:		
Combined final sales value ($120,000 + $240,000 + $90,000)		$450,000
Less costs of producing the end products:		
Cost of wool.	$200,000	
Cost of separating wool.	40,000	
Combined costs of dyeing ($60,000 + $10,000).	70,000	310,000
Profit		$140,000

Notice the revised profit of $140,000 is $10,000 higher than the profit of $130,000 computed earlier when the company further processes all three products. This $10,000 increase in profit equals the $10,000 financial disadvantage of further processing coarse wool computed earlier.

MCDONALD'S IS CLOSING MANY OF ITS WALMART LOCATIONS

McDonald's is closing hundreds of U.S. Walmart-based restaurants in the coming years, leaving only around 150 locations in the retail giant's stores. This is down from nearly 1,000 McDonald's stores at the peak of the partnership, which began in the early 1990s. With more customers shopping online and using drive-throughs, the in-store restaurant has lost much of its appeal to shoppers and retailers alike. This trend has been exacerbated by the COVID-19 pandemic, where indoor dining has become a much less attractive proposition for many patrons.

Source: Sarah Nassauer and Heather Haddon, "McDonald's Is Closing Hundreds of Its Walmart Restaurants," *The Wall Street Journal*, April 9, 2021, https://www.wsj.com/articles/mcdonalds-is-closing-hundreds-of-its-walmart-restaurants-11617960602?mod=trending_now_news_4.

Summary

This chapter's foundation is built on one powerful idea—only those costs and benefits that differ between alternatives are relevant in a decision. All other costs and benefits are irrelevant and should be ignored. In particular, sunk costs are irrelevant, as are future costs that do not differ between alternatives.

This simple idea was applied in a variety of situations including keep or drop decisions as well as sourcing, special order, volume trade-off, and sell or process further decisions. This list includes only a small sample of the possible applications of the differential cost concept. Indeed, any decision involving costs hinges on the proper identification and analysis of differential costs.

Data Analytics Exercise available in Connect to complement this chapter

Review Problem: Differential Analysis

Charter Sports Equipment manufactures round, rectangular, and octagonal trampolines. Sales and expense data for the past month follow:

	Total	Trampoline		
		Round	Rectangular	Octagonal
Sales	$1,000,000	$140,000	$500,000	$360,000
Variable expenses	410,000	60,000	200,000	150,000
Contribution margin	590,000	80,000	300,000	210,000
Fixed expenses:				
Advertising—traceable...............	216,000	41,000	110,000	65,000
Depreciation of special equipment ...	95,000	20,000	40,000	35,000
Line supervisors' salaries	19,000	6,000	7,000	6,000
General factory overhead*	200,000	28,000	100,000	72,000
Total fixed expenses.................	530,000	95,000	257,000	178,000
Net operating income (loss)	$ 60,000	$ (15,000)	$ 43,000	$ 32,000

*A common fixed cost that is allocated on the basis of sales dollars.

Given its apparent net operating loss, management is considering discontinuing the round trampolines. The special equipment used to produce the trampolines has no resale value. If the round trampoline model is dropped, the two line supervisors assigned to the model would be discharged.

Required:

What is the financial advantage (disadvantage) of discontinuing the round trampolines? The company has no other use for the capacity now being used to produce the round trampolines.

Solution to Review Problem

No, production and sale of the round trampolines should not be discontinued. Computations to support this answer follow:

Contribution margin lost if the round trampolines are discontinued		$(80,000)
Less fixed expenses that can be avoided:		
Advertising—traceable.	$41,000	
Line supervisors' salaries	6,000	47,000
Financial (disadvantage) of discontinuing the round trampolines		$(33,000)

The depreciation of the special equipment is a sunk cost, and therefore not relevant to the decision. The general factory overhead is allocated and will presumably continue regardless of whether or not the round trampolines are discontinued; thus, it is not relevant.

Glossary

Avoidable cost A cost that can be eliminated by choosing one alternative over another in a decision. This term is synonymous with *differential cost* and *relevant cost.* (p. 567)

Bottleneck A machine or some other part of a process that limits the total output of the entire system. (p. 577)

Constraint A limitation under which a company must operate, such as limited available machine time or raw materials, that restricts the company's ability to satisfy demand. (p. 577)

Differential cost A future cost that differs between any two alternatives. (p. 567)

Differential revenue Future revenue that differs between any two alternatives. (p. 567)

Incremental cost An increase in cost between two alternatives. (p. 567)

Joint costs Costs incurred up to the split-off point in a process that produces joint products. (p. 582)

Joint products Two or more products produced from a common input. (p. 582)

Opportunity cost The potential benefit given up when one alternative is selected over another. (p. 568)

Relaxing (or elevating) the constraint An action that increases the amount of a constrained resource. Equivalently, an action that increases the capacity of the bottleneck. (p. 581)

Relevant benefit A benefit that should be considered when making decisions. (p. 567)

Relevant cost A cost that should be considered when making decisions. (p. 567)

Sell or process further decision A decision as to whether a joint product should be sold at the split-off point or sold after further processing. (p. 582)

Sourcing decision A decision concerning whether a product or service should be produced or provided internally or purchased from an outside vendor. (p. 573)

Special order A one-time order not considered part of the company's normal ongoing business. (p. 576)

Split-off point That point in the manufacturing process where some or all of the joint products can be recognized as individual products. (p. 582)

Sunk cost A cost already incurred that cannot be changed by any decision made now or in the future. (p. 568)

Vertical integration The involvement by a company in more than one of the activities in the entire value chain from development through production, distribution, sales, and after-sales service. (p. 573)

Questions

13–1   What is a *relevant cost?*

13–2   Define the following terms: *incremental cost, opportunity cost,* and *sunk cost.*

13–3   Are variable costs always relevant costs? Explain.

13–4   "Sunk costs are easy to spot—they're the fixed costs associated with a decision." Do you agree? Explain.

13–5   "Variable costs and differential costs mean the same thing." Do you agree? Explain.

13–6   "All future costs are relevant in decision making." Do you agree? Why?

13–7   Prentice Company is considering dropping one of its product lines. What costs of the product line would be relevant to this decision? What costs would be irrelevant?

13–8   "If a product is generating a loss, then it should be discontinued." Do you agree? Explain.

13–9   What is the danger in allocating common fixed costs among products or other segments of an organization?

13–10   How does opportunity cost enter into a sourcing decision?

13–11   Give at least four examples of possible constraints.

13–12   How will relating product contribution margins to the amount of the constrained resource they consume help a company maximize its profits?

13–13   Define the following terms: *joint products, joint costs,* and *split-off point.*

13–14   From a decision-making point of view, should joint costs be allocated among joint products?

13–15   What guideline should be used in determining whether a joint product should be sold at the split-off point or processed further?

13–16   Airlines sometimes offer reduced rates during certain times of the week to members of a businessperson's family if they accompany that individual on trips. How does the concept of relevant costs enter into the decision by the airline to offer reduced rates of this type?

Mc Graw Hill connect   **Applying Excel**

The Excel worksheet form below recreates the example related to Santa Maria Wool Cooperative.   **LO13–7**
The workbook, and instructions on how to complete the file, can be found in Connect.

	A	B	C	D	E
1	Chapter 13: Applying Excel				
2					
3	Data				
4	Exhibit 13-5 Santa Maria Wool Cooperative				
5	Cost of wool	$200,000			
6	Cost of separation process	$40,000			
7	Sales value of intermediate products at split-off point:				
8	Undyed coarse wool	$120,000			
9	Undyed fine wool	$150,000			
10	Undyed superfine wool	$60,000			
11	Costs of further processing (dyeing) intermediate products:				
12	Undyed coarse wool	$50,000			
13	Undyed fine wool	$60,000			
14	Undyed superfine wool	$10,000			
15	Sales value of end products:				
16	Dyed coarse wool	$160,000			
17	Dyed fine wool	$240,000			
18	Dyed superfine wool	$90,000			
19					
20	Enter a formula into each of the cells marked with a ? below				
21	Example: Joint Product Costs and the Contribution Approach				
22					
23	Analysis of the profitability of the overall operation:				
24	Combined final sales value		?		
25	Less costs of producing the end products:				
26	Cost of wool	?			
27	Cost of separation process	?			
28	Combined costs of dyeing	?	?		
29	Profit		?		
30					
31	Analysis of sell or process further:				
32		Coarse Wool	Fine Wool	Superfine Wool	
33					
34	Final sales value after further processing	?	?	?	
35	Less sales value at the split-off point	?	?	?	
36	Incremental revenue from further processing	?	?	?	
37	Less cost of further processing (dyeing)	?	?	?	
38	Financial advantage (disadvantage) of further processing	?	?	?	
39					

Chapter 13 Form   Chapter 13 Formulas

Microsoft Excel

You should proceed to the requirements below only after completing your worksheet.

Required:

1. Check your worksheet by changing the cost of further processing undyed coarse wool in cell B12 to $30,000. The overall profit from processing all intermediate products into final products should now be $150,000 and the financial advantage of further processing coarse wool should now be $10,000. If you do not get these answers, find the errors in your worksheet and correct them. How should operations change in response to this change in cost?

2. In industries that process joint products, the costs of the raw materials inputs and the sales values of intermediate and final products are often volatile. Change the data area of your worksheet to match the following:

Data	
Exhibit 13–5 Santa Maria Wool Cooperative	
Cost of wool.	$290,000
Cost of separation process	$40,000
Sales value of intermediate products at split-off point:	
Undyed coarse wool.	$100,000
Undyed fine wool	$110,000
Undyed superfine wool	$90,000
Costs of further processing (dyeing) intermediate products:	
Undyed coarse wool	$50,000
Undyed fine wool	$60,000
Undyed superfine wool	$10,000
Sales value of end products:	
Dyed coarse wool.	$180,000
Dyed fine wool.	$210,000
Dyed superfine wool	$90,000

a. What is the overall profit if all intermediate products are processed into final products?

b. What is the financial advantage (disadvantage) from further processing each of the intermediate products?

c. With these new costs and selling prices, what recommendations would you make concerning the company's operations? If your recommendation is followed, what should be the company's overall profit?

The Foundational 15   Mc Graw Hill connect

LO13–2, LO13–3, LO13–4, LO13–5, LO13–6

Cane Company manufactures two products called Alpha and Beta that sell for $120 and $80, respectively. Each product uses only one type of raw material that costs $6 per pound. The company has the capacity to annually produce 100,000 units of each product. Its average cost per unit for each product at this level of activity is given below:

	Alpha	Beta
Direct materials	$ 30	$ 12
Direct labor.	20	15
Variable manufacturing overhead	7	5
Traceable fixed manufacturing overhead	16	18
Variable selling expenses	12	8
Common fixed expenses	15	10
Total cost per unit	$ 100	$ 68

The company's traceable fixed manufacturing overhead is avoidable, whereas its common fixed expenses are unavoidable and have been allocated to products based on sales dollars.

Required:

(Answer each question independently unless instructed otherwise.)

1. What is the total traceable fixed manufacturing overhead for each of the two products?
2. What is the company's total common fixed expenses?

3. Assume Cane expects to produce and sell 80,000 Alphas during the current year. One of Cane's sales representatives found a new customer willing to buy 10,000 additional Alphas for a price of $80 per unit. What is the financial advantage (disadvantage) of accepting the new customer's order?

4. Assume Cane expects to produce and sell 90,000 Betas during the current year. One of Cane's sales representatives found a new customer willing to buy 5,000 additional Betas for a price of $39 per unit. What is the financial advantage (disadvantage) of accepting the new customer's order?

5. Assume Cane expects to produce and sell 95,000 Alphas during the current year. One of Cane's sales representatives has found a new customer willing to buy 10,000 additional Alphas for a price of $80 per unit; however, pursuing this opportunity will decrease Alpha sales to regular customers by 5,000 units. What is the financial advantage (disadvantage) of accepting the new customer's order?

6. Assume Cane normally produces and sells 90,000 Betas per year. What is the financial advantage (disadvantage) of discontinuing the Beta product line?

7. Assume Cane normally produces and sells 40,000 Betas per year. What is the financial advantage (disadvantage) of discontinuing the Beta product line?

8. Assume Cane normally produces and sells 60,000 Betas and 80,000 Alphas per year. If Cane discontinues the Beta product line, its sales representatives could increase sales of Alpha by 15,000 units. What is the financial advantage (disadvantage) of discontinuing the Beta product line?

9. Assume Cane expects to produce and sell 80,000 Alphas during the current year. A supplier offered to manufacture and deliver 80,000 Alphas to Cane for a price of $80 per unit. What is the financial advantage (disadvantage) of buying 80,000 units from the supplier instead of making those units?

10. Assume Cane expects to produce and sell 50,000 Alphas during the current year. A supplier offered to manufacture and deliver 50,000 Alphas to Cane for a price of $80 per unit. What is the financial advantage (disadvantage) of buying 50,000 units from the supplier instead of making those units?

11. How many pounds of raw material are needed to make one unit of each of the two products?

12. What contribution margin per pound of raw material is earned by each of the two products?

13. Assume Cane's customers would buy a maximum of 80,000 units of Alpha and 60,000 units of Beta. Also assume the raw material available for production is limited to 160,000 pounds. How many units of each product should Cane produce to maximize its profits?

14. If Cane follows your recommendation in requirement 13, what total contribution margin will it earn?

15. If Cane uses its 160,000 pounds of raw materials as you recommended in requirement 13, up to how much should it be willing to pay per pound for additional raw materials?

 connect   **Exercises**

EXERCISE 13–1 Identifying Relevant Costs LO13–1
Kristen Lu purchased a used automobile for $8,000 at the beginning of last year and incurred the following operating costs:

Depreciation ($8,000 ÷ 5 years)	$1,600
Insurance	$1,200
Garage rent	$360
Automobile tax and license	$40
Variable operating cost	$0.14 per mile

The variable operating cost consists of gasoline, oil, tires, maintenance, and repairs. Kristen estimates, at her current rate of usage, the car will have zero resale value in five years, so the annual straight-line depreciation is $1,600. The car is kept in a garage for a monthly fee.

Required:

1. Kristen drove the car 10,000 miles last year. Compute the average cost per mile of owning and operating the car.

2. Kristen is unsure about whether she should use her own car or rent a car to go on an extended cross-country trip for two weeks during spring break. What costs above are relevant in this decision? Explain.

3. Kristen is thinking about buying an expensive sports car to replace the car she bought last year. She would drive the same number of miles regardless of which car she owns and would rent the same parking space. The sports car's variable operating costs would be roughly the same as the variable operating costs of her old car. However, her insurance, automobile tax, and license costs would go up. What costs are relevant in estimating the incremental cost of owning the more expensive car? Explain.

EXERCISE 13–2 Dropping or Retaining a Segment LO13–2

The Regal Cycle Company manufactures three types of bicycles—a dirt bike, a mountain bike, and a racing bike. Data on sales and expenses for the past quarter follow:

	Total	Dirt Bikes	Mountain Bikes	Racing Bikes
Sales	$300,000	$90,000	$150,000	$60,000
Variable manufacturing and selling expenses	120,000	27,000	60,000	33,000
Contribution margin	180,000	63,000	90,000	27,000
Fixed expenses:				
Advertising, traceable	30,000	10,000	14,000	6,000
Depreciation of special equipment	23,000	6,000	9,000	8,000
Salaries of product-line managers	35,000	12,000	13,000	10,000
Allocated common fixed expenses*	60,000	18,000	30,000	12,000
Total fixed expenses	148,000	46,000	66,000	36,000
Net operating income (loss)	$ 32,000	$17,000	$ 24,000	$ (9,000)

*Allocated on the basis of sales dollars.

Management is considering discontinuing the racing bikes. The special equipment used to produce racing bikes has no resale value and does not wear out.

Required:
1. What is the financial advantage (disadvantage) per quarter of discontinuing the Racing Bikes?
2. Should the production and sale of racing bikes be discontinued?

EXERCISE 13–3 Sourcing Decisions LO13–3

Troy Engines, Ltd., manufactures a variety of engines for use in heavy equipment. The company has always produced all of the parts for its engines, including the carburetors. An outside supplier offered to sell one type of carburetor to Troy Engines, Ltd., for a cost of $35 per unit. To evaluate this offer, Troy Engines, Ltd., summarized the cost of producing the carburetor internally as follows:

	Per Unit	15,000 Units per Year
Direct materials	$14	$210,000
Direct labor	10	150,000
Variable manufacturing overhead	3	45,000
Fixed manufacturing overhead, traceable	6*	90,000
Fixed manufacturing overhead, allocated	9	135,000
Total cost	$42	$630,000

*One-third supervisory salaries; two-thirds depreciation of special equipment (no resale value).

Required:
1. If the company has no alternative use for the facilities being used to produce the carburetors, what would be the financial advantage (disadvantage) of buying 15,000 carburetors from the outside supplier?
2. Should the outside supplier's offer be accepted?

3. Suppose if the carburetors were purchased, Troy Engines, Ltd., could use the freed capacity to launch a new product with a segment margin of $150,000 per year. Given this new assumption, what would be the financial advantage (disadvantage) of buying 15,000 carburetors from the outside supplier?

4. Given the new assumption in requirement 3, should the outside supplier's offer be accepted?

EXERCISE 13–4 Special Order Decision LO13–4

Imperial Jewelers manufactures and sells a gold bracelet for $189.95. The company's accounting system says the unit product cost for this bracelet is $149.00, as shown below:

Direct materials	$ 84.00
Direct labor	45.00
Manufacturing overhead	20.00
Unit product cost	$149.00

A wedding party has approached Imperial Jewelers about buying 20 gold bracelets for the discounted price of $169.95 each. The wedding party would like special filigree applied to the bracelets that would increase the direct materials cost per bracelet by $2.00. Imperial Jewelers would have to buy a special tool for $250 to apply the filigree to the bracelets. The special tool would have no other use once the special order is completed.

To analyze this special order, Imperial Jewelers determined most of its manufacturing overhead is fixed and unaffected by variations in how much jewelry is produced in any given period. However, $4.00 of the overhead is variable with respect to the number of bracelets produced. The company also believes accepting this order would have no effect on its ability to produce and sell jewelry to other customers. Furthermore, the company could fulfill the wedding party's order using existing manufacturing capacity.

Required:

1. What is the financial advantage (disadvantage) of accepting the wedding party's special order?

2. Should the company accept the special order?

EXERCISE 13–5 Volume Trade-off Decisions LO13–5

Outdoor Luggage, Inc., makes high-end hard-sided luggage for sports equipment. Data concerning three of the company's most popular models appear below:

	Ski Guard	Golf Guard	Fishing Guard
Selling price per unit	$200	$300	$255
Variable cost per unit	$60	$140	$55
Plastic injection molding machine processing			
time required to produce one unit.................	2 minutes	5 minutes	4 minutes
Pounds of plastic pellets per unit....................	7 pounds	4 pounds	8 pounds

Required:

1. If the total time available on the plastic injection molding machine is the constraint, how much contribution margin per minute of the constrained resource is earned by each product?

2. Which product offers the most profitable use of the plastic injection molding machine?

3. If a severe shortage of plastic pellets required the company to cut back production so much that its new constraint has become the total available pounds of plastic pellets, how much contribution margin per pound of the constrained resource is earned by each product?

4. Which product offers the most profitable use of the plastic pellets?

5. Which product has the largest contribution margin per unit? Why wouldn't this product be the most profitable use of the constrained resource in either case?

EXERCISE 13–6 Managing a Constrained Resource LO13–6

Portsmouth Company makes upholstered furniture. Its only variable cost is direct materials. The demand for the company's products far exceeds its manufacturing capacity. The bottleneck (or constraint) in the production process is upholstery labor-hours. Information concerning three of Portsmouth's products appears below:

	Recliner	Sofa	Love Seat
Selling price per unit.	$1,400	$1,800	$1,500
Variable cost per unit	$800	$1,200	$1,000
Upholstery labor-hours per unit	8 hours	10 hours	5 hours

Required:

1. Portsmouth is considering paying its upholstery laborers hourly compensation, in addition to their usual salaries, to work overtime. Assuming this extra time would be used to produce sofas, up to how much of an overtime rate per hour should the company be willing to pay to keep the upholstery shop open after normal working hours?

2. A small nearby upholstering company has offered to upholster furniture for Portsmouth at a price of $45 per hour. The management of Portsmouth is confident this upholstering company's work is high quality, and its craftsmen can work as quickly as Portsmouth's own craftsmen on the simpler upholstering jobs such as the Love Seat. How much additional contribution margin per hour can Portsmouth earn if it hires the nearby upholstering company to make Love Seats?

3. Should Portsmouth hire the nearby upholstering company? Explain.

EXERCISE 13–7 Sell or Process Further Decisions LO13–7

Dorsey Company manufactures three products from a common input in a joint processing operation. Joint processing costs up to the split-off point total $350,000 per quarter. For financial reporting purposes, the company allocates these costs to the joint products based on their relative sales value at the split-off point. Unit selling prices and total output at the split-off point are as follows:

Product	Selling Price	Quarterly Output
A.	$16 per pound	15,000 pounds
B.	$8 per pound	20,000 pounds
C.	$25 per gallon	4,000 gallons

Each product can be processed further after the split-off point. Additional processing requires no special facilities. The additional processing costs (per quarter) and unit selling prices after further processing are given below:

Product	Additional Processing Costs	Selling Price
A.	$63,000	$20 per pound
B.	$80,000	$13 per pound
C.	$36,000	$32 per gallon

Required:

1. What is the financial advantage (disadvantage) of further processing each of the three products beyond the split-off point?

2. Based on your analysis in requirement 1, which product or products should be sold at the split-off point and which should be processed further?

EXERCISE 13–8 Volume Trade-off Decisions LO13–5, LO13–6

Barlow Company manufactures three products—A, B, and C. The selling price, variable costs, and contribution margin for one unit of each product follow:

	Product		
	A	B	C
Selling price	$180	$270	$240
Variable expenses:			
Direct materials	24	80	32
Other variable expenses	102	90	148
Total variable expenses	126	170	180
Contribution margin	$ 54	$100	$ 60
Contribution margin ratio	30%	37%	25%

The same raw material is used in all three products. Barlow Company has only 6,000 pounds of raw material on hand and will not be able to obtain any more of it for several weeks due to a strike in its supplier's plant. Management is trying to decide which product(s) to concentrate on next week in filling its backlog of orders. The material costs $8 per pound.

Required:
1. Calculate the contribution margin per pound of the constraining resource for each product.
2. Assuming Barlow has unlimited demand for each of its three products, what is the maximum contribution margin the company can earn when using the 6,000 pounds of raw material on hand?
3. Assuming Barlow's estimated customer demand is 500 units per product line, what is the maximum contribution margin the company can earn when using the 6,000 pounds of raw material on hand?
4. A foreign supplier could furnish Barlow with additional stocks of the raw material at a substantial premium over the usual price. Assuming Barlow's estimated customer demand is 500 units per product line and the company has used its 6,000 pounds of raw material in an optimal fashion, what is the highest price Barlow Company should be willing to pay for an additional pound of materials? Explain.

EXERCISE 13–9 Special Order Decision LO13–4

Delta Company produces a single product. The cost of producing and selling a single unit of this product at the company's normal activity level of 60,000 units per year is:

Direct materials	$5.10
Direct labor.	$3.80
Variable manufacturing overhead	$1.00
Fixed manufacturing overhead	$4.20
Variable selling and administrative expense	$1.50
Fixed selling and administrative expense	$2.40

The normal selling price is $21 per unit. The company's capacity is 75,000 units per year. An order has been received from a mail-order house for 15,000 units at a special price of $14.00 per unit. This order would not affect regular sales or total fixed costs.

Required:
1. What is the financial advantage (disadvantage) of accepting the special order?
2. As a separate matter from the special order, assume the company's inventory includes 1,000 units that are inferior quality. The units must be sold through regular channels at a reduced price. The company does not expect the selling of these inferior units to affect regular sales. What unit cost is relevant for establishing a minimum selling price for the inferior units? Explain.

EXERCISE 13–10 Sourcing Decisions LO13–3

Futura Company purchases 40,000 starters from a supplier at $8.40 per unit that it installs in farm tractors. Due to a reduction in output, the company now has enough idle capacity to produce the starters rather than buying them from the supplier. However, the company's chief engineer is opposed to making the starters because the production cost per unit is $9.20, as shown below:

	Per Unit	Total
Direct materials	$3.10	
Direct labor	2.70	
Supervision	1.50	$60,000
Depreciation	1.00	$40,000
Variable manufacturing overhead	0.60	
Rent	0.30	$12,000
Total production cost	$9.20	

If Futura decides to make the starters, a supervisor would be hired (at a salary of $60,000) to oversee production. However, the company has sufficient idle tools and machinery such that no new equipment would have to be purchased. The rent charge above is based on space utilized in the plant. The total rent on the plant is $80,000 per period.

Required:
What is the financial advantage (disadvantage) of making the 40,000 starters instead of buying them from an outside supplier?

EXERCISE 13-11 Adding a Product Line LO13-2

Cabin Creek Company is considering adding a new line of kitchen cabinets. The company's accountant provided the following estimated data for these cabinets:

Annual sales.	800 units
Selling price per unit.	$3,500
Variable manufacturing costs per unit.	$1,500
Variable selling costs per unit.	$350
Incremental fixed costs per year:	
Manufacturing	$475,400
Selling	$55,000
Allocated common costs per year:	
Manufacturing	$80,000
Selling and administrative	$112,000

If the kitchen cabinets are added as a new product line, the company expects that the contribution margin earned from selling its other products will decrease by $200,000 per year.

Required:

1. What is the annual financial advantage (disadvantage) of adding the new line of kitchen cabinets?
2. What is the lowest selling price per unit that could be charged for the cabinets and still make it economically desirable for the company to add the new product line?

EXERCISE 13-12 Sourcing Decisions LO13-3

Han Products manufactures 30,000 units of part S-6 each year for use on its production line. At this level of activity, the cost per unit for part S-6 is:

Direct materials	$ 3.60
Direct labor	10.00
Variable manufacturing overhead	2.40
Fixed manufacturing overhead	9.00
Total cost per part	$25.00

An outside supplier has offered to sell 30,000 units of part S-6 each year to Han Products for $21 per part. If Han Products accepts this offer, the facilities now being used to manufacture part S-6 could be rented to another company for $80,000 per year. However, Han Products determined two-thirds of the fixed manufacturing overhead being applied to part S-6 would continue even if part S-6 were purchased from the outside supplier.

Required:

What is the financial advantage (disadvantage) of accepting the outside supplier's offer?

EXERCISE 13-13 Volume Trade-off Decisions LO13-5

Benoit Company produces three products—A, B, and C. Data concerning the three products follow (per unit):

	Product		
	A	B	C
Selling price	$80	$56	$70
Variable expenses:			
Direct materials	24	15	9
Other variable expenses	24	27	40
Total variable expenses	48	42	49
Contribution margin	$32	$14	$21
Contribution margin ratio	40%	25%	30%

The company estimates it can sell 800 units of each product per month. The same raw material is used in each product. The material costs $3 per pound with a maximum of 5,000 pounds available each month.

Required:

1. Calculate the contribution margin per pound of the constraining resource for each product.
2. Which orders would you advise the company to accept first, those for A, B, or C? Which orders second? Third?
3. What is the maximum contribution margin the company can earn per month if it makes optimal use of its 5,000 pounds of materials?

EXERCISE 13–14 Sell or Process Further Decision LO13–7

Wexpro, Inc., produces several products from processing 1 ton of clypton, a rare mineral. Material and processing costs total $60,000 per ton, one-fourth of which is allocated to product X15. Seven thousand units of product X15 are produced from each ton of clypton. The units can be either sold at the split-off point for $9 each or processed further at a total cost of $9,500 and then sold for $12 each.

Required:

1. What is the financial advantage (disadvantage) of further processing product X15?
2. Should product X15 be processed further or sold at the split-off point?

EXERCISE 13–15 Dropping or Retaining a Segment LO13–2

Thalassines Kataskeves, S.A., of Greece makes marine equipment. The company has been experiencing losses on its bilge pump product line for several years. The most recent quarterly contribution format income statement for the bilge pump follows:

Thalassines Kataskeves, S.A. Income Statement—Bilge Pump For the Quarter Ended March 31		
Sales		$850,000
Variable expenses:		
Variable manufacturing expenses	$330,000	
Sales commissions	42,000	
Shipping	18,000	
Total variable expenses		390,000
Contribution margin		460,000
Fixed expenses:		
Advertising (for the bilge pump product line)	270,000	
Depreciation of equipment (no resale value)	80,000	
General factory overhead	105,000*	
Salary of product-line manager	32,000	
Insurance on inventories	8,000	
Purchasing department	45,000†	
Total fixed expenses		540,000
Net operating loss		$ (80,000)

*Common costs allocated on the basis of machine-hours.
†Common costs allocated on the basis of sales dollars.

Discontinuing the bilge pump would not affect sales of other product lines and would have no effect on the company's total general factory overhead or total Purchasing Department expenses.

Required:

What is the financial advantage (disadvantage) of discontinuing the bilge pump?

EXERCISE 13–16 Identification of Relevant Costs LO13–1

Bill just returned from a duck hunting trip with eight ducks. Bill's friend, John, disapproves of duck hunting, and to discourage Bill from further hunting, John presented him with the following cost estimate per duck:

Camper and equipment:	
Cost, $12,000; usable for eight seasons; 10 hunting trips per season	$150
Travel expense (pickup truck):	
100 miles at $0.31 per mile (gas, oil, and tires—$0.21 per mile; depreciation and insurance—$0.10 per mile)	31
Shotgun shells (two boxes per hunting trip)	20
Boat:	
Cost, $2,320, usable for eight seasons; 10 hunting trips per season	29
Hunting license:	
Cost, $30 for the season; 10 hunting trips per season	3
Money lost playing poker:	
Loss, $24 (Bill plays poker every weekend whether he goes hunting or stays at home)	24
Bottle of whiskey:	
Cost, $15 per hunting trip (used to ward off the cold)	15
Total cost	$272
Cost per duck ($272 ÷ 8 ducks)	$ 34

Required:

1. Assuming the duck hunting trip Bill just completed is typical, what costs are relevant to a decision as to whether Bill should go duck hunting again this season?
2. Suppose Bill gets lucky on his next hunting trip and shoots 10 ducks using the same amount of shotgun shells he used on his previous hunting trip to bag 8 ducks. How much would it have cost him to shoot the last two ducks? Explain.
3. Which costs are relevant in a decision of whether Bill should give up hunting? Explain.

EXERCISE 13–17 Dropping or Retaining a Segment LO13–2
Bed & Bath, a retailing company, has two departments—Hardware and Linens. The company's most recent monthly contribution format income statement follows:

	Total	Department	
		Hardware	Linens
Sales	$4,000,000	$3,000,000	$1,000,000
Variable expenses	1,300,000	900,000	400,000
Contribution margin	2,700,000	2,100,000	600,000
Fixed expenses	2,200,000	1,400,000	800,000
Net operating income (loss)	$ 500,000	$ 700,000	$ (200,000)

A study indicates $340,000 of the fixed expenses being charged to Linens are sunk costs or allocated costs that will continue even if the Linens Department is dropped. In addition, the elimination of the Linens Department will result in a 10% decrease in the sales of the Hardware Department.

Required:
What is the financial advantage (disadvantage) of discontinuing the Linens Department?

EXERCISE 13–18 Special Order Decisions LO13–4
Shortt Company has been approached by a customer who is offering a one-time-only special order to buy 4,000 units of a customer-designed part. Each one of these parts requires 4 units of raw material A10 and 4 units of raw material C70. Data concerning these two raw materials follow:

	Units in Raw Materials Inventory	Cost per Unit in Raw Materials Inventory	Current Market Price per Unit	Disposal Value per Unit
A10	1,800	$5.50	$6.50	$2.00
C70	14,000	$6.00	$7.00	$2.50

The current market price per unit mentioned above reflects the prices currently charged by Shortt Company's raw materials supplier. The disposal value per unit mentioned above reflects the price that a recycling company would pay Shortt to purchase any unused raw materials that it wishes to liquidate. Material A10 is used by many of the company's products and is routinely replaced. Material C70 is no longer used by the company in any of its normal products.

Required:

1. What is the relevant cost of the raw materials that the company should include in its analysis when deciding whether to accept or reject the special order?
2. Assume that A10 and C70 are both no longer used in any of the company's normal products. What is the relevant cost of the raw materials that the company should include in its analysis when deciding whether to accept or reject the special order?

 Problems

PROBLEM 13–19 Relevant Cost Analysis in a Variety of Situations LO13–2, LO13–3, LO13–4

Andretti Company has a single product called a Dak. The company normally produces and sells 60,000 Daks each year at a selling price of $32 per unit. The company's unit costs at this level of activity are given below:

Direct materials	$10.00	
Direct labor	4.50	
Variable manufacturing overhead	2.30	
Fixed manufacturing overhead	5.00	($300,000 total)
Variable selling expenses	1.20	
Fixed selling expenses	3.50	($210,000 total)
Total cost per unit	$26.50	

A number of questions relating to the production and sale of Daks follow. Each question is independent.

Required:

1. Assume Andretti Company has sufficient capacity to produce 90,000 Daks each year without any increase in fixed manufacturing overhead costs. The company could increase its unit sales by 25% above the present 60,000 units each year if it increased fixed selling expenses by $80,000. What is the financial advantage (disadvantage) of investing an additional $80,000 in fixed selling expenses? Would the additional investment be justified?
2. Assume Andretti Company has sufficient capacity to produce 90,000 Daks each year. A customer in a foreign market wants to purchase 20,000 Daks. If Andretti accepts this order, it would pay import duties on the Daks of $1.70 per unit and an additional $9,000 for permits and licenses. The only selling costs associated with the order would be $3.20 per unit shipping cost. What is the break-even price per unit on this order?
3. The company has 1,000 Daks on hand with some irregularities that make it impossible to sell them at the normal price through regular distribution channels. What unit cost figure is relevant for setting a minimum selling price to liquidate these units? Explain.
4. Due to a strike in its supplier's plant, Andretti Company is unable to purchase more material for the production of Daks. The strike is expected to last for two months. Andretti Company has enough material on hand to operate at 30% of normal levels for the two-month period. As an alternative, Andretti could close its plant down entirely for the two months. If the plant were closed, fixed manufacturing overhead costs would continue at 60% of their normal level during the two-month period and the fixed selling expenses would be reduced by 20% during the two-month period.
   a. How much total contribution margin will Andretti forgo if it closes the plant for two months?
   b. How much total fixed cost will the company avoid if it closes the plant for two months?
   c. What is the financial advantage (disadvantage) of closing the plant for the two-month period?
   d. Should Andretti close the plant for two months?

5. An outside manufacturer offered to produce 60,000 Daks and ship them directly to Andretti's customers. If Andretti Company accepts this offer, the facilities it uses to produce Daks would be idle; however, fixed manufacturing overhead costs would be reduced by 75%. Because the outside manufacturer would pay for all shipping costs, the variable selling expenses would be only two-thirds of their present amount. What is Andretti's avoidable cost per unit it should compare to the price quoted by the outside manufacturer?

PROBLEM 13–20 Sourcing Decisions LO13–3

Express Delivery Company (EDC) is considering outsourcing its Payroll Department to a payroll processing company for an annual fee of $220,000. An internally prepared report summarizes the Payroll Department's annual operating costs as follows:

Supplies	$ 30,000
Payroll clerks' salaries	120,000
Payroll supervisor's salary.................................	58,000
Payroll employee training expenses	10,000
Depreciation of equipment................................	20,000
Allocated share of common building operating costs	15,000
Allocated share of common administrative overhead	28,000
Total annual operating cost...............................	$281,000

EDC currently rents overflow office space for $36,000 per year. If the company closes its Payroll Department, the employees occupying the rented office space could be brought in-house and the lease agreement on the rented space could be terminated with no penalty.

If the Payroll Department is outsourced, the payroll clerks will not be retained; however, the supervisor would be transferred to the company's Human Resource Management Department. As a result of this transfer, the company would discontinue its efforts to hire a new Human Resource Manager for whom it expected to pay an annual salary of $56,000.

The Payroll Department's equipment would be transferred to other departments within the company to replace outdated equipment that would be recycled for zero salvage value.

Required:

What is the financial advantage (disadvantage) of outsourcing the Payroll Department?

PROBLEM 13–21 Dropping or Retaining a Segment LO13–2

Jackson County Senior Services is a nonprofit organization providing three services to seniors who live in their own homes—home nursing, Meals on Wheels, and housekeeping. Revenue and expense data for the past year follow:

	Total	Home Nursing	Meals on Wheels	House-keeping
Revenues	$900,000	$260,000	$400,000	$240,000
Variable expenses	490,000	120,000	210,000	160,000
Contribution margin	410,000	140,000	190,000	80,000
Fixed expenses:				
Depreciation	68,000	8,000	40,000	20,000
Liability insurance	42,000	20,000	7,000	15,000
Program administrators' salaries	115,000	40,000	38,000	37,000
General administrative overhead* ...	180,000	52,000	80,000	48,000
Total fixed expenses	405,000	120,000	165,000	120,000
Net operating income (loss)	$ 5,000	$ 20,000	$ 25,000	$ (40,000)

*Allocated on the basis of program revenues.

The head administrator of Jackson County Senior Services, Judith Miyama, is considering discontinuing the housekeeping program.

The depreciation in housekeeping is for a small van used to carry the housekeepers and their equipment from job to job. If the program were discontinued, the van would be donated to a charitable organization. None of the general administrative overhead would be avoided if the housekeeping program was dropped, but the liability insurance and the salary of the program administrator would be avoided.

Required:
What is the financial advantage (disadvantage) of discontinuing the Housekeeping program? Should the Housekeeping program be discontinued? Explain.

PROBLEM 13–22 Sell or Process Further Decision LO13–7

(Prepared from a situation suggested by Professor John W. Hardy.) Lone Star Meat Packers is a major processor of beef and other meat products. The company has a large amount of T-bone steak on hand and is deciding whether to sell the T-bone steaks as they are initially cut or process them further into filet mignon and the New York cut.

If the T-bone steaks are sold as initially cut, the company figures a 1-pound T-bone steak yields the following profit:

Selling price ($7.95 per pound)	$7.95
Less joint costs incurred up to the split-off point where T-bone steak can be identified as a separate product...	3.80
Profit per pound	$4.15

If the company further processes the T-bone steaks, then one 16-ounce T-bone steak will yield one 6-ounce filet mignon, one 8-ounce New York cut, and two ounces of waste. It costs $0.55 to further process one T-bone steak into the filet mignon and New York cuts. The filet mignon can be sold for $12.00 per pound, and the New York cut can be sold for $8.80 per pound.

Required:
1. What is the financial advantage (disadvantage) of further processing one T-bone steak into filet mignon and New York cut steaks?
2. Would you recommend the T-bone steaks be sold as initially cut or processed further? Why?

PROBLEM 13–23 Dropping or Retaining a Flight LO13–2
In an effort to increase profits, Pegasus Airlines is thinking about dropping several flights that appear to be unprofitable.

A typical income statement for one round trip of one such flight (flight 482) is as follows:

Ticket revenue (175 seats × 40% occupancy × $200 ticket price)	$14,000	100.0%
Variable expenses ($15 per person)	1,050	7.5
Contribution margin	12,950	92.5%
Flight expenses:		
Salaries, flight crew	1,800	
Flight promotion	750	
Depreciation of aircraft	1,550	
Fuel for aircraft	5,800	
Liability insurance	4,200	
Salaries, flight assistants	1,500	
Baggage loading and flight preparation	1,700	
Overnight costs for flight crew and assistants at destination	300	
Total flight expenses	17,600	
Net operating loss	$ (4,650)	

The following additional information is available about flight 482:
a. Members of the flight crew are paid fixed annual salaries, whereas the flight assistants are paid based on the number of round trips they complete.
b. One-third of the liability insurance is a special charge assessed against flight 482 because, in the opinion of the insurance company, the destination of the flight is in a "high-risk" area. The remaining two-thirds would be unaffected by a decision to drop flight 482.

c.   The baggage loading and flight preparation expense is an allocation of ground crews' salaries and depreciation of ground equipment. Dropping flight 482 would have no effect on these expenses.

d.   If flight 482 is dropped, Pegasus Airlines will not replace it with another flight.

e.   Wear and tear on the aircraft caused by this flight is negligible.

f.   Dropping flight 482 would not allow Pegasus Airlines to reduce the number of aircraft in its fleet or the number of flight crew on its payroll.

Required:

1.   What is the financial advantage (disadvantage) of discontinuing flight 482?

2.   The airline's scheduling officer has been criticized because only 50% of the seats on Pegasus's flights are being filled compared to an industry average of 60%. The scheduling officer explained that Pegasus's average seat occupancy could be improved by eliminating 10% of its flights, but doing so would reduce profits. Explain how this could happen.

PROBLEM 13–24 Special Order Decisions LO13–4

Polaski Company manufactures and sells a single product called a Ret. Operating at capacity, the company can produce and sell 30,000 Rets per year. Costs associated with this level of production and sales are given below:

	Unit	Total
Direct materials	$15	$ 450,000
Direct labor	8	240,000
Variable manufacturing overhead	3	90,000
Fixed manufacturing overhead	9	270,000
Variable selling expense	4	120,000
Fixed selling expense	6	180,000
Total cost	$45	$1,350,000

The Rets normally sell for $50 each. Fixed manufacturing overhead is $270,000 per year within the range of 25,000 through 30,000 Rets per year.

Required:

1.   Assume due to a recession, Polaski Company expects to sell only 25,000 Rets through regular channels next year. A large retail chain offered to purchase 5,000 Rets if Polaski will accept a 16% discount off the regular price. There would be no sales commissions on this order; thus, variable selling expenses would be slashed by 75%. However, Polaski Company would have to purchase a special machine for $10,000 to engrave the retail chain's name on the 5,000 units. Polaski Company has no assurance that the retail chain will purchase additional units in the future. What is the financial advantage (disadvantage) of accepting the special order?

2.   Refer to the original data. Assume Polaski Company expects to sell 25,000 Rets through regular channels next year. The U.S. Army would like to make a one-time-only purchase of 5,000 Rets. The Army would reimburse Polaski for all of the variable and fixed production costs assigned to the units by the company's absorption costing system, plus it would pay an additional fee of $1.80 per unit. Because the army would pick up the Rets with its own trucks, there would be no variable selling expenses associated with this order. What is the financial advantage (disadvantage) of accepting the U.S. Army's special order?

3.   Assume the same situation as described in (2) above, except the company expects to sell 30,000 Rets through regular channels next year. Thus, accepting the U.S. Army's order would require giving up regular sales of 5,000 Rets. Given this new information, what is the financial advantage (disadvantage) of accepting the U.S. Army's special order?

PROBLEM 13–25 Sourcing Decisions LO13–3

Silven Industries, which manufactures and sells summer lotions and insect repellents, has decided to diversify in order to stabilize sales throughout the year. A natural area for the company to consider is the production of winter lotions and creams to prevent dry and chapped skin.

After considerable research, Silven developed a new lip balm called Chap-Off that is sold to wholesalers in boxes of 24 tubes for $8 per box. Because of excess capacity, no additional fixed manufacturing overhead costs will be incurred to produce Chap-Off. However, a $90,000 charge for fixed manufacturing overhead will be absorbed by the product under the company's absorption costing system.

Using estimated sales and production of 100,000 boxes of Chap-Off, the Accounting Department developed the following manufacturing cost per box:

Direct material	$3.60
Direct labor	2.00
Manufacturing overhead	1.40
Total cost	$7.00

The costs above include the lip balm and the tube containing it. As an alternative to making the tubes for Chap-Off, Silven is considering buying them from an outside supplier for $1.35 per box of 24 tubes. If Silven Industries stops making the tubes and buys them from the outside supplier, its direct labor and variable manufacturing overhead costs per box of Chap-Off would decrease by 10% and its direct materials costs would drop by 25%.

Required:
1. If Silven buys its tubes from the outside supplier, how much of its own Chap-Off manufacturing costs per box will it avoid? (Hint: You need to separate the manufacturing overhead of $1.40 per box shown above into its variable and fixed components.)
2. What is the financial advantage (disadvantage) per box of Chap-Off if Silven buys its tubes from the outside supplier?
3. What is the financial advantage (disadvantage) in total (not per box) if Silven buys 100,000 boxes of tubes from the outside supplier?
4. Should Silven Industries make or buy the tubes?
5. What is the maximum price Silven should be willing to pay the outside supplier for a box of 24 tubes? Explain.
6. Instead of sales of 100,000 boxes, revised estimates show a sales volume of 120,000 boxes. At this higher sales volume, Silven would need to rent extra equipment at a cost of $40,000 per year to make the additional 20,000 boxes of tubes. Assuming the outside supplier will not accept an order for less than 120,000 boxes, what is the financial advantage (disadvantage) in total (not per box) if Silven buys 120,000 boxes of tubes from the outside supplier? Given this new information, should Silven Industries make or buy the tubes?
7. Refer to the data in (6) above. Assume the outside supplier will accept an order of any size for the tubes at a price of $1.35 per box. How many boxes of tubes should Silven make? How many boxes of tubes should it buy from the outside supplier?
8. What qualitative factors should Silven Industries consider in this sourcing decision?

(CMA, adapted)

PROBLEM 13–26 Shutting Down or Continuing to Operate a Plant LO13–2
Birch Company normally produces and sells 30,000 units of RG-6 each month. The selling price is $22 per unit, variable costs are $14 per unit, fixed manufacturing overhead costs total $150,000 per month, and fixed selling costs total $30,000 per month.

Employment-contract strikes in the companies that purchase the bulk of the RG-6 units have caused Birch Company's sales to temporarily drop to only 8,000 units per month. Birch Company estimates the strikes will last for two months, after which time sales of RG-6 should return to normal. Due to the current low level of sales, Birch Company is thinking about closing its own plant during the strike, which would reduce fixed manufacturing overhead costs by $45,000 per month and fixed selling costs by 10%. Start-up costs at the end of the shutdown would total $8,000. Because Birch Company uses Lean Production methods, no inventories are on hand.

Required:
1. What is the financial advantage (disadvantage) if Birch closes its own plant for two months?
2. Should Birch close the plant for two months? Explain.
3. At what level of unit sales for the two-month period would Birch Company be indifferent between closing the plant or keeping it open? (Hint: This is a type of break-even analysis, except the fixed cost portion of your break-even computation should include only those fixed costs that are relevant [i.e., avoidable] over the two-month period.)

PROBLEM 13–27 Volume Trade-off Decisions LO13–5, LO13–6

The Walton Toy Company manufactures four dolls and a sewing kit. It provided the following data for next year:

Product	Demand Next Year (units)	Selling Price per Unit	Direct Materials	Direct Labor
Debbie	50,000	$16.70	$4.30	$6.40
Trish	42,000	$7.50	$1.10	$4.00
Sarah	35,000	$26.60	$6.44	$11.20
Mike	40,000	$14.00	$2.00	$8.00
Sewing kit	325,000	$9.60	$3.20	$3.20

The following additional information is available:

a.   The company's plant has a capacity of 130,000 direct labor-hours per year on a single-shift basis. Each employee and piece of equipment are capable of making all five products.
b.   Next year's direct labor pay rate will be $16 per hour.
c.   Fixed costs total $520,000 per year. Variable overhead costs are $2 per direct labor-hour.
d.   All of the company's nonmanufacturing costs are fixed.
e.   The company's finished goods inventory is negligible and can be ignored.

Required:

1.   How many direct labor-hours are used to manufacture one unit of each of the company's five products?
2.   How much variable overhead cost is incurred to manufacture one unit of each of the company's five products?
3.   What is the contribution margin per direct labor-hour for each of the company's five products?
4.   Assuming direct labor-hours is the company's constraining resource, what is the highest total contribution margin the company can earn next year if it makes optimal use of its constrained resource?
5.   Assuming next year the company makes optimal use of its 130,000 direct labor-hours, what is the highest direct labor rate per hour Walton Toy Company should be willing to pay for additional capacity (that is, for added direct labor time)?
6.   Identify changes the company could make to enable it to satisfy the customers' demand for *all* of its products.

(CMA, adapted)

PROBLEM 13–28 Close or Retain a Store LO13–2

Superior Markets, Inc., operates three stores in a large metropolitan area. A segmented absorption costing income statement for the company for the last quarter is given below:

	Superior Markets, Inc. Income Statement For the Quarter Ended September 30			
	Total	North Store	South Store	East Store
Sales	$3,000,000	$720,000	$1,200,000	$1,080,000
Cost of goods sold	1,657,200	403,200	660,000	594,000
Gross margin	1,342,800	316,800	540,000	486,000
Selling and administrative expenses:				
Selling expenses	817,000	231,400	315,000	270,600
Administrative expenses	383,000	106,000	150,900	126,100
Total expenses	1,200,000	337,400	465,900	396,700
Net operating income (loss)	$ 142,800	$ (20,600)	$ 74,100	$ 89,300

The North Store has consistently shown losses over the past two years, so management is considering closing this store.

a. A detailed breakdown of the selling and administrative expenses shown above is as follows:

	Total	North Store	South Store	East Store
Selling expenses:				
Sales salaries	$239,000	$ 70,000	$ 89,000	$ 80,000
Direct advertising	187,000	51,000	72,000	64,000
General advertising*	45,000	10,800	18,000	16,200
Store rent	300,000	85,000	120,000	95,000
Depreciation of store fixtures ...	16,000	4,600	6,000	5,400
Delivery salaries	21,000	7,000	7,000	7,000
Depreciation of delivery				
equipment................	9,000	3,000	3,000	3,000
Total selling expenses	$817,000	$231,400	$315,000	$270,600

*Allocated on the basis of sales dollars.

	Total	North Store	South Store	East Store
Administrative expenses:				
Store managers' salaries	$ 70,000	$ 21,000	$ 30,000	$ 19,000
General office salaries*	50,000	12,000	20,000	18,000
Insurance on fixtures and inventory	25,000	7,500	9,000	8,500
Utilities	106,000	31,000	40,000	35,000
Employment taxes	57,000	16,500	21,900	18,600
General office—other*	75,000	18,000	30,000	27,000
Total administrative expenses	$383,000	$106,000	$150,900	$126,100

*Allocated on the basis of sales dollars.

b. The North Store's rental agreement can be broken with no penalty.
c. The North Store's fixtures would be transferred to the other two stores if it were closed.
d. The North Store's general manager would be transferred to another position in the company if it were closed. She would fill a position that otherwise would have required hiring a new employee at a salary of $11,000 per quarter. The general manager of the North Store would continue to earn her normal salary of $12,000 per quarter. All other managers and employees in the North Store would be discharged.
e. The company has one delivery crew that serves all three stores. One delivery person could be discharged if the North Store were closed. This person's salary is $4,000 per quarter. The delivery equipment would be distributed to the other stores. The equipment does not wear out through use.
f. The company pays employment taxes equal to 15% of their employees' salaries.
g. One-third of the North Store's insurance relates to its fixtures.
h. The "General office salaries" and "General office—other" relate to the overall management of Superior Markets, Inc. If the North Store were closed, one person in the general office could be discharged because of the decrease in overall workload. This person's compensation is $6,000 per quarter.

Required:
1. How much employee salaries will the company avoid if it closes the North Store?
2. How much employment taxes will the company avoid if it closes the North Store?
3. What is the financial advantage (disadvantage) of closing the North Store?
4. Assuming the North Store's floor space can't be subleased, would you recommend closing the North Store?
5. Assume the North Store's floor space can't be subleased. However, let's introduce three more assumptions. First, if the North Store were closed, one-fourth of its sales would transfer to the East Store due to strong customer loyalty to Superior Markets. Second, the East Store has enough capacity to handle the increased sales that would arise from closing the North Store. Third, the increased sales in the East Store would yield the same gross margin as a percentage of sales as present sales in the East Store. Given these new assumptions, what is the financial advantage (disadvantage) of closing the North Store?

PROBLEM 13–29 Sell or Process Further Decisions LO13–7

Come-Clean Corporation produces a variety of cleaning compounds including Grit 337 and Sparkle silver polish. Grit 337 is a coarse cleaning powder that costs $1.60 a pound to make and sells for $2.00 a pound. A small portion of Grit 337 is combined with several other ingredients and further processed into Sparkle silver polish. The silver polish sells for $4.00 per jar.

This further processing requires one-fourth pound of Grit 337 per jar of silver polish. The additional variable manufacturing costs per jar of silver polish are:

Other ingredients	$0.65
Direct labor	1.48
Additional variable manufacturing cost	$2.13

Overhead costs associated with processing the silver polish are:

Variable manufacturing overhead cost	25% of direct labor cost
Fixed manufacturing overhead cost (per month):	
Production supervisor	$3,000
Depreciation of mixing equipment	$1,400

The production supervisor has no duties other than overseeing production of the silver polish. The mixing equipment is special-purpose equipment acquired specifically to produce the silver polish. It can produce up to 15,000 jars of polish per month. Its resale value is negligible and it does not wear out through use.

Advertising costs for the silver polish total $4,000 per month. Variable selling costs for the silver polish are 7.5% of sales.

Due to a decline in the demand for silver polish, the company is considering selling all of its Grit 337 for $2.00 per pound and discontinuing Sparkle silver polish.

Required:

1. How much incremental revenue does the company earn per jar of polish by further processing Grit 337 rather than selling it as a cleaning powder?
2. How much incremental contribution margin does the company earn per jar of polish by further processing Grit 337 rather than selling it as a cleaning powder?
3. How many jars of silver polish must be sold each month to exactly offset the avoidable fixed costs incurred to produce and sell the polish? Explain.
4. If the company sells 9,000 jars of polish, what is the financial advantage (disadvantage) of choosing to further process Grit 337 rather than selling it as a cleaning powder?
5. If the company sells 11,500 jars of polish, what is the financial advantage (disadvantage) of choosing to further process Grit 337 rather than selling it as a cleaning powder?

(CMA, adapted)

PROBLEM 13–30 Sourcing Decisions LO13–3

"We ought to stop making our own drums and accept that outside supplier's offer," said Wim Niewindt, managing director of Antilles Refining, N.V., of Aruba. "At a price of $18 per drum, we would be paying $5.20 less than it costs us to manufacture the drums in our own plant. Because we use 60,000 drums a year, that equals an annual cost savings of $312,000." Antilles Refining's current cost to manufacture one drum is given below (based on 60,000 drums per year):

Direct materials	$10.35
Direct labor	6.10
Variable overhead	1.60
Fixed overhead ($2.80 general company overhead, $1.60 depreciation, and $0.75 supervision)	5.15
Total cost per drum	$23.20

A decision about whether to make or buy the drums is especially important at this time because the equipment used to make the drums is completely worn out and must be replaced. The choices facing the company are:

Alternative 1: Rent new equipment and continue to make the drums. The equipment would be rented for $135,800 per year.

Alternative 2: Purchase the drums from an outside supplier at $18 per drum.

The new equipment is more efficient than the company's worn out equipment and would reduce direct labor and variable overhead costs by 30%. The old equipment has no resale value. Supervision cost ($45,000 per year) and direct materials cost per drum would not be affected by the new equipment. The new equipment's capacity is 100,000 drums per year.

The company's total general company overhead would be unaffected by this decision.

Required:

1. Assuming 60,000 drums are needed each year, what is the financial advantage (disadvantage) of buying the drums from an outside supplier?
2. Assuming 80,000 drums are needed each year, what is the financial advantage (disadvantage) of buying the drums from an outside supplier?
3. Assuming 100,000 drums are needed each year, what is the financial advantage (disadvantage) of buying the drums from an outside supplier?
4. What other factors should the company consider before making a decision?

Mc Graw Hill **connect**   **Cases**

Select cases are available in Connect.

CASE 13–31 Sell or Process Further Decision LO13–7

The Scottie Sweater Company produces sweaters under the "Scottie" label. The company buys raw wool and processes it into wool yarn from which the sweaters are woven. One spindle of wool yarn is required to produce one sweater. The market for sweaters is temporarily depressed due to unusually warm weather in the western states where the sweaters are sold. This has made it necessary for the company to discount the selling price of the sweaters to $30 from the normal $40 price. The company's cost system reports the profit per sweater as shown below:

		Per Sweater
Selling price		$30.00
Cost to manufacture:		
Raw materials:		
Buttons, thread, lining	$2.00	
Wool yarn	16.00	
Total raw materials	18.00	
Direct labor	5.80	
Manufacturing overhead	8.70	32.50
Manufacturing profit (loss)		$ (2.50)

Originally, the company used all of its wool yarn to produce sweaters, but in recent years a market has developed for the wool yarn itself. Current cost and revenue data per spindle of yarn are given below:

		Per Spindle of Yarn
Selling price		$20.00
Cost to manufacture:		
Raw materials (raw wool)	$7.00	
Direct labor	3.60	
Manufacturing overhead	5.40	16.00
Manufacturing profit		$ 4.00

Because the market for wool yarn has remained strong, the sales manager thinks production of sweaters should be discontinued. She is upset about having to sell sweaters at a $2.50 loss when the yarn could be sold for a $4.00 profit. However, the production manager does not want to close a large portion of the factory. He argues the company is in the sweater business, not the yarn business, and should focus on its core strength.

Manufacturing overhead is applied to products based on 150% of direct labor cost. However, the manufacturing overhead costs are fixed and would not be affected even if sweaters were discontinued. Materials and direct labor costs are variable.

Required:

1. What is the financial advantage (disadvantage) of further processing one spindle of wool yarn into a sweater?
2. Would you recommend the wool yarn be sold outright or processed into sweaters? Explain.
3. What is the lowest price the company should accept for a sweater? Why?

CASE 13–32 Ethics and the Manager; Shut Down or Continue Operations LO13–2

Haley Romeros had just been appointed vice president of the Rocky Mountain Region of the Bank Services Corporation (BSC). The company provides check processing services for small banks. The banks send checks presented for deposit or payment to BSC, which records the data on each check in a computerized database. BSC then sends the data electronically to the nearest Federal Reserve Bank check-clearing center, where the appropriate transfers of funds are made between banks. The Rocky Mountain Region has three check processing centers, which are located in Billings, Montana; Great Falls, Montana; and Clayton, Idaho. Prior to her promotion to vice president, Ms. Romeros had been the manager of a check processing center in New Jersey.

After assuming her new position, Ms. Romeros requested a complete financial report for the just-ended fiscal year from the region's controller, John Littlebear. Ms. Romeros specified the financial report should follow the standardized format required by corporate headquarters for all regional performance reports. That report follows:

Bank Services Corporation (BSC) Rocky Mountain Region Financial Performance				
			Check Processing Centers	
	Total	Billings	Great Falls	Clayton
Sales	$50,000,000	$20,000,000	$18,000,000	$12,000,000
Operating expenses:				
Direct labor	32,000,000	12,500,000	11,000,000	8,500,000
Variable overhead	850,000	350,000	310,000	190,000
Equipment depreciation	3,900,000	1,300,000	1,400,000	1,200,000
Facility expense*	2,800,000	900,000	800,000	1,100,000
Local administrative expense[†]	450,000	140,000	160,000	150,000
Regional administrative expense[‡]	1,500,000	600,000	540,000	360,000
Corporate administrative expense[§]	4,750,000	1,900,000	1,710,000	1,140,000
Total operating expense	46,250,000	17,690,000	15,920,000	12,640,000
Net operating income (loss)	$ 3,750,000	$ 2,310,000	$ 2,080,000	$ (640,000)

*Includes building rental expense for the Billings and Great Falls locations and building depreciation for the Clayton location.
[†]Local administrative expenses are the administrative expenses incurred at the check processing centers.
[‡]Regional administrative expenses are allocated to the check processing centers based on sales.
[§]Corporate administrative expenses are charged to segments of the company such as the Rocky Mountain Region and the check processing centers at the rate of 9.5% of their sales.

Upon seeing this report, Ms. Romeros summoned John Littlebear for an explanation.

Romeros: What's the story on Clayton? It didn't have a loss the previous year did it?

Littlebear: No, the Clayton facility has had a nice profit every year since it opened six years ago, but Clayton lost a big contract this year.

Romeros: Why?

Littlebear: One of our national competitors entered the local market and bid very aggressively on the contract. We couldn't afford to meet the bid. Clayton's costs—particularly their facility expenses— are just too high. When Clayton lost the contract, we had to lay off a lot of employees, but we could not reduce the fixed costs of the Clayton facility.

Romeros: Why is Clayton's facility expense so high? It's a smaller facility than either Billings or Great Falls and yet its facility expense is higher.

Littlebear: We are able to rent suitable facilities very cheaply at Billings and Great Falls. No such facilities were available at Clayton; we had them built. Unfortunately, there were big cost overruns. The contractor we hired was inexperienced and went bankrupt before the project was completed. After hiring another contractor to finish the work, we were way over budget. The large depreciation charges on the facility didn't matter at first because we didn't have much competition and could charge premium prices.

Romeros: Well, we can't do that anymore. The Clayton facility will obviously have to be shut down. Its business can be shifted to the other two check processing centers in the region.

Littlebear: I would advise against that. The $1,100,000 in facility depreciation at the Clayton location is misleading. That facility should last indefinitely with proper maintenance. And it has no resale value; there is no other commercial activity around Clayton.

Romeros: What about the other costs at Clayton?

Littlebear: If we shifted Clayton's sales over to the other two processing centers in the region, we wouldn't save anything on direct labor or variable overhead costs. We might save $90,000 in local administrative expense, but we would not save any regional administrative expense, and corporate headquarters would still charge us 9.5% of our sales as corporate administrative expense.

In addition, we would have to rent more space in Billings and Great Falls in order to handle the work transferred from Clayton; that would probably cost us $600,000 a year. And don't forget it will cost us additional money to move the equipment from Clayton to Billings and Great Falls. And the move will disrupt service to customers.

Romeros: I understand all of that, but a money-losing processing center on my performance report is completely unacceptable.

Littlebear: And if you shut down Clayton, you are going to throw some loyal employees out of work.

Romeros: That's unfortunate, but we have to face hard business realities.

Littlebear: And you would have to write off the investment in the facilities at Clayton.

Romeros: I can explain a write-off to corporate headquarters; hiring an inexperienced contractor to build the Clayton facility was my predecessor's mistake. But they'll have my head at headquarters if I show operating losses every year at one of my processing centers. Clayton has to go. At the next corporate board meeting, I am going to recommend the Clayton facility be closed.

Required:

1. From the standpoint of the company as a whole, what is the financial advantage (disadvantage) of closing the Clayton processing center and redistributing its work to other processing centers in the region? Explain.
2. Why might it be in Haley Romeros's self-interest to shut down the Clayton facility? Do you think Haley Romeros is conducting herself in an ethical fashion? Explain.
3. What influence should the depreciation on the facilities at Clayton have on prices charged by Clayton for its services?

CASE 13–33 Integrative Case: Relevant Costs; Pricing LO13–1, LO13–4

Wesco Incorporated's only product is a combination fertilizer/weedkiller called GrowNWeed. GrowNWeed is sold nationwide to retail nurseries and garden stores.

Zwinger Nursery plans to sell a similar fertilizer/weedkiller compound through its regional nursery chain under its own private label. Zwinger does not have manufacturing facilities of its own, so it has asked Wesco (and several other companies) to submit a bid for manufacturing and delivering a 20,000-pound order of the private brand compound to Zwinger. While the chemical composition of the Zwinger compound differs from GrowNWeed, the manufacturing processes are very similar.

The Zwinger compound would be produced in 1,000-pound lots. Each lot would require 25 direct labor-hours and the following chemicals:

Chemicals	Quantity in Pounds
AG-5	300
KL-2	200
CW-7	150
DF-6	175

The first three chemicals (AG-5, KL-2, and CW-7) are all used in the production of GrowNWeed. DF-6 was used in another compound Wesco discontinued several months ago. The supply of DF-6 Wesco had on hand when the other compound was discontinued was not discarded. Wesco could sell its supply of DF-6 at the prevailing market price less $0.10 per pound selling and handling expenses.

Wesco also has on hand a chemical called BH-3, which was manufactured for use in another product no longer produced. BH-3, which cannot be used in GrowNWeed, can be substituted for AG-5 on a one-for-one basis without affecting the quality of the Zwinger compound. The BH-3 in inventory has a salvage value of $600.

Inventory and cost data for the chemicals that can be used to produce the Zwinger compound are shown below:

Raw Material	Pounds in Inventory	Actual Price per Pound When Purchased	Current Market Price per Pound
AG-5	18,000	$1.15	$1.20
KL-2	6,000	$1.10	$1.05
CW-7	7,000	$1.35	$1.35
DF-6	3,000	$0.80	$0.70
BH-3	3,500	$0.90	(Salvage)

The current direct labor wage rate is $14 per hour. The predetermined overhead rate is based on direct labor-hours (DLH). For the current year, based on a two-shift capacity with no overtime, the rate is as follows:

Variable manufacturing overhead	$ 3.00 per DLH
Fixed manufacturing overhead	10.50 per DLH
Combined predetermined overhead rate	$13.50 per DLH

Wesco's production manager says the present equipment and facilities are adequate to manufacture the Zwinger compound. Therefore, the order would have no effect on total fixed manufacturing overhead costs. However, Wesco is within 400 hours of its two-shift capacity this month. Any additional hours beyond the 400 hours must be done in overtime. If need be, the Zwinger compound could be produced on regular time by shifting a portion of GrowNWeed production to overtime. Wesco's direct labor wage rate for overtime is $21 per hour. There is no allowance for any overtime premium in the predetermined overhead rate.

Required:
1. Wesco decided to submit a bid for the 20,000-pound order of Zwinger's new compound. The order must be delivered by the end of the current month. Zwinger noted this is a one-time order that will not be repeated. Calculate the lowest price Wesco could bid for the order and still exactly cover its incremental manufacturing costs.
2. Refer to the original data. Assume Zwinger Nursery plans to place regular orders for 20,000-pound lots of the new compound. Wesco expects the demand for GrowNWeed to remain strong. Therefore, the recurring orders from Zwinger would put Wesco over its two-shift capacity. However, production could be scheduled so that 90% of each Zwinger order could be completed during regular hours. As another option, some GrowNWeed production could be shifted temporarily to overtime so the Zwinger orders could be produced on regular time. Current market prices are the best available estimates of future market prices. Wesco's standard markup percentage for new products is 40% of the full manufacturing cost, including fixed manufacturing overhead. Calculate the price Wesco, Inc., would quote Zwinger Nursery for each 20,000-pound lot using the standard markup percentage.

(CMA, adapted)

CASE 13–34 Sourcing Decisions; Volume Trade-off Decisions LO13–1, LO13–3, LO13–5
TufStuff, Inc., sells a wide range of drums, bins, boxes, and other containers used in the chemical industry. One of the company's products is a heavy-duty corrosion-resistant metal drum, called the WVD drum, used to store toxic wastes. Production is constrained by the capacity of an automated welding machine used to make precision welds. A total of 2,000 hours of welding time is available annually on the machine. Because each drum requires 0.4 hour of welding machine time, annual production is limited to 5,000 drums. At present, the welding machine is used exclusively to make the WVD drums. The accounting department has provided the following financial data concerning the WVD drums:

WVD Drums		
Selling price per drum		$149.00
Cost per drum:		
Direct materials	$52.10	
Direct labor ($18 per hour)	3.60	
Manufacturing overhead	4.50	
Selling and administrative expense	29.80	90.00
Margin per drum		$ 59.00

Management believes 6,000 WVD drums could be sold each year if the company had sufficient manufacturing capacity. As an alternative to adding another welding machine, management has considered buying additional drums from an outside supplier. Harcor Industries, Inc., a supplier of quality products, would be able to provide up to 4,000 WVD-type drums per year at a price of $138 per drum, which TufStuff would resell to its customers at its normal selling price after appropriate relabeling.

Megan Flores, TufStuff's production manager, suggested the company could make better use of the welding machine by manufacturing bike frames, which would require only 0.5 hour of welding machine time per frame and yet sell for far more than the drums. Megan believes TufStuff could sell up to 1,600 bike frames per year at a price of $239 each. The accounting department provided the following data concerning the proposed new product:

Bike Frames		
Selling price per frame		$239.00
Cost per frame:		
Direct materials	$99.40	
Direct labor ($18 per hour)	28.80	
Manufacturing overhead	36.00	
Selling and administrative expense	47.80	212.00
Margin per frame		$ 27.00

The bike frames could be produced with existing equipment and personnel. Manufacturing overhead is allocated to products based on direct labor-hours. Most of the manufacturing overhead consists of fixed common costs such as rent on the factory building, but some of it is variable. The variable manufacturing overhead is $1.35 per WVD drum and $1.90 per bike frame. The variable manufacturing overhead cost would not be incurred on drums acquired from the outside supplier.

Selling and administrative expenses are allocated to products on the basis of revenues. Almost all of the selling and administrative expenses are fixed common costs, but variable selling and administrative expenses amount to $0.75 per WVD drum whether made or purchased and would be $1.30 per bike frame.

All of the company's employees—direct and indirect—are paid for full 40-hour work weeks, and the company has a policy of laying off workers only in major recessions.

Required:

1. Would you be comfortable relying on the financial data provided by the accounting department for making decisions related to the WVD drums and bike frames? Why?
2. Assuming direct labor is a fixed cost, compute the contribution margin per unit for:
   a. Purchased WVD drums.
   b. Manufactured WVD drums.
   c. Manufactured bike frames.
3. Assuming direct labor is a fixed cost, compute the contribution margin per welding hour for:
   a. Manufactured WVD drums.
   b. Manufactured bike frames.
4. Assuming direct labor is a fixed cost, determine the number of WVD drums (if any) that should be purchased and the number of WVD drums and/or bike frames (if any) that should be manufactured. What is the increase (decrease) in net operating income resulting from this plan over current operations?

As soon as your analysis was shown to the top management team at TufStuff, several managers got into an argument concerning how direct labor costs should be treated when making this decision. One manager argued direct labor is always treated as a variable cost in textbooks and in practice and has always been considered a variable cost at TufStuff. After all, "direct" means you can directly trace the cost to products. "If direct labor is not a variable cost, what is?" Another manager argued just as strenuously direct labor should be considered a fixed cost at TufStuff. No one had been laid off in over a decade, and for all practical purposes, everyone at the plant is on a monthly salary. Everyone classified as direct labor works a regular 40-hour workweek and overtime has not been necessary since the company adopted Lean Production techniques. Whether the welding machine is used to make drums or frames, the total payroll would be exactly the same. There is enough slack, in the form of idle time, to accommodate any increase in total direct labor time that the bike frames would require.

5. Assuming direct labor is a variable cost, compute the contribution margin per unit for:
   a. Purchased WVD drums.
   b. Manufactured WVD drums.
   c. Manufactured bike frames.
6. Assuming direct labor is a variable cost, compute the contribution margin per welding hour for:
   a. Manufactured WVD drums.
   b. Manufactured bike frames.
7. Assuming direct labor is a variable cost, determine the number of WVD drums (if any) that should be purchased and the number of WVD drums and/or bike frames (if any) that should be manufactured. What is the increase (decrease) in net operating income resulting from this plan over current operations?
8. What do you think is the correct way to treat direct labor cost in this situation—as variable or as fixed? Explain.

Appendix 13A: Pricing Decisions

Some products have an established market price. Consumers will not pay more than this price, and there is no reason for a supplier to charge less—the supplier can sell all it produces at this price. Under these circumstances, the supplier simply charges the prevailing market price for the product. Markets for basic raw materials such as farm products and minerals follow this pattern.

In this appendix, we are concerned with the more common situation in which a business needs to set its own prices. For example, Delta Airlines has to establish ticket prices for all of its flights. Accenture needs to establish bid prices when it responds to inquiries from prospective consulting clients. Procter & Gamble has to set prices for Bounty, Tide, Pampers, Crest, and its many other product lines. If these companies choose prices that are too high or too low, it can dramatically decrease profits.

Factors That Influence Pricing Decisions

Many factors influence how companies establish their selling prices. In this section, we'd like to discuss three of those factors—customers, competitors, and costs.

Customers   Customers usually possess two things—latitude and private information—that complicate the pricing process. In terms of latitude, the customer can choose to buy your product, or a competitor's product, or nothing at all. Customers also have private information regarding their level of interest in your product or service and how much they might be willing to pay for it.

For example, consider a scenario where a prospective customer invites numerous suppliers to place competitive bids in hopes of winning a contract. The customer has access to private information because it can compare and choose among the bids submitted by each supplier. If a particular supplier sets a bid price that is too high, the customer will award the contract to a competitor. Conversely, if that same supplier is awarded the contract based on a bid price that is much lower than its competitors' it may forgo revenue the customer would have been willing to pay.

Many companies do not continuously set bid prices for individual contracts; instead, they sell products and services to large volumes of diverse customers who do not have an identical willingness to pay a particular price for a given product. In these situations, companies are keenly interested in quantifying the customers' *price elasticity of demand*. The **price elasticity of demand** measures the degree to which a change in price affects unit sales. Demand for a product or service is *inelastic* if a change in price has little effect on the number of units sold. On the other hand, demand for a product or service is *elastic* if a change in price has a substantial effect on the volume of units sold. Generally speaking, managers should set higher prices when demand is inelastic and lower prices when demand is elastic.

Competitors   Competitors have an important effect on a company's pricing decisions because they provide *reference prices* that influence the price elasticity of demand. For example, gasoline buyers usually have readily available reference prices when buying fuel. If a gas station raises its prices higher than the reference price of its competitor across the street, then demand is likely to drop significantly. In this instance, demand is elastic because gasoline is a commodity; therefore, customers are unwilling to pay more than the competitor's reference price. If the same gas station lowered its prices expecting elastic demand to create market share gains, the competitor across the street would probably match the price reduction, thereby holding each gas station's market share constant while lowering both competitors' profits.

If a company wants to charge higher prices than its competitors, then the company must differentiate its products or services from competing choices in a manner that motivates its customers to accept higher prices. For example, brands such as Prada, Rolex, and Rolls Royce have created product quality and an elite social status that differentiates their products from competitors' and creates inelastic demand among wealthy customers willing to pay extremely high prices.

Costs   Customers and competitors play important roles in determining the *price ceiling* for a company's products and services. The price ceiling represents the highest price customers are willing to pay. A company's *price floor* is determined by its incremental costs. The price floor represents the lowest price a company can charge and still make incremental profit on the sales transaction.

It is important to recognize if a company prices all of its products above the price floor, it does not guarantee the company will earn a profit. This is because the total sales revenue earned minus incremental costs may not cover the company's fixed costs. A company increases its likelihood of covering all of its costs and maximizing profits if it is capable of choosing optimal prices based on customer demand data rather than arbitrarily computing prices without the benefit of customer feedback.

Cost-Plus Pricing

Companies frequently use a pricing approach where they *mark up* cost.[5] A product's **markup** is the difference between its selling price and its cost and is usually expressed as a percentage of cost.

$$\text{Selling price} = (1 + \text{Markup percentage}) \times \text{Cost}$$

---

[5] There are some legal restrictions on prices. Antitrust laws prohibit "predatory" prices, which are generally interpreted by the courts to mean a price below average variable cost. "Price discrimination"—charging different prices to customers in the same market for the same product or service—is also prohibited by the law.

For example, a company using a markup of 50 percent adds 50 percent to the costs of its products to determine selling prices. If a product costs $10, then the company would apply a markup of $5 to derive a selling price of $15. This approach is called **cost-plus pricing** because a predetermined markup percentage is applied to a cost base to determine the selling price.

Companies can define the cost base they use for cost-plus pricing in a variety of ways. For example, some companies may use absorption costing to define a cost base that includes direct materials, direct labor, variable manufacturing overhead, and fixed manufacturing overhead, whereas other companies may rely on a product's variable cost as the cost base. Furthermore, companies can use various types of cost systems, such as normal costing or standard costing, when quantifying the cost base. If a company uses normal costing for its absorption approach, it would calculate unit product costs based on actual direct materials and direct labor costs plus applied overhead. A company using standard costing for its absorption approach would derive unit product costs based on standard direct materials and direct labor costs per unit plus the applied overhead *allowed* per unit produced.

In the next section, we discuss the absorption costing approach to cost-plus pricing. As the name implies, the absorption approach uses an absorption-based unit product cost for the cost base when calculating the markup percentage.

The Absorption Costing Approach to Cost-Plus Pricing

LO13–8

Compute the selling price of a product using the absorption costing approach to cost-plus pricing.

Surveys consistently reveal many managers use the absorption costing approach to cost-plus pricing. This method can be explained in a three-step process.

First, a company needs to calculate its *unit product costs* (including direct materials, direct labor, variable manufacturing overhead, and fixed manufacturing overhead). Second, it needs to determine its markup percentage on absorption cost. Third, it needs to multiply a product's unit product cost by the sum of one plus the markup percentage to determine the product's selling price.

Ritter Company: An Example

Let's assume Ritter Company wants to set the selling price on a product that has undergone some design modifications. The company invested $100,000 in operating assets to sell an estimated sales volume of 10,000 units. Its required return on investment (ROI) in its operating assets is 20 percent. The accounting department provided the following cost estimates for the redesigned product:

	Per Unit	Total
Direct materials	$6	
Direct labor	$4	
Variable manufacturing overhead	$3	
Fixed manufacturing overhead		$70,000
Variable selling and administrative expenses	$2	
Fixed selling and administrative expenses		$60,000

In step one of its absorption cost-plus pricing process, Ritter Company would compute the redesigned product's unit product cost as follows (absorption basis):

Direct materials	$ 6
Direct labor	4
Variable manufacturing overhead	3
Fixed manufacturing overhead ($70,000 ÷ 10,000 units)	7
Unit product cost	$20

Ritter's second step would be to determine the markup percentage as follows:

$$\text{Markup percentage on absorption cost} = \frac{(\text{Required ROI} \times \text{Investment}) + \text{Selling and administrative expenses}}{\text{Unit product cost} \times \text{Unit sales}}$$

Referring to Ritter's background information, the markup percentage on absorption cost would be calculated as follows:

$$\text{Markup percentage on absorption cost} = \frac{(20\% \times \$100,000) + (\$2 \text{ per unit} \times 10,000 \text{ units} + \$60,000)}{\$20 \text{ per unit} \times 10,000 \text{ units}}$$

$$= \frac{(\$20,000) + (\$80,000)}{\$200,000}$$

$$= 50\%$$

Notice the 50 percent markup on absorption cost is designed to provide the company's required return on investment (20% × $100,000 = $20,000) and cover the product's selling and administrative expenses ($2 per unit × 10,000 units + $60,000 = $80,000).

The third step is to establish the selling price per unit using the cost-plus pricing equation introduced earlier:

$$\text{Selling price} = (1 + \text{Markup percentage}) \times \text{Cost}$$

$$= (1 + 50\%) \times \$20$$

$$= \$30$$

The selling price of $30 covers the unit product cost of $20 and provides $10 more to cover selling and administrative expenses and provide the required ROI.

As shown in Exhibit 13A–1, *if Ritter actually realizes its forecasted sales of 10,000 units*, the product will indeed earn a net operating income of $20,000 and an ROI of

Direct materials	$ 6
Direct labor	4
Variable manufacturing overhead	3
Fixed manufacturing overhead ($70,000 ÷ 10,000 units)	7
Unit product cost	$20

EXHIBIT 13A–1
Income Statement and ROI Analysis—Ritter Company
Actual Unit Sales = 10,000 Units;
Selling Price = $30

Absorption Costing Income Statement

Sales ($30 per unit × 10,000 units)	$300,000
Cost of goods sold ($20 per unit × 10,000 units)	200,000
Gross margin	100,000
Selling and administrative expenses ($2 per unit × 10,000 units + $60,000)	80,000
Net operating income	$ 20,000

ROI

$$\text{ROI} = \frac{\text{Net operating income}}{\text{Average operating assets}}$$

$$= \frac{\$20,000}{\$100,000}$$

$$= 20\%$$

20 percent. However, if more than 10,000 units are sold at this price, the ROI will be greater than 20 percent. If less than 10,000 units are sold, the ROI will be less than 20 percent. *The required ROI will be attained only if the forecasted unit sales volume is attained.*

Problems with the Absorption Costing Approach

The absorption costing approach makes pricing look deceptively simple. All a company needs to do is compute its unit product cost, decide how much profit it wants, and then set its price. It appears a company can ignore customer demand and arrive at a price that will safely yield whatever profit it wants. Given the absorption approach forecasts unit sales *before* establishing a selling price, it appears to operate on the faulty assumption that customers have no latitude—they are required to buy the product at whatever price the seller deems appropriate. That is not true! Customers have a choice. If the price is too high, they can buy from a competitor or they may choose not to buy at all.

Suppose, for example, when Ritter Company sets its price at $30, it sells only 7,000 units rather than the forecasted volume of 10,000 units. As shown in Exhibit 13A–2, this lower sales volume causes the unit product cost to increase from $20 to $23. Furthermore, and as also shown in Exhibit 13A–2, the company would have a loss of $25,000 on the product instead of a profit of $20,000.

If Ritter responds to this situation by raising its price in an effort to restore profitability at a sales volume of 7,000 units, it would recalculate the markup percentage on absorption cost as follows:

$$\frac{\text{Markup percentage}}{\text{on absorption cost}} = \frac{(20\% \times \$100,000) + (\$2 \text{ per unit} \times 7,000 \text{ units} + \$60,000)}{\$23 \text{ per unit} \times 7,000 \text{ units}}$$

$$= \frac{(\$20,000) + (\$74,000)}{\$161,000}$$

$$= 58.4\%$$

EXHIBIT 13A–2
Income Statement and ROI Analysis—Ritter Company
Actual Unit Sales = 7,000 Units;
Selling Price = $30

Direct materials	$ 6
Direct labor	4
Variable manufacturing overhead	3
Fixed manufacturing overhead ($70,000 ÷ 7,000 units)	10
Unit product cost	$23

Absorption Costing Income Statement	
Sales ($30 per unit × 7,000 units)	$210,000
Cost of goods sold ($23 per unit × 7,000 units)	161,000
Gross margin	49,000
Selling and administrative expenses ($2 per unit × 7,000 units + $60,000)	74,000
Net operating loss	$ (25,000)

ROI

$$\text{ROI} = \frac{\text{Net operating income}}{\text{Average operating assets}}$$

$$= \frac{-\$25,000}{\$100,000}$$

$$= -25\%$$

This higher markup percentage would in turn raise the price on the redesigned product from $30.00 to $36.43, which is calculated as follows:

$$\text{Selling price} = (1 + \text{Markup percentage}) \times \text{Cost}$$
$$= (1 + 58.4\%) \times \$23$$
$$= \$36.43$$

While Ritter may hope a price increase of $6.43 (= $36.43 − $30.00) will restore profitability, in all likelihood, the price hike will cause additional customer defections and lower profits. This is because Ritter's customers are not required to pay whatever price is necessary for Ritter to meet its financial goals. The customers have the latitude to reject Ritter's price and spend their money elsewhere.

Pricing and Customer Latitude

As discussed in the previous section, customers have latitude in their purchasing decisions. They can purchase a competitor's product or allocate their spending budget to some other product altogether. This latitude should be taken into account when setting prices. To illustrate, consider Nature's Garden, a company that sells many products including Apple-Almond Shampoo. The company provided the following data regarding this product:

LO13–9
Understand how the customers' sensitivity to changes in price should influence pricing decisions.

	Apple-Almond Shampoo
Unit sales (a)	200,000
Selling price per unit	$5.00
Variable cost per unit	2.00
Contribution margin per unit (b)	$3.00
Total contribution margin (a) × (b)	$600,000
Traceable fixed expenses	570,000
Net operating income	$ 30,000

Management is considering increasing the price of Apple-Almond Shampoo from $5.00 to $5.50 but is fully aware that this 10 percent increase in price [= ($5.50 − $5.00) ÷ $5.00] will result in a decline in unit sales because of the latitude customers have in their purchasing decisions. If unit sales drop too much, profit (i.e., net operating income) may actually decline despite the increase in the selling price. The company's marketing managers estimated this price hike could decrease unit sales by as much as 15 percent, from 200,000 units to 170,000 units.

The question the company would like to answer is which price ($5.00 or $5.50) will generate higher profits? To answer this question, the company can use the following equation to calculate Apple-Almond Shampoo's profit at each price:

$$\text{Profit} = (P - V) \times Q - \text{Fixed expenses}$$

where P is the selling price per unit, V is the variable cost per unit, and Q is the unit sales.

At a price of $5.00 and a sales volume of 200,000 units, Apple-Almond Shampoo earns a profit of $30,000, as shown below:

$$\text{Profit} = (P - V) \times Q - \text{Fixed expenses}$$
$$= (\$5.00 - \$2.00) \times 200,000 - \$570,000$$
$$= \$3.00 \times 200,000 - \$570,000$$
$$= \$600,000 - \$570,000$$
$$= \$30,000$$

At a price of $5.50 and a sales volume of 170,000 units, assuming that fixed expenses are not affected by the decrease in unit sales, Apple-Almond Shampoo earns a profit of $25,000, as shown below:

$$\text{Profit} = (P - V) \times Q - \text{Fixed expenses}$$
$$= (\$5.50 - \$2.00) \times 170,000 - \$570,000$$
$$= \$3.50 \times 170,000 - \$570,000$$
$$= \$595,000 - \$570,000$$
$$= \$25,000$$

Given these results, Nature's Garden should not raise the price of this product to $5.50 because its profits would be $5,000 higher (= $30,000 − $25,000) at the lower price of $5.00.

Customer Latitude: A Closer Look

Thus far, our example assumed management has only two options: either keep the price of Apple-Almond Shampoo at $5.00 or increase it to $5.50 with a resulting drop in unit sales of 15 percent. However, keep in mind the 15 percent figure is an estimate, not a certainty. Based on our previous calculations, we know increasing the price from $5.00 to $5.50 would reduce profits if unit sales decrease by 15 percent. If unit sales decrease by more than 15 percent, profits will decline even more. But what would be the financial implications if unit sales actually decreased by something *less than* 15 percent?

Management could explore this possibility by calculating the unit sales (Q) needed at the higher price ($5.50) to achieve the same profit ($30,000) earned at the lower price ($5.00). Assuming fixed expenses remain unchanged, the required unit sales (Q) can be derived as follows:

$$\text{Profit} = (P - V) \times Q - \text{Fixed expenses}$$
$$\$30,000 = (\$5.50 - \$2.00) \times Q - \$570,000$$
$$\$600,000 = \$3.50Q$$
$$Q = 171,429 \text{ units (rounded)}$$

This calculation tells us if the company sells 171,429 units at the selling price of $5.50, the company will earn the same profit it earned at the lower price of $5.00. But if the company sells *more* than 171,429 units, then increasing the selling price by 10 percent will *increase* profit. However, if the company sells *fewer* than 171,429 units, then increasing the selling price by 10 percent will *decrease* profit. The critical value of 171,429 units is sort of a break-even in this situation.

The sales volume of 171,429 units reflects a percentage change in sales of −14.3 percent [= (171,429 − 200,000) ÷ 200,000]. Thus, if management believes unit sales will drop by *less* than 14.3 percent, it should choose a price of $5.50. If management believes unit sales will drop by *more* than 14.3 percent, it should choose a price of $5.00. Let's suppose management believes unit sales will drop by less than 14.3 percent and therefore the selling price is increased to $5.50. Further suppose management is correct and after increasing the price, unit sales drop by only 13 percent—from 200,000 units to 174,000 units. Then Apple-Almond Shampoo would earn a profit of $39,000, as shown below:

$$\text{Profit} = (P - V) \times Q - \text{Fixed expenses}$$
$$= (\$5.50 - \$2.00) \times 174,000 - \$570,000$$
$$= \$3.50 \times 174,000 - \$570,000$$
$$= \$39,000$$

In this case, because unit sales drop by only 13 percent, the higher price of $5.50 causes profits to increase by $9,000 (= $39,000 − $30,000).

Choosing Optimal Prices: The Influence of Customer Latitude

If we assume a 10 percent increase in the price of Apple-Almond Shampoo causes a 13 percent decrease in unit sales, then a price of $5.50 will generate $9,000 (= $39,000 − $30,000) of additional profit compared to a price of $5.00. However, it would be incorrect to conclude that $5.50 is the *optimal price* for Apple-Almond Shampoo; in other words, the price that maximizes profit.

A price of $5.50 is not necessarily the optimal price because Nature's Garden is not limited to choosing a price of either $5.00 or $5.50. Perhaps the company would be better off considering an 8 percent or 12 percent price increase rather than a 10 percent increase. For that matter, the company can establish any price it wants for Apple-Almond Shampoo. It could establish a very low price, such as $2.00 per unit, or a very high price, such as $50 per unit, or anything in between. The low price of $2.00 would be a bad idea because it equals the product's variable cost per unit and would lead to a loss of $570,000, whereas the high price of $50 per unit may be a bad idea because very few customers, if any, would pay $50 for a bottle of shampoo. Thus, the management challenge becomes leveraging knowledge of how customers will respond to changes in price to determine the selling price that will maximize profits—keeping in mind this optimal price could be higher or lower than the current price of $5.00.

Exhibit 13A–3 uses Microsoft Excel to illustrate a pricing model that calculates an optimal price for any product or service once the percentage change in price and percentage change in unit sales have been specified.[6] The specific calculations shown in Exhibit 13A–3 relate to Nature Garden's Apple-Almond Shampoo assuming a 10 percent increase in price causes a 13 percent decrease in unit sales.

EXHIBIT 13A–3
Nature's Garden Apple-Almond Shampoo: An Optimal Pricing Model

	A	B	C	D	E	F
1		Optimal Pricing Model				
2	Apple-Almond Shampoo:					
3	Current unit sales	200,000				
4	Current selling price per unit	$5.00				
5	Variable cost per unit	$2.00				
6	Traceable fixed costs	$570,000				
7						
8	Percentage change in selling price	10%				
9	Percentage change in unit sales	-13%				
10						
11		Per Unit		Unit Sales		Total
12	Sales	$ 6.34 ×		141,467 =		$ 896,481
13	Variable expenses	2.00 ×		141,467 =		282,934
14	Contribution margin	$ 4.34 ×		141,467 =		613,547
15	Traceable fixed expenses					570,000
16	Net operating income					$ 43,547
17						

Microsoft Excel

Note: The price shown in cell B12 is rounded to the nearest penny, whereas Excel used the unrounded price (which is approximately $6.337) to compute the total sales in cell F12.

---

[6] This pricing model assumes a constant elasticity demand curve and fixed expenses that are unaffected by the changes in unit sales. Other demand curves, such as a linear demand curve, could be assumed. While there is some empirical support for using the constant elasticity demand curve, it should be acknowledged the "optimal" selling price will depend on the demand curve that is assumed. Because of this, as well as the uncertainty that usually surrounds estimates of customer responses to price changes, the "optimal" price produced by this model should be viewed as an estimate and not taken too literally.

The first thing to notice with respect to the output from our optimal price calculations shown in Exhibit 13A–3 is the optimal price is not $5.00 or $5.50. It is $6.34, as shown in cell B12. At this price, the company earns a profit of $43,547 (cell F16), which is $4,547 (= $43,547 − $39,000) higher than the previously computed profit obtained at a price of $5.50. While the mathematics underlying this pricing model are beyond the scope of this course, if you choose to download the model and familiarize yourself with it, we want you to understand how to input data into the model and how to interpret the results.[7]

To input data into the model, you should follow a four-step process. First, input the product's current unit sales (cell B3), current selling price (cell B4), variable cost per unit (cell B5), and traceable fixed costs (cell B6). Second, input the percentage change in selling price (cell B8) and the percentage change in unit sales (cell B9). Third, input the current selling price in cell B12. Fourth, click on the Data tab in Microsoft Excel and select Solver in the upper right-hand portion of your screen.[8] When the Solver window opens, click "Solve" and the optimal price will be calculated and automatically inserted into cell B12. In addition, the optimal profit will be automatically calculated in cell F16.

A Visual Perspective of the Optimal Pricing Model

Exhibit 13A–4 plots Apple-Almond Shampoo's net operating income as a function of the selling price when we assume a 10 percent increase in price decreases unit sales by 13 percent.[9]

This plot provides a visual aid in understanding what the optimal pricing model is doing. Essentially, Excel Solver efficiently searches along this graph for the price that maximizes the profit, which in this case is a selling price of $6.34 that results in a total profit of $43,547.

For a variety of reasons, this optimal selling price should not be taken too literally. A prudent manager would make a small change in price in the direction of the optimal price and then observe what happens to unit sales and net operating income. Nevertheless, the Excel workbook provides us with important insights into pricing. If we wanted to adjust the percentage change in unit sales or the percentage change in selling price, we could rerun the Solver function to automatically compute the revised optimal selling price.[10] For example, the table below summarizes the results for three scenarios illustrating different customer sensitivities to a 10 percent increase in price for Apple-Almond Shampoo:

Percentage change in selling price	+10%	+10%	+10%
Percentage change in unit sales	−12%	−13%	−15%
Optimal selling price	$7.86	$6.34	$4.84
Unit sales	109,009	141,467	211,685
Net operating income	$68,908	$43,547	$30,390

In general, the more sensitive customers are to price, the lower the optimal selling price will be, and the less sensitive customers are to price, the higher the optimal selling price will be. For example, when customers respond to a 10 percent increase in price with a 12 percent decrease in unit sales, the optimal price is $7.86, which is $2.86 above the current price of $5.00. Conversely, when customers respond to a 10 percent increase in price with a 15 percent decrease in unit sales, the optimal price is $4.84, which is $0.16 below the current price of $5.00. This large swing in prices illustrates how a small change in the customers' sensitivity to price can have a big impact on the optimal selling price.

---

[7] To obtain a copy of this Excel-based pricing model, go to www.mhhe.com/garrison_opm.

[8] Solver is an Add-in offered within Microsoft Excel. To activate Solver if you do not see it in your Data tab, click the File tab and select Options. Within the Excel Options menu that appears on your screen, click Add-ins and then select Solver Add-in and click OK.

[9] As with the Solver solution to the optimal pricing problem, this graph assumes a constant elasticity demand curve and that the fixed expenses are constant throughout the entire range of unit sales that result from the various prices.

[10] If Solver is unable to find a solution, the most likely cause is that the combination of the percentage change in price and the percentage change in unit sales that you have inputted has resulted in an infinite optimal price. For example, if a 10% increase in price always leads to only a 5% decrease in units sold and fixed costs are constant, then profits always go up when the price is increased. This obviously cannot happen in practice. At some point customers will stop buying the product altogether.

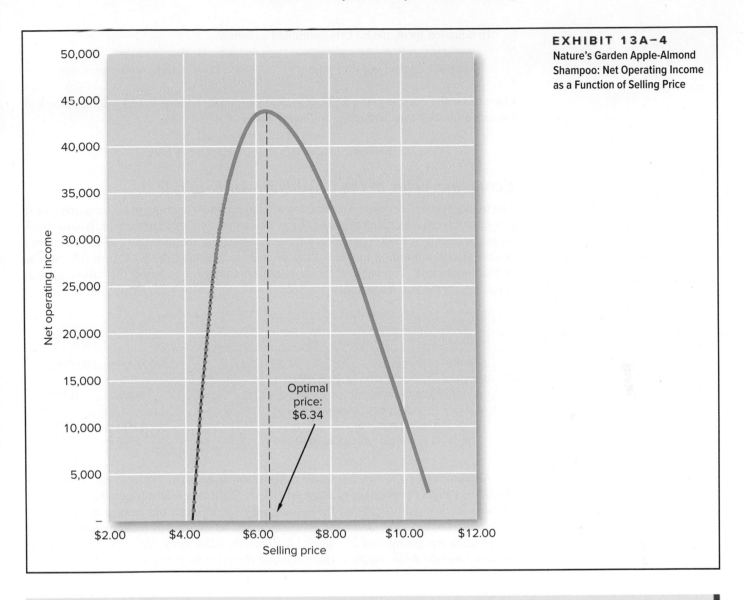

EXHIBIT 13A–4
Nature's Garden Apple-Almond
Shampoo: Net Operating Income
as a Function of Selling Price

Value-Based Pricing

An alternative to cost-plus pricing is *value-based pricing*. Companies using **value-based pricing** establish selling prices based on the economic value of the benefits their products and services provide to customers.

One approach to value-based pricing relies on a concept known as the *economic value to the customer (EVC)*. A product's **economic value to the customer** is the price of the customer's best available alternative plus the value of what differentiates the product from that alternative. The price of the best available alternative is known as the *reference value,* whereas the value of what differentiates a product from the best available alternative is known as the *differentiation value.*[11]

A product's differentiation value can arise in either of two ways. First, a product may differentiate itself by enabling customers to generate more sales and contribution margin than the best available alternative. Second, a product may differentiate itself by enabling customers to realize greater cost savings than the best available alternative.

LO13–10
Analyze pricing decisions using value-based pricing.

---

[11] The terms *reference value* and *differentiation value,* as well as the forthcoming example grounded in the magazine publishing industry, were adapted from *The Strategy and Tactics of Pricing: A Guide to Profitable Decision Making* by Thomas T. Nagle and Reed K. Holden (Upper Saddle River, NJ: Pearson Education, 2002).

In equation form, the EVC is computed as follows:

Economic value to the customer = Reference value + Differentiation value

Once the seller computes the EVC, it seeks to negotiate a value-based selling price with the customer that falls within the following range:

Reference value ≤ Value-based price ≤ EVC

Economic Value to the Customer: An Example

The managers of *Hike America* magazine want to establish a selling price for a one-month full-page advertisement in their magazine. While their primary competitor, *Hiking Trails* magazine, charges $5,000 per month for a full-page ad, the managers of *Hike America* believe they can justify a higher selling price by quantifying the EVC of a full-page ad in their magazine. To enable their analysis, the managers gathered the following data pertaining to the two magazines:

	Hike America	Hiking Trails
Number of readers	200,000	300,000
Percent of readers who buy advertised products each month	0.2%	0.1%
Monthly spending per reader who buys advertised products	$100	$80
Contribution margin ratio of advertisers	25%	25%

Although *Hike America* has fewer readers than *Hiking Trails* magazine (200,000 vs. 300,000), a higher percentage of *Hike America*'s "hard core" subscribers buy advertised products each month (0.2% vs. 0.1%), and they spend more per person on advertised products ($100 vs. $80). Given the assumption that advertisers in both magazines earn a contribution margin ratio of 25 percent on all merchandise sales, *Hike America*'s managers computed the differentiation value of an ad placed in their magazine as follows:

	Hike America	Hiking Trails
Number of readers (a)	200,000	300,000
Percent of readers who buy advertised products each month (b)	0.2%	0.1%
Number of readers per month buying advertised products (a) × (b)	400	300
Monthly sales per reader who buys advertised products (a)	$100	$80
Contribution margin ratio (b)	25%	25%
Monthly contribution margin per reader who buys advertised products (a) × (b)	$25	$20
Number of readers per month buying advertised products (a)	400	300
Monthly contribution margin per reader who buys advertised products (b)	$25	$20
Contribution margin per month provided by a full-page ad (a) × (b)	$10,000	$6,000
Differentiation value	$4,000	

Given that *Hike America*'s reference value is $5,000—the price charged by *Hiking Trails* for a full-page ad—the EVC would be computed as follows:

$$\text{Economic value to the customer} = \text{Reference value} + \text{Differentiation value}$$
$$= \$5,000 + \$4,000$$
$$= \$9,000$$

Hike America would seek to negotiate a value-based selling price for a full-page advertisement within the following range:

$$\text{Reference value} \leq \text{Value-based price} \leq \text{EVC}$$
$$\$5,000 \leq \text{Value-based price} \leq \$9,000$$

It bears emphasizing the EVC of $9,000 does not necessarily represent the price *Hike America* should charge customers for a full-page advertisement. Instead, it provides the magazine's managers a starting point for understanding the economic benefit (in terms of additional contribution margin) a full-page ad in their magazine can offer to prospective customers. In fact, the data shown below suggest *Hike America* probably needs to establish a price less than $9,000.

	Hike America		
	Price = $9,000	Price = $8,000	Hiking Trails
Contribution margin provided by the ad	$10,000	$10,000	$6,000
Investment in the ad (a)	9,000	8,000	5,000
Incremental profit from the ad (b)	$ 1,000	$ 2,000	$1,000
Return on investment (b) ÷ (a)	11%	25%	20%

Notice the right-hand column of numbers shows *Hiking Trails* magazine provides its customers with a 20 percent ROI for a full-page advertisement. Conversely, the left-hand column of numbers shows *Hike America*'s customers would only earn an 11 percent ROI if they paid $9,000 for a full-page ad. Thus, if *Hike America* established a price of $9,000, it would provide advertisers with a lower ROI than they could earn by placing a full-page ad in *Hiking Trails* magazine. However, *Hike America* might consider touting a lower price, such as $8,000, to its prospective customers. As shown in the middle column of data, this lower price provides prospective advertisers with an ROI of 25 percent, which compares favorably with *Hiking Trails*' ROI of 20 percent.

Target Costing

LO13–11
Compute the target cost for a new product or service.

Our discussion thus far has presumed a product has already been developed, has been costed, and is ready to be marketed as soon as a price is set. In many cases, the sequence of events is just the reverse. That is, the company already *knows* what price should be charged, and the problem is to *develop* a product that can be marketed profitably at the desired price. Even in this situation, where the normal sequence of events is reversed, cost is still a crucial factor. The company can use an approach called *target costing*. **Target costing** is the process of determining the maximum allowable cost for a new product and then developing a prototype that can be profitably made for that maximum target cost figure. A number of companies have used target costing, including Compaq, Culp, Cummins Engine, Daihatsu Motors, Chrysler, Ford, Isuzu Motors, ITT Automotive, Komatsu, Matsushita Electric, Mitsubishi Kasei, NEC, Nippondenso, Nissan, Olympus, Sharp, Texas Instruments, and Toyota.

The target cost for a product is computed by starting with the product's anticipated selling price and deducting the desired profit, as follows:

$$\text{Target cost} = \text{Anticipated selling price} - \text{Desired profit}$$

The product development team is then given the responsibility of designing the product so it can be made for no more than the target cost.

Reasons for Using Target Costing

The target costing approach was developed in recognition of two important characteristics of markets and costs. The first is that many companies have less control over price than they would like to think. The market (i.e., supply and demand) really determines price, and a company that attempts to ignore this does so at its peril. Therefore, the anticipated market price is taken as a given in target costing.

The second observation is most of a product's cost is determined in the design stage. Once a product has been designed and has gone into production, not much can be done to significantly reduce its cost. Most of the opportunities to reduce cost come from designing the product so it is simple to make, uses fewer parts, and is robust and reliable. If the company has little control over market price and little control over cost once the product has gone into production, then it follows the major opportunities for affecting profit come during a product's design stage. So that is where the effort is concentrated—in designing and developing cost-effective products that possess features valued by customers.

The difference between target costing and other approaches to product development is profound. Instead of designing the product and then finding out how much it costs, the target cost is set first and then the product is designed so the target cost is attained.

An Example of Target Costing

To provide a simple example of target costing, assume. Handy Company wishes to invest $2,000,000 to design, develop, and produce a new hand mixer. The company's Marketing Department surveyed the features and prices of competing products and determined a price of $30 would enable Handy to sell an estimated 40,000 hand mixers per year. Because the company desires a 15 percent ROI, the target cost to manufacture, sell, distribute, and service one mixer is $22.50, as computed below:

Projected sales (40,000 mixers × $30 per mixer)	$1,200,000
Less desired profit (15% × $2,000,000)	300,000
Target cost for 40,000 mixers	$ 900,000
Target cost per mixer ($900,000 ÷ 40,000 mixers)	$22.50

This $22.50 target cost would be broken down into target costs for the various functions: manufacturing, marketing, distribution, after-sales service, and so on. Each functional area would be responsible for keeping its actual costs within target.

Summary (Appendix 13A)

Pricing involves a delicate balancing act. Higher prices result in more revenue per unit but drive down unit sales. Exactly where to set prices to maximize profit is a difficult problem.

Managers often rely on cost-plus pricing to establish selling prices. The absorption approach to cost-plus pricing applies a markup to the absorption costing unit product cost that is intended to cover nonmanufacturing costs and to provide an adequate return on investment. With the absorption approach, costs will be covered and the return on investment will be adequate *only* if the unit sales forecast is accurate. If applying the cost-plus formula results in a price that is too high, the unit sales forecast will not be attained.

Customers have latitude in their purchasing decisions. They can choose to buy your product, a competitor's product, or nothing at all. This latitude should be taken into account when setting prices. The customers' sensitivity to price is *inelastic* if a change in price has little effect on the number of units sold. On the other hand, the customers' sensitivity to price is *elastic* if a change in price has a substantial effect on the volume of units sold. In general, the more sensitive customers are to price, the lower the optimal selling price will be and the less sensitive customers are to price, the higher the optimal selling price will be.

Value-based pricing is an alternative to cost-plus pricing. Companies using value-based pricing establish selling prices based on the economic value of the benefits their products and services provide to customers. One approach to value-based pricing relies on quantifying the *economic value to the customer (EVC)*. A product's EVC is the price of the customer's best alternative (the reference value) plus the value of what differentiates the seller's product from that alternative (the differentiation value). Once the seller computes the EVC, it establishes a value-based selling price that falls between the reference value and the EVC.

Companies that use target costing estimate what a new product's market price is likely to be based on its anticipated features and the prices of products already on the market. They subtract desired profit from the estimated market price to arrive at the product's target cost. The design and development team is then given the responsibility of ensuring the actual cost of the new product does not exceed the target cost.

Glossary (Appendix 13A)

Cost-plus pricing A pricing method in which a predetermined markup is applied to a cost base to determine the target selling price. (p. 612)

Economic value to the customer (EVC) The price of a customer's best alternative (called the reference value) plus the value of what differentiates a product from that alternative (called the differentiation value). (p. 619)

Markup The difference between the selling price of a product or service and its cost. The markup is usually expressed as a percentage of cost. (p. 611)

Price elasticity of demand A measure of the degree to which a change in price affects the unit sales of a product or service. (p. 611)

Target costing The process of determining the maximum allowable cost for a new product and then developing a prototype that can be profitably made for that maximum target cost figure. (p. 621)

Value-based pricing A pricing method in which a company establishes selling prices based on the economic value of the benefits their products and services provide to customers. (p. 619)

connect Appendix 13A: Exercises and Problems

EXERCISE 13A–1 Absorption Costing Approach to Cost-Plus Pricing LO13–8
Martin Company uses the absorption costing approach to cost-plus pricing. It is considering the introduction of a new product. To determine a selling price, the company gathered the following information:

Number of units to be produced and sold each year	14,000
Unit product cost	$25
Estimated annual selling and administrative expenses	$50,000
Estimated investment required by the company	$750,000
Desired return on investment (ROI)	12%

Required:
1. Compute the markup percentage on absorption cost required to achieve the desired ROI.
2. Compute the selling price per unit.

EXERCISE 13A–2 Customer Latitude and Pricing LO13–9

Maria Lorenzi owns an ice cream stand she operates during the summer months in West Yellowstone, Montana. She is unsure how to price her ice cream cones and has experimented with two prices in successive weeks during the busy August season. The number of people who entered the store was roughly the same each week. During the first week, she priced the cones at $3.50 and 1,800 cones were sold. During the second week, she priced the cones at $4.00 and 1,400 cones were sold. The variable cost of a cone is $0.80 and consists solely of the costs of the ice cream and the cone itself. The fixed expenses of the ice cream stand are $2,675 per week.

Required:

1. What profit did Maria earn during the first week when her price was $3.50?
2. At the start of the second week, Maria increased her selling price by what percentage? What percentage did unit sales decrease? (Round your answers to one-tenth of a percent.)
3. What profit did Maria earn during the second week when her price was $4.00?
4. What was Maria's increase (decrease) in profits from the first week to the second week?

EXERCISE 13A–3 Value-Based Pricing LO13–10

McDermott Company developed a new industrial component called IC-75 that offers superior performance relative to the comparable component sold by McDermott's primary competitor. The competing part sells for $1,200 and needs to be replaced after 2,000 hours of use. It also requires $200 of preventive maintenance during its useful life.

The IC-75's performance capabilities are similar to its competing product with two important exceptions—it needs to be replaced after 4,000 hours of use and it requires $300 of preventive maintenance during its useful life.

Required:

From a value-based pricing standpoint:

1. What is the reference value McDermott should consider when pricing IC-75?
2. What is the differentiation value offered by IC-75 relative the competitor's offering for each 4,000 hours of usage?
3. What is IC-75's economic value to the customer over its 4,000-hour life?
4. What range of possible prices should McDermott consider when setting a price for IC-75?

EXERCISE 13A–4 Target Costing LO13–11

Shimada Products Corporation of Japan plans to introduce a new electronic component to the market at a target selling price of $15 per unit. The company is investing $5,000,000 to purchase the equipment it needs to produce and sell 300,000 units per year. Its required rate of return on all investments is 12%.

Required:

Compute the component's target cost per unit.

EXERCISE 13A–5 Customer Latitude and Optimal Pricing LO13–9

Northport Company manufactures numerous products, one of which is called Sea Breeze Skin Cleanser. The company provided the following data regarding this product:

Unit sales (a)	120,000
Selling price per unit	$20.00
Variable cost per unit.............................	13.00
Contribution margin per unit (b)	$ 7.00
Total contribution margin (a) × (b)	$840,000
Traceable fixed expenses	800,000
Net operating income	$ 40,000

Management is considering increasing the price of Sea Breeze by 20%, from $20.00 to $24.00. The company's marketing managers estimate this price hike could decrease unit sales by as much as 30%, from 120,000 units to 84,000 units.

Required:

In all of the below requirements, assume the traceable fixed expenses are not affected by the pricing decision.

1. Assuming the marketing managers' estimate is accurate, what profit will Sea Breeze Skin Cleanser earn at a price of $24.00?

2. How many units would Northport need to sell at a price of $24.00 to earn the exact same profit it currently earns at a price of $20.00? (Round your answer up to the nearest whole number.)

3. If Northport raises the price of Sea Breeze Skin Cleanser to $24.00, what percentage decrease in unit sales could be absorbed while still providing the same profit currently being earned at a price of $20.00? (Round your answer to the nearest one-tenth of a percent.)

4. Download the optimal pricing model from www.mhhe.com/garrison_opm. Input all of the pertinent data related to Sea Breeze Skin Cleanser into the model (including the assumptions that a 20% increase in selling price will cause a 30% decrease in unit sales). Be sure to input the current price in cell B12. Click on the Data tab in Microsoft Excel and select Solver in the upper-right-hand portion of your screen. When the Solver window opens, click "Solve."
   a. What is the optimal selling price?
   b. What profit is earned at the optimal selling price?
   c. How much additional profit is earned at the optimal price compared to a price of $24.00?

5. Assume a 20% increase in selling price actually causes a 35% decline in unit sales instead of a 30% drop. Using the optimal pricing model, answer the following questions:
   a. What are the optimal selling price and optimal profit if unit sales decline by 35% instead of 30%?
   b. Is the optimal price from requirement 5a higher or lower than your answer in requirement 4a? Why?
   c. If a 20% increase in price causes unit sales to decrease by 35% instead of 30%, would you recommend retaining a price of $20 or implementing your optimal price from requirement 5a? Why?

EXERCISE 13A–6 Value-Based Pricing; Absorption Costing Approach to Cost-Plus Pricing LO13–8, LO13–10

Valmont Company developed a new industrial piece of equipment called the XP-200. The company is considering two methods of establishing a selling price for the XP-200— absorption cost-plus pricing and value-based pricing.

Valmont's cost accounting system reports an absorption unit product cost for XP-200 of $8,400. Its markup percentage on absorption cost is 85%. The company's marketing managers have expressed concerns about the use of absorption cost-plus pricing because it seems to overlook the fact that the XP-200 offers superior performance relative to the comparable piece of equipment sold by Valmont's primary competitor. More specifically, the XP-200 can be used for 20,000 hours before replacement. It only requires $1,000 of preventive maintenance during its useful life and it consumes $120 of electricity per 1,000 hours used.

These figures compare favorably to the competing piece of equipment that sells for $15,000, needs to be replaced after 10,000 hours of use, requires $2,000 of preventive maintenance during its useful life, and consumes $140 of electricity per 1,000 hours used.

Required:

1. If Valmont uses absorption cost-plus pricing, what price will it establish for the XP-200?
2. What is XP-200's economic value to the customer (EVC) over its 20,000-hour life?
3. If Valmont uses value-based pricing, what range of possible prices should it consider when setting a price for the XP-200?
4. What advice would you give Valmont's managers when choosing between absorption cost-plus pricing and value-based pricing?

EXERCISE 13A–7 Customer Latitude and Pricing LO13–9

The postal service of St. Vincent, an island in the West Indies, obtains a significant portion of its revenues from sales of special souvenir sheets to stamp collectors. The postal service purchases the souvenir sheets from a supplier for $0.80 each. St. Vincent has been selling the souvenir sheets for $8.00 each and ordinarily sells about 80,000 units. To test the market, the postal service recently priced a new souvenir sheet at $7.00 and sales increased to 93,600 units.

Required:

1. What total contribution margin did the postal service earn when it sold 80,000 sheets at a price of $8.00 each?
2. By what percentage did the St. Vincent post office decrease its selling price? By what percentage did unit sales increase? (Round your answers to one-tenth of a percent.)
3. What total contribution margin did the postal service earn when it sold 93,600 sheets at a price of $7.00 each?
4. What was the postal service's increase (decrease) in total contribution margin going from the higher price of $8.00 to the lower price of $7.00?
5. How many sheets would the postal service have to sell at the lower price of $7.00 to equal the total contribution margin earned at the higher price of $8.00? (Round your answer up to the nearest whole number.)
6. What percentage increase in the number of sheets sold at $7.00 must be achieved to equal the total contribution margin earned at the higher price of $8.00? (Round your answer up to the nearest one-tenth of a percent.)
7. A financial manager at the postal service has suggested that a more accurate comparison of the two pricing alternatives ($8.00 vs. $7.00) should include an allocation of the postal service's common fixed costs. A portion of the common fixed costs would be allocated to each alternative using total sales dollars as the cost allocation base. He contends this approach would help ensure the postal service's common fixed costs are covered by the prices it charges customers. Do you agree?

PROBLEM 13A–8 Standard Costs; Absorption Costing Approach to Cost-Plus Pricing LO13–8

Wilderness Products, Inc., has designed a self-inflating sleeping pad for use by backpackers and campers. The following information is available about the new product:

a. An investment of $1,350,000 will be necessary to carry inventories and accounts receivable and to purchase some new equipment needed in the manufacturing process. The company's required rate of return is 24% on all investments.
b. A standard cost card has been prepared for the sleeping pad, as shown below:

	Standard Quantity or Hours	Standard Price or Rate	Standard Cost
Direct materials	4.0 yards	$2.70 per yard	$10.80
Direct labor	2.4 hours	$8.00 per hour	19.20
Manufacturing overhead (20% variable) . .	2.4 hours	$12.50 per hour	30.00
Total standard cost per pad			$60.00

c. The only variable selling and administrative expense will be a sales commission of $9 per pad. The fixed selling and administrative expenses will be $732,000 per year.
d. Because the company manufactures many products, no more than 38,400 direct labor-hours per year can be devoted to production of the new sleeping pads.
e. Manufacturing overhead costs are allocated to products on the basis of direct labor-hours.

Required:

1. Assume the company uses the absorption approach to cost-plus pricing.
    a. Compute the markup percentage the company needs on the pads to achieve a 24% return on investment (ROI) if it sells all of the pads it can produce.
    b. What selling price per sleeping pad will the company establish if it uses a markup percentage on absorption cost?
    c. Assume the company is able to sell all of the pads it can produce. Prepare an income statement for the first year of activity. Compute the company's ROI based on the first year of activity.
2. After marketing the sleeping pads for several years, the company is experiencing a falloff in demand due to an economic recession. A large retail outlet will make a bulk purchase of pads if its label is sewn in and if an acceptable price can be worked out. What is the minimum acceptable price for this special order?

PROBLEM 13A–9 Absorption Costing Approach to Cost-Plus Pricing LO13–8

Aldean Company wants to use absorption cost-plus pricing to set the selling price on a new product. The company plans to invest $200,000 in operating assets to produce and sell 16,000 units. Its required return on investment (ROI) in operating assets is 18%. The accounting department provided cost estimates for the new product as shown below:

	Per Unit	Total
Direct materials	$7	
Direct labor	$5	
Variable manufacturing overhead	$2	
Fixed manufacturing overhead		$116,000
Variable selling and administrative expenses . . .	$1	
Fixed selling and administrative expenses		$50,000

Required:
1. What is the unit product cost for the new product?
2. What is the markup percentage on absorption cost for the new product?
3. What selling price would the company establish for its new product using a markup percentage on absorption cost? (Round your answer to the nearest penny.)

PROBLEM 13A–10 Absorption Costing Approach to Cost-Plus Pricing LO13–8

Currington Company wants to use absorption cost-plus pricing to set the selling price on a newly remodeled product. The company plans to invest $150,000 in operating assets to produce and sell 12,000 units. Its required return on investment (ROI) in operating assets is 16%. The accounting department provided cost estimates for the new product as follows:

	Per Unit	Total
Direct materials	$4	
Direct labor	$3	
Variable manufacturing overhead	$1	
Fixed manufacturing overhead		$66,000
Variable selling and administrative expenses . . .	$1	
Fixed selling and administrative expenses		$45,000

Required:
1. What is the unit product cost for the remodeled product?
2. What is the markup percentage on absorption cost for the remodeled product?
3. What selling price would the company establish for its remodeled product using a markup percentage on absorption cost?
4. Suppose the company actually sold only 10,000 units (instead of its planned sales volume of 12,000 units) at the selling price you derived in requirement 3. What ROI did the company actually earn at this lower sales volume?
5. Assume the company wants to raise the price of its newly remodeled product with the intention of achieving the product's desired ROI at the lower sales volume of 10,000 units. Using absorption cost-plus pricing, what would be the revised selling price at this lower sales volume? How might customers react to this new price?

PROBLEM 13A–11 Target Costing LO13–11

National Restaurant Supply, Inc., sells restaurant equipment and supplies throughout the United States. Management is considering adding a machine that makes sorbet to its line of ice cream–making machines. Management will negotiate the purchase price of the sorbet machine with its Swedish manufacturer.

Management of National Restaurant Supply believes the sorbet machine can be sold to its customers in the United States for $4,950. At that price, annual sales of the sorbet machine should be 100 units. If the sorbet machine is added to National Restaurant Supply's product lines, the company will have to invest $600,000 in inventories and special warehouse fixtures. The variable cost of selling the sorbet machines would be $650 per machine.

Required:

1. If National Restaurant Supply requires a 15% return on investment (ROI), what is the maximum amount the company would be willing to pay the Swedish manufacturer for the sorbet machines?

2. The manager is flying to Sweden to negotiate the purchase price of the machines and would like to know how the purchase price of the machines would affect National Restaurant Supply's ROI. Construct a chart showing National Restaurant Supply's ROI as a function of the purchase price of the sorbet machine. Put the purchase price on the *X*-axis and the resulting ROI on the *Y*-axis. Plot the ROI for purchase prices between $3,000 and $4,000 per machine.

3. After many hours of negotiations, management concluded the Swedish manufacturer is unwilling to sell the sorbet machine at a low enough price to enable National Restaurant Supply to earn its 15% required ROI. Apart from simply giving up on the idea of adding the sorbet machine to National Restaurant Supply's product lines, what could management do?

PROBLEM 13A–12 Absorption Costing Approach to Cost-Plus Pricing; Customer Latitude and Pricing LO13–8, LO13–9

Messina Company wants to use absorption cost-plus pricing to establish the selling price for a new product. The company plans to invest $650,000 in operating assets that provide the capacity to make 30,000 units. Its required return on investment (ROI) in operating assets is 20%. Messina's Accounting Department set a goal of producing and selling 20,000 units during the new product's first year of availability. It also provided the following cost estimates for the new product:

	Per Unit	Total
Direct materials	$12	
Direct labor	$8	
Variable manufacturing overhead	$3	
Fixed manufacturing overhead		$100,000
Variable selling and administrative expenses	$1	
Fixed selling and administrative expenses		$60,000

Required:

1. If the company plans to produce and sell 20,000 units, what is the absorption unit product cost for its new product?

2. At a planned sales volume of 20,000 units, what is the markup percentage on absorption cost for the new product?

3. Using absorption cost-plus pricing and assuming a planned sales volume of 20,000 units, what selling price would the company establish for its new product?

4. Using an absorption format, calculate Messina's net operating income if it actually produces and sells only 19,000 units (instead of 20,000 units) at the absorption cost-plus price from requirement 3. Calculate the ROI at this lower sales volume.

5. Assume Messina's controller recommends raising the new product's selling price in an effort to achieve the desired ROI at the lower sales volume of 19,000 units.
    a. What would become the new markup percentage? (Round your answer to the nearest one-tenth of a percent.)
    b. What would become the new selling price? (Round your calculations and answer to the nearest penny.)

6. Download the optimal pricing model from www.mhhe.com/garrison_opm. Suppose Messina's Marketing Department surveyed its customers and estimated an 8% increase in the price of this new product would cause unit sales to decrease by 22%. The company's marketing managers also believe Messina's total fixed costs will be unaffected by the pricing decision. Assuming the new product's actual sales volume was 19,000 units and the marketing managers' estimates and assumptions are correct, input all of the pertinent data into the pricing model. Be sure to input the current price (as calculated in requirement 3) in cell B12. Click on the Data tab in Microsoft Excel and select Solver in the upper right-hand portion of your screen. When the Solver window opens, click "Solve."
    a. What is the optimal selling price?
    b. What profit is earned at the optimal selling price?
    c. Comment on the wisdom of the controller's recommendation to increase the new product's selling price.

PROBLEM 13A–13 Value-Based Pricing LO13–10

The managers of *Midwest Whitetails* magazine (a magazine dedicated to deer hunters) want to establish a price for customers wishing to place a full-page advertisement in their magazine for one month. To help with the price-setting decision, the managers intend to compute the economic value to the customer (EVC) of a full-page ad in their magazine. They have gathered the following data pertaining to *Midwest Whitetails* magazine, as well as their primary competitor, *Trophy Whitetails* magazine:

	Midwest Whitetails	Trophy Whitetails
Number of readers	130,000	200,000
Percent of readers who buy advertised products each month	0.7%	0.5%
Monthly spending per reader who buys advertised products	$120	$100
Contribution margin ratio of advertisers	40%	40%

Trophy Whitetails magazine charges $4,000 per month for a full-page ad. *Midwest Whitetails'* managers believe they can charge more than $4,000 by quantifying the economic value to its customers of placing an ad in their magazine.

Although *Midwest Whitetails* has fewer readers than *Trophy Whitetails* (130,000 vs. 200,000), *Midwest Whitetails* attracts a segment of hunters more likely to buy advertisers' products than the casual hunters subscribing to *Trophy Whitetails*. Therefore, a higher percentage of *Midwest Whitetails* subscribers buy advertised products (0.7% vs. 0.5%), and they spend more per person on advertised products ($120 vs. $100). The managers of *Midwest Whitetails* assume advertisers in both magazines earn an average contribution margin ratio of 40% on all their merchandise sales.

Required:

From a value-based pricing standpoint:
1. What is the reference value *Midwest Whitetails* should consider when setting the price of a full-page ad in its magazine?
2. What is the differentiation value offered by a full-page ad placed in *Midwest Whitetails* magazine?
3. What is the EVC of a full-page ad in *Midwest Whitetails* magazine?
4. What range of possible prices should *Midwest Whitetails* consider when setting a price for a full-page ad?

lighthouse image: Martin73/Shutterstock;
big data image: INGARA/Shutterstock

LEARNING OBJECTIVES

After studying Chapter 14, you should be able to:

LO14–1 Calculate the payback period for an investment.

LO14–2 Evaluate the acceptability of an investment project using the net present value method.

LO14–3 Evaluate the acceptability of an investment project using the internal rate of return method.

LO14–4 Evaluate an investment project that has uncertain cash flows.

LO14–5 Rank investment projects in order of preference.

LO14–6 Compute the simple rate of return for an investment.

LO14–7 *(Appendix 14A) Understand present value concepts and the use of present value tables.*

LO14–8 *(Appendix 14C) Include income taxes in a net present value analysis.*

Data Analytics Exercise available in Connect to complement this chapter

Capital Budgeting Decisions

littlenySTOCK/Shutterstock

ENTREPRENEUR SPOTLIGHT

In 1989, Vera Wang was a bride-to-be who found herself frustrated by the limited selection of available bridal wear. She decided to solve this problem by designing her own wedding gown. A year later, she opened her first bridal boutique on Madison Avenue in New York City. Today Vera Wang is regarded as a fashion design icon whose designs are sold at more than 45 upscale stores worldwide. The Vera Wang Group LLC has also diversified into other product lines, such as eyewear, fragrance, and jewelry.

Applying Managerial Accounting

When the Vera Wang Group contemplates expanding its brand, such as introducing jewelry or eyewear, it could use capital budgeting techniques to assist in the decision-making process. For example, the company could estimate a new product's future cash inflows and outflows over a 10-year time horizon and then discount those cash flows to their present value. If the net present value is greater than zero, it suggests the investment is worthy of further consideration.

Serving All Stakeholders

Having raised two daughters of her own, Vera Wang was keenly aware of the anxiety that can plague teenagers and young adults. To help respond to this problem, she met with psychiatrist David Shaffer and eventually "one thing led to another and the New York Presbyterian Youth Anxiety Center was established in collaboration with Weill Cornell Medical College and Columbia College of Physicians and Surgeons." Beyond her efforts to address the anxiety challenges of people aged 16 to 28, Wang was chosen by the Breast Cancer Research Foundation as a recipient of the Sandra Taub Humanitarian Award. ■

Sources: www.biography.com/fashion-designer/vera-wang, www.verawang.com/stores, https://variety.com/2016/biz/news/vera-wang-childhood-anxiety-youth-center-1201745494/.

Managers often make decisions that require investing money now to realize future profits and cash inflows over a multiyear time horizon. For example, Yum! Brands, Inc., must decide when and where to open a new Pizza Hut restaurant. Ford must decide when to introduce new vehicles and redesign existing ones. The term **capital budgeting** refers to the planning and decision-making processes companies use to evaluate investment projects with multiyear profit and cash flow implications.

This chapter discusses four methods for making capital budgeting decisions—the *payback method, net present value method, internal rate of return method,* and *simple rate of return method.*

Capital Budgeting—An Overview

Typical Capital Budgeting Decisions

Any decision requiring a cash outlay now to earn returns over a multiyear time horizon is a capital budgeting decision. Typical capital budgeting decisions include:

1. Cost reduction decisions. Should new equipment be purchased to reduce costs?
2. Expansion decisions. Should a new plant, warehouse, or other facility be acquired to increase capacity and sales?
3. Equipment selection decisions. Which of several available machines should be purchased?
4. Lease or buy decisions. Should new equipment be leased or purchased?
5. Equipment replacement decisions. Should old equipment be replaced now or later?

Capital budgeting decisions fall into two broad categories—*screening decisions* and *preference decisions.* **Screening decisions** relate to whether a proposed project is acceptable—whether it passes a preset hurdle. For example, a company may have a policy of accepting projects only if they provide a return of at least 20 percent on the investment. The required rate of return is the minimum rate of return a project must yield to be acceptable. **Preference decisions,** by contrast, relate to selecting from among several acceptable alternatives that all exceed the preset hurdle.

Cash Flows versus Net Operating Income

The first three capital budgeting methods discussed in the chapter—the payback method, net present value method, and internal rate of return method—all focus on analyzing the *cash flows* associated with capital investment projects, whereas the simple rate of return method focuses on *incremental net operating income.* To better prepare you to apply the payback, net present value, and internal rate of return methods, we'd like to define the most common types of cash outflows and cash inflows that accompany capital investment projects.

Typical Cash Outflows   Most projects have at least three types of cash outflows. First, they often require an immediate cash outflow in the form of an initial investment in equipment, other assets, and installation costs. Any salvage value realized from the sale of old equipment can be recognized as a reduction in the initial investment or as a cash inflow.

Second, it is important to include the *total cost of ownership* associated with any initial investments in plant and equipment. These costs, also referred to as *life-cycle costs,* may include cash outflows such as annual operating costs, preventive maintenance costs, environmental impact costs, and disposal costs.

Third, some projects require a company to expand its *working capital.* **Working capital** is current assets (e.g., cash, accounts receivable, and inventory) less current liabilities. When a company invests in a new project, the balances in the current asset accounts often increase. For example, opening a new Nordstrom's department store requires additional cash in sales registers and more inventory. These additional working capital needs are treated as part of the initial investment in a project.

Typical Cash Inflows   Most projects also have at least three types of cash inflows. First, a project will normally increase revenues or reduce costs. Either way, the amount involved should be treated as a cash inflow. Notice from a cash flow standpoint, a reduction in costs is equivalent to an increase in revenues. Second, cash inflows are also frequently realized from selling equipment for its salvage value when a project ends. Third, any working capital tied up in the project can be released for use elsewhere at the end of the project and should be treated as a cash inflow at that time. Working capital is released, for example, when a company sells off its inventory or collects its accounts receivable.

The Time Value of Money

Beyond defining a capital project's cash outflows and inflows, it is also important to consider when those cash flows occur. For example, if someone offered to give you $1,000 today that you could save toward your eventual retirement or $1,000 a year from now that you could save toward your future retirement, which would you choose? In all likelihood, you would choose to receive $1,000 today because you could invest it and have more than $1,000 a year from now. This simple example illustrates an important capital budgeting concept known as *the time value of money*. The **time value of money** recognizes a dollar today is worth more than a dollar a year from now if for no other reason than you could put the dollar in a bank today and have more than a dollar a year from now. Because of the time value of money, capital investments promising earlier cash flows are preferable to those promising later cash flows.

Although the payback method focuses on cash flows, it does not recognize the time value of money. In other words, it treats a dollar received today as being of equal value to a dollar received at any point in the future. Conversely, the net present value and internal rate of return methods not only focus on cash flows, but they also recognize the time value of those cash flows. These two methods use a technique called *discounting cash flows* to translate the value of future cash flows to their present value. If you are not familiar with the concept of discounting cash flows and the use of present value tables, you should read Appendix 14A: The Concept of Present Value, at the end of the chapter, before studying the net present value and internal rate of return methods.

The Payback Method

LO14–1

Calculate the payback period for an investment.

The payback method of evaluating capital budgeting projects focuses on the *payback period*. The **payback period** is the length of time needed for a project to recover its initial cost from the net cash inflows it generates. The payback method assumes the more quickly the cost of an investment can be recovered, the more desirable the investment.

The payback period is expressed in years. *When the annual net cash inflow is the same every year,* the following formula can be used to compute the payback period:

$$\text{Payback period} = \frac{\text{Investment required}}{\text{Annual net cash inflow}} \qquad (1)$$

To illustrate the payback method, consider the following data:

Example A: York Company needs a new milling machine. The company is considering two machines: machine A and machine B. Machine A costs $15,000, has a useful life of ten years, and will reduce operating costs by $5,000 per year. Machine B costs only $12,000, will also reduce operating costs by $5,000 per year, but has a useful life of only five years.

Required:
Which machine should be purchased according to the payback method?

$$\text{Machine A payback period} = \frac{\$15,000}{\$5,000} = 3.0 \text{ years}$$

$$\text{Machine B payback period} = \frac{\$12,000}{\$5,000} = 2.4 \text{ years}$$

According to the payback calculations, York Company should purchase Machine B because it has a shorter payback period than Machine A.

Evaluation of the Payback Method

The payback method is not a true measure of the profitability of an investment. Rather, it simply tells a manager how many years are required to recover the original investment. Unfortunately, a shorter payback period does not always mean one investment is more desirable than another.

To illustrate, refer back to Example A. Machine B has a shorter payback period than machine A, but it has a useful life of only 5 years rather than 10 years for machine A. Machine B would have to be purchased twice—once immediately and then again after the fifth year—to provide the same service as just one machine A. Under these circumstances, machine A would probably be a better investment than machine B, even though machine B has a shorter payback period. Unfortunately, the payback method ignores all cash flows occurring after the payback period.

A further criticism of the payback method is that it does not consider the time value of money. A cash inflow to be received several years in the future is weighed the same as a cash inflow received right now. To illustrate, assume for an investment of $8,000 you can purchase either of the two following streams of cash inflows:

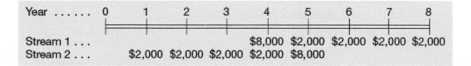

Which stream of cash inflows would you prefer to receive in return for your $8,000 investment? Each stream has a payback period of 4.0 years. Therefore, if payback alone is used to make the decision, the streams would be considered equally desirable. However, from a time value of money perspective, Stream 2 is much more desirable than Stream 1.

On the other hand, under certain conditions, the payback method can be very useful. For one thing, it can help identify which investment proposals are in the "ballpark." That is, it can be used as a screening tool to help answer the question, "Should I consider this proposal further?" If a proposal doesn't provide a payback within some specified period, then there may be no need to consider it further. In addition, the payback period is often important to new companies that are "cash poor." When a company is cash poor, a project with a short payback period but a low rate of return might be preferred over another project with a high rate of return but a long payback period. The reason is that the company may simply need a faster return of its cash investment. And finally, the payback method is sometimes used in industries where products become obsolete very rapidly—such as consumer electronics. Because products may last only a year or two, the payback period on investments must be very short.

An Extended Example of Payback

When new equipment replaces old equipment, the old equipment's salvage value should be deducted from the cost of the new equipment. Thus, only the *incremental* investment is used in the payback computation. In addition, any depreciation deducted in arriving at the project's net operating income must be added back to obtain the project's expected annual net cash inflow. To illustrate, consider the following data:

Example B: Goodtime Fun Centers, Inc., operates amusement parks. Some of the vending machines in one of its parks provide very little revenue, so the company is considering removing the machines and installing equipment to dispense soft ice cream. The equipment would cost $80,000 and have an eight-year useful life with no salvage value. Incremental annual revenues and costs associated with the sale of ice cream would be as follows:

Sales		$150,000
Variable expenses		90,000
Contribution margin		60,000
Fixed expenses:		
Salaries	$27,000	
Maintenance	3,000	
Depreciation	10,000	40,000
Net operating income		$ 20,000

The vending machines can be sold for a $5,000 scrap value. The company will not purchase the equipment unless it has a payback period of three years or less. Does the ice cream dispenser pass this hurdle?

Exhibit 14–1 computes the payback period for the ice cream dispenser. Several things should be noted. First, depreciation is added back to net operating income to obtain the

---

EXHIBIT 14–1
Computation of the Payback Period

Step 1: *Compute the annual net cash inflow.* Because the annual net cash inflow is not given, it must be computed before the payback period can be determined:

Net operating income	$20,000
Add: Noncash deduction for depreciation	10,000
Annual net cash inflow	$30,000

Step 2: *Compute the payback period.* Using the annual net cash inflow from above, the payback period can be determined as follows:

Cost of the new equipment	$80,000
Less: Salvage value of old equipment	5,000
Investment required	$75,000

$$\text{Payback period} = \frac{\text{Investment required}}{\text{Annual net cash inflow}}$$

$$= \frac{\$75,000}{\$30,000} = 2.5 \text{ years}$$

annual net cash inflow from the new equipment. Depreciation is not a cash outlay; thus, it must be added back to adjust net operating income to a cash basis. Second, the payback computation deducts the salvage value of the old machines from the cost of the new equipment so that only the incremental investment is used in computing the payback period.

Because the proposed equipment's payback period is less than three years, the company's payback requirement has been met.

Payback and Uneven Cash Flows

When the cash flows associated with an investment project change from year to year, the simple payback formula we outlined earlier cannot be used. Instead, the payback period can be computed as follows (assuming cash inflows occur evenly throughout the year): Payback period = Number of years up to the year in which the investment is paid off + (Unrecovered investment at the beginning of the year in which the investment is paid off ÷ Cash inflow in the period in which the investment is paid off). To illustrate how to apply this formula, consider the following data:

Year	Investment	Cash Inflow
1	$4,000	$1,000
2		$0
3		$2,000
4	$2,000	$1,000
5		$500
6		$3,000
7		$2,000

What is the payback period on this investment? The answer is 5.5 years, computed as follows: 5 + ($1,500 ÷ $3,000) = 5.5 years. In essence, we are tracking the unrecovered investment year by year as shown in Exhibit 14–2. By the middle of the sixth year, sufficient cash inflows will have been realized to recover the entire investment of $6,000 ($4,000 + $2,000).

Year	Investment	Cash Inflow	Unrecovered Investment*
1	$4,000	$1,000	$3,000
2		$0	$3,000
3		$2,000	$1,000
4	$2,000	$1,000	$2,000
5		$500	$1,500
6		$3,000	$0
7		$2,000	$0

*Year X unrecovered investment = Year X-1 unrecovered investment + Year X investment − Year X cash inflow

EXHIBIT 14–2
Payback and Uneven Cash Flows

COMMUNICATING WITH DATA VISUALIZATIONS

Predictive analytics answer the question: What will happen? This visualization depicts the pay-back period from Exhibit 14–2. Once the company estimates its future investments and cash inflows, it can predict a payback period of 5.5 years.

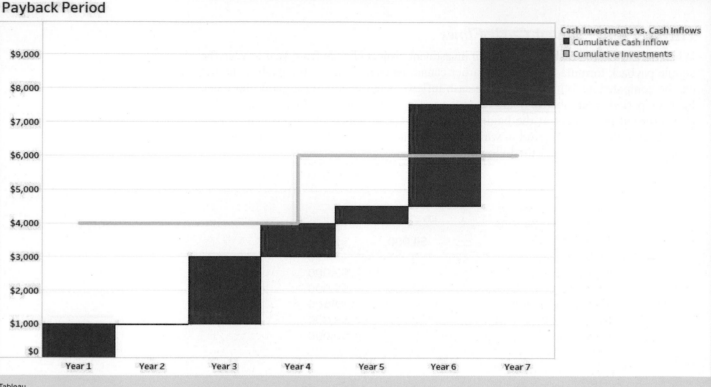

Payback Period

Tableau

The Net Present Value Method

LO14–2
Evaluate the acceptability of an investment project using the net present value method.

The *net present value method* and the *internal rate of return method* use discounted cash flows to analyze capital budgeting decisions. The net present value method is discussed in this section followed by a discussion of the internal rate of return method.

The Net Present Value Method Illustrated

The net present value method compares the present value of a project's cash inflows to the present value of its cash outflows. The difference between the present value of these cash flows, called the **net present value,** determines whether or not a project is an acceptable investment.

When performing net present value analysis, managers usually make two important assumptions. First, all cash flows other than the initial investment occur at the end of periods. This assumption is somewhat unrealistic because cash flows typically occur *throughout* a period rather than just at its end; however, it simplifies the computations considerably. Second, all cash flows generated by an investment project are immediately reinvested at a rate of return equal to the rate used to discount the future cash flows, also known as the *discount rate*. If this condition is not met, the net present value computations will not be accurate.

To illustrate net present value analysis, consider the following data:

Example C: Harper Company is contemplating buying a new machine that will cost $50,000 and last five years. The new machine will enable the company to reduce its labor costs by $18,000 per year. At the end of the five-year period, the company will sell the machine for its salvage value of $5,000. Harper Company requires a minimum pretax return of 18% on all investment projects.[1]

Should the machine be purchased? Harper Company must determine whether a cash investment now of $50,000 can be justified if it will result in an $18,000 cost reduction in each of the next five years. The answer may seem obvious given the total cost savings is $90,000 ($18,000 per year × 5 years); however, the company can earn an 18 percent return by investing its money elsewhere. It is not enough that the annual cost reductions cover just the original cost of the machine; they must also yield a return of at least 18% or the company would be better off investing the money elsewhere.

To determine whether the investment is desirable, the stream of annual $18,000 cost savings and the machine's salvage value of $5,000 should be discounted to their present values and then compared to the cost of the new machine. Exhibits 14–3, 14–4, and 14–5 demonstrate three distinct but equivalent ways of performing these calculations. The approaches in Exhibits 14–3 and 14–4 rely on the discount factors shown in Appendix 14B that have been rounded to three decimal places. The method shown in Exhibit 14–5 derives its answer using unrounded discount factors.

Cell B8 of Exhibit 14–3 calculates the present value of Harper Company's initial cash outlay of $(50,000) by multiplying $(50,000) by 1.000, the present value factor for any cash flow that occurs immediately. Cell C8 calculates the present value of the annual cost savings of $56,286 by multiplying $18,000 by 3.127, the present value factor of a five-year annuity at the discount rate of 18 percent (see Exhibit 14B–2). Cell D8 calculates the present value of the machine's salvage value of $2,185 by multiplying $5,000 by 0.437, the present value factor of a single sum to be received in five years at the discount rate of 18 percent (see Exhibit 14B–1). Finally, cells B8 through D8 are added together to derive the net present value in cell B9 of $8,471.

Exhibit 14–4 shows another way to calculate the net present value of $8,471. Under this approach Cell B8 calculates the present value of the initial cash outlay of $(50,000) by multiplying $(50,000) by 1.000—just as was done in Exhibit 14–3. However, rather than calculating the present value of the annual cost savings using a discount factor of 3.127 from Exhibit 14B–2, Exhibit 14–4 discounts the annual cost savings in Years 1–5 *and* the machine's salvage value in Year 5 to their present values using the discount factors from Exhibit 14B–1. For example, the $18,000 cost savings in Year 3 (cell E6) is multiplied by the discount factor of 0.609 (cell E7) to derive its present value of $10,962 (cell E8). As another example, the $23,000 of total cash flows in Year 5 (cell G6) is multiplied by the discount factor of 0.437 (cell G7) to determine its present value of $10,051 (cell G8). The present values in cells B8 through G8 are then added together to compute the project's net present value of $8,471 (cell B9).

EXHIBIT 14–3
Net Present Value Analysis Using Discount Factors from Exhibits 14B–1 and 14B–2 in Appendix 14B

	A	B	C	D	
1			Year(s)		
2		Now	1-5	5	
3	Initial investment	$ (50,000)			
4	Annual cost savings		$ 18,000		
5	Salvage value of the new machine			$ 5,000	
6	Total cash flows (a)	$ (50,000)	$ 18,000	$ 5,000	
7	Discount factor (18%) (b)	1.000	3.127	0.437	
8	Present value of the cash flows (a) × (b)	$ (50,000)	$ 56,286	$ 2,185	
9	Net present value (SUM B8:D8)	$ 8,471			
10					
11	Note: The discount factors come from Exhibits 14B-1 and 14B-2 in Appendix 14B.				
12					

Exhibit 14-3 | Exhibit 14-4 | Exhibit 14-5 | Exhibit 14-

Microsoft Excel

---

[1] For simplicity, we ignore inflation and taxes. The impact of income taxes on capital budgeting decisions is discussed in Appendix 14C.

EXHIBIT 14–4
Net Present Value Analysis Using Discount Factors from Exhibit 14B–1 in Appendix 14B

	A	B	C	D	E	F	G
1						Year	
2		Now	1	2	3	4	5
3	Initial investment	$ (50,000)					
4	Annual labor cost savings		$ 18,000	$ 18,000	$ 18,000	$ 18,000	$ 18,000
5	Salvage value of new machine						$ 5,000
6	Total cash flows (a)	$ (50,000)	$ 18,000	$ 18,000	$ 18,000	$ 18,000	$ 23,000
7	Discount factor (18%) (b)	1.000	0.847	0.718	0.609	0.516	0.437
8	Present value of cash flows (a) × (b)	$ (50,000)	$ 15,246	$ 12,924	$ 10,962	$ 9,288	$ 10,051
9	Net present value (SUM B8:G8)	$ 8,471					
10							
11	Note: The discount factors come from Exhibit 14B-1 in Appendix 14B.						
12							

Exhibit 14-4 / Exhibit 14-5 / Exhibit 14-6 / Exhibit 14-7 / Exhibit 14-i

Microsoft Excel

The methods described in Exhibits 14–3 and 14–4 are mathematically equivalent—they both produced a net present value of $8,471. The only difference between these two exhibits relates to the discounting of the annual labor cost savings. In Exhibit 14–3, the labor cost savings are discounted to their present value using the annuity factor of 3.127, whereas in Exhibit 14–4, these cost savings are discounted using five separate factors that sum to 3.127 (0.847 + 0.718 + 0.609 + 0.516 + 0.437 = 3.127).

The net present values in Exhibits 14–3 and 14–4 are calculated using the *rounded* discount factors from Appendix 14B. However, net present value calculations can also be performed using *unrounded* discount factors. One approach to using unrounded discount factors would be to replace the rounded discount factors shown in row 7 of Exhibits 14–3 and 14–4 with formulas that compute unrounded discount factors. Another approach, as shown in Exhibit 14–5, is to use Microsoft Excel's NPV function to perform the calculations. The NPV function automatically calculates the net present value after specifying three parameters—the discount rate (0.18), the annual cash flows (C6:G6), and the initial cash outlay (+B6). Notice the net present value in Exhibit 14–5 of $8,475 is $4 higher than the net present value shown in Exhibits 14–3 and 14–4. The trivial $4 difference arises because Microsoft Excel's NPV function uses unrounded discount factors.

EXHIBIT 14–5
Net Present Value Analysis Using Microsoft Excel's NPV Function

	A	B	C	D	E	F	G
1						Year	
2		Now	1	2	3	4	5
3	Initial investment	$ (50,000)					
4	Annual labor cost savings		$ 18,000	$ 18,000	$ 18,000	$ 18,000	$ 18,000
5	Salvage value of new machine						$ 5,000
6	Total cash flows (a)	$ (50,000)	$ 18,000	$ 18,000	$ 18,000	$ 18,000	$ 23,000
7	Net present value (SUM B8:G8)	$ 8,475					
8							
9	Note: The net present value is computed using the formula: =NPV(0.18,C6:G6)+B6						
10							

Exhibit 14-5 / Exhibit 14-6 / Exhibit 14-7 / Exhibit 14-8 / Exhibit 14-9 / Exi

Microsoft Excel

During your career, you should feel free to use any of the methods discussed thus far to perform net present value calculations. However, throughout this chapter and its forthcoming exercises and problems, we'll be using the approaches illustrated in Exhibits 14–3 and 14–4 accompanied by the rounded discount factors in Appendix 14B.

Once you have computed a project's net present value, you'll need to interpret your findings. For example, because Harper Company's proposed project has a positive net present value of $8,471, it implies the company should purchase the new machine. A positive net present value indicates the project's return exceeds the discount rate. A negative net present value indicates the project's return is less than the discount rate. Therefore, if the company's minimum required rate of return is used as the discount rate, a project with a positive net present value has a return that exceeds the minimum required rate of return and is acceptable. Conversely, a project with a negative net present value has a return less than the minimum required rate of return and is unacceptable. In sum:

If the Net Present Value Is . . .	Then the Project Is . . .
Positive	Acceptable because its return is greater than the required rate of return.
Zero	Acceptable because its return is equal to the required rate of return.
Negative	Not acceptable because its return is less than the required rate of return.

A company's *cost of capital* is usually regarded as its minimum required rate of return. The **cost of capital** is the average rate of return the company must pay to its long-term creditors and its shareholders for the use of their funds. If a project's rate of return is less than the cost of capital, the company does not earn enough to compensate its creditors and shareholders. Therefore, any project with a rate of return less than the cost of capital should be rejected.

The cost of capital serves as a *screening device.* When the cost of capital is used as the discount rate in net present value analysis, any project with a negative net present value does not cover the company's cost of capital and should be discarded as unacceptable.

Recovery of the Original Investment

The net present value method automatically provides for return of the original investment. Whenever the net present value of a project is positive, the project will recover the original cost of the investment plus sufficient excess cash inflows to compensate the organization for tying up funds in the project. To demonstrate this point, consider the following situation:

Example D: Carver Hospital is considering the purchase of an attachment for its X-ray machine that will cost $3,170. The attachment's useful life is four years with no salvage value. It will increase net cash inflows by $1,000 per year in the X-ray department. The hospital's board of directors requires a rate of return of at least 10% on such investments.

Exhibit 14–6 shows a net present value analysis for the X-ray attachment (using a discount factor of 3.170 from Exhibit 14B–2). Notice the attachment has exactly a 10 percent return on the original investment because the net present value is zero at a 10 percent discount rate.

Each annual net cash inflow of $1,000 is made up of two parts. One part represents a recovery of a portion *of* the original $3,170 paid for the attachment, and the other part represents a return *on* this investment. The breakdown of each year's $1,000 cash inflow between recovery *of* investment and return *on* investment is shown in Exhibit 14–7.

The first year's $1,000 cash inflow consists of a return *on* investment of $317 (a 10 percent return *on* the $3,170 original investment), plus a $683 return *of* the investment. Because the amount of the unrecovered investment decreases each year, the dollar amount of the return on investment also decreases each year. By the end of the fourth year, all $3,170 of the original investment has been recovered.

EXHIBIT 14–6

Carver Hospital—Net Present Value Analysis of X-Ray Attachment

	A	B	C	D
1			Years	
2		Now	1-4	
3	Initial investment	$ (3,170)		
4	Annual cost savings		$ 1,000	
5	Total cash flows (a)	$ (3,170)	$ 1,000	
6	Discount factor (10%) (b)	1.000	3.170	
7	Present value of the cash flows (a) × (b)	$ (3,170)	$ 3,170	
8	Net present value (SUM B7:C7)	$ 0		
9				
10	Note: The discount factor comes from Exhibit 14B-2 in Appendix 14B.			
11				

Exhibit 14-6 | Exhibit 14-7 | Exhibit 14-8 | Exhi

Microsoft Excel

EXHIBIT 14–7

Carver Hospital—Breakdown of Annual Cash Inflows

	A	B	C	D	E	F
1		(1)	(2)	(3)	(4)	(5)
2	Year	Investment Outstanding during the Year	Cash Inflow	Return on Investment (1) × 10%	Recovery of Investment during the Year (2) – (3)	Unrecovered Investment at the End of the Year (1) – (4)
3	1	$3,170	$1,000	$317	$683	$2,487
4	2	$2,487	$1,000	$249	$751	$1,736
5	3	$1,736	$1,000	$173	$827	$909
6	4	$909	$1,000	$91	$909	$0
7	Total investment recovered				$3,170	
8						

Exhibit 14-4 | Exhibit 14-5 | Exhibit 14-6 | Exhibit 14-7 | Exhibit 14- ...

Microsoft Excel

An Extended Example of the Net Present Value Method

Example E provides an extended example of the net present value method that reinforces many of the ideas discussed thus far.

Example E: Under a special licensing arrangement, Swinyard Corporation has an opportunity to market a new product for a five-year period. The product would be purchased from the manufacturer, with Swinyard responsible for promotion and distribution costs. The licensing arrangement could be renewed at the end of the five-year period. After careful study, Swinyard estimated the following costs and revenues for the new product:

Cost of equipment needed	$60,000
Working capital needed	$100,000
Overhaul of the equipment in four years	$5,000
Salvage value of the equipment in five years	$10,000
Annual revenues and costs:	
Sales revenues	$200,000
Cost of goods sold	$125,000
Out-of-pocket operating costs (for salaries, advertising, and other direct costs)	$35,000

At the end of the five-year period, if Swinyard decides not to renew the licensing arrangement the working capital would be released for investment elsewhere. Swinyard uses a 14 percent discount rate.

Exhibit 14–8 calculates the net present value ($31,410) of Swinyard's new product opportunity. Notice the working capital is counted as a cash outflow at the beginning of the project (cell B4) and as a cash inflow when released at the end of the project (cell G10). Also notice how the sales revenues, cost of goods sold, and out-of-pocket costs are handled. **Out-of-pocket costs** are actual cash outlays for salaries, advertising, and other operating expenses. Because the net present value is positive, the new product is acceptable.

EXHIBIT 14–8
The Net Present Value Method—An Extended Example

	A	B	C	D	E	F	G
1					Year		
2		Now	1	2	3	4	5
3	Purchase of equipment	$ (60,000)					
4	Investment in working capital	$ (100,000)					
5	Sales		$ 200,000	$ 200,000	$ 200,000	$ 200,000	$ 200,000
6	Cost of goods sold		$ (125,000)	$ (125,000)	$ (125,000)	$ (125,000)	$ (125,000)
7	Out-of-pocket costs for salaries, advertising, etc.		$ (35,000)	$ (35,000)	$ (35,000)	$ (35,000)	$ (35,000)
8	Overhaul of equipment					$ (5,000)	
9	Salvage value of the equipment						$ 10,000
10	Working capital released						$ 100,000
11	Total cash flows (a)	$ (160,000)	$ 40,000	$ 40,000	$ 40,000	$ 35,000	$ 150,000
12	Discount factor (14%) (b)	1.000	0.877	0.769	0.675	0.592	$ 0.519
13	Present value of cash flows (a) × (b)	$ (160,000)	$ 35,080	$ 30,760	$ 27,000	$ 20,720	$ 77,850
14	Net present value (SUM B13:G13)	$ 31,410					
15							
16	Note: The discount factors come from Exhibit 14B-1 in Appendix 14B.						
17							

Exhibit 14-8 / Exhibit 14-9 / Exhibit 14-10 / Exhibit 14-11 / Exhibit

Microsoft Excel

OAK VIEW GROUP INVESTS IN NEW ARENAS

Oak View Group is a Los Angeles–based company that plans to invest $3.9 billion to build eight new arenas throughout the United States. Rather than relying on professional sports teams to generate revenues at six of these eight venues, the company will rely on concerts from touring musicians such as the Eagles and Harry Styles. Oak View claims that an "arena can generate twice as much net income from hosting a concert than a National Basketball Association or National Hockey League game." While PricewaterhouseCoopers estimates that the live music industry currently generates $28 billion in annual revenues, Oak View expects that figure to grow to $38 billion by 2030.

Source: Anne Steele, "For New Arenas, It's Showtime," *The Wall Street Journal,* November 20, 2019, p. B3.

The Internal Rate of Return Method

LO14–3
Evaluate the acceptability of an investment project using the internal rate of return method.

The **internal rate of return** is an investment project's rate of return over its useful life. It is computed by finding the discount rate that equates the present value of a project's cash outflows with the present value of its cash inflows. In other words, the internal rate of return is *the discount rate that results in a net present value of zero.*

The Internal Rate of Return Method Illustrated

To illustrate the internal rate of return method, consider the following data:

Example F: Glendale School District is considering the purchase of a large tractor-pulled lawn mower. At present, the lawn is mowed using a small hand-pushed gas mower. The large, tractor-pulled mower will cost $16,950, have a useful life of 10 years, and have negligible scrap value. The tractor-pulled mower would do the job faster than the old mower, resulting in labor savings of $3,000 per year.

To compute the new mower's internal rate of return, we must find the discount rate that results in a zero net present value. *When the net cash inflow is the same every year,* the formula below calculates the factor from Exhibit 14B–2 needed to identify the internal rate of return:

$$\text{Factor of the internal rate of return} = \frac{\text{Investment required}}{\text{Annual net cash inflow}} \qquad (2)$$

Using the data for the Glendale School District's proposed project, we get a factor of:

$$\frac{\text{Investment required}}{\text{Annual net cash inflow}} = \frac{\$16,950}{\$3,000} = 5.650$$

Next, we scan along the 10-period line in Exhibit 14B–2 to find that a factor of 5.650 represents a 12 percent internal rate of return. Exhibit 14–9 verifies the project's internal rate of return by confirming the project's net present value is zero when using a discount rate of 12 percent.[2] Once the Glendale School District computes the project's internal rate of return of 12 percent, it would accept the project if this rate is equal to or greater than the school district's minimum required rate of return. It would reject the project if this rate is less than the minimum required rate of return. For example, if we assume Glendale's minimum required rate of return is 15 percent, then the school district would reject this project because the 12 percent internal rate of return does not clear the 15 percent *hurdle rate.*

Comparison of the Net Present Value and Internal Rate of Return Methods

This section compares the net present value and internal rate of return methods in two ways. First, both methods use the cost of capital to screen out undesirable investment projects. When the internal rate of return method is used, the cost of capital is used as

---

[2]   We can also verify the 12% internal rate of return using the IRR functionality within Microsoft Excel. To do this, you would depict the annual cost savings as 10 single sums rather than a 10-year annuity. In other words, you would create 11 cells of data—one cell would contain the initial investment of $(16,500) and ten cells would each contain an annual cost savings of $3,000. Then put your cursor in a 12th cell where you would like the internal rate of return to appear. Select the "Formulas" tab in Excel, followed by the "Financial" tab. Scroll down to select IRR. Insert the range of cells that contain your 11 distinct cash flows in the "Values" field that will appear on your screen and then click OK. Microsoft Excel will automatically calculate the IRR and insert it into your chosen cell.

EXHIBIT 14–9
Evaluation of the Mower Using a 12 percent Discount Rate

	A	B	C	
1			Years	
2		Now	1-10	
3	Initial investment	$ (16,950)		
4	Annual cost savings		$ 3,000	
5	Total cash flows (a)	$ (16,950)	$ 3,000	
6	Discount factor (12%) (b)	1.000	5.650	
7	Present value of the cash flows (a) × (b)	$ (16,950)	$ 16,950	
8	Net present value (SUM B7:C7)	$ 0		
9				
10	Note: The discount factor comes from Exhibit 14B-2 in Appendix 14B.			
11				

Exhibit 14-8   **Exhibit 14-9**   Exhibit 14-10   E

Microsoft Excel

the hurdle rate that a project must clear for acceptance. If the internal rate of return of a project is not high enough to clear the cost of capital hurdle, then the project is ordinarily rejected. When the net present value method is used, the cost of capital is the discount rate used to compute the net present value of a proposed project. Any project yielding a negative net present value is usually rejected.

Second, the internal rate of return method makes a questionable assumption. Both methods assume cash flows generated by a project during its useful life are immediately reinvested elsewhere. However, the two methods make different assumptions concerning the rate of return earned on those cash flows. The net present value method assumes the rate of return is the discount rate, whereas the internal rate of return method assumes the rate of return earned on cash flows is the internal rate of return on the project. Specifically, if the internal rate of return of the project is high, this assumption may not be realistic. It is generally more realistic to assume cash inflows can be reinvested at a rate of return equal to the discount rate—particularly if the discount rate is the company's cost of capital or an opportunity rate of return. For example, if the discount rate is the company's cost of capital, this rate of return can be actually realized by paying off the company's creditors and buying back the company's stock with cash flows from the project. In short, when the net present value method and the internal rate of return method do not agree concerning the attractiveness of a project, it is best to go with the net present value method. Of the two methods, it makes the more realistic assumption about the rate of return that can be earned on cash flows from the project.

Expanding the Net Present Value Method

So far, all of our examples involved an evaluation of a single investment project. In the following section we use the *total-cost approach* to explain how the net present value method can be used to evaluate two alternative projects.

The total-cost approach is the most flexible method for comparing competing projects. To illustrate, consider the following data:

Example G: Harper Ferry Company operates a high-speed passenger ferry service across the Mississippi River. One of its ferryboats is in poor condition. This ferry can be renovated at an immediate cost of $200,000. Further repairs and an overhaul of the motor will be needed three years from now at a cost of $80,000. In all, the ferry will be usable for 5 years if this work is done. At the end of 5 years, the ferry will have to be scrapped at a salvage value of $60,000. The scrap value of the ferry right now is $70,000. It will cost $300,000 each year to operate the ferry, and revenues will total $400,000 annually.

As an alternative, Harper Ferry Company can purchase a new ferryboat at a cost of $360,000. The new ferry will have a life of 5 years but will require some repairs costing $30,000 at the end of 3 years. At the end of 5 years, the ferry will have a scrap value of $60,000. It will cost $210,000 each year to operate the ferry, and revenues will total $400,000 annually.

Harper Ferry Company requires a return of at least 14% on all investment projects.

Exhibit 14–10 uses the total-cost approach and discount factors from Exhibit 14B–1 to compare the net present values of both alternatives.

Two points should be noted from the exhibit. First, *all* cash inflows and *all* cash outflows are included in the solution under each alternative. No effort has been made to include relevant cash flows and exclude irrelevant cash flows. The inclusion of all cash flows associated with each alternative gives the approach its name—the *total-cost* approach.

EXHIBIT 14–10
The Total-Cost Approach to Project Selection

	A	B	C	D	E	F	G
1	Keep the old ferry:				Year		
2		Now	1	2	3	4	5
3	Renovation	$(200,000)					
4	Annual revenues		$ 400,000	$ 400,000	$ 400,000	$ 400,000	$ 400,000
5	Annual cash operating costs		$(300,000)	$(300,000)	$(300,000)	$(300,000)	$(300,000)
6	Repairs in three years				$ (80,000)		
7	Salvage value of old ferry						$ 60,000
8	Total cash flows (a)	$(200,000)	$ 100,000	$ 100,000	$ 20,000	$ 100,000	$ 160,000
9	Discount factor (14%) (b)	1.000	0.877	0.769	0.675	0.592	0.519
10	Present value of cash flows (a) × (b)	$(200,000)	$ 87,700	$ 76,900	$ 13,500	$ 59,200	$ 83,040
11	Net present value (SUM B10:G10)	$ 120,340					
12							
13	Buy the new ferry:				Year		
14		Now	1	2	3	4	5
15	Initial investment	$(360,000)					
16	Salvage value of the old ferry	$ 70,000					
17	Annual revenues		$ 400,000	$ 400,000	$ 400,000	$ 400,000	$ 400,000
18	Annual cash operating costs		$(210,000)	$(210,000)	$(210,000)	$(210,000)	$(210,000)
19	Repairs in three years				$ (30,000)		
20	Salvage value of new ferry						$ 60,000
21	Total cash flows (a)	$(290,000)	$ 190,000	$ 190,000	$ 160,000	$ 190,000	$ 250,000
22	Discount factor (14%) (b)	1.000	0.877	0.769	0.675	0.592	0.519
23	Present value of cash flows (a) × (b)	$(290,000)	$ 166,630	$ 146,110	$ 108,000	$ 112,480	$ 129,750
24	Net present value (SUM B23:G23)	$ 372,970					
25							
26	Net present value in favor of buying the new ferry (B24-B11)	$ 252,630					
27							
28	Note: The discount factors come from Exhibit 14B-1 in Appendix 14B.						
29							

| ◄ ◄ ► ►| | Exhibit 14-8 | Exhibit 14-9 | **Exhibit 14-10** | Exhibit 14-11 | Exhibit 14C-| ◄ | | IIII | ► | |

Microsoft Excel

Second, notice a net present value is computed for each alternative. This is a strength of the total-cost approach because an unlimited number of alternatives can be compared side by side to determine the best option. For example, another alternative for Harper Ferry Company would be to get out of the ferry business entirely. If management desired, the net present value of this alternative could be computed to compare with the alternatives shown in Exhibit 14–10. Given the two alternatives at hand, the net present value in favor of buying the new ferry is $252,630.[3]

Least-Cost Decisions

Some decisions do not involve any revenues. For example, a company may be trying to decide whether to buy or lease an executive jet. In situations such as these, where no revenues are involved, the most desirable alternative is the one with the *least total cost* from a present value perspective. To illustrate a least-cost decision, consider the following example:

Example H: Val-Tek Company is considering replacing an old threading machine with a new threading machine that would reduce annual operating costs. Selected data relating to the old and new machines are presented below:

	Old Machine	New Machine
Purchase cost when new	$200,000	$250,000
Salvage value now	$30,000	—
Annual cash operating costs	$150,000	$90,000
Overhaul needed immediately	$40,000	—
Salvage value in six years	$0	$50,000
Remaining life	6 years	6 years

Val-Tek Company uses a 10% discount rate.

Exhibit 14–11 analyzes the alternatives using the total-cost approach and discount factors from Exhibits 14B–1 and 14B–2. Because this is a least-cost decision, the present values are negative for both alternatives. However, the present value of buying the new machine is $109,500 lower than the other alternative. Therefore, buying the new machine is the less costly alternative.

---

[3] The alternative with the highest net present value is not always the best choice, although it is the best choice in this case. For further discussion, see the section Preference Decisions—The Ranking of Investment Projects.

EXHIBIT 14–11
Least-Cost Decision: A Net Present Value Analysis

	A	B	C	D
1	Keep the old machine:		Year(s)	
2		Now	1-6	6
3	Overhaul needed now	$ (40,000)		
4	Annual cash operating costs		$ (150,000)	
5	Total cash flows (a)	$ (40,000)	$ (150,000)	
6	Discount factor (10%) (b)	1.000	4.355	
7	Present value of the cash flows (a) × (b)	$ (40,000)	$ (653,250)	
8	Net present value (SUM B7:C7)	$ (693,250)		
9				
10	Buy the new machine:		Year(s)	
11		Now	1-6	6
12	Initial investment	$ (250,000)		
13	Salvage value of old machine	$ 30,000		
14	Annual cash operating costs		$ (90,000)	
15	Salvage value of new machine			$ 50,000
16	Total cash flows (a)	$ (220,000)	$ (90,000)	$ 50,000
17	Discount factor (10%) (b)	1.000	4.355	0.564
18	Present value of the cash flows (a) × (b)	$ (220,000)	$ (391,950)	$ 28,200
19	Net present value (SUM B18:D18)	$ (583,750)		
20				
21	Net present value in favor of buying the new machine	$ 109,500		
22				

Exhibit 14-9   Exhibit 14-10   **Exhibit 14-11**   Exhibit 14C-1

Microsoft Excel

Uncertain Cash Flows

LO14–4
Evaluate an investment
project that has uncertain
cash flows.

Thus far, we have assumed all future cash flows are known with certainty. However, future cash flows are often uncertain or difficult to estimate. A number of techniques are available for handling this complication. Some of these techniques are quite technical—involving computer simulations or advanced mathematical skills—and are beyond the scope of this book. However, we can provide some very useful information to help managers deal with uncertain cash flows without getting too technical.

An Example

Consider the case of investments in automated equipment where the up-front costs and tangible benefits, such as reductions in operating costs and waste, are relatively easy to estimate. However, the equipment's intangible benefits, such as greater reliability, greater speed, and higher quality, are more difficult to quantify in terms of future cash flows. These intangible benefits certainly impact future cash flows—particularly in terms of increased sales and perhaps higher selling prices—but the cash flow effects are difficult to estimate.

Suppose, for example, a company with a 12 percent discount rate is considering purchasing automated equipment with a 10-year useful life. Also suppose a discounted cash flow analysis of just the *tangible* costs and benefits shows a negative net present value of $226,000. Clearly, if the *intangible* benefits are large enough, they could turn this negative net present value into a positive net present value. The formula for computing the value of the intangible benefits required to increase the net present value to zero is as follows:

Net present value excluding the intangible benefits (negative)	$(226,000)
Present value factor for an annuity at 12% for 10 periods (from Exhibit 14B–2 in Appendix 14B)	5.650

$$\frac{\text{Negative net present value to be offset, } \$226,000}{\text{Present value factor, } 5.650} = \$40,000$$

Thus, if the intangible benefits of the automated equipment are worth at least $40,000 a year, then the automated equipment should be purchased. If, in the judgment of management, these intangible benefits are not worth $40,000 a year, then the automated equipment should not be purchased.

This technique can also be used in other situations where future cash flows are difficult to estimate. For example, this technique can be used when the salvage value is difficult to estimate. To illustrate, suppose all cash flows from an investment in a supertanker have been estimated—other than its salvage value in 20 years. Using a discount rate of 12 percent, management determined the net present value of all of these cash flows is a negative $1.04 million. This negative net present value would be offset by the salvage value of the supertanker. How large would the salvage value have to be to raise the net present value of this investment to zero?

Net present value excluding salvage value (negative)	$(1,040,000)
Present value factor at 12% for 20 periods (from Exhibit 14B–1 in Appendix 14B)	0.104

$$\frac{\text{Negative net present value to be offset, } \$1,040,000}{\text{Present value factor, } 0.104} = \$10,000,000$$

Thus, if the salvage value of the tanker in 20 years is at least $10 million, its net present value would be positive and the investment should be made. However, if management believes the salvage value is unlikely to be as large as $10 million, the investment should not be made.

Preference Decisions—The Ranking of Investment Projects

When considering investment opportunities, managers must make two types of decisions—screening decisions and preference decisions. Screening decisions pertain to whether or not a proposed investment is acceptable. Preference decisions come *after* screening decisions and answer the following question: "How do all the acceptable investment proposals rank in terms of preference? That is, which one(s) would be *best* for the company to accept?"

LO14–5
Rank investment projects in order of preference.

Internal Rate of Return Method

When using the internal rate of return method to rank competing investment projects, the preference rule is: *The higher the internal rate of return, the more desirable the project.* For example, an investment project with an internal rate of return of 18 percent is preferable to another project with a return of only 15 percent.

Net Present Value Method

The net present value of one project cannot be directly compared to the net present value of another project unless the initial investments are equal. For example, assume a company is considering two competing investments, as shown below:

	Investment	
	A	B
Investment required*	$(10,000)	$(5,000)
Present value of cash inflows	11,000	6,000
Net present value	$ 1,000	$ 1,000

The investment required includes investments in working capital and is reduced by the salvage value realized from the sale of old equipment.

Although each project has a net present value of $1,000, the projects are not equally desirable if the funds available for investment are limited. The project requiring an investment of only $5,000 is much more desirable than the project requiring an investment of $10,000. This fact can be highlighted by dividing the present value of each project's cash inflows by its investment required. The result, shown below in equation form, is called the **profitability index.**

$$\text{Profitability index} = \frac{\text{Present value of cash inflows}}{\text{Investment required}} \qquad (3)$$

The profitability indexes for the two investments above would be computed as follows:

	Investment	
	A	B
Present value of cash inflows (a)	$11,000	$6,000
Investment required (b)	$10,000	$5,000
Profitability index, (a) ÷ (b)	1.10	1.20

When using the profitability index to rank competing investment projects, the preference rule is: *The higher the profitability index, the more desirable the project.*[4] Applying this rule to the two investments above, Investment B should be chosen over Investment A.

---

[4] Because of the "lumpiness" of projects, the profitability index ranking may not be perfect. Nevertheless, it is a good starting point.

STANLEY BLACK & DECKER MOVES PRODUCTION TO THE UNITED STATES

Stanley Black & Decker is investing $90 million to move production from China to a new manufacturing facility in Fort Worth, Texas. The newly constructed plant will employ 500 people to annually produce 10 million Craftsman wrenches and ratchets as well as 50 million sockets. The Fort Worth facility will rely on robots and fast-forging presses to "boost output about 25 percent above the older machinery used to make Craftsman wrenches in China." These automation-driven efficiencies coupled with rising tariff costs are also causing other companies, such as Whirlpool and Caterpillar, to bring overseas production back to the United States.

Source: Bob Tita, "Stanley to Make More Craftsman Tools in U.S.," *The Wall Street Journal,* May 16, 2019, p. B2.

The Simple Rate of Return Method

The **simple rate of return** method is the final capital budgeting technique discussed in the chapter. This method is often referred to as the accounting rate of return or the unadjusted rate of return. We will begin by explaining how to compute the simple rate of return followed by a discussion of this method's limitations and its impact on the behavior of investment center managers.

LO14–6
Compute the simple rate of return for an investment.

To obtain the simple rate of return, the annual incremental net operating income generated by a project is divided by the initial investment in the project, as shown below.

$$\text{Simple rate of return} = \frac{\text{Annual incremental net operating income}}{\text{Initial investment}} \quad (4)$$

The annual incremental net operating income in the numerator should be reduced by the depreciation charges that result from making the investment. Furthermore, the initial investment in the denominator should be reduced by any salvage value realized from the sale of old equipment.

Example I: Brigham Tea, Inc., is a processor of low-acid tea. The company is contemplating purchasing equipment for an additional processing line that would increase revenues by $90,000 per year. Incremental cash operating expenses would be $40,000 per year. The equipment would cost $180,000 and have a nine-year life with no salvage value.

To apply the formula for the simple rate of return, we must first determine the annual incremental net operating income from the project:

Annual incremental revenues		$90,000
Annual incremental cash operating expenses . . .	$40,000	
Annual depreciation ($180,000 − $0) ÷ 9	20,000	
Annual incremental expenses		60,000
Annual incremental net operating income		$30,000

Given the annual incremental net operating income from the project is $30,000 and the initial investment is $180,000, the simple rate of return is 16.7 percent, as shown below:

$$\text{Simple rate of return} = \frac{\text{Annual incremental net operating income}}{\text{Initial investment}}$$

$$= \frac{\$30,000}{\$180,000}$$

$$= 16.7\%$$

Example J: Midwest Farms, Inc., hires people on a part-time basis to sort eggs. The cost of hand sorting is $30,000 per year. The company is investigating an egg-sorting machine that would cost $90,000 and have a 15-year useful life. The machine would have negligible salvage value, and it would cost $10,000 per year to operate and maintain. The egg-sorting equipment currently being used could be sold now for a scrap value of $2,500.

This project is slightly different from the preceding project because it involves cost reductions with no additional revenues. Nevertheless, the annual incremental net operating income can be computed by treating the annual cost savings as if it were incremental revenues as follows:

Annual incremental cost savings		$ 30,000
Annual incremental cash operating expenses	$10,000	
Annual depreciation ($90,000 − $0) ÷ 15	6,000	
Annual incremental expenses		16,000
Annual incremental net operating income		$ 14,000

Thus, even though the new equipment would not generate any additional revenues, it would reduce costs by $14,000 a year, thereby increasing net operating income by the same amount.

Finally, the salvage value of the old equipment offsets the initial cost of the new equipment as follows:

Cost of the new equipment	$90,000
Less: Salvage value of the old equipment	2,500
Initial investment	$87,500

Given the annual incremental net operating income of $14,000 and the initial investment of $87,500, the simple rate of return is 16.0 percent, computed as follows:

$$\text{Simple rate of return} = \frac{\text{Annual incremental net operating income}}{\text{Initial investment}}$$

$$= \frac{\$14,000}{\$87,500}$$

$$= 16.0\%$$

The simple rate of return has two important limitations. First, it focuses on accounting net operating income rather than cash flows. Thus, if a project does not have constant incremental revenues and expenses over its useful life, the simple rate of return fluctuates from year to year, thereby possibly causing the same project to appear desirable in some years and undesirable in others. Second, the simple rate of return method does not involve discounting cash flows. It considers a dollar received 10 years from now to be as valuable as a dollar received today.

Given these limitations, it is reasonable to wonder why we bothered discussing this method. First of all, in spite of its limitations, some companies use the simple rate of return to evaluate capital investment proposals. Therefore, you should be familiar with this approach so you can properly critique it in the event that you encounter it in practice. More importantly, you need to understand how the simple rate of return method influences thc behavior of investment center managers who are evaluated and rewarded based on their return on investment (ROI).

For example, assume the following three facts. First, you are an investment center manager whose pay raises are based solely on ROI. Second, last year your division had an ROI of 20 percent. Third, your division has the chance to pursue a capital budgeting project with a positive net present value and a simple rate of return of 17 percent. Given these three assumptions, would you choose to accept this project or reject it? Although the company would want you to accept it because of its positive net present value, you would probably reject it because the simple rate of return of 17 percent is less than your prior year's ROI of 20 percent. This basic example illustrates how a project's simple rate of return can influence the decisions made by investment center managers. It also highlights an important challenge faced by organizations, namely designing performance measurement systems that align employee actions with organizational goals.

Postaudit of Investment Projects

After an investment project has been approved and implemented, a *postaudit* should be conducted. A **postaudit** involves checking whether or not expected results are actually realized. This is a key part of the capital budgeting process because it helps keep managers honest in their investment proposals. Any tendency to inflate the benefits or downplay the costs in a proposal should become evident after a few postaudits have been conducted. The postaudit also provides an opportunity to reinforce and possibly expand successful projects and to cut losses on floundering projects.

The same capital budgeting method should be used in the postaudit as was used in the original approval process. That is, if a project was approved on the basis of a net present value analysis, then the same procedure should be used in performing the postaudit. However, the data used in the postaudit analysis should be *actual observed data* rather than estimated data. This gives management an opportunity to make a side-by-side comparison to see how well the project has succeeded. It also helps assure that estimated data received on future proposals will be carefully prepared because the people submitting the data know that their estimates will be compared to actual results in the postaudit process. Actual results that are far out of line with original estimates should be carefully reviewed.

IN BUSINESS

THE FUTURE OF FAST FOOD IS HERE

With upwards of a million unfilled jobs in the wake of the pandemic, the fast-food industry is desperately seeking reliable help. Enter Miso Robotics' Flippy 2.0—a robot using artificial intelligence, powerful image processing, and machine learning to help restaurants such as White Castle prepare a variety of food items, including French fries, cheese sticks, and chicken tenders. While robots are unlikely to completely replace people, fast-food industry executives are nonetheless attracted to Flippy's resume: works 23 hours a day seven days a week; provides reliable, consistent production; is immune from disease, stress, and distractions; requires no benefits package; and never asks off on the weekend.

Source: Christopher Mims, "The Fry Cook That Never Calls in Sick," *The Wall Street Journal*, August 7, 2021, https://www.wsj.com/articles/restaurant-robots-kitchen-labor-shortage-11628290623, and Danielle Weiner-Bronner, "White Castle Thinks a Robot Can Make Better French Fries," CNN Business, November 2, 2021, https://www.cnn.com/2021/11/02/business/flippy-2-white-castle/index.html.

Summary

The payback method of evaluating capital investment projects focuses on the payback period. The payback period is the length of time it takes for a project to recover its initial cost from the net cash inflows it generates. The basic premise of the payback method is that the more quickly the cost of an investment can be recovered, the more desirable is the investment.

Investment decisions should take into account the time value of money because a dollar received today is more valuable than a dollar received in the future. The net present value and internal rate of return methods both reflect this fact. In the net present value method, future cash flows are discounted to their present value. The difference between the present value of the cash inflows and outflows is called a project's net present value. If the net present value of a project is negative, the project is rejected. The discount rate in the net present value method is usually based on a minimum required rate of return such as a company's cost of capital.

The internal rate of return is the rate of return that equates the present value of the cash inflows and outflows, resulting in a zero net present value. If the internal rate of return is less than a company's minimum required rate of return, the project is rejected.

After rejecting projects whose net present values are negative or whose internal rates of return are less than the minimum required rate of return, more projects may remain than can be supported with available funds. The remaining projects can be ranked using either the profitability index or internal rate of return. The profitability index is computed by dividing the present value of a project's cash inflows by its required initial investment.

The simple rate of return is determined by dividing a project's annual incremental net operating income by the initial investment in the project. While this method has important limitations, it can influence the decision-making process of investment center managers who are evaluated and rewarded based on their return on investment (ROI).

 Data Analytics Exercise available in Connect to complement this chapter

Review Problem: Comparison of Capital Budgeting Methods

Lamar Company is considering a project with a five-year life requiring a $2,400,000 investment in equipment. At the end of five years, the project would terminate and the equipment would have no salvage value. The project would provide net operating income each year as follows:

Sales		$3,200,000
Variable expenses		1,800,000
Contribution margin		1,400,000
Fixed expenses:		
Advertising, salaries, and other fixed out-of-pocket costs	$700,000	
Depreciation	300,000	
Total fixed expenses		1,000,000
Net operating income		$ 400,000

The company's discount rate is 12%.

Required:
1. Compute the annual net cash inflow from the project.
2. Compute the project's net present value. Is the project acceptable?
3. Find the project's internal rate of return to the nearest whole percent.
4. Compute the project's payback period.
5. Compute the project's simple rate of return.

Solution to Review Problem

1. The annual net cash inflow can be computed by deducting the cash expenses from sales:

Sales	$3,200,000
Variable expenses	1,800,000
Contribution margin	1,400,000
Advertising, salaries, and other fixed out-of-pocket costs	700,000
Annual net cash inflow	$ 700,000

Or the annual net cash inflow can be computed by adding depreciation back to net operating income:

Net operating income	$400,000
Add: Noncash deduction for depreciation	300,000
Annual net cash inflow	$700,000

2. The net present value is computed as follows:

	A	B	C	D	E	F	G
					Year		
1							
2		Now	1	2	3	4	5
3	Initial investment	$ (2,400,000)					
4	Sales		$ 3,200,000	$ 3,200,000	$ 3,200,000	$ 3,200,000	$ 3,200,000
5	Variable expenses		$(1,800,000)	$(1,800,000)	$(1,800,000)	$(1,800,000)	$(1,800,000)
6	Fixed out-of-pocket costs		$ (700,000)	$ (700,000)	$ (700,000)	$ (700,000)	$ (700,000)
7	Total cash flows (a)	$ (2,400,000)	$ 700,000	$ 700,000	$ 700,000	$ 700,000	$ 700,000
8	Discount factor (12%) (b)	1.000	0.893	0.797	0.712	0.636	0.567
9	Present value of cash flows (a) × (b)	$(2,400,000)	$ 625,100	$ 557,900	$ 498,400	$ 445,200	$ 396,900
10	Net present value (SUM B9:G9)	$ 123,500					
11							
12	Note: The discount factors come from Exhibit 14B-1 in Appendix 14B.						
13							

Sheet1 / Sheet2 / Sheet3

Microsoft Excel

Or it can also be computed as follows:

	A	B	C	D
2		Now	1-5	
3	Initial investment	$ (2,400,000)		
4	Sales		$ 3,200,000	
5	Variable expenses		$ (1,800,000)	
6	Fixed out-of-pocket costs		$ (700,000)	
7	Total cash flows (a)	$ (2,400,000)	$ 700,000	
8	Discount factor (12%) (b)	1.000	3.605	
9	Present value of the cash flows (a) × (b)	$ (2,400,000)	$2,523,500	
10	Net present value (SUM B7:C7)	$123,500		
11				
12	Note: The discount factor comes from Exhibit 14B-2 in Appendix 14B.			
13				

Sheet1 **Sheet2** / Sheet3

Microsoft Excel

Yes, the project is acceptable because it has a positive net present value.

3. The formula for computing the factor of the internal rate of return is:

$$\text{Factor of the internal rate of return} = \frac{\text{Investment required}}{\text{Annual net cash flow}}$$

$$= \frac{\$2,400,000}{\$700,000} = 3.429$$

Looking in Exhibit 14B–2 in Appendix 14B at the end of the chapter and scanning along the 5-period line, we find a factor of 3.429 is closest to a factor of 3.433, which corresponds to a rate of return of 14%.

4. The formula for the payback period is:

$$\text{Payback period} = \frac{\text{Investment required}}{\text{Annual net cash flow}}$$

$$= \frac{\$2,400,000}{\$700,000}$$

$$= 3.4 \text{ years (rounded)}$$

5. The formula for the simple rate of return is:

$$\text{Simple rate of return} = \frac{\text{Annual incremental net operating income}}{\text{Initial investment}}$$

$$= \frac{\$400,000}{\$2,400,000}$$

$$= 16.7\%$$

Glossary

Capital budgeting The planning and decision-making processes companies use to evaluate investment projects with multiyear profit and cash flow implications. (p. 631)

Cost of capital The average rate of return a company must pay to its long-term creditors and shareholders for the use of their funds. (p. 639)

Internal rate of return The discount rate at which the net present value of an investment project is zero; a project's rate of return over its useful life. (p. 642)

Net present value The difference between the present value of an investment project's cash inflows and the present value of its cash outflows. (p. 636)

Out-of-pocket costs Actual cash outlays for salaries, advertising, repairs, and similar costs. (p. 641)

Payback period The length of time it takes for a project to fully recover its initial cost out of the net cash inflows it generates. (p. 632)

Postaudit The follow-up after a project has been approved and implemented to determine whether expected results were actually realized. (p. 651)

Preference decision A decision in which the acceptable alternatives must be ranked. (p. 631)

Profitability index The present value of a project's cash inflows divided by the investment required. (p. 648)

Screening decision A decision as to whether a proposed investment project is acceptable. (p. 631)

Simple rate of return The rate of return computed by dividing a project's annual incremental net operating income by the initial investment required. (p. 649)

Time value of money The concept that a dollar today is worth more than a dollar a year from now. (p. 632)

Working capital Current assets less current liabilities. (p. 631)

Questions

14–1 What is the difference between screening decisions and preference decisions?

14–2 What is the *time value of money?*

14–3 What is meant by *discounting?*

14–4 Why isn't accounting net income used in the net present value and internal rate of return methods of making capital budgeting decisions?

14–5 Why are discounted cash flow methods of making capital budgeting decisions superior to other methods?

14–6 What is net present value? Can it ever be negative? Explain.

14–7 Identify two simplifying assumptions associated with discounted cash flow methods of making capital budgeting decisions.

14–8 If a company has to pay interest of 14% on long-term debt, then its cost of capital is 14%. Do you agree? Explain.

14–9 What is meant by an investment project's internal rate of return? How is the internal rate of return computed?

14–10 Explain how the cost of capital serves as a screening tool when using (*a*) the net present value method and (*b*) the internal rate of return method.

14–11 As the discount rate increases, the present value of a given future cash flow also increases. Do you agree? Explain.

14–12 Refer to Exhibit 14–8. Is the return on this investment exactly 14%, more than 14%, or less than 14%? Explain.

14–13 How is the profitability index computed, and what does it measure?

14–14 What is the *payback period?* How is the payback period calculated? How can the payback method be useful?

14–15 What is the major criticism of the payback and simple rate of return methods of making capital budgeting decisions?

Mc Graw Hill connect **Applying Excel**

The Excel worksheet appearing below recreates Example E and Exhibit 14–8. The workbook, and instructions on how to complete the file, can be found in Connect.   **LO14–2, LO14–3**

	A	B	C	D	E	F	G
1	Chapter 14: Applying Excel						
2							
3	**Data**						
4	**Example E**						
5	Cost of equipment needed	$60,000					
6	Working capital needed	$100,000					
7	Overhaul of equipment in four years	$5,000					
8	Salvage value of the equipment in five years	$10,000					
9	Annual revenues and costs:						
10	Sales revenues	$200,000					
11	Cost of goods sold	$125,000					
12	Out-of-pocket operating costs	$35,000					
13	Discount rate	14%					
14							
15	*Enter a formula into each of the cells marked with a ? below*						
16	**Exhibit 14-8**						
17					Years		
18		Now	1	2	3	4	5
19	Purchase of equipment	?					
20	Investment in working capital	?					
21	Sales		?	?	?	?	?
22	Cost of goods sold		?	?	?	?	?
23	Out-of-pocket operating costs		?	?	?	?	?
24	Overhaul of equipment					?	
25	Salvage value of the equipment						?
26	Working capital released						?
27	Total cash flows (a)	?	?	?	?	?	?
28	Discount factor (14%) (b)	?	?	?	?	?	?
29	Present value of cash flows (a) x (b)	?	?	?	?	?	?
30	Net present value	?					
31							
32	*Use the formulas from Appendix 14B:						
33	Present value of $1 = 1/(1+r)^n						
34	Present value of an annuity of $1 = (1/r)*(1-(1/(1+r)^n))						
35	where n is the number of years and r is the discount rate						
36							

|◄ ◄ ► ►| **Chapter 14 Form** / Filled in Chapter 14 Form / Chapter 14 Formula ◄ |

Microsoft Excel

You should proceed to the requirements below only after completing your worksheet. Note you may get a slightly different net present value from that shown in the text due to the precision of the calculations.

Required:

1. Check your worksheet by changing the discount rate to 10%. The net present value should now be between $56,495 and $56,518—depending on the precision of the calculations. If you do not get an answer in this range, find the errors in your worksheet and correct them.

    Explain why the net present value has increased as a result of reducing the discount rate from 14% to 10%.

2. The company is considering another project involving the purchase of new equipment. Change the data area of your worksheet to match the following:

Data	
Example E	
Cost of equipment needed	$120,000
Working capital needed	$80,000
Overhaul of equipment in four years	$40,000
Salvage value of the equipment in five years	$20,000
Annual revenues and costs:	
Sales revenues	$255,000
Cost of goods sold	$160,000
Out-of-pocket operating costs	$50,000
Discount rate	14%

a. What is the net present value of the project?
b. Experiment with changing the discount rate in one percent increments (e.g., 13%, 12%, 15%, etc.). At what interest rate does the net present value turn from negative to positive?
c. The internal rate of return is between what two whole discount rates (e.g., between 10% and 11%, between 11% and 12%, between 12% and 13%, between 13% and 14%, etc.)?
d. Reset the discount rate to 14%. Suppose the salvage value is uncertain. How large would the salvage value have to be to result in a positive net present value?

The Foundational 15   Mc Graw Hill connect

LO14–1, LO14–2, LO14–3, LO14–5, LO14–6

Cardinal Company is considering a five-year project requiring a $2,975,000 investment in equipment with a useful life of five years and no salvage value. The company's discount rate is 14%. The project would provide net operating income in each of five years as follows:

Sales		$2,735,000
Variable expenses		1,000,000
Contribution margin		1,735,000
Fixed expenses:		
Advertising, salaries, and other fixed		
out-of-pocket costs	$735,000	
Depreciation	595,000	
Total fixed expenses		1,330,000
Net operating income		$ 405,000

Required:

Answer each question by referring to the original data unless instructed otherwise.

1. Which item(s) in the income statement shown above will not affect cash flows?
2. What are the project's annual net cash inflows?
3. What is the present value of the project's annual net cash inflows?

4. What is the project's net present value?
5. What is the profitability index for this project? (Round your answer to the nearest whole percent.)
6. What is the project's internal rate of return to the nearest whole percent?
7. What is the project's payback period?
8. What is the project's simple rate of return for each of the five years?
9. If the company's discount rate was 16% instead of 14%, would you expect the project's net present value to be higher than, lower than, or the same as your answer to requirement 4? No computations are necessary.
10. If the equipment had a salvage value of $300,000 at the end of five years, would you expect the project's payback period to be higher than, lower than, or the same as your answer to requirement 7? No computations are necessary.
11. If the equipment had a salvage value of $300,000 at the end of five years, would you expect the project's net present value to be higher than, lower than, or the same as your answer to requirement 3? No computations are necessary.
12. If the equipment had a salvage value of $300,000 at the end of five years, would you expect the project's simple rate of return to be higher than, lower than, or the same as your answer to requirement 8? No computations are necessary.
13. Assume a postaudit showed all estimates (including total sales) were exactly correct except for the variable expense ratio, which actually turned out to be 45%. What was the project's actual net present value?
14. Assume a postaudit showed all estimates (including total sales) were exactly correct except for the variable expense ratio, which actually turned out to be 45%. What was the project's actual payback period?
15. Assume a postaudit showed all estimates (including total sales) were exactly correct except for the variable expense ratio, which actually turned out to be 45%. What was the project's actual simple rate of return?

Exercises

EXERCISE 14–1 Payback Method LO14–1

Unter Corporation, an architectural design firm, is considering an investment with the following cash flows:

Year	Investment	Cash Inflow
1	$15,000	$1,000
2	$8,000	$2,000
3		$2,500
4		$4,000
5		$5,000
6		$6,000
7		$5,000
8		$4,000
9		$3,000
10		$2,000

Required:
1. Determine the payback period of the investment.
2. Would the payback period be affected if the cash inflow in the last year were several times as large?

EXERCISE 14–2 Net Present Value Analysis LO14–2

Kunkel Company is considering the purchase of a $27,000 machine that would reduce operating costs by $7,000 per year. At the end of the machine's five-year useful life, it will have zero salvage value. The company's required rate of return is 12%.

Required:
1. Calculate the net present value of the investment in the machine.
2. What is the difference between the total, undiscounted cash inflows and cash outflows over the entire life of the machine?

EXERCISE 14–3 Internal Rate of Return LO14–3

Wendell's Donut Shoppe is investigating the purchase of an $18,600 donut-making machine with a six-year useful life. The new machine would reduce labor costs by $3,800 per year. In addition, it would allow the company to produce one new style of donut, resulting in the sale of 1,000 dozen more donuts each year. The company realizes a contribution margin of $1.20 per dozen donuts sold.

Required:
1. What are the new machine's total annual cash inflows?
2. What discount factor should be used to compute the new machine's internal rate of return?
3. Using Exhibit 14B–2 in Appendix 14B as a reference, what is the new machine's internal rate of return to the nearest whole percent?
4. In addition to the data given previously, assume the machine will have a $9,125 salvage value at the end of six years. Under these conditions, what is the internal rate of return to the nearest whole percent? (Hint: You may find it helpful to use the net present value approach; find the discount rate that will cause the net present value to be closest to zero.)

EXERCISE 14–4 Uncertain Future Cash Flows LO14–4

Lukow Products is investigating the purchase of automated equipment that will save $400,000 each year in direct labor and inventory carrying costs. This equipment costs $2,500,000 and is expected to have a 15-year useful life with no salvage value. The company's required rate of return is 20% on all equipment purchases. Management expects this equipment to provide intangible benefits such as greater flexibility and higher-quality output that will increase future cash inflows.

Required:
1. What is the net present value of the piece of equipment *before* considering its intangible benefits?
2. What minimum dollar value per year must be provided by the equipment's intangible benefits to justify the $2,500,000 investment?

EXERCISE 14–5 Preference Ranking LO14–5

Information on four investment proposals is given below:

	Investment Proposal			
	A	B	C	D
Investment required	$(90,000)	$(100,000)	$(70,000)	$(120,000)
Present value of cash inflows	126,000	138,000	105,000	160,000
Net present value	$ 36,000	$ 38,000	$ 35,000	$ 40,000
Life of the project	5 years	7 years	6 years	6 years

Required:
1. Compute the profitability index for each investment proposal.
2. Rank the proposals in terms of preference.

EXERCISE 14–6 Simple Rate of Return Method LO14–6

Ballard MicroBrew is considering the purchase of an automated bottling machine for $120,000. The machine would replace an old piece of equipment that costs $30,000 per year to operate. The new machine would cost $12,000 per year to operate. The old machine currently in use is fully depreciated and could be sold now for a salvage value of $40,000. The new machine would have a useful life of 10 years with no salvage value.

Required:
1. What is the annual depreciation expense associated with the new bottling machine?
2. What is the annual incremental net operating income provided by the new bottling machine?
3. What is the initial investment used for calculating the machine's simple rate of return?
4. What is the simple rate of return on the new bottling machine?

EXERCISE 14–7 Net Present Value Analysis of Two Alternatives LO14–2
Perit Industries has $100,000 to invest in one of the following two projects:

	Project A	Project B
Cost of equipment required	$100,000	$0
Working capital investment required	$0	$100,000
Annual cash inflows	$21,000	$16,000
Salvage value of equipment in six years	$8,000	$0
Life of the project	6 years	6 years

The working capital needed for Project B will be released at the end of six years for investment elsewhere. Perit Industries' discount rate is 14%.

Required:
1. Compute the net present value of Project A.
2. Compute the net present value of Project B.
3. Which investment alternative (if either) would you recommend that the company accept?

EXERCISE 14–8 Payback Period and Simple Rate of Return LO14–1, LO14–6
Nick's Novelties, Inc., is considering the purchase of new electronic games to place in its amusement houses. The games would cost a total of $300,000, have an eight-year useful life, and have a total salvage value of $20,000. The company estimates annual revenues and expenses associated with the games as follows:

Revenues		$200,000
Less operating expenses:		
Commissions to amusement houses	$100,000	
Insurance	7,000	
Depreciation	35,000	
Maintenance	18,000	160,000
Net operating income		$ 40,000

Required:
1. What is the payback period for the new electronic games? Assume Nick's Novelties, Inc., will not purchase new games unless they provide a payback period of five years or less. Would the company purchase the new games?
2. What is the simple rate of return promised by the games? If the company requires a simple rate of return of at least 12%, will the games be purchased?

EXERCISE 14–9 Net Present Value Analysis and Simple Rate of Return LO14–2, LO14–6
Derrick Iverson is a divisional manager for Holston Company. His annual pay raises are largely determined by his division's return on investment (ROI), which has been above 20% each of the last three years. Derrick is considering a capital budgeting project requiring a $3,000,000 investment in equipment with a useful life of five years and no salvage value. Holston Company's discount rate is 15%. The project would provide net operating income each year for five years as follows:

Sales		$2,500,000
Variable expenses		1,000,000
Contribution margin		1,500,000
Fixed expenses:		
Advertising, salaries, and other fixed		
out-of-pocket costs	$600,000	
Depreciation	600,000	
Total fixed expenses		1,200,000
Net operating income		$ 300,000

Required:
1. Compute the project's net present value.
2. Compute the project's simple rate of return.
3. Would the company want Derrick to pursue this investment opportunity? Would Derrick be inclined to pursue this investment opportunity? Explain.

EXERCISE 14–10 Net Present Value Analysis LO14–2

Kathy Myers frequently purchases stocks and bonds, but she is uncertain how to determine the rate of return she is earning. For example, three years ago she paid $13,000 for 200 shares of Malti Company's common stock. She received a $420 cash dividend on the stock at the end of each year for three years. At the end of three years, she sold the stock for $16,000. Kathy would like to earn a return of at least 14% on all of her investments. She is not sure whether the Malti Company stock provides a 14% return and would like some help with the necessary computations.

Required:
1. Compute the net present value Kathy earned on her investment in Malti Company stock.
2. Did the Malti Company stock provide a 14% return?

EXERCISE 14–11 Preference Ranking of Investment Projects LO14–5

Oxford Company has limited funds available for investment and must ration the funds among the four competing projects shown below:

Project	Investment Required	Present Value of Cash Inflows	Life of the Project (years)	Internal Rate of Return
A	$160,000	$204,323	7	18%
B	$135,000	$177,000	12	16%
C	$100,000	$135,035	7	20%
D	$175,000	$213,136	3	22%

The net present values above have been computed using a 10% discount rate.

Required:
1. Compute the profitability index for each project.
2. In order of preference, rank the four projects in terms of:
    a. Net present value.
    b. Profitability index.
    c. Internal rate of return.
3. Which ranking do you prefer? Why?

EXERCISE 14–12 Uncertain Cash Flows LO14–4

The Cambro Foundation, a nonprofit organization, is planning to invest $104,950 in a project that will last for three years. The project will produce net cash inflows as follows:

Year 1	$30,000
Year 2	$40,000
Year 3	?

Required:
Assuming the project will yield exactly a 12% rate of return, what is the expected net cash inflow for Year 3?

EXERCISE 14–13 Payback Period and Simple Rate of Return Computations LO14–1, LO14–6

Mitsui Electronics, Ltd., is considering buying a labor-saving pierce of equipment and provided the following data:

Purchase cost of the equipment	$432,000
Annual cost savings that will be provided by the equipment	$90,000
Life of the equipment	12 years

Required:

1. What is the payback period for the equipment? If the company requires a payback period of four years or less, would it buy the equipment?
2. What is the simple rate of return on the equipment? Use straight-line depreciation based on the equipment's useful life. Would the company buy the equipment if its required rate of return is 14%?

EXERCISE 14–14 Comparison of Projects Using Net Present Value LO14–2

Labeau Products, Ltd., of Perth, Australia, has $35,000 to invest in one of the following two projects:

	Project X	Project Y
Investment required	$35,000	$35,000
Annual cash inflows	$12,000	
Single cash inflow at the end of 6 years		$90,000
Life of the project	6 years	6 years

The company's discount rate is 18%.

Required:

1. Compute the net present value of Project X.
2. Compute the net present value of Project Y.
3. Which project should the company accept?

EXERCISE 14–15 Internal Rate of Return and Net Present Value LO14–2, LO14–3

Henrie's Drapery Service is investigating the purchase of a new machine for cleaning and blocking drapes. The machine would cost $137,320, including freight and installation. Henrie's estimated the new machine would increase the company's cash inflows, net of expenses, by $40,000 per year. The machine would have a five-year useful life and no salvage value.

Required:

1. What is the machine's internal rate of return to the nearest whole percent?
2. Using a discount rate of 14%, what is the machine's net present value? Interpret your results.
3. Suppose the new machine would increase the company's annual cash inflows, net of expenses, by only $37,150 per year. Under these conditions, what is the internal rate of return to the nearest whole percent?

 Problems

PROBLEM 14–16 Net Present Value Analysis LO14–2

Windhoek Mines, Ltd., of Namibia, is contemplating the purchase of equipment to exploit a mineral deposit on land to which the company has mineral rights. The company estimated the following cash flows related to opening and operating a mine in the area:

Cost of new equipment and timbers	$275,000
Working capital required	$100,000
Annual net cash receipts	$120,000*
Cost to construct new roads in three years	$40,000
Salvage value of equipment in four years	$65,000

*Receipts from sales of ore, less out-of-pocket costs for salaries, utilities, insurance, and so forth.

The mineral deposit would be exhausted after four years of mining. At that point, the working capital would be released for reinvestment elsewhere. The company's required rate of return is 20%.

Required:

What is the net present value of the proposed mining project? Should the project be accepted? Explain.

PROBLEM 14–17 Net Present Value Analysis; Internal Rate of Return; Simple Rate of Return LO14–2, LO14–3, LO14–6

Casey Nelson is a divisional manager for Pigeon Company. His annual pay raises are largely determined by his division's return on investment (ROI), which has been above 20% each of the last three years. Casey is considering a capital budgeting project requiring a $3,500,000 investment in equipment with a useful life of five years and no salvage value. Pigeon Company's discount rate is 16%. The project would provide net operating income each year for five years as follows:

Sales		$3,400,000
Variable expenses		1,600,000
Contribution margin		1,800,000
Fixed expenses:		
Advertising, salaries, and other fixed		
out-of-pocket costs	$700,000	
Depreciation	700,000	
Total fixed expenses		1,400,000
Net operating income		$ 400,000

Required:

1. What is the project's net present value?
2. What is the project's internal rate of return to the nearest whole percent?
3. What is the project's simple rate of return?
4. Would the company want Casey to pursue this investment opportunity? Would Casey be inclined to pursue this investment opportunity? Explain.

PROBLEM 14–18 Net Present Value Analysis LO14–2

Oakmont Company has an opportunity to manufacture and sell a new product for a four-year period. The company's discount rate is 15% and it estimated the following costs and revenues for the new product:

Cost of equipment needed	$130,000
Working capital needed	$60,000
Overhaul of the equipment in two years	$8,000
Salvage value of the equipment in four years	$12,000
Annual revenues and costs:	
Sales revenues	$250,000
Variable expenses	$120,000
Fixed out-of-pocket operating costs	$70,000

When the project concludes in four years, the working capital will be released for investment elsewhere within the company.

Required:

Calculate the net present value of this investment opportunity.

PROBLEM 14–19 Simple Rate of Return; Payback Period LO14–1, LO14–6

Paul Swanson has an opportunity to acquire a franchise from The Yogurt Place, Inc., to dispense frozen yogurt products under The Yogurt Place name. He assembled the following information relating to the franchise:

a. A suitable location in a large shopping mall can be rented for $3,500 per month.
b. Remodeling and necessary equipment would cost $270,000. The equipment would have a 15-year life and an $18,000 salvage value. Straight-line depreciation would be used, and the salvage value would be considered in computing depreciation.
c. Based on similar outlets elsewhere, Mr. Swanson estimates sales would total $300,000 per year. Ingredients would cost 20% of sales.

d. Annual operating costs would include $70,000 for salaries, $3,500 for insurance, $27,000 for utilities, and a commission paid to The Yogurt Place, Inc., of 12.5% of sales.

Required:

1. Prepare a contribution format income statement showing the expected net operating income each year from the franchise.
2. Compute the simple rate of return promised by the franchise. If Mr. Swanson requires a simple rate of return of at least 12%, should he acquire the franchise?
3. Compute the payback period on this investment. If Mr. Swanson wants a payback of four years or less, will he acquire the franchise?

PROBLEM 14–20 Net Present Value Analysis; Uncertain Cash Flows LO14–2, LO14–4

"I'm not sure we should lay out $250,000 for that automated welding machine," said Jim Alder, president of the Superior Equipment Company. "It would cost us $80,000 for software and installation, and another $36,000 per year just to maintain. In addition, the manufacturer admits it would cost $45,000 more at the end of three years to replace worn-out parts."

"I admit it's a lot of money," said Franci Rogers, the controller. "But you know the turnover problem we've had with the welding crew. This machine would replace six welders at a cost savings of $108,000 per year. And we would save another $6,500 per year in reduced material waste. When you figure the automated welder would last six years, I'm sure the return would be greater than our 16% required rate of return."

"I'm still not convinced," countered Mr. Alder. "We can only get $12,000 scrap value for our old welding equipment if we sell it now, and in six years the new machine will only be worth $20,000 for parts."

Required:

1. Compute the annual net cost savings promised by the automated welding machine.
2. Using the data from (1) above and other data from the problem, compute the automated welding machine's net present value. Would you recommend purchasing the automated welding machine? Explain.
3. Assume management can identify several intangible benefits associated with the automated welding machine, including greater flexibility in shifting from one type of product to another, improved quality of output, and faster delivery as a result of reduced throughput time. What minimum dollar value per year would management have to attach to these intangible benefits to make the new welding machine an acceptable investment?

PROBLEM 14–21 Preference Ranking of Investment Projects LO14–5

Revco Products is exploring the following four investment opportunities:

	Project Number			
	1	2	3	4
Investment required	$(270,000)	$(450,000)	$(360,000)	$(480,000)
Present value of cash inflows	336,140	522,970	433,400	567,270
Net present value	$ 66,140	$ 72,970	$ 73,400	$ 87,270
Life of the project	6 years	3 years	12 years	6 years
Internal rate of return	18%	19%	14%	16%

The net present values above have been computed using a 10% discount rate. Limited funds are available for investment, so the company can't accept all of the available projects.

Required:

1. Compute the profitability index for each investment project.
2. Rank the four projects according to preference, in terms of:
   a. Net present value
   b. Profitability index
   c. Internal rate of return
3. Which ranking do you prefer? Why?

PROBLEM 14–22 Net Present Value Analysis LO14–2

The Sweetwater Candy Company would like to buy a new machine for $120,000 that automatically "dips" chocolates. The manufacturer estimates the machine would be usable for five years but would require replacement of several key parts costing $9,000 at the end of the third year. After five years, the machine could be sold for $7,500.

    The company estimates the cost to operate the machine will be $7,000 per year. The present labor-intensive method of dipping chocolates costs $30,000 per year. In addition to reducing costs, the new machine will increase production by 6,000 boxes of chocolates per year. The company realizes a contribution margin of $1.50 per box. A 20% rate of return is required on all investments.

Required:

1. What are the annual net cash inflows provided by the new dipping machine?
2. Compute the new machine's net present value.

PROBLEM 14–23 Comprehensive Problem LO14–1, LO14–2, LO14–3, LO14–5, LO14–6

Lou Barlow, a divisional manager for Sage Company, has an opportunity to manufacture and sell one of two new products for a five-year period. His annual pay raises are determined by his division's return on investment (ROI), which has exceeded 18% each of the last three years. He computed the following cost and revenue estimates for each product:

	Product A	Product B
Initial investment:		
Cost of equipment (zero salvage value)	$170,000	$380,000
Annual revenues and costs:		
Sales revenues	$250,000	$350,000
Variable expenses	$120,000	$170,000
Depreciation expense	$34,000	$76,000
Fixed out-of-pocket operating costs	$70,000	$50,000

The company's discount rate is 16%.

Required:

1. Calculate each product's payback period.
2. Calculate each product's net present value.
3. Calculate each product's internal rate of return.
4. Calculate each product's profitability index.
5. Calculate each product's simple rate of return.
6. Which of the two products should Lou's division pursue? Why?

PROBLEM 14–24 Simple Rate of Return; Payback Period; Internal Rate of Return LO14–1, LO14–3, LO14–6

The Elberta Fruit Farm of Ontario is considering buying a cherry-picking machine to replace the part-time workers it usually hires to harvest its annual cherry crop. The machine shakes the cherry tree, causing the cherries to fall onto plastic tarps that funnel the cherries into bins. The company gathered the following information:

a. The farm pays part-time workers $40,000 per year to pick the cherries.
b. The cherry picker would cost $94,500, have a 12-year useful life with no salvage value, and be depreciated using the straight-line method.
c. The cherry picker's annual out-of-pocket costs would be the cost of an operator and an assistant, $14,000; insurance, $200; fuel, $1,800; and a maintenance contract, $3,000.

Required:

1. Calculate the annual savings in cash operating costs provided by the cherry picker.
2. Compute the cherry picker's simple rate of return. Would Elberta Fruit Farm buy the cherry picker if its required rate of return is 16%?

3. Compute the cherry picker's payback period. Would Elberta Fruit Farm purchase the cherry picker if it requires a payback period of five years or less?
4. Compute the cherry picker's internal rate of return (to the nearest whole percent). Does it appear the simple rate of return is an accurate guide in investment decisions?

PROBLEM 14–25 Net Present Value Analysis of a Lease or Buy Decision LO14–2

The Riteway Ad Agency provides cars for its sales staff. Its present fleet of cars is three years old and will be sold very shortly. To provide a replacement fleet, the company is considering two alternatives:

Purchase alternative: The company can purchase the cars and sell them in three years. Ten cars would be purchased for $17,000 each. If this alternative is chosen, the entire fleet will incur the following costs:

Annual cost of servicing, taxes, and licensing	$3,000
Repairs, first year	$1,500
Repairs, second year	$4,000
Repairs, third year	$6,000

At the end of three years, the fleet could be sold for one-half of the original purchase price.

Lease alternative: The company can lease the cars under a three-year lease contract costing $55,000 per year (the first payment due at the end of Year 1). As part of this lease agreement, the owner would provide all servicing and repairs, license the cars, and pay the taxes. Riteway would make a $10,000 security deposit at the beginning of the lease period, which would be refunded at the end of the lease contract.

Riteway Ad Agency's required rate of return is 18%.

Required:
1. What is the purchase alternative's net present value?
2. What is the lease alternative's net present value?
3. Which alternative should the company accept?

PROBLEM 14–26 Simple Rate of Return; Payback LO14–1, LO14–6

Sharkey's Fun Center is considering building a water slide for its customers and gathered the following information:
a. The water slide would cost $330,000, have a 12-year useful life with no salvage value and be depreciated using the straight-line method.
b. To make room for the water slide, several rides would be dismantled and sold. These rides are fully depreciated, but they could be sold for $60,000 to a nearby amusement park.
c. The water slide would attract 50,000 more customers per year who each pay the company's usual admission price of $3.60 per person.
d. The water slides' annual incremental operating expenses would be salaries, $85,000; insurance, $4,200; utilities, $13,000; and maintenance, $9,800.

Required:
1. Prepare an income statement showing the water slides' expected annual net operating income.
2. Compute the water slides' simple rate of return. Would the company purchase the water slide if it requires a simple rate of return of at least 14%?
3. Compute the water slides' payback period. Would the company purchase the water slide if it requires a payback period of five years or less?

PROBLEM 14–27 Net Present Value Analysis LO14–2

Kent Duncan is exploring the possibility of opening a self-service car wash and operating it for the next five years until he retires. He has gathered the following information:
a. A building for the car wash is available under a five-year lease for $1,700 per month.
b. The car wash equipment costs $200,000 and could be sold in five years for 10% of its original cost.

c. The car wash requires a working capital investment of $2,000 for cleaning supplies, change funds, and so forth. After five years, this working capital would be released for investment elsewhere.

d. Each customer would pay $2.00 for a wash and $1.00 for access to a vacuum cleaner.

e. The only variable costs are 20 cents per wash (for water) and 10 cents per use of the vacuum (for electricity).

f. Additional monthly operating costs include cleaning, $450; insurance, $75; and maintenance, $500.

g. Gross receipts from the wash would be $1,350 per week and 60% of the customers using the wash would also use the vacuum.

Mr. Duncan will not open the car wash unless it provides at least a 10% return.

Required:

1. Assuming the car wash will be open 52 weeks a year, compute the expected annual net cash inflows (gross cash receipts less cash disbursements) from its operation. (Do not include the cost of the equipment, the working capital, or the salvage value in these computations.)

2. What is the net present value of the investment in the car wash? Should Mr. Duncan open the car wash?

PROBLEM 14–28 Net Present Value Analysis LO14–2

Bilboa Freightlines, S.A., of Panama, uses a truck for intracity deliveries that has worn out and must be overhauled or replaced. The company assembled the following information:

	Present Truck	New Truck
Purchase cost (new)	$21,000	$30,000
Remaining book value	$11,500	
Overhaul needed now	$7,000	
Annual cash operating costs	$10,000	$6,500
Salvage value–now	$9,000	
Salvage value–five years from now	$1,000	$4,000

If the company overhauls its present delivery truck, then it will be usable for five more years. If a new truck is purchased, it will be used for five years and then traded in for another truck. The new truck would be diesel-operated, resulting in lower annual operating costs, as shown above.

The company computes depreciation on a straight-line basis and uses a 16% discount rate.

Required:

1. What is the net present value of the "keep the old truck" alternative?

2. What is the net present value of the "purchase the new truck" alternative?

3. Should Bilboa Freightlines keep the old truck or purchase the new one?

PROBLEM 14–29 Net Present Value Analysis LO14–2

Linda Clark received $175,000 from her mother's estate. She placed the funds into the hands of a broker, who purchased the following securities on Linda's behalf:

a. Common stock was purchased at a cost of $95,000. The stock paid no dividends and was sold for $160,000 at the end of three years.

b. Preferred stock was purchased at its par value of $30,000. The stock paid a 6% dividend (based on par value) each year for three years. At the end of three years, the stock was sold for $27,000.

c. Bonds were purchased at a cost of $50,000. The bonds paid annual interest of $6,000. After three years, the bonds were sold for $52,700.

The securities were all sold at the end of three years so that Linda would have funds available to open a new business venture. The broker said the investments earned more than a 16% return, and he gave Linda the following computations to support his statement:

Common stock:	
Gain on sale ($160,000 – $95,000)	$65,000
Preferred stock:	
Dividends paid (6% × $30,000 × 3 years)	5,400
Loss on sale ($27,000 – $30,000)	(3,000)
Bonds:	
Interest paid ($6,000 × 3 years)	18,000
Gain on sale ($52,700 – $50,000)	2,700
Net gain on all investments	$88,100

$$\frac{\$88,100 \div 3 \text{ years}}{\$175,000} = 16.8\%$$

Required:

1. Using a 16% discount rate, compute the net present value of each of the three investments. On which investment(s) did Linda earn a 16% rate of return?
2. Considering all three investments together, did Linda earn a 16% rate of return? Explain.
3. Linda wants to use the $239,700 proceeds ($160,000 + $27,000 + $52,700 = $239,700) from sale of the securities to open a retail store under a 12-year franchise contract. What minimum annual net cash inflow must the store generate for Linda to earn a 14% return over the 12-year period?

PROBLEM 14–30 Net Present Value Analysis; Uncertain Future Cash Flows; Postaudit LO14–2, LO14–4

Saxon Products, Inc., is investigating the purchase of a robot for use on its assembly line. Selected data relating to the robot are provided below:

Cost of the robot	$1,600,000
Installation and software	$450,000
Annual savings in inventory carrying costs	$210,000
Annual increase in power and maintenance costs	$30,000
Salvage value in 5 years	$70,000
Useful life	5 years

Using the robot will save 25,000 direct labor-hours each year. The labor rate is $16 per hour. Also, the automated work flow will reduce inventories by $400,000. This inventory reduction will take place at the end of the first year of operation; the released funds will be available for use elsewhere in the company. Saxon Products has a 20% required rate of return.

Required:

1. Determine the *annual net* cost savings if the robot is purchased. (Do not include the $400,000 inventory reduction or the salvage value in this computation.)
2. Compute the net present value of the proposed investment in the robot. Should the robot be purchased? Explain.
3. Assume the robot is purchased. However, due to unforeseen problems, software and installation costs were $75,000 more than estimated and direct labor could only be reduced by 22,500 hours per year, rather than the original estimate of 25,000 hours. Assuming all other cost data are accurate, what would a postaudit suggest is the actual net present value of this investment? Did the company make a wise investment?
4. Upon seeing your analysis in (3) above, Saxon's president stated, "That robot is the worst investment we've ever made. And now we'll be stuck with it for years."
   a. Explain to the president what benefits other than cost savings might accrue from using the new automated equipment.
   b. Compute the minimum dollar amount of annual cash inflow that would be needed from the benefits in (a) above for the automated equipment to yield a 20% rate of return.

Cases  connect

Select cases are available in Connect.

CASE 14–31 Ethics and the Manager

Fore Corporation's executives frequently use the company's airplanes to visit its domestic facilities and 24 international facilities. The company owns two business jets with international range and six smaller turboprop aircraft for shorter flights. When these airplanes are idle, the company generates extra revenue by allowing other organizations to charter them. While company policy requires assigning the aircraft to trips in a manner that minimizes cost, the executives have been ignoring this policy and booking planes based on organizational rank.

William Earle, Fore's vice president of finance, wants the company to buy a a third business jet. The people outranking Earle keep the two business jets busy, causing him to fly in the smaller turboprop aircraft. The cost of the jet is $11 million and its purchase would require the board of directors' approval.

Earle asked Rachel Arnett, assistant corporate controller, to analyze this investment opportunity, so she gathered the following data:

- Acquisition cost of the aircraft.
- Operating cost of the aircraft.
- Projected avoidable commercial airfare and other avoidable costs from company use of the plane.
- Projected value of executive time saved by using the third business jet.
- Projected contribution margin from incremental charter activity.
- Estimated resale value of the aircraft.

When Earle reviewed Arnett's completed proposal and saw the large negative net present value, he returned the proposal to her. With a glare, Earle commented, "You must have made an error. The proposal should look better than that."

Feeling some pressure, Arnett went back and checked her computations; she found no errors. However, Earle's message was clear. Arnett discarded her projections and replaced them with figures more favorable to the proposal but less realistic. For example, she used first-class airfares to refigure the avoidable commercial airfare costs, even though company policy requires flying coach. She found revising the proposal to be distressing.

The revised proposal still had a negative net present value. Earle's anger was evident as he told Arnett to revise the proposal again, starting with a $100,000 positive net present value and working backwards to compute supporting projections.

Required:

1. Explain whether Rachel Arnett's revision of the proposal was in violation of the IMA's Statement of Ethical Professional Practice.
2. Was William Earle in violation of the IMA's Statement of Ethical Professional Practice by telling Arnett specifically how to revise the proposal? Explain your answer.
3. Identify specific internal controls Fore Corporation could implement to prevent unethical behavior on the part of the vice president of finance.

(CMA, adapted)

CASE 14–32 Net Present Value Analysis of a New Product LO14–2

Matheson Electronics developed a new electronic device it believes will have broad market appeal. The company gathered the following estimates:

a. The equipment needed to make the device would cost $315,000 and have a six-year useful life with a salvage value of $15,000.
b. Sales in units over the next six years are projected to be as follows:

Year	Sales in Units
1	9,000
2	15,000
3	18,000
4–6	22,000

c. Production and sales of the device would require working capital of $60,000 to be released at the end of the project's life.
d. The device would sell for $35 each with a variable cost of $15 per unit.
e. Fixed costs for salaries, maintenance, property taxes, insurance, and straight-line depreciation on the equipment would total $135,000 per year. (Depreciation is based on cost less salvage value.)
f. To gain rapid entry into the market, the company would invest heavily in advertising as follows:

Year	Amount of Yearly Advertising
1–2	$180,000
3	$150,000
4–6	$120,000

g. The company's required rate of return is 14%.

Required:

1. Compute the device's estimated net cash inflow (incremental contribution margin minus incremental fixed expenses) for each year over the next six years.
2. Calculate the net present value of the proposed investment. Should Matheson invest in the new device?

Appendix 14A: The Concept of Present Value

A dollar received today is more valuable than a dollar received a year from now because if you have a dollar today, you can put it in the bank and have more than a dollar a year from now. Because dollars today are worth more than dollars in the future, cash flows received at different times must be valued differently.

LO14–7
Understand present value concepts and the use of present value tables.

The Mathematics of Interest

If a bank pays 5% interest, then a deposit of $100 today will be worth $105 one year from now. This can be expressed as follows:

$$F_1 = P(1 + r) \qquad (1)$$

where F_1 = the balance at the end of one period, P = the amount invested now, and r = the rate of interest per period.

In the case where $100 is deposited in a savings account that earns 5% interest, $P = \$100$ and $r = 0.05$. Under these conditions, $F_1 = \$105$.

The $100 present outlay is called the **present value** of the $105 amount to be received in one year. It is also known as the *discounted value* of the future $105 receipt. The $100 represents the value in present terms of $105 received a year from now when the interest rate is 5%.

Compound Interest   What if the $105 is left in the bank for a second year? In that case, by the end of the second year the original $100 deposit will have grown to $110.25:

Original deposit	$100.00
Interest for the first year: $100 × 0.05	5.00
Balance at the end of the first year	105.00
Interest for the second year: $105 × 0.05	5.25
Balance at the end of the second year	$110.25

Notice the interest for the second year is $5.25, compared to only $5.00 for the first year. This difference arises because interest is being paid on interest during the second year. That is, the $5.00 interest earned during the first year has been left in the account and added to the original $100 deposit when computing interest for the second year. This is known as **compound interest.** In this case, the compounding is annual. Interest can be compounded on a semiannual, quarterly, monthly, or even more frequent basis. The more frequently compounding is done, the more rapidly the balance will grow.

We can determine the balance in an account after n periods of compounding using the following equation:

$$F_n = P(1 + r)^n \qquad\qquad (2)$$

where n = the number of periods of compounding.

If $n = 2$ years and the interest rate is 5% per year, then the balance in two years is computed as follows:

$$F_2 = \$100\,(1 + 0.05)^2$$
$$F_2 = \$110.25$$

Present Value and Future Value   Exhibit 14A–1 shows the relationship between present value and future value. As shown in the exhibit, if $100 is deposited in a bank at 5% interest compounded annually, it will grow to $127.63 by the end of five years.

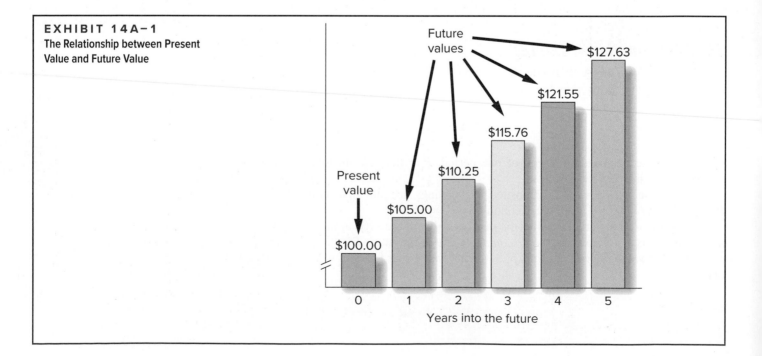

EXHIBIT 14A–1
The Relationship between Present Value and Future Value

Computation of Present Value

An investment can be viewed in two ways—in terms of its future value or its present value. We have seen from our computations above if we know the present value of a sum (such as our $100 deposit), the future value in n years can be computed by using equation (2). But what if the situation is reversed and we know the *future* value of some amount but we do not know its present value?

For example, assume you are to receive $200 two years from now but want to know its present value—what is it worth *right now?* The present value of any sum to be received in the future can be computed by turning equation (2) around and solving for P:

$$P = \frac{F_n}{(1 + r)^n} \tag{3}$$

In our example, $F_n = \$200$ (the amount to be received in the future), $r = 0.05$ (the annual rate of interest), and $n = 2$ (the number of years in the future that the amount will be received).

$$P = \frac{\$200}{(1 + 0.05)^2}$$

$$P = \frac{\$200}{1.1025}$$

$$P = \$181.40$$

The present value of $200 received two years from now is $181.40 if the interest rate is 5%. In effect, $181.40 received *right now* is equivalent to $200 received two years from now.

The process of finding the present value of a future cash flow is called **discounting.** We have *discounted* $200 to its present value of $181.40. The 5% interest used to compute the present value is called the **discount rate.**

Exhibit 14B–1 in Appendix 14B shows the discounted present value of $1 to be received at various periods in the future at various interest rates. The table indicates the present value of $1 to be received two periods from now at 5% is 0.907. Because in our example we want to know the present value of $200 rather than just $1, we need to multiply the factor in the table by $200:

$$\$200 \times 0.907 = \$181.40$$

This answer is the same as we obtained earlier using the formula in equation (3).

Present Value of a Series of Cash Flows

Although some investments involve a single sum to be received (or paid) at a single point in the future, other investments involve a *series* of cash flows. A series of identical cash flows is known as an **annuity.** To provide an example, assume a company purchased some government bonds that yield interest of $15,000 each year for five years. What is the present value of the stream of interest receipts from the bonds? As shown in Exhibit 14A–2, if the discount rate is 12%, the present value of this stream is $54,075. The discount factors used in this exhibit were taken from Exhibit 14B–1 in Appendix 14B.

Exhibit 14A–2 illustrates two important points. First, the present value of the $15,000 interest declines the further it is into the future. The present value of $15,000 received a year from now is $13,395, but only $8,505 if received five years from now. This point underscores the time value of money.

The second point is that the computations used in Exhibit 14A–2 involved unnecessary work. The same present value of $54,075 can be obtained more easily by referring to Exhibit 14B–2 in Appendix 14B. Exhibit 14B–2 contains the present value of $1 to be

EXHIBIT 14A-2
Present Value of a Series of Cash Receipts

Year	Factor at 12% (Exhibit 14B-1)	Interest Received	Present Value
1	0.893	$15,000	$13,395
2	0.797	$15,000	11,955
3	0.712	$15,000	10,680
4	0.636	$15,000	9,540
5	0.567	$15,000	8,505
			$54,075

received each year over a *series* of years at various interest rates. Exhibit 14B–2 has been derived by simply adding together the factors from Exhibit 14B–1, as follows:

Year	Factors at 12% (from Exhibit 14B-1)
1	0.893
2	0.797
3	0.712
4	0.636
5	0.567
	3.605

The sum of these five factors is 3.605. Notice from Exhibit 14B–2 the factor for $1 to be received each year for five years at 12% is also 3.605. If we use this factor and multiply it by the $15,000 annual cash inflow, we get the same $54,075 present value obtained earlier in Exhibit 14A–2.

$$\$15,000 \times 3.605 = \$54,075$$

Therefore, when computing the present value of a series of equal cash flows that begins at the end of period 1, Exhibit 14B–2 should be used.

To summarize, the present value tables in Appendix 14B should be used as follows:

Exhibit 14B–1: This table should be used to find the present value of a single cash flow (such as a single payment or receipt) occurring in the future.

Exhibit 14B–2: This table should be used to find the present value of a series of identical cash flows beginning at the end of the current period and continuing into the future.

The use of both of these tables is illustrated in various exhibits in the main body of the chapter. *When a present value factor appears in an exhibit, you should take the time to trace it back into either Exhibit 14B–1 or Exhibit 14B–2.*

Appendix 14A: Review Problem: Basic Present Value Computations Mc Graw Hill connect·

Consider each situation independently.

1. John plans to retire in 12 years. Upon retiring, he would like to take an extended vacation, which he expects will cost at least $40,000. What lump-sum amount must he invest now to have $40,000 at the end of 12 years if the rate of return is:
   a. Eight percent?
   b. Twelve percent?

2. The Morgans would like to send their daughter to a music camp at the end of each of the next five years. The camp costs $1,000 a year. What lump-sum amount would they have to invest now to have $1,000 at the end of each year if the rate of return is:
   a. Eight percent?
   b. Twelve percent?
3. You just received an inheritance from a relative. You can either receive a $200,000 lump-sum amount at the end of 10 years or receive $14,000 at the end of each year for the next 10 years. If your discount rate is 12%, which alternative would you prefer?

Solution to Review Problem

1. a. The amount that must be invested now would be the present value of the $40,000, using a discount rate of 8%. From Exhibit 14B–1 in Appendix 14B, the factor for a discount rate of 8% for 12 periods is 0.397. Multiplying this discount factor by the $40,000 needed in 12 years will give the amount of the present investment required: $40,000 × 0.397 = $15,880.
   b. We will proceed as we did in (a) above, but this time we will use a discount rate of 12%. From Exhibit 14B–1 in Appendix 14B, the factor for a discount rate of 12% for 12 periods is 0.257. Multiplying this discount factor by the $40,000 needed in 12 years will give the amount of the present investment required: $40,000 × 0.257 = $10,280.

   Notice that as the discount rate (desired rate of return) increases, the present value decreases.

2. This part differs from (1) above in that we are now dealing with an annuity rather than with a single future sum. The amount that must be invested now is the present value of the $1,000 needed at the end of each year for five years. Because we are dealing with an annuity, or a series of annual cash flows, we must refer to Exhibit 14B–2 in Appendix 14B for the appropriate discount factor.
   a. From Exhibit 14B–2 in Appendix 14B, the discount factor for 8% for five periods is 3.993. Therefore, the amount that must be invested now to have $1,000 available at the end of each year for five years is $1,000 × 3.993 = $3,993.
   b. From Exhibit 14B–2 in Appendix 14B, the discount factor for 12% for five periods is 3.605. Therefore, the amount that must be invested now to have $1,000 available at the end of each year for five years is $1,000 × 3.605 = $3,605.

   Again, notice that as the discount rate increases, the present value decreases. When the rate of return increases, less must be invested today to yield a given amount in the future.

3. For this part we will need to refer to both Exhibits 14B–1 and 14B–2 in Appendix 14B. From Exhibit 14B–1, we will need to find the discount factor for 12% for 10 periods, then apply it to the $200,000 lump sum to be received in 10 years. From Exhibit 14B–2, we will need to find the discount factor for 12% for 10 periods, then apply it to the series of $14,000 payments to be received over the 10-year period. Whichever alternative has the higher present value is the one that should be selected.

$$\$200,000 \times 0.322 = \$64,400$$
$$\$14,000 \times 5.650 = \$79,100$$

Thus, you should prefer to receive the $14,000 per year for 10 years rather than the $200,000 lump sum. This means that you could invest the $14,000 received at the end of each year at 12% and have *more* than $200,000 at the end of 10 years.

Glossary (Appendix 14A)

Annuity A series of identical cash flows. (p. 671)
Compound interest The process of paying interest on interest in an investment. (p. 670)
Discount rate The rate of return used to find the present value of a future cash flow. (p. 671)
Discounting The process of finding the present value of a future cash flow. (p. 671)
Present value The value now of an amount to be received in some future period. (p. 636)

Appendix 14A: Exercises   Mc Graw Hill connect

EXERCISE 14A–1 Basic Present Value Concepts LO14–7

Annual cash inflows from two competing investment projects are given below:

Year	Investment A	Investment B
1	$ 3,000	$12,000
2	6,000	9,000
3	9,000	6,000
4	12,000	3,000
	$30,000	$30,000

The discount rate is 18%.

Required:

Compute the present value of the cash inflows for each investment.

EXERCISE 14A–2 Basic Present Value Concepts LO14–7

Julie just retired and has two options for receiving her retirement benefits. Under the first option, she would immediately receive a lump sum of $150,000. Under the second option, she would receive $14,000 each year for 20 years plus a lump-sum payment of $60,000 at the end of the 20-year period.

Required:

If she can invest money at 12%, which option should she choose?

EXERCISE 14A–3 Basic Present Value Concepts LO14–7

In three years, when he is discharged from the Air Force, Steve wants to buy an $8,000 power boat.

Required:

What lump-sum amount must Steve invest now to have $8,000 at the end of three years if he can invest money at:
1. Ten percent?
2. Fourteen percent?

EXERCISE 14A–4 Basic Present Value Concepts LO14–7

Fraser Company will need a new $500,000 warehouse in five years.

Required:

What lump-sum amount should the company invest now to have $500,000 available at the end of five years period? Assume the company can invest money at:
1. Ten percent.
2. Fourteen percent.

EXERCISE 14A–5 Basic Present Value Concepts LO14–7

The Atlantic Medical Clinic can purchase a new computer system that will save $7,000 annually in billing costs. The computer system will last for eight years and have no salvage value.

Required:

What is the maximum price (i.e., the price that exactly equals the present value of the annual savings in billing costs) Atlantic Medical Clinic should be willing to pay for the new computer system if the clinic's required rate of return is:
1. Sixteen percent?
2. Twenty percent?

EXERCISE 14A–6 Basic Present Value Concepts LO14–7

The *Caldwell Herald* newspaper reported the following story: Frank Ormsby of Caldwell is the state's newest millionaire. By choosing the six winning numbers on last week's state lottery, Mr. Ormsby won the week's grand prize totaling $1.6 million. The State Lottery Commission indicated Mr. Ormsby would receive his prize in 20 annual installments of $80,000 each.

Required:

1. If Mr. Ormsby can invest money at a 12% rate of return, what is the present value of his winnings?
2. Is it correct to say that Mr. Ormsby is the "state's newest millionaire"? Explain your answer.

EXHIBIT 14B-1

Present Value of $1; $\frac{1}{(1+r)^n}$

Periods	4%	5%	6%	7%	8%	9%	10%	11%	12%	13%	14%	15%	16%	17%	18%	19%	20%	21%	22%	23%	24%	25%
1	0.962	0.952	0.943	0.935	0.926	0.917	0.909	0.901	0.893	0.885	0.877	0.870	0.862	0.855	0.847	0.840	0.833	0.826	0.820	0.813	0.806	0.800
2	0.925	0.907	0.890	0.873	0.857	0.842	0.826	0.812	0.797	0.783	0.769	0.756	0.743	0.731	0.718	0.706	0.694	0.683	0.672	0.661	0.650	0.640
3	0.889	0.864	0.840	0.816	0.794	0.772	0.751	0.731	0.712	0.693	0.675	0.658	0.641	0.624	0.609	0.593	0.579	0.564	0.551	0.537	0.524	0.512
4	0.855	0.823	0.792	0.763	0.735	0.708	0.683	0.659	0.636	0.613	0.592	0.572	0.552	0.534	0.516	0.499	0.482	0.467	0.451	0.437	0.423	0.410
5	0.822	0.784	0.747	0.713	0.681	0.650	0.621	0.593	0.567	0.543	0.519	0.497	0.476	0.456	0.437	0.419	0.402	0.386	0.370	0.355	0.341	0.328
6	0.790	0.746	0.705	0.666	0.630	0.596	0.564	0.535	0.507	0.480	0.456	0.432	0.410	0.390	0.370	0.352	0.335	0.319	0.303	0.289	0.275	0.262
7	0.760	0.711	0.665	0.623	0.583	0.547	0.513	0.482	0.452	0.425	0.400	0.376	0.354	0.333	0.314	0.296	0.279	0.263	0.249	0.235	0.222	0.210
8	0.731	0.677	0.627	0.582	0.540	0.502	0.467	0.434	0.404	0.376	0.351	0.327	0.305	0.285	0.266	0.249	0.233	0.218	0.204	0.191	0.179	0.168
9	0.703	0.645	0.592	0.544	0.500	0.460	0.424	0.391	0.361	0.333	0.308	0.284	0.263	0.243	0.225	0.209	0.194	0.180	0.167	0.155	0.144	0.134
10	0.676	0.614	0.558	0.508	0.463	0.422	0.386	0.352	0.322	0.295	0.270	0.247	0.227	0.208	0.191	0.176	0.162	0.149	0.137	0.126	0.116	0.107
11	0.650	0.585	0.527	0.475	0.429	0.388	0.350	0.317	0.287	0.261	0.237	0.215	0.195	0.178	0.162	0.148	0.135	0.123	0.112	0.103	0.094	0.086
12	0.625	0.557	0.497	0.444	0.397	0.356	0.319	0.286	0.257	0.231	0.208	0.187	0.168	0.152	0.137	0.124	0.112	0.102	0.092	0.083	0.076	0.069
13	0.601	0.530	0.469	0.415	0.368	0.326	0.290	0.258	0.229	0.204	0.182	0.163	0.145	0.130	0.116	0.104	0.093	0.084	0.075	0.068	0.061	0.055
14	0.577	0.505	0.442	0.388	0.340	0.299	0.263	0.232	0.205	0.181	0.160	0.141	0.125	0.111	0.099	0.088	0.078	0.069	0.062	0.055	0.049	0.044
15	0.555	0.481	0.417	0.362	0.315	0.275	0.239	0.209	0.183	0.160	0.140	0.123	0.108	0.095	0.084	0.074	0.065	0.057	0.051	0.045	0.040	0.035
16	0.534	0.458	0.394	0.339	0.292	0.252	0.218	0.188	0.163	0.141	0.123	0.107	0.093	0.081	0.071	0.062	0.054	0.047	0.042	0.036	0.032	0.028
17	0.513	0.436	0.371	0.317	0.270	0.231	0.198	0.170	0.146	0.125	0.108	0.093	0.080	0.069	0.060	0.052	0.045	0.039	0.034	0.030	0.026	0.023
18	0.494	0.416	0.350	0.296	0.250	0.212	0.180	0.153	0.130	0.111	0.095	0.081	0.069	0.059	0.051	0.044	0.038	0.032	0.028	0.024	0.021	0.018
19	0.475	0.396	0.331	0.277	0.232	0.194	0.164	0.138	0.116	0.098	0.083	0.070	0.060	0.051	0.043	0.037	0.031	0.027	0.023	0.020	0.017	0.014
20	0.456	0.377	0.312	0.258	0.215	0.178	0.149	0.124	0.104	0.087	0.073	0.061	0.051	0.043	0.037	0.031	0.026	0.022	0.019	0.016	0.014	0.012
21	0.439	0.359	0.294	0.242	0.199	0.164	0.135	0.112	0.093	0.077	0.064	0.053	0.044	0.037	0.031	0.026	0.022	0.018	0.015	0.013	0.011	0.009
22	0.422	0.342	0.278	0.226	0.184	0.150	0.123	0.101	0.083	0.068	0.056	0.046	0.038	0.032	0.026	0.022	0.018	0.015	0.013	0.011	0.009	0.007
23	0.406	0.326	0.262	0.211	0.170	0.138	0.112	0.091	0.074	0.060	0.049	0.040	0.033	0.027	0.022	0.018	0.015	0.012	0.010	0.009	0.007	0.006
24	0.390	0.310	0.247	0.197	0.158	0.126	0.102	0.082	0.066	0.053	0.043	0.035	0.028	0.023	0.019	0.015	0.013	0.010	0.008	0.007	0.006	0.005
25	0.375	0.295	0.233	0.184	0.146	0.116	0.092	0.074	0.059	0.047	0.038	0.030	0.024	0.020	0.016	0.013	0.010	0.009	0.007	0.006	0.005	0.004
26	0.361	0.281	0.220	0.172	0.135	0.106	0.084	0.066	0.053	0.042	0.033	0.026	0.021	0.017	0.014	0.011	0.009	0.007	0.006	0.005	0.004	0.003
27	0.347	0.268	0.207	0.161	0.125	0.098	0.076	0.060	0.047	0.037	0.029	0.023	0.018	0.014	0.011	0.009	0.007	0.006	0.005	0.004	0.003	0.002
28	0.333	0.255	0.196	0.150	0.116	0.090	0.069	0.054	0.042	0.033	0.026	0.020	0.016	0.012	0.010	0.008	0.006	0.005	0.004	0.003	0.002	0.002
29	0.321	0.243	0.185	0.141	0.107	0.082	0.063	0.048	0.037	0.029	0.022	0.017	0.014	0.011	0.008	0.006	0.005	0.004	0.003	0.002	0.002	0.002
30	0.308	0.231	0.174	0.131	0.099	0.075	0.057	0.044	0.033	0.026	0.020	0.015	0.012	0.009	0.007	0.005	0.004	0.003	0.003	0.002	0.002	0.001
40	0.208	0.142	0.097	0.067	0.046	0.032	0.022	0.015	0.011	0.008	0.005	0.004	0.003	0.002	0.001	0.001	0.001	0.000	0.000	0.000	0.000	0.000

EXHIBIT 14B–2
Present Value of an Annuity of $1 in Arrears; $\frac{1}{r}\left[1 - \frac{1}{(1+r)^n}\right]$

Periods	4%	5%	6%	7%	8%	9%	10%	11%	12%	13%	14%	15%	16%	17%	18%	19%	20%	21%	22%	23%	24%	25%
1	0.962	0.952	0.943	0.935	0.926	0.917	0.909	0.901	0.893	0.885	0.877	0.870	0.862	0.855	0.847	0.840	0.833	0.826	0.820	0.813	0.806	0.800
2	1.886	1.859	1.833	1.808	1.783	1.759	1.736	1.713	1.690	1.668	1.647	1.626	1.605	1.585	1.566	1.547	1.528	1.509	1.492	1.474	1.457	1.440
3	2.775	2.723	2.673	2.624	2.577	2.531	2.487	2.444	2.402	2.361	2.322	2.283	2.246	2.210	2.174	2.140	2.106	2.074	2.042	2.011	1.981	1.952
4	3.630	3.546	3.465	3.387	3.312	3.240	3.170	3.102	3.037	2.974	2.914	2.855	2.798	2.743	2.690	2.639	2.589	2.540	2.494	2.448	2.404	2.362
5	4.452	4.329	4.212	4.100	3.993	3.890	3.791	3.696	3.605	3.517	3.433	3.352	3.274	3.199	3.127	3.058	2.991	2.926	2.864	2.803	2.745	2.689
6	5.242	5.076	4.917	4.767	4.623	4.486	4.355	4.231	4.111	3.998	3.889	3.784	3.685	3.589	3.498	3.410	3.326	3.245	3.167	3.092	3.020	2.951
7	6.002	5.786	5.582	5.389	5.206	5.033	4.868	4.712	4.564	4.423	4.288	4.160	4.039	3.922	3.812	3.706	3.605	3.508	3.416	3.327	3.242	3.161
8	6.733	6.463	6.210	5.971	5.747	5.535	5.335	5.146	4.968	4.799	4.639	4.487	4.344	4.207	4.078	3.954	3.837	3.726	3.619	3.518	3.421	3.329
9	7.435	7.108	6.802	6.515	6.247	5.995	5.759	5.537	5.328	5.132	4.946	4.772	4.607	4.451	4.303	4.163	4.031	3.905	3.786	3.673	3.566	3.463
10	8.111	7.722	7.360	7.024	6.710	6.418	6.145	5.889	5.650	5.426	5.216	5.019	4.833	4.659	4.494	4.339	4.192	4.054	3.923	3.799	3.682	3.571
11	8.760	8.306	7.887	7.499	7.139	6.805	6.495	6.207	5.938	5.687	5.453	5.234	5.029	4.836	4.656	4.486	4.327	4.177	4.035	3.902	3.776	3.656
12	9.385	8.863	8.384	7.943	7.536	7.161	6.814	6.492	6.194	5.918	5.660	5.421	5.197	4.988	4.793	4.611	4.439	4.278	4.127	3.985	3.851	3.725
13	9.986	9.394	8.853	8.358	7.904	7.487	7.103	6.750	6.424	6.122	5.842	5.583	5.342	5.118	4.910	4.715	4.533	4.362	4.203	4.053	3.912	3.780
14	10.563	9.899	9.295	8.745	8.244	7.786	7.367	6.982	6.628	6.302	6.002	5.724	5.468	5.229	5.008	4.802	4.611	4.432	4.265	4.108	3.962	3.824
15	11.118	10.380	9.712	9.108	8.559	8.061	7.606	7.191	6.811	6.462	6.142	5.847	5.575	5.324	5.092	4.876	4.675	4.489	4.315	4.153	4.001	3.859
16	11.652	10.838	10.106	9.447	8.851	8.313	7.824	7.379	6.974	6.604	6.265	5.954	5.668	5.405	5.162	4.938	4.730	4.536	4.357	4.189	4.033	3.887
17	12.166	11.274	10.477	9.763	9.122	8.544	8.022	7.549	7.120	6.729	6.373	6.047	5.749	5.475	5.222	4.990	4.775	4.576	4.391	4.219	4.059	3.910
18	12.659	11.690	10.828	10.059	9.372	8.756	8.201	7.702	7.250	6.840	6.467	6.128	5.818	5.534	5.273	5.033	4.812	4.608	4.419	4.243	4.080	3.928
19	13.134	12.085	11.158	10.336	9.604	8.950	8.365	7.839	7.366	6.938	6.550	6.198	5.877	5.584	5.316	5.070	4.843	4.635	4.442	4.263	4.097	3.942
20	13.590	12.462	11.470	10.594	9.818	9.129	8.514	7.963	7.469	7.025	6.623	6.259	5.929	5.628	5.353	5.101	4.870	4.657	4.460	4.279	4.110	3.954
21	14.029	12.821	11.764	10.836	10.017	9.292	8.649	8.075	7.562	7.102	6.687	6.312	5.973	5.665	5.384	5.127	4.891	4.675	4.476	4.292	4.121	3.963
22	14.451	13.163	12.042	11.061	10.201	9.442	8.772	8.176	7.645	7.170	6.743	6.359	6.011	5.696	5.410	5.149	4.909	4.690	4.488	4.302	4.130	3.970
23	14.857	13.489	12.303	11.272	10.371	9.580	8.883	8.266	7.718	7.230	6.792	6.399	6.044	5.723	5.432	5.167	4.925	4.703	4.499	4.311	4.137	3.976
24	15.247	13.799	12.550	11.469	10.529	9.707	8.985	8.348	7.784	7.283	6.835	6.434	6.073	5.746	5.451	5.182	4.937	4.713	4.507	4.318	4.143	3.981
25	15.622	14.094	12.783	11.654	10.675	9.823	9.077	8.422	7.843	7.330	6.873	6.464	6.097	5.766	5.467	5.195	4.948	4.721	4.514	4.323	4.147	3.985
26	15.983	14.375	13.003	11.826	10.810	9.929	9.161	8.488	7.896	7.372	6.906	6.491	6.118	5.783	5.480	5.206	4.956	4.728	4.520	4.328	4.151	3.988
27	16.330	14.643	13.211	11.987	10.935	10.027	9.237	8.548	7.943	7.409	6.935	6.514	6.136	5.798	5.492	5.215	4.964	4.734	4.524	4.332	4.154	3.990
28	16.663	14.898	13.406	12.137	11.051	10.116	9.307	8.602	7.984	7.441	6.961	6.534	6.152	5.810	5.502	5.223	4.970	4.739	4.528	4.335	4.157	3.992
29	16.984	15.141	13.591	12.278	11.158	10.198	9.370	8.650	8.022	7.470	6.983	6.551	6.166	5.820	5.510	5.229	4.975	4.743	4.531	4.337	4.159	3.994
30	17.292	15.372	13.765	12.409	11.258	10.274	9.427	8.694	8.055	7.496	7.003	6.566	6.177	5.829	5.517	5.235	4.979	4.746	4.534	4.339	4.160	3.995
40	19.793	17.159	15.046	13.332	11.925	10.757	9.779	8.951	8.244	7.634	7.105	6.642	6.233	5.871	5.548	5.258	4.997	4.760	4.544	4.347	4.166	3.999

Appendix 14C: Income Taxes and the Net Present Value Method

This appendix discusses the impact of income taxes on the net present value method of making capital budgeting decisions. We ignored income taxes throughout the chapter for two reasons. First, many organizations do not pay income taxes. Nonprofit organizations, such as hospitals and charitable foundations, and government agencies are exempt from income taxes. Second, capital budgeting is complex and best absorbed in small doses. Now that we have a solid foundation in the concept of discounting cash flows, we can explore the impact of income taxes on the net present value method.

LO14–8
Include income taxes in a net present value analysis.

To keep this discussion within reasonable bounds, we make three simplifying assumptions. First, although the tax law allows companies to expense the entire cost of some fixed assets in the year the assets are placed into service, we will assume a company's taxable income equals its net income for financial reporting purposes and the company always uses straight-line depreciation with zero salvage value. Second, we assume a flat tax rate of 30 percent (a 21 percent federal income tax rate plus 9 percent for state and local income taxes). Third, we assume there are no gains or losses on the sale of noncurrent assets.

Key Concepts

This appendix takes everything you have already learned about the net present value method and adds one more type of cash flow to the computations—it adds income tax expense as a *cash outflow*. To calculate the amount of income tax expense associated with a capital budgeting project, we'll be using a two-step process. The first step is to calculate the incremental net income earned during each year of the project. The second step is to multiply each year's incremental net income by the tax rate to determine the income tax expense. Each year's income tax expense is then discounted to its present value along with all other cash flows realized over the life of the project.

A capital budgeting project's incremental net income computation *includes* annual revenues minus annual cash operating expenses (including variable expenses and fixed out-of-pocket costs), annual depreciation expense, and any one-time expenses. Notice *depreciation expense is included in the computation of incremental net income*. Although depreciation expense is a noncash expense, it does impact the computation of taxable income, which in turn affects the cash outflows pertaining to income tax expense. A capital budgeting project's incremental net income computation *does not include* immediate cash outflows in the form of initial investments in equipment, other assets, and installation costs. It also *does not include* investments in working capital, the release of working capital at the end of a project, and the proceeds from selling a noncurrent asset when no gain or loss is realized on the sale.

To summarize, the items that should be included and excluded from a capital budgeting project's incremental net income computations are as follows:

Include in the computation of incremental net income:
Annual revenues
Annual cash operating expenses
Annual depreciation expense
One-time expenses

Exclude from the computation of incremental net income:
Initial investments in equipment, other assets, and installation costs
Investment in working capital
Release of working capital at the end of a project
Proceeds from selling noncurrent assets when no gain or loss is realized

Income Taxes and Net Present Value Analysis: An Example

Holland Company owns the mineral rights to land that has a deposit of ore. The company is uncertain if it should purchase equipment and open a mine on the property. After careful study, the company gathered the following data:

Initial investment in equipment	$275,000
Initial investment in working capital	$50,000
Estimated annual sales of ore	$250,000
Estimated annual cash operating expenses	$150,000
Cost of road repairs needed in 3 years	$30,000

The ore in the mine would be exhausted after five years, at which time the mine would be closed and the working capital released and redeployed by the company. The equipment has a useful life of five years and a salvage value of zero. The company uses straight-line depreciation for financial reporting and tax purposes. Its after-tax cost of capital is 12 percent and its tax rate is 30 percent. To be consistent, when we take the net present value of after-tax cash flows, we use the *after-tax* cost of capital as the discount rate.

Should Holland Company purchase the equipment and open a mine on the property? Exhibit 14C–1 shows a net present value analysis that incorporates the impact of income taxes on this decision. The top portion of the exhibit computes the project's incremental net income for Years 1–5 and the income tax expense for each of those years. The incremental net income computations include the annual sales ($250,000), the annual cash operating expenses ($150,000), the road repairs in Year 3 ($30,000), and the annual depreciation expense of $55,000 ($275,000 ÷ 5 years = $55,000 per year). Each year's incremental net income is multiplied by the tax rate of 30 percent to determine the income tax expense.

The bottom portion of Exhibit 14C–1 calculates the net present value of the mining project. The cash flows summarized in this portion of the exhibit include the initial

EXHIBIT 14C–1

Holland Company:
Income Taxes and Net
Present Value Analysis

	A	B	C	D	E	F	G
1					Year		
2		Now	1	2	3	4	5
3	*Calculate the annual tax expense:*						
4	Sales		$ 250,000	$ 250,000	$ 250,000	$ 250,000	$ 250,000
5	Cash operating expenses		$ (150,000)	$ (150,000)	$ (150,000)	$ (150,000)	$ (150,000)
6	Road repairs				$ (30,000)		
7	Depreciation expense		$ (55,000)	$ (55,000)	$ (55,000)	$ (55,000)	$ (55,000)
8	Incremental net income		$ 45,000	$ 45,000	$ 15,000	$ 45,000	$ 45,000
9	Tax rate		30%	30%	30%	30%	30%
10	Income tax expense		$ (13,500)	$ (13,500)	$ (4,500)	$ (13,500)	$ (13,500)
11							
12	*Calculate the net present value:*						
13	Purchase of equipment	$ (275,000)					
14	Investment in working capital	$ (50,000)					
15	Sales		$ 250,000	$ 250,000	$ 250,000	$ 250,000	$ 250,000
16	Cash operating expenses		$ (150,000)	$ (150,000)	$ (150,000)	$ (150,000)	$ (150,000)
17	Road repairs				$ (30,000)		
18	Release of working capital						$ 50,000
19	Income tax expense	_____	$ (13,500)	$ (13,500)	$ (4,500)	$ (13,500)	$ (13,500)
20	Total cash flows (a)	$ (325,000)	$ 86,500	$ 86,500	$ 65,500	$ 86,500	$ 136,500
21	Discount factor (12%) (b)	1.000	0.893	0.797	0.712	0.636	0.567
22	Present value of cash flows (a) × (b)	$ (325,000)	$ 77,245	$ 68,941	$ 46,636	$ 55,014	$ 77,396
23	Net present value (SUM B22:G22)	$ 231					
24							
25	Note: The discount factors come from Exhibit 14B-1 in Appendix 14B.						
26							

Exhibit 14-10   Exhibit 14-11   **Exhibit 14C-1**

Microsoft Excel

outlays for the purchase of equipment ($275,000) and the investment in working capital ($50,000), the annual sales ($250,000), the annual cash operating expenses ($150,000), the road repairs in Year 3 ($30,000), the release of working capital in Year 5 ($50,000), and the annual income tax expense. Notice the amounts of income tax expense shown in cells C19 through G19 come directly from the calculations previously performed in cells C10 through G10. Each year's total cash flows in cells B20 through G20 are multiplied by the appropriate discount factor for 12 percent to compute their present value. The present values in cells B22 through G22 are combined to determine the project's net present value of $231. Because the net present value is positive, it indicates Holland Company should proceed with the mining project.

Summary (Appendix 14C)

Unless the organization is tax-exempt, such as a nonprofit school or a governmental body, income taxes should be considered when using net present value analysis to make capital budgeting decisions. Calculating the amount of income tax expense associated with a capital budgeting project is a two-step process. The first step is to calculate the incremental net income earned during each year of the project. The second step is to multiply each year's incremental net income by the tax rate to determine the income tax expense. Each year's income tax expense is then discounted to its present value along with all other cash flows realized over the life of the project.

A capital budgeting project's incremental net income computation includes annual revenues minus annual cash operating expenses, annual depreciation expense, and any one-time expenses. It does not include immediate cash outflows in the form of initial investments in equipment, other assets, and installation costs, as well as investments in working capital, the release of working capital at the end of a project, and the proceeds from selling a noncurrent asset where no gain or loss is realized on the sale.

Mc Graw Hill connect Appendix 14C: Exercises and Problems

EXERCISE 14C–1 Income Taxes and Net Present Value Analysis LO14–8

Gaston Company is considering a capital budgeting project requiring a $2,000,000 investment in equipment with a useful life of five years and no salvage value. The company's tax rate is 30% and its after-tax cost of capital is 13%. It uses the straight-line depreciation method for financial reporting and tax purposes. The project would provide annual net operating income over five years as follows:

Sales		$2,800,000
Variable expenses		1,600,000
Contribution margin		1,200,000
Fixed expenses:		
Advertising, salaries, and other fixed		
out-of-pocket costs	$500,000	
Depreciation	400,000	
Total fixed expenses		900,000
Net operating income		$ 300,000

Required:

Compute the project's net present value.

EXERCISE 14C–2 Income Taxes and Net Present Value Analysis LO14–8

Winthrop Company has an opportunity to manufacture and sell a new product for a five-year period. The company would need to purchase a piece of equipment for $130,000 that has a useful life of five years and zero salvage value. It would be depreciated for financial reporting and tax purposes using the straight-line method. Winthrop estimated the following annual costs and revenues for the new product:

Annual revenues and costs:	
Sales revenues	$250,000
Variable expenses	$120,000
Fixed out-of-pocket operating costs	$70,000

The company's tax rate is 30% and its after-tax cost of capital is 15%.

Required:
1. Calculate the annual income tax expense arising from this investment.
2. Calculate the net present value of this investment opportunity.

PROBLEM 14C–3 Income Taxes and Net Present Value Analysis LO14–8
Lander Company has an opportunity to pursue a capital budgeting project with a five-year time horizon. Lander estimated the following costs and revenues for the project:

Cost of equipment needed	$250,000
Working capital needed	$60,000
Repair of the equipment in two years	$18,000
Annual revenues and costs:	
Sales revenues	$350,000
Variable expenses	$180,000
Fixed out-of-pocket operating costs	$80,000

The piece of equipment mentioned above has a useful life of five years and zero salvage value. Lander uses straight-line depreciation for financial reporting and tax purposes. The company's tax rate is 30% and its after-tax cost of capital is 12%. When the project concludes in five years, the working capital will be released for investment elsewhere within the company.

Required:
1. Calculate the annual income tax expense for each of years 1 through 5 arising from this investment opportunity.
2. Calculate the net present value of this investment opportunity.

PROBLEM 14C–4 Income Taxes and Net Present Value Analysis LO14–8
Rosman Company has an opportunity to pursue a capital budgeting project with a five-year time horizon. Rosman estimated the following costs and revenues for the project:

Cost of new equipment needed	$420,000
Sale of old equipment no longer needed	$80,000
Working capital needed	$65,000
Equipment maintenance in each of Years 3 and 4	$20,000
Annual revenues and costs:	
Sales revenues	$410,000
Variable expenses	$175,000
Fixed out-of-pocket operating costs	$100,000

The new piece of equipment mentioned above has a useful life of five years and zero salvage value. The old piece of equipment mentioned above would be sold at the beginning of the project and there would be no gain or loss realized on its sale. Rosman uses the straight-line depreciation method for financial reporting and tax purposes. The company's tax rate is 30% and its after-tax cost of capital is 12%. When the project concludes in five years, the working capital will be released for investment elsewhere within the company.

Required:
1. Calculate the annual income tax expense for each of years 1 through 5 arising from this investment opportunity.
2. Calculate the net present value of this investment opportunity.

PROBLEM 14C–5 Income Taxes and Net Present Value Analysis LO14–5, LO14–8

Shimano Company has an opportunity to manufacture and sell one of two new products for a five-year period. The company's tax rate is 30% and its after-tax cost of capital is 14%. The cost and revenue estimates for each product are as follows:

	Product A	Product B
Initial investment in equipment	$400,000	$550,000
Initial investment in working capital	$85,000	$60,000
Annual sales	$370,000	$390,000
Annual cash operating expenses	$200,000	$170,000
Cost of repairs needed in three years	$45,000	$70,000

The equipment pertaining to both products has a useful life of five years and no salvage value. The company uses the straight-line depreciation method for financial reporting and tax purposes. At the end of five years, each product's working capital will be released for investment elsewhere within the company.

Required:

1. Calculate the annual income tax expense for each of years 1 through 5 that will arise if Product A is introduced.
2. Calculate Product A's net present value.
3. Calculate the annual income tax expense for each of years 1 through 5 that will arise if Product B is introduced.
4. Calculate Product B's net present value.
5. Calculate the profitability index for Product A and Product B. Which of the two products should the company pursue? Why?

Chapter 15

LEARNING OBJECTIVES

After studying Chapter 15, you should be able to:

LO15–1 Classify cash inflows and outflows as relating to operating, investing, or financing activities.

LO15–2 Compute net cash provided by (used in) operating activities using the indirect method.

LO15–3 Compute net cash provided by (used in) investing activities.

LO15–4 Compute net cash provided by (used in) financing activities.

LO15–5 Prepare a statement of cash flows using the indirect method to calculate the net cash provided by operating activities.

LO15–6 Compute free cash flow.

LO15–7 (*Appendix 15A*) Use the direct method to calculate the net cash provided by operating activities.

 Data Analytics Exercise available in Connect to complement this chapter

Statement of Cash Flows

Bennett Raglin/Getty Images

ENTREPRENEUR SPOTLIGHT

Kendra Scott started making jewelry in her spare bedroom with a mere $500 following the birth of her first child. Within five years, her pieces were gracing the runways of Paris and New York. With over 100 retail stores, a booming e-commerce business, and her collections available in stores such as Nordstrom, Neiman Marcus, and Bloomingdale's, Kendra Scott has developed a brand encompassing fashion jewelry, fine jewelry, home décor, and beauty product lines worth over $1 billion and growing.

Applying Managerial Accounting

Kendra Scott can analyze its operating, investing, and financing cash flows to help make numerous decisions such as whether and when to open new stores and whether it needs to borrow money to invest in developing and producing new products. The company can also glean useful insights by comparing numbers within the statement of cash flows. For example, if the additions to property, plant, and equipment in the investing activities section of the statement exceed the depreciation charges in the operating activities section, it suggests the company is making adequate investments to maintain its noncurrent assets.

Serving All Stakeholders

In 2015, Kendra Scott launched the Kendra Cares Program to support pediatric hospitals across the country. In 2019, she initiated the Kendra Scott Women's Entrepreneurial Leadership Institute with a $1 million donation to the University of Texas, with the goal of creating a "pipeline of courageous, creative female leaders who will change the world." Since 2010, her charitable efforts have exceeded $30 million in gifts to various causes. Kendra Scott also employs and mentors women, with a staff of more than 2,000 people, 95 percent of whom are female. Kendra says, "they call me Mama K around the office and you could say I have a couple thousand daughters." ∎

Sources: https://www.dallasnews.com/business/retail/2019/09/12/retail-therapy-why-kendra-scott-won-t-give-up-control-of-her-1-billion-brand/, https://www.statesman.com/story/business/2021/02/01/kendra-scott-steping-down-ceo-austin-based-jewelry-company/4339950001/, https://www.thelist.com/171550/the-untold-truth-of-kendra-scott/, https://www.inc.com/magazine/201902/tom-foster/austin-texas-kendra-scott-jewelry-2018-surge-cities.html.

Three major financial statements are required for external reports—an income statement, a balance sheet, and a statement of cash flows. The **statement of cash flows** highlights the major activities impacting cash flows and the overall cash balance. Managers focus on cash for a good reason—without sufficient cash at the right times, a company may miss golden investment opportunities or even go bankrupt.

The statement of cash flows answers questions not easily answered by looking at the income statement and balance sheet. For example, where did Delta Airlines get the cash to pay a dividend of $140 million in a year when it lost more than $1 billion? How was The Walt Disney Company able to invest $800 million to expand and renovate its theme parks despite a loss of more than $500 million on its investment in EuroDisney? Where did Microsoft get $25.9 billion to acquire other companies in a year when its net income was only $21.2 billion? The answers to such questions found on the statement of cash flows.

The statement of cash flows is a valuable analytical tool for managers as well as investors and creditors, although managers focus more on forecasting future cash flows as part of the budgeting process. The statement of cash flows answers crucial questions such as:

1. Is the company generating sufficient positive cash flows from its ongoing operations to remain viable?
2. Will the company be able to repay its debts?
3. Will the company be able to pay its usual dividend?
4. Why do net income and net cash flow differ?
5. To what extent will the company have to borrow money to make needed investments?

Managers prepare the statement of cash flows by applying a fundamental principle of double-entry bookkeeping—the change in the cash balance must equal the changes in all other balance sheet accounts besides cash.[1] This principle ensures that properly analyzing the changes in all noncash balance sheet accounts always quantifies the cash inflows and outflows that explain the change in the cash balance. Our goal in this chapter is to translate this fairly complex principle into a few concepts that simplify preparing a statement of cash flows.

As a starting point, we need to review two basic equations that apply to all asset, contra-asset, liability, and stockholders' equity accounts:

Basic Equation for Asset Accounts
Beginning balance + Debits − Credits = Ending balance

Basic Equation for Contra-asset, Liability, and Stockholders' Equity Accounts
Beginning balance − Debits + Credits = Ending balance

These equations will help you compute various cash inflows and outflows reported in the statement of cash flows, and they'll be referred to throughout the chapter.

---

[1] The statement of cash flows is based on the following fundamental balance sheet and income statement equations:

(1) Change in cash + Changes in noncash assets = Changes in liabilities + Changes in stockholders' equity

(2) Net cash flow = Change in cash

(3) Changes in stockholders' equity = Net income − Dividends + Changes in capital stock

These three equations can be used to derive the following equation:

(4) Net cash flow = Net income − Changes in noncash assets + Changes in liabilities − Dividends + Changes in capital stock

Essentially, the statement of cash flows, which explains net cash flow, is constructed by starting with net income and then adjusting it for changes in noncash balance sheet accounts.

TAKING A LOOK AT KROGER'S CASH FLOWS

In 2020, The Kroger Company, the largest food and drug retailer in the United States, reported net income of $2.6 billion. During the same year, the company spent $2.9 billion for plant and equipment, paid dividends totaling $534 million, paid off $747 million of long-term debt, and spent $1.3 billion to purchase shares of its own common stock. At first glance, these figures may seem confusing because Kroger is spending amounts of money that far exceed its net income. In this chapter you'll learn about the statement of cash flows that explains the relationship between a company's net income and its cash inflows and outflows.

Source: The Kroger Company, 2020 Form 10-K Annual Report, www.sec.gov/edgar/searchedgar/companysearch.html.

The Statement of Cash Flows: Key Concepts

The statement of cash flows summarizes all of a company's cash inflows and outflows thereby explaining the change in its cash balance. In a statement of cash flows, cash is broadly defined to include both cash and cash equivalents. **Cash equivalents** consist of short-term, highly liquid investments such as Treasury bills, commercial paper, and money market funds made solely for the purpose of generating a return on temporarily idle funds. Because such assets are equivalent to cash, they are included with cash in a statement of cash flows.

The remainder of this section discusses five key concepts you'll use to prepare the statement of cash flows. These concepts include organizing the statements of cash flows into three sections—operating activities, investing activities, and financing activities—as well as distinguishing between the direct and indirect methods of calculating the net cash provided by operating activities and completing the three-step process that underlies the indirect method. The two remaining sections explain how to calculate gross cash flows in the investing and financing sections of the statement.[2]

Organizing the Statement of Cash Flows

To make it easier to compare data from different companies, U.S. generally accepted accounting principles (GAAP) and International Financial Reporting Standards (IFRS) require companies to follow prescribed rules when preparing the statement of cash flows. One of these rules requires organizing the statement into three sections that report cash flows resulting from *operating activities, investing activities,* and *financing activities.* **Operating activities** generate cash inflows and outflows related to revenue and expense transactions affecting net income. **Investing activities** generate cash inflows and outflows related to acquiring or disposing of noncurrent assets such as property, plant, and equipment; long-term investments; and loans to another entity. **Financing activities** generate cash inflows and outflows related to borrowing from and repaying principal to creditors and completing transactions with the company's owners, such as selling or repurchasing shares of common stock and paying dividends. The most common types of cash inflows and outflows resulting from these three activities are summarized in Exhibit 15–1.[3]

---

[2] Another concept related to the statement of cash flows is direct exchange transactions, which refer to transactions where noncurrent balance sheet items are swapped. For example, a company might issue common stock in a direct exchange for property. Direct exchange transactions are not reported on the statement of cash flows; however, they are disclosed in a separate schedule that accompanies the statement. More advanced accounting courses cover this topic in greater detail. We will not include direct exchange transactions in this chapter.

[3] Operating cash inflows can also include interest income and dividend income; however, in this chapter we limit our scope to cash receipts from sales to customers.

	Cash Inflow	Cash Outflow
Operating activities		
Collecting cash from customers.........................	√	
Paying suppliers for inventory purchases................		√
Paying bills to insurers, utility providers, etc...............		√
Paying wages and salaries to employees.................		√
Paying taxes to governmental bodies....................		√
Paying interest to lenders		√
Investing activities		
Buying property, plant, and equipment...................		√
Selling property, plant, and equipment...................	√	
Buying stocks and bonds as a long-term investment.......		√
Selling stocks and bonds held for long-term investment....	√	
Lending money to another entity.........................		√
Collecting the principal on a loan to another entity	√	
Financing activities		
Borrowing money from a creditor	√	
Repaying the principal amount of a debt		√
Collecting cash from the sale of common stock	√	
Paying cash to repurchase your own common stock.......		√
Paying a dividend to stockholders.......................		√

Operating Activities: Direct or Indirect Method?

U.S. GAAP and IFRS allow companies to compute the net amount of cash inflows and outflows resulting from operating activities, which is known formally as the **net cash provided by operating activities,** using either the *direct* or *indirect* method. Both of these methods have the same purpose, which is to translate accrual-based net income to a cash basis. However, they approach this task in two different ways.

Under the **direct method,** the income statement is reconstructed on a cash basis from top to bottom. For example, cash collected from customers is listed instead of sales, and payments to suppliers is listed instead of cost of goods sold. In essence, cash receipts are counted as sales and cash disbursements pertaining to operating activities are counted as expenses. The difference between the cash receipts and cash disbursements is the net cash provided by operating activities.

Under the **indirect method,** net income is adjusted to a cash basis. That is, rather than directly computing cash sales, cash expenses, and so forth, these amounts are derived *indirectly* by removing from net income any items not affecting cash flows. The indirect method has an advantage over the direct method because it shows the reasons for any differences between net income and net cash provided by operating activities.

Although net cash provided by operating activities is the same under both methods the overwhelming majority of companies use the indirect method for external reporting purposes. If a company uses the direct method to prepare its statement of cash flows, then it must also provide a supplementary report using the indirect method. However, if a company uses the indirect method, there is no requirement that it also report results using the direct method. Because the direct method requires more work, very few companies choose this approach. Therefore, we explain the direct method in Appendix 15A and cover the indirect method in the main body of the chapter.

LO15–2
Compute net cash provided
by (used in) operating
activities using the indirect
method.

The Indirect Method: A Three-Step Process

The indirect method adjusts net income to net cash provided by operating activities using a three-step process.

Step 1   The first step is *add depreciation charges* to net income. Depreciation charges are the credits to the Accumulated Depreciation account—the sum total of the entries that increased Accumulated Depreciation. Why do we do this? Because Accumulated Depreciation is a noncash balance sheet account and we must adjust net income for all changes in noncash balance sheet accounts.

To compute the credits to Accumulated Depreciation, we use the equation for contra-assets mentioned earlier:

Basic Equation for Contra-asset Accounts

Beginning balance − Debits + Credits = Ending balance

For example, assume Accumulated Depreciation had beginning and ending balances of $300 and $500, respectively. Also, assume the company sold equipment with accumulated depreciation of $70 during the period. Because we debit Accumulated Depreciation to record accumulated depreciation on assets that have been sold or retired, the depreciation added to net income is computed as follows:

$$\text{Beginning balance} - \text{Debits} + \text{Credits} = \text{Ending balance}$$
$$\$300 - \$70 + \text{Credits} = \$500$$
$$\text{Credits} = \$500 - \$300 + \$70$$
$$\text{Credits} = \$270$$

The same logic can be depicted using an Accumulated Depreciation T-account. Given the account's beginning and ending balances the and $70 debit recorded for the sale of equipment, the credit side of the T-account must equal $270.

Accumulated Depreciation

		Beg. Bal.	$300
Sale of equipment	70		270
		End. Bal	$500

For service and merchandising companies, the credits to Accumulated Depreciation equal the debits to the Depreciation Expense account. For these companies, the adjustment in step one consists of adding depreciation expense to net income. However, for manufacturing companies, some of the credits to Accumulated Depreciation relate to depreciation on production assets that are debited to work in process inventories rather than depreciation expense. For these companies, the depreciation charges do not simply equal depreciation expense.

Because depreciation is added back to net income on the statement of cash flows, some people erroneously believe a company can increase its cash flow by increasing its depreciation expense. This is false; a company cannot increase its net cash provided by operating activities by increasing its depreciation expense. If it increases its depreciation expense by X dollars, then net income will decline by X dollars and the amount of the adjustment in step one of this process will increase by X dollars. The decline in net income and the increase in the amount of the adjustment in step one exactly offset each other, resulting in zero impact on the net cash provided by operating activities.

Step 2 The second step is *analyze net changes in noncash balance sheet accounts* that impact net income. Exhibit 15–2 provides general guidelines for analyzing current asset and current liability accounts.[4] For each account shown in the exhibit, refer to the balance sheet to compute the change in the account balance from the beginning to the end of the period. Then, either add each of these amounts to net income or subtract them from net income as shown in Exhibit 15–2. Notice changes in all current asset accounts (Accounts Receivable, Inventory, and Prepaid Expenses) require the same adjustment to net income. If an asset account balance increases, then the increase is subtracted from net income. If an asset account balance decreases, then the decrease is added to net income. The current liability accounts (Accounts Payable, Accrued Liabilities, and Income Taxes Payable) are handled in the opposite fashion. If a liability account balance increases, then the increase is added to net income. If a liability account balance decreases, then the decrease is subtracted from net income.

Keep in mind the purpose of these adjustments is to translate net income to a cash basis. For example, the change in the Accounts Receivable balance measures the difference between credit sales and cash collections from customers who purchased on account. When Accounts Receivable increases, it means the credit sales exceed the cash collected from customers. In this case, the change in Accounts Receivable is subtracted from net income because it reflects the amount by which credit sales exceed cash collections from customers. When Accounts Receivable decreases, it means cash collected from customers exceeds credit sales. In this case, the change in Accounts Receivable is added to net income because it reflects the amount by which cash collections from customers exceed credit sales.

The other accounts shown in Exhibit 15–2 have a similar underlying logic. The Inventory and Accounts Payable adjustments translate cost of goods sold to cash paid for inventory purchases. The Prepaid Expenses and Accrued Liabilities adjustments translate selling and administrative expenses to a cash basis. The Income Taxes Payable adjustment translates income tax expense to a cash basis.

Step 3 The third step in computing the net cash provided by operating activities is *adjust for gains/losses* included in the income statement. Under U.S. GAAP and IFRS rules, the cash proceeds from the sale of noncurrent assets must be included in the investing activities section of the statement of cash flows. To comply with these rules, the gains and losses pertaining to the sale of noncurrent assets must be removed from net income as reported in the operating activities section of the statement of cash flows. To make this adjustment, subtract gains from net income and add losses to net income in the operating activities section.

	Increase in Account Balance	Decrease in Account Balance
Current Assets		
Accounts receivable..............	Subtract	Add
Inventory........................	Subtract	Add
Prepaid expenses.................	Subtract	Add
Current Liabilities		
Accounts payable.................	Add	Subtract
Accrued liabilities	Add	Subtract
Income taxes payable.............	Add	Subtract

EXHIBIT 15–2
General Guidelines for Analyzing How Changes in Noncash Balance Sheet Accounts Affect Net Income on the Statement of Cash Flows

---

[4] Other accounts such as Interest Payable can impact these computations. However, for simplicity, in this chapter we focus on the accounts shown in Exhibit 15–2.

Investing Activities: Gross Cash Flows

U.S. GAAP and IFRS require the investing section of the statement of cash flows to disclose gross cash flows. To illustrate, suppose Macy's Department Stores purchases $50 million in property and sells other property for $30 million. Instead of showing the net change of $20 million, the company must show the gross amounts of both the purchases and sales. The $50 million purchase would be disclosed as a cash outflow and the $30 million sale would be reported as a cash inflow in the investing section of the statement.

IN BUSINESS

FG/Bauer-Griffin/Getty images

NETFLIX TACKLES ITS CASH FLOW PROBLEMS

Netflix is investing heavily in creating its own original programming in an effort to attract more subscribers and increase profits. The challenge inherent in this strategy is that it "takes roughly two years to get a new show from production to screen, and Netflix's investment is tied up for that period with no returns." In October of 2018 and 2019, the company had $3 billion in negative cash flows and relied on increasing its debt load to cover the shortfall. Netflix believes it can handle a capital structure that is up to 25 percent debt; however, the company's investors worry that a decline in stock price could threaten the aforementioned debt ceiling.

Source: Tatyana Shumsky, "New Netflix CFO to Tackle Cash-Flow Issues," *The Wall Street Journal*, January 4, 2019, p. B4.

The gross method of reporting cash flows is not used in the operating activities section of the statement of cash flows, where debits and credits are netted against each other. For example, if REI adds $600 million to its accounts receivable as a result of sales during the year and $590 million of accounts receivable are collected, only the net increase of $10 million is reported on the statement of cash flows.

To compute gross cash flows for the investing activities section of the statement of cash flows, start by calculating the changes in the balance of each applicable balance sheet account. As with current assets, when a noncurrent asset account balance (including Property, Plant, and Equipment; Long-Term Investments; and Loans to Other Entities) increases, it signals the need to subtract cash outflows. If the balance in a noncurrent asset account decreases, it signals the need to add cash inflows. Exhibit 15–3 summarizes these general guidelines.

While these guidelines provide a helpful starting point, to properly calculate each account's *gross* cash inflows and outflows, you'll need to analyze the transactions that occurred within that account during the period. We will illustrate how to do this using Property, Plant, and Equipment.

Property, Plant, and Equipment   When a company purchases property, plant, or equipment, it debits Property, Plant, and Equipment for the amount of the purchase. When it sells or disposes of these kinds of assets, it credits Property, Plant, and Equipment for the original cost of the asset. To compute the cash outflows related to Property, Plant, and Equipment, we use the basic equation for assets mentioned earlier:

Basic Equation for Asset Accounts
Beginning balance + Debits − Credits = Ending balance

For example, assume a company's beginning and ending balances in Property, Plant, and Equipment are $1,000 and $1,800, respectively. In addition, the company sold a piece of equipment for $40 cash that originally cost $100 and had accumulated depreciation of $70. The company recorded a gain on the sale of $10, which had been included in net income.

We start by calculating the $800 increase in Property, Plant, and Equipment, which, according to Exhibit 15–3, signals the need to subtract cash outflows. While it may be tempting to immediately record this $800 increase as an $800 cash outflow, that would

	Increase in Account Balance	Decrease in Account Balance	EXHIBIT 15-3
Noncurrent Assets			General Guidelines for Analyzing How Changes in Noncash Balance Sheet Accounts Affect the Investing Section of the Statement of Cash Flows
Property, plant, and equipment...............	Subtract	Add	
Long-term investments......................	Subtract	Add	
Loans to other entities	Subtract	Add	

only be correct if the company did not sell any property, plant, and equipment during the year. Because the company did sell equipment, we must use the basic equation for asset accounts to compute the cash outflows as follows:

$$\text{Beginning balance} + \text{Debits} - \text{Credits} = \text{Ending balance}$$
$$\$1,000 + \text{Debits} - \$100 = \$1,800$$
$$\text{Debits} = \$1,800 - \$1,000 + \$100$$
$$\text{Debits} = \$900$$

The same logic can be depicted using a Property, Plant, and Equipment T-account. Given the account's beginning and ending balances and the $100 credit recorded to write off the *original cost* of the sold equipment, the additions to the account, as summarized on the debit side of the T-account, must equal $900.

Property, Plant, and Equipment

Beg. Bal.	$1,000		
Additions	900	Sale of equipment	100
End. Bal.	$1,800		

So, instead of reporting an $800 cash outflow pertaining to Property, Plant, and Equipment, the proper accounting requires subtracting the $10 gain on the sale of equipment from net income in the operating activities section of the statement. It also requires disclosing a $40 cash inflow from the sale of equipment and a $900 cash outflow for additions to Property, Plant, and Equipment in the investing activities section of the statement.

Financing Activities: Gross Cash Flows

Similar to investing activities, U.S. GAAP and IFRS require reporting financing activities using gross cash flows. For example, if Alcoa receives $80 million from selling long-term bonds and then pays out $30 million to retire other bonds, the two transactions must be reported separately rather than being netted against each other.

LO15-4
Compute net cash provided by (used in) financing activities

To compute gross cash flows related to financing activities, start by calculating changes in the Bonds Payable and Common Stock accounts. As shown in Exhibit 15–4, if the balance increases, it signals the need to add cash inflows, whereas if the balance decreases, it signals the need to subtract cash outflows.

While these guidelines provide a helpful starting point, to properly calculate each account's financing cash flows, you may need to analyze the transactions occurring within that account during the period. We will illustrate how to do this using Retained Earnings.

Retained Earnings   When a company earns net income, it credits Retained Earnings, and when it pays a dividend, it debits Retained Earnings. To compute the amount of a

EXHIBIT 15–4
General Guidelines for Analyzing How Changes in Noncash Balance Sheet Accounts Affect the Financing Section of the Statement of Cash Flows

	Increase in Account Balance	Decrease in Account Balance
Liabilities and Stockholders' Equity		
Bonds payable........................	Add	Subtract
Common stock.......................	Add	Subtract
Retained earnings	*	*

*Requires further analysis to quantify cash dividends paid.

cash dividend payment, we use the basic equation for stockholders' equity accounts mentioned earlier:

Basic Equation for Stockholders' Equity Accounts
Beginning balance − Debits + Credits = Ending balance

For example, assume a company's beginning and ending balances in Retained Earnings are $2,000 and $3,000, respectively. In addition, the company reported net income of $1,200 and paid a cash dividend. To determine the amount of the dividend, we start by calculating the $1,000 increase in the Retained Earnings account. However, given this amount reflects the net income earned during the period as well as the dividend payment, we must use the equation above to calculate the dividend payment as follows:

$$\text{Beginning balance} - \text{Debits} + \text{Credits} = \text{Ending balance}$$

$$\$2,000 - \text{Debits} + \$1,200 = \$3,000$$

$$\$3,200 = \$3,000 + \text{Debits}$$

$$\text{Debits} = \$200$$

The same logic can be depicted using a Retained Earnings T-account. Given the account's beginning and ending balances and the net income recorded on the credit side of the T-account, the dividend, as reported on the debit side of the T-account, must equal $200.

Retained Earnings

		Beg. Bal.	$2,000
Dividend	200	Net income	1,200
		End. Bal.	$3,000

So, instead of erroneously reporting a $1,000 cash flow pertaining to the overall change in Retained Earnings, the proper accounting requires disclosing net income of $1,200 within the operating activities section of the statement of cash flows and a $200 cash dividend in the financing activities section of the statement.

Summary of Key Concepts

Exhibit 15–5 summarizes the five key concepts just discussed. The first key concept is that the statement of cash flows is divided into three sections: operating activities, investing activities, and financing activities. The net cash used or provided by these three types of activities is combined to derive the net increase/decrease in cash and cash equivalents, which explains the change in the cash balance. The second key concept is the operating activities section of the statement of cash flows can be prepared using the direct or indirect method. The direct method translates sales, cost of goods sold, selling and administrative expenses, and income tax expense to a cash basis. The indirect method begins with accrual-based net income and adjusts it to a cash basis. The third key concept is the

EXHIBIT 15–5
Summary of Key Concepts Needed to
Prepare a Statement of Cash Flows

Key Concept #1		Key Concept #2	
The statement of cash flows is divided into three sections:		U.S. GAAP and IFRS allow two methods for preparing the operating activities section of the statement of cash flows:	
Operating activities		**Direct Method (Appendix 15A)**	
Net cash provided by (used in) operating activities	$xx	Cash receipts from customers	$ xx
Investing activities		Cash paid for inventory purchases	(xx)
Net cash provided by (used in) investing activities	xx	Cash paid for selling and administrative expenses	(xx)
Financing activities		Cash paid for income taxes	(xx)
Net cash provided by (used in) financing activities	xx	Net cash provided by (used in) operating activities	$ xx
		Indirect Method	
Net increase/decrease in cash and cash equivalents	xx	Net income	$ xx
Beginning cash and cash equivalents	xx	Various adjustments (+/−)	xx
Ending cash and cash equivalents	$xx	Net cash provided by (used in) operating activities	$ xx

Key Concept #3			Key Concepts #4 and #5	
Computing the net cash provided by operating activities using the indirect method is a three-step process:			The investing and financing sections of the statement of cash flows must report gross cash flows:	
	Operating activities		Net cash provided by (used in) operating activities	$xx
	Net income	$xx	**Investing activities**	
	Adjustments to convert net income to a cash basis:		Purchase of property, plant, and equipment	(xx)
			Sale of property, plant, and equipment	xx
Step 1	Add: Depreciation	xx	Purchase of long-term investments	(xx)
			Sale of long-term investments	xx
	Analyze net changes in noncash balance sheet accounts:		Net cash provided by (used in) investing activities	(xx)
Step 2	Increase in current asset accounts	(xx)	**Financing activities**	
	Decrease in current asset accounts	xx	Issuance of bonds payable	xx
	Increase in current liability accounts	xx	Repayment of principal on bonds payable	(xx)
	Decrease in current liability accounts	(xx)	Issuance of common stock	xx
			Purchase of own shares of common stock	(xx)
	Adjust for gains/losses:		Payment of a dividend	(xx)
Step 3	Gain on sale	(xx)	Net cash provided by (used in) financing activities	xx
	Loss on sale	xx	Net increase/decrease in cash and cash equivalents	xx
	Net cash provided by (used in) operating activities	$xx	Beginning cash and cash equivalents	xx
			Ending cash and cash equivalents	$xx

indirect method requires three steps to compute net cash provided by operating activities. The first step is to add back depreciation to net income. The second step is to analyze net changes in noncash balance sheet accounts that impact net income. The third step is to adjust for gains or losses included in the income statement. The fourth and fifth key concepts relate to recording gross (rather than net) cash inflows and outflows in the investing and financing activities sections of the statement of cash flows.[5]

[5] This chapter adopts two simplifications related to common stock transactions. First, it always assumes companies issue no-par value common stock; thus, the chapter excludes Additional Paid-In Capital. Second, the chapter assumes stock repurchases are recorded with a debit to the Common Stock account rather than a debit to the contra-equity account called Treasury Stock.

An Example of a Statement of Cash Flows

LO15–5

Prepare a statement of cash flows using the indirect method to calculate the net cash provided by operating activities.

To illustrate the ideas introduced in the preceding section, we will now construct a statement of cash flows for a merchandising company called Apparel, Inc. The company's income statement and balance sheet are shown in Exhibits 15–6 and 15–7.

Let's also assume the following facts with respect to Apparel, Inc.:

1. The company sold a store that had an original cost of $15 million and accumulated depreciation of $10 million. The cash proceeds from the sale were $8 million. The gain on the sale was $3 million.
2. The company did not issue any new bonds during the year.
3. The company did not repurchase any of its own common stock during the year.
4. The company paid a cash dividend during the year.

Notice the balance sheet in Exhibit 15–7 includes the amount of the change in each balance sheet account. For example, the beginning and ending balances in Cash and Cash Equivalents are $29 million and $91 million, respectively. This is a $62 million increase in the account balance. A similar computation is performed for all other balance sheet accounts. Study the changes in these account balances because we will be referring to them later. For example, keep in mind the purpose of Apparel's statement of cash flows is to disclose the operating, investing, and financing cash flows underlying the $62 million increase in Cash and Cash Equivalents shown in Exhibit 15–7. *Also, please be advised although the changes in account balances are computed for you in Exhibit 15–7, you'll ordinarily need to compute these amounts yourself before attempting to construct the statement of cash flows.*

Operating Activities

This section uses the three-step process explained earlier to construct Apparel's operating activities section of the statement of cash flows.

Step 1 The first step in computing Apparel's net cash provided by operating activities is *add depreciation* to net income. The balance sheet in Exhibit 15–7 shows Apparel's Accumulated Depreciation account had beginning and ending balances of $561 million and $654 million, respectively. We also know from the assumptions mentioned earlier that Apparel sold a store during the year with $10 million of accumulated depreciation.

EXHIBIT 15–6
Apparel, Inc., Income Statement

Apparel, Inc. Income Statement (dollars in millions)	
Sales	$ 3,638
Cost of goods sold	2,469
Gross margin	1,169
Selling and administrative expenses	941
Net operating income	228
Nonoperating items: Gain on sale of store	3
Income before taxes	231
Income taxes	91
Net income	$ 140

EXHIBIT 15-7
Apparel, Inc., Balance Sheet

Apparel, Inc.
Comparative Balance Sheet
(dollars in millions)

	Ending Balance	Beginning Balance	Change
Assets			
Current assets:			
Cash and cash equivalents	$ 91	$ 29	+62
Accounts receivable.	637	654	−17
Inventory.	586	537	+49
Total current assets.	1,314	1,220	
Property, plant, and equipment.	1,517	1,394	+123
Less accumulated depreciation	654	561	+93
Net property, plant, and equipment. . .	863	833	
Total assets.	$2,177	$2,053	
Liabilities and Stockholders' Equity			
Current liabilities:			
Accounts payable	$ 264	$ 220	+44
Accrued liabilities	193	190	+3
Income taxes payable	75	71	+4
Total current liabilities.	532	481	
Bonds payable.	479	520	−41
Total liabilities.	1,011	1,001	
Stockholders' equity:			
Common stock.	157	155	+2
Retained earnings	1,009	897	+112
Total stockholders' equity	1,166	1,052	
Total liabilities and stockholders' equity	$2,177	$2,053	

Given these facts, we can use the basic equation for contra-assets to calculate Apparel needs to add $103 million of depreciation to its net income:

$$\text{Beginning balance} - \text{Debits} + \text{Credits} = \text{Ending balance}$$
$$\$561 \text{ million} - \$10 \text{ million} + \text{Credits} = \$654 \text{ million}$$
$$\text{Credits} = \$654 \text{ million} - \$561 \text{ million} + \$10 \text{ million}$$
$$\text{Credits} = \$103 \text{ million}$$

Step 2 The second step in computing net cash provided by operating activities is to *analyze net changes in noncash balance sheet accounts* that impact net income. Exhibit 15–8 explains the five adjustments Apparel needs to make to complete this step. For your ease of reference, the top half of Exhibit 15–8 reproduces an excerpt of the general guidelines for completing this step previously summarized in Exhibit 15–2. The bottom half of Exhibit 15–8 applies the general guidelines from the top half of the exhibit to Apparel's balance sheet. For example, Exhibit 15–7 shows Apparel's Accounts Receivable balance decreased by $17 million. The top half of Exhibit 15–8 says decreases in accounts receivable are added to net income. This explains why the bottom half of Exhibit 15–8 includes a plus sign in front of Apparel's $17 million decrease in Accounts Receivable. Similarly, Exhibit 15–7 shows Apparel's Inventory balance increased by $49 million. When inventory increases, the amount of the increase is subtracted from net income. This explains why the bottom half of Exhibit 15–8 includes a minus sign in front of Apparel's

EXHIBIT 15–8

Apparel, Inc.: Analyzing How Net Changes in Noncash Balance Sheet Accounts Affect Net Income on the Statement of Cash Flows

	Increase in Account Balance	Decrease in Account Balance
General Guidelines from Exhibit 15–2		
Current Assets:		
Accounts receivable	Subtract	Add
Inventory	Subtract	Add
Current Liabilities:		
Accounts payable	Add	Subtract
Accrued liabilities	Add	Subtract
Income taxes payable	Add	Subtract
	Increase in Account Balance	Decrease in Account Balance
Apparel's Account Analysis		
Current Assets:		
Accounts receivable		+17
Inventory	−49	
Current Liabilities:		
Accounts payable	+44	
Accrued liabilities	+3	
Income taxes payable	+4	

$49 million increase in Inventory. Similar logic can be used to explain why the increases from Exhibit 15–7 in Accounts Payable (+44), Accrued Liabilities (+3), and Income Taxes Payable (+4) all result in the additions to Apparel's net income shown in the bottom half of Exhibit 15–8.

Step 3 The third step in computing the net cash provided by operating activities is *adjust for gains/losses* included in the income statement. Apparel reported a $3 million gain on its income statement in Exhibit 15–6; therefore, this amount needs to be subtracted from net income. Subtracting the gain on sale removes it from the operating activities section of the statement of cash flows. The entire amount of the cash proceeds related to this sale will be recorded in the investing activities section of the statement.

Exhibit 15–9 shows the operating activities section of Apparel's statement of cash flows. Take a moment to trace each of the numbers we just computed to this exhibit.

EXHIBIT 15–9

Apparel, Inc.: Operating Activities Section of the Statement of Cash Flows

Apparel, Inc.
(dollars in millions)

Operating Activities			
Net income			$140
Adjustments to convert net income to a cash basis:			
Step 1 → Depreciation		$103	
Step 2 → Decrease in accounts receivable		17	
Increase in inventory		(49)	
Increase in accounts payable		44	
Increase in accrued liabilities		3	
Increase in income taxes payable		4	
Step 3 → Gain on sale of store		(3)	119
Net cash provided by (used in) operating activities ...			$259

The total amount of the adjustments to net income is $119 million, which results in net cash provided by operating activities of $259 million.

Investing Activities

Apparel's investing cash flows pertain to its Property, Plant, and Equipment account, which according to Exhibit 15–7 had beginning and ending balances of $1,394 million and $1,517 million, respectively, for an increase of $123 million. This increase suggests Apparel purchased equipment; however, it does not capture the gross cash flows that need to be reported in the statement of cash flows.

The previously defined assumptions say Apparel sold a store with an original cost of $15 million for $8 million in cash. The cash inflow from this sale needs to be recorded in the investing activities section of the statement of cash flows. To compute the cash outflows related to purchases of property, plant, and equipment, we use the basic equation for assets mentioned in the beginning of the chapter:

$$\text{Beginning balance} + \text{Debits} - \text{Credits} = \text{Ending balance}$$

$1,394 million + Debits − $15 million = $1,517 million

Debits = $1,517 million − $1,394 million + $15 million

Debits = $138 million

Notice the credits in the equation above include the original cost of the store that was sold. When the cash outflows of $138 million for purchases of property, plant, and equipment are combined with the $8 million of cash proceeds from the sale of the store, Apparel's net cash used in investing activities is $130 million.

Financing Activities

Exhibit 15–10 explains how to compute Apparel's financing cash flows related to its Bonds Payable and Common Stock balance sheet accounts. The top half of the exhibit reproduces an excerpt of the general guidelines for analyzing financing cash flows previously summarized in Exhibit 15–4. The bottom half of Exhibit 15–10 applies the general guidelines from the top half of the exhibit to these two accounts from Apparel's balance sheet. We will analyze each account in turn.

Exhibit 15–7 shows Apparel's Bonds Payable balance decreased by $41 million. Because, as stated earlier, Apparel did not issue any bonds during the year, we can conclude the $41 million decrease in the account is due solely to retiring bonds payable. The top half of Exhibit 15–10 says a decrease in Bonds Payable signals the need to

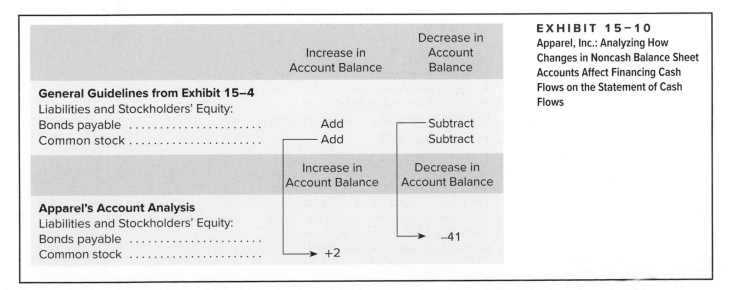

EXHIBIT 15–10
Apparel, Inc.: Analyzing How Changes in Noncash Balance Sheet Accounts Affect Financing Cash Flows on the Statement of Cash Flows

subtract cash outflows in the financing activities section of the statement of cash flows. This explains why the bottom half of the exhibit includes a minus sign in front of Apparel's $41 million decrease in Bonds Payable. Similarly, Exhibit 15–7 shows Apparel's Common Stock balance increased by $2 million. Because, as stated earlier, Apparel did not repurchase any of its own stock during the year, we can conclude the $2 million increase in the account is due solely to issuing common stock. The top half of Exhibit 15–10 says increases in common stock signal the need to add cash inflows in the financing activities section of the statement of cash flows. This explains why the bottom half of the exhibit includes a plus sign in front of Apparel's $2 million increase in Common Stock.

The final financing cash outflow for Apparel is its dividend payment to common stockholders. The dividend payment can be computed using the basic equation for stockholders' equity accounts mentioned at the beginning of the chapter:

$$\text{Beginning balance} - \text{Debits} + \text{Credits} = \text{Ending balance}$$

$$\$897 \text{ million} - \text{Debits} + \$140 \text{ million} = \$1{,}009 \text{ million}$$

$$\$1{,}037 \text{ million} = \$1{,}009 \text{ million} + \text{Debits}$$

$$\text{Debits} = \$28 \text{ million}$$

When the cash outflows of $69 million (= $41 million + $28 million) are combined with the cash inflows of $2 million, Apparel's net cash used in financing activities is $67 million.

Exhibit 15–11 shows Apparel's statement of cash flows. The operating activities section of this statement is carried over from Exhibit 15–9. Take a moment to trace the investing and financing cash flows just discussed to Exhibit 15–11. Notice the net change in cash and cash equivalents ($62 million) is calculated using the following equation:

EXHIBIT 15–11
Apparel, Inc., Statement of Cash Flows

Apparel, Inc.
Statement of Cash Flows—Indirect Method
(dollars in millions)

Operating Activities

Net income....................................		$140
Adjustments to convert net income to a cash basis:		
Depreciation	$103	
Decrease in accounts receivable..................	17	
Increase in inventory	(49)	
Increase in accounts payable.....................	44	
Increase in accrued liabilities	3	
Increase in income taxes payable	4	
Gain on sale of store	(3)	119
Net cash provided by (used in) operating activities		259
Investing Activities		
Additions to property, plant, and equipment	(138)	
Proceeds from sale of store	8	
Net cash provided by (used in) investing activities.....		(130)
Financing Activities		
Retirement of bonds payable	(41)	
Issuance of common stock	2	
Cash dividends paid..............................	(28)	
Net cash provided by (used in) financing activities.....		(67)
Net increase in cash and cash equivalents		62
Beginning cash and cash equivalents................		29
Ending cash and cash equivalents		$ 91

$$\begin{array}{l} \text{Net change in} \\ \text{cash and cash} \\ \text{equivalents} \end{array} = \begin{array}{l} \text{Net cash provided} \\ \text{by (used in)} \\ \text{operating activities} \end{array} + \begin{array}{l} \text{Net cash provided} \\ \text{by (used in)} \\ \text{investing activities} \end{array} + \begin{array}{l} \text{Net cash provided} \\ \text{by (used in)} \\ \text{financing activities} \end{array}$$

$$\begin{array}{l} \text{Net change in} \\ \text{cash and cash} \\ \text{equivalents} \end{array} = \$259 \text{ million} + \$(130) \text{ million} + \$(67) \text{ million}$$

$$\begin{array}{l} \text{Net change in} \\ \text{cash and cash} \\ \text{equivalents} \end{array} = \$62 \text{ million}$$

This amount agrees with the $62 million change in the Cash and Cash Equivalents account shown on the balance sheet in Exhibit 15–7.

Seeing the Big Picture

In the beginning of the chapter, we mentioned a statement of cash flows is prepared by analyzing the changes in noncash balance sheet accounts. We then presented a method of preparing a statement of cash flows. This method simplified the process of creating the statement of cash flows, and now we will show it is equivalent to analyzing the changes in noncash balance sheet accounts.

Exhibit 15–12 uses T-accounts to summarize how the changes in Apparel, Inc.'s noncash balance sheet accounts quantify the cash inflows and outflows that explain the change in its cash balance. The top portion of the exhibit is Apparel's Cash T-account and the bottom portion provides T-accounts for the company's remaining balance sheet accounts. Notice the net cash provided by operating activities of $259 million and the net increase in cash and cash equivalents of $62 million shown in the Cash T-account agree with the corresponding figures in the statement of cash flows shown in Exhibit 15–11.

We will explain Exhibit 15–12 in five steps. Entry (1) records Apparel's net income of $140 million in the credit side of the Retained Earnings account and the debit side of the Cash account. The net income of $140 million shown in the Cash T-account will be adjusted until it reflects the $62 million net increase in cash and cash equivalents. Entry (2) adds the depreciation of $103 million to net income. Entries (3) through (7) adjust net income for the changes in the current asset and current liability accounts. Entries (8) through (11) summarize the cash outflows and inflows related to the additions to property, plant, and equipment; the retirement of bonds payable; the payment of the cash dividend; and the issuance of common stock. Entry (12) records the sale of the store.

EXHIBIT 15-12
T-Accounts after Posting of Account
Changes—Apparel, Inc. (in millions)

Cash

Net income	(1)	140	49	(4)	Increase in inventory
Depreciation	(2)	103	3	(12)	Gain on sale of store
Decrease in accounts receivable	(3)	17			
Increase in accounts payable	(5)	44			
Increase in accrued liabilities	(6)	3			
Increase in income taxes payable	(7)	4			
Net cash provided by operating activities		259			
Proceeds from sale of store	(12)	8	138	(8)	Additions to property, plant, and equipment
Increase in common stock	(11)	2	41	(9)	Decrease in bonds payable
			28	(10)	Cash dividends paid
Net increase in cash and cash equivalents		62			

Accounts Receivable		Inventory		Property, Plant, and Equipment		Accumulated Depreciation	
Bal. 654		Bal. 537		Bal. 1,394			561 Bal.
	17 (3)	(4) 49		(8) 138	15 (12)	(12) 10	103 (2)
Bal. 637		Bal. 586		Bal. 1,517			654 Bal.

Accounts Payable		Accrued Liabilities		Income Taxes Payable	
	220 Bal.		190 Bal.		71 Bal.
	44 (5)		3 (6)		4 (7)
	264 Bal.		193 Bal.		75 Bal.

Bonds Payable		Common Stock		Retained Earnings	
	520 Bal.		155 Bal.		897 Bal.
(9) 41			2 (11)	(10) 28	140 (1)
	479 Bal.		157 Bal.		1,009 Bal.

Notice the gain on the sale of $3 million is recorded in the credit side of the Cash T-account. This is equivalent to subtracting the gain from net income so the entire amount of the cash proceeds from the sale of $8 million can be recorded in the investing activities section of the statement of cash flows.

Interpreting the Statement of Cash Flows

Managers derive many useful insights from the statement of cash flows. In this section, we discuss two guidelines managers should use when interpreting the statement of cash flows.

Consider a Company's Specific Circumstances

A statement of cash flows should be evaluated in the context of a company's specific circumstances. To illustrate this point, let's consider two examples related to start-up companies and companies with growing versus declining sales. Start-up companies usually are unable to generate positive cash flows from operations; therefore, they rely on issuing stock and taking out loans to fund investing activities. This means start-up companies often have negative net cash provided by operating activities and large spikes in net cash used for investing activities and net cash provided by financing activities. However, as a start-up company matures, it should begin generating enough cash to sustain day-to-day operations and maintain its plant and equipment without issuing additional stock or borrowing money. This means the net cash provided by operating activities should swing from a negative to a positive number. The net cash used for investing activities should decline somewhat and stabilize and the net cash provided by financing activities should decrease.

A company with growing sales would understandably have an increase in its accounts receivable, inventory, and accounts payable balances. On the other hand, if a company with declining sales has increases in these account balances, it could signal trouble. Perhaps accounts receivable is increasing because the company is attempting to boost sales by selling to customers who can't pay their bills. Perhaps the increase in inventory suggests the company is stuck with large amounts of obsolete inventory. Accounts payable may be increasing because the company is deferring payments to suppliers to inflate its net cash provided by operating activities. Notice the plausible interpretations of these changes in account balances depend on the company's circumstances.

Consider the Relationships among Numbers

While each number in a statement of cash flows provides useful information, managers derive the most meaningful insights by examining the relationships among numbers.

For example, some managers study their company's trends in cash flow margins by comparing the net cash provided by operating activities to sales. The goal is to continuously increase the operating cash flows earned per sales dollar. If we refer back to Apparel's income statement in Exhibit 15–6 and its statement of cash flows in Exhibit 15–11, we can determine its cash flow margin is about $0.07 per dollar of sales (= $259 ÷ $3,638). Managers also compare the net cash provided by operating activities to the ending balance of current liabilities. If the net cash provided by operating activities is greater than (less than) the current liabilities, it indicates the company did (did not) generate enough operating cash flow to pay its bills at the end of the period. Apparel's net cash provided by operating activities of $259 million (see Exhibit 15–11) was not enough to pay its year-end current liabilities of $532 million (see Exhibit 15–7).

As a third example, managers compare the additions to property, plant, and equipment in the investing activities section of the statement of cash flows to the depreciation included in the operating activities section of the statement. If the additions to property, plant, and equipment are consistently less than depreciation, it suggests the company is not investing enough money to maintain its noncurrent assets. If we refer back to Apparel's statement of cash flows in Exhibit 15–11, its additions to property, plant, and equipment ($138 million) are greater than its depreciation ($103 million). This suggests Apparel is investing more than enough money to maintain its noncurrent assets.

Free Cash Flow *Free cash flow* looks at the relationship among three numbers from the statement of cash flows—net cash provided by operating activities; additions to property, plant, and equipment (also called capital expenditures); and dividends. **Free cash flow** measures a company's ability to fund its capital expenditures for property, plant, and equipment and its cash dividends from its net cash provided by operating activities.[6] The equation for computing free cash flow is as follows:

LO15–6
Compute free cash flow.

$$\text{Free cash flow} = \begin{array}{c} \text{Net cash provided} \\ \text{by operating} \\ \text{activities} \end{array} - \text{Capital expenditures} - \text{Dividends}$$

---

[6] For a summary of alternative definitions of free cash flow, see John Mills, Lynn Bible, and Richard Mason, "Defining Free Cash Flow," *CPA Journal*, January 2002, pp. 36–42.

Using this equation and the statement of cash flows shown in Exhibit 15–11, we can compute Apparel's free cash flow (in millions) as follows:

$$\text{Free cash flow} = \$259 - \$138 - \$28$$
$$= \$93$$

The interpretation of free cash flow is straightforward. A positive number indicates the company generated enough cash flow from its operating activities to fund its capital expenditures and dividend payments. A negative number suggests the company needed to obtain cash from other sources, such as borrowing money from lenders or issuing shares of common stock, to fund its investments in property, plant, and equipment and its dividend payments. Negative free cash flow does not automatically signal poor performance. As previously discussed, a new company with enormous growth prospects would be expected to have negative free cash flow during its start-up phase. However, even new companies eventually need to generate positive free cash flow to survive.

COMMUNICATING WITH DATA VISUALIZATIONS

Descriptive analytics answer the question: What happened? This visualization uses a doughnut chart to describe, Apparel, Inc.'s free cash flow (in millions). The total net cash provided by operating activities, as stated in the middle of the circle, is $259. The doughnut chart breaks this total into three pieces: (1) capital expenditures of $138, (2) dividends of $28, and (3) free cash flow of $93.

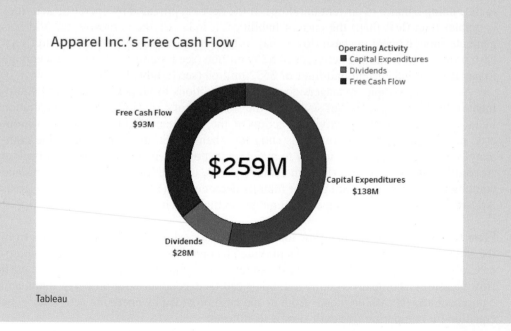

Tableau

Earnings Quality   Managers and investors look at the relationship between net income and net cash provided by operating activities to assess the extent to which a company's earnings truly reflect operational performance. Managers generally perceive earnings are of higher quality, or more indicative of operational performance, when the earnings (1) are not unduly influenced by inflation, (2) are computed using conservative accounting principles and estimates, and (3) are correlated with net cash provided by operating activities. When a company's net income and net cash provided by operating activities move in tandem with one another (in other words, are correlated with one another), it suggests earnings result from changes in sales and operating expenses. Conversely, if a company's net income is steadily increasing and its net cash provided by operating activities is declining, it suggests net income is being influenced by factors unrelated to operational performance, such as nonrecurring transactions or aggressive accounting principles and estimates.

COMPANIES SIT ON PILES OF CASH

Due to the uncertainty created by the COVID-19 pandemic, many companies dramatically increased their cash balances. For example, while only operating 23 of its 91 ships, cruise-line operator Carnival Corporation bumped its cash balance to $9 billion, compared to a usual balance of $2.5 billion. United Airlines Holdings "had $23 billion of liquidity at the end of the second quarter, more than quadruple the same period of 2019." Volkswagen's cash balance grew to $41 billion, an 88 percent increase over the prior year. S&P Global estimates companies across the globe are sitting on $6.84 trillion in cash, which is 45 percent higher than the five-year average preceding the pandemic.

Source: Anna Hirtenstein, "Companies Hold Tight with Their Piles of Cash," *The Wall Street Journal*, August 17, 2021, pp. B1–B2.

Summary

The statement of cash flows is one of three major financial statements prepared by organizations. It explains how cash was generated and how it was used during a period. The statement of cash flows is widely used as a tool for assessing the financial health of organizations.

For external reporting purposes, the statement of cash flows must be organized in terms of operating, investing, and financing activities. The net cash provided by operating activities is an important measure because it indicates how successful a company is in generating cash on a continuing basis. The indirect method of computing the net cash provided by operating activities is a three-step process. The first step is to add depreciation to net income. The second step is to analyze net changes in noncash balance sheet accounts that impact net income. The third step is to adjust for gains or losses included in the income statement.

The investing and financing sections of the statement of cash flows must report gross cash flows. The statement of cash flows summarizes the net increase/decrease in cash and cash equivalents during the period, which explains the change in the cash balance.

 Data Analytics Exercise available in Connect to complement this chapter

Review Problem

Rockford Company's comparative balance sheets for this year and last year and its income statement for this year follow:

Rockford Company Comparative Balance Sheet (dollars in millions)	This Year	Last Year
Assets		
Current assets:		
Cash and cash equivalents	$ 26	$ 10
Accounts receivable	180	270
Inventory	205	160
Prepaid expenses	17	20
Total current assets	428	460
Property, plant, and equipment	430	309
Less accumulated depreciation	218	194
Net property, plant, and equipment	212	115
Long-term investments	60	75
Total assets	$700	$650
Liabilities and Stockholders' Equity		
Current liabilities:		
Accounts payable	$230	$310
Accrued liabilities	70	60
Income taxes payable	15	8
Total current liabilities	315	378
Bonds payable	135	40
Total liabilities	450	418
Stockholders' equity:		
Common stock	140	140
Retained earnings	110	92
Total stockholders' equity	250	232
Total liabilities and stockholders' equity	$700	$650

Rockford Company Income Statement For This Year Ended December 31 (dollars in millions)	
Sales	$1,000
Cost of goods sold	530
Gross margin	470
Selling and administrative expenses	352
Net operating income	118
Nonoperating items:	
Loss on sale of equipment	4
Income before taxes	114
Income taxes	48
Net income	$ 66

Additional data:
1. This year Rockford paid a cash dividend.
2. The $4 million loss on sale of equipment reflects a transaction in which equipment with an original cost of $12 million and accumulated depreciation of $5 million was sold for $3 million in cash.
3. Rockford did not purchase any long-term investments during the year. There was no gain or loss on the sale of long-term investments.
4. This year Rockford did not retire any bonds payable, or issue or repurchase any common stock.

Required:
1. Using the indirect method, calculate the net cash provided by operating activities for this year.
2. Construct a statement of cash flows for this year.

Solution to Review Problem

The first task you should complete before turning your attention to the problem's specific requirements is to compute the changes in each balance sheet account as shown below (all amounts are in millions):

Rockford Company Comparative Balance Sheet (dollars in millions)			
	This Year	Last Year	Change
Assets			
Current assets:			
Cash and cash equivalents	$ 26	$ 10	+16
Accounts receivable	180	270	−90
Inventory	205	160	+45
Prepaid expenses	17	20	−3
Total current assets	428	460	
Property, plant, and equipment	430	309	+121
Less accumulated depreciation	218	194	+24
Net property, plant, and equipment	212	115	
Long-term investments	60	75	−15
Total assets	$700	$650	
Liabilities and Stockholders' Equity			
Current liabilities:			
Accounts payable	$230	$310	−80
Accrued liabilities	70	60	+10
Income taxes payable	15	8	+7
Total current liabilities	315	378	
Bonds payable	135	40	+95
Total liabilities	450	418	
Stockholders' equity:			
Common stock	140	140	+0
Retained earnings	110	92	+18
Total stockholders' equity	250	232	
Total liabilities and stockholders' equity	$700	$650	

Requirement 1:

You should perform three steps to compute the net cash provided by operating activities.

Step 1: Add depreciation to net income.

To complete this step, apply the following equation:

$$\text{Beginning balance} - \text{Debits} + \text{Credits} = \text{Ending balance}$$

$$\$194 \text{ million} - \$5 \text{ million} + \text{Credits} = \$218 \text{ million}$$

$$\text{Credits} = \$218 \text{ million} - \$194 \text{ million} + \$5 \text{ million}$$

$$\text{Credits} = \$29 \text{ million}$$

Step 2: Analyze net changes in noncash balance sheet accounts that affect net income. To complete this step, apply the logic from Exhibit 15–2 as follows:

	Increase in Account Balance	Decrease in Account Balance
Current Assets:		
Accounts receivable		+90
Inventory	−45	
Prepaid expenses		+3
Current Liabilities:		
Accounts payable		−80
Accrued liabilities	+10	
Income taxes payable	+7	

Step 3: Adjust for gains/losses included in the income statement.
Rockford's $4 million loss on the sale of equipment must be added to net income.

Having completed these three steps, the operating activities section of the statement of cash flows would appear as follows:

Rockford Company Statement of Cash Flows—Indirect Method For This Year Ended December 31 (dollars in millions)		
Operating Activities		
Net income		$66
Adjustments to convert net income to a cash basis:		
Depreciation	$29	
Decrease in accounts receivable	90	
Increase in inventory	(45)	
Decrease in prepaid expenses	3	
Decrease in accounts payable	(80)	
Increase in accrued liabilities	10	
Increase in income taxes payable	7	
Loss on sale of equipment	4	18
Net cash provided by (used in) operating activities		$84

Requirement 2:
To finalize the statement of cash flows, we must complete the investing and financing sections of the statement. This requires analyzing the Property, Plant, and Equipment; Long-Term Investments; Bonds Payable; Common Stock; and Retained Earnings accounts. The table below is based on Exhibits 15–3 and 15–4 and it captures the changes in four account balances for Rockford.

	Increase in Account Balance	Decrease in Account Balance
Noncurrent Assets		
Property, plant, and equipment	− 121	
Long-term investments		+15
Liabilities and Stockholders' Equity		
Bonds payable	+95	
Common stock	No change	No change
Retained earnings	*	*
*Requires further analysis to quantify cash dividends paid.		

The data at the beginning of the problem state Rockford did not purchase any long-term investments during the year and there was no gain or loss on the sale of long-term investments. This means the $15 million decrease in Long-Term Investments corresponds with a $15 million cash inflow from the sale of long-term investments that is recorded in the investing section of the statement of cash flows. The data also state Rockford did not retire any bonds payable during the year; therefore, the $95 million increase in Bonds Payable must be due to issuing bonds payable. This cash inflow is recorded in the financing section of the statement of cash flows.

The Common Stock account had no activity during the period, so it does not impact the statement of cash flows. This leaves two accounts requiring further analysis—Property, Plant, and Equipment and Retained Earnings.

The company sold equipment with an original cost of $12 million for $3 million in cash. The cash proceeds from the sale need to be recorded in the investing activities section of the statement of cash flows. The cash outflows related to Rockford's investing activities can be computed using the following equation:

$$\text{Beginning balance} + \text{Debits} - \text{Credits} = \text{Ending balance}$$
$$\$309 \text{ million} + \text{Debits} - \$12 \text{ million} = \$430 \text{ million}$$
$$\text{Debits} = \$430 \text{ million} - \$309 \text{ million} + \$12 \text{ million}$$
$$\text{Debits} = \$133 \text{ million}$$

Rockford's Retained Earnings account and the basic equation for stockholders' equity can be used to compute the company's dividend payment as follows:

$$\text{Beginning balance} - \text{Debits} + \text{Credits} = \text{Ending balance}$$
$$\$92 \text{ million} - \text{Debits} + \$66 \text{ million} = \$110 \text{ million}$$
$$\$158 \text{ million} = \$110 \text{ million} + \text{Debits}$$
$$\text{Debits} = \$48 \text{ million}$$

The company's complete statement of cash flows is shown below. Notice the net increase in cash and cash equivalents of $16 million equals the change in the Cash and Cash Equivalents account balance.

Rockford Company Statement of Cash Flows—Indirect Method For This Year Ended December 31 (dollars in millions)		
Operating Activities		
Net income		$66
Adjustments to convert net income to a cash basis:		
Depreciation	$29	
Decrease in accounts receivable	90	
Increase in inventory	(45)	
Decrease in prepaid expenses	3	
Decrease in accounts payable	(80)	
Increase in accrued liabilities	10	
Increase in income taxes payable	7	
Loss on sale of equipment	4	18
Net cash provided by (used in) operating activities		84
Investing Activities		
Additions to property, plant, and equipment	(133)	
Proceeds from sale of long-term investments	15	
Proceeds from sale of equipment	3	
Net cash provided by (used in) investing activities		(115)
Financing Activities		
Issuance of bonds	95	
Cash dividends paid	(48)	
Net cash provided by (used in) financing activities		47
Net increase in cash and cash equivalents		16
Beginning cash and cash equivalents		10
Ending cash and cash equivalents		$26

Glossary

Cash equivalents Short-term, highly liquid investments such as Treasury bills, commercial paper, and money market funds, that generate a return on temporarily idle cash. (p. 684)

Direct method A method of computing the net cash provided by operating activities in which the income statement is reconstructed on a cash basis from top to bottom. (p. 685)

Financing activities These activities generate cash inflows and outflows related to borrowing from and repaying principal to creditors and completing transactions with the company's owners, such as selling or repurchasing shares of common stock and paying dividends. (p. 684)

Free cash flow A measure of a company's ability to fund its capital expenditures and dividends from its net cash provided by operating activities. (p. 699)

Indirect method A method of computing the net cash provided by operating activities that starts with net income and adjusts it to a cash basis. (p. 685)

Investing activities These activities generate cash inflows and outflows related to acquiring or disposing of noncurrent assets such as property, plant, and equipment; long-term investments; and loans to another entity. (p. 684)

Net cash provided by operating activities The net result of the cash inflows and outflows arising from day-to-day operations. (p. 685)

Operating activities These activities generate cash inflows and outflows related to revenue and expense transactions that affect net income. (p. 684)

Statement of cash flows A financial statement highlighting the major activities impacting cash flows and the overall cash balance. (p. 683)

Questions

15–1 What is the purpose of a statement of cash flows?

15–2 What are *cash equivalents,* and why are they included with cash on a statement of cash flows?

15–3 What are the three major sections on a statement of cash flows, and what type of cash inflows and outflows should be included in each section?

15–4 What general guidelines can you provide for interpreting the statement of cash flows?

15–5 If an asset is sold at a gain, why is the gain subtracted from net income when computing the net cash provided by operating activities under the indirect method?

15–6 Why aren't transactions involving accounts payable considered to be financing activities?

15–7 Assume a company repays a $300,000 loan from its bank and then later in the same year borrows $500,000. What amount(s) would appear on the statement of cash flows?

15–8 How do the direct and the indirect methods differ in computing the net cash provided by operating activities?

15–9 A business executive once stated, "Depreciation is one of our biggest operating cash inflows." Do you agree? Explain.

15–10 If the Accounts Receivable balance increases, how will this increase be recognized using the indirect method of computing the net cash provided by operating activities?

15–11 Would a sale of equipment for cash be a financing activity or an investing activity? Why?

15–12 What is the difference between net cash provided by operating activities and free cash flow?

The Foundational 15

LO15–1, LO15–2, LO15–3, LO15–4, LO15–5

Ravenna Company is a merchandiser using the indirect method to prepare the operating activities section of its statement of cash flows. Its balance sheet for this year is as follows:

	Ending Balance	Beginning Balance
Cash and cash equivalents	$ 48,000	$ 57,000
Accounts receivable	41,000	44,000
Inventory	55,000	50,000
Total current assets	144,000	151,000
Property, plant, and equipment	150,000	140,000
Less accumulated depreciation	50,000	35,000
Net property, plant, and equipment	100,000	105,000
Total assets	$244,000	$256,000
Accounts payable	$ 32,000	$ 57,000
Income taxes payable	25,000	28,000
Bonds payable	60,000	50,000
Common stock	70,000	60,000
Retained earnings	57,000	61,000
Total liabilities and stockholders' equity	$244,000	$256,000

During the year, Ravenna paid a $6,000 cash dividend and sold a piece of equipment for $3,000 that originally cost $6,000 and had accumulated depreciation of $4,000. The company did not retire any bonds or repurchase any of its own common stock during the year.

Required:

1. What net change in cash and cash equivalents would be shown on the company's statement of cash flows?
2. What net income would the company include on its statement of cash flows?
3. How much depreciation would the company add to net income on its statement of cash flows?
4. (To help answer this question, create an Accounts Receivable T-account and insert the beginning and ending balances.) If the company debited Accounts Receivable and credited Sales for $600,000 during the year, what is the total amount of credits recorded in Accounts Receivable during the year? What does the amount of these credits represent?
5. What are the amount and direction (+ or −) of the accounts receivable adjustment to net income in the operating activities section of the statement of cash flows? What does this adjustment represent?
6. (To help answer this question, create T-accounts for Inventory and Accounts Payable and insert their beginning and ending balances.) If the company debited Cost of Goods Sold and credited Inventory for $400,000 during the year, what is the total amount of inventory purchases recorded on the debit side of the Inventory T-account and the credit side of the Accounts Payable T-account? What is the total amount of the debits recorded in the Accounts Payable T-account during the year? What does the amount of these debits represent?
7. What is the combined amount and direction (+ or −) of the inventory and accounts payable adjustments to net income in the operating activities section of the statement of cash flows? What does this amount represent?
8. (To help answer this question, create an Income Taxes Payable T-account and insert the beginning and ending balances.) If the company debited Income Tax Expense and credited Income Taxes Payable $700 during the year, what is the total amount of the debits recorded in the Income Taxes Payable account? What does the amount of these debits represent?
9. What are the amount and direction (+ or −) of the income taxes payable adjustment to net income in the operating activities section of the statement of cash flows? What does this adjustment represent?
10. Would the operating activities section of the company's statement of cash flows contain an adjustment for a gain or a loss? What would be the amount and direction (+ or −) of the adjustment?
11. What is the company's net cash provided by operating activities?
12. What are the gross cash outflows in the investing section of the company's statement of cash flows?

13. What is the company's net cash provided by (used in) investing activities?
14. What are the gross cash inflows in the financing section of the company's statement of cash flows?
15. What is the company's net cash provided by (used in) financing activities?

Exercises   Mc Graw Hill connect

EXERCISE 15–1 Classifying Transactions LO15–1

The following transactions occurred at Hazzard, Inc., last year:

a. Collected cash from customers.
b. Paid cash to repurchase its own stock.
c. Borrowed money from a creditor.
d. Paid suppliers for inventory purchases.
e. Repaid the principal amount of a debt.
f. Paid interest to lenders.
g. Paid a cash dividend to stockholders.
h. Sold common stock.
i. Loaned money to another entity.
j. Paid taxes to the government.
k. Paid wages and salaries to employees.
l. Purchased equipment with cash.
m. Paid bills to insurers and utility providers.

Required:
Prepare an answer sheet with the following headings:

| | Activity | | |
Transaction	Operating	Investing	Financing
a.			
b.			
Etc.			

For each transaction, place an X under the appropriate heading to indicate whether it is an Operating, Investing, or Financing activity.

EXERCISE 15–2 Net Cash Provided by Operating Activities LO15–2

Hanna Company's current asset and current liability account balances at the beginning and end of the year were as follows:

| | December 31 | |
	End of Year	Beginning of Year
Current assets:		
Cash and cash equivalents	$30,000	$40,000
Accounts receivable	$125,000	$106,000
Inventory	$213,000	$180,000
Prepaid expenses	$6,000	$7,000
Current liabilities:		
Accounts payable	$210,000	$195,000
Accrued liabilities	$4,000	$6,000
Income taxes payable	$34,000	$30,000

The Accumulated Depreciation account had total credits of $20,000. Hanna Company's net income was $35,000 and it did not record any gains or losses on the sale of noncurrent assets.

Required:
Using the indirect method, calculate the net cash provided by operating activities for the year.

EXERCISE 15–3 Net Cash Provided by (Used in) Investing Activities LO15–3
Assume the following excerpts from a company's balance sheet:

	Beginning Balance	Ending Balance
Property, plant, and equipment	$3,500,000	$3,700,000
Long-term investments	$1,100,000	$800,000

During the year, the company did not sell any property, plant, and equipment or purchase any long-term investments. Its income statement did not report any gains or losses.

Required:
Calculate the company's net cash provided by (used in) investing activities.

EXERCISE 15–4 Net Cash Provided by (Used in) Financing Activities LO15–4
Assume the following excerpts from a company's balance sheet:

	Beginning Balance	Ending Balance
Bonds payable	$500,000	$650,000
Common stock	$950,000	$950,000
Retained earnings	$375,000	$440,000

During the year, the company's net income was $120,000 and it did not retire any bonds or issue or repurchase any common stock.

Required:
Calculate the net cash provided by (used in) financing activities.

EXERCISE 15–5 Statement of Cash Flows LO15–5
Assume the following information:

Item	Amount	Item	Amount
Beginning cash and cash equivalents	$110,000	Gain on sale of equipment	$(11,000)
Additions to plant and equipment	$(180,000)	Change in accounts receivable	$11,000
Depreciation	$40,000	Change in accounts payable	$5,000
		Proceeds from sale of	
Cash dividends	$(25,000)	equipment	$70,000
Additions to long-term investments	$(60,000)	Issuance of bonds payable	$80,000
		Change in income taxes	
Change in inventory	$(21,000)	payable	$(4,000)
Change in accrued liabilities ...	$7,000	Change in prepaid expenses	$(5,000)
Increase in common stock	$30,000	Net income	$115,000

During the year, the company did not sell any long-term investments, retire any bonds payable, or repurchase any common stock.

Required:
1. Calculate the net cash provided by operating activities.
2. Calculate the net cash provided by (used in) investing activities.
3. Calculate the net cash provided by (used in) financing activities.
4. Calculate the cash and cash equivalents ending balance.

EXERCISE 15–6 Calculating Free Cash Flow LO15–6

Apex Company prepared the statement of cash flows shown below:

Apex Company Statement of Cash Flows—Indirect Method		
Operating activities		
Net income		$ 40,000
Adjustments to convert net income to cash basis:		
Depreciation	$ 22,000	
Increase in accounts receivable	(60,000)	
Increase in inventory	(25,000)	
Decrease in prepaid expenses	9,000	
Increase in accounts payable	55,000	
Decrease in accrued liabilities	(12,000)	
Increase in income taxes payable	5,000	(6,000)
Net cash provided by (used in) operating activities		34,000
Investing activities		
Proceeds from the sale of equipment	14,000	
Loan to Thomas Company	(40,000)	
Additions to plant and equipment	(110,000)	
Net cash provided by (used in) investing activities		(136,000)
Financing activities		
Increase in bonds payable	90,000	
Increase in common stock	40,000	
Cash dividends	(30,000)	
Net cash provided by (used in) financing activities		100,000
Net decrease in cash and cash equivalents		(2,000)
Beginning cash and cash equivalents		27,000
Ending cash and cash equivalents		$ 25,000

Required:

Compute Apex Company's free cash flow.

EXERCISE 15–7 Prepare a Statement of Cash Flows LO15–1, LO15–2, LO15–3, LO15–4, LO15–5

The following changes took place last year in Pavolik Company's balance sheet accounts:

Asset and Contra-asset Accounts			Liabilities and Stockholders' Equity Accounts		
Cash and cash equivalents	$5	D	Accounts payable	$35	I
Accounts receivable	$110	I	Accrued liabilities	$4	D
Inventory	$70	D	Income taxes payable	$8	I
Prepaid expenses	$9	I	Bonds payable	$150	I
Long-term investments	$6	D	Common stock	$80	D
Property, plant, and equipment ...	$185	I	Retained earnings	$54	I
Accumulated depreciation	$60	I			

D = Decrease; I = Increase

Long-term investments costing $6 were sold for $16 and land costing $15 was sold for $9. In addition, the company paid $30 in cash dividends. Besides the sale of land, no other sales or retirements of plant and equipment took place during the year. Pavolik did not retire any bonds or issue common stock.

The company's income statement for the year follows:

Sales		$700
Cost of goods sold		400
Gross margin		300
Selling and administrative expenses		184
Net operating income		116
Nonoperating items:		
Loss on sale of land	$(6)	
Gain on sale of investments	10	4
Income before taxes		120
Income taxes		36
Net income		$ 84

The company's beginning cash balance was $90 and its ending balance was $85.

Required:
1. Use the indirect method to determine the net cash provided by operating activities.
2. Prepare a statement of cash flows.

EXERCISE 15–8 Net Cash Provided by Operating Activities LO15–2

Changes in various accounts and gains and losses on the sale of assets for Argon Company are given below:

Item	Amount
Accounts receivable	$90,000 decrease
Inventory	$120,000 increase
Prepaid expenses	$3,000 decrease
Accounts payable	$65,000 decrease
Accrued liabilities	$8,000 increase
Income taxes payable	$12,000 increase
Sale of equipment	$7,000 gain
Sale of long-term investments	$10,000 loss

Required:

Prepare an answer sheet using the following column headings:

Item	Amount	Add	Subtract

For each item, place an X in the Add or Subtract column to indicate whether the dollar amount should be added to or subtracted from net income under the indirect method when computing the net cash provided by operating activities.

EXERCISE 15–9 Net Cash Provided by (Used in) Investing Activities LO15–3

Assume the following excerpts from a company's balance sheet:

	Beginning Balance	Ending Balance
Property, plant, and equipment	$3,400,000	$3,750,000
Long-term investments	$950,000	$1,100,000

During the year, the company sold a piece of equipment for $200,000. The equipment originally cost $500,000 and had accumulated depreciation of $270,000. The company did not sell any long-term investments during the period.

Required:

Calculate the company's net cash provided by (used in) investing activities.

EXERCISE 15–10 Net Cash Provided by (Used in) Financing Activities; Statement of Cash Flows LO15–2, LO15–4, LO15–5

Assume a company's balance sheet included the following long-term liabilities and stockholders' equity accounts:

	Beginning Balance	Ending Balance
Bonds payable	$500,000	$590,000
Common stock	$900,000	$900,000
Retained earnings	$375,000	$450,000

Also assume the company's beginning and ending cash balances are $270,000 and $240,000, respectively; its net income is $125,000; and its net cash provided by (used in) investing activities is $(220,000). The company did not retire any bonds payable during the year.

Required:
1. Calculate the company's dividend payment.
2. Calculate the net cash provided by (used in) financing activities.
3. Calculate the net cash provided by operating activities.

EXERCISE 15–11 Prepare a Statement of Cash Flows; Free Cash Flow LO15–1, LO15–2, LO15–3, LO15–4, LO15–5, LO15–6

Comparative financial statement data for Carmono Company follow:

	This Year	Last Year
Assets		
Cash and cash equivalents	$ 3	$ 6
Accounts receivable	22	24
Inventory	50	40
Total current assets	75	70
Property, plant, and equipment	240	200
Less accumulated depreciation	65	50
Net property, plant, and equipment	175	150
Total assets	$250	$220
Liabilities and Stockholders' Equity		
Accounts payable	$ 40	$ 36
Common stock	150	145
Retained earnings	60	39
Total liabilities and stockholders' equity	$250	$220

For this year, the company reported net income as follows:

Sales	$275
Cost of goods sold	150
Gross margin	125
Selling and administrative expenses	90
Net income	$ 35

This year Carmono paid a cash dividend but it did not sell any property, plant, and equipment or repurchase any of its own stock.

Required:
1. Using the indirect method, prepare a statement of cash flows for this year.
2. Compute Carmono's free cash flow for this year.

EXERCISE 15–12 Net Cash Provided by Operating Activities LO15–2
Assume a company's net cash provided by operating activities is $81,000. It provided the following excerpts from its balance sheet:

	This Year	Last Year
Current assets:		
Accounts receivable	$41,000	$46,000
Inventory	$53,000	$44,000
Prepaid expenses	$13,000	$11,000
Current liabilities:		
Accounts payable	$40,000	$44,000
Accrued liabilities	$18,000	$15,000
Income taxes payable	$13,000	$10,000

Also assume the company incurred a loss on the sale of equipment of $7,000 and the credits to its accumulated depreciation account are $22,000.

Required:
1. Calculate the adjustment that would appear in the operating activities section of the statement of cash flows for each of the following (use parentheses for amounts that would decrease net income):
   a. Depreciation
   b. Accounts receivable
   c. Inventory
   d. Prepaid expenses
   e. Accounts payable
   f. Accrued liabilities
   g. Income taxes payable
   h. Loss on the sale of equipment
2. Calculate the company's net income.

EXERCISE 15–13 Net Cash Provided by (Used in) Financing Activities LO15–4
Assume the following excerpts from a company's balance sheet:

	Beginning Balance	Ending Balance
Bonds payable	$500,000	$630,000
Common stock	$900,000	$920,000
Retained earnings	$380,000	$450,000

During the year, the company did not retire any bonds or repurchase any common stock. Its net cash provided by financing activities is $65,000.

Required:
1. Calculate the adjustments that would appear in the financing activities section of the statement of cash flows for each of the following (use parentheses to indicate decreases):
   a. Bonds payable
   b. Common stock
   c. Dividends
2. Calculate the company's net income.

Problems   Mc Graw Hill connect

PROBLEM 15–14 Prepare a Statement of Cash Flows LO15–1, LO15–2, LO15–3, LO15–4, LO15–5

Comparative financial statements for Weaver Company follow:

Weaver Company Comparative Balance Sheet at December 31	This Year	Last Year
Assets		
Cash and cash equivalents	$ 9	$ 15
Accounts receivable	340	240
Inventory	125	175
Prepaid expenses	10	6
Total current assets	484	436
Property, plant, and equipment	610	470
Less accumulated depreciation	93	85
Net property, plant, and equipment	517	385
Long-term investments	16	19
Total assets	$1,017	$840
Liabilities and Stockholders' Equity		
Accounts payable	$ 310	$230
Accrued liabilities	60	72
Income taxes payable	40	34
Total current liabilities	410	336
Bonds payable	290	180
Total liabilities	700	516
Common stock	210	250
Retained earnings	107	74
Total stockholders' equity	317	324
Total liabilities and stockholders' equity	$1,017	$840

Weaver Company Income Statement For This Year Ended December 31		
Sales		$800
Cost of goods sold		500
Gross margin		300
Selling and administrative expenses		213
Net operating income		87
Nonoperating items:		
Gain on sale of investments	$7	
Loss on sale of equipment	(4)	3
Income before taxes		90
Income taxes		27
Net income		$ 63

During this year, Weaver sold some equipment for $20 that had cost $40 and on which there was accumulated depreciation of $16. In addition, the company sold long-term investments for $10 that had cost $3 when purchased several years ago. Weaver paid a cash dividend and repurchased $40 of its own stock but did not retire any bonds.

Required:
1. Using the indirect method, determine the net cash provided by operating activities for this year.
2. Prepare a statement of cash flows for this year.

PROBLEM 15–15 Classification of Transactions LO15–1

Below are several transactions that took place in Seneca Company last year:

a.   Paid suppliers for inventory purchases.

b.   Bought equipment for cash.

c.   Paid cash to repurchase its own stock.

d.   Collected cash from customers.

e.   Paid wages to employees.

f.   Sold equipment for cash.

g.   Sold common stock to investors.

h.   Paid cash dividends.

i.   Made long-term loan to a supplier.

j.   Paid income taxes to the government.

k.   Paid interest to a lender.

l.   Retired bonds by paying the principal amount due.

Required:

Prepare an answer sheet with the following headings:

Transaction	Activity			Cash Inflow	Cash Outflow
	Operating	Investing	Financing		
a.					
b.					
Etc.					

Indicate how each of the above transactions would be classified on a statement of cash flows. As appropriate, place an X in the Operating, Investing, or Financing column. Also, place an X in the Cash Inflow or Cash Outflow column.

PROBLEM 15–16 Understanding a Statement of Cash Flows LO15–1, LO15–2, LO15–3, LO15–4, LO15–5

Brock Company is a merchandiser that prepared the statement of cash flows and income statement provided below:

Brock Company		
Statement of Cash Flows—Indirect Method		
Operating Activities		
Net income		$275
Adjustments to convert net income to a cash basis:		
Depreciation	$140	
Increase in accounts receivable	(24)	
Decrease in inventory	39	
Decrease in accounts payable	(45)	
Decrease in accrued liabilities	(5)	
Increase in income taxes payable	6	
Gain on sale of equipment	(4)	107
Net cash provided by (used in) operating activities		382
Investing Activities		
Additions to property, plant, and equipment	(150)	
Proceeds from sale of equipment	19	
Net cash provided by (used in) investing activities		(131)
Financing Activities		
Issuance of bonds payable	40	
Issuance of common stock	4	
Cash dividends paid	(35)	
Net cash provided by (used in) financing activities		9
Net increase in cash and cash equivalents		260
Beginning cash and cash equivalents		170
Ending cash and cash equivalents		$430

Brock Company Income Statement	
Sales	$5,200
Cost of goods sold	2,980
Gross margin	2,220
Selling and administrative expenses	1,801
Net operating income	419
Nonoperating items: Gain on sale of equipment	4
Income before taxes	423
Income taxes	148
Net income	$ 275

Required:

Assume you have been asked to teach a workshop to the employees within Brock Company's Marketing Department. The purpose of your workshop is to explain how the statement of cash flows differs from the income statement. Your audience is expecting you to explain the logic underlying each number included in the statement of cash flows. Prepare a memo explaining the format of the statement of cash flows and the rationale for each number included within it.

PROBLEM 15–17 Prepare a Statement of Cash Flows; Free Cash Flow LO15–1, LO15–2, LO15–3, LO15–4, LO15–5, LO15–6

Joyner Company's income statement for Year 2 follows:

Sales	$900,000
Cost of goods sold	500,000
Gross margin	400,000
Selling and administrative expenses	328,000
Net operating income	72,000
Nonoperating items:	
Gain on sale of equipment	8,000
Income before taxes	80,000
Income taxes	24,000
Net income	$ 56,000

Its balance sheet amounts at the end of Years 1 and 2 are as follows:

	Year 2	Year 1
Assets		
Cash and cash equivalents	$ 4,000	$ 21,000
Accounts receivable	250,000	170,000
Inventory	310,000	260,000
Prepaid expenses	7,000	14,000
Total current assets	571,000	465,000
Property, plant, and equipment	510,000	400,000
Less accumulated depreciation	132,000	120,000
Net property, plant, and equipment	378,000	280,000
Loan to Hymans Company	40,000	0
Total assets	$989,000	$745,000
Liabilities and Stockholders' Equity		
Accounts payable	$310,000	$250,000
Accrued liabilities	20,000	30,000
Income taxes payable	45,000	42,000
Total current liabilities	375,000	322,000
Bonds payable	190,000	70,000
Total liabilities	565,000	392,000
Common stock	300,000	270,000
Retained earnings	124,000	83,000
Total stockholders' equity	424,000	353,000
Total liabilities and stockholders' equity	$989,000	$745,000

Equipment costing $40,000 with accumulated depreciation of $30,000 was sold during Year 2 for $18,000. The company paid a cash dividend during Year 2 but did not retire any bonds or repurchase any of its own stock.

Required:

For Year 2:

1. Compute the net cash provided by operating activities using the indirect method.
2. Prepare a statement of cash flows.
3. Compute the free cash flow.
4. Briefly explain why cash declined so sharply.

PROBLEM 15–18 Missing Data; Statement of Cash Flows LO15–1, LO15–2, LO15–3, LO15–4, LO15–5

Yoric Company listed the net changes in its balance sheet accounts for the past year as follows:

	Debits > Credits by:	Credits > Debits by:
Cash and cash equivalents	$ 17,000	
Accounts receivable	110,000	
Inventory		$ 65,000
Prepaid expenses		8,000
Long-term loans to subsidiaries		30,000
Long-term investments	80,000	
Plant and equipment	220,000	
Accumulated depreciation		5,000
Accounts payable		32,000
Accrued liabilities	9,000	
Income taxes payable		16,000
Bonds payable		400,000
Common stock	170,000	
Retained earnings		50,000
	$ 606,000	$606,000

The following additional information is available about last year's activities:
a. Net income for the year was $ _____?_____ .
b. The company sold equipment during the year for $15,000. The equipment originally cost $50,000 and had $37,000 in accumulated depreciation.
c. Cash dividends of $20,000 were paid during the year.
d. The beginning and ending balances in the Plant and Equipment and Accumulated Depreciation accounts are given below:

	Beginning	Ending
Plant and equipment	$1,580,000	$1,800,000
Accumulated depreciation	$675,000	$680,000

e. The balance in the Cash account at the beginning of the year was $23,000; the balance at the end of the year was $ _____?_____ .
f. If data are not given explaining the change in an account, make the most reasonable assumption as to the cause of the change.

Required:

Using the indirect method, prepare a statement of cash flows.

PROBLEM 15–19 Prepare a Statement of Cash Flows LO15–1, LO15–2, LO15–3, LO15–4, LO15–5

A comparative balance sheet and an income statement for Burgess Company are given below:

Burgess Company Comparative Balance Sheet (dollars in millions)	Ending Balance	Beginning Balance
Assets		
Current assets:		
Cash and cash equivalents	$ 49	$ 79
Accounts receivable	645	580
Inventory	660	615
Total current assets	1,354	1,274
Property, plant, and equipment	1,515	1,466
Less accumulated depreciation	765	641
Net property, plant, and equipment	750	825
Total assets	$2,104	$2,099
Liabilities and Stockholders' Equity		
Current liabilities:		
Accounts payable	$ 250	$ 155
Accrued liabilities	190	165
Income taxes payable	76	70
Total current liabilities	516	390
Bonds payable	450	620
Total liabilities	966	1,010
Stockholders' equity:		
Common stock	161	161
Retained earnings	977	928
Total stockholders' equity	1,138	1,089
Total liabilities and stockholders' equity	$2,104	$2,099

Burgess Company Income Statement (dollars in millions)	
Sales	$3,600
Cost of goods sold	2,550
Gross margin	1,050
Selling and administrative expenses	875
Net operating income	175
Nonoperating items: Gain on sale of equipment	3
Income before taxes	178
Income taxes	63
Net income	$ 115

Burgess also provided the following information:
1.   The company sold equipment for $8 million that originally cost $13 million with accumulated depreciation of $8 million. The gain on the sale was $3 million.
2.   The company did not issue any new bonds, pay a dividend, or complete any common stock transactions during the year.

Required:
1.   Using the indirect method, prepare a statement of cash flows.

2. Assume Burgess had sales of $3,800, net income of $135, and net cash provided by operating activities of $150 in the prior year (all numbers are stated in millions). Prepare a memo summarizing your interpretations of Burgess's financial performance.

PROBLEM 15–20 Prepare and Interpret a Statement of Cash Flows; Free Cash Flow LO15–1, LO15–2, LO15–3, LO15–4, LO15–5, LO15–6

Mary Walker, president of Rusco Company, considers $14,000 to be the minimum cash balance for operating purposes. As can be seen from the following statements, only $8,000 in cash was available at the end of this year. Because the company reported a large net income for the year, and also issued both bonds and common stock, the sharp decline in cash is puzzling to Ms. Walker.

Rusco Company Comparative Balance Sheet at July 31	This Year	Last Year
Assets		
Current assets:		
Cash and cash equivalents	$ 8,000	$ 21,000
Accounts receivable	120,000	80,000
Inventory	140,000	90,000
Prepaid expenses	5,000	9,000
Total current assets	273,000	200,000
Long-term investments	50,000	70,000
Plant and equipment	430,000	300,000
Less accumulated depreciation	60,000	50,000
Net plant and equipment	370,000	250,000
Total assets	$693,000	$520,000
Liabilities and Stockholders' Equity		
Current liabilities:		
Accounts payable	$123,000	$ 60,000
Accrued liabilities	8,000	17,000
Income taxes payable	20,000	12,000
Total current liabilities	151,000	89,000
Bonds payable	70,000	0
Total liabilities	221,000	89,000
Stockholders' equity:		
Common stock	366,000	346,000
Retained earnings	106,000	85,000
Total stockholders' equity	472,000	431,000
Total liabilities and stockholders' equity	$693,000	$520,000

Rusco Company Income Statement For This Year Ended July 31		
Sales		$500,000
Cost of goods sold		300,000
Gross margin		200,000
Selling and administrative expenses		158,000
Net operating income		42,000
Nonoperating items:		
Gain on sale of investments	$10,000	
Loss on sale of equipment	(2,000)	8,000
Income before taxes		50,000
Income taxes		20,000
Net income		$ 30,000

The following additional information is available for this year.
a. The company paid a cash dividend.
b. Equipment costing $20,000 with accumulated depreciation of $10,000 was sold for $8,000.
c. Long-term investments costing $20,000 were sold for $30,000.
d. The company did not retire any bonds payable or repurchase any of its common stock.

Required:

For this year:
1. Compute the net cash provided by operating activities using the indirect method.
2. Prepare a statement of cash flows.
3. Compute free cash flow.
4. Explain the major reasons for the decline in the company's cash balance.

PROBLEM 15–21 Prepare and Interpret a Statement of Cash Flows LO15–1, LO15–2, LO15–3, LO15–4, LO15–5

A comparative balance sheet for Lomax Company containing data for the last two years is as follows:

Lomax Company Comparative Balance Sheet		
	This Year	Last Year
Assets		
Current assets:		
Cash and cash equivalents	$ 61,000	$ 40,000
Accounts receivable	710,000	530,000
Inventory	848,000	860,000
Prepaid expenses	10,000	5,000
Total current assets	1,629,000	1,435,000
Property, plant, and equipment	3,170,000	2,600,000
Less accumulated depreciation	810,000	755,000
Net property, plant, and equipment	2,360,000	1,845,000
Long-term investments	60,000	110,000
Loans to subsidiaries	214,000	170,000
Total assets	$4,263,000	$3,560,000
Liabilities and Stockholders' Equity		
Current liabilities:		
Accounts payable	$ 970,000	$ 670,000
Accrued liabilities	65,000	82,000
Income taxes payable	95,000	80,000
Total current liabilities	1,130,000	832,000
Bonds payable	820,000	600,000
Total liabilities	1,950,000	1,432,000
Stockholders' equity:		
Common stock	1,740,000	1,650,000
Retained earnings	573,000	478,000
Total stockholders' equity	2,313,000	2,128,000
Total liabilities and stockholders' equity	$4,263,000	$3,560,000

The following additional information is available about the company's activities during this year:
a. Paid a cash dividend this of _____?_____ .
b. Retired bonds with a principal balance of $350,000.
c. Equipment costing $130,000 with accumulated depreciation of $40,000 was sold for $70,000.
d. Sold long-term investments for $110,000. These investments cost $50,000 when purchased several years ago.

e. The subsidiaries did not repay any outstanding loans.
f. Lomax did not repurchase any of its own stock.

The company reported net income this year as follows:

Sales		$2,000,000
Cost of goods sold		1,300,000
Gross margin		700,000
Selling and administrative expenses . . .		490,000
Net operating income		210,000
Nonoperating items:		
Gain on sale of investments	$60,000	
Loss on sale of equipment	(20,000)	40,000
Income before taxes		250,000
Income taxes		80,000
Net income		$ 170,000

Required:
1. Using the indirect method, prepare a statement of cash flows for this year.
2. What problems relating to the company's activities are revealed by the statement of cash flows?

Appendix 15A: The Direct Method of Determining the Net Cash Provided by Operating Activities

To compute the net cash provided by operating activities under the direct method, we reconstruct the income statement on a cash basis from top to bottom. Exhibit 15A–1 shows the adjustments that translate sales, expenses, and so forth, to a cash basis. To illustrate, we have included in the exhibit the Apparel, Inc., data from the chapter.

Note the net cash provided by operating activities of $259 million agrees with the amount computed in the chapter by the indirect method. The two amounts agree because the direct and indirect methods are just different roads to the same destination. The investing and financing activities sections of the statement will be exactly the same as shown for the indirect method in Exhibit 15–11. The only difference between the indirect and direct methods is in the operating activities section.

LO15–7
Use the direct method to calculate the net cash provided by operating activities.

Similarities and Differences in the Handling of Data

Although we arrive at the same destination under either the direct or indirect method, not all data are handled the same way in the two adjustment processes. Stop for a moment, flip back to the bottom half of Exhibit 15–8, and compare the adjustments described in that exhibit to the adjustments made for the direct method in Exhibit 15A–1. The adjustments for accounts that affect sales (which includes only accounts receivable in our example) are handled the same way in the two methods. In either case, increases in the accounts are subtracted and decreases are added. However, the adjustments for accounts that affect expenses (which include all remaining accounts in Exhibit 15–8) are handled in opposite ways in the indirect and direct methods. This is because under the indirect method the adjustments are made to *net income,* whereas under the direct method the adjustments are made to the *expense accounts* themselves.

EXHIBIT 15A–1
General Model: Direct Method of Determining the Net Cash Provided by Operating Activities

Revenue or Expense Item	Add (+) or Deduct (−) to Adjust to a Cash Basis	Illustration— Apparel, Inc. (in millions)	
Sales (as reported)		$3,638	
Adjustments to a cash basis:			
Increase in accounts receivable	−		
Decrease in accounts receivable	+	+17	$3,655
Cost of goods sold (as reported)		2,469	
Adjustments to a cash basis:			
Increase in inventory	+	+49	
Decrease in inventory	−		
Increase in accounts payable	−	−44	
Decrease in accounts payable	+		2,474
Selling and administrative expenses (as reported)		941	
Adjustments to a cash basis:			
Increase in prepaid expenses	+		
Decrease in prepaid expenses	−		
Increase in accrued liabilities	−	−3	
Decrease in accrued liabilities	+		
Depreciation	−	−103	835
Income tax expense (as reported)		91	
Adjustments to a cash basis:			
Increase in income taxes payable	−	−4	
Decrease in income taxes payable	+		87
Net cash provided by (used in) operating activities ...			$ 259

To illustrate this difference, note the handling of inventory and depreciation in the indirect and direct methods. Under the indirect method (Exhibit 15–8), an increase in the inventory account ($49) is *subtracted* from net income to compute net cash provided by operating activities. Under the direct method (Exhibit 15A–1), an increase in inventory is *added* to cost of goods sold. The reason for the difference can be explained as follows: An increase in inventory means the period's inventory purchases exceeded the cost of goods sold included in the income statement. Therefore, to adjust net income to a cash basis, we either subtract this increase from net income (indirect method) or add it to cost of goods sold (direct method). Either way, we end up with the same figure for net cash provided by operating activities. Similarly, depreciation is added to net income under the indirect method to cancel out its effect (Exhibit 15–9), whereas it is subtracted from selling and administrative expenses under the direct method to cancel out its effect (Exhibit 15A–1). These differences in the handling of data are true for all other expense items in the two methods.

For gains and losses on sale of assets, no adjustments are needed under the direct method. These gains and losses are simply ignored because they are not part of sales, cost of goods sold, selling and administrative expenses, or income taxes. Observe in Exhibit 15A–1, Apparel's $3 million gain on the sale of the store is not listed as an adjustment in the operating activities section.

Special Rules—Direct and Indirect Methods

When the direct method is used, U.S. GAAP and IFRS require a reconciliation between net income and the net cash provided by operating activities, as determined by the indirect method. Thus, *when a company elects to use the direct method, it must also present the indirect method* in a separate schedule accompanying the statement of cash flows.

On the other hand, if a company elects to use the indirect method to compute the net cash provided by operating activities, then it also must provide a special breakdown of data. The company must provide a separate disclosure of the amount of interest and the amount of income taxes paid during the year. This separate disclosure enables users to take the data provided by the indirect method and make estimates of what the amounts for sales, income taxes, and so forth, would have been if the direct method had been used instead.

Mc Graw Hill connect   Appendix 15A: Exercises and Problems

EXERCISE 15A–1 Adjust Net Income to a Cash Basis LO15–7
Refer to the data for Pavolik Company in Exercise 15–7.

Required:
Use the direct method to convert the company's income statement to a cash basis.

EXERCISE 15A–2 Net Cash Provided by Operating Activities LO15–7
Wiley Company's income statement for Year 2 follows:

Sales	$150,000
Cost of goods sold	90,000
Gross margin	60,000
Selling and administrative expenses	40,000
Income before taxes	20,000
Income taxes	8,000
Net income	$ 12,000

The company's selling and administrative expense for Year 2 includes $7,500 of depreciation expense. Selected balance sheet accounts for Wiley at the end of Years 1 and 2 are as follows:

	Year 2	Year 1
Current Assets		
Accounts receivable	$40,000	$30,000
Inventory	$54,000	$45,000
Prepaid expenses	$8,000	$6,000
Current Liabilities		
Accounts payable	$35,000	$28,000
Accrued liabilities	$5,000	$8,000
Income taxes payable	$2,000	$2,500

Required:
1. Using the direct method, convert the company's income statement to a cash basis.
2. Assume that during Year 2 Wiley had a $9,000 gain on sale of investments and a $3,000 loss on the sale of equipment. Explain how these two transactions would affect your computations in (1) above.

EXERCISE 15A–3 Net Cash Provided by Operating Activities LO15–7
Refer to the data for Carmono Company in Exercise 15–11.

Required:
Using the direct method, convert the company's income statement to a cash basis.

EXERCISE 15A–4 Net Cash Provided by Operating Activities LO15–7
Refer to the data for Hanna Company in Exercise 15–2. The company's income statement for the year appears below:

Sales	$350,000
Cost of goods sold	140,000
Gross margin	210,000
Selling and administrative expenses	160,000
Income before taxes	50,000
Income taxes	15,000
Net income	$ 35,000

Required:
Using the direct method (and the data from Exercise 15–2), convert the company's income statement to a cash basis.

PROBLEM 15A–5 Prepare and Interpret a Statement of Cash Flows LO15–1, LO15–7
Refer to the financial statements for Rusco Company in Problem 15–20. Because the Cash account decreased so dramatically during this year, the company's executive committee is anxious to see how the income statement would appear on a cash basis.

Required:
1. Using the direct method, adjust the company's income statement for this year to a cash basis.
2. Using the data from (1) above, and other data from the problem as needed, prepare a statement of cash flows for this year.
3. Briefly explain the major reasons for the sharp decline in cash during this year.

PROBLEM 15A–6 Prepare a Statement of Cash Flows LO15–1, LO15–7
Refer to the financial statement data for Weaver Company in Problem 15–14.

Required:
1. Using the direct method, adjust the company's income statement for this year to a cash basis.
2. Using the information obtained in (1) above, along with an analysis of the remaining balance sheet accounts, prepare a statement of cash flows for this year.

PROBLEM 15A–7 Prepare and Interpret a Statement of Cash Flows LO15–1, LO15–7
Refer to the financial statement data for Joyner Company in Problem 15–17. Sam Conway, president of the company, considers $15,000 to be the minimum cash balance for operating purposes. As can be seen from the balance sheet data, only $4,000 in cash was available at the end of the current year. The sharp decline is puzzling to Mr. Conway, particularly because sales and profits are at a record high.

Required:
1. Using the direct method, adjust the company's income statement to a cash basis for Year 2.
2. Using the data from (1) above and other data from the problem as needed, prepare a statement of cash flows for Year 2.
3. Explain why cash declined so sharply during the year.

Financial Statement Analysis

OntheRun photo/Alamy Stock Photo

lighthouse image: Martin73/Shutterstock;
big data image: INGARA/Shutterstock

ENTREPRENEUR SPOTLIGHT

When Randy Goldberg and David Heath heard socks are the most requested clothing item by homeless shelters, they founded Bombas as a buy-one-donate-one sock company. Considered one of TV show *Shark Tank*'s biggest successes, analysts estimate the company has grown to more than 120 employees and annual sales in excess of $100 million. More recently, Bombas has expanded into t-shirts, underwear, and slippers. It has also announced product partnerships with Sesame Street and Disney and extended operations into the United Kingdom.

Applying Managerial Accounting

Bombas could use financial statement analysis in a variety of ways to manage its operations. For example, it could monitor inventory turnover to make optimal use of working capital. It could review trends in gross margin percentage and net profit margin percentage to ensure sales are translating into profits. It could also track return on total assets to motivate efficient use of current and noncurrent assets.

Serving All Stakeholders

Bombas has donated more than 50 million clothing items to more than 3,500 community organizations, across all 50 of the United States. The company maintains a keen focus on helping the African American community, noting, "Black people [make] up 40 percent of the homeless population compared with 13 percent of the general population in the US." In addition, for every clothing item sold from The Bombas Pride Collection, the company donates one item to an organization dedicated to those experiencing homelessness in the LGBTQ+ community. ■

Sources: https://bombas.com/pages/about-us, https://www.dnb.com/business-directory/company-profiles.bombas_llc, https://finance.yahoo.com/news/bombas-billon-dollar-brand-exit-strategy-202751737.html, https://www.workhuman.com/resources/globoforce-blog/the-bombas-story-changing-the-world-one-sock-at-a-time, https://www.modernretail.co/startups/weve-built-this-infrastructure-of-giving-bombas-co-founder-randy-goldberg-on-expanding-into-new-regions-and-categories/.

LEARNING OBJECTIVES

After studying Chapter 16, you should be able to:

LO16–1 Prepare and interpret financial statements in comparative and common-size form.

LO16–2 Compute and interpret financial ratios managers use to assess liquidity.

LO16–3 Compute and interpret financial ratios managers use for asset management purposes.

LO16–4 Compute and interpret financial ratios managers use for debt management purposes.

LO16–5 Compute and interpret financial ratios managers use to assess profitability.

LO16–6 Compute and interpret financial ratios managers use to assess market performance.

Data Analytics Exercise available in Connect to complement this chapter

Stockholders, creditors, and managers are examples of stakeholders that use *financial statement analysis* to evaluate a company's financial health and future prospects. Stockholders and creditors analyze a company's financial statements to estimate its potential for earnings growth, stock price appreciation, making dividend payments, and paying principal and interest on loans. Managers use financial statement analysis for two reasons. First, it enables them to better understand how their company's financial results will be interpreted by stockholders and creditors when making investing and lending decisions. Second, it provides them with valuable feedback regarding their company's performance. For example, managers may study trends in their company's financial statements to assess whether performance has been improving or declining. Or they may use financial statement analysis to benchmark their company's performance against world-class competitors.

In this chapter, we'll explain how managers prepare financial statements in comparative and common-size form and how they use financial ratios to assess their company's liquidity, asset management, debt management, profitability, and market performance.

Limitations of Financial Statement Analysis

This section discusses two limitations of financial statement analysis managers should always keep in mind—comparing financial data across companies and looking beyond ratios when formulating conclusions.

Comparing Financial Data across Companies

Comparisons of one company with another can provide valuable clues about the financial health of an organization. Unfortunately, differences in accounting methods between companies sometimes make it difficult to compare their financial data. For example, if one company values its inventories by the LIFO method and another company by the average cost method, then direct comparisons of their financial data such as inventory valuations and cost of goods sold may be misleading. Sometimes enough data are presented in footnotes to the financial statements to restate data to a comparable basis. Otherwise, managers should keep in mind any lack of comparability. Even with this limitation in mind, comparing key ratios with other companies and with industry averages often helps managers identify opportunities for improvement.

Looking beyond Ratios

Ratios should not be viewed as an end, but rather as a *starting point*. They raise many questions and point to opportunities for further analysis, but they rarely answer any questions by themselves. In addition to financial ratios, managers should consider various internal factors, such as employee learning and growth, business process performance, and customer satisfaction as well as external factors like industry trends, technological changes, changes in consumer tastes, and changes in broad economic indicators.

Statements in Comparative and Common-Size Form

LO16–1
Prepare and interpret financial statements in comparative and common-size form.

An item on a balance sheet or income statement has little meaning by itself. Suppose a company's sales for a year were $250 million. In isolation, that is not particularly useful information. How does that stack up against last year's sales? How do the sales relate to the cost of goods sold? In making these kinds of comparisons, three analytical techniques are widely used:

1. Dollar and percentage changes on statements (*horizontal analysis*).
2. Common-size statements (*vertical analysis*).
3. Ratios.

The first and second techniques are discussed in this section; the third technique is discussed in the remainder of the chapter. Throughout the chapter, we will illustrate these analytical techniques using the financial statements of Brickey Electronics, a producer of specialized electronic components.

Dollar and Percentage Changes on Statements

Horizontal analysis (also known as **trend analysis**) involves analyzing financial data over time, such as computing year-to-year dollar and percentage changes within a set of financial statements. Exhibits 16–1 and 16–2 show Brickey Electronics' financial statements in

EXHIBIT 16–1

	Brickey Electronics Comparative Balance Sheet (dollars in thousands)			
			Increase (Decrease)	
	This Year	Last Year	Amount	Percent
Assets				
Current assets:				
Cash	$ 1,200	$ 2,350	$(1,150)	(48.9)%*
Accounts receivable, net	6,000	4,000	2,000	50.0%
Inventory	8,000	10,000	(2,000)	(20.0)%
Prepaid expenses	300	120	180	150.0%
Total current assets	15,500	16,470	(970)	(5.9)%
Property and equipment:				
Land	4,000	4,000	0	0.0%
Buildings and equipment, net	12,000	8,500	3,500	41.2%
Total property and equipment	16,000	12,500	3,500	28.0%
Total assets	$31,500	$28,970	$ 2,530	8.7%
Liabilities and Stockholders' Equity				
Current liabilities:				
Accounts payable	$ 5,800	$ 4,000	$ 1,800	45.0%
Accrued liabilities	900	400	500	125.0%
Notes payable, short term	300	600	(300)	(50.0)%
Total current liabilities	7,000	5,000	2,000	40.0%
Long-term liabilities:				
Bonds payable, 8%	7,500	8,000	(500)	(6.3)%
Total liabilities	14,500	13,000	1,500	11.5%
Stockholders' equity:				
Common stock, $12 par	6,000	6,000	0	0.0%
Additional paid-in capital	3,000	3,000	0	0.0%
Total paid-in capital	9,000	9,000	0	0.0%
Retained earnings	8,000	6,970	1,030	14.8%
Total stockholders' equity	17,000	15,970	1,030	6.4%
Total liabilities and stockholders' equity	$31,500	$28,970	$ 2,530	8.7%

*The changes between this year and last year are expressed as a percentage of the dollar amount for last year. For example, Cash decreased by $1,150 between this year and last year. This decrease expressed in percentage form is computed as follows: $1,150 ÷ $2,350 = 48.9%. Other percentage figures in this exhibit and Exhibit 16–2 are computed in the same way.

EXHIBIT 16-2

Brickey Electronics Comparative Income Statement and Reconciliation of Retained Earnings (dollars in thousands)				
	This Year	Last Year	Increase (Decrease) Amount	Percent
Sales	$52,000	$48,000	$4,000	8.3%
Cost of goods sold	36,000	31,500	4,500	14.3%
Gross margin	16,000	16,500	(500)	(3.0)%
Selling and administrative expenses:				
Selling expenses	7,000	6,500	500	7.7%
Administrative expenses	5,860	6,100	(240)	(3.9)%
Total selling and administrative expenses	12,860	12,600	260	2.1%
Net operating income	3,140	3,900	(760)	(19.5)%
Interest expense	640	700	(60)	(8.6)%
Net income before taxes	2,500	3,200	(700)	(21.9)%
Income taxes (30%)	750	960	(210)	(21.9)%
Net income	1,750	2,240	$ (490)	(21.9)%
Dividends to common stockholders, $1.44 per share	720	720		
Net income added to retained earnings	1,030	1,520		
Beginning retained earnings	6,970	5,450		
Ending retained earnings	$ 8,000	$ 6,970		

this *comparative form.* The dollar changes highlight the changes that are most important economically; the percentage changes highlight the changes that are most unusual.

Horizontal analysis can be even more useful when data from a number of years are used to compute *trend percentages.* To compute **trend percentages,** a base year is selected and the data for all years are stated as a percentage of that base year. To illustrate, consider the sales and net income of Katy Company:

	Year 1	Year 2	Year 3	Year 4	Year 5	Year 6	Year 7	Year 8	Year 9	Year 10
Sales	$18,818	$18,196	$19,260	$21,605	$22,054	$22,485	$21,953	$20,330	$19,698	$18,256
Net income......	$3,450	$3,641	$3,957	$4,402	$4,372	$4,469	$3,806	$3,623	$3,750	$4,154

By simply looking at these data, you can see that sales increased every year from Year 2 through Year 6 and then declined every year afterwards. Net income steadily climbed from Year 1 through Year 4, plateaued through Year 6, declined in Years 7 and 8, and started to rebound in Years 9 and 10. However, recasting these data into trend percentages aids interpretation:

	Year 1	Year 2	Year 3	Year 4	Year 5	Year 6	Year 7	Year 8	Year 9	Year 10
Sales	100%	97%	102%	115%	117%	119%	117%	108%	105%	97%
Net income	100%	106%	115%	128%	127%	130%	110%	105%	109%	120%

In the above table, both sales and net income have been restated as a percentage of the Year 1 sales and net income. For example, the Year 7 sales of $21,953 are 117 percent of the Year 1 sales of $18,818. This trend analysis is easier to analyze when the data are plotted as in Exhibit 16–3. Katy experienced constant sales growth from Year 2 through Year 6 and then sales declined each year afterwards. Net income grew pretty consistently from Year 1 through Year 6, plummeted in Years 7 and 8, and resumed an upward trend in Years 9 and 10.

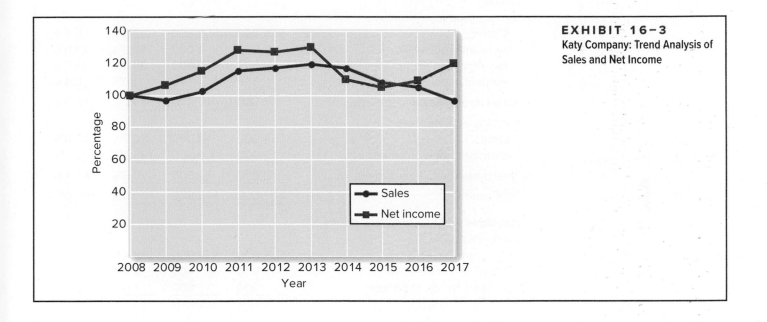

EXHIBIT 16–3
Katy Company: Trend Analysis of Sales and Net Income

Common-Size Statements

Horizontal analysis, which was discussed in the previous section, examines changes in financial statement accounts over time. **Vertical analysis** focuses on the relations among financial statement accounts at a given point in time. A **common-size financial statement** is a vertical analysis in which each financial statement account is expressed as a percentage. In income statements, all items are usually expressed as a percentage of sales. In balance sheets, all items are usually expressed as a percentage of total assets. Exhibit 16–4 contains Brickey Electronics' common-size balance sheet and Exhibit 16–5 contains its common-size income statement.

Notice from Exhibit 16–4 that placing all assets in common-size form clearly shows the relative importance of the current assets as compared to the noncurrent assets. It also shows significant changes have taken place in the composition of the current assets over the last year. For example, accounts receivable have increased in relative importance and both cash and inventory have declined in relative importance. Judging from the sharp increase in accounts receivable, the deterioration in the cash balance may be a result of an inability to collect from customers.

The common-size income statement in Exhibit 16–5 states each line item as a percentage of sales. For example, the administrative expenses were 12.7 percent of sales last year and 11.3 percent of sales this year. If the quality and efficiency of Brickey's administrative services is holding constant or improving over time, then these two percentages suggest this year Brickey managed its administrative resources more cost-effectively than last year. Beyond administrative expenses, managers also have a keen interest in other percentages disclosed in a common-size income statement, and those will be discussed in a later section related to profitability ratios.

EXHIBIT 16–4

Brickey Electronics
Common-Size Comparative Balance Sheet
(dollars in thousands)

	This Year	Last Year	Common-Size Percentages* This Year	Last Year
Assets				
Current assets:				
Cash	$ 1,200	$ 2,350	3.8%	8.1%
Accounts receivable, net	6,000	4,000	19.0%	13.8%
Inventory	8,000	10,000	25.4%	34.5%
Prepaid expenses	300	120	1.0%	0.4%
Total current assets	15,500	16,470	49.2%	56.9%
Property and equipment:				
Land	4,000	4,000	12.7%	13.8%
Buildings and equipment, net	12,000	8,500	38.1%	29.3%
Total property and equipment	16,000	12,500	50.8%	43.1%
Total assets	$31,500	$28,970	100.0%	100.0%
Liabilities and Stockholders' Equity				
Current liabilities:				
Accounts payable	$ 5,800	$ 4,000	18.4%	13.8%
Accrued liabilities	900	400	2.9%	1.4%
Notes payable, short term	300	600	1.0%	2.1%
Total current liabilities	7,000	5,000	22.2%	17.3%
Long-term liabilities:				
Bonds payable, 8%	7,500	8,000	23.8%	27.6%
Total liabilities	14,500	13,000	46.0%	44.9%
Stockholders' equity:				
Common stock, $12 par	6,000	6,000	19.0%	20.7%
Additional paid-in capital	3,000	3,000	9.5%	10.4%
Total paid-in capital	9,000	9,000	28.6%	31.1%
Retained earnings	8,000	6,970	25.4%	24.0%
Total stockholders' equity	17,000	15,970	54.0%	55.1%
Total liabilities and stockholders' equity	$31,500	$28,970	100.0%	100.0%

*Each asset account on a common-size statement is expressed as a percentage of total assets, and each liability and equity account is expressed as a percentage of total liabilities and stockholders' equity. For example, the percentage figure above for this year's Cash balance is computed as follows: $1,200 ÷ $31,500 = 3.8%. All common-size percentages have been rounded to one decimal place; therefore, the figures as shown may not fully reconcile down each column.

			Common-Size Percentages*	
Brickey Electronics Common-Size Comparative Income Statement (dollars in thousands)	This Year	Last Year	This Year	Last Year
Sales	$52,000	$48,000	100.0%	100.0%
Cost of goods sold	36,000	31,500	69.2%	65.6%
Gross margin	16,000	16,500	30.8%	34.4%
Selling and administrative expenses:				
Selling expenses	7,000	6,500	13.5%	13.5%
Administrative expenses	5,860	6,100	11.3%	12.7%
Total selling and administrative expenses	12,860	12,600	24.7%	26.3%
Net operating income	3,140	3,900	6.0%	8.1%
Interest expense	640	700	1.2%	1.5%
Net income before taxes	2,500	3,200	4.8%	6.7%
Income taxes (30%)	750	960	1.4%	2.0%
Net income	$ 1,750	$ 2,240	3.4%	4.7%

EXHIBIT 16–5

*Note the percentage figures for each year are expressed as a percentage of total sales for the year. For example, the percentage figure for this year's cost of goods sold is computed as follows: $36,000 ÷ $52,000 = 69.2%. All common-size percentages have been rounded to one decimal place; therefore, the figures as shown may not fully reconcile down each column.

IN BUSINESS

CORONAVIRUS HAZARD PAY CURTAILS PROFITS

Amid the coronavirus pandemic, many of America's largest companies struggled to balance the needs of two important stakeholders—employees and stockholders. On the one hand, many companies, such as Kroger, Home Depot, Amazon.com, and CVS Health Corporation, supported their employees during the pandemic with "hazard pay" in the form of higher hourly wages and bonuses. For example, Home Depot spent $850 million in one quarter on extra pay, benefits, and safety measures for its employees. On the other hand, many of these same companies decided to end their "hazard pay" policies a few months after implementing them because the higher expenses were lowering profits. Jackie Mayoral, an employee at a Kroger-owned supermarket, expressed her displeasure when the company ended its "hazard pay" by saying, we "are still putting [our lives] on the line . . . It's a slap in the face." Ten percent of the employees at her grocery store had tested positive for COVID-19.

Source: Jaewon Kang and Sharon Terlep, "Workers Push Back against Plans to Curtail Coronavirus Hazard Pay," *The Wall Street Journal*, May 20, 2020, p B2.

Ratio Analysis—Liquidity

Liquidity refers to how quickly an asset can be converted to cash. Liquid assets can be converted to cash quickly, whereas illiquid assets cannot. If a company's liquid assets are not enough to support timely payments to short-term creditors, it can lead to bankruptcy.

This section uses Brickey Electronics' financial statements to explain one measure and two ratios managers use to analyze their company's liquidity and its ability to pay

LO16–2
Compute and interpret financial ratios managers use to assess liquidity.

short-term creditors. *As you proceed through this section, keep in mind that all calculations are performed for this year rather than last year.*

Working Capital

Working capital is the excess of current assets over current liabilities.

$$\text{Working capital} = \text{Current assets} - \text{Current liabilities}$$

For Brickey Electronics, it is computed as follows:

$$\text{Working capital} = \$15,500,000 - \$7,000,000 = \$8,500,000$$

Managers need to interpret working capital from two perspectives. On one hand, if a company has ample working capital, it provides some assurance the company can pay its creditors in full and on time. On the other hand, maintaining large amounts of working capital isn't free. Working capital must be financed with long-term debt and equity—both of which are expensive. Furthermore, a large and growing working capital balance may indicate troubles, such as excessive growth in inventories. Therefore, managers often want to minimize working capital while retaining the ability to pay short-term creditors.

Current Ratio

The **current ratio** expresses working capital in ratio form:

$$\text{Current ratio} = \frac{\text{Current assets}}{\text{Current liabilities}}$$

For Brickey Electronics, it is computed as follows:

$$\text{Current ratio} = \frac{\$15,500,000}{\$7,000,000} = 2.21$$

Although widely regarded as a measure of short-term debt-paying ability, the current ratio must be interpreted with great care. A *declining* ratio might be a sign of a deteriorating financial condition, or it might arise from eliminating obsolete inventories or other stagnant current assets. An *increasing* ratio might indicate improving financial performance, or it might arise from stockpiling too much inventory.

The general rule of thumb calls for a current ratio of at least 2. However, many companies successfully operate with a current ratio below 2. The adequacy of a current ratio depends heavily on the *composition* of the assets. For example, as we see in the table below, both Worthington Corporation and Greystone, Inc., have current ratios of 2. However, they are not in comparable financial condition. Greystone is more likely to have difficulty meeting its current financial obligations because almost all of its current assets consist of inventory rather than more liquid assets such as cash and accounts receivable.

	Worthington Corporation	Greystone, Inc.
Current assets:		
Cash	$ 25,000	$ 2,000
Accounts receivable, net	60,000	8,000
Inventory	85,000	160,000
Prepaid expenses	5,000	5,000
Total current assets (a)	$175,000	$175,000
Current liabilities (b)	$ 87,500	$ 87,500
Current ratio, (a) ÷ (b)	2	2

Acid-Test (Quick) Ratio

The **acid-test (quick) ratio** is a more rigorous test of a company's ability to meet its short-term debts than the current ratio. Inventories and prepaid expenses are excluded from total current assets, leaving only the more liquid (or "quick") assets to be divided by current liabilities.

$$\text{Acid-test ratio} = \frac{\text{Cash} + \text{Marketable securities} + \text{Accounts receivable}}{\text{Current liabilities}}$$

The acid-test ratio measures how well a company can meet its obligations without having to liquidate inventory. Ideally, each dollar of liabilities should be backed by at least $1 of quick assets. However, acid-test ratios as low as 0.3 are common.

The acid-test ratio for Brickey Electronics is computed below:

$$\text{Acid-test ratio} = \frac{\$1,200,000 + \$0 + \$6,000,000}{\$7,000,000} = 1.03$$

Although Brickey Electronics' acid-test ratio is within the acceptable range, a manager might be concerned about several trends revealed in the company's balance sheet. Notice in Exhibit 16–1 short-term debts are rising, while the cash balance is declining. Perhaps the lower cash balance is caused by the increase in accounts receivable. In short, as with the current ratio, the acid-test ratio should be interpreted with care.

Ratio Analysis—Asset Management

A company's assets are funded by lenders and stockholders, both of whom expect those assets to be deployed efficiently and effectively. In this section, we'll describe various measures and ratios managers use to assess their company's asset management performance. *All forthcoming calculations will be performed for this year.*

LO16–3
Compute and interpret financial ratios managers use for asset management purposes.

Accounts Receivable Turnover

The *accounts receivable turnover* and *average collection period* ratios measure how quickly credit sales are converted into cash. The **accounts receivable turnover** is computed by dividing sales on account (i.e., credit sales) by the average accounts receivable balance for the year:

$$\text{Accounts receivable turnover} = \frac{\text{Sales on account}}{\text{Average accounts receivable balance}}$$

Assuming all of Brickey Electronics' sales were on account, its accounts receivable turnover is computed as follows:

$$\text{Accounts receivable turnover} = \frac{\$52,000,000}{(\$6,000,000 + \$4,000,000)/2} = 10.4$$

The accounts receivable turnover can then be divided into 365 days to determine the average number of days required to collect an account (known as the **average collection period**).

$$\text{Average collection period} = \frac{365 \text{ days}}{\text{Accounts receivable turnover}}$$

The average collection period for Brickey Electronics is computed as follows:

$$\text{Average collection period} = \frac{365 \text{ days}}{10.4} = 35.1 \text{ days}$$

This means on average it takes 35 days to collect a credit sale. Whether this is good or bad depends on the credit terms Brickey Electronics is offering its customers. Many customers will tend to withhold payment for as long as the credit terms allow. If the credit terms are 30 days, then a 35-day average collection period would usually be viewed as very good. On the other hand, if the company's credit terms are 10 days, then a 35-day average collection period is worrisome. A long collection period may result from having too many old uncollectible accounts, failing to bill promptly or follow up on late accounts, lax credit checks, and so on. In practice, average collection periods ranging all the way from 10 days to 180 days are common, depending on the industry.

Inventory Turnover

The **inventory turnover ratio** measures how many times a company's inventory has been sold and replaced during the year. It is computed by dividing the cost of goods sold by the average level of inventory [(Beginning inventory balance + Ending inventory balance) ÷ 2]:

$$\text{Inventory turnover} = \frac{\text{Cost of goods sold}}{\text{Average inventory balance}}$$

Brickey's inventory turnover is computed as follows:

$$\text{Inventory turnover} = \frac{\$36,000,000}{(\$8,000,000 + \$10,000,000)/2} = 4.0$$

The number of days needed on average to sell the entire inventory (called the **average sale period**) can be computed by dividing 365 by the inventory turnover:

$$\text{Average sale period} = \frac{365 \text{ days}}{\text{Inventory turnover}}$$

$$= \frac{365 \text{ days}}{4 \text{ times}} = 91.3 \text{ days}$$

The average sale period varies from industry to industry. Grocery stores, with significant perishable stocks, turn over their inventory quickly. On the other hand, jewelry stores turn over their inventory slowly. In practice, average sale periods of 10 days to 90 days are common, depending on the industry.

A company whose inventory turnover ratio is much slower than the average for its industry may have too much inventory or the wrong sorts of inventory. Some managers argue they must buy in large quantities to take advantage of quantity discounts. But these discounts must be compared to the added costs of insurance, taxes, financing, and risks of obsolescence and deterioration resulting from greater inventories.

Operating Cycle

The **operating cycle** measures the elapsed time from when inventory is received from suppliers to when cash is received from customers. It is computed as follows:

$$\text{Operating cycle} = \text{Average sale period} + \text{Average collection period}$$

Brickey Electronics' operating cycle is computed as follows:

$$\text{Operating cycle} = 91.3 \text{ days} + 35.1 \text{ days} + 126.4 \text{ days}$$

A manager's goal is to reduce the operating cycle because it puts cash receipts in the company's possession sooner. In fact, if a company can shrink its operating cycle to fewer days than its average payment period for suppliers, it means the company is receiving cash from customers before it has to pay suppliers for inventory purchases. For example, if a company's operating cycle is 10 days and its average payment period to suppliers is 30 days, the company is receiving cash from customers 20 days before it pays its suppliers. In this example, the company could earn interest income on cash collections for 20 days before paying a portion of those receipts to suppliers. Conversely, if a company's operating cycle is longer than its average payment period for suppliers, it creates the need to borrow money to fund inventories and accounts receivable. In the case of Brickey Electronics, its operating cycle is very high, thereby suggesting it needs to borrow money to fund its working capital.

Total Asset Turnover

The **total asset turnover** is a ratio comparing total sales to average total assets. It measures how efficiently a company's assets are being used to generate sales. This ratio expands beyond current assets to include noncurrent assets, such as property, plant, and equipment. It is computed as follows:

$$\text{Total asset turnover} = \frac{\text{Sales}}{\text{Average total assets}}$$

Brickey Electronics' total asset turnover is computed as follows:

$$\text{Total asset turnover} = \frac{\$52,000,000}{(\$31,500,000 + \$28,970,000)/2} = 1.72$$

A company's goal is to increase its total asset turnover by increasing sales or reducing investment in assets. If a company's accounts receivable turnover and inventory turnover are increasing, but its total asset turnover is decreasing, it suggests the problem may relate to noncurrent asset utilization and efficiency. It also bears emphasizing if all else holds constant, a company's total asset turnover will increase over time because the accumulated depreciation on plant and equipment grows over time.

IN BUSINESS

FORD LOOKS TO REDUCE INVENTORIES

Ford Motor Company is trying to grow its build-to-order sales model, where customers order the exact vehicle they want online and pick it up at a dealership 6–8 weeks later. While this approach is familiar to European customers, it contradicts American car shopping norms where customers get the instant gratification of buying a vehicle and driving it home all in the same day. If successful, the new sales model would lower the company's inventory carrying costs and increase its inventory turnover. On the other hand, if the customers' desire for instant gratification exceeds the appeal of ordering a customized vehicle, Ford will lose customers to competing dealerships with larger selections of on-site inventories.

Source: Mike Collas, "Ford to Test New Way of Selling Cars," *The Wall Street Journal,* August 18, 2021, pp. B1, B4.

Ratio Analysis—Debt Management

LO16–4
Compute and interpret financial ratios managers use for debt management purposes.

Managers need to evaluate their company's debt management choices from the vantage point of two stakeholders—long-term creditors and common stockholders. Long-term creditors are concerned with a company's ability to repay its loans over the long run. For example, if a company paid out all of its available cash in the form of dividends, then nothing would be left to pay back creditors. Consequently, creditors often seek protection by requiring that borrowers agree to various restrictive covenants, or rules. These covenants typically include restrictions on dividend payments as well as rules requiring the company to maintain certain financial ratios at specified levels. Although restrictive covenants are widely used, they do not ensure creditors will be paid when loans come due. The company still must generate sufficient earnings to cover payments.

Stockholders look at debt from a *financial leverage* perspective. **Financial leverage** refers to borrowing money to acquire assets in an effort to increase sales and profits. A company can have either positive or negative financial leverage depending on the difference between its rate of return on total assets and the rate of return it must pay creditors. If the company's rate of return on total assets exceeds the rate of return paid to creditors, *financial leverage is positive.* If the rate of return on total assets is less than the rate of return the company pays its creditors, *financial leverage is negative.* We will explore whether Brickey Electronics has positive or negative financial leverage later in the chapter. For now, you need to understand if a company has positive financial leverage, having debt can benefit common stockholders. Conversely, if a company has negative financial leverage, common stockholders suffer. Given the potential benefits of positive financial leverage, managers do not try to avoid debt; rather, they seek to maintain a level of debt considered normal within their industry.

In this section, we explain three ratios managers use for debt management purposes— times interest earned ratio, debt-to-equity ratio, and the equity multiplier. *All calculations are performed for this year.*

Times Interest Earned Ratio

The most common measure of a company's ability to protect its long-term creditors is the **times interest earned ratio.** It is computed by dividing earnings before interest expense and income taxes (i.e., net operating income) by interest expense:

$$\text{Times interest earned ratio} = \frac{\text{Earnings before interest expense and income taxes}}{\text{Interest expense}}$$

For Brickey Electronics, the times interest earned ratio for this year is computed as follows:

$$\text{Times interest earned} = \frac{\$3,140,000}{\$640,000} = 4.91$$

The times interest earned ratio is based on earnings before interest expense and income taxes because that is the amount of earnings available for making interest payments. Interest expenses are deducted *before* income taxes are determined; creditors have first claim on the earnings before taxes are paid.

A times interest earned ratio less than 1 is inadequate because interest expense exceeds the earnings available for paying that interest. In contrast, a times interest earned ratio of 2 or more usually provides sufficient protection for long-term creditors.

Debt-to-Equity Ratio

The **debt-to-equity ratio** indicates the relative proportions of debt and equity at one point in time on a company's balance sheet. As the debt-to-equity ratio increases, it indicates a company's financial leverage is increasing. In other words, it is relying on a greater proportion of debt rather than equity to fund its assets. The debt-to-equity ratio is measured as follows:

$$\text{Debt-to-equity-ratio} = \frac{\text{Total liabilities}}{\text{Stockholders' equity}}$$

Brickey's debt-to-equity ratio for this year is computed as follows:

$$\text{Debt-to-equity ratio} = \frac{\$14,500,000}{\$17,000,000} = 0.85$$

At the end of this year, Brickey Electronics' creditors were providing 85 cents for each $1 provided by stockholders.

Creditors and stockholders have different views about the optimal debt-to-equity ratio. Stockholders like a lot of debt to take advantage of positive financial leverage. On the other hand, because equity represents the excess of total assets over total liabilities, and hence a buffer of protection for creditors, creditors like less debt and more equity. In practice, debt-to-equity ratios from 0.0 (no debt) to 3.0 are common. In industries with little financial risk, managers maintain high debt-to-equity ratios. In industries with more financial risk, managers maintain lower debt-to-equity ratios.

Equity Multiplier

The **equity multiplier** indicates the portion of a company's assets funded by equity. Similar to the debt-to-equity ratio, as the equity multiplier increases, it indicates a company's financial leverage is increasing. In other words, it is relying on more debt rather than equity to fund its assets. Instead of measuring amounts in the numerator and denominator at one point in time (as is done with the debt-to-equity ratio), the equity multiplier focuses on average amounts maintained throughout the year and is measured as follows:

$$\text{Equity multiplier} = \frac{\text{Average total assets}}{\text{Average stockholders' equity}}$$

Brickey's equity multiplier for this year is computed as follows:

$$\text{Equity multiplier} = \frac{(\$31,500,000 + \$28,970,000)/2}{(\$17,000,000 + \$15,970,000)/2} = 1.83$$

Ratio Analysis—Profitability

When profits are stated as a percentage of another number, such as sales or total assets, it helps managers draw informed conclusions about how the organization is performing over time. For example, if a company had profits in Years 1 and 2 of $10 and $20, respectively, it would be naïve to immediately assume the company's performance improved. In other words, if we further assume sales in Year 1 are $100 and sales in Year 2 are $1,000, it would be troubling to see the company converted $900 of additional sales into only $10 of additional profit. In this section, we further develop this idea by discussing four profitability ratios commonly used by managers—gross margin percentage, net profit margin percentage, return on total assets, and return on equity. *All forthcoming calculations are performed for this year.*

> **LO16–5**
> Compute and interpret financial ratios managers use to assess profitability.

Gross Margin Percentage

Exhibit 16–5 shows Brickey's cost of goods sold as a percentage of sales increased from 65.6 percent last year to 69.2 percent this year. Or looking at this from a different viewpoint, the *gross margin percentage* declined from 34.4 percent last year to 30.8 percent this year. The **gross margin percentage** is computed as follows:

$$\text{Gross margin percentage} = \frac{\text{Gross margin}}{\text{Sales}}$$

The gross margin percentage should be more stable for retailing companies than for other companies because the cost of goods sold in retailing excludes fixed costs. When fixed costs are included in the cost of goods sold, the gross margin percentage should increase and decrease with sales volume. With increases in sales volume, fixed costs are spread across more units and the gross margin percentage should improve.

IN BUSINESS

Ezra Shaw/Getty Images

PELOTON STRUGGLES TO EARN A PROFIT

Peloton Interactive hopes to eventually put its $2,000 exercise bikes into 45 million homes. With a gross margin percentage hovering around 36 percent and sales and marketing expenses equal to 18 percent of sales, it may be tempting to conclude that Peloton earns a net profit margin percentage of 18 percent. However, this incomplete perspective overlooks additional expenses related to paying fitness instructors, renting space to sell bikes, and paying royalties for the rights to play the latest workout songs. After accounting for all of Peloton's expenses, the company's loses total $456 million over the previous three years.

Sources: Peloton 2021 Annual Report, Lauren Silva Laughlin and Dan Gallagher, "Peloton Has a Tough Ride Ahead," *The Wall Street Journal*, September 6, 2019, p. B12; and Stephen Gandel, "Peloton's CEO Said the Hot Fitness Company Makes Money—Not Even Close," *CBS News*, August 29, 2019, https://www.cbsnews.com/news/why-would-the-ceo-of-hot-ipo-peloton-say-it-was-profitable-when-it-was-not.

Net Profit Margin Percentage

Exhibit 16–5 shows Brickey's *net profit margin percentage* decreased from 4.7 percent last year to 3.4 percent this year. The **net profit margin percentage** is computed as follows:

$$\text{Net profit margin percentage} = \frac{\text{Net income}}{\text{Sales}}$$

The gross profit margin percentage and net profit margin percentage state the gross margin and net income as a percentage of sales. The gross margin percentage focuses on only one type of expense (cost of goods sold), whereas the net profit margin percentage also looks at how selling and administrative expenses, interest expense, and income tax expense have influenced performance. The remaining ratios in this section look at profitability relative to amounts on the balance sheet rather than sales.

Return on Total Assets

The **return on total assets** is calculated as follows:

$$\text{Return on total assets} = \frac{\text{Net income} + [\text{Interest expense} \times (1 - \text{Tax rate})]}{\text{Average total assets}}$$

Interest expense is added back to net income to show what earnings would have been if the company had no debt. With this adjustment, a manager can evaluate the company's return on total assets over time without the analysis being influenced by changes in the company's mix of debt and equity. Furthermore, this adjustment enables managers to

COMMUNICATING WITH DATA VISUALIZATIONS

Diagnostic analytics answer the question: Why did it happen? The visualization below is a combo chart showing Brickey Electronics' sales dollars and gross margin percentage for each of the last five years. It uses the data from Exhibit 16–5 for Last Year and This Year (referred to as Years 4 and 5 in the visualization below) along with assumed data for years 1–3 to explain why the company's profits are declining despite continuous sales growth. Notice the upward trend in sales dollars is not leading to growing profits, at least in part because of the downward trend in gross margin percentage.

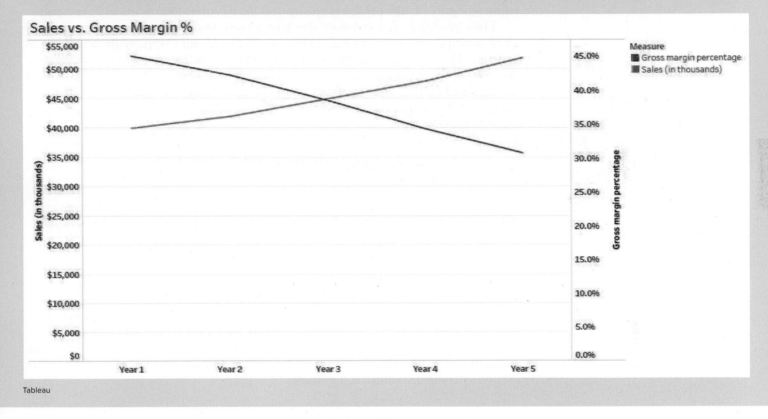

Tableau

draw more meaningful comparisons with other companies having different amounts of debt. Notice the interest expense is placed on an after-tax basis by multiplying it by the factor (1 − Tax rate).

The return on total assets for Brickey Electronics is computed as follows (from Exhibits 16–1 and 16–2):

$$\text{Return on total assets} = \frac{\$1,750,000 + [\$640,000 \times (1 - 0.30)]}{(\$31,500,000 + \$28,970,000)/2} = 7.3\%$$

Brickey Electronics has earned a return of 7.3 percent on average total assets employed during this year.

Return on Equity

The return on total assets looks at profits relative to total assets, whereas the *return on equity* looks at profits relative to the book value of stockholders' equity. The **return on equity** is computed as follows:

$$\text{Return on equity} = \frac{\text{Net income}}{\text{Average stockholders' equity}}$$

Brickey Electronics' return on equity for this year is computed as follows:

$$\text{Return on equity} = \frac{\$1,750,000}{(\$17,000,000 + \$15,970,000)/2} = 10.6\%$$

Now that we have computed return on total assets and return on equity, we can see financial leverage in operation for Brickey Electronics. Notice from Exhibit 16–1 the company pays 8 percent interest on its bonds payable. The after-tax interest cost of these bonds is only 5.6 percent [8% interest rate × (1 − 0.30) = 5.6%]. As shown earlier, the company's after-tax return on total assets is 7.3 percent. Because the return on total assets of 7.3 percent is greater than the 5.6 percent after-tax interest cost of the bonds, leverage is positive and the difference goes to the stockholders. This explains in part why the return on equity of 10.6 percent is greater than the return on total assets of 7.3 percent.

Many managers and investors also take a more in-depth look at return on equity using principles pioneered by E.I. du Pont de Nemours and Company (better known as DuPont). This approach recognizes return on equity is influenced by three elements—operating efficiency (as measured by net profit margin percentage), asset usage efficiency (as measured by total asset turnover), and financial leverage (as measured by the equity multiplier). The following equation computes Brickey Electronics' return on equity using these three elements:

$$\text{Return on equity} = \frac{\text{Net profit margin}}{\text{percentage}} \times \frac{\text{Total asset}}{\text{turnover}} \times \frac{\text{Equity}}{\text{multiplier}}$$

$$\text{Return on equity} = \frac{\text{Net income}}{\text{Sales}} \times \frac{\text{Sales}}{\text{Average total assets}} \times \frac{\text{Average total assets}}{\text{Average stockholders' equity}}$$

$$\text{Return on equity} = 3.37\% \times 1.72 \times 1.83 = 10.6\%$$

Notice the sales and average total asset figures cancel, so we are left with net income divided by average stockholders' equity. While this equation is a little more complex, its return on equity of 10.6 percent agrees with the initial return on equity computation performed earlier. Also notice this equation uses a net profit margin percentage of 3.37 percent rather than the rounded net profit margin percentage of 3.4 percent shown in Exhibit 16–5. The total asset turnover of 1.72 and the equity multiplier of 1.83 were previously computed earlier in the chapter.

Ratio Analysis—Market Performance

LO16–6
Compute and interpret financial ratios managers use to assess market performance.

This section summarizes five ratios common stockholders use to assess a company's performance. Because common stockholders own the company, it logically follows that managers should have a thorough understanding of the measures their owners use to judge their performance. *All calculations are performed for this year.*

Earnings per Share

An investor buys a stock in the hope of realizing a return in the form of either dividends or future increases in the value of the stock. Because earnings form the basis for dividend payments and future increases in the value of shares, investors monitor a company's *earnings per share.*

Earnings per share divides net income by the average number of common shares outstanding during the year.

$$\text{Earnings per share} = \frac{\text{Net income}}{\text{Average number of common shares outstanding}}$$

Using the data in Exhibits 16–1 and 16–2, Brickey Electronics' earnings per share is computed as follows:

$$\text{Earnings per share} = \frac{\$1,750,000}{(500,000 \text{ shares*} + 500,000 \text{ shares})/2} = \$3.50 \text{ per share}$$

_____
*$6,000,000 total par value ÷ $12 par value per share = 500,000 shares.

Price-Earnings Ratio

The **price-earnings ratio** divides a stock's market price per share by its earnings per share. If we assume Brickey Electronics' stock has a market price of $40 per share at the end of this year, then its price-earnings ratio would be computed as follows:

$$\text{Price-earnings ratio} = \frac{\text{Market price per share}}{\text{Earnings per share}}$$

$$= \frac{\$40 \text{ per share}}{\$3.50 \text{ per share}} = 11.43$$

The price-earnings ratio is 11.43; that is, the stock is selling for about 11.43 times its current earnings per share.

A high price-earnings ratio means investors are willing to pay a premium for the company's stock—presumably because the company is expected to have higher-than-average future earnings growth. Conversely, if investors believe a company's future earnings growth prospects are limited, the company's price-earnings ratio would be relatively low.

IN BUSINESS

GROWGENERATION'S EARNINGS PROSPECTS ARE BRIGHT

As more U.S. states have legalized cannabis, businesses like Colorado-based GrowGeneration have boomed. The company, which sells equipment used for growing plants without the need for soil, has seen sales growth of 60 percent and a 12-month price gain of 140 percent, outpacing Amazon and Netflix on the stock market. GrowGeneration benefitted from a strong cannabis industry during the pandemic, which was boosted by dispensaries remaining open during lockdowns as well as added stimulus cash in buyers' hands. The company's price-earnings ratio in excess of 52 suggests investors see immense earnings growth on its horizon.

Source: Carol Ryan, "Cannabis Gives Boost to a Garden Supplier," *The Wall Street Journal,* August 17, 2021, https://www.wsj.com/articles/a-garden-supply-stock-with-a-fast-growing-cannabis-patch-11629110445.

Dividend Payout and Yield Ratios

In general, earnings should be retained in a company and not paid out in dividends as long as the rate of return on funds invested inside the company exceeds the rate of return stockholders could earn on alternative investments outside the company. Therefore, companies with excellent prospects of profitable growth often pay little or no dividend. Companies with little opportunity for profitable growth, but with steady, dependable earnings, pay out a higher percentage of their cash flow from operations as dividends.

The Dividend Payout Ratio The **dividend payout ratio** quantifies the percentage of current earnings paid out in dividends and is computed as follows:

$$\text{Dividend payout ratio} = \frac{\text{Dividends per share}}{\text{Earnings per share}}$$

For Brickey Electronics, the dividend payout ratio is computed as follows:

$$\text{Dividend payout ratio} = \frac{\$1.44 \text{ per share (see Exhibit 15–2)}}{\$3.50 \text{ per share}} = 41.1\%$$

There is no such thing as a "right" dividend payout ratio, although the ratio is usually similar for companies within the same industry. As noted above, companies with ample growth opportunities at high rates of return have low payout ratios, whereas companies with limited reinvestment opportunities have higher payout ratios.

The Dividend Yield Ratio   The **dividend yield ratio** divides dividends per share by the market price per share:

$$\text{Dividend yield ratio} = \frac{\text{Dividends per share}}{\text{Market price per share}}$$

Because the market price for Brickey Electronics' stock is $40 per share, its dividend yield is computed as follows:

$$\text{Dividend yield ratio} = \frac{\$1.44 \text{ per share}}{\$40 \text{ per share}} = 3.6\%$$

The dividend yield ratio measures the rate of return (in the form of cash dividends only) an investor earns when buying common stock at the current market price. A low dividend yield ratio is neither bad nor good by itself.

Book Value per Share

Book value per share measures the amount per share distributed to common stockholders if all assets were sold at their balance sheet carrying amounts (i.e., book values) and if all creditors were paid off. Book value per share is based on historical costs. The formula for computing it is:

$$\text{Book value per share} = \frac{\text{Total stockholders' equity}}{\text{Number of common shares outstanding}}$$

The book value per share of Brickey Electronics' common stock is computed as follows:

$$\text{Book value per share} = \frac{\$17,000,000}{500,000 \text{ shares}} = \$34 \text{ per share}$$

If this book value is compared with the $40 market value of Brickey Electronics' stock, then the stock may appear to be overpriced. However, market prices reflect expectations about future earnings and dividends, whereas book value is based on historical results. Ordinarily, the market value of a stock exceeds its book value. For example, in one year, Microsoft's common stock traded at over 4 times its book value, and Coca-Cola's market value was 17 times its book value.

Summary of Ratios and Sources of Comparative Ratio Data

Exhibit 16–6 summarizes this chapter's ratios. The formula for each ratio and a summary comment on each ratio's significance are included in the exhibit.

Exhibit 16–7 contains a listing of public sources that provide comparative ratio data organized by industry. These sources are used extensively by managers, investors, and analysts. The EDGAR database listed in Exhibit 16–7 is a particularly rich source of data. It contains copies of all reports filed by companies with the SEC since about 1995—including annual reports filed as Form 10-K.

EXHIBIT 16–6
Summary of Ratios

Ratio	Formula	Significance
Liquidity:		
Working capital	Current assets − Current liabilities	Measures the company's ability to repay current liabilities using only current assets
Current ratio	Current assets ÷ Current liabilities	Test of short-term debt-paying ability
Acid-test ratio	(Cash + Marketable securities + Accounts receivable) ÷ Current liabilities	Test of short-term debt-paying ability without having to rely on inventory
Asset Management:		
Accounts receivable turnover	Sales on account ÷ Average accounts receivable balance	Measures how many times a company's accounts receivable have been turned into cash during the year
Average collection period	365 days ÷ Accounts receivable turnover	Measures the average number of days taken to collect an account receivable
Inventory turnover	Cost of goods sold ÷ Average inventory balance	Measures how many times a company's inventory has been sold during the year
Average sale period	365 days ÷ Inventory turnover	Measures the average number of days taken to sell the inventory one time
Operating cycle	Average sale period + Average collection period	Measures the elapsed time from when inventory is received from suppliers to when cash is received from customers
Total asset turnover	Sales ÷ Average total assets	Measures how efficiently assets are being used to generate sales
Debt Management:		
Times interest earned ratio	Earnings before interest expense and income taxes ÷ Interest expense	Measures the company's ability to make interest payments
Debt-to-equity ratio	Total liabilities ÷ Stockholders' equity	Measures the amount of assets being provided by creditors for each dollar of assets being provided by the stockholders
Equity multiplier	Average total assets ÷ Average stockholders' equity	Measures the portion of a company's assets funded by equity
Profitability:		
Gross margin percentage	Gross margin ÷ Sales	Measures profitability before selling and administrative expenses
Net profit margin percentage	Net income ÷ Sales	A broad measure of profitability
Return on total assets	{Net income + [Interest expense × (1 − Tax rate)]} ÷ Average total assets	Measures how well assets have been employed by management
Return on equity	Net income ÷ Average stockholders' equity	When compared to the return on total assets, measures the extent to which financial leverage is working for or against common stockholders
Market Performance:		
Earnings per share	Net income ÷ Average number of common shares outstanding	Affects the market price per share, as reflected in the price-earnings ratio
Price-earnings ratio	Market price per share ÷ Earnings per share	An index of whether a stock is relatively cheap or relatively expensive in relation to current earnings
Dividend payout ratio	Dividends per share ÷ Earnings per share	An index showing whether a company pays out most of its earnings in dividends or reinvests the earnings internally
Dividend yield ratio	Dividends per share ÷ Market price per share	Shows the return in terms of cash dividends being provided by a stock
Book value per share	Total stockholders' equity ÷ Number of common shares outstanding	Measures the amount that would be distributed to common stockholders if all assets were sold at their balance sheet carrying amounts and if all creditors were paid off

EXHIBIT 16–7
Sources of Financial Ratios

Source	Content
Almanac of Business and Industrial Financial Ratios, Aspen Publishers; published annually	A source containing common-size income statements and financial ratios by industry and by the size of companies within each industry.
RMA Annual Statement Studies, Risk Management Association; published annually	A publication containing common-size statements and financial ratios on individual companies; the companies are arranged by industry.
EDGAR, Securities and Exchange Commission; website that is continually updated; www.sec.gov	An Internet database containing reports filed by companies with the SEC; these reports can be downloaded.
D&B Hoovers Online, D&B Hoovers; website that is continually updated; www.dnb.com/products/marketing-sales/dnb-hoovers.html	A site providing capsule profiles for 10,000 U.S. companies with links to company websites, annual reports, stock charts, news articles, and industry information.
Industry Norms & Key Business Ratios, Dun & Bradstreet; published annually	Fourteen commonly used financial ratios are computed for over 800 major industry groupings.
Mergent Industrial Manual and Mergent Bank and Finance Manual; published annually	A source containing financial ratios on all companies listed on the New York Stock Exchange, the American Stock Exchange, and regional American exchanges.
Standard & Poor's Industry Survey, Standard & Poor's; published annually	Various statistics, including some financial ratios, are given by industry and for leading companies within each industry grouping.

Summary

The data contained in financial statements represent a quantitative summary of a company's operations and activities. Managers skilled at analyzing these statements can learn much about their company's strengths, weaknesses, emerging problems, operating efficiency, profitability, and so forth.

Many techniques are available to analyze financial statements and assess the direction and importance of trends and changes. In this chapter, we discussed three such analytical techniques—dollar and percentage changes in statements (horizontal analysis), common-size statements (vertical analysis), and ratio analysis. Refer to Exhibit 16–6 for a detailed listing of the ratios.

 Data Analytics Exercise available in Connect to complement this chapter

Review Problem: Selected Ratios and Financial Leverage

Mulligan Corporation's financial statements are as follows:

Mulligan Corporation Comparative Balance Sheet (dollars in millions)		
	This Year	Last Year
Assets		
Current assets:		
Cash	$ 281	$ 313
Marketable securities	157	141
Accounts receivable	288	224
Inventories	692	636
Other current assets	278	216
Total current assets	1,696	1,530
Property and equipment, net	2,890	2,288
Other assets	758	611
Total assets	$5,344	$4,429
Liabilities and Stockholders' Equity		
Current liabilities:		
Accounts payable	$ 391	$ 341
Short-term bank loans	710	700
Accrued liabilities	757	662
Other current liabilities	298	233
Total current liabilities	2,156	1,936
Long-term liabilities	904	265
Total liabilities	3,060	2,201
Stockholders' equity:		
Common stock and additional paid-in capital	40	40
Retained earnings	2,244	2,188
Total stockholders' equity	2,284	2,228
Total liabilities and stockholders' equity	$5,344	$4,429

Mulligan Corporation Income Statement (dollars in millions)	
	This Year
Sales	$9,411
Cost of goods sold	3,999
Gross margin	5,412
Selling and administrative expenses:	
Store operating expenses	3,216
Other operating expenses	294
Depreciation and amortization	467
General and administrative expenses	489
Total selling and administrative expenses	4,466
Net operating income	946
Plus: Interest and other income	110
Interest expense	0
Net income before taxes	1,056
Income taxes (about 36%)	384
Net income	$ 672

Required:
1. Compute the return on total assets.
2. Compute the return on equity.
3. Is Mulligan's financial leverage positive or negative? Explain.
4. Compute the current ratio.
5. Compute the acid-test ratio.
6. Compute the inventory turnover.
7. Compute the average sale period.
8. Compute the debt-to-equity ratio.
9. Compute the total asset turnover.
10. Compute the net profit margin percentage.

Solution to Review Problem

1.   Return on total assets:

$$\text{Return on total assets} = \frac{\text{Net income} + [\text{Interest expense} \times (1 - \text{Tax rate})]}{\text{Average total assets}}$$

$$= \frac{\$672 + [\$0 \times (1 - 0.36)]}{(\$5,344 + \$4,429)/2} = 13.8\% \text{ (rounded)}$$

2.   Return on equity:

$$\text{Return on equity} = \frac{\text{Net income}}{\text{Average stockholders' equity}}$$

$$= \frac{\$672}{(\$2,284 + \$2,228)/2} = 29.8\% \text{ (rounded)}$$

3.   The company has positive financial leverage because the return on equity of 29.8% is greater than the return on total assets of 13.8%. The positive financial leverage was obtained from current and long-term liabilities.

4.   Current ratio:

$$\text{Current ratio} = \frac{\text{Current assets}}{\text{Current liabilities}}$$

$$= \frac{\$1,696}{\$2,156} = 0.79 \text{ (rounded)}$$

5.   Acid-test ratio:

$$\text{Acid-test ratio} = \frac{\text{Cash} + \text{Marketable securities} + \text{Accounts receivable}}{\text{Current liabilities}}$$

$$= \frac{\$281 + \$157 + \$288}{\$2,156} = 0.34 \text{ (rounded)}$$

6.   Inventory turnover:

$$\text{Inventory turnover} = \frac{\text{Cost of goods sold}}{\text{Average inventory balance}}$$

$$= \frac{\$3,999}{(\$692 + \$636)/2} = 6.0 \text{ (rounded)}$$

7.   Average sale period:

$$\text{Average sale period} = \frac{365 \text{ days}}{\text{Inventory turnover}}$$

$$= \frac{365 \text{ days}}{6.0} = 60.8 \text{ days (rounded)}$$

8.   Debt-to-equity ratio:

$$\text{Debt-to-equity ratio} = \frac{\text{Total liabilities}}{\text{Stockholders' equity}}$$

$$= \frac{\$3,060}{\$2,284} = 1.34 \text{ (rounded)}$$

9. Total asset turnover:

$$\text{Total asset turnover} = \frac{\text{Sales}}{\text{Average total assets}}$$

$$\text{Total asset turnover} = \frac{\$9{,}411}{(\$5{,}344 + \$4{,}429)/2} = 1.93 \text{ (rounded)}$$

10. Net profit margin percentage:

$$\text{Net profit margin percentage} = \frac{\text{Net income}}{\text{Sales}}$$

$$\text{Net profit margin percentage} = \frac{\$672}{\$9{,}411} = 7.1\% \text{ (rounded)}$$

Glossary

(Note: Definitions and formulas for all financial ratios are shown in Exhibit 16–6. These definitions and formulas are not repeated here.)

Acid-test (quick) ratio a more rigorous test of a company's ability to meet its short-term debts than the current ratio. Inventories and prepaid expenses are excluded from total current assets, leaving only the more liquid (or "quick") assets to be divided by current liabilities (p. 733)

Current ratio A company's current assets divided by its current liabilities (p. 732)

Common-size financial statements A statement showing each account in percentage and dollar form. On the income statement, the percentages are based on total sales; on the balance sheet, they are based on total assets. (p. 729)

Financial leverage A difference between the rate of return on assets and the rate paid to creditors. (p. 736)

Horizontal analysis A side-by-side comparison of two or more years' financial statements. (p. 727)

Liquidity Refers to how quickly an asset can be converted to cash. Liquid assets can be converted to cash quickly, whereas illiquid assets cannot. (p. 731)

Trend analysis See *Horizontal analysis*. (p. 727)

Trend percentages Several years of financial data expressed as a percentage of a base year. (p. 728)

Vertical analysis The presentation of a company's financial statements in common-size form. (p. 729)

Working capital Current assets less current liabilities. (p. 732)

Questions

16–1 Distinguish between horizontal and vertical analysis.

16–2 What is the purpose for examining trends in a company's financial ratios and other data? What other kinds of comparisons might a manager make?

16–3 Assume two companies in the same industry have equal earnings. Why might these companies have different price-earnings ratios? If a company has a price-earnings ratio of 20 and reports earnings per share for the current year of $4, what is its market price per share?

16–4 Would you expect a company in a rapidly growing technological industry to have a high or low dividend payout ratio?

16–5 What does *dividend yield* mean?

16–6 What is *financial leverage?*

16–7   The president of a plastics company said, "We haven't had a dollar of interest-paying debt in over 10 years. Not many companies can say that." As a stockholder in this company, how would you feel about its policy of not taking on debt?

16–8   Is a company's stock overpriced if its market price per share exceeds its book value per share?

16–9   Why might a bank decline a loan to a company with a seemingly adequate current ratio of 2.0?

The Foundational 15   Mc Graw Hill connect

LO16–2, LO16–3, LO16–4, LO16–5, LO16–6

Markus Company's common stock sold for $2.75 per share at the end of this year. The company paid a common stock dividend of $0.55 per share this year. It also provided the following *data excerpts* from this year's financial statements:

	Ending Balance	Beginning Balance
Cash	$35,000	$30,000
Accounts receivable	$60,000	$50,000
Inventory	$55,000	$60,000
Current assets	$150,000	$140,000
Total assets	$450,000	$460,000
Current liabilities	$60,000	$40,000
Total liabilities	$130,000	$120,000
Common stock, $1 par value	$120,000	$120,000
Total stockholders' equity	$320,000	$340,000
Total liabilities and stockholders' equity	$450,000	$460,000

	This Year
Sales (all on account)	$700,000
Cost of goods sold	$400,000
Gross margin	$300,000
Net operating income.................	$140,000
Interest expense	$8,000
Net income..........................	$92,400

Required:
1. What is the earnings per share?
2. What is the price-earnings ratio?
3. What are the dividend payout ratio and the dividend yield ratio?
4. What is the return on total assets (assuming a 30% tax rate)?
5. What is the return on equity?
6. What is the book value per share at the end of this year?
7. What are the working capital and current ratio at the end of this year?
8. What is the acid-test ratio at the end of this year?
9. What are the accounts receivable turnover and the average collection period?
10. What are the inventory turnover and the average sale period?
11. What is the company's operating cycle?
12. What is the total asset turnover?
13. What is the times interest earned ratio?
14. What is the debt-to-equity ratio at the end of this year?
15. What is the equity multiplier?

Exercises

EXERCISE 16–1 Common-Size Income Statement   LO16–1

A comparative income statement is given below for McKenzie Sales, Ltd., of Toronto:

McKenzie Sales, Ltd. Comparative Income Statement		
	This Year	Last Year
Sales	$8,000,000	$6,000,000
Cost of goods sold	4,984,000	3,516,000
Gross margin	3,016,000	2,484,000
Selling and administrative expenses:		
Selling expenses	1,480,000	1,092,000
Administrative expenses	712,000	618,000
Total expenses	2,192,000	1,710,000
Net operating income	824,000	774,000
Interest expense	96,000	84,000
Net income before taxes	$ 728,000	$ 690,000

The company's board of directors is surprised to see net income increased by only $38,000 when sales increased by $2,000,000.

Required:

1. Express each year's income statement in common-size percentages.
2. Interpret the changes between the two years.

EXERCISE 16–2 Financial Ratios for Assessing Liquidity   LO16–2

Comparative financial statements for Weller Corporation, a merchandising company, for the year ending December 31 appear below. The company did not issue any common stock during the year. A total of 800,000 shares of common stock were outstanding. The interest rate on the bond payable was 12%, the income tax rate was 40%, and the dividend per share of common stock was $0.75 last year and $0.40 this year. The market value of the company's common stock at the end of this year was $18. All of the company's sales are on account.

Weller Corporation Comparative Balance Sheet (dollars in thousands)		
	This Year	Last Year
Assets		
Current assets:		
Cash	$ 1,280	$ 1,560
Accounts receivable, net	12,300	9,100
Inventory	9,700	8,200
Prepaid expenses	1,800	2,100
Total current assets	25,080	20,960
Property and equipment:		
Land	6,000	6,000
Buildings and equipment, net	19,200	19,000
Total property and equipment	25,200	25,000
Total assets	$50,280	$45,960

(Continued on next page)

(Continued)	This Year	Last Year
Liabilities and Stockholders' Equity		
Current liabilities:		
Accounts payable	$ 9,500	$ 8,300
Accrued liabilities	600	700
Notes payable, short term	300	300
Total current liabilities	10,400	9,300
Long-term liabilities:		
Bonds payable	5,000	5,000
Total liabilities	15,400	14,300
Stockholders' equity:		
Common stock	800	800
Additional paid-in capital	4,200	4,200
Total paid-in capital	5,000	5,000
Retained earnings	29,880	26,660
Total stockholders' equity	34,880	31,660
Total liabilities and stockholders' equity	$50,280	$45,960

Weller Corporation Comparative Income Statement and Reconciliation (dollars in thousands)		
	This Year	Last Year
Sales	$79,000	$74,000
Cost of goods sold	52,000	48,000
Gross margin	27,000	26,000
Selling and administrative expenses:		
Selling expenses	8,500	8,000
Administrative expenses	12,000	11,000
Total selling and administrative expenses	20,500	19,000
Net operating income	6,500	7,000
Interest expense	600	600
Net income before taxes	5,900	6,400
Income taxes	2,360	2,560
Net income	3,540	3,840
Dividends to common stockholders	320	600
Net income added to retained earnings	3,220	3,240
Beginning retained earnings	26,660	23,420
Ending retained earnings	$29,880	$26,660

Required:

Compute the following financial data and ratios for this year:
1.   Working capital.
2.   Current ratio.
3.   Acid-test ratio.

EXERCISE 16–3 Financial Ratios for Asset Management LO16–3
Refer to the data in Exercise 16–2 for Weller Corporation.

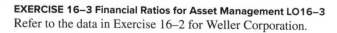

Required:
Compute the following financial data for this year:
1. Accounts receivable turnover. (Assume all sales are on account.)
2. Average collection period.
3. Inventory turnover.
4. Average sale period.
5. Operating cycle.
6. Total asset turnover.

EXERCISE 16–4 Financial Ratios for Debt Management LO16–4

Refer to the data in Exercise 16–2 for Weller Corporation.

Required:
Compute the following financial ratios for this year:
1. Times interest earned ratio.
2. Debt-to-equity ratio.
3. Equity multiplier.

EXERCISE 16–5 Financial Ratios for Assessing Profitability LO16–5

Refer to the data in Exercise 16–2 for Weller Corporation.

Required:
Compute the following financial data for this year:
1. Gross margin percentage.
2. Net profit margin percentage.
3. Return on total assets.
4. Return on equity.

EXERCISE 16–6 Financial Ratios for Assessing Market Performance LO16–6

Refer to the data in Exercise 16–2 for Weller Corporation.

Required:
Compute the following financial data for this year:
1. Earnings per share.
2. Price-earnings ratio.
3. Dividend payout ratio.
4. Dividend yield ratio.
5. Book value per share.

EXERCISE 16–7 Trend Percentages LO16–1

Rotorua Products sells agricultural products in the Asian market. The company's current assets, current liabilities, and sales over the last five years (Year 5 is the most recent year) are as follows:

	Year 1	Year 2	Year 3	Year 4	Year 5
Sales	$1,800,000	$1,980,000	$2,070,000	$2,160,000	$2,250,000
Cash	$ 50,000	$ 65,000	$ 48,000	$ 40,000	$ 30,000
Accounts receivable, net	300,000	345,000	405,000	510,000	570,000
Inventory	600,000	660,000	690,000	720,000	750,000
Total current assets	$ 950,000	$1,070,000	$1,143,000	$1,270,000	$1,350,000
Current liabilities.......................	$ 400,000	$ 440,000	$ 520,000	$ 580,000	$ 640,000

Required:
1. Express all of the asset, liability, and sales data in trend percentages. (Show percentages for each item.) Use Year 1 as the base year.
2. Interpret the company's trends.

EXERCISE 16–8 Selected Financial Ratios LO16–2, LO16–3, LO16–4
The financial statements for Castile Products, Inc., are given below:

	Castile Products, Inc. Balance Sheet December 31	
Assets		
Current assets:		
Cash		$ 6,500
Accounts receivable, net		35,000
Merchandise inventory		70,000
Prepaid expenses		3,500
Total current assets		115,000
Property and equipment, net		185,000
Total assets		$300,000
Liabilities and Stockholders' Equity		
Liabilities:		
Current liabilities		$ 50,000
Bonds payable, 10%		80,000
Total liabilities		130,000
Stockholders' equity:		
Common stock, $5 par value		30,000
Retained earnings		140,000
Total stockholders' equity		170,000
Total liabilities and stockholders' equity		$300,000

	Castile Products, Inc. Income Statement For the Year Ended December 31
Sales	$420,000
Cost of goods sold	292,500
Gross margin	127,500
Selling and administrative expenses	89,500
Net operating income	38,000
Interest expense	8,000
Net income before taxes	30,000
Income taxes (30%)	9,000
Net income	$ 21,000

Account balances at the beginning of the year were accounts receivable, $25,000, and inventory, $60,000. All sales were on account.

Required:
Compute the following financial data and ratios:
1. Working capital.
2. Current ratio.
3. Acid-test ratio.
4. Debt-to-equity ratio.
5. Times interest earned ratio.
6. Average collection period.
7. Average sale period.
8. Operating cycle.

EXERCISE 16–9 Financial Ratios for Assessing Profitability and Managing Debt LO16–4, LO16–5
Refer to the financial statements for Castile Products, Inc., in Exercise 16–8. Assets at the beginning of the year totaled $280,000, and the stockholders' equity totaled $161,600.

Required:
Compute the following:
1. Gross margin percentage.
2. Net profit margin percentage.
3. Return on total assets.
4. Return on equity.
5. Was financial leverage positive or negative for the year? Explain.

EXERCISE 16–10 Financial Ratios for Assessing Market Performance LO16–6
Refer to the financial statements for Castile Products, Inc., in Exercise 16–8. In addition to the data in these statements, assume Castile Products, Inc., paid dividends of $2.10 per share during the year. Also assume the company's common stock had a market price of $42 at the end of the year and there was no change in the number of outstanding shares of common stock during the year.

Required:
Compute financial ratios as follows:
1. Earnings per share.
2. Dividend payout ratio.
3. Dividend yield ratio.
4. Price-earnings ratio.
5. Book value per share.

EXERCISE 16–11 Financial Ratios for Assessing Profitability and Managing Debt LO16–4, LO16–5
Selected financial data at the end of this year for Safford Company are given below:

Total assets	$3,600,000
Long-term debt (12% interest rate)	$500,000
Total stockholders' equity	$2,400,000
Interest paid on long-term debt	$60,000
Net income	$280,000

Total assets at the beginning of the year were $3,000,000; total stockholders' equity was $2,200,000. The company's tax rate is 30%.

Required:
1. Compute the return on total assets.
2. Compute the return on equity.
3. Is financial leverage positive or negative? Explain.

EXERCISE 16–12 Selected Financial Measures for Assessing Liquidity LO16–2
Norsk Optronics had a current ratio of 2.5 on June 30 of the current year. On that date, the company's assets were:

Cash	$ 90,000
Accounts receivable, net	260,000
Inventory	490,000
Prepaid expenses	10,000
Plant and equipment, net	800,000
Total assets	$1,650,000

Required:
1. What was the company's working capital on June 30?
2. What was the company's acid-test ratio on June 30?
3. The company paid an account payable of $40,000 immediately after June 30.
    a. What effect did this transaction have on working capital? Show computations.
    b. What effect did this transaction have on the current ratio? Show computations.

Problems Mc Graw Hill connect

PROBLEM 16–13 Effects of Transactions on Various Financial Ratios LO16–2, LO16–3, LO16–4, LO16–5, LO16–6

The table below summarizes 18 business transactions or events, each accompanied by one financial measure or ratio.

Business Transaction or Event	Ratio
1. Declared a cash dividend.	Current ratio
2. Sold inventory on account at cost.	Acid-test ratio
3. Issued bonds with an interest rate of 8%. The company's return on assets is 10%.	Return on equity
4. Net income decreased by 10% between last year and this year. Long-term debt remained unchanged.	Times interest earned
5. Paid a previously declared cash dividend.	Current ratio
6. The market price of the company's common stock dropped from $24.50 to $20.00. The dividend paid per share remained unchanged.	Dividend payout ratio
7. Obsolete inventory totaling $100,000 was written off as a loss.	Inventory turnover ratio
8. Sold inventory for cash at a profit.	Debt-to-equity ratio
9. Changed customer credit terms from 2/10, n/30 to 2/15, n/30 to comply with a change in industry practice.	Accounts receivable turnover ratio
10. Issued a stock dividend to common stockholders.	Book value per share
11. The market price of the company's common stock increased from $24.50 to $30.00.	Book value per share
12. Paid $40,000 on accounts payable.	Working capital
13. Issued a stock dividend to common stockholders.	Earnings per share
14. Paid accounts payable.	Debt-to-equity ratio
15. Purchased inventory on account.	Acid-test ratio
16. Wrote off an uncollectible account against the Allowance for Bad Debts.	Current ratio
17. The market price of the company's common stock increased from $24.50 to $30.00. Earnings per share remained unchanged.	Price-earnings ratio
18. The market price of the company's common stock increased from $24.50 to $30.00. The dividend paid per share remained unchanged.	Dividend yield ratio

Required (consider each transaction independently):

Indicate whether each business transaction or event will increase, decrease, or have no effect on its corresponding measure or ratio. Give the reason for each answer. In all cases, assume the current assets exceed the current liabilities both before and after the event or transaction.

Effect on Ratio	Reason for Increase, Decrease, or No Effect
1.	
Etc.	

PROBLEM 16–14 Effects of Transactions on Various Ratios LO16–2

Denna Company's working capital accounts at the beginning of the year follow:

Cash	$50,000
Marketable securities	$30,000
Accounts receivable, net	$200,000
Inventory	$210,000
Prepaid expenses	$10,000
Accounts payable	$150,000
Notes due within one year	$30,000
Accrued liabilities	$20,000

During the year, Denna Company completed the following transactions:

a. Issued shares of common stock for cash, $100,000.

b. Sold inventory costing $50,000 for $80,000, on account.

c. Wrote off uncollectible accounts in the amount of $10,000, reducing the accounts receivable balance accordingly.
d. Paid a cash dividend, $15,000.
e. Paid accounts payable, $50,000.
f. Borrowed cash on a short-term note with the bank, $35,000.
g. Sold inventory costing $15,000 for $10,000 cash.
h. Purchased inventory on account, $60,000.
i. Paid off all short-term notes due, $30,000.
j. Purchased equipment for cash, $15,000.
k. Sold marketable securities costing $18,000 for cash, $15,000.
l. Collected cash on accounts receivable, $80,000.

Required:

1. Compute the following amounts and ratios as of the beginning of the year:
   a. Working capital.
   b. Current ratio.
   c. Acid-test ratio.
2. Indicate whether each of the above transactions will *increase, decrease,* or have *no effect* on working capital, the current ratio, and the acid-test ratio.

| | The Effect on | | |
Transaction	Working Capital	Current Ratio	Acid-Test Ratio
a. Issued shares of common stock for cash, $100,000			

PROBLEM 16–15 Comprehensive Ratio Analysis LO16–2, LO16–3, LO16–4, LO16–5, LO16–6
Lydex Company's financial statements for the last two years are as follows:

Lydex Company Comparative Balance Sheet	This Year	Last Year
Assets		
Current assets:		
Cash	$ 960,000	$ 1,260,000
Marketable securities	0	300,000
Accounts receivable, net	2,700,000	1,800,000
Inventory	3,900,000	2,400,000
Prepaid expenses	240,000	180,000
Total current assets	7,800,000	5,940,000
Plant and equipment, net	9,300,000	8,940,000
Total assets	$17,100,000	$14,880,000
Liabilities and Stockholders' Equity		
Liabilities:		
Current liabilities	$ 3,900,000	$ 2,760,000
Note payable, 10%	3,600,000	3,000,000
Total liabilities	7,500,000	5,760,000
Stockholders' equity:		
Common stock, $78 par value	7,800,000	7,800,000
Retained earnings	1,800,000	1,320,000
Total stockholders' equity	9,600,000	9,120,000
Total liabilities and stockholders' equity	$17,100,000	$14,880,000

Lydex Company		
Comparative Income Statement and Reconciliation		
	This Year	Last Year
Sales (all on account)	$15,750,000	$12,480,000
Cost of goods sold	12,600,000	9,900,000
Gross margin	3,150,000	2,580,000
Selling and administrative expenses ...	1,590,000	1,560,000
Net operating income	1,560,000	1,020,000
Interest expense	360,000	300,000
Net income before taxes	1,200,000	720,000
Income taxes (30%)	360,000	216,000
Net income	840,000	504,000
Common dividends	360,000	252,000
Net income retained	480,000	252,000
Beginning retained earnings	1,320,000	1,068,000
Ending retained earnings	$ 1,800,000	$ 1,320,000

The following financial data and ratios are typical of companies in Lydex Company's industry:

Current ratio	2.3
Acid-test ratio	1.2
Average collection period	30 days
Average sale period	60 days
Return on assets	9.5%
Debt-to-equity ratio	0.65
Times interest earned ratio	5.7
Price-earnings ratio	10

Required:

1. To assess the company's performance in terms of debt management and profitability, compute the following for this year and last year:
   a. The times interest earned ratio.
   b. The debt-to-equity ratio.
   c. The gross margin percentage.
   d. The return on total assets. (Total assets at the beginning of last year were $12,960,000.)
   e. The return on equity. (Stockholders' equity at the beginning of last year totaled $9,048,000. There has been no change in common stock over the last two years.)
   f. Is the company's financial leverage positive or negative? Explain.
2. To assess the company's stock market performance, compute the following for this year and last year. Assume Lydex's stock price at the end of this year and last year was $72 and $40, respectively.
   a. The earnings per share.
   b. The dividend yield ratio.
   c. The dividend payout ratio.
   d. The price-earnings ratio. How do investors regard Lydex Company as compared to other companies in the industry? Explain.
   e. The book value per share of common stock. Does the difference between market value per share and book value per share suggest the stock's current price is a bargain? Explain.

3. To assess the company's liquidity and asset management, compute the following for this year and last year:
   a. Working capital.
   b. The current ratio.
   c. The acid-test ratio.
   d. The average collection period. (The accounts receivable at the beginning of last year totaled $1,560,000.)
   e. The average sale period. (The inventory at the beginning of last year totaled $1,920,000.)
   f. The operating cycle.
   g. The total asset turnover. (The total assets at the beginning of last year totaled $12,960,000.)
4. Prepare a brief memo summarizing how Lydex is performing relative to its competitors.

PROBLEM 16–16 Common-Size Financial Statements LO16–1
Refer to the financial statement data for Lydex Company given in Problem 16–15.

Required:
For this year and last year:
1. Present the balance sheet in common-size format.
2. Present the income statement in common-size format down through net income.
3. Interpret the common-size financial statements.

PROBLEM 16–17 Interpretation of Financial Ratios LO16–2, LO16–3, LO16–6
Pecunious Products, Inc.'s financial results for the past three years are summarized below:

	Year 3	Year 2	Year 1
Sales trend	128.0	115.0	100.0
Current ratio	2.5	2.3	2.2
Acid-test ratio	0.8	0.9	1.1
Accounts receivable turnover	9.4	10.6	12.5
Inventory turnover	6.5	7.2	8.0
Dividend yield	7.1%	6.5%	5.8%
Dividend payout ratio	40%	50%	60%
Dividends paid per share*	$1.50	$1.50	$1.50

*There have been no changes in common stock outstanding over the three-year period.

Required:
Review the results above and answer the following questions:
1. Is it becoming easier for the company to pay its bills as they come due?
2. Are customers paying their accounts at least as fast now as they were in Year 1?
3. Are the accounts receivable increasing, decreasing, or remaining constant?
4. Is inventory increasing, decreasing, or remaining constant?
5. Is the market price of the company's stock going up or down?
6. Is the earnings per share increasing or decreasing?
7. Is the price-earning ratio going up or down?

PROBLEM 16–18 Common-Size Statements and Financial Ratios for a Loan Application LO16–1, LO16–2, LO16–3, LO16–4
Paul Sabin organized Sabin Electronics 10 years ago to produce and sell several electronic devices. Due to a cash shortage, the company is requesting a $500,000 long-term loan from Gulfport State Bank. The company's financial statements for the two most recent years follow:

Sabin Electronics Comparative Balance Sheet	This Year	Last Year
Assets		
Current assets:		
Cash	$ 70,000	$ 150,000
Marketable securities	0	18,000
Accounts receivable, net	480,000	300,000
Inventory	950,000	600,000
Prepaid expenses	20,000	22,000
Total current assets	1,520,000	1,090,000
Plant and equipment, net	1,480,000	1,370,000
Total assets	$3,000,000	$2,460,000
Liabilities and Stockholders' Equity		
Liabilities:		
Current liabilities	$ 800,000	$ 430,000
Bonds payable, 12%	600,000	600,000
Total liabilities	1,400,000	1,030,000
Stockholders' equity:		
Common stock, $15 par	750,000	750,000
Retained earnings	850,000	680,000
Total stockholders' equity	1,600,000	1,430,000
Total liabilities and stockholders' equity ..	$3,000,000	$2,460,000

Sabin Electronics Comparative Income Statement and Reconciliation	This Year	Last Year
Sales	$5,000,000	$4,350,000
Cost of goods sold	3,875,000	3,450,000
Gross margin	1,125,000	900,000
Selling and administrative expenses ...	653,000	548,000
Net operating income	472,000	352,000
Interest expense	72,000	72,000
Net income before taxes	400,000	280,000
Income taxes (30%)	120,000	84,000
Net income	280,000	196,000
Common dividends	110,000	95,000
Net income retained	170,000	101,000
Beginning retained earnings	680,000	579,000
Ending retained earnings	$ 850,000	$ 680,000

During the past year, the company introduced several new products and raised the selling prices on a number of existing products to improve its profit margin. The company also hired a new sales manager, who expanded sales into several new territories. Sales terms are 2/10, n/30. All sales are on account.

Required:

1. To assist in approaching the bank about the loan, Paul asked you to compute the following ratios for both this year and last year:
   a. The amount of working capital.
   b. The current ratio.
   c. The acid-test ratio.
   d. The average collection period. (The accounts receivable at the beginning of last year totaled $250,000.)

 e. The average sale period. (The inventory at the beginning of last year totaled $500,000.)

 f. The operating cycle.

 g. The total asset turnover. (The total assets at the beginning of last year were $2,420,000.)

 h. The debt-to-equity ratio.

 i. The times interest earned ratio.

 j. The equity multiplier. (The total stockholders' equity at the beginning of last year totaled $1,420,000.)

2. For both this year and last year:

 a. Present the balance sheet in common-size format.

 b. Present the income statement in common-size format down through net income.

3. Paul Sabin also gathered the following financial data and ratios typical of companies in the electronics industry:

Current ratio	2.5
Acid-test ratio	1.3
Average collection period	18 days
Average sale period	60 days
Debt-to-equity ratio	0.90
Times interest earned ratio	6.0

Comment on the results of your analysis in (1) and (2) above and compare Sabin Electronics' performance to the benchmarks from the electronics industry. Do you think the company will get its loan application approved?

PROBLEM 16–19 Financial Ratios for Assessing Profitability and Market Performance LO16–5, LO16–6

Refer to the financial statements and other data in Problem 16–18. Assume Paul Sabin asked you to assess his company's profitability and stock market performance.

Required:

1. You decide first to assess the company's stock market performance. For both this year and last year, compute:

 a. The earnings per share. There has been no change in common stock over the last two years.

 b. The dividend yield ratio. The company's stock is currently selling for $40 per share; last year it sold for $36 per share.

 c. The dividend payout ratio.

 d. The price-earnings ratio. How do investors regard Sabin Electronics as compared to other companies in the industry if the industry norm for the price-earnings ratio is 12? Explain.

 e. The book value per share of common stock. Does the difference between market value and book value suggest the stock is overpriced? Explain.

2. You decide next to assess the company's profitability. Compute the following for both this year and last year:

 a. The gross margin percentage.

 b. The net profit margin percentage.

 c. The return on total assets. (Total assets at the beginning of last year were $2,420,000.)

 d. The return on equity. (Stockholders' equity at the beginning of last year was $1,420,000.)

 e. Is the company's financial leverage positive or negative? Explain.

3. Comment on the company's profit performance and stock market performance over the two-year period.

PROBLEM 16–20 Ethics and the Manager LO16–2, LO16–4

Venice InLine, Inc., was founded by Russ Perez to produce a specialized in-line skate he had designed for doing aerial tricks. Up to this point, Russ has financed the company with his own savings and with cash generated by his business. However, Russ now faces a cash crisis. In the year just ended, an acute shortage of high-impact roller bearings developed just as the company was beginning production for the Christmas season. Russ had been assured by his suppliers the roller bearings would be delivered in time to make Christmas shipments, but the suppliers were unable to deliver on this promise. As a consequence, Venice InLine had large stocks of unfinished skates at the end of the year and was unable to fill all of the orders from retailers for the Christmas season. Consequently, sales were below expectations for the year, and Russ does not have enough cash to pay his creditors.

Well before the accounts payable were due, Russ visited a local bank and inquired about obtaining a loan. The loan officer at the bank assured Russ there should not be any problem getting a loan to pay off his accounts payable—providing the current ratio is above 2.0, the acid-test ratio is above 1.0, and net operating income is at least four times the interest on the proposed loan. Russ promised to return later with a copy of his financial statements.

Russ would like to apply for an $80,000 six-month loan with an interest rate of 10% per year. The unaudited financial reports of the company appear below:

Venice InLine, Inc.
Comparative Balance Sheet as of December 31
(dollars in thousands)

	This Year	Last Year
Assets		
Current assets:		
Cash	$ 70	$150
Accounts receivable, net	50	40
Inventory	160	100
Prepaid expenses	10	12
Total current assets	290	302
Property and equipment	270	180
Total assets	$560	$482
Liabilities and Stockholders' Equity		
Current liabilities:		
Accounts payable	$154	$ 90
Accrued liabilities	10	10
Total current liabilities	164	100
Long-term liabilities	—	—
Total liabilities	164	100
Stockholders' equity:		
Common stock and additional paid-in capital	100	100
Retained earnings	296	282
Total stockholders' equity	396	382
Total liabilities and stockholders' equity	$560	$482

Venice InLine, Inc.
Income Statement
For the Year Ended December 31
(dollars in thousands)

	This Year
Sales (all on account)	$420
Cost of goods sold	290
Gross margin	130
Selling and administrative expenses:	
Selling expenses	42
Administrative expenses	68
Total selling and administrative expenses	110
Net operating income	20
Interest expense	—
Net income before taxes	20
Income taxes (30%)	6
Net income	$ 14

Required:

1. Based on the unaudited financial statements and the statement made by the loan officer, would the company qualify for the loan?

2. Last year Russ purchased new equipment to replace an older plastic injection molding machine. Russ had planned to sell the old machine but found it is still needed whenever the plastic injection molding process is a bottleneck. When Russ discussed his cash flow problems with his brother-in-law, he suggested to Russ the old machine be reclassified as inventory on the balance sheet because it could be readily sold. At present, the machine is carried in the Property and Equipment account and could be sold for its net book value of $45,000. The bank does not require audited financial statements. What advice would you give to Russ concerning the machine?

PROBLEM 16–21 Incomplete Statements; Ratios Analysis LO16–2, LO16–3, LO16–4, LO16–5, LO16–6

Incomplete financial statements for Pepper Industries follow:

Pepper Industries Balance Sheet March 31	
Current assets:	
Cash	$?
Accounts receivable, net	?
Inventory	?
Total current assets	?
Plant and equipment, net	?
Total assets	$?
Liabilities:	
Current liabilities	$320,000
Bonds payable, 10%	?
Total liabilities	?
Stockholders' equity:	
Common stock, $5 par value	?
Retained earnings	?
Total stockholders' equity	?
Total liabilities and stockholders' equity	$?

Pepper Industries Income Statement For the Year Ended March 31	
Sales	$4,200,000
Cost of goods sold	?
Gross margin	?
Selling and administrative expenses......	?
Net operating income	?
Interest expense	80,000
Net income before taxes	?
Income taxes (30%)	?
Net income	$?

The following additional information is available about the company:

a. All sales during the year were on account.

b. There was no change in the number of shares of common stock outstanding during the year.

c. The interest expense on the income statement relates to the bonds payable; the amount of bonds outstanding did not change during the year.

d. Selected balances at the *beginning* of the current year were:

Accounts receivable	$270,000
Inventory	$360,000
Total assets	$1,800,000

e. Selected financial ratios computed from the statements above for the current year are:

Earnings per share	$2.30
Debt-to-equity ratio	0.875
Accounts receivable turnover	14.0
Current ratio	2.75
Return on total assets	18.0%
Times interest earned ratio	6.75
Acid-test ratio	1.25
Inventory turnover	6.5

Required:

Compute the missing amounts on the company's financial statements. (*Hint:* What's the difference between the acid-test ratio and the current ratio?)

Integration Exercises: An Overview

Successful managers rely on an integrated set of managerial accounting competencies to solve complex real-world problems. Therefore, we have created 20 integration exercises to help you develop these critically important managerial skills. This collective group of exercises enables you to see how the learning objectives throughout the book interrelate with one another. As you begin to understand "how it all fits together," you will start the exciting evolution from "number cruncher" to a manager-in-training.

Mc Graw Hill connect   Integration Exercises

INTEGRATION EXERCISE 1 Activity Variance, Spending Variance, Materials Price Variance, Materials Quantity Variance LO9–1, 9–2, LO9–3, LO10–1

Southside Pizzeria wants to improve its ability to manage the ingredient costs associated with making and selling its pizzas. For the month of June, the company plans to make 1,000 pizzas. It created a planning budget including a cost formula for mozzarella cheese of $2.40 per pizza. At the end of June, Southside actually sold 1,100 pizzas and the actual cost of the cheese used during the month was $2,632.

Required:

1. What is the mozzarella cheese activity variance for June?
2. What is the mozzarella cheese spending variance for June?
3. Assume the company establishes a price standard of $0.30 per ounce for mozzarella cheese and a quantity standard of eight ounces of cheese per pizza. Also, assume Southside actually used 9,400 ounces of cheese during the month to make 1,100 pizzas.
   a. What is the materials price variance for mozzarella cheese for June?
   b. What is the materials quantity variance for mozzarella cheese for June?
   c. What is the materials spending variance for mozzarella cheese for June?

INTEGRATION EXERCISE 2 Different Costs for Different Purposes, Cost-Volume-Profit-Relationships LO1–1, LO1–2, LO1–3, LO1–4, LO1–5, LO 1–6, LO5–1, LO5–2, LO5–3, LO5–4, LO5–5

Hixson Company manufactures and sells one product for $34 per unit. The company maintains no beginning or ending inventories and its relevant range of production is 20,000 units to 30,000 units. When Hixson produces and sells 25,000 units, its unit costs are as follows:

	Amount Per Unit
Direct materials	$8.00
Direct labor	$5.00
Variable manufacturing overhead	$1.00
Fixed manufacturing overhead	$6.00
Fixed selling expense	$3.50
Fixed administrative expense	$2.50
Sales commissions	$4.00
Variable administrative expense	$1.00

Required:

1. For financial accounting purposes, what is the total amount of product costs incurred to make 25,000 units? What is the total amount of period costs incurred to sell 25,000 units?

2. If 24,000 units are produced, what is the variable manufacturing cost per unit produced? What is the average fixed manufacturing cost per unit produced?
3. If 26,000 units are produced, what is the variable manufacturing cost per unit produced? What is the average fixed manufacturing cost per unit produced?
4. If 27,000 units are produced, what are the total amounts of direct and indirect manufacturing costs incurred to support this level of production?
5. What total incremental manufacturing cost will Hixson incur if it increases production from 25,000 to 25,001 units?
6. What is Hixson's contribution margin per unit? What is its contribution margin ratio?
7. What is Hixson's break-even point in unit sales? What is its break-even point in dollar sales?
8. How much will Hixson's net operating income increase if it can grow production and sales from 25,000 units to 26,500 units?
9. What is Hixson's margin of safety at a sales volume of 25,000 units?
10. What is Hixson degree of operating leverage at a sales volume of 25,000 units?

INTEGRATION EXERCISE 3 Absorption Costing, Variable Costing, Cost-Volume-Profit-Relationships
LO5–4, LO5–5, LO5–7, LO6–1, LO6–2

Newton Company manufactures and sells one product. The company assembled the following projections for its first year of operations:

Variable costs per unit:	
Manufacturing:	
Direct materials	$20
Direct labor.	$16
Variable manufacturing overhead	$4
Variable selling and administrative	$2
Fixed costs per year:	
Fixed manufacturing overhead.	$450,000
Fixed selling and administrative expenses.	$70,000

During its first year of operations Newton expects to produce 25,000 units and sell 20,000 units. The budgeted selling price of the company's only product is $66 per unit.

Required *(answer each question independently by referring to the original data):*

1. Assuming Newton's projections are accurate, what will be its absorption costing net operating income in its first year of operations?
2. Newton is considering investing in a higher quality raw material that increases its direct materials cost by $1 per unit. It estimates the higher quality raw material will increase sales by 1,000 units. What will be the company's revised absorption costing net operating income if it invests in the higher quality raw material and continues to *produce* 25,000 units?
3. Newton is considering raising its selling price by $1.00 per unit with an expectation it will lower unit sales by 1,500 units. What will be the company's revised absorption costing net operating income if it raises its price by $1.00 and continues to *produce* 25,000 units?
4. Assuming Newton's projections are accurate, what will be its variable costing net operating income in its first year of operations?
5. Newton is considering investing in a higher quality raw material that increases its direct materials cost by $1 per unit. It estimates the higher quality raw material will increase sales by 1,000 units. What will be the company's revised variable costing net operating income if it invests in the higher quality raw material and continues to *produce* 25,000 units?
6. Newton is considering raising its selling price by $1.00 per unit with an expectation it will lower unit sales by 1,500 units. What will be the company's revised variable costing net operating income if it raises its price by $1.00 and continues to *produce* 25,000 units?
7. What is Newton's break-even point in unit sales? What is its break-even point in dollar sales?
8. What is the company's projected margin of safety in its first year of operations?

INTEGRATION EXERCISE 4 Cash Budget, Income Statement, Balance Sheet, Statement of Cash Flows, Ratio Analysis LO8–2, LO8–3, LO8–4, LO8–8, LO8–9, LO8–10, LO15–2, LO16–3

Millen Corporation is a merchandiser preparing a master budget for the month of July. The company's balance sheet as of June 30 is shown below:

Millen Corporation Balance Sheet June 30	
Assets	
Cash	$120,000
Accounts receivable............................	166,000
Inventory......................................	37,200
Plant and equipment, net of depreciation	554,800
Total assets	$878,000
Liabilities and Stockholders' Equity	
Accounts payable	$ 93,000
Common stock...................................	586,000
Retained earnings...............................	199,000
Total liabilities and stockholders' equity	$878,000

Millen's managers made the following additional assumptions and estimates:

1. Estimated sales for July and August are $310,000 and $330,000, respectively.
2. Each month's sales are 20% cash sales and 80% credit sales. Each month's credit sales are collected 30% in the month of sale and 70% in the month following the sale. All of the accounts receivable at June 30 will be collected in July.
3. Each month's ending inventory must equal 20% of the cost of next month's sales. The cost of goods sold is 60% of sales. The company pays for 40% of its merchandise purchases in the month of the purchase and the remaining 60% in the month following the purchase. All of the accounts payable at June 30 will be paid in July.
4. Monthly selling and administrative expenses are always $70,000. Each month $10,000 of this total amount is depreciation expense and the remaining $60,000 relates to expenses paid in the month they are incurred.
5. The company does not plan to buy or sell any plant and equipment during July. It will not borrow any money, pay a dividend, issue any common stock, or repurchase any of its own common stock during July.

Required:

1. Calculate the expected cash collections for July.
2. Calculate the expected cash disbursements for merchandise purchases for July.
3. Prepare a cash budget for July.
4. Prepare a budgeted income statement for the month ended July 31. Use an absorption format.
5. Prepare a budgeted balance sheet as of July 31.
6. Calculate the estimated accounts receivable turnover and inventory turnover for the month of July.
7. Calculate the estimated operating cycle for the month of July. (*Hint:* Use 30 days in the numerator to calculate the average collection period and the average sales period.)
8. Using the indirect method, calculate the estimated net cash provided by operating activities for July.

INTEGRATION EXERCISE 5 Statement of Cash Flows; Ratio Analysis LO15–1, LO15–2, LO15–3, LO15–4, LO15–5, LO15–6, LO16–2, LO16–3, LO16–4, LO16–5, LO16–6

A comparative balance sheet and an income statement for Rowan Company are given below:

Rowan Company
Comparative Balance Sheet
(dollars in millions)

	Ending Balance	Beginning Balance
Assets		
Current assets:		
Cash and cash equivalents......................	$ 70	$ 91
Accounts receivable...........................	536	572
Inventory.....................................	620	580
Total current assets............................	1,226	1,243
Property, plant, and equipment....................	1,719	1,656
Less accumulated depreciation	640	480
Net property, plant, and equipment...............	1,079	1,176
Total assets.....................................	$ 2,305	$ 2,419
Liabilities and Stockholders' Equity		
Current liabilities:		
Accounts payable.............................	$ 205	$ 180
Accrued liabilities	94	105
Income taxes payable	72	88
Total current liabilities.........................	371	373
Bonds payable....................................	180	310
Total liabilities..................................	551	683
Stockholders' equity:		
Common stock.................................	800	800
Retained earnings.............................	954	936
Total stockholders' equity	1,754	1,736
Total liabilities and stockholders' equity	$ 2,305	$ 2,419

Rowan Company
Income Statement
For the Year Ended December 31
(dollars in millions)

Sales	$4,350
Cost of goods sold	3,470
Gross margin	880
Selling and administrative expenses..................	820
Net operating income..............................	60
Nonoperating items: Gain on sale of equipment........	4
Income before taxes...............................	64
Income taxes	22
Net income.......................................	$ 42

Rowan also provided the following information:

1. The company sold equipment with an original cost of $16 million and accumulated depreciation of $9 million. The cash proceeds from the sale were $11 million. The gain on the sale was $4 million.
2. The company did not issue any new bonds during the year.
3. The company paid a cash dividend during the year.
4. The company did not complete any common stock transactions during the year.

Required:
1. Using the indirect method, prepare a statement of cash flows for the year.
2. Calculate the free cash flow for the year.
3. To help Rowan assess its liquidity at the end of the year, calculate the following:
   a. Current ratio
   b. Acid-test (quick) ratio
4. To help Rowan assess its asset management, calculate the following:
   a. Average collection period (assuming all sales are on account)
   b. Average sale period
5. To help Rowan assess its debt management, calculate the following:
   a. Debt-to-equity ratio at the end of the year
   b. Equity multiplier
6. To help Rowan assess its profitability, calculate the following:
   a. Net profit margin percentage
   b. Return on equity
7. To help Rowan assess its market performance, calculate the following (assume the par value of the company's common stock is $10 per share):
   a. Earnings per share
   b. Dividend payout ratio

INTEGRATION EXERCISE 6 Plantwide and Departmental Overhead Allocation; Activity-Based Costing; Segmented Income Statements LO2–1, LO2–2, LO2–3, LO2–4, LO6–4, LO6–5, LO7–1, LO7–3, LO7–4

Koontz Company manufactures two models of industrial components—a Basic model and an Advanced model. The company considers all of its manufacturing overhead costs to be fixed and uses plantwide manufacturing overhead cost allocation based on direct labor-hours. Koontz's controller prepared the segmented income statement shown below for the most recent year (he allocated selling and administrative expenses to products based on sales dollars):

	Basic	Advanced	Total
Number of units produced and sold	20,000	10,000	30,000
Sales	$3,000,000	$2,000,000	$5,000,000
Cost of goods sold	2,300,000	1,350,000	3,650,000
Gross margin	700,000	650,000	1,350,000
Selling and administrative expenses	720,000	480,000	1,200,000
Net operating income (loss)	$ (20,000)	$ 170,000	$ 150,000

Direct laborers are paid $20 per hour. Direct materials cost $40 per unit for the Basic model and $60 per unit for the Advanced model. Koontz is considering a change from plantwide overhead allocation to a departmental approach. The overhead costs in the company's Molding Department would be allocated based on machine-hours and the overhead costs in its Assemble and Pack Department would be allocated based on direct labor-hours. To enable further analysis, the controller gathered the following information:

	Molding	Assemble and Pack	Total
Manufacturing overhead costs	$787,500	$562,500	$1,350,000
Direct labor-hours:			
Basic	10,000	20,000	30,000
Advanced	5,000	10,000	15,000
Machine-hours:			
Basic	12,000	—	12,000
Advanced	10,000	—	10,000

Required:

1. Using the plantwide approach:
    a. Calculate the plantwide overhead rate.
    b. Calculate the amount of overhead assigned to each product.
2. Using a departmental approach:
    a. Calculate the departmental overhead rates.
    b. Calculate the total amount of overhead assigned to each product.
    c. Using your departmental overhead cost allocations, redo the controller's segmented income statement (continue to allocate selling and administrative expenses based on sales dollars).
3. Koontz's production manager suggested using activity-based costing instead of either the plantwide or departmental approaches. To facilitate the necessary calculations, she assigned the company's total manufacturing overhead cost to five activity cost pools as follows:

Activity Cost Pool	Activity Measure	Manufacturing Overhead
Machining	Machine-hours in Molding	$ 417,500
Assemble and pack	Direct labor-hours in Assemble and Pack	282,500
Order processing	Number of customer orders	230,000
Setups	Setup hours	340,000
Other (unused capacity)		80,000
		$1,350,000

She also determined the average order size for the Basic and Advanced models is 400 units and 50 units, respectively. The molding machines require a setup for each order. One setup hour is required for each customer order of the Basic model and three hours are required to setup for an order of the Advanced model.

The company pays a sales commissions of 5% for the Basic model and 10% for the Advanced model. Its traceable fixed advertising costs include $150,000 for the Basic model and $200,000 for the Advanced model. The remainder of the company's selling and administrative costs are organization-sustaining in nature.

Using the additional information provided by the production manager, calculate:

a. An activity rate for each activity cost pool.
b. The total manufacturing overhead cost allocated to the Basic model and the Advanced model using the activity-based approach.
c. The total selling and administrative cost traced to the Basic model and the Advanced model using the activity-based approach.
4. Using your activity-based cost assignments from requirement 3, prepare a contribution format segmented income statement adapted from Exhibit 6–8. (*Hint:* Organize all of the company's costs into three categories: variable expenses, traceable fixed expenses, and common fixed expenses.)
5. Using your contribution format segmented income statement from requirement 4, calculate the break-even point in dollar sales for the Advanced model.
6. Explain how Koontz's activity-based costing approach differs from its plantwide and departmental approaches.

INTEGRATION EXERCISE 7 Normal Costing versus Actual Costing LO2–1, LO2–2, LO2–3, LO3–3, LO3–4, LO6–1, LO6–2

Darwin Company manufactures only one product that it sells for $200 per unit. The company uses plantwide overhead cost allocation based on the number of units produced. It provided the following estimates at the beginning of the year:

Number of units produced	50,000
Total fixed manufacturing overhead costs	$1,000,000
Variable manufacturing overhead per unit produced	$12

During the year, the company had no beginning inventories and no ending raw materials or work in process inventories. All raw materials were used in production as direct materials. An unexpected business downturn caused annual sales to drop to 38,000 units. In response to the decline in sales, Darwin decreased its annual production to 40,000 units. The company's actual costs for the year were as follows:

Variable costs per unit:		
Manufacturing:		
Direct materials		$78
Direct labor.		$60
Variable manufacturing overhead		$12
Variable selling and administrative		$15
Fixed costs per year:		
Fixed manufacturing overhead.	$1,000,000	
Fixed selling and administrative expenses.	$350,000	

Required:

1. Assuming the company uses normal costing (as described in Chapters 2 and 3):
   a. Compute the plantwide predetermined overhead rate.
   b. Compute the unit product cost for each unit produced during the year.
   c. Prepare a schedule of cost of goods manufactured and a schedule of cost of goods sold. Assume any underapplied or overapplied overhead is closed entirely to cost of goods sold.
   d. Compute absorption costing net operating income for the year.
2. Assuming the company uses actual costing (as described in Chapter 6):
   a. Compute the unit product cost for each unit produced during the year.
   b. Compute absorption costing net operating income for the year.
3. Are your normal costing and actual costing net operating incomes the same? Why? Support your answer with computations.

INTEGRATION EXERCISE 8 Capital Budgeting, Return on Investment, Residual Income LO11–1, LO11–2, LO14–2

Simmons Company is a merchandiser with multiple store locations. One of its store managers is considering a shift in her store's product mix in anticipation of a strengthening economy. Her store would invest $800,000 in more expensive merchandise (an increase in its working capital) with the expectation it would increase annual sales and variable expenses by $400,000 and $250,000, respectively for three years. At the end of the three-year period, the store manager believes the economic surge will subside; therefore, she will release the additional investment in working capital. The store manager's pay raises are largely determined by her store's return on investment (ROI), which has exceeded 22% each of the last three years.

Required:

1. Assuming the company's discount rate is 16%, calculate the net present value of the store manager's investment opportunity.
2. Calculate the annual margin, turnover, and return on investment (ROI) provided by the store manager's investment opportunity.
3. Assuming the company's minimum required rate of return is 16%, calculate the residual income earned by the store manager's investment opportunity for each of years 1 through 3.
4. Do you think the store manager would choose to pursue this investment opportunity? Do you think the company would want the store manager to pursue it? Why?
5. Using a discount rate of 16%, calculate the present value of your residual incomes for years 1 through 3. Is your answer greater than, less than, or equal to the net present value that you computed in (1) above? Why? Support your explanation with computations.

INTEGRATION EXERCISE 9 Variance Analysis and Internal Business Process Performance Measures LO10–1, LO10–2, LO10–3, LO12–3

"I thought lean production was supposed to make us more efficient," commented Ben Carrick, manufacturing vice president of Vorelli Industries. "But just look at June's manufacturing variances for Zets. The labor efficiency variance was $240,000 unfavorable—four times higher than it's ever been before. If you add on the $102,000 unfavorable materials price variance, that's $342,000 down the drain in a single month on just one product."

"Now take it easy, Ben," replied Sandi Shipp, the company's purchasing manager. "We knew the switch to lean production was going to increase our material costs. But now we're partnering with top-notch suppliers who deliver raw materials to our plant three times a day. In a few months, we'll be able to offset most of our higher purchasing costs by vacating three rented warehouses."

"And I know our labor efficiency variance looks bad," responded Raul Duvall, the company's production manager, "but it doesn't tell the whole story. The just-in-time flow in our production lines has made our plant more efficient than ever before. Plus our investment in automation is reducing our materials waste each month."

"How can you say you're being more efficient when you took 90,000 direct labor-hours to produce just 30,000 Zets last month?" asked Ben Carrick. "That's an average of 3 hours per unit, whereas the Zets' standard cost card only allows 2.5 hours per unit."

Raul explained, "Part of our lean transformation requires cutting back production to reduce excess finished goods inventories. In a few months our finished goods inventories will be depleted and we'll be able to match production with demand. In the meantime, don't forget our line people aren't just standing around when their machines are idle. Under the lean approach, they're doing their own inspections and equipment maintenance."

Ben replied, "We can't let this go on a few more months . . . at least not if you want to earn a bonus this year. I've been looking at these reports for 30 years, and I know inefficiency when I see it. Let's get things back under control."

After leaving Ben's office, Raul asked for your help in developing some performance measures highlighting the benefits of the company's lean transformation. Working with Raul, you gathered the following information:

a. A standard cost card for Zets (one of the company's many products) is given below:

	Standard Quantity or Hours	Standard Price or Rate	Standard Cost
Direct materials............................	18 feet	$3.00 per foot	$ 54.00
Direct labor................................	2.5 hours	$16.00 per hour	40.00
Variable manufacturing overhead	2.5 hours	$2.80 per hour	7.00
Total standard cost			$101.00

b. During June the company purchased 510,000 feet of material for production of Zets at a cost of $3.20 per foot. All of this material was used to make 30,000 units during the month.

c. The company maintains a stable workforce to produce Zets. Employees who previously performed inspections and maintenance have been reassigned as direct labor workers. During June, direct laborers worked 90,000 hours on the Zets production lines at an average pay rate of $15.85 per hour.

d. Variable manufacturing overhead cost is allocated to products based on direct labor-hours. During June, the company incurred $207,000 in variable manufacturing overhead costs associated with the manufacture of Zets.

e. As workers have become more familiar with lean production methods, the following trends (per unit) have emerged over the last three months:

	April	May	June
Processing time.............	2.6 hours	2.5 hours	2.4 hours
Inspection time	1.3 hours	0.9 hour	0.1 hour
Move time..................	1.9 hours	1.4 hours	0.6 hour
Queue time.................	8.2 hours	5.2 hours	1.9 hours

Required:

1. For direct materials:
    a. Compute the price and quantity variances.
    b. Is the decrease in waste that was mentioned by Raul apparent from your variance calculations? Explain.
    c. What standard price per foot should the company use going forward to compute the materials price variance? Why?

2. For direct labor:
   a. Compute the rate and efficiency variances.
   b. Is the company's labor efficiency variance a useful performance measure in its lean environment? Why?
3. For variable manufacturing overhead:
   a. Compute the rate and efficiency variances.
   b. Is direct labor-hours an appropriate cost driver for variable manufacturing overhead in the company's lean environment? Explain.
4. Compute the following for April, May, and June:
   a. The throughput time per unit.
   b. The manufacturing cycle efficiency (MCE).
5. Which performance measures are more appropriate in the company's lean environment—the labor efficiency variance or throughput time per unit and manufacturing cycle efficiency?

INTEGRATION EXERCISE 10 Segmented Income Statements; Activity Rates and Activity-Based Cost Allocation LO6–4, LO7–3, LO7–4

Morley Products is a wholesale distributor competing in three markets—Commercial, Home, and School. It prepared the following segmented income statement:

	Total Company		Commercial Market	Home Market	School Market
Sales	$20,000,000	100.0%	$8,000,000	$5,000,000	$7,000,000
Less expenses:					
Cost of goods sold	9,500,000	47.5%	3,900,000	2,400,000	3,200,000
Sales support	3,600,000	18.0%	1,440,000	900,000	1,260,000
Order processing	1,720,000	8.6%	688,000	430,000	602,000
Warehousing	940,000	4.7%	376,000	235,000	329,000
Packing and shipping	520,000	2.6%	208,000	130,000	182,000
Advertising	1,690,000	8.5%	676,000	422,500	591,500
General management	1,310,000	6.5%	524,000	327,500	458,500
Total expenses	19,280,000	96.4%	7,812,000	4,845,000	6,623,000
Net operating income	$ 720,000	3.6%	$ 188,000	$ 155,000	$ 377,000

Although the Commercial Market has the highest sales, it reports much lower profit than the School Market. Therefore, management is considering shifting attention and resources away from the Commercial Market and towards the School Market. They have asked for your recommendation how to proceed. You decided to create a properly formatted segmented income statement. To assist in this endeavor, you have gathered the following information:

a. The cost of goods sold figures shown in the income statement above are traceable to their respective markets.
b. Sales support, order processing, and packing and shipping are variable costs. Warehousing, general management, and advertising are fixed costs. In the income statement above, all of these costs have been allocated to the three markets on the basis of sales dollars.
c. Using your knowledge of activity-based costing, you compiled the following data:

		Amount of Activity			
Cost Pool and (Allocation Base)	Total Cost	School Market	Commercial Market	Home Market	Total
Sales support (number of calls)	$3,600,000	11,000	8,000	5,000	24,000
Order processing (number of orders)	$1,720,000	1,650	1,750	5,200	8,600
Warehousing (square feet of space)	$940,000	17,500	35,000	65,000	117,500
Packing and shipping (pounds shipped)	$520,000	64,000	24,000	16,000	104,000

d.   You also determined the following breakdown of the company's advertising expense and general management expense:

	Total	Commercial Market	Home Market	School Market
Advertising:				
Traceable	$1,460,000	$700,000	$180,000	$580,000
Common......................	$230,000			
General management:				
Traceable salaries..............	$410,000	$150,000	$120,000	$140,000
Common......................	$900,000			

Required:

1. Refer to the data in part (c) above. Calculate an activity rate for each cost pool. Then, using those rates, allocate each cost pool to the company's three markets.
2. Prepare a revised contribution format segmented income statement for the company. Include an "Amount" column and a "Percent" column for the company as a whole and for each market segment.
3. What insights from your segmented income statement should be brought to management's attention? Explain.

INTEGRATION EXERCISE 11 Transfer Pricing and Differential Analysis LO11–3, LO13–1

Bend Corporation consists of three decentralized divisions—Grant Division, Able Division, and Facet Division. The division managers are evaluated and rewarded based on their division's profit. They each can choose to sell their products to outside customers or to sell their products to other divisions within the company. They also have the authority to set their own selling prices to outside customers and to negotiate transfer prices with other divisions.

The manager of the Able Division is considering two alternative orders:

Alternative 1:

The Able Division could sell 2,000 motors to the Facet Division for a transfer price of $1,600 per motor. To manufacture each motor, Able would buy one component part from Grant Division at a transfer price of $400 per unit. Able would further process each part received from Grant at a variable cost of $450 per unit. In addition, Able would use five machine-hours to complete each motor. It's fixed manufacturing overhead rate is $23 per machine-hour.

Grant incurs a variable cost of $200 per unit before selling each part to Able for $400. It also uses 2.5 machine-hours to manufacture each part sold to Able. Grant has a fixed manufacturing overhead rate of $38 per machine-hour.

If Able declines this opportunity (and pursues alternative 2 as described in the next paragraph), the Facet Division will buy 2,000 motors from Waverly Coporation for a price of $1,600 per motor. To produce each motor, Waverly would buy a component part from Grant Division for $350 per unit. Grant would use 2.5 machine-hours to make each part; however, because the part differs from the one it would produce for Able, the variable cost per unit is only $175 per unit.

Alternative 2:

The Able Division could sell 2,500 motors to Tech Corporation for a price of $1,200 per motor. To manufacture each unit of this particular motor, Able would buy one component part from Grant Division at a transfer price of $200 per unit. From Grant's perspective, this part would have a variable cost per unit of $100 and would require two machine-hours to produce. Able would further process each part received from Grant at a variable cost of $470 per unit. Able would also use four machine-hours to complete each motor.

Able Division's plant capacity is limited; therefore, it can only choose one of the two alternatives. The company's total general fixed overhead would not be affected by this decision.

Required:

1. If the manager of the Able Division wants to maximize the division's profits, which alternative should be accepted—the order from the Facet Division or the order from Tech Corporation? Support your answer with computations.
2. Which of the two alternatives will maximize profits for the company as a whole? Support your answer with computations.

INTEGRATION EXERCISE 12 Service Department Cost Allocation; Step-Down Method; Variable and Fixed Costs LO4–11, LO11–4

The Bayview Resort has three operating departments—the Convention Center, Food Services, and Guest Lodging—supported by three service departments—General Administration, Cost Accounting, and Laundry. For billing and management control purposes, the resort manager wants to calculate each operating department's direct costs plus its allocated share of service department costs.

The company uses the step-down method of service department cost allocation beginning with the General Administration Department, followed by Cost Accounting, and Laundry. The allocation bases for each department are as follows:

	Allocation Base
General Administration:	
Fixed costs	Long-run average number of employees
Cost Accounting:	
Variable costs	Number of transactions processed each period
Fixed costs	Percentage of peak-period transaction processing needs
Laundry:	
Variable costs	Pounds of laundry washed each period
Fixed	Percentage of peak-period laundry washing needs

The following additional data is available for a recent quarter:

	Service Departments			Operating Departments			
	General Administration	Cost Accounting	Laundry	Convention Center	Food Services	Guest Lodging	Total
Variable costs.	$ 0	$ 70,000	$143,000	$ 0	$ 52,000	$ 24,000	$ 289,000
Fixed costs	200,000	110,000	65,900	95,000	375,000	486,000	1,331,900
Total overhead cost	$200,000	$180,000	$208,900	$95,000	$427,000	$510,000	$1,620,900
Percentage of peak-period resource usage		10%	4%	30%	16%	40%	100%
Number of transactions processed			800	1,200	3,000	9,000	14,000
Percentage of peak-period transaction processing needs . . .			7%	13%	20%	60%	100%
Pounds of laundry washed				20,000	15,000	210,000	245,000
Percentage of peak-period laundry washing needs				10%	6%	84%	100%

Required:

1. Using the step-down method, allocate the service department variable costs to the operating departments. What is the total amount of direct and allocated variable costs within each operating department?
2. Using the step-down method, allocate the service department fixed costs to the operating departments. What is the total amount of direct and allocated fixed costs within each operating department?
3. Calculate each operating department's total direct and allocated variable costs plus its total direct and allocated fixed costs.

INTEGRATION EXERCISE 13 Service Department Cost Allocation; Direct Method; Plantwide and Departmental Overhead Rates LO2–1, LO2–2, LO4–10, LO11–4

Hobart Company manufactures attaché cases and suitcases. It has five manufacturing departments. The Molding, Component, and Assembly departments convert raw materials into finished goods; hence, they are treated as operating departments. The Power and Maintenance departments are treated as service departments because they support the three operating departments.

Hobart has always used a plantwide predetermined overhead rate with direct labor-hours as the allocation base for product costing purposes. The overhead rate is computed by dividing the company's total estimated overhead cost (across the five manufacturing departments) by the total estimated direct labor-hours to be worked in the three operating departments.

The company has been experiencing declining profits; therefore, it is considering switching from plantwide overhead allocation to a departmental approach. Under the departmental approach, the service department costs would be allocated to the three operating departments. Then each operating department would compute its own overhead rate. The overhead rate in Molding would be based on machine-hours and the rates in Component and Assembly would be based on direct labor-hours.

The service departments' estimated costs for the coming year are as follows:

	Service Departments	
	Power	Maintenance
Variable overhead cost	$ 640,000	$ 25,000
Fixed overhead cost	1,200,000	375,000
Total overhead cost	$1,840,000	$400,000

The Power Department would allocate its variable costs to the operating departments based on estimated kilowatt hours used and its fixed costs based on the percentage of peak-period capacity required. The Maintenance Department would allocate its variable costs to the operating departments based on estimated maintenance hours used and its fixed costs based on the percentage of peak-period capacity required.

The corresponding data for allocating service department costs to operating departments are as follows:

	Operating Departments		
	Molding	Component	Assembly
Power department:			
Estimated kilowatt hours used	36,000	32,000	12,000
Percentage of peak-period capacity	50%	35%	15%
Maintenance Department:			
Estimated maintenance hours used	9,000	2,500	1,000
Percentage of peak-period capacity	70%	20%	10%

The company also provided the following estimated data for its three operating departments:

	Operating Departments		
	Molding	Component	Assembly
Departmental costs:			
Direct materials	$1,630,000	$3,000,000	$ 25,000
Direct labor	350,000	2,000,000	1,300,000
Manufacturing overhead	1,960,500	1,620,000	2,399,500
Total departmental costs	$3,940,500	$6,620,000	$3,724,500
Allocation bases:			
Direct labor-hours	50,000	200,000	150,000
Machine-hours	87,500	12,500	0

Required:

1. Compute the company's predetermined plantwide overhead rate.
2. Assume the company decides to use departmental overhead rates.

a. Using the direct method, allocate the variable and fixed service department costs to the operating departments.

b. Calculate the predetermined departmental overhead rates for each of the three operating departments.

3. One of Hobart's products is a small attaché case that uses the following machine-hours and direct labor-hours in the three operating departments:

	Machine-Hours	Direct Labor-Hours
Molding Department	3,000	1,000
Component Department	800	2,500
Assembly Department	0	4,000
Total hours	3,800	7,500

a. Calculate the amount of overhead applied to this attaché case using the plantwide approach.

b. Calculate the amount of overhead applied to this attaché case using the departmental approach.

4. Is the plantwide approach overcosting or undercosting the attaché case compared to the departmental approach? If the company uses cost-plus pricing, how would plantwide overhead allocation affect its price-setting decisions?

INTEGRATION EXERCISE 14 Service Department Cost Allocation; Step-Down Method versus Direct Method; Plantwide and Departmental Overhead Rates LO2–1, LO2–2, LO4–10, LO4–11

Sendai Company has budgeted costs in its various departments as follows for the coming year:

Factory Administration	$270,000
Custodial Services	68,760
Personnel	28,840
Maintenance	45,200
Machining—overhead	376,300
Assembly—overhead	175,900
Total cost	$965,000

The company allocates service department costs to other departments in the order listed below.

Department	Number of Employees	Total Labor-Hours	Square Feet of Space Occupied	Direct Labor-Hours	Machine-Hours
Factory Administration	12	—	5,000	—	—
Custodial Services	4	3,000	2,000	—	—
Personnel	5	5,000	3,000	—	—
Maintenance	25	22,000	10,000	—	—
Machining................	40	30,000	70,000	20,000	70,000
Assembly	60	90,000	20,000	80,000	10,000
	146	150,000	110,000	100,000	80,000

Machining and Assembly are operating departments; the other departments are service departments. Factory Administration is allocated based on labor-hours; Custodial Services based on square feet occupied; Personnel based on number of employees; and Maintenance based on machine-hours.

Required:

1. Allocate service department costs to consuming departments by the step-down method. Then compute predetermined overhead rates in the operating departments using machine-hours as the allocation base in Machining and direct labor-hours as the allocation base in Assembly.

2. Repeat (1) above, this time using the direct method. Again compute predetermined overhead rates in Machining and Assembly.

3. Assume the company doesn't bother with allocating service department costs but simply computes a plantwide overhead rate that divides the total overhead costs (both service department and operating department costs) by the total direct labor-hours. Compute the plantwide overhead rate.

4. Suppose a job requires machine-hours and labor-hours as follows:

	Machine-Hours	Direct Labor-Hours
Machining Department........	190	25
Assembly Department	10	75
Total hours	200	100

Using the overhead rates from requirements (1), (2), and (3), compute the amount of overhead cost assigned to the job.

INTEGRATION EXERCISE 15 Segmented Income Statements; Contribution Margin Ratio; Activity-Based Cost Allocation LO5–1, LO6–4, LO7–4

Diversified Products, Inc., recently acquired a small publishing company offering three books for sale—a cookbook, a travel guide, and a handy speller. Each book sells for $10. The publishing company's most recent monthly income statement is shown below:

			Product Line	
	Total Company	Cookbook	Travel Guide	Handy Speller
Sales	$300,000	$90,000	$150,000	$60,000
Expenses:				
Printing costs......................	102,000	27,000	63,000	12,000
Advertising.......................	36,000	13,500	19,500	3,000
General sales.....................	18,000	5,400	9,000	3,600
Salaries..........................	33,000	18,000	9,000	6,000
Equipment depreciation.............	9,000	3,000	3,000	3,000
Sales commissions	30,000	9,000	15,000	6,000
General administration..............	42,000	14,000	14,000	14,000
Warehouse rent....................	12,000	3,600	6,000	2,400
Depreciation—office facilities	3,000	1,000	1,000	1,000
Total expenses......................	285,000	94,500	139,500	51,000
Net operating income (loss)	$ 15,000	$ (4,500)	$ 10,500	$ 9,000

The following additional information is available:

a. Only printing costs and sales commissions are variable; all other costs are fixed. The printing costs (which include materials, labor, and variable overhead) are traceable to the three product lines as shown in the income statement above. Sales commissions are 10% of sales.

b. The same equipment is used to produce all three books, so the equipment depreciation expense has been allocated equally among the three product lines. An analysis of the company's activities indicates the equipment is used 30% of the time to produce cookbooks, 50% of the time to produce travel guides, and 20% of the time to produce handy spellers.

c. The warehouse is used to store finished units of product, so the rental cost has been allocated to the product lines on the basis of sales dollars. The warehouse rental cost is $3 per square foot per year. The warehouse contains 48,000 square feet of space, of which 7,200 square feet is used by the cookbook line, 24,000 square feet by the travel guide line, and 16,800 square feet by the handy speller line.

d. The general sales cost above includes the salary of the sales manager and other sales costs not traceable to any specific product line. This cost has been allocated to the product lines on the basis of sales dollars.

e. The general administration cost and depreciation of office facilities both relate to administration of the company as a whole. These costs have been allocated equally to the three product lines.

f. All other costs are traceable to the three product lines in the amounts shown on the income statement above.

The management of Diversified Products, Inc., is anxious to improve the publishing company's 5% return on sales.

Required:

1. Prepare a new contribution format segmented income statement for the month. Adjust allocations of equipment depreciation and of warehouse rent as indicated by the additional information provided.

2. Based on the segmented income statements given in the problem, management plans to eliminate the cookbook because it is not returning a profit and to focus all available resources on promoting the travel guide. However, based on the new contribution format segmented income statement that you prepared:

    a. Do you agree with management's plan to eliminate the cookbook? Explain.

    b. Do you agree with the decision to focus all available resources on promoting the travel guide? Assume an ample market is available for all three product lines. (*Hint:* Compute the contribution margin ratio for each product.)

INTEGRATION EXERCISE 16 Master Budgeting LO8–2, LO8–3, LO8–4, LO8–5, LO8–6, LO8–7, LO 8–8, LO8–9, LO8–10

Endless Mountain Company manufactures a single product popular with outdoor recreation enthusiasts. The company sells its product to retailers throughout the northeastern quadrant of the United States. It is in the process of creating a master budget for next year and reports a beginning balance sheet as follows:

	A	B	C
1	**Endless Mountain Company**		
2	**Balance Sheet**		
3	**December 31, This Year**		
4			
5	**Assets**		
6	Current assets:		
7	Cash	$ 46,200	
8	Accounts receivable	260,000	
9	Raw materials inventory (4,500 yards)	11,250	
10	Finished goods inventory (1,500 units)	32,250	
11	Total current assets		$349,700
12	Plant and equipment:		
13	Buildings and equipment	900,000	
14	Accumulated depreciation	(292,000)	
15	Plant and equipment, net		608,000
16	Total assets		$957,700
17			
18	**Liabilities and Stockholders' Equity**		
19	Current liabilities:		
20	Accounts payable		$158,000
21	Stockholders' equity:		
22	Common stock	$ 419,800	
23	Retained earnings	379,900	
24	Total stockholders' equity		799,700
25	Total liabilities and stockholders' equity		$957,700
26			

Beginning Balance Sheet / Budgeting Assum[ ]

Microsoft Excel

The company's chief financial officer (CFO), in consultation with various managers across the organization, developed the following set of assumptions to help create next year's budget:

1. The budgeted unit sales are 12,000 units, 37,000 units, 15,000 units, and 25,000 units for quarters 1–4, respectively. Notice the company experiences peak sales in the second and fourth quarters. The budgeted selling price for the year is $32 per unit. The budgeted unit sales for the first quarter of the following year is 13,000 units.

2. All sales are on credit. Uncollectible accounts are negligible and can be ignored. Seventy-five percent of all credit sales are collected in the quarter of the sale and 25% are collected in the subsequent quarter.

3. Each quarter's ending finished goods inventory should equal 15% of the next quarter's unit sales.

4. Each unit of finished goods requires 3.5 yards of raw material that costs $3.00 per yard. Each quarter's ending raw materials inventory should equal 10% of the next quarter's production needs. The estimated ending raw materials inventory on December 31 of next year is 5,000 yards.

5. Seventy percent of each quarter's purchases are paid for in the quarter of purchase. The remaining 30% of each quarter's purchases are paid in the following quarter.

6. Direct laborers are paid $18 an hour and each unit of finished goods requires 0.25 direct labor-hour to complete. All direct labor costs are paid in the quarter incurred.

7. The budgeted variable manufacturing overhead per direct labor-hour is $3.00. The quarterly fixed manufacturing overhead is $150,000 including $20,000 of depreciation on equipment. The number of direct labor-hours is used as the allocation base for the budgeted plantwide overhead rate. All overhead costs (excluding depreciation) are paid in the quarter incurred.

8. The budgeted variable selling and administrative expense is $1.25 per unit sold. The fixed selling and administrative expenses per quarter include advertising ($25,000), executive salaries ($64,000), insurance ($12,000), property tax ($8,000), and depreciation expense ($8,000). All selling and administrative expenses (excluding depreciation) are paid in the quarter incurred.

9. The company plans to maintain a minimum cash balance at the end of each quarter of $30,000. Assume any borrowings take place on the first day of the quarter. To the extent possible, the company will repay principal and interest on any borrowings on the last day of the fourth quarter. The company's lender imposes a simple interest rate of 3% per quarter on any borrowings.

10. Dividends of $15,000 will be declared and paid in each quarter.

11. The company uses a last-in, first-out (LIFO) inventory flow assumption. This means the most recently purchased raw materials are the "first-out" to production and the most recently completed finished goods are the "first-out" to customers.

Required:

The company's CFO asked you to use Microsoft Excel to prepare next year's master budget. Your Excel file should include a tab containing the beginning balance sheet, a tab summarizing the budgeting assumptions, and tabs corresponding to the following budget schedules and financial statements:

1. Quarterly sales budget including a schedule of expected cash collections.
2. Quarterly production budget.
3. Quarterly direct materials budget including a schedule of expected cash disbursements for purchases of materials.
4. Quarterly direct labor budget.
5. Quarterly manufacturing overhead budget.
6. Ending finished goods inventory budget at December 31 of next year.
7. Quarterly selling and administrative expense budget.
8. Quarterly cash budget.
9. Income statement for next year ended December 31.
10. Balance sheet at December 31 of next year.

INTEGRATION EXERCISE 17 Statement of Cash Flows LO15–1, LO15–2, LO15–3, LO15–4, LO15–5

Refer to the information pertaining to Endless Mountain Company that is provided in Integration Exercise 16. In addition to the budget schedules that you prepared in Integration Exercise 16, insert a new tab in your Microsoft Excel worksheet titled "Statement of Cash Flows."

Required:

1. Using the indirect method, calculate Endless Mountain Company's estimated net cash provided by operating activities for next year.
2. Prepare the company's budgeted statement of cash flows for the year ended December 31 of next year.

INTEGRATION EXERCISE 18 Financial Statement Ratio Analysis LO16–2, LO16–3, LO16–4, LO16–5

Refer to the information pertaining to Endless Mountain Company provided in Integration Exercise 16. In addition to the budget schedules you prepared in Integration Exercise 16, insert a new tab in your Microsoft Excel worksheet titled "Ratio Analysis."

Required (For all questions, be sure to use formulas that link to the other tabs in your Microsoft Excel worksheet when performing your calculations):

1. To help assess the company's liquidity, calculate the following at December 31 of next year:
   a. Working capital
   b. Current ratio
2. To help assess the company's asset management, calculate the following for next year:
   a. Accounts receivable turnover
   b. Average collection period
   c. Inventory turnover
   d. Average sale period
   e. Operating cycle
3. To help assess the company's debt management, calculate the following for next year:
   a. Times interest earned ratio
   b. Equity multiplier
4. To help assess the company's profitability, calculate the following for next year:
   a. Net profit margin percentage
   b. Return on equity
5. For each of the measures and ratios computed in requirements 1 through 4, indicate whether, generally speaking, management would prefer to see it increase or decrease over time. Support each answer with an explanation.

INTEGRATION EXERCISE 19 Cost-Volume-Profit Relationships, Variable Costing LO1–4, LO5–2, LO5–3, LO5–4, LO5–5, LO6–1, LO6–2, LO6–3

Refer to the information pertaining to Endless Mountain Company provided in Integration Exercise 16. In addition to the budget schedules you prepared in Integration Exercise 16, insert two new tabs in your Microsoft Excel worksheet titled "CVP Analysis" and "Variable Costing."

Required (For all questions, be sure to use formulas that link to the other tabs in your Microsoft Excel worksheet when performing your calculations):

1. Calculate the following budgeted figures for next year:
   a. The total fixed cost.
   b. The variable cost per unit sold.
   c. The contribution margin per unit sold.
   d. The break-even point in unit sales and dollar sales.
   e. The margin of safety.
   f. The degree of operating leverage.
2. Calculate the following budgeted figures for next year:
   a. A variable costing income statement. Stop your computations at net operating income.
   b. A reconciliation explaining the difference in the absorption costing and variable costing net operating incomes.

INTEGRATION EXERCISE 20 Master Budgeting, Statement of Cash Flows, Ratio Analysis, Cost-Volume-Profit Relationships, Variable Costing LO5–4, LO6–2, LO8–5, LO8–6, LO8–8, LO8–9, LO8–10, LO15–2, LO16–3

Refer to the information pertaining to Endless Mountain Company provided in Integration Exercise 16 as well as the schedules you prepared in answering Integration Exercises 16 through 19.

Required:

1. Assume the company expects to collect all of its credit sales in the quarter of sale rather than the original assumption it will collect 75% of credit sales in the quarter of sale and the remaining 25% in the subsequent quarter. *Without changing any of the underlying assumptions in your budgeting assumptions tab,* calculate the following revised figures related to next year's budget:
   a. Net income (absorption basis)
   b. Accounts receivable turnover
   c. Net cash provided by operating activities

2. Go to the Budgeting Assumptions tab in your Microsoft Excel worksheet. Change the percentage of sales collected in the quarter of sale to 100% and the percentage of sales collected in the quarter after sale to 0%. Do your answers to 1a through 1c match the numbers appearing in your Excel worksheet? If not, why?

3. Refer to the original budgeting assumptions from Integration Exercise 16. Assume the company expects to pay its direct laborers $19 per hour instead of the original estimate of $18 per hour. *Without changing any of the underlying assumptions in your budgeting assumptions tab,* calculate the following revised figures related to next year's budget:
   a. Ending finished goods inventory at December 31 of next year.
   b. The break-even point in unit sales.
   c. Variable costing net operating income

4. Go to the Budgeting Assumptions tab in your Microsoft Excel worksheet. Change the direct labor cost per hour from $18 to $19. Do your answers to 3a through 3c match the numbers appearing in your Excel worksheet? If not, why?

Index